Modern Indian History

Eighteenth Edition

Modern Indian History

Eighteenth Edition

V D MAHAJAN
MA (Honours.), LLB, PhD
Formerly Professor
History and Political Science
Punjab University, Lahore
and
Faculty of Law
University of Delhi

S Chand And Company Limited
(ISO 9001 Certified Company)

S Chand And Company Limited
(ISO 9001 Certified Company)

Head Office: D-92, Sector–2, Noida – 201301, U.P. (India), Ph. 91-120-4682700
Registered Office: A-27, 2nd Floor, Mohan Co-operative Industrial Estate,
New Delhi – 110 044, Phone: 011-49731800
www.schandpublishing.com; e-mail: info@schandpublishing.com

Marketing Offices:

Chennai	: Ph: 23632120; chennai@schandpublishing.com
Guwahati	: Ph: 2738811, 2735640; guwahati@schandpublishing.com
Hyderabad	: Ph: 40186018; hyderabad@schandpublishing.com
Jalandhar	: Ph: 4645630; jalandhar@schandpublishing.com
Kolkata	: Ph: 23357458, 23353914; kolkata@schandpublishing.com
Lucknow	: Ph: 4003633; lucknow@schandpublishing.com
Mumbai	: Ph: 25000297; mumbai@schandpublishing.com
Patna	: Ph: 2260011; patna@schandpublishing.com

© S Chand And Company Limited, 1990

All rights reserved. No part of this publication may be reproduced or copied in any material form (including photocopying or storing it in any medium in form of graphics, electronic or mechanical means and whether or not transient or incidental to some other use of this publication) without written permission of the copyright owner. Any breach of this will entail legal action and prosecution without further notice.

Jurisdiction: All disputes with respect to this publication shall be subject to the jurisdiction of the Courts, Tribunals and Forums of New Delhi, India only.

S. CHAND'S Seal of Trust

In our endeavour to protect you against counterfeit/fake books, we have pasted a hologram over the cover of this book. The hologram displays full visible effect, emboss effect, relief effect, mirror lens effect, pearl effect, motion effect, animated text, kinetic effect, concealed effect, micro structure, multicolour small text 'S.CHAND', nanotext '50 micron' 'ORIGINAL' 'S.CHAND', mirror strip '6.5 mm', mirror lens 3 mm with text 'SC', microtext 'OK', scratch strip '7 mm', color sparkling effect under scratch and QR code size 10 mm x 10 mm, etc.

A fake hologram does not display ALL these effects.

First Edition 1990
Subsequent Editions and Reprints 1993, 94, 95, 97, 98, 99, 2000, 2001, 2003, 2004, 2005, 2006, 2007, 2008, 2009, 2010, 2012, 2013, 2014, 2015, 2016, 2017
Eighteenth Edition 2020; Reprint 2021 (Twice), 2022 (Thrice)

Reprint 2023 (Twice)

ISBN: 978-93-528-3619-2   **Product Code:** H5MIH41HIST10ENAR20O

PRINTED IN INDIA

By Vikas Publishing House Private Limited, Plot 20/4, Site-IV, Industrial Area Sahibabad, Ghaziabad – 201 010 and Published by S Chand And Company Limited, A-27, 2nd Floor, Mohan Co-operative Industrial Estate, New Delhi – 110 044.

Preface to the Eighteenth Edition

This revised edition continues to engage the readers with its unique narrative style of writing. It comprises the history of British India from the late eighteenth century until 1947 and of the Republic of India, thereafter. The new edition caters to the syllabi requirements of various universities in India. It also incorporates the topics keeping in view the UGC Choice Based Credit System syllabus requirements. Students of Arts and Law courses would find the book suitable for their programmes and it would be equally useful for the preparation of various competitive examinations. Also incorporated are the chapter-end questions for the students to review and discuss the learning gained in the text.

As in the previous edition, the book is divided into two parts. Part One gives an account of the decline and disintegration of the Mughal Empire and, subsequently, the rise of autonomous states in India. It discusses in detail the society and culture of India during the eighteenth century. Part Two deals extensively with the advent of Europeans in India and how they consolidated their inroads in the country. It explains how the British established their supremacy over the French in the Anglo-French struggle. The book goes in greater depth by giving a chronological account of British expansion from Bengal to all parts of India under various British generals, the concept of colonialism and its impact on Indian agriculture and industries. It also delves with the topics of critical relevance such as the rise of nationalism, phases of Indian nationalist movement and contributions made by Indian leaders.

The Publishers invite suggestions for further improvement in the book.

Preface to the Seventeenth Edition

I have a great pleasure in placing the Seventeenth Edition of the book in the hands of the readers. In this edition, Chapter 1 on "Decline and Disintegration of the Mughal Empire" has been re-written. It contains a lot of new material which did not exist in the last edition. Chapter 2 on "Rise of Autonomous States" is a new one. It discusses in detail the various States which came into existence or became stronger as a result of the decline and disintegration of the Mughal Empire. Chapter 41 dealing with "Changes in Land Revenue Settlement" is a new one. I have no doubt that these additions have added to the utility of the book. I avail of this opportunity to thank all those who have patronised the book in the past and it is hoped that they will continue to do so in the future. All suggestions for its improvement will be gratefully acknowledged.

I want the readers of *Modern Indian History* to note that what made India weak and a prey to foreign conquest, was the lack of unity among the people of this country. Every one quarrelled with every one. Brothers fought against brothers. Brothers killed brothers. They were prepared to lose all and be destroyed but were not willing to compromise with their brothers and other countrymen. This was particularly so during the eighteenth century. I would like the Indians to learn a lesson. They should subordinate everything to the higher interests of their country. No sacrifice should be considered high to make India strong. It should never be forgotten that it is only if India lives, that we also live and prosper and can claim respect in the world.

D-805, New Friends Colony
New Delhi-110065

V D MAHAJAN

Disclaimer: While the author of this book has made every effort to avoid any mistakes or omissions and has used his skill, expertise and knowledge to the best of his capacity to provide accurate and updated information, the author and S Chand do not give any representation or warranty with respect to the accuracy or completeness of the contents of this publication and are selling this publication on the condition and understanding that they shall not be made liable in any manner whatsoever. S Chand and the author expressly disclaim all and any liability/responsibility to any person, whether a purchaser or reader of this publication or not, in respect of anything and everything forming part of the contents of this publication. S Chand shall not be responsible for any errors, omissions or damages arising out of the use of the information contained in this publication. Further, the appearance of the personal name, location, place and incidence, if any; in the illustrations used herein is purely coincidental and work of imagination. Thus the same should in no manner be termed as defamatory to any individual.

Brief Contents

PART A

1. Decline and Disintegration of the Mughal Empire — 2–39
2. Rise of Autonomous States — 40–65
3. Society and Culture in the Eighteenth Century — 66–80

PART B

1. The Advent of Europeans in India — 82–89
2. Rise and Growth of the English and French East India Companies — 90–93
3. Anglo-French Struggle for Supremacy in the Deccan — 94–107
4. The English in Bengal from 1757 to 1772 — 108–129
5. Warren Hastings (1772-85) — 130–145
6. Lord Cornwallis and Sir John Shore — 146–159
7. Lord Wellesley (1798-1805) — 160–171
8. Lord Hastings and Amherst — 172–181
9. Rise and Fall of the Peshwas — 182–205
10. William Bentinck to Auckland — 206–215
11. Ellenborough and Hardinge — 216–221
12. Maharaja Ranjit Singh and His Successors — 222–239
13. Lord Dalhousie (1848-56) — 240–251
14. The Revolt of 1857 — 252–267
15. Canning to Lytton — 268–277
16. Ripon to Elgin(1880-98) — 278–287
17. Lord Curzon (1899-1905) — 288–299
18. India since Lord Minto — 300–311
19. Constitutional Development (1773-1950) — 312–417
20. Growth of Central and Provincial Legislatures — 418–425
21. The Nationalist Movement in India — 426–463
22. Establishment of Pakistan — 464–479
23. Leaders of Modern India — 480–491
24. Decentralisation of Finance — 492–499
25. Public Services in India — 500–511

26.	Growth of Local Self-Government in India	512–521
27.	History of the Press in India	522–533
28.	History of Education	534–543
29.	Religious and Social Development	544–555
30.	Anglo-Afghan Relations	556–569
31.	The North-Western Frontier Policy	570–575
32.	The Indian States	576–613
33.	Legacy of British Rule in India	614–621
34.	Economic Impact of British Rule in India	622–629
35.	Famines in India and Development of Famine Policy	630–635
36.	Peasants' Movement and Uprisings	636–645
37.	The Left Movements in India	646–655
38.	Role of Mahatma Gandhi in the Nationalist Movement	656–661
39.	The Renaissance in India	662–675
40.	Political, Cultural and Social Impact of British Rule	676–681
41.	Changes in Land Revenue Settlement	682–691

Chronological Table   692–696
Index   697–700

Detailed Contents

PART A

1. **Decline and Disintegration of the Mughal Empire** — 2–39
   Condition of India at the Time of Death of Aurangzeb 2
   Successors of Aurangzeb 4
      Bahadur Shah I (1707-12) 4
      Jahandar Shah (1712-13) 7
      Farrukh-siyar (1713-19) 9
      Rafi-ud-Darajat 12
      Rafi-ud-Daulah 12
      Muhammad Shah (1719-48) 12
      Ahmed Shah (1748-54) 26
      Alamgir II (1754-59) 27
      Shah Alam II (1759-1806) 27
      Akbar II (1806-37) 28
      Bahadur Shah II (1837-57) 28
   Causes of the Downfall of the Mughals 28

2. **Rise of Autonomous States** — 40–65
   Bengal Subah 40
   Avadh 43
   Hyderabad 45
   Rohilkhand 47
   The Jats 49
   The Rajput States 52
   The Sikhs 54
   Jammu and Kashmir 59
   The Marathas 60

3. **Society and Culture in the Eighteenth Century** — 66–80
   Social Condition 66
   Education 70
   Religious Condition 72
   Economic Condition 75

PART B

1. **The Advent of Europeans in India** — 82–89
   The Portuguese in India 82
   The Dutch in India 88
   The Danes in India 88

(xi)

2. **Rise and Growth of the English and French East India Companies**   90–93
   The English East India Company   90
   The French East India Company   92

3. **Anglo-French Struggle for Supremacy in the Deccan**   94–107
   First Carnatic War (1746-48)   95
   Rise of Hyderabad State   97
   Second Carnatic War (1748-54)   98
   Third Carnatic War (1756-63)   99
   Causes of English Success   100
   Estimate of Dupleix   103

4. **The English in Bengal from 1757 to 1772**   108–129
   Black-hole Tragedy   109
   Battle of Plassey   109
   Mir Jafar (1757-60)   110
   Invasion of Ali Gohour   111
   Deposition of Mir Jafar   111
   Mir Kasim (1760-63)   112
   Clive's Second Governorship of Bengal (1765-67)   118
   Bengal from 1767 to 1772   127

5. **Warren Hastings (1772-85)**   130–145
   Warren Hastings' Reforms   130
   The Rohilla War   132
   Trial of Nand Kumar   133
   Case of Chet Singh   133
   Begums of Oudh   134
   Regulating Act and Council   134
   Warren Hastings and Supreme Court   135
   Foreign Policy of Warren Hastings   136
   Estimate of Warren Hastings   142
   Pitt's India Act (1784)   145
   Sir John Macpherson (February 1785-September 1786)   145

6. **Lord Cornwallis and Sir John Shore**   146–159
   Lord Cornwallis (1786-93)   146
   Sir John Shore (1793-98)   157

7. **Lord Wellesley (1798-1805)**   160–171
   Condition of India in 1798   160
   Subsidiary System   161
   Fourth Mysore War (1799)   163
   Character of Tipu   164
   Tanjore, Surat and Carnatic   165
   Oudh   165
   Steps against the French Danger   166
   Second Maratha War (1802-04)   166
   War with Holkar   167
   Estimate of Wellesley   167

Lord Cornwallis (1805) *169*
Sir George Barlow (1805-07) *170*
Lord Minto (1807-13) *170*

8. Lord Hastings and Amherst — 172–181
Lord Hastings (1813-23) *172*
John Adams (1823) *178*
Lord Amherst (1823-28) *179*

9. Rise and Fall of the Peshwas — 182–205
Balaji Vishwanath (1714-20) *182*
Baji Rao (1720-40) *185*
Balaji Baji Rao (1740-61) *188*
Third Battle of Panipat (1761) *188*
Madhavrao I (1761-72) *192*
Narayanrao (1772) *194*
Madhavrao Narayan (1774-95) *194*
Bajirao II (1796-1818) *194*
Mahadji Scindhia (1727-94) *194*
Nana Phadnavis (1742-1800) *197*
Maratha Administration under Peshwas *197*
Causes of the Downfall of the Marathas *201*

10. William Bentinck to Auckland — 206–215
Lord William Bentinck *206*
Sir Charles Metcalfe (1835-36) *214*
Lord Auckland (1836-42) *214*

11. Ellenborough and Hardinge — 216–221
Lord Ellenborough (1842-44) *216*
Lord Hardinge (1844-48) *220*

12. Maharaja Ranjit Singh and His Successors — 222–239
Rise of Ranjit Singh *222*
Anglo-Sikh Relations (1809-39) *223*
Civil Administration of Ranjit Singh *225*
Territorial Divisions and Local Administration *227*
Ranjit Singh's Government *228*
Army of Ranjit Singh *228*
Personality of Ranjit Singh *231*
First Sikh War (1845-46) *234*
Treaty of Lahore (1846) *236*
Annexation of the Punjab *237*

13. Lord Dalhousie (1848-56) — 240–251
Conquests of Dalhousie *240*
Wajid Ali Shah (1822-57) *245*
Abolition of Titles and Pensions *247*
Administrative Reforms of Dalhousie *247*
Dalhousie's Responsibility for the Mutiny *248*
Estimate of Dalhousie *249*

14. The Revolt of 1857 — 252–267
Its Character 252
Causes of Revolt 255
Causes of Failure of the Revolt 262
Effects of the Revolt 264

15. Canning to Lytton — 268–277
Lord Canning (1856-62) 268
Lord Elgin (1862-63) 270
Lord Lawrence (1864-69) 271
Lord Mayo (1869-72) 272
Lord Northbrook (1872-76) 273
Lord Lytton (1876-80) 274
Estimate of Lytton 275

16. Ripon to Elgin (1880-98) — 278–287
Lord Ripon (1880-84) 278
Lord Dufferin (1884-88) 283
Lord Lansdowne (1888-93) 285
Lord Elgin II (1894-99) 286

17. Lord Curzon (1899-1905) — 288–299
Curzon's Foreign Policy 288
Internal Administration of Curzon 292
Estimate of Lord Curzon 298

18. India since Lord Minto — 300–311
Lord Minto II (1905-10) 300
Lord Hardinge (1910-16) 301
Lord Chelmsford (1916-21) 303
Lord Reading (1921-26) 304
Lord Irwin (1926-31) 304
Lord Willingdon (1931-36) 305
Lord Linlithgow (1936-44) 305
Lord Wavell (1944-47) 306
Lord Mountbatten (March 1947 to June 1948) 306

19. Constitutional Development (1773-1950) — 312–417
The Regulating Act, 1773 312
Judicature Act of 1781 318
Dundas's Bill (1783) 319
Fox India Bill (1783) 319
Provisions of Pitt's India Act 320
Act of 1786 322
Declaratory Act of 1788 322
Charter Act of 1793 322
Charter Act of 1813 323
Charter Act of 1833 324
Charter Act of 1853 327
Government of India Act, 1858 328
Queen's Proclamation of 1858 331

Indian Councils Act, 1861 *332*
Indian Councils Act, 1892 *335*
Minto-Morley Reforms (1909) *338*
Circumstances Leading to Montagu-Chelmsford Reforms (1919) *343*
August Declaration *345*
Proposals for Reforms *345*
Memorandum of the Nineteen (1916) *346*
Congress-League Scheme (1916) *347*
Gokhale's Political Testament *350*
The Round Table Group *351*
Recommendations of 1918 *353*
Main Provisions of the Act of 1919 *359*
Constitutional Development from 1919 to 1935 *368*
The Home Government *385*
Constitutional Development from 1937 to 1950 *397*

20. Growth of Central and Provincial Legislatures — 418–425
Growth of the Central Legislature *418*
Growth of Provincial Legislatures *422*

21. The Nationalist Movement in India — 426–463
Its Nature *426*
Causes *426*
Genesis of Indian National Congress *430*
First Session of Congress *432*
Second Session of Congress *432*
Lahore Session *432*
The Moderates (1885-1905) *433*
Attitude of the Government *435*
Achievements of the Moderates *436*
The Surat Split (1907) *437*
Rise of Extremism or Militant Nationalism *439*
Partition of Bengal *440*
The Home Rule Movement *443*
Revolutionary and Terrorist Movement: Causes *444*
Maharashtra *444*
Bengal *445*
Punjab *446*
The Ghadar Party *446*
Post-war Movement *447*
Kakori Case *448*
Contribution of Revolutionaries *449*
India and World War I (1914-18) *449*
Jallianwala Bagh Tragedy *450*
Non-Cooperation Movement *451*
The Swarajist Party *453*
The Civil Disobedience Movement *454*
The Second World War and the Congress *457*
"Quit India" Movement *457*
Why England gave India Independence? *460*

22. Establishment of Pakistan — 464–479
Condition of Muslims before 1871 464
Work of Sir Syed Ahmed Khan 465
Work of Beck 466
Partition of Bengal and Its Effects 466
Lucknow Pact, 1916 469
Pakistan 472
Pakistan Resolution (1940) 473
Causes of Pakistan Demand 474
Dr. Latif's Scheme 476
The Aligarh Scheme 476
Formula of Rajagopalachari 477
Cabinet Mission 477

23. Leaders of Modern India — 480–491
Dadabhai Naoroji (1825-1917) 480
Gopal Krishan Gokhale (1866-1915) 481
Lokmanya Bal Gangadhar Tilak (1856-1920) 483
Mahatma Gandhi (1869-1948) 486

24. Decentralisation of Finance — 492–499
Mayo's Resolution (1870) 493
Lytton's Change 493
Ripon (1882) 494
Curzon 494
Decentralisation Commission 495
Resolution of 1912 495
Meston Settlement 496
Reforms of 1935 497
New Constitution 497

25. Public Services in India — 500–511
Reforms of Cornwallis 500
Lord Wellesley 501
Indian Civil Service Act 501
Aitchison Commission 502
Resolution of 1893 503
Islington Commission 503
Recommendations of 1918 Report 503
Lee Commission (1923) 504
Government of India Act, 1935 505
Services under the New Constitution of India 506
Public Service Commissions 507
Functions of Public Service Commissions 508
Shortcomings 510

26. Growth of Local Self-Government in India — 512–521
Presidency Towns 513
Non-Presidency Towns 514
Mayo's Resolution of 1870 514
Ripon's Resolution of 1881 514

Resolution of 1882   515
Decentralisation Commission Report (1909)   518
Resolution of 1918   518
Under Dyarchy   519
Defects in the Present System   520

27. History of the Press in India   522–533
Early History of the Press up to 1822   522
Munro's Recommendations   523
Licensing Act of 1857   524
Act of 1867   524
Vernacular Press Act, 1878   524
The Newspapers (Incitement to Offences) Act, 1908   525
The Indian Press Act, 1910   526
Criticism of the Act of 1910   527
The Indian Press (Emergency Powers) Act, 1931   528
Foreign Relations Act, 1932   529
Indian States (Protection) Act, 1934   530
Press Trust of India Ltd.   530
Press Laws Inquiry Committee, 1948   530
The Indian Constitution   531
Press (Objectionable Matter) Act, 1951   531
Press Commission   532

28. History of Education   534–543
Early history of education   534
Wood's Despatch of 1854   537
The Hunter Commission, 1882   538
Universities Act of 1904   539
Resolution of 1913   540
Calcutta University Commission   540
Sergeant Scheme for Education   541
Radhakrishnan Commission   541
University Grants Commission   542
Secondary Education Commission   542
Kothari Commission   542

29. Religious and Social Development   544–555
Raja Ram Mohan Roy (1774-1833)   544
Brahmo Samaj   546
Prarthana Samaj   547
The Theosophical Society   547
Ramakrishna Mission   547
Dev Samaj   548
Arya Samaj   548
Islam   549
Sikhs   550
Parsees   550
Christianity   550
Social Development   550

30. Anglo-Afghan Relations — 556–569
Afghan War I 558
Criticism of the Afghan War I 561
Lord Lawrence's Policy of Masterly Inactivity 562
Lord Mayo (1869-72) 565
Lord Northbrook (1872-76) 566
Lord Lytton 566
Criticism of the Second Afghan War 567

31. The North-Western Frontier Policy — 570–575
Sind Frontier 570
The Punjab Frontier 572
The Forward Policy 573

32. The Indian States — 576–613
Ring-Fence Policy (1757-1813) 576
Policy of Subordinate Isolation (1813-58) 577
Policy of Subordinate Union 578
British Paramountcy in India 579
The Gazette Notification Number 579
Minto's Udaipur Speech (November 1909) 582
Chamber of Princes 583
The Butler Committee 584
Government of India Act, 1935 587
Accession of States 593
Integration and Democratisation of States 605
The States Reorganisation Commission 607
The States Reorganisation Act, 1956 609
Border Disputes between Maharashtra and Mysore 612

33. Legacy of British Rule in India — 614–621

34. Economic Impact of British Rule in India — 622–629
Peasantry 622
Zamindars 623
Agriculture 623
Industries 623
India a Colony 624
Economic Condition 624
Economic Drain 625
Favours to British industries 626
Railways 627
The Civil Services 628
Famines 628

35. Famines in India and Development of Famine Policy — 630–635
Bengal Famine of 1769-70 630
Famine of 1860-61 631
Famine of 1865-66 631
Campbell Committee 631
Famine of 1868-70 631

Famine of 1873-74   632
Famine of 1876-78   632
Strachey Commission   632
Lyall Commission   633
Famine of 1900   633
MacDonnel Commission   634
Bengal Famine (1943)   634

36. Peasants' Movement and Uprisings 636–645
The Santhals' Rebellion (1855-73)   636
The Revolt of 1857-58   637
Strike of Bengal Indigo Cultivators   637
East Bengal (1872-76)   638
Maharashtra (1875)   638
Moplah Peasants   639
Riots in Assam   639
The Punjab Land Alienation Act, 1900   639
South India in Ferment   640
Champaran (1917-18)   640
Satyagraha of Kaira (1918)   641
Moplah Rebellion (1921)   641
Chauri Chaura (1922)   641
Vizag Revolution (1923)   642
Satyagraha Struggle between 1921-30   642
Bardoli Satyagraha (1929-30)   642
Revolts of Peasants in Indian States   642
Revolts under Communists   643
Revolt of Veera Gunnamma (1940)   643
August Revolution and Peasants   644
Revolt of Telengana   644

37. The Left Movements in India 646–655
The Communist Party of India   646
Meerut Conspiracy Case   648
The Communists and Government of India   650
Telengana   651
First General Elections and Communists   651
PEPSU   652
Split in Communist Party   652
The Congress Socialist Party   652
Forward Bloc   654

38. Role of Mahatma Gandhi in the Nationalist Movement 656–661

39. The Renaissance in India 662–675
Meaning of Renaissance in India   662
Sri Aurobindo on the Renaissance in India   663
Condition of India Before Renaissance   663
British Impact   664
Indologists   666
Indian Writers   667

  Rammohan Roy and Brahmo Samaj *668*
  Prarthana Samaj *669*
  Arya Samaj *670*
  Theosophical Society *670*
  Ramakrishna Paramhans *671*
  Swami Vivekananda (1863-1902) *671*
  Vernacular Literature *672*
  Spirit of Research and Discovery *673*
  Fine Arts *673*

40. Political, Cultural and Social Impact of British Rule **676–681**
  Political Effects *676*
  Impact in Cultural and Social Fields *679*

41. Changes in Land Revenue Settlement **682–691**
  Permanent Settlement of Bengal *682*
  Ryotwari System *685*
  Mahalwari System *688*
  Taluqdari System *690*

Chronological Table **692–696**
Index **697–700**

PART A

1. Decline and Disintegration of the Mughal Empire
2. Rise of Autonomous States
3. Society and Culture in the Eighteenth Century

1 Decline and Disintegration of the Mughal Empire

 LEARNING OBJECTIVES

- Know about the condition of India at the time of Aurangzeb's death
- Discuss the activities and achievements of Aurangzeb's successors
- Examine the causes of decline and disintegration of the Mughal empire

CONDITION OF INDIA AT THE TIME OF DEATH OF AURANGZEB

The Mughal Empire which had earned the admiration of contemporaries for its extensive territories, military might and cultural accomplishments disintegrated after the death of Aurangzeb. Within a short span of about 50 years, nine Mughal Emperors occupied the throne in quick succession and were not able to provide any effective government. Taking advantage of their weakness, many adventurers carved out independent principalities of their own and freed themselves from the central control.

Aurangzeb had created more problems during his reign than he was able to solve. It is true that some of them he inherited, but many of them were his creation. Those together shook the Mughal Empire to its very foundation. No wonder, the political and financial horizon at the time of his death betokened the dark prospects of decline, decay and dissolution. The glory of the Mughal Empire was becoming past history and its tragic end was in the offing. Stanley Lanepoole writes. "Even before the end of his reign, Hindustan was in confusion and the signs of coming dissolution had appeared. As some imperial corpse, preserved for ages in its dread seclusion, crowned and armed and still majestic, yet falls into dust at the mere breath of heaven, so fell the Empire of the Mughals when the great name that guarded it was no more. It was as though some splendid palace reared with infinite skill with the costliest stones and precious metals of the earth had attained its perfect beauty only to collapse in undistinguishable ruin when the insidious roots of the creeper sapped the foundation. Even if Aurangzeb had left a successor of his own mantle and moral stature, it may be doubted whether the process of disintegration could have been stayed. The disease was too far advanced for even the heroic surgery".

At the time of the death of Aurangzeb on 20 February 1707, the Mughal Empire consisted of 21 Subahs (provinces): one in Afghanistan, 14 in North India and 6 in Deccan. It embraced in the North Kashmir and all Afghanistan from the Hindukush southwards to a line 36 miles North of Ghazni, on the West coast stretched in theory to the Northern frontier of Goa and inland to Belgaum and the Tungabhadra river'. No Emperor of India since the death of Asoka had ruled over such extensive territories. The years 1686-89 which saw the annexation of Bijapur and Golkunda and the apparent collapse of the Maratha power, marked the zenith of Mughal political ascendancy. However, the vast extent of his Empire was a source of weakness and not strength. It was too large to be ruled by one man from one centre.

The religious policy of Aurangzeb affected the fortunes of the Mughal Empire. Religious persecution acted as a provocation in the risings of the Satnamis, the Bundelas and the Sikhs. The fear of suppression of Hinduism was an important factor. The urge to uphold Hindu Dharma stiffened the resistance of the Marathas. The imposition of Jizya offer ended the sentiments and injured the material interests of the Hindus. Aurangzeb's zeal for Islam weakened the foundations of his multi-religious imperial structure. The attempt to annex Marwar was a grave mistake. It led to a long and costly war in Rajasthan. It alienated the Rajputs whose political and military support had played a vital role in the consolidation and maintenance of Mughal power for a century.

The Deccan war of Aurangzeb contributed substantially to the decline of the Mughal Empire. That endless war exhausted the treasury. The Government became bankrupt. The soldiers starving from arrears of pay, mutinied. The Maratha country became "devoid of trees and bare of crops, their place being taken by the bones of men and beasts". In two years (1702-04), plague and famine took a toll of over two million souls. The Deccan war affected the administration and economy of North India. Aurangzeb's long absence from his capital weakened the Central Government in its relations with the provinces. The provincial Governors (Subahdars), largely free from his supervision and control, ceased to have respect or fear for imperial authority. The administrative machinery in the provinces was weakened because their best soldiers, highest officers and all their collected revenues were sent to in the Deccan. The older and more settled, peaceful and prosperous provinces in the North were left to be governed by minor officers with small contingents and incomes quite inadequate for maintaining central authority. All classes of lawless men began to raise their heads. Desultory war ruined large parts of Rajasthan. Some Rajput Zamindars created disturbances in Malwa. The plundering Maratha bands penetrated into Malwa and Gujarat. The Jats carried on raids in the Agra region. The Sikhs fought against the Mughal and the hill Rajas in the Punjab. In Bengal, there were hostilities between the English traders and the Mughal officers. In his exile in the Deccan, Aurangzeb lost his grip over the administration of those provinces which formed the backbone of the Mughal Empire.

A large portion of the income of the Mughal state was spent on the army on account of constant warfare. The number of Mansabdars rose from 8000 under Shah Jahan to 14,449 under Aurangzeb. The army bill of Aurangzeb was roughly double of that of Shah Jahan. Out of 14,449 Mansabdars under Aurangzeb, about 7,000 were paid through Jagirs and 7,450 were paid in cash. The Mansabdari system reached a crisis as a result of the enormous increase in the number of the Mansabdars who had to be paid through Jagirs. As the number of Jagirs was not adequate, many Mansabdars had to wait for some time before they could get Jagirs. Even when Jagirs were available in the Deccan, the Government could not always ensure security of tenure because those were often exposed to the risk of sudden occupation by the Marathas Constant military operations in the Deccan and disturbances and lawlessness in the North Indian provinces, reduced cultivation in both regions and the peasants were not able to pay their full dues to the Jagirdars. The uncertainty about the income from their Jagirs weakened the numerical strength of the army. Large-scale corruption crept into the Mansabdari system and sapped the foundations of the Mughal military power.

War, disorder and official exactions injured trade and industry. Trade almost ceased in the Deccan. The Maratha raiders made it almost impossible for caravans to travel North of the Narmada without strong escorts.

The Mughal nobles who were the pillars of the Empire, succumbed to the fatal vice of love of ease and luxury and became "pale persons in muslin petticoats". Immigration from Persia and Central Asia almost came to a stop. Alienated by Aurangzeb's policy of suspicion and hostility the

Rajputs were reluctant to serve the Mughal Empire. Moreover, Rajput society no longer produced warrior-statesmen like Man Singh and Raja Jai Singh. High-spirited, talented and energetic officers found themselves checked, discouraged and driven to sullen inactivity. Aurangzeb, in his later years, could bear no contradiction, could hear no unpalatable truth, but surrounded himself with smooth-tongued and pompous echoes of his own voice. His ministers became no better than clerks passively registering his edicts. Such nobles could not carry the burden of a great Empire. The only survivor of the old nobility in the last years of Aurangzeb's reign was Asad Khan about whom Aurangzeb said, "There is not, nor will there ever be, any Wazir better than Asad Khan".

There was 'inefficiency' in the Mughal army. It was composed of diverse racial elements and religious group such as Turks, Afghans, Rajputs and Hindustanis. It was a mercenary force. The real allegiance of the troops was not to the imperial throne but to the persons in immediate command. If a prince, or a Mansabdar or a tributary chief rebelled against the Mughal monarch, he usually carried his troops with him. The infantry was practically useless. There was no naval wing. The proportion of officers to men on active service was very low. The Mughal army moved like an unwieldy city and was incapable of swift action or brilliant adventure. The camp-followers were more than the combatants. Luxuries of camp life demoralised the nobles who were the leaders of the army. Ease-loving commanders could not maintain a high standard of discipline among the troops. There was no commissariat service. Each man had to make his own arrangement for transport. Supplies were provided by large Bazars marching with the army. Antiquated weapons were used and antiquated methods of warfare were followed. Aurangzeb made no attempt to improve the Mughal army except that he doubled the number of Mansabdars and added to the number *of* troops.

At the end of Aurangzeb's reign, the Mughal Empire "was in a state of hopeless decay: administration, culture, economic life military strength and social organisation— all seemed to be hastening to utter ruin and dissolution".

SUCCESSORS OF AURANGZEB

Bahadur Shah I (1707-12)

In the closing years of his life, Aurangzeb was perturbed by the gloomy prospects of a bloody war among his sons. Therefore, he attempted an equitable distribution of the Empire among his sons. He intended that his eldest son Muazzam should receive 12 Subahs with his capital at Delhi. Mohammad Azam should have Agra, the Subahs of the Deccan, Malwa and Gujarat. His youngest son Kam Baksh was to have the provinces of Bijapur and Hyderabad. Though the will of Aurangzeb is considered to be of doubtful veracity, the presence of Muazzam in Kabul, deputation of Kam Baksh by his father to Bijapur and that of Mohammad Azam to Malwa, lend support to the presumption that Aurangzeb did not want his sons to fight among themselves after his death.

However, the wish of Aurangzeb was not respected. When Aurangzeb died, Wazir Asad Khan who was the master of the situation, assembled the other Amirs and in consultation with them, sent messengers to Mohammad Azam asking him to return post-haste to Ahmednagar. Mohammad Azam arrived there and was proclaimed king on 14 March 1707. Most of the officers and commanders tendered their submission to the new Emperor but there were others who were indifferent towards him. Even Asad Khan became lukewarm later on. The disqualification of Mohammad Azam was that he had Shia inclinations. Unmindful of the attitude of the nobles, Mohammad Azam decided to march straight to Agra.

Muazzam was not sitting idle. He left Kabul and arrived at Pul-i-Shah Daulah where he celebrated his accession and took up the title of Bahadur Shah. He had already conciliated Budh

Singh Hada of Bundi and Bijay Singh Kachhwaha of Amber and through them had enlisted a large number of Rajputs. His second son lost no time and marched towards Agra where he joined his father. The capital fell into the hands of Muazzam who thereby scored a march over his rival. The rival armies of Muazzam and Azam faced each other at Jajau near Samugarh. There was a bloody battle in which Azam and his two sons Bidar Bakht and Wala Jah were killed.

Muazzam had still to fight against Kam Baksh who had already got the Khutba recited and coins struck in his name in the Deccan. Bahadur Shah at first followed a policy of conciliation towards Kam Baksh, but when that failed, he marched to Hyderabad and arrived there in January 1709. On the eve of the decisive battle which occurred on 13 January 1709, the position of Kam Baksh was pitiable. He had neither men nor money. However, both Kam Baksh and his son fought bravely. They were wounded and captured. Kam Baksh was brought to Bahadur Shah in a palanquin and Bahadur Shah was very affectionate towards him, but Kam Baksh died at night. Thus ended the war of succession and Bahadur Shah became the undisputed lord of the Mughal Empire.

Immediately after his victory, Mohammad Azam Bahadur Shah conferred new titles and higher ranks on his supporters, Munim Khan and his son Naim Khan. Munim Khan was appointed Wazir. However, being a man of conciliatory nature, Bahadur Shah invited to his court the associates of his rival and not only forgave them for their opposition to him but also gave them their due share in the Government. Asad Khan, the Wazir of Aurangzeb, was offered a new office of Wakil-i-Mutlaq and his son Zulfiqar Khan was made the Bakshi. However, by investing the office of the Chief Minister in two persons, Bahadur Shah opened the flood gates of intrigue and contest for supreme power in the Government. Though in keeping with the nature of the new Emperor, this compromise gave birth to a tradition which was pregnant with potentialities of harm. The rivalry of Munim Khan and Asad Khan was relieved for the time being by sending Asad Khan to Delhi and heaping on him a further appointment of the Governor of that city. Asad Khan's family had also been in possession of the Subadari of the Deccan to which the Wakil-i-Mutlaq and his son clung.

When Bahadur Shah ascended the throne, he was more than 63 and he had passed the age when he could be expected to show initiative in any work. He was a man of mild and equitable temper, learned, dignified and generous. He was incapable of saying no to anybody and his idea of statesmanship was to let matters drift and patch up a temporary peace by humouring everybody without facing issues and saving future trouble by making decisions promptly and courageously. Though he did not suffer from any vice, his complacency and negligence earned for him the title of Shah-i-Bekhabar (Heedless King). It was during his reign that intrigues began to increase at the royal court and he felt that he was too weak to suppress them. Though not a great sovereign, he was still more successful than his successor in maintaining the dignity of the Empire. He was profuse in the grant of titles and rewards and did not keep tight control over the administration.

Dr. A.L. Srivastava writes about Bahadur Shah, "He followed his father's policy of religious intolerance, retained the Jizya and did not appoint the Hindus to high posts". This is considered to be an extreme view of Bahadur Shah. He was better than his father in his religious policy. If he had been in the prime of his life, he might have done much to arrest the progress of the dissolution of the Mughal Empire by his conciliatory and tolerant policy.

Bahadur Shah was a Shia by faith and that led to the growth of two parties in the court. The Irani party consisted of nobles like Asad khan and his son Zulfiqar Khan who professed the Shia faith. The Turani party consisted of powerful nobles like Chin Qilch Khan and Ghazi-ud-din Feroz Jang who followed the Sunni beliefs of Islam. This political strife between the parties further weakened the Mughal Empire.

The Rajputs. Bahadur Shah had to deal with many problems. As regards the Rajputs, the embers of disaffection were still there. The Rathor ruler, Ajit Singh, had expelled the imperial officers after the death of Aurangzeb and occupied his capital Jodhpur. The Rajput ruler of Amber, Jay Singh, had offended Bahadur Shah by helping Muhammad Azam. Rana Amar Singh of Udaipur was not friendly towards Bahadur Shah. The ruler of Kotah was in the Deccan with Zulfiqar Khan and the ruler of Bundi was with Bahadur Shah. The strategic position of Rajput states demanded immediate action. Bahadur Shah resolved to march to Jodhpur by way of Amber and Ajmer. His departure from Agra cowed down the spirits of the Rana of Udaipur who sent his brother to Bahadur Shah along with a letter of congratulations and numerous costly presents. As regards Amber, it was given to Bijay Singh who was a rival claimant to Amber. Ajit Singh of Jodhpur was defeated and the fort of Merta was captured. Ajit Singh surrendered and he was not only pardoned but also given a special robe of honour and title of Maharaja and his rank was fixed at 3500 Zat and 3000 Sawar. His two sons were also enrolled Mansabdars. However, the peace restored in Rajputana did not prove to be enduring. Ajit Singh, Jay Singh and Amar Singh formed a confederacy with the object of completely rooting out the Mughal influence from Rajputana. The allies invested Jodhpur and compelled its Faujdar to abandon the fort. They marched towards Agra and defeated the Faujdar of Hindaun and Bayana. However, they were defeated by the Faujdars of Mewat and Narnaul. Bahadur Shah assembled armies against the Rajputs but at the same time followed a policy of conciliation. The result was that Jay Singh and Ajit Singh were restored to their former ranks. Bahadur Shah might have taken action against the Rajputs but the situation in the Punjab precipitated his departure. In his Rajput policy, Bahadur Shah was firm in suppressing the insurgents but he was not against a compromise with them.

The Sikhs. Bahadur Shah had to deal with the Sikhs in the Punjab. Under the leadership of Gobind Singh, the Sikhs had carried a fierce struggle against Aurangzeb, but after his death, Bahadur Shah became friendly with the Sikh Guru. The Guru met Bahadur Shah at Agra and was received with honours due to him. He was successfully persuaded to accompany the Mughal army to the Deccan. On reaching Nander, the Guru separated himself from the Emperor and decided to pass the rest of his life there. However, he was murdered on 17 November 1708. Banda Bahadur assumed the military leadership of the Sikhs at that stage. He collected thousands of Sikhs from various parts of the Punjab to fight against the Muslims and captured Kaithal, Samana, Shahabad, Ambala, Kapuri and Sadhura. His greatest victory was against Wazir Khan, Governor of Sirhind whom he defeated and killed. After a wholesale massacre of the Muslim population of Sirhind, Banda Bahadur captured Saharanpur. In this way, the entire territory between the Sutlej and Jamuna passed into the hands of the Sikhs. The Sikh forces reached the outskirts of Delhi and took to plunder.

When the inhabitants of Sirhind, Thaneshwar etc. represented their tales of woe and misery to Bahadur Shah, he hurried to the scene of trouble in June 1710. He bypassed Delhi, prohibited his soldiers from visiting the capital and issued orders to the Hindus in his train to shave off their beards so that they may be distinguished from the enemy. Extensive preparations were made to suppress the insurrection. In the face of the heavy odds against them, the Sikhs were unable to keep firm to their ground. They were driven out of Thaneshwar, ousted from Sirhind, expelled from Lahore, closely invested at Lohgarh and were made to suffer crushing defeats at numerous places. However, they did not give up their plan of harassing the imperialists and plundering those who sided with them. On account of the differences between the two Mughal generals, Banda was able to effect his escape. There were fresh disturbances in the Bari Doab; but the Sikhs were defeated. Banda was exposed to a grave danger. However, the preoccupation of the Mughals elsewhere saved the Sikhs for the time being.

The Deccan. As regards the Deccan policy of Bahadur Shah, it appears that he was not able to formulate a clear-cut and decisive policy. After the death of Kam Baksh, Zulfiqar Khan was appointed the Viceroy of the Deccan. He favoured conciliation with the Marathas, but the Vazir Munim Khan made a different approach. Bahadur Shah released Sahu, son of Sambhaji and grandson of Shivaji. That was done on the suggestion of Zulfiqar Khan. Sahu was given his former Mansab but the Emperor was reluctant to recognise his claims to Chauth and Sardeshmukhi on the six Sabahs of the Deccan. This did not work and the Marathas restarted their plundering raids. They ravaged even the Jagirs of Zulfiqar Khan. His representative secretly concluded a pact with Sahu by which his claims were conceded but that was not confirmed by the Emperor. The result was that the Deccan remained a scene of confusion and lawlessness.

Bahadur Shah died on 27 February 1712 and with him disappeared over the last semblance of the glory and greatness of the Mughals. He held the reins of administration in his hand. His word was final in the state. He rose high above party factions and court intrigues. Unlike his successors, he cannot be said to have played the role of a mere puppet. When Banda escaped capture, Bahadur Shah reprimanded his favourite Prime Minister Munim Khan. He showed firmness and discretion in his dealings with the Rajputs but he failed to solve the Rajput problem. He might have succeeded in suppressing the Sikhs but before he could do so he died. Though his attitude towards the Hindus was less intolerant than that of Aurangzeb, he did not abolish Jizya or cancel discriminatory regulation against the Hindus. He failed to arrest the acceleration of the financial crisis. He granted Jagirs recklessly and gave promotions and rewards to all and sundry. The result was that before his death, the royal treasury was empty and the salary of artillery men had fallen into arrears.

About Bahadur Shah, Sidney Owen writes, "He was the last Emperor of whom anything favourable can be said. Henceforth, the rapid and complete abasement and practical dissolution of the Empire are typified in the incapacity and political insignificance of its sovereigns". Khafi Khan observes, "For generosity, munificence, boundless good nature, extenuation of faults and forgiveness of offences, very few monarchs have been found equal to Bahadur Shah in the histories of past times and especially in the race of Taimur. But though he had no vice in his character, such complacency and such negligence were exhibited in the protection of the state and in the Government and management of the country, that witty sarcastic people found the date of his accession in the words. 'Shah-i-Bekhabar (Heedless King)'". According to Irvine, "Bahadur Shah was a man of mild and equitable temper, learned, dignified and generous to a fault".

Jahandar Shah (1712-13)

The death of Bahadur Shah was followed by a civil war among his four sons, Jahandar Shah, Azim-ush-Shan, Jahan Shah and Rafi-ush-Shan. The contestants were in such indecent haste about deciding the question of succession that the dead body of Bahadur Shah was not buried for about a month. Jahandar Shah came out successful with the help of Zulfiqar Khan. Azim-ush-Shan was defeated and he disappeared in a sand-storm which swept the bed of the Ravi. Jahan Shah was killed in the encounter with Zulfiqar Khan. Rafi-ush-Shan was deserted and received but he fought valiantly and faced death with the supreme courage of a soldier.

Jahandar Shah was about 52 years of age at the time of his accession to the throne. He celebrated his success by making new appointments and distributing largesses to his supporters. Zulfiqar Khan became the Chief Minister. His father Asad Khan retained the title of Wakil-i-Mutlaq. The friends of Zulfiqar Khan were introduced into other high offices. The new reign did not stop with merely rewarding friends and supporters, but also took to execution, imprisonment and confiscation of property of those who had joined the vanquished princes. The new Wazir fortified his position by surrounding himself with his supporters and eliminated opposition by destroying the unfriendly ones.

The new Emperor moved from Lahore to Delhi and the next few months in the capital "were given up to dissipation" and the city "for a time fell under the domination of the Lord of Misrule. Grand illuminations took place three times in every month. So much oil was used that it rose to be half seer weight the rupee; then all the oil being expended, they had recourse to clarified butter until it too ceased to be procurable. Grain also grew very dear".

Sidney Owen writes, "Jahandar Shah was an utterly degenerate representative of the house of Timur, Babar and Akbar. Frivolous, profligate, cruel and cowardly, servilely devoted to a favourite lady Lal Kanwar whose relatives he promoted wholesale to high honours to the disgust of the old nobles and the able and experienced servants of the state, he soon became generally odious and despicable". Jahandar Shah indulged in acts which for their impropriety, indecency and even cruelty, were unprecedented and helped considerably to bring down the prestige of royalty. The Emperor did not even desist from visiting the vegetable market in the company of Lal Kanwar in a bullock cart and exposed himself to the abuses of the women selling vegetables. On one of them, Zuhra, was bestowed high rank and Jagirs were assigned to her. Her retinue came into clash with that of Chin Qilch Khan who later became Nizam-ul-Mulk. The behaviour of Lal Kanwar and her hold over the Emperor caused anger and estrangement in the royal family. The lack of decorum which the Emperor exhibited in the company of Lal Kanwar and her relations, the low musicians who gathered every night to drink with the Emperor in the palace, created a strong feeling of resentment and all respect or fear for the Emperor ceased. The nobles and men of position shunned the company of the Emperor.

The Emperor set the evil example of a licentious and effeminate court life and vitiated the morals of the ruling class. His influence made the recovery of the old imperial glory impossible. He was reduced to a puppet. All authority was wielded by the Wazir, Zulfiqar Khan and the ministers who passed on their duties to their deputies. Responsibilities were divided and offices were transferred from person to person according to the whim and fancy of the minister in power. The temporary incumbents used those opportunities to make rapid gains. The result was that administration was neglected and disorder spread. All sense of loyalty vanished. During his reign of eleven months, Jahandar Shah squandered away most of the treasures accumulated by his predecessors. The gold and silver and other precious articles collected since the time of Babar were thrown away.

The Emperor was not alone in introducing chaos and disaffection. Zulfiqar Khan followed suit and left most of his official work to a favourite, Subhag Chand, who by his overbearingness offended all and sundry. A feud developed between Zulfiqar Khan and Khan Jahan Kokaltash, the foster-brother of Jahandar Shah, who exploited the affection of the Emperor for him to supplant the former in the ministership. All this was happening at the capital, aggravating the weakness of the central authority.

Zulfiqar Khan was overtaken with senile decay. By delegating all his authority to Subhag Chand, he lost all the influence he had built up. He was bitterly hated like his master. With such persons at the helm of affairs, the fate of the Empire can better be imagine than described.

When such was the state of affairs at the capital, Farrukh-siyar, the second son of Azim-ush-Shan, took advantage of it. He won over the support of Sayyid Hussain Ali, the Governor of Patna and Sayyid Abdullah, the Governor of Allahabad. He advanced with a large following to contest the throne with his uncle. He overcame the opposition of his cousin Aziz-ud-din who blocked his way at Khajuha. Near Agra, he confronted Jahandar Shah. Jahandar Shah deserted the army and fled from the battlefield in the company of Lal Kanwar to Delhi in a bullock cart. Zulfiqar Khan was already making fast for the capital. Jahandar Shah took protection with Asad Khan, the Vakil-i-Mutlaq, who betrayed him to his enemies. For such an act of treachery, Asad Khan and his son Zulfiqar Khan, had to pay dearly. Asad Khan suffered disgrace and Zulfiqar Khan was put to death. Jahandar Shah was also put to death on 11 February 1713.

Irvine writes, "Jahandar Shah was the first sovereign of the house of Timur who proved himself absolutely unfitted to rule because of his extreme profligacy, cruel nature, shallowness of mind and cowardice". Iradat Khan, a contemporary historian, wrote about Jahandar Shah, "He was a weak man, devoted to pleasure, who gave himself no trouble about state affairs, or to gain the attachment of any of the nobility". Warid attributed the fall of Jahandar Shah to the "morning slumbering and mid-night carousing". In the reign of Jahandar Shah, "the owl dwelt in the eagle's nest and the crow took the place of the nightingale". Khafi Khan wrote, "In the brief reign of Jahandar Shah, violence and debauchery had full sway. It was a fine time for minstrels and singers and all the tribes of dancers and actors. There seemed to be a likelihood that Qazis would turn tosspots, and Muftis became tipplers. All the brothers and relatives, close and distant, of Lal Kanwar, received Mansabs of four or five thousand, presents of elephants, drums and jewels, and were raised to dignity in their tribe. Worthy; talented and learned men were driven away and bold and impudent wits and tellers of fictitious anecdotes gathered round".

Farrukh-siyar (1713-19)

At the time of his accession to the throne, Farrukh-siyar was a youngman of 30. Although he was extremely handsome, he was utterly weak, thoughtless and devoid of physical and moral courage. He was faithless to promises, ungrateful to benefactors, tortuous in intrigues, cowardly and cruel. He was led by personal favourites, Mir Jumla and Khan Dauran Khan. He started picking up quarrels with the Sayyid Brothers and tried to exercise real power. As the Sayyid Brothers had put him on the throne, they demanded complete control over the Government, particularly in the matter of appointments and distribution of the spoils of victory. From day to day the conflict became more and more bitter. Farrukh-siyar resorted to treachery and intrigue, of the dirtiest type to dispose of the Sayyid Brothers.

When Farrukh-siyar ascended the throne, he appointed Sayyid Abdullah as Prime Minister with the title of Qutb-ul-Mulk. He appointed Husain Ali as Mir Bakshi with the title of Amir-ul-Umara. During his rule of about seven years, Farrukh-siyar was constantly afflicted by mental conflict caused by his will to assert his power and prerogative and by his concern not to wound the susceptibilities of his benefactors, the Sayyid Brothers. His weakness of will prevented him from taking bold decisions and suppressing his enemies. He proved himself unfit to be a sovereign.

Military Campaigns. Three military campaigns were undertaken during his reign to suppress the spirit of defiance prevailing in Northern India. In Marwar, Ajit Singh had reasserted his independence and even occupied Ajmer. Husain Ali marched against him and pursued him from pillar to post. In the end, Ajit Singh begged for peace which was granted on the condition that he gave one of his daughters in marriage to the Emperor, sent his son Abhay Singh to the court and promised to attend in person whenever summoned.

One of the greatest achievements of Farrukh-siyar was the defeat of the Sikhs under Banda Bahadur. Taking advantage of the chaos which prevailed after the death of Bahadur Shah, the Sikhs under Banda Bahadur had increased their power. Farrukh-siyar decided to suppress their power. He appointed Abdul Samad as the Governor of Lahore in 1714 with specific instructions to crush the Sikhs. In the meanwhile, dissensions occurred in the ranks of the Sikhs with the result that a large number of Sikh soldiers withdrew their support from Banda Bahadur. The Mughal Governor took full advantage of the new development and compelled Banda Bahadur to evacuate Lohgarh and retreat to Gurdaspur. Even there he was not allowed to live in peace. The place was stormed and Banda was forced to surrender in December 1715. Along with his 740 followers, he was taken prisoner and brought to Delhi where he was brutally put to death. V.A. Smith writes, "Banda was executed with fiendish tortures".

The third military project related to the suppression of the Jats who had become strong under the leadership of Churaman who had started levying unauthorised road-tolls, terrorised the local Jagirdars and constructed a stronghold at Thun. Raja Jay Singh pressed him hard and Churaman approached the Wazir to secure pardon for him and the same was given.

Party Politics. Party politics formed an important phase in the court life during the reign of Farrukh-siyar. There was jealousy and rivalry among the nobles belonging to different factions, particularly the Turan's, the Irans, the Afghans and Hindustanis. The Turanis had come from Transoxiana and they professed the Sunni faith. The Iranis had migrated from the Eastern and Western provinces of Iran and were Shias. The Afghans had come from the mountainous border regions across the Indus and many of them belonged to the Rohilla tribe. They were mostly Sunnis. Among the Hindustani nobles were Muslim families who had settled in India for many generations and were jealous of the new arrivals. These factions remained under control till the death of Bahadur Shah I. However, after that, their importance and influence increased because every rival claimant to the imperial throne asked for their help. Each faction tried to establish its control over the person of the Emperor and was prepared to adopt any means to achieve its objective. These parties conformed neither to religion nor to race nor even to nationality. As to principles, there were none whatsoever. It was the individuals and their satellites who mattered. Their governing passion was self-interest and their guiding maxim was personal aggrandisement. None cared for the fairness or foulness of the means to achieve its end. The repercussions of such display of rivalry and disunity were far-reaching on the fortunes of the Empire and disastrous for Farrukh-siyar.

The Mughal imperial court was the centre of intrigues and counter-intrigues by one party against the other. The palace revolutions of king-making were the work of the Hindustani party under the leadership of the Sayyid Brothers, while the more effective and real revolution by which was brought about the fall of the Sayyid Brothers was the work of the Irani or Turani party, also called "Emperor's friends". This triumph of the king's friends over the kingmakers was of very great importance in history. Asaf Jah and his brother Mohammad Amin Khan thus gained ascendancy later in the court and became the pillars of the Mughal imperial court. None of these parties had any solid national programme before them which could have given them the name of political parties. They were only party factions which concerned themselves merely with efforts for their personal ascendancy and achievement of their selfish ends. The worst consequence of this party politics was that the Mughal imperial Court became a hotbed of intrigues which produced confusion and chaos in the Court and thus resulted in corruption and inefficiency in the entire governmental machinery of the Empire.

Plot against the Sayyid Brothers. Farrukh-siyar participated in three plots against the Sayyid Brothers. When Husain Ali was deputed to lead the imperial forces to quell the insurrection in Rajputana, secret letters were written to Ajit Singh Rathor, the rebel Raja of Jodhpur, promising him rich reward if he did away with Husain Ali. However, the plot failed. Ajit Singh submitted and passed on the letters of Farrukh-siyar to Husain Ali.

Another plot was hatched. Nizam-ul-Mulk, the Viceroy of the Deccan, was recalled and the province was put under the charge of Husain Ali. When Husain Ali was to the way to the South, Daud Khan, Deputy Governor of the Deccan, was secretly instigated to obstruct him. However, Daud Khan was defeated and killed and the plot failed.

An attempt was made on the life of Saiyad Abdullah Khan under the very nose of the Emperor. At the Nauroz ceremonies, the Wazir Abdullah Khan was to be surrounded and assassinated or imprisoned. However, the plot miscarried. Abdullah Khan came to know of the trap and overawed Farrukh-siyar by a large massing of the troops in advance.

Professor S.R. Sharma writes, "In the face of such persistent dangers, the Sayyid Brothers would have been fools if they also did not make efforts to weaken, outwit or overawe their enemies". The result was that there were manoeuvre and counter-manoeuvres. Farrukh-siyar tried one trusted noble after another to lay hold of Abdullah Khan while his brother Husain Ali was in the Deccan, but none had the courage to carry out his nefarious design. Raja Ajit Singh, the father-in-law of Farrukh-siyar, was called for help by the Emperor. The Raja knew the character of his son-in-law. He came to Delhi but he threw in his lot with Abdullah Khan. Even Nizam-ul-Mulk and his cousin Muhammad Amin Khan turned against the Emperor. When the imperial officers were fighting against the rebellious Jats, their chieftain Churaman Jat was helped secretly by Abdullah Khan.

The relations between the Emperor and the Sayyid Brothers were very much strained. There was an improvement for some time when Mir Jumla, the favourite of the Emperor, was sent away to Patna and Husain Ali left for the Deccan as the Subedar of the six Subahs of the Deccan. However, the fire of misunderstanding was fanned to full fury again when Mir Jumla came back from Patna and Nizam-ul-Mulk from the Deccan and Inayatullah Kashmiri was appointed Diwan-i-Khalsa, much against the wishes of Sayyid Abdullah Khan. The quest by Farrukh-siyar of a substitute for Abdullah Khan brought the quarrel to a head. Abdullah Khan succeeded in weaning away from the side of the Emperor all his supporters. He then sent express messages to his brother Husain Ali in the Deccan asking him to return to Delhi as quickly as possible.

To provide against all eventualities, Husain Ali opened negotiations with Peshwa, Balaji Vishwanath who demanded the recognition of Sahu's succession to Shivaji's kingdom, the right of levying Chauth and Sardesh-mukhi on the six provinces of the Deccan, confirmation of recent Maratha conquests in Berar, Gondwana, Karnatak and the return of Sahu's mother and his family to the Deccan. In lieu of those concessions, the Peshwa promised to pay a tribute or Peshkush for Sardeshmukhi, to preserve and guard peace in the Deccan and in return for Chauth place 15,000 Maratha horsemen at the disposal of Husain Ali. As the terms were advantageous to both the parties, the bargain was struck. When those were placed before the Emperor, he rejected them. When Husain Ali reached Delhi in 1719, he resolved to end the sorry state of affairs. In his army were 11,000 Maratha troops led by Peshwa Balaji Vishwanath, Senapati Khande Rao Dabhade, Santaji Bhonsle and others. The city was thrown into a state of alarm and so was the Emperor. He made desperate efforts to undo the mischief by placating the Sayyid Brothers, but they were impervious' to tears and threats alike. The Emperor was completely isolated. Even his father-in-law, Ajit Singh, deserted him. The fort and palace in Delhi were cleared of the partisans of the Emperor who had taken refuge in women's compartments. He was overpowered, dragged out, blinded and confined in a "bare, dark unfurnished hole". He was subjected to all sorts of tortures by his jailors. Bitter and over-salted dishes were served to him. Even slow poisoning was attempted for some time. However, he survived. At last, executioners were sent and they strangled him to death on 28 April 1719. This was the first instance of a Mughal sovereign losing his life at the hands of a noble and the Sayyid Brothers had to pay for their crime with their blood.

About Farrukh-siyar, Irvine writes, "Farrukh-siyar was feeble, cowardly and contemptible and strong neither for evil nor for good and his attempt to assert his own power made his reign throughout an agitated and perplexing one, ending in another imperial tragedy". Again, "The Way of doing what had become almost a necessity was unduly harsh, too utterly regardless of the personal dignity of the fallen monarch. Blinding a deposed king was the fixed usage, for that the Sayyids are not especially to blame. But the severity of the subsequent confinement was excessive and the taking of the captive's life was an extremity entirely uncalled for". Khafi Khan says, "Farrukh-siyar had no will of his own. He was young, inexperienced in business and inattentive to business of state. He had grown up in Bengal far away from his grandfather and father. He was entirely dependent on the opinions of others for he had no resolution or discretion. By the help of fortune, he had seized the crown. The timidity of his character contrasted with the vigour of the race of Timur and he was not cautious in listening to the words of artful men". It is said of Farrukh-siyar that "like all weak men, he was swayed by the latest adviser and having resolved to do a thing could never hold to it long but soon sank into despair and went back on his undertakings. Constitutionally incapable of governing by his own will and controlling others, he would not trust any able agent, but was easily inspired by a childish suspicion of his ministers and enticed to enter into plots for their overthrow". Dr. A.L. Srivastava observes about Farrukh-siyar, "He had proved to be the most incapable ruler of the house of Babar that had so far occupied the throne of Delhi".

It is worthy of notice that during the reign of Farrukh-siyar, the Mughal Empire drifted towards dissolution. There was disorder everywhere. Chiefs, landholders and leaders of tribal bands began to defy the authority of the Government. There were fights in the streets of Delhi among the followers of different nobles. Roads became infested with thieves and robbers. The Emperor himself set the example of misappropriating provincial revenues on their way to the imperial treasury and his example was followed by ambitious adventurers. The orders of the Government began to be openly flouted. Officers left their posts without permission. Rules and regulations were neglected. Corruption and inefficiency prevailed. As troops were not paid, they mutinied.

Rafi-ud-Darajat

From the deposition of Farrukh-siyar on 28 February 1719 to the accession of Muhammad Shah on 24 September 1719, three princes were raised to the throne like bubbles of water rising to the surface, only to end their ephemeral existence in a very short time.

After the deposition of Farrukh-siyar, the Sayyid Brothers raised to the throne a puppet named Rafi-ud-Darajat. The Marathas were permitted to return to the Deccan. They carried with them three Farmans granting the concessions demanded by them.

The cruelty of the Sayyid Brothers towards Farrukh-siyar was resented by the people of Delhi. Ajit Singh was subjected to insult and ridicule. The rivals of the Sayyid Brothers set up Niku-siyar, another puppet Emperor, at Agra. Added to that was the growing mistrust and rivalry between the Sayyid Brothers themselves. Abdullah Khan favoured settlement with Niku-siyar but Husain Ali insisted upon a fight with him and his view prevailed. Meanwhile, the health of Rafi-ud-Darajat began to decline fast and on his suggestion the Sayyid Brothers raised to the throne his elder brother Rafi-ud-Daulah on 6 June 1719.

Rafi-ud-Daulah

The new Mughal Emperor was virtually a prisoner in the charge of Sayyid Himmat Khan Barha. He was not permitted to attend the Friday prayers, not to go out hunting nor even to converse with any nobles, except in the presence of his custodian. He fell ill and died on 17 September 1719.

Muhammad Shah (1719-48)

After the death of Rafi-ud-Daulah, Muhammad Shah was put on the throne by the Sayyid Brothers. He was the fourth son of Emperor Bahadur Shah I. It is said of him that never before a more carefree sovereign had sat on the throne of Delhi. He was a young boy of 17 who had passed most of his time within the four walls of the palace, in the society of eunuchs and ladies of the harem. None had cared for his education because none thought that he would sit on the throne of Delhi. Though fairly intelligent, he never attempted to make use of his wits. He was of a generous disposition. He never gave his consent to the shedding of blood or doing harm to the creatures of God. He was timid and wavering. He was a lover of pleasure, indolent and addicted to loose habits. He made it a rule of his life never to decide anything for himself. He left that work for his favourites. He readily listened to the advice of others without pausing to reflect upon the consequences of accepting it. He had no initiative, nor even the dash of his predecessors. He was utterly ignorant of the elementary rules of the game of politics and the pity was that he was not anxious to know them. Rustam Ali writes, "Muhammad Shah was negligent of his duties; but the fact is that he did not know if he had any duties to perform".

Muhammad Shah took no interest in the affairs of the Government. He spent his time in frivolous pursuits surrounded by favourites. He left everything to his Wazir Qamar-ud-din Khan, son of Mir Muhammad Amin Khan. Unfortunately, the Wazir was also an indolent, procrastinating and pleasure-loving person. Delhi was left without a Government. The provincial governments got no help from the Centre in the hour of their need. When Nadir Shah threatened Afghanistan and the Mughal Governor of Kabul asked for help, nobody cared for his request. The leading nobles were jealous of the power of the Wazir and intrigued against the Mughal Empire with its enemies. They shirked all military tasks involving any risk. None of them was willing to face the Marathas. They invented excuses when they were asked to proceed against the Raja of Jodhpur. The results were disastrous. The Mughal Empire began to disintegrate. Many provinces virtually became independent. Murshid Quli Khan in Bengal, Bihar and Orissa (now Odisha) and Saadat Khan in Avadh paid only nominal allegiance to the Mughal Emperor at Delhi. The Nizam set up an independent dynasty of his own in the Deccan. In the Doab, the Rohillahas set up autonomous chieftainships. The Marathas occupied Gujarat, Malwa and a part of Bundelkhand. The Governors of Kabul and Lahore were left to their own resources.

For full one year after his accession. Muhammad Shah remained a virtual prisoner in the hands of the Sayyid Brothers. He was surrounded by "numbers of their trusted adherents; and when occasionally, in the course of two or three months, he went out of hunting and for an excursion into the country, they went with him and brought him back". Even after the disappearance of the Sayyid Brothers, Muhammad Shah fell into the clutches of Rahmat-un-Nisa Koki Jiu, eunuch Hafiz Khidmatgar Khan, Shah Abdul Ghaffar and Turrabaz Raushan-ud-Daulah Zafar Khan Panipati. In 1739, they were supplanted by Khan Dauran Samsamud-Daulah and his brother Muzaffar Khan. After their death in 1739, they were succeeded by Amir Khan, Muhammad Ishaq, Asad Yar and Safdarjang.

For about 13 years, Koki Jiu and her associates brought havoc in the kingdom. She was authorised by Muhammad Shah to impress the official documents with the royal seal and extract money from all sources for him. The regret of the Emperor was that he could not make her Wazir on account of her sex. Her four brothers were given high ranks. Their total annual income from the Jagirs amounted to ₹25 lakhs. Shah Abdul Ghafur, her companion, pillaged the public purse without fear or shame. His income from Jagirs and other sources was ₹25,000 daily, apart from his equal share in the bribes with Koki Jiu. He boasted that money was power which could control clouds and check the rains. He got for his son a Mansab of 6000 and for himself a rare exemption from customary prostration in the court. His son became a nuisance to the public. He committed many acts of high handedness. The result was that both the father and son were hated. There was a storm of protests against their activities and ultimately they were removed with great difficulty.

Muhammad Shah spent most of his time in watching animal fights. On account of his indifference towards public affairs and addiction to wine and women, he was called Muhammad Shah *"Rangila"*.

The reign of Muhammad Shah can be divided into two periods, the dividing point being the invasion of Nadir Shah in 1739. The main interest in the political sphere centres round the steady expansion of Maratha power and influence and its pressure on Mughal territory. They spread the network of their activity from Gujarat to Bengal and from the Narmada to the Jamuna, and even up to the river Ravi in the Punjab. Their leader was Peshwa Baji Rao I. It was under him that the Marathas cut across the limits of the Deccan and carried their arms right to the very heart of the Mughal Empire.

Fall of the Sayyid Brothers. Muhammad Shah resented the authority of the Sayyid Brothers. The leaders of the Turani faction, Nizam-ul-Mulk, Subedar of the Deccan, Mir Muhammad Amin Khan, head of the Mughal soldiery and his cousin Abdus Samad Khan, Governor of Lahore, as well as the chiefs of the Irani faction were tired of the Sayyids and they decided to destroy them. The Sayyid Brothers conciliated Jay Singh who never made a secret of his pro-Farrukh-siyar sympathy by assigning to him the Sarkar Sorath in the Subah of Ahmedabad. They suppressed and killed Budh Singh and seated their ally Bhim Singh on the throne of Bundi. They attempted to disperse the Turani group by sending away Nizam-ul-Mulk to Malwa. They sent forces against Chhabela Ram, the rebellious Governor of Allahabad who was devoted to Farrukh-siyar. On his death, his nephew Girdhar Bahadur was persuaded to surrender Allahabad. He was made the Governor of Avadh and was given ₹30 lakhs.

After reaching Malwa, Nizam-ul-Mulk gave free play to his ambitions. He marched to the South, defeated and killed in two separate battles Dilawar Ali Khan and Alam Ali Khan and seized the Deccan Subah. The Sayyid Brothers did not know what to do. Abdullah did not trust Husain Ali and neither of the two could count upon the support of a few faithful supporters. After prolonged discussion, they decided that Abdullah should remain at Delhi and Husain Ali and the Emperor should go to the Deccan to deal with Nizam-ul-Mulk.

Husain Ali and the Emperor left Delhi for the Deccan. They chose the Ajmer route in the hope of meeting Raja Ajit Singh and reinforcing the imperial army by Rajput soldiers. Nothing happened up to Agra but after that, the conspirators became more active. Mohammad Amin Khan, Qamar-ud-din Khan, Haidar Quli Khan, Mir Jumla, Sayyid Muhammad Amin and Saadat Khan started making schemes for the assassination of Husain Ali. They won over the mother of the Emperor to their side. On 8 October 1720, their plans were successful and Hasain Ali was stabbed to death. This was followed by the arrest of Ratan Chand and Muhkham Singh Jat who were the supporters of Sayyid Abdullah. A day after the murder of Husain Ali, the Emperor appointed Mohammad Amin Khan as Minister. The other conspirators were also rewarded and given higher ranks or offices. The conspirators then marched against Sayyid Abdullah. Sayyid Abdullah demanded from the Emperor that the conspirators be punished but there was no response. He set up a rival at Delhi in the person of Prince Ibrahim and proceeded to fight against the advancing imperial army. Abdullah was defeated in the battle of Hasanpur. He was made a prisoner and handed over to the charge of Haidar Quli Khan. He was poisoned and killed after two years.

The Sayyid Brothers. The Sayyid Brothers, Abdullah Khan and Husain Ali Khan, claimed their descent from Abdul Farh, an adventurer from Mesopotamia who had settled down in India many centuries ago. The father of the Sayyid Brothers was a Subahdar of Bijapur and Ajmer. Later on, he joined Prince Muazzam. During the war of succession, the Sayyid Brothers fought on the side of Prince Muazzam who became Mughal Emperor as Bahadur Shah. The new Emperor rewarded the two brothers. In 1708, Prince Azim-us-Shan gave an important assignment to Husain Ali in Bihar. In 1711, he appointed Abdullah Khan as his Deputy in the province of Allahabad. In lieu of those favours, the Sayyid Brothers supported Farrukh-siyar, a son of Azim-us-Shan, for the throne of Delhi. They killed Emperor Jahandar Shah in the battle and offered the throne to Farrukh-siyar. In recognition of the services rendered to him. Farrukh-siyar appointed Abdullah Khan as Wazir and Husain Ali as Mir Bakshi. That caused great jealousy in the minds of Turani and Irani nobles, who started instigating the Emperor to remove them. The chief figure in the whole drama was Mir Jumla who had been authorised by Farrukh-siyar to sign on his behalf. That was resented by the Sayyid Brothers. Khafi Khan writes, "The two brothers were not inclined to bear patiently Mir Jumla's invidious and provoking interference in their affairs".

Farrukh-siyar took part in at least three plots against the Sayyid Brothers. The Emperor sent Husain Ali against the Rajputs but also sent secret instructions to Raja Ajit Singh to help him in getting rid of Husain Ali in return for tempting gifts. The plot failed. In the second plot, the Emperor sent Hussian Ali to the South as Subahdar of the Deccan and at the same time instigated Daud Khan to kill Husain Ali on the way. He promised to hand over the viceroyalty of the Deccan to Daud Khan after the successful implementation of the plan. The third plot was directed against the life of Abdullah Khan. Abdullah Khan was to be surrounded and assassinated at the time of Nauroz ceremony. However, Abdullah Khan got scent of the plot and posted a large number of troops to overawe Farrukh-siyar. That plot also failed.

The Sayyid Brothers joined hands with the Jats and also entered into an alliance with Raja Ajit Singh by making him promises of reward. Husain Ali Khan came to Delhi along with troops to help his brother. The fort and the palace in Delhi were cleared of the supporters of Farrukh-siyar and he himself was dragged out from the harem, insulted and strangled.

After the death of Farrukh-siyar, the Sayyid Brothers became the masters of the whole show. They really became "kingmakers". They put Rafi-ud-Darajat, Rafi-ud-Daulah and Muhammad Shah on the throne of Delhi. As the new Emperor was young and inexperienced, he left the entire administration in the hands of the Sayyid Brothers. Khafi Khan writes, "All the officers and servants around the Emperor were, as before, the servants of Sayyid Abdullah. When the Emperor went out for a ride, he was surrounded, as with a halo, by a number of the Sayyid's adherents, and when occasionally he went out hunting or for an excursion into the country, they went with him and brought him back".

The Sayyid Brothers not only believed in but also acted upon the policy of religious toleration. It was under their influence and at their suggestion that the Jizya was abolished at the accession of Farrukh-siyar. It was again on their suggestion that Mohammad Shah also abolished it. The result was that the Sayyid Brothers were able to win over the sympathies of the Rajputs. It was on their suggestion that Rattan Chand, a grain merchant, was appointed Diwan in place of Inayat Ullah Khan. From a rebel, Raja Ajit Singh was won over and he agreed to give his daughter in marriage to Farrukh-siyar. Under the influence of Husain Ali Khan, the Marathas were won over by granting them their demands of Chauth and Sardeshmukhi. The Sayyid Brothers mediated on behalf of Churaman Jat to allow him to retain his post on the condition of submitting to the Emperor. Jai Singh who was besieging the Jat fort of Thuri was directed to raise the siege. The result was that Churaman visited Delhi in April 1718. In order to counteract the moves of the Turani and Irani nobles, the Sayyid Brothers formed the Hindustani party which consisted of Mohammadans born in India, Rajput and Jat chiefs and other powerful Hindu landowners. It is contended that if the high officials had carried on the liberal policy of the Sayyid Brothers, the course of Indian history would have been different. They could have established a strong state on a national and tolerant basis with the support of Indian Mohammadans and Hindu Princes. By establishing a strong central Government, they would have avoided the invasions of Nadir Shah and Ahmad Shah Abdali. They would have checked the rapid rise of the Marathas and the British to power. They would have maintained the power and prestige of the Mughals intact.

It is unfortunate that there were differences between the Sayyid Brothers. They quarrelled over the sharing of the spoils of victory and political power. They differed over the attitude to be adopted towards the old nobles in general and Nizam-ul-Mulk in particular. Husain Ali contended that Abdullah Khan had taken advantage of his position as Wazir and taken possession of all the buried treasures of Farrukh-siyar and the goods in his jewel house, imperial establishments etc. He also maintained that Abdullah Khan had resumed the Jagirs of more than 200 nobles and distributed them among his followers. There was great tension but a compromise was arrived at through the good offices of Ratan Chand. When Agra was captured, most of the booty fell into the hands of Husain Ali. Trouble arose when Abdullah Khan demanded his share. In spite of the intervention of Ratan Chand, Abdullah Khan was not satisfied.

There were other differences between them. Husain Ali was more energetic than Abdullah Khan. He was of a haughty and hasty temperament and he failed to weigh all the pros and cons before coming to a conclusion or taking action. Khafi Khan writes that Husain Ali "deemed himself superior in military governmental matters to his brother though he was forgetful of the real matter and unacquainted with stratagem". Husain Ali overestimated the strength and stability of his own position and did not appreciate the wisdom and moderation of his brother. The misfortunes of the Sayyid Brothers were very much due to the haste of Husain Ali in putting down the potential rivals. The view of Abdullah Khan was that Nizam-ul-Mulk should be appointed the Governor of Bihar which province was notorious for its turbulent Zamindars and brought practically no revenue, but Husain Ali insisted on the appointment of Nizam-ul-Mulk to Malwa and the same was done. It was from Malwa that Nizam-ul-Mulk was able to consolidate his position and raise the standard of revolt which ultimately led to the fall of the Sayyid Brothers.

When Nizam-ul-Mulk was incharge of Malwa, it was reported that he was collecting men and materials of war in excess of his requirements as Governor of Malwa. It was suspected that he had an eye on the Deccan. The Sayyid Brothers were afraid of him and decided to shift him from Malwa to Agra or Allahabad or Multan or Burhanpur. When Nizam-ul-Mulk did not accept the new offer, the Sayyid Brothers sent a mace-bearer to bring him to the capital. Instead of obeying, he revolted and crossed the Narmada into the Deccan. He was joined by the Governors of Berar, Khandesh and Asirgarh. In order to win over the Muslims to his side, he declared that whatever he was doing was for the honour and prestige of the royal house. He had revolted because the Sayyid Brothers were determined to ruin and disgrace all Turani and Irani nobles. He also contended that the Sayyid Brothers had allied themselves with the Hindus and were pursuing anti-Islamic policies. Those sentiments became the rallying cry of the movement against the Sayyid Brothers led by the Nizam.

Abdullah Khan realised the gravity of the situation. He was in favour of winning over the Nizam by making concessions. He was supported by Khan-i-Dauran and Ratan Chand. However, Husain Ali rejected the proposal for a compromise and accused his brother Abdullah Khan of lack of initiative and courage. Dilawar Ali was ordered to march against the Nizam from the North and Alam Ali from the South. The Nizam fell upon Dilawar Ali and routed him in June 1720 before he was joined by Alam Ali. Alam Ali and his Maratha supporters were also defeated by the Nizam in August 1720. Husain Ali was assassinated when he was on the way to the Deccan with the Emperor. Abdullah Khan was defeated in the battle of Hasanpur and was taken prisoner. He was killed two years after.

The fall of the Sayyid Brothers was due to many causes. They were not able to win over an important section of the old nobles belonging to the time of Aurangzeb and Bahadur Shah who looked upon the Sayyid Brothers as upstarts and were not prepared to be over-shadowed by them in the conduct of the affairs of the state. They did not approve of the policy of the Sayyid Brothers to conciliate the Marathas, Rajputs and Jats. They were themselves ambitious people and could not be expected to tolerate the usurpation of all power by the Sayyid Brothers. They declared that the Sayyid Brothers were anti-Mughal and wanted to monopolies all power into their hands.

The Sayyid Brothers committed a blunder in deposing and murdering Farrukh-siyar. Abdullah Khan was not in favour of deposing Farrukh-siyar and the blame must rest on the shoulders of Husain Ali. The deposition of Farrukh-siyar created an apprehension in the minds of many nobles about the ultimate intentions of the Sayyid Brothers who came to be regarded as tyrants and traitors. The deposition of Farrukh-siyar was a political blunder because it enabled the Chin group to appear as the champions of Timurid monarchy and exploit the public feeling against the Sayyid Brothers for their own ends.

Another cause of their failure was that they overestimated their own strength and resources. They should have followed a policy of caution and conciliation as advocated by Abdullah Khan. It was the determination of Husain Ali to destroy Nizam-ul-Mulk, Amin Khan and others at the earliest possible moment that brought about the fall of the Sayyid Brothers. The dependence of the Sayyid Brothers on their subordinates such as Ratan Chand, made them unpopular. Their Government became corrupt. They failed to maintain law and order. They did not receive timely help from the Marathas, Rajput and Jats.

The Sayyid Brothers acted as king-makers and they brought about the deaths of Farrukh-siyar and many other royal princes. Those heinous crimes alienated the sympathies of the people and they did not get any support from them at the time of their crisis.

Emperor Mohammad Shah highly resented the control of the Sayyid Brothers over him. He was anxious to get rid of them. In order to achieve his end, he joined the party opposed to the Sayyid Brothers. The alliance between the Emperor and the party opposed to the Sayyid Brothers, was an important factor which brought about the fall of the Sayyid Brothers.

Work of the Sayyid Brothers. As regards the work of the Sayyid Brothers, it is contended that if they had remained in power for long, they would have established a strong state on a national and tolerant basis with the support of Indian Muslims and Hindu Princes. By establishing a strong Central Government, they would have avoided the invasions of Nadir Shah and Ahmad Shah Abdali. They would have checked the rapid rise of the Marathas and the British in India. They would have maintained the power and prestige of the Mughals intact. The Mughal Emperor did not gain anything from the deaths of Husain Ali and Abdullah Khan. He fell under the influence of evil counsellors and Nizam-ul-Mulk retired to the Deccan in disgust.

The Sayyid Brothers exercised their influence on the Emperor to get the Jizya abolished in 1713. They cultivated cordial relations with the Hindus and offered them positions of trust. They won over Raja Ajit Singh who was a rebel and succeeded in arranging a marriage between his daughter and Farrukh-siyar. They also won over the Jats and Marathas. If the high officials had carried out the liberal policy of the Sayyid Brothers, the course of Indian history would have been different. The Sayyid Brothers had certain qualities of their own. Khafi Khan writes thus about the Sayyid Brothers, "In the course of this narrative, upon some points, the pen has been used to condemn the two brothers, the martyrs of misfortune, and this cannot now be rectified; but in at one movement I will now write a few words upon the excellence and beauty of character, the love of justice and the liberality of both brothers. Both the Brothers were distinguished in their day for their generosity and leniency towards all mankind. The inhabitants of those countries which were innocent of contumacy and selfishness made no complaint of the rule of the Sayyids. In liberality and kindness to the learned men and to the needy and in protection of men of merit, Husain Ali excelled his elder brother and was the Hatim suited to his day. Numbers owed their comforts to the cooked food and raw grain which he gave away. At the time of the scarcity at Aurangabad, he appropriated large sum of money and a great quantity of grain to supply the wants of the poor and of widows. The reservoir at Aurangabad was begun by him which, in summer, when water is scarce, relieved the sufferings of the inhabitants. In their native country of Barha, they built Sarais, bridges and other buildings for the public benefit. Sayyid Abdullah was remarkable for his patience and wise sympathy".

About the rule of the Sayyid Brothers, Dr. Satish Chandra writes, "The Sayyids made a definite break with narrow, exclusionist policy and moved in the direction of establishing a state essentially secular in approach and national in character. Their downfall did not imply the automatic negation of this process which they had stimulated and strengthened; it continued to work apace and influenced the political and cultural developments of the succeeding period".

Nadir Shah's Invasion of India (1739). One of the most important events of the reign of Muhammad Shah was the invasion of India by Nadir Shah in 1739. Nadir Shah had become the ruler of Iran in 1736. He was warlike and ambitious and keen to earn a name and fame and to raise his country to high glory. He entertained aggressive designs both eastward and westward. He came into conflict with the Turks and sent his troops to punish the Governors of Balkh and Andkhud. He then decided to conquer Qandhar which was the running sore to the security of his Eastern possessions and won remarkable success. He captured Qandhar by storming his way into it in March 1738. He had to pay heavily for his victory in Qandhar. In his hour of triumph, financial stringency impeded his further conquests. In order to implement his future plans, Nadir Shah had to replenish his treasury as quickly as possible. That could be done by invading India which was reputed to have enormous wealth. Lockhart observes, "With the spoils of India, he could raise and pay more the Afghan and Uzbeg levies and so renew war with Turks; besides by invading the Punjab, he would be following the example of Alexander the Great, Mahmood Ghazni and thereby merit the title of "World Conqueror".

The immediate pretext for the invasion of India was the alleged disregard for Nadir Shah's repeated requests to the Mughal Emperor not to give asylum to the Afghan rebels. Even after the siege of Qandhar had begun, the Mughal authorities did nothing to close the Western frontier against the refugees. When the Persian envoy Muhammad Khan Turkman delivered in person the protest of his master to Muhammad Shah, instead of giving a straight reply, the envoy was unduly detained inspite of the explicit direction of Nadir Shah not to prolong his stay beyond 40 days. Muhammad Khan Turkman had been preceded by two other envoys who had brought similar requests but received evasive replies. What infuriated Nadir Shah was the murder of two Persian couriers who had been sent to Delhi under escort to bring the news of Muhammad Khan Turkman.

Nadir Shah used Qandhar as a vital base for his Indian expedition. He arrived at Ghazni from where he marched to Kabul which he occupied after a brief resistance. He professed his friendly intentions towards the Mughal Emperor saying that his sole object was to punish the rebel Afghans and he had no territorial designs. He sent an envoy to Delhi, but he was killed at Jalalabad. Nadir Shah ruthlessly avenged the murder and sacked the town of Jalalabad.

Nasir Khan, the Governor of Peshawar and Kabul, sent a note of warning to the Mughal Emperor and appealed for reinforcements. The Mughal court was surcharged with intrigues, neglect and indifference and hence no action was taken. Nadir Shah left Jalalabad and marched towards Peshawar. Nasir Khan by his own efforts collected 20,000 Afghans to meet the Persian army. Nadir Shah defeated them and Nasir Khan and a number of his officers were taken prisoners. Peshawar was occupied. A bridge was constructed at Attock and the Persian army crossed over to the other side. The river Jhelum was crossed. An Indian army led by Qalandar Khan barred his advancement, but the general was killed. Zakariyah Khan, the Mughal Governor of Lahore, made an abject surrender and by offering a gift of ₹20 lakhs and several elephants, he saved himself and the property and honour of the people of Lahore. Nadir Shah stayed at Lahore for 12 days. He appointed Zakariyah Khan the Governor of Lahore and Nasir Khan the Governor of Kabul and Peshawar. Nadir Shah reached Sirhind on 16 February 1739. From Sirhind, he set out for Ambala. From Ambala he marched to Azimabad and then to Karnal.

The Mughal Emperor summoned Burhan-ul-Mulk Saadat Khan from Awadh but did not wait for his arrival. He immediately held a council of war with Nizam-ul-Mulk, Khan-i-Dauran and Itimad-ud-Daulah and decided that the nobles should march to Karnal. The number of combatants in the Indian army at that moment was about 75,000. Saadat Khan arrived with his troops but his baggage was plundered by the Persians. Saadat Khan attacked them. A minor action developed into the battle of Karnal. The Persians slaughtered a considerable number of Saadat Khan's men. Saadat Khan was wounded and taken prisoner. Khan-i-Dauran was fatally wounded.

It appears strange that the Emperor Muhammad Shah, his Wazir Qamar-ud-din and his adviser Nizam-ul-Mulk should have complacently watched the terrible carnage which was going on before their very eyes. The Indian left wing under their commands remained intact to the last without helping the hard-pressed imperial forces. Either Nizam-ul-Mulk was taking a malicious pleasure in the humiliation of his two rivals or he considered it futile to fight against the superior tactics of Nadir Shah. Whatever the reason, his conduct could not be defended.

When Saadat Khan was led into the audience of Nadir Shah, he tactfully answered the questions put to him. He impressed upon Nadir Shah that there were still vast resources at the disposal of Muhammad Shah with which he could continue the fight on equal terms and advised him to send for Nizam-ul-Mulk and negotiate with him. The invitation was sent and Nizam-ul-Mulk accepted the invitation, went to the Persian camp and succeeded in negotiating a settlement with Nadir Shah. According to the settlement, the Persian army was not to advance towards Delhi provided an indemnity of ₹50 lakhs was paid to Nadir Shah. Out of that amount, ₹20 lakhs were to be paid immediately—₹10 lakhs at Lahore, ₹10 lakhs at Attock and the balance at Kabul. No territorial annexations were to be made. The Mughal Emperor went to the Persian camp where he was received with great honour and consideration.

When the Emperor Muhammad Shah learnt of the death of Khan-i-Dauran, he immediately conferred on Nizam-ul-Mulk the rank and title of Amir-ul-Umara which the deceased Khan-i-Dauran had worn. This was bitterly resented by Saadat Khan who had himself been coveting the post of Mir Bakshi. Enraged at the preference shown to Nizam-ul-Mulk, Saadat Khan impressed upon Nadir Shah that he had been duped by Nizam-ul-Mulk who would have agreed to pay much more. He suggested to him to take Muhammad Shah, the Nizam and others into custody, march to Delhi and make himself master of the immense treasures in store there. Nadir Shah accepted the suggestion. Nizam-ul-Mulk was again invited to the Persian camp and was asked to furnish 20 crores of rupees in addition to 20,000 cavalries to serve under Nadir Shah. When he pleased his inability, he was placed under surveillance. Likewise, the Emperor Muhammad Shah, Wazir Qamar-ud-din and the royal harem were also placed in custody. Saadat Khan was elevated to the post of Vakil-i-Mutlaq and sent to Delhi with instructions to the Governor to hand over the keys of the imperial palaces and establishments.

Nadir Shah and the Mughal Emperor left Karnal on 12 March 1739. On 20 March, Nadir Shah entered Delhi. Nadir Shah took up his residence near the Diwan-i-Khas in the palace occupied by Shah Jahan. On 21 March, the Khutba was read in all the mosques of Delhi in the name of Nadir Shah and coins were also struck in his name. As Saadat Khan could not collect the large amount promised by him, he committed suicide.

Unfortunately, rumours were spread in the city that Nadir Shah had met with untimely death or had been seized or imprisoned by the orders of the Emperor. Nobody cared to verify the truth. Mobs collected at various places and attacked the Persian troops and about 3000 of them were killed. At first, Nadir Shah refused to believe the reports of the disturbance but when he rode through the streets in Chandni Chowk, a bullet missed him but killed one of his officers. Red with anger, he ordered a general massacre of the inhabitants of Delhi. The Persian soldiers forced their way into shops, and houses killing the occupants and looting everything. The money-changers Bazar and the shops of jewellers and merchants were set on fire and destroyed, all the occupants perishing in the flames. No distinction was made between the innocent and the guilty, male and female, old and young. The massacre continued for about six hours. Sir Jadunath Sarkar puts the number of those dead at 20,000 besides several hundred women who committed suicide. The streets of Delhi remained littered with corpses for several days till they were burnt with the timber from the wrecked houses. Nadir Shah obtained from the Emperor, his nobles and the people of Delhi about ₹70 lacs. Nadir Shah demanded the hand of a Mughal princess for his son Nasrullah and a great grand-daughter of Aurangzeb was married to him. To celebrate the occasion, Nadir Shah ordered illumination, display of fireworks and other entertainments. All this was done when the people of Delhi were in a state of mourning. The Peacock throne of Shah Jahan was seized by Nadir Shah. Likewise, elephants, horses and precious stuffs were seized.

Nadir Shah left Delhi after a stay of 57 days. Before his departure, he put the crown on the head of Muhammad Shah, the Mughal Emperor who offered to Nadir Shah the provinces of the Mughal Empire West of the river Indus from Kashmir to Sind and in addition the Subah of Thatta and the forts subordinate to it. The view of Sir Wolseley Haig is that the departure of Nadir Shah left the Mughal Emperor and his courtiers stupefied with the blow which had fallen on them. For two months, nothing was done or proposed in regard to the state of affairs in the Empire. However, even this blow did not change the attitude of the Mughal Emperor and his courtiers.

Nadir Shah marched out of Delhi on 16 May 1739. His long and richly-laden baggage train consisting of, besides costly jewels and cash, hundreds of camels, mules and elephants, was subjected to plunder and loot by the peasants of the Punjab. Nadir Shah killed some of them but they would not desist. It was in this manner that he returned home via Peshawar and Kabul.

There is a difference of opinion among historians regarding the factors responsible for Nadir Shah's invasion of India. Some attribute it to the non-observance of the accepted standards of diplomatic niceties on the part of Empero Muhammad Shah who failed to felicitate Shah Tahmasp II on the occasion of his restoration. Some put emphasis on the failure of the Mughal Emperor to drive out the Afghans beyond the Indian borders in spite of his promises. Another view is that the invitations of Saadat Khan and Nizam-ul-Mulk to Nadir Shah were responsible for the invasion. Those who accuse the Mughal Emperor of lack of polite disposition and breach of faith, try to justify Nadir Shah's act of unprovoked aggression. Some of the Afghans who had been defeated by Nadir Shah made their way into India through difficult passes and unknown roads and came into contact with those sections of the people who were sympathetic towards them for their sufferings. It is possible that some of the Afghans might have eluded the frontier guards and entered India. The Iranian officers could not pursue them beyond their own frontiers and Nadir Shah asked the Mughal Emperor to take effective steps to drive out the Afghan refugees from India. The Mughal Emperor received Nadir Shah's embassies with every mark of respect, provided them with princely comforts and gave them lakhs of rupees in the form of gifts. He also promised to take necessary action against the enemies of Nadir Shah. He never asserted his claim over Qandhar. He did not oppose Nadir Shah when he was conquering it. He gave no encouragement to Afghan resistance in Qandhar. No official support was given to them to enter India. However, any effort to chastise the Afghans meant the launching of a military expedition which he could not afford at a time when his own difficulties were on the increase. On account of his continued war against the Marathas, the Mughal Emperor admitted his inability to meet the demands of Nadir Shah. The truth is that the obligation of repelling the Afghans was "beyond the capacity of his power and Government". The insistence of Nadir Shah on the expulsion of the Afghan refugees from India creates doubts about his real intentions to invade India. It appears that Nadir Shah was using this as a pretext to prepare the ground for his invasion of India. He was certainly aware of the limited resources of the Mughal Government and the serious crisis it was facing. That situation encouraged Nadir Shah "to invade India and pave the way for another military success". It is difficult to determine the number of Afghans who had taken shelter in India. However, they were scattered and stripped of their resources and hence could not be a source of danger to Nadir Shah. There could not be any apprehension that the Mughal Emperor in collusion with Afghan fugitives would be able to defy the might of Nadir Shah. There is no truth in the assertion that the Mughal Emperor did not want to risk a break with the Afghans and hence kept himself aloof from the war between Nadir Shah and the Afghans. His active participation was not called for as it had no direct bearing on his fortunes. In the light of this fact, there is no element of truth in the charge of breach of faith and lack of courtesy levelled against Muhammad Shah. The real cause of his invasion of India was that Nadir Shah was attracted by the fabulous wealth of India. Prolonged war had made Persia virtually bankrupt. Money was required to maintain the army.

As regards the effect of Nadir Shah's invasion of India, it was in the nature of a holocaust. There was wholesale destruction, plunder and rapine. It gave a severe blow to the Mughal Empire. It proved to be the harbinger of future invasions of India by Ahmad Shah Abdal. It shook the nerves of many Indian politicians and statesmen. The French, the English and the Dutch trading Companies were also frightened. Peshwa Baji Rao was so alarmed that he asked Chimnaji Appa to give up his campaign against the Portuguese. He made peace with his enemy in Central India. Raja Jay Singh of Amber sent his family to Udaipur. By the invasion of Nadir Shah, the glamour and wealth of India which had dazzled even the foreigners, was gone. Nizam-ul-Mulk was called away to the Deccan to meet the Maratha pressure on his possessions. Saadat Khan was dead. Qamar-ud-din Khan, on account of his indolence and licentiousness, was like a broken reed. The young men who stepped into the political void were a band of self-seekers who were unfit to discharge their responsibilities in the prevailing atmosphere of strife and struggle.

Nadir Shah's invasion gave a severe blow to the already tottering Mughal Empire and expedited the process of disintegration. The quick victory of Nadir Shah demonstrated the hollowness of the authority of the Mughal Emperor and encouraged the Governors of the provinces to assert their independence. The Mughal Emperor surrendered to Nadir Shah the territories lying to the West of the river Indus and that was a permanent loss to the Mughal Empire. The Mughal Emperor lost not only the provinces of Western Punjab and Sind but also lost permanently Kabul which was annexed to Afghanistan.

Nadir Shah's invasion paved the way for the future invasions of India from the North-West. As a result of the loss of the territories to the West of the river Indus, the natural defence boundaries of the Mughal Empire were weakened and that made the job of future invaders of India easy. The demonstration of the weakness of the Mughal Empire encouraged, future invaders to come to India. The complete political chaos and confusion which prevailed in North-West frontier after the invasion of Nadir Shah led to a series of foreign invasions after 1739. The invasion also ruined the country financially. Nadir Shah not only caused large-scale destruction of life and property but also carried away with him a lot of wealth from India. V.A. Smith writes, "Nadir Shah proceeded systematically and remorselessly to collect from all classes of population the wealth of Delhi, the accumulation of nearly three centuries and a half".

According to Irvine, "Nadir Shah's occupation of Delhi and massacre of the people carried men's memories 300 years back to a similar calamity at the hands of Timur. But there was a great difference between the results of these two foreign invasions. Timur left the state of Delhi as he had found it, impoverished no doubt, but without any dismemberment; Nadir Shah on the other hand, annexed the Trans-Indus provinces and the whole of Afghanistan and thus planted a strong foreign power constantly impinging on our Western frontier. Timur's destructive work and the threat of further invasion from his country ended with his life. But the Abdali and his dynasty continued Nadir's work in India as the heir to his Empire. With the Khyber Pass and the Peshawar District in foreign hands, the Punjab became a starting point for fresh expeditions against Delhi".

The view of Dr. Bisheshwar Prasad is that "the defeat at the hands of Nadir Shah exposed the incapacity and lustful luxuriousness of the nobles who commanded the army. It showed the inanity of the central authority with its factious and impotent jealousies in the court circles. This exposure was a death-knell of the Empire, the central edifice which had kept the centrifugal forces in restraint. The consequence was the disintegration of the Mughal Empire into a large number of provincial or local states, which, while maintaining the facade of obedience to the Crown, strengthened their autonomy. The Central Government was soon reduced to a mere shadow, its authority scarcely prevailing beyond the suburbs of Delhi in time to come". (*Bondage and Freedom*, Vol. I, p. 20.)

Dr. Satish Chandra writes that the effects of the invasion continued to be felt long after the departure of Nadir Shah. The invasion proclaimed the real weakness of the Mughal Empire to the entire world, particularly to the European adventurers who were gradually increasing their commercial activities and were watching the political situation in the country with keen interest. The invasion of Nadir Shah demonstrated forcefully that a new political situation had been created in Northern India. The loss of Kabul and the areas to the West of the Indus deprived India of an advance post for the country's defence and a vantage point for following West Asian affairs. All the Indian powers including the Marathas were made aware that a new force had arisen in West Asian and the Indians could no longer bank on their North-West regions being safe from recurrent foreign invasions. Whether those invasions would be in the nature of plundering raids only or would also aim at the creation of a dynastic empire remained to be seen. The parties at the Mughal court were also affected by the invasion of Nadir Shah. Among the old leaders, Saadat Khan and Khan-i-Dauran were dead. Nizam-Mulk and Qamar-ud-Din had forfeited the confidence of the Emperor for their sorry part in the battle of Karnal. Nizam-ut-Mulk decided once again to leave the Mughal court and sought an agreement with the Marathas for maintaining his position in the Deccan. Safdarjang, Amir Khan and a number of other nobles gradually rose into prominence. The decline in the imperial prestige led to a resumption of the old struggle for Wizarat. The wealth extorted by Nadir Shah from the Emperor, his nobles, the commercial classes and the citizens of Delhi represented a big drain on the resources of the country. It not only dealt crippling blow to the power and authority of the Emperor who was left with no cash reserves for an emergency, but also affected the position of Delhi as one prime commercial mart of Northern India. The general impoverishment of the nobles led to a sharpening of the struggle for the possession of Jagirs. The tendency towards rack-renting of the peasantry became more marked. The realisation of land revenue became more and more a kind of military operation and a large number of peasants were massacred. The invasion of Nadir Shah also led to the introduction of the quick-firing musket and improved light artillery in India. The Rohilla Afghans were the first to adopt them but the Marathas continued with very light cavalry warfare. The rise of Nadir Shah and his invasion of India ended the close cultural contact between India and Persia which had subsisted between the two preceding centuries. The Indian frontier no longer marched with Iran and Turan so that the adventurers from these countries into India finally stopped. It had an indirect bearing on India and its social and cultural development. The Irani and Turani immigrants who had settled down in India found it difficult to stand aside as a separate cultural and social group or to adopt an attitude of social and cultural superiority. The result was that the forces making for the a creation of a composite culture and society in the country were strengthened in the long run. (*Parties and Politics at the Mughal Court, 1707-40.*)

Invasions of Ahmad Shah Abdali. Ahmad Shah Abdali or Durrani was an important general of Nadir Shah. Of him, Nadir Shah had once remarked, "I have not found in Iran, Turan or Hindustan any man equal to Ahmad Shah Abdali in capacity and character". When after the conquest of Qandhar, Nadir Shah decided to settle all his Abdali subjects there, the relatives of Ahmad Shah also settled there. After the murder of Nadir Shah on 9th June 1747 by some of his nobles, all the Afghans proceeded towards Qandhar and chose Ahmad Shah Abdali as their leader. On reaching Qandhar, they had to fight against the local garrison which was captured. Ahmad Shah Abdali was declared Emperor and coins were struck in his name. After Qandhar, he occupied Ghazni, Kabul and Peshawar. All that added to his personal glory and the morale of his troops.

When Nadir Shah had attacked India in 1739, Ahmad Shah Abdali was with him. He saw with his own eyes the weakness of the Mughal Emperor and the Empire. No wonder, he was tempted to attack India to take advantage of the prevailing situation.

Ahmad Shah Abdali led as many as seven expeditions against India between 1748 and 1767. He undertook those invasions mainly with a view to establish Afghan supremacy over India. There were many factors which encouraged him to undertake those invasions. The weak and precarious condition of the Mughal Empire encouraged him in his designs. He had seen the weakness of the Mughal Empire when he came to India along with Nadir Shah. In subsequent years, the Mughal Empire became weaker all the more. Ahmad Shah Abdali wanted to take advantage of that position. The neglect of the North-Western borders by the later Mughals encouraged him to launch so many invasions. The Mughal rulers completely neglected the roads, passes etc., on the border. They did not employ any intelligence to keep the court informed about the developments on the border. This indifferent attitude of the later Mughal rulers towards the defence of their border was fully exploited by Ahmad Shah Abdali. The view of Elphinstone is that Ahmad Shah Abdali invaded India so many times with a view to make financial gains and realise his political ambitions. He carried with him a lot of money and gifts from India which were utilised by him for increasing his military strength and improving its organisation. The immediate cause of his invasion of India was that he was invited by Shah Nawaz Khan, the Governor of the Punjab, to undertake an invasion of India. That invitation fitted very well into the ambitious plans of Ahmad Shah Abdali.

Ahmad Shah Abdali crossed the Indus and the Jhelum to invade the Punjab in 1748. Lahore and Sirhind were occupied but he was defeated by the Mughal army near Sirhind and was forced to withdraw.

Ahmad Shah Abdali was not prepared to put up with the insult and he led another attack on India in 1749. Muin Khan, Governor of the Punjab, resisted the advance of Abdali and asked for reinforcements. As he did not get any help, he agreed to pay ₹14,000 as annual tribute to Abdali.

Ahmad Shah Abdali led the third invasion of India towards the dose of 1751 as the promised tribute was not paid to him. After defeating the Governor of the Punjab, Abdali advanced towards Delhi. The Mughal Emperor offered to transfer Multan and Punjab to Abdali. The view of some scholars is that Ahmad Shah Abdali also conquered Kashmir during his third invasion and appointed his own Governor. He had to go back because there was the possibility of opposition at home at that time.

Ahmad Shah Abdali invaded India for the fourth time to punish Imad-ul-Mulk who had appointed his own man as the Governor of the Punjab. Ahmad Shah Abdali had appointed Mir Mannu as his agent and Governor of the Punjab. In 1753, after the death of Mir Mannu, his infant son, under the Regency of his mother Mughlani Begum, succeeded him. In May 1754, even this successor of Mir Mannu died. After that, there was chaos and confusion in the Punjab. Mughlani Begum invited Imad-ul-Mulk, the Wazir of Delhi and he appointed Mir Munim as the Governor of the Punjab after imprisoning Mughlani Begum. When Ahmad Shah Abdali came to know of these developments, he decided to attack India. He came to India in November 1756. As soon as he reached Lahore. Mir Munim ran away to Delhi. After capturing the Punjab, Ahmad Shah Abdali marched towards Delhi. He reached Delhi on 23 January 1757 and captured the city. He stayed in Delhi for about a month and repeated the carnage and arson of the type of Nadir Shah's invasion. The rich and poor, noblemen and commoners, men and women, all suffered torture and disgrace indiscriminately.

After pillaging Delhi, the Afghan army marched out leaving a trail of burning villages, rotting corpses and desolation. Crushing the Jats on the way, they proceeded to Mathura, Brindaban and Gokul. The carnage and destruction that visited these sacred towns beggars description. For 7 days following the general slaughter, "the water (of the Jamuna) flowed of a blood-red colour". Temples were desecrated, priests and Sadhus were put to the sword. Women were dishonoured and children were cut to pieces. There was no atrocity which was not perpetrated.

The cry of anguish which arose from Delhi, Mathura, Agra and a thousand towns and villages in Northern India remained unheard. However, the outbreak of cholera halted the Afghan army. The soldiers clamoured for returning home. Abdali was forced to retire but not before he had collected a booty estimated at 3 to 12 crores of rupees and inflicted unspeakable indignities upon the Mughal Emperor.

Before his departure from Delhi, Abdali compelled the Mughal Emperor to cede to him Kashmir, Lahore, Sirhind and Multan. He appointed his son Timur Shah to look after the government of those regions. Mughlani Begum was not given Kashmir or Jullunder Doab which had been promised to her. She was imprisoned, caned and disgraced. Abdali appointed Najib Khan Rohilla as Mir Bakshi and he remained in Delhi as the agent of Ahmad Shah.

After the departure of Abdali, the situation in India became critical. Najib Khan was forced to leave Delhi along with all his men and Ahmed Bangash was appointed Mir Bakshi in his place. Najib Khan complained to Abdali and asked for a fresh invasion by him. Sirhind and Lahore fell into the hands of the Marathas in 1758. Abdali sent Jahan Khan to the Punjab but he was defeated. When that happened, Abdali himself attached India. The Marathas could not stand against him and were forced to withdraw from Lahore, Multan and Sirhind. Before the end of 1759, the Punjab was once again brought under his control by Abdali.

Abdali was full of anger against all those who had dared to defy his authority. He rushed to the Doab. He fought against Dattaji and defeated and killed him. Malharrao was able to escape with great difficulty. The Peshwa took up the challenge and sent Sadasiva Rao Bhau to the North in 1760. Many other Maratha generals were sent to fight against Abdali. The Marathas had not ,a single friend or ally in the North on account of their previous treatment of the Rajputs, Jats and others. There were differences within their own ranks in regard to the tactics to be employed against Abdali. The only success of their army was their entry into Delhi because Ahmad Shah Abdali was campaigning in the Doab. The Marathas were forced to leave Delhi on account of scarcity of food for men and horses. It was under these circumstances that the third battle of Panipat was fought on 14 January 1761 between the Marathas and Ahmad Shah Abdali. In spite of their best efforts, the Marathas were defeated. Holkar fled and the contingents of Sindhia followed him. The defeat turned into a rout and terrific slaughter ensued. On the battlefield, there lay the corpses of 28,000 men. Most of the officers were killed. Both Vishwas Rao, the son of the Peshwa and Sadasiva Rao Bhau died fighting heroically.

The defeat at Panipat was a disaster of the first magnitude but it was by no means decisive. For Abdali, it was an empty victory. As soon as his back was turned, his conquests fell to pieces. He and his successors were pestered by rebellions at home. They were not able to give adequate support to their agents in India. The Sikhs drove out the Afghan officers and plundered their baggages. In a few years, not a trace of Abdali's conquest was left on this side of the Indus. The Marathas received a severe blow but within ten years they were back in the North, acting as the guardians of the Mughal Emperor Shah Alam whom they escorted from Allahabad to Delhi in 1771. The defeat of Panipat was not conclusive. The battle which was really decisive was the battle of Plassey which was fought in 1757.

After the battle of Panipat, Ahmad Shah Abdali recognised Shah Alam II as the Emperor of Delhi. Munir-ud-Daulah and Najib-ud-Daulah promised to pay a tribute of ₹40 lakhs per annum to Ahmad Shah Abdali on behalf of the Mughal Emperor. After that, Ahmad Shah Abdali left India.

Ahmad Shah Abdali came to India for the sixth time in March 1764. The Sikhs had increased their power in the Punjab. They had captured considerable property and also killed Khawaja Abid, the Afghan Governor of Lahore. The object of Abdali's invasion was to punish the Sikhs. He stayed in India only for about a fortnight. He had to retreat in view of the possibility of a revolt among his soldiers. As soon as Ahmad Shah Abdali left India, the Sikhs captured Lahore. They also captured Majha and Central Punjab. However, Abdali was able to retain his control over Peshawar and the country West of Attock.

As regards the effects of the invasions of Ahmad Shah Abdali, it is true that Abdali could not stay in India for a long time on the occasion of any of his invasions and he had to hurry back to his country for one reason or the other, but in spite of that his invasions had many effects on the history of India. One of the effects of his invasions was that they paved the way for the rise of the Sikh power in the Punjab. From 1752 to 1761, there were frequent wars among the four great powers to gain ascendancy in the Punjab viz., the Durranis, the Mughals, the Marathas and the Sikhs. The invasions of Abdali so much weakened the Mughal Empire that he was able to take away the two provinces of the Punjab and Sind from the Mughal Empire. Ahmad Shah Abdali defeated the Marathas in 1761 in the third battle of Panipat. The result was that the Marathas lost an opportunity to set up their Empire in the Punjab. After the elimination of the Mughals and the Marathas from the Punjab only the Afghans and the Sikhs remained in the field. In spite of his many invasions, Abdali was not able to crush the Sikhs of the Punjab which was occupied by the Sikhs. In this way the invasions of Abdali Paved the way for the rise of the Sikh power in the Punjab. It is rightly said that the career of Ahmad Shah Abdali in India "is very intimately a part of the Sikh struggle for independence".

The invasions of Ahmad Shah Abdali hastened the downfall of the Mughal Empire. The invasions gave stunning blows to the already crumbling Mughal Empire. There was great anarchy and confusion in the Mughal administration on account of the frequency of Abdali's invasions of India. That anarchy destroyed the internal organisation and vitality of the Mughal Government. That gave rise to insubordination and indiscipline towards the Mughal Government on the part of Mughal officers and officials. The Mughal Empire was already confined to the city of Delhi as the rest of the provinces had become independent. Whatever was left was finished by Ahmad Shah Abdali.

The attempts of the Marathas to oust the Afghans from Delhi and the Punjab ended in the catastrophe to themselves and not to the Mughal Empire. The latter had already ceased to exist in 1759. What was accomplished by the third battle of Panipat in 1761 was that the dream of the Marathas to establish a Hindu Empire from the Deccan right upto the Punjab came to nothing.

After their defeat in 1761, the Marathas had to face a lot of difficulty before they could recover from the deadly effects of the battle of 1761. Their prestige fell down very low. The charm of their invincibility was gone. The organisation and authority of the Marathas became weak and their enthusiasm and initiative practically died out.

In the middle of the eighteenth century, two powers dashed with each other in India. One was the declining power of the, Mughals and second was the rising power of the Marathas. The third battle of Panipat in 1761 weakened the Mughals and the Marathas to such an extent that the English people came forward as the legal heirs to the Mughal Empire. The invasions of Nadir Shah had given a rude shock to the Mughal Empire by depriving it of Sind, Kabul and the Western Punjab and by giving an opportunity to the other nobles to become independent. The invasions of Ahmad Shah Abdali put an end to the Mughal Empire and frustrated the attempts of the Marathas to establish s Hindu Empire in India by crushing their power in the third battle of Panipat. In other words, the invasions of Abdali prepared the field for the British to establish their authority because the Marathas and to Muslims had considerably weakened each other on account of their deadly conflict. Thus, the significant result of the invasions of Nadir Shah and Ahmad Shah Abdali was the rise of the English power in India. Sydney Owen writes, "With the Battle of Panipat, the local rule in Indian history comes to an end and that after this, the centre of interest begins to revolve around the rise of Western commercial princes in this country".

Ahmed Shah (1748-54)

After the death of his father Muhammad Shah "Rangila" in April 1748 Ahmed Shah was put on the throne of Delhi. He was the only son of his father. He was "a good-natured imbecile" who had received no training for war or administration. "From his infancy to the age of 21, he had been brought up among the women of harem in neglect and poverty and often subjected to his father's brow-beating". According to the writer of *Tarikh-i-Alamgir Sani*, "Ahmed Shah was not a man of great intellect, all the period of his youth till manhood had been spent in the harem and he had absolutely no experience whatever of the affairs of a kingdom or of the cares of the Government. Besides these, he was surrounded by all sorts of youthful pleasures which every person, seeing the turn of his mind, was anxious to display before him to entice his fancy. As a natural consequence, he gave himself up entirely to pastime and sports, and bestowed no thought on the weighty affairs of the kingdom. To manage a country and wield a sceptre is a matter full of difficulty, and until an Emperor understands thoroughly himself the good and bad tendency of every measure, he cannot be fit for rule. For this reason, Ahmed Shah was unable to govern the Empire entrusted to him". Again, "He gave himself up to useless pursuits, to pleasure and enjoyment, and his reign was brought to an end after six years, three months and nine days by the enmity which he showed to Nizam-ul-Mulk, Asaf Jah".

The affairs of the state fell into the hands of "a cabal of eunuchs and women" headed by the Queen mother Udham Bai, who before her marriage with Muhammad Shah, was a public dancing girl. She promoted worthless men into high offices, receiving large presents in money for every appointment. No one cared for the administration and the Governors and nobles misappropriated the royal revenues. Their example was followed by powerful landlords who usurped the lands of their weak neighbours.

Ahmed Shah excelled his predecessors in his sensual pursuits. His harem extended over a full Kos where from all males were excluded and the Emperor spent a week and sometimes a month in the company of those women.

In the field of administration, the Emperor did many foolish things. He appointed his one and a half years old son Mahmud as the Governor of the Punjab and named Muhammad Amin, a one year old boy, as the Deputy under him. The Governorship of Kashmir was conferred on Tala Said Shah, a one year old boy and a boy of 15 years of age was appointed his deputy. Those appointments were made at a time when the danger of Afghan invasions was very great.

Ahmed Shah favoured Javid Khan, his chief eunuch who became the leader of the court party. Javid Khan came to be known as Nawab Bahadur and he dominated the whole of the administration. He plotted against the Wazir Safdarjang. There was utter confusion in the country. In 1749, Ahmad Shah Abdali invaded the Punjab but retired after getting a heavy indemnity. In 1752, Abdali attacked the Punjab again. The Governor of the Punjab was defeated and Abdali marched towards Delhi. With a view to avoid destruction at Delhi, the Mughal Emperor made peace by ceding the Punjab and Multan to Ahmad Shah Abdali.

Delhi became a hot bed of intrigues and rival factions. The most important Minister at the court at that time was Safdarjang, the Nawab Wazir of Avadh. He became so arrogant that he began to give orders without consulting the Emperor. The Emperor retaliated by forming a court party headed by Javid Khan. When Javid Khan was assassinated, the Mughal Emperor chose Ghazi-ud-Din Imad-ul-Mulk, grandson of Nizam-ul-Mulk, as his Wazir. There was a struggle for power between Imad-ul-Mulk and Safdarjang. Ghazi-ud-Din convened the Mughal Darbar and proposed the following resolution : "This Emperor has shown his unfitness for rule. He is unable to cope with the Marathas. He is false and fickle towards his friends. Let him be deposed and a worthier son of Timur raised to the throne". The resolution was passed and immediately acted upon. Ahmed Shah was deposed and blinded and consigned to the state prison of Salimgarh. Alamgir II was put on the throne.

Alamgir II (1754-59)

Alamgir II was the second son of Jahandar Shah. He was 55 at the time of his accession to the throne. As he had spent almost all his life in prison, he had practically no experience of administration. He was a very weak person and was merely a puppet in the hands of his Wazir Ghazi-ud-Din Imad-ul-Mulk. The Wazir was a man of no principles. He was extremely selfish. He put all the royal revenues into his own pocket and starved the royal family. He persecuted Ali Gauhar, the eldest son of the Mughal Emperor. He tried to form an anti-Maratha coalition with a view to drive out the Marathas from Northern India but he failed. The relations between Alamgir II and Imadul-Mulk were not satisfactory and the latter got him assassinated in 1759. His body was thrown out of the window and was found lying stark naked on the banks of the river Jamuna.

Shah Alam II (1759-1806)

Ali Gauhar was the son of Alamgir II. He became the Mughal Emperor in 1759 and took up the title of Shah Alam II. At the time of the death of his father, he was in Bihar. Although he was declared the Mughal Emperor, he did not proceed to Delhi for 12 years. He reached Delhi in January 1772 with the help of the Marathas. During that period, he tried to conquer Bihar and Bengal but failed. He was defeated in 1764 in the Battle of Buxar and made a prisoner along with the Nawab Wazir of Avadh. In 1765, he gave the Diwani of Bengal, Bihar and Orissa (now Odisha) to the English East India Company and the latter promised to pay him an annual sum of ₹26 lacs.

Throughout his long life, Shah Alam II remained a puppet in the hands of his ministers, the Marathas and the British. The Rohilla leader Najib-ud-Daulah and later on his son Zabita Khan and grandson Ghulam Qadir ransacked the palace. The floors of the houses of the grandees in the city were dug out. The princesses were turned out and their Jewellery was snatched by Ghulam Qadir. Ghulam Qadir, also blinded Snah Alam and deposed him and put Bidar Bakht on the Mughal throne. However, the Marathas brought out Shah Alam from his captivity and restored him to the throne. Ghulam Qadir was defeated and hanged. In 1803, the English captured Delhi and Shah Alam II, became a pensioner of the English East India Company and he died in 1806.

It is said about Shah Alam II that he was a religious man. He Was affectionate as a father and humane as a master. As a prince, he was weak, indolent, irresolute and easily swayed by self-interested men. To these weaknesses were added idleness, superstitiousness, sloth, indolence and excess of the harem after his return to Delhi. He was indecisive in his measures and did not trust his able ministers. These failings aggravated the situation and the Mughal Empire hastened to its doom.

Akbar II (1806-37)

After the death of Shah Alam II, his son succeeded as Akbar II. Like his father, he was also a pensioner of the British. He was the head of the royal establishment in the Red Fort of Delhi and enjoyed the imperial title only by courtesy. He died in 1837.

Bahadur Shah II (1837-57)

After the death of Akbar II, Bahadur Shah II became the Emperor. He was allowed to retain the imperial title. He was fond of poetry and had the title of "Zafar". He took part in the Revolt of 1857. He was captured and tried by the British. He was deported to Rangoon where he died in 1862. Thus ended the Mughal dynasty.

CAUSES OF THE DOWNFALL OF THE MUGHALS

The cause of the downfall of the Mughals are as follows:

1. The downfall of the Mughal Empire was not due to any single factor but was the result of a combination of a number of factors. According to certain scholars, the decline of the Mughal Empire was largely due to the *policies and character of Aurangzeb*. Aurangzeb alienated the sympathy and support of the Hindus by his religious policy towards them. He imposed Jizya on all the Hindus in the country. Even the Rajputs and Brahmans were not spared. He dismissed Hindu officials from state service and allowed only those Hindus to continue in service who were prepared to embrace Islam. An order banning the building of new Hindu temples in the areas directly under Mughal control was promulgated early in his reign. Though old temples were not to be destroyed under that order, it was decreed that the temples built since the rime of Akbar should be treated as newly built temples and on that plea those temples were desecrated in different parts of the Mughal Empire. Those temples included the temples of Vishwanath at Kashi and Bir Singh Deo at Mathura. In 1679 when the State of Marwar was under- direct imperial control and the Rajputs prepared themselves to resist Mughal authority, old as well as new temples were destroyed in different parts of the Empire. Thousands of artisans and labourers were employed to pull down Hindu temples and mosques were built with the material of those temples. After the death of Raja Jaswant Singh, Aurangzeb tried to keep his son Ajit Singh under his control. Durga Das Rathore managed to remove him and his mother to Rajputana in spite of all the precautions taken by Aurangzeb. That led to the Rajput War which continued from 1679 to 1681. Although peace was restored, Aurangzeb could not depend upon the Rajputs. It proved to be a, great handicap during his Deccan war. Instead of depending upon the support of the Rajputs, he had to set apart Mughal troops to meet any possible trouble from them. The execution of Guru Teg Bahadur was a blunder of Aurangzeb. That led to the alienation of the Sikhs who became a strong military power under Guru Gobind Singh. Later on, those very Sikhs gave trouble to the Mughal Emperors. Although Banda was captured and put to death, Sikh resistance was not crushed. It kept on growing day by day and ultimately the Sikhs were able to drive out the Mughals from the Punjab. The same policy of religious persecution led to the rise of the Marathas under Shivaji. The persecution of the Hindus hardened their character and they became the bitter enemies of the Mughals. Lane-Poole writes about Aurangzeb, "His mistaken policy towards Shivaji provided the foundation of a power that was to prove a successful rival to his

own Empire". 'According to V.A. Smith, "The powerful Hindu support of the throne won so cleverly by Akbar, was weakened by the erroneous policy of Shah Jahan and in a still greater degree, by the austere fanaticism of Aurangzeb".

In defence of the religious policy of Aurangzeb, it is contended that Aurangzeb never intended to Hindus to accept Islam. As an orthodox Muslim king, he wanted to rule in accordance with the orthodox interpretation of the Holy Quran. While reimposing Jizya, he formally abolished about 80 taxes not sanctioned by Islamic law. Aurangzeb wanted to emphasize the Islamic character of the state and to rally the Muslims more closely round the throne. However, he did not realise that his policy would lead to a strong reaction, among the Hindus and alienate such sections as the Rajputs who had been generally loyal to the Mughal throne. The reign of Aurangzeb witnessed armed resistance from many quarters. The Jats revolted in 1669 and 1688-91. The Satnamis revolted in 1672. Sikh and Maratha resistance continued not only during the reign of Aurangzeb but even after that.

The Deccan policy of Aurangzeb was also responsible for the downfall of the Mughal Empire. Aurangzeb was bent upon crushing the power of the Maratha. He found that the states of Bijapur and Golcunda were a source of great help to the Marathas who were employed in large numbers in those states. They got not only money but also military training from those states. The conclusion of Aurangzeb was that if those states were annexed to the Mughal Empire, the source strength of the Marathas would be stopped. Moreover, the rulers of those states were Shias and for a fanatical Sunni Muslim like Aurangzeb; their very existence was intolerable. Aurangzeb annexed Bijapur in 1686 and Golcunda in 1687. He might have claimed credit for the destruction of the Shia states but he had committed a blunder. He should have followed a buffer state policy towards them and subordinated his religious zeal to statesmanship. If Aurangzeb had helped Bijapur and Golcunda against the Marathas, he would have been able to keep the Marathas in check with much less expense and waste of energy and resources.

After the annexation of Bijapur and Golcunda, Aurangzeb tried to crush the power of the Marathas. War was declared against Sambhaji, the son of Shivaji. He was captured and put to death under the orders of Aurangzeb. His son, Sahu, was captured and made a prisoner. He continued to be in prison till the death of Aurangzeb in 1707. However, the Marathas carried on their struggle against Aurangzeb first under the leadership of Raja Ram and after his death, his widow Tara Bai. When Aurangzeb died in 1707, the power of the Marathas was still not crushed. As a matter of fact, they were stronger than before.

About the Deccan policy of Aurangzeb, V.A. Smith observes, "The Deccan was the grave of his reputation as well as of his body". Aurangzeb had to remain away from Northern India for a quarter of a century on account of his involvement in, the wars in the Deccan. The result was that the whole of Mughal administration was thrown out of gear. There was complete confusion everywhere. As the Emperor was busy in the Deccan, the provincial Governors did not send land revenue to the Central Government. At a time when more money was required for the wars in the Deccan, very little was coming from the provinces. When Bahadur Shah succeeded to the throne, the treasury was empty. The Mughal Government being a centralised despotism, the absence of Aurangzeb from the North for a long period encouraged centrifugal tendencies among the Governors. After the death of Aurangzeb, those tendencies continued to grow and the result was that ultimately the various provinces became independent. It was in this way that Avadh, Bengal, the Punjab and the Deccan became independent. The Rohillas became independent in Rohilkhand. The Jats also asserted their independence. Gradually, the Mughal Empire broke up. The failure of Aurangzeb in the Deccan wars destroyed the military prestige of the Mughals. Too much of expenditure made the Mughal Government bankrupt.

It was a mistake on the part of Aurangzeb not to have come to terms with Shivaji or Sambhaji. Although Aurangzeb gave high ranks (Mansabs) to a large number of Maratha Sardars (chiefs), he had no following among the Marathas. The conflict with the Marathas had far reaching consequences. The military prestige of the Mughals was damaged. The Mughals were prevented from consolidating their position in the Deccan. A feeling of tension was created among the Hindus and Muslims. A considerable harm was done to trade and industry on the Western coast and in the Deccan.

Aurangzeb was a man of suspicious nature. He did not trust even his sons and relatives. That is why he kept the whole of the administration under his personal supervision. That deprived his sons of the necessary training in the art of administration and practical experience in the art of statesmanship and diplomacy. As it was difficult for one man sitting at the Centre to control the whole of administration personally, the whole of the administration fell a prey to corruption and inefficiency, especially when the means of transport and communication were not fully developed in those days. Any attempt on the part of a single individual to control the vast Empire was destined to failure. Even during the lifetime of Aurangzeb, it was not possible to control the entire administration personally, but after his death, there was disorder, confusion and chaos.

Under Aurangzeb, the Mughal Empire became unwieldy. With the conquest and annexation of Bijapur and Golcunda, it became so huge in size and extent that it was difficult to keep it intact. The means of transport and communication during those days were not developed and hence the maintenance of the central control over the distant parts of the Empire was a difficult problem. Rebellions in distant provinces were often witnessed even during the life-time of Aurangzeb who was admittedly a strong man. Under his weak successors, it became impossible to maintain control over the distant provinces which, one by one, drifted away from the control of the Central Government. Saadat Ali Khan became independent in Avadh. Ali Vardi Khan declared his independence in Bengal, Bihar and Orissa (now Odisha). The Rohillas and the Rajputs took advantage of the weakness of the distant Central Government and set up their independent states in their own regions. Nizam-ul-Mulk set up his own independent state in the Deccan.

2. Another cause of the downfall of the Mughal Empire was the *financial bankruptcy of the Mughal Government* for which Aurangzeb alone was not responsible, although he contributed to it and did nothing to check it. It is true that Akbar had set up a well-organised economic system but the same was not maintained by his successors. The economic system of the Empire was strained, almost to the breaking point, by the end of the reign of Shah Jahan on account of his extravagance on the construction of magnificent buildings and palaces. He increased the state demand of land revenue to one-half. The long, expensive and Wasteful wars of Aurangzeb in the Deccan and the North-West Frontier rained the treasury. After the death of Aurangzeb, the system of farming of taxes was resorted to. Although the Government did not get much by that method, the people were ruined. The financial collapse, came in the time of Alamgir II who was practically starved by his Wazir Imad-ul-Mulk. It is stated that Alamgir II had no conveyance to take him to the Idgah and he had to walk on foot. Sir Jadunath Sarkar points out that on one occasion, no fire was kindled in the royal kitchen for three days and one day the princesses could bear starvation no longer and in frantic disregard of Purdah rushed out of the palace to the city. The gates of the fort being closed, they sat down in the men's quarters for a day and a night after which they were persuaded to go back to their rooms. That happened in 1775. The continuance of such a Government was not possible.

3. Another cause of the downfall of the Mughal Empire was the *weak successors of Aurangzeb*. If they had been intelligent and brilliant, they may have stopped the decline of the Empire which had set in during the reign of Aurangzeb. Unfortunately, most of them were worthless. They were busy in their luxuries and intrigues and did nothing to remedy the evils which had crept into the

Mughal body politic. Bahadur Shah I was 63 when he ascended the throne and he did not possess the energy to perform the onerous duties of the Government. He tried to keep the various parties and courtiers satisfied by offering them liberal grants, titles, rewards etc. Bahadur Shah earned the nickname of *Shah-i-Bekhabar* (Heedless King). Jahandar Shah was a dissolute profligate who fell under the vicious influence of a court dancer, Lal Kanwar, a lady descendant of Tansen family. Farrukh-siyar was "contemptible and cowardly" and a shameless debauchee. He was "strong neither for evil nor for good," Muhammad Shah was rightly called *"Rangila"* and he could not be expected to check the rot. In the time of Ahmad-Shah, the Mughal Empire had shrunk to a small area round Delhi. Shah Alam II was blinded and he suffered terribly. Akbar II and Bahadur Shah II were no better. Edwards and Garret write, "The chronicles of the court of Delhi after the death of Aurangzeb offer an unbroken tale of plots and counter-plots on the part of powerful nobles, culminating at intervals in open disorder and fighting, with the titular Emperor serving as the sport and plaything of contending groups".

4. Another cause was the *absence of the law of primogeniture* or any other settled law of succession to the Mughal throne. The result was that every Mughal prince considered himself to be equally fit to become the next ruler and was prepared to fight out his claim. In the world of Erskine, "The sword was the grand arbiter of right and every son was prepared to try his fortune against his brothers". After the death of Aurangzeb, there was a war of succession among his four sons and Bahadur Shah came out successful. After the death of Bahadur Shah, the various claimants to the throne were used as tools by the leaders of the various factions in the court to promote their personal interests. Zulfikar Khan acted as the king-make Likewise, the Sayyid Brothers acted as king-makers from 1713 to 1720. They were instrumental in the appointment of four kings to the throne. After their disappearance from the scene, Mir Mohammad Amin and Asif Jah Nizam-ul-Mulk acted as king-makers. It is not incorrect to say that the absence of a law of succession led to frequent wars of succession and contributed to the decline of the Mughal Empire.

5. Another cause was the gradual deterioration in the court of the Mughal kings. When Babar attacked India, he swam all the rivers on the way. He was so strong that he could run on the wall of a fort while carrying man in his arms. Unmindful of the difficulties confronting him, Humayun was able to win back his throne after the lapse of many years. The same hardy character enabled Akbar to conquer the whole of Northern India and a part of the Deccan. No amount of riding on horse-back exhausted him. He could walk miles and miles on foot. He is said to have walked from Agra to Delhi. He could kill a lion with one stroke of his sword. After the death of Aurangzeb, the Mughal Emperors became ease-loving. Their harems were full. They went about in palanquins. They were hardly fit to rule a country where the mass of the people detested their rule. Prof. S.R. Sharma writes, "Kam Baksh as a captive on his deathbed regretted that a descendant of Timur was captured alive. But Jahandar Shah and Ahmad Shah were not ashamed to be caught up in the tresses of their concubines who came between them and their duties as Emperors.

> They looked on beauty,
>
> And turned away from duty!

The former fooled himself in public with his Lal Kanwar and the latter buried himself in his seraglio—which extended over four square miles— for weeks together without seeing the face of a male".

6. There was the *degeneration of the Mughal nobility*. When the Mughals came to India, they had a hardy character. Too much of wealth, luxury and leisure softened their character. Their harems became full. They got wine in plenty. They went in palanquins to the battle-field. Such nobles were

not fit to fight against the Marathas, the Rajputs and the Sikhs. The Mughal nobility degenerated at a very rapid pace. Sir Jadunath Sarkar writes that no Mughal noble family retained its importance for more than one or two generations. If the achievements of a nobleman were mentioned in three pages, the achievements of his son occupied nearly a page and the grandson was dismissed in a few lines such as "he did nothing worthy of being recorded here". The Mughal nobility was taken from the Turks, the Afghans and the Persians and the climate of India was not suitable for their growth. They began to degenerate during their stay in India.

The truth of this argument is challenged. It is pointed out that there is no reason to believe that the people belonging to colder climates are better warriors. Among the many well-known administrators and distinguished warriors produced by the Mughal Empire, there were many Hindustanis and immigrants who had lived in India for a long time. The eighteenth century also produced a large number of capable nobles and distinguished generals. Their personal ambitions were unlimited and they preferred to carve out independent principalities for themselves rather than serve the Mughal Emperors loyally and devotedly. The chief reason for the degeneration of the nobility was that gradually it became a closed corporation. It gave no opportunity of promotion to capable men belonging to other classes as had been the case earlier. The offices of the state became hereditary and the preserve of people belonging to a few families. Another reason was their incorrigible habit of extravagant living and pompous display which weakened their morale and drained their limited financial resources. Most of the nobles spent huge sums on keeping large harems, maintaining a big staff of servants etc., and indulged in other forms of senseless show. The result was that many of the nobles became bankrupt in spite of their large Jagirs. Dismissal from service or loss of Jagirs spelt ruin for most of them. That prompted many of them to form groups and factions for securing large and profitable Jagirs. Others turned themselves into grasping tyrants who mercilessly fleeced the peasants of their Jagirs. Many nobles became ease-loving and soft. They dreaded war and became so much accustomed to an extravagant way of life that they could not do without many of the luxuries even when they were on military campaigns.

The Mughal nobility was corrupt and faction-ridden. By giving suitable bribes, any Government rule could be evaded or any favour secured. The interests of the Mughal Empire did not appeal to them. The British regularly bribed Mughal nobles for getting their work done. Even the highest nobles took bribes which were called *Peshkash* or presents. That lowered the tone of administration. With the passage of time, corruption and bribery increased. Later on, even some of the Mughal Emperors shared the money which their favourites charged as Peshkash from people desirous of getting a post or seeking a transfer. Factionalism kept on growing till it extended to all branches of administration. The two major causes of factionalism were struggle for Jagirs and personal advancement and struggle for supremacy between the Wazir and the monarch. Thus, faction fights weakened the monarchy, gave a chance to the Marathas, Jats etc., to increase their power and to interfere in the court politics and prevented the Emperors from following a consistent policy. Factionalism became the most dangerous bane of the Mughal rule from 1713 onwards. To save themselves from these faction fights, the Mughal Emperors depended upon unworthy favourites that worsened the situation.

Sir Jadunath Sarkar writes, "All the surplus produce of a fertile land under a most bounteous Providence was swept into the coffers of the Mughal nobility and pampered them in a degree of luxury not dreamt of even by kings in Persia or Central Asia. Hence, in the houses of the Delhi nobility, luxury was carried to an excess. The harems of many of them were filled with a large number of women of an infinite variety of races, intellect and character. Under Muslim Law the sons of concubines are entitled to their matrimony equally with sons born sons in wedlock, and they occupy no inferior position in society. Even the sons of lawfully married wives became, at a precocious age, familiar with vices from what they saw and heard in the harem while their mothers were insulted by the higher splendor and influence enjoyed in the same household by younger and fairer rivals of servile origin or easier virtue. The proud spirit and majestic dignity of a Cornelia are impossible in the crowded harem of a polygamist; and without Cornelias among the mothers there cannot be Grachhi among the sons".

Where wealth accumulates, men decay;
And disloyalty on the Empire did prey.

A reference may also be made to the moral degeneration among the Mughal nobles. "In a mean spirit of jealousy, they insulted and thwarted new men drawn from the ranks and ennobled for the most brilliant public services, and yet they themselves had grown utterly worthless. We have a significant example of the moral degeneration of the Mughal peerage. The Prime Minister's grandson, Mirza Tafakhur, used to sally forth from his mansion in Delhi with his ruffians, plundered the shops in the bazar, kidnapped Hindu women passing through the public streets in litters or going to the river, and dishonoured them; and yet there was no judge strong enough to punish him, no police to prevent such crimes. Every time such an occurrence was brought to the Emperor's notice by the newsletters or official reports, he referred it to the Prime Minister and did nothing more".

7. Another cause of Mughal downfall was the *deterioration and demoralisation in the Mughal army*. The abundance of riches of India, the use of wine and comforts had their evil effects on the Mughal army and nothing was done to stop the deterioration. The soldiers cared more for personal comforts and less for winning battles. In the words of Irvine, "Excepting want of personal courage, every other fault in the list of military vices may be attributed to the degenerate Mughals; indiscipline, want of cohesion, luxurious habits, inactivity and commissariat and cumbrous equipment". The impotence of the Mughal armies was declared to the world when the Mughals failed to recapture Qandhar in spite of three determined efforts made by them. In 1739, Nadir Shah not only plundered the whole of Delhi but also ordered wholesale massacre. When such a thing happens without any effort on the part of the ruler to stop it, he forfeits the right to command allegiance from the people. The Mughal state was a police state and when it failed to maintain internal order and external peace, the people lost all their respect for the Government. The view of Sir Wolseley Haig is that the demoralisation of the army was one of the principal factors in the disintegration of the Mughal Empire. The source of the weakness was the composition of the army which consisted chiefly of contingents maintained by the great nobles from the revenues of assignments held by them for that purpose. As the authority of the sovereign relaxed, the general tendency among the great nobles was naturally to hold as their own those assignments which maintained their troops. The general laxity of discipline converted the army into a mob. Drill was unknown and a soldier's training which he might undergo or not as he liked, consisted in muscular exercise and in individual practice in the use of the weapons with which he was armed. He mounted guard or not as he liked. There was no 'regular punishment for military crimes. Aurangzeb himself habitually overlooked, as matters of course, acts of treason, cowardice and deliberate neglect of duty before the enemy.

About the military system of the Mughals, it is contended that their weapons and methods of war had become frost-grown and outmoded. They put too much reliance on artillery and armoured cavalry. The artillery was local in action and ponderous in movement. It was rendered stationary by huge tail of camp which looked like a city with its markets, tents, stores and baggage. All kinds of people, men and women, old and young, combatants and non-combatants, besides elephants, cattle and beasts of burden, accompanied the Mughal army. On the other hand, the Maratha cavalry was swift and elusive like wind. They suddenly erupted on Mughal camps and launched damaging attacks on their posts. Before the Mughals could get time for recovery, the Marathas "like water parted by the oar," closed and fell on them. At the turn of the 18th century, musketry made rapid progress and became prominent in the methods of warfare. Swift running cavalry of matchlock-men was superior to army equipped with heavy artillery and armour-clad cavalry. In spite of that, the Mughals refused to change their old methods of warfare and no wonder they were defeated by the Marathas and the Afghan.

8. The *Mughals neglected the development of the navy* and that proved suicidal for them. They never realised the importance of a fully equipped navy for the defence of their Empire. They neither gave any importance to naval power nor took any measures to develop it. The result was that the Mughals could not stand before the rising European powers which were expert in naval tactics of war. It was the strength of their naval power which enabled the European powers, particularly the British, to establish their commercial and political supremacy in India. In course of time, they struck a deadly blow to the already tottering Mughal Empire.

9. The Mughals suffered from intellectual bankruptcy. That was partly due to the lack of an efficient system of education in the country which alone could produce leaders of thought. The result was that the Mughals failed to produce any political genius or leader who could "teach the country a new philosophy of life and to kindle aspirations after a new heaven on earth. They all drifted and dozed in admiration of the wisdom of their ancestors and shook their heads at the growing degeneration of the moderns". Sir Jadunath Sarkar points out that there was no good education and no practical training of the Mughal nobility. They were too much patted by eunuchs and maid servants and passed through a sheltered life from birth to manhood. Their domestic tutors were an unhappy class powerless to do any good except by love of their pupils, brow-beaten by eunuchs, disobeyed by the lads themselves and forced to cultivate the arts of the courtier or to throw up their thankless office. Not much could be expected from such teachers and their words.

10. Another of cause of Mughal downfall was *the prevalence of corruption in every department of the Government.* The exaction of official perquisites from the public by the officials and their subordinates was universal and an admitted practice. Many officials from the highest to the lowest took bribes for doing undeserved favours. Even the Emperor was not above it. Aurangzeb is stated to have asked an aspirant to a title: "Your father gave to Shah Jahan one lakh of rupees for adding Alif to his title and making him Amir Khan. How much will you pay me for the title I am giving you ?" The ministers and influential courtiers around the Emperor made fortunes. Qabil Khan in one and a half years of personal attendance on Aurangzeb amassed ₹12 lakhs of rupees in cash, besides articles of value and a new house. Offices were reserved for old families of clerks and accountants and outsiders were not allowed to come in. Such a state of affairs was detrimental to the highest interests of the state.

11. The Mughal Government received no *popular support*. The Mughals came to India from foreign lands and their rule came to be considered as alien. With the exception of Akbar, no Mughal ruler made any effort to bring the Hindus and Muslims together and create a composite nation. Akbar did some pioneering work, but his work was undone by his successors. Aurangzeb particularly behaved in a bigoted way and always considered himself as the ruler of the Muslims only. His policies naturally offended the sentiments of the Hindus and encouraged them to revolt against him. The Mughal rulers did not pay any attention to the welfare of the people. They were mainly concerned with the collection of revenue and maintenance of law and order. The result was that the Hindus continued to look upon the Muslim rulers as foreigners and enemies of their religion and country. They were keen for an opportunity to overthrow the alien rule of the Mughals. The result was that when the Mughal Empire grew weak in the 18th century, the Hindus, particularly the Marathas, Jats and Rajputs, did everything possible to bring about its fall.

12. The Mansabdari system degenerated in the time of Aurangzeb and his successors. Jagirs were in short supply. Transfers were frequent and the allotment of a new Jagir took long time. Even when a Jagir was allotted, its real income was generally far below its paper income, The result was that many nobles could not keep their quota of troops. That weakened the army and affected adversely the administrative efficiency. The practice of farming lands to the highest bidder made the position of the peasants miserable. The old landed nobility (Zamindars) were replaced by a new type of business-cum-oppressor class.

13. Another cause of Mughal downfall was the stoppage of adventurers from Persia, Afghanistan and Turkistan. While the Mughals in India ruined themselves through luxuries and pleasures, there was a dearth of men who could shoulder the responsibilities of the Government. It is the adventurers, particularly from Persia, who had given able administrators and generals to the Muslim rulers of India and when that source stopped, the Mughal administrative machinery became like a corpse. It was not able to deliver the goods.

14. There was the general loss of nerve on the part of the Muslim community in India. They forgot that they had a mission to fulfil in India. Those who counted in the country, cared more for personal aggrandisement than for the glory of Islam in, India. The ablest among them were keen to set up kingdoms of their own and thereby perpetuate their names. Theologians like Shah Wali Ullah took refuge in the concept of the community of the faithful looking only to God instead of calling upon the Muslims to rally round the throne. What was to be seen was not patriotism or bravery but cynicism, opportunism and indulgence. Much could not be expected in those circumstances.

15. The invasions of India by Nadir Shah and Ahmad Shah Abdali gave a serious blow to the already tottering Mughal Empire. The easy victory of Nadir Shah and the repeated invasions of Ahmad Shah Abdali exposed to the world the military weakness of the Mughal state. The prestige of the Mughal Empire was adversely affected. The people lost all faith in the capacity of the Mughal rulers to protect them against foreign invaders. That encouraged them to revolt and set up their independent states.

16. Probably one of the most important factors which contributed to the decline of the Mughal Empire was the rise of the Marathas under the Peshwas. After consolidating their position in Western India, they started entertaining plans for a Hindu Empire covering Northern India also. That dream could be realised only at the cost of the Mughals. The Marathas made their gains at the cost of the Mughals and emerged. As the strongest power in Northern India in the mid 18th century. They not only played the role of kingmakers at the Delhi court but also acted as the defenders of the country against foreign invaders like Ahmad Shah Abdali. Though the Marathas did not succeed in setting up their Empire in Northern India, they certainly gave a death blow to the Mughal Empire.

17. The rise of the British power in India was also responsible for the downfall of the Mughal Empire. Although, the English East India Company started merely as a commercial adventure, it became powerful in course of time and acquired political power. By the middle of the eighteenth century, it was successful in ousting other European rivals in the commercial and political spheres. By their victories in the battles to Plassey and Buxar in 1757 and 1764 respectively, the English East India Company became the virtual master of Bengal, Bihar and Orissa (now Odisha). The Mughal Emperors had no naval power of their own to meet the danger from the English East India Company. In course of time, the English East India Company got a perfect mastery of the whole of India which once formed the Mughal Empire. Sir Jadunath Sarkar writes, "The English conquest of the Mughal Empire is only a part of the inevitable domination of all Africa and Asia by the European nations... which is only another way of saying that the progressive races are supplanting the conservative ones, just as enterprising families are constantly replacing sleepy and self-satisfied ones in the leadership of our society".

18. Another important factor which hastened the downfall of the Mughal Empire was that in the eighteenth century, there was a revival of political consciousness among the martial races of the Hindus. Those races were the Rajputs, the Sikhs and the Marathas. They set up their independent states in their own areas on the ruins of the Mugal Empire. Their attacks on the Mughal Empire rendered it hollow from within.

19. Another cause of the downfall of the Mughal Empire was that it could no longer satisfy the minimum needs of the people. The condition of the Indian peasant gradually worsened during the 17th and 18th centuries. In the 18th century, his life was "poor, nasty, miserable and uncertain". The constant transfer of nobles from their Jagirs led to great evil. They tried to extract as much from a Jagir as possible in the short period of their tenure as Jagirdars. They made heavy demands on the peasants and cruelly oppressed them, often in violation of official regulations. After the death of Aurangzeb, the practice of Ijarah or farming the land revenue to the highest bidder became more and more common both on Jagir and Khalisah (Crown) lands. That led to the rise of a new class of revenue farmers and Talukdars whose extortions from the peasantry often knew no bounds. There was stagnation and deterioration in agriculture and impoverishment of the peasant. Peasant discontent increased and came to the surface. There were instances of the peasants leaving the land in order to avoid the payment of taxes. Peasant discontentment found an outlet in a series of uprisings such as the Satnamis, the Jats and the Sikhs and that weakened the stability and strength of the Empire. Many peasants formed roving bands of robbers and adventurers and thereby undermined law and order and efficiency of the Government.

Bhimsen writes thus about the oppressive officers: "There is no limit to the oppression of these men... of their oppression and cruelty what may one write? For no description can suffice". To quote Khafi Khan, "The cruelty, oppression and injustice of the officials, who have no thought of God, has reached such a degree that if one wishes to describe a hundredth part of it, will still defy description".

Professor Irfan Habib writes thus in his book entitled *The Agrarian System of Mughal India*: "But the Mughal Empire had its own grave digger and what Sadi said of another great Empire might well serve as its epitah:

> The Emperors of Persia
> Who oppressed the lower classes;
> Gone is their glory and Empire;
> Gone their tyranny over the peasant!"

View of Dr. Satish Chandra. A reference may be made to some of the views of Dr. Satish Chandra regarding the downfall of the Mughal Empire. He points out that Aurangzeb has been criticised for having failed to unite with the Deccai states against the Marathas, or for having conquered them thereby making the Empire "so large that it collapsed under its own weight". A unity of hearts between Aurangzeb and the Deccai states was "a psychological impossibility", once the treaty of 1636 was abandoned, a development which took place during the reign of Shah Jahan himself. After his accession, Aurangzeb desisted from pursuing a vigorous forward policy in the Deccan. In fact, he postponed as long as possible the decision to conquer and annex the Deccai states. His hand was virtually forced by the growing Maratha power, the support extended to Shivaji by Madanna and Akhanna from Golconda and fear that Bijapur might fall under the domination of Shivaji and the Maratha-dominated Golconda. By giving shelter to the rebel Prince Akbar, Sambhaji virtually threw a challenge to Aurangzeb who quickly realised that the Marathas could not be dealt with without first subduing Bijapur and possibly Golconda.

Dr. Satish Chandra points out that the impact of the Deccai and other wars of the Mughal Empire and of the prolonged absence of Aurangzeb from Northern India, should not be over-estimated. Despite the mistakes of policy and some of the personal shortcomings of Aurangzeb, the Mughal Empire was still a powerful and vigorous military and administrative machinery. The Mughal army might fail against the elusive and the highly mobile bands of the Marathas in the mountainous region of the Deccan. Maratha forts might be difficult to capture and still more difficult to retain. But in the plains of Northern India and the vast plateau extending up to the Karnatak, the Mughal artillery was still the master of the field. Thirty or forty years after the death of Aurangzeb when the Mughal artillery had declined considerably in strength and efficiency, the Marathas could still not face it in the field of battle. In Northern India which was the heart of the Empire and was of decisive economic and political importance in the country, the Mughal administration still retained much of its vigour. The administration at the district level proved amazingly tenacious and a good deal of it survived and found its way indirectly into the British administration. Despite the military reverses and mistakes of Aurangzeb, the Mughal dynasty still retained a powerful hold on the mind and imagination of the people.

Dr. Satish Chandra further points out that as far as the Rajputs were concerned, the breach with Marwar was not due to any attempt on the part of Aurangzeb to undermine the Hindus by depriving them of a recognised head. That was due to a miscalculation on his part. He wanted to divide the Marwar state between the two principal claimants, and in the process alienated both, as also the ruler of Mewar who considered Mughal interference in such matters to be a dangerous precedent. The breach with Mewar and the long-drawn-out war which followed damaged the moral standing of the Mughal state. However, the fighting was not of much consequence militarily after 1681. It may be doubted whether the presence of Rathor Rajputs in large numbers in the Deccai between 1681 and 1706 would have made much difference in the outcome of the conflict with the Marathas. In any case, the demands of the Rajputs related to the grant of high Mansabs as before and restoration of their homelands. Those demands having been accepted within half a dozen years of the death of Aurangzeb, the Rajputs ceased to be a problem for the Mughals. They played no role in the subsequent disintegration of the Mughal Empire.

Dr. Satish Chandra maintains that the religious policy of Aurangzeb should be seen in the social, economic and political contexts. Aurangzeb was orthodox in his outlook and he tried to remain within the framework of Islamic law. That was developed outside. India in vastly dissimilar situations and could hardly be applied rigidly to India. The failure of Aurangzeb to respect the susceptibilities of his non-Muslim subjects on many occasions, his adherence to the time-worn policy towards temples and re-imposition of Jizya as laid down by the Islamic law did not help him to rally the Muslims to his side or generate a greater sense of loyalty towards a state based on Islamic Law. On the other hand, it alienated the Hindus and strengthened the hands of those sections which were opposed to the Mughal Empire for political or other reasons. By itself, religion was not at issue. Jizya was scrapped within half a dozen years of the death of Aurangzeb and restrictions on the building of new temples were eased, but they had no effect on the decline and disintegration of the Mughal Empire.

The conclusion of Dr. Satish Chandra is that in the ultimate resort, the decline and downfall of the Mughal Empire was due to economic, social, political and institutional factors. Akbar's measures helped to keep the forces of disintegration in check for some time, but it was not possible for him to effect fundamental changes in the structure of society. By the time Aurangzeb came to the throne, the socioeconomic forces of disintegration were already strong. Aurangzeb lacked the foresight and statesmanship necessary to effect fundamental changes in the structure or to pursue policies which could reconcile the various competing elements. Aurangzeb was both a victim of circumstances and helped to create the circumstances of which he became a victim.

The view of Dr. Satish Chandra is that India lagged behind the world in the field of science and technology and the Mughal ruling class remained blind to this development. It was more concerned with matters of immediate concern than matters which would shape the future. The Mughal Empire had already reached the limits of its development. The feudal aristocratic nature of the state and the neglect of science and technology by the ruling class were placing limits to the economic development of the country.

Dr. Satish Chandra concludes, "Thus, the roots of the disintegration of the Mughal empire may be found in the Medieval Indian economy; the stagnation of trade, industry and scientific development within the limits of that economy; the growing financial crisis which took the form of a crisis of the Jagirdari system and affected every branch of state activity; the inability of the nobility to realise in the circumstances their ambitions in the service of the state and, consequently, the struggle of factions and the bid of ambitious nobles for independent dominion: the inability of the Mughal emperors to accommodate the Marathas and to adjust their claims within the framework of the Mughal Empire, and the consequent breakdown of the attempt to create a composite ruling class in India; and the impact of all these developments on politics at the court and in the country, and upon the security of the north-western passes. Individual failings and faults of character also played their due role but they have necessarily to be seen against the background of these deeper, more impersonal factors". (*Parties and Politics at the Mughal Court,* p. 268.)

Sir Jadunath Sarkar writes, "The Mughal Empire and with it the Maratha overlordship of Hindustan fell because of the rottenness at the core of Indian society. The rottenness showed itself in the form of military and political helplessness. The country could not defend itself; royalty was hopelessly depraved or imbecile; the nobles were selfish and short-sighted; corruption, inefficiency and treachery disgraced all branches of public service. In the midst of this decay and confusion, our literature, art and even true religion had perished". (*Fall of the Mughal Empire,* Vol. 4, pp. 343-44.)

REVIEW QUESTIONS

1. Throw light on the social, political and religious conditions of India at the time of Aurangzebn's death.
2. Discuss the condition of India at the end of Aurangzeb's region.
3. Explain the activities and achievements of the successors of Aurangzeb.
4. Write a detailed note on the achievements and fall of the Sayyid Brothers.
5. Assess the factors responsible for Nadir Shah's invasion of India.
6. The religious policy of Aurangzeb affected the fortunes of the Mughal empire. Comment.
7. Critically analyse the causes of the decline and disintegration of the Mughal empire.
8. Write short notes on the following:
    (a) Bahadur Shah I and II
    (b) Invasions of Ahmad Shah Abdali
    (c) Akbar II
9. At the end of Aurangzeb's reign, the Mughal empire was in a state of hopeless decay. Examine.
10. Discuss the view of Dr. Satish Chandra regarding the downfall of the Mughal empire.

SUGGESTED READINGS

Athar Ali: *The Mughal Nobility under Aurangzeb.*

Bisheshwar Prasad: *Bondage and Freedom,* Vol. I, New Delhi, 1981.

Faruki, Zahiruddin: *Aurangzeb and His Times.*

Frazer, J.: *History of Nadir Shah.*

Gupta, Hari Ram: *Studies (in the Later Mughal History of the Punjab.*

Habib, Irfan: *The Agrarian System of Mughal India.*

Irvine, William: *Later Mughals,* Vols. I and II.

Kashiraj, Pandit: *Battle of Panipat,* Ed. by Rawlinson (1926 Edition).

Lockhart, L.: *Nadir Shah,* 1938.

Keene, H.G.: *The Fall of the Mughal Empire,* 1887.

Majumdar, R.C.: (Ed.). *The Maratha Supremacy,* Bhartiya Vidya Bhavan, Bombay, 1977.

Malleson, G.B.: *The Decisive Battles of India.*

Owen, Sidney: *The Fall of the Mughal Empire.*

Sarkar, Sir Jadunath: *The Fall of the Mughal Empire,* 4 Vols.

Satish Chandra: *Parties and Politics at the Mughal Court, 1707-40.*

Spear, Percival: *Twilight of the Mughals,* 1951.

Srivastava, A.L.: *The First Two Nawabs of Oudh.*

Srivastava, A.L.: *Shuja-ud-Daulah.*

Tara Chand: *History of the Freedom Movement in India,* Vol. I, Government of India, 1961.

2 Rise of Autonomous States

LEARNING OBJECTIVES

- Throw light on the emergence of various autonomous states with the disintegration of the Mughal empire
- Explain the activities and achievements of the rulers of the autonomous states

BENGAL SUBAH

Murshid Quli Khan. When the Mughal Empire began to disintegrate, many provinces virtually became independent. The Subah of Bengal was the first to become autonomous and the first to pass under British rule. It became autonomous under Murshid Quli Khan, a South Indian Brahman convert to Islam. He was educated in Persia. He served his apprenticeship in Mughal administration in the Deccan. He won the confidence of Aurangzeb by honest and efficient discharge of his duties. He was appointed Diwan of Bengal Subah in 1700 A.D. In 1701, the Diwani of Orissa (now Odisha) was added to his charge. In 1704, the Diwani of Bihar was also given to him. He kept Aurangzeb satisfied by regular transmission of large amounts of money for the Deccan War. On account of his disagreement with the Subahdar Azim-ush-Shan, the grandson of Aurangzeb, Murshid Quli Khan transferred Diwani office from Dacca, the provincial capital, to Maqsudabad whose name was later on changed to Murshidabad.

At the time of the death of Aurangzeb, Murshid Quli Khan was Naib Nazim or Deputy Governor of Bengal and full Governor of Orissa (now Odisha) and Diwan of Bengal and Orissa (now Odisha). In February 1713, Farrukh-siyar conferred on him the Diwani of Bengal. In September 1713, he made him also Deputy Governor of Bengal. On 6 May 1714, he received Subahdari of Orissa. In September 1717, he was made full Subahdar of Bengal.

Murshid Quli Khan was a strict ruler. He established an efficient administration. He effectively reorganised the revenue system by converting all the Jagirs of the officers in Bengal into Khalsa directly under the Crown collectors and by introducing the *Ijara* system according to which contracts were given for collection of revenue. Later on, those contractors became Zamindars and many of them got the title of Rajas and Maharajas. Thus, a new landed aristocracy was created in Bengal whose "position was confirmed and made hereditary by Lord Cornwallis". Increase of revenue was also due to economy in administration and maintenance of internal peace.

Although he freed himself from central control, he continued to send regularly his tribute to the Mughal Emperor. He established peace by freeing Bengal of internal and external dangers. Bengal was relatively free of uprisings by Zamindars. The only three major uprisings during his rule were by Sitaram Ray of Bhusna Pargana, Udai Narayan and Ghulam Muhammad and then by Shujat Khan and finally by Najat Khan. After defeating them, he gave their Jagirs to Ramjivan, his own favourite. He was a good administrator and he improved the finances of the state. He also helped the growth of trade and gave all possible help and incentives to traders. He was a man of puritan character who despised all kinds of luxury. He succeeded in bringing prosperity to the province of Bengal. He died in June 1727.

Sir Jadunath Sarkar writes about Murshid Quli Khan, "A puritan in his private life, strictly attentive to his public duties as he understood them, gravely decorous and rigidly orthodox as befitted a favourite disciple of Aurangzeb, and a propagator of his faith as ordained in his scriptures, Murshid Quli Khan presents one side of his character in a brilliant light. But his heart was cold and his sympathies narrow, his calculating vindictiveness, his religious bigotry, and his utter lack of warm, all-embracing benevolence, denied this conscientious civil servant the right to be ranked as a statesman or even as a truly great soul." (*History of Bengal*, Vol. I, edited by Jadunath Sarkar, 1948, pp. 420-21.)

Shuja-ud-Din. When Murshid Quli Khan died in 1727, without leaving any male issue, his son-in-law Shuja-ud-din Mohammad Khan who had been Deputy Governor of Orissa (now Odisha), ascended the Masnad of Bengal. He appointed his friends and kinsmen to the principal offices of the Government. In managing all important affairs of administration, Shuja-ud-din followed the counsel of Ali Vardi Khan, of his brother Haji Ahmad, of Alam Chand, a loyal officer and able financiar and of Jagat Seth Fateh Chand, the famous banker of Murshidabad.

During the early part of his rule, Shuja-ud-Din paid due attention the affairs of administration and sought to promote the welfare of his subjects. He was, charitable to his old friends, kind and bountiful towards his officers and hospitable to those who happened to come to Murshidabad. He dispensed justice impartially. He strictly asserted his authority over the European trading Companies in Bengal. The English did not consider it advisable to risk an open rupture with him and paid him occasionally large sums of money. However, towards the end of his life, some vices in the private character of Shuja-ud-Din impaired the efficiency of his administration and supreme power fell into the hands of his advisers, Haji Ahmad, Alam Chand and Jagat Seth Fateh Chand who degenerated into a clique of self-seekers who tormented intrigues and conspiracies to serve their own interests.

Sarfaraz Khan (1739-40). When Shuja-ud-Din died in March 1739, he was succeeded by his son Sarfaraz Khan. He retained old officers like Haji Ahmad and Alam Chand. Sarfaraz Khan was excessively addicted to debauchery and he did not possess the essential qualities needed for the ruler of a state. He had to pay a very heavy price by losing his life and the Masnad of Bengal. The weakness of Delhi authority, inefficiency of Sarfaraz Khan and machinations of Haji Ahmad excited Ali Vardi's ambition to seize the Masnad of Bengal for himself. With that object, he left Patna for Murshidabad. Sarfaraz was killed in the battle of Gheria on 10 April 1740. Ali Vardi Khan ruled Bengal from 1740 to 1756.

Ali Vardi Khan. Ali Vardi Khan rose gradually to higher and higher posts by dint of his tact and ability. In 1728, Shuja-ud-Din appointed him Faujdar of the Chakla Akbarnagar. He governed that area efficiently and brought peace and prosperity to the people. His brother Haji Ahmad was at Murshidabad as one of the chief advisers of Shuja-ud-Din. His eldest son Muhammad Raza was appointed Paymaster of Nawab's troops and Superintendent of Customs at Murshidabad. His second son Aga Muhamrnad Said was appointed Faujdar of Rungpur. In 1733, Ali Vardi Khan was appointed Deputy Governor of Bihar and he restored peace in that province by vigorous steps and measures of reconciliation. He suppressed the disturbances with firmness. The Zamindars were reduced to submission. He also took strong action against the turbulent Banjaras who were devastating different parts of Bihar. In 1740 Ali Vardi seized the Masnad of Bengal by defeating and killing Sarfaraz Khan.

The rule of Ali Vardi Khan was disturbed by frequent military operations. He had to subjugate Orissa by force of arms in 1741. Safdarjang, the Nawab of Avadh, entered Bihar and occupied Patna for some time (1742). The Afghans of Bihar rose in revolt in 1745 and 1748 and they received support from Afghan adventurers from different parts of Northern India. However, the Marathas were the greatest menace to Ali Vardi Khan. There were as many as five Maratha invasions in 1742, 1743, 1744, 1745 and 1748. Raghuji Bhonsle of Nagpur found in the rich province of Bengal a profitable field for plunder and extension of his political influence. In 1742, his general Bhaskar Ram invaded Bengal and his troops ravaged the Western Districts of Bengal and parts of Bihar and Orissa (now Odisha). In 1743, Raghuji Bhonsle himself marched at the head of a large army on the plea of realising the Chauth of Bengal, Bihar and Orissa. At the same time, Peshwa Balaji Baji Rao entered at the head of another Maratha army. Ali Vardi Khan conciliated the Peshwa by promising payment of Chauth to Sahu and by making an immediate payment of ₹22 lacs. The allied troops of the Peshwa and Ali Vardi Khan expelled Raghuji Bhonsle. The Peshwa also left Bengal. Bhaskar Ram invaded again in 1744. Ali Vardi Khan got rid of him by treacherous murder and his troops fled. In 1745, Raghuji Bhonsle again attacked Bengal, but he was defeated by Ali Vardi Khan and forced to retreat to Nagpur. In 1748, a Maratha army from Nagpur, led by Janoji Bhonsle, advanced into Bengal and the operations continued till 1751. Worn out with incessant toil and weighed down with age at the age of 75, Ali Vardi Khan concluded a treaty with the Marathas in May/June 1751. The river Subarnarekha was fixed as the boundary of the Bengal Subah and the Marathas agreed never to cross it again. Orissa (now Odisha) was ceded to the Bhonsle ruler. From October 1751, ₹12 lakhs of rupees were to be paid annually to the Marathas from Bengal revenues as the Chauth of that Subah in two installments on the condition that the Marathas would never set their foot again in the Subah of Bengal.

Apart from territorial loss, the Nawab of Bengal suffered serious economic loss. Agriculture, industry, trade and commerce were dislocated. There was social dislocation as a large number of people migrated from the ravaged Western Districts of Bengal to the Northern and Eastern Districts. The English merchants of Calcutta took measures for the Defence of the town against apprehended Maratha raids and provided shelter for many people. That earned for them the goodwill and confidence of the Indians. Ali Vardi was generally conciliatory. He was aware of their growing strength and the political developments connected with the Anglo-French conflict in the Deccan alarmed him. That fear came out to be true in the time of his successor.

Ali Vardi Khan governed Bengal ably and with prudence and foresight. In his private life, he was free from the prevailing vices of the ruling and aristocratic classes of those days. He was a tactful and strong Governor who tried to infuse spirit and vigour into every branch of his administration.

Siraj-ud-Daulah. Ali Vardi Khan died on 10 April 1756 and he was succeeded by his grandson and heir-designate Siraj-ud-Daulah. He had enemies among his near relations who coveted the Bengal Masnad or influence through it. They were his cousin Shaukat Jung and his mother's eldest sister Ghasiti Begum who had amassed immense wealth. Siraj-ud-Daulah's most formidable enemy was Mir Jafar, the Commander-in-Chief of the army.

Soon after his accession, Siraj-ud-Daulah seized the huge wealth of Ghasiti Begum. He removed Mir Jafar from the post of the commander of the army and appointed in his place Mir Madan. Mohan Lal was made Peshkar of the Diwan-i-Khanah. Siraj-ud-Daulah defeated and killed Shaukat Jung in October 1756.

Siraj-ud-Daulah had three specific grievances against the English East India Company. The Company had built strong fortifications and dug a large ditch in the King's dominion contrary to the laws of the country. The second grievance was that the English had abused the privilege of their *Dastaks* by granting them to such men as were in no way entitled to them and the Nawab lost the revenue. The third complaint was that they had given protection in Calcutta to some of the King's subjects and instead of giving them up on demand, they allowed such persons to shelter themselves within their bounds from the hands of justice. The charges were not baseless, but the English in Calcutta insulted the messenger of Siraj-ud-Daulah. On 4 June 1756, the English factory at Kasim Bazar was stormed by the soldiers of the Nawab. The Nawab captured Calcutta on 20 June 1756. The story of *"Blackhole"* has been proved to be untrue. The Madras Council sent reinforcement of troops under Admiral Watson and Colonel Clive to recover Calcutta by the first week of February 1757. Adverse circumstances forced Siraj-ud-Daulah to conclude a treaty with the English on 9 February 1757 by which the trade rights and factories of the English East India Company were restored to them and restitution and compensation money were promised by the Nawab to the Company, its servants and tenants. The English were granted permission to fortify Calcutta and coin sicca rupees. In return for these concessions, the English Company promised to help Siraj-ud-Daulah against the Afghans.

However, peace between Siraj-ud-Daulah and the English did not last long. The Nawab was suspicious of the designs of the English Company and the English Company was also convinced that the Nawab would try to destroy them. The result was that the English decided to overthrow the Nawab. A conspiracy was hatched and it was decided to put Mir Jafar on the Manad of Bengal. In pursuance of that conspiracy, the battle of Plassey was fought on 23 June 1757 in which the English were victorious. Siraj-ud-Daulah ran away from the battlefield but he was captured and put to death. Mir Jafar was made the Nawab of Bengal.

Mir Jafar. Mir Jafar ruled from 1757 to 1760. He was merely a figurehead and the real power was in the hands of Clive. Ultimately, in 1760 he was removed by the English Company and Mir Qasim was made the Nawab in 1760. He ruled from 1760 to 1763. He was also removed in 1763 and replaced by Mir Jafar. Mir Jafar remained the Nawab of Bengal for the second time from July 1763 to February 1765. When Mir Jafar died in 1765, his second son Najam-ud-Daulah was put on the throne but all power passed into the hands of the English Company. In 1765, Clive set up what is known as Dual Government of Bengal which lasted upto 1772 when the administration of Bengal was taken over directly by the English East India Company.

AVADH

Saadat Ali Khan. Avadh became independent under Saadat Ali Khan who was the leader of the Irani faction in the court of Muhammad Shah. After being in the service of Sarbuland Khan (1710-12), Saadat Ali Khan joined the service of Farrukh-siyar. He became Faujdar of Hindaun and Bayana and was made a noble on 9 October 1720. He was appointed Governor first of Agra (1720-22) and then of Avadh. He extended the jurisdiction of Avadh over Banaras, Ghazipur, Jaunpur and Chunar. He gradually acquired power and fame. He was summoned to Delhi at the time of invasion of Nadir Shah in 1739 but he committed suicide in March 1739 as he could not fulfil the promise made by him to Nadir Shah. During his long tenure, the people began to look upon him as their real master and thus the foundations of the Shia dynasty in Avadh were securely laid.

Safdarjang. The next Governor of Avadh was Safdarjang (1739-54). He was the nephew and son-in-law of Saadat Ali Khan. In 1742, Emperor Muhammad Shah asked Safdarjang to protect Bihar. Safdarjang went to Bihar and entered Patna city in December 1742. However, the Mughal Emperor asked him to come back and he did so in February 1743.

When Ahmed Shah became the Emperor in 1748, he appointed Safdarjang as his Wazir. The position of Safdarjang was "one of unusual difficulty". He was considered as an interloper by the old nobility. He had to meet opposition from Nizam-ul-Mulk's son and grandson, of Javid Khan and the sons of the late Wazir Qamar-ud-Din. He had contests with the Afghans (1748-52). He was defeated at Ramchatauni in 1750 and he made peace with the Rohillas and Bangashes under the orders of the Mughal Emperor in April 1752. In 1753, Safdarjang got Javid Khan murdered. He tried to grasp everything and became extremely domineering. A conspiracy was hatched against Safdarjang. There was a civil war between the Emperor and Safdarjang from March to November 1753. He left for Avadh in November and died in 1754. He gave lasting peace to Avadh and Allahabad.

Shuja-ud-Daula (1754-75). After the death of Safdarjang in October 1754, his son Shuja-ud-Daulah became the Subedar of Avadh and he occupied that position till 1775. His personal character was not at all commendable. He was occupied with nothing but pleasure, hunting and the most violent exercises. He did not possess the genius of a soldier. He was wanting in valour and courage. He specialised in treachery. He was rapacious in acquiring and preserving wealth.

The relations of Shuja-ud-Daula with Imad-ul-Mulk, the imperial Wazir, were extremely bitter and that resulted in plots and counterplots. Prince Ali Gauhar became a friend of Shuja-ud-Daula who encouraged the Prince to invade Bihar. During the Maratha-Afghan contests (1759-61), Shuja-ud-Daula fought as an ally of Ahmad Shah Abdali. In February 1762, Shah Alam II appointed Shuja-ud-Daula as the Wazir.

When Mir Qasim was driven out from Bengal in 1763, he took refuge with Shuja-ud-Daula who agreed to help him to recover his lost province. Mir Qasim helped Shuja-ud-Daula in subduing the rebels of Bundelkhand and promised to pay the Mughal Emperor and Shuja-ud-Daula ten and seventeen lakhs of rupees respectively. In October 1764 was fought the battle of Buxar in which Shuja-ud-Daula and Mir Qasim were defeated. After running from one place to another, Shuja-ud-Daula was finally defeated in the battle, of Kora in May 1765. Colonel Fletcher overran the territory of Shuja-ud-Daula and occupied Banaras, Buxar and Allahabad. Avadh fell completely under British control. Shah Alam threw himself under the protection of the English who gave him residence in the Allahabad fort. Lord Clive who had returned to Bengal as Governor of the English East India Company in May 1765 met Shuja-ud-Daula at Banaras and the Mughal Emperor at Allahabad. By the treaty of Allahabad dated 16 August 1765, all the territories of Shuja-ud-Daula were restored to him with the exception of Kora and Allahabad which were given to the Mughal Emperor, Chunar and the Zamindari of Banaras. Shuja-ud-Daula agreed to pay ₹50 lakhs to the English East India Company as compensation for the expenses of the recent war. He entered into a defensive treaty with the British for mutual support in the defence of his territories and agreed to defray the cost of the troops maintained for that purpose. This treaty made Shuja-ul-Daula completely dependent on the British.

In July 1766, Clive called a congress at Chapra in Bihar which was attended by Shuja-ud-Daula and others. A treaty was signed for mutual defence and security from the attacks of the Marathas. Under pressure from Clive, Shuja-ud-Daula was appointed the Wazir by the Mughal Emperor. In order to check the anti-English designs of Shuja-ud-Daula, the English concluded a treaty with him on 29 November 1768 which "checked the strength and progress of the Wazir's army and freed the English from apprehension from their ally". This treaty was resented by Shuja-ud-Daulah and hence it was cancelled in September 1773.

The relations of Shuja-ud-Daula with the Mughal Emperor were not cordial between 1765-68 as he wanted to have complete control over the imperial court as *de facto* Wazir by eliminating the influence of Munir-ud-Daula in whom the Emperor had confidence. Through the efforts of the British, a reconciliation was arranged between the Emperor and Shuja-ud-Daulah and their relations were cordial from 1769 to 1771. When the Mughal Emperor returned to Delhi with Maratha help in 1771, he was deprived of Kora and Allahabad which were transferred to Shuja-ud-Daula in lieu of ₹50 lakhs and an annual subsidy for the maintenance of a garrison of the troops of the English Company for the protection of Nawab Shuja-ud-Daula. This arrangement was ratified by the treaty of Banaras on 7 September 1773. Warren Hastings promised to help Shuja-ud-Daula to conquer Rohilkhand. Shuja-ud-Daula agreed to receive an English gentleman having the confidence of Warren Hastings who was to act as Political Resident in Avadh.

The Nawab of Avadh wanted to occupy Rohilkhand. To prevent the attacks of the Marathas into Rohilkhand, a treaty was concluded between Shuja-ud-Daula and the Rohillas. The Rohillas promised to pay ₹40 lakhs to Shuja-ud-Daula if he expelled the Marathas from their territory. When the Marathas invaded Rohilkhand in 1773, they were defeated by the combined forces of the English

Company and Avadh. Shuja-ud-Daula demanded from Hafiz Rahmat Khan, leader of the Rohillas, the payment of the sum of ₹40 lacs. Rahmat Khan evaded payment. Shuja-ud-Daula demanded help from the English Company. British army was sent under Colonel Champion in February 1774. The combined forces of Shuja-ud-Daula and the English Company marched into Rohilkhand in April 1774. Hafiz Rahmat Khan was killed. About 20,000 Rohillas were expelled beyond the Ganges and their province became a part of the kingdom of Avadh. A part of it was given to Rampur. Shuja-ud-Daula died on 26 January 1775 and he was succeeded by his eldest son Asaf-ud-Daulah (1775-97).

Asaf-ud-Daula (1775-97). The accession of Asaf-ud-Daula marked the beginning, of the degradation and exploitation of Avadh by the English Company. This was due to the fact that Asaf-ud-Daula was weekend dependent on the British. Warren Hastings forced the Nawab of Avadh to accept another brigade and pay for it. The British got the right of nominating the ministers of Asaf-ud-Daula. Private British merchants entered Avadh and started exploiting the people. The result was that there was a rapid decline in the prosperity of Avad and steady deterioration in its administration. The treasury was exhausted on account of the extravagance of the Nawab. The Nawab had also to pay for the subsidiary force. Asaf-ud-Daula pleaded and protested against the heavy expenses of the subsidiary force but without any result. British control over Avadh continued to grow and there was more and more exploitation of Avadh. Asaf-ud-Daula died in 1797 and his son Wazir Ali was recognised by Sir John Shore but he was deposed and Saadat Ali was put on the throne.

Lord Wellesley put pressure on Saadat Ali to sign the annexation of Avadh by the British but the Nawab refused. However, by the treaty of 1801 the British, took away from Avadh Rohilkhand and the Eastern Districts to pay the expenses of the subsidiary force. This was an act of high-handedness. The British attitude towards Avadh was one of exploitation. When Saadat Ali made any saving, it was taken away in the form of loans which were never returned. However, in lieu of them, Nawab Wazir of Avadh got the title of king of Avadh. During the regime of Lord William Bentinck, there was a danger to the very existence of the state of Avadh on account of its misgovernment.

Nasir-ud-Din died in 1837 and he was succeeded by Muhammad Ali who was forced to pay for another British brigade. In 1842, Muhammad Ali was succeeded by Amjad Ali who was succeeded by Wajid Ali Shah his 1856, Avadh was annexed to the English Company and Wajid Ali Shah was given a pension and sent to Calcutta.

HYDERABAD

Hyderabad was formed by the six Deccan Subahs of the Mughal Empire. The Deccan was a newly conquered region in which Mughal authority could not be consolidated on account of the struggle with the Marathas. Zulfiqar Khan, the most powerful and reputed general of Aurangzeb, formed plans to seize the Deccan Subahs after the death of Aurangzeb. In order to achieve his aim, he entered into a secret understanding with the Marathas. He was a Shia and his aim was to build up a Shia kingdom on the ruins of Bijapur and Golcunda. Another powerful Mansabdar who aspired to set up an independent state in the Deccan was Chin Qilich Khan who later on became Nizam-ul-Mulk Asaf Jah. Zulfiqar Khan and Chin Qilich Khan belonged to two rival factions in the Mughal court, Irani and Turani. For some years after the death of Aurangzeb, Zulfiqar Khan and his father Asad Khan who had held the office of Wazir under Aurangzeb, continued to exercise great influence in the Mughal court. In 1708, Zulfiqar Khan managed to secure the vice-royalty of the Deccan from Bahadur Shah I and held that post till 1713 when he was murdered by Farrukh-siyar.

At the time of the death of Aurangzeb, Chin Qilich Khan was at Bijapur and he observed neutrality during the war of succession among the sons of Aurangzeb. Bahadur Shah removed Chin Qilich Khan from the Deccan and made him the Governor of Avadh and Faujdar of Gorakhpur on 9 December 1707. For some time, he retired from public service but joined it again towards the close of the reign of Bahadur Shah. In 1713, Farrukh-siyar appointed Nizam-ul-Mulk the Governor of the six Subahs by investing him with the titles of Khan Nizam-ul-Mulk Bahadur Fatehjang as a reward for his services having espoused his cause. Nizam-ul-Mulk was extremely ambitious and he wanted to rule over the Deccan independently of Delhi.

Nizam-ul-Mulk was an astute diplomat. He tried to check the growing power of the Marathas by stopping the payment of Chauth and instigating the self-seeking and ambitious Maratha leaders against Sahu. The intrigues at the Delhi court led to Nizam-ul-Mulk's recall from the Deccan by the end of 1715 and in his place Husain Ali was appointed Governor of the Deccan. Nizam-ul-Mulk was transferred to Muradabad and subsequently it was decided to move him to Bihar. Before he could assume charge of the new office, the regime of Farrukh-siyar came to an end and Nizam-ul-Mulk was transferred to Malwa. He started for Ujjain after receiving the pledge that he would not be transferred again.

While in Malwa, Nizam-ul-Mulk was able to lay the foundation of his future greatness. His activities aroused the jealousy of the Sayyid Brothers and he was recalled. Nizam-ul-Mulk decided to act in self-defence by the use of arms. He occupied Asirgarh in May 1720 and three days later Burhanpur fell. The Sayyid Brothers ordered Sayyid Dilawar Ali Khan and Alam Ali Khan to oppose the march of Nizam-ul-Mulk. Dilawar Ali Khan was defeated in June 1720. Alam Ali Khan was defeated and killed in the battle. While Husain Ali was on the way to the Deccan, he was stabbed to death on 8 October 1720. Sayyid Abdullah was also defeated and killed.

After the fall of the Sayyid Brothers, Nizam-ul-Mulk made himself the master of the six Subahs of the Deccan and began his operations against the Marathas. In February 1722, he was appointed Wazir of the Mughal Empire and he occupied that office upto 1724. He tried to put things in order but he was unsuccessful on account of opposition from the Emperor and his flatterers. His strict discipline provoked dislike and jealousy. He was extremely unhappy. As Wazir, he added Malwa and Gujarat to the Subedari of the Deccan. When he found that he was not liked in the court, he marched away to the Deccan without the permission of the Emperor. That was not liked by the Emperor who appointed Mubariz Khan as the Viceroy of the Deccan and directed him to send the Nizam to the court, dead or alive. Mubariz Khan was defeated and killed by the Nizam who sent his head to the Emperor. Nizam-ul-Mulk defeated the son of Mubariz Khan and took possession of Hyderabad by the beginning of 1725. Irvine writes, "From this period may be dated Nizam-ul-Mulk's virtual independence and the foundation of the present Hyderabad state." He bestowed offices in the Deccan. He made promotions in rank and conferred titles. He issued assignments on land revenue at his own will and pleasure. The only attributes of sovereignty from which he refrained were the use of scarlet or imperial umbrella, the recitation of the Friday prayer in his own name and the issue of coins stamped with his own superscription.

Nizam-ul-Mulk correctly realised that the activities of Peshwa Baji Rao I were opposed to his own policy of establishing an independent kingdom in the Deccan and hence he decided to oppose him. There were many Maratha chiefs who were not satisfied with the Peshwa and they joined the Nizam against him. For five years, Peshwa Baji Rao I had to fight against them from 1727 to 1732. The Nizam was defeated at Palkhed in 1728 and his ally Senapati Trimbak Rao Dabhade was killed in 1731. Nizam-ul-Mulk decided to come to terms with the Peshwa who was also anxious to settle with the Nizam so that he could carry on his campaigns in the North. A compromise was arrived at in December 1732 by which the Nizam was to be free to satisfy his ambition in the South and the Peshwa in the North.

After the sudden dash of Pesshwa Baji Rao on Delhi, the Mughal Emperor summoned the Nizam from the Deccan and he reached Delhi in July 1737. The Mughal Emperor conferred the title of Asaf Jah on the Nizam. The Nizam marched towards Malwa but he was defeated by Peshwa Baji Rao near Bhopal and was compelled to conclude a humiliating peace in January 1738. The Nizam promised to grant to Baji Rao the Subedari of Malwa and rights over the territory between the Narmada and the Chambal.

When Nadir Shah attacked India, the Mughal Emperor called Nizam-ul-Mulk to Delhi to negotiate the terms of agreement with the invader. The agreement was actually made by the Nizam but the same was upset by Saadat Ali Khan.

Nizam-ul-Mulk ruled the Deccan independently till his death in 1748. He continued to profess his allegiance to the Mughal Emperor. He rejected the offer of Nadir Shah to make him the ruler of Delhi. Nizam-ul-Mulk was not only the foremost general of his time in India and a careful and honest administrator but also a master of statecraft and diplomacy. He was universally regarded as the sole representative of the spacious times of Aurangzeb. The rich provinces under his administration prospered during his long reign. The refractory chiefs, ambitious officers and robber leaders were suppressed. The revenue assessment was moderate. His taxation policy promoted trade. He followed a policy of religious toleration. He appointed Puran Chand as his Diwan.

After the death of Nizam-ul-Mulk, there was a war of succession which became linked with the Anglo-French conflict in the Deccan. Political stability was restored in 1762 by the accession of Nizam Ali who had a long reign of more than four decades. In the time of Lord Wellesley, the Nizam entered into a subsidiary alliance with the English East India Company and virtually became their subordinate ally.

ROHILKHAND

In the first half of the eighteenth century, there was a fresh wave of Afghan immigration into Northern India. Afghan adventurers found military employment in many places. Many of them settled in a solid bloc between Delhi and Agra on the West and Avadh and Allahabad on the East and became a serious menace to the Mughal Empire by the middle of the eighteenth century. Their Indian settlement, formerly known as Katehar, now came to be known as Rohilkhand because it was populated mainly by the Rohillas. The Rohillas, first came into prominence under *Daud*, an Afghan soldier of fortune, who came from Qandhar. He and his party of Afghan adventurers hired themselves out first to the landowners and then to the imperial Governor of that place. Daud "laid the foundations of an estate." On his death in 1721, his adopted son Ali Muhammad Khan obtained command of his retainers and sought to implement his ambitious plans. *Ali Muhammad Khan* was able to raise an army of his own. In 1727, he defeated a Khawajasara of the Mughal Emperor and seized all his property. That raised his prestige and he took up the title of Nawab. He started living in royal style and held his court like an independent prince. He was able to get the right of collecting taxes from the region under his authority. In 1737, he got the title of Nawab from the Emperor. The adverse effects of the invasion of Nadir Shah on the Mughal Empire emboldened Ali Muhammad Khan to seize territories right and left. He extended his influence to Muradabad and occupied most of the region. His authority extended to the whole of Bareilly and Muradabad and portions of Hardoi and Badaun. He was appointed the Governor of Katehar by the Emperor. In due course, he was able to occupy Pilibhit, Bijnor and Kumaon. In 1745, the Emperor Muhammad Shah was persuaded by Safdar Jang to lead an expedition against Ali Muhammad Khan. After three months campaigning, it "achieved only a superficial and ephemeral victory and that too more by persuasion than by compulsion". Apprehending trouble during the ensuing rainy season, the Mughal Emperor was persuaded to make peace with Ali Muhammad Khan who agreed to dismantle the fortifications of Bangarh and to surrender the fiefs reserved, by him to the Mughal authorities. Soon he received a Mansab of 4000 and was sent to Sirhind as the Mughal Faujdar of that place. On hearing of the capture of Lahore by Ahmad Shah Abdali and his intention to march towards Delhi, Ali Muhammad Khan left his post at Sirhind in the middle of February 1748 and returned to Rohilkhand with his full contingent of Afghans and re-established his authority by March/April 1748. In this way, the Mughal rule was ended in Rohilkhand.

Ali Muhammad Khan died on 15 September 1748 and his possessions were divided into three parts, to one of which Hafiz Rahmat Khan succeeded as the leader. Shaikh Qutb-ud-Din tried to get back the Faujdari of Rohilkhand which his grandfather had once enjoyed but he was defeated in the battle at Dhampur near Muradabad.

Wazir Safdarjang formed a new plan to suppress the Rohillas whom he considered as serpents infesting his road to Delhi. Safdar Jang instigated Qaim Khan, the Bangash chief, to drive out the Afghans by appointing him the Faujdar of Rohilkhand. After some success at the beginning, Kaim Khan's army met with disaster and he himself was shot dead. All the possessions of the Bangash chief on the left or Eastern bank of the Ganges were annexed by Hafiz Rahmat. However, Hafiz Rahmat dissuaded his troops from crossing the river and invading the territories of Qaim Khan's territories on the West bank. The reason given was that the Afghans could not destroy one another. Within a few months, Safdarjang became unpopular with the Bangash Afghans and was defeated at the battle of Ram Chatauni on 13 September 1750. He was also disgraced at the Delhi court. However, he was able to reestablish his position and form an alliance with the Marathas and Jats for invading Rohilkhand. In April 1751, the allies won a resounding victory over the Rohillas. When the Emperor heard of the invasion of the Punjab by Ahmad Shah Abdali in early 1752, the Emperor asked the Wazir to make peace with the Afghans of Rohilkhand. Farrukhabad and some other Mahals worth ₹16 or ₹22 lakhs a year were left to Ahmad and other sons of Muhammad Khan Bangash while the sons of Ali Muhammad Khan were confirmed in the possession of Mirabad and some other Mahals which they had seized after the death of Qaim Khan, but they were subjected to the payment of revenue for them. Safdarjang kept a few of the places for himself. The Rohillas and the Bangashes emerged with very little permanent loss. By rendering good services to Ahmad Shah Abdali in the third battle of Panipat in January 1761, the Rohillas and the Bangashes made some gains. After that, Rohillas became independent. For some time, they were able to capture Delhi also but they had to vacate it on account of opposition from the Marathas and Nawab of Avadh.

In the time of Warren Hastings, British troops were sent to Rohilkhand to help the Nawab Wazir of Avadh to conquer Rohilkhand. Hafiz Rahmat Khan was killed while fighting bravely. About 20,000 Rohillas were expelled beyond the Ganges. Their province was annexed to Avadh. Only a fragment of it, together with Rampur, was left in the possession of Faizullah Khan, son of Ali Muhammad Khan.

Farrukhabad

Muhammad Khan Bangash, an Afghan adventurer, established his control over the territory around Farrukhabad, between Aligarh and Kanpur, during the reigns of Farrukh-siyar and Muhammad Shah. Muhammad Khan raised a band of Afghans whom he employed in plundering raids and fighting the battle of local Jagirdars on payment. In 1713, he was appointed a courtier by Farrukh-siyar. In 1714, he founded the town of Farrukhabad. He was able to acquire a large Jagir whose area was about 75,000 square miles. His influence became so great that he was appointed the Governor of Allahabad and Malwa. He was so faithful to the Emperor that he never thought of independence. When he died in 1743, he was succeeded by his son Qayam Khan.

Bundelkhand

Bundelkhand was an absolutely wild tract and difficult of access in the rainy season. Its dense forests, rapid streams and steep hills shielded it from all outside invaders. The Bundelas gathered strength, extended their territories and were forged into a formidable force under Madhukar Shah who was ruling at Orchha. He was forced into submission in 1578 after repeated Mughal expeditions. After the death of Madhukar Shah in 1592, his son Bir Singh became the head of Bundelkhand. In 1602, at the instigation of Prince Salim, Bir Singh Bundela murdered Abul Fazl. During the reign of Akbar, Bir Singh Bundela was pursued by Mughal forces, but when Jahangir became Emperor, Bir Singh was given a Mansab of 3000. He was made the ruler of Orchha state. The Bundela power reached its zenith under Bir Singh. He grew in wealth and power. He brought under his rule vast neighbouring fertile tracts. He was a great builder. He built a temple in Mathura at a cost of ₹33 lacs. He was a patron of Hindi poet Keshav. Bir Singh died in 1627 and he was succeeded by Jujhar Singh. In the reign of Shah Jahan, Jujhar Singh was forced into submission. He died in 1635. He was succeeded by Champat Rai Bundela. He was a brave fighter and a courageous leader of men. He fought for Aurangzeb in the battle of Samugarh, but later on left him. Aurangzeb sent a Mughal force to suppress him. He was relentlessly pursued and he ultimately committed suicide in October 1661.

Champat Rai was succeeded by Chhatra Sal. He was enlisted the Mughal army at the request of Mirza Raja Jai Singh and he accompanied him to the Deccan. He fought well in the Purandhar campaign of 1665 and the invasion of Deogarh in 1667. However, Chhatra Sal did not feel happy while serving the Mughals. He wanted to live a life of adventure and independence like Shivaji. He visited Shivaji and sought to enter his service in 1670. However, Shivaji advised him to go back to his own country and promote local risings against Aurangzeb. The efforts of Chhatra Sal to win over the Bundela leaders to fight against the Mughal Empire did not succeed. However, Aurangzeb launched upon a policy of temple destruction which aroused universal indignation among the Hindus. The Hindus of Bundelkhand and Malwa made preparations to defend their places of worship. When Chhatra Sal appeared in their midst to oppose the Mughal army, he was hailed as the champion of Hindu faith and Bundela liberty. He was elected their leader by the rebels. Many petty chiefs joined Chhatra Sal. As Aurangzeb became more and more entangled in the Deccan, Chhatra Sal took full advantage of the opportunity. He captured Kalinjar and Dhamuni and even looted Bhilsa. He extended his raids upto Malwa. In 1699, Chhatra Sal was defeated by Sher Afghan. A year later, Sher Afghan was killed. There was none to oppose Chhatra Sal. In 1705, Chhatra Sal was made a Mansabdar of 4000 and he met Aurangzeb in the Deccan. He returned to Bundelkhand after the death of Aurangzeb. For 14 years, Chhatra Sal fully cooperated with the Mughal Empire. In May 1708, the sons of Chhatra Sal met Bahadur Shah and they were given Mansabs. In April 1710, Chhatra Sal presented himself before the Emperor and joined the Mughal army which was marching against Banda, the Sikh leader. He participated in the assault on the Sikh fortress of Lohgarh. He retained imperial favour during the reign of Farrukh-siyar. On 21 January 1714, he got the rank of 6000 Zat. In May 1718, three of his sons and some grandsons attended the Imperial Court and received presents. In 1720, the Bundelas revolted. They sacked Kalpi and killed the local Amil. In a fierce fight on 25 May 1721 between Chhatra Sal and his men with those of Dilir Khan, 500 men of Chhatra Sal were killed. After the death of Dilir Khan, Chhatra Sal had to be suppressed. In 1723, Muhammad Khan was asked to lead an expedition into Bundelkhand to check the growing power of Chhatra Sal. In May 1727, Muhammad Khan encountered the entrenched position of the Bundelas at Ijoli in Pargana Mahoba. Chhatra Sal and his party sought refuge in the fort of Salhat. He was pursued by the enemy. Active hostilities were resumed in April 1728. In December 1728, the fortress of Jaitpur fell in the hands of the Mohammadans. The Bundelas renewed their activities in February 1729. Muhammad Khan met with difficulties and reverses! Chhatra Sal asked the Peshwa to come to his help. Peshwa Baji Rao responded and he attacked Muhammad Khan in March 1729. Muhammad Khan and his troops suffered terribly. The Marathas defeated Qaim Khan who had come to help Muhammad Khan. Muhammad Khan appealed to the Mughal Emperor and the great nobles for help but without any success. On account of the outbreak of epidemic in the Maratha camp, the Marathas raised the siege and returned to the Deccan. Chhatra Sal came to terms with Muhammad Khan in August 1729. Muhammad Khan signed a written agreement that he would not attack Bundelkhand again. Chhatra Sal died in December 1731 at the age of 82. His sons divided the state among themselves.

THE JATS

The Jats lived in the region around Delhi, Agra and Mathura. They were a hardy tribe, pre-eminently agricultural and well-known for their valour, indefatigable energy, martial spirit and untiring perseverance. The tribal feeling was very strong among them. They professed different religions, viz.,

Hinduism, Sikhism and Islam, but they clung tenaciously to their tribal name as a proud heritage. The Mughal Government had been following a policy "which left behind it a legacy of undying hatred". Murshid Quli Khan Turkman, Faujdar of Mathura, offended the Jats by abduction of women from villages and religious gatherings at Govardhan on the birthday of Lord Krishna. Abdun Nabi Khan, another Faujdar of Mathura (1660-69), built a Jama Masjid in the heart of the city of Mathura on the ruins of a Hindu temple. He forcibly removed the carved stone railing presented by Dara Shikoh to Keshab Rai's temple. All these goaded the Jats to break out into open revolt. In 1669, the Jat peasants revolted under their leader Gokla, the Zamindar of Tilpat. There was bitter fighting and ultimately Gokla was killed at Agra and the members of his family were converted to Islam. However, the spirit which he had infused into his men did not die with him and after several years, other capable leaders stepped into his place. They were *Raja Ram and Ram Chehra.* They gave military training to the Jat peasants, equipped them with five-arms and gave them the semblance of an organised and regular army. They built small forts in the midst of deep forests and erected mud walls around them for defence against artillery. Those forts served as refuges in times of necessity, bases for military operations and places for the storage of their booty. The road from Delhi to Agra and Dholpur and thence via Malwa to the Deccan lay through the Jat country and the Jats carried on plundering raids on that highway and the suburbs of Agra. The long absence of Aurangzeb from Northern India and his stay in the Deccan encouraged the Jats to plunder the rich convoys passing through their country. The Governor of Agra was not able to check the lawless activities of Raja Ram who closed the roads to traffic and sacked many villages. Raja Ram became more and more daring and attacked even influential persons, Aurangzeb sent his grandson Bidar Bakht against Raja Ram and two important strongholds of the Jats were taken by the Mughal troops.

Churaman. Another leader of the Jats was *Churaman* (1695-1721) who was the younger brother of Raja Ram. Churaman started his career as a freebooter. Within a short time, he brought under his leadership 1000 infantry and 500 horsemen. To begin with, he plundered wayfarers and merchant caravans, but later on he sacked Parganas also. He built a palace in the midst of a thick forest about 48 Kos from Agra and dug a deep moat which was gradually made into a mud fort, subsequently known Bharatpur. He had great capacity for organisation. He was a practical politician who made "clever use of opportunities" whenever possible. Many of his activities and the full development of his power were seen after the death of Aurangzeb. He took full advantage of the war of succession among the sons of Aurangzeb to strengthen his position. After the victory of Bahadur Shah, he professed allegiance to him and received a Mansab of 1500 Zat, 500 Sawar. He joined the Mughal forces at Ajmer and fought against the Sikhs at Sadhaura and Lohgarh (1710).

There was another war of succession after the death of Bahadur Shah in 1712. Jahandar Shah came out successful but he was totally unfit to rule. Ghuraman went back to his country and devoted his energy to increase his power. When Farrukh-siyar approached Agra to contest the throne, Churaman did not render any help to Jahandar Shah and looted the baggage of both parties. The Mughal Subahdar of Agra tried to subdue Churaman, but he failed. The next Subahdar followed a policy of conciliation and was able to bring Churaman to the Imperial Court. He was cordially received and placed incharge of the royal highway from Barapula near Delhi to the crossing on the Chambal. Churaman constructed a fortress at Thun in the midst of a thick and thorny forest.

The Mughal Emperor did not approve of the attitude of Churaman and deputed Sawai Jai Singh of Jaipur to punish Churaman. Sawai Jai Singh besieged the fort of Thun in November 1716. Churaman made proposals of peace to Sayyid Abdullah and offered to pay a tribute of ₹30 lakhs of rupees to the Imperial Government and a present of ₹20 lakhs of rupees to Sayyid Abdullah. The proposal was accepted and Sawai Jai Singh raised the siege. Churaman visited Delhi in April 1718. When differences arose between Sayyid Abdullah and the Emperor Muhammad Shah, Churaman took the side of Sayyid Abdullah. Churaman also entered into an alliance with Ajit Singh of Jodhpur against the interests of the Imperial Government. He also helped the Bundelas against the Mughal

Governor of Allahabad. The Emperor Muhammad Shah ordered the Governor of Agra to take action against Churaman. Churaman made a mistake in having quarrels with his relations. He committed suicide.

Badan Singh. Churaman was succeeded by Badan Singh (1722-56) who was his nephew. He was recognised as the chief of the Jats by Jai Singh and the same was confirmed by the Imperial Court. It was a very critical time for the Jats and Badan Singh had to start everything afresh. By his conduct, he won over the support of Jai Singh who bestowed on him the title of Brajaraj, but Badan Singh abstained from assuming the title of Raja. Throughout his life, he called himself only a Thakur or baron and represented himself in public as a vassal of the ruler of Jaipur. He was a capable leader with indefatigable energy. He united the scattered units of the Jats. All lands and wealth held by Jat village headmen were brought under his control. He strengthened his position by the application of force where necessary and by matrimonial alliances with some influential families of Mathura. He organised a strong army consisting of infantry and cavalry. He constructed four strong forts including Bharatpur and Dig and provided them with ample provisions and sufficient artillery. He laid the foundations of a new ruling house of Bharatpur with an enlarged territory. In 1752, he was created a Raja by the Mughal Emperor, Ahmad Shah. He was a patron of architecture. He constructed a temple at Brindaban, fine palaces in the fort of Dig and palaces at Kamar and Sahar. He was succeeded by his adopted son, Suraj Mal.

Suraj Mal (1756-63). During the later half of the reign of his father, Suraj Mal had acted as Regent on account of his inactivity and growing blindness. During that period, he earned a name for himself as an able warrior, efficient leader and able statesman. As a ruler, he extended his authority over a large area which extended from the Ganges in the East to Chambal in the South, the province of Agra in the West and the province of Delhi in the North. His state included, among others, the Districts of Agra, Mathura, Meerut and Aligarh. For his political sagacity, steady intellect and clear vision, he is remembered as "the Jat Ulysses". A contemporary historian described Suraj Mal in these words: "Though he wore the dress of a farmer and could speak only his Brij dialect, he was the Plato of the Jat tribe. In prudence and skill, and ability to manage the revenue and civil affairs, he had no equal among the grandees of Hindustan except Asaf Jah Bahadur." Sayyid Ghulam Husain writes that Suraj Mal was "the eye and shining taper of the Jat tribe—a prince who rendered himself famous by his good manners and civil department, as well as by his conquests and his superior knowledge in the arts of Government." He gave his state peace and prosperity. He was loved and respected by his subjects. He was admired and feared by foreigners. At the time of his death, his army consisted of 15,000 cavalry and 25,000 infantry besides fort garrisons. He left behind a reserve fund of 10 crores. The view of Thornton is that the palaces constructed by him "are surpassed in India for elegance of design and perfection of workmanship only by the Tajmahal of Agra". By his tactful and efficient guidance of affairs of the state, Suraj Mal not only proved his political foresight and sagacity, but remained "the strongest potentate in India with absolutely unimpaired forces and an overflowing treasury, while every other chief had been more or less ruined. He wrested considerable portions of the Doab from the Marathas, recovered his lost places in Aligarh and Bulandshahr Districts from the possession of Ahmad Shah Abdali and also conquered some places of the Agra District and Haryana.

Jawahir Singh (1764-68). Suraj Mal was succeeded by his son Jawahir Singh. He made preparations against Najib-ud-Daulah in order to take revenge of the death of his father. He marched to Delhi and laid siege to it. However, he could not reap the desired benefit due to the faithlessness of Malhar Rao and treacherous conduct of a section of the Jat officers. Jawahir Singh took action against those influential and powerful Jat leaders whom he considered to be refractory. He was involved in a quarrel with the Marathas who had supported his brother Nahar Singh in his claim to the throne of his father. He defeated his enemies in March 1766 and captured Dholpur. He also raided the Maratha possessions in Northern Malwa. However, he brought misfortune upon himself by his quarrel with Madho Singh, Raja of Jaipur. Madho Singh invaded the Jat territory and defeated Jawahir Singh in 1768. He was assassinated by one of his soldiers.

Jawahir Singh was a strong ruler. He centralised all powers in his own hands. However, he did not possess the foresight, tact and wisdom of his father. But, his finances were in good order and he maintained a magnificent court.

Jawahir Singh was succeeded by Ratan Singh (1768-69), Kesari Singh (1768-75), Ranjit Singh (1775-1805) and Randhir Singh. About them, Jadunath Sarkar writes, "Brain and character alike were wanting among the successors of Jawahir Singh, and in addition, the lack of a strong man at the head of the state let loose all the selfishness and factiousness among the other members of the royal family which completed the national downfall in a few years." (*Fall of the Mughal Empire*, Vol. III, p. 4). Ranjit Singh entered into a defensive and offensive alliance with the English in September 1803 and fought with them in the battle of Laswari against Daulat Rao Scindia. However, in 1804, he joined Yashwant Rao Holkar in his attack on Delhi against the English. The English besieged Dig and captured it. They then laid siege to Bharatpur but Ranjit Singh repulsed four successive assaults of General Lake. However, he made peace with the English East India Company in April 1805. He promised to pay an indemnity of ₹20 lakhs and desist from holding any communication with the enemies of the English or employing any European without their permission. Dig was restored to him afterwards.

THE RAJPUT STATES

The Rajput states took advantage of the growing weakness of the Mughal Empire and freed themselves from imperial control and increased their influence in the rest of the Empire. During the reigns of Farrukh-siyar and Muhammad Shah, the rulers of Amber and Marwar were appointed the Governors of the Mughal provinces like Gujarat, Malwa and Agra. However, the rulers of the Rajput states were divided among themselves. Bigger Rajput states tried to expand themselves at the cost of their weaker neighbours. Most of them were constantly involved in petty quarrels and civil wars. In most of the Rajput states, there was corruption, intrigues and treachery. Ajit Singh of Marwar was killed by his own son. At one stage, the Rajputs controlled the entire territory extending from South of Delhi to Surat on the Western coast. However, they failed to consolidate their position on account of their internal dissensions. Their outlook was essentially parochial. Clan traditions fostered isolation, rivalry and conflict. The disappearance of the imperial authority intensified clan rivalry. There was no longer imperial control over inter-state disputes. Every state was free to strike at its neighbours. Succession disputes led to civil wars which often invited external intervention. The situation was worsened by the expansionist policy of the Marathas. Instead of using the Rajput princes as useful allies, the Marathas exploited them for money and fostered dissensions among them to serve their own interests.

Marwar (Jodhpur)

The two leading Rajput clans at the beginning of the reign of Bahadur Shah I were the Rathors of Marwar and Bikaner and the Kach-chhwahas of Amber (Jaipur). Aurangzeb's intolerance and persecution had alienated the Rajputs. The result was that, the prominent Rajput rulers like Ajit Singh of Marwar, Amar Singh of Mewar (Udaipur) and Jay Singh of Amber sought to cast off their allegiance to the Mughal Empire and assert their independence. When Bahadur Shah proceeded to subdue them, Amar Singh sent his brother to Agra with a letter of congratulations, 100 gold coins, one thousand rupees and some costly presents. Bahadur Shah also brought Amber under his control and made it over to Bijay Singh who was the younger brother of Jai Singh. Ajit Singh of Jodhpur also tendered submission. He received the title of Maharaja and the rank of 3500 Zat and 3000 Sawar. In view of the Sikh rising in the Punjab, Bahadur Shah adopted a policy of conciliation in relation to the Rajputs between October 1708 and June 1710. In October 1708, Jai Singh and Ajit Singh were restored to their ranks in the Mughal service.

During the confusion which followed the death of Bahadur Shah, Ajit Singh "after forbidding cow-killing and the call of prayer from the Alamgiri mosque, besides ejecting the Imperial officers from Jodhpur and destroying their houses, entered the Imperial territory and took possession of Ajmer". Sayyid Husain Ali was sent to subdue Ajit Singh. However, letters were also sent to Raja Ajit Singh asking him to make away with Husain Ali in any way he could and if he did so, he would receive rewards and also the whole of the property of Husain Ali. Ajit Singh did not offer any opposition and concluded a treaty according to one article of which he agreed to marry one of his daughters to Farrukh-siyar.

During the reign of Farrukh-siyar, the houses of Jodhpur and Jaipur played a conspicuous part in the politics of Delhi and added to their kingdoms a large portion of the Empire. Ajit Singh was the governor of Ajmer and Gujarat which he held till 1721. Ajit Singh secretly assisted the Marathas in their movements in Western India. After the fall of the Sayyid Brothers, Ajit Singh was removed from the Government of Gujarat. Ajit Singh met with tragic death at the hands of his son Bakht Singh in 1724. Ajit Singh had cooperated with the Sayyid Brothers in the overthrow of Farrukh-siyar and the people of Delhi called him *Damad Kush* (Slayer of son-in-law).

Abhai Singh, the eldest son of Ajit Singh, ruled over Marwar till his death in 1749. He served as the Mughal Governor of Gujarat. His invasion of Bikaner involved him in a struggle with Sawai Jai Singh of Amber. Abhai Singh secured a complete victory in the battle of Gangwana in 1741.

With, the death of Abhai Singh, Marwar lost its internal political stability and the state suffered from a protracted civil war on the issue of succession, during the long reign of Bijay Singh (1752-92), Marwar came to the verge of dissolution. For that sorry state, the Maratha invasions and the growing power of the turbulent Rathor nobility were responsible.

Amber (Jaipur)

The greatest Rajput ruler of the first half of the eighteenth century was *Sawai Jai Singh* of Amber (1699-1743). To describes him as "a statesman, legislator and man of science". He founded the city of Jaipur which was "the only city in India built upon a regular plan with streets bisecting each other at right angles." While building the new city of Jaipur, Jai Singh utilised the plans of several European cities collected by him. He was deeply interested in mathematics and astronomy. He studied Greek and modern European treatises on mathematics in addition to Indian books on the subject. At his instance, some Greek and European works on mathematics and some Arabic works on astronomy were translated into Sanskrit. He built well-equipped observatories m Jaipur, Delhi, Ujjain, Banaras and Mathura. He invited to Jaipur the Jesuit Father Boudier from Bengal and Father Andre Strobl and Antoine Gabelsperguer from Germany to help him in the task of building those observatories. He procured astronomical tables from Portugal. The instruments put in the above observatories were very accurate. His own astronomical observations were remarkably accurate. He prepared a set of tables to enable people to make astronomical observations he got translated into Sanskrit Euclid's *Elements of Geometry.* Napier's work on the construction and use of Logarithms was also translated into Sanskrit. Jai Singh was also a social reformer. He tried to reduce the expenditure incurred in connection with the marriages of daughters.

Sawai Jai Singh played an important part in Imperial politics and served as Subahdar of Agra and Malwa but he did not make any contribution to the preservation of the disintegrating Mughal Empire. He found that it was not possible to resist the Marathas in Malwa and hence "he only made a show of fight and preferred the policy of buying them off for the time with a part of the money given to him by the Mughal Government, pocketing the balance". As the Subahdar of Agra, he used his power and influence in extending and consolidating his hereditary dominion. He intervened in a disputed succession in Bundi. He was defeated by the Rathors in the battle of Gangwana in 1714. He performed the Asvamedha sacrifice.

The Maratha advance into Malwa served as a "convenient starting point for raids into Rajputana". The Marathas defeated and killed Girdhar Bahadur, its Subahdar on 29 November 1729. His cousin Daya Bahadur was also killed. On 22 April 1734, Malhar Rao Holkar and Ranoji Sindia attacked Bundi. That caused alarm in the whole of Rajasthan to prepare a concerted plan for checking Maratha spoliation of their countries. However, nothing came out of it.

Sawai Jai Singh died on 21 September 1743. There was a struggle between Ishwari Singh and his younger brother Madho Singh. Ishwari Singh tried to keep Madho Singh satisfied by heavy concessions to him. Ishwari Singh's reign of seven years (1743-50) was one long struggle with his younger brother Madho Singh and his Rajput and Maratha allies. Jagat Singh supported the claim of his nephew Madho Singh and advanced towards Jaipur. However, with the support of the Marathas, Ishwari Singh defeated the Rana in February 1745. The Rana managed to secure the help of Malhar Rao Holkar. In March 1747, a combined army consisting of the troops of Marwar and Bundi assisted by Holkar's troops under his son Khande Rao was defeated in the battle of Rajmahal. At the end .of 1750, Jaipur had to suffer from "a new and disastrous visitation of the Marathas" and saw a revolution in its affairs. Ishwari Singh committed suicide in December 1750 and Madho Singh occupied the throne of Jaipur. In the war of succession, the Marathas became the arbiters of Rajputana. After ascending the throne of Jaipur, Madho Singh adopted an anti-Maratha Policy.

Mewar (Udaipur)

Mewar was great when it was ruled by Rana Sangram Singh who was known as Hindupat. After his defeat in 1527 and death in 1528, Mewar was weakened by internal dissensions and external invasions. Its long resistance to Akbar and Jahangir also weakened her. Although Mewar accepted Mughal suzerainty in 1615, it remained isolated from the Imperial court. Amber and Marwar were in the limelight. In the seventeenth century, the only capable ruler of Mewar was Raj Singh who fought against Aurangzeb. In the eighteenth century, the weak rulers of Mewar were not able to control the ambitious and factious nobility and resist external invasions. Sangram Singh II ruled from 1710 to 1733. In his reign, symptoms of internal disintegration came to the surface. Jagat Singh II ruled from 1734 to 1751. In January 1736, Peshwa Baji Rao I appeared at the Southern frontier of Mewar. Jagat Singh welcomed him at Udaipur and signed a treaty by which he promised to pay an annual tribute. Jagat Singh had no strength of character. In the reign of his successor Pratap Singh II (1751-54), the Marathas exacted large contributions from Mewar which was tormented by disputed successions. During the reign of Raj Singh II (1754-61), the repeated invasions of his country by the Marathas so exhausted it that the Rana was compelled to ask pecuniary aid from the Brahman Collector of revenue, to enable him to marry the Rathor chieftain's daughter. Even after 1761, the Maratha raids into Rajasthan sucked its life-blood and added to the woes of its unhappy people. The Maratha invasions resulted in anarchy, plunder, economic ruin and humiliation of the Rajputs who entered into subsidiary alliances with the English East India Company during the Governor-Generalship of Lord Hastings in 1818.

THE SIKHS

The Sikhs were transformed into a militant and fighting community under Guru Har Govind (1606-1645). The execution of Guru Teg Bahadur forced the Sikhs to fight against the Mughals. Guru Gobind Singh (1664-1708) showed considerable organisational ability and founded the military brotherhood called the Khalsa in 1699. Before that, he had set up his headquarters at Makhowal or Anandpur Sahib in the foothills of the Punjab. A series of clashes took place between

Guru Govind Singh and the Hill Rajas in which the Guru generally came out successful. The organisation of the Khalsa further strengthened his hands. An open breach between the Guru and the Hill Rajas took place only in 1704 when the combined forces of a number of Hill Rajas attacked the Guru at Anandpur. The Rajas retreated and pressed the Mughal Government to take action against the Guru.

Aurangzeb was concerned with the growing power of the Guru and had asked the Mughal Faujdar earlier "to admonish the Guru". Aurangzeb wrote to the Governor of Lahore and the Faujdar of Sirhind, Wazir Khan, to help the Hill Rajas against Guru Govind Singh. The Mughal forces assaulted Anandpur but the Sikhs fought bravely and beat off all assaults. When starvation began inside the fort, the Guru was forced to open the gate apparently on a promise of safe conduct by Wazir Khan. However, when the forces of the Guru were crossing a swollen stream, Wazir Khan suddenly attacked them. Two of the sons of Guru Govind Singh were captured and on their refusal to embrace Islam, they were beheaded at Sirhind. The Guru lost two of his remaining sons in another battle. After that, he retired to Talwandi.

It is contended that Aurangzeb was not keen to destroy the Guru and he wrote to the Governor of Lahore to "conciliate the Guru". When the Guru wrote to Aurangzeb in the Deccan apprising him of the events, Aurangzeb invited him to meet him. Towards the end of 1706, the Guru set out for the Deccan and when he was still on the way, Aurangzeb died in 1707.

After the death of Aurangzeb, Guru Govind Singh joined Bahadur Shah's camp as a noble of the rank of 5000 Zat and 5000 Sawar and accompanied him to the Deccan where he was treacherously murdered in 1708 by one of his Pathan employees.

After the death of Guru Govind Singh, Banda became the leader of the Sikhs. He had met Guru Govind Singh just before his death and he was sent to the Punjab to continue the struggle against the Mughals. When Banda arrived in the Punjab, he called upon the Sikhs to join him telling them that he would punish Wazir Khan who had cruelly murdered the sons of Guru Govind Singh and chastise the Hill Rajas who had fought against the Guru for many years. The Sikh peasantry took up arms and marched under the leadership of Banda in the direction of Sirhind. Banda had with him about 40,000 well-armed Sikhs. He overpowered the Mughal authorities in the neighbourhood of Sirhind and captured Sirhind for wreaking vengeance on Wazir Khan who was the murderer of the sons of Guru Govind Singh. Wazir Khan was killed by a musket-shot. "The baggage was plundered, the elephants captured. Not a single Mohammadan escaped with anything but the clothes upon his back". Banda committed great atrocities at Sirhind. One Bar Singh was appointed the Governor of Sirhind. Banda occupied the area between the Sutlej and the Jamuna and built the strong fort of Lohgarh at Mukhlispur, half way between Nahan and Sadhaura. He became the *Sachcha Padshah*. He established his headquarters at Mukhlispur and after repairing its old fort, named it Lohgarh (Iron Castle). He assumed the position of a king, counting his regnal year from the date of his conquest of Sirhind and issuing a seal for his official documents. He did not assume any royal title. In his seal, he attributed his power to his master.

Banda removed the Zamindars and the tillers of the soil became masters. Every Sikh felt that he was superior to others and entitled to rule over them. The new political order was a signal for the general rising of the Sikhs against the Mughals. "They started on a career of conquest and every method, including loot and sabotage, which would cripple the resources of the enemy, was considered justified."

After invading the Gangetic Doab and occupying a large tract in the Saharanpur area, Banda retreated to the Jullundar Doab where his presence provoked a general rebellion of the Sikhs against Mughal authorities. By the end of 1710, Jullundar and Hoshiarpur were occupied without striking a blow. The Sikh rising spread to Central Punjab and took the form of a religious crusade. The Manjha fell into the hands of the Sikhs who carried their arms to the very gates of Lahore.

The Mughal Emperor Bahadur Shah was alarmed by the reports relating to the movements of Banda and he hastened to the Punjab. Banda was besieged in the fort of Lohgarh, but he managed to escape with many of his followers to the hills of Nahan, the struggle continued. The Sikhs won temporary successes and the Mughal Government tried to crush them. When Bahadur Shah reached Lahore, he died there on 28 February 1712, The happenings in the Mughal court after the death of Bahadur Shah offered a favourable opportunity to Banda to restore his control over the lost territories. He occupied Sadhaura and Lohgarh. He built a fort of considerable size with high and thick walls at Gurdaspur between the Beas and the Ravi. The Viceroy of Lahore marched against Banda but he was defeated. A party of the Sikhs advanced towards Sirhind. Its Governor marched forward to oppose Banda but he was overpowered along with his followers.

Under the orders of Farrukh-siyar, Abdus Samad Khan and his son Zakariya Khan, Governor of Lahore and Faujdar of Jammu respectively, started operations against the Sikhs who were obliged to evacuate Sadhaura and Lohgarh in October 1713. Banda retreated from post to post. He fought valiantly and inflicted heavy losses on the Mughals. However, he was compelled to shelter himself in the fort of Gurdaspur. He was besieged by the Mughal army and was not able to collect provisions. His troops suffered terribly on account of hunger. In eight months, about 8,000 of them died. The remaining fighters were reduced to skeletons. When the Mughal troops entered the fort, Banda and his famished followers were taken prisoners on 17 December 1715. Banda and his followers were sent to Delhi and severe tortures were inflicted upon them. Banda was kept in an iron cage. He was placed on the back of an elephant. His own son was killed before his eyes. He himself was tortured to death on 10 June 1716.

As regards the contribution of Banda, it can safely be said that he converted the Khalsa into a political instrument for the overthrow of the Mughal Empire. During his time, the slogan *"Raj Karega Khalsa"* became the battle-cry of the Sikhs. He made a bid for the establishment of Sikh rule in the Punjab. It was a revolutionary step in the history of the Sikhs. However, he failed because the Mughal Empire was deeply rooted and its power at that time was not exhausted. It is true that he was able to mobilise the enthusiasm of the Sikh masses, but the upper classes had not the courage to come forward and help him openly.

The Mughals were helped by the Hill Rajas of the Punjab, the Jats and the Bundelas. Banda did not inherit any military organisation to fight against the professional Mughal army. It is rightly pointed out that when he occupied Sirhind, he had no artillery, no elephants and not given a sufficient number of horses for his followers. It is true that he failed, but he left an important legacy for the Sikhs. A new will was created among the Sikhs to resist the Mughals and to set up a state of their own in the Punjab. It was this new spirit which enabled the sikhs to create a state of their own in the Punjab after many ups and downs. About Banda, Dr. Ganda Singh writes, "It was through him that the path of conquest and freedom was discovered by the people of the Punjab. He was the first man to deal a severe blow at the intolerant rule of the Mughals in the Punjab and to break the first sod in the conquest of that province by the Sikhs".

After the death of Banda, there was a division among the Sikhs. The Bandais were the followers of Banda. The orthodox Sikhs were called the Tat Khalsa. Through the efforts of Bhai Mani Singh and Mata Sundri, widow of Guru Govind Singh the differences between the two were composed in 1721.

Zakariya Khan was the Mughal Governor of the Punjab from 1726 to 1745. He followed a policy of harassing and persecuting the Sikhs in every possible way. Tara Singh Van and his 21 followers were, killed by the Mughal troops. Zakariya Khan appealed to Muslim fanaticism and the Haidari flag was hoisted. However, the Sikhs were able to defeat the Mughal forces at a place near Bhilowal. After that, Zakariya Khan tried to placate the Sikhs who organised themselves into the Dal Khalsa under the leadership of Kapur Singh. The Dal Khalsa was the army of the Sikhs. Its two main divisions were the Budha Dal and the Taruna Dal. The Budha Dal consisted of the army of grown-up Sikhs. The members of the Taruna Dal were a source of nuisance to the Mughal forces. They overran the whole of the Bari Doab and some of them crossed the Sutlej and helped Ala Singh to set up a small state in Malwa.

Even before the invasion of India by Nadir Shah in 1739, the Sikhs assembled at Amritsar in large numbers on the occasion of Baisakhi and Diwali. They sat together with the Holy Granth called Guru Granth in their midst, discussed questions of common interest and issued decisions in the form of resolutions called Gurmatta. Those decisions were accepted by all the Sikhs as the decisions of the Guru and disobedience was looked upon as an act of sacrilege. Those meetings were called Sarbat Khalsa and were held twice a year on the occasion of Baisakhi and Diwali. The Mughal Government took possession of the temple of Amritsar and the Sikhs were prevented from assembling there. Moving columns were sent round to haul up the Sikhs. The greatest martyr of that period was the Granthi of the Golden Temple. Bhai Mani Singh who had compiled the writings of Guru Govind Singh (*Dasam Padshah Ka Granth*). Many Sikhs left the plains and sought shelter in the Siwalik hills, the jungles of the Punjab and the desert of Rajasthan.

The invasion of Nadir Shah helped the recovery of the Sikhs. It enfeebled the strong Government of Zakariya Khan in the Punjab. The confusion and disorder created by Nadir Shah in the country also helped the rise of the Sikhs. They used that opportunity to increase their financial resources and military strength. The result was that the suppression of the Sikhs became a very difficult one.

The Sikhs organised themselves at a place called Dalewal and built a fort there. From that place, they carried on their depredations around the country and extended them upto the very neighbourhood of Lahore. Nadir Shah confirmed Zakariya Khan in the Nizamat of Lahore and the Sikhs withdrew from Lahore and its neighbourhood and carried on their activities in the Jullundar Doab. The Sikhs fell upon the rear of the army of Nadir Shah when he was retreating from Delhi. They were able to snatch away a lot of booty from the Afghans. The result was that Zakariya Khan decided to destroy the Sikhs root and branch. He placed Adina Beg incharge of Jullundar Doab and authorised him to take strong action against the Sikhs. The Sikhs were hunted like wild beasts and they retired to the hills and jungles. In 1742, Haqiqat Rai was put to death. Mahtab Singh. Buta Singh and Bhai Taru Singh were executed. The Sikhs also hit back. They attacked Sialkot and murdered all those Qazis and Mullahs who had a hand in the execution of Haqiqat Rai. They plundered Gondlanwala and its Faujdar was killed. Jassa Singh Ahluwalia raided Kasur with the help of other Sikh Chiefs. However, they were defeated near Basoli hills and about 7,000 of them were killed and 300 were taken prisoners. This happened in 1746 and is known as the *first Ghalughara* (Great Holocaust).

After the death of Zakariya Khan in 1745, intrigues of the rival parties in the Mughal Court prevented immediate appointment of a Governor of the Punjab. The result was that disorder broke out. Everywhere lawless men, plunderers and adventurers who were in hiding so long, came out in the open and began to desolate the realm. No only the Sikhs gave trouble, even the Raja of Jammu rebelled. At last, Yahya Khan, son of Zakariya Khan, was appointed the Deputy Governor of the Punjab. Yahya Khan tried to suppress the Sikhs. Many Sikhs lost their lives at Shahidganj. Yahya Khan passed an order for general massacre of the Sikhs but that was prevented by a quarrel between Yahya Khan and Shah Nawaz who was another son of Zakariya Khan. Whenever Yahya Khan sent troops against the Sikhs, Shah Nawaz helped the latter in various ways. The result was that the Sikhs got breathing time so badly needed by them.

Yahya Khan lost power in 1747 and a year later Mir Mannu became the Governor. The Sikhs took full advantage of the political confusion in the Punjab created by the struggle for the Governorship of Lahore dissensions among nobles in Delhi and the invasions of Ahmad Shah Abdali. They occupied Amritsar and elected Jassa Singh Ahluwalia as supreme commander of Dal Khalsa in 1748. To serve as a base of military operations and to ensure the security of the central shrine, they built a small mud fort, Ram Rauni or Ramgarh, about a mile to the South of the Golden Temple. A territorial base of the Sikh political power was created by the occupation of different parts of Central Punjab by different Sikh leaders.

It has rightly been said that Ahmad Shah Abdali's career in India is very intimately a part of the Sikh struggle for independence. His repeated invasions between 1748 and 1767 "exercised a very decisive influence on the history of the rise of the Sikh power."

When Abdali attacked India in 1748, the Sikhs pursued the retreating Afghan army upto the banks of the Indus and plundered the baggage of Abdali. Ahmad Shah Abdali invaded the Punjab again in 1750. Mir Mannu stopped his advance by promising to pay him ₹14 lakhs of rupees. In 1752, the Punjab ceased to be a part of the Mughal Empire as a result of the third invasion of India by Abdali. Mir Mannu became the Governor of Lahore and Multan on behalf of Ahmad Shah Abdali. After the death of Mir Mannu in 1753, power was seized by his widow Mughlani Begam. There was complete chaos in the Punjab. Ahmad Shah Abdali invaded India for the fourth time in 1756-57 and placed the provinces of Lahore, Sirhind, Kashmir, Thatta and Multan in the charge of his minor son Taimur with the title of Shah. He plundered Amritsar, and demolished the sacred buildings and the tank. The Sikhs pounced upon his tents and looted his baggage without engaging in any pitched battle.

During the administration of Mir Mannu and Taimur Shah, Adina Beg played a dubious role. Though he was outwardly opposed to the Sikhs, he was not prepared to crush them because that would reduce his own importance in the eyes of his Mughal and Afghan suzerains. He hoped to make himself the master of the Punjab by driving out the Afghans with the help of the Marathas. He invited Raghunath Rao, the Maratha chief, who was stationed near Delhi with a large army and promised to pay him a liberal financial subsidy. Raghunath Rao advanced to the Punjab and occupied Sirhind and Lahore in March-April 1758. He was helped by Adina Beg and the Sikhs. Raghunath Rao left Lahore immediately leaving the government incharge of Adina Beg in return for an annual tribute of 75 lakhs. Adina Beg died within four months and the Marathas took charge of the Punjab early in 1759. By that time, the Sikhs had established themselves in a commanding position. Ahmad Shah Abdali invaded India in October 1759. He defeated the Marathas in the third battle of Panipat in January 1761. In the course of his return journey, Abdali was harassed by the Sikhs who began to plunder the stragglers. Ahmad Shah Abdali could do nothing as his army was loaded with plunder. The Sikhs followed him all the way upto Attock. When he crossed the Attock, the Sikhs returned to blockade Lahore.

Ahmad Shah Abdali appointed one Governor after another to hold charge of the Punjab, but the Sikhs made a bold bid for sovereignty. They occupied Lahore. Jassa Singh Ahluwalia was proclaimed king with the title of Sultan-ul-Qaum. He coined money in the name of the Guru. Practically the whole of the Punjab from the Indus to the Sutlej passed into the hands of the Sikhs. Only a few pockets remained.

In the sixth invasion of Ahmad Shah Abdali, the Sikhs suffered fearful carnage in a pitched battle in February 1762. This is known as *Wadda Ghalughara* (Second Great Holocaust). Amritsar was occupied. The sacred temple was blown up with gunpowder. The sacred tank was desecrated and filled up with refuse and debris. A wholesale massacre of the Sikhs was ordered. However, the Sikhs regained their prestige by defeating Ahmad Shah Abdali in the battle of Amritsar and the latter was obliged to run away.

After the departure of Abdali in December 1763, the Sikhs set out under different leaders to make conquests in different areas. Sirhind was occupied, plundered and devastated in January 1764. In 1764, the Sikhs assembled at Amritsar and struck there the first coins of good pure silver with the inscription *"Degh, Tegh, Fateh"*. This was the first public proclamation of the establishment of the sovereignty of the Sikh community. Realising that his agents would not be able to suppress the Sikhs, Abdali invaded India for the seventh time in October 1764. He ravaged and plundered the country and placed Ala Singh of Patiala incharge of Sirhind and left for Afghanistan. (1765).

The Sikhs occupied Lahore, extended their territories in the Punjab, plundered the territory of Najibuddaula and entered into an alliance with the Jat chief Jawahir Singh and raided the territory of Madho Singh of Jaipur. Abdali came to India for the eighth time in 1766-67 and tried to crush the Sikhs. He came twice again, up to the Chenab in 1768 and upto Peshawar in 1769, but he had to retreat on account of the rebellion of his own troops. Abdali died in 1772.

On the final retreat of Abdali from the Punjab, the Sikhs reappeared in their full strength. Lahore was reoccupied and also the entire open country. Between 1767 and 1773, the Sikhs extended their power from Saharanpur in the East to Attock in the West and from Multan in the South to Kangra and Jammu in the North. They organised themselves into twelve Misls or confederacies: The Bhangi Misl, Ahluwalia Misl, Faizullapuria Misl, Ramgarhia Misl, Kanheya Misl, Sukerchakiya Misl, Nakhai Misl, Dalewalia Misl, Karorasinghia Misl, Nishanwalia Misl, Phulkia Misl and Shahids' Misl or Nihangs' Misl. It is difficult to calculate the exact fighting strength of the Sikh Misls. It is generally estimated that their total strength was about one lakh. Cavalry was the backbone of the armies of the Misls. There was no regular training for the soldiers. The weapons commonly used by them were swords, spears, match-locks, sabres etc. The soldiers of the Misls believed more in guerilla warfare than in pitched battles. Most of the Misls were annexed by Maharaja Ranjit Singh and some of them accepted the protection of the English East India Company. It was under the leadership of Maharaja Ranjit Singh that the Sikhs were able to establish a strong sovereign state in the Punjab. He died in 1839 and after the two Sikh Wars the Punjab was annexed by Lord Dalhousie in 1849.

The success of the Sikhs was due to many reasons. One reason was the method of their warfare. The Sikhs were weak in organisation, equipment and arms and could not face the well-equipped Mughal and Afghan armies. They adopted hit and run tactics. They took full advantage of their knowledge of local geography. They had unparalleled capacity for endurance. Another cause was their moral ardour. The Sikhs were dedicated soldiers who were fighting for their freedom. They fought against the disintegrating, but cruel and oppressive Mughal power. The religious fervour of the Sikhs gave them an inexhaustible fountain of strength and a perennial stimulant to sacrifice. It was the spirit infused in the Sikhs by Guru Govind Singh which enabled them to establish a sovereign state in the Punjab. The Sikh war of independence was not a war led by an individual. It was a people's war. The victory was not won by the genius of a single great leader. It was the reward of the sacrifices made by all the Sikhs.

JAMMU AND KASHMIR

Jammu was under the rule of a Hindu Rajput dynasty for a long time. The Mughal Emperors kept a Muslim Faujdar at Jammu to realise tributes from the hill states and to suppress any revolt in the region. So long as the tribute was paid, he did not interfere in their internal affairs.

Farrukh-siyar appointed Zakartya Khan as the Faujdar of Jammu in 1713. Banda had recovered Lohgarh by that time. He was besieged by the Mughal army. He held his ground for 6 months and then escaped to the hills. Zakariya Khan pursued him, captured a number of Sikhs and sent their heads to Delhi where they were produced before Farrukh-siyar on 13 December 1713. Zakariya Khan was given a robe of honour and the rank of 3,000 Zat and 1,000 Sawar. Zakariya Khan was present in the siege of Banda at Gurdas Nangal near Gurdaspur. Banda faced the Mughal army for 8 months and surrendered on 17 December 1715 along with 740 followers. Zakariya Khan accompanied those prisoners first to Lahore and then to Delhi and participated in their procession in the streets of Delhi.

With the decline of the Mughal Empire, the Raja of Jammu began to assert his independence. In about 1746, he started paying tribute to the Mughals. Jammu was under Raja Ranjit Deo from 1750 to 1781. He took full advantage of the confused political condition in the Punjab and extended his authority over all the hills between the Chenab and Ravi and over some of those lying to the West of the Chenab. Ranjit Deo was a dependable ally of Ahmad Shah Abdali. He helped him in conquering Kashmir in 1752 and again in 1762. In April 1757, Ahmad Shah Abdali granted him three Paraganas of Zafarwal, Sankhatra and Aurangabad. He struck coins in his own name. During his reign, the city of Jammu prospered and became a centre of trade. Even rich bankers, merchants and high officials of Lahore and Delhi found refuge at Jammu. During the third invasion of India by Ahmad Shah Abdali in 1751-52. Mir Mannu sent his family and treasures to the care of Raja Ranjit Deo. In about 1770, Ranjit Deo submitted to Jhanda Singh Bhangi and agreed to pay tribute. Ranjit Deo died in 1781. He was succeeded by his son Brij Raj Deo. During his reign, the Jammu state came completely under the control of the Sikhs.

As regards Kashmir, Abdus Samad Khan was the Governor of Kashmir under Bahadur Shah and Jahandar Shah. He was transferred to the Punjab by Farrukh-siyar. The decline of the Mughal Empire after Aurangzeb affected the political condition of Kashmir which remained disturbed upto 1752. No Mughal Emperor visited Kashmir after Aurangzeb. Ahmad Shah Abdali conquered Kashmir in 1752 and the Afghan rule lasted for 67 years upto 1819. The Afghan kings were mainly interested in getting annual tribute and so long as that was paid, the kings left the Governors with full powers and did not care how they ruled, whether ably or tyrannically. There were 28 Governors during the Afghan rule and only one of them was a Hindu. Sukhjiwan took charge of the state and conveyed his submission to Ahmad Shah Abdali. Ahmad Shah Abdali confirmed him and appointed another person as his deputy. Sukhjiwan was a brave soldier, wise administrator, scholar, linguist and a poet. He engaged five good scholars to compile a history of Kashmir. Each writer was provided with ten assistants. His Government was the best and most efficient for the Hindus and Muslims, Sunnis and Shias.

Ahmad Shah Abdali demanded from Sukhjiwan an exorbitant tribute equal to ten times the revenue of the country. Sukhjiwan ignored the demand as it was beyond his capacity. He offered allegiance to the Mughal Emperor Alamgir II (1754-59) who conferred on him the title of Raja. In June 1762, Ahmad Shah Abdali sent an expedition against Sukhjiwan but it failed. Another expedition was sent and the Afghan forces entered Kashmir. Sukhjiwan was captured, blinded and sent to Lahore where he was trampled to death by horses.

In 1793, Mir Hazar Khan sewed up Hindu leaders in gunny bags and threw them into the Dal Lake to be drowned. Abdullah Khan (1796-1800) collected one crore of rupees as his personal wealth. Ata Muhammad Khan forcibly seized petty girls to satisfy his lust. There was great unrest in the province. It was conquered by Ranjit Singh in 1819.

THE MARATHAS

The most important challenge to the decaying Mughal Empire came from the Marathas who produced a number of brilliant commanders and statesmen at that time. However, they lacked unity and hence failed to replace the Mughals. They waged a continuous war against the Mughal Empire till it was completely destroyed.

When Aurangzeb died in 1707, Sahu was a prisoner since 1689. He was released in 1707. A civil war broke out between Sahu at Satara and Tara Bai, widow of Raja Ram, at Kolhapur. The Maratha chiefs sided with one party or the other. They took full advantage of the situation and increased their influence by bargaining. Many of them even intrigued with the Mughal Viceroys of the Deccan. A new system of Maratha Government was evolved under the leadership of Balaji Vishwanath who was the Peshwa of Sahu.

Balaji Vishwanath. Balaji Vishwanath (1714-20) rose to power step by step. He rendered loyal and useful service to Sahu and suppressed his enemies and rivals. He excelled in diplomacy and won over many Maratha chiefs to the side of Sahu. In recognition of his services, Sahu made him his Peshwa. Gradually, Balaji Vishwanath consolidated Sahu's hold and also his own over the Maratha chiefs. The Peshwa concentrated all power in his office. As a matter of fact, Balaji Vishwanath and his son Baji Rao made the Peshwa the functional head of the Maratha Empire.

Balaji Vishwanath took full advantage of the internal conflicts of the Mughal officials and increased the Maratha power. He induced Zulfiqar Khan to pay Chauth and Sardeshmukhi of the

Deccan. He signed a pact with the Sayyid Brothers. All the territories which had formed the kingdom of Shivaji, were restored to Sahu who was given the right to Chauth and Sardeshmukhi of the six provinces of the Deccan. In return, Sahu recognised Mughal suzerainty. He agreed to place a body of 15,000 cavalry at the service of the Mughal Emperor to prevent rebellions and plundering in the Deccan. He was also to pay an annual tribute of ₹10 lakhs. In 1719. Balaji Vishwanath accompanied Sayyid Husain Ali to Delhi at the head of a Maratha force and helped the Sayyid Brothers in overthrowing Farrukh-siyar. While in Delhi, he and the other Maratha Chiefs saw with their own eyes the weakness of the Mughal Empire and they were filled with the ambition to expand Maratha power in Northern India. For the efficient collection of Chauth and Sardeshmukhi of the Deccan. Balaji Vishwanath assigned separate areas to Maratha chiefs who kept the greater part of the collection for their expenses. An increasing number of Maratha chiefs began to flock to the side of the Peshwa. They gradually settled down in various regions as more or less autonomous chiefs. The conquests by the Marathas outside their original kingdom were not made by a central army directly controlled by the Maratha kings or the Peshwa but by the Maratha chiefs with their private armies. Their interests dashed with one another. If the Peshwa strictly enforced his authority over them, they did not hesitate to join the Mughals, the Nizam or the English East India Company.

Baji Rao I. Balaji Vishwanath was succeeded as Peshwa by his son Baji Rao I (1720-40). He was a bold and brilliant commander and an ambitious and clever statesman. Under his leadership, the Marathas waged numerous campaigns against the Mughal Empire to compel the Mughal officials first to give them the right to collect Chauth of the vast areas and then to cede those areas to the Maratha kingdom. He defeated the Nizam in the battle near Bhopal in 1738. By the time of his death in 1740, the Marathas had established their control over Malwa, Gujarat and parts of Bundelkhand. The Maratha families of Sindhia, Holkar, Gaekwad and Bhonsle came into prominence. Baji Rao changed the character of the Maratha state. From the kingdom of Maharashtra, it was transformed into an Empire expanding in Northern India. New territories were conquered and occupied but little attention was paid to their administration. The Maratha chiefs were mainly concerned with the collection of revenue and not the welfare of the people.

Balaji Baji Rao. Baji Rao was succeeded by Balaji Baji Rao and he was Peshwa from 1740 to 1761. He was as able as his father, but not so energetic. When Sahu died in 1749, the work of management of the affairs of the state fell into the hands of the Peshwa who became the official head of the administration. He shifted the Government to Poona. He extended the Maratha Empire in different directions. Maratha armies overran the whole of Northern India. Maratha control over Malwa, Gujarat and Bundelkhand was consolidated. Bengal was repeatedly invaded. In 1751, the Nawab of Bengal had to give Orissa (now Odisha) to the Marathas. In the South, the state of Mysore and other minor principalities were forced to pay tribute. In 1760, the Nizam of Hyderabad was defeated at Udgir and was compelled to cede vast territories yielding an annual revenue of 62 lacs. In the North, the Marathas became the power behind the Mughal throne. In 1752, the Marathas helped Imad-ul-Mulk to become the Wazir who became a puppet in their hands. From Delhi, the Marathas turned to the Punjab and brought it under their control after expelling the agent of Ahmad Shah Abdali. This brought them into conflict with Ahmad Shah Abdali. A struggle for supremacy over Northern India started. Ahmad Shah Abdali formed an alliance with Najib-ud-Daulah of Rohilkhand and Shuja-ud-Daulah of Oudh. Both of them had suffered at the hand of the Marathas. The Peshwa despatched a powerful army to the North under the nominal commands of his minor son, Vishwas Rao but the actual command was in the hands of his cousin Sadashiv Rao Bhau. The Marathas tried to find allies among the Northern powers but their earlier behaviour and political ambitions had antagonised all those powers. The Maraths had interfered in the internal affairs of the Rajput states and realised huge fines and tributes from them. They had made large territorial and monetary claims upon Oudh. Their action in the Punjab annoyed the Sikhs. The Jats did not trust them on account of the imposition of heavy fines. The result was that the Maratha had to fight their enemies all alone. On 14 January 1761 was fought the third battle of Panipat in which the Marathas were defeated. Vishwas Rao, Sadashiv Rao Bhau and many other Maratha commanders died in the battlefield. About 28,000 soldiers were killed. When the Peshwa heard the news of the defeat of the Marathas he died in June 1761.

Malwa

The old province of Malwa which is now merged into Madhya Pradesh was the connecting link between the Deccan and Hindustan proper. On account of its central position, this province had great strategic importance. The highways of commerce and military routes to the Deccan and Gujarat passed through it and armies based in Malwa could strike at Rajputana or Bundelkhand with the greatest ease.

Malwa was first conquered by Humayun and then by Akbar and it enjoyed peace for more than a century, but that peace was disturbed by Aurangzeb's policy of religious persecution. The result was that the provincial administration lost its efficiency. The discontented Rajput chiefs, Zamindars and their Hindu subjects refused to cooperate with the Mughal Subedar and they welcomed the Maratha invaders, gave them secret information about rivers, fords and mountain passes and facilitated their invasions.

According to Sir Jadunath Sarkar, the first invasion of Malwa by the Marathas took place in 1699. They crossed the Narmada and ravaged places near Dhamuni and retired. The path thus opened was never again closed till Malwa passed into the hands of the Marathas in the middle of the eighteenth century. In 1703. Nemaji Sindia burst into Malwa and plundered and burnt the villages. The Mughal Emperor had to despatch a special force to stop his advance. Maratha raids were repeated with greater boldness in the next decade.

When the Mughal Emperor granted the right of Chauth and Sardeshmukhi to the Marathas in 1719, Khandesh and Malwa were assigned to the Peshwa for making collection. The Peshwa looked upon the possession of Malwa as the best guarantee for the security of Maratha Motherland and the Deccan. Peshwa Baji Rao invaded Malwa in February 1723 and May 1724. He collected Chauth and met Nizam-ul-Mulk who was the Governor of Malwa at that time. In June 1725, Girdhar Bahadur was appointed the Subedar of Malwa. The new Subedar was a man of strong character and he refused to compromise with the Marathas and chased them beyond the Narmada. It was after the defeat of Nizam-ul-Mulk at Palkhed in February 1728 that the Peshwa was able to take action against Girdhar Bahadur. A big army led by Peshwa's brother Chimnaji Appa invaded Malwa. Girdhar Bahadur was defeated and killed. Bhavani Ram, the son of Girdhar Bahadur, held up Maratha advance for some time but failed. There was utter confusion in Malwa. No money or reinforcements could be obtained from the Mughal Emperor. The troops clamoured for their arrears. The mountain passes into Malwa were lost to the Marathas and within a decade, Malwa passed into the hands of Marathas.

Towards the end of 1729, Sawai Jai Singh was appointed the Governor of Malwa. Realising the difficulty of resisting the Marathas, he adopted the policy of appeasement. The Mughal Emperor got suspicious of his motives and he was replaced by Muhammad Khan Bangash who was opposed to the Marathas. The policy of Muhammad Khan Bangash failed and Sawai Jai Singh was again appointed the Subedar of Malwa in 1732. He pursued his old policy of appeasing the Marathas. He purchased peace by sharing with the Marathas the large sums sent to him from Delhi for the defence of the province. The Mughal campaigns in 1734-36 failed to keep Malwa free from the aggression of the Marathas. The policy of appeasement was not successful and fresh concessions called forth fresh aggression. In 1738, after his defeat at Bhopal, Nizam-ul-Mulk offered to the Peshwa the whole of Malwa and the complete sovereignty of the territory between the Narmada and the Chambal. The Nizam was not able to secure the approval of the Mughal Emperor and the matter remained unsettled. In 1741, Peshwa Balaji Baji Rao advanced to Gwalior and a settlement was made with the Mughal Emperor through the mediation of Sawai Jai Singh who was then the Subedar of Agra. Emperor Muhammad Shah bestowed the Deputy Governorship of Malwa on the Peshwa. This was merely a device for saving the face of the Emperor as otherwise Malwa ceased to be a part of the Empire of Delhi.

Gujarat

Internal strife among the Mughals in Gujarat gave the Marathas a chance to fish in troubled waters and establish themselves firmly in that province. Civil war among the Mughals began in 1724 when the Nizam was replaced by Sarbuland Khan as the Subedar of Gujarat. At that time, "Hamid Khan, the uncle of the Nizam, was acting as the Deputy of the Nizam in Gujarat. Sarbuland Khan himself stayed at Delhi and sent his Deputy Shujat Khan to take charge from Hamid Khan." Hamid Khan also wanted to become the ruler of Gujarat and got the support of the Marathas by conceding them the right to collect Chauth and Sardeshmukhi. With the help of Kanthaji, Hamid Khan defeated and killed Shujat Khan and his brother Rustam Ali who came from Surat. Sarbuland Khan himself marched to Gujarat and expelled Hamid Khan, but he could not expel the Marathas. In 1727, Sarbuland Khan agreed to pay the Marathas Chauth and Sardesh mukhi in Gujarat. The Mughal Emperor did not approve of the arrangement, recalled Sarbuland Khan and sent Raja Abhay Singh as the Governor of Gujarat with orders to turn out the Marathas from Gujarat. In order to overawe the Marathas, Abhay Singh got Pilaji Gaikwar, a Maratha leader, killed. That resulted in a widespread upheaval among the local population. Damaji, the eldest son of Pilaji, renewed the struggle, recovered Baroda and harassed Abhay Singh so much that the latter left for Jodhpur without any success. Damaji even invaded Jodhpur. Gujarat was finally lost to the Empire in 1737.

Mysore

Another important state which emerged in South India was Mysore under Hyder Ali. The kingdom of Mysore had preserved its precarious independence ever since the end of the Vijayanagar Empire. Early in the eighteenth century, two ministers Nanjaraj and Devaraj seized power in Mysore and reduced the king Chikka Krishna Raj to a mere puppet.

Hyder Ali started his career as a petty officer in the Mysore army. Though uneducated, he possessed a keen intellect. He was a man of great energy, daring and determination. He was also a brilliant commander and shrewd diplomat. By dint of his military skill and qualities of leadership, he became the Faujdar of Dindigal in 1755. He misappropriated the revenues of Dindigal and managed to raise an independent army of his own. In 1761, he overthrew Nanjaraj and Devaraj and established his own authority in the state of Mysore. In 1763, he occupied Bednore. He strengthened his financial position by the booty that fell into his hands. He conquered Canara. He set up his capital at Seringapatarn. He created a strong war machine within a short time.

From the very beginning, Hyder Ali had strained relations with the English East India Company. He had secured valuable help from the French. For his help against the British. Count Lally had agreed to pay ₹10,000/- per month to Hyder Ali and also the forts of Thaigur and Elvanasore. After the expulsion of the British, Hyder Ali was expected to get Trichinopoly, Madurai, Tinnevelly etc. A British force under Major More was routed. However, Sir Eyre Coote captured Villenore. When Pondicherry surrendered to the British in 1761. Hyder Ali took about 300 French soldiers in his service. There was also hostility between Hyder Ali and Muhammad Ali, the Nawab of Carnatic. There were many districts in Carnatic which were claimed both by Hyder Ali and Muhammad Ali. Muhammad Ali allowed British troops to be stationed at Vellore but the same was resented by Hyder Ali. Hyder Ali took into service Raja Sahib, son of Chanda Sahib and gave protection to Mahfuz Khan, brother and rival of Muhammad Ali.

After the collapse of the French power in Southern India, Hyder Ali tried to patch up, with the English East India Company but failed. The Madras Government encouraged the Nizam to take up arms against Hyder Ali and offered to give necessary military help for that purpose. The Nizam had the support of the Marathas. In November 1767, the Madras Government concluded a treaty with the Nizam by which it agreed to pay him a tribute of ₹5 lakhs for the Northern Circars. It also promised not to acquire the Circar of Guntoor so long as Balasat Jang lived. The British promised military help to the Nizam against his enemies. The Madras Government was keen to acquire Carnatic and Balaghat which were held by Hyder Ali and agreed to pay ₹7 lakhs to the Nizam for its Diwani.' This was impliedly acknowledgement of the sovereignty of the Nizam over the dominions of Hyder Ali. Both the Nizam and the English Company were keen to prey upon the territories of Hyder Ali and the British Government agreed to help him. The Nizam advanced into Mysore in August 1767. Hyder Ali was able, to win over the Marathas and the Nizam and the British were left alone. The opposition of Hyder Ali and his son Tipu was formidable. Tipu was able to reach near Madras itself and the Madras authorities entered into a peace treaty with Hyder Ali in April 1769. Both the parties agreed to give up the territories conquered by them.

In 1770, Mysore was invaded by Peshwa Madhav Rao. Hyder Ali approached the Madras Government for help but the same was refused. In August 1778, the British attacked Pondicherry (now Puducherry) and after its occupation, they sent an expedition against Mahe. Hyder Ali sent his troops to defend Mahe but in spite of that, it was captured by the British in March 1779.

The Second Mysore War started in 1780 and continued up to 1784. The army of Hyder Ali was so near Madras that many of its residents ran away. The towns of Porto Novo and Conjeevaram were plundered. Hyder Ali occupied Arcot, capital of Carnatic. However, Hyder Ali was defeated by Sir Eyre Coote. Hyder Ali died in December 1782, but the war was continued by his son Tipu. The Second Mysore War was ended by the treaty of Mangalore in May 1784. Both parties agreed to restore the conquests made by them.

The Third Mysore War was fought from 1790 to 1792 in the time of Lord Cornwallis. Tipu was defeated. By the treaty of Seringapatam signed in March 1792. Tipu had to give up half of his territory.

The Fourth Mysore War was fought in the time of Lord Wellesley. Lord Wellesley demanded absolute submission from Tipu and as he refused to do so, war was declared. Tipu died fighting at Seringapatam in May 1799. After the war Lord Wellesley annexed large and important territories of Mysore. Some territory was given to the Nizam as a reward. A child of the Hindu family ousted by Hyder Ali in 1761 was placed on the throne of Mysore. Mysore continued to flourish under the control of the Government of India during the nineteenth century. The state of Mysore was still there when India became independent in 1947. Now its name has been changed into Karnatak.

Carnatic

Carnatic was one of the Subahs of the Deccan and was under the authority of the Nizam. As the Nizam became independent of Mughal control, the Deputy Governor of Carnatic, known as the Nawab of Carnatic, freed himself from the control of the Viceroy of the Deccan and made his office hereditary. Nawab Saadatullah Khan of Carnatic made his nephew Dost Ali his successor without the approval of his superior, the Nizam.

The Peshwa wanted to occupy Carnatic but the Nizam was equally determined to defend it as it was a part of the Deccan Subah. To begin with, the Nizam tried to undermine the position of Raja Sahu by granting Jagirs to those Maratha officers who turned hostile to their master. The Nizam also entered into a league with Sambhaji, the rival of Sahu. In 1727 when the Peshwa was proceeding to Carnatic, the Nizam wrote to Sahu that until his dispute with Sambhaji was settled, he would not pay Chauth and he must accept his mediation in it. Without waiting for reply, the Nizam invaded the Maratha kingdom and did a lot of destruction. Peshwa Baji Rao hit back and inflicted a crushing defeat on the Nizam in 1728 at Palkhed. This defeat unnerved the Nizam and he sued for peace. After 1740, the affairs of Carnatic deteriorated on account of the repeated struggles for its Nawabship. That gave the British an opportunity to interfere in Carnatic.

REVIEW QUESTIONS

1. Write an essay on the emergence of the autonomous states as a result of the decay of the Mughal empire.
2. What are the common features of the three regional states of Bengal, Awadh and Hyderabad?
3. Who were the rulers of the Avadh state? Throw light on their achievements.
4. Discuss the impact of the Jat kings on the history of India.
5. Describe in detail the history of Bengal under the leadership of Murshid Quli Khan, Sarfaraz Khan and Ali Vardi Khan.
6. Write a detailed note on the administration of the Marathas.
7. Write short notes on the following:
   (a) Siraj-ud-Daulah
   (b) Safdarjang
   (c) The Rajput states
   (d) The Sikhs
8. Trace the history of evolution of Sikh community. What was the nature of their relationship with the Mughal state?

SUGGESTED READINGS

Datta. K.K.: *Ali Vardi and His Times,* 1939.
Datta. K.K.: *Bengal Subah.*
Dighe, V.G.: *Peshwa Baji Rao I and Maratha Expansion,* 1944.
Hill, S.C.: *Bengal in 1756-57.*
Keith, Feiling: *Warren Hastings,* 1954.
Majumdar, R.C. (Ed.): *The Maratha Supremacy,* Bhartiya Vidya Bhavan, Bombay, 1977.
Malgoankar, M.: *Kanhoji Angrey.*
Mohibul Husain Khan: *History of Tipu Sultan.*
Moon, Penderel: *Warren Hastings and British India,* 1947.
Niggar; Bakshis Singh. *Punjab under the Great Mughals.*
Qanungo. K.R.: *History of the Jats.*
Raghubir Singh: *Malwa in Transition.*
Sardesai, G.S.: *New History of the Marathas,* 3 Vols., 1950.
Sinha, N.K.: *Rise of the Sikh Power.*
Sinha, N.K.: *Haidar Ali,* 1941.
Spear, Percival: *Master of Bengal,* 1975.
Spear, Percival: *India, A Modern History.*
Srinivasan, C.K.: *Peshwa Baji Rao I.*
Srivastava, A.L.: *Shuja-ud-Daula,* 2 Vols.
Srivastava, A.L.: *First Two Nawabs of Oudh,* 1933.
Yusuf Husain Khan: *Nizam-ul-Mulk Asaf Jah,* 1963.

3 Society and Culture in the Eighteenth Century

 LEARNING OBJECTIVES

- Discuss the social, religious and economic conditions of the people in the eighteenth century
- Describe the development of art, literature, science and technology during the eighteenth century

The political instability in the country after the death of Aurangzeb had its effect on the social, religious and economic condition of the people. For a long time, there was practically no authority, no administration, no law and no security in vast areas of the country. Anarchy was the order of the day. The strong prevailed over the weak. The Indians had very bad time in every way.

SOCIAL CONDITION

Social life in the eighteenth century was marked by stagnation and dependence on the past. There was no uniformity of culture and social patterns all over the country. People were divided by religion, region, tribe, language and caste. The social life of the upper classes was different in many ways from the life of the lower classes. There were pronounced social disparities. The higher classes and castes were overconscious of their supremacy and superiority. The entire wealth of the country was concentrated in the hands of the higher classes while the masses lacked the barest necessities of life. The Muslim concept of equality and fraternity had vanished so completely that a Muslim Sharif could not bear to see a Muslim Radhil trying to come in any way near him in social status. The different castes among the Hindus were jealous of their rights and each caste and every group was isolated within its own customs and social traditions. Any deviation from established laws and conventions resulted in excommunication. The people were so much absorbed in the celebration of marriages, feasts, festivals and other family ceremonies that they had no urge to create new social values.

The social system in the eighteenth century had two aspects. One aspect was a grading on the basis of official power and position. The second aspect was an ordering based on religion and the traditional divisions of society. The first was a reflection of the political system. The second comprised the castes and sub-castes among the Hindus and rigid grading in Muslim society on the basis of Kufr.

Four Castes

The Hindu society was divided into four parts, viz., the Brahmans, Kshatriyas, Vaisyas and Sudras. The Brahman was the priest, the sole exponent of religion as well as the teacher and guide. To quote Craufurd, "Their caste is the only repository of the literature that yet remains; to them alone is entrusted the education of youth; they are the sole interpreters of the law and the only expounders of their religion." Both the ignorant and the educated were superstitious and the Brahmans exploited the innate human fear of the unknown. The hereditary occupation of the Kshatriyas was to wield temporal power. The kings, ministers and soldiers generally belonged to this class. The question whether the Kshatriyas were actually doing in this period what they were supposed to do is aptly answered by Nagari Dass, the Hindi poet, who has observed that the Kshatriyas were greedy and selfish. They never did any good to anybody and were not compassionate. If they saw a beautiful woman in the house of a poor man, their strength of arm lay only in their effort to grab her for themselves. The Vaisyas were the community of businessmen. They had two broad divisions. One branch took to trade and the other to agriculture. It was the former who were typical of their class. They were the usurers and the sole aim of their life was to live on the interest of the money that they gave as loans. A Bania was notorious for his love of money. He was looked down upon by the society for that reason. The Sudras comprised the mass of the people. They included the aborigines admitted to the Hindu community. Their salvation was supposed to lie in the direct and indirect service rendered by them to the three upper classes. Below these four castes were the Antyajas with their eight guilds of craftsmen. They had to live at a distance from the higher castes and still rendered their services to them. The lowest of the low were the Hadis, Doms and Chandalas.

The Brahmanas, Kshatriyas and Vaisyas were all divided and subdivided into a large number of castes and sub-castes. Each caste formed an endogamous group and it was only in this endogamous group that inter-dining was permissible. Restrictions on marriage, food and occupation distinguished and defined his social status. Any deviation from the customs of a locality was considered to be a sin and one who was guilty of such an offence was liable to be excommunicated. The caste Panchayat did not readmit him in his caste until he humbled himself publicly. The marriage had to be in the same caste in order to prevent the intermixture of blood and maintain the purity of descent.

In the eighteenth century, the people were very sensitive about the concept of Roti (bread) and Beti (daughter). Interdining among the people of different castes was non-existent. Only the Sikhs had their institution of Langar which was open to all. People of different castes could worship the same gods, observe the same manners and customs, but would not eat together. As a matter of fact, no one could ever think of it as the threat of excommunication was an effective deterrent.

The question of permissible and forbidden food was an important one. As a rule, the Brahmans had to abstain from meat and intoxicating liquors. The caste prescribed different codes for different groups. Meat was not a staple diet in India. Abstinence from meat was general practised in the areas dominated by Jain influence. The classes that came into contact with them were generally vegetarian, while the others took meat as a luxury and delicacy. Vegetarianism and non-vegetarianism was determined not so much by caste as by the religious sect to which an individual belonged. The Kshatriyas, Rajputs, Jats and other lower classes all ate meat.

Occupation was another decisive factor in the formation of caste. In spite of the general taboos, social and economic exigencies necessitated contacts between the twice-born and the artisan classes and the creation of relationship between the higher and lower castes. Those who practised the professions of barber, weaver, embroiderer, dyer, printer, gardener, potter, ivory-worker etc., were sometimes paid directly for the services rendered by them. More often, their remuneration was a fixed quantity of grain at the harvest time, or some money or clothes on occasions of celebration in the family.

There were certain occupations which were open to all. Trading, agriculture and even military service could be taken up by anybody who was eligible for it.

Caste regulations were strictly enforced by caste councils and Panchayats and caste chiefs through fines, penances (Prayaschitta) and expulsion from the caste. Caste was a major division force and an element of disintegration in the India of the eighteenth century. It often split Hindus living in the same village or region into many social atoms. However, it was possible for a person to acquire a higher social status by the acquisition of high office or power as was done by the Holkar family in the eighteenth century. Sometimes, an entire caste succeeded in raising itself in the caste hierarchy.

Family

The family system in the eighteenth century was primarily patriarchal. The family was dominated by the senior male member. Inheritance was through the male line. However, in Kerala, the family was matrilineal. Outside Kerala, women were subjected to nearly complete male control. They were expected to live as mothers and wives only. Women of that time possessed little individuality of their own. However, Ahilya Bai administered Indore with great success from 1766 to 1796. Many other Hindu and Muslim women played an important role in the politics of that time.

The *status of a woman* in the family depended entirely on her capacity to give births to sons and hence they were prepared to make any sacrifice for that purpose. A mother wielded tremendous influence in all important matters of the household. A daughter occupied a peculiar position in the family. Although theoretically she was considered Lakshmi (the goddess of prosperity) but her birth was not welcomed. She had no share in her father's and brother's property. If there were many daughters, they became a galling responsibility.

The custom of *female infanticide* was very much prevalent among the Rajputs and not in all the cases. Child marriage was prevalent in society. Child marriage was more for social security than as a sign of backwardness. The instability in the eighteenth century created great anxiety among the parents about the honour of their daughters and hence they were married at an early age. Women were excluded and the Purdah became an established custom both among the Hindus and Muslims. The general in security and lawlessness prevailing at that time made their exclusion more tight and that deprived the women of any opportunity to acquire education. Their physical and mental health also suffered. The custom of *Sati* mostly prevailed in Bengal, Central India and Rajputana. In the South, it was uncommon. The Peshwas discouraged Sati in their dominion with limited success.

Polygamy prevailed among the Kulin families of Uttar Pradesh and Bengal. Remarriage of widows was generally looked down upon though it prevailed in some places. The Peshwas imposed a tax called Patdam on remarriage of widows. The lot of the Hindu widows was usually pitiable. There were all sorts of restrictions on their clothing, diet, movements etc. They were expected to give up all the pleasures of the earth and serve selflessly the members of her husband's or brother's family. Raja Sawai Jai Singh of Amber and the Maratha General Parshuram Bhau tried to promote widow remarriage but failed.

Untouchability was prevalent in society. The untouchables were denied certain basic privileges of living. They could not use tanks, wells, inns or schools meant for upper class people, not to speak of places of a worship or public institutions.

The people performed many *superstitious rites*. The upper class Hindus resorted to human sacrifices on certain occasions. It was believed that the Goddess Kali requires human blood or heads and for the gratification of the Devi, a human victim was slaughtered. Self-immolation was another form of human sacrifice. In some cases, one could drown oneself in a river in order to escape a disease. In other cases, life could be taken by way of mortification had penance. In some cases, one's child was sacrificed. Under peculiar conditions, parents took a vow to offer their first-born child to the Ganges. Another superstitious rite was self-torture. Many devotees pierced their tongues and arms with pointed rods. This was done in the belief that good results followed self-torture.

Slavery

Slavery prevailed in the country. Broadly speaking, slaves could be divided into two parts, domestic slaves and serfs tied to the land. The second category of the slaves were transferred with the sale of the land to the buyer. In some cases, economic distress, natural calamities, extreme poverty and famines compelled parents to sell their children. The Rajputs, the Kshatriyas and Kayasthas usually kept slave women for domestic work. Slaves in India were treated better than the slaves in Europe and America. They were usually treated as hereditary servants of the family and were allowed to marry among themselves.

The practice of slavery increased with the coming of the Europeans in India, particularly the Portuguese, the Dutch and the English. The European Companies purchased slaves in the open market. There were reports of Europeans at Surat, Madras and Calcutta purchasing Abyssinian slaves and employing them for domestic work.

Muslim Family

In the eighteenth century, it became difficult to differentiate between the practices of a Muslim family and a Hindu family although the Muslims conformed to the Shariat. A polygamous household was the fashion among the royalty and the nobility and all those who could afford it. The wives, concubines, slave-girls, dancing and singing girls all had their share in the rich or powerful man's life. The individual Muslim, man or woman, was a complete and self-sufficient unit of society. Marriage was a civil contract and the family found legal recognition only in connection with inheritance. The first wife enjoyed the privileges of seniority. She was considered to be the head of the female establishment and she was given precedence over all the other wives. However, the children of the subsequent wives enjoyed equal status.

The mother in a Muslim family had a status of her own. The father was the head of the family but he did not have absolute power in a Muslim family. The Muslim woman had the right to give or withhold her consent to marriage, but she could not exercise her right in the eighteenth century. In certain cases, a marriage in Islam could be even a temporary contract (Muta), having no higher motive than sexual gratification. Due to the influence of Hinduism, divorce in Muslim families was looked down upon and respectable people preferred to put up with all the differences and disputes in the family than to become objects of public discussion by trying to get a divorce. One cannot easily find an example among the higher classes to prove the prevalence of divorce in Muslim society. Muslim parents had to give dowries to their daughters which were generally beyond the means of the family. The son in a Muslim family was the source of much more pleasure than a daughter on account of the patriarchal form of society. The reason was mainly economic as the father of girls was considered to be a poor man.

Muslim women were kept in seclusion. The family dwelling was divided into a Zenanah (woman's quarter) and a Mardanah (man's quarter). Political insecurity might have prompted these measures but in the eighteenth century it was made a point of prestige to have the women of the family concealed in the innermost quarters of the house. The seclusion of women, both among the Muslims and Hindus, was mainly confined to the higher classes. Women of the lower classes had to appear in public because they had to work and earn. As they had to work like chattels for their menfolk, they could not be kept veiled. Those who lived in the countryside had to till the land and carry the produce to the market, while those in the towns had to pay the price of their existence by performing all the household duties and assisting their husbands in any business in which they were engaged.

Celibacy did not find any recognition as a virtue in Muslim society. Barring the princesses of the royal family and sometime the Sufi saints, marriage was an obligation to be fulfilled by every Muslim. The concept of the prohibited degree in marriage seems to have been obligatory on the Muslims in the eighteenth century. Among the orthodox Muslims, there was a prejudice amounting to prohibition in regard to marriages between Sunni Muslims and Shiahs.

Islam permitted plurality of wives upto four, but alongwith that it was enjoined that the wives should be treated in a very equitable manner. The number of wives almost determined the social status of a man. The leading noblemen kept regular harems while the lower classes were usually monogamous because polygamy was beyond their means.

No age limit was fixed for marriage but Muslims generally favoured early marriages. That may be due to the influence of Hinduism. Almost as a rule, boys were not allowed to see the girls before they were married. Manned writes, "Among the Mohammedans, it is the practice not to see their brides beforehand, but to marry upon reports, interests or respect."

The Mehr formed an important part in a Muslim marriage. It was usually fixed before the marriage. However, in the eighteenth century, in most of the cases, it was more form than reality. Mehr could be payable as soon as possible or its payment could be deferred. Match making among Muslims was generally the business of women except when the marriage took place for political reasons. There was a class of people whose occupation was to negotiate marriages. Though the custom of betrothal was opposed to Shariat, the Muslims were as particular as the Hindus.

Occasionally, there were inter-communal marriages. Farrukh-siyar was married to the daughter of Raja Ajit Singh. We do not find any other reference to inter-communal marriage.

EDUCATION

The educational system of both the Hindus and Muslims was unprogressive and hence both of them were equally backward educationally.

Neither of them had any idea of the progress sciences had made in the West. They also knew nothing about the new methods of observation, experiment and criticism. Although the Europeans dominated the seas around India and made landing stations and factories both on the Western and Eastern coasts, the Indians of Gujarat, Konkan, Kerala, Cholamandal, Orissa (now Odisha) and Bengal remained intellectually wholly unaffected by their presence. The princes and noblemen of India showed some interest in European animals and birds, mirrors, toys, wives and spirits, but they showed no interest in their social, economic or cultural affairs. Although almost every branch of knowledge of the Muslims was studied in the Christian universities of Spain, Italy and France, the new discoveries of Europe remained almost entirely unknown in India till the end of the eighteenth century. This was not due to the lack of schools in India and there were plenty of them. The real trouble was in the quality of education. Education was organised on communal basis. There were in fact two altogether different systems for the Hindus and Muslims. The Hindus used the regional language for elementary education and Sanskrit for higher learning. The medium of instruction in both the Hindu and Muslim schools was Persian.

The Hindu schools were divided into two watertight compartments. One section imparted elementary education. The schools catered for the needs of those pupils who would follow agricultural and commercial pursuits. The teachers largely belonged to the writer castes. In Murshidabad, out of 67 teachers in the same number of schools, 39 were Kayasthas, 14 Brahmanas and 14 members of other castes. In South Bihar, there were 285 schools and the same number of teachers. Out of these, 278 were Kayasthas and 7 came from other castes. None belonged to the Brahman caste.

The pupils in the primary schools spent from five to ten years in completing their course which included elements of reading, writing and arithmetic. The aim was to learn letter-writing and composing business correspondence—petitions, grants, leases etc. In arithmetic, the main object was to acquire proficiency in accounting, either agricultural or commercial. The emphasis was on tables such as multiplication, weights and measures etc. Education was purely utilitarian and extremely narrow. It did not awaken the mind and also did not free it from the trammels of tradition. Passions and affections were allowed to grow up wild without any thought of pruning their luxuriances or directing their exercise to good purposes.

The condition of the higher schools of learning was even worse. In those institutions, both the students and the teachers were Brahmanas because their courses were predominantly theological. Three main types of courses were taught, viz., grammar and general literature, law and logic. Studies extended from 2 to 12 and even 22 years. Most of the schools were in the house of the teacher.

The students of law devoted 8 to 23 years in mastering the various branches of Hindu law and rites. In Bengal the treatises of Raghunandan and Jimutavahan were studied. Manu and Mitakashara were taught in other schools. The study of logic required 12 to 22 years. In medicine and astronomy, studies were based on the ancient texts and their commentaries. These prolonged studies made the students narrow in their outlook. The disciplines of grammar, law and logic were largely formal and verbal.

The educational system of the Muslims was not very much better than that of the Hindus. It was intended only for the upper classes and did not offer any instruction to the Muslim masses. In all Muslim schools, Persian was the medium of instruction. Neither Urdu nor any other Indian spoken language was used. The Muslim masses were steeped in ignorance.

There were three types of instruction for the Muslims. The first type consisted of memorising the verses of the Quran without understanding the meaning. The second type of instruction was given in Persian schools. It concerned itself mainly with literature, grammar, computation and arithmetic In poetry, Firdausi, Sadi, Hafiz, Urfi, Jami, .Khaqani etc., were taught. In prose, Gulistan, Waqai Nimat Khan Ali, Bahar-i-Danish etc., were taught. In epistolary art, Abul Fazl, Alamgir, Madhoram Brahman etc. were taught. In grammar and rhetoric, Hadikat-ul-Balaghat, Dastur-ul-Mubtabi etc., were taught. Rules of arithmetic and geometry were included in the course.

The teaching of rational sciences, including medicine and astronomy, was wholly bookish. Laboratories and observatories were not available. The experimental method was not employed in study. The main emphasis was on theology and law and the authority of the great teachers of the past was held in great esteem. The Muslim mind was soaked in medievalism and it was intellectually quite unprepared to withstand the attack from the West.

Centres of higher education in Sanskrit literature were called Chatuspathis or Tols in Bengal and Bihar. Nadia, Kas, Tirhut and Utkala were reputed centres for Sanskrit education. Institutions for higher education in Persian and Arabic were called Madrasahs. As Persian was the court language, it was learnt both by the Muslims and the Hindus. Azimabad (Patna) was a great centre of Persian education.

Elementary education was widespread. Hindu elementary schools were called Pathshalas and those of the Muslims were called Maktabs. The schools were not attached to temples or mosques. The students were given instruction in the three R's of reading, writing and arithmetic. Moral instruction with emphasis on truth, honesty and obedience found a place in the school curriculum. Education was mainly popular with the higher castes. Female education received very little attention.

Literature

During the eighteenth century, Urdu spread to all corners of India. Urdu literary circles were established in every province of India. When the British dominion extended over Northern India, Urdu was employed by polite society of the Muslims and the Hindus.

The literature produced during this period was not of high order. Its poetry was dilettantish, weighed with euphemism and conceit. Its spirit was shackled by artificial limitations of rhyme. Its mood alternated between the sensuous and the spiritual, neither deeply experienced. Clouds of pessimism and despair hung over it. It was away from reality. The Urdu writers made Urdu a pliant instrument of expression.

Both Hindi and Urdu poets of this period were virtuosos. They were so much absorbed in their pursuit that they almost lost the awareness of the meaning of life and higher purpose of literature. It is worthy of notice that behind the diversities of language, race and creed, a deep cultural unity pervaded the whole of India.

Heer Ranjha, the famous romantic epic in Punjab, was written by Warris Shah. For Sindhi literature, the eighteenth century was a period of enormous achievement. Shah Abdul Latif composed his famous collection of poems, Risalo, Sachal and Sami were the other great Sindhi poets of the century. Daya Ram, one of the great lyricists of Gujarat, wrote during the second half of the eighteenth century. Tayaumanavar (1706-44) was one of the best exponents of Sittar poetry in Tamil. In line with other Sittar poets, he protested against the abuse of temple-rule and the caste system.

Dr. Varadarajan writes about Tamil, "The literature of this period is full of frigid conceits and pedantic exercises of the grammarians, and the simplicity, the directness and the restraint characteristic of the early literature are now lost. Most of the poets of this age seem imitative and repetitive not only in their narrative but also in their descriptions. Taste in poetry has become sophisticated and poets are judged by the jingle of their alliteration and the acrobatics of their meter. We come across really talented writers capable of original productions but they are only a very few. Even the works of these eminent poets evince a childish delight in riotous imaginations and hyperbolic utterances. There is, in many works of this period, not so much of art as artificiality, and therefore many of these works have fallen into oblivion."

Dr. Sitapati writes about Telugu literature that "good poetry vanished and a period of decadence prevailed." Shri Adya Rangacharya writes that "by the middle of the 18th century, Kannada ceased to exist". In Marathi, Lavanis (erotic poems) became common and even spiritual love and devotion was described in the degraded fashion of carnal love. Deshpande observes, "It was obvious that degeneration had set in. Metaphysical acumen was getting blunt. Devotional urge was on the wane and the verse and vigour of a soldier's life was also getting lost. Literature was settling down to the leisurely luxuriousness and erudite ornateness of the later days of the Peshwas." According to Trivedi, "Life was decadent from 1700 until the advent of the British." Regarding Bengali poetry in the 18th century, Dr. S.K. Banerjee says that it is "a colourless dragging in of the old patterns both in subject-matter and form". The predominantly secular tone prevailed in Assamese literature. Urdu and Hindi suffered from similar ills.

However, during this period appeared a large number of masters of rhetoric, style and diction who possessed supreme authority over language. They refined and developed the languages in which they wrote and made them instruments fit to meet the demands of the future. Their literary output indicates the cultural unity of India.

It was during the 18th century that the Christian missionaries set up printing presses in India and brought out vernacular editions of the Bible. Ziegenbelg, a Danish missionary, composed a Tamil grammar and published a Tamil version of the Bible. The missionaries also compiled a Tamil dictionary. The Baptist missionaries like Carey, Ward and Marshman set up a printing press at Serampur and published a Bengali version of the Bible.

Art

As there was a lack of patronage at Delhi, the artists migrated to the slate capitals like Hyderabad, Lucknow, Murshidabad, Jaipur etc. In 1784, Asaf-ud-Daula built the great Imambara. It has no pillars or supports. The view of Percy Brown is that it is a work of "outward show and tawdry pretence" whose "style has no spiritual values". The palace of Suraj Mal at Dig, the capital of Bharatpur, was planned to rival the imperial palaces at Agra. Work on its construction was started in 1725 but the construction was left unfinished.

Many painters of the Mughal school migrated to Hyderabad, Lucknow, Kashmir and Patna and flourished there. New schools of painting also achieved distinction. The paintings of Kangra and Rajput schools revealed new vitality and taste. Music continued to develop and flourish in the 18th century, particularly in the reign of Muhammad Shah.

Science

Throughout the 18th century, India remained far behind the Western countries in the spheres of science and technology. The Indian rulers of the 18th century did not show any interest in the developments in science and technology in the West except in weapons of war and techniques of military training. India had to pay very heavily for this weakness.

RELIGIOUS CONDITION

The Hindus believed in the trinity of Brahma, Vishnu and Mahesh— the three major powers of creation, sustenance and destruction. The worship of Brahma was not popular because he was alleged to have been cursed by a god on account of some sin.

Siva and Vishnu, alongwith their female counterparts—Parvati and Lakshmi—claimed the devotion of almost entire Hindu society. Their worship represented three distinct forms of belief and practice. The followers of Siva were called Shaivites. The followers of Vishnu were called Vaishnavites. The people who worshipped the female counterpart (Sakti) of Lord Siva were called Saktas. However, these divisions did not make any difference in the basic concepts of Hinduism.

The worship of Siva was generally the religion of the common people. His ritual could be performed without a priest. He appeared to be more terrible than benevolent and consequently more feared and revered than loved. His third eye could rain fire on the people who neglected him. He was the patron of craftsmen, cartwrights, smiths, potters, hunters and washermen. He was also the head of the armies, the god of the fighters in any mode of warfare. His name, Har Har Mahadev, was a war cry. Thieves and freebooters were devoted to him. The beggars and Faqirs showed their affinity with him by wearing long and matted hair or by shaving their heads clean. He was omnipotent but he was supposed to live on high mountains, dense forests and solitary places. The Rajputs were predominantly the followers of Siva. They built temples dedicated to Siva even outside Rajasthan—Gujarat and Bundelkhand. The image of Siva in the form of Lingam was carved out of stone and water was poured over it to give bath to the god.

Vishnu was the ideal god for the householder. He was the god recommended to him by the priestly class. The ascendancy of Vishnu over the other gods is shown by a painting of the Rajasthani school dated 1740 A.D. Vishnu is seated on a throne in heaven with Lakshmi on his knee. He is attended by the other gods, among whom Siva appears on the right as an ascetic alongwith Ganesh. On the left are seen Indra and Brahma with his four heads. It was both fashionable and respectable to be a devotee of Vishnu. His image was a complete image of a well-formed human being.

Both Siva and Vishnu held very prominent positions in the religious thought of the Hindus. It was not necessary to be either a follower of Siva or Vishnu. *Harihara* was the god representing both of them. Hari was the name of Vishnu and Hara of Siva. They could both be worshipped in this combined form.

The third important sect of the Hindus was the *Saktas*. They believed that the gods had relegated their more onerous and troublesome executive functions to their female counterparts. In difficult circumstances, the worshippers turned to the goddesses with greater devotion than to the gods. Mahadevi, the great goddess, was worshipped under a thousand designations and invested in an infinite variety of forms.

The religion of *Devi* and her designations were much more prevalent in the Eastern provinces of Northern India. Their worship was fairly widespread. The worship of the *Vam Marg* comprised the use of wine, meat, fish, various postures of the body and sexual intercourse. Their shrines could be the centres for bloody sacrifices and sensual obscenities.

All over Northern India, the goddesses were worshipped as the Great Mothers. These goddesses were sometimes very gracious and bounteous like Gauri whom the young girls worshipped in the hope of getting good husbands and a happy married life.

The Rajputs took their inspiration and courage from Shakti, Durga, Bhawani who had their shrines all over Rajasthan where the rulers were generally the followers of Siva. She was addressed by such names as Mahamaya, Kali Mata, Chamunda, Sakrai, Rai Mata, Naguechian, Sitala Mata, Karniji etc.

In addition to Siva, Vishnu and the female personifications of divine power, the Hindus also worshipped *Ganesa* or *Ganpati* as god of luck and good fortune and the Sun. This five-fold reverence was called *Panchayatan Puja* and was the most popular form of worship. Ganesa was believed to be the remover of all evil and was worshipped everywhere at the beginning of all auspicious ceremonies. In Rajasthan Ganesa was called *Vinayak*.

The worship of Surya or the Sun was also prevalent in the 18th century. The Sun being a very potent factor in their life, Sun worship was in the blood of the Hindu people. Every morning the Sun was saluted and offered water in the form of Arghya by the householders who prayed for his liberation in the event of an eclipse. The famous Gayatri Mantra was the invocation of the Sun god for bestowing his glorious brightness to sharpen the intellect of his worshippers.

The worship of nature had a very strong hold over the pastoral and agricultural people. They had always to go through the extremities of weather and were very susceptible to the effects of heat, cold, rain or drought.

The rivers, Ganga and Jamuna, were revered as the Great Mothers. Their entire course in the plains was dotted with holy cities. Tree worship was very common. Pipal was regarded as the Brahman among trees. Tulsi plant was held very sacred by the Hindus. Spirit worship was another major element in Hindu belief.

Sects

Separate religious communities were organised and consolidated within the pale of Saivism and Vaishnavism by particular teachers in order to restrict and ensure the entire devotion of the individual for either Siva or Vishnu. The most prominent Siva sect was that of the *Jogis*. They professed Vedantism with Jangamas. They practised severe austerities and physical mortifications like their god. The most important order of the Jogis was that of the Kanphatas or slit ears'. The Jogis were a common and prominent feature of society. They did not stick to one place but kept on roaming all over the area. They enjoyed great prestige and honour. Another class of the Jogis shaved all their hair and were called *Mundiyas*. The other sects were Gosains, Sannyasis, Dandins, with their ten branches. Some of them practised the most revolting rites. Many sold charms. Some became astrologers, jugglers or minstrels and some practised incantations and exorcisms.

Garibdas (1717-78), a Jat, was a saint-cum-householder. Keshavdas belonged to the same order. Ram Charan who was born in 1718 founded the sect of Ram Sanehis. This order consisted exclusively of Sadhus. The sect of Sivanarayanis was founded by Shiv Narayan in the year 1734.

The Muslims

The beliefs and practices of the Muslims in the 18th century were influenced by three main factors viz., the decline of the Mughal Empire the wide prevalence of the doctrine of Wahdat-ul-Wujud (Unity of Existence or Immanence) and the influence of Hinduism. The Muslim state was supposed to be Islamic state and Muslim rulers were responsible for the maintenance of the Shariat. However, his responsibility was hypothetical. The Muslims of the 18th century had neither the wish nor the power to follow the Shariat.

The doctrine of Wahdat-ul-Wujud encouraged an attitude of indifference towards moral laxity although its main aim was to establish a kind of positive tolerance of the beliefs and practices of non-Muslims, on the ground that God is immanent in His creation and Muslims and non-Muslims. Islam and other religions, are all one.

There was opposition to the doctrine of Wahdat-ul-Wujud. Shaikh Ahmed of Sirhind declared that those who believed in Wahdat-ul-Wujud were evading or undermining the Shariat, the concept of which was higher and could be realised through a spiritual awareness of the unity of phenomena. Shah Walliullah (1703-63) brought about the intellectual reconciliation of the two doctrines through his own spiritual experience. According to him, the two doctrines were the different stages on the road to spiritual knowledge. Shah Waliullah was also a religious reformer. He tried hard to bring Islam to the masses of India by translating the Quran into Persian.

The orthodox Muslims were involved in acute sectarianism. The party system at the Mughal court was strongly influenced by Shiah-Sunni differences. Mirza Mazhar Jani-Janan (1702-81), a leading religious and social personality, was murdered by the Shias as they suspected him of having made derogatory remarks about Tadhiahs.

Goga

The old make worship seems to have taken the form of veneration for Goga who was called a Chauhan by the Rajputs and a Pir by the Muslims. There was also the worship of *Khwaja Khizr*, the god of water.

There are references to certain sects in the 18th century. The *Bisnois* performed the Namaz five times a day with their faces towards the East. They repeated the names of God and all the angels and prophets Allah, Michael, Israel, Jibraeel, Muhammadaeel etc., and buried their dead. Whenever they uttered the name of Vishnu, they had to say Bismillah also. Untouchability was very common and they did not eat with one who did not belong to their fraternity.

Hussaini Brahmans claimed a mythical relationship with Imam Hussain. They accepted gifts and charity only from the Muslims and not from the Hindus. The *Shanwis* followed the religious practices of both the Hindu's and Muslims and abstained from eating beef and pork. They danced before the idol of Kalka and listened to Arti in Mathura and Brindaban. The sect of *Sivanarayanis* was popular with the Muslims. The cult of *Mian Bibi* found favour both with Hindus and Muslims equally although Mian Bibi was a deity of the female sex alone. Shah Daulah's mausoleum attracted people. The worship of Panjpir (five saints) was very common in the Punjab and adjacent areas.

The people in general believed in the power of amulets and charms for healing the sick, catching the thieves, casting out devils, establishing friendship between two persons, curing barrenness, ensuring, the birth of male children and identifying thieves etc. Charms were solicited from holy men. People's faith in astrology led to dependence on astrologers. The people consulted astrologers before undertaking a voyage, proposed purchase of a slave, the first wearing of clothes etc. There were lucky numbers and unlucky numbers. 13 was generally considered to be unlucky. The odd numbers were considered to be lucky. The number 52 was one of the Hindu favourite numbers. No. of 5 was considered sacred.

The people believed in acts of charity which carried special healing powers. It was common to release prisoners when a king ascended the throne or any member of the royal family was sick.

Fasts

The people believed in fasts of varying rigour and duration. The *Nirjala Ekadasi* was a rigorous fast as the devotee was not to take even a sip of water. The Janmashtmi fast was also popular. It was connected with the birth of Lord Krishna. *Nagapanchmi* was a day of fasting in honour of the Nagas. *Shivaratri* was observed in honour of Siva. It was a day of strict fasting and vigil. The full moon inspired the people to observe fast and worship *Sat Narayan,* that is, Vishnu. *Malpunya* was held on the full moon in September. *Kartika Purnima* fell on the full moon of Karttika (October-November). It was a fast in honour of Siva's victory over the demon called Tripurasura. Shraddhs were the days when the manes were propitiated by feeding the Brahmanas. Women fasted in the Navaratri which fell in March/April and September/October. Devi was worshipped and propitiated by sowing barley in small earthen vessels. The people also celebrated Durgashtmi and Ram Naumi. They also celebrated Makar Sankranti and Karak Sankranti.

The people also celebrated Rakshabandhan, Bhaiduj, Teej etc. Holi was a very popular festival. It was celebrated best in Mathura and Brindaban. It was celebrated both by the Hindus and the Muslims. Dussehra and Diwali were also celebrated by the Hindus.

Islam being a puritanical religion, the Muslims had very few festivals. Id-ul-Azha or Id-i-Qurban was the most important festival. Id-ul-Fiter was celebrated after the fasts of the month of Ramzan. It was celebrated for three days with great festivities, fireworks and banqueting. Nauroz was the Persian New Year day. On that date, the king received many presents from the nobles. Muharram was celebrated mainly by the Shias.

Shab-i-Barat was a Muslim festival. Houses were illuminated alongwith great display of fireworks.

ECONOMIC CONDITION

India of the 18th century was a land of contrasts. Extreme poverty existed side by side with extreme riches and luxury. While the nobles were rich and powerful and steeped in luxury and comfort, the peasants were oppressed and impoverished. The increasing revenue demands of the state, oppression of officials, greed and rapacity of the nobles, revenue farmers and Zamindars, marches and countermarches of the rival armies and the destruction brought about by foreign invaders, made the life of the people wretched. Many prosperous cities which were the centres of flourishing industry, were sacked and devastated. Delhi and Mathura were plundered by Ahmed Shah Abdali. Agra was plundered by the Jats. Surat and other cities of Gujarat and the Deccan were plundered by the Maratha chiefs. Sarhind was plundered by the Sikhs. On account of the disintegration of the Mughal Empire in the 18th century, there was practically no law and order and hence there could be no manufactures or trade. It is pointed out that by the close of the 18th century, the urban centres had become a "dead place." Nazir, a poet, gives a graphic picture of Agra of the 18th century in these words:

> Joblessness could show only one thing—poverty
> On the hovels of the poor there are no roofs
> Poverty covers the hovels
> Every one in Agra these days is ruined
> No one knows how he will live further
> Although they know thousands of arts and crafts
> Dust settles in bazar while shopkeepers sit in their empty shops
> As though thieves lined up in prison.

V.P.S. Raghuvanshi writes, "Civilised life cannot flourish amid conditions of insecurity and oppression. In the 18th century, the break-up of the Mughal monarchy released forces of political disintegration and anarchical conditions which destroyed the creative and cooperative spirit of man. They caused deterioration in every phase of national life. The regions which suffered most from the ravages of the soldiery became the scenes of uprooted humanity and epidemics. The period glorified war, bred anarchy and held civilisation in terror." (*Indian Society in the Eighteenth Century,* pp. 25-6.)

Ghulam Hussain, a historian of Bengal, calls the 18th century as "an age of senseless, slothful princes and of grandees, ignorant and meddling." He further writes, "It is in consequence of such wretched administration that every part of Hind has gone to ruin and every one of its discouraged urban inhabitants have broken their hearts. Life itself has become disgustful to most. So that, on comparing the present times with the past, one is apt to think that the world is overspread with blindness and that the earth is totally overwhelmed with an everlasting darkness."

In the 18th century, wars, invasions and other calamities wrought havoc and cities like Lahore, Delhi, Agra and Mathura in the North and large tracts of the country in the Deccan were destroyed. However, this adversity was compensated to some extent by the appearance of European merchants on the coasts of India. They purchased Indian goods in return for gold and silver and gave a stimulus to industry.

Particular group of artisans undertook distinct processes of production and the specialists worked in coordination to produce finished goods. Specialisation promote skill and Indian workmanship reached a perfection unrivalled in those times in the world. In industrial organisation and techniques, India was more advanced than the Western countries. The products of Indian industry fulfilled not only the needs of Asian and African countries but there was also a great demand in the markets of Europe. They readied the Western countries by sea and land routes.

The Indian merchants were well established all along the ports of the Persian Gulf and the Red Sea. They were also met in considerable numbers in Qandhar, Kabul, Balkh, Bukhara, Kashghar etc, in Afghanistan and Central-Asia. Peter, the Great wrote, "The commerce of India is the commerce of the world and he who can exclusively control it is the dictator of Europe," Indian goods found their way into the East-Asian countries, viz., Burma, Malaya, Indonesia, China and Japan.

The upper classes in India demanded luxury articles. Its volume was considerable. The rich created a great volume of demand for luxury goods as they loved good things of life and desired expensive articles of fine make. The producers of high quality luxury goods worked in their homes or in the state Karkhanas (workshops) in the towns. Some village artisans who had acquired special skill in their respective crafts also contributed to the supply of these articles.

As most of the craftsmen were poor, they had to work for merchants who advanced them money through brokers or dealt with them through agents. Money was paid to craftsmen for implements and raw materials and advance wages were given in return for finished goods. The finished articles were usually collected and placed in the market by middleman. Sometimes the nobles held direct dealings with the artisans.

The Indian village was a self-sufficient economic unit. The agricultural surplus went to the king in the form of land revenue and the peasant after meeting the Government demand, had little surplus left with him for purchasing the goods of the urban industry. The stream of exchange of goods between the village and the town was thin. Lack of capital, rigidity of caste restrictions and the meagerness of trade between the village and the town, were the factors which prevented the development of the traditional business classes engaged in trade and banking into a strong and well-knit middle class of the European type.

The tradesmen, bankers and moneylenders constituted the Indian mercantile community. They utilised their income in giving loans to the members of the ruling class. However, they lacked the spirit of enterprise.

Pyrard has written about the greatness and originality of Indian industry and culture. To quote him, "I have never seen men of wit so fine and polished as are these Indians; they have nothing barbarous and savage about them, as we are apt to suppose." Again, "No people in the world know so much about pearls and precious stones; and even at Goa, the goldsmiths, lapidaries and other workmen occupied with the finer crafts, are all banias and Bramenis (Brahmans) of Cambay and have their own streets and shops."

Merchant ships in the port towns and boats playing on the country's rivers were all manufactured in the country. There was a flourishing boatbuilding -industry at Dacca, Allahabad, Lahore, Thatta, Masulipatam. Pulicat, Calicut, Surat, Bassein and Goa. In the art of ship-building, India was ahead of European nations. Parkinson writes, "In shipbuilding, they probably taught the English far more than they learnt from them." The important shipbuilding centres were Goa, Bassein, Surat, Masulipatam, Satgaon, Dacca and Chittagong.

The important centres of textile industry were Dacca and Murshidabad in Bengal, Patna in Bihar, Surat, Ahmedabad and Broach in Gujarat, Chanderi in Madhya Pradesh, Burhanpur in Maharashtra, Jaunpur, Varanasi, Lucknow and Agra in Uttar Pradesh, Multan and Lahore in the Punjab, Masulipatam, Aurangabad, Chicacole and Vishakhapatnam in Andhra Pradesh, Bangalore (now Bengaluru) in Mysore (Karnataka) and Coimbatore and Madurai in Madras. Kashmir was a centre of woollen manufactures.

Indian was self-contained and generally self-sufficient in agricultural and industrial goods required for the consumption of her population. The imported materials included raw silk, ivory, coral, tortoiseshell and amber in addition to metals.

Indian industries not only met the home demand but also exported their goods. Indian industries catered for foreign markets also. India continued to be a sink of precious metals. Van Twist writes, "Although there were no gold or silver mines in India, large quantities of both were imported from foreign countries, and it was forbidden to export them." Similar views are expressed by Hawkins and Terry.

For centuries, India was known for the excellence of her cotton products. There was a large consumption of Indian manufactures in Rome in ancient times. The principal riches of India consisted chiefly of silk and cotton stuffs. Their great popularity was based upon the excellence of craftsmanship.

Among other articles of export, indigo was of importance. Limited quantities of iron and steel were exported from Masulipatam. Cotton yarn was exported from the Coromandel coast. Gujarat exported precious stones, marble, drugs, opium, *Hing* etc.

The trade and industry of India was organised and financed by Indian merchants. They were not confined to port towns but were spread in all cities and towns all along the trade routes of the country. Multan in the Punjab and the three Sing towns of Bukkur, Sukkur and Rohri were important centres of inland trade in the North-West. They had a flourishing community of merchants comprising mostly of Khattris, Lohanas and Bhatias. Lahore, Delhi and Agra were also great centres of commercial activity in Northern India. Malda, Rangpur and Kasimbazar were important trade centres in Bengal. In Rajasthan, Ajmer, Jodhpur, Pali and Jaisalmer were old centres. Ahmedabad in Gujarat and Poona and Nagpur in the Maratha country rose in importance after 1750. Hyderabad, Bangalore and Tanjore were flourishing centres of trade and commerce.

In addition to the merchants, there was a class of financiers, both big and small. The Jagat Seths of Bengal, the Nathjis of Gujarat and the Chettis of the South were famous financiers. The Jagat Seths possessed a capital of 10 crores of rupees in the first half of the 18th century. During their first invasion of Bengal, the Marathas carried away from their Kothi two crores of Arcot rupees but even that loss did not affect their resources appreciably. The Nathjis in Surat had similarly vast resources. The single family of Nathu Kothari Chettis monopolised business and was regarded the richest. Their business extended to Burma, Malaya and the Eastern Islands. The Chettis acted as bankers and supplied the British merchants with cash for their bills of exchange on Madras, Bombay and Calcutta. They had regular agencies in the Presidencies. The big bankers performed all the functions of a modern bank, viz., receiving deposits, giving loans and issuing Hundis. There were small bankers who gave loans to artisans and other producers. Every village had its own moneylender who advanced loans for agricultural operations and also to meet their other requirements. If the resources of all the bankers, financiers and moneylenders in India in the 18th century are taken into account, the aggregate capital resources of the country were substantial, though they were scattered.

The view of Dr. Tara Chand is that the peasant in the 18th century was better off than his successor in the 19th century. This was so not only in respect of the larger size of his holding, but also because the average productivity of land was higher at that time.

The most important item of agricultural produce was foodgrains. In the Deccan, wheat and gram, rice and millet were the crops grown. Khafi Khan states that Jowar and Bajra were the main support of the people of the Deccan and were extensively grown. In the North also, millets supplied the maJOR part of the articles of food of people and formed the principal crop. Wheat was not an important crop in Uttar Pradesh at that time. Next to foodgrains, cotton and sugar were the most widely grown crops. Tobacco, opium and indigo were the other commercial crops.

The country was not free from the danger of famines. Not less than 24 famines and deaths occurred over a period of 200 years from 1595 to 1792. Famines in those days were caused by the non-availability of food in the affected area although there may be surplus in some other parts of the country. This was partly due to the lack of efficient means of transport at that time.

There were wide variations of prices of foodgrains. Generally, foodgrains were cheaper in Bengal than in Northern India. Those were cheaper in Northern India than in Gujarat. The prices of commodities of daily consumption were very low.

The prices in India showed two types of fluctuations, viz., regional and periodical. The former was the result of the difficulties and heavy cost of transport of bulky agricultural produce from one place to another.

Every region and even every village tried to be self-sufficient in food supply. If the rains were deficient and crops failed, he could not supplement his stock from outside except at ruinous prices. The margin of fluctuations in prices in the same locality from year to year was very wide.

The price level was a matter of great importance to the wage earners. In the 18th century India, wage labour was exclusively an urban phenomenon. In the villages, the menials, and the agricultural labourers and artisans were remunerated for their work by giving them a share in the produce of the farm on which they worked. Money wages were paid to ordinary and skilled labourers employed in the town. By the middle of the 18th century, the prevailing rate of daily wages in Calcutta was five pice for ordinary labourers and ten pice for skilled workers.

European travellers and other contemporary writers have mentioned the poverty of the Indian masses. Their view was based on the scantiness of clothing, miserable dwellings, poor utensils and lack of furniture and not the lack of adequate quantities of nourishing diet. Fitch writes that in Northern India, the people go all naked save a little cloth bound about their middle. In the winter, the men wear quilted gowns of cotton and quilted caps with a slit to look out at and so tied down beneath their ears. The view of Dr. Tara Chand is that as far as the poor classes of the people were concerned, they had few wants and those were met adequately from what the country produced. There was no general starvation or inadequate nourishment except in periods of famine. They did not have any surplus even in normal years to accumulate and build up economic reserves for meeting calamities like famines. Their clothing was scanty and their dwellings poor, but in respect of those necessaries they probably did not feel the want of more than they had and they hardly ever made an effort to improve their lot. Life was simple and contented and the simple and few wants were easily met so that the struggle for existence was not hard. Their simplicity and contentment had its own advantages, but it had one great drawback also. The common people did not feel the urge for improvement and hence did not struggle for economic progress. (*History of the Freedom Movement in India,* Vol. I, pp. 194-95.)

Dr. Tara Chand also refers to the pattern of consumption of the upper classes which retarded the progress of the country in the economic field. The princes, nobles and the provincial chiefs lived in grand style and in great luxury. Mughal nobility has been described as "nothing but voluptuousness and wealth confusedly intermingled." A lot of money was spent on delicacies like costly imported fruit, on servants and retainers, on houses and elephants, on marriages and dowries and on building fort-like houses. A large part of the income was spent on jewellery, costly dresses and horses and elephants. Each noble kept hundreds of servants for his stables and his household. A large sum of money was spent on making presents to the king. The law of escheat required that all the accumulated wealth of a noble after his death would go to the royal treasury. The result was that there was no incentive to save and hence the nobles spent all that they had and something more. They were mostly under debt. Under the circumstances, there was no accumulation of capital. There was no opportunity for profitable investment of savings. The result was that even if some nobles accumulated large fortunes, they spent them in marriages, dowries and buildings rather than in investment in business or industry. (*Ibid,* pp. 195-96.)

While discussing the economic condition of the people in the 18th century, a reference may be made to what was done by the English East India Company in India in the second half of the 18th century. The servants of the English Company penetrated into all parts of the country and compelled the handicraftsmen to deal exclusively with them. The prices of the monopolised goods were arbitrarily fixed by the officials and the producers were fleeced mercilessly. The weavers were compelled to enter into engagements to work for the English Company and for a breach of the contract, they were punished with fine, imprisonment, flogging etc. Even the highest officials of the Company were engaged in private trade which brought them huge sums of money. Even the Directors of the English Company admitted that "the vast fortunes acquired in the inland trade have been obtained by a scene of the most tyrannical and oppressive conduct that was ever known in any age or country. Vansittart tells us that the English compelled the natives to buy or sell at just what rates they pleased on pain of flogging or confinement. It was estimated that between 1757 and 1766, the English East India Company and its employees received £ 6 millions from Indians as gifts. Clive himself was guilty of this offence. Trade monopolies, political corruption and exorbitant land taxes enabled the English Company to transfer large sums of money annually to Great Britain. There was a regular drain of wealth from India to Great Britain. Sir John Shore wrote in 1797. "The Company are merchants as well as sovereigns of the county. In the former capacity, they engross its trade, whilst in the latter they appropriate the revenues. The remittances to Europe of revenues are made in the commodities of the country which are purchased by them. Whatever allowance we may make for the increased industry of the subjects of the state, owing to the enhanced demand for the produce of it, there is reason to conclude that the benefits are more than counter-balanced by evils inseparable from the system of a remote foreign dominion." Lord Cornwallis wrote in 1790,

"The consequences of the heavy drain of wealth from the above causes, with the addition of that which has been occasioned by the remittances of private fortunes, having been for many years past and are now severely felt, by the great diminution of the current specie and by the langour which has thereby been thrown upon the cultivation and the general commerce of the country."

REVIEW QUESTIONS

1. Elaborate on the social condition of the people in the eighteenth century.
2. Write a detailed note on the education system of the eighteenth century.
3. Write an essay on the society and culture in the eighteenth century.
4. Discuss the development of art and literature in the eighteenth century.
5. Give an account of the religious and economic conditions of India during the eighteenth century.
6. Social life in the eighteenth century was marked by stagnation and dependence of the past. Comment.
7. Write short notes on the following:
    (a) Patriarchal family
    (b) Slavery
    (c) Sects

SUGGESTED READINGS

Craufurd, Q.: *Sketches Chiefly related to the History, Religion, Learning and Manner of Hindus*, London, 1790.
Grose, F. S.: *A Voyage to East Indies*, 2 Vols., London, 1772.
Hodges, William: *Travels in India*, London, 1793.
Irvine, William: *The Army of the Indian Mughals*, London, 1903.
Irvine, William: *Later Mughals*, 2 Vols., Calcutta, 1922.
Ives, Edward: *Voyage from England to India*, London, 1773,
Keene, H.G.: *The Great Anarchy or Darkness before Dawn*, London, 1901.
Keene, H.G.: *The Mughal Empire from the Death of Aurangzeb to Over-throw of the Mahnutta Power*, London, 1866.
Manucci, Niccolao: *Storia Do Mogor*, 4 Vols., London, 1907
Ojha, P.N.: *Some Aspects of North Indian Social Life*, Patna, 1961.
Orme, R.: *Historical Fragments of the Mughal Empire*, London, 1805.
Owen, S.J.: *India on the Eve of the British Conquest*, London, 1876.
Raghuvanshi, V.P.S.: *Indian Society in the Eighteenth Century.*
Sarkar, J.N.: *Fall of the Mughal Empire.*
Shukla, Ram Chandra: *Hindi Sahitya Ka Itihas* (in Hindi).
Sitat, Jit Singh (Ed.): *Heer Warris*, Delhi, 1963.
Stavorinus, John Splinter: *Voyage to the East Indies (1668-71)*, London, 1798.
Suri, Pushpa: *Social Conditions in Eighteenth Century Northern India*, University of Delhi, 1977.
Tara Chand: *History of the Freedom Movement in India*, Vol. I, Government of India, New Delhi, 1961.
Williams, Monier: *Religious Thought and Life in India*, London, 1883.
Wilson, H.H.: *Religious Sects of the Hindus*, London, 1861-62.
Wilson, John: *History of the Suppression of Infanticide in Western India*, Bombay, 1899.

PART B

1. The Advent of Europeans in India
2. Rise and Growth of the English and French East India Companies
3. Anglo-French Struggle for Supremacy in the Deccan
4. The English in Bengal from 1757 to 1772
5. Warren Hastings (1772-85)
6. Lord Cornwallis and Sir John Shore
7. Lord Wellesley (1798-1805)
8. Lord Hastings and Amherst
9. Rise and Fall of the Peshwas
10. William Bentinck to Auckland
11. Ellenborough and Hardinge
12. Maharaja Ranjit Singh and His Successors
13. Lord Dalhousie (1848-56)
14. The Revolt of 1857
15. Canning to Lytton
16. Ripon to Elgin (1880-98)
17. Lord Curzon (1899-1905)
18. India Since Lord Minto
19. Constitutional Development (1773-1950)
20. Growth of Central and Provincial Legislatures
21. The Nationalist Movement in India
22. Establishment of Pakistan
23. Leaders of Modern India
24. Decentralisation of Finance
25. Public Services in India
26. Growth of Local Self-Government in India
27. History of the Press in India
28. History of Education
29. Religious and Social Development
30. Anglo-Afghan Relations
31. The North-Western Frontier Policy
32. The Indian States
33. Legacy of British Rule in India
34. Economic Impact of British Rule in India
35. Famines in India and Development of Famine Policy
36. Peasants' Movement and Uprisings
37. The Left Movements in India
38. Role of Mahatma Gandhi in the Nationalist Movement
39. The Renaissance in India
40. Political, Cultural and Social Impact of British Rule
41. Changes in Land Revenue Settlement

1 The Advent of Europeans in India

LEARNING OBJECTIVES

- Throw light on the advent of Europeans in India, the Portuguese, the Dutch and the Danes, and discuss their activities here
- Examine the causes of the rise and fall of the Portuguese empire in India

THE PORTUGUESE IN INDIA

The coming of the Europeans to India was an event of very great importance in the history of our country as it ultimately led to revolutionary changes in her destiny in the future and the Portuguese were the first in this field.

It is a matter of common knowledge that Indian commodities were in great demand in European markets throughout the Middle Ages. These things used to reach Europe either completely by land or partly by land and partly by sea. However, difficulties began to arise on account of the rise to power of the Turks. As the land route was practically closed, there arose the necessity of finding a new route to India.

The Portuguese led the way in this matter. Prince Henry of Portugal (1393-1460), who is commonly known as the "Navigator", did a lot in this field. He set up a regular school for the training of seamen on scientific lines. He patronized all those who took up work of navigation. The result of the efforts of the Portuguese was that practically the whole of the coastline of Africa, came to be known to the Portuguese. They crossed the Equator in 1471 and reached the Congo river in 1481.

In 1487, Bartholomew Diaz was carried by storms past the Cape of Good Hope. He was patronized by King John II.

In 1497, Vasco da Gama started on his expedition under the patronage of King Emmanuel. To begin with, he covered the whole of the route which had been followed by Diaz and crossed the Cape of Good Hope. He reached Mozambique. He got help of an Indian pilot and set sail for India in April 1498. After a voyage of a month, he reached Calicut. He was cordially received by King Zamorin who gave him certain privileges also.

The arrival of Vasco da Gama on the Indian scene was not liked at all by the Arabs. They started rumours of many kinds against the Portuguese. Finding the situation hard, Vasco da Gama left India after a stay of about three months.

According to Dodwell, "In four respects the Portuguese were singularly fortunate. Arriving on the Malabar Coast, they found themselves in touch with a multitude of small princes divided by mutual jealousy, so that hostility in one was certain to be accompanied by friendship in another. Furthermore, the country round Cochin and Calicut did not at that time produce enough rice for the needs of the inhabitants, who were supplied by Muslim vessels with grain from the Coromandel Coast; the region was, therefore, peculiarly sensitive to a blockade by sea. Again, reaching India at the close of the fifteenth century, the Portuguese found no State which could make either great or sustained efforts to prevent their establishment. And lastly the difficulties which they had to meet and overcome implied that for purposes of war their vessels would be stouter and more formidable than any ships they would meet in Indian waters. This last was of all the most important, for the position which the Portuguese would occupy in the East certainly depended upon naval power. Their nation was too small, in view of the conditions of land warfare, for them to dream of establishing a military empire. They were vowed to the destruction (if they could possibly contrive it) of Muslim States, and therefore could not contemplate taking up the position of unarmed and helpless traders. Supremacy at sea was the essential condition of success. And the physical circumstances which had fostered the early development of eastern seafaring had not promoted sustained progress. The regular and periodic winds which blow in the Indian seas had permitted men to sail easily and regularly at certain seasons of the year from Aden and Basra to Gujarat, from Bengal to Malacca, from Malacca to Malabar; but their very strength and regularity had forbidden all attempts to sail against them, while cyclone and typhoon were too awful in their might for primitive sailors to dream of meeting and outliving them. Eastern mariners and vessels were, therefore, trained and built for voyaging with reliable and favourable winds. Their vessels were frail compared with the ships built to resist Atlantic storms. The consequence was firstly that Portuguese shipping could hold the seas in weather which would send all possible enemies fleeing for the first windward port and secondly that the Portuguese could mount cannon, the recoil of which would have shaken Indian vessels to pieces at the first discharge". (*The Cambridge Shorter History of India*, pp. 379-80.)

In 1501, Vasco da Gama came to India for the second time and founded a factory at Cannanore and returned to Portugal in 1503. In spite of the opposition from the Arabs, the Portuguese were able to establish their trading centres at Calicut, Cochin and Cannanore and they treated the Arabs with cruelty and oppression. After Vasco da Gama left India, the Portuguese, suffered. King Zamorin attacked the Portuguese in Cochin, but was defeated. This established the supremacy of the Portuguese.

De Almeida (1505-09)

De Almeida was the first Viceroy of the Portuguese possessions in India. He was not in favour of multiplying settlements on land. He wanted his countrymen to concentrate on the development of their naval power. According to him, "should it be known for certain that as long as you may be powerful at sea, you will hold India as yours; and if you did not possess this power, little will avail you a fortress on shore". This policy has rightly been called the "Blue water" policy. Both Almeida and his son were defeated and killed in 1509 by the Egyptians.

Albuquerque (1509-15)

He was the second Viceroy of the Portuguese in India. Mr. Stephens refers to four points on which his policy was based. In the first place, he desired to occupy certain important places for trading purposes, and to rule them directly. Secondly, he desired to colonize the selected districts by encouraging mixed marriages with the native inhabitants. In the third place, when Albuquerque could not conquer or colonise, he desired to build fortresses. Fourthly, when this was impracticable, he desired to induce the native merchants to recognize the supremacy of the King of Portugal and to pay him tribute.

Albuquerque was a great conqueror. He conquered and annexed Goa in 1510. This place became the headquarters of the Portuguese Empire. He conquered Malacca in the Far East and fitted out an expedition for the Spice Islands. In 1515, he conquered Ormuz, an Island in the Persian Gulf. He built a fort at Cochin with the permission of the Rajah.

He appointed a large number of Portuguese officers for the work of administration. While the Muslims were persecuted, the Hindus were welcomed in the various branches of administration. Schools were established for them. The Panchayats of the Hindus were not discarded. Indian soldiers commanded by Hindu officers were welcomed. He also encouraged the marriages of the Portuguese with Indian women.

Albuquerque was a great man. He can really be called the founder of the Portuguese Empire in India. "He had traits in his character that appeal peculiarly to orientals: his valour, his strict veracity, his integrity and charitableness. He was feared and at the same time loved. He was not a man to be daunted by one failure and never rested till he had achieved his resolve. A patriot every inch, his reputation for disinterestedness was very high". Again, "His lofty vision was accompanied by a commanding character and by a tenacity of purpose which few leaders have possessed; he had a genius for civil administration as well as for war, while in diplomacy he could meet orientals with their own weapon". No wonder, he was called by his countrymen Albuquerque, the Great. It is said that when he died in 1515, he was buried at Goa "amidst the regrets of Europeans and natives, by whom he was equally loved".

According to Dodwell, "In many ways he anticipated the qualities which were to mark out the great Englishman, Clive. Both were great military leaders, whose courage and insight rose with danger. Both were men of unshakable constancy, ready to meet any foe however numerous; of a high spirit, which imposed itself on their followers; of a good fortune, which daunted their enemies. Both were capable of acts of treachery; but both resorted to treachery so rarely that they never lost the confidence of other men. Both had the skill to discern essential conditions of success and to ignore all else. Albuquerque seems to have stood alone in his generation in perceiving that 'a dominion founded on a navy alone cannot last. He insisted against all opposition from Portugal on the importance of maintaining Goa as the centre of Portuguese power in the east, as a great dockyard in which vessels could always be refitted, remanned and revictualled, and as a great city whence reserves of troops could always be drawn. In this he was certainly justified. When a century afterwards the Portuguese found themselves involved in a war of life and death, they could not possibly have maintained the struggle for over fifty years but for the resources which had been accumulated at Goa". (*The Cambridge Shorter History of India*, p. 384.)

The power of the Portuguese kept on growing even after the death of Albuquerque. They got Diu and Bassein in 1534. Four years after, they conquered Daman. In the same year they got permission to establish a factory at Goa. In 1545, the fort of Diu was attacked by the King of Gujarat but was successfully defended. In 1571, the rulers of Bijapur, Ahmednagar and Calicut combined together against the Portuguese. However, they failed to take possession of Goa.

It is to be observed that the appearance of the Portuguese in India led necessarily to a conflict of interests. It was not, as it has occasionally been represented, a struggle between the Christians and Muslims, but one between importers and exporters. The Indian importers, many of whom were

Muslims, welcomed the Portuguese as new customers. The Arab and Egyptian customers objected to them as new competitors who might break existing monopoly. The result was that the Portuguese acquired from the ruler of Calicut the principal seaport on the Malabar Coast and established friendly relations at those centres which offered the largest supply of pepper.

The Portuguese were not satisfied with merely a share in the trade. They were determined to control the same. This they were able to accomplish by setting up a strong navy which helped them to command the seas. They also built fortresses to guard the narrow waters. They set up a central establishment from which operations could be directed on which the navy could be based.

As regards the methods adopted by the Portuguese to control the trade, some routes, and some commodities on all routes, were monopolised for the benefit of the Kingdom of Portugal. Subject to these restrictions, Indian or other ships could obtain licenses to ply between specified ports on payment of substantial fees... . An unlicensed vessel was liable to be captured and confiscated. The gun boats employed by the Portuguese to patrol the routes were more than a match for the cumbrous ships of their rivals. By these methods, the Portuguese controlled the main trade routes throughout the sixteenth century. It is true that some goods continued to reach Europe over land, but that was due mainly to the increasing corruption of the Portuguese officials who looked upon their posts as a source of private gain and could be bribed to allow the contraband goods to pass.

The possessions of the Portuguese on the west coast of India were an integral part of the kingdom of Portugal. However, settlements of less regular type cropped up on the east coast of India. At various places in Bengal and on the Coromandel Coast, Portuguese merchants settled with the consent of the local rulers. However, relying on the prestige of their nation, they fortified their settlements, assumed right of self-government and eventually in some cases repudiated the authority of the Portuguese Viceroy at Goa.[1] Thus Portuguese settlements became centres of lawlessness and in some cases nests of pirates.

The immediate effects produced by the Portuguese in India were not great. In the field of politics, their capture of Goa involved them in enmity with Bijapur. On the whole, they maintained friendly relations with Vijayanagar, but they did not render any material help to her in her struggle against the Muslims. From the point of view of the Indians, the appearance of the Portuguese merely added one more element in the confused politics of the time. In war, they introduced higher standards of efficiency in artillery and musketry. They created a legend of invincibility which immensely helped them in their work.

So far as commerce was concerned, it cannot be said that the diversion of trade was accompanied by any great expansion in the exports of Indian goods. It is probable that more pepper reached Western Europe than before. However, the only new development was the opening of new markets for Indian cotton goods in Western Africa and Brazil. The Portuguese were not successful in developing the import trade. The great bulk of their purchases were paid for in silver. They could sell little except luxuries and curiosities from Europe. The important service which they rendered to India was the effective policing of the coastal trade. There were nests of pirates along the Malabar Coast who lived mainly by attacks on the small vessels which plied in great numbers between Gujarat on the one side and Ceylon, Madras and Bengal on the other. The Portuguese provided gunboats to convoy the fleets of these vessels and thereby established a reasonable degree of security on the main line of Indian trade. However, we must not forget the toll, whether in licence fees or in bribes, which they levied on Indian commerce, both coastal and foreign.

---

[1] Cf. "Though the earliest in the East, Portugal could not establish any permanent dominion in India".

From the beginning of the 17th century, the power of the Portuguese began to decline. This was particularly due to the fact that in 1580 Portugal was made a part and parcel of Spain in the time of Philip II of Spain. Spain herself was not doing well at that time. She could hardly be expected to defend the interests of the Portuguese. The result was that one by one the Portuguese lost many of their possessions. They were turned out from Amboyna by the Dutch. In 1662, Ormuz was matched away by the Government of Iran. The Dutch got Malacca in 1640. They were also turned out from Ceylon in 1656. In 1739, the Marathas got Bassein.

Causes of Failure of Portuguese Empire in India.[2]

Many causes were responsible for the failure of the Portuguese empire in India.

1. After the death of Albuquerque, no strong person was sent by the Portuguese Government to India. The result was that the Portuguese empire began to disintegrate.

2. The Portuguese administration in India was corrupt. The salaries of the official were low and consequently they felt no hesitation in accepting bribes from any quarter. The bulk of the Portuguese officials were selfish. Unmindful of the sufferings of the people, they were bent upon making fortunes for themselves. The means did not matter to them.

3. The religious policy of the Portuguese was also responsible for their ruin[3]. The Portuguese introduced the Inquisition into India and they committed atrocities on those who were not Christians. They used all kinds of methods for the conversion of the people of India to Christianity. Their coercive methods created bitterness in the minds of the people. In 1540, all the Hindu temples in the Island of Goa were destroyed under the orders of their king. The Franciscan missionaries arrived in 1517 and Goa became the centre of an immense propaganda. The Portuguese authorities in India did not care for the people. The civil authorities at Goa wrote to their king in 1552 thus: "In India, there is no justice either in your Viceroy or in those who are to meet it out. The one object is gathering together of money by every means".

4. The establishment of the Mughal empire was also partly responsible for Portuguese failure. At the beginning of the 16th century, the Portuguese did not meet any great opposition. However,

---

[2] Cf. "Though the earliest in the East, Portugal could not establish any permanent dominion in India".

[3] Before the capture of Malacca, Albuquerque is said to have observed thus: "The first is the great service which we shall perform to our Lord in casting the Moors out of this country, and quenching the fire of this sect of Muhammad so that it may never burst out again hereafter; and I am so sanguine as to hope for this from our undertaking, that if we can only achieve the task before us, it will result in the Moors resigning India altogether to our rule, for the greater part of them increase its size or perhaps all of them-live upon the trade of this country, and are become great and rich, and lords of extensive treasures... .And the other reason is the additional service which we shall render to the King Dom Manoel in taking this city, because it is the headquarters of all the spices and drugs which the Moors carry every year hence to the Straits, without our being able to prevent them from so doing; but if we deprive them of this, their ancient market, there does not remain for them a single port nor a single situation as commodious in the whole of these parts, where they can on their trade in these things. For after we were in possession, the pepper of Malabar, never more did any reach Cairo, except that which the Moors carried thither from these parts, and the forty or fifty ships, which sail hence every year laden with all sorts of spices bound to Mecca, cannot be stopped without great expense and large fleets, which must necessarily cruise about continually in the offing of Cape Comorin; and the pepper of Malabar, of which they may hope to get some portion, because they have the King of Calicut on their side, is in our hands, under the eyes of the Governor of India, from whom the Moors cannot carry of so much with impunity as they hope to do; and I hold it as very certain that, if we take this trade of Malacca away out of their hands, Cairo and Mecca will be entirely ruined, and to Venice will no spices be conveyed, except what her merchants go and buy in Portugal".

after the accession of Akbar in 1556, the Mughal power began to grow. The Mughals were able to bring practically the whole of India under their control. Under these circumstances there was no scope for the growth of the Portuguese power on the mainland of India.

5. Portugal is a small country. Its resources were not sufficient for the conquest of a country like India. Moreover, the resources were divided between the Portuguese possessions in India and Brazil. After some time, Portuguese started caring more for Brazil than for India.

6. In 1580, Portugal came under the control of Spain. The result was that the Spanish interests predominated and that Portuguese interests were subordinated. Various restrictions were put on Portuguese enterprise in the interests of Spain. Lisbon, which was once the depot of Europe, lost all its importance. Worthless Spanish officers were sent to the Portuguese possessions in India and these persons tried to make as much money as possible unmindful of its effect on the people of the country. These Spanish favourites ruined the Portuguese cause in the country.

7. The rise of Dutch and the English power in India created strong rivals in the country. They were more than a match for the Portuguese. The result was that by slow degrees the Portuguese empire in India failed.

8. The Portuguese who came to India were characterised by great individual courage, enthusiasm for conquest, personal and national pride but many of them were cruel, factious and domineering. Their early success encouraged their inborn arrogance. No wonder, they came to regard the Asiatics in general as their natural subjects. As very few Portuguese women came from Europe, they were encouraged to marry Indian women. It was hoped that in this way the Portuguese settlements in India would become self-supporting in soldiers and sailors. Unfortunately, the mixed race which came into existence was inferior to the original stock, less brave, but not less arrogant, increasingly avaricious and corrupt. Records of gallant exploits became fewer, and instances of treachery and rapacity increased. The Portuguese came to be detested by the people of India and no wonder that in course of time their empire in India became an insignificant one.

Regarding the causes of Portuguese failure, Dodwell observes thus: "But by the close of the sixteenth century the Portuguese dominion was fast falling into decay. The officials were corrupt; the fortresses unrepaired and unarmed; trade was declining. Even more significant was the dissolution of Portuguese union and solidarity. When the Raja of Cochin had resolved to accept the Portuguese alliance, he had been moved by admiration for their discipline, which was such that, had a cabin-boy arrived with the king's orders to command them, he would have been obeyed. But when Francisco da Gama was Viceroy at Goa from 1597 to 1600, he was subjected to the grossest insults. The statue of his great ancestor Vasco was thrown down and broken; and on the day when he embarked for his homeward voyage, forty men went abroad and hung him in effigy from his own yardarm. Some of the causes of this decline are evident. Portugal was but a small country; she had undertaken two great enterprises —the occupation of Brazil and the conquest of Indian waters. Both took a heavy toll of her manhood. The mortality on board the ship and in tropical climates was extraordinary. Few of the gallant adventurous men who built up the Portuguese position in the east ever returned to their native country. The breed, robbed of its finest elements, decayed; and their successors were not the equals of the early adventurers. Even by 1538 difficulties were found in securing the necessary number of men. Outlaws were tempted by a general pardon to all, heretics and traitors excepted who would volunteer for Indian service. Criminals sentenced to death were respited and sent out into perpetual banishment; and lesser criminals were offered pardon in return for three or more years, service. The Portuguese settlements were being reinforced by men bringing little of civic virtue, who would probably mate, and breed with the lowest classes of the Indian population.

"At the same time the Portuguese were falling into a condition of mental stagnancy. The astonishing progress which they had made in the allied arts of shipbuilding and navigation ceased. They remained supreme in Indian waters but were doomed to succumb should they be called on to meet men who should have learnt to build or sail or fight their ships better than the Portuguese had learnt to do by the time of Vasco da Gama and the great Albuquerque. Goa was, in fact, destined to become the burial-place of reputations". (*The Cambridge Shorter History of India*, p. 391.)

THE DUTCH IN INDIA

The students of history are familiar with the revolt of the Netherlands against Philip II. It is also well known that in spite of all the efforts of Philip II, they were able to win their freedom. It was in the hour of their victory that the Dutch Company was started in 1592 by a group of Amsterdam merchants. Three years after, Cornelius Houtman set out for India and returned with large cargo in 1597. The Indian Archipelago was opened to the Dutch. The Dutch success was so great that many other companies were started. In 1602, all the Dutch companies were amalgamated into the Dutch East India Company. A Charter was also given. It gave a monopoly of eastern trade to the Company which was also empowered to wage war, make treaties, occupy territories and build fortresses.

The main object of the Dutch Company was trade. The Dutch concentrated their attention on the Spice Islands in the Far East. They tried to establish their exclusive monopoly. They made the chiefs of the islands accept the sovereignty of Holland. All other European nations were forbidden to trade with those islands. Every effort was made to maintain the monopoly of trade.

It is true that the Dutch and the English entered the East as friends. Both of them were the champions of Protestants against Catholic Spain and Portugal. However, differences arose between the two powers. The Dutch were determined to maintain their monopoly at all costs. The rivalry between the two countries increased to such an extent that in 1623 the Dutch perpetrated the massacre of Amboyna. After this tragedy, the English were forced to leave the Spice Islands and retire to the mainland of India.[4] The Dutch had to pay an indemnity of £85,000 in the time of Cromwell.

The Dutch conquered Malacca from the Portuguese in 1641. In 1658, they acquired Ceylon. In India, they had Negapatnam on the Madras Coast and Chinsurah in Bengal. From the beginning to the end, the Dutch position in India was insignificant.

THE DANES IN INDIA

Encouraged by the other European merchants the people of Denmark also thought of having a share in the Indian trade. For that purpose, they founded a settlement in 1620 at Tranquebar in the Tanjore District. In 1676, they occupied Serampore. However, the Danes did not find a foothold in India and consequently they sold their settlements in India to the British Government in 1845.

REVIEW QUESTIONS

1. Which European came to India first? What was his role in the history of India?
2. Write a detailed note on the expansion of the Portuguese empire in India. Discuss its impact on the trade of India.
3. Analyse the causes of the failure of the Portuguese empire in India.

---

[4] "The high-handed policy of the Dutch in the Malaya Archipelago was a blessing in disguise for the English".

4. Describe the establishment of the Portuguese empire in India and the causes for its decline.
5. Discuss the achievements of the Dutch and the Danes in India.
6. Write short notes on the following:
   (a) Vasco da Gama
   (b) Albuquerque
   (c) East India Company
7. Who was the founder of the Portuguese empire in India? Discuss his activities.
8. Describe the rise and fall of the Portuguese in India.

SUGGESTED READINGS

Danvers, F.C.: *History of the Portuguese in India* (1894).
Dodwell, H.H. (Ed.): *The Cambridge History of India,* Vol. V.
Jayne, K.G.: *Vasco da Gama and His Successors* (1910).
Ross, E.D.: *The Portuguese in India and Arabia between 1507 and 1517.*
Whiteway: *The Rise of the Portuguese Power in India (1497-1550).*

Rise and Growth of the English and French East India Companies

2

LEARNING OBJECTIVES

- Discuss the rise and growth of the English and French East India Companies
- Narrate the trade policies of the English and French East India Companies

THE ENGLISH EAST INDIA COMPANY

Like other Europeans, Englishmen also were desirous of getting the things produced in India and the Far East. After their victory over the Spanish Armada in 1588, their desire to trade directly began to increase. In September 1599, a resolution was passed under the chairmanship of Lord Mayor to form an association to trade directly with India. On 31st December 1600, Queen Elizabeth granted a Charter to the Governor and Company of Merchants of London trading into the East Indies. The Charter authorised the London Company to traffic and trade freely "into and from the East Indies, in the countries and parts of Asia and Africa, and into and from all islands, ports, havens, cities, creeks, towns and places of Asia and Africa and America, or any of them beyond the Cape of Bona Esperanza to the Straits of Migellan". The Charter was given for 15 years and the same could be cancelled after giving a notice of two years. It is true that James I gave a new Charter which made the Charter of 1600 perpetual, but the same could also be ended by giving a notice of 3 years if it was proved that the continuation of the monopoly was injurious to the interests of the people at large.

To begin with, the London Company organised separate voyages. What was actually done was that a large number of persons contributed money for the expedition and distributed among themselves the profits of victory. There was no dearth of subscribers as the profits made by the Company were enormous. In certain cases, the profits were as high as 500 or 600%. Joint stock enterprises began in 1612. The first two voyages were directly towards the Spice Islands. The English Company set up a factory at Bantam and also did some trade there. However, it met bitter opposition at the hands of the Dutch. Captain Hawkins was sent along with the third voyage. He landed at Surat and from there went to the Court of Jahangir to get certain concessions for the English. Hawkins was received favourably at the Court and the English were given the permission to settle at Surat. However, the concession was cancelled on account of the Portuguese influence at the Mughal Court.

In 1612, Captain Best defeated the Portuguese fleet off Swally near Surat. The result of this victory was that the Portuguese influence declined and the English Company got the permission to set up a factory at Surat.

In 1615, Sir Thomas Roe was sent to the Court of Jahangir by James I, King of England. He was successful in securing certain trading concessions for the English Company from the Mughal Emperor. This he did in spite, of the opposition from the vested interests.

In 1622, the English captured Ormuz from the Portuguese with the help of the King of Iran. The English also set up their trading stations at Aramgaon and Masulipatam. The site of Madras was bought by the English Company in 1640. Permission was also obtained to set up a fortified factory called Fort St. George. In 1633, factories were set up at Balasore and Hariharpore. In 1651, a factory was set up at Hugli. In 1661, London Company got the island of Bombay from Charles II at a nominal rent of £10 a year.

In 1688, there was a dispute between the English traders in Bengal and Governor Shayista Khan. At that time, Sir Josiah Child was the Governor of the English Company and he persuaded James II, King of England, to declare war against the Mughal Government. The English failed miserably. They were no match for the might of Aurangzeb. The English factory at Surat was captured and the English were ordered to leave the Mughal territory. Ultimately, peace was brought about. The English got permission to come back. They also got from Aurangzeb the permission to build a factory on the site of Calcutta in 1690. In 1696, a fort was built at that place and the same was called Fort William. The English Company also bought the villages of Sutanati, Kalikata and Govindapur. Thus, the city of Calcutta began to grow.

In 1714, the Presidencies of Calcutta (now Kolkata) Madras and Bombay (now Mumbai) sent a combined mission to the Court of Emperor of Farrukhsiyar under John Surman. With the help of William Hamilton who had cured the emperor of a disease, Surman was able to get three Firmans in July 1717. By these Firmans, the right of the Company to trade duty free in Bengal, in lieu of an annual payment of ₹3,000 was confirmed. The English Company was also allowed to settle wherever they pleased and to rent additional territories around Calcutta (now Kolkata). In the case of province of Hyderabad, the English Company was allowed freedom from all the dues except the rent paid for Madras. In the province of Gujarat, a yearly sum of ₹10,000 was accepted in the satisfaction of all customs due at Surat. The rupees coined by the English Company at Bombay (now Mumbai) were made current throughout the Mughal empire. It cannot be denied that the concessions obtained by Surman added to the powers and prosperity of the English Company.

A reference may be made at this stage to the various changes made in the London Company itself. In 1615, the Company was authorised to issue commissions to its captains. In capital offences a verdict was to be given by a jury alone. In 1623, the Company, was authorised to grant commissions to its Presidents and Chief Officers for the punishment of offences committed by the servants of the Company on land. In capital offences, the trial was to be by a jury.

The London Company met with opposition from the Assada Company. This Company got a licence to trade with the East Indies in 1635. It founded a settlement at Assada in Madagascar and carried on trade vigorously. It was able to inflict great losses on the London Company. Ultimately, a compromise was arrived at and the Assada Company was merged into the London Company.

London Company got a setback on account of the Civil War in England. However, she gained in the time of Cromwell. The Company got £85,000 as compensation for the massacre of Amboyna in 1623. The Charter of 1657 required the Company to have one continuous joint stock. According to Hunter, "The London Company was transformed from a feeble relic of the medieval trade-guild into a vigorous forerunner of the Modern Joint Stock Company". The Charter of 1657 provided that anyone would become a member of the Company by paying an entrance fee of £5 and by subscribing at least £100 to the stock of the Company. The member could vote in the general meeting only if he had stock worth £500. Those who held stock worth £1,000 or more could be elected as the members of the Committees. The term of the office of the Governor and Deputy Governor was reduced to 2 years.

A new Charter was issued to the Company by Charles II in 1661 after the Restoration. The Company was authorised to send ships of war, men and ammunition for the security of their factories. They could also erect forts. They could choose commanders and officers and give them commission under their seal. They were to exercise power and command over their fortresses. They were given power to appoint Governors and other officers. The Governor and his Council were given general judicial authority "to judge all persons belonging to the said Governor and Company or that shall live under them, in all cases, whether civil or criminal, according to the laws of this kingdom, and to execute judgment accordingly". Where there was no Governor, the Chief Factor and Council were empowered to send offenders for punishment either to a place where there was a Governor and a Council or to England.

The Charter of 1683 gave the Company full power to declare war and make peace with any other power. The Company was also given the power to raise, arm, train and muster sufficiently a strong army. The Charter also provided for the establishment of a Court consisting of one person learned in civil law and two assistants to be appointed by the Company.

The Charter of 1686 authorised the Company to appoint admirals and other sea officers. The Company was given a general power to coin any species of money.

The Charter of 1693 added £744,000 to the capital of the Company. No individual member was to be allowed to subscribe more than £510,000. For every one thousand pounds, the subscriber was given one vote, but no one could exercise more than 10 votes. The salaries of the Governor and Deputy Governors were fixed. The Charter of 1694 made the principle of rotation of offices compulsory. Neither Governor nor Deputy Governor could remain in office for more than two years. Eight Committees out of twenty-four were to be elected every year.

It is desirable to mention the case of East India Company vs. Sandys. In this case, the Company brought an action against Mr. Sandys on the ground that he had traded to the East Indies without their licence. The case ended in favour of the Company. The Company also detained the Redbridge which was lying in the Thames, but was believed to be bound for the East Indies. The action of the Company was challenged. It was contended that the Company had no such right to detain a ship. On 19th January 1694, the House of Commons passed a resolution that "all the subjects of England have equal right to trade to the East Indies unless prohibited by Acts of Parliament". Although a resolution of Parliament had not the force of law, it had undoubtedly the effect of encouraging the interlopers. As the Company was determined to stop them there was bound to be trouble.

At this time, Mr. Montagu was the Chancellor of the Exchequer. He was in need of money for the State and was finding out ways and means for the same. The monopoly in trade was virtually put up for auction among all those who could give the Government £2,000,000 at 8% p.a. The London Company offered £700,000 which was insufficient. But a new Company was willing to subscribe the amount needed. The result was that a Bill was passed in 1698 by the British Parliament. The Act provided for a subscription of £2,000,000 sterling as a loan to the State which in return was to grant "General Society" the exclusive right of trading to the East Indies. The London Company was to be given a notice of three years (expiring in 1701) to wind up its business.

In order to strengthen its position, the old Company bought shares worth £315,000 in the new Company. There was ruinous competition between the two Companies for some time. The result was that the new Company began to lose heavily. Ultimately, a compromise was arrived at in 1702. According to this compromise "the old Company was to maintain its separate existence for seven years, but the trade of the two companies was to be carried on jointly, in the name of the English Company, but for the common benefit of both under the direction of twenty-four managers, twelve to be selected by each Company. At the end of the seven years, the old Company was to surrender its Charters". The new Company was to carry on its trade in the name of "The United Company of Merchants of England trading to the East Indies". In March 1709, the London Company surrendered its Charters to Queen Anne.

THE FRENCH EAST INDIA COMPANY

When other European nations were desirous of trading with India and having a share of the profits, the French also thought of trying their luck. It was in 1611 that King Louis XII of France granted letters patent to a Company for the monopoly of the eastern trade. However, that attempt ended in smoke. In 1664, a new Company was started under the guidance of Colbert and Louis XIV. The Government of France undertook to defend the territories of the French Company. The French Company was to concentrate on India. Madagascar was to serve as a halfway house. In December 1667, the first French factory was established at Surat by Francis Caron who was nominated as Director-General. Another French factory was established at Masulipatam in December 1669. This was facilitated by a grant from the King of Golkunda which freed the Company from import and export duty. Caron Was called back in 1672 and his place was taken by Francis Martin.

Martin was one of the real founders of the French Company in India. In the year of his appointment, he founded the settlement of Pondicherry under a grant from Sher Khan Lodi, the King of Bijapur. In spite of the fact that Martin did not get help from the Home Government he was able to make Pondicherry the premier settlement of the French on the Indian mainland. It is true that Pondicherry had to be surrendered to the Dutch in 1693 on account of their superior forces, but the same was restored to the French in 1697 by the Treaty of Ryswick. Martin was once again appointed the Governor of Pondicherry. In 1706, Martin died.

The French had also their settlements at Chandranagar, Balasore and Qasim Bazar. On the Malabar Coast, the French got Mahe in 1725. In 1739, they got Karaikal on the Coromandel Coast.

After the death of Martin, there was confusion in the affairs of the French East India Company for some time. However, after 1726, things began to improve. In 1735, Dumas became the Governor of Pondicherry (now Puducherry). He got permission from Delhi to coin money. In 1739, he got Karaikal as a reward for his support of a pretender to the throne of Tanjore. This is where the French Company stood when it came into conflict with the English East India Company in the 1740's.

REVIEW QUESTIONS

1. Discuss the factors leading to the rise and growth of the English East India Company.
2. Assess the impact of the English East India Company on the trade of India.
3. Throw light on the rise and growth of the French East India Company.
4. Give a detailed account of the trade policies of the English and French East India Companies.
5. Write a detailed note on the arrival of the French East India Company.
6. Analyse the causes of the French failure in India.

SUGGESTED READINGS

Balkrishna: *Commercial Relations between India and England.*
Birdwood, Sir George: *Dawn of British Trade to the East Indies* (1886).
Bruce, John: *Annals of the East India Company* (1810).
Dodwell, H.H. (Ed.): *The Cambridge History of India,* Vol. V.
Foster, W.: *English Factories in India, 1618-69.*
Lyall, A.: *The Rise of the British Dominion in India* (1906).
Mukherjee, Ramkrishna: *The Rise and Fall of the East India Company* (1958).
Roberts, P.E.: *British India.*
Shafat Ahmed Khan: *East India Trade in the Seventeenth Century* (1923).
Wheeler, J.T.: *Early Records of British India* (1878).

3 Anglo-French Struggle for Supremacy in the Deccan

 LEARNING OBJECTIVES

- Throw light on the Carnatic Wars
- Discuss the causes of success of the English and failure of the French in the Deccan
- Elaborate on the establishment of the supremacy of the English in the Deccan
- Give an estimate of Dupleix

Before describing the struggle for supremacy between the English and French East India Companies[1], it is desirable to explain their respective positions on the eve of the Carnatic Wars. To put it briefly, the English East India Company was a private enterprise and consequently possessed a lot of initiative and vigour. It was a prosperous Company and carried on a lot of trade. The despatches of the Company point out to the large volume of trade carried on by it. Its officers were putting their very best into their jobs and the Englishmen were looking forward to their good prospects in the future. As compared with it, the French East India Company was more the "offspring of State patronage than

---

[1]. According to Ramkrishna Mukherjee, "While the English found a tougher rival in the Dutch than in the Portuguese, the French outrivalled both. Both the Powers, the English and the French, fought their utmost in the eighteenth century to obtain, in the end, India—the jewel of the East' as booty".

"Why was the Anglo-French rivalry so many times more virulent than the Anglo-Portuguese or the Anglo-Dutch rivalries? The reason appears to lie in the fact that in the first half of the seventeenth century, when the Portuguese and the English fought most seriously over India, the Mughal Power was strong and so it could resist any aggressive move of a foreign power. Hence, the rival merchant powers could only snipe at each other's trading advantages, while maintaining the facade of remaining 'peaceful traders' to the Mughal Emperor and his vassals and pleasing them with flattery and presents. In later years also, even though the Mughal Power had begun to disintegrate from the beginning of the eighteenth century, it was yet strong enough to punish any impudence on the part of foreign merchants; so the Anglo-Dutch rivalry reaching its climax in the second half of the seventeenth century, could also not come completely out in the open, although it was more virulent than the Anglo-Portuguese rivalry. The Anglo-French rivalry, however, took place mainly after the fourth decade of the eighteenth century, when after the death of the Mughal Emperor Aurangzeb in 1707 the disintegration of the Mughal Empire could not pass unnoticed even by a superficial observer. So, a serious contest with a view to control India for the supreme 'trading' advantages of one company at the expense of others, by means of subduing the power of the Indian rulers and using this power to the favour of one company only, a contest which could not unfold itself in the previous phase of 'commercial enterprises' of the European merchant bourgeoisie in India, now came out very openly.

"Neither the Portuguese nor the Dutch could avail themselves of this wonderful situation, as their powers were already broken. The English Company, therefore, found itself without any serious rival in India except the French. And the fight which ensued between them after the fourth decade of the eighteenth century was quite naked as regards the ultimate objective of merchant capital". (*The Rise and Fall of the East India Company*, pp. 109-10.)

the outcome of spontaneous mercantile activity". There was too much control of the Government and that destroyed all initiative on the part of the officials of the French Company. The volume of trade carried on by them was not much and consequently the French Company was poor. Moreover, the only important settlement of the French was at Pondicherry. Chandranagar was no good. There was nothing to compare with Bombay. The English Company had a brilliant record of progress and growth and consequently the people of England looked upon the English Company with a feeling of pride. However, that was not the case with the French Company which failed to fire the imagination of the Frenchmen. It is obvious that the French were handicapped in their race for supremacy with the English Company. All the resourcefulness of Dupleix could not change the state of affairs.

FIRST CARNATIC WAR (1746-48)

The French and the English Companies fought the three Carnatic Wars in the Deccan and these wars sealed the fate of the French in the Deccan. As regards the 1st Carnatic War, it was merely an echo of the war of Austrian Succession which broke out in Europe in connection with the succession of Maria Theresa to the throne of Austria. In spite of the pragmatic sanction, Frederick, the Great, of Prussia occupied Silesia. He ironically remarked that it would have been better for Maria Theresa's father to have left a few more battalions than the pragmatic sanction which was nothing better than a waste paper. The news of the War of Austrian Succession reached India in 1744. However, rumours of war were persisting ever since 1740 and both the parties were making preparations to oust each other.

At this time, Dupleix was the Governor of Pondicherry (now Puducherry). Finding his position not very strong, Dupleix is started to have suggested to the Madras (now Chennai) Governor to observe neutrality. Such a suggestion was not accepted by the English Governor. The latter was expecting reinforcements from Home Government and he hoped to drive out the French from India with their help. Dupleix still persisted his efforts to save the French. Ultimately, he appealed to Anwar-ud-Din, the Nawab of Carnatic. The Nawab told both the English and the French—Companies not to quarrel and thereby not to break the peace of the country. The English did not like the idea of challenging the authority of the Nawab of Carnatic and submitted to the orders. The British troops along with its squadron reached India but Commodore Barnett died soon after.

Dupleix had also sent a word to La Bourdonnais, Governor of Mauritius, asking him for help. The result was that La Bourdonnais hastened to India with a fleet and reached the Coromandel Coast in July 1746. The French and British squadrons faced each other for some time but the English squadron left for Ceylon after some time. Finding his position strong, Dupleix asked La Bourdonnais to besiege Madras (now Chennai). When the latter did so, the English approached Anwar-ud-Din, Nawab of Carnatic, to direct the French to leave Madras (Chennai) and maintain peace. However, Dupleix promised to hand over Madras to Anwar-ud-Din if the latter allowed the French to conquer it. The Nawab agreed. Madras[2] surrendered to the French in September 1746. Differences arose

---

[2] About Madras (now Chennai), Commodore Griffin wrote thus to Nizam-ul-Mulk 1747: "I shall not enter into a particular detail of the robberies, cruelties, and depredations, committed on shore upon the King my Master's subjects, by that insolent, perfidious nation the French; connived at, and abetted by those under your Excellency, (the Nabob of Arcot), whose duty it was to have preserved the peace of your country, instead of selling the interest of a nation, with whom you have had the strictest friendly time out of mind; a nation that has been the means not only of enriching this part of the country, but the whole dominions of the grand Mogul; and that to a people who are remarkable all over the world for encroaching upon, and giving disturbances and disquiet to all near them; a people who are strangers in your country, in comparison of those who have been robbed by them of that most important fortress and factory, Madras (now Chennai); and now they are possessed of it, have neither money nor credit to carry on the trade... . And now, excellent Sir, we have laid this before you, for your information and consideration; and must entreat you, in the name of the King of Great Britain, my Royal Master, to call the Nabob to an account for his past transactions, and interpose your power to restore as near as possible in its original state, what has been so unjustly taken from us".

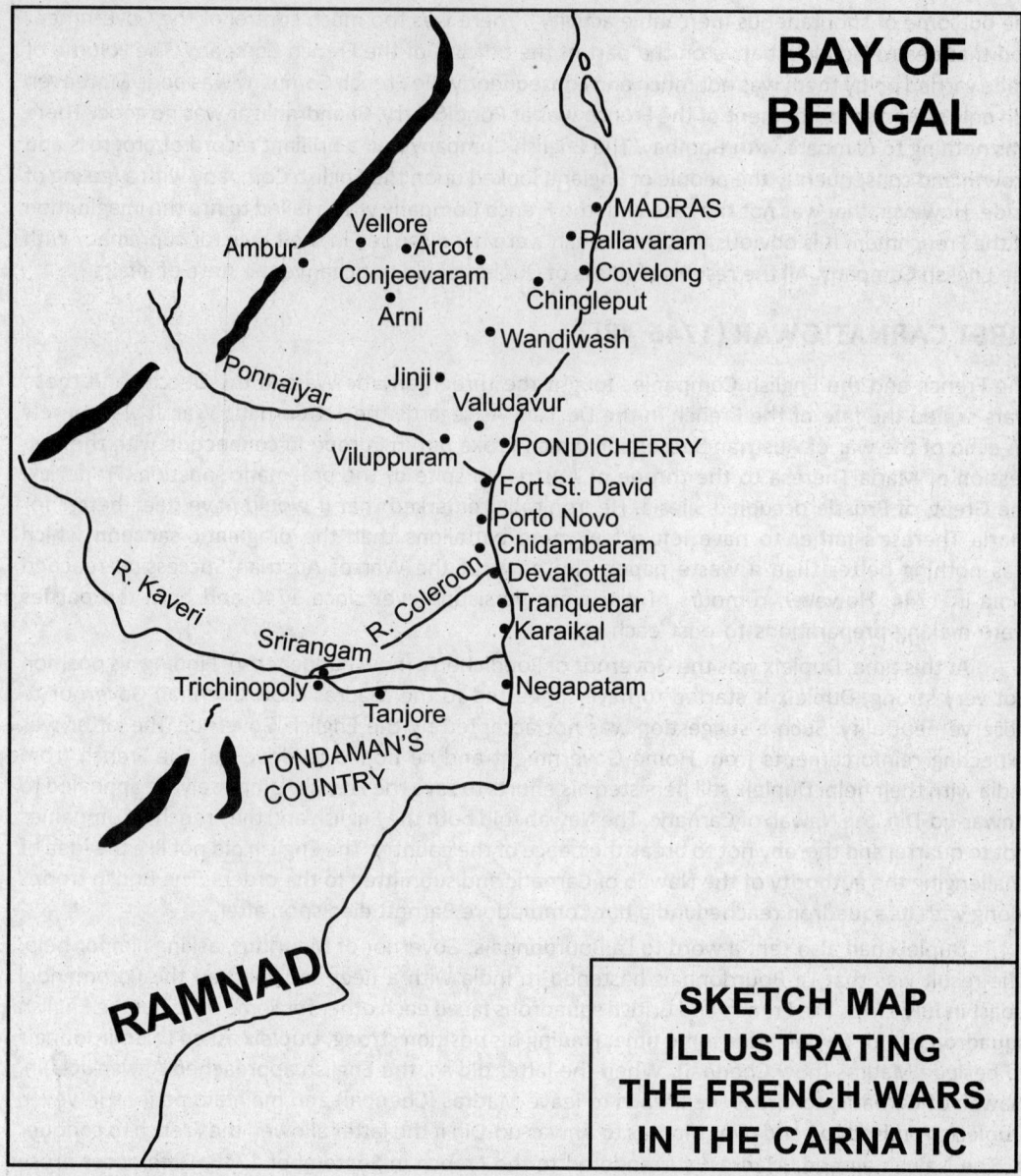

SKETCH MAP ILLUSTRATING THE FRENCH WARS IN THE CARNATIC

between Dupleix and La Bourdonnais. La Bourdonnais accepted a bribe of one lakh pagodas and restored Madras to the English for £40,000. Dupleix repudiated the action of La Bourdonnais and recaptured Madras. When Anwar-ud-Din asked for the restoration of Madras to him, Dupleix refused to do so Consequently, the Nawab sent an army to fight against the French. The army was defeated in the battle of St. Thomas or the battle of Adyar, a place near Madras. In this battle, the French were successful and the Nawab's army was defeated. The battle of Adyar is regarded to be one of the decisive battles of India. It demonstrated the superiority of disciplined infantry supported by artillery over cavalry.

Dupleix tried to capture Fort St. David also but failed. The English tried to capture Pondicherry, but the French defended the same successfully.

The first Carnatic War was ended by the Treaty of Aix La Chappelle of 1748. The net result of this treaty was that the English got back Madras and the French got back Louisburg in North America. Although the treaty did not bring about any changes, yet, according to Prof. Dodwell, this treaty marks an epoch in Indian history. To quote him, "It demonstrated the overwhelming influence of sea power, it displayed the superiority of European methods of war over those followed by Indian armies, and it revealed the political decay that had eaten into the heart of the Indian state".

RISE OF HYDERABAD STATE

Before describing the events of the Second Carnatic War, it is desirable to refer to the rise of the Hyderabad State. This State was created by Nizam-ul-Mulk. In 1713, he was appointed the Viceroy of the six Subahs of the Deccan. The Nizam was ambitious and unscrupulous and he decided to rule those Sabahs independently of the Mughal authority at Delhi. The Nizam had to pass through many ups and downs before he could finally achieve his objective. He was the Viceroy of the Deccan up to 1715 when he was called back to Delhi. He was appointed the Governor of different places. He was sent to Muradabad, then to Patna and Ujjain. From there he was also called back in 1719 and was asked to choose anyone out of the four provinces of Akbarabad, Allahabad, Multan and Burhanpur. He did not approve of the royal action and consequently began to prepare for self-defence. He made straight for the Narmada and crossed it in May 1720. He occupied the fortresses of Asirgarh and Burhanpur in May 1720. He defeated the Mughal forces sent against him in the battles of Khandwa and Balapur in June and July 1720 respectively. These victories left the Nizam the master of the six Subahs of the Deccan and the Viceroyalty was conferred on him by the Mughal emperor.

In 1722, he was appointed the Wazir of the Mughal empire. As Wazir, he tried to stop the rapid disintegration of the Mughal empire but finding his task hopeless, he left for the Deccan in 1724. That was considered to be an act of disloyalty and the Nizam had to fight successfully the battle of Shakar-kheda in October 1724 against the Mughal troops. The Nizam entered Hyderabad in 1725 as a victor. In June 1725 he was pardoned and a formal order appointing him the head of the Deccan was passed. However, he was removed from the Governorship of Malwa and Gujarat. After 1725, Nizam-ul-Mulk concentrated his attention on the Deccan and was able to develop the State of Hyderabad without any interference from the Mughal empire at Delhi. This he continued to do till his death in 1748. However, he had to fight against the Marathas who were determined to sweep everything before them. Between 1727 and 1731, the Nizam successfully created dissensions among the Marathas but ultimately he failed. Bajirao Peshwa defeated the Nizam in the battle of Palkhed and forced on him the treaty of Mungi-Shegaon. The Nizam agreed to allow the Marathas to collect Chauth and Sardeshmukhi.

In 1737,[3] the Nizam was appointed the Chief Minister of the Mughal empire and he was given the title of Asaf Jah ("Equal in dignity to Asaf, the Minister of King Solomon"). The immediate problem before the Nizam was to deal with the Marathas. However, he himself was defeated by Bajirao in a battle near Bhopal in 1738. He had to sign the treaty of Durai Sarai by which he had to give the whole of Malwa and the territory between the Narmada and Chambal to Bajirao. The Nizam was in Delhi when Nadir Shah attacked India. However, he went back to the Deccan and continued to consolidate his position there till his death in 1748. Before that, he was successful in putting the State of Hyderabad on a very stable footing.

According to J. N. Sarkar, "For a quarter of a century Asaf Jah had been the most outstanding personality in the Mughal empire. He was universally regarded as the sole representative of the spacious times of Aurangzeb and of the policy and traditions of that strenuous monarch. The higher

---

[3] He was the son of Asaf Joh's daughter.

minds among the younger generation of the court nobility looked up to him with the respect due to a father while fools and knaves hated him for his love of discipline and the honesty of administration. He was undoubtedly the foremost General of his time in India. In statecraft and diplomacy, he was no less eminent. He had the true statesman's length of vision and spirit of moderation, and of this we have many proofs. He won over the surviving partisans of Mubariz Khan by liberal provision for their support. After crushing the rebellion of his son Nasir Jung, he destroyed the unread rebel's despatch box which was reported to contain promises of adhesion from thirty-eight nobles of his own court. Still more strongly was his wisdom shown when in 1739, Nadir Shah, disgusted with the inability of Mohammad Shah, offered the throne of Delhi to Asaf Jah, but the latter refused to be disloyal to his master". (*The Cambridge History of India*, Vol. IV, p. 385.)

SECOND CARNATIC WAR (1748-54)

There are two aspects of the war between the English and the French. On the one hand, Asaf Jah Nizam-ul-Mulk died in May 1748. There was a struggle between his second son Nasir Jung and grandson Muzzafar Jung. Both of them aspired to the headship of the Deccan Muzzafar Jung joined hands with Chanda Sahib[4] who wanted to be Nawab of Arcot. Chanda Sahib also opened negotiations with Dupleix. The latter recognised the importance of future prospects if both Chanda Sahib and Muzzafar Jung were helped. It was not difficult to arrive at the advantages to be secured from the new move. Agreement was entered into and Muzzafar Jung and Chanda Sahib, helped by the French, defeated Anwar-ud-Din in August 1949 in the battle of Amber. Anwar-ud-Din was killed and his son Mohammad Ali took refuge in the fort of Trichinopoly. Chanda Sahib was able to establish his control over the rest of Carnatic. The siege of Pondicherry (now Puducherry) was not pressed vigorously. He wasted a lot of time in dealing with the Raja of Tanjore.

If the French had helped Muzzafar Jung and Chanda Sahib, the English helped Nasir Jung. Nasir Jung took the field in 1750. Muzzifar Jung was defeated, captured and imprisoned. However, there was a change of fortune. Nasir Jung was deserted by his troops and was captured and put to death. At this time, Muzzafar Jung gave £50,000 to the Company. He also gave Dupleix a Jagir worth £10,000 a year. Chanda Sahib was recognized as the Nawab of Arcot. When Muzzafar Jung was killed in January 1751, Salabat Jung was put on the throne by Bussy.

Within a few months, Bussy was able to set the forces of Salabat Jung on a sound footing by a strict discipline and incessant vigilance. He was able to train a large number of troops and paid them well and punctually. His discipline was so strict that even Salabat Jung began to tremble before him. The intrigues of the officials of the State were put an end to. For his own expenses, Bussy got possession of some districts which came to be known as the Northern Circars. Those were entirely managed by the French.

The English Company refused to accept the new situation. Governor Saunders was the leader of those who were opposed to change. Clive appeared on the scene and occupied Arcot. All efforts to dislodge him from Arcot failed. Even when Chanda Sahib sent half of his army under his own son

---

[4] Chanda Sahib was the son-in-law of Dost Ali, Nawab of Arcot. In 1732, he was sent by his father-in-law to occupy Trichinopoly. He was able to capture it by falling in love with the widow of the king of Trichinopoly. He also tried to capture Tanjore and Madura but failed on account of opposition from the Marathas. When his father-in-law was killed in 1740 by the Marathas, Chanda Sahib thought of capturing Arcot and marched towards the same. However, he failed in his objective. The Marathas also snatched away Trichinopoly from him. Chanda Sahib was captured by the Marathas and kept as a prisoner for seven years. The first three years he spent in Berar. In 1744, he was taken to Satara. The Marathas demanded lakhs of rupees for his release, He tried to make friends with the Peshwas but failed. In 1748, he escaped from Satara and was successful in raising an army.

to relieve Arcot, there was no better success than before. [5] As half the army of Chanda Sahib was sent away from Trichinopoly to Arcot, the siege of Trichinopoly had to be given up. Chanda Sahib was himself defeated and killed. The whole of the Carnatic fell into the hands of the English.

Dupleix tried to recover his position, but could not. Victory after victory was won by the English against the French. A conference was held between the English and French Commissioners. However, it failed in its objective. Soon after the conference, the war restarted. Before much could be done, Dupleix was recalled in 1754, and he died in 1764.

Dupleix was succeeded by Godeheu. The latter arranged terms of peace with the English. By the new treaty, both the nations agreed not to interfere in the internal affairs of the Indian States. Both the French and the English retained their old positions. However, the English got a town in Northern Circar. Bussy remained in the Deccan and continued to exercise his influence. It has been pointed out that by the treaty of 1755, Godeheu sacrificed everything for which Dupleix had fought. According to Dupleix himself "Godeheu had signed the ruin of the country and the dishonour of the nation". The French agreed to give away all that they had captured so far. Whether the treaty was (wise) or not, one thing is certain. It made the English stronger. It also gave them much needed rest before embarking upon the Third Carnatic War.

THIRD CARNATIC WAR (1756-63)

The peace between the French and the English Companies in India was a short-lived one. The Seven Years' war started in Europe in 1756 and before long the two nations started fighting in India also. The French Government sent Count Lally as the Governor and Commander-in-Chief. With great difficulty, Lally reached India on account of the naval supremacy of the English. He had some success at the start. He was able to capture Fort St. David. He recalled Bussy from the Deccan. This was a mistake on his part. As soon as Bussy left, the French influence ended. Salabat Jung went over to the English and gave them Northern Circars. Lally tried to get Madras (now Chennai) but failed. He was forced to retire to Pondicherry and was defeated by Sir Eyre Coote in the battle of Wandiwash in January 1760. It was a decisive battle. It sealed the fate of the French. Bussy was taken prisoner. Karaikal fell in April 1760. Lally surrendered at Pondicherry in January 1761. In April 1761, Jinji was captured. The French had lost practically everything. After the peace of Paris, there was an exchange of prisoners of war. Lally was returned to France but he was condemned and: executed.[6] The peace of Paris (1763) restored the French settlements to them but the French were not allowed to fortify them. It is true that in time of Lord Wellesley, the French gave some trouble to the English, but it cannot be denied that the three Carnatic wars completely destroyed their chances of founding French empire in India.

According to Furber, "From many points of view it was a misfortune for France ever to have striven for political power and prestige in India after the days of Dupleix. This story of Anglo-French

---

[5] "Clive's capture of Arcot proved to be the turning point in the contest between the French and the English'.

[6] It has rightly been pointed out that the possession of the military and financial resources of Bengal gave the English a decisive advantage over Lally. From this secure base they could send a constant supply of men and money to Madras (now Chennai) and create a diversion in its favour by attacking the French in the Northern Circars. Although it was not fully recognised at the time, the position of the English in Bengal made the struggle of the French a hopeless one from the very beginning of the Third Carnatic War. The Battle of Plassey may be truly said to have decided the fate of the French in India.... In spite of Lally's undoubted failings and shortcomings, it is only fair to remember that the difficulties confronting him were really insurmountable and that the French had no real chance of success against the English even under the best of leaders. There is a large element of truth in the remark of a historian, that "neither Alexander the Great nor Napoleon could have won the empire of India by starting from Pondicherry (now Puduchurry) as a base and contending with the power which held Bengal and command of the sea".

relations in Indian affairs after 1733 reveals the existence of 'rivets' of British power unappreciated and largely unknown to the great majority of Englishmen and Frenchmen. Utterly unable to carry on an East India trade without British assistance, completely powerless to reassert political dominance and military prestige with the resources she could then muster, France's only opportunity in India lay in turning Britain's increasing responsibilities in India to her own advantage. Bourdieu, with his advice to make 'golden' voyages during Britain's war with Tipu, had a truer grasp of realities than Vergennes. War and revolution intervened to make any fulfillment of Bourdieu's plans impossible. When the 'domestic situation' in France once more enabled French statesmen to think of India, they never thought of the commercial advantages that could be obtained in India without conquest. Napoleonic France thought only of Vergennes' old dream of re-creating by force of arms a French Indian empire which really never had existed and was desirable never to exist".

CAUSES OF ENGLISH SUCCESS

It is desirable to discuss the causes that were responsible for the success of the English Company and failure of French Company.

1. To begin with, it may be pointed out that the English Company was a private enterprise. This created a spirit of self-reliance among the people. They knew that if they worked hard, they would be able to get profits and if they slackened, they were to be ruined. The result was that the English Company became prosperous. Its condition was so sound that it could give loans to the Government. On the other hand, the French Company was merely a department of the Government. It lacked self-reliance and completely depended upon the Government which in itself was rotten during the 18th century. The corruption in the French Government was reflected in the French Company. Moreover, the French Government guaranteed a certain percentage of profit to the shareholders. This also was responsible for the destruction of initiative among those who were incharge of the French Company. On account of its private nature, the English Company gained in another way. The changes at home did not affect the fortunes of the English Company in India.

2. Another cause of English success was their naval supremacy. On account of this, the English could send help to India whenever they pleased. There was none to check them on the way. It was this factor that cut off the link between the French possessions in India and France. The French had to avoid the Englishmen on the way while coming to India. The result was that sometimes months and years were spent on the way. This happened particularly in the case of Count Lally. Although he started very early from France so as to be in India in time, he reached India very late on account of his forced halts on the way.

3. The English had their naval base in Bombay. The result was that they could keep their ships in safety in Bombay and could start their operations at once as soon as an opportunity offered itself. They could also repair their ships there. The French had their naval base in the Isle of France which was very far off. The result was that they could not take immediate action.

4. The English had three important places in India, viz., Calcutta (now Kolkata), Madras (now Chennai) and Bombay (now Mumbai). The result was that even if one of these places was conquered by the enemy, the other two remained. Even if two places were conquered by the enemy at one time, one place always remained with the English because the three places were far off from one another. All of them could not be conquered at one time. The French had only one important station in India and that was Pondicherry (now Puducherry). The other places like Mahi and Chandranagar could be conquered at any time and were always at the mercy of the English. The result was that with the fall of Pondicherry, the French lost their all.

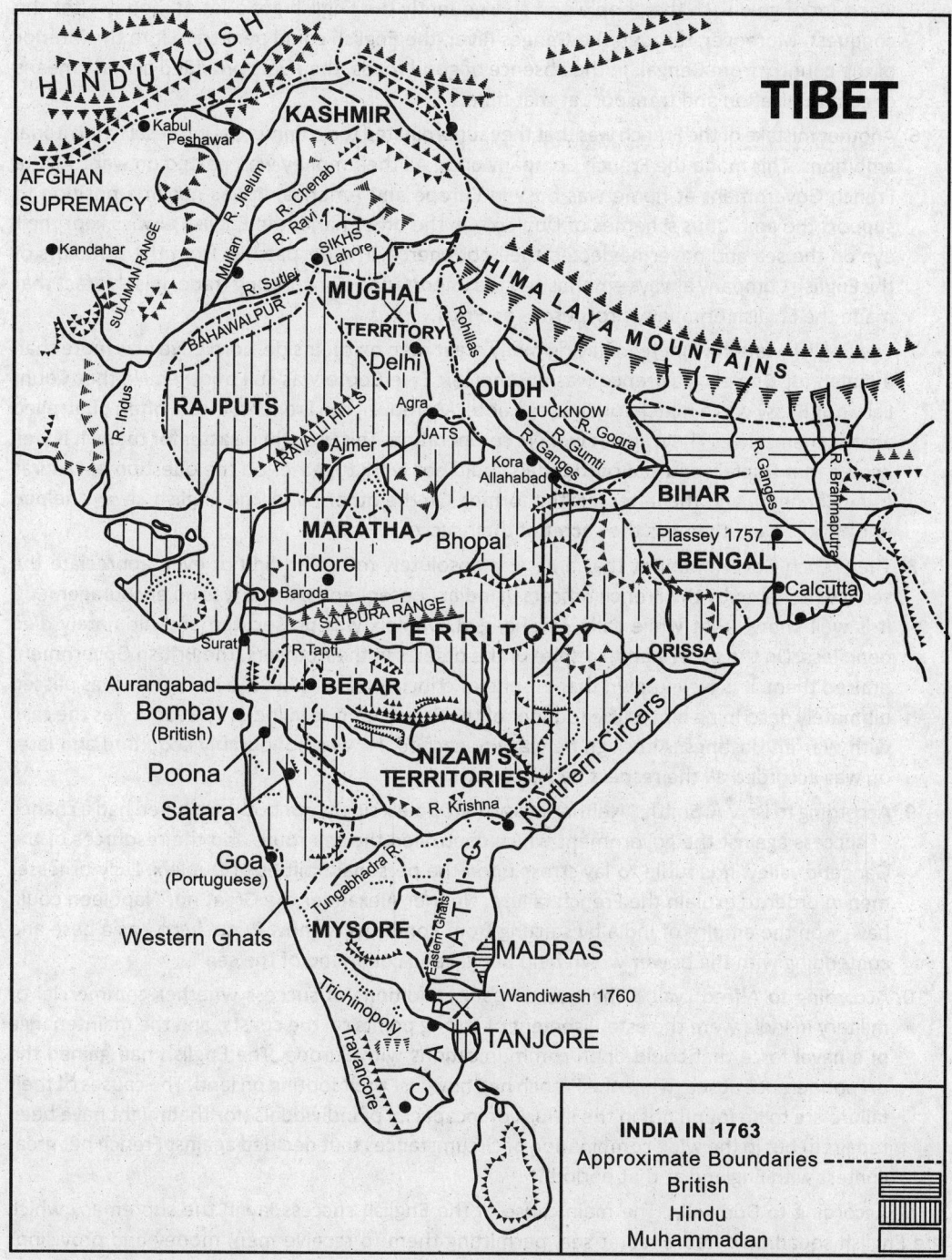

INDIA IN 1763
Approximate Boundaries ----------
British
Hindu
Muhammadan

5. The French entered India from the wrong quarter. The Deccan was not fertile. It was absolutely unproductive. The result was that the military conquest of the Deccan by the French did not compensate them. Their enterprise was a failure. On the other hand, the English entered India from the right quarter. They started from Bengal. It had a very productive soil. There

was a lot of gold with the people and consequently the English got a lot of money after the conquest. Moreover, through the Ganges River, the English could penetrate into the interior of the country from Bengal. In the absence of good roads, the rivers provided an easy means of communication and transport at that time.

6. Another mistake of the French was that they subordinated the commercial interests to territorial ambitions. This made the French Company poor. All their money was wasted on wars. As the French Government at home was busy in Europe and America, it was not in a position to support the ambitious schemes of Dupleix. On the other hand, the English always kept their eye on the sea and never neglected their commerce. The despatches from the Directors of the English Company always emphasised the importance of increasing trade. It is this fact that made the English Company prosperous and rich.

7. The English were fortunate in having many great men on their side. Lord Clive was more than a match for Dupleix. Lawrence was another. Sir Eyre Coote was still another. Neither Count Lally nor Bussy was a match for Sir Eyre Coote. Moreover, the French Officers often quarrelled among themselves. They did not work in co-operation. This brought disaster for them. It is well known that Dupleix and La Bourdonnais could not work together on the question of Madras (now Chennai), and the latter left the former. On the other hand, the English always helped one another and that was the secret of their success.

8. The French Government at that time was absolutely rotten. It did not even appreciate the service rendered by the French officers in India. Consequently, there was no encouragement. It is well-known that while Lally was hanged, Dupleix was prosecuted and ultimately died penniless. On the other hand, in spite of the defects in their officers, the British Government praised them. It is well-known that in spite of criticism of Lord Clive, a resolution was passed ultimately describing him as the founder of the British empire in India. The same was the case with Warren Hastings. Although he was impeached, he was honourably acquitted and later on was accorded all the respect by his countrymen.

9. According to Dr. V.A. Smith, "Neither Bussy nor Dupleix singly, nor both combined had a chance of success against the government which controlled the sea-route and the resources of the Gangetic valley. It is futile to lay stress upon the personal frailties of Dupleix, Lally or lesser men in order to explain the French failure. Neither Alexander the Great nor Napoleon could have won the empire of India by starting from Pondicherry (now Puducherry) as a base and contending with the power which held Bengal and command of the sea".

10. According to Alfred Lyall, "The two primary conditions of success whether commercial or military in India were the establishment of strong points on the coasts, and the maintenance of a naval force that could open communications with Europe. The English had gained the preponderance at sea, while the French had now lost their footing on land. The causes of their failure are to be found not in the ill-luck or incapacity of individuals (for that might have been repaired) but in the wide combination of circumstances that decided against French her great contest with England at that period".

According to Dodwell, "The main cause of the English success lay in the supremacy which the English squadron established at sea, permitting them to receive men, money and provisions from Bengal and England, enabling them to transport, and cover the operations of their forces, and depriving the French of their supplies. This placed Lally at a grievous disadvantage and the elusive authority which Dupleix had seized vanished at the first touch of that naval power which had not been applicable when he was projecting his schemes. Then, too, while Bussy's exploits had not contributed a man or a rupee to French aid, the English in Bengal were able at a critical time to send down both troops and money. Lastly, Lally himself was hampered by personal defects and confronted by an impossible task. As a leader he was hasty, inconsiderate, violent. He expected others to attend to the details of supplies, and never reflected on the hindrances which might be caused by the councillors whom he abused. Moreover, no man could at once conduct a war against the English and reform the Pondicherry (now Puducherry) methods of administration. The knowledge that he was charged with the latter duty made every servant of the Company desire to see him return to Europe discredited by defeat". (*The Cambridge Shorter History of India*, p. 334.)

ESTIMATE OF DUPLEIX

Undoubtedly, Dupleix was one of the greatest of the Frenchmen who were sent to India by the French Company. It was he who dreamt the dream of founding a French empire in India. He critically analysed the political condition in Indian and came to the conclusion that by helping one State against the other, the French could add to their resources and ultimately set up an empire of their own in the country. It has already been pointed out that to begin with, he did very well. He was able to put Chanda Sahib on the Carnatic throne. He was also able to put Muzzafar Jung on the Deccan throne. When Muzzafar Jung died, he was able to put Salabat Jung in his place. He got the Northern Circars from Salabat Jung. Bussy was stationed with Salabat Jung. It appeared that the French influence in South India was to be supreme. However, things changed. Clive appeared on the scene and captured Arcot. Chanda Sahib failed to carry out the instructions of Dupleix and wasted his time in Tanjore while he should have finished the opposition of Mohammed Ali in Trichinopoly at once. The delay on the part of Chanda Sahib gave the English time to prepare. The result was that ultimately Chanda Sahib was defeated and the plans of Dupleix miscarried.

It is true that Dupleix was as good a diplomat as Clive, but Clive was also a great soldier which Dupleix was not. The result was that Dupleix was no match for Clive. No wonder, while Dupleix failed, Clive succeeded.

It cannot be denied that Dupleix was handicapped throughout by lack of funds and an inadequate supply of soldiers. If he had enough of money, he could have recruited a large number of soldiers from the Indians, but the paucity of funds did not allow him to do so. It was impossible for anybody to fight with those soldiers whose salaries had been promised but not paid. The result was that the schemes of Dupleix could not be carried out.

Critics point out that the masters of Dupleix looked more to dividends and not to the prospects of a future French empire in India. It is true that Dupleix was also partly to blame because he did not unfold his plans and their prospects to the Home Government, but even when he did so, nobody felt enthusiastic about them. The only result was that he was called back.

Dupleix will always remain a tragic figure in history. He was let down both by his fortune and by his countrymen. He rightly pointed out that "he had sacrificed his youth, his fortune and his life". He had spent money out of his own pocket to finance the wars.

According to Elphinstone, "Dupleix was the first who made an extensive use of disciplined sepoys, the first who quitted the ports on the sea and marched an army into the heart of the continent, the first, above all, who discovered the illusion of the Mughal greatness and turned to his own purpose, the awe with which weaker minds still regarded that gigantic phantom".

According to Henri Martin, "The genius of a Richelieu had matured in a Factory. Dupleix was the first to realise the inevitable result of the contact between the static societies of the East and the progressive societies of Europe...; he had seen Asia, like America and like the whole world, destined to submit to the law of the European races... .Dupleix judged India destined to be conquered, not by other Asians, like those who had ravaged her before, but by Europeans; among the European powers, Portugal had fallen and Holland was declining; there remained only France and-England. Dupleix was determined to give India to France... .His plan was as much prudent in respect of means as audacious in respect of the final objective". For the failure of Dupleix to achieve this ambitious project, Martin put the entire blame on the French Government and the Company. "Asia would have been ours if, with Dupleix and Bussy in India, we could still have Louis XIV and Colbert Versailles, or if we could have only Law. But in place of Louis XIV and Colbert, we had Louis XV aid Madame de Pompadour and the inept merchants who directed the Company of the Indies". Again, "There is not a single instance in modern history of a nation being betrayed to this extent by its own Government".

On the other hand, Alfred Martineau asserts that Dupleix did not start with any conception of empire-building, that he was gradually driven to it by circumstances he had not foreseen earlier, and that the failure of his project was due at least as much to his own wrong moves and miscalculations as to the indifference of the home government. To quote Martineau, "If the psychologist could penetrate with certainty into the thoughts of statesmen, there would be little, very little indeed in their actions, which would appear to him inspired by high ideas, particularly by foresight and plans for the future'. Chance and self-interest guide them more than one would like generally to confess. Dupleix did not escape this common law. Coming to India with the sole object of making money, he was led unexpectedly by the course of events and by a sort of financial necessity to a policy of territorial expansion which he had not foreseen earlier, and even the vaguest idea of which he did not form for the first time till twenty-seven years after his arrival in the peninsula". Analysing the motive which prompted Dupleix to conceive the idea of a colonial empire, Martineau says, "Constantly embarrassed in his trading operations by the delay or insufficiency of funds coming from France, he came slowly to the idea that the only means to get rid of such embarrassment was to find money in India, without waiting for funds from Europe and without having to seek the assistance of bankers. That made it necessary to have a fixed territorial revenue, the collection of which could be assured only by the exercise of a political power. This was first conceived and later developed more fully in the mind of Dupleix the idea of creating for our advantage a sort of colonial empire in India where we would be practically the masters under the authority, more nominal than real, of Indian princes, who would owe their thrones or their security to us. But this idea, which was to change the face of India and in a certain measure that of the world, was not in his mind at any time before the year 1749 or perhaps before 1750". Discussing the causes of the failure of Dupleix, Martineau has emphasised the wrong judgment and blind obstinacy of Dupleix himself. "No doubt, at the beginning, the error was legitimate; but in the later stage, when came an unending series of misfortunes and disillusions, it became evident that the substance was being sacrificed for the shadow. The blindness or the obstinacy of Dupleix was the principal cause of his fall".

"Dupleix is a striking and brilliant figure in Indian history. His political conceptions were daring and imaginative, and he aroused a dread in his English contemporaries which is at once a tribute to his personal power and testimony to their sagacity". "Like all able men, he loved power both from policy and inclination, was not averse to a certain theatrical pomp and display". "It is my opinion that there never can be peace in the province while Dupleix stays in India. He neither values men nor money, nor anything but what can gratify his own ambition. The continued ill-success of his troops would have made anybody but him reflect and be glad of the terms offered; but he talks not like the Governor of Pondicherry (now Puducherry) but as Prince of the Province". (Major Lawrence in 1754.)

According to Malleson, Dupleix was a great administrator and diplomat with a wonderful capacity for organisation and great persistence and tenacity of purpose.

According to Roberts, "Dupleix is a striking and brilliant figure in Indian history. For even if we give up the old uncritical estimate, we need not deny his real claims to greatness. His political conceptions were daring and imaginative. He raised the prestige of France in the East for some years to an amazing height, he won a reputation among Indian princes and leaders that has never been surpassed, and he aroused a dread in his English contemporaries which is at once a tribute to his personal power and a testimony to their sagacity. (*British India*, pp. 118-19.)

According to Dodwell, "The policy of Dupleix indeed lacked the elements of permanent success, and could never have survived a European war. Had he never been recalled, Coote or some other English leaders would nonetheless have besieged, captured, and ruined Pondicherry (now Puducherry). The indispensable condition of political expansion in the East lay in the 18th century, as it had lain in the sixteenth and seventeenth, in predominance at sea. But this condition, as events were to prove, was not possessed by France. Dupleix's success was only obtained under temporary conditions of a most favourable nature. He launched his campaign after the War of the Austrian Succession. The most powerful weapon of the English, their naval power, was for the moment out of action. They could not pursue, intercept, or destroy the vessels which carried to Pondicherry (now Puducherry) recruits and munitions. Without this advantage it is unlikely that Dupleix would have obtained as high a degree of success as he in fact secured". (*The Cambridge Shorter History of India*, p. 427.)

It is usually contended that in conquering India, the English had to follow the path which the genius of French had opened out to her. While summarising the causes of British success, James Mill pointed out that the two important discoveries for conquering India were the weakness of the native armies against European discipline and the facility of imparting that discipline to natives in the service of the Europeans and "both these discoveries were made by the French". Many writers have maintained that the failure of Dupleix was due to the ineffective cooperation on the part of the French naval officers, the want of good military commanders, bad luck at critical moments of the campaign and the faintheartedness of the French Ministry.

Sir Alfred Lyall admitted that Dupleix was a man of genius and political vision who strove gallantly against all those obstacles. But he also pointed out that the English had in Clive and Lawrence commanders superior to any of the French military officers with Dupleix, except Bussy. Bussy was a very able man but he was intent much more upon building up his own fortunes, as a military dictator at Hyderabad than on sharing the unprofitable hard hitting struggle between the English and French commanders in the Carnatic. When misfortune overtook Dupleix and Lally he behaved ungenerously to both of them. Alfred agreed with Elphinstone that Dupleix was "the first who made an extensive use of disciplined sepoys; the first who quitted the ports on the sea and marched an army into the heart of the continent; the first, above all, who discovered the illusion of the Mughal greatness", but he maintained that Dupleix could not be ranked as an original discoverer in Asiatic warfare and politics. The weakness of all oriental States and armies had long been known. India had not shown the capacity to resist foreign invasions. The only soldiers upon which the princes of Southern India could rely were commonly mercenaries from the North. The view of Bernier was that a division of Turenne's men would have made short work of the whole of the Mughal army. It was a common knowledge with the European military men of that time that the loose levies of the Carnatic could be scattered by a few well-armed and disciplined battalions. There was no great novelty in the introduction by the French of the practice of drilling a few native regiments for their own service. The Mughal army had always contained some European officers and the same was the case with the Marathas.

Alfred was prepared to give due credit to Dupleix for having first started on the right road towards European conquest with energy, ability and patriotism, but he was not prepared to concede that but for the blindness of the French Government towards the ideas of Dupleix, the blunders of his colleagues or subordinates and the final disavowal of Dupleix himself, France might have supplanted England in India. Such a view, he pointed out, betrayed an incomplete survey of the whole situation. The extensive political changes did not hang on the event of a small battle or the behaviour at some critical moment of a provincial general or governor. That cannot be attributed to one cause but was due to many factors.

In spite of the above views, Alfred Lyall paid the following tribute to Dupleix: "Dupleix was a man of original and energetic political instincts of an imperious and morally intrepid disposition who embarked upon wide and somewhat audacious schemes of oriental dominion, and lost the stakes for which he played more through want of strength and continuous support than want of skill. He saw that so long as a European Company held their possessions or carried on trade at the pleasure of capricious and ephemeral Indian governments, the position was in the highest degree precarious. The right method, he argued, was to assert independence, to strike in for mastery, and to strike down any European rival who crossed his path; and if the English had not been too strong for him he might have succeeded. He made the commonplace mistake of affecting ostentatious display and resorting to astute intrigues in his dealings with the Indians; whereas a European should meet oriental not with their weapons, but with his own. His claim to be recognized as Nawab of the Carnatic, under patents of doubtful authenticity, was a grave political blunder, since it was quite impossible for the English to acquiesce in a position that would have placed their settlements in perpetual jeopardy". Again, "We may regard him, nevertheless, as the most striking figure in the short Indian episode of that long and arduous contest for transmarine dominion which was fought out between France and England in the eighteenth century, although it was far beyond his power to influence the ultimate destiny of either nation in India, and although the result of his plans was that 'we accomplished for ourselves against the French exactly everything that the French intended to accomplish for themselves against us. It is certain, moreover, that the conception of an Indian empire had already been formed by others beside Dupleix, and that more than one clearheaded observer had perceived how easily the whole country might be subdued by a European power".

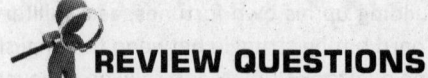

REVIEW QUESTIONS

1. Give an account of the three Carnatic Wars.
2. Explain the positions of the English and French on the eve of the Carnatic Wars.
3. When the state of Hyderabad was created? What was its importance?
4. Describe the causes that were responsible for the success of the English and failure of the French in the Deccan.
5. Give an estimate of Dupleix.
6. Write short notes on the following:
   (a) First Carnatic War
   (b) Second Carnatic War
   (c) Third Carnatic War
   (d) Dupleix
7. The French and English companies fought the three Carnatic Wars in the Deccan and these wars sealed the fate of the French in the Deccan. Comment.
8. Throw light on the establishment of the supremacy of the English in the Deccan.

SUGGESTED READINGS

Cambridge, R.O.: *Account of the War in India* (1761).
Cultru: *Dupleix* (1901).
Dodwell, H.H.: *Dupleix & Clive* (1920).
Jouveau-Dubreuil: *Dupleix* (1941).
Lawrence: *Narrative of Anglo-French Conflicts.*
Malleson, G.B.: *Final French Struggles in India and in the Indian Seas.*
Malleson, G.B.: *History of the French in India.*
Mukherjee, Rama Krishna: *The Rise and Fall of the East India Company.*
Sen, S.P.: *The French in India, 1763-1816.*
Thompson, Virginia: *Dupleix and His Letters* (1933).

4 The English in Bengal from 1757 to 1772

LEARNING OBJECTIVES

- Know about the Black-Hole Tragedy
- Review the policies and reforms of the Nawabs of Bengal from 1757 to 1772
- Assess the impact of the battles of Plassey and Buxar on the rise of the English in Bengal

After the death of Aurangzeb, the Mughal empire began to disintegrate and various parts of the empire became independent under different heads. In the case of Bangal, Ali Vardi Khan made himself independent.[1] He was possessed of a lot of resourcefulness, and uncommon ability. The Marathas gave him a lot of trouble but ultimately he made peace with them by handing over to them the province of Orissa (now Odisha). He also promised to pay a sum of ₹12 lakhs a year as Chauth. He maintained friendly relations with the Englishmen. However, he did not allow them to fortify their settlements. He continued to rule up to 1756.

After the death of Ali Vardi Khan, his grandson called Siraj-ud-Daula became the Nawab of Bengal. He was a young man of hardly 24. He was not only self-willed but also self-indulgent. Soon after his succession to the throne, the young Nawab came into conflict with the English in Bengal. There were many causes for this rupture. In anticipation of the breaking out of the Seven Years' War, the English in Bengal began to fortify their settlements. As they did so without the permission of the Nawab, the latter ordered them to demolish the same. However, the English refused to do so and this provided a ground of complaint to the Nawab. Moreover, the English took up the cause of Shaukat Jang who was a rival of Siraj-ud-Daula. The English also gave shelter to a rich merchant of Bengal and refused to hand him over to the Nawab even when the latter made a demand to that effect. It was also found that the Englishmen were abusing the trade privileges which were given to them by the Government.

---

[1] Ali Vardi Khan was a Turk, who had come to India and accepted service in Bengal in 1726. He was clever in the art of war and diplomacy. He was calculating in his manoeuvres. He soon rose to the position of a principal military officer of Bengal and secured for himself the Government of Bihar. He earned the good opinion of the Delhi Durbar by his work and was given the title of Mahabat Jung. He took advantage of the weakness of the Mughal Government and marched from Patna upon Murshidabad. A battle was fought in 1740 in which Ali Vardi Khan was successful. Thus, he became the Nawab of Bengal in 1740. After taking possession of the accumulated wealth at the Capital, he paid two crores of rupees to the Mughal emperor and got from him the confirmation of his appointment.

BLACK-HOLE TRAGEDY

"The result of all this was that Siraj-ud-Daula captured the English factory at Kasim Bazar and also took possession of the city of Calcutta (now Kolkata). One hundred and forty-six persons including one woman were captured and shut up in a very small room at night. The heat was so great and the space was so small that 123 of them were suffocated to death. Only 23 survived and one of them was Holwell. This incident is known as the Black-hole Tragedy.

There has been a lot of controversy as to whether the Black-hole tragedy was a reality or a myth. It is maintained by some historians that the so-called Black-hole tragedy never took place. It is pointed out that it is physically impossible to shut up 146 persons in a room which is only 22 ft. long and 14ft. wide. Moreover, the contemporary Muslim accounts such as Seir Mutaqhrein and Riyas-us-Salatin do not mention this incident at all. It is pointed out that That the of the Black-hole tragedy was invented merely for the purpose of arousing the indignation of the Englishmen in India and that purpose was amply served. Holwell is the only person who makes a mention of this tragedy and he is hardly reliable. Probably, he did so for the purpose of getting promotion.

Whatever the truth, when the news of the Black-hole tragedy reached Madras (now Chennai), the Englishmen were indignant. At once Admiral Watson and Clive were sent to Bengal to have revenge for the Black-hole tragedy. They were able to capture Calcutta without much difficulty. Siraj-ud-Daula attacked Calcutta and there was an indecisive battle. However, peace was restored and the Nawab restored the privileges of the English Company. The latter were also allowed to fortify Calcutta (now Kolkata). As the Seven Years' War had broken out, the English captured Chandranagar from the French.

Although outwardly Clive had made peace with Siraj-ud-Daula, he was determined to have revenge for the Black-hole tragedy. He hatched a conspiracy against the Nawab. Rai Durlab, the Treasurer of the Nawab, Mir Jafar, the Commander-in-Chief of the Nawab's forces, and Jagat Seth, the richest banker of Bengal, were induced to revolt against the Nawab. The details of the conspiracy were settled through Amin Chand. It was decided that Clive was to march at once to Plassey. Mir Jafar was to desert the Nawab and join Clive with all the forces under his command. The Nawab was to be deposed and Mir Jafar was to be put in his place.

However, when all the details were settled, Amin Chand threatened to divulge the whole conspiracy unless he was paid a sum of ₹30 lakhs. He also wanted that amount to be entered into the treaty. When Clive came to know of this demand, he made up his mind to deal with Amin Chand in the way he deserved. He got two copies of the treaty prepared. One was on white paper and the other was on red paper. In the treaty on the white paper there was no mention of the payment of ₹30 lakhs to Amin Chand. The treaty on the red paper provided for that amount. When Clive asked Admiral Watson to sign the false treaty, he refused. The result was that Clive himself forged the signatures of Watson on the false treaty. The action of Clive has been universally condemned but he defended it on the ground of expediency.

BATTLE OF PLASSEY

When everything was ready, Clive wrote a letter to Nawab Siraj-ud-Daula complaining of the grievances of the Englishmen in Bengal. He marched towards plassey at the head of his army. To begin with, the situation seemed to be very serious for Clive. He was advised not to fight. However, he made up his mind to give battle to the enemy. His artillery created confusion in the ranks of the enemy. At this time, Mir Jafar joined Clive. As soon as this happened, the battle was over. Clive got a cheap and decisive victory. Siraj-ud-Daula ran away to Murshidabad and from there to Patna. However, he was captured and put to death by Miran, the son of Mir Jafar.

The result of the battle of Plassey was that Mir Jafar was put on the throne of Bengal. He gave 24 Parganas and one crore of rupees to the Company. He also gave presents to other English officers of the Company. The share of Clive was £334,000.

According to Admiral Watson, the battle of Plassey was of "extraordinary importance not only to the Company but to British nation in general". The importance of the battle to the English has been described in these words by a contemporary: "Many of those who would have totally lost the fruits of long labour and various hardships, and who must have been beggars if subject to any other power, are again easy in their fortunes, and some of them have already transported their effects to their native country; the proper return for the assistance they derived from her maternal affection; and as these events have distinguished the present age and present administration, so their effects will probably be felt in succeeding times. The Company, by an accession of territory, has an opportunity of making an ample settlement; which under proper management, may not only be extremely serviceable to her, but also to the nation; and having a revenue from these lands, the mint at Calcutta (now Kolkata), and the lease of saltpetre at Patna, which amounts on the whole to one hundred thousand pounds a year, there is a provision against future dangers upon the spot, and without further expense".

The defeat and humiliation of the Governor of an Indian Province by the English Company added to its prestige and strength. Moreover, the battle of Plassey demonstrated the utterly corrupt political life in Bengal. It also shows that the Hindus were absolutely dissatisfied with the Muslim rule in the province and were prepared to make common cause with anybody who may be able to end the Muslim rule. However, when all has been said, it cannot be maintained that the battle of Plassey firmly established the British power in India or in Bengal. The British had still to fight for another 50 years or more to secure that position.

MIR JAFAR (1757-60)

Mir Jafar was the Nawab of Bengal from 1757 to 1760. He was neither brilliant nor active. He had not the capacity to carry on the administration of the province with his own hands. Throughout this period, he was merely a figurehead and the real power was in the hands of Clive. Moreover, he was surrounded on all sides by difficulties. He had no money in the treasury. When he ascended the throne, he had not enough even to meet his previous commitments. As a matter of fact, the English Company had to agree that one-half of the amount should be paid by 31st of October, 1757, and the "remainder to be paid within the compass of three years by equal payments every six months". At first, the Company received ₹72,71,660. On 9th August, 1757, ₹16,55,358 more were received. On 30th August 1957, gold, jewels and cash amounting to ₹15,99,737 were received by the Company. The other members of the Calcutta Council got huge amounts. The result of all this was that Mir Jafar was worried by the problem of finance. He had no money even to pay the soldiers and some of them mutinied. The English Company also pressed him for the payment of the instalments but he expressed his inability to do so.

Mir Jafar made a mistake in trying to crush such Hindu officers as Durlabhrai and Ramnarain. This led to a lot of discontentment in the country. Through the efforts of Clive, a conciliation was brought about between Mir Jafar on the one hand and Durlabhrai and Raja Ramnarain on the other.

Mir Jafar had to meet the danger from the Dutch. The real cause of the Dutch trouble was their jealousy of the British influence in Bengal. Although they had remained neutral when the English and the Nawab fought, they were feeling worried about their own future in the province. "The Dutch were in fact in the same position in Bengal now, as the English would have been in South India had Saunders done nothing to counteract the schemes of Dupleix. Bisdom and Vernet, the Dutch leaders, have therefore the same justification for attempting to overthrow the English supremacy as Saunders and Clive have for contesting that of the French in the South".

In 1759, six or seven Dutch vessels with 300 European and 600 Malayan soldiers appeared in the Ganges. The English also got ready to meet them. The Dutch were defeated at Bidderra by Colonel Forde. The Dutch fleet was also defeated and captured. They made peace with the English. They acknowledged themselves as the aggressors and agreed to pay costs and damages. At this stage, Miran, the son of Mir Jafar, also appeared on the scene. He was indignant against the Dutch. However, he "received their deputies; and after severe alteration forgave them and promised ample protection in their trade and privileges on the following terms that they shall never initiate war, introduce or enlist troops, or raise fortifications in the country; that they shall be allowed to keep up one hundred and twenty-five European soldiers, and no more, for the service of their factories at Chinsura, Kasimbazar and Patna; that they shall forthwith send their ships and remaining troops out of the country; and that a breach of any one of these articles shall be punished with utter expulsion".

After the battle of Bidderra, the Dutch were not able to make any headway in India. Their existence in India was absolutely dependent on the goodwill of the English.

INVASION OF ALI GOHOUR

Ali Gohour was the eldest son of the Mughal emperor, Alamgir. He revolted his father and invaded Bihar. He was assisted by Mohammad Quli Khan, the first cousin of Shuja-ud-Daula of Oudh and the Subedar of Allahabad. Ali Gohour advanced up to Patna and besieged the same. However, he was defeated by Clive. For this help, Clive got from Mir Jafar the revenues of the land south of Calcutta. This came to be known as Clive's Jagir. In 1760, Ali Gohour who had become Emperor Shah Alam, attacked again but was defeated. According to Sarkar, "All of his hopes of independence crushed, and in utter penury and lack of supporters, the sovereign of the Delhi empire now sued for the mercy of the English".

According to P. E. Roberts, "**A comparison of the position in 1756 with that, in 1760** reveals beyond all possibility of cavil the magnitude of his achievement. In 1756 the British in Bengal, though the most prosperous European community in that province of the empire, were regarded merely as a body of merchants with one rich settlement, a few territorial rights in the villages round Calcutta, and some up-country agencies or factories at Kasimbazar, Dacca, Balasore, Jagdea, and Patna. Though shrewd observers, such as Bernier the French physician at the end of the seventeenth century, and Colonel Mill about ten years before Plassey, had seen and recorded their opinions that Indian armies would be helpless before trained European troops, the British had never yet dreamt of challenging the power of the Nawab of Bengal. They had submitted with occasional protests to Ali Vardi Khan's strict and irksome control. It was necessary to keep on good terms with him, for the up-country factories were quite unfortified, and it was the practice of the Nawabs in any serious dispute to blockade them and stop all trade till submission ,was made. By 1760 the position was entirely altered. The British were supreme in Bengal. The French and Dutch were impoverished and reduced; their military and political power was gone. The titular Nawab of the province was little more than the creature and protege of the company. British influence extended outwards from Calcutta through Bengal and Bihar to the southern boundary of Oudh. The possession of this rich country also completely altered the English position in Madras. This tremendous change was almost entirely the work of Clive. He was throughout the moving spirit. The more closely the contemporary records are examined, the more clearly his immense energy, masterful will, and dominating influence over his colleagues stand out".

DEPOSITION OF MIR JAFAR

There were many causes which were responsible for the deposition of Mir Jafar in 1760. His treasury was empty and he had no money to pay either to the Company in the form of instalments or bribes to the servants of the Company. The servants of the Company also thought that if there was a change of Government in Bengal, there was every likelihood of their getting presents or bribes from the new successor. The invasions of Ali Gohour and the Dutch had also cost Mir Jafar a lot of money. When the Marathas attacked Bengal, he had again to ask for the English help. However, every intervention on the part of the English Company "made the control of the Company over Bengal more unmistakable and the restraining of its servants more difficult; while the burden of maintaining these troops formed a heavy drain on the Company's resources and Mir Jafar, whose treasury was exhausted, could not defray those charges".

The situation in Bengal became desperate after the death of Miran, the son of Mir Jafar. Mir Kasim, the son-in-law of Mir Jafar, began to aspire to be the Nawab of Bengal. He had already given proof of his intelligence as the Faujdar of Rangpur and Purniah. He was able to win over' the Calcutta Council. He entered into a treaty with the English Company in September 1760. By this treaty, he agreed to give to the English Company the three districts of Burdwan, Midnapore and Chittagong. He also agreed to pay immediately the arrears of money due from Mir Jafar to the English Company. He also promised to pay ₹5 lakhs towards the Carnatic wars. He agreed to pay £50,000 to Vansittart, £27,000 to Holwell and £25,000 to the other members of the Calcutta Council.

When all this was settled between the Calcutta Council and Mir Kasim, Vanittart went to Murshidabad to secure the consent of Mir Jafar. The latter strongly objected to the new arrangement. However, he found that his objections were of no avail. He declared, "His life would not be worth a day's purchase once Mir Kasim had been recognised and he would rather retire to Calcutta than continue to be the Nawab on such terms". Mir Jafar left the throne and went away to Calcutta. There he began to live as a pensioner of Mir Kasim. It cannot be denied that the deposition of Mir Jafar was "in breach of a treaty founded on the most solemn oaths". The members of the Calcutta Council deserve all the condemnation. They were bound to support him by "the most solemn ties". His deposition was "an indelible stain upon our national character". Perhaps, Mir Jafar deserved this fate. He himself had betrayed his master in 1757.

MIR KASIM (1760-63)

It is admitted on all hands that Mir Kasim was the most efficient of all the Nawabs of Bengal from 1756 onwards. He had given a proof of his administrative ability as a Faujdar. He was the man who could win over people by his personality. His contemporaries have praised his qualities of head and heart. According to Vansittart, "he discharged the Company's debt and the heavy arrears of his army, retrenched the expenses of his court which had consumed that income of his predecessors and secured his own authority over the country by reducing the power of the Zamindars who were before continual disturbers of the peace of the province". Ghulam Hussain has paid a tribute to Mir Kasim in these words: "In unraveling the intricacies of affairs of government and especially the knotty mysteries of finance; in examining and determining private differences; in establishing regular payment for his troops and for his household; in honouring and rewarding men of merit and men of learning, in conducting his expenditure exactly between the extremities of parsimony and prodigality; and in knowing intuitively where he must spend freely and where with moderation,—in all these qualifications, he was an incomparable man indeed and the most extraordinary prince of his age".

Mir Kasim made a very good beginning. He suppressed the rebellious zamindars of Bengal and Bihar, who had challenged the authority of the Nawab on previous occasions. He forced the old officers to give up the money which they had misappropriated. He levied some Abwabs or additional cesses. He tried to organise his army in the same way as the Europeans did. He made arrangements for the manufacture of fire locks and guns at Monghyr.

Mir Kasim transferred his capital from Murshidabad to Monghyr. Many reasons have been suggested for the change. The Nawab required a strongly fortified place for his permanent residence and Murshidabad did not serve that purpose. Monghyr could put at his disposal a satisfactory fort which by means of necessary improvement could be made stronger and more serviceable. The Nawab hoped to start at Monghyr with a clean slate as he would be absolutely free from the atmosphere of the old capital, its intrigues and corruption. Murshidabad was the centre of late Nawabs and was still associated with their names. The vanity of Mir Kasim required some new place where he could inaugurate his new regime. The transfer had both spectacular and psychological aspects. Moreover, there was a suspicion in the mind of Mir Kasim that Mir Jafar would be restored by the Company sooner or later and the attitude of Ellis and the members of the opposition in the Council deepened his suspicion. Under the circumstances, the Nawab may have considered it prudent to leave the old capital and settle at a place which was far away from Calcutta so that if Mir Jafar was reappointed; he may be able to offer resistance or escape to Oudh. The Nawab also wanted to remain at a safe distance from Calcutta so that there may be less of supervision and interference from the English side and he may be able to develop an army without hindrance with a view to establishing his complete independence by ultimately overthrowing the power of the English.

After removing his capital from Murshidabad to Monghyr, the Nawab seriously turned his attention to the subject of private inland trade of the servants of the Company. By a Firman of 1717, the English Company had been given the privilege of free seaborne trade. However, the servants of the Company had taken advantage of the chaotic condition in the country and started abusing the privilege by extending the same to the private trade of all kinds. As the Nawab was in need of money and he found that he was being deprived of a lot of his revenues on account of the illegal private trade carried on by the servants of the Company he decided to stop the same. Under instructions from the Nawab, his officers in the districts began to stop the boats belonging to the English merchants in spite of their having Dastaks with them. The English men protested. The Chief and Council at Dacca wrote thus in October 1762: "At every Chokey our boats are stopped, the people insulted, and the flag used with the utmost and most gross contempt". In the same month, the Chief and Council at Chittagong wrote thus: "Our business is entirely put to a stop by the Nawab's people and our boats not suffered to pass the Chokeys, the zamindars demanding very considerable duties to be paid to them, declaring that they have orders from Cossim Allee Cawn so to do". A report from Lakhipur was to the following effect: "Within these few days, every boat which we have sent out of the river has been stopped at the different Chokeys, notwithstanding they have the Chiefs Dustuck". The Faujdar of Katwa stopped 150 boats belonging to the English gentlemen although they had the Dustucks of the Company. All these facts indicated that the Nawab had decided to stop the duty-free trade of the servants of the Company.

All sorts of obstructions to the trade of the Company came to be reported. Ellis complained of the interference of the local Amil with the weavers and bleachers in their business at Jahanabad. The Ziladars of the Nawab were instructed to direct the ryots not to have any dealings with the English. The Nawab suddenly multiplied the number of customs stations in the country with a view to checking the private trade of the English. New stations were established in places where there was none before. The number of soldiers stationed at the Chaukis was increased so that English boats could be stopped effectively. The Nawab also complained of the increase in a number of factories of the company.

The most serious charge of the Nawab was against the rapacity of the Gumashtahs of the Company. About them, he wrote thus: "The Gumashtahs who have gone into the country on the part of your gentlemen, regardless of what anyone says to them, insolently use violent means to carry on their traffic, and whenever a gauge or golah has been established, they act as Zemindars, Taalookdars and renters, and leave my officers no authority; and besides this, they send other people's goods with their own, under the protection of their dustucks". The allegations of the Nawab were substantially correct. The Gumashtahs were generally a set of the worst type of rascals whose oppressive conduct was an open scandal. Their masters usually supported them. Assured of sympathy and assistance, the English agents practised the worst tyranny wherever they went. They compelled the ryots to sell their goods below the market rate and purchase the commodities they had brought at very high prices. They forcibly exacted large presents from the people and thus plundered them under this pretext. They sold dustucks to private merchants for money. Sergeant Brego wrote thus in May 1762: "A gentleman sends a Gumashtah here to buy or sell; he immediately looks upon himself as sufficient to force every inhabitant, either to buy his goods or sell him theirs, and on refusal a flogging, or confinement immediately ensues. Before justice was given in the public cutcherree, but now every Gumashtah has become a judge and every one's house a cutcherree; they even pass sentences on the Zemindars themselves and draw money from them by pretended injuries". The Faujdar of Dacca wrote thus in September 1762: "The Gumashtahs of Luckypoor and Dacca factories oblige the merchants, etc., to take tobacco, cotton, iron and sundry other things at a price exceeding that of the bazar and then extort the money from them by force; besides they take direct money from the peons and make them pay a fine for breaking their agreement. By these proceedings the Aurangs and other places are ruined. The Gumashtahs of Luckypoor factory have taken the taalookdars taalooks from "the tahsildar by force for their own use and will not pay the rent. By these disturbances, the country is ruined and the ryots cannot stay in their houses, not pay they malgujaree". In April 1762, Mr. Hastings wrote thus: "I beg leave to lay before you a grievance which calls for redress and will, unless duly attended to, render ineffectual any endeavours to create a firm or lasting harmony between the Nawab and the Company. I mean the oppressions committed under the sanction of the English name. This evil, I am well assured, is not confined to our dependents alone, but is practised all over the country by people falsely assuming the habits of our sepoys, or calling themselves our Gumashtahs". According to Verelst himself, "English agents or Gumashtahs, not contented with injuring the people trampled on the authority of the government, binding and punishing the Nawab officers wherever they presume to interfere".

The disputes arising out of the private trade of the English gentlemen became so serious and frequent that a conflict between the Nawab and the Company was imminent. There were complaints and counter-complaints. The only alternative to war was a compromise and Mr. Vansittart decided to visit Monghyr to settle the points of dispute amicably. When Vansittart reached Monghyr in November 1762, he and his party were treated "with all the usual marks of respect and friendship". The Nawab related to Vansittart his grievances. He contended that the private trade of the servants of the Company was not covered by the Firmans of Company. His administration was adversely affected by the private trade and it was difficult for him to maintain law and order in the country. He was suffering a heavy loss in his customs duty. Under the protection of the name of the Company innumerable persons passed their goods duty-free. The prestige of his government suffered on account of the irregularities of private trade. The Gumashtahs and servants of the Company oppressed the people. The gentlemen of the factories held farms, taaluqs, ganjs and golas. They borrowed from and lent to the people. They gave protection to his dependents. They coined money at different places. They used force in the purchase and sale of goods.

The Nawab demanded the total abolition of private trade of English gentlemen but Vansittart had no authority to give his approval without the consent of the Council. In spite of that, Vansittart agreed to surrender the right of the servants of the Company to trade duty-free. Vansittart also agreed that the Chiefs of the factories were to be instructed not to oppress their ryots and protect their dependents. The Faujdars were to be permitted to try any offending Gumashtah. The Chiefs of Chittagong and Lakhipur were not to work the saltpans themselves. The Chiefs and Gumashtahs of the factories were not to rent or purchase any land nor lend to or borrow from the zamindars and officers of the government. The Chiefs and Gumahstahs of the factories were not to obstruct the Dallals and weavers of the government. The billion of the English gentlemen and Gumashtahs was not to be coined in the English mints. It was agreed that only the export or import trade of the Company was to be duty-free. For the inland trade, the Dastak of the Company was not to be granted. Duties were to be paid according to the fixed rate on all goods meant for the inland trade. Duties were to be paid only once before the despatch of goods. The goods were not to be retained after the Dastak was examined by the Chaukidars. If any person was without a Dastak or used fraudulently the Dastak of the Company, his goods were to be confiscated. The Gumashtahs were not to use force in buying or selling and were to bring all their complaints to the Faujdars instead of taking the law into their own hands.

Dr. Nandlal Chatterji has criticised the deal made by Vansittart with the Nawab on many grounds. According to him, Vansittart showed great imprudence in divulging his plan to the Nawab before discussing it in the Council. He ought to have anticipated opposition from his colleagues. He should not have forgotten that he had no authority to make fundamental changes on behalf of the Council. He unwisely submitted to the desire of the Nawab to control the Gumashtahs and other subordinates of the Company through the Faujdars. He should not have agreed to the stoppage of the making of the coins of the Company at different mills. No clear-cut distinction was made between the trade of the Company and that of its servants. Vansittart made a mistake in accepting a gift from the Nawab and this could easily be interpreted as a bribe from the Nawab for the favours given to him.

The Council at Calcutta rejected the agreement arrived at between Vansittart and Mir Kasim. The result was that the Nawab decided to abolish the duties altogether. The English clamoured against this and insisted upon having preferential treatment as against other traders. Ellis, the chief of the English factory at Patna, asserted that he considered it to be the rights and privileges of the English and even made an attempt to capture the city of Patna. However, his attempt failed and the garrison was destroyed. This led to the outbreak of war between the English and Mir Kasim in 1763. According to Ramsay Muir, Ellis deliberately aimed at war "in order, that the obstacle to the private traffic of himself and his friends might be removed".

In June 1763 Major Adams was sent to fight against Mir Kasim. Many battles were fought with the Nawab's troops and most important of them were those at Katwah, Giria, Suti and Udaynala.

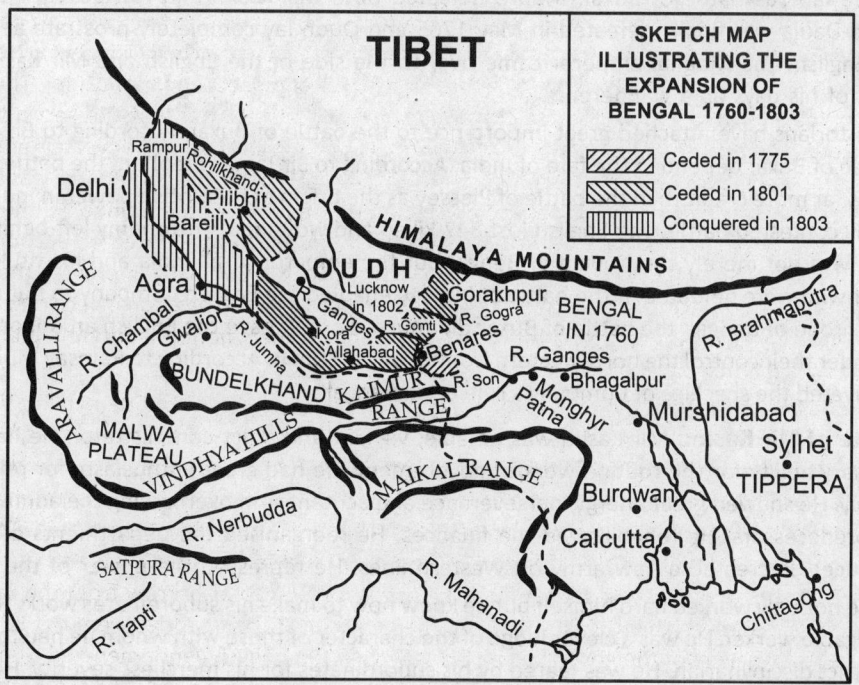

When Mir Kasim found his cause hopeless, he proceeded towards Patna. In despair, he ordered the Indian prisoners to be put to death and some of them were Raja Ramnarain, Raja Rajballabh, etc. Then came the turn of the European prisoners. He ordered his officers to kill all the European prisoners. However, their reply was as follows: "No. Turn them out with arms in their hands and we will fight them to death. We are soldiers and not executors". However, that work was done by a German named Walter Rheinhardt. He is better known by the name of Somru. He ordered his soldiers to mount the roofs of the prison and fire on the prisoners. The result was that not a single man was saved.

Even before the defeat of Mir Kasim, Mir Jafar had already been declared as the future Nawab of Bengal. This had been done in July 1763. The new Nawab agreed that "the English shall carry on their trade by means of their own Dustuks, free from all duties, taxes and impositions, in all parts of the country excepting the salt on which a duty of two and a halt per cent is to be levied on the Rowna of Hoogly market price; wherein, it is further agreed, that the late Perwannahs issued by Kossim Ally Khan granting to all merchants the exemption of all duties for the space of two years shall be reversed and called in and the duties collected as before". Mir Jafar also promised to make compensation for all losses incurred by the English Company. However, his throne was not a bed of roses. The evils of Dustuks began to increase. Even the revenues of the State could not be collected.

Battle of Buxar. After his defeat in 1763, Mir Kasim went away to Oudh. Emperor Shah Alam was also in Oudh. The Nawabs of Oudh looked forward to Bengal for their expansion and consequently a conflict between the Nawab of Oudh and the English was inevitable. Mir Kasim helped the Nawab Vazir of Oudh by suppressing the rebels of Bundelkhand. It was agreed between the parties that "on the Vazir's crossing the Ganga and entering the enemy's country, Mir Kasim from that day and for so long as the expedition might last, would pay him for the expenses of his army eleven lakhs of rupees per month". Some adventurous Frenchmen also joined. To begin with, there were some indecisive engagements. However, in October 1764, there took place the famous Battle of Buxar. Munro defeated both Mir Kasim and Nawab Vazir of Oudh. Shuja-ud-Daula was finally defeated in May 1765 and Oudh lay completely prostrate at the feet of the English. The Mughal emperor came over to the side of the English and Mir Kasim spent the rest of his days as a wanderer.

Historians have attached great importance to the battle of Buxar. According to Broome, on the battle of Buxar depended the fate of India. According to Sir James Stephen, the battle of Buxar deserves far more credit than the battle of Plassey as the origin of the British power in India. It was a fiercely contested battle. The English lost 847 killed and wounded. The enemy left behind 2,000 dead. It was not merely the Nawab of Bengal but the emperor of all India and his titular Prime Minister who were defeated. If the battle of Plassey enabled the English Company to put a puppet on the throne of Bengal, the battle of Buxar did much more. It gave the English an opportunity to bring under their control the northwestern frontier of the Subah. According to Ramsay Muir, "Buxar finally riveted the shackles of Company's rule upon Bengal".

Estimate of Mir Kasim. Mir Kasim was an able, vigilant and strict administrator. He had an extraordinary ability for the routine work of government. He had great enthusiasm for reform and efficiency. He showed great energy, perseverance and acuteness in overhauling the administration of his predecessors. He rehabilitated the finances. He reorganised the departments of revenue and justice. He created a new army on Western lines. He repressed the power of the barons.

He not only worked hard himself but he knew how to make his subordinates work. He was an indefatigable worker. He was a clever judge of the character of those with whom he had to deal. He was a strict disciplinarian. He was feared by his subordinates for his merciless severity. He tried to remove fraud, corruption and negligence with a heavy hand. He enforced regularity and discipline with an iron hand. According to Ghulam Hussain, the Nawab was the most remarkable prince of his age on account of his skill in technical problems of administration and finance, insight into man's character and motives, enforcement of a strict economy without appearance of parsimony and introduction of regularity in the payment of the troops.

If he had virtues, he had his shortcomings also. He lacked personal courage and a genius for war. He was vain and ambitious. At the same time he was timid and cowardly. He did not possess any military talents. In the hour of slightest danger, Mir Kasim became nervous. He could not face a crisis in a calm manner. He was a mixture of ambition and timidity.

He did not trust others. He suspected every official, high or low. Mere suspicion was enough to punish any person. Any subordinate could be imprisoned or executed for a very ordinary omission. The Nawab was so much undependable that nobody was sure of his future. Such a state of terrorism and repression could not be expected to strengthen the foundations of the State. The Nawab believed in duplicity, intrigue and treachery. Such important personalities as Ramnarain, Rajballabh, Naubatray, Sitaram, Saadullah and Gurgin suffered at the hands of the Nawab. It is difficult to estimate the number of smaller persons who suffered at the hands of the Nawab. Everything was centralised in the hands of the Nawab and that was bound to sap the very foundations of his government.

It is pointed out that the massacre of the English prisoners at Patna was not the worst piece of brutality. Batches of Indian political prisoners were drowned in the Ganges at Monghyr with sandbags tied to their necks. According to Gentil, the Nawab defended his massacre of the English prisoners in these words: "If I fall into the hands of the English, they would not spare my life. I lose my government, but I have at any rate this compensation that my enemies will derive no satisfaction from my fall, for I shall first of all put them all to death".

The Nawab systematically oppressed the wealthy people in his realm. As a matter of fact, very few monied people were left in his kingdom. The officials of the late regime were made to hand over to the Nawab whatever they had accumulated. Most of them were imprisoned or executed after the confiscation of their entire property. It was in this way that the Nawab was able to fill his coffers. The land revenue in the country was nearly doubled. The result was that the condition of the peasants became very unhappy. The condition of the people in general also became miserable.

The Nawab suffered from all the vices of his age. He did all that he could to add new recruits to his harem. The result was that excessive dissipation broke down his health and even the best of the physicians could not restore it.

It is said that the Nawab was absolutely unscrupulous. There cannot be greater proof than the way in which he managed to bring about the deposition of his own father-in-law.

The Nawab possessed a passionate and excitable nature. He became a heartless bully. No wonder, he had hardly any friends and was hated even by his relatives. He was inwardly feared and detested by everybody.

However, the Nawab was proficient in mathematics and astrology. He spent a lot of money on scholars, poets and pious men. He wanted to be known as a great patron of learning.

We may conclude with the following words of Dr. Nandlal Chatterji: ore inhuman and cynical than the much abused Siraj-ud-Daulah, more perfidious than Mir Jafar, more aspiring and persistent than Haidar Ali more calculating and greedy than Shuja-ud-Daulah, more suspicious and exacting than Muhammad Ali, more egoistical and literary than Shah Alam, more timid and nervous than Nizam Ali, Mir Qasim lacked the impetuosity of Siraj-ud-Daulah, the indolence of Mir Jafar, the bravery of Haidar Ali, the sagacity of Shuja-ud-Daulah, the extravagance of Muhammad Ali, the chivalry of Shah

Alam, and the prudence of Nizam Ali. Mir Kasim was obviously one of the most intriguing figures among the contemporary Muslim rulers in India".

It may be noted that Mir Jafar remained the Nawab of Bengal for the second time from July 1762 to February 1765. When he died in 1765, the Calcutta Council put his second son named Najam-ud-Daulah on the throne of Bengal. However, all power passed into the hands of the English Company. By the arrangement of February 1765, the new Nawab agreed to maintain troops only for the support of his dignity, the maintenance of internal peace and the collection of revenues. The English got the right of controlling the appointment of the officers of the Nawab. At this time, the condition of Bengal was chaotic. There was anarchy, confusion, bribery, corruption and extortion everywhere. Such was the state of affairs when Clive came to India in 1765 as the Governor of Bengal for the second time.

CLIVE'S SECOND GOVERNORSHIP OF BENGAL (1765-67)

The period of second Governorship of Bengal of Lord Clive is remarkable for the successful handling of the political and administrative problems which confronted the Company in 1765. His masterly handling of the situation silenced all opposition and created an atmosphere of calm and quiet at least for some time.

The administrative reforms were rather difficult. The covenanted servants of the English Company were demoralized by the conditions under which they had been working and the facility with which they were able to make fortunes. A kind of a tradition had grown that on the occasion of every change in the government in Bengal, presents should be made to the servants of the Company. On the occasion of the accession of Najam-ud-Daulah, the son of Mir Jafar, in 1765, presents were got even from the ministers. The worst thing about the whole affair was that all this was done in the face of the specific orders from the Company prohibiting the acceptance of presents and requiring its servants to sign covenants agreeing not to accept them in future. The servants were under the impression that as Clive himself had accepted present in the past, he would not be able to take action against them. However, they were mistaken in their calculations. Clive was determined to carry out the orders of the Company. He forgot altogether that he himself was enjoying £30,000 a year from the Jagir. Clive demanded of all the civil and military servants of the Company to enter into covenants to the effect that they would not accept presents. This they did under the impression that the zeal of Clive would cool down after some time and he would modify his own orders accordingly. However, the servants of the Company found that Clive was faithful in the performance of his duties towards the Company.

When Clive came to Calcutta, he found that there was a great lack of senior servants of the Company. The reason was that the salaries of the Company's servants were hopelessly low and efficient persons were not available on those terms. He found the junior servants occupying all important jobs and making profits by selling their passes to the Indian merchants. Clive found that the office of the secretary of a department was held by a writer of three years' standing. The paymaster of the army was merely a writer. The same was the case with the office of an accountant. The intention of Lord Clive was to regulate the private trade in such a way that out of the profits, higher salaries might be given and efficient persons might be forthcoming. Although Clive was in favour of raising the salaries of the servants of the Company, he failed in his objective on account of the opposition of the Court of Directors of the Company. The result was that he had to resort to some questionable methods in order to give effect to his own scheme.

Salt was a monopoly of the Company and Lord Clive decided to administer the same and employ the profits arising out of it for the payment of additional allowances to civil and military servants. Out of the profits, the Governor was to receive £17,500 per annum, a Colonel in the army or a member of the Council £7,000, and persons occupying lower ranks were to get less money.

The starting of a trading company with the object of giving higher salaries to the servants of the Company was contrary to the orders of the Company. Clive was under the impression that the Company would ignore this action of his. However, when the Directors came to know of it, they immediately ordered its abolition. But, Lord Clive kept those orders suspended so long as he was in Bengal and hoped to procure their reversal on his return to England. As the Directors insisted, the Company had to be wound up. According to Dodwell, "In this matter Clive had been unduly blamed. His proposals amounted in reality to the continuation of the monopoly which had been customary and the assignment of the revenues so raised to the payment of establishment". Lord Clive was condemned for what Lord Cornwallis was praised later on. The mistake which Clive made was probably one of tactics.

There was a strong resistance to his reforms from the servants of the Company. When Clive thundered against the rapacity and oppression universally prevalent and declared that "every spark of sentiment and public spirit was lost and extinguished in the inordinate lust of unmerited wealth," they failed to understand as to how Clive himself was above board. An association was formed by them. Clive's entertainments were boycotted. Memorials were prepared. However, when the servants of the Company found that Clive was adamant, they submitted to their lot. The result of this was that Clive was able to clear the Aegean stables of Company's establishment.

Lord Clive had to deal with the military side of the administration also. While doing so, he had to face a difficult situation. For many years, the English Company had been trying to cut down the Bhatta or field allowances of its military officers. Those allowances were made to make good the extra cost of living in the field as compared with living in garrison. The origin of the double Bhatta could be traced to the Carnatic Wars where Chanda Sahib and Mohammad Ali paid Bhatta to the French and English officers. Likewise, Mir Jafar paid double Bhatta to the English soldiers. Mir Kasim did likewise. However, when the English Company got the Diwani of Bengal, Bihar and Orissa (now Odisha), the duty of paying double Bhatta to the soldiers fell on the shoulders of the Company. No wonder, the Directors of the Company sent instructions to reduce expenditure on that account.

Lord Clive prepared a comprehensive scheme in this connection. The troops of the Company were divided into three Brigades each consisting of one regiment of European infantry, one Company of artillery, six battalions of sepoys, and one troop of black cavalry. One Brigade was stationed at Monghyr, another at Bankipore and the third one at Allahabad. Clive laid down that the officers in the cantonment at Monghyr or Patna were to draw half Bhatta as the officers did at Trichinopoly. When they took the field, they were to draw Bhatta while within the limits of Bengal and Bihar, but if they crossed into Oudh, they were entitled to double Bhatta. For a Captain, that amounted to three, six, twelve rupees a day.

A combination was formed among the military officers to resist the enforcement of the new regulations. It was decided to resign simultaneously their commissions. They were encouraged to take this action by Sir Robert Fletcher. However, Lord Clive was determined to crush all opposition and he carried out the new regulation. He at once accepted the resignations of those who offered them and got officers from Madras (now Chennai) to replace them. Clive visited the headquarters of the three brigades in person to assure himself that the men were under control. Gradually, the officers began to quarrel among themselves and the mutiny broke down. Fletcher and six others were turned out. Those who were considered to be not guilty were allowed to return to duty on condition of signing a three years' agreement.

Clive set up a fund known as Lord Clive's Fund with a view to helping the servants of the Company at the time of financial difficulty. That fund performed a useful function till the time the

Company adopted the system of pensioning its servants. The fund was created out of the sum of ₹5 lakhs left by Mir Jafar to be given to Clive.

Dual Government of Bengal (1765-72). The system of dual Government of Bengal which was set up by Clive is not easy to explain. It was not the simple division of control over the administration of Bengal between the English East India Company and the Nawab of Bengal. The position was somewhat as follows:

The Nawab or Subedar of Bengal, as Viceroy of the Mughal emperor, exercised two functions: (1) the Diwani, i.e., revenue, and civil justice, and (2) the Nizamat, i.e., military power and criminal justice. As Sir James Stephen points out, the Nawab granted practically the Nizamat to the Company in February 1765. In August 1765, the Emperor Shah Alam granted the Diwani to the Company. The Company thus held the Diwani from the emperor and the Nizamat from the Subedar. So far the position was clear. But the difficulty was created by the fact that the servants of the East India Company as yet did not undertake their duties as Diwan or Nizam in their own person. The nominal head of the administration was a Deputy Naib or Nawab whom the Nawab bound himself to appoint with their sanction. A similar Deputy was appointed for Bihar. But the whole administration was carried on for many years through the agency of the native servants. However, in 1769 English supervisors (afterwards called Collectors) were appointed to control the native revenue officers. But instead of improving matters, they only made confusion worse confounded and corruption also increased.

Such was the Dual system of Government set up in Bengal by Clive. It might be asked asked as to why it was that Clive hesitated to take over the administration of the province when the could have done that so easily. The Nawab was merely a puppet in the hands of the British. As a matter of fact, all power was in the hands of the British. As a matter of fact, all power was in the hands of the British. He was their creature and depended upon them for this existence. Clive would have rendered a great service by abolishing his office and assuming the control of the government directly, rather than agree to play the role of the wirepuller from behind the scene. As pointed out the Dodwell in **Cambridge History of India**, the great disadvantage of the scheme was that it separated power from responsibility. The English were given control over the province but they did not feel any responsibility for its administration and could not be held responsible for anything done badly. This thing was made clear when in 1770, a severe famine broke out in Bengal. The servants of the company did not feel any duty towards the people who were left to die in thousands. That appalling distress can be attributed to the system of Dual government set up by Clive. P. E. Roberts criticises the system in these words: "The unfortunate divorce of power from responsibility soon caused a recrudescence of the old abuses".

But as Dodwell points out, the system as set up in 1765 had certain immediate advantages. It was suited to the exigencies of the time. It secured that control over the Nawab which was regarded as the most pressing need of the time. It also secured protection against the complaints of the foreign powers and demands of the Home Government. Clive still remembered how the ostensible assumption of power contributed to produce the unyielding opposition of the English to the schemes of Dupleix. The writs of the emperor of Parwanas of the Nawab, though valueless without the support of the English power, could not be fully dominion at Paris or the Hague without a serious breach of diplomatic etiquette. It was thought that something less than the assumption of full dominion would be less likely to excite legal difficulties in England to provoke the interference of Parliament. "In short, the grant of the Diwani was designed to secure the full control of Bengal affairs so far as the Company's interests went without incurring the inconvenience of formal dominion". (**Dodwell**).

Lord Clive's own observations were as follows: "The first point in politics which I offer to your consideration is the form of Governments. We are sensible that since the acquisition of the Diwani the power formerly belonging to the Subah of these provinces is totally, in fact, vested in the East India Company. Nothing remains to him but the name and shadow of authority. This name, however, the shadow, it is indispensably necessary we should seem to venerate under the sanction of Subah, every encroachment that may be attempted by foreign powers can be effectively crushed, without any apparent interposition of our own authority and all real grievances complained of by them can, through the same channel, be examined into a redress. But it is, therefore, always remembered that there is a Subah and though the revenues belong to the Company, the territorial jurisdiction must still rest in the chiefs of the country, acting under him and this Presidency in conjunction".

Roberts says that even Clive would not have denied the charge that the system set up by him was not perfect. But he remarks that "Clive could not afford to indulge in counsels of perfection; he had to deal with actualities". He admitted that the Nawab had only "the name and shadow of authority," yet "this name, the shadow, it is indispensably necessary that we should venerate". Verelst tells us that it was impossible to take over the full government of the province. In the first place, the number of servants of the Company required for the task of administration was very limited. However, they were quite ignorant of the task of administration, for they were merely writers in the Company's service.

According to Dr. Nandalal Chatterji, "The double government which Clive established was both illogical and unworkable. He forgot that division of power was impossible without creating anarchy and confusion. The assumption of the Diwani of the Bengal Subah exhibited the cynical adroitness of an astute schemer rather than the foresight of a responsible administrator. It was a selfish contrivance for enjoying the spoils of office, without taking over its fundamental obligations. It was avowedly a device for hoodwinking the country powers and the foreign nations whom Clive did not want to give umbrage. He frankly justified it as an excellent screen for concealing the political revolution in Bengal. The Nawab was now a pensioner of State and had nothing but the name and shadow of authority; but Clive insisted that this name and shadow must be preserved and outwardly venerated as a convenient mask which, he thought, it would be unwise and even dangerous to throw off Diwani was therefore little more than a deceptive camouflage.

"The tragic inhumanity of the dual system resulted naturally in a complete breakdown of the internal administration. The Nawab had no power to enforce law and justice, while the English on their part disowned the responsibility of government. The result was disorder in the country. The villainy of the zamindars, and the rapaciousness of the Nawab's officials and the Company's servants knew no bounds; and the peasants, weavers and merchants were intimidated and fleeced to the utmost. The people were left virtually without appeal, and many were compelled to leave their hearths and homes in despair and became vagrants or freebooters. The country was, in short, reduced to a state of miserable desolation. At no period in the chequered annals of Bengal did the province suffer such flagrant spoliation as it did in the era of Clive".

From 1765 to 1772, the actual administration was in the hands of two Indian officials known as Naib Diwans, the Company itself being the actual Diwan. Mohammed Raza Khan was in Bengal and Raja Shitab Rai was in Bihar. In 1769 were appointed British supervisors who were given "a controlling, though not an immediate, power over the Collectors". The evil of the system was that while the Company itself was in serious financial straits, its servants were returning to England with big fortunes.

Becher, Resident at Murshidabad, wrote thus in 1769: "It must give pain as an Englishman to have reason to think, that since the accession of the Company to the Diwani, the condition of the people of this country has been worse than it was before; and yet I am afraid the fact is undoubted. The fine country which flourished under the despotic and arbitrary government, is verging towards its ruin, while the English have really so great a share in the administration".

Moreover, the Directors strongly suspected that the Naib Diwans were intercepting a large part of the revenue which would have filled the Company's treasury. Hastings was appointed in 1772 definity with a view to ending the Dual System. The Court of Directors had decided "to stand forth as Diwan". He was in fact selected to take the place of the three supervisors. "We now arm you with our full powers, wrote the Directors of the Company, "to make a complete reformation". Although he was given definite instruction on most points, it is to a certain extent true, as Lord Thinlow says, that he was ordered "to destroy the whole fabric of the double government—he was to form a system for the government of Bengal, under instructions so general, that I may fairly say the whole plan was left to his judgment and discretion".

Formally the abolition of the Dual Government did no more than that the Company should henceforth collect the revenues through the Agency of its own servants. But in reality, it meant becoming responsible for the whole of civil administration. Hastings hardly exaggerated it when he described it as "implanting the authority of the Company and the sovereignty of Great Britain, in the constitution of this country". The first step was the abolition of the offices of Naib Diwans of Bengal and Bihar, and the prosecution of Mohd. Raza Khan and Raja Shitab Rai for peculation. After undergoing a long trial and being kept in custody for rather more than a year, they were both acquitted. The trial was merely a formal affair designed indirectly to remove them. Although Warren Hastings was opposed to it, it served the purpose. "The retrospections and examinations are death to my views," said Hastings.

Thus, it was that the Dual System, which was set up by Clive, was abolished by Warren Hastings. It was not intended to last forever. It was a stop-gap. It was a make-shift agreement which aimed at tidying over the difficulties confronting the English in 1765. It was the creation of the genius of the Englishmen who believe in bit-by-bit advance. It was the policy of muddling through which, though often misunderstood, serves its purpose in the long run.

Dr. Nandalal Chatterji points out that Clive was the real founder of a regular postal system in British India. He laid the foundations on which the modern postal system was subsequently built up by his successors. The system introduced by him was mainly a continuation of the old Dak organisation of horse carriers or runners who carried letters and despatches by relays along the road from place to place. All that was required was to set up a permanent and efficient staff of runners and Clive entrusted this task to the zammdars along the postal routes. They were required to supply runners to carry the mails. However, they were allowed to claim deduction in their rents in proportion to the expenditure incurred by them for the maintenance of the runners.

In 1766, Clive arranged for a full-fledged organisation of Daks within the Bengal province and from Bengal to other presidencies. According to the new system, the Daks were to be controlled by a post-master with assistants under him. The mails from Calcutta (now Kolkata) were to be despatched from the Government House. Letters meant for despatch were to be sorted every night. The Daks were to be sent off personally by the postmaster or his assistants. Letters for different centres were to be packed in separate bags. The mail bags were to be sealed with the seal of the Company. None but chiefs of factories or Residents were to open the bags meant for their respective areas. The chiefs were to observe the same rule with respect to the letters sent down to Calcutta (now Kolkata).

The system of runners was defective and consequently there were delays in the delivery of mail bags. No wonder, new regulations were framed by Clive. According to them, the mail bags were to be numbered in regular succession. The day and hour of despatch and the number of the packets were to be noted on the tickets affixed to them. The Resident or Chief of factory was regularly to send advice of the receipt of each packet to the Resident of the stage from whence it came last. If any packets were found missing, the runners were to be punished if any one failed to give satisfactory explanation of the loss. All packets were to be sealed with the seal of the Governor and that of the Company with a view to preventing their being opened before arrival at the destination.

It is to be noted that the postal system set up by Clive was employed only for official purposes. The private individual could not make use of it.

Foreign Policy. According to Dr. Nandalal Chatterji, "The foreign policy promulgated by Clive and continued throughout the Diwani period was one of cautious moderation, based on a realistic grasp of the practical possibilities and dangers inherent in the situation facing Bengal on its vulnerable sides. The fundamental principle underlying this policy was the avoidance of conquest and dominion outside the existing limits of the province. The defence of Bengal itself was an arduous charge. 'To go farther' Clive maintained in one of his letters to the Directors, 'is in my opinion a scheme so extravagantly ambitious and absurd that no Governor and Council in their senses can adopt it, unless the whole system of the Company's interest be first entirely new-modelled'. 'The limits of the Nabob's dominions', he further argued, 'are sufficient to answer all your purposes. These, we think, ought to constitute the boundaries, not only of all your territorial possessions and influence in these parts, but of your commerce also since by grasping at more, you endanger the safety of those immense revenues, and that well-founded power, which you now enjoy, without the hopes of obtaining an adequate advantage'. This policy was grounded on the following consideration: Firstly, a distant dominion might prove to be a burden on Bengal, both financially and militarily. Secondly, hazards of war and conquest could not be conducive to the growth of the Company's trade. Thirdly, aggression outside Bengal was likely to stir up serious trouble with the country powers. Fourthly, Bengal itself produced, in the words of Clive, 'all the riches we are ambitious to possess'. Fifthly, a pacific policy alone could 'conciliate the affections of the country powers 'remove any jealousy they may entertain of our unbounded ambition,' and 'convince them that we aim not at conquest and dominion, but security of carrying on a free trade, equally beneficial to them and to us'. Sixthly, the security of Bengal was to be sought rather in the discordancy of the view and the interests of the neighbouring powers than in a policy of aggression, against them. Seventhly, if ideas of conquest were to be the basis of English policy, Clive apprehended that the Company would, by necessity, be led from one acquisition to another. Eighthly, when a sufficient number of competent English officials could not be for the administration of Bengal itself, it was out of the question to assume the responsibility of government outside the province. Lastly, Clive was aware of the fact that, owing to the enormous requirements of the Company's own trade investments, it was impossible to find money to undertake distant wars".

Clive had to deal with Nawab Wazir of Oudh and the Emperor Shah Alam. Both of them were at this time in the hands of the English and were asking for favours. Oudh lay defenceless before the British armies. On his arrival, Clive found that Vansittart had already promised Oudh to the Moghul Emperor. To Clive, it seemed to be a foolish step. It would have been impossible for Shah Alam to maintain his hold over Oudh. Negotiations were opened with Shuja-ud-Daula and ultimately the treaty of Allahabad was signed in August 1765. By this treaty, the Nawab Wazir of Oudh was confirmed in his kingdom with the exception of the districts of Kora and Allahabad, Chunar and the Zamindari of Banaras including Ghazipur. The Nawab Wazir also agreed to pay ₹15 lakhs as war indemnity. He also entered into a defensive alliance with the English Company by which the latter agreed to help him for the defence of his frontiers and the former promised to pay the cost of maintenance. The Nawab Wazir also agreed to allow the English Company to carry on trade, duty-free throughout-the whole of his dominions.

The result of the above provisions was that Oudh was created into a buffer State. The soundness of the policy of Clive with regard to Oudh can be proved from the fact that right from 1765 to 1856 this policy was continued by the successors of Clive. According to Ramsay. Muir, "It was a matter of fixed policy to maintain a close alliance with Oudh which was useful as a bulwark against the threatening power of the Marathas".

Lord Clive also made a settlement with Shah Alam. The latter was given the districts of Kora and Allahabad which were secured from the Nawab Wazir of Oudh. The English Company also promised to pay ₹26 lakhs a year as tribute. In return of all this, the Mughal emperor granted the Diwani of Bengal, Bihar and Orissa (now Odisha) to the English Company.[2]

The settlement with the Mughal Emperor was criticised from many quarters. It was pointed out that Lord Clive was over-generous to a political fugitive. Men like Sir Eyre Coote advocated a British march to Delhi and the conquest of India in the name of Shah Alam. It is true that from military point of view, such a conquest was a possibility, but Lord Clive regarded that venture to be dangerous. According to him, to go further was a scheme so extravagantly ambitious and absurd that no Governor and Council in their senses could even adopt it. The soundness of Clive's judgment was proved by the fact that it was with great difficulty that the Company was able to defend its existing frontiers against the foreigners. Had the British frontiers been extended unnecessarily in 1765, the problem of defence would have become hopeless.

According to Dr. Nandalal Chatterjee, "Clive had been sent out a second time specifically to reform the entire government of the Company, and to root out the glaring abuses in its affairs there. At the time of his arrival, he found the whole situation in the presidency to be unspeakably bad. There was nothing that bore the form or appearance of orderly administration, and gross self-seeking appeared to be rampant among all classes of the Company's servants. Luxury, rapacity and a want of principle were prevalent in every sphere. Sudden and, among many, unjustifiable acquisition of riches during the recent years seemed to have totally demoralised everybody from the senior most officials down to the writer and the ensign. Corruption was universal and contagious. Clive was fully cognisant of the extent and variety of the oppression which had brought a lasting reproach to the English name. He himself confessed that it was impossible to enumerate the complaints that had been laid before

---

[2] The text of the Firman granted by Shah Alam to the Company was as follows: "At this happy time our royal Firmaund, indispensably requiring obedience, is issued; that, whereas, in consideration of the attachment and services of the high and mighty, the noblest of exalted nobles, the chief of illustrious warriors, our faithful servants and sincere well-wishers, worthy of our royal favours, the English Company, we have granted them the Dewanny of the Provinces of Bengal, Bihar, and Orissa (now Odisha) from the beginning of the Fussel Rubby of the Bengal year 1172, as a free gift and ultumgan, without the association of any other person, and with an exemption of the payment of the customs of the Dewanny, which used to be paid by the Court. It is requisite that the said Company engage to be security for the sum of 26 lakhs of rupees a year for our royal revenue, which sum has been appointed from the Nabob Nudjum-ui-Dawla Behauder, and regularly remit the same to the royal Circar; and in this case, as the said Company are obliged to keep up a large Army for the Protection of the Provinces of Bengal, and we have granted to them whatsoever may remain out of the revenues of the said provinces, after remitting the sum of 26 lakhs of rupees to the royal Circar, and providing for the expenses of the Nizamut. It is requisite that our royal descendants, the Viziers, the bestowers of dignity, the Omrahs high in rank, the great officers, the Muttaseddees of the Dewanny, the manager of the business of the Sultanut, the Jaghirdars and Crocries, as well 'the future as the present using their constant endeavours for the establishment of this our royal command, leave the said office in possession of the said Company, from generation to generation for ever and ever. Looking upon them to be assured from dismissal or removal, they must, on no account whatsoever, give them any interruption, and they must regard them as excused and exempted from the payment of all the customs of the Dewanny and royal demands. Knowing our orders on the subject to be most strict and positive, let them not deviate therefrom".

him by the poor inhabitants of the country. There was no law and order in the province, and the Nawab's government was a mere mockery. The peasantry groaned under the merciless weight of taxation which drained the life blood from the land. Jobbery and bribery were the order of the day, and the whole burden thereof ultimately fell on the starving cultivator. The trade of Bengal was the unholy monopoly of the Company's servants and their gumashtahs, and thousands and thousands of Indian traders were reduced to poverty on account of the unashamed misuse and abuse of the privilege of the Dastak". According to the same writer, Clive was well fitted for the role of a reformer. He had the resolution of a taskmaster, the sternness of a dictator and the efficiency of a supervisor. He knew how to fight opposition, and had the capacity for enforcing obedience to himself. He could recognise merit and had the ability of choosing men with discrimination. He was energetic, courageous and well-balanced. Bold in action, he could be cool in judgment. His industry and application to business were prodigious. Possessed of the qualities that go to make a good administrator, Clive was also armed with very wide powers to deal with the situation in Bengal in any way he liked.

"But, with all his good intentions and marked abilities, Clive lamentably failed to achieve real success as an administrator. The reason is not far to seek. Being unscrupulous and devoid of a fine moral feeling, he could not set before himself a high ideal and allow himself to be guided always and in every matter by considerations of expediency alone. He took into his consideration nothing but the immediate present, and refused to look beyond it. He sought to provide for today, and he would leave tomorrow to take care of itself. If he committed grave errors, it was because he was narrow and illiberal in his outlook. The Company had secured a vast empire and an enormous revenue. It was to be expected that these circumstances should have called for a few and radical approach. Clive, however, viewed the Company's position from the point of view of a shopkeeper, and so he failed to recognise the fact that the people of Bengal had to be assured of good government".

Clive left India in 1767 when he was absolutely broken in health. He entered Parliament and was greatly admired to begin with. However, his critics started troubling him. In 1773, Colpnel Burgoyne moved a resolution in Parliament that Lord Clive, "through the influence of the powers with which he was entrusted as a member of the Select Committee and Commander-in-Chief of the British forces did obtain and possess himself of the sum of £234,000, and that in doing so the said Robert Clive abused the power with which he was entrusted to the evil example of the servants of the public and to the dishonour and detriment of the State". The resolution was not passed in this form. After a lengthy debate, the following resolution was unanimously carried: "That Robert Clive at the same time rendered great meritorious services to his country".

Estimate of Clive. A critical examination of the work done by Clive in India shows that his services to the British Empire in India were great. He was responsible for the capture and defence of Arcot in 1751. In collaboration with Lawerence, he was able to frustrate all the designs of Dupleix. He learnt his soldiering from General Lawerence and his diplomacy from Governor Saunders. In 1756, he co-operated with the Marathas to put down the pirate stronghold of Ghariah. By his victory of Plassey, he laid the foundations of the British power in Bengal and provided the basis for further expansion into the interior of the country. During his second Governorship of Bengal, he established Oudh as a Buffer State. He was not only a great warrior but also a great administrator and statesman. Lord Chatham compared Lord Clive with Frederick, the Great of Prussia. According to Burke, Lord Clive settled great foundations. When he "forded a deep water with an unknown bottom, he left a bridge for his successors over which the lame might hobble and the blind might grope their way". According to P.E. Roberts, in spite of his faults, there was the stamp of grandeur on all the words and actions of Clive. "His headlong valour

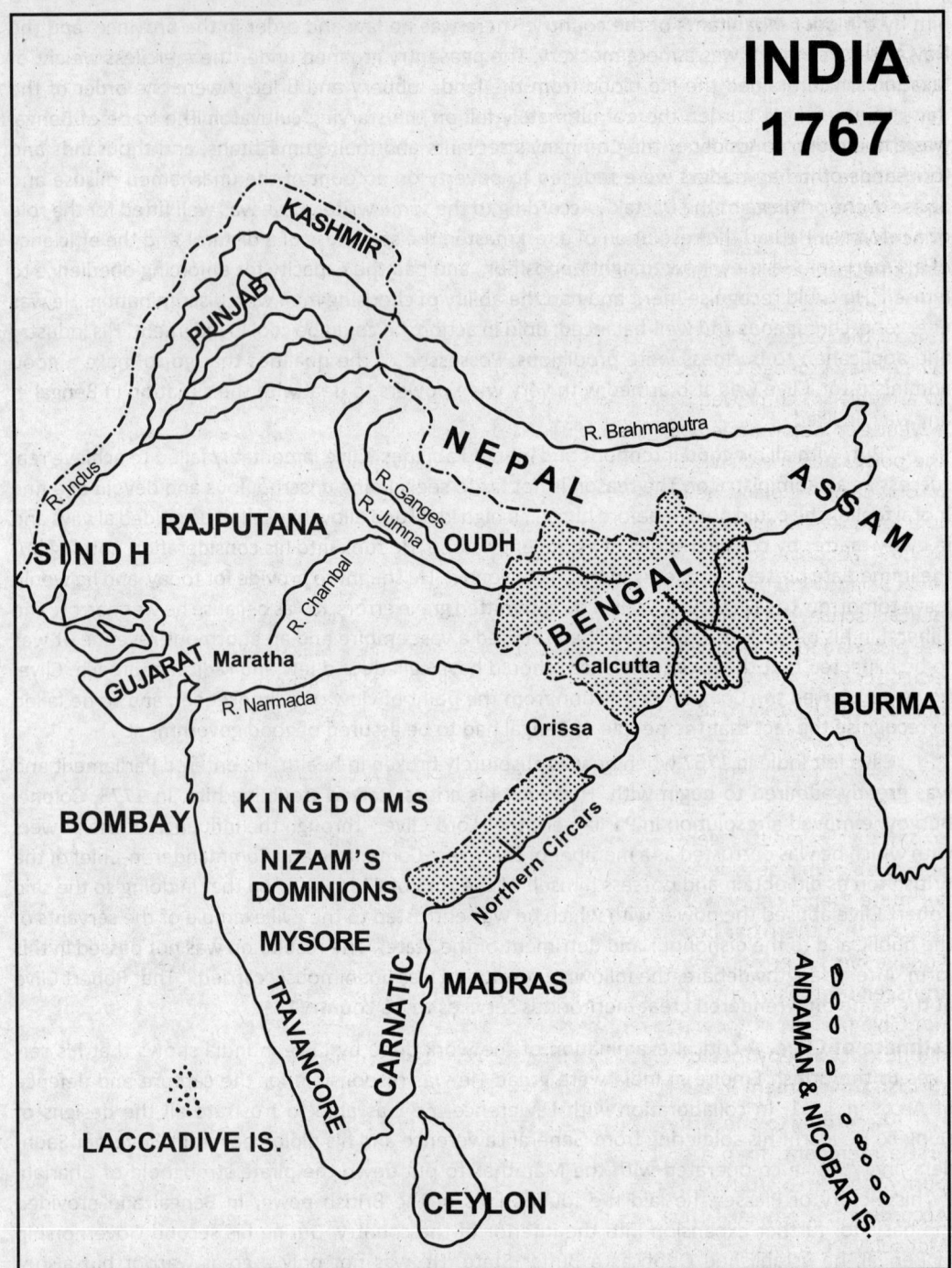

on the battlefield, his splendid daring and audacity in a political crisis, his moral courage in lacing disaffected and mutinous subordinates, his force and fire in debate, all justified the lofty verdict of Lord Macaulay that our Island scarcely ever produced a man more truly great, either in arms or in Council".

Reference may be made to two views which, however, do not do justice to Clive. According to Sir Charles Wilson, "There is little trace of skillfull combination in his plans, and on some occasions he appears to have neglected the most obvious military precautions. To seek the enemy and on finding him, to attack with headlong valour seems to have been his guiding principle, and his successes were due rather to his personal intrepidity, and to his power of inspiring large masses of men with confidence than to studied plans or dexterous manoeuvres". Horace Walpole referred to Clive in these words: "Though Lord Clive was so frank and high-spirited as to confess a whole folio of his Machiavellism, they were so ungenerous as to have a mind to punish him for assassination, forgery, and treachery and it makes him very indignant".

Lord Clive who was the founder of the British empire in India, was also the architect of the ruin of the people of Bengal. "The corruption; the oppression and the mal-administration under which they groaned for years were in no small measure due to him. His lust for gold amounted to a mania which proved contagious and Bengal was rifled of its treasures by a set of rapacious adventures whom none could control. He reduced the Nawab to a figurehead, deprived him of the power and means of doing good and shirked responsibility himself. There was nothing new or original in his plans; he followed in the footsteps of Dupleix and Bussy and his success was due to a fortuitous combination of circumstances and treachery than to genius". According to Dr. V. A. Smith: "It appears to me impossible for the impartial historian to deny that Clive was too willing to meet Asiatic intriguers on their own ground, too greedy of riches, and too much disposed to ignore delicate scruples in their acquisition. That verdict undoubtedly tarnishes his memory and precludes the historian from according to him the unqualified admiration which has heroic qualities seem to exact. His most outstanding characteristic was an inflexible will which guided his conduct to success in all affairs, whether military or civil. His military genius and his gift for leadership were abundantly manifested both in the Peninsula and in Bengal. His abilities as a statesman were exhibited chiefly in his second administration when he confronted extraordinary difficulties with unflinching courage".

According to Lord Curzon, "Great as a captain for good judges of warfare have been heard to say that in military genius he was equal to Marlborough and superior to Turenne—greater still as an administrator and statesman for he was the real founder of that Clive Service which for more than a century and a half has been the glory of British rule in India —to Clive we owe the fact that there has been an India for Englishmen to serve and for British Viceroys to govern. Forgive him his errors they were great, but never mean; remember his achievements they were transcendent; shed a tear over the final scene—it was tragic but not ignoble. After all, was not Clive the first of the Indian Pro-consuls to suffer from the ingratitude of his countrymen and did he not thereby inculcate a lesson and set an example that has taught others to endure?" (**British Government in India**, Vol. I, p. 144).

According to one writer, "Lord Clive's career in India may be briefly summed up as follows: first a merchant, then a soldier and then a statesman". "Although Clive did not completely purify the administration, yet he initiated and maintained reforms of considerable magnitude". According to Dodwell, "Clive was a man of insight rather than of foresight". According to Lord Macaulay, "Our island has seldom produced a man more truly great than Robert Clive, either in arms or in Council".

BENGAL FROM 1767 TO 1772

According to Roberts, two men of mediocre ability bridged over the interval between the departure of Clive said and the appointment of Warren Hastings as the Governor of Bengal. Those two persons were Verelst (1767-69) and Castier (1770-2). Under their weak rule, the people of Bengal suffered terribly. The defects of the double government of Bengal added to their sufferings. The English left everything to be done by the Nawab and the latter did nothing. The people suffered on account of the mistakes of omission and commission of the Company and the Nawab. It is stated that many cultivators left their fields and became vagabonds and dacoits.

The servants of the Company carried on their private trade and made fortunes for themselves. They also continued to enjoy the monopoly of trade in salt, betelnuts and other articles. There was none to interfere with the private trade of the servants of the Company and their Gomashtahs. The Government realized the seriousness of the situation but seemed to be helpless.

At the top of it, there came the great famine of 1770. Practically, one-third of the population was swept away. The famine was in a very violent form in Bihar. Raja Shitab Rai, the Deputy Governor, reported that more than fifty poor wretches died every day in the streets of Patna and sometimes the number of deaths was three times as great. Sir W. W. Hunter has described the effects of famine in these words: "The husbandmen sold their cattle; they sold their implements of agriculture; they devoured their seed-grain; they sold their sons and daughters till at length no buyers of children could be found. They ate the leaves of the trees and the grass of the fields; and in June 1770, the resident of the Darbar affirmed that the living were feeding on the dead".

When troubles come, they come in battalions. Famine was followed by fever and smallpox in a virulent form. The streets of Murshidabad were littered with heaps of the dying and the dead. Instead of helping the people of Bengal, the servants of the Company exploited the situation to the maximum. They sold the things as dear as they could. There was no remission of land revenue. If a certain portion could not be collected from certain individuals on account of their deaths, the deficiency was made up by charging the same from others. The result was that the people had to undergo untold sufferings. Nothing better could be expected from the merchants of London. This state of affairs continued till 1772 when Warren Hastings took up the reins of office as the Governor of Bengal.

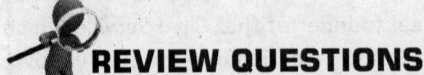

REVIEW QUESTIONS

1. What is Black-Hole Tragedy? Discuss in detail.
2. Who were the Nawabs of Bengal from 1757 to 1772? Discuss their achievements.
3. Review the policies of Mir Jafar in the history of Bengal.
4. Discuss the administrative reforms and foreign policy of Lord Clive.
5. Write a detailed note on the dual government of Bengal.
6. Analyse the condition of Bengal between 1757 and 1772.
7. Give an estimate of the work and achievement of Mir Kasim.
8. Write short notes on the following:
    (a) Battle of Plassey
    (b) Invasion of Ali Gohour
    (c) Deposition of Mir Jafar
    (d) Battle of Buxar
9. Discuss the comparative importance of the battles of Plassey and Buxar.
10. Describe how the battles of Plassey and Buxar were responsible for the rise of the English in India.

SUGGESTED READINGS

Auber, Pster: *Rise and Progress of the British Power in India* (1837).
Broome, A.: *Rise and Progress of the Bengal Army* (1850).
Chatterjj, N.L.: *Mir Qasim* (1935).
Chatterji, N.L.: *Verelst's Rule in India* (1929).
Datta, K.K.: *Bengal Subah, 1740-1770* (1936).
Dodwell, H.H.: *Dupleix and Clive* (1920).
Forrest: *Life of Clive* (1918).
Ghose, N.N.: *Memoirs of Nubkissen* (1901).
Malcolm, Sir J.: *Life of Robert Clive*.
Malleson, G.B.: *Lord Clive* (1907).
Mill, James: *History of British India*.
Muir, Ramsay: *Making of British India* (1915).
Roy, A.C.: *Mir Jafar Khan* (1953).
Sinha, N.K.: *Economic History of Bengal* (1956).
Sinha, S.C.: *Early Economic Annals in Bengal* (1927).
Sutherland, Lucy: *East India Company in 18th Century Politics* (1952).
Thornton, E.: *History of the British Empire in India* (1841).

5   Warren Hastings (1772-85)

LEARNING OBJECTIVES

- Evaluate the reforms and foreign policy of Warren Hastings
- Give an estimate of Warren Hastings as a ruler
- Throw light on the Regulating Act, 1773 and the Pitt's India Act, 1784

Warren Hastings joined the English East-India Company as a writer at the age of 18. Later on, he was appointed the Resident of Kassim Bazar where he showed that he was a man of parts. When the place was captured by Siraj-ud-Daula, he was captured but he managed to escape. In 1761, he was made a member of the Calcutta Council. He went home for a few years and came back as a member of the Madras Council. After the retirement of Cartier, he was appointed the Governor of Bengal in 1772. After the passing of the Regulating Act, he became the Governor-General of Bengal.

When Warren Hastings took up office as Governor of Bengal, he had to face many difficulties. There was chaos in the country. There was practically no administration. The servants of the Company were doing havoc to the people. While the Company was getting nothing and its treasury was empty, its servants were making fortunes. There was no administration of justice worth the name. Everything required overhauling. In addition to these troubles, the Marathas were a source of danger. The Emperor Shah Alam had left the protection of the British and gone to the Marathas. Haidar Ali in the Deccan was another threat. Warren Hastings had to meet all these difficulties.

WARREN HASTINGS' REFORMS

Administrative Reforms. Warren Hastings carried out a large number of reforms and those may be discussed under four heads, viz., administrative, revenue, commercial and judicial. As regards administrative reforms, Warren Hastings decided to put an end to the dual system of government in Bengal as established by Lord Clive in 1765. The Company was to take over the responsibility of administration of the province. It was to stand forth as Diwan and collect the revenue through the agency of its own servants. Mohammad Raza Khan and Raja Shitab Rai who were the deputy Nawabs of Bengal and Bihar were tried for peculation and removed from their offices. However, they were honorably acquitted, but the object was achieved. The treasury was shifted from Murshidabad to Calcutta (now Kolkata). The young Nawab of Bengal was put under the control of Munni Begum, the widow of Mir Jafar. His pension was reduced from 32 lakhs to 16 lakhs.

Revenue Reforms. Although the Company had got the Diwani of Bengal, Bihar and Orissa (now Odisha) in 1765, it had not taken over the work of collection of land revenue into its own hands.

The work had been left in the hands of functionaries called Amils. The Amils were no better than contractors and the tenants suffered a lot. Although supervisors had been appointed in 1769, no improvement was made. Warren Hastings appointed a Committee and its President toured certain parts of Bengal to collect information. His conclusion was that the Company must directly collect the revenue. Consequently, Warren Hastings appointed collectors for revenue collection and administration. They were to be helped by native officers. Settlement was made for 5 years with the highest bidders. To supervise the whole organisation, a Board of Revenue was established at Calcutta. The system of farming out the land to the highest bidders for 5 years was found to be defective and consequently in 1777 the old system of bidding for a year was resorted to.

As the Mughal Emperor Shah Alam had left the protection of the British, Warren Hastings stopped the payment of ₹26 lakhs of rupees a year. He also took over the districts of Kora and Allahabad from the Mugal Emperor and sold them to the Nawab Wazir of Oudh for ₹50 lakhs. He made the accounts of revenue simple and intelligible and made many provisions for the protection of the ryots. He also cut off from the list a large number of Abwabs. The Banyas were prevented from lending money to the ryots.

Commercial Reforms. He prohibited the use of Dustuks by the servants of the Company and thereby added to the revenues of the Company. A large number of custom houses or Chowkies were hampering the growth of trade in the country and consequently he abolished them. In future there were to be only 5 custom houses at Calcutta (now Kolkata), Hugli, Murshidabad, Patna and Dacca. The uniform reduction 2½ of per cent in duties on all goods except salt, betelnut and tobacco was ordered. The result of all these reforms was that trade improved. Warren Hastings boasted that "goods passed unmolested to the extremities of the province".

Judicial Reforms. Warren Hastings carried out a large number of reforms in the judicial sphere. In 1772, he provided for the collection in each district of a provincial Court of Diwani Adalat for all civil cases. Over this court presided the Collector. Provision was made for appeal to the Sadar Diwani Adalat at Calcutta which consisted of the Governor and at least two members of the Council. Provision was also made for criminal courts. In the Faujdari Adalat sat the Kadi and Mufti of the district with two Maulvis to expound the law. It was the duty of collector to see that in criminal cases evidence was duly submitted and weighed and the decision was not only fair and impartial but also given in the open court. The Faujdari Adalats were supervised by the Sadar Nizamat Adalat which was presided over by the Daroga Adalat appointed by the Nazim. The Daroga Adalat consisted of the Chief Kadi, the Chief Mufti and three Maulvis. The proceedings of the Sadar Nizamat Adalat were supervised by the Governor and the Council.

Provision was made for the improvement of procedure in the courts. The courts were not only to keep their records of proceedings but also send the same to the Sadar Diwani Adalat. The head farmers of the Parganas were empowered to try cases so that the ryots may not have to travel long distances in search of justice. Provision was made for arbitration by consent. In case of marriage, inheritance, caste and religious usage, the decision was to be given according to the Koran for the Mohammedans and Shastras for the Hindus. The decisions of the Mofussil Adalats were final up to ₹5,000. In other cases, an appeal could be taken. Faujdari Adalats were not allowed to pass death sentences. Fines over ₹100 were to be confirmed by the Sadar Adalat. Dacoits were to be executed in their own villages and their families were to be made slaves. Their villages were to be fined and the police officers who captured them, were to be given rewards. Warren Hastings made certain changes in 1774. The three provinces of Bengal, Bihar and Orissa (now Odisha) were divided into six divisions and in each of these divisions a Council consisting of 4 or 5 covenanted servants of the English Company was created. Each division consisted of many districts and a Diwan or Amil took the place of the Collector. He collected revenue but also acted as judge. Provision was also made for the Provincial Court of Appeal.

A further change in the judicial system was made in 1780. Provision was made for the establishment of a court of Diwani Adalat in every division. This court was to be presided over by the Superintendent of the Diwani Adalat. He was to be an Englishman and a covenanted servant of the Company. The Provincial Courts of Appeal were deprived of their judicial powers. Up to ₹1,000 the decision of the Courts of Diwani Adalat were to be final and if the amount involved was more, an appeal could be taken to the Sadar Diwani Adalat.

There was constant conflict between the Supreme Court of Calcutta (now Kolkata) and the executive and consequently Warren Hastings appointed Sir Elijah Impey, the Chief Justice of the Supreme Court, as the sole judge of the Sadar Diwani Adalat. Impey held this office for two years when he was made to resign on account of criticism at home. However, he was able to introduce a large number of reforms which improved the administration of justice in the Mofussil.

In 1781, it was provided that Superintendents of Diwani Adalats were also to act as magistrates. They were to assist those persons who were suspected to have committed crimes. After arrest, they were to be sent to the nearest Mofussil Faujdari Adalat for trial.

Warren Hastings created a new department at Calcutta (now Kolkata). Its head was known as the Remembrancer of Criminal Courts. He was to receive all the reports and returns from the Mofussil Faujdari Adalats. His duty was to analyse those reports and prepare extracts from them. However, that work was not very useful.

Warren Hastings' Oudh Policy. Warren Hastings continued the buffer State policy towards Oudh. He was determined to continue good relations with the Nawab on account of the danger from the Marathas. In 1772, he concluded the Treaty of Banaras by which Kora and Allahabad were sold to the Nawab of Oudh for ₹50 lakhs. If the Nawab paid a subsidy, the English Company was to lend him the aid of British troops whenever required.

THE ROHILLA WAR

The people of Rohilkhand were frequently attacked by the Marathas and consequently their ruler entered into a treaty with the Nawab Wazir of Oudh in 1772. It was agreed between the parties that if the Marathas invaded Rohilkhand, the Nawab Wazir was to help the Rohillas and get ₹40 lakhs as the price of his help. The very next year, the Marathas invaded Rohilkhand, but retired on account of the approach of British and Oudh troops. The Nawab Wazir of Oudh demanded money and the Rohillas evaded it. Ultimately, the Nawab Wazir of Oudh contracted with the English Company to bear all the expenses of war and to pay ₹50 lakhs in addition if he were given military help to conquer Rohikhand. Warren Hastings accepted the proposition. British troops were sent. Rohilkhand was conquered. Hafiz Rahmat Khan, their leader, was killed. About 20,000 Rohillas were turned out from the country. The soldier of the Nawab committed atrocities on the innocent people of Rohilkhand and the country was annexed to Oudh.

Hastings' policy towards Rohilkhand has been severely condemned and it was one of the points of his impeachment. Undoubtedly, Warren Hastings was moved by two considerations. He wanted more money for the Company and this he could get from the Nawab of Oudh. Rohilkhand occupied a strategic position and its occupation by Oudh would protect Oudh from the attacks of the Marathas. If a policy is judged by its results, Hastings' Rohilla policy was more than justified. Rohillas were not strong enough to protect themselves from the attacks of the Marathas and it would have been a folly to allow them to fall into the hands of the Marathas. That would have seriously jeopardised the safety of Bengal itself. However, it is pointed out that the Rohillas had done nothing against the Company and consequently there was no moral justification for the English help to Oudh merely for the sake of money. The British arms were prostituted for hire. Moreover, such an action was against the instructions of the Directors. Such an interference created an unfortunate precedent. Anybody could hire the services of British troops on payment of money. It is contended that "the Rohilla war should be beyond defence by any critic with principles".

TRIAL OF NAND KUMAR

Nand Kumar was a higher influential Brahman of Bengal. He not only moved in higher circles but also indulged in higher politics. He had been found guilty of carrying on intrigues with those zamindars who had revolted against the English Company.

When differences arose between Warren Hastings and the members of his Council, Nand Kumar tried to take advantage of them. He accused Warren Hastings of having been bribed to dismiss Mohd. Raza Khan and of having sold several public offices. Philip Francis read the paper of accusation in the presence of Warren Hastings. Nand Kumar requested to be heard in person in support of his accusation. Warren Hastings refused to be confronted with Nand Kumar at his own Council table. He refused to allow his Councillors to sit in judgment over him. He dissolved the meeting and departed. In his absence, the other members of the Council called in Nand Kumar and decided to go on with the charges.

However, Nand Kumar was suddenly arrested and committed to prison on a charge of forgery. The Council of the Governor-General protested and remonstrated, but a jury of the Supreme Court found Nand Kumar guilty of forgery and he was sentenced to be hanged and was actually hanged.

The legality of the trial and conviction of Nand Kumar has been questioned. The Supreme Court has been accused of committing "a judicial murder". Critics point out that both the trial and conviction were illegal. There is a controversy whether the English statute of 1728 relating to forgery was applicable to Calcutta (now kolkata) or not.

It was contended that there was a conspiracy between Sir Elijah Impey, the Chief Justice of the Supreme Court, and Warren Hastings. The conviction and execution of Nand Kumar were the outcome of that conspiracy. However, it is pointed out that Nand Kumar was not tried by the Chief Justice alone but by other judges of the Supreme Court as well. He was held guilty not only by all the judges of the Supreme Court but also by the members of the jury. However, it cannot be denied that the judges of Supreme Court examined the defence witnesses in such a way that the whole of the defence of Nand Kumar collapsed. That was an unusual procedure to adopt. Moreover, the judges of the Supreme Court rejected the application of Nand Kumar for leave to appeal to the King-in-Council. Although this was a very suitable case for leave to appeal, the same was refused. All these facts pointed out to the mala fides of the judges of Supreme Court.

According to P. E. Roberts, "It is very doubtful whether the Supreme Court had any jurisdiction over the natives and there is practically no doubt at all that the English law making forgery a capital crime was not operative in India till many years after Nand Kumar's alleged forgery had been committed".

CASE OF CHET SINGH

Balwant Singh, father of Chet Singh, was a vassal of the Nawab of Oudh. He was the first Raja of Banaras. In 1775, Banaras was transferred to the Company by the Nawab of Oudh and consequently the English Company became the overlord of Chet Singh. He paid annually rent of his land to the Company and the same could not be enhanced. However, he was bound to help his new masters in times of difficulty. In 1778, Warren Hastings asked for a special contribution of ₹5 lakhs from Chet Singh and the latter paid the same. Next year, a similar demand was made and was complied with after hesitation. In 1780, Chet Singh was asked to give two thousand horses. The Raja pleaded his inability and offered to provide one thousand horses. Although Hastings lowered his demand the Raja did not comply with the same. The Raja had also not paid his regular tribute. Warren Hastings was in great financial difficulty. He imposed a fine of ₹50 lakhs on Chet Singh and marched to Banaras to realise the same. Chet Singh submitted to Warren Hastings who got him arrested. However, the Raja managed to escape. There was rioting and bloodshed. Situation was brought under control with some difficulty. Ultimately the

Raja was deposed and his nephew was put in his place. The latter was required to pay tribute at double the rate.

Warren Hastings' treatment of Chet Singh has been severely condemned. It is pointed out that Chet Singh was not bound to help the English Company if the latter was in financial difficulty. Moreover, Warren Hastings was too exacting. His conduct was unjust, improper and highhanded. It was tyranny pure and simple. The very purpose for which Warren Hastings took all the tribute, was defeated because the treasury of Chet Singh was looted by the troops and nothing fell into the hands of Warren Hastings.

BEGUMS OF OUDH

The Nawab Wazir of Oudh owed a lot of money to the English Company and he was not in a position to pay. Warren Hastings wanted money very badly. The Nawab Wazir told Warren Hastings that he could pay the money only if he was allowed to resume the Jagirs and treasures held by his mother and grandmother, who were known as the Begums of Oudh. Although both the Jagirs and treasures were guaranteed to the Begums by the Calcutta Council by the Treaty of Chanar of 1781, Hastings allowed the Nawab of Oudh to take possession of them. The Nawab hesitated to take action against his own mother and grandmother but he was forced to do so by Warren Hastings. The result was that British troops were sent to do the job. The place of the Begums was surrounded. The two eunuchs, who acted as stewards, were tortured in every possible way and ultimately were forced to part with the money. With the money thus secured, the Nawab Wazir was able to pay off the debts of the Company.

Dr. V. A. Smith defended the action of Warren Hastings on the ground of expediency. According to him, "Urgent necessities of the time justified Hastings in cancelling treaty obligation and putting a certain amount of pressure on the Begums to make them disgorge". He also stated that the treatment meted out to the Begums was mild according to the Indian standards. Moreover, Warren Hastings had no personal knowledge of coercive measures adopted by the troops of the Company. However, such a defence is insufficient to convince any impartial leader. It has been proved that Warren Hastings was the moving spirit throughout the period when the tragedy was being enacted. As a matter of fact, it was Warren Hastings who forced the hands of Nawab Wazir when the latter hesitated to take action against his mother and grandmother. The doctrine of urgent necessity cannot be put forward to justify all the acts of high-handedness on the part of the English troops and the civil servants. According to Sir Alfred Lyall "The employment of personal severities under the superintendence of British officers in order to extract money from women and eunuchs is an ignoble kind of undertaking; to push him (Nawab) and actively assist in measure of coercion against women and eunuchs was conduct unworthy and indefensible". Moreover, there is nothing to prove that the Begums of Oudh were in league with Chet Singh. If such was the case it was the duty of Hastings to put forward evidence in his possession to support this allegation.

REGULATING ACT AND COUNCIL

The Regulating Act was passed in 1773 and it provided for the establishment of a Supreme Court of Calcutta (now Kolkata) and Governor-General's Council. This Council was to consist of four members and the Governor-General was given a casting vote only in the case of a tie. Out of the 4 members, 3 of them came from England and those were Clavering, Monson and Francis. Only Barwell was in India at the time of his appointment. From the very beginning, the three members who came from England started opposing Warren Hastings. The result was that on many occasions Warren Hastings was over-ruled and he was made to do things which he did not approve of at all. The majority of his Council condemned the Rohilla war. The British Resident at Lucknow was called back. Likewise, the Councillors recognised the claims of the Begums of Oudh to the Jagirs and the treasure. The same Council allowed Nand Kumar to denounce Warren Hastings in the Council itself.

The condition of Warren Hastings was so very difficult in his Council that on one occasion he instructed his agent to tender his resignation to the Company. However, things became better after a lapse of time. In 1776, Monson died a natural death. In 1777, Clavering died of dysentery. In 1780, Warren Hastings wounded Francis in a duel and the latter left for England. It has rightly been said that **"the members of the Council died, sickened and fled away"**.

WARREN HASTINGS AND SUPREME COURT

The Regulating Act also set up a Supreme Court at Calcutta. Unfortunately, the powers of the Supreme Court were not clearly defined and that led to a conflict of jurisdiction between the Supreme Court of Calcutta (now Kolkata) and the courts of the Company. There were frequent tussles between the two authorities. In the case of **Raja of Cossijurah**, the two authorities came into open conflict. In this case, the Supreme Court issued a writ of capias against the Raja for his arrest. The only way the defendant could save himself was by means of furnishing security. Instead of doing that, the Raja concealed himself and thereby avoided the service of the writ, and the same was returned without service. Warren Hastings was informed by the Collector that the Raja was a zamindar and was concealing himself to avoid the service of the writ and consequently the revenue of the Company was not being collected. Warren Hastings consulted the Advocate-General and directed the Raja not to appear or plead before the Supreme Court or in any way submit to its jurisdiction. A general notification was issued by the Government that zamindars were not subject to the jurisdiction of Supreme Court unless they accepted the same by their own consent.

The Supreme Court took up the challenge and issued another writ to sequester the land and property of the Raja. Sixty men, headed by a sergeant of the Supreme Court, were sent to execute the wife. The Raja complained that the persons deputed by the Supreme Court entered his house, beat and wounded his servants, broke open and forcibly entered his zenana, stripped his place of religious worship of its ornaments and prohibited his farmers from paying his rents.

The Governor-General and the Council instructed the Raja not to obey the process of the Supreme Court and ordered the troops of the Company to intercept the party of the Sheriff and retain them in custody. As a matter of fact, the troops of the Company caught hold of the party of the Court and brought them to Calcutta (now Kolkata). The Supreme Court took action against the Advocate-General and the officers who had seized the Sheriff's party. The result was that the Advocate-General was put into prison.

Baboo Cassinaut brought an action against the Governor-General and the members of the Council individually for trespass. To begin with, the Governor-General and the members of his Council appeared before the Supreme Court, but later on they retired and refused to submit to any process which the Supreme Court might issue. A petition was signed by the prominent British inhabitants of Bengal and sent to British Parliament against the exercise of its power by the Supreme Court of Calcutta (now Kolkata). The result was the passing of the Amending Act of 1781. One of the objects of the new Act was to give relief to certain "persons imprisoned at Calcutta under the judgment of the Supreme Court and also indemnifying the Governor-General and Council and all officers who have acted under their orders or authority in the undue resistance made to the process of the Supreme Court". The Act of 1781 reduced the powers of the Supreme Court and the conflict between the Supreme Court and the Court of the Company was avoided.

According to Prof. Davies. "The importance of the Regulating Act in Hastings' life can hardly be over-estimated. It marked a milestone in his career for the whole of the rest of his administration was to be spent under the sway of this Act, he being the only Governor-General of India to suffer that unhappy fate. Its consequences to India in general were to be serious but to him personally they were to be nothing less than catastrophic. For if ever a man has had his life ruined for him by Act of Parliament, that man was Warren Hastings. The story of his life during the next twenty years may be simply stated in two sentences, thus: Parliament by passing this Act was the prime cause of the troubles and difficulties in which he immediately became involved; and Parliament by impeaching him for the way he extricated himself from these difficulties shifted on to his shoulders the responsibility for its own negligence and folly... . Perhaps, if anybody deserved impeaching it was Lord North, the author and executor of the Act".

According to the same author, "Contemporary opinion on the merits of the Act was very varied. It naturally accorded with George the third's ideas, and the expressed pleasure at its smooth passage to the statute book. Equally, naturally, it was bitterly resented and condemned by the Company and its friends. Burke Renounced it as '*an infringement of national right, national faith, and natural justice*'. Others of them described it as a medley of inconsistencies, dictated by tyranny, yet bearing throughout each line the mark of ignorance".

"The mark of ignorance was, indeed, but too plainly visible, nor need it excite surprise. The framers of the Act were utterly ignorant of India and had not, it would seem, deemed it fit to consult those with the possible exception of Lord Clive, who could have given them good advice. Lord North might have paid heed to Hastings' views, but the Act was passed before he had time to deliver them. The suspicion rests upon ministers of thinking more about obtaining for the Crown a share in the extensive patronage rights of India than providing its government with a sound, workable constitution. In the eyes of both the supporters and the opponents of the Act, the chief point at issue was the rights of the East India Company.

"A recent verdict on the Act is that it was probably on the whole an honest attempt to deal with a difficult problem. Yet, even if conceivably this be so, the fact remains that by passing it Lord North very nearly achieved a double title to fame as the minister who lost Great Britain her Eastern as well as her Western Empire. The man who was to save him from this ignominy was Warren Hastings".

FOREIGN POLICY OF WARREN HASTINGS

First Maratha War (1778-82)

In 1772, Narayan Rao became the Peshwa after the death of Madho Rao. However, he was murdered at the instigation of Raghoba who himself wanted to become the Peshwa. Nana Phadnavis took up the cause of the posthumous son of Narayan Rao against Raghoba. The latter asked for English help. By the treaty of Surat (1775),[1] Raghoba agreed to give to the Government of Bombay Salsette and Bassein as the price of English help. This was done without the knowledge of the Governor-General. The English attacked Salsette and defeated the Marathas at Arass. Both the Governor-General and

---

[1] As regards the details of this treaty, the former treaties concluded between the Government of Bombay (now Mumbai) and the Marathas in 1739 and 1756 and all other agreements between the two Governments were ratified and confirmed. Both parties agreed to abstain from assisting the enemies of the other. The English were to assist Raghoba (Raghunath Rao) with a military contingent of 2,500 men of which at least 700 were to be Europeans. Those forces Were to be equipped with "proper guns and war-like stores as a field train of artillery". To begin with, the English were to send 1,500 men and the rest were to be sent afterwards, if asked for. Raghoba agreed to pay to the Company annually ₹75,000 from the revenues of Ankleshvar. He also agreed to pay ₹ 2½ lakhs every month for the military assistance which he was to receive. As a security for the payment, Raghoba made temporary assignment of the Districts of Amod, Hasot, Versaul and a part of Ankleshvar. He was to deposit jewels valued at ₹6 lakhs to the English "as a security for the promised advance, pledging himself to redeem them". He also agreed to give to the English in perpetuity Bassein, Salsette, Jambusar, Olpad and small islands adjacent to Bombay (now Mumbai). He also agreed to procure for the Company the Gaikwad's share of the revenue in the town and parganas of Broach. Maratha raids into Bengal and the Carnatic were to stop. Any peace made with the Poona Government was to include the English. Raghoba was to defray all expenses that might be incurred in taking possession of any of the places ceded to the Company. He was to assist the ships of the Company or of persons under their protection, if wrecked and to protect the cargoes. The Company agreed to establish Raghoba "at Poona in the Government of the Maratha Empire".

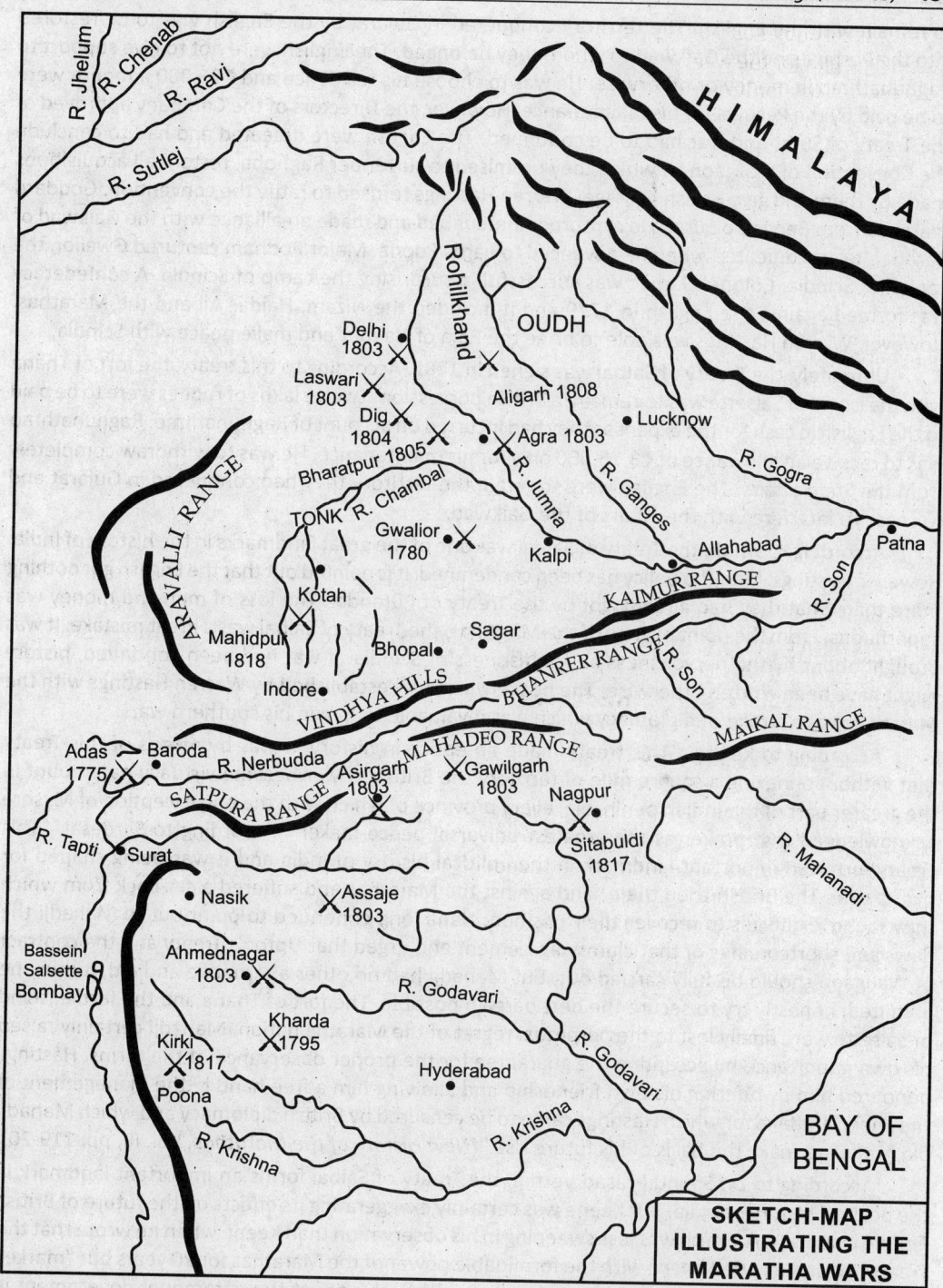

SKETCH-MAP ILLUSTRATING THE MARATHA WARS

the Calcutta Council disapproved of the treaty of Surat. A new treaty was concluded called the Treaty of Purandar (1776). According to it, all places including Bassein taken by the English during the war since the Treaty of Purandar were to be restored to the Peshwa. The island of Salsette and the small ones near Bombay were to remain in the possession of the English. The city of Broach was to remain with the English. The territory conquered in Gujarat by the English was to be restored into the Peshwa and the Gaikwad to whom they belonged. The English were not to give support to Raghunathrao in money or otherwise. He was to choose his residence and ₹25,000 a month were to be paid by the Peshwa for his maintenance. However, the Directors of the Company approved of the Treaty of Surat and war had to be continued. The English were defeated and had to conclude the Convention of Wargaon by which they promised to surrender Raghoba, restore all acquisitions made by them and give British hostage. Warren Hastings refused to ratify the convention. Goddard marched from Bengal to Surat. He captured Ahmedabad and made an alliance with the Gaikwad of Baroda. He was defeated when he advanced towards Poona. Major Podham captured Gwalior, the capital of Scindia. Colonel Gamac was successful in surprising the camp of Scindia. A confederacy was formed against the English in 1779 and it included the Nizam, Haidar Ali and the Marathas. However, Warren Hastings was able to bribe the Raja of Nagpur and make peace with Scindia.

Ultimately, the **Treaty of Salbai** was signed in 1782. According to this treaty, the fort of Thana with the island of Salsette was to remain in British possession. Twelve lakhs of rupees were to be paid to the English in cash for the expenses they had incurred on account of Raghunathrao. Raghunathrao was to receive an allowance of ₹3,15,000 only for his maintenance. He was to withdraw completely from the State affairs. The English were to retain the territory they had conquered in Gujarat and to cease to interfere with the affairs of the Gaikwad.

According to Smith, the Treaty of Salbai was one of the great landmarks in the history of India. However, Hastings' Maratha policy has been condemned. It is pointed out that the English got nothing more than what they had already got by the Treaty of Purandar. The loss of men and money was superfluous. From the point of view of the Marathas, the Treaty of Salbai was a great mistake. It was brought about by the nervousness and selfishness of Scindia. If war had been continued, history might have been written otherwise. The peace which was established by Warren Hastings with the Marathas was a stroke of diplomacy which was invaluable to him in his southern wars.

According to Keene, "This treaty made an epoch in history. It was by means of this Treaty that without annexing a square mile of territory the British power became virtually paramount in the greater part of the Indian peninsula, every province of which with the one exception of Mysore acknowledged that power as the greatest universal peace-maker". According to Sardesai, "This Treaty forms an important landmark in the political history of India and it was being shaped for over a year. The British tried their hand against the Marathas and suffered a set-back from which they found it difficult to recover their position. Nana long continued to point out to Mahadji the flaws and shortcomings of that clumsy agreement and urged that Upton's Treaty and the contract of Wadgaon should be fully carried out. But Mahadji had no other alternative and did, it must be admitted, honestly try to secure the best bargain possible. The fort of Thana and the fertile island of Salsette were finally lost to the perpetual regret of the Maratha nation. Mahadji certainly raised his own importance by accepting the guarantee for the proper observance of the terms. Hastings honoured him by offering his own friendship and allowing him a free hand in the management of the imperial affairs for which Hastings came to be censured by British diplomacy and which Mahadji did not fail to make the basis of his future rise" (*New History of the Marathas*, Vol. III, pp. 119-20).

According to Dr. Shanti Prasad Verma, the Treaty of Salbai forms an important landmark in the political history of India. But Keene was certainly exaggerating its effects on the future of British Empire in India. V. A. Smith was less sweeping in his observation than Keene when he wrote that this Treaty not only assured peace with the formidable power of the Marathas for 20 years but "marked the ascendancy of the English as the controlling, although not yet the paramount government in India". Lt. Col. Luard is right when he says that the Treaty "formed the turning point in the history of the English in India". But he is merely paraphrasing Keene and V.A. Smith when he adds that without the acquisition of any fresh territory, it established beyond dispute the dominance of the British controlling factor in Indian politics, their subsequent rise in 1818 to the position of the paramount power being an inevitable result of the position gained by the Treaty of Salbai. Warren Hastings took a more realistic view when he modestly described it as "a successful negotiation of peace... in the most desperate period of my distresses". For the English, the Treaty of Salbai was a clear acknowledgment of failure. According to Janse and Banaji, "the phrase 'annexing a square inch' smacks of historical travesty in the light of the appalling territorial and political sacrifices which the Governor-General consented to make.... Territories acquired by consent or Treaty were restored; indemnities which the Poona Darbar had promised to pay by the Treaty of Purandar were written off; the Treaty formally acknowledging the Gaikwad's political independence was torn up like a scrap of paper; Fateh Singh Gaikwad reverted to his pre-war state of quasi-vassalage; the Marathas attacked the British shipping with impunity. Yet we are asked to believe that by the Treaty of Salbai, British power virtually became paramount in the greater part of the Indian peninsula". According to Dr. Verma, "The loyalty of the Maratha chiefs had never been really put to the test before. It was now put to the test and not found wanting. With the exception of Raghoba not a single Maratha chieftain willingly colluded with the English. Everybody put his shoulder to the wheel and gave the confederacy whatever strength he could. All internal differences were set aside. There were grumblings but they were gracefully expressed. Weakness was tolerated; every little contribution made to the common cause was given its due recognition.... The Treaty of Salbai was the result of closest collaboration between the two leading figures of the Maratha State. Nana Phadnavis and Mahadji by their supreme exertions in war and peace saved the Maratha Empire for a period of 20 years by pushing back the rising tide of the English aggression from their territories and regaining their losses". (*A Study of Maratha Diplomacy*, p. 390.)

According to Dr. Sailendra Nath Sen, "The treaty of Salbai formed an important landmark in the history of India as it secured to the English the alliance of the most formidable power in the country. The foundation on which the British Empire in India rested in the last quarter of the eighteenth century was weak. The structure which Clive had created was not yet sufficiently strong to resist the sweep of the invasions of the Marathas and the Mysoreans. It was left to Hastings to turn the tide by converting the Marathas to an alliance with the English against Haidar Ali. In the political game of chess Hastings had won and in this respect the treaty of Salbai 'marked the ascendancy of the English as the controlling, although not yet the paramount Government in India". (*Anglo-Maratha Relations*, 1772-85, p. 210.)

Rise of Hyder Ali. Warren Hastings had also to fight against Hyder Ali (1722-82). Not much is known about the ancestors of Hyder Ali. One of his ancestors is said to have migrated to Southern India from the Punjab. His father was a Nayak in the army of Subedar of Sira. Later on, he became Faujdar of the Raja of Mysore who granted him the jagir of Budikota. It was at Budikota that Hyder Ali was born in 1721 or 1722. Hyder Ali did not receive any education and also did not accomplish much up to the age of 27. However, after that, he shot into prominence as a military leader. By dint of his military skill and qualities of leadership he became the Faujdar of Dindigal in 1755. By misappropriating the revenues of Dindigal, he managed to raise an independent army for himself. In 1763, he occupied Bednore. With the booty which fell into his hands, he strengthened his financial position. He also conquered Canara. He became the undisputed master of the Mysore State with Seringapatam as its capital. He was able to build up a strong war-machine within a short time.

There were many factors which were responsible for his unhappy relations with the English East India Company. In the earlier phase of his career, Hyder Ali had secured valuable aid from the French. In 1760, a Portuguese bishop had promoted an alliance between him and the French. For his aid against the English, Count Lally had agreed to pay Hyder Ali ₹10,000 per month and also the Forts of Thaigur and Elvanasore. After the expulsion of the English, Hyder Ali was expected to have Trichnopoly, Madurai, Tinnevelly, etc. The British force under Major More sent to prevent Hyder Ali from joining the French was routed. However, the capture of Villenore by Coote exercised a demoralising influence on Hyder Ali and weakened his alliance with the French. When Hyder Ali was busying in crushing his opponents in Mysore, the of English did much to discredit him. This was strongly resented by Hyder Ali. When Pondicherry (now Puducherry) surrendered to the English in January 1761, Hyder Ali took about 300 French soldiers in his service.

Another factor which strained the relations between Hyder Ali and the British was the hostility between Mohammed Ali, the Nawab of Carnatic and Hyder Ali. There were many districts in the Carnatic which were claimed by both. Mohammed Ali allowed British troops to be stationed at Vellore and this was not approved of by Hyder Ali. Hyder Ali also took into his service Raja Sahib, the son of Chanda Sahib and gave protection to Mahfuz Khan, brother and rival of Mohammed Ali.

It is true that after the collapse of the French power in Southern India, Hyder Ali tried to patch up with the British. As a matter of fact, he made an offer of friendship to the Madras authorities and the latter sent Pourchier to test his sincerity. However, he had to return without meeting Hyder Ali as the time and place of meeting could not be settled. The real reason seems to have been that the Madras authorities had a second thought and decided to check the expansionist activities of Hyder Ali. As a matter of fact, the Madras (now Chennai) Government encouraged the Nizam to take up arms against Hyder Ali and offered to give necessary military help for that purpose. A military alliance was entered into between the English Company and the Nizam. The Nizam already enjoyed the support of the Marathas and thus a triple alliance was formed against Hyder Ali. In November, 1767, the Madras Government concluded a treaty with the Nizam by which it agreed to pay him tribute of ₹5 lakhs for the three Northern Circars. The Madras Government also promised not to acquire the Circar his of Guntoor as long as Basalat Jang lived. The British promised military help to Nizam against his enemies. The Madras Government was eager to acquire Carnatic Balaghat which were then held by Hyder Ali and agreed to pay ₹ 7 lakhs to the Nizam for its Diwani. This engagement acknowledged sovereignty of the Nizam over the dominions of Hyder Ali. Both Nizam and the Poona Government were very keen to prey upon territories of Hyder Ali and the British Government also agreed to help them.

First Mysore War (1767-69)
The British alliance with the Nizam provoked Hyder Ali, the ruler of Mysore. With British forces under Col. Smith, the Nizam advanced into Mysore in August 1767. It is true that Hyder Ali was faced with a very serious situation but he rose to occasion and was able to win over the Marathas by promising them sum a of ₹23 lakhs. He also managed to win over the Nizam. The result was that the English were left alone. The British fought well but the opposition of Hyder Ali and his son Tipu was formidable. Tipu was able to reach near Madras itself and plundered its suburbs. The Madras authorities became panicky and begged for peace. Hyder Ali virtually dictated the terms of peace which were concluded on April 4, 1769. The treaty showed that Hyder Ali was both a strategist and a diplomat. His success was also due to the efficiency and superiority of vast cavalry which made it possible for him to campaign on an extensive scale. The Court of Directors had to admit that the war had been "very improperly conducted and most disadvantageously concluded".

The treaty of 1769 was based on the mutual restitution of conquests but the fort and the district of Kurur were to be retained by Hyder Ali. There was also a provision for an alliance for mutual aid in case either party was attacked by a third power. The Madras authorities had to agree to this clause as Hyder All insisted on this. This was advantageous to Hyder Ali as he was always in danger of attacks from the Marathas.

In 1770, Mysore was invaded by Peshwa Madhav Rao. The Madras Government was approached for help by Hyder Ali against the Peshwa, but it decided to remain neutral. Hyder Ali treated this as a violation of the terms of the Treaty of 1769. The Madras Government also refused to supply war material to Hyder Ali. The Bombay Government concluded a Treaty with Hyder Ali which allowed them trading privileges in Mysore in exchange for guns, saltpetre, lead, etc. However, that Treaty was disapproved by the Court of Directors in 1772. But that did not upset Hyder Ali. Bombay Government also concluded the Treaty of Surat in March, 1775 by which they committed themselves to support the claim of Raghoba who was contesting for the Peshwaship. The British were to get Salsette and Bassein. In spite of all this, Hyder Ali tried to establish friendly relations with the British and when ultimately he failed he was very bitter. He took possession of the Maratha State of Gooti. He took many Frenchmen in his service and also secured arms and stores from the French. He also made friends with the Dutch.

Things were very bad in Madras. Lord Pigot, its Governor, was confined by certain members of the Council and he died in detention in August, 1776. Sir Thomas Rumbold, his successor, was more interested in making money than looking after the interests of his nation. British relations with Hyder Ali took a turn for the worse. The British were getting involved in a war with the Poona Government on behalf of Raghoba. In August 1778, the British attacked Pondicherry and after its occupation, they sent an expedition against Mahe. Hyder Ali protested as he was getting his military supplies mostly through Mahe. Hyder Ali sent his troops to defend Mahe but in spite of that Mahe fell in March 1779. This embittered the relations between Hyder Ali and the British. The Nizam was also not happy with the Madras Government as they withheld tribute for the northern Circars. It was under these circum-stances that the Grand Quadruple Alliance consisting of Hyder Ali, the Nizam, the Poona Government and Bhonsle of Nagpur was formed against the British.

Second Mysore War (1780-84)

Hostilities started in 1780. Bhonsle of Nagpur who was the enemy of the Poona Government was won over by Warren Hastings and he left the alliance. The Nizam also deserted Hyder Ali. The Poona Government also left the alliance. The result was that Hyder Ali was left alone to fight against the British.

During the early phase of the war, the war-machine of Hyder Ali was superior to the British armies. The army of Hyder Ali burst like an avalanche and swept away many villages and towns. It carried fire and sword in the Carnatic. It was so near Madras that many of its residents ran away in panic. The towns of Porto Novo and Conjeevaram were plundered. The armies led by Col. Baillie and Col. Fletcher were hacked to pieces. Munro, the Commander-in-Chief, threw his artillery in a tank and retired to Madras. Hyder Ali occupied Arcot, the capital of Cranatic.

When Sir Eyre Coote took over the supreme command in the South, the situation was critical. However, things began to improve. Sir Eyre Coote was able to hold Hyder Ali and deal with him effectively at Porto Novo in July 1781. Hyder Ali was forced to recall Tipu who was besieging Wandiwash. The battle at Pollilure in August 1781 was a drawn one. In 1781, Sir Eyre Coote inflicted a crushing defeat to Hyder Ali at Solinger. Nagapatam and Trincomali were also captured by the British. In spite of these reverses, Hyder Ali continued to fight in a vigorous manner. He was suffering from cancer and he died on December 7, 1782.

It cannot be denied that Hyder Ali was a leader of outstanding merit, a soldier endowed with superb strategic insight, an efficient administrator, a diplomat of a high order, a man though unlettered, yet possessing a large measure of commonsense. He rarely lost his balance of mind, whether in victory or in defeat. He was both a strategist and a diplomat.

After the death of Hyder Ali, the war was continued by Tipu. He successfully wrested Bednore but failed to capture Mangalore. The British took the offensive and proceeded towards Seringapatam. Both sides were sick of the war and ultimately the treaty of Mangalore was concluded on May 11, 1784. Tipu tried to show that it was the English Company which had sued for peace. The English Commissioner who negotiated the peace treaty remained standing with his head uncovered and with a copy of the treaty on his outstretched hands for nearly two hours as indicating that they were "using every form of flattery and supplication to induce compliance". The Vakils of Poona and Hyderabad had also to undergo the same humiliation.

After the conclusion of the Second Mysore War, the old conflict between the Marathas and Mysore started. Nana Fadnis resumed the traditional policy of hostility towards Mysore. Grant Duff points out that Nana Fadnis was even eager to intervene in the final stages of the Second Mysore War to create an impression that Tipu was "a Mahratta dependent as well as a tributary". It was his jealousy of the growing influence of Scindia and the rivalry between Holkar and Scindia that kept him inactive. However, in 1784, Nana Fadnis and the Nizam concluded the convention of Yadgir to fight against Tipu. The Poona Government was eager to recover the territory south of the river Krishna ceded to Mysore by the Maratha-Mysore Treaty of 1780. In the Maratha-Mysore war of 1796, the English remained aloof. However, their sympathies were with the Marathas as they did not like the State of Mysore to become stable and powerful. In spite of that, Tipu was successful in his fight against the Marathas who were forced to accept his sovereignty over the territory between the Krishna and the Tungabhadra. Tipu took up the title of Padshah.

Tipu was aware of the British intrigues against him at Poona and Hyderabad and he tried to improve his position by coming to some understanding with foreign powers. His efforts to get help from Turkey and France failed.

When Tipu was occupied in the war with the Marathas and the rebellions of the chiefs in Coorg and Malabar, he could not think of disturbing his relations with the English Company. However, the Rajas of Travancore and the Nawab of Carnatic who were the allies of the English, were active against him. Martanda Varma, the Raja of Travancore, (1729-58), was dreaming of unifying Malabar under his flag. Ram Varma, his nephew, who ascended the throne in 1758, was equally ambitious. His kingdom was threatened by the rising power of Mysore and no wonder he helped the English Company in the Second Mysore War and was recognised as an ally of the English Company in the Treaty of Mangalore. In 1788, the English Company supplied the Raja two Battalions of infantry to be maintained at his expense and stationed on his frontiers as security against aggression from Tipu. Finding himself strong and secure, the Raja tried to incite the vassals of Mysore in Malabar.

ESTIMATE OF WARREN HASTINGS[2]

It goes to the credit of Warren Hastings that from an ordinary writer of the Company, he rose to the position of the Governor-General of Bengal. In spite of the difficulties which he had to encounter in the country he was able to accomplish a lot. It should not be forgotten that whatever he accomplished in India was done in spite of the opposition in India and the lack of support at home. His colleagues in the Council were always ready to outvote him and harass him in any manner they could. He had to fight many wars and that also at a time when he was practically getting no help from the mother of country as the latter was busy in a life and death struggle in North America. All the European States tried to exploit the situation created be the American War of Independence. While the Home Government lost the American colonies, it goes to the credit of Warren Hastings that he was able to consolidate the British position in India.

It is true that he made many mistakes of omission and commission and for those mistakes he was impeached on his return to England. The trial lasted from 1788 to 1795.[3] In spite of the inconvenience and expense to which he was subjected by the impeachment, he was ultimately honourably acquitted.

---

[2] "Warren Hastings had both the virtues and the unscrupulousness of an empire builder".

[3] Burke took a prominent part in the denunciation of Warren Hastings. According to Lord Morley, "Looking back across the ninety years that divide us from the memorable scene in the Westminster Hall, we may say that Burke had more success than at first appeared. If he did not convict the man, he overthrew a system and stamped its principle with lasting censure and shame. That Hastings was acquitted was immaterial. The lesson of his impeachment had been taught with sufficiently impressive force; the great lesson that Asiatics have rights, and that Europeans have obligations".

According to Lord Macaulay, Warren Hastings "dissolved the double government. He transferred the direction of affairs to the English hands. Out of a fruitful anarchy, he educed at least a rude and imperfect order. The only quarter in which Britain lost nothing was the quarter in which her interests had been committed to the care of Hastings. In spite the utmost exertions of both European and Asiatic enemies, the power our Company in the East greatly augmented".

In his reply to his impeachment, Warren Hastings declared thus: "The valour of others acquired, I enlarged and gave shape and consistency to the dominion which you held there; I preserved it; I sent forth it armies with an effectual but an economic hand, through unknown and hostile regions to the support of your possessions; to the retrieval of one (Bombay) from degradation and dishonour; and of the other (Madras from utter loss and subjection. I maintained the wars which were of you formation or that of others, not of mine".

Warren Hastings was the oldest of the able men who gave to Great Britain her Indian empire. He was a versatile genius. He had a limitless, energy and strong determination. He was the first foreign ruler who succeeded in gaining the confidence of the princes of India.

According to Lord Curzon, "I doubt if in the entire history of public affairs any man has been so cruelly persecuted or more persistently tried. Surrounded by vindictive enemies, daily outvoted and insulted in his own Council, accused by his colleagues of the meanest of crimes, confronted by a series of situations that might have daunted the most heroic spirit, with an empty treasury and a discontented service, and beset by frequent ill-health, Hastings showed a patience, fortitude, a fertility of resource, and a self-control that could only have proceeded from a character profoundly conscious both of its own integrity and its power to prevail". (*British Government of India,* Vol. I, p. 152.) Again, "Side by side with this deep tenacity of purpose, there was to be found in his nature a tender heartedness and generosity which, while it was constantly imposed upon by the crowd of blood-suckers, mendicant friends, and impoverished relatives who infested him on every side, and while it tempted him sometimes in its public aspect to repose undue confidence in quite unsuitable and unworthy persons (witness his unfortunate selection of Major Scott as his Parliamentary Agent in England), rendered him incapable of parsimony in his own interest, and left him almost alone among the higher civil servants of that time, in constant need of money, and, when he retired, in possession of a fortune which in those days might fairly be regarded as modest and which had been acquired by honourable means. Even Macaulay pauses in his full-throated declamation to offer a halting tribute to Hastings' general uprightness with respect to money".

"There were many other attractive features in the character of the Governor-General. He was almost the only one in the long list of the British rulers of India who took a real interest in literature; scholarship and the arts. His correspondence with the 'Great Cham which is referred to and in part quoted in Boswell's Life, is well-known. So is Boswell's appreciation of him as a man the extent of whose abilities was equal to that of his power, and who, by those who are fortunate enough to know him in private life, is admired for his literature and taste, and "beloved for the candour, moderation and mildness of his character. Hastings was well-versed in Persian and Arabic literature, and tried to establish a Persian Professorship at Oxford University. He founded with Sir William Jones the Asiatic Society of Bengal, instituted the Mohammedan Madrassa or College at Calcutta (now Kolkata), and patronised, even if he did not understand Sanskrit. His library, both in India, where it was constantly replenished, from England, and after his return, at Daylesford, testified to the wide range of his reading. Like most cultured men of that day he dabbled in versification, of a somewhat academic and pedestrian character, whether it took the form of translation from the classics or of poems of his wife. On the other hand, he was the master of a nervous and polished literary, style and even the author of 'Junius', no mean an authority, admitted that 'there was no contending against the pen of Hastings. Macaulay acclaimed him as the real founder of the school of official writing in

India. He was the friend and patron of painters, as was testified by the many portraits of him by the foremost artists of the day; and he encouraged the visits to India and the artistic work of Hodges, Zoffuny and Devis". (*Ibid.*, pp. 154-55.)

According to Prof. A.M. Davies, "Hastings has always been and will always remain the subject of controversy. He has suffered from friend and foe alike; from opponents who have used unmeasured and undeserved invective, from admirers who can see nothing but wisdom and ability in his career. The knowledge which most Englishmen have of Clive and Hastings has filtered through the rhetoric of Macaulay. But even admirers of Macaulay's famous essays, with their purple patches like those which describe the night Clive spent before Plassey and the great trial of Hastings in Westminster Hall, must admit that Macaulay took a partial and even a prejudiced view of some of the events, and those-whose sympathies are with Hastings must often wish that an historian with the pen and powers of Macaulay would have written in defence of Hastings."

"To some extent Clive's work was done once for all. Hastings' work is still being tested, for he laid some of the foundations of our rule and traditions in India. It was the work of a statesman and a scholar and his labours for research into the past history of Indian literature and religion were beyond praise".

According to the same writer, "The achievement of Warren Hastings in India is not to be estimated by the criteria usually applied to empire-builders—the number of battles won and enemies vanquished, the number of square miles of territory conquered and annexed, the plunder and the glory amassed. His generals gained few battles; only the Rohillas and Chait Singh were vanquished; there were no conquests or trophies of victory; there was no plunder and little glory; all the superficial evidences of success were strikingly lacking. To outward appearances he had done no more than justify his retention of his post and the trust, reposed in him, by bringing the Company safely through a great crisis with its territories intact and its resources unimpaired. Actually, however, he had achieved immeasurably more and to estimate what that more was we have only to recall the extent of British power in India at the beginning of his administration; and to compare it with what it was at the end. On the one hand, two weak footholds on the coast at Madras and Bombay, undisputed but undefined authority over the vast, chaotic, famine-stricken province of Bengal, a weak alliance with one native State, no friends, no security, bankrupt finances, demoralized officers, incompetent leaders. And on the other hand, an empire in being that had conclusively proved itself to be the most powerful State in India, an empire that was built on secure foundations, buttressed with treaties, and alliances, doubly strong because it had gained the respect and goodwill of no small part of the Indian world, and that only required a continuance of the same able statesmanship to become the paramount power. The contrast is a fair measure of Hastings' achievement".

According to J. S. Cotton, "Indians and Anglo-Indians alike venerate Hastings' name, the former as their first beneficent administrator, the latter the most able and the most enlightened of their own class. If Clive's sword acquired the Indian empire, it was the brain of Hastings that planned the system of civil administration and his genius that saved the empire in its darkest hour". "Hastings made no conquest, but his subsidiary system paved the way for the final overthrow or defeat of every power that sought to hinder the growth of our Eastern empire".

According to another writer, Hastings applied unreservedly the energy, boldness, tenacity and resource which enabled him to grapple successfully with his enemies. He may be described with justice as the Indian Pitt, the Chatham of the East.

We may conclude with the following words of P.E. Roberts: "Hastings was perhaps the greatest Englishman who ever ruled. A man who with some, ethical defect possessed in a super-abundant measure, the mobile and fertile brain, the tireless energy and the lofty fortitude which distinguishes only the supreme statesman".

PITT'S INDIA ACT (1784)

This Act was passed by the British Parliament in 1784. It provided for a Board of Control. A kind of dual control was established from the Home Government. This system continued up to 1858. The Pitt's India Act was changed in 1786 with a view to giving special powers to Lord Cornwallis.

SIR JOHN MACPHERSON (February 1785-September 1786)

When Warren Hastings left India in 1785, Sir Macpherson, the senior member of the Executive Council of the Governor-General became the Governor-General of Bengal. During the term of his office, he carried out many reforms, with a view to effecting economies in the expenditure of the Company. At this time, Mahadji Scindia was very strong. He got control over the Moghul emperor and was able to get from him the provinces of Agra and Delhi. He demanded Chouth even from the English Company, but the same was refused. Macpherson was relieved by Lord Cornwallis in 1786.

REVIEW QUESTIONS

1. Give a detailed account of the various reforms of Warren Hastings.
2. What was Warren Hastings' Oudh policy? Discuss in detail.
3. Write a detailed note on the Rohilla War.
4. Narrate the foreign policy of Warren Hastings.
5. Discuss the importance of the Regulating Act in the life of Warren Hastings.
6. Describe the impact of the Mysore Wars on the history of India.
7. What is the importance of the Pitt's India Act in the life of Warren Hastings? Discuss in brief.
8. Warren Hastings had both the virtues and the unscrupulousness of an empire builder. Analyse.
9. Evaluate the achievements and failures of the Warren Hastings.

SUGGESTED READINGS

Beveridge, H.: *Maharaja Nuncomar* (1896).
Bowring: *Hyder Ali and Sultan Tipu*.
Davies: *Warren Hastings and Oudh* (1939).
Dodwell, H.H. (Ed.): *Cambridge History of India,* Vol. V.
Jones, M.: *Warren Hastings in Bengal*.
Lyall, A.: Sir Alfred. *Life of Warren Hastings* (1902).
Lyall, A.: *Rise of the British Dominion in India*.
Mill, James: *History of British India* (1817).
Moon, P.: *Warren Hastings and British India* (1947).
Roberts, P.E.: *History of British India*.
Sinha, N.K.: *Haidar Ali* (1949).
Stephen, Sir J.: *The Story of Nuncomar and the Impeachment of Sir Elijah Impey* (1905).
Strachey, Sir John: *Hastings and the Rohilla War* (1892).
Thompson & Garret: *Rice and Fulfilment of British Rule in India*.
Weitzman, Sophia: *Warren Hastings and Philip Francis*.

6 Lord Cornwallis and Sir John Shore

LEARNING OBJECTIVES

- Review the foreign policy and internal reforms of Lord Cornwallis
- Throw light on the activities of Sir John Shore

LORD CORNWALLIS (1786-93)

Unlike Warren Hastings, Lord Cornwallis belonged to a high respectable family of England. Before his appointment as Governor-General of Bengal, he had acted as the Commander-in-Chief of the British armies in North America in the American War of Independence. It was he who had surrendered at York Town and thereby brought to a close the War of American Independence. He accepted the office of the Governor-General with great hesitation. It was for his sake that the Pitt's India Act was amended in 1786 so that he might combine in himself the powers of the Governor-General and the Commander-in-Chief. He was also given the power to over-rule the members of his Executive Council. Throughout the period of 7 years when he acted as Governor-General, he enjoyed the confidence of the Board of Control and the Prime Minister of England. No wonder, he was able to accomplish a lot. The work of Cornwallis can be discussed under two heads: foreign policy and internal reforms.

Foreign Policy. As regards his foreign policy, he was determined to follow a policy of non-intervention into the affairs of the Indian States as laid down in the Pitt's India Act. It may be pointed out that the Pitt's India Act contained the following clause: "Whereas to pursue schemes of conquest and extension of dominion in India are measures repugnant to the wish, honour and the policy of this nation, the Governor-General and his Council were not, without the express authority of the Court of Directors or of the Select Committee, to declare wars or commence hostilities or enter into any treaty for making war, against any of the country princes or States in India". In pursuance of this policy Cornwallis refused to help the son of Shah Alam to recover his throne of Delhi. He gave a stern warning to Mahadji Scindia against interfering into the affairs of Oudh. However, he could not avoid a war against Sultan Tipu.

Third Mysore War (1790-92)

Soon after taking charge, Lord Cornwallis in his letter of November, 1786 to the Court of Directors, anticipated the possibility of a rupture with Tipu because "the ambition and real inclination of Tipu are so well known that should, unluckily, any difference arise with the French nation, we must lay our account that the Carnatic will immediately after become the scene of a dangerous war". Cornwallis was careful not to give the impression that the English were the aggressors. He also did not want to expose the English to the risk of a war with Mysore without getting the help of the Indian States or checking them from joining hands with Tipu. Cornwallis followed a very questionable policy. In his effort to "conform to the letter of an Act of Parliament (Pitt's India Act) enforcing a system of neutrality, Lord Cornwallis violated its spirit, by not only entering into what was, to all intents and purposes, a new treaty but undertaking engagements which contemplated the dismemberment of the territories of an ally and thereby broke faith with him". (Beveridge).

The English had entered into a treaty of alliance with the Nizam in 1766 but that had become ineffective on account of the subsequent treaties which the English Company made with the rulers of Mysore. However, in his letter dated July 1, 1789, Lord Cornwallis stated that the treaty of 1766 was still binding and effective. This implied that the British Government did not question the claim of the Nizam to have sovereignty on Mysore and dispose of its territory in whatever manner he liked. This was virtually a declaration of war against Mysore. The Raja of Travancore began to take advantage of British hostility towards Tipu. In 1789, the Raja purchased the towns and forts of Cranganore and Ayacottah from the Dutch. These forts were very important for the safety of Mysore and Tipu was already negotiating for their purchase. The action of the Raja was obviously an unfriendly act. Tipu demanded the surrender of the forts on the ground that they belonged to his vassal, the Chief of Cochin. However, Lord Cornwallis directed the Madras (now Chennai) Government to support the Raja of Travancore. This made Tipu indignant.

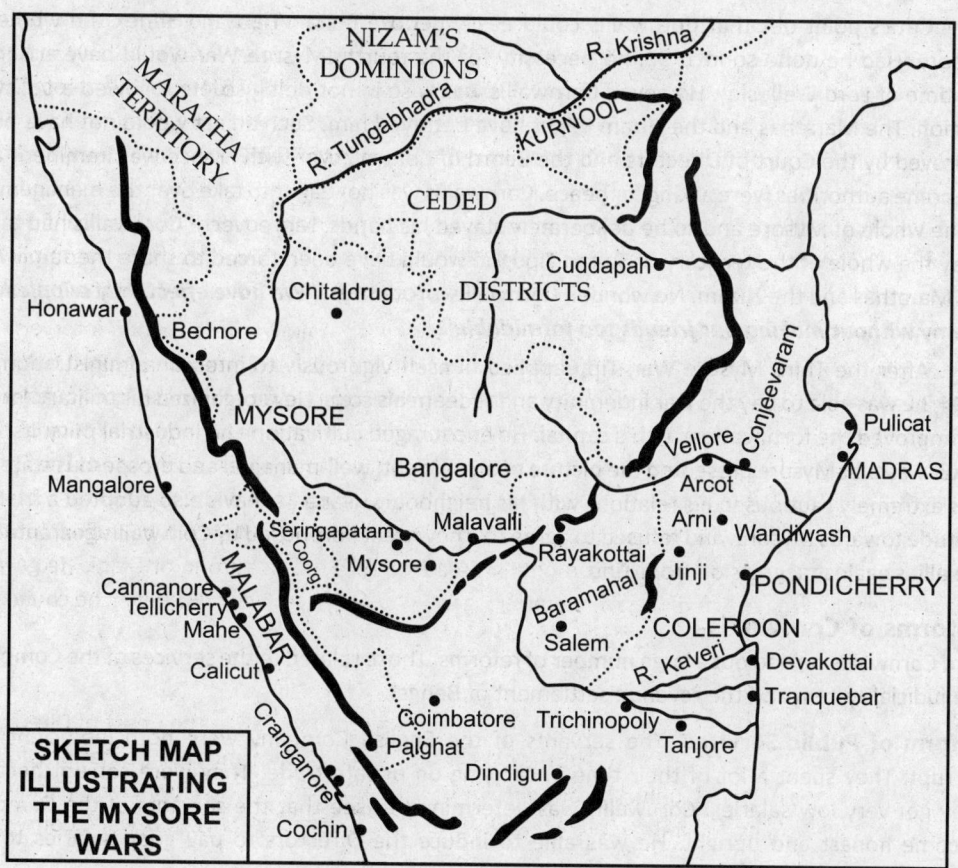

SKETCH MAP ILLUSTRATING THE MYSORE WARS

In his effort to win over the other Indian powers against Tipu, Lord Cornwallis sent instructions to Malet, the English Resident at Poona, to persuade the Peshwa to fight against Tipu. Very attractive terms were offered to the Marathas. They were given the hope of recovering what they had lost to Mysore. A treaty of alliance was signed on June 1, 1790 with the Peshwa. The Nizam signed a treaty with the British on July 4, 1790. Both the treaties were defensive alliances against Tipu and provided for an equal share of conquests. The English Company also concluded defensive alliances with the Raja of Coorg and the Bibi of Cannanore; It is true that Tipu was aware of the gravity of the situation and he tried to secure French help, but he failed on account of the Revolution in France. He also failed to win over the Nizam and the Peshwa to his side. He appealed to Cornwallis for peace but that appeal also failed and the Third Mysore War started.

To begin with, things did not go in favour of the English Company in spite of the help from the Marathas and the Nizam. In 1790, Cornwallis himself took the command. He captured Bangalore (now Bengaluru) and defeated Tipu but was forced to withdraw on account of shortage of supplies. In 1792, Cornwallis captured the hill forts of Tipu and advanced upon Seringapatam. The Marathas completely destroyed the Mysore territory. Finding his position helpless, Tipu sued for peace and the Treaty of Seringapatam was concluded in 1792. By this treaty, Sultan Tipu had to give up half of his territory. He was to pay a war indemnity of 2.5 crores of rupees. He was to surrender two of his sons as hostages. The English, the Nizam and the Marathas divided the acquired territory among themselves. The English got Malabar, Coorg, Dindigul and Baramahal. The Marathas got territory on the north-west and Nizam on the north-east of Mysore.

Critics point out that Cornwallis could easily depose Sultan Tipu and annex the whole of Mysore. Had he done so in 1792, no necessity for the fourth 'Mysore War would have arisen in the time of Lord Wellesley. However, Cornwallis was wise in not doing so. He followed a policy of caution. The Marathas and the Nizam might have betrayed him. Such an act would not have been approved by the Court of Directors and the Board of Control. War with France was imminent and the home authorities were asking for peace. Cornwallis was not eager to take over the management of the whole of Mysore and so he deliberately stayed his hands. Moreover, if Cornwallis had taken away the whole of the territory of Sultan Tipu, he would have been forced to share the same with the Marathas and the Nizam. No wonder, Cornwallis wrote thus: **"We have effectually crippled our enemy without making our friends too formidable".**

After the Third Mysore War, Tipu applied himself vigorously to internal administration. By 1794, he was able to pay the war indemnity and redeem his sons. He reorganized his military forces. He improved the fortifications of his capital. He encouraged cultivation and industrial pursuits. The result was that Mysore presented the picture of an efficient, well-managed and prosperous state. He was extremely cautious in his relations with his neighbours. Nana Fadnavis also adopted a friendly attitude towards Mysore, and refused to agree to a new treaty proposed by Cornwallis guaranteeing the allies against aggression from Tipu.

Reforms of Cornwallis

Lord Cornwallis carried out a large number of reforms. Those related to the services of the Company, the judicial system and the revenue settlement of Bengal.

Reform of Public Services. The servants of the English Company were both inefficient and corrupt. They spent a lot of their time in carrying on private trade. They were corrupt because they got very low salaries. Cornwallis was determined to see that the servants of the Company become honest and upright. He was able to induce the Directors to pay good salaries to the servants of the Company. He reduced the number of officers but increased the salaries of others. He demanded whole-time service from the servants of the Company. Private trade was completely prohibited. Cornwallis refused to oblige those Englishmen who came to India with chits from the Directors and members of the Board of Control. On one occasion, he refused to oblige so great a person as Dundas, President of the Board of Control.

While making appointments, he gave the best jobs only to the Europeans in general and the Englishmen in particular. He was convinced that the Indians were unworthy of trust and they could not be allowed to fill in any but the humblest offices in the government. The exclusion of the Indians from all effective share of the Government of their own country was almost without a parallel. Cornwallis treated the Indians with scorn. He stigmatized the whole nation as unworthy of trust and incapable of honourable conduct. The Cornwallis system was calculated to debase rather than uplift the people fallen under the dominion, of the Company. He would have got the same amount of loyalty, efficiency and uprightness from the Indian officers as he got from, the Europeans and Englishmen if he had given them the same salaries.

Judicial Reforms. Cornwallis carried out his judicial reforms in 1787, 1790 and 1793. The reforms made by him in Bengal, Bihar and Orissa served as model for Madras (now Chennai) and Bombay (now Mumbai).

The main object of the reforms of 1787 was *economy*. The number of districts was reduced from 36 to 23 and for each district an Englishman who was a covenanted servant of the English Company, was made the Collector. The latter was not only to collect revenue, but was also to act as a magistrate and judge. The Collector was required to perform the three duties separately in three different capacities and not to combine them and exercise them all at one time. While sitting in the revenue court, he was not to exercise the powers of a magistrate and vice versa. Appeals were to be taken to the Board of Revenue at Calcutta from the decisions of the Maal Adalats. The final appeal in Revenue cases was to be taken to the Governor-General-in-Council.

As regards civil cases, an appeal could be taken to the Sadar Diwani Adalat if the amount involved was more than ₹1,000. Ordinarily the decision of Sadar Diwan Adalat was final. However, if the amount involved was more than ₹5,000 an appeal was to be taken to the King in-Council.

Provision was made for the creation of the office of the Registrar. The Collector as a judge of the Mofussil Diwani Adalat was given the power to forward the cases up to ₹200 to the Registrar. The decisions of the Registrar became valid only when they were countersigned by the Collector as a judge.

The one great defeat of the system of 1787 was the concentration of too many powers in the hands of the Collector. Those powers were not only uncontrollable but in actual practice uncontrolled. The combination of the functions of the collector, magistrate and judge in the hands of one person was against the theory of separation of powers. The judiciary could not be independent of the executive.

Cornwallis made certain reforms in the criminal justice of the country in 1790. The Sadar Nizamat Adalat was shifted to Calcutta. It was provided that that court was to meet at least once a week to transact business. It might meet more than once. It was required to keep a regular record of the work done by it. It was given the authority to recommend cases to Governor-General-Council for mercy. The control of the Nawab over the Sadar Nizamat Adalat was completely abolished. This work was to be done by the Governor-General-in-Council with the help of chief Kadi and two Mufties.

Lord Cornwallis provided for the establishment of four courts of circuit. The three provinces of Bengal, Bihar and Orissa (now Odisha) were divided into four divisions and for each of those divisions a court of circuit was provided. Each circuit court was presided over by two covenanted servants of the English Company. It was held by the chief Kadi and Mufties who were appointed and removed by the Governor-General-in-Council on the ground of misconduct or incapacity for the performance of their functions. Each circuit court was required to move in its division for the disposal of cases. The decisions of the circuit court were to be executed by the magistrates. In the case of punishment of death or perpetual imprisonment, the decision of the circuit court had to be confirmed by the Sadar Nizamat Adalat.

The Collector of the district was made a magistrate. He was given the duty of apprehending murderers, robbers, thieves, housebreakers and other disturbers of peace. If after preliminary enquiry, the Collector found that there was no *prima facie* case against the accused, he acquitted him. If he found the accused guilty in a petty case, he convicted him. But in serious cases, it was his duty either to put the accused in Faujdari jail to stand his trial before the circuit court or let him off on bail till the time the court of circuit met at the district headquarters. There were certain cases in which the Magistrate was not allowed to let off the prisoners on bail, e.g., murder and robbery.

Cornwallis had found that on account of low salaries the judicial officers were taken from the dregs of society. They were also tempted to accept bribes. Cornwallis provided for liberal salaries so that men of character and ability might join the judicial service. He defended the additional expenditure on the ground that it was necessary for the administration of justice.

Other changes were made by Cornwallis in 1793. The Maal Adalats or revenue courts were abolished and all revenue cases were transferred to the ordinary civil courts known as Diwani Adalats. Provision- was made for the establishment of a court of Diwani Adalat in every district of the three provinces Every such court was to be presided over by a covenanted servant of the Company. At the time of taking office, the judge was required to take a prescribed oath. Diwani Adalats tried both civil and revenue cases, but they had nothing to do with criminal cases. Ordinarily, cases were to be tried according to Hindu law or Mohammedan law. However, if there was no specific provision on any point, the same was to be disposed of according to justice, equity and good conscience.

A regulation of the same year made the servants of the Company liable before the courts of justice. It was provided that the natives of India were to be allowed to bring cases against British subjects in the Diwani Adalats. If the amount involved was not more than ₹500. If it was more than ₹500, the suit had to be filed in the Supreme Court at Calcutta.

Even those cases in which the Government was a party were to be tried by the ordinary civil courts.

Provision was made for four provincial courts of appeals for the three presidencies. Their headquarters were to be at Calcutta, Murshidabad, Dacca and Patna. Every provincial court of appeal was to be presided over by three covenanted servants of the English Company. These courts were given both original and appellate jurisdiction. Their decisions were final in cases involving ₹1,000 or less. If the amount was more, an appeal could be taken to the Sadar Diwani Adalat.

The Sadar Diwani Adalat was to hear appeals involving more than ₹1,000. Up to ₹5,000 its decisions were final. If the amount involved was more, an appeal could be taken to the King-in-Council. The Sadar Diwani Adalat was also given the power of supervising and controlling the working of the lower courts.

Provision was made for the appointment of Munsiffs to try petty cases involving not more than ₹50. The number of Munsiffs was to depend upon the volume of work. The proceedings of the Munsiffs were to be submitted to the court of Diwani Adalat for approval. They did their work honorarily and consequently there were complaints of corruption and bribery.

In 1793, Cornwallis abolished the court fees which were previously paid by the litigants. His view was that arrears of work were due to the dilatoriness and inefficiency of administration of justice. The Collector was deprived of his magisterial powers. The result was that he was to do only the work of rent collection.

Cornwallis tried to regulate the legal profession. It was provided that lawyers in future were to charge only moderate fees prescribed by Government. If they violated this law, they were liable to be disqualified. Formerly, the system of issuing regulations was not systematic and consequently it was difficult to ascertain the exact law of the country. It was provided that in future all the regulations issued in any year were to be printed and put in one volume. This facilitated reference.

Cornwallis deserves high praise for the judicial reforms carried out by him. Although he was criticised for adding to the expenses of administration, he defended the reforms on the ground that those were absolutely necessary for the efficient administration of justice and the peace and prosperity of the country. His view was that as the English Company was getting a lot of money from the people of India in the form of revenue, it was criminal to make economy in the administration of justice. However, his system suffered from certain shortcomings. He avoided the appointment of Indians to jobs of responsibility and position in the judicial hierarchy. Indians were appointed only Munsiffs. This policy continued up to the time of Lord William Bentinck, when the same was reversed.

Police Reforms. Formerly, the zamindars exercised police powers. It was their duty to maintain law and order and arrest the suspected persons. They also commanded the local police forces. The reform of Cornwallis took away the police powers of the zamindars. He also divided the districts into small areas and each of these areas was placed under a Darogha or superintendent under the supervision of a representative of the Company in the district. The police services were Europeanised with fixed salaries and functions.

Permanent Settlement of Bengal (1793)

Another great achievement of Cornwallis was the permanent settlement of Bengal, Bihar and Orissa (now Odisha). When in 1765 the English Company secured the Diwani of Bengal, Bihar and Orissa, it was found that the ryot or the cultivator paid a fixed share of the produce of his land either in cash or in kind to the zamindar. The latter was merely the collector of revenue. However, his office gradually had become hereditary. Thus, the zamindari, which was originally contract agency, became something resembling a landed estate. Zamindar received the revenue, paid 9/10ths to Viceroy and 1/10th to himself. He inherited his zamindari, and could sell or give away his office on obtaining permission and could demand compensation if the State deprived him of it. He was responsible for maintaining peace within his jurisdiction. In 1765, the work of collection of revenue was left in the hands of the natives, but in 1769, British supervisors were appointed to control them. Things did not improve in spite of this change. In 1772, Warren Hastings set up the quinquennial settlement but the same was discontinued in 1777 on account of the failure of the experiment. The old system of annual settlements was resorted to. In 1784, an Act of Parliament directed the Court of Directors to abandon the annual settlement and frame permanent rules for the collection of land revenue.

When Lord Cornwallis came to India he found "agriculture and trade decaying, zamindars and ryots sinking into poverty and money-lenders the only flourishing class in the community". The Directors of the Company were also alarmed at the steady deterioration of the revenue collection. It was found that annual collection left the zamindars in arrears and did not benefit any class. They recommended a moderate permanent assessment as more beneficial both to the Government and the people. They condemned the employment of temporary renters and farmers who had no interest either in the State or in the ryots. They oppressed the latter as much as they could. Cornwallis got these, instructions but felt that it was not possible to carry them out certain changes had already been brought about in revenue administration with the object of decentralization: The Board of Revenue controlled the collectors who were in charge of land revenue collections. In 1787 and 1788, annual settlements were made by the Collectors. In 1789, a decennial settlement was made.

It was found that there were two schools of thought with regard to the revenue settlement. The school led by James Grant emphasized the fact that the zamindars had no permanent rights whether as proprietors of the soil or as officials who collected and paid the rent. The State was not bound by any definite limit in its demands from them. The other school of thought was led by Sir John Shore. Its view was that the proprietary rights in the land belonged to the zamindars and that the State was entitled only to a customary revenue from them. For an accurate settlement, the proportion of rent actually paid and the actual collections and payments made by zamindars and farmers should both be ascertained. He was in favour of a direct settlement with the zamindars for 10 years. There were other officials who were in favour of a permanent settlement with the zamindars. Cornwallis was of the opinion that a decennial settlement would have all the disadvantages of an annual settlement. It would not give the zamindars sufficient inducement to ensure the clearance of the extensive jungles in the provinces. Sir John contended that a permanent settlement would result in an unfair distribution of the assessment particularly when there was no survey. In 1790, the rules for the decennial settlement were published and it was stated that at the end of that period, the settlement would probably be made permanent. In accordance with the orders of the Court of Directors, the settlement of Bengal, Bihar and Orissa (now Odisha) was made permanent in March 1793. The settlement was made as high as possible. As a matter of fact, it was practically double of what it was in 1765. "It was possible to raise it so high because it was declared to be final and permanent".

It is to be noted that the permanent settlement was not a hastily devised measure. It did not emanate solely from Cornwallis. Many of the permanent officials recommended such a change. The new settlement was based on the information acquired during many years of enquiry. It had also the full support of the home authorities as it was sanctioned by Pitt, Prime Minister of England, Dundas, President of Board of Control and the Court of Directors.

Provisions. The permanent settlement created a limited proprietary right in the land in the zamindars. All rights of the State in the nature of Nazrana and permission to sell fees were given up. Magisterial powers were taken away from zamindars. They were left with no police work. As long as they paid revenue to the Government in time they were left free in their relation with their tenants. If they did not pay the land revenue, a part of their land was to be disposed of to recover the land revenues.

Historians have passed conflicting judgments with regard to the merits and demerits of permanent settlement. According to Marshman, "It was a bold, brave and wise measure. Under the genial influence of this territorial charter, which for the first time created indefeasible rights and interests in the soil, population has increased, cultivation has been extended and a gradual improvement has become visible in the habits and comforts of the people". According to R. C. Dutt, "If the prosperity and happiness of a nation be the criterion of wisdom arid success, Lord Cornwallis's Permanent Settlement of 1793 is the wisest and most successful measure which the British nation had ever adopted in India". He further added that the permanent settlement was "the one act of British nation within the century and a half of their rule in India which has most effectually safeguarded the economic welfare of the people". On the other hand, Holmes condemned the permanent settlement in these words: "The permanent settlement was a sad blunder. The interior tenants derived from it no benefit whatever. The zamindars again and again failed to pay their rent charges, and their estates were sold for the benefit of the Government". In spite of these judgments, it is desirable to discuss the merits and demerits of the settlement separately.

Merits

1. The State was assured of a certain amount of land revenue from the people. It was not to depend upon the results of annual bidding. If a zamindar did not pay the land revenue, the same could be realised by settling a portion of his land.

2. The landlords knew that they had to pay a specific amount of money as land revenue to the Government. If they put more labour, and capital in the land and got more profit out of it, they stood to gain because Government share was not to increase proportionately. It was absolutely fixed whether the landlord cultivated their lands more or less. At the time of the settlement, many parts of the land were covered with jungles and the same were cleared after the settlement.

3. Cornwallis thought that the permanent settlement of Bengal would play the same part in creating a loyal class which the establishment of the Bank of England had played in the case of William III and Mary. The zamindars who were made the owners of land could be counted upon to defend the rule of the English Company against their rivals and opponents. It was found that these very zamindars were loyal to the British Government during the days of the Mutiny. No wonder, Setton Carr observes that the political benefits of the settlement balanced its economic defects.

4. The permanent settlement gave popularity and Stability to the British Government and thus helped to make the province the healthiest and most flourishing in India.

5. The permanent settlement set free the ablest servants of the Company for judicial work. Formerly, they had to waste a lot of their time every year in offering the collection of revenue to the highest bidder and realising the same amount.

6. The permanent settlement avoided the evils of periodical settlements which, in spite of long intervals, produced economic dislocation, evasion, concealment of worth and the deliberate throwing of land out of cultivation.

7. It is true that the Government could not increase the land revenue in the future but it gained in an indirect manner. As the people became richer, the Government got money by taxing them in various ways.

8. A permanent land tax is inexpensive, uniform and certain. It has all the advantages mentioned by Adam Smith in his **Canons of Taxation.**

Demerits

1. The immediate effect of the permanent settlement on the zamindars was disastrous. Many of them could not realise the land revenue from their tenants and consequently could not pay the money to the Government in time. The result was that their lands were sold.

2. Contrary to the expectations, the landlords did not take much interest in the development of their lands. They became merely absentee landlords living in Calcutta (now Kolkata) or at the district towns on the income derived from the tenants. It has rightly been pointed out that although Cornwallis intended to create a class of English landlords in Bengal, what he actually created was a class of Irish landlords.

3. The permanent settlement ignored the rights of the tenants. They were left absolutely at the mercy of the landlords who could oust them at any time. The landlord could charge any amount of money from the tenants he pleased. It is true that Cornwallis had laid down that

"the zamindar should keep a register of his tenants and grant them Pattahs or leases, specifying the rents they were to pay, and that in case of any infringement of these rules, the ryot was to seek a remedy in an action against him in the civil court," but unfortunately the registers were not kept and the Pattahs were rarely given. The remedy of the civil court was a very expensive one and the poor tenants felt that they could not take advantage of it. This state of affairs continued till the Government came to the rescue of the tenants and safeguarded their interests by passing tenancy legislation.

4. The Government lost forever a share of the unearned increment. The deficit was estimated at ₹4.5 crores.
5. Bengal did not possess cadastral records till 1893 and consequently there was expensive litigation between the tenants and the landlords.

Setton Carr sums up his criticism thus: "The permanent settlement somewhat secured the interests of the zamindars, postponed those of the tenants and permanently sacrificed those of the State". According to P.E. Roberts, "Had the permanent settlement been postponed for another 10 to 20 years, the capacities of the land would have been better ascertained. Many mistakes and anomalies would have been avoided, and the reforms brought about by Cornwallis himself in the civil service would have trained up a class of officials far more competent to deal with so vast a subject".

According to Baden-Powell, "The permanently settlement disappointed many expectations and produced several results that were not anticipated". "A very great blunder as well as gross injustice was committed when a settlement was made with the zamindars alone and the rights of property every bit as good as theirs were ignored". "He (Cornwallis) committed himself to a policy which in regard to the three interested parties—the zamindar, the ryot and the ruling power—assured the welfare of the first, somewhat postponed the claims of the second and sacrificed the interests of the third". "The permanent settlement in contrast to the chaotic system which it supplanted, had many fairly obvious advantages".

According to Dr. Tara Chand, "The Permanent Settlement deprived the State of a share in the increase of rent which resulted from the general improvement of the economic conditions and handed over the entire unearned increment to the zamindars. In the second place, while the settlement favoured a handful of landholders, it completely ignored the interests to that vast mass of the oppressed cultivators, whose resentment and dissatisfaction seemed to evoke no sympathy. Munro wrote, "It seems extraordinary that it should ever have been conceived that a country could be as much benefited by giving up a share of the public rent to a small class of zamindars or mootadars as...by giving it to ryots, from whom all rent is derived'".

Cornwallis Completed the Work of Hastings

Dr. Aspinall rightly remarks that it is no disparagement of Cornwallis's work to point out that he completed what Hastings had begun. In 1772, Warren Hastings had abolished the double government of Bengal, Bihar and Orissa which was set up in 1765 by Lord Clive. The judicial and police reforms of Cornwallis completed that constitutional change.

Warren Hastings had come to the conclusion that the servants of the Company were not likely to become honest in their work unless their salaries were increased and their private trade was prohibited. In 1774, he had prohibited the members of the Supreme Council from engaging in trade and had increased their remuneration by means of a commission. In 1781, he introduced fixed salaries for the members of the Committee of Revenue and commission of one per cent of net revenue. Cornwallis was able to take the reform a step further. He extended the improved scales of pay and allowances to all the senior servants. However, he was not in a position to extend the prohibition of trade to all officials.

Warren Hastings had realised the danger of entrusting power into the hands of the Indian officials who were as a rule corrupt. He had made the Collector the superintendent of the district criminal court. To substitute English for Indian judges was merely the next step. The appointment by Warren Hastings of Indian magistrates charged with the supervision of the Mofussil police and with the duty of arresting and committing for trial did not prove a success. Consequently, these offices were abolished by Warren Hastings. While doing so, he gave the magisterial powers to the judges of the civil courts.

The separation of revenue administration from civil jurisdiction, which was accomplished by Cornwallis, was foreseen by Warren Hastings who began the change in 1780. The judges whom he appointed in charge of new civil courts were not at all connected with revenue work. The bifurcation of functions was only partial because the Collectors were still authorised to decide cases relating to revenue and consequently the jurisdiction of the civil judge and the Collector was continually clashing. It is probable that if Warren Hastings had stayed longer in India, he would have remedied the situation in the same way as Cornwallis did in 1793.

In the matter of substituting English criminal law for Mohammedan law, Cornwallis went only a little further than Warren Hastings. The latter was of opinion that until the constitution of Bengal "shall have attained the same perfection" as the English, "no conclusion can be drawn from the English that can be properly applied to the manners and state of this country". The only legislative change made by Warren Hastings was to give very severe punishment to dacoits and their families. In many cases, the Supreme Court intervened to alter the unsuitable punishments prescribed by Mohammedan law. Undoubtedly Cornwallis made more use of the legislative power than Warren Hastings did. But even he was cautious in making changes in Mohammedan criminal law. Although he had very strong views regarding the superiority of the criminal law of Great Britain, he did not radically alter the Mohammedan criminal law. Generally, Cornwallis carried on the work which Hastings had started. He met with much less interference, criticism and obstruction than his predecessor did.

The Code of Civil Procedure of Cornwallis was based on the earlier codes which Warren Hastings and Sir Elijah Impey had compiled and for which James Stephen had a word of praise.

It is for these reasons that it has been stated that **"if the foundation of the civil administration had been laid by Warren Hastings, the structure was raised by Lord Cornwallis."**[1]

According to Lord Curzon, Lord Cornwallis was a man with quite ordinary abilities but with a sterling character, a great fund of commonsense and a superb and untiring devotion to duty—who left a considerable mark upon the Indian administration. Cornwallis was one of those men upon whom Government rely to do their business straightforwardly, efficiently and well. For twenty years he was the dues ex-machine to whom successive ministries turned to extricate them from muddles or to place disordered affairs upon a stable basis. Even his failures never counted against him. The surrender of York Town brought with it no censure, but was followed by other and higher employments. Twenty years later the Treaty of Amiens which Cornwallis was sent out to negotiate, proved to be obsolete almost as soon as it had been signed. But no one blamed its author. It was

---

[1] Cf. "It must remain the verdict of history that Cornwallis merely developed under happier auspices what Warren Hastings had begun that in that part of this policy which was his own, he embarked from the false premises that reform in India meant making it like the England of his ideals; and that he made serious abiding mistakes from the best of motives in the world".

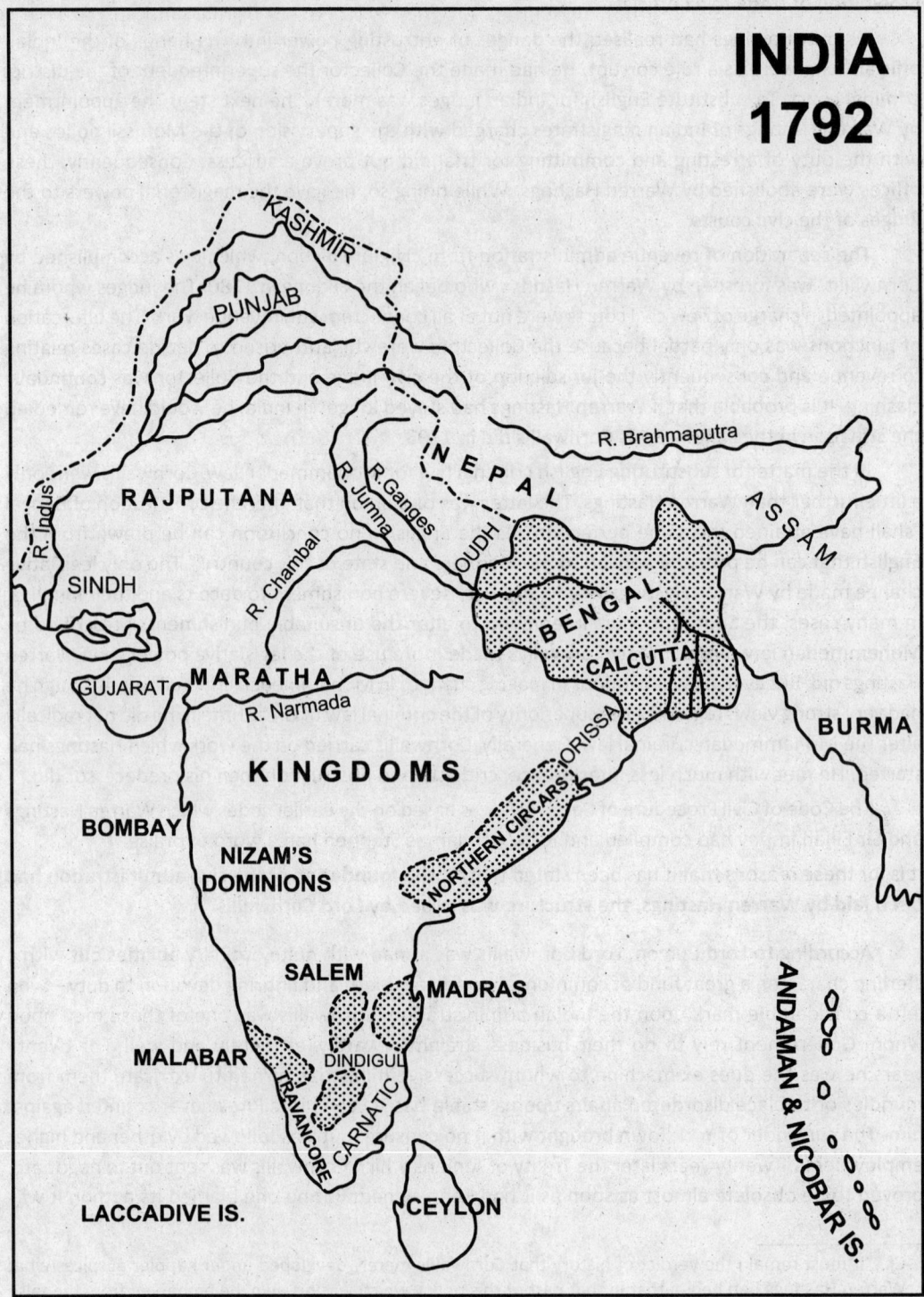

always felt that Cornwallis had done his best in an honest, capable, commonsense way, and that no lower consideration than the honour of his country had guided his action. Thus, although destitute of any pretension to genius and with quite mediocre intellectual gifts he filled post after post in the internal and external services of Britain and was regarded as having comported himself in each with credit and success". (*British Government in India*, Vol. 1, pp. 166-67.) Again, "The administration of Cornwallis, which was prolonged for seven years in spite of his frequently expressed desire to return, was remarkable for his internal reforms, in which, with a courage that cannot be over-praised, he set his face against the jobbery and corruption that still permeated the civil service, carrying the now forgotten crusade of Clive to its logical conclusion by the grant of decent salaries to the "writers in return for the prohibition of private trade. The civil and criminal courts were reformed, and the inefficiency in the military services, which had reached the dimensions of a scandal, was severely taken in hand. The permanent settlement in Bengal, which is invariably associated with the name of Cornwallis, but which was really the work of his civilian advisers (albeit the best of them, Sir John Shore, who advocated a decennial term, was unfortunately overruled, is now generally regarded as having been a mistake, and has happily not been followed in any other province. Perhaps, however, the most characteristic as also the most creditable, of Cornwallis's achievements was the fearless rage with which he fought against jobbery in any form, refusing to yield a jot to the shameless pressure that was brought to bear upon him from the highest quarters in London, including the Prince of Wales. Sir John Shore wrote of him: "The honesty of his principles is inflexible; he is manly, affable, and good natured, of an excellent judgment, and he has a degree of application to business beyond what you would suppose'; and again: 'His situation was uncomfortable on arrival; he now receives the respect due to his zeal, integrity and indefatigable application'.

"A study of Cornwallis's character and a survey of his administration leave us with a very pleasant impression of the service that can be rendered in an oriental dependency—or, indeed, anywhere— by **transparent honesty** of purpose, a total absence of self-seeking and unswerving devotion to duty. Cornwallis neither did nor attempted anything brilliant but he never spared himself in making things better than he found them and in diffusing a general sense of contentment and stability. (*Ibid.*, pp 170-71.)

According to Dodwell, "Lord Cornwallis was a public servant who upheld national and not private traditions. His service was to the Crown and the people whom he governed, and he thus embodied fitly the new spirit of Indian rule".

SIR JOHN SHORE (1793-98)

It is true that Lord Cornwallis was opposed to the appointment of a civil servant of the English Company as the Governor-General of Bengal, but when in 1793 Cornwallis left India he was succeeded by Sir John Shore who was a senior member of the Supreme Council and was also intimately connected with him in connection with the land reform. During the term of his office, Sir John Shore followed the policy of neutrality as laid down in the Pitt's India Act. This policy was carried to such as extreme point that it lowered the prestige of the English Company in India. According to Sir John Malcolm, "It was proved from the events of this administration that no ground of political advantage could be abandoned without being instantly occupied by an enemy; and that to resign influence, was not merely to resign power, but to allow that power to pass into the hands hostile to the British Government". The most important event of Sir John Shore's time was the attack of the Marathas on the Nizam and the defeat of Nizam in the battle of Kharda in March 1795. The Nizam begged for British help but the same was refused by Sir John Shore on the ground that such help was likely to entangle the English Company into the internal affairs of the Indian States. Such a treatment made the Nizam bitter and he had to submit to humiliating terms of the Marathas. However, the Nizam was able to recover his position on account of dissensions among the Marathas and on the whole the Nizam did not lose much. Anyhow, the Nizam was not in a mood to forget and forgive the British betrayal of his cause.

Sir John Shore interfered in the affairs of Oudh. The Nawab died in 1797 and was succeeded by a son of worthless character. To begin with, Sir John sanctioned the succession. However, where he came to know that the son was the offspring of a menial servant, he reversed his decision, and set up a brother of the late Nawab on the throne. He also entered into a treaty with the new Nawab. By the new treaty, the English Company was made responsible for the defence of Oudh. The Nawab was to pay an annual subsidy of 76 lakhs of rupees. He also gave up the Fort of Allahabad to the English Company. He bound himself to hold no communication with any foreign State. This treaty was probably due to the fear of the attack of Zaman Shah of Kabul who was in the Punjab at that time.

In 1795, there occurred a dangerous mutiny of the European officers of Bengal who threatened to seize the administration. The situation was so serious that Sir John Shore was forced to make many concessions to the rebels. On account of his failure to deal with the situation, Sir John Shore was called back in 1798 and was succeeded by Lord Wellesley.

According to Lord Curzon, "It cannot be said that in his five year's rule Shore left any mark. He was a typical Bengal civilian of the best type, a great revenue expert, an upright, dull, respectable, friendly kind of man, hating pomp of any sort, loving peace and economy, very pious, declining to work on Sundays though not attending the services of the Church, and ultimately joining the Clapham sect after his return to England. As Major Toone, who had been one of Hastings' A.D.C.'s, remarked: 'A **good man, but as cold as a greyhound's nose**'. Shore had the strong tastes of a scholar, being a student of Urdu, Persian and Arabic; he wrote a journal in Latin, kept up his knowledge of Greek and composed mediocre verses and translations in the decorous 18th century fashion. While in India he did not enjoy good health and was always chafing at the absence of his wife and family.

"Shore's strong views about economy had made him a strenuous critic of Hastings' regime, and he was popularly regarded as a member of the Opposition or Francis's camp, until he was won over by personal contact with Hastings, notably on the return journey of the latter to England. This conversion excited the not too kindly comment of William Hickey, who wrote in his Memoirs : "Mr. John Shore suddenly and most unaccountably from an inveterate and bitter enemy became that gentleman's (i.e., Hastings') sworn bosom friend". (*British Government in India*, Vol. I, pp. 171-72.)

REVIEW QUESTIONS

1. Give a detailed account of the work of Lord Cornwallis with respect to his foreign policy and internal reforms.
2. Write a note on the third Mysore War.
3. Review the reforms of Lord Cornwallis.
4. Discuss the achievements of Lord Cornwallis.
5. Narrate the features of the Permanent Settlement of Bengal.

6. Describe the merits and demerits of the Permanent Settlement of Bengal.
7. Write a detailed note on the administration of Cornwallis.
8. Explain the achievements of Sir John Shore.
9. Sir John Shore interfered in the affairs of Oudh. Comment.
10. Write short notes on the following:
    (a) Permanent settlement of Bengal
    (b) Sir John Shore

SUGGESTED READINGS

Aspinall, A.: *Cornwallis in Bengal* (1931).
Dodwell, H.H.: *Cambridge History of India*, Vol. V.
Seton Karr: *The Marquis Cornwallis* (1898).

7   Lord Wellesley (1798-1805)

LEARNING OBJECTIVES

- Know the condition of India at the advent of Lord Wellesley
- Discuss the merits and demerits of the subsidiary system
- Throw light on the administration and achievements of Lord Wellesley
- Give an account of the character of Tipu Sultan
- Know about the successors of Lord Wellesley

Lord Wellesley, "the great Pro-Consul", was appointed the Governor-General of Bengal at the age of 37. He was one of the greatest of the British rulers of India. The only persons who can stand comparison with him are Lord Clive, Warren Hastings and Lord Dalhousie. In the matter of actual achievements, he beat all of them.

CONDITION OF INDIA IN 1798

When Lord Wellesley came to India as Governor-General, the condition of India was very critical. The Nizam was angry because the English Company had not helped him when he was attacked by the Marathas in the time of Sir John Shore. He was organizing a body of regular troops under a French officer named Raymond. He was not in a mood to come to terms with the English Company. The Marathas were also feeling a sense of importance on account of their victory over the Nizam. They had huge resources and were controlling practically the whole of Central India. Scindia had a powerful army which was trained and commanded by a Frenchman called Perron. Undoubtedly, the key positions occupied by the French officers in the Indian States were a source of real danger to the English Company. Sultan Tipu had not forgotten the humiliation to which he was subjected by Lord Cornwallis when he was forced to give up half of his territory, pay a huge war indemnity and also surrender his two sons as hostages. He was the deadly enemy of the English Company and openly so. He was carrying on negotiations with the French Governor of Mauritius and Reunion. He had employed French officers to drill his soldiers and train them. There was the danger of the invasion of Napoleon. He was already on his way to the East.

Thus, the political situation in the country was not an easy one. The English Company had not much of resources and it was left to the intelligence, bravery and resourcefulness of Lord Wellesley to tackle the situation in a masterly manner. Within the next 7 years, Lord Wellesley was able to defeat and humble the enemies of the English Company. Many of them submitted without striking a blow. However, before he could finish his work, he was forced to resign in 1805.

The one thing to be noted with regard to Lord Wellesley is that when he came to India, he felt that the policy of non-intervention was not at all practicable. That was due to the political condition in the country. On account of the absence of a paramount power each State could do whatever it pleased. There was no guarantee of peace. There was no supreme power to which an aggrieved State could appeal for help. Under the circumstances, Lord Wellesley came to the conclusion that either the English Company must become the Supreme power in the country or quit the country. There was absolutely no half-way. It was with this conviction in mind that Lord Wellesley started his work.

SUBSIDIARY SYSTEM

One of the great master strokes of Lord Wellesley was the application of the system of subsidiary alliances to a large number of Indian States. It was in this way that he was able to add to the resources

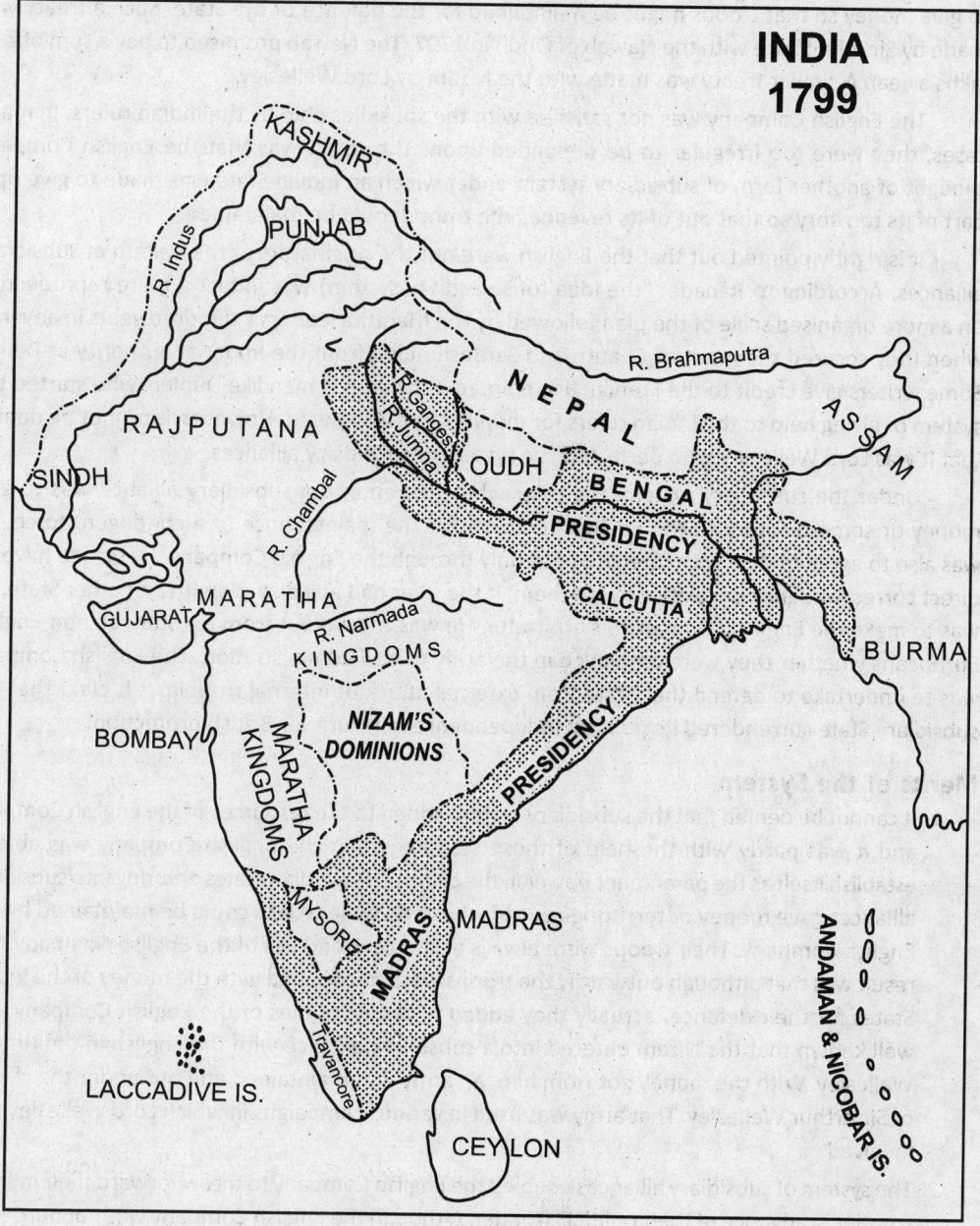

of the English Company, oust the foreigners from the Indian States and make the English Company the arbiter in the affairs of the Indian States. However, it is wrong to say that Lord Wellesley was the author of the system of subsidiary alliances.

According to Sir Alfred Lyall, there were four stages in the evolution of the subsidiary system. To begin with, the English Company contented itself with lending a military contingent to help some Indian princes. This was done by Warren Hastings when he lent British troops to the Nawab of Oudh to fight against the Rohillas. The second stage came when the English Company took the field on its own account. It was usually assisted by the army of some Indian prince who was not strong enough to do the job single-handed. In the third stage, the English Company asked the ruler of the State to give money so that troops might be maintained for the defence of the State. Such a treaty was made by Sir John Shore with the Nawab of Oudh in 1797. The Nawab promised to pay a sum of ₹76 lakhs a year. A similar treaty was made with the Nizam by Lord Wellesley.

The English Company was not satisfied with the subsidies paid by the Indian rulers. In many cases, they were too irregular to be depended upon. The result was that the English Company thought of another form of subsidiary system under which an Indian State was made to give up a part of its territory so that out of its revenues the troops could be maintained.

It is rightly pointed out that the English were not the originators of the system of subsidiary alliances. According to Ranade, "the idea (of subsidiary system) was in fact a mere reproduction on a more organised scale of the plan followed by the Maratha leaders a hundred years in advance when they secured the grant of Chauth and Sardeshmukhi from the Imperial authority at Delhi". Some writers give credit to the French. It is pointed out that it is men like Dupleix who started the system of giving help to the Indian rulers for money or other reward. However, it cannot be denied that it was Lord Wellesley who perfected the system of subsidiary alliances.

Under the subsidiary system, the ruler who entered into a subsidiary alliance was to give money or some territory to the English Company for the maintenance of a contingent force. He was also to agree to deal with foreign States only through the English Company. He was to have no direct correspondence or relations with them. If the ruler had any dispute with any other State, he was to make the English Company his arbitrator. He was to turn out from his State all non-English Europeans whether they were employed in the army or civil administration. The English Company was to undertake to defend that State from external attack or internal trouble. It is clear that the subsidiary State surrendered its political independence in return for British protection.

Merits of the System

1. It cannot be denied that the subsidiary system added to the resources of the English Company and it was partly with the help of these resources that the English Company was able to establish itself as the paramount power in the country. The Indian States entering into subsidiary alliances gave money or territories out of whose revenue troops could be maintained by the English Company. Their troops were always at the beck and call of the English Company. The result was that although outwardly the troops were maintained with the money of the Indian States for their defence, actually they added to the resources of the English Company. It is well known that the Nizam entered into a subsidiary alliance with the English in the time of Wellesley. With the money got from him, an army was maintained and put under the charge of Sir Arthur Wellesley. That army was used in various campaigns in which Lord Wellesley was involved.

2. The system of subsidiary alliances enabled the English Company to throw forward their military frontier in advance of their political frontier. Although the English Company was not burdened

with the responsibility of the administration of the States joining the subsidiary system, its influence was enhanced.

3. The evils of war were kept at a distance from the territories of the English Company. The territories under the English Company did not suffice because the battles were fought, in most cases in the territories of the States joining the subsidiary alliance.
4. The system of subsidiary alliance did not arouse the jealousy of other European nations. The reason was that outwardly the independence of the States was maintained.
5. The English Company was able to exclude the influence of the French from the Indian States. Whenever a State entered into a subsidiary alliance, the ruler had to drive out all Europeans who were not Englishmen.

Demerits of the System

1. The one great demerit of the system was that the amount of money demanded from the rulers of the Indian States was out of all proportion to their resources. The result was that the rulers of the States paid the money to the Company even at the expense of the welfare of their people. All kinds of methods were adopted to collect the money so that the English Company might not have an excuse to demand territory from that State. However, in certain cases even when the subsidy was paid regularly, the English Company forced the ruler to hand over certain territory for the maintenance of the army. This was done by Wellesley when he forced the Nawab of Oudh to give Gorakhpur, Rohilkhand and the Doab for the maintenance of troops by the Company.
2. The subsidiary system resulted in the internal decay protected States.[1] It destroyed the initiative of the ruling princes. It made them dependent on the English Company. The result was that the Indian princes led lives of vice and corruption on account of the assurance that the English Company was always there to help them in times of trouble. The people of the States were deprived of the natural remedy of revolution. They had no chance of success even if they dared to revolt against their corrupt ruler.
3. The Court of Directors did not approve of the subsidiary system because it created jealousy among the Indian States against the English Company. Moreover, the Directors were also opposed to the policy of annexing territories.

On the whole, the system of subsidiary alliances helped the English Company to tide over its difficulties and emerge as a great power in the country.

FOURTH MYSORE WAR (1799)

It has already been pointed out that Sultan Tipu had not forgotten the humiliating treatment which had been meted out to him by Cornwallis. He was determined to have his revenge. He sent his emissaries to Kabul, Constantinople, Arabia and Mauritius. The Sultan planted the tree of liberty at Seringapatam. He was elected a member of the Jacobin Club of France. He tried to correspond with Napoleon who was in Egypt at that time. French generals were drilling his forces. The situation was serious and Lord Wellesley at once made up his mind to deal with it with a firm hand.

Before taking action against Tipu, Wellesley tried to win over the Nizam and the Marathas and succeeded so far as the Nizam was concerned. The Nizam entered into a subsidiary alliance

---

[1] According to Thomas Munro, "Wherever subsidiary system is introduced, the country will soon bear the marks of it in decaying villages and decreasing population".

with the English Company in September 1798. He agreed to make a payment for the maintenance of the contingent force. He agreed to turn out the officers of other European nations. The French army of the Nizam was disbanded.

Having got the support of the Nizam on his side, Lord Wellesley[2] demanded absolute submission from Sultan Tipu. As the latter did not carry out the command, war was declared. The main army was under General Harris and he proceeded towards Mysore. Arthur Wellesley, the younger brother of the Governor-General and later known as the Duke of Wellington, was incharge of the Nizam's contingent. A force from Bombay (now Mumbai) also marched towards Mysore. The armies carried everything before them and reached Seringapatam. Sultan Tipu refused to accept the humiliating terms offered to him and died fighting in the ramparts of Seringapatam. This was in May 1799. After the victory, Wellesley annexed large and important territories which included Kanara, Coimbatore and Seringapatam. Mysore was surrounded on all sides by British territory. The Nizam was given some territory as a reward for the help given by him. Certain territories were offered to the Marathas also on certain conditions which they refused to accept. A child of the Hindu family who had been turned out by Haidar Ali was placed once again on the throne of Mysore.

Many critics have condemned the Fourth Mysore War as unnecessary and unjustified. It is pointed out that the French danger was needlessly magnified by Wellesley. There is a lot of truth in this criticism. Wellesley was a full-blooded imperialist to whom Tipu was a formidable hurdle in the expansion of the British empire in Southern India and consequently the liquidation of Tipu was a top priority in his political calculation. Wellesley knew that with the disappearance of Tipu from the political scene, the steamroller of British imperialism would be able to crush very easily any opposition from the Marathas. The Nizam was too weak a power to create any difficulty. Wellesley considered Tipu as the real enemy of the British and hence took action against him. Otherwise, there was no moral justification for the war.

It cannot be denied that the Fourth Mysore War placed on the throne of Mysore a safe and dependable vassal who was shorn of former prestige and glory. The British became the strongest power in Southern India. They had no fear of rival combinations. The capture of Seringapatam was an event of great importance after Plassey and Buxar.

CHARACTER OF TIPU

It is wrong to say that Sultan Tipu was a savage, barbarous and cruel fanatic. He was an industrious ruler who himself attended to every branch of administration. He was not cruel by nature. He was cruel only towards his enemies and he hated the English from the very core of his heart. He could never reconcile himself to co-operate with the English Company. He fought against the British tooth and nail and died fighting, but could not think of coming to a compromise with them. He was inclined towards the French and his preference for them continued all his life.

The English hated him and dreaded him. According to Kirkpatrik, Sultan Tipu was "the cruel and relentless enemy...the oppressive and unjust ruler and what not". According to Wilks, Haidar was seldom wrong and Tipu seldom right. Unlimited persecution united in detestation of his rule every Hindu in his dominion. He was barbarous where severity was vice and indulgent where it was

---

[2] It is pointed out that before starting the war, Lord Wellesley made full preparations. He personally went to Madras (now Chennai) towards the end of 1798 to direct the political and military arrangements. The Madras Army of 20,000 men under General Harris was joined by 16,000 troops from Hyderabad under Arthur Wellesley. General Stuart commanded the Bombay (now Mumbai) force of more than 6,000 men and it assembled in Malabar. Another large army commanded by Col. Reed and Brown marched from Trichinopoly.

virtue. If he had qualities fitted for empire, they were strangely equivocal. There is a Mysore proverb that "Haidar was born to create an Empire, Tipu to lose one."[3]

However, there are other writers who have paid tributes to the intelligence and other qualities of head and heart of Sultan Tipu. According to Mill, "As a domestic ruler, he sustains an advantageous comparison with the greatest princes of the East". According to Moor, "When a person travelling through a strange country finds it well cultivated, populous with industrious inhabitants, cities newly founded, commerce extending, towns increasing, and everything flourishing so as to indicate happiness, he will naturally conclude it to be under a form of government congenial to the minds of the people. This is a picture of Tipu's country, and this is our conclusion respecting its government". Major Dirom remarked thus: "His country was found everywhere full of inhabitants, and apparently cultivated to the utmost extent to which the soil was capable; while the discipline and fidelity of his troops in the field, until their last overthrow, were testimonies equally strange of the excellent regulations which existed in his army. His government, though strict and arbitrary, was despotism of a politic and able sovereign".

There is not much to condemn the character of Sultan Tipu. His misfortune was that he was pitted against the British Government which had endless resources. He could not find anybody to help him in his hour of difficulty. While the English were able to win over the Marathas and the Nizam on the occasion of the third Mysore War and the Nizam in the fourth Mysore War, Tipu had to fight alone. The French on whom he depended failed him completely.

TANJORE, SURAT AND CARNATIC

Lord Wellesley had to deal with Tanjore, Surat and Carnatic. In October 1799, Wellesley entered into a subsidiary treaty with the Raja of Tanjore. The Raja practically gave up the administration into the hands of the English Company in lieu of the payment of £40,000 a year. In the case of Surat, Wellesley abolished the double government, granted a pension to the Nawab and took over the supreme control of the country into his own hands. As regards Carnatic, its government was rotten and scandalous. It was alleged that the Nawab of Carnatic and his son had entered into correspondence with Sultan Tipu. Although the evidence was not conclusive, Wellesley took over the civil and military government of Carnatic in July 1801, when the Nawab died. The Nawab was allowed to retain his title and he was to be paid 20 per cent of the revenue of his State.

OUDH

Wellesley's treatment of Oudh was altogether high-handed. The Nawab of Oudh was asked to disband a part of his army and receive a bigger subsidiary force. The Nawab resisted and even expressed his willingness to abdicate. When Wellesley showed his readiness to accept the offer of abdication, the Nawab withdrew the offer. He declared that he was prepared to abdicate provided his son was allowed to succeed him. The indignation of Wellesley knew no bounds and he was disgusted with the duplicity and insincerity of the Nawab. Wellesley prepared a new draft treaty by which the size of the contingent force was to be increased and the subsidy was increased to 2½ million sterling. Wellesley did not care at all for the protests of the Nawab. The result was that the Nawab gave way.

---

[3] "The contrast in character and policy between father and son explains why Haidar Ali was successful in founding kingdom and Tipu contrived to lose it".

However, in spite of this, Wellesley made new demands on the Nawab. Although the Nawab had paid his subsidies regularly, Wellesley demanded and got the surrender of Rohilkhand and the southern districts between the Ganges and the Jamuna. All this amounted to about one-half of his dominions. Naturally, the Nawab resented. Sir Alfred Lyall says that Wellesley "subordinated the feelings and interests of his ally to paramount considerations of British policy in a manner that showed very little patience, forbearance or generosity. The only justification for such a policy was expediency".

STEPS AGAINST THE FRENCH DANGER

Wellesley also took certain steps to meet the French menace. He was in favour of an expedition against Mauritius but the English Admiral refused to cooperate and the scheme had to be given up. He urged the ministry at home to capture Ceylon and Batvia from the Dutch, but failed to secure their assent. He sent Indian troops to Egypt to cooperate in the expulsion of the French from that country. Wellesley also sent John Malcolm to Persia to counteract the French and Russian advance in that direction.

SECOND MARATHA WAR (1802-04)

The Maratha State was not a unified State. It was merely a confederacy. The Peshwa was weak and not in a position to control and direct the other Maratha chiefs. The important Maratha chiefs were Scindhia, Holkar, Gaikwad and Bhonsla. The Marathas were not very strong on account of the mutual jealousies of the Maratha chiefs.

In March 1800, Nana Fadnavis died at Poona and **with him departed "all the wisdom and moderation of the Maratha government"**. Both Scindhia and Holkar tried to establish their control over the Peshwa and started fighting with each other. The Peshwa submitted to the control of Scindhia but Holkar would not tolerate this. He attacked and defeated Scindhia and tried to establish his control over the Peshwa. This was too much for the Peshwa who ran away to Bassein to secure help from the English Company. It was in the circumstances that the **Treaty of Bassein** was signed on 31st December 1802. Both the Peshwa and the English agreed that the friends and enemies of the one should be treated as the friends and enemies of the other. The British were to protect the territory of Peshwa as their own. For that purpose, a subsidiary force of not less than 6,000 regular infantry with the usual proportion of field artillery was to be permanently stationed in the territory of the Peshwa. For the expenses of that force, the Peshwa was to give to the British districts yielding ₹26 lakhs a year. The Peshwa was not to entertain in his service any European hostile to the British. In the case of a dispute arising with the Nizam, the Peshwa was to accept British arbitration. The Peshwa was to respect the treaty of friendship contracted by the Gaikwad with the British and accept British arbitration in the case of a dispute. The British and the Peshwa were to give each other more military help whenever necessary. The Peshwa bound himself to negotiate in no hostilities with other States without a previous consultation with the British Government. As soon as the treaty was signed the British took the Peshwa to Poona and put him on his throne in May 1803. Holkar retired.

A lot of importance has been attached to the treaty of Bassein. It has been regarded as one of the important landmarks of British dominion in India. The English Company was able to bring the head of the Marathas under its control. It must have been understood that such a state of affairs would not be acceptable to the other Maratha chiefs. Those who entered into the treaty must have known that war was inevitable. According to Arthur Wellesley, the treaty of Bassein was made "with a cipher".

The expected happened. The Maratha chiefs gave expression to their feelings of resentment and anger. Scindhia and Bhonsla at once combined. Gaekwad and Holkar stood apart. Scindhia and Bhonsla attacked, but they met with stiff resistance at the hands of the British troops. The important battles were fought at Assaye, Aragaon and Laswari. The power of both Scindhia and Bhonsla was smashed and they both entered into separate treaties.

The treaty of Deogaon was made with the Raja of Berar and that of Surji Arjangaon was made with Scindhia. By the treaty of Deogaon, Bhonsla gave Cuttack to the English and accepted a subsidiary alliance. By the treaty of Surji Arjangaon, Scindhia accepted a subsidiary alliance and surrendered Broach, Ahmednagar and the territory between the Ganges and the Jamuna including Agra and Delhi.

WAR WITH HOLKAR

Holkar had his differences with Scindhia and consequently did not join hands with him when the latter was fighting against the British, but when Scindhia and Bhonsla were defeated, Holkar made up his mind to continue the fight. He attacked the territories of the Rajputs and demanded Chauth from the English Company. As was to be expected, Wellesley rejected those demands and war was declared. Holkar forced Colonel Monson to retreat and inflicted upon him a crushing defeat in Rajputana. The Raja of Bharatpur defied British authority. He also joined Holkar in an attack on Delhi, but their attempt failed. Later on, Holkar himself was defeated. The efforts of Lake to conquer Bharatpur failed and he suffered heavy losses. Lake made peace with the Raja of Bharatpur. When such was the condition, Lord Wellesley was called back by the Home Government which was tired of his aggressive and expensive wars.

ESTIMATE OF WELLESLEY

Lord Wellesley was one of the greatest of the Governors-General of the English Company. He has rightly been called a great pro-consul. One cannot help recalling to one's mind the great work done by him. In 1798, the position of the English Company was precarious. By 1805, Wellesley had foiled all the designs of the French, defeated and killed Tipu and humbled the Marathas. Had he been given a little more time he would have completely crushed the resistance of Holkar.

Dr. V. A. Smith gives his estimate of Wellesley in these words: "The Marquess of Wellesley is undoubtedly entitled to a place in the front rank of the Governors-General by the side of Warren Hastings, Marques of Hastings and Lord Dalhousie. Some authors would award him the first place, but in my judgment that honour belongs to Warren Hastings. Lord Wellesley, like Lords Lytton and Dufferin in later times, looked upon the affairs of India as seen by a British nobleman and politician from a Foreign Office point of view. He was a statesman rather than an administrator, concerned chiefly with matters of high policy and little inclined to examine closely the details of departmental administration. His policy was directed to two main objects: The first was the elevation of the British Government to the position of paramount power in India; or, to use his stately words to establishing a comprehensive system of alliance and political relation over every region of Hindustan and the Deccan'. The second object was the full utilisation of Indian strength so that it might play a proper part in resistance to the menace of Napoleon's world-wide ambition, which avowedly aimed at the overthrow of British power in the whole of India".

According to Lord Curzon, "There hardly exists in the gallery of British celebrities a man upon whose character and achievements more opposite verdicts have been passed, or whose career more fairly justifies such a clash of opinion. One class of writers has seen in Wellesley the courageous and farsighted architect of the empire, who carried out and expanded the great work of Warren Hastings and reared the central edifice, lofty and strong, of British dominion in the East. The opposite school regards him, if not as the 'brilliant incapacity' of Croker, at any rate as embodiment of vanity in high places, the 'Sultanised Englishmen' of mackintosh, who, by an excess of arrogance and self-esteem failed in India, as later in England, to attain the goal which his self-confident ambition had marked out for him. The truth does not lie midway between these extremes. It is to be found in both of them. Wellesley was at the same time both great and small, a man of noble conceptions and petty conceits, a prescient builder of empire and a rather laughable person. On the Indian side of his career the balance is, however, decidedly in his favour; and if his letters had not been published, which reveal him in his most petulant as well as in his most majestic moods, the credit balance would probably have been even larger". (*British Government in India*, Vol. I, p. 173.) Again, "Many of Wellesley's enterprises in India, apart from the Mysore and other campaigns, which added so much both to the glory and the territory of the empire, and which incidentally laid the foundations of his younger brother's fame, were characterised both by wisdom and imagination. But there was always a flavour of self-advertisement about them, and they were as a rule too expensive, particularly in a country like India which is liable to such sharp oscillations of policy to be sure of a prolonged existence. These remarks apply to his project for a College of Fort William for the education of the young European cadets, which was first vetoed by the Directors and then only sanctioned in a very modified form, and to his schemes for the encouragement of agriculture and horticulture and the study of the flora and fauna of India (which led to the institution of Gardens and Menagerie at Barrackpore).

"But, unquestionably in all that he did or planned in India Wellesley was actuated by the highest sense of public and personal duty, always operating, however, as a gracious dispensation from a benign Providence. His administration was conscientious, laborious and upright, and was untouched by any of those public scandals that had disfigured the reign of some of his predecessors. Even his pomp and show were dictated by the desire to full justice to a great station and a supreme responsibility". (*Ibid.*, p. 175.)

According to Warren Hastings, "Lord Wellesley has constructed a political system of vast strength and extent, but of a weight which will require that it should be continually upheld by an arm as strong as his; but that if they nominate a successor to him, of abilities much inferior to him, and of an activity of mind not equal to his, the whole structure will fall to pieces and all that we formerly possessed be lost in the same ruin". Again, "The Governor-General has committed the heinous crime of using expressions of Ridicule and Contempt about the Company at his table and the words have been carried home. If I were in his confidence, I would tell him that civility costs little".

According to Lord Holland, "He (Wellesley) had more genius than prudence, more spirit than principle, and manifestly despised his colleagues as much as they dread him. Unlike most English politicians, he was rather a statesman than a man of business, and more capable of doing extraordinary things well, than conducting ordinary transactions with safety or propriety". Again, "Yet there was a smack, a fancy of greatness in all he did; and though in his speeches, his manners and his actions he was very open to ridicule, those who smiled and even laughed could not despise him".

According to Alfred Lyall, Wellesley "crushed in a single brief campaign the Sultan of Mysore; he disarmed and disbanded the formidable *corps darmes* of fourteen thousand sepoys under French officers that was maintained by the Nizam; he took possession of the Carnatic, annexed half the dominions of the Oudh vizier, forced all the great military States into subjection or subsidiary alliance, and by completely breaking down the power of the Maratha confederacy he removed the last important obstacle to the accomplishment of our undisputed supremacy.

"We may regard with just admiration the high qualities shown by the Governor-General in the prosecution of this magnificent career, his rapid apprehension of a complicated political situation, and the vigour and address with which he carried out not only military operations and diplomatic strokes, but also the reforms of internal administration, and the organization of government in the ceded or conquered provinces. No man was ever a better subject for panegyric; nor is it worthwhile to scan too closely, at this distance of time, the defects of a great public servant by whose strenuous qualities the nation has very largely profited. It is essential, however, to lay stress, for historical purposes, on the peculiar combination of circumstances which gave scope and encouragement to Lord Wellesley's ardent and masterful statesmanship, and which enabled him to treat those who opposed him or criticized him with the supreme contempt that his home correspondence inability discloses. He had left England and reached India in the darkest hour of the fierce struggle between the French and English nations, when Bonaparte's star was in the ascendant over Europe, when he was invading Egypt and meditating Asiatic conquests, and when at home a powerful Tory Ministry was governing by measures that would in these days be denounced as the most arbitrary coercion. At such a conjuncture there was little time or inclination to look narrowly into Wellesley's declarations that the intrigues of the French in India and the incapacity or disaffection of the native rulers reduced him to the necessity of dethroning or disarming them, and that for our rule to be secure it must be paramount. As a matter of fact, he was applauded and supported in measures many times more high-handed and dictatorial than those for which Hastings had been impeached a dozen years earlier. During that interval the temper of the English Parliament had so entirely changed, that he could afford to ride roughshod over all opposition in India, and to regard the pacific Directors of the East India Company as a 'pack of narrow-minded old women".

To quote Lyall again, "The avowed object of Lord Wellesley had been to enforce peace throughout India, and to provide for the permanent security of the British possessions by imposing upon every native State the authoritative superiority of the British Government, binding them down forcibly or through friendly engagement to subordinate relations with a paramount power, and effectively forestalling any future attempts to challenge our exercise of arbitration or control. In short, whereas up to his time the British Government had usually dealt with all States in India upon a footing of at least nominal political equality, Lord Wellesley revived and proclaimed the imperial principle of political supremacy. All his views and measures pointed towards the reconstruction of another empire in India, which he rightly believed to be the natural outcome of our position in the country, and the only guarantee of its lasting consolidation. It must be acknowledged that Wellesley's trenchant operations only accelerated the sure and irresistible consequences of establishing a strong civilized government among the native States that had risen upon the ruins of the Moghul empire; for by swift means or slow, by fair means or forcible, the British dominion was certain to expand, and the armed opposition of its rivals could not fail to be beaten down at each successive collision with a growing European power".

LORD CORNWALLIS (1805)

Lord Cornwallis was sent to India for the second time with the object of undoing the mischief which Lord Wellesley was considered to have done. He came to India with the determination to revert to the policy of non-intervention. He tried to end the hostilities with Holkar and pacify Scindhia. He decided to restore Gwalior and Gohud to Scindhia. He also decided to give up all territory west of the Jamuna and withdraw the protection of the English Company from the Rajput States. However, Cornwallis could not carry out his policy as he died in October, 1805. He was in India for a few months only.

SIR GEORGE BARLOW (1805-07)

When Lord Cornwallis died in 1805, Sir George Barlow, the senior member of the Governor-General's Council, was appointed the Governor-General. Like a typical civil servant, Sir George Barlow strictly followed the policy of non-intervention. He gave back Gwalior and Gohud to Scindhia. He withdrew British protection from the Rajputs. He also agreed to fix the Chambal river as the boundary line between Scindhia's territory and the possessions of the English Company. He also offered very advantageous terms to Holkar although his position had become very weak on account of the action of Lord Lake. He was asked to enter into a subsidiary alliance.

However, Sir George Barlow forced the Nizam to abide by the terms of the subsidiary alliance and refused to allow him to make any alteration. The directors of the English Company asked Sir George Barlow to withdraw from the treaty of Bassein and allow the Peshwa to resume his old position. However, he resisted the orders of the Directors and the treaty of Bassein continued.

Another event of Sir George Barlow's tenure of office was the mutiny of the sepoys at Vellore. Certain orders had been passed demanding the putting on of certain kinds of military uniforms. New regulations also prescribed the fashion of wearing the hair. The people considered it to be an interference into their religious affairs. British officers were massacred. Lord William Bentinck, the Governor of Madras (now Chennai), could not handle the situation satisfactorily and was consequently recalled.

LORD MINTO (1807-13)

Lord Minto succeeded Sir George Barlow in 1807. Before coming to India as Governor-General, Minto was the President of Board of Control. He came to India with the firm conviction that the policy of non-intervention was in the best interests of the English Company. However, he had to modify his policy in certain cases.

In 1809, a Pathan chief called Amir Khan invaded Berar and he had with him 40,000 horsemen and more than 20,000 Pindaris. The British Government had no obligation, moral or legal, to help Berar because the Raja had refused to enter into a subsidiary alliance with the Company. In spite of this Lord Minto intervened to put an end to the anarchy in the country. Amir Khan was defeated and turned out from Berar and thus peace was maintained. In 1809, Lord Minto entered into the Treaty of Amritsar with Maharaja Ranjit Singh. Sir Charles Metcalfo played the most important part in this connection. The Sikh territory was to be on the other side of the Sutlej. This treaty was observed by both the parties for 30 long years.

John Malcolm was sent by Lord Wellesley to Tehran on account of its critical position. The Home Government also sent Sir Harford Jones to do the same job. The Indian Government accepted the treaty entered into by the envoy of the Crown.

Elphinstone was sent to Kabul on a similar mission. However, he met Shah Shuja, the King of Afghanistan, at Peshawar. He agreed to oppose the French and the Persians if they attacked India. However not much came out of it because Shah Shuja was himself turned out from his country.

Lord Minto took up the offensive against the French. He sent a naval expedition against the French colonies of Bourbon and Mauritius. These islands were captured. Another expedition was sent to Java.

In 1813, the Charter of the English East India Company was renewed for 20 years. The same year Lord Minto was succeeded by Lord Hastings.

According to Lord Curzon, "Lord Minto was one of the class of Governors-General who leave no particular mark on history and cease to be remembered either for good or ill. Coming out to pursue the policy of peacefully isolation which had been unsuccessfully practised by his immediate predecessors, he soon found himself driven into courses which even Wellesley would have approved". (*British Government in India,* p. 184.)

REVIEW QUESTIONS

1. Discuss the condition of India in the year 1798.
2. What is subsidiary system? Describe its merits and demerits.
3. Write in detail about the Fourth Mysore War and the Second Maratha War.
4. Throw light on the achievements and policies of Lord Wellesley.
5. Make an estimate of Lord Wellesley as one of the greatest Governor-Generals of the British Company.
6. Elaborate on the political condition of India at the time of Lord Wellesley.
7. Review the expansionist policy of Lord Wellesley.
8. Discuss the administration of Lord Wellesley.
9. Who were the successors of Lord Wellesley? Write in brief about their achievements.
10. Write short notes on the following:
    (a) Character of Tipu Sultan
    (b) Steps of Wellesley against the French danger
    (c) Lord Cornwallis

SUGGESTED READINGS

Hutton, W.H.: *Marquess Wellesley* (1897).
Malcolm, Sir John: *Political History of India from 1784 to 1823* (1826),
Minto: *Lord Minto in India* (1880).
Mohibbul Hasain Khan: *History of Tipu Sultan* (1952)
Roberts, P.E.: *India under Wellesley* (1929).
Tonres, W.M.: *Marquess Wellesley* (1850).

8 Lord Hastings and Amherst

LEARNING OBJECTIVES

- Discuss the events that took place during the regime of Lord Hastings
- Examine the reforms and policies of Lord Hastings
- Throw light on the events that took place in the tenure of Lord Amherst

LORD HASTINGS (1813-23)

Lord Hastings or Earl of Moira was appointed the Governor-General of Bengal in 1813 and he occupied that exalted office for a decade. He completed the work which was started by Warren Hastings and continued by Lord Wellesley. He came to India with a determination to follow a policy of non-intervention into the affairs of the country, but later on felt that the situation of the country was such that it was not possible to follow that policy. There were dangers from many quarters and only a policy of intervention could suit.

War with Nepal (1814-16)

Lord Hastings had first of all to deal with Nepal. This country was inhabited by the Gorkhas who were very hardy warriors. They had grown in strength by slow degrees and established their control over the whole of the hilly region from the frontier of Bhutan in the east to the Sutlej on the west. The Gorkhas were determined to extend their territory over the plains and that could be done only at the cost of territory of the English East India Company.

The non-intervention policy of some of the Governors-General of Bengal encouraged them to attack and occupy certain villages on the British side of the frontier. The climax was reached when the Gorkhas occupied the districts of Butwal and Sheoraj. As the Marathas refused to restore them even when a demand was made on them, war had to be declared in 1814.

All military strategists[1] agree on the point that Nepal is a very difficult country from the military point of view. It is true that elaborate plans were prepared in advance, but most of them were ill-executed. The fighting qualities of the Gorkhas also made victory over them a difficult task. General Gillespie who had fought heroically in Java, was defeated and killed by the Gorkhas. Three more generals were defeated. However, things improved under the command of Ochterloney. The English were able to occupy Almora. Amar Singh, the Gorkha leader, was defeated and surrendered. Thereafter the **Treaty of Sagauli** was signed in March 1816.

---

[1] Cf. "Lord Hastings conceived and carried through the greatest strategical operation ever undertaken in India".

By the treaty, the Gorkhas gave up most of their claims in the Tarai along their southern border. The provinces of Garhwal and Kumaon were also surrendered and the English thus got the site of Simla. The north-western frontier of the English company was carried right up to the mountains. The Gorkhas were to accept a resident in their capital.

The importance of the Treaty of Sagauli cannot be over-emphasized. The friendship established between the two countries in 1816 has continued since then. The Gorkha soldiers have been welcomed in the Indian army. They are employed in very large numbers in many other jobs by the Indians. The treaty of 1816 thus established an abiding friendship between India and Nepal.

Pindari War (1817-18)

After the Gorkhas, Lord Hastings had to deal with the Pindaris. Their origin is not known but in the time of Peshwa Baji Rao I, they were attached to the Maratha army as irregular horsemen. After the third battle of Panipat in 1761, the Pindaris settled themselves in Malwa and they attached themselves to Scindhia and Holkar. Their two branches came to be known as the Scindhia Shahi and Holkar Shahi Pindaris. As the power of the Maratha chief declined, the Pindaris began to do things independently. Wherever they went, they carried fire and sword with them. Particularly in the time of Wellesley, their number multiplied. This led to lawlessness in the country. The people suffered and the Pindaris gained.

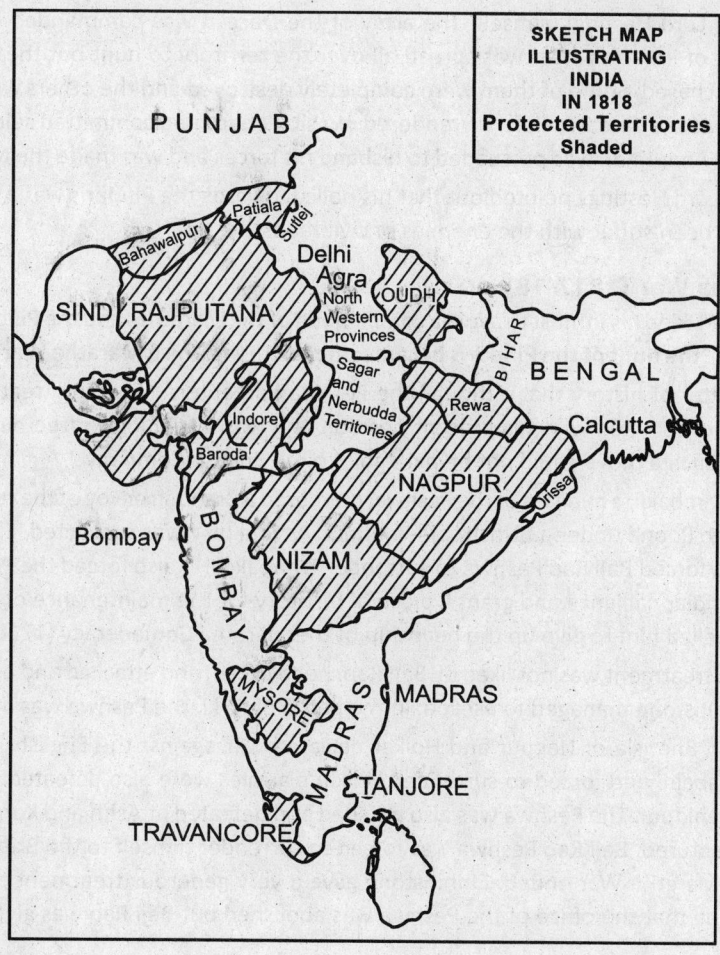

The Pindaris did not form a regular army. The only link between the Pindari chief and his followers was the prospect of plunder. Even loyalty to the chief was not continuous. The Pindaris were prepared to follow anybody who promised to get them booty. They did not form any homogeneous body. All kinds of elements joined the ranks of the Pindaris. There was no distinction between Hindu or a Muslim. All were welcomed to the brotherhood. In most cases, the Pindaris came from the ranks of the disbanded leaders and fugitives from justice, idlers, profligates and unscrupulous persons from every caste and creed were welcomed. The Pindaris had their special technique of fighting. They scrupulously avoided to give battle to the enemy. They were always on the lookout for their victims. They attacked their target with the speed of lightning and managed to run away with all their booty. The Pindaris have been compared to the swarms of the locusts. As the Pindaris followed the Maratha armies, they have been called the **scavengers of Marathas**.

The Pindaris were getting emboldened by the official policy of nonintervention. In 1812, they attacked Bundelkhand. In 1815 and 1816, they attacked and plundered the territories of the Nizam. In 1816, they led an attack on Northern Circars. This was too much for the English to put up with. Lord Hastings made elaborate preparations for it. By diplomacy, Lord Hastings was able to detach the Marathas from the Pindaris. He made a subsidiary alliance with Apa Sahib, the Regent of Bhonsla's territory. He also forced Scindhia to sign a treaty binding him to help English against Pindaris. Then comprehensive preparations were made to hunt out the Pindaris. The army of Hindustan was commanded by Lord Hastings himself. The army of the Deccan was commanded by Sir Thomas Hislop. The ring of iron and steel was spread all over the territory to hunt out the Pindaris. They were ruthlessly chased. Some of them were completely destroyed and the others were broken up. Karim Khan one of the Pindari chiefs, surrendered. Wasil Mohammed committed suicide. Chitu was eaten by a tiger. Amir Khan was persuaded to disband his forces and was made the Nawab of Tonk.

Critics of Lord Hastings pointed out that his policy towards the Pindaris was a generous one. He should have been stiffer with the enemies of civilization.

Third Maratha War (1817-18)

Lord Hastings had tried his utmost to avoid a combination of the Marathas and the Pindaris. In spite of this precaution, **"the hunt of the Pindaris became merged in the Third Maratha War"**. (V. A. Smith.)

It is a matter of history that although the Peshwa had entered into the treaty of Bassein in 1802, he was not satisfied with his present position and was intriguing to free himself from the British control. Such a move could not be palatable to the English Company.

In 1815, Trimbakji, a minister of the Peshwa, murdered a Brahmin envoy of the ruler of Gaekwar who had gone to Poona under a British safe-conduct. As foul play was suspected, Elphinstone, the British resident, forced Baji Rao Peshwa to surrender Trimbakji. He also forced the Peshwa to enter into a new subsidiary alliance and grant a piece of territory for the maintenance of the contingent force. He compelled him to give up the headship of the Maratha Confederacy (1718).

As such a treatment was not liked by Baji Rao, he revolted, and attacked and burnt the British Residency. Elphinstone managed to escape. In the battle of Kirki, the Peshwa was defeated.

Apa Sahib Bhonsla of Nagpur and Holkar declared war against the English. Apa Sahib was defeated at Sitabaldi and forced to surrender. Holkar's armies were also defeated and crushed in the battle of Mahidpur. The Peshwa was also pursued and defeated at Ashti and Koregaon. In 1819. Asirgarh was captured. Baji Rao Peshwa was forced to surrender himself to the British in 1818 and thus the third Maratha War ended. Elphinstone gave a very generous treatment to the defeated Peshwa. It is true that the office of the Peshwa was abolished but Baji Rao was given a pension of

₹8 lakhs a year for his life. A representative of the line of Shivaji was put on the throne of Sitara. Apa Sahib of Nagpur was deposed and a new Raja was put in his place. The Narbada territories of Bhonsla were annexed. Holkar was forced to enter into a subsidiary alliance and grant some territory for the maintenance of the contingent army. He was also forced to give up all his claims on the Rajput States.

It is evident that the power of the Marathas was completely crushed and henceforth they were not in a position to raise their head again. Marshman has described the results of the above wars in these words: "The wars subdued not only the native armies, but the native mind and taught the princes and people of India to regard the supreme command in India as indisputably transferred to a foreign power. It placed the Company on the Moghul throne with a more absolute authority than Akbar or Aurangzeb had ever enjoyed".

According to Dodwell, "The settlement of 1818 marks the beginning of the paramountcy of the East India Company. No State remained which could challenge its supremacy. No State remained which could reject its alliance. The project of Wellesley had been realised. All the principal States of India had been brought into agreement with the Company, and had placed in its hands the conduct of political relations. Many had accepted a subsidiary force, which implied a position of dependency. The peace of India had been assured. The wars which for a century and a half had desolated India had been brought to an end. But if the political project of Wellesley had been completed one aspect at least had been neglected. The treaties into which Moira had entered had not been treaties such as Wellesley would have ratified, for they all omitted those stipulations on which he would have set a high importance. Moira's treaties all included some clause intended to avoid all possibility of interference on the part of the Company's government in matters of internal administration. Unlike Wellesley, Moira limited his views to the regions under the direct control of the East India Company, while Wellesley had envisaged the good of India as a whole. Consequently, the Company found itself committed to a number of alliances by which it was bound to support the reigning prince without much regard for the quality of his administration. The relations which had characterised the alliance with the Nawab of Arcot or with the Nawab of Oudh were perpetuated over a wide field. The Governor-General, to whom it was given to establish the paramountcy of the Company, did not choose with it to recognise the responsibility of the Company for the general well-being of India. While, therefore, Moira's conduct of relations with the Maratha princes was marked by an exact and vigorous estimate of political forces, he shrank from the more extended responsibility which Wellesley sought, and which, if Wellesley had been left for another year in power, he would probably have assumed. In short, the settlement of 1818 imposed upon the Company all those ambiguities and uncertainties which were afterwards to mark its relations with the native states". (*The Cambridge Shorter History of India*, pp. 485-87.)

Internal Reforms

Judicial. Many reforms were carried out during the regime of Lord Hastings. The problem facing the country was the ever-growing number of undecided cases in the courts of justice. As the cases were not disposed of for years, parties were forced in many cases to take the law in their own hands. The problem could be tackled by increasing the number of courts, but the Company was reluctant to increase the number of courts because such a step involved additional expenditure Publicists like Mill attacked the miserliness of the Company.

In 1814, Lord Hastings provided that there was to be a Munsif in every Thana. These Munsifs were to be appointed by the judges of the Diwani Adalat although the power of approval was left with the Provincial Court of Appeal. Munsifs were empowered to try cases up to the value of ₹64 and their own decisions were to be confirmed by the judges of the Diwani Adalat. Appeals could be taken to the Diwani Adalat from the decisions of the Munsifs. The Munsifs could be removed on grounds of misconduct, incapacity or neglect of duty. In addition to Munsifs, Sadar Amins were also appointed in every zila or city. The number of the Sadar Amins depended upon the requirement of the area. Appointments were to be made by the judges of the Diwani Adalat bur the approval of the Provincial Court of Appeal was necessary. They were empowered to try cases up to ₹150. However, Sadar Amins were not allowed to try cases in which British subjects, Americans or Europeans were involved. Appeals could be taken against the decisions of the Diwani Adalat.

An attempt was made to decrease the arrears of work by abolishing the right of appeal in certain cases. Generally, only one appeal was allowed. It was provided in 1814 that appeals were to be taken from the Diwani Adalat to the Provincial Court of Appeal. However, if the latter tried a case in its original jurisdiction, an appeal could be taken to the Sadar Diwani Adalat.

Lord Hastings also increased the powers of the Registrars. Cases up to the value of ₹50 were to be sent to the Registrars for disposal. In exceptional cases, the Diwani Adalats were empowered to refer cases involving more than ₹500 to the Registrars. Provision was made for the taking of appeals directly to the Provincial Court of Appeal against the decisions of the Registrars.

It was further provided that in future all cases whose value was not more than ₹5,000 were to be instituted in the City Diwani Adalat or Zilla Diwani Adalat. The Sadar Diwani Adalat was given the power to transfer cases from the District or City Diwani Adalat to the Provincial Court of Appeal. If the amount involved was more than ₹5,000, provision was made for the institution of those cases directly in the Provincial Court of Appeal. Sometimes, those cases could be transferred to the Sadar Diwani Adalat also.

It was provided in 1821 that if one Munsif was considered to be insufficient for the work in hand, more Munsifs were to be appointed for that purpose. They were allowed to try cases up to the value of ₹150. Sadar Amins were also allowed to try cases up to the value of ₹500.

In 1815, it was laid down that no person was to be deemed to be qualified to be appointed to the office of a judge of the Sadar Diwani Adalat unless he had previously officiated as a judge of the Provincial Court of Appeal, for a period of not less than three years or had worked nor less than 9 years in judicial capacity.

Lord Hastings provided in 1818 that the magistrates were to – powered to give the punishment of imprisonment with hard labour up to two years corporal punishment of not more than 30 stripes.

Another regulation of 1821 provided that it should be competent for the Governor-General-in-Council to authorise a Collector of Revenue or other officers employed in the management or superintendence of any branch of the territorial revenues to exercise the whole or any portion the powers and duties vested in the magistrates or to employ a magistrate in the collection of public revenue and also invest the person so employed with the whole or any portion of the powers of the Collector of Revenue. The powers of the Collector were increased tremendously.

Revenue Reforms. Lord Hastings appealed to the Directors of the Company for a Permanent Settlement. However, his suggestion was not accepted. Arrangements were made with the representatives of every village community for the adjustment of shares of the individuals.

The Bengal Tenancy Act was passed in 1822. Provisions were made very stringent.

Sir Thomas Munro was the Governor of Madras in 1820. He introduced the Ryotwari system. There were to be no intermediaries. Elphin stone fixed the rights and rents of each ryot after a survey.

Education. Efforts were made to promote education among the people. A college was opened at Calcutta (now Kolkata) for the spread of English language. Similar measures were adopted by the various provincial Governments.

Press. To begin with, more liberty of action was given to the press and censorship was abolished. However, restrictions were imposed soon after on ground of their necessity.

Estimate

Undoubtedly, Lord Hastings completed the work of Lord Wellesley. After his departure in 1823, there was no serious rival of the English East India Company in India. Not only was the office of the Peshwa abolished, Holkar was deprived of half of his territory. Bhonsla Raja became a vassal of the English Company. Scindhia was humbled and made impotent. He established law and order in the country after crushing the power of the Pindaris. Both his military achievements and internal reforms accomplished a great deal. According to Mill, "The administration of the Marquess of Hastings may be regarded as the completion of the great scheme of which Clive had laid the foundations, and Warren Hastings and Marquess of Wellesley had reared the super-structure. The growing pinnacle was the work of Lord Hastings and by him was the supremacy of the British empire in India proper finally established. Of the soundness of the work no better proof could be afforded than the fact that there has been no national warfare since his administration. Rajputs, Marathas and Mohammedans have remained at peace with one another under the shade of British power. The wars in which the latter had been engaged have carried that power beyond the frontiers of Hindustan, but no interruption of internal tranquillity from the Himalayas to the sea has been suffered or attempted".

Roberts has drawn a comparison between Lord Hastings and Lord Wellesley in these words: "His material achievements challenged comparison with those of Lord Wellesley, but he was of course not so great or commanding a figure. He owed much to the success of his administration to a brilliant band of subordinates, men who had been trained and inspired by his great predecessor. Hastings did not possess Wellesley's dignity, eloquence or originality; there was an element of vanity in his otherwise estimable character, and signs are not lacking that he would hardly have shown Wellesley's equanimity in the face of reverses or his noble consideration of defeated generals. On the other hand, he conceived and carried through the grandest strategical operations ever undertaken in India, in the course of which twenty-eight actions were fought and a hundred and twenty fortresses taken without a single reverse. He was less precipitate than Lord Wellesley, less harsh to errant native rulers, and he did not proceed against them till his case was very strong".

According to Lord Curzon, "This excellent and hard-working ruler deserves recollection for two other achievements. It was he who made up for the loss of Java, foolishly given back to the Dutch, by the purchase of Singapore, which has since become the most important naval base and coasting station in the East. He earned the undying gratitude of Calcutta (now Kolkata) by his efforts to cleanse and beautify the city which commemorated the service by attaching his name or titles to more streets or quarters than preserve the fame of any other Governor-General. Loudoun Street, Rawdon Street, Hungerford Street, Moira Street (Hastings Street had already received the title in honour of an earlier and more famous Hastings), the colony of Hastings in the south-west corner of the Maidan, **Hastings Bridge**, erected by public subscription over Tolly's Nullah in honour of his administration—all keep alive his name. With the proceeds of a great lottery he built the Strand Road along the river bank, and added greatly to the amenities of both the City and the Maidan. Perhaps he rendered a more doubtful service in removing the historic pipal tree, under which Job, Charnock was said to have sat and smoked his hookah, as well as the battered pillar which Governor Holwell had set up over the remains of the victims of the Black Hole and which it was left to me, 80 years later to replace.

"Lord Hastings was a man of strong domestic affections; and he felt very deeply the prolonged separation from his wife and family. Lady Loudoun and their children had to go home in January

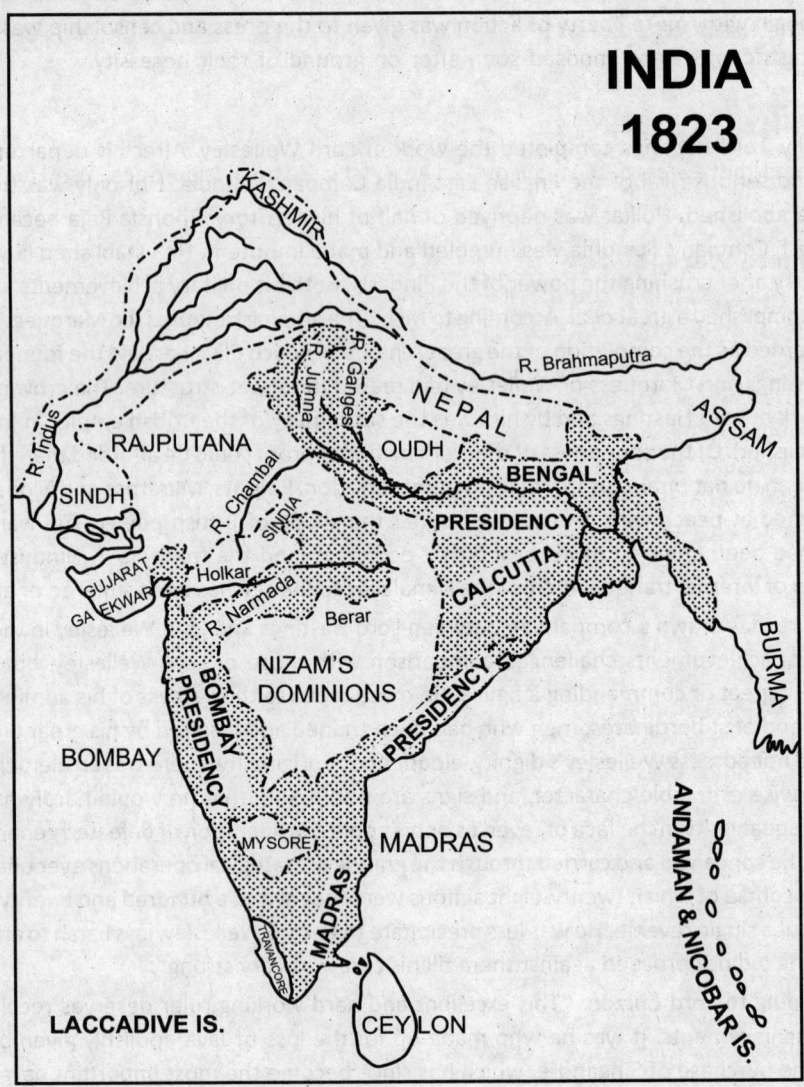

1816. She returned alone in 1819 to be with him during the remainder of his stay. When dying, he directed that his right hand should be cut off and clasped in that of his wife when she should follow him. This strange but pathetic request was faithfully carried out. The hand, enclosed in a small box, was deposited in the family vault at Loudoun in Ayrshire, and when Lady Hastings died, fourteen years later, it was placed in her coffin".

JOHN ADAMS (1823)

The interval between Lord Hastings and Lord Amherst was covered by John Adams who was the senior member of the Calcutta Council. His rule lasted for 7 months. Adams' name is notorious for his censorship of the press. He also put an end to the disgraceful affairs of Palmer & Co. He took action against Mr. Buckingham, editor of the Calcutta Journal, who was critical of the work of the Government. The editor was deported. He also passed orders that Palmer & Co. was not to lend any more money to the Nizam. The English East India Company owed a lot of money to the Nizam on account of the of annual tribute for Northern Circars. Adams ordered the payment to the Nizam who was thus able to pay off Palmer & Co.

LORD AMHERST (1823-28)

The most important events of the reign of Lord Amherst were the First Burmese War and the capture of Bharatpur.

First Burmese War (1824-26)

Burma was an independent country. Its inhabitants were a source of threat to the security and tranquillity of the possessions of the English East India Company. In 1817-18, the Burmese forces threatened Assam. They also sent a letter to the Indian Government demanding the surrender of Chittagong, Dacca, Murshidabad and Kossimbazar. However, the danger was avoided on account of the defeat of the Burmese at the hands of the Siamese. Peace did not last long. In 1822, Siam was conquered. The security of India was threatened and the English Company had to take action. The Burmese believed that no troops could stand against them. From the king to the beggar, they were hot for a war with the English. The Burmese tried to provoke the English as much as they could. In 1823, they attacked Shahpuri, a small island near Chittagong and commenced the war. Lord Amherst declared war in February 1824.

It is rightly pointed out that Lord Amherst did not make adequate preparations for the war in Burma. The work done by his subordinates was also not up to the mark. The war in Burma was fought leisurely. The Company failed to take the initiative in the war. The result was that war was prolonged, but ultimately the Burmese were defeated. A treaty was signed in 1826 between the Government of India and Burma. By the **Treaty of Yandaboo (1826)**, the Burmese king agreed to give to the English Company the province of Arakan and Tenasserim. Burmese forces were to be withdrawn from Assam and Cachar. They recognised the independence of Manipur and entered into a commercial treaty. They also agreed to take a British Resident at their capital and pay a war indemnity of one million pounds.

It cannot be denied that the Burmese War was a very expensive one. It lasted for two years. It is stated that if Lord Amherst had spent more time on preparations, he might have been able to avoid many a pitfall but unfortunately Lord Amherst could not do otherwise. He was a man of mediocre ability and never showed his firm grasp of the problems of the country.

Capture of Bharatpur

There was a dispute at Bharatpur after the death of the Raja. The British Government recognised the claims of the minor. Durjan Sal, the other claimant, started war preparations to vindicate his right. The fort of Bharatpur was captured. A large number of persons were captured by the British troops. Sir Charles Metcalfe wrote thus: "Our plundering here has been very disgraceful.... until I can get rid of the price agents, I cannot establish the sovereignty of the young Raja whom we came professedly to protect but have been plundering to the last Lotah since he fell into our hands".

A reference may also be made to the mutiny at Barrackpore. A Sepoy regiment was ordered to go to Burma. The Sepoys thought that they would be losing their caste by doing so and refused to obey. However, the mutiny was crushed and the soldiers were killed. A number of mutineers were hanged. The 47th regiment was disbanded and its Indian officers were dismissed.

The Burmese war had made the Governor-General very unpopular and the story of the mutiny at Barrackpore made him all the more so. From the end of 1825, the ship of Amherst was labouring in very heavy waters. He was saved for a time by the intervention of the Duke of Wellington. However,

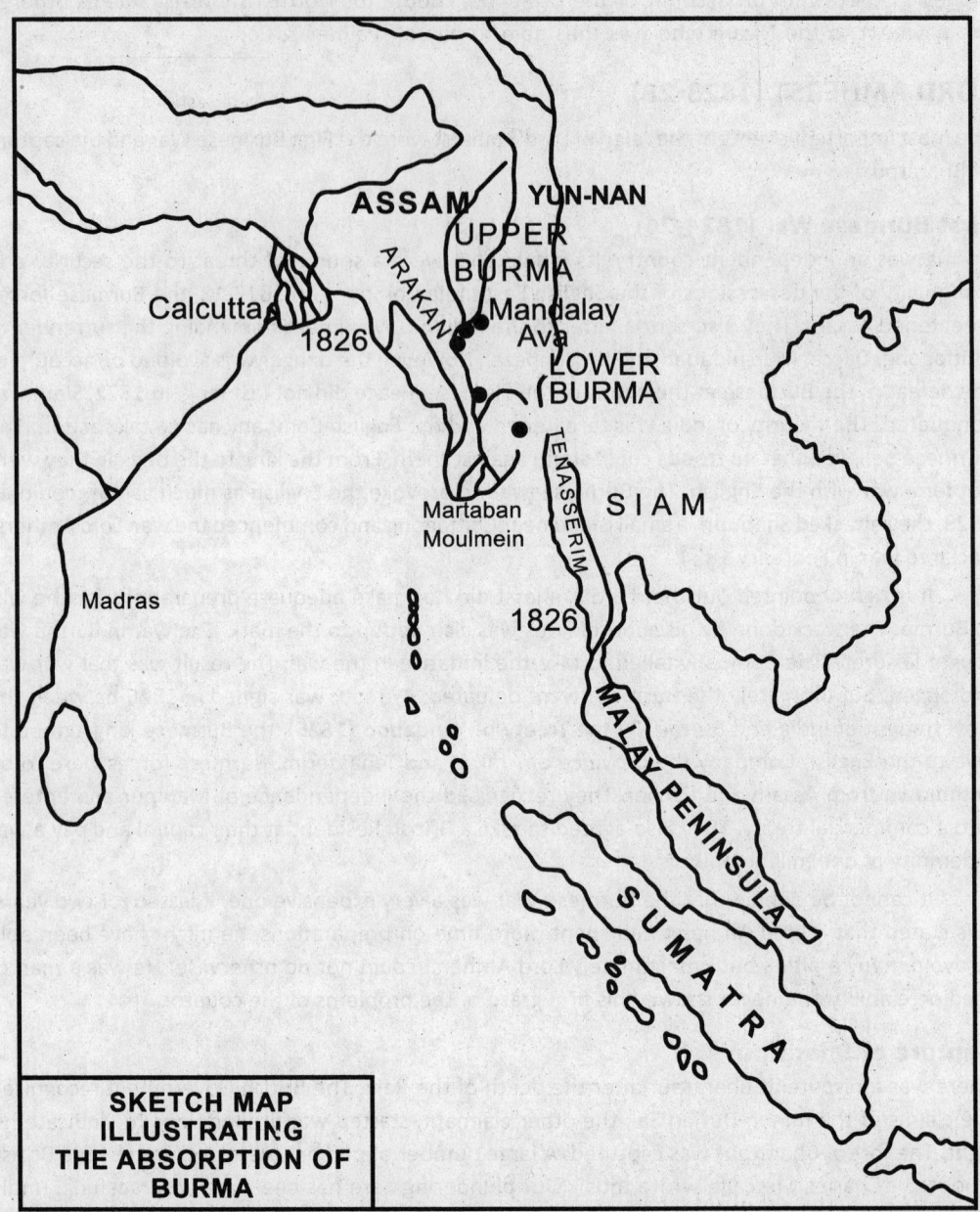

SKETCH MAP ILLUSTRATING THE ABSORPTION OF BURMA

in March 1826, the news reached the Governor-General that he was about to be recalled. Calcutta took his side and so also did the Home cabinet. For months together, the unhappy Governor-General was left in almost daily expectation of being recalled. In August 1826, he made up his mind to resign. However, in May 1827, there arrived a resolution of thanks and compliments from the Court of Directors. In spite of that, his resignation which was submitted on the score of ill health, was accepted. In March 1828, Lord and Lady Amherst left Calcutta (now Kolkata) after a chequered reign. Among the British rulers of India, Lord Amherst left one of the most inconspicuous and impalpable of impressions.

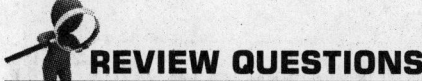
REVIEW QUESTIONS

1. Write an essay on the main events that took place during the regime of Lord Hastings.
2. Assess the impact of Lord Hastings' War with the Gorkhas and the Pindaris.
3. Describe the administration and policies of Lord Hastings.
4. Write a detailed note on the treaty of Sagauli.
5. What was the policy of Lord Hastings towards the Pindaris? Discuss in detail.
6. Explain the reforms carried out during the regime of Lord Hastings.
7. Assess the role of Lord Hastings as a ruler.
8. Write short notes on the following:
    (a) Treaty of Sagauli
    (b) Pindari War
    (c) First Burmese War (1824-26)
9. Who was Lord Amherst? Discuss the important events of his regime.

SUGGESTED READINGS

Laurie, W.F.B.: *Our Burmese Wars and Relations with Burma* (1880).
Mehta, M.S.: *Lord Hastings and the Indian States.*
Nisbet, J.: *Burma Under British Rule and Before* (1901).
Phayre, Sir A.: *History of Burma* (1883).
Prinsep, H.T.: *History of the Political and Military Transactions in India during the Administration of the Marquess of Hastings* (1825).
Snodgrass, Major: *Narrative of the Burmese War* (1827).
Roy, M. P.: *Origin, Growth and Suppression of the Pindaris.* New Delhi.
Sinha, B. K.: *The Pindaris* (Calcutta).

9

Rise and Fall of the Peshwas

LEARNING OBJECTIVES

- Critically examine the causes of the rise and fall of the Peshwas
- Throw light on the Third Battle of Panipat (1761)
- Discuss the Maratha administration under the Peshwas

According to Dr. Sinha, "The difficulties of Sahu and the great political unrest of Maharashtra are the chief factors in the rise of the Peshwas. Their rise is neither phenomenal nor accidental. They gradually worked their way up from an ordinary position to the headship of the State and eventually to *de facto* sovereignty. Balaji Vishwanath is the founder of the House of the Peshwas, who made the office hereditary in their family, paralysed the power of their colleagues and ultimately that of the king. To start with, they occupied a rank second to the Pratinidhi's. They had first to sweep him aside before they could make their position supreme in the State, and once supreme in the State, the king automatically yielded place to them. And all these they achieved on account of their superior ability. Thus, in the attainment of supremacy they had first to eclipse the Pratinidhi and the rest of their colleagues, and then the king. These two phases should be clearly noticed as the reader proceeds with the narrative, for this transfer of authority from the masters to the servant is so gradually, silently, carefully accomplished that the successive steps important as they were in relation to the whole move, escaped all contemporary notice". (*Rise of the Peshwas,* p. 9.)

BALAJI VISHWANATH (1714-20)

Balaji Vishwanath enjoyed the trust and confidence of his master, Sahu, and no wonder he was appointed to the post of Senakarte or Organiser of Forces. Balaji's ancestors were Deshmukhs. He himself was employed as a clerk in the salt works at Chiplun. In 1689, he worked as a revenue clerk and later on was appointed as Sar-Subah of Poona and Daulatbad. He seems to have come into contact with the Mughals and Sahu about 1705. Sahu had a very high opinion of the ability, loyalty and character of Balaji. The latter was one of those persons who joined Sahu after his release. He also played a very important part in crushing the opposition to Sahu.

Taking full advantage of the dissensions and intrigues at the Mughal court at Delhi, the Marathas gained strength and influence. In 1719, Balaji Vishwanath was invited to Delhi to help the Sayyid Brothers. Although Farrukh Sayyar was killed in 1719, Balaji Vishwanath got three grants from Mohammad Shah, the new Mughal emperor. The three grants are considered to be the foundation-stone of the great fabric of the Maratha empire in India. The first grant gave to the Marathas the right of Chauth or one-fourth share of the revenues of the Deccan and Southern India including

Hyderabad, the Karnatak and Mysore. The second grant gave the right of Sardeshmukhi or one-tenth share of the produce over and above the Chauth. The third grant recognised the right of Swaraj or the entire sovereignty of the Marathas over their country. Sahu was not to molest Sambhaji of Kolhapur and he was to pay an annual tribute of ₹10 lakhs to the Mughal emperor. The emperor was to release and send back from Delhi Sahu's mother, his wife, his brother and the members of the Maratha royal family detained at Delhi.

According to Dr. Sinha, "This journey of the Marathas to Delhi produced far-reaching consequences in their history. Besides its immediate advantages it deeply coloured the later policy of the Marathas, and came as an eye-opener to them in many respects. For long the Marathas, who had looked upon the imperial power and prestige with awe, witnessed at Delhi what that power actually meant. The halo of glory that surrounded the names of the descendants of Babar and Akbar, whom the president of Fort William addressed as 'the Absolute Monarch and Prop of the Universe', vanished into the lurid light of utter contempt when the Marathas found them reduced to mere tools at the hands of the unscrupulous courtiers, and dragged to dishonour and ignominious death. Delhi reeking with blood, courtiers thriving in machination, the emperor an instrument of the ambitious nobles, the central authority levelled to the dust all these revealed the realities about the Mughal empire. Long before, their great king Shivaji had proved to his people that the Mughal army was not invincible, and the Mughal territory not inviolable. Further they had been sufficiently disillusioned with regard to the real strength of the Mughals during their War of independence (1690-1707). Now they realized full well that the Mughal empire was rotten to the core, that it could never sustain its pristine glory and perhaps, who knows, it might fall to the powerful blows of the Marathas. Balaji Vishwanath, a shrewd man of affairs as he was, must have seen with the eyes of a statesman that the splendid structure of the Mughal empire was tottering to its fall, and was a prize worth attempting, and worth fighting for. He and his other Maratha leaders must have conjured up a glorious picture of Hindustan, the homeland of Hinduism and the treasure house of Asia, a land consecrated by a thousand memories of Shri Ram and Shri Krishna so dear to the Hindu heart. This holy land, this rich country, they must have thought, would be theirs, if they could but overthrow the Mughals. And then what a difference it would make to Maharashtra. Maharashtra, sterile and rugged, where "nature enforces a spartan simplicity, would flow in riches, milk and honey. The gorgeous paraphernalia of the nobles, the polished luxury of the inhabitants, their graceful manners and customs, health and beauty, bearing and speech, all testifying to a cultured society; the verdant plains of the Ganges and the Jamuna, the flower and foliage, the delightful sun and shade—all these must have captivated the eyes and imagination of the rough, crude but intelligent Chitpavan Brahmin, Balaji Vishwanath".

"And was this all? The prestige of their presence at the imperial capital, not as mercenaries, but as the allies and supporters of the kingmakers held out to them a promise that they might someday make and un-make emperors. Indeed it was the surest basis on which Balaji Vishwanath could confidently build his policy of founding a Maratha empire on the ruins of the Mughal empire". (*Rise of the Peshwas,* pp. 67-68.)

Balaji Vishwanath was able to accomplish a lot for the Marathas. When he came to power, he found his country torn with a civil war, but he left it peaceful and prosperous. He won for his people Shivaji's Swarajya from the Mughals without a battle and he impressed the Mughal capital with the prestige of the Maratha arms. He strengthened the position of Sahu on his throne. At a time when the Maratha chiefs were playing a waiting game and loyalty was a rare commodity, he by his devotion and sincerity, was able to win the confidence of Sahu and the respect of the people.

Balaji Vishwanath laid the foundations of the future *Maratha Confederacy.* He was helped in this task by the circumstances prevailing at that time. As a result of the Deccan wars of Aurangzeb, the Mughal empire was completely disintegrated and that helped the Marathas to acquire the right of Chauth and Sardeshmukhi over the six Subahs of the Deccan. The Maratha State set up by Shivaji was also completely destroyed and the system of Jagirs came into existence in Maharashtra. Both these factors changed the very nature of the Maratha State and laid the foundations of the Maratha Confederacy.

When Shivaji created the Astapradhans, he paid their salaries in cash. There were no jagirs and no hereditary offices. No change was made by Sambhaji, his son. It was during the time of Rajaram that a change was made in the old system. Rajaram decided to follow a policy of systematically plundering the Mughal territories and for that purpose he assigned the different parts of the Deccan to his commanders or those who professed obedience to him. Thus the Maratha commanders harassed the Mughals in every possible way. Rajaram allowed them to establish their headquarters in their own areas and also to rule over them. Out of their revenues, the commanders paid a share to Rajaram and kept the rest to themselves. They acted on their own initiative and did not depend upon Rajaram for anything except the grant of territory to them. They considered the parts of the country granted to them as their Jagirs which were won and maintained by them entirely by their own strength. The commanders did whatever suited their interests and were not in any way obedient to Rajaram. They took pride in their independence. This system continued not only under Rajaram but also under Tara Bai and Sahu. It is pointed out that the Sawants of Wadi, Kanhoji Angre, Damaji Thorat, etc., did not care for the authority of Tara Bai or Sahu. When after 1707, Sahu wanted to strengthen his hands, he had to ask for the help of the Maratha chiefs who held big jagirs under him. These jargirdars supported Sahu on the condition that their jagirs were not to be touched. As a matter of fact, when Sahu came out victorious, he gave more jagirs to those who had helped him. The policy of Sahu was not to change anything that was old and not to create anything that was new. The result was that the old jagirs were allowed to remain in the hands of their holders. Had he tried to confiscate their jagirs, that might have resulted in trouble. All the high officials surrounding Sahu themselves had big jagirs and obviously they were not prepared to part with the same. Balaji Vishwanath himself had huge jagirs and no wonder he did not raise his finger to abolish the system of jagirs. These jagirs had become hereditary.

The grant of the right of collecting Chauth and Sardeshmukhi from the six Subahs of the Deccan to the Marathas by the Mughals in 1719 also favoured the growth of the Maratha Confederacy. The Marathas were given the right of collecting the above taxes but they were also required to maintain peace and order in their territories. That seemed to be a very big job for the Marathas. Balaji solved the problem by dividing the different parts of the Deccan excluding the Swarajya to the various jagirdars of feudatories, ministers of state or his favourites. Balaji himself was to collect money from Khandesh and parts of Balaghat. He assigned Balgam and Gujarat to the Senapati. He gave portions of Gondwana, the Painghat and Berar to Senasaheb Subah Kanhoji Bhonsla. He gave Gangathadi and Aurangabad to the Sarlaskar. He gave the Karnatic to Fateh Singh Bhonsla. He gave Hyderabad, Bedar and the territories between the Nira and Warna to the Pratinidhi. The above officials were allowed to collect Chauth and Sardeshmukhi from their territories. They were allowed to keep a part of the revenues for the maintenance of their establishments and send the rest to the royal treasury. They were independent in their territories to all intents and purposes. They were not in any way subordinate to the Peshwa or Sahu. They collected a lot of money from the territories assigned to them and thereby added to their resources. The possession of a lot of money and large armies enabled them to think in terms of their independence and to all intents and purposes they were actually independent. It was under these circumstances that the State formed by Balaji Vishwanath was later on called *Maratha Confederacy*. The nature of the confederacy remained the same. The only change made later on was that with the conquest of the various parts of India by the Marathas the territories under the Maratha commanders became larger and in the same proportion they began to assert their independence more and more.

The financial arrangements made by Balaji Vishwanath also made the Peshwa and Sahu dependent upon the Maratha military leaders. They had to depend upon the money which they were to get from the Maratha chiefs. According to Dr. Sinha, "The king lived as a pensioner of the feudatories, expecting only his 25% besides the Sardeshmukhi income. The military power had passed out of his hands and by this arrangement he was made dependent on the big Sardars for the maintenance of his office. Balaji did not realise the gravity of this mistake and he further weakened the position of the king by making it a rule that the different establishments of the royal households should be maintained by different Sardars. The Sardars and the Astapradhans like the Bhonsla and Angre were called upon to maintain the royal establishments by monthly payments. The Sachiv had to pay for the upkeep of the royal stables; the Pratinidhi had to pay for that of the royal stores, and the Peshwa, for that of the royal palaces. The officers appointed to see whether every feudatory was sending his contribution every month regularly or not was called the Rajajnya. This arrangement rendered the king only a pensioner of the feudatories in all but name. The discredit of having thus undermined the strength of royal authority goes to Balaji Vishwanath". (*Rise of the Peshwas,* pp. 79-80.)

Sir Richard Temple has described the character and achievements of Balaji Vishwanath in these words: "He was more like a typical Brahmin than any of his successors. He had a calm, comprehensive and commanding intellect, an imaginative and aspiring disposition, an aptitude for ruling rude nature by moral force, a genius for diplomatic combinations and a master of finance. His political destiny propelled him into affairs, wherein his misery must have been acute. More than once, he was threatened with death for which he doubtlessly prepared himself with all the stoicism of his race when a ransom opportunity arrived. He wrung by power of menace and argument from the Mughals, a recognition of Maratha sovereignty. He carried victoriously all his diplomatic points and sank into premature death with the consciousness that a Hindu empire had been created over the ruins of Muhammedan power and that of this empire the hereditary chiefship had been secured for his family".

According to Sardesai, "The services and achievements of this first Peshwa have not yet received proper recognition in history, since they are matters of only recent research. Sahu in one of his letters styles him *atula parakrami-sevaka.* i.e., 'a servant of incomparable capacity' showing thereby that Sahu did not bestow his Peshwaship on a mere clerk in the employ of the Senapati but on a worthy person of proved merit after a full trial of 5 years and a close personal acquaintance going back to a much longer period. In fact, although sufficient details of this first Peshwa's life and work have not yet been discovered: we have enough ground for asserting that his father and grandfather had been in Shivaji's service, that he possessed long and varied experience obtained by him during the Mughal. Maratha struggle and consequently a secure grasp of the circumstances and the situation in which Sahu and the whole nation came to be placed upon the death of Aurangzeb. He also evinced rare foresight and statesmanship in utilizing all available resources towards completing the task of constructing a Hindu empire, which the Great Shivaji had set before himself and which had all but crumbled away during the troubles of the two preceding reigns. Balaji had to look to the north as his path to the south was permanently closed by the independent existence of Tarabai's kingdom". (*Main Currents of Maratha History,* p. 93.)

BAJI RAO (1720-40)

After the death of Balaji Vishwanath, his eldest son, Baji Rao, was appointed the Peshwa by Sahu. This was done in spite of the opposition of his advisers and chiefs. At the time of coming to power, Baji Rao was hardly a young man of 19. In spite of his youth, Baji Rao possessed plenty of commonsense, intelligence and very good physique. He was well-versed in diplomacy and administration. He correctly came to the conclusion that the Mughal power was declining and it was possible to snatch away the provinces from it. Baji Rao made the following observation in that connection: "Now is our time to drive the strangers from the country of the Hindus, and acquire immortal renown. *Let us strike at the trunk of the withering tree, and the branches will fall off themselves.* By directing our efforts to Hindustan, the Maratha flag shall fly from the Krishna to Attock". Sahu approved of his policy in these words: "You shall plant it beyond the Himalayas. You are, indeed, a noble son of a worthy father". Baji Rao reorganised the armies of the State and started his campaigns in 1731. The Marathas' claim, to Chauth and Sardeshmukhi was recognised in that year. In 1732, the Maratha armies over-ran the province of Malwa. Bundelkhand was conquered; and in 1737, Baji Rao appeared before the very walls of Delhi. Nizam-ul-Mulk advanced from the Deccan to help the Mughal emperor, but he himself was defeated near Bhopal and had to agree to a formal cession of Malwa and Gujrat. According to Dr. Dighe, "The victory of Bhopal marks the zenith of the Peshwa's triumphant career.... . By defeating the confederate armies at Bhopal, the Peshwa established the supremacy of Maratha arms in India and announced the birth of a New Imperial Power". The Nizam also promised to pay a war indemnity of ₹50 lakhs to Baji Rao. In 1739, the Island of Bassein was taken from the Portuguese. Baji Rao died in 1740 after putting the Maratha power on secure footing.

Baji Rao loved a Muslim dancing girl named Mastani. She was an exceedingly accomplished lady and was the most charming lady of her time in India. She was a good musician and looked after Baji Rao like a devoted wife. It is said that Baji Rao's addiction to meat and wine was due to her influence. Both of them died in 1740.

All his life Baji Rao tried to accomplish two things. He tried to expand the Maratha power in the north and also tried to ensure harmonious co-operation of the Maratha Confederacy by a process of inter-dependence of its various members. As pointed out above, he succeeded in his mission of extending the Maratha power in the north but in his second mission he failed. His attitude towards the Maratha Confederacy was one of domination. What he aimed at was that the members of the Maratha Confederacy should be guided by the Peshwa. Their internal and external relations should be scrutinized and controlled by him. They should not make war and peace without his approval. His foreign conquests were also meant to include the conquest of the Maratha Confederacy. He did not want actually to rule over Maharashtra but he wanted to the dominate over the whole of Maharashtra.

Baji Rao has been criticized for his aggressive attitude towards the Maratha Confederacy. It is pointed out that he should have followed a policy of conciliation towards them. However, it appears that his own experience during the first 11 years of office had brought him to the conclusion that he could not expect sympathy and co-operation from his colleagues or the Maratha chiefs. The result of his policy was that a deep resentment was created against his domination.

Baji Rao enjoyed the confidence of Chhatrapati Sahu. The result was that Sahu left everything into the hands of the Peshwa, Baji Rao had his way in everything. This directly resulted in undermining the authority of the Chhatrapati. The Peshwa decided to make Poona the city of his power. In 1730, he started building a castle there and later on the same was strongly fortified. The other Maratha chiefs also followed the example of Baji Rao. Pratinidhi established his power at Karhad, Sachiv at Bhore, Senapati at Telegaon and Bhonsla at Nagpur. Each of them regarded himself independent of the King or the Peshwa. Such a spirit led to the defiance of royal authority. Dr. Sinha points out that the policy of domination ensured the rise of the Peshwa but enfeebled the unity among the various members of the Maratha Confederacy and indirectly hastened its fall.

Baji Rao was a great general and soldier. He possessed an indomitable courage and extraordinary personal bravery. He was incomparable as a soldier. No amount of hardship or fatigue was too much for his iron constitution. In guerilla warfare, he had no equal. He was next only to Shivaji. The way he humbled the pride of Nizam-ul-Mulk shows his ability. He inspired his followers with confidence and commanded their loyalty. He led them from victory to victory. His mobility and brilliant tactics were responsible for his success. His originality of plan, boldness of execution and eye for strategy show that he was a great commander. He stands head and shoulders above his contemporaries in Maharashtra. He had the head to plan and the hand to execute.

According to Sardesai, "It is not necessary to write separately about Baji Rao's character and achievements. His deeds speak for him. He stands next only to Shivaji in a military genius. Sahu's discernment in selecting him for the Peshwaship at the early age of nineteen was more than justified. That a boy in his teens assuming the highest position under the Maratha Chhatrapati, should be able within twenty years to extend the Maratha dominion in all directions, north, south, east and west and to overcome great antagonists both at home and abroad is an achievement which stands to the permanent credit of the Maratha race. Twenty years spent in breathless activity and tireless journeys across the Indian continent from Srirangpattam to Delhi and from Ahmedabad to Hyderabad, wore out the iron constitution of this great man of action. The twenty years of his active career witnessed a complete revolution in the character of the Maratha State and an entire redistribution of political power throughout India. *At his death in 1740 the political centre of gravity shifted from the Court of Delhi to that of Sahu.* The system introduced by Baji Rao's father and executed by him and his son, equally transformed the constitution laid down by Shivaji and dotted the map of India with numerous centres of Maratha power. Thus, Baji Rao became the creator of greater Maharashtra". (*New History of the Marathas* Vol. II, p. 182.)

Sir Richard Temple has summed up the character of Baji Rao in these words: "Baji Rao was hardly surpassed as a rider and was ever forward in action, eager to expose himself under fire if the affair was arduous. He was endured to fatigue and prided himself in enduring the same hardship as his soldiers and shared their scanty fare. He was moved by ardour for success in national undertakings by a patriotic confidence in the Hindu cause as against its old enemies Mohammedans and its new rival Europeans, then rising above the political horizon. He lived to see the Marathas spread terror over the Indian continent from the Arabian Sea to the Bay of Bengal. He died as he had lived in camp under canvas among his men and he is remembered to this day among the Marathas as the fighting Peshwa and an incarnation of Hindu energy".

According to H.G. Rawlinson, "He was the most remarkable man next to Shivaji himself that his nation had produced. In the words of the historian of the Marathas, his was 'the head to plan and the hand to execute'. Tall and commanding in appearance he was like all his family, famous for his good looks. He was equally great as a soldier and as a statesman. He understood to perfection the peculiar tactics of the Maratha horse, and his campaigns against the Nizam were masterpieces of strategy. He was as chivalrous in the hour of victory as he was brave in the field. As politician he had the lofty and far-reaching ambitions of his father, and he lived to see the tiny Maratha race once 'a cloud no bigger than a man's hand', spread all over India, from Delhi to Tanjore. He was an eloquent and inspiring orator, and if in private life he had something of the haughty and imperious reserve of the Chitpavan; he was a generous master to those who served him faithfully". (*Cambridge History of India*, Vol. IV, p. 407.)

According to Sinha, "Despite his great talents as a soldier and a leader of men, Baji Rao lacked some of the sterling qualities of a statesman. He was domineering in his attitude towards others and overbearing in his manners. He was a soldier to the core, and could never bear opposition. Fortunately, he possessed resourcefulness in plenty and, therefore, he could bear down all opposition. *It is said that he had the head to plan and the hand to execute.* True, but too much masterfulness cuts at the root of statesmanship. A little elasticity of temper adds salt to statecraft. Hence, Baji Rao made many enemies in his lifetime and left as many behind. He did not know how to conciliate. He knew how to domineer. But domination even when dictated by absolutely selfless or disinterested motives antagonises people more often than we suppose; and Baji Rao's domination was not disinterested. There is no gainsaying the fact that he was deeply imbued with a love of self-glory though he was also deeply loyal to his chief Sahu and to the cause of his country. He firmly believed that all he did, was for the good of Maharashtra and that his lead was not only desirable but indispensable. Naturally he gave offence to many by such an attitude as this. At the beginning of his regime he met with much opposition, and as he succeeded in overcoming it step-by-step he gained greater and greater self-confidence. His brilliant victories made him a terror to his enemies and a trust-worthy friend to Sahu. His attitude towards the Maratha Confederacy was stern and unrelenting. He wanted that its members should work in harmony, under the guidance of the Peshwas. He would not let them go their own way, and would not brook any other's authority than his own. Thus, actuated he incurred the jealousy and hostility of many of the prominent members of the Confederacy. The Pratinidhi, Dabhade, Raghoji Bhonsla, Fatteh Singh Bhonsla, and Angre—all these nourished a jealousy against Baji Rao because he was both ambitious and domineering. He tried to suppress the same faults in others, and, therefore, incurred the implacable hostility of others. Had he been a little more conciliating and considerate, he would have won over many of those, who became his avowed enemies". (*Rise of the Peshwas*, pp. 202-3.)

BALAJI BAJI RAO (1740-61)

After the death of Baji Rao in 1740, his son Balaji Baji Rao became Peshwa.[1] There was not much opposition from his brothers. It is true that Balaji Baji Rao was not a man of parts himself, but he took advantage of the worth of his own cousin, Sadasiva Bhao. Balaji consulted him in every important affair of the state and did nothing without his advice. It was under the guidance of Sadasiva that the Maratha power reached its climax in 1760.

Raghoji Bhonsla over-ran the whole of Central India and attacked Bengal many a time. He forced Ali Vardi Khan in 1751 to give Orissa (now Odisha) to the Marathas and also give Chauth of the Provinces of Bengal and Bihar to the Marathas. Between 1752 and 1756, the Peshwa secured a promise of the Chauth of the Imperial revenues of Northern India. In 1758, the Marathas occupied the Punjab and the Maratha flag was unfurled over the fort of Attock. According to Elphinstone, "Their frontier extended on the north to the Indus and Himalayas, and on the south nearly in the extremity of the Peninsula: all the territory within those limits which was not their own paid tribute".

THIRD BATTLE OF PANIPAT (1761)

The conquest and occupation of the Punjab by the Marathas brought them into conflict with Ahmed Shah Abdali who started from Afghanistan to recover the same from the Marathas. The Marathas were also ready to meet him, and thus the famous Battle of Panipat was fought in January 1761. Ahmad Shah Abdali had under his command about 40,000 cavalry and 35,000 infantry. Sadasiva Bhao had under his command 55,000 cavalry, 15,000 infantry and 15,000 Pandaris. Both sides had artillery and other auxiliaries. Sadasiva Bhao was proud of his artillery strength and against the advice of his generals, decided to fight a pitched battle. Abdali was able to cut off the lines of communication of the Marathas. To begin with, the Marathas had the upper hand, but later on the Afghans carried the day. Sadasiva Bhao was killed. Visvas Rao, the son of the Peshwa, was also killed. Malhar Rao Holkar saved his life by running away from the battlefield. Mahadji Scindhia was able to save his life but

---

[1] He was also known as Nana Sahib.

he became lame. There was a terrible loss of life among the Marathas. The losses of the Marathas army were reported to the Peshwa in these words: "Two Pearls have been dissolved, twenty-seven gold mohars have been lost, and of the silver and copper the total cannot be reckoned". The news was received by Balaji Baji Rao when he was coming to Panipat with reinforcements. However, he was too late. He retired broken-hearted to Poona and died in 1761, a few days later.

There is no unanimity of opinion among the historians with regard to the effects of the Battle of Panipat in 1761. According to Sardesai, "Notwithstanding the terrible losses in manpower suffered on that field by Marathas, the disaster decided nothing. In fact, it pushed forward in the distant sequal two prominent members of the dominant race. Nana Phadnavis and Mahadji Scindhia, both miraculously escaping death on that fatal day, who resuscitated that power to its former glory... . The disaster of Panipat was indeed like a natural visitation destroying life but leading to no decisive political consequences. To maintain that the disaster of Panipat put an end to the dreams of supremacy cherished by the Marathas, is to misunderstand the situation as recorded in contemporary documents".

However, this view is not accepted by other historians. According to Sir Jadunath Sarkar, "A dispassionate survey of Indian history will show how unfounded this (Maratha) chauvinistic claim is. A Maratha army did, no doubt, restore the exiled Mughal emperor to the capital of his fathers in 1772, but they came then not as kingmakers, but as the dominators of the Mughal empire and the real masters of his nominal ministers and generals. That proud position was secured by Mahadji Scindhia only in 1789 and by the British in 1803". There is a lot to be said for this view. The battle of Panipat was a decisive battle. The flower of the Maratha army was cut off.[2] After this battle, the Maratha dream of establishing the empire over the whole of India vanished. The Maratha defeat had a great demoralising effect. The Indians after 1761 felt that they could not depend upon the protection and friendship of the Marathas. On account of the death of most of the Maratha captains and statesmen, the pain was left open for the "guilty ambition of Raghunath Dada, the most infamous character in Maratha history. Other losses time could have made good, but this was the greatest mischief done by the debacle at Panipat". The internal dissensions in the Peshwa family were responsible for the weakening of the Maratha power. It is this fact which helped the English to rise to power. To quote Sardesai, "It is significant that while the two combatants, the Marathas and the Mussalmans were locked in deadly combat on the field of ancient Kurukshetra, Clive, the first founder of the British empire in India, was on his way to England to explain the feasibility of his dreams of an Indian empire to the Great Commoner, Lord Chatham, the then Prime Minister. Panipat indirectly ushered in a new participant in the struggle for Indian supremacy. This is indeed the direct outcome of that historical event, which on that account marks a turning point in the history of India".

The Third Battle of Panipat "decided the fate of India". "The Marathas and the Mohammedans weakened each other in that deadly conflict, facilitating the aims of the British for Indian supremacy". Again, "If Plassey had sown the seeds of British supremacy in India, Panipat afforded time for the maturing and striking roots".

According to Elphinstone, "Never was a defeat more complete, and never was there a calamity that diffused so much consternation. Grief and despondency spread over the whole Maratha people; most had to mourn relations and all felt the destruction of the army as a death-blow to their national greatness. The Peshwa never recovered the shock. He slowly retreated from his frontier towards Poona and died in a temple which he had himself erected near that city. The wreck of the army

---

[2.] According to Sir J.N. Sarkar, "It was, in short, a nation-wide disaster like Flodden Field; there was not a home in Maharashtra that had not to mourn the loss of a member and several houses their very heads. An entire generation of leaders was cut off at one stroke".

retired beyond the Narbada, evacuating almost all their acquisitions in Hindustan. Dissensions soon broke out after the death of Balaji and the government of the Peshwa never recovered its vigour. Most of the Maratha conquests were recovered at a subsequent period; but it was by independent chiefs, with the aid of European officers and disciplined sepoys. The Confederacy of the Maratha princes dissolved on the cessation of their common danger".

Causes of Maratha Defeat in the Battle of Panipat. The defeat of the Marathas was due to many causes. Almad Shah Abdali had a stronger military force than that of the Marathas. Sadasiva Bhao, the commander of the Maratha forces, was no match for Ahmad Shah Abdali who was admittedly the ablest Asiatic general of his time: The latter was a general *par excellence*. After the death of Vishwasrao, he plunged into the battlefield like an ordinary soldier and lost his life. Sadasiva Bhao could not maintain his lines of communication with Delhi. The result was that for two months before the battle, the Maratha army was practically starving. The Marathas fought with hungry bellies in the battle-field. The Marathas had alienated the sympathies of the Rajputs and the Jats and consequently they could not rely upon anybody's support. No wonder, nobody raised his finger in defence of the Marathas. The troops of Ahmad Shah Abdali were better armed than those of the Peshwa. While the Marathas had lances and swords, the Afghans were armed with muskets. In the hand to hand fight, the Maratha artillery could not play its part but the Afghan muskets helped the Afghans to win the battle. While the Afghans possessed discipline of a very high order, the Marathas lacked the same. They were individualists and refractory. They hated discipline with the hatred of lesser breeds without law. They extolled lawless caprice as liberty and howled against discipline, self-control and organised teamwork of a true army or schools as the mark of a 'slave mentality' and the 'destroyer of their clan'. The ill-disciplined Marathas lost the day to the well organised and well disciplined Afghan troops.

Sardesai has attributed the Maratha defeat at Panipat to the following causes: Raghunathrao failed to maintain order and discipline among the Maratha agents in the north. Holkar failed to restrain Najib Khan from doing mischief. The Peshwa failed to go to the north and adjust matters when it was yet time to mend them. Bhau Saheb failed to keep women and non-combatants behind at Bharatpur or at Delhi. As soon as the two armies came face to face, Bhau should have at once attacked and maintained communications with his base at Delhi. After the death of Vishvasrao, Bhau Saheb should not have rushed headlong into the fight. Most of the Maratha horses had died on account of starvation in the camp at Panipat and the Marathas had to fight without their horses. They were accustomed to fight only with their horses and not without them and no wonder they failed. Sardesai thinks that it is wrong to say that the Marathas lost the battle of Panipat because they gave up guerilla warfare.

Balaji Bajirao was a man of refined tastes, fond of luxurious life and enjoying splendour and fine arts. During his regime, the social life of Maharashtra underwent great changes, in many directions. The camp life of the Marathas lost its original rudeness and simplicity. The Peshwa was an expert in accounts and penmanship and exercised strict control over receipts and expenditure. Public servants were drawn in a special institution of the Secretariat called the Phad. The Peshwa used persuasive methods both in diplomacy and war. There is no substance in the allegation that he favoured the Brahmans. He treated all castes equally. He distributed patronage equally.

According to a contemporary writer, "Balajipant Nana secured the affection of the great Chhatrapati Shahu and promoted in the service of the State all those who had been selected and raised to high positions by his father and uncle. He encouraged talent wherever he detected it and bestowed titles, gifts and honours upon those who exhibited valour and capacity. With a heart pressed towards public welfare, he manned the services with highly qualified individuals. Sardars and people undertook adventures and carried out grand conquests. His sweet, conciliatory and forgiving ways conquered the hearts even of his enemies. His conquests extended from Rameshwar to Indraprasta. Nana Saheb and Bhau Saheb were both incarnations of divine qualities.

According to Kincaid, "the fame of Balaji Peshwa resounded from the Indus river to the southern seas".

According to Sir Richard Temple, "Balaji's character was formed on the same lines as that of his father and his disposition moved in the same direction. But though a man of skillful address, of influence in counsel and of ability in the field, he was inferior to his father both as soldier and as a politician. He well knew how to utilise the talents of those about him, and some of his greatest successes were won for him by his lieutenants. Still he was ever to the front, organizing or supervising, and he saw the Maratha power attain its zenith. It was under him that the Maratha cavalry fully one hundred thousand strong could truly boast that they had slaked their thirst in every stream that flowed between Cape Comorin and the Himalayas. But he did not take, perhaps he was not capable of taking, any step for rendering this widely extended dominion advantageous to the people. He allowed Maratha rule to continue to be what it had been from the first, more an organization of plunder than a system of administration. Personally, he was unscrupulous in this respect, morally inferior to his father and grandfather".

According to Grant Duff, "Balaji Bajirao was one of those princes whose good fortune originating in causes anterior to their time, obtained in consequences of national prosperity, a higher degree of celebrity than they may fully merit. He was a man of considerable political sagacity, of polished manners and of great address. The territory under the immediate care of the Peshwa had been in a progressive state of improvement. Balajirao appointed fixed Mamlatdars or Subedars each of whom had charge of several districts. They had absolute charge of the police, the revenue and the civil and criminal judicature and in most cases had power of life and death. The commencement of a better system of administration particularly for Maharashtra is ascribed to Ramchandra Baba Shenwee and after his death Sadashivrao improved on his suggestions. A Shastree of respectability named, Balkrishna Gadgil was appointed head of the Poona Nyayadhisi or court of justice and the police was much invigorated at the capital. Under the Government of Balajirao, Panchayats, the ordinary tribunals of civil justice, began to improve. The Maratha dominion attained its greatest extent under Balajirao's administration and most of the principal Brahman families can only date their rise from that period. In short, the condition of the whole population was in his time improved and the Maratha peasantry, sensible of the comparative amelioration which they began to enjoy, have ever since blessed the days of Nana Saheb Peshwa".

Sardesai points out two serious mistakes committed by Balaji Bajirao. In the first place, Balaji made a mistake in taking British help to crush the Maratha navy headed by Angria, his own navy commander. Secondly, he neglected to support Bhonsla's claims in Bengal when Siraj-ud-Daula was being hard pressed by the British before the battle of Plassey (1757). Bengal had been acquired by Raghunathji and subjected to the annual payment of Chauth in return for which the Marathas were bound to help its Subedar. When the Englishmen turned their arms against Siraj-ud-Daula, it was the duty of the Peshwa to help him. In 1776, the position of the Peshwa was secure. At that time, he was the most powerful ruler in India. A move on his part against the British, both in Karnatak and in Bengal, would have at once checked their advance. Unfortunately, the Peshwa paid undue attention to the politics of Delhi and contracted unnecessary enmity with Ahmad Shah Abdali and brought about the disaster of Panipat in 1761. He had no business to go beyond the Sutlej into the Punjab. It appears that the Peshwa did not understand the real nature of the British game and side-tracked his attention to the Punjab. He was found wanting in sagacity and length of vision at a crucial moment. If he had understood all-India politics, he would have acted otherwise. The result of his folly was that the Britishers were able to establish themselves in Bengal, Oudh and the Deccan.

MADHAVRAO I (1761-72)

Peshwa Balajirao left behind two sons, Madhavrao and Narayanrao, and one brother Raghunathrao. Madhavrao was 16 years old at the time of the death of his father and became the Peshwa. His uncle Raghunathrao had hoped to conduct the affairs of the State but that was not tolerated by Madhavrao who is known as the greatest of the Peshwas. Although young, he possessed a mature judgment, a high spirit and the talents of both a soldier and a statesman. To begin with, there was friction between Madhavrao and Raghunathrao which later on developed into an open rupture. Raghunathrao demanded half the share of the Maratha State. Then started a civil war which ended in 1768 in the victory of Madhavrao. Raghunathrao was captured and was confined in his palace at Poona.

The enemies of the Marathas tried to take advantage of the Maratha defeat in Panipat in 1761 and the civil war in the country. Nizam Ali marched with all speed towards Poona but after a struggle for two years he was defeated at Raksasbhuvan and was forced to surrender.

On account of Maratha failure at Panipat, Hyder Ali of Mysore tried to extend his influence in the Karnatak and thereby destroyed all traces of Maratha influence in that region. The result was that Madhavrao had to spend the best part of his time and resources in capturing his former territories and exacting complete submission from Hyder Ali.

The Peshwa also subdued the Bhonslas of Nagpur, and forced them to accept him as the Peshwa and the head of the Maratha State. They were also forced to support him against all rivals and enemies. The treaty of Kankapur of 1769 with the Bhonslas is known as a masterstroke of Madhavrao's valour and capacity in organising the united power of the Maratha State.

The Peshwa also sent a strong expedition under two Maratha and Brahman commanders to restore the Maratha prestige and claims at the court of Delhi which had received a setback after the battle of Panipat. Mahadji Scindhia was one of the four leaders who were sent to Delhi. They won remarkable success in that undertaking. They restored the Mughal emperor to the Delhi throne. They humbled the Rohillas and carried out all the commitments usually understood by the terms Hindupad-padshahi.

Madhavrao improved the moral tone of the Maratha administration. Corruption was put down with a heavy hand. The revenue system was reformed in the interests of all the people. The judiciary began to function efficiently under the famous Ram Shastri. The complaints of the public were welcomed and attended to. The wrong doers were punished. Many vexatious taxes were removed. Definite rules and conditions of service were framed for the jagirdars and their military equipment. The system of Veth or exaction of forced labour from the lower classes was abolished. Every kind of service had to be paid for in cash. Spies were appointed to gather information from all over the country. A new generation of honest and efficient officials, clerks, accountants, supervisors, revenue collectors and military suppliers came into existence. Commanders had to give up their lethargy and learn obedience. A special branch for the manufacture of firearms and ammunition was set up and it worked under the personal supervision of the Peshwa himself. Madhavrao was not only a great administrator but also a great commander of large armies. He often showed exemplary valour and skill in strategy. He was a benevolent despot. He devoted his whole life to the service of the people.

A mere reference to a large number of great personalities shows that the Peshwa had brought into existence a large number of honest officers. Some of them were Ram Shastri, Govind Shivram,

Tatya, Naro Appaji, Mahadji Ballal Guruji, Trimbakrao Pethe, Gopalrao Patwardhan, Ramchandra Ganesh, Visaji Krishna, Nana Phadnavis, Moroba and Haripant Phadke.

According to Sir Richard Temple, "In some of the characters just depicted there has been found virtue of the secondary type, energy, courage, enthusiasm, patriotism and the like; but in none of them is to be seen virtue of the purer, nobler, loftier quality. In Madhavrao there is virtue of the best stamp. In trying moments he evinced not only presence of mind but also a proud consciousness that by him an example should be set to all around. He chose ministers with discrimination, some of whom justified his choice by their subsequent achievements. He enforced strictness in the service of the State and strove to procure honesty so far as that was procurable in a corrupt age. If an instance occurred of bad faith in high place, he would denounce it with a frankness surprising to those who lived in evil times. Though obliged to keep the uncle out of positions which afforded opportunities of doing harm, yet he showed the utmost consideration towards his relative. When two of his officers during a siege wanted to fight a duel over a quarrel, he told them, instead, to scale a deadly breach, promising to decree in favour of the disputant who should first plant the national flag upon the rampart. His care extended to the fiscal, the judicial, and the general departments. All men in his day knew that the head of the State was personally master of the work, was the friend of the oppressed and the foe of the oppressor, and was choosing agents who would carry out his beneficent orders. His thoughtfulness and considerateness were untiring and were often shown in a signal or graceful manner. For instance, he conferred benefits upon the descendants of the cavalry leader Santaji Ghorpade, who had been assassinated by Shivaji's son and successor, in order that such tardy justice as might be possible after the lapse of a generation, should be done. All the while, he was engaged in war and politics. He had to hold his own against the Nizam of the Deccan, to drive back Hyder Ali of Mysore, to retrieve that disaster at Panipat which had grieved his father to death. While greatly superior to his predecessors as a civil ruler, he was not inferior to them as a war like commander. His lieutenants were just retrieving the Panipat disaster when his own health, always delicate, gave way... .

"That Madhavrao, a Hindu prince, should have done so much in so brief a life as his, under such disadvantages and despite such temptations that, before being cut off, in the heyday of his career, he should have evinced such capacity as this, not only in affairs susceptible of management by youthful genius, but also in matters ordinarily demanding the experience of ripe years, is truly astonishing. Indeed, he is forever to be revered as the model prince, 'the flos regum' and as *one of the finest characters that the Hindu nationality has ever produced*".

According to Kincaid, "Threatened both by domestic and foreign enemies, Madhavrao triumphed signally over all. Yet his triumph had brought him no rest. Victorious over his foes he had spent his years in tireless labour to better the condition of his people. Every department was quickened by his supervision, his industry and his example. His secret intelligence was faultless; and no matter how remote the officer guilty of acts of tyranny, he rarely escaped punishment. The Peshwa's armies went well-equipped on service, for the entire military organization was under his direct control. Quick to anger, he was no less quick to forgive. And the only fault that the harshest critic can find in this admirable ruler is, that he shortened a life precious to his people by his arduous and unceasing toil".

According to Grant Duff, "Although the military talents of Madhavrao were very considerable, his character as a sovereign is entitled to far higher praise and to much greater respect than that of any of his predecessors. He is deservedly celebrated for his firm support of the weak against the oppressive, of the poor against the rich, and, as far as the constitution of society admitted, for his equity to all".

NARAYANRAO (1772)

When Madhavrao died of consumption in 1772, he was succeeded by his younger brother Narayanrao. His uncle Raghunath Rao, who was still in confinement, tried to escape. The attempt having failed, he was put under severer vigilance. A plot was prepared to make Raghunath Rao the Peshwa and put Narayanrao in confinement. However, Narayanrao was cut to pieces in the presence of Raghunath Rao and the latter became the Peshwa. There was a lot of resentment against the cruel murder and the enquiry which was held by Ram Shastri showed that Raghunath Rao was the prime author of the murder. The result was that the responsible ministers and leaders of Maharashtra formed a Council of State known as the *Bara Bhai* for the conduct of the affairs. In 1774, a posthumous son was born to the widow of Narayanrao and he was named Madhavrao Narayan.

MADHAVRAO NARAYAN (1774-95)

Madhavrao Narayan who is also known as Sawai Madhavrao II was declared the Peshwa and Raghunath Rao had to run away. The new Peshwa reigned for 21 years and died in 1795.

Although Raghunath Rao had to go into exile, he did not keep quiet. He sought the help of the English East India Company and the result was the Maratha War I. The war dragged on for many years and was ended by the treaty of Salbai in 1782. As a result of that treaty, Raghunath Rao had to give up all claims to the Peshwaship but he was given a pension. During the Maratha War I, Mahadji Scindhia and Nana Phadnavis distinguished themselves. In 1795, the Nizam was defeated by the Marathas.

BAJIRAO II (1796-1818)

When Madhavrao II died in 1795, there was a lot of confusion in Maratha politics. There were many intrigues for the appointment of a successor. To begin with, Nana Phadnavis was in favour of making Chimnaji Appa as the Peshwa. However, later on he changed his front and began to support Bajirao. Ultimately in 1796, Bajirao II became the Peshwa. The new Peshwa was the son of Raghunath Rao.

Bajirao was a worthless man. He was thoroughly unscrupulous. He had no training or competence for the high office to which he was called. He believed in intrigues. Nana Phadnavis who had helped him to come to power was put in jail but later on was restored to his previous position. However, the old man died in 1800.

It was during his tenure of office that the Maratha War II was fought in the time of Lord Wellesley. In 1802, Bajirao II entered into treaty of Bassein with the English East India Company. The net result of that was that the Peshwa came under the control of the Company. It was later on that he realised that the control exercised by the English Company was too much for him. The result was that he began to make efforts to release himself from the British control. This led to his participation in Maratha War III in the time of Lord Hastings. Peshwa was defeated by the East India Company. In 1818 he surrendered. The Peshwaship was abolished by the English Company. However, Bajirao was given a pension and he spent the rest of his days in Uttar Pradesh in religious pursuits. He died on 28th January 1851.

MAHADJI SCINDHIA (1727-94)

It seems desirable to refer to two great personalities of this period: Mahadji Scindhia and Nana Phadnavis. Both of them were contemporaries and both of them played an important part during the Maratha War I and came into prominence in Maratha politics. Nana Phadnavis controlled the Maratha affairs at Poona and Mahadji busied himself in the north. Both of them served the Maratha State faithfully. It is pointed out by Sardesai that if Mahadji and Nana Phadnavis had not acted in concert and brought all their resources to bear on the First Maratha War, there would have been an end of the Maratha power.

Mahadji and Nana Phadnavis differed from each other in their physical features as in their mental cast. "Nana, a Brahman, tall and thin, brownish in complexion with a long oval face marked with large piercing eyes and a long nose, the other a Kshatriya, of middle stature, dark, thickset, stout and athletic, a typical Maratha soldier of his time. While Nana was by nature strict and serious, regular and hard-working, abstemious in words and action, difficult of approach and never given to sport, mirth or company, hardly ever seen to laugh and of an extremely delicate and thin constitution, Mahadji was, on the other hand, of a jovial and merry temperament, ever surrounded by crowd of people, talking, joking, laughing and enjoying company, taking counsel with all, but always so cautious as to set people entirely on a wrong scent, never to let others fathom his real intentions or plans; in fact, an exact antithesis of Nana".

The life of Mahadji was one long period of strenuous activity. His life can be divided into 4 parts. During the first part up to 1761, he was an obscure figure over-shadowed by his brilliant brothers from 1761 to 1772. His life was one of apprenticeship in which he acquired the supreme fitness which later on helped him to co-operate with Nana Phadnavis to defeat the English during the Maratha War I. During the third part, he gained valuable experience of war and diplomacy on his own initiative which he put it in actual test later on. During the 4th part, he created the kingdom which he left for his children.

According to Keene, "Mahadji was easily provoked and not easily appeased. If he seldom forgave an injury, he never forgot the benefit. If he was severe in punishment, when punishment seemed requisite, he was not implacable or given to cause needless pain; while in conferring rewards for service rendered, his gratitude admitted neither stint nor oblivion. Consequently, he was served with fidelity and affection. It is impossible to read the memoirs of De Boigne without seeing how great a part of Scindhia's success was due to the admiration inspired by his moral character, and the confidence with which his subordinates trusted to his consistency of conduct, good faith and tenacity of purpose. He was good humoured, not exactly good tempered, and his countenance, in spite of an usually dark complexion, was full of amiability and intelligence. His correct expression was happily caught by a young Italian artist (Wales) who painted his portrait at Poona shortly before his death. His personal habits were simple and abstemious. Better educated than was usual among men of his class, he was not only able to read and write but was a good accountant and had a colloquial knowledge of Persian and Urdu. He was versed in business and without caring for the details either of war or civil administration, invariably chose good agents, whom he trusted thoroughly, and who repaid him for his confidence. The officers whom he employed at Ujjain and Gwalior were not less successful in fighting his battles and managing his affairs. He was an Indian ruler of successful capacity in times of exceptional difficulty. He was coldly regarded if not positively disliked for his abandonment of old Maratha warfare and favouring Muslims, such as chief adviser Ranakhan and his religious guide Mansur Shah".

The private life of Mahadji was pure and free from blemish. He was free from caste and religious bias. He was equally respected by the Muslims and the Hindus. He employed Brahmans, the Prabhus, Marathas and Maharas. The Saraswat Brahmans attained special distinction in his service as soldiers and diplomats. Mahadji was always careful and faithful to the Peshwa family. He never tried to assert his independence. It was unfortunate that Nana Phadnavis was jealous of Mahadji and always tried to keep him away from Poona.

Mahadji did not manage his financial affairs properly. He borrowed a large amount of money from all sources. A lot of money was pocketed by unscrupulous middlemen. There was confusion and misappropriation. Money was poured into useless channels. Lands were deserted and cultivation was stopped at many places. Robberies became frequent. Life became insecure. Mahadji agreed to pay the expenses of the Mughal empire and his armies but he had no money to do so.

According to Malleson, "By the death of Mahadji Scindhia, the Marathas lost their ablest warrior, and their most foreseeing statesman. In his life he had two main objects, the one to found a kingdom, the other to prepare for the contest for empire with the English. In both, it may be said he succeeded. The kingdom he founded still lives; and if the army which he formed was annihilated by Lake and Wellesley eight years after, it was because of the loss of his guiding hand. Had he lived, Mahadji would have brought under one standard the horseman and the French contingent of Tipu, the powerful artillery of the Nizam, the whole force of the Rajputs and every spear which Maratha influence could have collected from Poona, from Indore, from Baroda and from Nagpur. Even if the final result might not have been attained, the great problem of contest between a united India and the English would have been fairly fought out. As it was, his death settled it. Thenceforth the sinister result was only a question of time".

According to J.N. Sarkar, "Mahadji Scindhia, a heroic personality, dominates the North Indian history of his time like a colossus. His resources were defective, his instruments and allies often played him false; many an anxious crisis he had to face. Even sympathetic Residents like James Anderson and William Palmer predicted his sure downfall. And yet in the end he triumphed over all. We see the intense religious feeling, modern nationalists may call it superstition, which formed the essence of his being. We see the deep family affection, the habitual meekness of spirit, the respect for venerable persons, which this strong and busy man of action displayed even at the height of his earthly glory.

"In establishing Maratha control over the Imperial Government of Delhi and wiping off the disgrace of Panipat, Mahadji Scindhia had to labour alone, nay in the teeth of pinpricks and covert opposition by the Court of Poona. The supreme glory of the Regency of the Empire of Delhi that he gained, with the superlative titles of Wakil-i-Mutlab, Bakhshi-ul-Mamalik, Amir-ul-Umra, Alija, Infant of the Throne, was to him but a crown of thorns: the Muslim peers and former captains of the decadent Delhi State and their North Indian Hindu underlings, the Rajput vassals and even some British Residents, exalted at each disaster, each rebuff that he met with, and they counted the days of his sure extinction. And the Poona Government denied to him money and armed help in his sorest need and even insulted him in public The Khilats and costly presents that he had won from the Emperor for the Peshwa (in December 1784), were refused and left to rot at Ujjain for years together, as a brand of public humiliation put by his master on the greatest and most successful Maratha general then living. He was called in the Poona Minister's letters, a cheat, a disloyal servant, a selfish upstart bent on aggrandising himself by robbing his holy Brahman Shrimant of the fabulous wealth of Delhi.

"All this Mahadji bore with infinite patience, just as he broke through the successive nets of intrigue woven round him by his foreign enemies and nominal allies. He triumphed in the end, but that triumph was clearly purchased at the expense of years of frustration, of swaying fortune, and of immense personal suffering. *He towers over Maratha history in solitary grandeur, a ruler of India without an ally, without a party.* He reared a devoted band of his own captains, and he triumphed in the end no doubt and confounded his enemies and candid friends, but after what a tremendous loss of valuable time and avoidable waste of resources. If Nana Phadnavis had backed Mahadji at the outset, then the unchallengeable position which the great Scindhia gained for the Maratha race in January 1789, would have been achieved fully four years earlier;' and if such an early consummation had, as its natural effect, prolonged Mahadji's life by sparing the needless agonies of the intervening four years' time of struggle and reverses, then the whole course of Maratha history might have become different".

NANA PHADNAVIS (1742-1800)

Nana Phadnavis was born in 1742 and he died at the age of 58. He was thin in body and half fair in complexion. He was always serious and was hardly seen laughing. He was very studious and regular in his habits. He worked very hard at his desk. He attended to all the details of the administration. He did not like the open methods of Mahadji and always worked in secret. He was usually reasonable and fair in his dealings. He was afraid to commit treachery or wrong. He was strict in punctually carrying on the work. However, he did not possess self-sufficiency of Mahadji. He took counsel with all separately, but acted according to his own considered judgment. He was not at all loved as he was a stern task master. He was often in danger of assassination. On about 20 occasions, he had a miraculous escape from attempts on his life.

Nana lacked military leadership and that was a great disadvantage in the rough times in which he lived.

Nana did not possess a conciliatory spirit. He gradually removed all the members, one by one, of the Bara-Bhai Council and concentrated all power in his own hands. If instead of that, Nana had shared powers with others, there would have been better prospects for the future of the Marathas. It has been suggested that if Nana Phadnavis had taken into confidence all the Maratha chiefs and pooled together all the resources of the Marathas, the Marathas would not have fallen as they did under Bajirao II.

Nana had too much love for power. It is suggested that if he had retired from politics in 1795, he would have rendered a great service to the Maratha cause.

Another criticism of Nana Phadnavis is that he loved money too much. It is estimated that his private property amounted to several lakhs. It was with a view to safeguarding his own money that he opposed to the nomination of Bajirao Peshwa at the beginning.

According to Sardesai, Nana would have acquired a much higher place in history if he had subordinated his love of power and monetary interest to the service of the nation.

Reference may be made to some of the tributes paid to Nana after his death. According to Captain Browning, "Nana is gone and with him the Brahman raj. Poona has fallen". According to Palmer, "With Nana has departed all the wisdom and moderation of the Maratha Government". According to Sir Richard Temple, "Maratha administration lost all vestige of honesty and efficiency by the death of its great Minister". According to Grant Duff, "Nana Phadnavis was certainly a great statesman. His principal defects originated in the want of personal courage and in an ambition not always restrained by principles. His life was entirely public. In private he was a man of strict veracity, humane, frugal and charitable. His whole time was regulated with the strictest order and the business personally transacted by him almost exceeds credibility. *Nana doubtless shines out as the last genius produced by the Maratha nation".*

MARATHA ADMINISTRATION UNDER PESHWAS

The Maratha administrative system under the Peshwa was a compound of the principles laid down in the books of Hindu polity, arrangements made by Shivaji and his successors and the modifications introduced by the Peshwas themselves.

The Peshwas rose to power as the power and prestige of Raja of Satara declined. From 1714 onwards, the office of the Peshwa became hereditary in the family of Balaji Vishwanath. To begin with, the Peshwa was one of the Astha Pradhan of Shivaji and that was not a hereditary appointment. Gradually, the position of the Peshwa became supreme. The genius of Balaji Vishwanath made the office of the Peshwa both supreme and hereditary.

Although the Peshwa showed to the Raja of Satara on public occasions the attention due to a ruler, they virtually controlled the whole administration and even usurped the power of the Raja as the religious head of the State. However, these powers were not granted to him merely because he was a Brahman. The high position of Peshwa was recognised by the Maratha feudal nobility. He divided the revenues of each district among several Maratha chiefs. This system of sub-division of revenue gave rise to complications in accounts and the Peshwa and his Brahmin Secretariat took advantage of the same. Perpetual feuds and jealousies were also created among the Maratha chiefs.

Hazur Daphtar. The centre of the Maratha administration was the Peshwa Secretariat at Poona and it was known as the Hazur Daphtar. It was divided into many departments. It dealt with the revenues and expenditure of all the districts, the accounts submitted by the village and district officials, the pay and rights of all grades of public servants and the budgets of civil, military and religious servants. The daily register recorded all revenue income, all grants and payments and all payments received from foreign territory. These records became valueless in the time of Bajirao II on account of the chaotic state of affairs.

Village. The unit of Peshwa's administrative system was the self-contained and self-supporting village community. At the head of each village was a headman called Patel. He was not paid by the Government. His post was hereditary and that was the subject of sale and purchase. The Patel was helped by Kulkarni or village clerk and record-keeper who was always a Brahman. He was second in importance to the Patel and was paid in the same way as the Patel. The communal duties and wants of the village were performed and supplied by *Bara-Baluth* or 12 hereditary village servants who received a share of the crops and other requisites. They were also helped by other 12 village servants called *Bara-Baluth*. The carpenters, blacksmiths and other village mechanics and artisans gave *Begar* or forced labour.

Mamlatdar was in charge of a division called Sarkar, Suba or Prant. He was helped by Kama Vistar who was in charge of a similar area called Pargana. The Kama Vistar was subordinate to the Peshwa's Secretariat except in the case of Khandesh, Gujarat and Karnatak. Originally, Mamlatdar and Kama Vistar were appointed for short terms, but they got renewals. They were responsible for every branch of district administration including agriculture, industries, civil and criminal justice, control of police and investigation of Social and religious questions. They received the State revenues and fixed the revenues of each village after consultation with the Patel. They heard and decided the complaints of village official. Under the existing system, there were many opportunities for bad administration. In theory, the accounts of Mamlatdars were not passed by the Secretariat at Poona until they tallied with the accounts of the local officers. In all disputes regarding land, the Deshmukh was expected to produce ancient records with the history of all Inams and grants and the register to transfer of property which he maintained. The registers of the Deshmukh were irregularly maintained and were often incomplete. These registers were checked by the Mamlatdars. There were in all 9 officers in each district.

In order to prevent wholesale misappropriation of public money, the Maratha Government was accustomed to demand from the Mamlatdars and other officials the payment of a heavy sum (Rasad) on their first appointment to a district. The Hazur Daphtar prepared for them estimates of probable income and expenditure of the district. In time of Bajirao II, the posts of the Mamlatdars and others were auctioned. The clerks and menials were paid for 10 or 11 months in a year because it was thought that every servant got so much leave in a year.

Judicial System. The Judicial System was very imperfect. There were no rules of procedure and no codified law. In several cases, the main object was to bring about an amicable settlement between the parties. Arbitration was considered to be the first step in the disposal of a suit. If arbitration failed, the case was transferred for decision to a Panchayat appointed by the Patel in the village and by the leading merchants in urban areas. An appeal lay from the decision of the Panchayat to the Mamlatdar who usually upheld the verdict of the Panchayat. In spite of its primitive character, the Panchayat was a popular institution. If the Panchayat did not decide the case properly, a retrial took place. The peasant obtained fair justice from the village Panchayat. However, there was no justice if the big guns were involved in a case.

In criminal cases, the procedure of the other courts was repeated. However, the Panchayat was less frequently appointed. The chief authorities were the Patel in the village, the Mamlatdar in the district, and Sarsubedar in the province and the Peshwa and the Nyayadhish at the headquarters. They administered justice according to the popular custom tempered by the notions of the presiding officers. No regular form of trial of the accused persons was prescribed. Flogging was frequently inflicted with the object of extorting confession. Torture was also allowed. After 1761, capital punishment and mutilation of limbs were inflicted upon persons convicted of dacoity and theft, murder or treason. The usual methods of execution were hanging, cutting to pieces with a sword or crushing the skull. In the case of Brahmans, they were starved to death or poisoned. The ruler alone had the power of life and death. False evidence figured in criminal inquiries and the only notice taken of false evidence was a mild reproof from the Nyayadhish. The members of the family were taken away from the convict so that they might not be spoiled. Prisoners were kept in hill forts and gold often unlocked their gates.

Police System. The method employed was one of setting a thief to catch a thief. Every village kept its own watchmen who belonged to the degraded Mahar tribe under the direct control of the Patel. Watchmen were helped by gangs of hereditary criminal tribesmen. Each group was under the control of its own Nayak or headman who was answerable to the Patel for theft or robbery committed in the village. The system failed to prevent crimes. Umeji Nayak, the famous Ramosi outlaw, committed many crimes against persons and property when he was actually in receipt of a salary from the Bombay (now Mumbai) Government for performing police duties in the Poona district. His methods showed that there was nothing to prevent the village police from committing crimes settling them upon the innocent. Even the petty chiefs and the estate-holders plundered the villages of their rivals. Whenever the crime was on the increase, Government strengthened the village police with irregular infantry from the neighbouring hill forts and levied a house-tax on the residents of the disturbed area. The duty of the irregular infantry was to support the village police under the Patel and to oppose violence by force of arms. It did not include the work of detection of crime.

In the time of Bajirao II, the district police system was changed by the appointment of additional police officials whose duty was to discover and seize offenders. In the case of urban areas, magisterial and police powers were given to the Kotwal. The latter also regulated prices, took a census of the inhabitants, investigated and decided disputes regarding immovable property, supplied labour to Government, levied fees from the professional duties given to the Nagaraka or police superintendent.

Army. The Maratha army consisted of the mercenary forces of the feudal chiefs and regiments under the control of the Peshwa. In the time of Shivaji they were national in character, but later on they assumed a professional character. The Marathas were sent to the cavalry and their knowledge of horse-breeding proved very useful. The infantry was mostly drawn from Northern India. The artillery was manned and commanded by the Portuguese and Indian Christians. The military services of the Marathas were secured by the grant of fiefs. As the fiefs of the rival chiefs were in the same areas, there was a lot of internal strife and dissensions and that stood in the way of the solidarity of the State.

The Maratha Government did practically nothing for the economic improvement and intellectual advancement of the people. A large proportion of the revenues of the Government came from robbing the territories of the neighbours. The Marathas did not construct works of public utility. The only thing they did in the field of education was to give money to the deserving Pandits. The Marathas maintained "Jasuds" (spies) and "Harkaras" (messengers) for political and military performance and not for the convenience of the public.

Sources of Revenue. The most important source of revenue was in the form of Chauth and Sardeshmukhi. The Chauth was divided into (1) 25 per cent for ruler, (2) 66 per cent for Maratha Sardars and chiefs for the maintenance of troops, (3) 6 per cent for the Pant Sachiv, and (4) 3 per cent for other persons according to the pleasure of the ruler. Such a division of Chauth continued under the Peshwas.

Another important source of revenue was agricultural income from the village belonging to original settlers who acquired the forests and who could not be deprived of their lands. The assessment was based on a careful survey. Land was divided into three classes, viz., according to the character of the crop, facilities for irrigation and productivity of land. The Patel was the only official authority who could speak for the rights of the villagers against the higher authorities. The cultivator had practically no hearing.

Dr. S.N. Sen has described the system of revenue collection in these words: When the time for collection came, the Mahar called the ratepayers to the village Chawdi where the Patel held his office. The Kulkarni of the village, accounts-keeper, was present there with his records to assist the Patel in his work, and so were Potdars. The latter assayed and stamped the money when paid, for which the rent-payer got a receipt from the Kulkarni. When the collection was over, the money was sent to the Kamavisdar with a letter under the charge of the Chaugula, and a similar letter, often a duplicate copy, was sent to the Deshmukh, under the charge of the Mahar. The Chaugula got a receipt from the Mamlatdar for the sum paid, which was carefully preserved in the Kulkarni's bundle of village account. Sometimes Shibandi was sent by the officer incharge of the district or Tarf to help the Patel in his work of collection. The revenue was generally paid in four installments and sometimes in three".

Another source of a revenue was the miscellaneous taxes such as tax of one year's rent in 10 years on the lands held by the Deshmukh and Deshpande, a tax on land kept for the village Mahars, a tax on lands irrigated by wells, a house-tax levied from everyone except Brahmans and village officers, an annual fee for the testing of weights and measures, a tax on the re-marriage of widows, a tax on sheep and she-buffaloes, a pasturate fee, a tax on melon cultivation in river beds, succession duty, a duty on the sale of houses, etc. When the Maratha Government was in financial difficulty, it did not mind levying on all landholders *Kurja-Patti* or *Tasti-Patti* equal to one year's income of the tax-payer.

Customs duties also brought some revenue. They were in the form of taxes on trades and professions, taxes on projects and sale and octroi and ferry charges. Brahmans were exempted from duty on things imported for their own use. They were also exempted from house tax and other small taxes.

Another source of income was from the forests. Permits were sold for cutting timber. Some money was also got from the sale of grass, bamboos, fuel, honey and pastures.

The Government also got some money by giving licences to approved goldsmiths for private mints. The goldsmiths undertook to maintain a certain standard. In spite of this, the goldsmiths turned out spurious and faulty coins. Such a thing happened in 1760 in a certain division. On such an occasion, all private mints were closed and central mint was established which charged a fee of 7 coins for every licence.

The administration of justice also brought some money, although the income was not stable. A fee of 25% was charged on money bonds. Succession fee was charged and large sums of money were taken away from persons suspected or found guilty of adultery.

No definite estimate of the total revenues of Maratha State can be given. The revenue depended upon the robbing expeditions and could not be certain. On account of the unsettled condition of the country, the Maratha Government raised large sums of money on the security of its revenue. The people were impoverished on account of too much looting. The Constitution of the Maratha Government and army was intended more to destroy than to create an Empire.

CAUSES OF THE DOWNFALL OF THE MARATHAS

It goes without saying that after the disintegration and fall of the Mughal Empire, power fell into the hands of the Marathas. Their empire was vast. Their armies were big. The Marathas themselves were great warriors and in fearlessness and bravery they were second to none in the world. However, in spite of these qualities, the Marathas failed to hold their own against the British. This was due to many causes.

1. It is true that the Maratha Empire was a vast one, but it was not well-knit. It was not a unitary State and all power was not in the hands of the Peshwa. The Maratha Empire was a confederacy. Power was shared by many Maratha chiefs and most important of them were Holkar, Scindhia, Bhonsla and Gaikwad. It is true that nominally the Peshwa was the head of the Maratha confederacy but, as a matter of fact, he had no substantial control over the various Maratha chiefs. Every one of them was independent in his own territory and did whatever he pleased. They did not hesitate to intrigue against one another. It was not a happy phenomenon to see Holkar, Scindhia or Bhonsla helping another power against one another. Evidently, there was no discipline and solidarity among the Marathas. They were not brought together even by a national emergency. They failed to help one another against their common enemies and the result was that all of them were defeated one by one by the English East India Company.

2. The Marathas did not bother about finance. Such a vital department was absolutely ignored. The result was that the Marathas were always in need of money. This need they tried to satisfy by plundering the country. Plundering raids by the Maratha chiefs in search of money were common. But such a system can hardly bring any credit to the Government. No country can grow under such circumstances. Even the people cannot have any devotion or loyalty to such a State. The Maratha empire was bound to fall. The Marathas could plunder others when their own territory was small, but when their own empire began to grow, they could not adopt the old device of plundering. This resulted in shortage of finance. The Marathas did not set up an efficient system of administration. Nothing was done to safeguard the interests of the people. Their rule was positively oppressive.

3. Another cause of Maratha failure was that they gave up their old method of fighting. The Marathas were experts in guerilla warfare. They were not accustomed to pitched battles. However, guerilla tactics were possible only so long as the Marathas had not set up an Empire of their own. When they established their own Empire, it became absolutely necessary for them to protect the people from foreign invasion. Consequently, by the force of circumstances, the Marathas were forced to give up their old method of fighting and that brought about their ruin.

4. The Marathas were poor students of geography. They did not bother to understand the geography of the country which was indispensable for successful military operations. The result was that their lack of knowledge of the geography of the country landed them into

difficulties. If the Maratha armies were moving to a destination, they might not be knowing that they would have to cross a big river or mountain on the way. Such a handicap was suicidal for successful military operations. If such was the condition of the Marathas, the Englishmen knew all about the Maratha territory. This knowledge helped the Englishmen in their military operations.

5. The English Company had enormous resources at its disposal and the Marathas were no match for them. The English were also the masters of diplomacy and the Marathas were merely children before them in that difficult art.

6. Another cause of Maratha failure was the neglect of the study of science and of military training and organization. Those who conducted the affairs of the Maratha State did not take note of what their European neighbours were doing in India. When Bajirao and his brother Chimnaji conquered the Island of Bassein from the Portuguese after a heroic fight they failed to take the logical step of founding a naval arsenal and shipbuilding base as a measure of self-defence. The Portuguese had docks and foundries for making guns and experts to work them on scientific lines. These could have been continued under Maratha management at Bassein. If that had been done, the Peshwas would not have been helpless in naval matters. They would not have been forced to apply to Europeans for the supply of shot, cannon, power, ships, etc. The Peshwas and their advisers were intelligent and it is a pity that they utterly neglected the study and development of sciences which were absolutely necessary for the preservation of their organization, artillery and trained infantry and no wonder the Marathas ran away before the European guns. It is pointed out that no Maratha leader had the courage to face the British gunmen even if they were very few in number. Sardesai points out if the Maratha Government had possessed the necessary foresight and perseverance to organize their fighting on the European lines they would have been able to resist the British advance successfully.

7. Another cause of Maratha failure was the lack of organization or system in whatever they did. There was no unity of command, no distribution of work and power, no clear-cut assignment of duties, no methods, no system and no rule. Each Maratha chief pulled in his own direction. There was want of attention to details and pre-arrangement. It is true that the Marathas saw the necessity of uniting for a common purpose but no one came forward to do the needful in the matter. They never joined together against a common enemy. The result was that they were individually defeated.

8. It is pointed out that the downfall of the Marathas synchronised with the end of the 18th and the beginning of the 19th century. At that time, the position of the Marathas was the weakest and that of the Englishmen was the strongest. Between 1794 and 1800, most of the experienced and able persons in the Maratha kingdom were removed by the cruel hand of death. The old Ram Shastri had already died in November, 1789. Mahadji Scindhia died in February 1794. Hari Pant Phadka died in June 1794. Ahalya Bai Holkar died in August 1795. Peshwa Mahadeo Rao lost his life in October 1795 by an accidental fall from the balcony of his palace. Tukoji Holkar died in August 1797. Parshuram Bhan Patwardhan died on 18th September 1799. Nana Phadnavis died on 13th March 1800. Before the Marathas were able to put their house in order, they were called upon to oppose the formidable British power, strong in science, constitution, unity and naval supremacy. The supreme power at this time fell into the hands of Bajirao II and Daulatrao Scindhia. Their misdeeds brought the Poona court and society to such a moral degradation that no one's life, liberty or honour was safe. People even in the distant parts of the country had to suffer terrible misery through misrule,

oppression, plunder and devastation. The Sardars and Jagirdars, particularly of the southern Maratha country, were so completely alienated that they rushed for escape into the arms of the English. Bajirao was unscrupulous and incapable. It is true that Yashwantrao Holkar tried his best to remove Bajirao and put in his place his brother Amritrao. If he had succeeded in his objective, there would have been no chance for the British to establish their supremacy. However, the British did not allow that to be done and the result was that Bajirao II ruined everything. Bajirao II did not trust those who had been brought up under the old regime and selected his advisers from menials, selfish priests or intriguing up-starts like Arajerao Ghatge. Persons like Bajirao II surrounded by men of small minds and poor character could not hold their own against eminent personalities on the English side. Lord Wellesley and his two brothers Arthur Wellesley and Henry Wellesley were men of extraordinary capacity and talent. The same could be said about men like Elphinstone, Sir John Malcolm, Sir Barry Close, Col. Collins, Jonathan, Duncan and Sir Thomas Munro. Sardesai says that a nation possessing such able personalities for its agents is bound to win success at any time.

9. Another cause of success of the British was their inquisitive nature and their superior diplomacy. During the First Maratha War, the British had full and detailed information in their possession regarding the Maratha Raj, its armies, the comparative worth of the various Jagirdars, their mutual relations and their family disputes. The British knew who could be won over and who were loyal to the Peshwa. When they started the war, they were prepared for any eventuality. Apart from Hornby, Warren Hastings, Mostyn, Anderson, Upton, Malet and Goddard who were actively participating in war, there were other British agents who were obtaining all kinds of information about the Maratha forts and their positions, paths leading to them, the condition of the people, local disputes and political happenings. For seven years, Mostyn supplied useful information about Poona to Bombay and Calcutta. Indeed, it can be said that he was the prime agent who provoked the war. On the other hand, the Marathas had practically no information about the English. They knew practically nothing about England, her resources, her strength in India, etc. Even Nana Phadnavis did not at all possess such details. We do not know any Hindu who had learned the English language during the Maratha regime and who could talk and correspond freely in that language. On the other hand, there were a large number of Englishmen who had learned Indian languages and could freely speak the same. It is pointed out that even Nana Phadnavis was ignorant not only of the geography of the outside world but even of India. The maps used by him were fantastic, incorrect and useless. No wonder the Marathas failed.

10. According to Rajwade, the want of scientific study by the Marathas was the main cause of their failure. To quote him, "If any of the Maratha troopers accompanying Peshwa Bajirao II in his fight before the British regiments of General Smith and others during the early months of 1818, were asked why he ran away and what particular fright had seized him, he would have unhesitatingly answered that he was not at all afraid of white bipeds but of the wonderful long range guns which they handled and the superior scientific equipment that they possessed in the art of conducting war". According to Ranade, "If the innovation (of Scindhia's trained brigade) had been accompanied by the acquisition of the requisite knowledge of military strategy and the scientific processes in the use and manufacture of superior arms, the helplessness which paralyzed the native armies when their European officers left them might have been avoided; but no care seems to have been bestowed in this direction and they were more helpless than ever on the battlefield".

11. According to Sardesai the untimely and unexpected deaths of many of its great men at different times were responsible for the failure of the Marathas. The untimely death of Shivaji brought

the Mughal Emperor down upon Maharashtra. The untimely death of Bajirao I in 1740 freed the Nizam from extinction and made his dynasty permanent in the Deccan. The death of Peshwa Madhavrao let loose the latent dissolving forces upon Maharashtra and hastened its ruin. The death of Madhavrao II in 1795 brought to the Maratha leadership the evil genius of Bajirao II. According to Elphinstone, "It was the good fortune of the British that neither Bajirao nor Scindhia possessed the strength and spirit to stand forth boldly at a critical moment. If there was any other more intrepid man occupying the Peshwa's position at the time, it is not difficult to conceive how the British would have fared. The Marathas had at their command ample means of waging a successful war—arms, money, army and ammunition. Everything was ready. They only lacked a leader. Both Bajirao in the south and Daulatrao in the north became traitors to their nation and lost the game".

12. Another cause of Maratha failure was the narrow conservatism and racial arrogance inherent in the traditional system of caste. The Brahman rulers set in motion reactionary forces and revived old customs instead of supporting bold reforms for the regeneration of society. Men like Bajirao II cared more for earning religious merit by distributing jobs among the Brahmans than for the security of the State. According to Rajwade, "An Englishman is a born political animal possessing the glittering polish of a gentleman, but diabolic at heart. Where politics is concerned, he will not respect even his own father, much less anyone else. It was no wonder, therefore, that with our high talk of spiritual greatness, we went down in a short moment before the Englishmen".

Khare has given certain reasons for the failure of the Marathas. According to him, the Marathas did not possess any national sentiment. The internal jealousy and selfish treachery among them triumphed over the public interest. While individually the Marathas were clever and brave, they lacked the corporate spirit so essential for national independence. The scientific spirit of inquiry and improvement was entirely absent among them. They neglected to develop artillery as the main support of defence. The pernicious system of allowing lands in lieu of pay for Military service proved ruinous. After the death of Madhavrao I no capable leader appeared in Maharashtra. The Marathas as a race lacked the virtue of discipline and methodical pre-arrangement. The British were past masters in the art of diplomacy and the Marathas could not stand against them.

In his despatch dated 17th August 1817, Sir Thomas Munro pointed out some of the defects of the Marathas in these words: "When I consider the weakness of the native States and the character of the chiefs under whose sway they now are, I see little chance of a protracted resistance from them. They have no force to turn our armies and lengthen out the contest by a predatory invasion of our territories. They may run ahead of a few days but will have no time to rest or plunder. They will be exhausted and overtaken. It is not that they want resources, that they have not men and horses, but that there is no one amongst them possessed of those superior talents which are necessary to direct them to advantage".

"There is so little system or subordination in native governments that much more energy is required under them than under the more regular governments of Europe to give full effect to their resources. Daulatrao Scindhia was never formidable even in the height of his power. The great means which he possessed were lost in his feeble hands. The exertions of Holkar against Lord Lake were still weaker than those of Scindhia. The power of Holkar's as well as Scindhia's government has so much declined since that time (1805) that it is scarcely credible they would venture to oppose us. The superiority of our Government is so great that the event of any struggle is no longer doubtful".

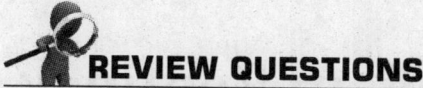

REVIEW QUESTIONS

1. What were the chief factors in the rise and fall of the Peshwas? Discuss in detail.
2. Discuss the policies and reforms of the Peshwas.
3. Write a detailed note on the Third battle of Panipat (1761).
4. Describe the administrative system of the Marathas under the Peshwas.
5. Highlight the salient features of the Maratha administration.
6. Review the causes of the defeat of the Marathas in the Battle of Panipat.
7. Analyse the causes of the downfall of the Marathas.
8. Write short notes on the following:
   (a) Baji Rao
   (b) Madhavrao
   (c) Narayanrao
   (d) Nana Phadnavis

SUGGESTED READINGS

Dodwell, H.H. (Ed.): *Cambridge History of India*, Vol. V, Chapter 23.
Duff, Grant: *History of the Marathas*.
Joshi, V.V.: *Clash of Three Empires*.
Kincaid and Parasnis: *History of the Maratha People*.
Mahamahopadhyaya: *Prof. D.V. Potdar Commemoration Volume* (1950).
Sardesai, G.S.: *New History of the Marathas* (1946)
Sardesai, G.S.: *Main Currents of Maratha History*.
Sen, S.N.: *Administrative System of the Marathas* (1925)
Sen, Surendra Nath: *Anglo-Maratha Relations* (1772-85)
Sinha: *Rise of the Peshwas*.

10 William Bentinck to Auckland

LEARNING OBJECTIVES

- Throw light on the conquests and reforms of William Bentinck
- Give an estimate of William Bentinck
- Discuss the reforms carried out by Charles Metcalfe and Lord Auckland

LORD WILLIAM BENTINCK

The arrival of Lord William Bentinck marked the beginning of a new era in many ways. He was a man of resolution, capacity and spirit. Helped by his previous experience in Madras (now Chennai) and an efficient staff of officials, he consolidated and reorganised the administrative machinery. He was a true liberal of his day and was thoroughly in accord with the ideals that inspired the era of Catholic Emancipation and parliamentary reform. He was the first Governor-General who acted on the theory that the welfare of the people was the main duty of the British in India. He infused into oriental despotism the spirit of British freedom. Although he was considered to be unsuccessful as the Governor of Madras he is considered to be one of the greatest of the Governors-General of India. He is famous not for his conquests but for the large number of reforms carried out by him in various fields.

It is a matter of common knowledge that the wars of Lord Hastings and Lord Amherst cost a good deal to the Indian exchequer. The Nepal War, the Third Maratha War, the First Burmese War and the action against the Pindaris practically exhausted the Indian treasury. When William Bentinck reached India he found a deficit budget. The time for the renewal of the Charter of the Company was coming near and the Directors wanted to present a favourable picture of Indian administration with a view to convincing the people. No wonder, *economy, reduction* and *increase in the total revenues* of the State became the watchwords of Bentinck's policy.

Financial Reforms. William Bentinck appointed two committees to inquire into the expenditure on civil and military affairs of the Company and make recommendations for its reduction. The committees went into the whole matter and made their recommendations. Accepting their recommendations, William Bentinck abolished many sinecure jobs, cut down the allowances and reduced the salaries of the civil servants. In the case of the military establishment, much could not be attempted. However, he halved the Bhatta allowances paid to the military personnel. Even before William Bentinck, the Directors of the English Company had tried to reduce the allowances but they had failed. Now, they ordered William Bentinck to reduce the Bhatta immediately. Consequently, in November 1828 an order was issued by which the Bhatta was required by fifty per cent at all stations within four hundred miles of Calcutta (now Kolkata). There was a lot of agitation against the Governor-General who was openly insulted and condemned by the Anglo-Indian press. In spite of this opposition, William Bentinck stuck to his guns and ultimately the opposition died out.

He abolished the Provincial Courts of Appeal and Circuit. According to Bentinck, these courts served as "resting places for those members of the services who were deemed unfit for higher responsibilities". A lot of saving was made from this account.

An attempt was made to increase the revenues of the Company by regulating the opium trade. Bentinck evolved the system of licences for the direct conveyance of opium from Malwa to Bombay (now Mumbai) and thereby added to the revenues of the Company.

Even before the assumption of Diwani of Bengal, Bihar and Orissa (now Odisha) by the Company, grants of revenue-free lands had been made to individuals and institutions. The English Company also confirmed those grants. A regulation of 1793 and another of 1819 empowered the Collectors to examine the validity of the grants. There was a suspicion that many grants were fictitious and illegal. A Regulation of 1828 directed the Collectors to look into the legality or otherwise of those grants. Special Commissioners were appointed to hear appeals from the decisions of the Collectors. The parties concerned pleaded that they could not produce their Documents on account of the passage of time. The Government did not accept this plea and consequently many revenue-free lands were resumed by the Government. This resulted in a lot of discontentment among the people, but William Bentinck was able to add to the revenues of the Company.

At this time, the revenue settlement of the North-Western Province was carried out. We are told that William Bentinck attended to this problem as soon as he came to India. He personally went on a tour of the province and consulted the best brains on the subject. He evolved a plan of settlement which became law in 1833. Land was surveyed. A classification of the soil was made. Settlement was fixed for thirty years. It was made either with ryots or the zamindars or the village community. Undoubtedly the revenue settlement encouraged the improvement of the soil and guaranteed the Government a definite amount of revenue.

The employment of Indians in the service of the Company also resulted in some economy. The salaries paid to the Indians were much lower than those paid to the Europeans.

The result of the above reforms was that the finances of the English Company were rehabilitated. Instead of a deficit of one million, Bentinck left behind a surplus of two millions.

Judicial Reforms. The judicial system of the Company suffered from three evils, viz., delay, expense and uncertainty, Calcutta (now Kolkata) had become too distant for the newly acquired territories. In the work of judicial reforms, Bentinck was assisted by Sir Charles Metcalfe, Butterworth Bayley and Holt Mackenzie.

In 1829, William Bentinck abolished the Provincial Courts of Appeal and Circuit. These courts were not doing their work enthusiastically. Their work was falling in arrears. These judges did not acquire sufficient knowledge and acquaintance with the people of the country. They failed to protect the people from the oppression of the police. The undertrials were made to live in prison for months before their cases were heard and disposed of. No wonder William Bentinck decided to abolish these courts. However, he appointed Commissioners of Revenue and Circuits. The Bengal Presidency was divided into twenty divisions and a Commissioner was appointed for each division.

These Commissioners were required to perform the same duties which were formerly performed by the judges of the Provincial Courts of Appeal and Circuit. The Commissioners were also given the duty of supervising the Collectors of Revenue and the police within their areas. However, these Commissioners were themselves placed under the control of the Sadar Nizamat Adalat and Board of Revenue for their criminal and revenue functions respectively.

In 1829, a Regulation provided that the magistrates were to have the power of awarding punishment of two years' imprisonment with labour. Appeals were to be taken to the Commissioners.

A Regulation of 1831 provided for the summary disposal of cases relating to rent. Collectors were given the power to decide those cases summarily. Their decisions were to be final. Those could be reversed only by means of regular suits in civil courts.

Another Regulation of 1831 provided that respectable Indians were to be appointed in the Zila Courts and City Courts. Indian judges were to try cases up to the value of ₹300. These judges were known as Munsifs. They were to get fixed salaries from the Government.

It was provided in 1831 that principal Sardar Ameens were to be appointed by the Governor-General-in-Council. Respectable Indians were to hold these offices. They were to get regular salaries. Appeals were to be taken from their decisions to the Zila or City Courts. Neither the Ameens nor the Munsifs were empowered to try cases in which Americans and European British subjects were involved.

Bentinck decided to set up a separate Sadar Diwani Adalat and Sadar Nizamat Adalat at Allahabad and these courts started working from the beginning of 1832.

A Regulation of 1832 introduced the jury system in Bengal. Its object was to help the European judges to take advantage of the assistance of respectable Indians for the disposal of cases before them. European judges were given the power to refer a case to a Panchayat of the Indians and the latter was required to make inquiries regarding the matter in question, and send a report to the judge. Provision was made for the appointment of Indian assessors to help the judges. They were required to give their opinions individually.

William Bentinck abolished the use of Persian as court language and ordered the use of vernacular for that purpose. This was a great boon to litigants who could express their grievances in their language.

Administrative Reforms. Lord William Bentinck reversed the policy of Lord Cornwallis with regard to the employment of Indians in the service of the English East India Company. Cornwallis had no faith in Indians and consequently insisted upon the employment of Europeans. It was found that it was very expensive to employ Europeans while Indians could be employed on much cheaper wages. Indians were available for clerical jobs on account of the spread of English language. Bentinck introduced three grades of Indian judges and the highest of them called Sadar Amins were given a salary of ₹750. The employment of Indians removed one of their grievances. This new policy was in accordance with the principle laid down in the Charter Act of 1833. That Act laid down that "no native of India nor any natural born subject of His Majesty should be disabled from holding any place, office of employment by reason of his religion, place, of birth, descent or colour". William Bentinck followed the lines suggested by Sir Charles Metcalfe, viz., "native functionaries in the first instance of all departments. The European superintendents, uniting the local powers of judicature, police and revenue in all their branches, through the districts over which they preside; Commissioners over them and a Board over them communicating with and subject to the immediate control of the Government".

William Bentinck appointed a Board of Revenue at Allahabad for the North-Western Province.

Educational Reforms. It is well known that the Charter Act of 1813 allotted a sum of ₹1 lakh a year for the "revival and promotion of a acknowledge of the sciences among the inhabitants of the British territories". The Government of India could not make up its mind as to how the money was to be spent and the same was allowed to accumulate every year. In 1823, Mr. Adams appointed a Committee of Public Instruction to make suggestions. However, much could not be done on account of pre-occupation with the First Burmese War. William Bentinck had to tackle this problem. There were two schools of thought on this question. H.H. Wilson was the leader of the Orientalists and Sir Charles Trevelyan was the leader of the Anglicists. The arrival of Lord Macaulay as Law Member strengthened the hands of those who stood for the expenditure of money on English education. Ultimately, the issue was decided in favour of the English language. Practical considerations were responsible for deciding the issue. It was felt that not only the Government of India would get cheap clerks but there would be greater demand for English goods. Even Indians like Raja Rammohan Roy were in favour of the English language. By a resolution of March 1835, William Bentinck declared that "the great object of British Government ought to be the promotion of literature and science among the natives and that the funds appropriated for education should be best employed on English education alone".

It cannot be denied that the English education gave the Indians a *lingua franca* and thereby helped the cause of nationalism in the country. The Indians were introduced to the treasures of western knowledge.

In 1835, a Medical College was opened at Calcutta (now Kolkata). Thus the knowledge of the western theory of medicine began to be given to the students in India.

Social Reforms. William Bentinck was responsible for the abolition of Sati and Thugee. Both these customs involved death. The only difference was that death in the case of Sati took place voluntarily and in the case of Thugee was inflicted by Thugs on others. Nobody knows the origin of the custom of Sati. Undoubtedly, it was an old custom which prevailed among the higher castes. It was considered to be a privilege and honour and that is why it was accompanied by the recitation of sacred hymns. The widowed woman burnt herself along with her husband. She was made to put on all her clothes and ornaments and after the act of burning was over the Brahmans were able to put all the gold into their pocket. This created vested interests and hence the custom was continued in spite of protests from time to time. It is well-known that Akbar tried to suppress the custom of Sati. Albuquerque had done the same. The Peshwas also prohibited this custom within their territories. In 1823 the Court of Directors made an inquiry into the custom and hinted at the possibility of prohibiting it by law if there was no danger of any great opposition. Lord Amherst had invited opinions on this question and it was found that there was no unanimity. William Bentinck came to the conclusion that there was no possibility of any serious consequences if the Sati was made a penal offence. He was helped in this task by Raja Rammohan Roy. By a regulation of December 1829, Bentinck declared the practice of Sati as illegal and punishable as "culpable homicide". There was strong opposition from the orthodox sections of society but William Bentinck had the courage of a reformer and he carried out the reform. There was agitation for sometime but the same died out after passage of time.

As regards the Thugs they were bands of hereditary robbers and murderers who carried out their crimes in a uniform manner. The existence of the associations of Thugs first came to the notice of the British after the capture of Seringapatam in 1799. A few hundred of them were captured in the Mysore territory where they particularly flourished. A few years later further arrests in the Arcot district led to the discovery that the Thugs operated in many parts of India and enjoyed the protection of petty chieftains and zamindars in many places. It was found that they worked in gangs, and confined their attention to travellers. Their customary method of murdering was by strangling. Their children were regularly trained in their profession. They robbed the poor and the rich and were ready to commit murder for the sake of a few rupees. The gangs of Thugs often contained as many as 300 men. In such cases, they worked as sub-gangs and gathered as a body only when it was absolutely necessary.

Thornton has explained the method of the working of the Thugs in these words: "Some variations have existed in the manner of perpetrating the murders; but the following seems to be the most general: While travelling along, one of the gang suddenly throws a rope or cloth round the neck of the devoted individual and retains hold of one end, the other end being seized by an accomplice. The instrument of death, crossed behind the neck, is then drawn very tight, the two Thugs who hold it pressing the head of the victim forward: a third villain, who is in readiness behind the traveller, seizes him by the legs, and he is thus thrown on the ground. In this situation there is little opportunity of resistance. The operation of the noose is aided by kicks inflicted in the manner most likely to produce vital injury, and the sufferer is thus quickly despatched.... Such are the perseverance and caution of Thugs that, in the absence of a convenient opportunity, they have been known to travel in company with persons whom they have devoted to destruction, for several days before they executed their intention. If circumstances favour them, they generally commit the murder in a jungle, or an unfrequented part of the country, near a sandy place or dry water-course. Particular tracts are chosen, in every part of India, where they may exercise their horrid profession with the greatest convenience and security. Much-frequented roads, passing through extensive jungles, where the ground is soft for the grave, or the jungle thick to cover them, and where the local authorities take no notice of the bodies, are favourite spots. The Thugs speak of such places with the same affection and enthusiasm as other men would of the most delightful scenes of their early life".

Inside each band of Thugs there were regular ranks and gradations. A Thug with a great reputation as a strangler or whose ancestors had been Thugs from time immemorial or who could bribe or hoodwink the local officials, or who was a natural leader of men, became a Jamadar. A person who was an outstanding member of the profession became a Subedar. Whatever things were captured by the Thugs, had to be divided among many persons. The leader was given a special share of the plunder. First of all portions were set aside for the local polygars or chieftains whose connivance was important. Something was set apart for the performance of religious ceremonies. After that two shares were given to the actual murderer and a share each was given to the ordinary member of the gang. The Thugs had great faith in religious superstitions. They believed that if they acted according to the rules and observed the omens, the Hindu Goddess Kali would not desert them. One of the Thugs told Sleeman thus: "That Davy (or Kali) instituted Thugi and supported it, as long as we attended to her omens and observed the rules framed by the wisdom of our ancestors, nothing can ever make us doubt".

The English East India Company did something in this field to remove the curse of Thugee, but there was not much progress. In 1829, the agent of the Governor-General in Narbada territories was instructed to take action against all the Thugs wherever they might be. Captain Sleeman was appointed as the Assistant of the Agent. The officials of the Company throughout India were directed to send to him not only reports of all cases of Thugee, but also all facts which might help to unearth the secrets of the Thugs. A study of the reports showed that in Mysore alone, hundreds of persons were murdered annually by the Thugs.

There were four main difficulties in the way of successful operations against the Thugs. The first difficulty arose from the very nature of the crime which was usually done in secret. The magistrate of Chittoor observed thus: "It is only necessary to consider the habits of the phansigors to be convinced of the extreme difficulty of discovering and convicting them and how inadequate the ordinary measures of State and the operation of the present laws are for effecting those objects. The scene of their crimes is always out of their own districts, seldom within thirty miles of their usual places of abode; they have sometimes left their homes for several months together and faced journeys of many hundreds of miles. Their victims are generally travellers with whose circumstances they become acquainted at public choultries; they frequently change their names and sometimes go by several names, the latter to prevent detection; murder their victims at a distance from towns or large villages in public roads leading through jungles or uncultivated land, in which they bury their bodies; they sometimes take with them some of their children (boys under twelve years of age) the less to attract notice and suspicion. The headman of the gang sometimes rides on a horse; they generally have with them some bullocks or tattoo ponies to carry the plundered property; by these means they normally pass for merchants, the character they frequently assume. A gang is always sufficiently numerous to allow several persons belonging to it being stationed at a short distance from the places where their victims are put to death, to give alarm in the case of approaching danger. They never commit robbery unaccompanied with murder; they first strangle their victims and then plunder them".

Another difficulty in the way of the Government was that the Thugs enjoyed the protection of the chiefs, zamindars and officials and consequently could do whatever they pleased without any fear of punishment. The Thugs were required to pay lot of money in the form of Nazrana. A Thug approver stated that not he alone but his father also was a Thug. The approver also produced a list of the Thugs who paid tribute to the Gwalior State. All the houses of the Thugs were taxed and one of the Thugs was required to collect the money. When the Thugs returned from expeditions, they made presents to their leaders. According to another approver, the Thug leaders "keep up a direct understanding with the local authorities in Bundelkhand, in whose limits they and their followers reside invariably on their return from an excursion, conciliate their forbearance and favour by suitable Nazranas". Connivance by local rulers perhaps the rule rather than the exception.

Another difficulty was that many Thugs had alternative sources of livelihood. They spent most of their time in a respectable occupation and practised Thugee occasionally. It was difficult to suspect such persons.

Another difficulty arose from the new standards of proof demanded by the courts under English officials. Many persons, known to the people of the locality to be Thugs, were acquitted for want of rigorous evidence. Sometimes an honest informer was punished because his case was not proved in a legal sense.

To meet the above difficulties, two measures were adopted. An Act was passed by which the mere fact of belonging to a gang of Thugs was made an offence punishable with imprisonment for life. It was often possible to prove association where evidence of a commission of a specific offence was not forthcoming. Moreover, Sleeman and his colleagues made skilful and discriminating uses of approvers. A Thug against whom evidence was clear was pardoned after making a full confession.

That helped the authorities to know more about the Thugs and their whereabouts. It is stated that within six years, about 200 Thugs were arrested, about 1,500 were put to death or transported for life and the rest were confined to a reformatory at Jubbulpore.

According to Hindu law, if a Hindu became a convert to Christianity, he was not entitled to a share in the property of his family. The law was changed in such a way that even if a Hindu was converted to Christianity, he was to be entitled to his share in the paternal property.

Public Works Reforms. The irrigation schemes started in the time of Lord Minto were taken up in the time of William Bentinck. Canals were dug for the distribution of water in the North-Western Province. Roads were improved. The Grand Trunk Road from Calcutta to Delhi was built and from Bombay to Agra was started.

Relations with Indian States. The Mughal Emperor complained of the inadequate allowance given to him. Although Raja Rammohan Roy went to England to plead the cause of the Mughal Emperor, nothing came out of it. This created bitterness.

William Bentinck followed a policy of non-intervention with regard to the dependent States. After the death of Nizam Sikandar Shah of Hyderabad in 1829, Nazir-ud-Daula became the Nizam and the latter requested the British Government to remove the British officers. The request was granted.

There were disturbances in Jaipur. The Rani and her lover were executed in 1835. The British Resident was assailed. However, the policy of non-intervention was followed.

In the case of Bhopal, Sikandar Begum took over the administration into her hands. There was a lot of confusion and trouble in the State. In spite of that, the British Government remained neutral.

In the case of Gwalior and Sind, no consistent policy was followed. Sometimes a policy of intervention was followed and sometimes that of non-intervention.

As regards Mysore, there was a lot of confusion and misgovernment in the State. The people revolted against the ruler. William Bentinck intervened and took over the administration of the State in his own hands. This arrangement continued up to 1881.

William Bentinck was responsible for the annexation of the State of Coorg. The ruler of Coorg became insane and put to death every male member of the royal family. He oppressed his subjects. The result was that the British Government denied him its protection. As this had no effect, war was declared against the Raja. He was defeated and captured, and the State was annexed.

William Bentinck sent Colonel Pottinger with instructions to enter into a commercial treaty with the Amirs of Sind. Although the latter hesitated, they were forced to enter into a treaty on account of the danger of Sikhs.[1]

Bentinck met Maharaja Ranjit Singh at a Durbar held at Rupar in 1831. The object of this meeting was to bring the two countries together so that they might cooperate with each other in the event of a Russian advance.

Charter Act of 1833. The Charter renewed the monopoly of the English Company for 20 years. It centralised legislation.

---

[1] According to Alfred Lyall, Bentinck's treaties with Ranjit Singh and the Amirs of Sindh "were in point of fact the preliminary steps that led us, a few years later on, upon the wide and perilous field of Afghan politics". (*British Dominion in India*, p. 313.)

Estimate of Bentinck. The glories of William Bentinck were the glories of peace and not of war[2]. He was responsible for rehabilitating the finances of the English Company. He removed the legitimate grievances of the Indians by admitting them into the service of the Company. He carried out many useful reforms in the social, administrative and judicial fields. He introduced the steamship navigation on the Ganges. R.C. Dutt has summed up his achievements in these words: "William Bentinck's seven years' rule was an era of peace, retrenchment and reform. He secured tranquility in the East India Company's dominions and lived at peace with the Indian powers. He reduced the public debt, decreased the annual expenditure and showed a surplus. He commenced that revised settlement of land revenue in Northern India which gave relief to landlords and cultivators. He admitted the educated people of India to the higher appointments in the revenue and judicial departments. He abolished the practice of *sati* and suppressed the crime of *thugee.* He promoted English education in India and endeavoured to carry out the maxim that the administration of India was primarily for the interest of the people".

"Lord William Bentinck infused into oriental despotism the spirit of British freedom". "William Bentinck's part in consolidating British authority in India was a great and honourable one".

Lord Macaulay wrote on the base of Bentinck's statute at Calcutta the following inscription: "To William Cavendish Bentinck, who during seven years ruled India with eminent prudence, integrity and benevolence; who, placed at the head of a great empire, never laid down the simplicity and moderation of a private citizen; who infused into oriental despotism the spirit of British freedom; who never forgot that the end of government is the happiness of the governed; who abolished cruel rites; who effaced humiliating distinctions; who gave liberty to the expression of public opinion; whose constant study it was to elevate the intellectual and moral character of the nation committed to his charge". Macaulay also referred in another place to "the veneration with which the latest generation of Hindus will contemplate the statue of Lord William Bentinck".

According to Grenville, "He (Bentinck) is a man whose success in life has been greater than his talents warrant, for he is not right-headed and has committed some great blunder or other in every public situation in which he has been placed but he is simple in his habits, popular in his manners, liberal in his opinions, and magnificently hospitable in his mode of life".

H.T. Prinsep who *knew* William Bentinck intimately wrote thus about him: "It was not in Lord William Bentinck's nature to give his implicit confidence to anybody except his wife, and he never took any important step without consulting her. She had been trained to diplomacy at Naples and in Sicily, and I cannot say that her advice and influence was other than beneficial". Again, "He had a great love of change and desire to meddle with every institution of practice that he found in work or prevailing. It is impossible to deny that some of his changes were beneficial, but *he as often muddled what he meddled with as improved it,* and he left a great deal to be done by those who succeeded him in order to bring the machine of Government back into good working order". Again, "Lord William Bentinck wrote more Minutes than all the other Governors-General of India put together, but they were mostly on subjects of little moment. If he had to discuss a great question, he did not bring to it any originality of view or commanding intelligence and power of reasoning that carried with it the conviction of those who read and had to carry out the ideas and propositions he desired to see adopted. But there never was a more honest man in his intentions, and in the distribution of his patronage".

---

[2] "Peace hath her victories no less renowned than war".

SIR CHARLES METCALFE (1835-36)

Lord William Bentinck was succeeded by Sir Charles Metcalfe who was one of the ablest servants of the English East India Company. It was he who had negotiated the Treaty of Amritsar with Ranjit Singh in 1809. He had also worked as Lieutenant-Governor of the North-Western Province. The only important event of his time was the abolition of the restrictions on the Indian Press. The Home Government was so much annoyed at this act of the Governor-General that it decided to recall him. His period of office lasted for a few months.

LORD AUCKLAND (1836-42)

The most important event of his reign was the First Afghan War which has been discussed at length in Chapter XXXI. His Afghan policy has been universally condemned.

However, Lord Auckland carried out a few reforms. Before his time, the English in India enjoyed certain privileges with regard to their dealings with the Indians. They had the power to take their cases to the Supreme Court at Calcutta. Lord Minto was of the opinion that the discrimination was unjust and must be abolished. An Act was passed by which Englishmen in civil suits were put on the same footing as the Indians. This Act was called by the Englishmen by the name of "The Black Act".

Lord 'Auckland set up a large number of scholarships for the various Government schools in India. He also announced that the medium of instruction in all primary schools was to be the vernacular language of the area concerned. He set up medical colleges at Bombay and Madras.

With a view to meeting the menace of famines, Auckland sanctioned a large scheme of irrigation for the people of Doab. On account of the outbreak of the First Afghan War, the scheme could not be carried out as no money was available.

Relations with Indian States. Lord Auckland threatened the ruler of Indore to depose him in case he did not improve his administration. The warning proved effective and the administration was improved.

The Raja of Satara resented his weak position and carried on negotiations with other interested and disaffected elements. The Government of Bombay asked him to admit his fault but the latter refused to do so. The result was that he was deposed and sent as a state prisoner to Banaras. His brother was put on the throne.

As regards Oudh, Lord Auckland entered into a treaty with its ruler. The treaty was disallowed by the Home Government. Although Lord Auckland knew the true state of affairs, he concealed the same from the ruler of Oudh and merely informed him that only a part of the treaty had been changed by the Home Government. Such an act of duplicity was unpardonable.

According to Trotter, "Cold-mannered, reticent, shy, good-natured robust of figure, disliking all pomp or parade, and delighting in regular official work, Lord Auckland was eminently fitted by temperament and long experience to discharge the most exacting duties of quiet times". According to Grenville, "He (Auckland) was a man without shining qualities or showy accomplishments, austere and almost forbidding in his manner. Silent and reserved in society, unpretending both in public and in private life, and in the House of Lords taking a rare and modest part in debate... . Nevertheless he was universally popular... . His understanding was excellent, his temper placid, his taste and tact exquisite, his disposition notwithstanding his apparent gravity, cheerful; and under his cold exterior there was a heart overflowing with human kindness".

According to H.T. Prinsep, "He was a good man of business, an assiduous reader of all papers, and very correct and careful in any of the drafts he approved and passed but he was much wanting in promptness of decision and had an overweening dread of responsibility which caused the instructions he gave which were often penned by himself, to be so unsatisfactory that his agents had generally to decide for themselves what to do in the difficulty". Again, "Lord Auckland was much esteemed by the society of Calcutta, native as well as European. He had many amiable, qualities, and his two sisters, especially the elder, contributed much to establish his popularity. But he was the author of no great measure to Improve the internal administration, and in his general policy he showed a hesitation and want of decision that prevented his being looked upon as a Governor-General of whom India might be proud. He was considered to have yielded too much to his Private Secretary (John Colvin), who on occasions when the Governor-General called his Members of Council and others into private consultation with himself, would take the whole initiative of the discussion while his Lordship sat listening with his hands at the back of his head; and from having thus so much thrown upon him he got the nickname of Lord Colvin among the younger Civil Servants".

REVIEW QUESTIONS

1. Write a detailed note on the conquests of William Bentinck.
2. Discuss the reforms carried out by William Bentinck in various fields.
3. Describe the policies of William Bentinck.
4. William Bentinck is famous for his social reforms in India. Elaborate.
5. William Bentinck was responsible for the abolition of *Sati* and *Thugee* in society. Comment.
6. The glories of William Bentinck were the glories of peace and not of war. Comment.
7. Describe the important events that took place in the reign of Lord Auckland.
8. Write short notes on the following:
    (a) Social reforms of William Bentinck
    (b) The Charter Act of 1833
    (c) Sir Charles Metcalfe
9. William Bentinck was a man of resolution, capacity and spirit. Analyse.
10. Assess the role of William Bentinck as a ruler.

SUGGESTED READINGS

Bearce, George D.: *British Attitudes Towards India.*
Boulger, D.C.: *Lord William Bentinck* (1897).
Evans, R.: *Lord Amherst* (1894).
More, R.W.: *Hindu Infanticide* (1860).
Sleeman, W.H.: *Rambles and Recollections.*
Strokes, Eric: *The English Utilitarians and India.*
Taylor, Meadows: *Confessions of a Thug.*
Thompson, E.: *Sutee* (1928).
Trotter, L.J.: *Earl of Auckland* (1905).

11

Ellenborough and Hardinge

LEARNING OBJECTIVES

- Throw light on the events and reforms that took place during the reign of Ellenborough
- Discuss the reforms undertaken by Lord Hardinge

LORD ELLENBOROUGH (1842-44)

Lord Ellenborough was appointed at a time when the situation in India was very serious on account of the British bungling in Afghanistan in the time of Auckland. He was a man of vigour and decision. Before his coming to India, he had acted as the President of Board of Control.

The first work done by Lord Ellenborough was that he brought the first Afghan War to a successful close. The credit may be shared by various English generals who actually conducted the campaigns but he also can claim his share.

Annexation of Sindh (1843)

Another important event of the Governor-Generalship of Lord Ellenborough was the conquest and annexation of Sindh in 1843. It seems desirable to discuss at this place the Anglo-Sindh relations from the beginning of the 19th century up to its annexation.

Sindh was ruled by a number of chiefs or Amirs of the Talpura tribe who had originally come from Baluchistan. The important Amirs were at khairpur, Hyderabad and Mirpur. The Amir of Khairpur claimed suzerainty over other Amirs.

In 1890, the English Company entered into a treaty with the Amirs by which the latter undertook not to allow any settlement of "the tribe of the French" in Sindh. In 1831, Burnes went on a mission to Lahore and he passed through the river Indus. It is stated that when a Syed saw the ship of Burnes passing through the river Indus, he remarked thus: "Alas, Sindh is now gone since the English have seen the river".

In 1831, Maharaja Ranjit Singh suggested to William Bentinck the partition of Sindh between himself and the British. The Governor-General did not accept the suggestion. However, the English Company forced the Amir of Hyderabad to enter into a treaty in April 1832 on the following terms:

1. "That the two contracting powers bind themselves never to look with the eye of covetousness on the possessions of each other".
2. "That the British Government has requested a passage for the merchants and traders of Hindustan by the rivers and roads of Sind by which they may transport their goods and

merchandise from one country to another and the said Government of Hyderabad hereby acquiesces in the same request on the following conditions: (a) that no person shall bring any description of military stores by the above river and roads, (b) that no armed vessel or boats shall come by the said river".

3. "That no English merchant shall be allowed to settle the Scinde, but shall come as occasion requires and having stopped to transact their business, shall return to India".

This treaty was renewed in 1834.

Maharaja Ranjit Singh was very anxious about the conquest of Sindh but the British Government refused to allow him to do so. As a matter of fact the British Government took the Amirs under its own protection. As a result of the favour done to them, Lord Auckland forced the Amirs in 1838 to have a British Resident at Hyderabad.

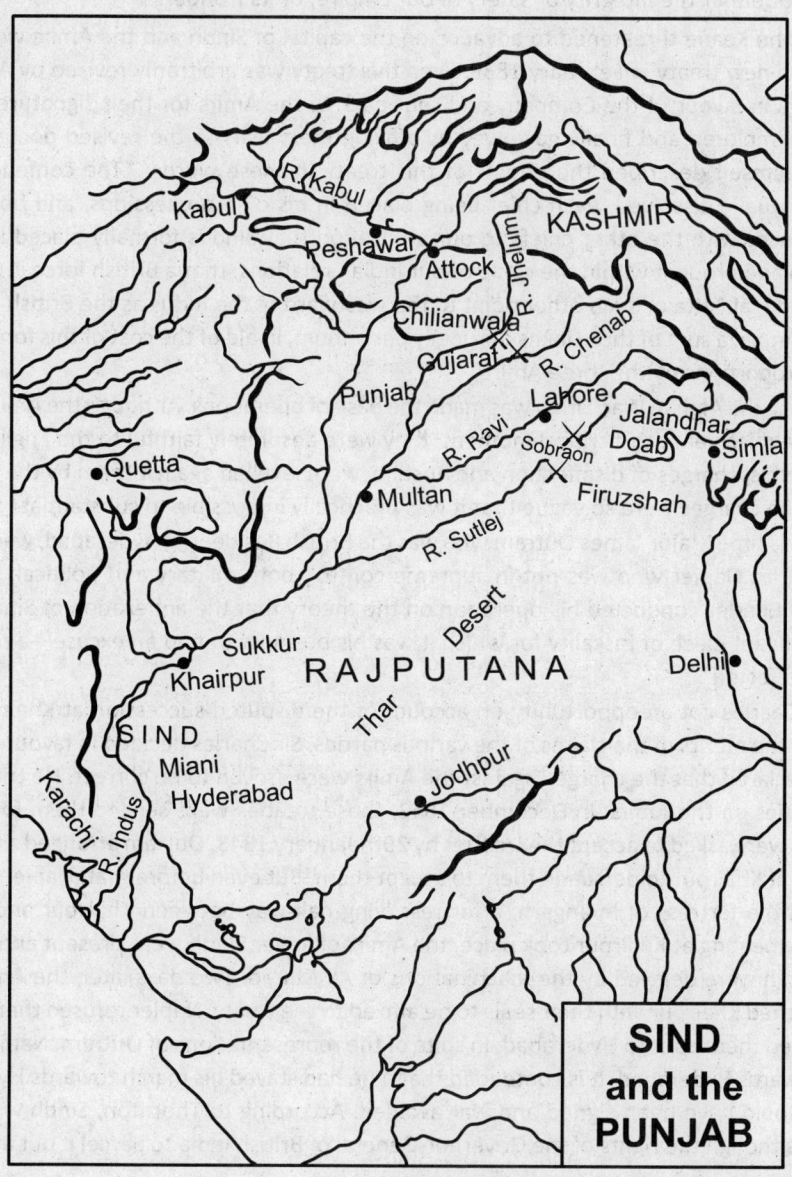

SIND and the PUNJAB

When the first Afghan War broke out and Maharaja Ranjit Singh refused to allow the British forces to pass through the Punjab Lord Auckland decided to send the British troops through Sindh. The British Government did not care at all for the treaty of 1832. As a matter of fact, the Amirs were merely informed that "while the present exigency lasts...the article of the treaty prohibiting the use of the Indus for the conveyance of military stores must necessarily be suspended". Not contented with this, a demand was made for a large sum of money in commutation of Shah Shuja's claim for tribute. The Amirs argued that they had ceased paying any tribute to Shah Shuja during his 30 years exile from Kabul. Shah Shuja himself had exempted them from all claims in 1833. At this the British Resident remarked thus: "How this is to be got over, I do not myself see". In spite of this difficulty, the money was exacted from them. They were also warned that "we have the ready power to crush and annihilate them, and we will not hesitate to call it into action, should it appear requisite however remotely for either the integrity or safety of our Empire, or its frontiers".

Sir John Keane threatened to advance on the capital of Sindh and the Amirs were forced to enter into a new treaty in February 1839. Even this treaty was arbitrarily revised by Auckland and his advisers in favour of the Company and sent back to the Amirs for their signatures. The latter "objected, implored and finally gave way by affixing their seals to the revised documents". Lord Auckland himself described the effects of this treaty in these words: "The confederacy of the Amirs is virtually dissolved, each chief being placed in his own possessions, and bound to refer his differences with the other chiefs to our arbitration that Sind is formally placed under British protection and brought within the circle of our Indian relations; that a British force is to be fixed in lower Scinde, at Tatta or such other point to the westward of the Indus as the British Government may determine, a sum of three lakhs of rupees per annum, in aid of the cost of this force being paid in equal proportions by the three Amirs".

During the Afghan War, Sindh was made the base of operations. Although the Amirs could have done some mischief at this critical moment, they were absolutely faithful to the English Company. In spite of this, charges of disaffection and hostility were levelled against them by the Government of India. The charges were so vague that it was practically impossible to substantiate them.

At this time Major James Outram who was the British Resident at Hyderabad, was superseded by Sir Charles Napier who was put in supreme control, both military and political. According to Innes, "Sir Charles conducted his operation on the theory that the annexation of Sind would be a very beneficent piece of rascality for which it was his business to find an excuse—a robbery to be plausibly effected".

Sir Charles got an opportunity on account of the disputed succession at Khairpur. Without going into the merits of the claims of the various parties, Sir Charles decided in favour of Ali Murad, He also declared that the charges against the Amirs were proved to be correct. He tried to impose fresh treaties on the Amirs. In December 1842, those treaties were sent to them for ratification. The Amirs were asked to accept the treaties by 20th January 1843. Outram arranged a meeting with the Amirs at Khairpur to persuade them to accept them. But even before that, Napier attacked and destroyed the fortress of Imangarh, a fortress lying half-way between Khairpur and Hyderabad. When the meeting at Khairpur took place, the Amirs of lower Sindh were present and the Amirs of Upper Sindh were delayed by the machinations of Ali Murad. Two days later, the Amirs of Upper Sindh reached Khairpur with their seals to be affixed to the treaty. Napier refused them permission and ordered them back to Hyderabad. In spite of the representations of Outram, Napier started his march towards Hyderabad. It is contended that if he had stayed his march towards Hyderabad, the treaties would have been signed and war avoided. According to Thornton, Sindh was treated by Napier "as though the rights of the Governor-General of British India to parcel it out at his pleasure were unquestioned and unquestionable and, moreover, as if it were desired to exercise this right in a manner as offensive as possible to those who were to suffer privation from the exercise".

It may be mentioned that by the new treaties required to be signed, the Amirs were to give important territories to the English Company in lieu of tribute. They were to provide fuel to the English steamers navigating the Indus. They were also to give up their right of coining money in favour of the British Government.

The acts of highhandedness on the part of Napier excited the war like Baluchis who attacked the residence of Outram on 15th February, 1843. Outram managed to escape to a steamer. Regular war started. The important battles were fought at Miani and Dabo in February and March respectively. On 27th March, 1843, Napier occupied Mirpur. Napier communicated his victory to Lord Ellenborough in the well-known phrase: *"Peccavi, I have Sindh".* Sindh was annexed in August 1843. The Annirs were exiled. Napier got £70,000 as his share of the prize money. Outram was given £3,000 but he distributed the same among charitable institutions. Outram wrote to Napier thus: "I am sick of policy; I will not say yours is the best, but it is undoubtedly the shortest—that of the sword. Oh! How I wish you had drawn it in a better cause".

The Sindh policy of Lord Ellenborough and Sir Charles Napier has been universally condemned. The Directors of the Company disapproved of it although they had no courage to restore the same to the Amirs. It cannot be denied that the Amirs had given absolutely no provocation to the English. They were absolutely loyal throughout. They did not merit the treatment which was actually meted out to them. According to Innes, '"If the Afghan episode is the most disastrous in our Indian annals, that of Sindh is morally even less excusable". Napier himself wrote thus in his diary, *"We have no right to seize Sind, yet we shall do so and a very advantageous, useful, humane piece of rascality it will be... .* My present position is not, however, to my liking, we had no right to come here and are tarred with the Afghan brush". On this, Dr. Marshman remarks thus: "The rascality is more apparent than the advantage except to the captors to whom it brought a real draught of prize money of which seven lakhs fell to the share of the General-in-Chief".

The conquest of Sindh was in every respect the aftermath of the Afghan disaster. According to Elphinstone, "Coming after Afghanistan, it put one in mind of a bully who had been kicked in the streets and went home to beat his wife in revenge, it was the tail of the Afghan storm".

According to Dodwell, "In this Ellenborough's policy has almost universally been condemned. The Directors of the Company made it a pretext for an embittered attack on a man who had offended them in other ways; and the Whigs naturally were glad to attack the man who had not hesitated to expose Auckland's misconduct. Napier's phrase, 'a good, honest, useful piece of rascality,' represents the common judgment. But the notion that the Amirs were attacked and their country annexed simply because they were weak is scarcely tenable. The main culpability lies with Auckland. Ellenborough's responsibility is limited to his treatment of the situation which he inherited. He found the rulers of this frontier state engaged in intrigues which were hostile though certainly not in themselves dangerous. He was clearly entitled to decide whether or not to exact the penalty. That was a question not of political morals but of political expediency. The size of the state, the immediate danger of its intrigues, are not relevant matters. Viewed broadly, the annexation of Sind seems comparable with the assumption of the Carnatic. In both cases advantage was taken of foolish and hostile conduct to secure a considerable political advantage. Ellenborough, like Wellesley, was more concerned to consolidate and strengthen the position of the East Indian Company than to make benevolent gestures in the idle hope that others would follow so futile an example". (*The Cambridge Shorter History of India,* pp. 520-21.)

According to Ramsay Muir, "Sindh is the only British acquisition in India of which it may fairly be said that it was not necessitated by circumstances and that it was, therefore, an act of aggression". According to P.E. Roberts, 'The conquest of Sindh followed in the wake of the first Afghan War and it was morally and politically its sequel".

War with Gwalior

Another event of the reign of Ellenborough was the war with Scindhia. In 1843, Jankaji Scindhia died without any issue. His widow, Tarabai, adopted a son and a regent was appointed with the permission of the Governor-General. The regent was dismissed and a kind of civil war started in the territory. There was the danger of the revolt of the army. The Governor-General demanded the reduction of the troops. Negotiations failed and hostilities started. The Scindhia army was defeated at Maharajpur and Paniar. A new treaty was made by which the army was cut down to 9,000 men. A British contingent of 10,000 was enlisted. The affairs of the minor rulers were placed under a Council of Regency which was to follow the advice of the Resident.

Recall of Ellenborough

The Court of Directors was not at all happy with the way in which things were being managed in India by Lord Ellenborough. They also highly disapproved of the insubordinate and hectoring tone in which they were addressed by their Governor-General. The Duke of Wellington warned the Governor-General of the gathering storm and blamed him for his long absence from the seat of Government. Ellenborough himself was conscious that recall was in the air. There was an exchange of unpleasant letters between the Governor-General and the Court of Directors in which the former declined to resign, and challenged the Directors to remove him. In June 1844, the Directors took him at his word and although he was supported by the Board of Control he was ordered by the unanimous vote of the Court of Directors to return. By identifying himself at every stage with the army and the military policy, Ellenborough had not merely alienated but exasperated the European Civil Service. Although he was much esteemed by the army whose side he had so openly taken, his departure was witnessed without regret.

According to Lord Curzon, "With better judgment and less vanity Ellenborough might have been a considerable ruler; for he had conspicuous talents, and I remember Mr. Gladstone telling me that he thought him the best Speaker of his day in the House of Lords. As it is, he was the shortest-lived and the least successful of all the Governors-General". Lord Macaulay observed thus in the House of Commons on 19th March, 1843, about Ellenborough: *"We have sometimes sent them, Governors whom they love, and sometimes Governors whom they feared, but they never before had a Governor at whom they laughed".*

LORD HARDINGE (1844-48)

Hardinge was a brave soldier and was well acquainted with the arts of war and peace. He was a hero of the Peninsular War and had participated in the battle of Waterloo. Before coming to India as Governor-General, he had remained in Parliament for 20 years and worked as Secretary of War.

The most important event of his reign was the first Sikh War. The war started in December, 1845. The important battles of the war were fought at Mudki, Firozshah, Aliwal and Subraon. The war was ended by Treaty of Lahore (1846). The English got the Doab and an indemnity of 2½ crores of rupees. The Sikh army was reduced to 22,000 infantry and 12,000 cavalry. Henry Lawrence was left as Resident.

Hardinge also carried out certain reforms. He issued an order that all appointments in public services were to be given to those persons who had received English education. Salt duty was reduced and many octroi duties were abolished. Free trade was encouraged. Expenditure on the military was reduced. The native states were asked to abolish *Sati* within their territories. He made arrangements for the preservation of ancient monuments in India. He suppressed the practice of human sacrifice prevalent among the Gonds in the hilly tracts of Orissa (now Odisha).

REVIEW QUESTIONS

1. What was the first work done by Lord Ellenborough? Discuss the another important events of the his Governor-Generalship.
2. Discuss the Sindh policy of Lord Ellenborough.
3. Describe the reforms of Lord Hardinge.
4. Lord Ellenborough was a man of vigour and decision. Review.
5. Write short notes on the following:
    (a) Annexation of Sindh
    (b) Recall of Ellenborough
    (c) Lord Hardinge

SUGGESTED READINGS

Colchester, Lord: *The History of the Indian Administration of Lord Ellenborough* (1874).
Lambrick, H.T.: *Sir Charles Napier and Sind* (1952).
Law, A.L.: *India under Ellenborough* (1926).
Napier, William: *The Conquest of Sindh* (1845).
Outram, Sir J.: *Conquest of Sind* (1846).
Young, Keith: *Sinde in the Forties*.

12 Maharaja Ranjit Singh and His Successors

LEARNING OBJECTIVES

- Analyse the causes of the rise of Maharaja Ranjit Singh
- Bring out the relations between the English and Maharaja Ranjit Singh
- Discuss the administrative system of Ranjit Singh and assess his personality
- Know about the history of Ranjit Singh's successors

RISE OF RANJIT SINGH

The Sikhs who were originally a religious sect were hammered into a military power by their conflict with the Afghans. When Ahmed Shah Abdali withdrew in 1767, they occupied the country between the Jamuna and Rawalpindi. It is true that for some time that progress was checked by the Marathas, but when the Maratha power was broken by Lord Lake in 1803, the Sikhs began to entertain new hopes of progress and growth in the future.

Ranjit Singh was born in 1780. At the age of 19, he helped Zaman Shah, the Afghan ruler of Kabul, in invading the Punjab. Out of gratitude, Zaman Shah appointed Ranjit Singh the Governor of Lahore in 1799. He was also given the title of Raja. In 1802, he made himself master of Amritsar. By and by, he brought under his control the Sikh Misls or fraternities west of Sutlej.

Ranjit Singh was encouraged by the policy of non-intervention followed by Sir George Barlow (1805-7). He intended to extend his authority over the territory known as the Cis-Sutlej states. These Sikh states were formerly under Scindhia, but when the latter was turned out from Hindustan, they informally came under British protection. In 1806, some Sikhs chiefs of these states quarrelled among themselves and asked for the intervention of Maharaja Ranjit Singh. The latter accepted the invitation, crossed the Sutlej and occupied Ludhiana. When this happened, the Sikh chiefs were alarmed and they appealed to the British Government for protection. At that time, Lord Minto was the Governor-General and he was determined to keep the power of Maharaja Ranjit Singh to the line west of the Sutlej. The British Government declared that they would not allow Ranjit Singh to establish his control over the Cis-Sutlej states, and there was every possibility of war between the two powers. At this time, Ranjit Singh hesitated. Negotiations were started and Charles Metcalfe was sent for that purpose. After many delays, the Treaty of Amritsar was signed in 1809. This treaty fixed the river Sutlej as the boundary line between Maharaja Ranjit Singh's territory and that of the English Company. It established perpetual amity between the two powers.

If Maharaja Ranjit Singh could not extend his territory in the East, he tried to extend the same in the West. In 1810, he led an expedition against Multan which was ultimately annexed in 1818. He got Kangra from the Gurkhas and Attock from the Afghans in 1813. He took advantage of the lawlessness that prevailed in Afghanistan and became independent of that territory. In 1814, he gave shelter to Shah Shuja and relieved him of his Koh-i-Noor. In 1819, Ranjit Singh conquered Kashmir and in 1823 Peshawar passed into his hands. It was formally annexed in 1834. He had his designs on Sindh but could not achieve them on account of the British opposition. He died in 1839 at the age of 50.

ANGLO-SIKH RELATIONS (1809-39)

It seems desirable to discuss at length the relations between the English and Maharaja Ranjit Singh from the time of the signing of the Treaty of Amritsar to the death of the Lion of the Punjab. It has already been pointed out that one of the effects of the treaty of Amritsar was that the British Government was able to take the Cis-Sutlej states under its protection. Ranjit Singh's advance in the East was checked but he was given a *carte blanche* so far as the region to the west of the Sutlej was concerned. Metcalfe is said to have told Ranjit Singh that in 20 years he would reap the fruits of his alliance with the British. In 1827, the Maharaja told Wade that "His words have been verified".

Up to 1812, there were some doubts and suspicions. A small fort was raised at Phillaur near the British frontier and Muhkam Chand was put in charge of it. It served as a frontier outpost, a station of defence and a watchtower. Even deserters from the British army were received by Muhkam Chand. However, after some time, the relations between Ranjit Singh and the English Company began to improve and continued to be cordial up to 1823. During this period the English were busy with the Gurkhas and the Marathas and Ranjit Singh was busy in conquering Multan, Derajat, Kashmir, Peshawar and the hills and plains of the Punjab.

There was a change in the British attitude. That was due to the fact that Ranjit Singh came to be considered as a rival of the British in India and consequently an attempt was made to check and curb his power. There were certain disputes with regard to the indefinite Cis-Sutlej frontier. Out of the 47 territories claimed by Ranjit Singh, 12 were disputed. In 1827, the British Government decided most of these 12 cases practically in their own favour. The claim of Ranjit Singh to Ferozepur was disallowed although he claimed that the Sikhs of Ferozepur were among the oldest of his subjects. The reason for this given was by Murray in these words: "The capital Lahore is distant only 40 miles with a single river to cross, fordable for 6 months in the year. The post of Ferozepur from every point of view seems of the highest importance to the British Government whether as a check on the growing ambition of Lahore or as a post of consequence". Ferozepur was occupied by the British in 1835 and a military cantonment was made in 1838. There were protests against this but the British Government ignored them.

Between 1822 and 1828, British attitude was to watch very carefully the activities of Maharaja Ranjit Singh. According to Murray, "The British Government must not lose sight in a moment of repose and tranquility of one of the principal and original motives of the advance of our troops to the frontier".

In 1815, Pirthi Bilas, the Vakil of the Gurkhas, and Seo Dat Rai, a reliable person of the Raja of Bilaspur, approached Maharaja Ranjit Singh and requested him to help the Gurkhas in their war with the British, to speak to the bankers to lend them 5 lakhs of rupees and to help the Gurkhas to cross the Jamuna and the Ganges. The Maharaja expressed his inability to help the Gurkhas against the British although he was very unhappy when the Gurkhas were defeated. Likewise, he did not respond to the appeal of the ex-Peshwa Baji Rao in 1822. He also ignored the requests of the ex-king of Nagpur in 1820. He did not adopt any hostile attitude towards the English Company when it was busy in the Burmese War. In 1825-26, he did not go to the help of the people of Bharatpur. The ruler of Bharatpur offered ₹1 lakh for every day's march and ₹50,000 if he brought 20,000 troops to his assistance.

Between 1827—1831, there was an insurrection at Peshawar led by Syed Ahmed against Ranjit Singh. It is true that the British Government did not give any help to the Syed either directly or indirectly but undoubtedly it connived at the help given to the Syed by his own subjects.

In the case of Sindh, Ranjit Singh wanted to have Shikarpur which was regarded as the gate of Khorasan, and of great importance to the industry of Asia. It had a commercial connection with many remote marts. The possession of Shikarpur could give Ranjit Singh some control over Afghanistan and Baluchistan. More than half of the population of Shikarpur was that of the Sikhs and only about one-tenth of the people were Muslims. Before taking any action, Maharaja Ranjit Singh sounded the British Government. However, the latter was reticent. Although Pottinger was negotiating at that time a commercial treaty with the Amirs of Sindh, that fact was not mentioned to Ranjit Singh at the time of his meeting with William Bentinck at Rupar. Ranjit Singh did not oppose the British Government on the point of commercial treaty and also did not press his claims on Shikarpur.

In 1835, Ranjit Singh once again began to make preparations for the defence of Shikarpur and an attack on Sindh. In September 1836, the Maharaja held his Durbar and gave a Khilat to Nao Nihal Singh and directed him to proceed to Multan and from there to Mithankot. He was also to inform the rulers of Sindh that if they did not pay the tribute to the Maharaja, Shikarpur would be occupied. Hari Singh Nalwa was sent to join the prince. Diwan Sohan Mal, Governor of Multan, also advanced. War seemed to be imminent, but Ranjit Singh did not precipitate matters on account of the stiff attitude of the British Government. He was not prepared to give up his British alliance for the sake of Sindh.

Ranjit Singh and William Bentinck met at Rupar. So far as the British Government was concerned, its underlying motive for the interview was to give the world an impression that there was complete amity between Ranjit Singh and the British Government in India. Ranjit Singh also wanted to emphasize the fact that he was acknowledged as the head of the Khalsa by the British Government.

It is well known that when Burnes was sent to Kabul to negotiate a treaty with Dost Mohammad, the latter expressed his willingness to enter into an alliance on the condition that the British Government helped him to get Peshawar from Ranjit Singh. Burnes's view was that if the British Government asked Maharaja Ranjit Singh, the latter would be only too glad to give up Peshawar because that was not a profitable affair. In spite of this suggestion, Lord Auckland refused to ask Ranjit Singh to give Peshawar to Dost Mohammad. The result was that negotiations with Dost Mohammad fell through and Burnes had to come back empty-handed. Lord Auckland made it clear that he was not prepared to do anything which was likely to create any suspicion in the mind of Ranjit Singh.

In 1838, the Tripartite Treaty was signed between Maharaja Ranjit Singh, Shah Shuja and the English Company. Ranjit Singh at first showed hesitation to enter into this treaty. He was an unwilling partner because he felt that he was going to have in Kabul a dependent ally of the British in Shah Shuja but he also knew that he could not improve his position by remaining aloof. There was a meeting of Ranjit Singh and Auckland in November 1838 at Ferozepur and Ranjit Singh got an undertaking that the British troops would not pass through the Punjab. However, on account of the death of Ranjit Singh in 1839, and the disorder and confusion that prevailed in the Punjab, the British Government was able to take its troops and convoys through the Punjab during the First Afghan War. It is pointed-out that one of the objects of the Tripartite treaty was to check the power of Ranjit Singh in Sindh. One of the articles of the treaty provided that Shah Shuja was to give up his claims of supremacy and arrears of tribute over the Amirs of Sindh and matters were to be left to the mediation of the British Government. The British Government was preparing the way for the annexation of Sindh.

It is pointed out that in the last decade of his carrier, Ranjit Singh did not deal with the British Government in a firm manner. Probably that was due to the fact that he felt the English to-be too strong for him. He feared to expose his kingdom to the risk of war and consequently decided to follow a policy of surrender before the British Government.

According to Dr. Sinha, a political alliance means a rider and a horse. "In this Anglo-Sikh alliance, the British Government was the rider and Ranjit Singh was the horse. The English limited Ranjit's power on the East, on the South and would have limited him on the West if that were possible. Evidently, a collision between his military monarchy and British imperialism was imminent. Ranjit Singh, the Massinissa of British Indian history, hesitated and hesitated forgetting that in politics as in war, time is not on the side of the defensive. When the crash came after his death under far less able men, chaos and disorder had already supervened and whatever hope there had been when he was living, there was no more when he was dead. In his relations with the British Government, Ranjit Singh is seen at his worst. He never grandly dared. He was all hesitant and indecision".

CIVIL ADMINISTRATION OF RANJIT SINGH

According to Dr. G.L. Chopra, "The only administrative plan which could serve as a precedent for the organisation of civil departments was that of the Mughals".— (*The Punjab as a Sovereign State*). There was a close resemblance between the Mughal system of administration and that of Ranjit. Singh. In all essential matters there was no departure. The Maharaja did not avail himself of European intelligence and experience in civil administration as he did in the case of military organisation. A very limited number of Europeans were employed in civil capacity. In 1805, the Maharaja was advised by Holkar to organise a regular treasury, but he did not do so till 1808 on account of his military pre-occupation. In 1808, Diwan Bhawani Das was appointed Finance Minister and it is the Diwan who divided the financial transactions of the State among the following Daftars:

(i) **Daftar-i-Abwab-il-Mal.** This Department dealt with the accounts of the revenue receipts, and was subdivided into (a) Jama Kharch-i-Taaluqat, and (b) Jama Kharch-i-Sairat. The Taaluqat section comprised entries referring to the land revenue; while the Sairat included all other sources of income, the most important being Nazrana, Zabti, Abkari, Wajihati-i-Moqarai and Chaukiyat.

Nazrana was a tribute paid to the supreme ruler of the state on different occasions under various circumstances by his subjects, specially by prominent *vassals* and dignitaries. Sometimes, it was in the form of fixed annual charge from a subordinate chieftain. Sometimes it was the price paid to the conqueror for the retention of a piece of territory by a defeated prince. *Zabti* formed a source of considerable income to the Sikh ruler, who often punished his delinquent officials with fines or forfeitures of property or both. Besides, in several cases, he withdrew grants of land from the descendants of his deceased Sardars. They were sometimes retained by the state while sometimes they were regranted to others in lieu of cash payment.

Abkari included all charges made on the sale of opium, bhang, spirits and other drugs. The income derived from this source was comparatively insignificant.

Wajuhat-i-Moqarari included both the profits of justice and charges corresponding to the stamp duties of modern times. The receipts under this head were collected in different ways. First, certain charges were made for the redress of grievances by means of judicial decisions. Fines paid for criminal acts may be put under this head. Then there were proceeds from various charges levied on petitions addressed by the people either to the Sikh ruler or to one of his ministers.

Lastly, we may include the payments made for the affixation of the Royal seals on all kinds of private contracts.

Chaukiyat. There, was a very comprehensive scale of duties which were levied, under forty-eight different heads, and on most articles of daily consumption. No discrimination was made between articles of luxury, and those which formed the necessaries of life. Charges were generally made in cash. Griffin writes that the mode of collection was extremely vexatious, the country was covered with custom houses at which merchants were treated with insolence and oppression. An article paid duty on being taken into a town, a second time on being taken into a shop, and a third time on re-export.

Land Revenue System. In India, land revenue has been the mainstay of every government. In the beginning of Ranjit's career, the system known as Batai was re-introduced on the old Mughal plans to regulate apportionment of produce between the cultivator and the government. This system continued until 1823 and constituted the first period.

In the second period, which began in 1824 and extended over nearly a decade, the Batai system was replaced by a system of assessments known as Kankut. According to this, the share of the government was reckoned out of a standing crop, the value of which was estimated in terms of money. The portion for the state was now collected in cash. It was a distinct improvement on the old method, because it saved the officials from twofold responsibility, viz., guarding the grain from being stolen by the peasantry and carrying it to distant markets for sale. The adjustment of expenditure to income was made much easier and far more certain than before, owing to the ability of the government to estimate its share in money beforehand. Even the Kankut system was found partly ineffective because it enabled the government to estimate its income only just before the end of a harvest. Hence it was difficult to make a correct forecast in advance. After 1834, Ranjit Singh began to encourage the practice of farming out the revenues of large area of irrigable lands to the highest bidders for period varying from three to six years. By these contracts, the farmers were required to present detailed accounts of the extent of the cultivated area and the total amount of produce in their districts. This practice of leasing was developed by selling the farms of the village, as a whole, to the villagers themselves.

As a rule, the state demand may be said to have varied from two-fifths to one-third of the year's produce. This proportion prevailed in all districts which had been fully conquered and which were fairly cultivated.

On further investigations, we come to the conclusion that the share of the gross produce which belonged to the government was never rigidly fixed at one uniform rate. It varied from place to place, according to the productivity of the crops, the means of irrigation and other facilities of cultivation.

In addition to the regular share of the produce the state claimed a number of Abwabs (cesses). These were collected along with the land revenue, of which they formed a fixed proportion. The percentage, however, differed, the usual rate varying from 5 per cent to 15 per cent of revenue.

The revenue was collected twice a year, a month or so after the reaping of the two harvests called *Rabi* and *Kharif*. The chief officer incharge of the collection in a district was the Kardar (collector) and he was assisted by subordinate officials like Muqadams (foremen), Patwaris (revenue assessors) and Kanungos (hereditary registrars) The proceeds of revenue were kept in the district treasury under the control of the Kardar and were either transmitted to Lahore or disposed of according to the wishes of the ruler.

(ii) **Daftar-i-Abwab-il-Tahwil.** This was the second department and was concerned with the records of accounts of income and expenditure sent by officials. The cashiers were called Tahwildars. At first, this department dealt with accounts of a varied nature. But when separate offices of record, income and expenditure were set up, the work of this office became more limited.

(iii) **Daftar-i-Taujhihat.** This attended to the accounts of the royal household, such as the expenses of the Zanana, presents and Khilats, entertainments of guests, and Tosha-Khana.

(iv) **Daftar-i-Mawajib.** In this office were kept the accounts of pay and other emoluments in the various governmental services, such as the army, the civil staff, and the clerical establishment. This department was gradually divided into several branches to deal with the ever-increasing volume of work.

(v) **Daftar-i-Roznamcha-i-ikharjat.** This office was set up to register accounts of daily expenditure under various heads. Hence it dealt with various items from this standpoint.

These Daftars passed through several changes concerning details of organisation in subsequent years. Each of them was subdivided into branches to cope with the administrative developments.

TERRITORIAL DIVISIONS AND LOCAL ADMINISTRATION

The Punjab was divided into four Subas: Lahore, Multan, Kashmir and Peshawar.

Each Suba was divided into Parganas, each Pargana into Taluqas and every Taluqa was made of 50 to 100 Mauzas. This division followed largely the system of the Mughals. The administration of a Suba was entrusted to a Nazim (Governor) whose duties were analogous to those of the Lieutenant-Governor before the Reforms of 1919. He had under him number of Kardars. There was one Kardar for every Taluqa. The Kardars differed in position and importance according to the extent of territory under their charge. The Nazim occupied a higher position than that of an average Kardar, but his functions were largely of an appellate character and of a more general nature. The Kardar came into immediate contact with the people in their daily activities. He was a revenue collector, a treasurer and an accountant, a judge and a magistrate, an excise customs officer, and a general supervisor of the people on behalf of government.

Judicial Arrangements. There were no written laws in existence in days of Ranjit Singh. Judicial decisions were made in accordance with customary principles. The procedure was crude and simple and no distinction was made between civil and criminal cases. The settlement of disputes rested with the Panchayat. This was a body of five men who were the eiders of the village. The qualification for its membership was the possession of land and a certain amount of local influence and prestige. The Panchayat was more like an arbitration court. Hence its decisions were revised by the Kardars, whenever they were rejected by either party. In towns, justice was administered by the Kardars who also decided the more important cases within their Taluqas. In the cities, cases were decided by the Nazims or by more important Kardars and sometimes separate officials were appointed to devote themselves entirely to judicial work. They were known as Adaltis (justices). A distinct court was set up at the capital town known as Adalat-i-Ala (exalted). Its functions resembled those of a High Court of present day.

Civil cases were of a varied nature. First of all, there were cases of betrothals and matrimonial engagements, which were decided by the Panchayats. There were breaches of contracts, sales on credit and the like. In these decisions, great importance was attached to the sworn testimony of witnesses. In such matters, the government of Ranjit Singh levied fees on the successful party. Civil suits regarding landed property were decided on evidence obtained from records which were regularly kept in Qazikhanas.

As regards crimes, the infliction of capital punishment was reserved to the ruler himself. The punishment for murder or other physical injuries was meted out to the offenders more often in the form of fines than bodily chastisement. Mutilation was employed in exceptional circumstances. On the whole, it may be said that the rigour of punishment depended upon the nature of the crime, the personal disposition of the magistrate and likelihood of his action being reported to the ruler.

Though to all intents and purposes Ranjit's judicial system was crude and simple, yet in actual practice it suited to the social and political environments of the people of the Punjab. The abuse of authority on the part of local officials was limited by several considerations. *Firstly*, the term of office of Ranjit Singh's officials depended on good behaviour. The consciousness that their dignity, prestige and social status and even their private wealth and property depended solely on the favour of their master, acted as a restraining influence on their arbitrary actions. *Secondly*, the Maharaja's frequent and unexpected tours introduced a real risk of complaints of bribery and corruption reaching his ears. Another factor contributing to the same result was the practice of deputing special justices to tour in different districts for the purpose of hearing complaints and deciding cases of particular importance. The greatest merit of the system lay, however, in its simplicity and in the absence of those legal intricacies and technicalities which, if introduced among the Sikh peasantry, would have beset the path of justice with difficulties.

RANJIT SINGH'S GOVERNMENT

He established in the Punjab a pure and unmitigated despotism. He transformed the whole constitution of the Sikhs from an irregular commonwealth of a loose federal type into a military monarchy based on personal rule.

Under Ranjit Singh's personal despotism, the Punjab was governed in a manner which generally suited the existing state of society. Village life throughout was little interfered with. Its local affairs were mostly subject to the Panchayats. One great secret of the popularity of the Maharaja's rule was that it kept open to the humblest citizen the possibilities of acquiring position and wealth. Another great merit of Ranjit's authority was that he never based it upon his own inherent superiority, or any Divine Right Theory of Supremacy. He never arrogated to himself any high-sounding titles, or claimed supernatural powers. On the contrary, he always showed that his actions were directed to the glory of the Khalsa. Under Ranjit Singh, the Sikhs had achieved brilliant triumphs, city after city had acknowledged their authority, until a large kingdom had been created, whose military resources now commanded awe and arid reverence alike from the neighbouring States and distant rulers.

The despotism of Ranjit Singh may be described as benevolent. He was no alien ruler from the point of view of race and religion. Under his authority, the economic resources were wholly utilized in the kingdom. Through the blessing of his rule, the people of the Punjab evolved a degree of law and order, and entered upon a period of peace and prosperity which had not been enjoyed for several generations.

ARMY OF RANJIT SINGH

There has been considerable confusion among writers about the year in which Ranjit Singh first raised regular units. Most of them state that the idea originally struck the prince in 1809, while observing the discipline of Metcalfe's escort. In 1805, Holkar had entered the Punjab and in the course of conversation with Ranjit Singh, he urged upon him the desirability of organising the treasury, constructing defensive fortifications and disciplining forces. Ranjit Singh visited Lake's camp in disguise and observed the drill of the Company's troops. Yet the greater incentive to reforming activities came from the agreement with Metcalfe. This agreement created great anxiety in Ranjit Singh's mind as to the safety of his kingdom. Experience led him to decide that the maintenance of a strong standing army was indispensable for triumphs of diplomacy and war.

In the Khalsa Darbar, records of the army of Ranjit Singh were divided into two sections—the Fauj-i-Am or the regular army, and the Fauji-i-be-Qawaid or the irregular force.

Fauj-i-Am or Regular Army. The regular army may be sub-divided into three parts: (*a*) Infantry, (*b*) Cavalry, and (*c*) Artillery.

(a) **Infantry.** The creation of the *infantry* was a gradual process which began soon after 1805 and continued throughout Maharaja's reign. The Sikhs looked upon service with contempt and refused to join its ranks. But Ranjit Singh persisted in his efforts and ultimately succeeded in overcoming; their traditional prejudices. The result was visible in 1818, when the inhabitants of the Punjab, both Sikhs and others, began to dominate the service. In 1822, the Maharaja employed French officers in his service. Most of them had taken part in the Napoleonic campaigns, and were fully conversant with the latest methods of Western tactics and drill. Under the personal supervision of Ranjit Singh, they performed their duties energetically, and in a few years organised and trained an efficient force.

The early organisation of the infantry was simple. It consisted of a number of Paltans, to each of which two horse-guns were attached on an average, to form them into separate units. Each of these was put under a Commandant. This organisation was expanded later on as the strength of a battalion increased. Later, the Paltan or battalion became a part of a large organisation called a brigade. On an average, a brigade contained four battalions of infantry, a small varying strength of cavalry, and a battery of eight to ten horse-guns. A company of Beldars was generally attached to it.

At the time of Ranjit Singh's death, eight hundred formed the minimum strength of a battalion, which was divided into eight companies each of which in turn was composed of four sections. The average strength of a company was one hundred, while a section comprised roughly twenty-five men. As regards officers, the Commandant was assisted by an Adjutant and a Major. Each company was under a Subedar who was assisted by two Jamedars. Each section of a company was commanded by a Hawildar, who also had a Naik for his assistance. The officers of the battalions were sons or relatives of Sirdars, or members of the landed gentry. When the Sirdar had two or more sons the Maharaja usually took one while young, and trained him for service. The non-combatant establishment of each battalion included a Munshi, a Mutassaddi, and a Granthi, in addition to the manual workers, such as Khalasis, Saqqas, Gharyalis, Beldars, Jhanda Bardars, Mistris, Kannas, and Tahilyas.

The uniform of the infantry was scarlet. There were, however, different coloured facings to distinguish the regiments. The trousers were of the blue cotton cloth; and the turbans were of same colour. The belts were of black leather. The men were usually armed with sword, musket and bayonet.

Fauj-i-Khas or French Legion. This was the model brigade of the Sikh army. It was raised in 1822 by Generals Ventura and Allard. Its normal strength was four battalions of infantry, two regiments of cavalry, and one troop of artillery comprising twenty-four guns. Special efforts were made in its training, and in point of discipline and equipment, it grew to be the best organised section of regular army. The infantry section of the brigade consisted of the Khas battalion, a Gurkha battalion, and two more commanded by Deva Singh and Sham Sota. The cavalry portion comprised a Khas regiment, and a dragoon regiment. The artillery was known as the corps of General Ilahi Baksh.

As regards the officers of the Khas brigade, Dr. Murray says: "To each company in these battalions there is attached one Subedar, one Jamedar, four Hawildars, and four Naiks; and to each battalion one Commandant and one Adjutant."

"The Fauj-i-Khas had, as its emblems, the eagle and the tri-colour flag, with an inscription of the Martial Guru Govind Singh embroidered upon it. It used French words of command. Thus it has been often called the French Brigade or the French Legion."

Captain Wade saw parades of the infantry section of the Fauj-i-Khas in 1827, five years after it had been constituted, and described his impressions thus: "They were all dressed, armed, and equipped like the Raja's other regular battalions but in a neater and superior style. It was indeed impossible not to admire the high degree of perfection to which M. Ventura had brought his Legion".

(b) **Cavalry.** When Ranjit Singh began reforming his troops after 1805, his idea was to create a disciplined force of all the three branches. He accordingly attempted to introduce the European drill among irregular horsemen. The proud Ghorcharas regarded the new practices as the tricks of a dancing girl, and refused to abandon their old method of warfare. This led to the raising of new recruits, which, coupled with Ranjit's preoccupation in organising the foot service, hindered rapid progress. Until the arrival of Allard in 1822, there were only four trained regiments of cavalry in Sikh service. The total number of drilled horsemen was one thousand against ten thousand foot. After 1822, the progress was rapid in 1829, seven years after Allard's arrival, the strength of the regular horse increased more than four times.

A cavalry regiment was, at first, composed of men of different creeds like the Pathans, Rajputs, Dogras, and others. Its number varied from one hundred to more than five hundred men. Later on, this service became popular among the Sikhs themselves; and the number of regiments increased. Regiments of large numerical strength were divided into Risalas, the strength of which ranged from one hundred and fifty to two hundred. The officers in the cavalry were similar to those as in an infantry battalion; and similar was the arrangement of nom-combatants. The pay of the carvalry regiment was much higher than in the infantry.

The regular horsemen have been described as "mean-looking, ill-dressed an wretchedly mounted," and their horse trappings as "of the leather of worst quality". In the field, their conduct corresponded with their general appearance.

(c) **Artillery.** In the beginning two guns were usually attached to infantry battalion, there being no distinct detachment of artillery in existence. In 1810, however, a separate corps was raised and placed under an officer called Darogha-i-Topkhana. Two years later, this corps formed the principal unit of the artillery, and as such was called Topkhana-i-Khas. It was commanded by a Muslim officer, named Mian Ghuas Khan. The entire Topkhana was now divided into four sections, the first comprising Aspi guns, and the second Gavi guns. The third consisted of a separate horse battery; while the last comprised a number of guns which were distributed over various battalions of infantry. The Ghubaras and Zambyraks were organised into Deras called Dera-i-Zamburkhana. In 1814 a fresh battery was raised, but the separate battery of the earlier period was signed to the regular army. As a result of the reforming efforts of both these officers, General Court and Colonel Gardner, the entire Tophkhana was reorganised. It was divided into three sections, (i) Topkhana-i-Jinsi, (ii) Topkhana-i-Aspi, (iii) Zamburkhanas. The mixed batteries of the first were composed of Aspi guns, and Gavi guns and howitzers. The Top-khana-i-Khas was amalgamated with other batteries to form one of the three principal sections of the regular army. In 1835 when the army was organised into brigades, the artillery branch underwent further modifications.

There was a close resemblance between the internal organisation of a battery and a battalion of infantry, the average strength of a ten-gun battery being two hundred and fifty men, including non-combatants. Each battery was sub-divided into sections, every section comprising two guns and eight to ten gunners. The ten-gun battery was officered by a Commandant, assisted by an Adjutant and a Major; while each section was under a Jamedar, with a Hawildar and a Naik to assist him.

The training and organisation of the artillery on European lines was accomplished in less than a decade. General Court, to whom this task, was chiefly assigned, joined the Sikhs in 1827, and within a few years, he "raised the corps to a high pitch of efficiency.

Fauj-i-be-Qawaid or the Irregular Army. It was composed chiefly of horsemen. These were divided, into two sections—Ghorchara Khas and Misaldar. The former was a single organisation, and was recruited amongst the yeomen or landed gentry. Many members were relatives of the dignitaries of the court. They supplied their own equipment, and regularly paid at first in Jagirs but later on in cash. The Misaldars comprised all the petty chiefs who, having been recently dispossessed of their territories by Ranjit Singh, had consented to serve under him at the head of their respective bands of horsemen. The latter thus represented all classes of society, and were regarded as inferior in social status to the Khas troops. This difference was visible in their horses and equipment. The Misaldars grew in numbers, and at the end of the reign, formed by far the greater proportion of the irregular cavalry. For administrative purposes, the Ghorcharas were divided into several Deras, each Dera comprising several minor groups of horsemen, which were called Misls. The men in a Misl belonged to a single clan. Their leader was usually the descendant of one under whom they had originally joined Ranjit Singh's Army. These Misls were of varying strength, ranging from twenty-five to seventy-five men. In 1822, the Deras were grouped into bigger divisions, each of which was put in charge of a high dignitary of State. In these appointments, care was taken to keep these clans intact. Lord Auckland saw the Ghorcharas during his visit to the Punjab in 1838 and considered them to be "the most picturesque troops in the world".

Recruitment and Pay. Enlistment in the army was voluntary and recruits could always be found in abundance. This was due to several causes. In the *first* place, many of the tribes inhabiting the Punjab possessed martial traditions of a higher order. *Secondly,* a considerable social prestige was attached to the profession of arms. *Thirdly,* Ranjit Singh's personal attitude to the fighting forces secured an abundant supply of men who sought military careers.

In the days of the Misls, the troops were paid either out of the plunder or by grant of land, usually liable to the payment of revenue. The latter system continued under Ranjit Singh. It was, however, found unsuitable for the needs of a standing army. Hence the system of cash payments in the form of monthly salaries was introduced.

Though the salaries were fixed at a monthly rate, in practice they were never paid at regular intervals. The army remained in arrears on an average from four to six months, and payments were made three or four times a year. This was partly due to the inefficiency of the pay department, but to a greater extent to the deliberate policy on the part of the Sikh ruler, who thereby checked the insubordination and desertion of his men. For purposes of distribution of pay, the army was divided into three branches—Fauj-i-Sowari, Fauj-i-Am, and Fauj-i-Filajat. The irregulars were paid at first by the commanding officer of each unit, and after wards by a Dewan attached to each division. The regulars were always paid through a Bakshi. Payments to the third branch were made through Thanedars. The paymasters of all three branches submitted an estimate based on the approximate strength of the units under their sway, to the central treasury at the capital.

The pay in the regular army of the cavalry was higher than the infantry; but the artillery and the infantry were paid much the same. The emoluments of the Ghorcharas were still better than those of the regular horsemen. Instead of a regular system of pensions for long service, occasional jagirs and donations of money were bestowed, but no systematic provision was made for the widows or children of those who lost their lives in the field.

PERSONALITY OF RANJIT SINGH

Ranjit Singh is known as the Lion of the Punjab. He was so popular with his subjects that Sir Repel Griffin, who wrote fifty years after the death of the Maharaja, was constrained to remark thus: "Although half a century has passed since his death, his name is still a household word in the province; his portrait is still preserved in castle and cottage. It is a favourite subject with the ivory painters of Amritsar and Delhi".

As regards the physical features of the Maharaja, he was not handsome at all. According to Baron Hugel, "I must call him (Maharaja Ranjit Singh) the most ugly and unexpressing man I saw throughout the Punjab. His left eye which is quite closed disfigures him less than the other, which is always rolling about wide open and is much distorted by disease. The scars of the small-pox on his face do not run into one another but form so many dark pits in his grayish brown skin; his short straight nose is swollen at the tip; the skinny lips are stretched tight over his teeth which are still good.... He has a thick muscular neck, thin arms and legs, the left foot and left arm drooping, and small well-formed hands".

According to Griffin, the Maharaja was "the beau ideal of a soldier—strong, spare, active, courageous and enduring". He was excellent as a horseman and a swordsman. He had great capacity for work and he worked from early morning till late in the evening. With his indefatigable capacity for work, he could give suggestions and guidance on very minute points. He had a wonderful memory. According to Jacquemont, "He knew the name, position and history of from ten to twelve thousand villages in his kingdom". He was so inquisitive that he put hundreds of questions to those who came to see him. According to Sinha, "His conversation was a nightmare even to a man of the intellectual capacity of Jacquemont". The topics he discussed ranged "from war to wine, and from learning to hunting with breathless rapidity". He was a great patron of learning. He gave rent free lands to the Pathshalas and Madrasas. He also gave them monthly grants. He patronised scholars like Munshi Sohan Lal, Mian Shah Muhammad, Diwan Amar Nath and Ganesh Dass. Munshi Sohan Lal wrote his famous book known as Umdat-ut-Tawarikh in Persian. Amar Nath was the author of Zafar Nama. Ganesh Dass wrote Fateh Nama Guru Khalsa Ji Ka.

The Maharaja followed a policy of religious toleration. In spite of his love for his own religion, he treated the other religions generously. This is evident from the fact that he employed the Faquir Brothers, the Dogra Rajas, and Brahmin Khushal Singh and Tej Singh. According to Griffin, "The tolerance of the Maharaja was due rather to indifference and selfishness than to any enlightened sentiment," but whatever the origin, his liberalism had an excellent effect on his administration.

The Maharaja was a great statesman. He cleverly came to the conclusion that it was practically impossible to make any headway against the Englishmen, It was with this conviction that he entered into a treaty of Amritsar with the English in 1809. Not only that, he hesitated throughout his long reign from fighting with the English. He tried to get as much as he could from the British Government but did not strain the relations to the breaking point.

Critics point out to some of his faults. He loved opium, wine and dancing girls. He had his weakness for Moran and Gul Begum. He was greedy and unscrupulous. This is clear from the way he got the Kohinoor from Shah Shuja.

In spite of his shortcomings, he was a great man in many ways. He was a born ruler of men. In the words of Griffin, "Men obeyed him by instinct and because they had no power to disobey. The control which he exercised, even in the closing years of his life over the whole Sikh people, nobles and priests, was the measure of his greatness". Again, "He was great because he possessed in an extraordinary degree the qualities without which the highest success cannot be attained; and the absence of the commonplace virtues which belong to the average citizen, neither diminished nor affected in any way the distinction of his character".

Estimate of Ranjit Singh. Ranjit Singh was a great warrior and statesman. The establishment of authority all over the Punjab, Kashmir and Peshawar is a proof positive of the qualities of head and heart possessed by Ranjit Singh. His genius helped him to create a centralised State. Although he was supreme, he styled himself as the first servant of the Khalsa. He always used the word Sarkar or Khalsaji instead of Maharaja. He collected together generals and administrators and with their help was able to make the Punjab a powerful State. His employment of the Muslims and Europeans shows that he had no religious bias in him. Although he was absolutely illiterate, he possessed a lot of commonsense. He was the master of details and no wonder he was able to set up a strong State in the Punjab.

According to Cunningham, "Ranjit Singh found the Punjab a waning confederation, a prey to the factions of its chiefs, pressed by the Afghans and the Marathas, and ready to submit to English supremacy. He consolidated the numerous petty States into a kingdom, he wrested from Kabul the fairest of its provinces, and he gave the potent English no cause for interference. He found the military array of his country a mass of horsemen, brave indeed but ignorant of war as an art, and he left it mustering fifty thousand disciplined soldiers, fifty thousand well-armed yeomanry and militia, and more than three hundred pieces of cannon for the fiel. His rule was founded on the feelings of a people, but it involved the joint action of the necessary principles of military order and territorial extension and when a limit had been set to Sikh dominion, and his own commanding genius was no more the vital spirit of his race began to consume itself in domestic contention". (*History of the Sikhs,* p. 200).

Ranjit Singh's Responsibility for Ultimate Decline of Sikh Power. According to Dr. G.L. Chopra, "Ranjit Singh has been held responsible for the ultimate decline of his kingdom. It is generally said that he committed the grave blunder of allowing the acquisition of vast territorial power and influence by the Dogra chiefs. This view, on the whole, has a substantial element of truth. Nevertheless, it must not be supposed that the Maharaja was blind to the dangers of his policy. We have already seen how he whittled down the possession of his Sirdars, even to the point of incurring blame for ingratitude to his servants. In the consistent pursuit of such a policy, however, the Maharaja felt a characteristic difficulty of destroying vested interests, which he himself had once created. It is, indeed, very difficult if not almost impossible, for a despot, much of whose power depends on the maintenance of a semi-feudal nobility, to curtail the size of their holdings. Thus, Ranjit failed to follow consistently the policy of reducing the people of the Punjab to a more or less uniform political level; the most glaring example of such a failure was the grant of an extensive and contiguous territory to a single Dogra family".

Dr. Chopra also points out that the despotic and personal character of Maharaja's rule was also responsible for the ultimate decline of the Sikh power. To quote him, "That he was a 'State in person' is more particularly true of him than of several other despots known to history. Hence his death was certain to bring a rapid paralysis of the central authority in the kingdom. His court also, as has already been discussed in the previous chapter, was composed of diverse elements and conflicting interests; and the harmonious cooperation of its members was only possible under his own unifying authority. His ministers were mostly favourites and adventurers, who had never been allowed to exercise much personal initiative, and were always taught to reflect in their actions the sole will of their monarch. Consequently, when that monarch died their efforts were directed to individual gain and advantage rather than to collective benefit while the absence of any competent successor revealed the inherent weakness of all States based on personal absolutism".

After pointing out the above two factors, Dr. Chopra refers to the threat from the side of the English East India Company and says that the annexation of the Punjab was inevitable as the Company was determined to annex the whole of India. Dr. Chopra says that "such subtle and fundamental causes were working against the independence of the Punjab, as the ruler of Sikhs could not possibly provide against even if he had displayed a better political genius".

The Punjab Politics from 1839 to 1845. After the death of Maharaja Ranjit Singh in 1839, the whole of the superstructure raised by him fell to pieces. The army became all powerful. It made and unmade kings. Confusion and disorder reigned everywhere. The hostility between the Dogras and the Sindhianwalas added to the confusion. For six long years, there was absolutely no law and order in the country.

Maharaja Ranjit Singh was succeeded by his eldest son known as Kharak Singh. Dhian Singh became his Wazir. He was opposed by Sher Singh, another son of Ranjit Singh, and Nao Nihal Singh, his own son. Chet Singh, a favourite of Kharak Singh, was murdered. Kharak Singh died in November 1840. His son Nao Nihal Singh also was killed by a fall of a gateway in the Lahore fort. There arose some difficulty with regard to the succession to the throne and ultimately it was decided that Mai Chand Kaur should become the regent for the expected son of Nao Nihal Singh. Dhian Singh was to act as Wazir and Sher Singh was to work as Viceroy. Sher Singh did not approve of the new arrangement and consequently usurped power in January 1841 and proclaimed himself as Maharaja. It was during the reign of Sher Singh that English troops and convoys were allowed to pass through the Punjab on their way to Kabul to participate in the First Afghan War. In June 1842, Chand Kaur was murdered. In September 1843, Sher Singh was murdered. Then came the turn of Dhian Singh who was disposed of similarly. Dhian Singh's son, Hira Singh, made up his mind to have revenge for the death of his father. He put Dalip Singh, a minor, on the throne and himself became the Wazir. Rani Jindan, mother of Dalip Singh, became regent. Hira Singh was assisted in his work by one Pandit Jalla. Throughout this period, it was suspected, that the English had their hand in the anarchy prevailing in the Punjab. In December, 1844, Hira Singh was murdered. After this, power fell into the hands of Jawahar Singh and Lal Singh, the brother and paramour of Rani Jindan. In September, 1845, Jawahar Singh was shot dead and Lal Singh became the Wazir. On 11th December 1845, the Sikh army crossed the Sutlej and on 13th December, the war was declared by the British.

FIRST SIKH WAR (1845-46)

The most important cause of First Sikh War was the problem of the Khalsa army which was facing Lal Singh and Rani Jindan. The army had become independent of the civil authority and for six long years had acted as kingmakers. This very army was responsible for the conquest of the whole of the Punjab in the time of Ranjit Singh; but after his death there was absolutely no one to control it. It is rightly said that fire is a good servant but a bad master. Likewise, when the Khalsa army could not be controlled by anybody, it began to kill all those who came in its way. The French Generals like Ventura were turned out and the country was helpless before the tyranny of the army. Various sections managed to win it over by means of presents and gifts, but there could be no stability under such circumstances.

The main problem facing the Punjab was how to deal with the Khalsa army. No wonder, both Rani Jindan and Lal Singh felt that the only way to deal with the Khalsa army was to make it fight against the British. If it was successful, it would have the whole of India to conquer and thereby it would be kept busy. If it was defeated by the English, its number and strength would be reduced. It was with that idea that the Sikh army was ordered to cross the Sutlej.

An effort was made to convince the Khalsa army that the English were bent upon invading the Punjab. It was pointed out to them that after the annexation of Sindh, the turn of the Punjab was sure to come. The English were massing their troops on the Sutlej. The military post of Ludhiana had more than 35,000 troops. A similar number of British troops was stationed at Ferozepur. Likewise, a large number of troops were concentrated at Ambala. All this military activity alarmed the Khalsa army. It came to believe that the only motive of the English was to attack the Punjab. The English had built a brigade of boats for crossing the Sutlej. They had also increased their troops in Sindh. The Sikh leaders were also aware of the scheme of men like Burnes, Macnaughten and Napier for the dismemberment of the Punjab.

The British collected pontoons near Ferozepore for a bridge of boats for the convenience of the British army to march into the Sikh territory. They established a ground supply depot at Basian near Rajkot. This was an unmistakable sign of the readiness of the British to undertake the threatened operations against the Sikhs at an early date. Broadfoot, the British envoy at Ludhiana, was a man of boundless ambition. Presuming that the Sikhs were not likely to give any cause for offence, he tried to provoke them and with that object in view, he treated the Cis-Sutlej territories of the Punjab as if those were under British jurisdiction. That was a clear violation of the Treaty of Amritsar. He adopted an arrogant and overbearing attitude towards the officials of the Lahore Durbar. At one time, Lal Singh, a Judge in the service of the Lahore Durbar, who was crossing the Sutlej on official duty, was made under duress to recross the river and his party was even fired at. The insulting and provocative behaviour of the British annoyed the Lahore Durbar.

Raja Suchet Singh, the youngest brother of Dhian Singh and Gulab Singh, had secretly deposited at Ferozepore a large quantity of coins and bullions worth about 15 lakhs of rupees. After his death, the Lahore Durbar claimed the treasure. Legally and morally, the treasure belonged to the Lahore Durbar, but the British Government refused to hand over the treasure to the Lahore Durbar.

A village named Moron in the Nabha territory had been given by Raja Jaswant Singh of Nabha to Maharaja Ranjit Singh in 1819. The latter gave the same to Sardar Dhanna Singh. In 1843, Jaswant Singh's son Raja Devinder Singh, became displeased with S. Dhanna Singh and resumed the gift. The soldiers of Joginder Singh even plundered the property of Dhanna Singh that was absolutely illegal and high-handed. The gift had been made to Ranjit Singh and not to Dhanna Singh and therefore the Raja of Nabha had no right to resume it. The British Government justified the action of the ruler of Nabha in spite of the protests of Lahore Durbar. There was a certain island in the river Sutlej near Ferozepore. That belonged to the Lahore Durbar but the same was occupied by the British.

The British Government carried on propaganda against the Lahore Durbar. They sent spies and agents provocateurs to the Punjab. British officials and the press started intensive propaganda in order to prepare the people of India and England for a war between the British Government and the Lahore Durbar and to cover their war-like preparations. A speech of Sir Charles Napier was published in the Delhi Gazette wherein he openly and threateningly stated that the British were going to declare war against the Sikhs.

Under the circumstances, the war was inevitable and it actually broke out in December, 1844. According to the British, the immediate cause of the war was the crossing of the river Sutlej by the Sikh army on December 11, 1845. However, considering the fact that the British army had already left Ambala for the Sutlej on December 6, 1845, it cannot be denied that the British wanted only an excuse to start the war. It is also to be remembered that when Lord Hardinge declared war against the Lahore Durbar on December 13, 1845, the Lahore army was still encamped on its own territory.

The most important battles of the First Sikh War were those of Mudki, Ferozshah, Aliwal and Sabraon. The Sikhs were defeated in the battle of Mudki. That was partly due to the treachery on the part of Lal Singh who left his followers just at the time when victory was in sight. The Sikhs also committed the folly of not destroying 7,000 British troops under Sir John Little who were absolutely at their mercy.

The battle of Ferozshah was fought on 21st December, 1845. The Sikhs put up a very stiff resistance and the position of the English was really critical. Sir Hugh Gough wrote that "during that night of horrors, we were in a critical and perilous state". This time the treachery of Teja Singh helped the British. He ran away from the battlefield leaving the Sikh armies without a commander.

For more than a month, there was practically no fighting. That was partly due to the fact that the Khalsa army was without a leader and the British were so much stunned that they did not know what to do. The Sikhs found a leader in Ranjhor Singh and he defeated Sir Henry Smith at Buddiwal on 21st January 1846. Ranjhor Singh not only gave up the pursuit of the enemy but also left Buddiwal and the same was reoccupied by Sir Henry Smith. The Sikhs were defeated in the battle of Aliwal and Ranjhor Singh ran away.

At this time, Gulab Singh managed to become supreme at Lahore and he started negotiations with the British Government with a view to achieving his own selfish ends. It was settled between the parties that the Sikh army should be attacked by the English and when beaten it was to be openly disbanded by its own Government. The passage of the Sutlej was not to be opposed and the road to the capital was to be kept open to the victors. For all this service to the British Government, Gulab Singh was to receive Kashmir. It was under these circumstances that the battle of Sabraon was fought. Lal Singh also had sent a plan of the Sikh position at Sabraon to the English three days before the battle. It was in this atmosphere of treachery and shameful treason that the Sikh soldiers fought against the British. Soon after the first attack, Teja Singh ran away and "either accidentally or by design sank a boat in the middle of the bridge of communication". The Sikhs were without a leader and no wonder, were defeated. The battle of Sabraon has been called the bloodiest battle of the war. The whole of the river Sutlej at that place ran red on account of the blood of the Sikh soldiers. After Sabraon, British armies marched on to Lahore and occupied the same on 20th February, 1846. The *Treaty of Lahore* was signed in March 1846.

Lord Hardinge decided not to annex the Punjab and four reasons have been put forward for the same. It was thought that the existence of a Hindu State between Afghanistan and British India would be advantageous to the Company. Another reason was that the annexation of the Punjab would not be profitable on account of the large amount of money that would be required to be spent on the newly acquired province. Another reason given is that Lord Hardinge doubted the strength of the English to occupy the whole country. Still another reason that is put forward is that the English did not annex the Punjab out of their respect for the memory of Ranjit Singh who was their faithful ally for many decades.

The rival claims of Lal Singh and Gulab Singh who had helped the English in winning the First Sikh War, gave some headache to Lord Hardinge. Both of them wanted to be supreme at Lahore.,

Ultimately, a way was found to reward both of them. Lal Singh was to be recognised as the Chief Minister of Maharaja Dalip Singh and Gulab Singh got the State of Jammu and Kashmir on the payment of a sum of one million sterling. The amount was reduced by one-fourth by the British Government.

TREATY OF LAHORE (1846)

By the Treaty of Lahore the British got the Cis-Sutlej States, the Jullundur Doab Hazara. The Sikhs were to pay an indemnity of $1\frac{1}{2}$ crores of rupees. They were able to pay only half a crore out of their treasury and for the balance of it the State of Jammu and Kashmir was sold to Gulab Singh. The Sikh army was reduced to 25 battalions of infantry and 12,000 cavalry. The Sikhs were deprived of all those guns which were used by them against the English. The Sikh Government agreed not to employ British subjects or subjects of any European State without the concurrence of the British Government. Passage was to be allowed to the British troops through the Punjab. Maharaja Dalip Singh was recognised the ruler of the Punjab. A British force was to be stationed at Lahore and was to be withdrawn only by the end of the year. Henry Lawrence was appointed the British Resident at Lahore.

After the Treaty of Lahore, things did not work smoothly in the Punjab. Lal Singh and other Sikh leaders were opposed to the handing over of Jammu and Kashmir to Gulab Singh and their territory was given to them only after the intervention of the British troops. Rani Jindan and Lal Singh were accused of creating the trouble. An enquiry was made into their conduct and they were found guilty. Lal Singh was sent to Banaras.

In December 1846, another treaty known as the *Treaty of Bhairowal* was made by the British Government with the Lahore Durbar. By this treaty, Council of Regency consisting of 8 pro-British Sikh chiefs was appointed and the council was to act under the advice and guidance of the British Resident. A British force was to be maintained at Lahore and the Sikhs were to pay ₹22 lakhs every year. This arrangement was to continue up to 1854 when Maharaja Dalip Singh was expected to become major. By this treaty, the Sikhs became virtually the masters of the Punjab.

In 1847 and 1848, many reforms were carried out in the Punjab which were against the interests of the Sikh nobility. This added to their discontent. The disbanded soldiers were naturally discontented because they had lost their salaries and other allowances. The Sikhs bitterly resented their defeat particularly because those were due to treachery on the part of their leaders. They also resented the activities of the British agents who were carrying on negotiations with the tribesmen on the frontier. They did not approve of the concessions given to the Muslims in the matter of Azan or call for prayer and cow slaughter. Rani Jindan was bitter at the loss of her power and was determined to have her revenge. She was accused of conspiracy and sent away to Chunar. Her deportation was resented by the Sikhs.

SECOND SIKH WAR (1848-49)

There is no doubt that discontentment prevailing in the Punjab would have resulted in a war sooner or later, but the revolt of Mul Raj, Governor of Multan, precipitated matters. He was the Governor of Multan since 1844. Previous to that, his father Sawan Mal was the Governor of Multan. Mul Raj was asked by the Lahore Durbar to pay the succession duty of one crore of rupees. He expressed his inability and was asked to pay ₹18 lakhs. On account of the intervention of the First Sikh War, Mul Raj was able to postpone the payment, but demand was renewed after the war. The sum now demanded was ₹19 lakhs. As the payment was not made by him, he was ordered to pay ₹20 lakhs and give up one-third of his territory. His annual tribute of ₹12 lakhs was increased to ₹18 lakhs. The Lahore Durbar also tried to interfere in the internal affairs of Multan. Mul Raj expressed his desire to resign provided the whole matter was kept a secret and no charges were brought against him and he was asked to render one year's accounts. The British Resident refused to accept these terms and ordered him to resign unconditionally and render accounts for 10 years. The demand for 10 years' accounts was simply stupid as he had not been the Governor of Multan for more than 4 years. The British Resident sent Anderson and Agnew with Sardar Khan Singh to take over the administration. Mul Raj handed over the Multan fort to them on 19th April 1848. The people of Multan got infuriated at the sight of Englishmen. There was a revolt on 20th April and the two British officers were murdered.

The British Government could have taken action at once but they waited for months and during that interval rebellion spread all over the Punjab. Sir Hugh Gough, the Commander-in-Chief, was of the opinion that the heat of the Punjab at the time was not favourable to large scale operations. It was decided to have a winter "hunt" after the rains.

On 10th October, 1848, Lord Dalhousie declared thus: *"Unwarranted be precedents, uninfluenced by example, the Sikh nation has called for war, and on my word, sirs, they shall have it with a vengeance"*. On 16th November, Gough crossed the river Ravi and on 22nd November was fought the battle of Ramnagar. In December 1848, the siege of Multan was started, and it surrendered in January 1849. On 13th January 1849, was fought the *battle of Chillianwala*. It was a drawn battle. In February 1849 was fought the *battle of Gujarat* which has been called the "battle of guns". The Sikhs were defeated and the war ended on 13th March 1849. On 29th March 1849, the Punjab was annexed. Maharaja Dalip Singh was deposed and given a pension. Lord Dalhousie rejected the suggestion of administering the Punjab with Dalip Singh on the throne. According to him, "By maintaining the pageant of a throne we should leave just enough sovereignty to keep alive among the Sikhs the memory of their nationality and serve as constant nucleus for intrigue". Again, "When I am forcibly convinced that the sovereignty of our State requires us to enforce subjection of the Sikh people, I cannot abandon that necessary measure merely because the effectual subjection of the nation involves in itself the deposition of their prince... . While deeply sensible of the responsibility I have assumed, I have an undoubting conviction of the expediency of the justice and of the necessity of my act. What I have done, I have done with a clear conscience, in the honest belief that it was imperatively demanded of my duty to the State".

ANNEXATION OF THE PUNJAB

The annexation of the Punjab by Lord Dalhousie has been condemned by many writers. According to Trotter, the policy of Dalhousie was "unprincipled and unjustifiable". When Diwan Mul Raj and Chattar Singh revolted, it was the duty of the British Government to suppress them. Dalhousie had no business to wait for months to allow the other Sikh elements to revolt. It was a dirty plan "deliberately adopted by the Resident and the Governor-General, contrary to the advice of the Council of Regency".

According to Bell, the annexation of the Punjab was "a violent breach of trust". Dalhousie "violated treaties, abused a sacred trust, threw away the grandest opportunity ever offered to the British Government of planting solid and vital reform up to the northern limits of India; and by an acquisition as unjust as it was imprudent, weakened our frontier, scattered our military strength and entailed a heavy financial burden upon the Empire. That, I believe, will be the verdict of posterity and history upon the transactions which have just passed under our review".

It is pointed out that after the Treaty of Bhairowal of December 1846, the British Government had become responsible for the administration of the Punjab during the minority of Maharaja Dalip Singh who was a ward of the British Government. It was the duty of the Governor-General and the British Resident at Lahore, Sir Frederick Currie, to crush the revolts of Diwan Mul Raj, Chattar Singh and Sher Singh. They had no business to delay matters. If they failed in their duty, Maharaja Dalip Singh was not to blame. The latter had absolutely no power in his hands. It was the Khalsa army and not the Lahore Government which began the Sikh War and the Khalsa army alone should have been punished after its defeat. There was absolutely no justification for dethroning Maharaja Dalip Singh. He was absolutely innocent.

Some of the British officers were also opposed to the annexation of the Punjab, Sir Henry Lawrence was one of them. However, he failed to convince Lord Dalhousie. Major Edwards was also opposed to annexation. To quote him, "It was my own belief at the time that had the Multan rebellion been put down at once, the Sikh insurrection would never have grown out of it; it was a belief shared, moreover (as well as I remember), by every political officer in the Punjab, and I for one still think so now". Again, "With respect to the Sardars, I believe them to be heart and soul on our side".

We may conclude by saying that Dalhousie's annexation of the Punjab was based on a policy of expediency and necessity. According to Bell, the Second Sikh War could have been avoided. To quote him, "I can perceive no advantage, material or moral, that has been gained by any person or class that could not have been more fully and effectually conferred and secured without annexation than with it".

After the annexation of the Punjab in March 1849, the administration of the province was put under the control of a Board of three members. Lord Dalhousie was himself to control the whole of it through the Board. After some time, the Board was disbanded. Henry Lawrence was asked to go to Rajputana as an agent for Governor-General. John Lawrence was appointed the Chief Commissioner of the Punjab. The Punjab was divided into four divisions and each of them was put under a Commissioner. The divisions were subdivided and put under the control of Deputy Commissioners and the latter controlled the Tehsildars and Naib Tehsildars. The Sikh army was completely disarmed and disbanded. Arms were taken away from the people of the Punjab. The Jagirs of the Sikh nobles were confiscated. A strong police force was raised and put under the supervision of English officers. Village watchmen were appointed. The landlords were given police powers to maintain law and order within their localities. A frontier force was raised from the tribes. The judiciary was reorganised under the supreme control of the Judicial Commissioner. Under him were the Commissioners, Deputy Commissioners, Tehsildars, etc. A code of law was prepared to give rough and ready justice to the people. Roads, bridges and canals were constructed. Agriculture was improved. Loans were given to the people for the improvement of land.

The result of all these reforms was that law and order was established in the Punjab within a short period. The people got contented. So great was the measure of their contentment that when after the lapse of eight years, the mutiny broke out in 1857, the Sikhs did not join it. On the other hand, the Sikh soldiers went to Delhi to crush the mutiny.

REVIEW QUESTIONS

1. Assess the causes of the rise of Maharaja Ranjit Singh.
2. Examine the relations between the English and Maharaja Ranjit Singh.
3. Throw light on the administration of Ranjit Singh.
4. Write in brief about the army of Ranjit Singh.
5. Ranjit Singh has been held responsible for the ultimate decline of his Kingdom. Analyse.
6. Who were the successors of Ranjit Singh? Discuss their historical achievements.
7. Ranjit Singh was a great warrior and statesman. Comment.
8. Write short notes on the following:
    (a) Ranjit Singh's government
    (b) Army of Ranjit Singh
    (c) Punjab politics from 1839 to 1845
    (d) Sikh Wars
    (e) Treaty of Lahore

SUGGESTED READINGS

Banerjee, A.C.: *Anglo-Sikh Relations*.
Bell, Evans: *Annexation of the Punjab*.
Chopra, G.L.: *The Punjab as a Sovereign State* (*1779-1889*).
Cunningham, H.S.: *History of the Sikhs*.
Gough and Innes: *The Sikhs and the Sikh Wars* (1897).
Griffin, L.: *Ranjit Singh*.
Khushwant Singh: *Ranjit Singh, Maharajah of Punjab* (*1780-1839*).
Latiff, S.M.: *History of the Punjab* (1891).
Mahajan, Jagmohan: *Annexation of the Punjab*.
Osborne, W.G.: *Court and Camp of Ranjit Singh* (1840).
Sinha, N.K.: *Ranjit Singh* (1945).
Sinha, N.K.: *The Rise of the Sikh Power* (1956).

13   Lord Dalhousie
(1848-56)

 LEARNING OBJECTIVES

- Throw light on the conquests of Lord Dalhousie
- Discuss the policies and reforms of Lord Dalhousie
- Give an estimate of Lord Dalhousie

Lord Dalhousie was born in 1812 and came to India as Governor-General at the age of 35. He had entered Parliament in 1837 and acted as President of the Board of Trade in the Ministry of Peel. He was a great imperialist and did all that he could to add to the British dominion in India. He is rightly called the *builder of the British Empire* in this country. Undoubtedly, he was one of the greatest of the Governors-General of India. Neither in ambition nor in hard work, could he be defeated by anyone. His eight years of office are full of important events in every field.

He was a great annexationist. He annexed territories for the uniformity of administration, consolidation and addition to the resources of the treasury. To quote him, "No man can deprecate more than I do any extension of the frontiers of our territory which can be avoided or which may not become indispensably necessary for considerations of our own safety, and of the maintenance of tranquility of our provinces. But I cannot conceive it possible for anyone to dispute the policy of taking advantage of every *just opportunity* which presents itself for consolidating the territories which already belong to us by taking possession of States which may lapse in the midst of them; for thus getting rid of those petty intervening principalities which may be made a means of annoyance, but which can never, I venture to think, be a source of strength for adding to the resources of the public treasury and for extending the uniform application of our system of Government to those whose best interests we sincerely believe will be protected thereby".

CONQUESTS OF DALHOUSIE

Punjab (1849)
The First Sikh War was fought in the time of Hardinge and the Second War was fought in the time of Lord Dalhousie. The real cause was that although the Sikhs were defeated in the First war, their power was not crushed and they were determined to have revenge for their previous defeat.

Mul Raj, the Governor of Multan, revolted and put to death the English officers who were sent there. For many reasons, Lord Dalhousie did not interfere at once. He wanted the Lahore Durbar to take action. Moreover, he preferred to take action against the rebels after the rainy season. Two important battles of the Second Sikh War were those of Chilianwala and Gujarat. The first was a drawn battle and the second was decisive. The Sikhs were completely defeated and they laid down their arms. The Punjab was annexed in March 1849. Dalip Singh, the Sikh Maharaja, was given a pension. The Punjab was put under a Board of three Commissioners. However, the Board was abolished later on and Sir John Lawrence was appointed Chief Commissioner. It was he who was responsible for the settlement of the province.

Second Burmese War (1852)

The real cause of the Second Burmese War was the determination of Dalhousie to exclude all European powers from Burma. He could not tolerate the idea of France or any other country capturing any part of Burma. However, he got an excuse to interfere into the affairs of Burma.

Under the Treaty of Yandaboo, the English merchants were allowed to settle in Burma and carry on trade. As their commercial rights were not defined precisely, each party interpreted them in its own way. The English merchants had their grievances but they stuck on to the trade on account of the high profits made by them.

The imperialist character of Dalhousie encouraged the English traders to appeal to him for the removal of their grievances. They sent him long petition in which they narrated all the wrongs suffered by them. Dalhousie welcomed the petition as God-sent. He declared that the Treaty of Yandaboo had been violated and the Burmese Government must pay damage for the wrongs done to the Englishmen. Commodore Lambert was sent to Rangoon for this purpose. On account of the behaviour Lambert, the Burmese Government could not satisfy the demands of the Government of India. The result was that there was the exchange of guns and the Second Burmese War started. Even before the declaration of war, a British force was sent under General Godwin. Martaban was taken, Rangoon and Bassein also fell into the hands of the English. Later on, Prome was occupied. Thus, the British were able to bring whole of lower Burma under their control. Negotiations were started by no treaty was signed. Lord Dalhousie, declared the annexation of Pegu by a Proclamation issued in 1852. According to Arnold, "The Second Burmese War was neither just in its origin nor marked by strict equity in its conduct or issue". Dalhousie's view was that the annexation of Pegu was "unavoidably demanded by sound views of general policy". Again, "Although this conquest be an evil it will not be an evil altogether without mitigation. If conquest is contemplated by me now, it is not a positive good but solely as the least of those evils before us from which we must of necessity select one".

Doctrine of Lapse

The name of Dalhousie is famous for his application of the Doctrine of Lapse in very many cases. However, it is wrong to say that he was the creator of this doctrine. The Directors of the English Company had declared in 1834 that permission to adopt on the failure of natural heirs "should be the exception and not the rule, and should never be granted but as a special mark of favour or approbation". It was declared in 1841 that every effort should be made to abandon "no just and honourable annexation of territory or revenue". The only thing done by Dalhousie was that he employed the Doctrine of Lapse in as many cases as possible. The basis of the Doctrine of Lapse was that as the English Company was the paramount power in India, the dependent States could not pass to the adopted son without the sanction of the paramount power and the latter had the right to withhold the sanction.

It has been contended that Dalhousie applied the Doctrine of Lapse only to dependent States. However, no precise distinction was drawn between independent, allied, dependent and subordinate States. The omission might have been intentional. The result of this was that any State could be annexed by merely stating that it was a dependent State although there was nothing to prove that. It is well known that Dalhousie annexed Karauli on the ground that it was a dependent State. He was overruled by the Directors on the ground that it was a protected ally and not a dependent State. No wonder, Sir John Strachey came to the conclusion that the distinction between dependent and allied States was mythical.

Lord Dalhousie wrote thus on the subject: "I take occasion of reordering my strong and deliberate opinion that in exercise of a wise and sound policy, the British Government is bound not to put aside or neglect such rightful opportunities of acquiring territory or revenue as may from time to time present themselves, where they arise from the lapse of subordinate States, by the failure of all heirs, of every description whatsoever or from the failure of natural heirs where the succession can be sustained only by the sanction of the Government being given to the ceremony of adoption by Hindu law". Lord Dalhousie applied the Doctrine of Lapse in the case of Satara in 1848, Jaitpur and Shambalpur in 1849, Baghat in 1850, Udaipur in 1852, Jhansi in 1853 and Nagpur in 1854.

As regards Satara, its Rajah died in 1848 without leaving any natural son. However, he adopted a son before his death. Dalhousie declared the adoption as invalid because his sanction was not taken. The Court of Directors declared that "By the general law and custom of India, a dependent principality like that of Satara cannot pass to an adopted son without the consent of the paramount power; that we are under no pledge direct or constructive to give such consent; and that the general interest committed to our charge is best consulted by withholding it". According to Arnold, the annexation of Satara was "a rich but not a lawful prize". It is wrong to maintain that the State of Satara was a British creation. The English Company entered into a treaty with Satara in 1819 with a view to conciliating the Marathas. The treaty was made between the two powers on the basis of equality. No amount of quibbling can justify the action of Dalhousie.

As regards Nagpur, its Raja, died in 1853. He did not adopt any son before his death. However, he had directed his queen to adopt a son. Under the Hindu law, such an adoption is perfectly valid. The Rani adopted Yaswant Rao. However, instead of recognising Yaswant Rao as the adopted son of Rajah of Nagpur, the British Resident took possession of the territory. It was declared that on account of the absence of legal heirs, the State lapsed to the English Company. According to Dalhousie, the case of Nagpur "stands wholly without precedent. We have before us no question of inchoate or incomplete or irregular adoption. The Rajah has died and has deliberately abstained from adopting an heir. His widow has adopted no successor. The State of Nagpur conferred by the British Government in 1818 on the Rajah and his heir has reverted to the British Government on the death of the ruler without any heir. Justice and custom and precedent leave the Government wholly unfettered to decide as it thinks best. Policy alone must decide the question". According to Arnold, "The real law by which Nagpur was added to the British Dominion was, it must be pronounced, the old but not on that account more respectable, the law of the strongest".

As regards Jhansi, it was given by the Peshwa to the English in 1817. In the same year, Lord Hastings put Rao Ramchandra on the throne of Jhansi and by a treaty guaranteed the right of succession in perpetuity. Rao Ramchandra died in 1835. His adopted son was not recognised and Raghunath Rao was put on the throne. The latter died in 1838 and was succeeded by Gangadhar Rao who also died in 1853 without leaving any child behind. Before his death, he adopted Anand Rao as his son and requested the English Company to recognise him as such. Dalhousie refused to recognise him and annexed the State. Rani Laxmibai of Jhansi had her revenge in the mutiny.

Annexation of Berar (1853)
Dalhousie annexed Berar in 1853. The reason was that the Nizam owed a lot of money to the English Company on account of the charge of the contingent forces. As the Nizam had not made payments, the debt reached the figure of £780,000. A new treaty was made with the Nizam by which he gave Berar to the English for the maintenance of the contingent force and the payment of the debts.

Anglo-Oudh Relations (1765-1856)
Before referring to the annexation of Oudh in 1856 by Lord Dalhousie, it is desirable to refer to the relations of the rulers of Oudh with the English Company from 1765 to 1856. It has already been pointed out that the Nawab Wazir of Oudh was defeated in 1765 in the battle of Buxar and taken prisoner along with Shah Alam. British troops also marched into Lucknow. The whole of Oudh was at

the mercy of the British troops. In spite of this, Lord Clive decided to restore to the Nawab of Oudh his conquered territories. He was made to part with only Kora and Allahabad. These districts were given to Shah Alam to maintain his dignity. Lord Clive followed a buffer State policy towards Oudh.

In 1773, Warren Hastings got back Kora and Allahabad from the Mughal Emperor who had gone over to the side of the Marathas. Both these districts were sold to the Nawab of Oudh for ₹50 lakhs. The Nawab of Oudh got British help in the Rohilla war and annexed Rohilkhand. In January 1775, a new treaty was imposed by the anti-Hastings majority in the Council on the new ruler of Oudh. The Nawab was forced to give up the sovereignty of Banaras. He was also made to agree to the increase of the subsidy to be paid for the British troops. It is well-known that Warren Hastings was instrumental in the maltreatment of the Begums of Oudh. He has been rightly condemned for his attitude. His conduct was absolutely high-handed.

In the time of Cornwallis, the Nawab requested the English Company to relieve him of the expenses of the British troops in Oudh. There were two brigades in Oudh at that time. One of them was a permanent Brigade of Kanpur and the other was known as the temporary Brigade stationed at Fatehgarh. The Nawab appealed again in 1781 and 1784 for the withdrawal of the temporary Brigade. Although Cornwallis did not grant the request of the Nawab in full, he reduced the subsidy to ₹50 lakhs a year.

In 1797, Sir John Shore intervened in a disputed succession in Oudh. He put Sadat Ali on the throne and made a new treaty with him. By the new treaty, the English Company became responsible for the defence of Oudh in return for an annual tribute of ₹70 lakhs. The Allahabad fort was given to the English Company. It was also provided that there was to be no increase in the subsidy except in the case of necessity. The Governor-General was given the discretion to add to the troops in the case of necessity.

When Lord Wellesley came as Governor-General, the condition of Oudh was deplorable. Its administration was a by word for inefficiency, corruption and oppression. The problem was a complicated one. While inefficiency and corruption demanded action, the loyalty of the Nawab to the English Company did not allow the English to intervene effectively. Moreover, the Nawab paid regularly and punctually the instalments of the subsidy. Although the amount already paid by the Nawab was too much for his paying capacity, Lord Wellesley demanded the increase of the British troops in Oudh and also demanded an increase in the subsidy.

Lord Wellesley made further demands on the Nawab. First of all, the Nawab agreed and then withdrew his consent. He even agreed to abdicate on the condition that his son was allowed to succeed him. The British Government did not accept his offer. British troops were ordered to march into Oudh and the Nawab was ordered to find money for paying them.

The real desire of Wellesley was to force upon the Nawab the cession of territory in lieu of revenue payments. Consequently, the Nawab was confronted with entirely new demands. He was either to cede the whole of his dominions retaining only a nominal sovereignty or cede as much territory as would yield revenue equal to the subsidy to be paid for. Practically, half of the Nawab's dominions were annexed by Wellesley. The treaty was signed in November 1801 and the territory surrendered was Rohilkhand and the Lower Doab.

The result of Lord Wellesley's policy was that Oudh was entirely surrounded by British territory except on the north. The policy of maintaining Oudh as a buffer State was given up. With regard to the territory left in the hands of the Nawab, he was required to act in accordance with the direction of the Company. It cannot be denied that the ceded territory was violently and compulsorily snatched away from the Nawab. The introduction of additional troops into Oudh was a violation of the existing treaties.

"It has been said that the Oudh action was the most high-handed of all Wellesley's despotic actions. He would hardly have denied all this but he would have justified it. The tangle of conflicting interests could only be cut by the sword, and he did not hold the sword in vain".

In the time of Lord Hastings, the Nawab of Oudh paid huge sums of money to the English Company towards the expenses incurred by the English Company in the Gurkha War. It was contended that the Nawab should pay because the defeat of the Gurkhas had added to his security. As an appreciation of the contribution made by the Nawab, the latter was allowed by the English Company to assume the title of king. However, this outraged the Muslim loyalty to the Mughal Emperor. Leonard says in *Cambridge History of India* that "in the Governor-General's opinion this act would benefit the British Government by causing a division between these important leaders of Mohammedan community. It also met with approval of all experienced British officials".

William Bentinck tried to fill his empty treasury from Oudh. He visited Lucknow and warned the king that "unless his territories were governed upon other principles than those hitherto followed and the prosperity of the people made the principal object of his administration, the precedents afforded by the principalities of Carnatic and Tanjore would be applied to the kingdom of Oudh and the entire management of the country would be assumed by the Company and the king would be transmitted into a State prison".

In the time of Lord Auckland, Nasir-ud-Din died in 1837 under very suspicious circumstances. The Dowager Queen put a son on the throne. However, the English put Mohammed Ali Shah as its ruler. A new treaty was made with Mohammed Ali Shah in 1837 by which the English Company got the right of assuming the management of the Company in the case of gross misrule. He also agreed to pay ₹16 lakhs for the maintenance of an auxiliary force. This treaty was disallowed by the Directors of the English Company and the Governor-General was directed to inform the ruler of Oudh accordingly. Unfortunately, Lord Auckland did not communicate this fact to the ruler of Oudh. The latter was merely informed that he would not have to pay for the auxiliary force. It was an act of treachery on the part of a Governor-General and he should not have gone so low in his action. The result was that the King of Oudh and many others remained under the impression that the Treaty of 1837 was in force. This Treaty was included in Government publications and was referred to Sir John Lawrence in 1844. Lord Hardinge also referred to the Treaty of 1837.

Lord Dalhousie was determined to deal with Oudh in a very effective manner. The Government of Oudh was rotten and openly so. The country would have been annexed long ago but for the consistent loyalty of the king.

In 1848, Sleeman was sent to Lucknow by Dalhousie as a Resident to undertake the reconstruction of an oppressed country. In 1849, he was instructed to make a tour and report on the conditions prevailing in the country. Sleeman reported that the people killed their female children and buried them alive. Lucknow was in perpetual turmoil of processions, illuminations and festivities. The only companions of the king were fiddlers and buffoons. The ambition of the king was limited to the reputation of being known as the best drumbeater, dancer and poet of the day. Most of his associates were outcasts from the low classes. The king was always in need of money and used the military aid to squeeze as much as he could. The peasantry grew swift-footed. The governing classes had no sympathy for the subjects and the latter suffered terribly under the tyranny of the officials. The officials took delight in plundering the peasants.

Although the condition of Oudh was far from satisfactory, Sleeman was opposed to the annexation of the country. His view was that "the annexation of Oudh would cost the British power more than the value of such kingdom and would inevitably lead to a mutiny of the sepoys". Moreover, the native States were "the breakwaters, and when they are all swept away, we shall be left to the mercy of our native army which may not be always sufficiently under control". Sleeman stressed the educational value of the native States in so far as they afforded an opportunity to those Indians "whose habits unfitted them to become humbler and accept low jobs and swagger with their sword and matchlock in the States". In 1851, Lord Dalhousie himself journeyed on the borders of Oudh and he tells us that he heard the use of heavy cannon for the purpose of collecting revenues by the servants of the king. In spite of this, Dalhousie hesitated to take action.

In 1854, Sleeman was replaced by Outram as Resident. The new Resident reported that the administration of the country was an orgy of massacre and corruption set to music.

Lord Dalhousie's recommendation was that while the King of Oudh be allowed to retain his title, the entire administration of the country be vested in the Company in perpetuity. On account of the consistent loyalty of the King, Dalhousie did not recommend his forcible abdication and annexation of his territory. The members of the Executive Council of Lord Dalhousie were divided with regard to the future of the Oudh. The majority was opposed to Dalhousie's views. In January 1856, Dalhousie got the orders of the Directors with regard to the future of Oudh. He was to offer to the King a kind of Vatican sovereignty, the title of king, adequate funds and full jurisdiction short of death over Lucknow palace parks: Outram was sent back to Lucknow and a brigade followed him. The king refused to accept the new position and was deposed. He was sent to Calcutta (now Kolkata). In justification of the act, Lord Dalhousie wrote thus: "The British Government would be guilty in the sight of God and man if it were any longer to aid in sustaining by its' countenance an administration fraught with suffering to millions". The Indians do not seem to have cared for the material gains which followed in the wake of the annexation of Oudh. They preferred their own misrule to the strict rule of the British with the insolence of the Chaprasis and other petty officials.

The annexation of Oudh created a feeling of awe and despair in the minds of the rulers of the Indian States. They began to fear their safety. They could say to themselves:

"Another year, another deadly blow,

Another mighty Empire overthrown.

And we are left, or shall be left alone".

Sleeman's opinion was that annexation of Oudh was a political blunder. According to him, the English used their giant's strength like a giant and injured their reputation in the eyes of the Indians. During the mutiny the sepoys of Oudh brought about havoc and added to the difficulties of the British. It has rightly been maintained that the forced abdication of Wajid Ali Shah and the annexation of Oudh were offences against good faith and public conscience.

WAJID ALI SHAH (1822-57)

The character of Wajid Ali Shah, the last ruler of Oudh, demands a detailed treatment. He was born in 1822 and he ascended the throne in 1847 at the age of 25. He was jolly and good-natured and the gayest of the gay rulers. He studied Persian, rode horses, shot tigers, started loving at an early age and also composed love poems in Urdu. All efforts to train him as a ruler failed.

He was a man of high tastes. He loved architecture. He had a flair for landscape gardening. Under his inspiration, the Nuzurbagh garden was constructed with canals on two sides from which fountains played. He planned and supervised the construction of three palaces, one for summer, one for winter and one for the rainy season. However, the supreme passion of his life was *Ishq* or love. He surrounded himself with *Paris* or fairies and put them all in a special palace called *Parikhana*. They were handsomely paid and richly dressed and they were his special property. He sang and danced with them. He held inquiries into their petty thefts. He watched over their loyalty and turned out anyone whom he did not like. The *Parikhana* was guarded by a band of women who were trained to carry out his, commands. *Ishqnama* or the diary of Wajid Ali begins thus: "The Lord of the world has bestowed the taste of love on every human being, and everyone has had his growth in the ever-blooming garden of love. Hence, I too have been nourished with the spring and flowers of love. And as I got this woe of love from the very beginning, I have noted down my own tale of romance and love from the beginning up to the present time".

From the time of his succession to the throne, Wajid Ali Shah did not show any interest in the administration of his territory. He was raw, impulsive arid irresponsible. He did things in a hurry and later on repented for having done so. There are many interesting stories about the follies of the ruler. It is stated that once upon a time, a complaint was made to him that a particular Jain jeweller had sacrificed a Brahmin boy while building a temple of Parsnath. Without making any enquiry, the temple was demolished. There were protests and ultimately Wajid Ali Shah admitted that he had absolutely no administrative experience and that was why the mistake had been made. The house of the officer who was responsible for the trouble was pulled down. It is also stated that once upon a time when his Chief Minister was going to see him, he was caught by four ruffians and he was not let off till they were paid ₹50,000 ransom.

Wajid Ali Shah had a command of the Persian language and he was also a master of Urdu. He wrote over 100 books in those languages. His poems fill several big volumes. He was an expert in music. He was the greatest patron of Indian music and dance of his time. Music and dance were the breath of the *Parikhana* and its master was the patron of the well-known Lucknow Thumri. Wajid Ali was also fond of drama. His troupe consisted of 361 persons, out of which 84 were women. Their total salary amounted to ₹11,859 per month.

Wajid Ali was the father of modern Urdu stage. Amanat, the well-known Urdu poet of Lucknow, wrote his famous *Inder Sabha* under his patronage.

As the administration of Oudh was not efficient. Lord Dalhousie gave Wajid Ali Shah a warning. The king was so much affected that he left the whole administration in the hands of the Resident and himself joined the company of poets, eunuchs, musicians and dances. His companions took the law into their own hands. They robbed the people of their money and set free their friends from jails. When the Resident gave him a warning, Wajid Ali entered into an agreement by which it was agreed that "eunuchs, singers, and other improper persons should not be employed either directly or indirectly, nor would they interfere with the matters of administration".

Wajid Ali Shah was surrounded by gay persons. His ministers lacked ability and character. The officials were corrupt and quarrelsome. The landed aristocracy had no respect for the court. The Resident wanted an efficient government but nobody knew what efficiency was.

In Ayodhya, there was a shrine of Hanuman called Hanumangarhi. This shrine was under the charge of Bairagis. Some Muslims forcibly entered the shrine and offered prayers. English troops intervened to stop the trouble which was taking the shape of a Jehad.

By the end of 1855, the administration of Oudh had completely collapsed, but Wajid Ali Shah continued to play Krishna to his *Paris*. The peasantry groaned. The communal situation was unsatisfactory. The patience of the Governor-General was exhausted. On 23rd January, 1856, General Outram was directed by the Governor-General to take over Oudh. The Resident was ordered to get a treaty signed from Wajid Ali Shah and if the latter refused to do so, the Resident was to take over the administration. On 30th January 1856, the Resident conveyed his directions to the Minister. The king expressed his desire to discuss the matter with the Resident. The Resident declined to do so but conveyed his instructions to the mother of the king.

On 4th February 1856, when General Outram went to see Wajid Ali, he found the palace deserted and surrounded by gloom. The guards had laid aside their arms and removed their turbans. The artillery had been dismantled. When Outram presented the letter of the Governor-General to Wajid Ali, his innocent question was: "What wrong have I committed?" The Resident assured the king that the Government had provided for his maintenance, honour and dignity. The king read the treaty and asked: "Who am I now? Treaties are necessary only between equals. Who am I now that the British Government should enter into a treaty with me? The kingdom is the creation of the British. They have to issue the commands to ensure their fulfilment". And then he added, "I am not in a position to sign the treaty. I would not even ask for maintenance. Let me go straight to England and throw myself at the feet of the British throne for mercy".

On 5th February 1856, Wajid Ali Shah discharged all his troops. On 7th February 1856, he finally refused to sign the treaty and, consequently, the Resident took over the administration of Oudh as Chief Commissioner.

When Wajid Ali Shah left Lucknow, thousands of persons accompanied him. In spite of all his failings, he was loved by the people of Lucknow. The parting scenes were pathetic. Everyone shed tears. It was thus that Wajid Ali Shah disappeared from the scene. He died on September 1, 1857. One may feel pity for him but probably he got what he richly deserved.

ABOLITION OF TITLES AND PENSIONS

Dalhousie was not content with the annexation of territories. He also tried to abolish titles and pensions. The first victim of his policy was Dhondu Pant or Nana Sahib who was the adopted son of Peshwa Baji Rao II. Baji Rao had been given a pension of ₹8 lakhs a year. He adopted Nana Sahib as his son and asked for the recognition of the Company. Baji Rao died in 1852 and Lord Dalhousie rejected the claim of Nana Sahib. According to Sir John Kaye, the action of Dalhousie was harsh. Arnold described it as grasping.

In 1855, the *Nawab of Carnatic* died without leaving any male issue. Azimjah was the heir and he applied to the Madras (now Chennai) Government for recognition. The view of the Governor was that the title and pension were personal and "the semblance of royalty without power is mockery of authority which must be pernicious—that it is impolitic and unwise to allow pageant to continue which, though it has been politically harmless, may at any time become a nucleus for sedition and agitation". Lord Dalhousie endorsed the views of the Madras Governor in these words: "I entirely agree with Lord Harris in holding that the treaty of 1801 confers no right of hereditary succession. It is purely a personal treaty. There is no mention of heirs and successors in any part of the treaty and no grant of anything is made by it of anyone except to the Nawab Azim-ud-Dowla himself".

The *Raja of Tanjore* died in 1855 and left a widow and two daughters. He was a king without a kingdom and enjoyed a pension and some jagirs. Consequently, on the death of the Rajah, Dalhousie stopped the pension and confiscated the jagirs. The case went to the Privy Council and was decreed in favour of the Company. Lord Kingsdown made the following observations in his judgment: "It is extremely difficult to discover in these papers any grant of legal right on the part of the East India Company into the possession of this Raja, or of any part of the property of the Raja on his death. The Raja was an independent sovereign of territories undoubtedly minute and bound by treaties to a powerful neighbour, which left him practically little power of free action, but we did not hold, his territory such as it was, as chief of the British Crown, or of the East India Company, nor does there appear to have been any pretence for claiming it on the death of the Rajah without a son, by any legal title, either as an escheat or as *Bona Vacantia*".

ADMINISTRATIVE REFORMS OF DALHOUSIE

Lord Dalhousie carried out many reforms in various fields. The keynotes of his reforms was centralisation. The object of the reforms was to gather all the threads of power into his own hands. Dalhousie organised the non-regulation system to meet the new needs of the Indian Empire. Under this system, the administration was to be carried on by a Commissioner who was to be responsible directly to the Governor-General-in-Council. Its chief merit was economy of personnel. It did not make any distinction between civil and military government. The District Magistrate was given all the powers in various fields. The unfortunate effect of this system was that it demoralised the people.

Military Reforms. Lord Dalhousie carried out a large number of reforms in the military field. He started the general movement of troops from Bengal towards the west. The headquarters of the Bengal artillery were shifted from Calcutta (now Kolkata) to Meerut. The Army Headquarters were gradually shifted to Simla. He also started the policy of reduction, disintegration and distribution. He encouraged the enlistment of Gurkha regiments in the Indian army. He raised a new irregular force in the Punjab. He asked the home authorities to increase the number of British troops in

India so that there might be no possibility of revolt by the Indian troops. Dalhousie was always afraid of a conspiracy among the Indian troops.

Telegraphs and Railways. These two departments got a great impetus from Dalhousie. Their development was considered to be necessary from the point of view of the defence of the Indian empire and also for the encouragement of British investments in India. He entered into contracts with English corporations for the construction of railways. All kinds of facilities were given to them for construction work. They were also guaranteed interest by the government irrespective of the profits. A few strategic lines were constructed at an enormous cost to the Indian revenues, but this helped the English capitalists to make huge profits. Telegraph wire linked up the various parts of India and this fact helped the English a great deal during the mutiny.

Commercial Reforms. In the interests of the British traders and manufacturers, Lord Dalhousie followed the policy of free trade. All ports of India were declared free. Improvements were made in lighthouses and harbours. All hindrances in the way of the flow of goods and capital were removed. All the coastal trade of India fell into the hands of English capitalists. This led to the economic exploitation of the country.

Public Works Department. Before Dalhousie, the Military Member was in charge of the Public Works Department. The work on the civil side was neglected. Consequently, Lord Dalhousie appointed a commission in every Presidency to report on the state of affairs. The result was that public works were withdrawn from the control of the military. A separate Public Works Department was started in every Presidency and its important officers were the Chief Engineer and Executive Officers. They were all imported from England. The recognised Department of Public Works took up the task of constructing roads, canals and bridges.

Postal System. Dalhousie also removed the defects in the postal system. He reorganised the system on the recommendations of a commission. He started a uniform rate of half anna for letters not exceeding half a tola in weight for the whole of India. The sender of the letter was to pay the charges in the form of stamps. Dalhousie's reforms removed corruption from Postal Department.

Wood's Despatch of 1854. Sir Charles Wood, President of Board of Control, sent his famous despatch on education. According to this despatch, education was entitled to the first claim of the government. At the apex of the educational structure were to be universities on the model of the London University in the Presidencies. These universities were to be merely examining bodies and not teaching institutions. Colleges were to be affiliated to the universities and were to provide education for intermediate and degree classes. There were also to be high schools and Anglo-vernacular schools. Their medium of instruction was to be the vernacular of the province. Private enterprise in the field of education was to be encouraged by the Government. There was to be a Director-General of Education for the whole of India. Education was to be entirely secular. Universities were established in 1857 in Bombay, Calcutta and Madras.

DALHOUSIE'S RESPONSIBILITY FOR THE MUTINY

Dalhousie left India in 1856 and the mutiny broke out in 1857. Naturally, the critics attributed the mutiny to the acts of omission and commission of Lord Dalhousie. It was stated that Lord Dalhousie was in a hurry to annex States to the Indian Empire. He should have been more considerate towards the sentiments of the Indians. It is true that the various annexations and conquests brought more money into the coffers of the English Company, but it cannot be denied that they created the unfortunate impression that the territory of no Indian prince was safe. It was feared that the unscrupulous Government of the Company was ready to find out an excuse for whatever it did. The people lost faith in the sense of justice of the English. The application of the Doctrine of Lapse made matters worse. It created a large number of discontented persons who were ready to avail of any opportunity to hit back against the English Company. No wonder, Rani Jhansi brought about havoc. Likewise, the refusal to pay the pension to Nana Sahib turned him into a bitter enemy. The abolition of pensions of the Raja of Tanjore and the Nawab of Carnatic was unfortunate. It was during his time that a very large number of British troops were sent to fight in the Crimean War. The proportion of the British troops as compared with the Indian troops became very low. Lord Dalhousie asked the Home Government to fill in the gap, but the same was not done in spite of many reminders. The result was that when the mutiny broke out the Indian soldiers found themselves in a very advantageous position on account of the shortage of British troops in India. However, for this not Dalhousie but the Home Government was to blame.

Dalhousie himself was not in favour of the annexation of Oudh. He was overruled by the Directors in this matter and it is they who should share the blame for its annexation.

Dalhousie carried out his reforms with the best of motives but every move of his was suspected. It was feared that every effort was being made by the Indian Government to convert the people to Christianity or otherwise to injure their sentiments.

On the whole, we may say that Lord Dalhousie was partly responsible for the mutiny of 1857. His policy towards the Indian States created a sense of despair among the Indian Princes and that led to revolt. He should have tried to carry his people with him and also avoid all those measures which could in any way create misunderstanding and suspicion in the minds of the innocent Indians.

Continued Sickness of Dalhousie. Dalhousie suffered throughout his Indian career from an ill-health that was partly responsible for his fretfulness and which also made his manifold exertions truly heroic. He wrote in July 1849 that he was broken in health when he started from England and he landed in Calcutta an invalid and almost a cripple. As time passed on and Dalhousie strained himself under the stress of circumstances, he became a prey to a lamentable combination of maladies. He practically lost his voice. He became lame in the right leg and thus developed inside an open and incurable sore of the shin-bone. There were frequent attacks in the head and many other subsidiary ailments. Dr. Alexander Grant who was the surgeon of Dalhousie in India has written a faithful account of the sufferings and ailments of Dalhousie. On every day of the eight years which he spent in India, the life-blood of Dalhousie was drop by drop being drained away.[1]

ESTIMATE OF DALHOUSIE

According to Lord Curzon, Lord Dalhousie left a mark upon India inferior to none of his predecessors and acquired "a reputation second only to that of Warren Hastings. The career of Dalhousie did, indeed, provoke at the time and has ever since aroused, though in a diminishing degree as time has proceeded, a controversy that recalls the fate of his famous predecessor. The formidable fighters of Gough and Napier, whom he encountered and overthrew, the forceful personality of the two Lawrences, whom he alternately conciliated and coerced, the tremendous sweep of his territorial acquisitions, and the range of his administrative reforms, the masterful character of the man himself and the appealing nature of the convulsion with which India was shaken to its foundations almost immediately after his retirement, and which might, not without plausibility, be in some measure regarded as the consequence of his rule—all of these combined to make the reign of Dalhousie a theme of legitimate and even embittered disputation which did not die down till long after the subject of the controversy, at once too ill and too proud to defend himself, was in the grave. The

---

[1] The fiery soul, which working out its way,
   Crippled the puny body to decay,
   And O'er informed its tenement of day.

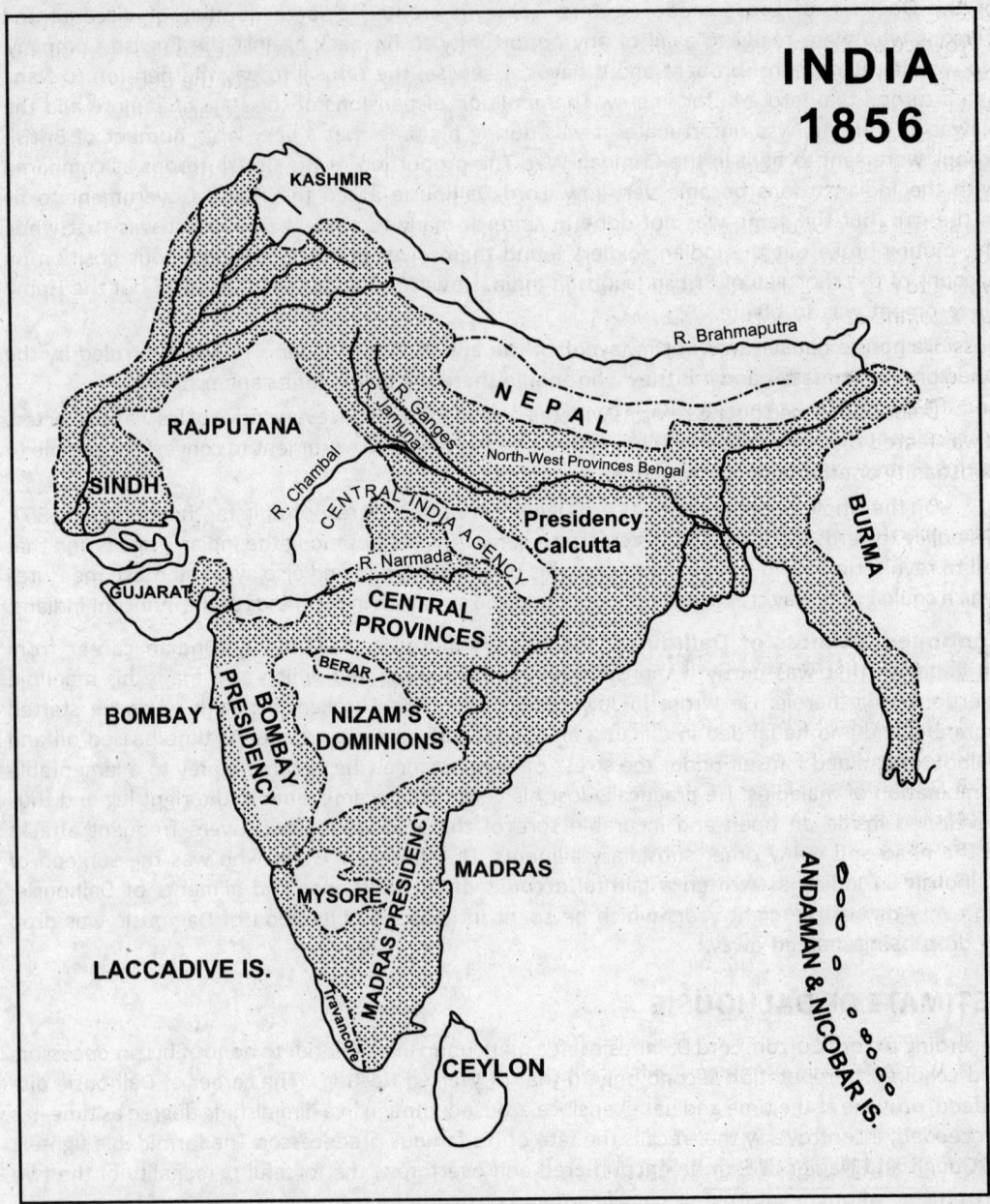

protagonists in this furious polemic, Sir John Kaye and Edwin Arnold on the one side, the Duke of Argyll and Sir Charles Louis Jackson on the other, filled the arena with their vehement denunciation of defence. Later the ranks of the defenders were strengthened by the powerful aid of Captain L.J. Trotter, Sir William Hunter, and Sir Richard Temple, while the biographer of Sir John Lawrence held a midway position between. Dalhousie himself looked for his vindication to the subsequent publication of his own papers and correspondence, although, with a self-restraint that perhaps had in it more of dignity than of wisdom, he left in his will a direction that no portion of his private papers should be made public until at least fifty years after his death". Again, "As an Imperial administrator, Dalhousie was not inferior to the greatest of the great men whose genius for organisation has built the British Empire in the East. He was splendid in his organisation of war, an Abraham Lincoln in the Orient. But he was even more splendid in his organisation of peace; and no sooner had he annexed a Province or confiscated a State than his plans for the new regime, elaborated in the most minute detail, were ready, and he began to erect the new structure almost before the debris of the old had been removed. Whether such a man, after his eight years of Indian autocracy, would ever have bent his neck to the yoke of official life in England, even though he had excelled it in his pre-Indian career, is more than doubtful. He himself again and again repudiated both the capacity and the desire. Public life on a lower plane than that on which he had moved, and on what he considered the sordid stage of British politics, possessed for him no attraction. Whether the retention or the recovery of health would have altered his attitude it is impossible to say; that he would have been willing to rust from idleness, is unbelievable; that some form of public service would have claimed his incomparable talents is more than likely. While on his return journey he even discussed the possibility of accepting the War Office if offered to him, but this would only be on terms which he could hardly expect to be conceded; since he was, he confessed, 'a curious compound of the radical and the despot'. That he would have re-entered a Cabinet or, had he done so, that he would have succeeded in showing that a Governor-General of India can also be a Prime Minister of Great Britain seems to me improbable".

According to Ramsay Muir, "The distinctive features of modern India have been far more influenced by Dalhousie's work than by the Mutiny itself or by the constitutional adjustments which followed it".

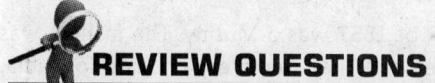

REVIEW QUESTIONS

1. Write a detailed note on the conquests of Lord Dalhousie.
2. Explain the doctrine of lapse.
3. Bring out the relations between the rulers of Oudh and the British.
4. Bring out the main features of the administrative reforms of Lord Dalhousie.
5. Make an estimate of Lord Dalhousie.
6. Lord Dalhousie was a great annexationist. Comment.
7. Write short notes on the following:
    (a) Second Burmese War
    (b) Doctrine of Lapse
    (c) Wajid Ali Shah
8. Comment on Dalhousie's policy of abolition of titles and pensions.
9. Was Lord Dalhousie responsible for the mutiny of 1857? Analyse.

SUGGESTED READINGS

Arnold, E.: *Dalhousie's Administration of British India* (1861).
Hunter, W.W.: *The Marquis of Dalhousie*.
Lee-Warner: *Life of Marquis of Dalhousie*.
Malleson: *The Indian Mutiny of 1857*.
Sleeman, W.H.: *Journey Through the Kingdom of Oudh* (1885).
Trotter, L.J.: *Life of Marquis of Dalhousie*, 1889.

14   The Revolt of 1857

LEARNING OBJECTIVES

- Know the causes, nature and character of the Revolt of 1857
- Analyse the causes of the failure of the Revolt of 1857
- Assess the administrative, political and social impact of the Revolt on India

ITS CHARACTER

The view of the British historians was that the outbreak of 1857 was a Mutiny. The fashion was originally set by the Government of the day. Earl Stanley, the then Secretary of State for India, while reporting the events of 1857 to Parliament, used the term "Mutiny" and most of the English writers on the subject followed his lead and writers like Charles Ball, G.W. Forrest, T.R. Holmes, M. Innes, J.W. Kaye, G.F. Macmunn, G.B. Malleson, C.T. Metcalfe, Earl Roberts and others used the term "Mutiny" in this connection. Sir John Lawrence was of the opinion that the Mutiny had its origin in the army and its cause was the greased cartridges and nothing else. It was not attributable to any antecedent conspiracy whatsoever, although it was taken advantage of by the mutineers to increase their number. The view of Sir John Seeley was that the Mutiny was a "wholly unpatriotic and selfish sepoy mutiny with no native leadership and no popular support". The British officers conducting the trial of Bahadur Shah II held him responsible for originating the Mutiny in conspiracy with the Shah of Iran and other Muslim rulers of the Middle East. Sir Theophilius Metcalfe deposed in the trial of Bahadur Shah that six weeks before the outbreak, a seditious poster was found pasted on the walls of Jama Masjid proclaiming that the Shah of Iran would invade India and all the Muslims should be ready to join the Jehad. British historians are of the view that Nana Sahib organised the revolution long before its outbreak at Meerut. To quote Kaye, "For months, for years, indeed ever since the failure of the mission to England had been apparent, they had been quietly, spreading their network of intrigue all over the country. From one native court to another, from one extremity to another of the Great Continent of India, the agents of Nana Sahib had passed with overtures and invitations, discretely perhaps mysteriously worded, to princes and chiefs of different races and religions, but most hopeful of all to the Marathas. Nana Sahib's two most important agents were Rungo Bapoji in the South and Azimullah in the North".

There were also writers who considered the revolt of 1857 the result of a Hindu conspiracy. The Hindus were said to have a genius for conspiracy. "They possess a power of patience of foreseeing results, of carefully weighing chances, of choosing time and weapon, of profiting by circumstances, never losing sight of the object desired, taking advantage of every turn of fortune—all qualities invaluable for success in intrigue". It was contended that the circulation of the *Chapatis* was originated by the Hindus and the rebellion was successfully engineered by the emissaries of the Peshwa under the guidance of Nana Sahib.

The view of Dr. Alexander Duff was that the revolt was neither Hindu nor Muslim in character. It was the spontaneous outcome of the fraternising sepoys of all castes and creeds.

The view of Lord Canning, the then Governor-General of India, was that, "The struggle which we have had has been more like a national war than a local insurrection. In its magnitude, duration, scale of expenditure and in some of its moral features, it partakes largely of the former characters".

The view of Thompson and Garratt is that for four months during summer of 1857, it seemed that the Mutiny might develop into a real War of Independence, but by September 1857, it was clear that the Indians who were in revolt were incapable of working to any settled plan or of subordinating themselves to a national leader. Their prestige was waning and their commanders had proved themselves incompetent except in guerrilla warfare. They conclude by observing that the Mutiny may be considered either as a military revolt, or as a bid for the recovery of their property and privileges by dispossessed princes and landlords or as an attempt to restore the Mughal Empire or as a peasants' war.

Professor P.E. Roberts accepts the view of John Lawrence and Seeley and observes that the Mutiny was mainly military in origin but it occurred at a time when for various reasons there was social and political discontent in the country and the mutineers took advantage of the same.

Many Indian writers have described the events of 1857 as a War of Independence. V. D. Savarkar wrote his book called "War of Indian Independence" in which he tried to show how the Mutiny was really a War of Indian Independence. Asoka Mehta has pointed out to the national character of mutiny in his book entitled "1857, The Great Rebellion". He admits that the sepoys were the mainstay of the rebellion and they bore the brunt of the struggle to break the chains that imprisoned India. They gave the backbone to the resistance and became its shield and spear. However, besides the sepoys millions of Indians took part in the rebellion. The number of the civilians killed was as large as that of the sepoys. They joined the struggle to free their country and to redress their grievances. The rapidity with which the revolt spread shows that in some areas at least, the rebellion enjoyed strong mass support. At many stations, the sepoy were egged on to action by the citizens. Those who sided with the British had to face social ostracism. Those who could not join openly, non-cooperated with the British. General Havelock could not get boats and boatmen to ferry his soldiers across the river. Although labourers at Kanpur were pressed into service by the British, they managed to escape at night. At many places, the natives of all classes tried to keep aloof from the British. The decisive evidence showing the national character of the rebellion is the note of common harmony it struck in both the Hindus and Muslims. Even the British Government found it difficult to separate the two communities. The Mughal Emperor prohibited the cow slaughter throughout the country to conciliate the Hindus. In a letter to Rajas of Rajputana, the Mughal Emperor wrote, "It is my ardent wish to see that the Feringi is driven out of Hindustan by all means and at any cost. It is my ardent wish that the whole of Hindustan should be free, but the Revolutionary War that is being waged for the purpose will not be crowned with success unless a man capable of sustaining the whole burden of the movement, who can organise and concentrate the different forces of the nation and unify the whole people in himself, comes forward to guide the rising. I have no desire left of ruling over India after the expulsion of the English for my own aggrandizement. If all of your native Rajas are ready to unsheathe your sword to drive away the enemy, then I am willing to resign imperial powers and authority in the hands of any confederacy of native princes who are chosen to exercise it". The Hindus responded to the offer of the Muslims. Nana Saheb declared his allegiance to the Mughal Emperor. It was only after the fall of Delhi that the Sikhs joined the British army in large numbers. All this shows that the Mutiny was a national rising, although on a limited scale.

In his book entitled "Eighteen Fifty Seven", Dr. S. N. Sen says that the story of the *chapatis* lends some colour to the theory of prior preparation, propaganda and conspiracy. The view of Wilson was that a date and time had been fixed for a simultaneous rising at all the military stations of India, but he did not give any evidence in support of his view. His view is contradicted by the known facts. The rising at Meerut was not pre-meditated and the same was the case at other places. The sepoys and their leaders were not in league with any foreign power. The only foreign power which was approached by the rebels was that of Nepal and that was done after the collapse of the mutiny and not during it. The remarkable thing about the mutiny was that it had its recruits from many sources. The movement began as a military Mutiny, but it was not confined to the army. Moreover, the army as a whole did not join the revolt and a considerable section of the army actively fought on the side of the government. Every disarmed regiment was not necessarily disloyal and every deserter was not a mutineer. The rebels came from every section of the population. At all stages, both Hindus and Muslims were well represented in the rebel army. Nana had his Azimullah Khan, Bahadur Khan his Sobha Ram and the Rani of Jhansi her trusted Afghan guards. Outside Avadh and Shahabad, there was no evidence of that general sympathy which would invest the mutiny with the dignity of a national war. At the same time, it is wrong to dismiss it as a military rising. The mutiny became a revolt and assumed a political character when the mutineers of Meerut placed themselves under the king of Delhi and a section of the landed aristocracy and civil population declared in his favour. "What began as a fight for religion, ended as a war of independence; for there was not the slightest doubt that the rebels wanted to get rid of the alien governments and restore the old order of which the King of Delhi was the rightful representative". The revolt assumed national dimensions in Avadh although in a limited sense. The Mutiny was not a war between the white and the black. No normal issue was involved. Truth was the first casualty and both sides were guilty of false propaganda. According to Dr. Sen, the struggle may be described as "a war of fanatic religionists against Christians". The Mutiny was not a conflict between barbarism and civilisation. It was an inhuman fight between the people driven mad by hatred and fear. Burning and hanging expeditions were an important routine and no distinction was made between the innocent and the guilty. The Mutiny was inevitable because no dependent nation could have ever reconciled itself to foreign domination. A despotic government must ultimately rule by the sword and in India sword was in the custody of the sepoy army. Between the sepoys and the English masters, there were no common ties of race, language and religion. The Mutiny was inherent in the constitution of the Empire.

In "History of the Freedom Movement in India," Dr. Tara Chand says that it is misleading to use the term Mutiny to describe the upheaval of 1857-58. There was no doubt that the army was abundantly involved in the revolt. It was equally true that the drive was supplied by the Bengal Army, although there were signs of disaffection in some regiment in the other Presidencies also. However, the outbreak was not confined to the army. It was not a Mutiny in the ordinary sense of the term. Its causes were deeper than those involved in usual breaches of military discipline. Dr. Tara Chand has referred to various authorities in support of his view.

Dr. Tara Chand comes to the conclusion that while it is inappropriate to give the designation "Mutiny" to the events of 1857, it was also not proper to call them "The national war of independence". It has to be admitted that the war against the British was not inspired by any sentiment of nationalism because in 1857 India was not yet politically a nation. It is true that the Hindus and Muslims cooperated, but the leaders and followers of the two communities were moved by personal loyalties rather than by loyalty to a common motherland. Nonetheless, the upheaval of 1857 was a war for the liberation of India from the yoke of the foreigner because he had given mortal offence of the dignity and self-respect of the ruling class which exercised social influence and carried the burden to administration. He had also antagonised the masses by his oppressive land revenue policy and by his economic measures which ruined their arts and crafts. On the whole, the rising of 1857 was an attempt to halt the process of dissolution of the medieval order. The uprising of 1857 was a general movement of the traditional elite of the Muslims and the Hindus—princes, landholders, soldiers, scholars and theologians (Pandits and Maulavis). The Emperor of Delhi, the King of Avadh, some Nawabs and Rajas, Talukdars and Zamindars and the soldiers, whether Pathans, Mughals, Rajputs or Brahmins of northern India, comprised the main body of the rebels. The class composition of the insurgents reflected the geographical disposition of the movement and sheds light upon the motives of the participants. There is no doubt that practically all those who belonged to this order were disaffected although some of them abstained from active participation on account of their peculiar circumstances. The chiefs and landlords constituted the leadership of this rebellious host, the regular and irregular troops of the English East India Company and of the princes, its fighting arm and their dependents and peasants became followers. They had common traditions and common grievances. They sympathised with one another in their misfortune. The loss of territory and political power affected them all. If the higher section was deprived of the titles of authority, the others had lost avenues of employment and position of influence and profit. Scholars, theologians, poets, craftsmen and artists were left without patronage. Many of those whose hereditary occupation was fighting, were rendered jobless and many were Obliged to drift into the army of the English East India Company. Dr. Tara Chand refers to the charge sheets drawn by the leaders of the movement against the British Government in support of his view.

The view of Dr. R.C. Majumdar is that the revolt of 1857 was not at all a national movement. He has given many facts and figures to show that its leaders had their own axes to grind. They were not inspired by any feelings of nationalism as such. There was no cordiality between the Hindus and the Muslims. Bahadur Shah did not heartily cooperate with the mutineers. Rani Jhansi also did not side with them at the beginning and actually did so when she was faced with a trial by the British Government. The Muslim Nawabs did not treat their Hindu subjects properly even during the days of the mutiny. Dr. Majumdar points out that the Muslims as a community had their special grievances against the British who had deprived them of their former paramountcy. In spite of that Muslim swords were pointed against the Hindus rather than against the British and many Hindus prayed for the collapse of the mutiny. The mutineer sepoys of both the communities freely sacked Indian towns and murdered their fellow countrymen. Not one voice was heard to cry: "Let me die so that India be free!" Once the British launched their campaign of ruthless suppression and reprisal, all "rebels" were obliged to fight on to save their skin. The view of Dr. Majumdar is that the true significance of "1857" lies in the inspiration which its memory afforded to the later freedom movements and for such inspirational purpose, it matters nothing that the sordid and unhappy facts have become shrouded in a fog of pious make-beliefs.

We may conclude with the following words of Asoka Mehta: "The rebellion of 1857 was more than a mere sepoy mutiny and was an eruption of the social volcano wherein many pent-up forces found vent. After the eruption, the whole social topography had changed. The scars of the rebellion remained deep and shining".

CAUSES OF REVOLT

Political
The Revolt of 1857 can be attributed to many causes. As regards the political cause, Dalhousie's doctrine of lapse and annexation of the territories of the native rulers had created a spirit of uneasiness and suspicion throughout India. The Punjab was annexed in 1849. The Raja of Satara

died in 1848 and Dalhousie did not recognise the adoption of a son made by him before his death and annexed the state of Satara. The Raja of Nagpur died in 1853. Dalhousie did not recognise the adopted son and the British resident took possession of the territory. The ruler of Jhansi died in 1853 and Dalhousie refused to recognise his adopted son and annexed the state. In 1853, Berar was annexed. In 1856, the state of Avadh was annexed although its ruler had always been faithful to the British Government. This annexation angered the soldiers of the English East India Company most of whom came from Avadh. They had now to pay higher taxes on the lands held by their families in Avadh. The British Government confiscated the estates of a majority of the Taluqdars or Zamindars and they became the opponents of the British rule in India. The annexation of Avadh was resented not only by the Muslims but also by the other rulers of India. It created among them a spirit of despair. Even the most faithful and loyal among them could not be sure of their future. The British Government had ordered that on the death of the last Mughal Emperor, his successor was to give up his ancestral palace and leave something of its royal splendour. Remarks made by high British officials created the impression that the Government had made up its mind to put an end to the native states. Sir Charles Napier is said to have observed, "Were I the Emperor of India for 12 years, no Indian prince should exist. The Nizam should be no more heard of—Nepal would be ours". By stopping the annual pension of £80,000 to Nana Sahib, the adopted son of the last Peshwa Baji Rao II, the British made him their deadly enemy. The Hindus regarded him as the legitimate successor of Baji Rao and his exclusion was considered to be unjust. He proved himself to be a prince among conspirators.

The annexation of a native state not only deposed the King, but also limited the scope of the Indians to get higher administrative jobs. That created bitterness among the higher strata of the Indian society. At the time of the settlement of newly acquired territories, the old claims of the native aristocracy were severely scrutinized by the officials who favoured the peasants against the landlords. That also created bitterness. Lord Bentinck's resumption of rent-free lands brought a lot of money to the government, but reduced to poverty many landowners whose title deeds had been lost or who had held land by long prescriptive right. In the five years preceding the mutiny, the famous Inam Commission in Bombay (now Mumbai) confiscated about 20,000 estates. After the annexation of Avadh, Jackson was appointed Chief Commissioner for Settlement. He critically examined the titles of the Taluqdars and most of them were left without any means of subsistence. The native army was disbanded and about 60,000 men lost their livelihood. The discontented soldiers and Taluqdars joined the ranks of the rebels.

The English officers were aloof, exacting and unimaginative. Even the best among them "insulted the native gentry whenever they had the opportunity to do so. The administrative machinery was inefficient and insufficient. The strain on it was so great that whenever a new territory was conquered and annexed it roused a very bad feeling and led to many agrarian outrages". Even the landlords were refused the right of adoption and their estates were confiscated by the government. The lot of the landlords was so bad that it was difficult for them to raise loans even at 30 per cent or 40 per cent of the value of the land. There was a lot of uncertainty about land. The government officials very often cancelled private transfers of land and interfered even with the decisions of the courts. The Raja of Manipur was deprived of 116 out of 158 villages. Another Raja had his Taluka curtailed by the severance of 138 villages out of 216 villages. The Collector was ordered by the Sadar Board not to carry the decree passed in his favour into effect. Many Taluqdars lost half of their villages and the others lost their all. Heavy assessments and increased duties made them frantic.

Courts of law tried to bring all the people on the same footing. The British officials took pride in introducing the principle of civil equality among the people. It was found that the principle of civil equality was not applied to Europeans. The caste spirit permeated the whole administration. When the system of flogging for civil offences was abolished, a period of imprisonment was substituted for the same. These changes were not approved by the people.

Religious

One of the causes of the revolt was the fear among the Hindus that their religion will be destroyed by Christianity. Both the army and civil population were under the fear that the Government intended to make everybody a Christian as the Mohammedans had done before. Missionary activity was extended by the Englishmen in all parts of the country. On many occasions, the meetings of the missionaries were held at the headquarters of the districts under the chairmanship of the Collectors. The Hindu law of property was changed with a view to facilitate the conversion of the Hindus to Christianity. Formerly, a convert from Hinduism was not allowed to inherit property but that hurdle was removed by the enactment of the Converts' Inheritance Act in 1850. The British made no secret of their intention to convert the Indians to Christianity. Mr. Mangles, Chairman of the Directors of the East India Company, made the following statement in the House of Commons: "Providence has entrusted the extensive Empire of Hindustan to England in order that the banner of Christ should wave triumphant from one end of India to the other. Everyone must exert all his strength that there may be no dilatoriness on any account in continuing in the country the grand work of making all Indians Christians". Rev. M. A. Sherring stated thus in 1858-59 in "The Indian Church during the Great Rebellion". "The whole land has been shaken by the missions to its innermost centre. The Hindu trembles for his religion, the Mohammedan for his". The Friend of India, a Calcutta newspaper, published the following extract from a correspondent, "All classes of natives imagine that they are to be converted by force. Amongst the native soldiery this erroneous imagination dangerously exists". The sepoys in the Bengal army had come to believe that the foreigners wanted to make them Christians. The Bengal Hurkaru wrote that the sepoys had come to believe that the Governor-General of India had promised the Home Government to convert them all in three years. Lt. Col. Wheeler distributed tracts and was considered unfit for his post. When asked to explain his conduct, he admitted that he was in the habit of speaking to the natives of all classes about Christianity and he did that "from a conviction that every converted Christian is expected or commanded by the scriptures to make known the glad tidings of salvation to his lost fellow-creatures". Answering the charge of preaching conversion, he categorically admitted, "As to the question whether I have endeavoured to convert sepoys and others to Christianity, I would humbly reply: that has been my object". Lord Canning, Governor-General of India, passed the following orders on the conduct of Wheeler, "I allude the rumours which reached the government that Col. Wheeler had lately addressed the men of his regiment on religious subjects. Col. Wheeler's answers were not satisfactory but no punishment was given". No wonder, a lot of dissatisfaction was created. There was bitter controversy on the subject of conversion in the Calcutta Press. Even the Governor-General was accused of conniving at the conversion of Indians to Christianity. He was guilty of subscribing to every society which had for its object the conversion of the natives. Lord Canning's subscriptions to the Bible Societies and missionary associations were a matter of common knowledge. Col. Sykes refuted in the House of Commons the charge that Christianity was not encouraged by the Government of the East India Company. He quoted reliable figures to show the ever-increasing employment of chaplains and Bishops in India from, 1836-37 to 1855-56. He drew his information from a return read before the House of Commons and asserted that "It will be borne in mind that all this outlay of £2,453,882 in 20 years for Christian purposes was from taxes paid by heathens". He further observed, "Why in India the Company proclaimed its Christianity at the cannon's mouth by saluting the Bishops when they arrived at military stations? The sepoys necessarily asked the cause of the salute and were told it was to do honour to the Head of the Christian Church, the Lord Padre Sahib!" Even Lord Dalhousie wrote thus, "It is announced as a certain fact of very great significance that the young

Prince, Maharaja Duleep Singh had entered into the Christian Community and it is announced also as a matter of great significance that the daughter of the Raja of Coorg had been baptised and that our Gracious Sovereign was her god-mother".

The Commissioner at Fatehpur had put up at his own expense, four pillars at each entrance to the city inscribed in Urdu and Hindi with the "Ten Commandments".

Most of the missionaries who came to India were intolerant, dogmatic and fired by the Victorian zeal and they quoted the Old Testament more often than the New. They regarded the conversion of the whole country to Christianity as only a matter of time and they considered it "ripe for the harvest". They were everywhere, not only in their churches but in prisons, schools and market places. The Indians did not object to their propagating their religion, but they found that they were not content with explaining Christ, but were also busy ridiculing the rites and practices of the Indians. The missionaries claimed a "monopoly of truth" for Christianity. They regarded it not only as their vocation but also their positive duty to convert everyone with a dark skin. India was to be not only a jewel in the British Crown, but also a Christian jewel. They believed that the country was being governed for the good of its inhabitants and Christianity was a part of it.

No wonder, the leaders of the revolution of 1857 raised the cry of religion and faith in danger and the Indian sepoys rallied round their banner. The famous Delhi Proclamation issued between 11 May and 15 May 1857 declared that all Europeans were united on the point of depriving the Army of their religion and to convert them to Christianity by the force of strong measures. In his Proclamation of 6 July 1857 Nana Sahib declared that the Englishmen had calculated that seven or eight thousand Europeans would be sufficient to convert all the people of India to Christianity. A Proclamation issued by Bahadur Shah on 25 August 1857 called upon the Pandits, Fakirs and other learned persons to join the holy war against the English, who stood condemned by the Sunnah and the Sastras. It was declared that the people of Hindustan, both Hindus and Muslims, had been ruined under the tyranny and oppression of the Englishmen. In his circular letter dated 2 January 1858 addressed to the Chiefs of Bundelkhand, Shrimant Maharaja Peshwa Bahadur, the nephew of Nana Sahib, called upon them to defend their faith. The Rani of Jhansi accused Englishmen of having overthrown our religions. They had caused books to be written and circulated throughout the country and brought a number of pressures to spread their religion. Maulvi Liaquat Ali of Allahadbad openly declared Jehad and incited the Muslims to massacre all the Christians. A similar call was made to the Muslims by Birjees Kudur Wali of Oudh in his Proclamation. In his proclamation dated 17 February 1858 Mirza Feroz Shahzada accused the English of committing all kinds of excesses and tyrannies with the object of converting Indians to Christianity by force and of subverting and doing away with the religions of the Hindus and Muslims. He called upon the people to join Jehad against the British.

Military

As regards, the Military cause, there was lot of discontentment among the Indian soldiers. The highest pay attainable by a Sepoy as Subedar of the infantry was less than the minimum pay of a raw European recruit. Very often there was no promotion of an Indian soldier. He may enter as a Risaldar and retire as a Risaldar. The Government did not trust the Indian soldiers. "In every company there are two or three native officers who, when they are too good, are discharged from service with full pay on retirement, on the pretext of rewarding them. So soon as Sepoys become attached to them, so soon as they encroach upon the admiration and respect which must be the exclusive property of European officers, they are immediately discharged". The self respect of the Sepoys was trampled upon at every step. "It is by no means uncommon for an officer to curse and swear at his men on parade and use most disgusting terms of abuse to them". A contemporary

English observer wrote: "The Sepoy is esteemed as an inferior creature. He is swored at. He is treated roughly. He is spoken as a 'Nigger'. He is addressed as 'Suar' or pig. The younger men treated him as an inferior animal".

The number of British troops in India was never very large but the Company was able to recruit without trouble from the native Indians. With the British in the ratio of one in four thousand, the ratio of troops had been fixed by a former Governor-General as one British soldier to three native soldiers and had never been less than one to four. On account of the Crimean War and the trouble in Burma, China and Persia, the ratio had been allowed to become almost one to eight. There were 40,160 European troops as against 3,11,000 native troops and among them were 5,362 British officers.

Originally, the native soldiers were low-caste Afghan or Turkish mercenaries. With a view to make the army more national, the sons of the landowners and peasants were deliberately recruited. In the army of Bengal, three-fifths of the men serving in the 63 infantry regiments came from Avadh, "the nursery of soldiers". As the servants of the British in their home, they were treated there as nothing or even with contempt as the British against the corrupt native government. However, when Avadh was annexed in 1856, all their privileges disappeared. When they went home, they were treated there as nothing or even with contempt as the slaves of the British. Many of them were Brahmins while the cavalry consisted of Muslims.

It is true that the native soldiers seemed to be loyal to the British, but there had been previous instances of trouble among them. In 1806, there had been a mutiny of the native soldiers at Vellore when they were ordered to wear a new style of head-dress which included a leather cockade believed to be made of cow hide or pig skin. In 1824, a regiment which was ordered to go to Burma defied the orders on account of a dispute over cooking pots and also because they believed they were to be transported by sea in defiance of their caste feelings. In 1852, the 38th Native Infantry refused to cross the sea to Burma. However, in 1856, the General Service Enlistment Act was passed to give the authorities absolute power to take the soldiers out of India. To cross the Kala Pani was pollution to the orthodox Hindus who considered themselves to be reduced in caste. No Indian soldier would eat salt pork or ship's biscuits. This was very much resented as the new law was to apply to all the future entrants to the army, which was considered to be a monopoly of a class of people in the country.

The increased ratio of Indian troops to British troops gave a sense of self-confidence to the Indians. There were small mutinies or near-mutinies at different places. These were signs of hatred between the white and coloured people. Almost all of them were caused by the fear that the British were trying to break caste and convert the sepoys to Christianity. Rumours started circulating among the native soldiers. It was rumoured that all the Company's armies had been killed in Burma and all the British in the Crimea. It was said that English women were to be brought to India to marry Indian princes whose children would then become Christians and all sepoys would be baptised. There was to be a mass murder of sepoys by a mine under the parade ground. The British had polluted the sugar and mixed ground bullox's bones with flour and the sepoys were to be forced to eat cow's flesh. Although the government heard all these rumours, it did nothing to discount them. Ignoring the fact that the Indian soldiers regarded service in the form of a trade guild in which son followed father in the handling of weapons, the government officers continued to disregard their customs and religions. Though outwardly all seemed to be calm, below the surface, there was a highly inflammable situation and some common cause was required to unite the different religions against the British and that was provided by the introduction of the greased cartridges.

The Greased Cartridges

The Government of India decided to replace the old heavy brown Bess smooth-broke musket with which most of the Company's army was equipped with new Enfield rifle which had proved very effective in the 'Crimean War'. To load the new rifle entailed extracting from a pouch a cartridge with a greased patch at the top, which was torn off with the teeth, and then used to assist in ramming the bullet down the barrel. The sepoys began to believe that the grease used in this case was made from the fat of a cow or that of a pig. To both the Hindus and the Muslims the use of the greased cartridge was something which was against their religion. The sepoys saw in it an attempt to break their caste and force them to become Christians. At first slowly and then with increasing anger as the stories were spread by agitators, the Indian regiments refused to accept the greased cartridges. General Hearsey and others warned the government against the use of the greased cartridges which seemed to be causing so much anger and distress among the sepoys and suggested that the sepoys be allowed to make their own grease, but they were over-ruled by Adjutant-General who felt that it might make the sepoys think that the old cartridges which they had been using were contaminated. On his advice, Lord Canning decided that the concession would be weakness and he ordered that the cartridges must be used. The British officers who understood their men, were astonished. It is stated that Captain Edward Martineau, musketry instructor at Ambala, angrily pointed out to a member of the staff of the Commander-in-Chief that the order had produced "all the elements of combustion". Loyal servants began to drop hints of sepoys meeting to plot mutiny. The information was passed on to Anson who was the Commander-in-Chief of India, but nothing was done to redress the grievance of the people.

In the following couplet, Bahadur Shah described how the mighty Englishmen who boasted of having defeated Russia and Iran, had been overthrown in India by a simple cartridge:

"Na Iran ne kiya na Shah Russne,

Angrez ko Tabah Kiya Kartoos (Cartouche) ne".

On 26 February 1857, the 19th Native Infantry at Behrampur refused to use the cartridges and was marched to Barrackpore to be disbanded under the eyes of a British regiment specially brought back from Burma. On 29 March 1857 Mangal Pande, a young officer of 34th native infantry, fired at his British Adjutant and Sergeant-Major and called upon his comrades to join him. The guards did not join but also did not disarm him. The result was that Mangal Pande wounded both the Englishmen with his sword and they were also struck by the guards with their muskets, General Hearsey interfered. He roared, "The first man who refuses to march when I give the order is a dead man". The guards submitted and followed him. Mangal Pande lost his nerve. He was caught and hanged. The 34th native infantry was disbanded on 6 May 1857 and its soldiers left for their homes which in many cases was Avadh.

At this critical time when the Bengal Army was simmering with revolt, there was no one in command. As was usual in the hot weather, General Anson and the whole of his headquarters staff had taken themselves off to Simla. With the British troops and officers on leave, the whole military area of the Bengal command was virtually without central direction. The command was left to the seven Divisional Commanders. Major-General William Hewitt of the Meerut Division was almost 70 and unfit for active service. The British troops had been thinned out even more with the recent conquest of the Punjab in 1849 and more troops had to be sent to the North-Western Frontier. Most of them were now north of Meerut and Ambala. At Calcutta, there was one infantry battalion, the next was 400 miles away at Dinapur and there were others at Agra and Lucknow. The result was that in an area half as much as Europe, there were only four battalions and a few reliable batteries of artillery. It was not difficult for the troublemakers to see that their opportunity to strike had come.

On 23 April 1857 the Commanding Officer of the 3rd Light Cavalry, Colonel Smyth, ordered a parade of the regimental skirmishers, 85 picked men, and demanded of them, one after the other, if they would accept the cartridges. One after the other, the men refused, only 5 of them agreeing. When Smyth made his report to Hewitt, he had no option but to set up a Court of Inquiry and when the findings were passed on to Anson, the Commander-in-Chief, he insisted that all the 85 men must be Court-martialled for mutiny. A Court of 15 Indian officers of both Hindu and Muslim faiths was assembled. On 8 May all of them were found guilty sentenced to 10 years' imprisonment with hard labour on the roads. On 10 May the excited cavalry men attacked the jail where the 85 persons were imprisoned. The guard made no resistance and all of them were set free. There was a general revolt. The British officers were killed and the mutineers set off for Delhi.

The Revolt

When the Meerut soldiers appeared in Delhi the next morning, the local infantry joined them, killed their own European officers and seized the city. Bahadur Shah, the Mughal Emperor of Delhi, was put on the throne. Delhi became the centre of the revolt and Bahadur Shah its symbol. The rebellious sepoys from all over the country turned towards Delhi and all the Indian chiefs who took part in the revolt proclaimed their loyalty to the Mughal Emperor. Bahadur Shah also wrote letters to all the Chiefs and rulers of India, asking them to organise a confederacy of Indian states to fight and replace the British regime.

The entire Bengal Army rose in revolt. Avadh, Rohilkhand, the Doab, Bundelkhand, Central India, large parts of Bihar and East Punjab shook off British authority. In many Indian States, the rulers remained loyal to the British Government but their soldiers revolted or were on the brink of revolt. Many of the soldiers of Indore State rebelled and joined the sepoys. More than 20,000 troops of the ruler of Gwalior went over to Tantia Tope and Rani of Jhansi. Many small chiefs of Rajasthan and Maharashtra revolted with the support of the people who were hostile to the British Government. There were local rebellions in Hyderabad and Bengal. Both in Northern and Central India, the mutiny of the sepoys was followed by the popular revolts of the civilian population. After the sepoys had destroyed British authority, the common people rose up in arms and fought with their spears and axes, bows and arrows, lathis and scythes and crude muskets. At many places, the people revolted even before the sepoys did or even when no sepoy regiments were present. In Uttar Pradesh and Bihar the peasants and zamindars attacked the moneylenders and the new zamindars and destroyed the account books and records of debts of the moneylenders. They also attacked the law courts, revenue offices, police stations and revenue records. Even where the people did not revolt, they showed strong sympathy for the rebels. They were happy at the success of the rebels and organised social boycott of those sepoys who remained loyal to the British. They showed active hostility to the British forces, refused to give them help or information and in some cases, even misled them with wrong information.

The revolt at Kanpur was led by Nana Sahib, the adopted son of Bajirao II. Nana Sahib expelled the English from Kanpur with the help of the sepoys and proclaimed himself the Peshwa. He also recognised Bahadur Shah as the Emperor of India and himself his Governor. The chief burden of fighting on behalf of Nana Sahib fell on the shoulders of Tantia Tope. The British garrison at Kanpur surrendered and all of them, except 4 persons, were killed. Later on, Kanpur was captured by Campbell.

The revolt at Lucknow was led by the Begum of Avadh, who declared her son Birjis Kader as the Nawab of Avadh. Helped by the sepoys at Lucknow and the zamindars and peasants of Avadh, the Begum organised an all-out attack on the British. Sir Henry Lawrence was killed during the course of the siege of the Residency. Later on, General Outram and Havelock forced their way into the Residency. They were also besieged but were relieved later on.

Rani Lakshmibai of Jhansi joined the rebels when the British refused to acknowledge her right to adopt an heir to the Gaddi of Jhansi and threatened to treat her as an instigator of the rebellion of the sepoys at Jhansi. She vacillated for some time but later on decided to throw in her lot with the rebels. She was driven out of Jhansi by the British forces after a fierce battle in which "even women were seen working the batteries and distributing ammunition". She captured Gwalior with the help of Tantia Tope and her trusted Afghan guards. Maharaja Sindhia tried to fight against Rani of Jhansi but most of his troops deserted to her and he took refuge at Agra. Rani Jhansi died fighting on 17 June 1858.

Kunwar Singh was the chief organiser of the revolt in Bihar. Although he was nearly 80 years of age at that time, he was perhaps the most outstanding military leader and strategist of the revolt. He fought the British in Bihar and also campaigned in Avadh and Central India. He defeated the British forces near Arrah where he sustained a fatal wound while fighting. He died on 27 April 1858.

CAUSES OF FAILURE OF THE REVOLT

Many causes were responsible for the failure of the revolt of 1857. In the first place, the mutiny was localised. There were many parts of India which were not affected by it at all. Particularly, the territory south of the river Narbada remained undisturbed. Sindh was quiet. Rajputana was loyal. Dost Mohammed remained friendly. Central and Eastern Bengal remained undisturbed. Instead of joining the rebels, the Gurkhas of Nepal rendered meritorious services to the British. In spite of the fact that the Punjab had been conquered from the Sikhs only 8 years before the revolt, it remained quiet. If the people of the Punjab had joined the rebels, the story of the revolt would have been absolutely different. As a matter of fact, the rule of Sir John Lawrence was not very popular and he himself was not certain about the loyalty of the people. Anyhow, the loyalty of the Punjab is made the matter easier for the British. Not only they remained loyal themselves, they helped the government in disarming and guarding the Bengal troops at Lahore, Peshawar and Multan. Those regiments which mutinied were put down. It was, the tranquility of the province that enabled the provincial government to send reinforcements to Delhi. So great was the loyalty of the Punjab, that practically all the troops left the Punjab and even then, there was no trouble. It is contended that if the revolt had not been localised and had spread in every nook and corner of the country, the fate of the country would have been different.

The chief Sirhind rendered excellent help to the British. Sir Dinkar Rao and Salar Jung were responsible for maintaining peace in the territories of Sindhia and the Nizam. Without their devotion and sincerity, things might have been too hard for the British. It is contended that the name of Salar Jung deserves to be mentioned forever by Englishmen with gratitude and admiration.

The rebels failed on account of the lack of leadership among them. It is true that the Rani of Jhansi was a capable woman, but she was neither the head of all the forces nor an experienced general. General Bakht Khan was a brilliant man, but he was not incharge of the whole show. The rebels worked without any common plan. They were short of modern weapons and other materials of war. They fought with ancient weapons such as pikes and swords. They were brave and selfless, but they were ill-disciplined. Sometimes they behaved more like a riotous mob than a disciplined army. There was no centralised leadership. There was no coordination among them in various parts of the country. The rebels were joined together with a common feeling of hatred against foreigners and when British power was overthrown from any area, they did not know what sort of power to create in its place. They were suspicious and jealous of one another and often indulged in suicidal quarrels. The Begum of Avadh quarrelled with Maulavi Ahmedullah and the Mughal princes with the sepoy generals, Azimullah asked Nana Sahib not to visit Delhi lest he be over-shadowed by Bahadur Shah. Selfishness of the leaders sapped the strength of the revolt and prevented its consolidation. The peasantry having destroyed the revenue records and the account books of the moneylenders, became passive and did not know what to do next. The British succeeded in crushing the leaders of the revolt one by one.

The rebels had no forward-looking programme to be implemented after the capture of power. The absence of a modern and progressive programme enabled the reactionary princes and Zamindars to seize the levers of power of the movement. It is these people who had already been defeated by the British and there was nothing new in them which could help them to succeed against the British.

The moneylenders were the targets of the attacks by the villagers. They were naturally hostile to the revolt. The merchants also gradually became unfriendly towards the rebels, who were compelled to impose heavy taxes on them in order to finance the war or to seize their stocks of foodstuffs to feed the army. The merchants often concealed their wealth and goods and refused to give free supply to the rebels. The Zamindars of Bengal remained loyal to the British. The hostility of Bihar peasants towards the Zamindars frightened the Bengal Zamindars. The big merchants of Bombay, Calcutta and Madras supported the British because their main profits came from foreign trade and economic connections with the British merchants.

The educated Indians also did not support the revolt. They stood for ending the backwardness of their country and they believed that the British government in India was destroying the feudal forces in the country and bringing in a new era of progress in the country. Their view was that the rebels of 1857 stood for the old order along with its superstitions.

The British had great personalities in Sir John Lawrence, Outram, Havelock, Nicholson, Edwardes, Neil, etc., who controlled the situation from the beginning to the end and the Indians were no match for them.

The personal character of the Bengal troops was also responsible for the failure of the revolt. They were arrogant and were hated in every part of India to which they were sent. At many places, the rebels were crushed by the people themselves.

The year 1857 was favourable to the British in many ways. The Crimean War was over in 1856. The Chinese War was just over. The British armies were free to throw their weight against the mutineers. Russia was defeated in the Crimean War and there was no danger from that quarter. Internationally, the Indian rebels were isolated.

As the British had control over the seas, they were in a position to pour men and materials into India with practically no difficulty. A large number of troops were at once sent to India. The Indians fighting with primitive weapons were no match for the British with the Enfield rifles.

The only hope of success for the rebels was to have quick victories. Time factor was against them. It could be taken for granted that the English would be able to get reinforcements from outside and when that happened, the revolt collapsed.

The rebels appealed to all other sections of society, but no appeal was made to the peasants or tillers of the soil. While all other classes were promised a better deal, the peasants were ignored altogether. The inability of rebel leaders to rally the peasants to their side doomed their cause. The revolt got its strength from the princes, ruined noblemen and other feudal interests and those forces were incapable of overthrowing the British Government in India.

The view of Dr. A.R. Desai is that while England was a capitalist country, India was essentially feudal, and the victory of the former was a foregone conclusion. To quote him, "A capitalist nation is socially, politically, economically and culturally stronger than a feudal people. A capitalist nation has a high sense of patriotism and nationalism since, unlike the feudal people who are physically separated, socially disunited and politically unamalgamated, it is socially, economically and politically high integrated, living under one political regime and single economic system. This is why throughout the whole history of British conquest, we hardly come across Britons who betrayed the interests of Britain in India, in contrast to hundreds of Indians, Princes, Generals and merchants who went over to the British and assisted them to dominate India". R.P. Dutt says, "The rising of 1857 was in its essential character and dominant leadership the revolt of the old conservative and feudal forces and dethroned potentates for their rights and privileges which they saw in process for destruction. The reactionary character of the rising, prevented any wide measure of popular support and doomed it to failure". (*India Today*, p. 274).

About the causes of the failure of the revolt of 1857 Dr. Tara Chand says that its failure was almost a foregone conclusion. It was actuated by pure negations. It was not inspired by any positive creative idea. It did not entertain either the vision of a higher social order or of a higher political system. It was a transient intoxication and not a settled, permanent transformation of the will of the people. As it was an almost spontaneous episodic outburst, there was no stable well-ordered organisation behind the movement as a whole. It lacked plan, programme and funds. The only thing which united the rebels was the desire to eliminate foreign rule and that was equated with the physical destruction of the foreign personnel. There was no understanding of the character of the political organisation of the enemy, no realisation that the extermination of the individuals was not tantamount to the break-up of the system. It was dimly perceived that Hindu-Muslim cooperation was necessary, but it was not realised that the nation was an organic unity, that no mere temporary cooperation of independent units was enough and that a fusion of communication into a political organism alone could guarantee success against a modern power. The cause for which they fought was not unjust, but its ethos was inadequate. There was little discipline among the rebels and their loyalties were fragile. Intellectually they were no match for their enemies whose military technique was based upon science. In strategy and tactics, the British forces were far superior to the Indians and the British Commanders were well-trained men and many of them possessed extensive experience of war. These forces worked under the orders of a highly organised Government in India which was backed by ample resources in men and money of the British people and the British Government. So long as the central organs of the Company's administration continued to function, the loss of peripheral territories was not fatal and so long as reinforcements could be supplied from across the seas, the citadel of the British rule in India was safe from the storms that blew all round.

EFFECTS OF THE REVOLT

The Revolt of 1857 did not leave India unaffected. It is contended that "Perhaps a more fortunate occurrence than the Mutiny of 1857 never occurred in India". It swept the Indian sky clear of many clouds. It disbanded a lazy, pampered army which thought that in its 100 years of life, it had done splendid service. It showed to the world that the English possessed courage and national spirit which made light of disaster and which did not care for the heavy odds.

As a direct result of the Revolt of 1857, the English East India Company was ended and the Government of India was taken over by the Crown. The Board of Control and the Court of Directors were abolished and their place was taken by the Secretary of State for India and the India Council.

There was a change in the policy of the Government of India towards the Indian Princes. The loyalty of the Rajput, Maratha and Sikh Chiefs and of the Nizam had been of very great value in preventing the spread the revolt. An attempt was now made to integrate as well as reward them. Their territories were guaranteed and some received material recognition for special service. The most significant change was psychological. They were now regarded as members of an order and not just survivals and anachronisms. They were an integral part of the Indian Empire and had personal relation with the monarch. Men like Lord Mayo and Lytton saw them as props of British Imperialism in India. They were to be encouraged to become enlightened despots. Lord Lytton even proposed an Indian Peerage for them. Queen Victoria declared in her Proclamation of 1858 that the British Government in future would not annex the Indian States. The Indian Princes were assured the right of adoption and succession. They were given Sanads and certificates of recognition of their status. The Government of India began to rely more and more on the Indian princes on account of the alienation of the feelings of the Indians.

There was a change in the land policy of the Government. The tactless treatment of the Taluqdars (zamindars) of Avadh had, at one time, confronted the British with a whole province in revolt. It was noted that it was the dispossessed landlords in Bihar who turned the Mutiny into something like an agrarian revolt. There was the aristocratic reaction in land policy. The extension of the Permanent Settlement of Bengal was seriously considered. Short of this, their estates were safeguarded. They themselves were cherished with such devices as Honorary Magistrates. The tendency to come between them and their tenants was checked. They were treated as an important prop to the administration. An attempt was made to revise the Punjab Settlement in favour of the dispossessed landlords.

There was a change in the policy of the Government of India to Westernise the Indians. The British view that all good things came from the West and more of them the better, received a rude shock. The revolt was considered in one respect as a resurgence of the old order against Western innovations. It was now thought that the upper classes must be conciliated as the humbler classes followed them. The upper classes were the most conservative in a conservative country and all interference was given up in the future.

There was an extensive reorganisation of the army in India. The Bengal Army virtually ceased to exist. The separation of the three armies of Bengal, Bombay and Madras was retained because each group had its own tradition and their distinctness had prevented the spread of the Mutiny virus from the Bengal Army to the other armies. However, the Bengal Army was completely recast. The Company's European troops, 16,000 strong, were paid off or absorbed into the British army. The rest of the army was reformed into community regiments, two battalions of which were always bridged with a British battalion. The personnel of the army was modified. The Brahmin element from Uttar Pradesh was heavily reduced and its place was taken by Gurkhas, Sikhs, Jats and Rajputs of the Punjab. The northern element was later increased with infusions of Pathans and Punjabis at the expense of men from the South. The ratio of European to Indian troops in the Bengal Army was increased to parity and nearly the to two for the army as a whole (65,000 to 1,40,000). The artillery of the old army was abolished except for a few mountain batteries. Officers continued to be Europeans but more of them were appointed and they lived in far closer touch with their men than before. As the cost of a European soldier was 4 or 5 times than that of sepoy, the military budget of India swelled as a result of reorganisation. Military positions and strategic points were transferred to the European troops. Sir Richard Temple wrote thus: "At every large military station in the Empire, there are (now) enough Europeans to hold their own even in the event of a Mutiny". In the new native army, men of higher caste were excluded. The Bengal army virtually became the Punjab army and new army was organised on the basis of division and counterpoise. Jawaharlal Nehru says that "The policy of balance and counter-poise was deliberately furthered in the Indian army. Various groups were so arranged as to prevent any sentiment of national unity growing amongst them, and tribal and communal loyalties were encouraged. Every effort was to isolate the army from the people and even ordinary newspapers not allowed to reach the Indian troops. All the key positions were kept in the hands of the Englishmen and no Indian could hold the King's Commission. No Indian could be employed at the Army Headquarters, except as a petty clerk in the Accounts Department. For additional protection, the more effective weapons of warfare were not given to the Indian forces; they were reserved for the British troops in India. These British troops were always kept with the English regiments in all the vital centres of India to serve as 'Internal Security Troops', for suppression of disorder and to over-awe the people". The exclusion of the Indians from the artillery minimised the dangers. The British view was that an artillery manned exclusively by Europeans "is to India what a Channal Fleet is to England. As long as it is strong, we are all but secure against any attempts at disturbance. It will keep all in check, Sikhs included". The attitude of the Government of India towards the Indian soldiers is clear from the following passage in a Despatch to the Secretary of State for India in the time of Lord Lawrence while recommending the supply of inferior type of rifles to Indian soldiers: "After the events of 1857, which it is impossible to forget and which it would be unwise to ignore, blind and implicit confidence in a mercenary native army liable to be swept by a sudden, almost unaccountable impulses and prejudices, is out of the question and the show or prevalence of such a feeling would more probably be viewed as symptom of weaknesses than as a proof of trust".

The Revolt of 1857 created a lot of bitterness between the Indians and the Englishmen. Garratt says, that "the English killed their prisoners without trial and in a manner held by all Indians to be the height of barbarity—sewing Mohammedans in pig skins, smearing them with pork fat before execution and burning their bodies and forcing Hindus to defile themselves. They also massacred thousands of civilian population not only in Delhi, but also in the country. Certain guilty villages were marked out for destruction and all the men inhabiting them were slaughtered and the indiscriminate burning of their inhabitants occurred wherever our armies moved". (*An Indian Commentary*, p. 112.)

The revolt resulted in the tightening of the control of India from London. The English foreign policy was linked up with European politics. The centre of interest in India shifted from external policy to the internal development.

Another effect of the Mutiny was that the Muslim renaissance which had been growing in Delhi before the Mutiny got an irreparable set-back. The cultural blossoms were blighted. C.F. Andrews says, "It is not difficult to trace the fatal havoc to budding spiritual life which one year of Mutiny wrought. Decay immediately overtook the revival of learning in Delhi from which it never recovered". Calcutta (now Kolkata), the centre of Hindu renaissance escaped the horrors of Mutiny and was saved.

When the rebellion started, both the Hindus and Muslims took part in it in large numbers. However, the Muslims were more violently anti-British than the Hindus and the British feared the Muslims more than the Hindus. The result was that the hand of repression fell more heavily on the Muslims than on the Hindus. Many of the leading Muslims were hanged or exiled, e.g., Nawab Sahibs of Jhajjar, Ballabhgarh, Faruknagar and Farukabad. 24 Shahzadas were hanged in Delhi on 18 November 1857 alone. Muslim quarters were everywhere the target. Muslim property was widely confiscated. The result of all this was that the Muslims came to have a grievance against the Hindus. The differences between the two began to develop and they drifted away from each other. The problem of Hindu-Muslim unity became impossible to tackle and ultimately that led to the Partition of India in 1947.

REVIEW QUESTIONS

1. What was the character of the Revolt of 1857?
2. Examine the causes that led to the Revolt of 1857.
3. Examine the significance of the Revolt of 1857.
4. Throw light on the causes of the failure of the Revolt of 1857.
5. Critically analyse the impact of the Revolt of 1857 on India.
6. What was the result of the Revolt of 1857?
7. Discuss the nature of the Revolt of 1857. Why did it fail?

SUGGESTED READINGS

Ball, Charles: *History of the Indian Mutiny.*
Edwardes, Michael: *Battles of the Indian Mutiny,* London, 1963.
Forbes, Mitchell, W.: *The Relief of Lucknow,* London, 1962.
Forest, Sir G.W.: *History of the Indian Mutiny.*
Griffiths, Charles: *A Narrative of the Siege of Delhi,* London, 1910.
Harris, John: *The Indian Mutiny.* London, 1973.
Hilton, Maj. Gen. R.: *The Indian Mutiny,* London, 1957.
Holmes, T. Rice: *The Indian Mutiny,* London, 1904.
Innes: *The Sepoy Revolt.*
Joyce, M.: *Ordeal at Lucknow* (1938).
Kay and Malleson: *History of the Indian Mutiny.*
Kaye, J.W.: *History of the Sepoy War.* London, 1880.
Khan, Sir Syed Ahmed: *The Causes of the Indian Revolt* (1873).
Kincaid, C.A.: *Laxmi Bai, Rani of Jhansi.*
Majumdar, R.C.: *History of the Freedom Movement in India,* Vol. I.
Majumdar, R.C.: *The Mutiny and Revolt of 1857.*
Malleson, Col. G.B.: *The Indian Mutiny of 1857,* London, 1912.
McMunn, Sir G.: *The Indian Mutiny in Perspective,* London, 1931.
Mehta, Asoka: *1857.*
Nigam, N.K.: *Delhi in 1857.*
Palmer. J.A.B.: *The Mutiny Outbreak at Meerut in 1957.*
Pearson, Hesketh: *The Hero of Delhi,* London, 1939.
Sen, S.N.: *Eighteen Fifty-seven.*
Smith, Bosworth: *Life of Lord Lawrence.*
Spear, T.G.P.: *Twilight of the Mughals* (1951).
Thompson, E.: *The Other Side of the Medal* (1925).
Trevelyan, G.S.: *Cawnpore.*
Trotter, L.J.: *Life of John Nicholson* (1905).

15   Canning to Lytton

LEARNING OBJECTIVES

- Give an account of the events, policies and reforms in the reigns of all the administrators from Lord Canning to Lord Lytton
- Give an estimate of Lord Lytton

LORD CANNING (1856-62)

The most important event of the reign of Lord Canning was the Mutiny which broke out in 1857 and was suppressed in 1858. This subject has already been discussed at length.

In spite of the fact that the mutineers were responsible for a lot of destruction of English property and lives and there was a demand for retaliation, Lord Canning kept his head cool and refused to follow that course. He continued to follow a policy of pacification even at the risk of personal unpopularity. In a letter to Lord Grenville, Lord Canning defended his policy in these words: "As long as I have any breath in my body, I will pursue no other policy than that which I have been following; not only for the reason of expediency and policy above stated but because it is just. I will not govern in anger. Justice, and that as stern and inflexible as law and might can make it, I will deal out. But I will never allow an angry or indiscriminating act or word to proceed from the Government of India as long as I am responsible for it. I don't care two-straws for the abuse of the papers, British or Indian. I am forever wondering at myself for not doing so, but it really is the fact. Partly from want of time to care, partly because with an enormous task before me all other cares look small... .

"I don't want you to...do more than defend me against unfair or mistaken attack. But do take up and assert boldly that, whilst we are prepared, as the first duty of all, to strike down resistance without mercy, wherever it shows itself, we acknowledge that, resistance over deliberate justice and calm patient reason are to resume their way; that we are not going, either in anger or from indolence, to punish wholesale, whether by wholesale hangings or burnings, or by the less violent but not one jot less offensive course of refusing trust and countenance and favour and honour to any man because he is of a class or creed. Do this and get others to do it, and you will serve India more than you would believe".

When there was a demand for his recall, he wrote thus to the Home Government: "No taunts or sarcasm, come from what quarter they may, will turn me from the path which I believe to be that of my public duty. I believe that a change in the head of the Government of India at this time (1858), if it took place under circumstances which indicated a reputation on the part of the Government of England of the policy which has hitherto been pursued towards the rebels of Oudh, would seriously retard the pacification of the country. I believe that *that policy has been from the beginning merciful without weakness, and indulgent without compromise of the dignity of the Government... .*

"Firm in these convictions I will not, in a time of unexampled difficulty, danger, and toil, down of my own act the high trust which I have the honour to hold".

One of the effects of the Mutiny was that the English East India Company was ended and the Government of India was taken over by the Crown. This happened in 1858 when a formal declaration to that effect was made. Lord Canning was thus the last Governor-General of the English East India Company and the first Viceroy under the Crown.

In 1861 was passed the famous Indian Councils Act. This Act provided for the setting up of legislatures in the Presidencies and the extension of the Viceroy's Executive Council by the addition of additional members for legislative purposes.

In 1861 was passed a law by which Chartered High Courts were set up in place of Supreme Courts and Adalats of the English Company.

In 1859 was passed the Bengal Rent Act. It applied to Bihar, Agra and C.P. According to it, every ryot who had held his land at the same rent for 20 years was to be treated as if he had held it since 1793. Tenants who had held land for 12 years were to enjoy occupancy rights and their rents could be enhanced only after due enquiry by a court of law.

In 1861, Baird Smith proposed the extension of the principles of the permanent settlement of Bengal to the whole of India. In 1862, Sir Charles Wood, Secretary of State for India, approved of the proposal. However, in the time of Lord Mayo, the proposal was opposed and in the time of Lord Ripon, it was completely given up.

Lord Canning's Government had to face the problem of finance. There was a deficit of 36 million. That was partly due to the expenditure involved on the suppression of the Mutiny and partly due to the disorganisation of society and administration. The great need of the moment was economy, retrenchment and the increase in the proceeds of revenue. A large number of troops were disbanded as they were no longer required. James Wilson, a great economist of England, came to India in 1859 and was entrusted with the work of rehabilitating the finances of the country. He died within less than a year of his arrival in India and his work was carried on by Samuel Laing. Before his death, Wilson had recommended the imposition of three new taxes and those were income-tax, license duty on trades and professions and an excise duty on home-grown tobacco. The proposal of income-tax was accepted as an experimental measure. It was to be at the rate of 5 per cent for five years on incomes of ₹500 and more a year. Wilson also established a uniform import duty of 10 per cent. He also provided for economies in civil and military expenditure. Salt duties were to be raised. The result of the reforms of Wilson and Laing was that by the time Lord Canning left India, there was no deficit budget.

Certain reforms were made in the army. The British learnt a lesson from the Mutiny. Rules were laid down for a definite proportion between the Indian and European soldiers. British officers were organised into three staff-corps for the three Presidencies. The European regiments of the English Company were amalgamated with the forces of the Queen. During this period, laws were codified. The Indian Penal Code which was drafted by Lord Macaulay, became law in 1858 after the necessary changes. It was followed by the Code of Criminal Procedure next year.

In 1861, a very severe famine visited North-Western Provinces of Agra and Oudh and some parts of the Punjab and Rajputana. Mortality was about ten per cent of the population. The famine was partly due to the after-effects of the Mutiny. There was also a failure of rain and consequently of crops. A lot of money was spent by the Government to give relief to the people.

In 1859 and 1860, there took place disputes between the European indigo planters and the Bengal peasantry. The situation became very serious and disturbances took place. A commission was appointed to investigate into the matter. It was ultimately settled by the Secretary of state that a tenant should not be liable to criminal prosecution for refusal to fulfil a civil contract to grow indigo.

As regards Lord Canning himself, it has rightly been pointed out that no Governor-General could excel him in intellectual qualities. He worked so hard that he practically killed himself. He did not care either for physical exercise or for mental relaxation. Although he was very cold and reserved in his manners, he was dutiful, noble and generous. He was responsible for suppression of the Mutiny with great tact and energy. He was "a nobleman who never, in the midst of greatest peril, allowed his judgment to be swayed by passion or his fine sense of honour and justice to be tarnished by even a passing feeling of revenge". According to Trotter, "After all deductions, his name will stand fair in English memories as that of a fearless, true-hearted Englishman who encountered on the whole with credit the two-fold misfortune of a Great Sepoy Revolt and a predecessor unmatched in Indian history".

According to Lord Elgin, "Poor Canning certainly never gave himself a good chance; at least not during the last year or two of his reign here. He took no exercise and not even such relaxation of the mind as was procurable, though that is not much in the situation of Governor-General. When I told him that I should ask two or three people to dine with me daily, in order to get acquainted with all the persons I ought to know, and to talk matters over with them by candlelight, so as to save daylight for other work, he said: 'I was always so tired by dinner-time that I could not speak".

According to Alexander Grant, "A cultivated man of patient thought and perseverance of most genial yet inflexible mind, his great defect was want of decision in time of emergency; but his irresolution and vacillation were undoubtedly the result of high conscientiousness, of almost morbid scruples, which on some occasions during the Mutiny were extremely perilous. The strength of his character and of his true devotion to his work was best seen on the establishment of order and in his dealing generously with the Native chiefs".

According to Lord Curzon, Lord Canning "stands in Indian history as one of the most pathetic but also one of the most heroic figures that have represented the name and upheld the honour of England".

LORD ELGIN (1862-63)

Lord Elgin was the son-in-law of Lord Durham, the famous author of the Durham Report. Before his coming to India, he had already worked as Governor of Canada and jamindar. His period of office was a brief one as he died at Dharamsala after 18 months. He merely tried to follow in the footsteps of his predecessor. He avoided levying new taxes. He tried to keep down the military expenditure.

Lord Elgin held a large number of Durbars at Benaras, Kanpur, Agra and Ambala. The object of these Durbars was to bring the Indian States nearer the British Government.

In his time, the Wahabis gave trouble. They were defeated and their stronghold at Malka was completely destroyed in 1861. The Wahabis were a fanatical sect of the Muslims living on the North-West Frontier.

According to Lord Curzon, "Lord Elgin was a sagacious, industrious, cheerful man who did all that he had to do conscientiously and without ever giving offence, but withal he possessed courage and no small common sense".

LORD LAWRENCE (1864-69)

Sir John (afterwards) Lord Lawrence came into prominence when he was appointed the Chief Commissioner of the Punjab after its annexation. It was through his tact that the Punjab remained calm during the Mutiny. He is rightly called "the saviour of India and organiser of victory". He was a very hard-working man and hardly any clerk would have worked harder than he did. His appointment was an exception to the general rule that no Indian civil servant should be appointed the Governor-General of India. His period of office was a success in every way.

Sir John Lawrence followed the so-called policy of masterly inactivity with regard to Afghanistan. He would not like to interfere into the internal affairs of that country unless some other power tried to interfere in the same country. In that case, the Indian armies were to go to Afghanistan to help the Afghans. He refused to side with any party in the struggle for succession to the throne after the death of Dost Mohammad. He was always prepared to accept the *de facto* ruler of the country. This policy was followed by Lord Mayo and Lord Northbrook. It was reversed by Lord Lytton with disastrous consequences.

He had to fight the Bhutan War. The Bhutanese used to make raids into the British territory. Mr. Ashley Eden was deputed to negotiate on the question of raids. The Bhutanese forced Mr. Eden to sign a humiliating treaty by which the Duars were surrendered to them. When the British Government came to know of it, it repudiated the treaty and sent a huge force. To begin with, the English were defeated. However, later on they were able to recover their position. Ultimately, a treaty was made by which Bhutanese surrendered Duars and they were to get an annual.

In 1866, there was a famine in Orissa. There was a terrible loss of life. The Government utterly failed to come to the rescue of the people. There was another famine in 1868-69. It affected Rajputana and Bundelkhand. A Famine Commission was appointed to consider the best means of fighting famines. Every effort was to be made by the Government to prevent deaths by starvation.

Lawrence did a lot for the economic progress of the country. A large number of railways, canals and public works were started. He also started the principle of raising money for reproductive works.

John Lawrence was an advocate of the cause of the peasantry. By the Punjab Tenancy Act, the occupancy rights of the tenants were recognised in certain cases. This law is known as the "bulwark and a charter of a contented peasantry". By the Oudh Tenancy Act, about one-fifth of the total number of ryots were granted occupancy rights at fair rents was to be increased only through a court of law. Both these laws were passed in 1868.

V.A. Smith gives his estimate of John Lawrence in these words: "The validity of the arguments against the appointment of a member of the civil service of India to the office of the Governor-General was confirmed rather than discredited by the history of viceroyalty of Sir John Lawrence. He was never able to shake off the habits of the Punjab official of old days and admittedly was too indifferent to the ordinary daily maintenance of the dignity of great office. His reputation rests upon his administration of the Punjab after the annexation and on the invaluable services rendered by him at the time of the Mutiny, not on his work as Viceroy, which could have been done as well or better by a worse man".

According to Temple, "The prevailing sentiment in his public life was a love for duty. Though his temper was strong, and on occasions warm, yet in his nature judgment and reason reigned supreme. As a subsidiary element caution was present with him in the highest degree and there never was in India a more cautious statesman than he. It being an object of the first importance with him to foresee the course of all affairs, he remembered that prescience could be required only by careful reflection..... . To weigh both sides of every question evenly and strike the balance, to eliminate passion, favour, prejudice or misleading sentiment, and fixed the gaze on exact justice alone, were maxims uppermost in his mind. He acted according to this principle in judging of the conduct and character of officers whose fates he held in the hollow of his hands. To those who, notwithstanding their gifts and accomplishments, lacked the fundamental condition of zeal for public duty he would show no consideration. In equitable discrimination of the diverse moral and intellectual qualities of the numerous subordinates under his command he has not been surpassed by any man of his generation in India. He did not at that time arouse so much enthusiasm as his brother (Henry) among large numbers of men, nor win so extensive a popularity. But he was respected by all, admired by most and beloved by many".

According to Lord Lytton, "No statesman since Warren Hastings has administered the Government of India with a genius and an experience as exclusively trained and developed in her service, as those of the illustrious man whose life now closed in the fullness of time, though not of age, bequeaths to his country a bright, example of all that is noblest in the high qualities for which the civil service of India has justly been renowned, and in which, with such examples before it, it will never be deficient".

According to Lord Curzon, "the fact is that Lawrence was unfitted both by temperament and training for work in the peculiar conditions by which the Viceroy is bound. Essentially a man of action rather than of speech, he was intolerant of discussion and debate, and could not accustom himself to the slow and ponderous procession of the departmental files. All his life he had been used to give orders and to be obeyed; now he was in harness with a troublesome and factious team whom he could not in general overrule, and moreover, he found himself not merely thwarted but widely traduced. He was exceedingly sensitive under attack, had not the resilience of temper to make him react to the situation as it developed, and in common with many other Viceroys, thought himself insufficiently supported at home". Again, "The reign of Sir John Lawrence, honourable and strenuous as it was, generally regarded as demonstrating the undesirability of raising even the most eminent of Indian civilians to the Viceregal throne. Allowing that personal idiosyncrasies were the most potent factor in his particular case, the administration of Lawrence did incidentally suggest that the potential danger of the experiment exceeded its advantages, and it has never since been repeated".

LORD MAYO (1869-72)

Lord Mayo succeeded Sir John Lawrence. Although he was selected by Disraeli, he was not disturbed by Gladstone when he became Prime Minister. He was popular with the Indian princes and the European community. He had a charming personality.

As regards Afghanistan, he continued the policy of Sir John Lawrence. It is true that he met Sher Ali, the Afghan ruler, at Ambala in 1869, but he refused to commit himself. He was able to win over Sher Ali by his tact and personal charm.

Lord Mayo was responsible for the foundation of the Mayo College at Ajmer for the education of the children of the Indian princes. Duke of Edinburgh, the second son of Queen Victoria, visited India in 1869.

The Red Sea cable was laid in 1870. This brought about a lot of change in the position of the Governor-General *vis-à-vis* the Home Government. According to Lord Curzon, "The introduction of the electric telegraph marked the beginning of the change. The Governor-General both lost and gained in the process. On the one hand, a very necessary check was placed upon his initiative, and he could no longer wage war or make treaties, or commit his employers in England behind their backs, conscious that even if a year after the event, they censured the agent, they could not reverse the act. The Governor-General ceased henceforward to be a quasi-independent potentate. A Wellesley or a Hastings, perhaps even a Dalhousie, became impossible. On the other hand, though the Viceroy was still exposed to the curb of Whitehall, sometimes pulled in his mouth with quite unnecessary violence, he was freed from the tempestuous caprice of the Court of Directors and the internecine conflict between the rival authorities in London. The loss of concrete power was compensated by the greater security of position. Viceroys may still be obliged or may elect to resign. But we no longer read of the acrimonious exchange of affronts, almost of insults, of abrupt dismissals, and petulant recalls" (*British Government in India*, Vol. I, p. 108.)

Lord Mayo started the process of decentralisation of finance in India. He took the first step in this direction in 1870. The provinces were given a certain amount of money and also certain departments for management.

Lord Mayo was assassinated in 1872 by a fanatical Pathan in the Andaman Islands. According to Dr. Smith, "Lord Mayo during his three years of office justified the hopes of the statesmen who had appointed him, and proved himself to be a thoroughly efficient Governor-General and Viceroy. His exceptional personal charm endeared him especially to the rulers of the protected States who regarded him as the ideal representative of the sovereign. He worked hard at all the problems of administration and lost his life owing to his zealous efforts to improve the defective system of government in the convict settlements of the Andaman Islands". According to P.E. Roberts, "His winning manners and universal popularity were more than engaging personal attributes—they became imperial assets of great value. They won for him the real regard and willing co-operation of the protected chiefs and enabled the complicated mechanism of Indian bureaucracy during his viceroyalty, to work with a minimum of friction and maximum of efficiency". In the words of Rushbrook Williams, "With the Governor-Generalship of Lord Mayo, we may trace the beginning of that steady development of India along lines leading inevitably to the direction of responsible Government within the British Commonwealth".

LORD NORTHBROOK (1872-76)

Lord Northbrook was a man of caution. He was possessed of a high character and sound administrative experience. He did not try to introduce anything new and merely followed the policy of his predecessors. To quote him, "The main object of my policy was to let things go quietly on-to give the land rest". He declared in 1873 that "my aim has been to take off taxes and stop unnecessary legislation". He was not a fluent writer or speaker but possessed considerable independence of judgment.

As regards Afghanistan, he continued the policy of Lawrence and Mayo. He held a conference with the Afghan envoy at Simla in 1873 but refused to commit himself. He resigned in 1876 as his views differed from the Government of Disraeli with regard to the policy in Afghanistan.

In his time, the Kuka movement got a momentum in the Punjab. The Kukas were very daring and murdered many Muslims. Every punishment awarded to the Kukas added to their fanaticism and strength. In 1878, a band of these Kukas attacked the Fort of Malodh near Ludhiana. Another band tried to enter the town of Malerkotla. An attempt was made to capture the treasury and make the people revolt. The Government took timely action. The Deputy Commissioner was able to suppress the rebels. After a summary trial, 50 persons were blown away by guns. There was a lot of agitation and both the Commissioner and Deputy Commissioner were dismissed.

During his period of office, the Gaekwad of Baroda was tried by a commission on the charge of torture of women, attempt to poison the British Resident, spoliation of merchants and banks and mal-treatment of the relatives of his late brother. The result of the trial was unfortunate. The official members held the Gaekwad of Baroda guilty, while the non-nofficial members held him to be non-guilty. In spite of this, the Gaekwad was removed from his *Gaddi* on ground of misgovernment and misconduct. The Rajah was sent away to Madras (now Chennai).

In 1873-74, a famine broke out in Bihar and a part of Bengal. A lot of money was spent to lessen the sufferings of the people.

According to Lord Curzon, "Lord Northbrook was a quite sound man of what in England would be termed the Whig type mind, just and humane in his administration and conscientious in all his acts. He was as unlike his predecessor as the latter had been unlike Lawrence, for he was difficult in manner, disliked all parade and pageantry, and was not a good speaker. I often heard him in later years in the House of Lords, where he was greatly respected but left no impression of power. He never lost his regard for India, and of all the ex-Viceroys was the one who showed the most continuous interest in Indian affairs, corresponding with me regularly during my term of office, as he had done with my predecessors, even though he had left the country for thirty years. Of all the British rulers of India he was also the one with the keenest taste for art. Himself the owner in England of a fine collection of paintings, and possessing artistic susceptibilities of no mean order, he took seriously in hand the completion of the Government House collection of pictures and, under the mistaken idea that the Indian genius could be or ought to be trained in Western schools of painting, accumulated a number of European pictures in the Museum at Calcutta, which in the succeeding quarter of a century were gradually dispersed, having exercised no influence whatever upon the Eastern mind".

LORD LYTTON (1876-80)

Lord Lytton had great administrative experience at the time of his appointment. He was a great writer and a brilliant speaker. He was specially sent by Disraeli to inaugurate a new spirited foreign policy towards Afghanistan. Suffice it to say that he precipitated the Second Afghan War and was responsible for the disasters which the Indian troops met there. He has been universally condemned for his Afghan policy.

He was responsible for passing the Vernacular Press Act. The details of this Act are given in the chapter on the history of the Press. This Act was a discriminatory one and no wonder the Indians condemned him for that.

Lord Lytton suggested the formation of an Indian Privy Council of ruling chiefs to advise the Viceroy. His suggestion was not accepted, but a similar thing was later on set up in India after the passing of the Government of India Act, 1919 in the form of Narendra Mandal or Chamber of Princes.

Lord Lytton was opposed to the tendency of the courts of India to pass lenient punishments in those cases in which the Europeans were involved.

The British Parliament passed the Royal Titles Act which conferred upon the sovereign of England the title of Kaisar-i-Hind. Lord Lytton held in 1877 a magnificent Durbar at Delhi and Queen Victoria was proclaimed the Empress of India. The effect of this was the lowering of the position of the native princes. However, it was merely a formal declaration of a patent fact.

In 1876-78, a very severe famine visited Madras, Bombay, Mysore, Hyderabad and some parts of the Punjab and C.P. Famine was followed by cholera and fever. Owing to the mismanagement and defective relief measures of the Madras Government, there was a terrible loss of life. It took two years to check the famine. The sufferings of the people forced the Government to examine thoroughly the whole question of famine relief whenever it occurred. A Famine Commission was appointed to go into the whole question of famine relief. The Commission submitted a report which forms the foundation of the existing relief measures. The main principles adopted were the employment of the able-bodied persons on relief works. Those who were unable to do any work were to be given gratuitous help by the Government. A Famine Fund was to be set up in every province and the object of every province was to contribute every year towards that Fund. That Fund was to be allowed to grow so that the same may be used at the time of emergency. Railways were constructed and canals were to be dug to meet the danger of famines. According to Smith, "Lord Lytton deserves high credit for sound views on foreign policy, thoroughly thought out and expressed with forceful lucidity. The whole existing system of famine administration rests on the foundation well and truly laid by him".

Many financial reforms were carried out in the time of Lord Lytton. These were partly due to the efforts of John Strachy who became the Finance Member after giving up the Lieutenant-Governorship of North-Western Province. Before Lytton, salt tax was levied at different rates in different provinces. Negotiations were made with the various native States which were producing salt and they were asked to give up their right of manufacturing salt in return for some compensation. The result of this was that salt duties were equalised in all the parts of India. The customs lines or hedges created for the purpose of preventing the import of untaxed salt from native States into British India were abolished.

Lord Lytton followed a policy of free trade. He abolished import duties on 29 commodities. He removed 5 per cent duties on cotton cloth. The result was that there was a lot of expansion in the overseas trade.

Lord Mayo had taken the first step towards financial decentralisation. In 1877, Lord Lytton took the second step. Some more departments were given to the provinces and more sources of revenues were given to them. The object was to give to provinces incentive for efficiency and economy.

Lord Lytton opened the Mohammedan Anglo-Oriental College at Aligarh. Later on, it grew into the Aligarh University.

It had been declared in 1833 that no native of British India was to be debarred from holding any office or place on account of his nationality, race and religion, but nothing had been done to redeem these promises. In 1789, Lord Lytton founded the Statutory Civil Service. It was provided that one-sixth of the posts hitherto held by the members of the Covenanted Civil Service were in future to be filled by men of Indian birth nominated by the Local Governments in India with the approval of the Viceroy-in-Council and the Secretary of State. Candidates were to serve two years of probation and pass special tests before their final appointment. The Statutory Civil Service held a position mid-way between the Covenanted and un-Covenanted Service. The new scheme was not a success. It did not succeed in attracting persons from the higher classes. The service was recruited from men and who would ordinarily have entered the subordinate service. No wonder, it was abolished after 8 years.

ESTIMATE OF LYTTON

No Viceroy has been subjected to so much criticism as Lord Lytton. His Afghan policy was condemned not only by the people of India but also by the leaders of the Liberal Party and a majority of the Englishmen. It was undoubtedly "a calamitous and unrighteous blunder and on that head alone Lord Lytton's claims to statesmanship are justly forfeit". He is held guilty for the terrible loss of life on account of the famine. While the people were dying of famine, he was busy in holding the Durbar at Delhi. However, it cannot be denied that he was a man of great ideas. Some of his schemes could not be realised because they were before time. He was in favour of a gold standard for India and the country would have gained if his suggestion would have been accepted. He was in favour of separating the North-Western Frontier Province from the Punjab and putting the same under the direct control of the Central Government. His reform was actually carried out by Lord Curzon. It has already been pointed out that his scheme of an Indian Privy Council was given a practical shape in the form of a Chamber of Princes. He also wanted that the Europeans should not be given any lenient treatment when they were involved in cases.

Dr. Smith sums up his estimate of Lytton in these words "His reputation has been obscured by the lack of adequate biography; by certain foreign peculiarities of manner and habits which offended conventional opinion; and above all by reason of the bitter partisan controversies aroused by his Afghan policy executed by him under the instruction of Lords Beaconsfield and Salisbury, the equally venomous criticism of the Vernacular Press Act further discredited him in the popular opinion. These causes have prevented Lytton from attaining the enduring fame promised by the Prime Minister and perhaps may be said to have left a general impression that he was a failure as a ruler of India. If such an opinion exists, it is based upon insufficient grounds. The best parts of his internal policy were of a permanent value, and served as the basis of developments effected by his successors; while the most essential measures of his Afghan policy, by which I mean, the occupation of Quetta and the securing of the Khurram Valley, either remained undisturbed or if reversed for a time, had to be reaffirmed a few years later".

According to Lord Curzon, "A study of the papers, however, both as published at the time and later on in the official records in India, let me admire the extraordinary ability and resourcefulness with which Lord Lytton conducted his case on paper, and the perfection of the English prose in which his Minutes and Despatches were clothed. Of all the Governors-General and Viceroys, he seemed to me to have the greatest literary gift, not indeed excelling Warren Hastings or Dalhousie in lucidity of exposition or vigour of phrase but superior to both in the artistic quality of his writing". Again, "It has been said that his picturesque and poetic figure—for Lytton was picturesque in appearance as well as in fact—was in reality out of date and that he ought to have been born and to have lived in Elizabethan times. There is pertinence in this observation, for certainly in the picture gallery of Indian Viceroys there is no more singular or indeed startling portrait than his. In the Embassy at Paris he found a more congenial stage for his social and diplomatic accomplishment".[1]

REVIEW QUESTIONS

1. What was the most important event in the reign of Lord Canning? Explain.
2. Describe the administrative systems of Lord Canning and Lord Lytton.
3. Throw light on the policies and reforms of Lord Elgin, Lord Lawrence and Lord Mayo.
4. Northbrook brook was a man of caution. Comment.
5. Give an estimate of the character and personality of Lord Lytton.
6. Write short notes on the following:
    (a) Lord Canning
    (b) Lord Mayo
    (c) Lord Lytton

---

[1] "Though often hasty and impulsive, he brought some new fruitful conceptions into the field of Indian politics".

SUGGESTED READINGS

Aitchison, C.S.: *Lord Lawrence.*
Balfour, B.: *Lord Lytton's Indian Administration* (1899).
Cunningham, H.S.: *Earl Canning.*
Dharam Pal: *The Administration of Sir John Lawrence in India.*
Hunter, W.W.: *Life of Lord Mayo* (1876).
Mallet, B.: *Northbrook, a Memoir* (1908).
Smith, B.: *Life of Lord Lawrence.*
Strachey, Sir J.: *India, its Administration* (1911).
Temple, Sir Richard: *The Life of Lord Lawrence.*
West, A.: *Sir Charles Wood's Administration* (1867).

16 Ripon to Elgin (1880–98)

LEARNING OBJECTIVES

- Throw light on the administration, policies and reforms of all the administrators from Lord Ripon to Lord Elgin II
- Know about the Hunter Commission and Ilbert Bill

LORD RIPON (1880-84)

Lord Ripon resembled Lord William Bentinck in many ways. His political outlook was the very antithesis of Lords Lytton and Curzon. He was a true Liberal of the Gladstonian era and had firm faith in peace, self-government and *laissez faire*. So far, the Government of India had merely been doing what it considered to be in the best interests of the country without consulting the people as to what their aspirations and feelings were. According to Burke, "The English nation in India is nothing but a seminary for the succession of officers. They are a nation of placemen. They are a republic, a commonwealth without a people. They are a State made up wholly of magistrates". According to Montgomery, "In India, we set aside the people altogether; we devise and say that such a thing is a good thing to be done and we carry it out without asking them very much about it". The Indians who were receiving western education and who had come into contact with western democratic institutions, aspired to introduce the same in their country. Lord Ripon sympathised with their aspirations and took steps in that direction. In his famous resolution on Local Self-Government, Lord Ripon declared that his object was to give popular and political education to the people of India. He sincerely desired them to take their first lessons in democracy in the Local Boards which were to be set up in every part of the country. It is true that many Englishmen did not share his views and as a matter of fact opposed him, but Lord Ripon continued to do what he thought to be in the best interests of the people of India.

Lord Ripon brought the Second Afghan War to a close. He also repealed in 1881 the Vernacular Press Act which had been passed by Lord Lytton and which was severely criticised by the Indians.

In his letter dated 19th February 1881, to Lord Hartington communicating his decision to repeal the Act, Lord Ripon wrote thus: "The fact is that the official in India regards the press as an evil, necessary perhaps, but to be kept within as narrow limits as possible. He has no real feeling of the benefits of free discussion".

In the time of Lord Ripon, the entrance of Indians to the Indian Civil Service was very difficult as the examinations were held in England and the age-limit of candidates was fixed at 18. Ripon was in favour of simultaneous examinations but he could not persuade the Council as well as the Home Government to agree to the change. He, however, succeeded in getting the age-limit raised from 18 to 21, thus affording better facilities for Indian to compete at the examination in London.

When Sir Richard Garth, the Chief Justice of the Calcutta (now Kolkata) High Court went on leave, Ripon appointed Sir Romesh Chunder Mitter to act as the Chief Justice. There was great opposition from the Europeans against this appointment and even Sir Richard Garth himself objected to the appointment.

Local Self-Government

As regards Local Self-Government, Lord Ripon passed a resolution in 1881. It was stated therein that time had come when further steps should be taken to develop the idea of Lord Mayo's Government. Agreements with Provincial Governments regarding finance should not ignore the question of Local Self-Government. Provincial Governments were directed to transfer considerable revenues to the local bodies and the latter were to deal with those matters which concerned their localities. The Provincial Governments were asked to make a careful study of the provincial, local and municipal Acts. The object of the inquiry was to find out as to what sources of revenues could be transferred from the provincial heads to the local heads so that the same could be administered by municipal committees. It was also to be determined as to what subjects could be given specially to the local bodies. Only those items were to be transferred which could be understood and appreciated by the people.

In accordance with the resolution of 1881, letters were issued to the Provincial Governments. In those letters, the Government of India hinted on those items of expenditure which could be conveniently transferred to the local bodies. The Provincial Governments were asked to suggest other objects that could be transferred to the local bodies. Provincial Governments were told that "it would be hopeless to expect any real development of self-government if the local bodies were subject to check or interference in matters of detail". It was also pointed out that the Governor-General was anxious to give the fullest possible liberty of action to the local bodies.

The next step was taken by Ripon in 1882 when he issued his famous resolution. In that resolution, Lord Ripon made it clear that the expansion of Local Self-Government was not expected to bring about a change for the better from the point of view of efficiency. To quote him, "It is not primarily with a view to improvement in administration that this measure is put forward and supported. It is chiefly desirable as an instrument of political and popular education". However, he hinted at the possibility of improved efficiency after some time. There were to be failures at the beginning. Success was possible if the people got encouragement and support from the officials of the Government.

Lord Ripon declared that he was not prepared to admit that the people of India were indifferent towards self-government. As a matter of fact, a large number of intelligent and public-spirited persons were required to lend their services for the cause of the people. Ripon's view was that the system of Local Government had not been satisfactorily tried in the country. The old system was overridden and practically crushed initiative by direct official interference. He emphasized the necessity of putting more faith in the non-official members of the local bodies.

Provincial Governments were directed to maintain and extend a network of Local Boards in every district. The area of jurisdiction of every Local Board was to be so small that both local knowledge and local interest on the part of the people could be secured. The number of non-official members was to be very large and the official element was not to exceed one-third of the whole. Whenever possible, the system of election was to be introduced in Local Boards in as many places as possible.

With regard to the control of the Government, it was stated that it should be exercised from *without* and not from *within*. The Government should revise and check the acts of the local bodies and not dictate them. The sanction of the Government should be made necessary to legalise certain acts of the local bodies. The number of the cases, where sanction was required, was to be large at the beginning but the same was to be reduced later on. The Government was to be given the authority to set aside altogether the proceedings of the Local Boards or to suspend them temporarily in the case of crisis and continued neglect of duty. The power of absolute supersession was to be exercised only with the consent of the Government of India. To quote him, "It should be the general function of the executive officers of Government to watch, especially at the outset, the proceedings of the Local Boards, to point out to them matters calling for their consideration, to draw their attention to any neglect of duty on their part, and to check by official remonstrance any attempt to exceed their proper functions or to act illegally or in any arbitrary or unreasonable manner".

The Indians were to be encouraged to become members of the local bodies and the Government was to do its utmost to help them in the efficient discharge of their duties.

For his reforms in the field of Local Self-Government, Lord Ripon is rightly called the *Father of Local Self-Government* in the country.

Hunter Commission on Education

In 1882, Lord Ripon appointed the Hunter Commission to inquire into the manner in which the principles of Wood's Dispatch of 1854 had, worked in the country and also to recommend the future course of action: The Hunter Commission recommended the withdrawal of the State from direct support and management of institutions of higher education. This work was to be given to the Indians if there was any reasonable prospect of its being done efficiently. Ordinary and special grants were to be made to colleges. The Professors of the colleges were to give series of lectures on the duties of men and citizens. Some special steps were to be taken to spread education among the Muslims. All elementary schools were to be inspected and supervised by the educational officers of the Government. A part of the provincial revenues was to be earmarked for purposes of education. The recommendations of the Commission were accepted by the Government and carried out.

Decentralisation of Finance

In 1882, Lord Ripon introduced the system of Imperial, Divided and Provincial heads of revenue. Income from the Imperial heads was to go to the Central Government. Province were to get all the incomes from Departments under their control. Income from the Divided heads was to be divided between the Imperial Government and Provincial Governments. The deficit in the provincial budgets was to be made good by the Imperial Government by giving a fixed percentage of land revenue. The settlement was made for 5 years and was renewed in 1887, 1892 and 1897.

Lord Ripon took keen interest in the welfare of the people. In 1881 was passed the First Factory Act to regulate and improve the conditions of labour in Indian factories. Children between the ages of 7 and 12 were not to work for more than 9 hours a day. Dangerous machinery was to be properly fenced and inspectors were to be appointed for the purpose of inspection.

Another popular step taken up by Lord Ripon was that he restored in 1881 the Raja of Mysore. However, certain restrictions were put on the exercise of powers by the Raja. All laws in force at the time of rendition of Mysore were to remain in force and efficiently administered. No material change was to be made by the Raja in the system of government without consulting the Governor-General.

As regards Kolhapur, its Raja became insane in 1882. When the Raja died, he was succeeded by the other prince.

Lord Ripon completed the free trade policy initiated by Lord Northbrook and Lord Lytton. In 1882, the Finance Minister removed from the tariff all the 5 per cent *ad valorem* import duties. Duties were left on things like salt, wines, spirits, etc. These duties were retained for purely political reasons.

In 1882, salt tax was lowered throughout India. In the field of revenue, Ripon was not successful. His view was that in the districts which had once been surveyed and assessed, the Government should pledge itself to make no other increase of revenue except on the sole ground of a rise in prices. His suggestion was not accepted.

Ilbert Bill

Sir Courtenay Ilbert was the Law Member of the Government of India. He attempted to change the law of the country with regard to the trial of the Europeans. The Criminal Procedure Code of 1873 laid down that except in the presidency towns, no magistrate or Sessions Judge could try a European British subject unless he himself was a European by birth. By this time many Indian members of the covenanted civil service were occupying posts of responsibility and dignity. Justice demanded that the Indian magistrates should be given the same authority as their European counterparts. The Government of India made up its mind to abolish the judicial disqualification based on race distinction.

Ilbert prepared the bill in 1883 to bring the Indian and European magistrates on the same footing.

The bill in draft was generally approved by Lord Ripon's Executive Council as well as by almost all the provincial governments and was introduced in the Imperial Legislative Council in February 1882. Within a few weeks, the whole of the British community joined in a vigorous denunciation of the bill. A monster public meeting was held in the Calcutta (now Kolkata) Town Hall where speeches were delivered which went beyond all limits of decency. Similar meetings were held all over the Bengal presidency. The Anglo-Indian and European Defence Association was formed. The non-official European community boycotted Ripon's levies. It was proposed to boycott the government loan. On his return to Calcutta (now Kolkata) from Simla Ripon was openly insulted in the streets by planters who had come from the mofussil.

A correspondent in the *Englishman* wrote thus: "The only people who had any right in India are the British. The so-called Indians have no right whatever". The cry of European women in danger was raised. Meredith Townshend wrote thus in the *Spectator*: "*Would you like to live in a country where at any moment your wife would be liable to be sentenced on a false charge of slapping an Ayah to three days' imprisonment, the magistrate being a copper-coloured pagan who probably worships the Linga, and certainly exults any opportunity of showing that he can insult white persons with impunity?*" The Ladies Committee was also formed to oppose the bill.

Lord Ripon and some of the members of his Executive Council as well as the Home Government remained firm. However, the bill was ultimately modified by extending the power to try European offenders only to Indian Sessions Judges and District Magistrates and giving such European offenders the right to be tried by a jury if they so pleased. Lord Ripon and his Government were largely influenced in accepting the compromise by the desire to avoid the risk of a street row in Calcutta organised by Europeans. In his letter dated 22nd December 1883, to Lord Kimberley, Lord Ripon wrote thus: "I do not deny, however, that the great weakness of Government for dealing with a European disturbance weighed with me as it did with my colleagues. I had no idea till I came to Calcutta, that the European police force at the disposal of the Bengal Government was so very small (between 60 and 70 men all told). In any riot, the least serious, we should have had at once to call out the troops and I felt and feel still that to employ European soldiers against Europeans in this country would be a step of the gravest kind".

According to Thompson and Garratt, "No educated Indian has ever forgotten the lesson of the Ilbert Bill. They were accustomed to rulers who should be influenced by cajolery and entreaty, bribery or threats of revolt, but it was an entirely new experience to see a government, and especially the aloof and powerful British Government, deflected from its purpose by newspaper abuse and an exhibition of bad manners. In later days Indian nationalism was to acquire some of its techniques from the suffrage movement in England, and more from Irish Home Rulers, but it was the successful agitation against the Ilbert Bill which decided the general lines upon which the Indian politician was to run his campaigns. It is significant that the two years which followed this agitation saw the foundation of the Indian National Congress and the European Association". Again, "Political interest received a great stimulus from the European opposition to the Ilbert Bill. This unhappy disputes served to emphasize the inferior state of Indians. The point was driven home by a succession of cases where manslaughter of Indians was alleged against British soldiers and civilians. These cases were often treated by the courts in a manner suggesting the half-conscious recognition that an Indian life was not so valuable as that of a European. The nationalist movement began to take shape".

According to Robert, if "Lord Ripon had forfeited popularity among his countrymen, he had at any rate won by his championship of their cause, the enthusiastic devotion and support of men of Indian birth. On his resignation in 1884, the route of his journey to Bombay (now Mumbai) was lined with acclaiming and admiring crowds and his name has ever since been enshrined in the hearts of the nationalist party in India as the great champion of their cause on the Viceregal throne". (*British India*, p. 470.)

According to Lord Curzon, "Lord Ripon was personally liked and esteemed, for he was an indefatigable worker, a conciliatory colleague, and a perfectly straightforward and consistent man. His friends trembled under the voluminous correspondence which he showered upon them, but this was a feature of his willingness to argue and his anxiety to convince. He held rigidly to what he regarded as the orthodox and fundamental principles of Indian Government; and many years later, when I was involved in the struggle to uphold the supremacy of the civil as against the military authority in Indian administration, he made, without any communication to me, a powerful speech in the House of Lords on my behalf, and must have suffered considerable pangs when his colleague, Lord Morley, hauled down the flag which a little earlier he had so defiantly planted on the walls of the fortress". Again, "The Viceroyalty of Lord Ripon only lasted for four years and if its termination was viewed without regret by the British community, it excited the most fervid and overwhelming demonstrations from Indians of all classes, who have ever since canonised him as the foremost saint in their political calendar, and still regard him as the real author of that advance towards self-government and nationhood which has in recent times progressed at such a dizzy rate of speed".

According to Meredith Townshend, after the (Lord Ripon) had ceased to be able to promote to punish any man, all northern and western India, including the pick of the fighting races, prostrated itself at his feet. His journey from Simla to Bombay (now Mumbai) was a triumphal march such as India had never witnessed—a long procession in which seventy million Indians sang *bosanna* to their friend. Lord Ripon had done nothing, had taken off no tax, had removed no burden, had not altered the mode of government a hair's breadth. He was only supposed to be for Indians and against Europeans, and that sufficed to bring every Indian in a favour of friendship to his side". (*Asia and Europe*, p. 108.)

Referring to Lord Ripon, Lord Dufferin observed that no Viceroy had laboured so conscientiously or so uninterruptedly for the good of the millions entrusted to his care as Lord Ripon did. Ability, industry, conscientiousness, moderation, good sense and noble and lofty spirit characterised the control of affairs.

According to S. Gopal, Ripon "was idolized by Indians and detested by the vast majority of Englishmen. And the controversy started then has continued to rage. The starched society of Anglo-Indians ever viewed his activities with bewilderment and pain, and found it difficult to forgive him. As late as 1915, when a statue of his was set up in Calcutta, no subscriptions were forthcoming from English sources, and the monument was paid for entirely by Indians". (*The Viceroyalty of Lord Ripon*, p. 219.) Again, "He whom the English condemned as Indophile became to Indians the most English of all Viceroys in that he was the prophet and champion of their freedom. Raja Sir Sahib Dyal, an old friend of Lord Lawrence, said that if ever British power in India were in danger the authorities should send for Lord Ripon. 'He will do more for you than regiments of soldiers, and our women will sell their jewels and lay them at his feet'. Like Gladstone Ripon was one of the great apostles of reconciliation between peoples. If Indian nationalism never acquired an exclusive and uncompromising character, if during the many years of struggle the number of British lives lost can be counted on one's fingers, the credit to some extent belongs to Ripon. His activities and experience laid the foundations of that free association and broad community of purpose and ideals which today characterize the relations between Great Britain and India. The legacy of these four years could never be wholly lost.

"If often he was wrong and at times absurd,

To us he is no more a person,

Now but a whole climate of opinion.

"Ripon, in short, was not so much the wrecker of an empire as a builder of the Commonwealth. His place in history is alongside Lord Durham and Sir Henry Campbell Bannerman. But his task was even more difficult than theirs". (*Ibid.,* p. 224.)

According to Lucien Wolfe, "He was not a showy statesman. He hated the 'Palaver, and the limelight. He was not a great speaker or a good writer. But he was industrious, painstaking, honest, and shrewd. He had high purposes and far more than average ability, which, joined with a character of singular nobility and lovableness, once—in the Indian Viceroyalty—almost touched the high watermark of genius. He served his country through nearly sixty years with such simplicity and so little self-assertion that, at the end, he seemed to fall quite easily into the ruck of political mediocrity. For at that time even his Indian work was only beginning to emerge from the distorting atmosphere of party controversy. The re-reading of his Life today in the light of an ample material, and more especially of the lessons of the Great War and of its political and social concomitants, must, I think, reverse this judgment and give to Lord "Ripon a high place in the constructive statesmanship of the Victorian and Edwardian epochs". (*Preface, Life of Lord Ripon,* Vol. I, pp. v-vi.)

When Ripon relinquished his office in December 1884, there was a spontaneous outburst of demonstrations of goodwill. His journey from Calcutta to Bombay was one triumphant progress in which Indian gratitude expressed itself with touching and tumultuous unanimity and sincerity. In his letter dated 28th November 1884 to Lord Northbrook, Lord Ripon wrote thus: "I have been overwhelmed with addresses since I left Simla and the task of replying to them has been in many ways difficult. I do not think that I have said anything calculated to give offence to anyone. But I could not honestly speak well of the principles or proceedings of any unscrupulous opponents of last year, or of the lamentable weakness which marked the conduct of the civil service as a body". During his stay in Bombay, Lord Ripon performed the ceremony of laying the foundation-stone of the present Municipal Building opposite to the Victoria Terminus station. The address of welcome was read out by Pheroze-shah Mehta who was the President of the Bombay Municipal Corporation. At Town Hall, addresses from many towns in the presidency were presented to Lord Ripon. On the platform behind Lord Ripon, there rose a regular mountain of silver caskets, carved boxes, volumes of parchments, rolls of signatures and illustrative addresses on silks and satins. On the day of his departure from Bombay, the whole town was be flagged and decorated and a solid mass of humanity lined the streets of the way from Parel to Apollo Bunder. In one bazar, the merchants hung up garlands of pearls and diamonds. Ripon's carriage was stopped at the Bhuleshwar and Mumbadevi temples and the Brahmin priests blessed him and applied *kumkum* and rice to his forehead. They presented silver trays to him with coconuts placed in them.

LORD DUFFERIN (1884-88)

At the time of his appointment as Viceroy, Lord Dufferin had a great administrative and diplomatic experience at his back. He had acted as British Ambassador in Turkey and Russia. He was also Governor-General of Canada from 1875 to 1878. He was an eloquent speaker and a man of great personal charm. As he was old, he did not introduce any new reforms and was contented to continue the old ones. According to Lecky, "He was a great diplomatist and a great statesman; a man who possessed a degree what was hardly equalled by any of his contemporaries, the qualities of brilliance and the qualities of charm; a man of unqualified tact and versatility, and who combined with these gifts rare sagacity of judgment and a singularly firm and tenacious will. His rare gift of carrying out great works with the minimum of friction was perhaps the distinctive feature of his great Indian career".

Panjdeh Affair (1884)

Reference may be made to the famous Panjdeh incident which brought Russia and Great Britain on the brink of war. In 1884, the Russians annexed Mery. This caused great anxiety in the mind of the Government of India and that of Great Britain. A Commission was appointed to fix the northern boundary line of Afghanistan. A difficulty arose with regard to the position of Panjdeh which was under the Afghan rule. The Russian General ordered the Afghans to leave Panjdeh and when his order was not carried out, he drove the Afghans away forcibly. Finding the situation serious, the Indian armies were assembled at Quetta and the Russian armies at Herat. However, "the disastrous issue of war was averted by the labours of diplomats, the tact of Lord Dufferin and above all by the shrewd commonsense of Abdur Rahman". Abdur Rahman, the Amir of Afghanistan, declared that he was not sure whether Panjdeh belonged to him or not and he was also not very desirous of keeping the same in his possession. He declared his willingness to give up his claim to Panjdeh if he was given compensation anywhere else. The Amir was determined to avoid a clash between Great Britain and Russia. He knew fully well that in the event of a war between the two countries, his country was to suffer because it was to become the theatre of war. Abdur Rahman rightly pointed out that "Afghanistan was between two mill-stones and it had been already ground to powder". To quote Abdur Rahman again, "My country is like a poor goat on whom the lion and the bear have both fixed their eyes and without the protection and help of Almighty Deliverer the victim cannot escape very long".

When such was the attitude of the Amir, there was no justification for British troops to clash with the Russian troops. There were lengthy negotiations between Russia, Great Britain, India and Afghanistan and ultimately the line of demarcation was settled in July 1887. Abdur Rahman was not a loser in any way. He did not lose either money or territory.

Lord Dufferin entertained Abdur Rahman at a Durbar at Rawalpindi and assured him of British help against foreign aggression.

Third Burmese War (1885)

The real cause of the third Burmese War was the attempt of King Theebaw of Burma to secure French help against the British by giving them special privileges and concessions. The Burmese mission visited Paris in 1883 and in 1885 a French envoy went to Mandalay. King Theebaw was a savage and cruel despot and he imposed a heavy fine upon the Bombay (now Mumbai) and Burma Trading Company and ordered the arrest of its officials. Lord Dufferin insisted on an enquiry to be made into the matter. King Theebaw refused to reopen the question. Lord Dufferin sent an ultimatum demanding that King Theebaw should admit a British envoy at Mandalay, suspend proceedings against the Company till the arrival of the envoy, have no external relations with foreign countries except on the advice of the Government of India and grant the British the right to trade with the Chinese through his dominions. King Theebaw refused to accept the terms of the ultimatum and consequently war was declared. The Burmese could not stand before the British armies and surrendered. King Theebaw was sent to India and Upper Burma was annexed to India in 1886.

British preference in Upper Burma has been the subject of criticism from many quarters. It is contended that it was no business of the British Government to interfere in Upper Burma even if its ruler was a despot and a savage. The British Government had no justification to interfere into the internal affairs of a neighbouring country whose ruler was absolutely independent to follow any policy he liked. If King Theebaw wanted to have friendly relations with France, it was no business of the British to intervene. It seems that the British Government was determined to check the advance of France into Upper Burma. To quote Lord Dufferin: "If the French proceedings should eventuate in any serious attempt to forestall us in Upper Burma, I should not hesitate to annex the country". According to Roberts, "The ethics of the relations between powerful western empires and weak eastern nations are admittedly difficult to disentangle but it is to be feared that the abstract rights of semi-civilized countries receive scant recognition, which great colonizing powers converge upon them".

Reference may be made to some other events of the time of Lord Dufferin. It was in 1885 that the first session of the Indian National Congress was held at Bombay. On 16th February 1887 was celebrated the silver jubilee of Queen Victoria. Many Indian princes went to London to see the celebrations in June 1887.

Three Tenancy Acts were passed in the time of Lord Dufferin. The Bengal Tenancy Act of 1885 gave greater security of tenure to the tenants. Their rents were not to be increased arbitrarily. The Oudh Tenancy Act of 1886 aimed at strengthening the position of the tenants by granting them a statutory holding for 7 years with a right to compensation for improvements. The Punjab Tenancy Act of 1887 gave the tenants a limited guarantee against eviction and enhancement of rent.

The Age of Consent Act was passed in the time of Lord Dufferin. By this Act, the age-limit within which protection was given to young girls was raised from 10 to 12. This was intended to improve the lot of women in the country.

In 1886, Lord Dufferin gave the Fort of Gwalior to Maharaja Scindhia. Morar was given up in exchange for the town of Jhansi.

According to Lord Curzon, "In his conduct of affairs the Viceroy exhibited a curious mixture of application and indifference. He laboured hard to obtain a mastery of all essential features of the administration and wrote or inspired long and eloquent Minutes and Despatches. He took a great deal of trouble about his public addresses, which in common with all his speeches were carefully elaborated. He devoted weary hours to the study of Persian, under the quite mistaken impression that it was the language of the educated classes and of the Indian Princes, with whom he hoped to be able to converse in their own tongue. But he was careless about detail, interfered very little in departmental business, and left the conduct of all minor matters to his private secretary and the officials".

LORD LANSDOWNE (1888-93)

Lord Lansdowne belonged to the forward school of thought. He devoted special attention to the question of frontier defence. Between the territory of Afghanistan and that of British India, there was the area known as the tribal territory. The British wanted to conquer it although it was a difficult task. This was not liked by the Afghans. Certain events brought Afghanistan and the Government of India on the brink of war. The Afghans saw with suspicion the completion of the British railway up to the Bolan Pass. The Commander-in-Chief of India, Lord Roberts, behaved in an aggressive way towards the tribal people. In 1890, a British envoy went to Chitral. Happily, the clash between the two countries was avoided and a satisfactory agreement was arrived at. Sir Mortimer Durand was sent to Kabul. Durand travelled without any escort of his own to Kabul and showed that he had complete faith in the Afghans. Arrangements were made to demarcate the boundary line between India and Afghanistan. This line is known as *Durand Line*.

The Amir of Kabul agreed not to interfere into the affairs of the tribal area. As a result of the demarcation of the boundary line, the Amir got certain districts and bound himself not to interfere in Swat, Dir, Chitral and Rajaur. The Amir also gave up his claim to Chaman. His subsidy was increased from ₹12 lakhs to 18 lakhs a year. He was to be allowed to purchase and import munitions of war and the Government of India was not to raise any objection.

In the case of Manipur, there was a disputed succession. The Commissioner of Assam was deputed to settle the matter, but he was treacherously murdered by the Commander-in-Chief of Manipur. The result was that the Government of India sent its troops to Manipur. The Commander-in-Chief and his accomplices were captured and hanged. A boy Raja was placed on the throne under the guardianship of the Political Resident during his minority.

After the death of Sir Robert Sandeman, the Khan of Kalat was found guilty of many acts of violence including the murder of his Wazir, his father and son. He was summoned to Quetta and asked to abdicate. His son was put on the throne and acknowledged as a ruler.

In the case of Kashmir, certain charges were brought against its Maharaja. Those charges were vague and unsubstantiated. In spite of this, the Maharaja was asked to abdicate. The work of administration was put into the hands of a Council of Regency. Kashmir was restored to its ruler in 1905 after the lapse of 16 years.

In 1892 was passed the famous Indian Councils Act which was in some ways an improvement on the Act of 1861.

The new factory law was passed which made certain improvements on the Factory Act of 1881 which was passed in the time of Lord Ripon. According to the Act, the hours of employment for women were limited to 11 hours a day. The minimum age for children was raised from 7 to 9 and their hours of work were restricted to 7 hours. Night work was absolutely forbidden for children. A weekly holiday was prescribed for all factory hands.

On account of the depreciation in the value of silver, there was a dislocation of the Indian finance. The Government of India closed the mints against the unrestricted coinage of silver and made gold the legal tender. The rate of exchange was fixed at ₹15 to a sovereign.

The armies of the Indian States were organised and came to be known as the Imperial Service Troops.

LORD ELGIN II (1894-99)

Lord Elgin II was a sound and cautious administrator but there was a lot of trouble during the tenure of his office on account of famine, plague and frontier wars.

Reference may be made first of all to the affairs of Chitral which lies to the north-east of Kashmir. In 1895, the Mehtar or ruler of Chitral was assassinated and there was a disputed succession. The British Political Agent was besieged. The Government of India sent an army of 15,000 men. However, a new Ministry came to power in England and ordered the evacuation of the country. But before that decision could be carried out, another Ministry came to power and that reversed the order of evacuation.

In 1897, the Afridis closed the Khyber Pass. The activities of the British in that area had created strong suspicions in the minds of the Afridis and no wonder a kind of Jehad was started against the British. There was a general revolt throughout that part of the country. The expeditions were sent and a large number of troops were employed. The result was that the rebels surrendered, laid down their arms and paid fines imposed on them.

In 1896, the bubonic plague started at Bombay (now in Mumbai). By slow degrees, it spread to the various parts of the country and resulted in a very heavy loss of life. The measures adopted by the Government to check it led to a lot of misunderstanding and unpleasantness among the people. Two British officers at Poona were murdered.

Between 1896 and 1898, there took place a severe famine in U.P., C.P. Bihar and the Hissar district of the Punjab. A Commission was appointed in 1898 to go into the question of famines once again.

During this period, the Government of India was required to tackle the problem of opium production. A Commission known as the Opium Commission had been appointed in 1893 to inquire and report on the effects of the use of opium on the health of the people. As the production of opium was the monopoly of the Government, the Government of India was making huge profits by exporting the same to China. Protests were raised against the practice. The report of the Commission was that the evil effects of opium were exaggerated. The Government of India could not afford to give up its revenue from the production of opium. It was also pointed out that if opium was not imported from India into China, the people of China would use a substitute of an inferior quality and that would have a worse effect. Ultimately, it was decided to reduce the quantity of opium to be sent to China.

A reform was also made in the army. Formerly, there used to be separate Commanders-in-Chief of the three Presidencies. According to the new arrangement, there was to be one Commander-in-Chief of India and under him were put Lieutenant-Generals in the various provinces.

REVIEW QUESTIONS

1. Throw light on Lord Ripon's resolution on local self-government.
2. Lord Ripon is rightly called the 'Father of Local Self-Government' in the country. Critically analyse.
3. Sketch the policy and reforms of Lord Dufferin.
4. What was the real cause of the third Burmese War? Assess its impact on India.
5. Describe in brief about Panjdeh Affair.
6. What is meant by decentralisation of finance? Describe.
7. Write short notes on the following:
   (a) Hunter Commission
   (b) Ilbert Bill
   (c) Lord Lansdowne
   (d) Lord Elgin II
8. Lord Ripon resembled Lord William Bentinck in many ways. Evaluate.

SUGGESTED READINGS

Blunt, W.S.: *India under Ripon*.
Forrest, Sir, G.W.: *The Administration of Lord Lansdowne* (1894).
Gopal, S.: *Viceroyalty of Lord Ripon* (1953).
Lyall, Alfred: *Life of Marquis of Dufferin and Ava*.
Wolfe, L.: *Life of Lord Ripon*.
Keeton, C.L.: *King Thebaw and the Ecological Rape of Burma*, Delhi, 1974.
Mathur, L.P.: *Lord Ripon's Administration in India* (1880-84).

17

Lord Curzon
(1899-1905)

LEARNING OBJECTIVES

- Throw light on Curzon's foreign policy
- Elucidate the reforms carried out by Lord Curzon
- Give an account of the administrative system of Lord Curzon
- Give an estimate of Lord Curzon

Lord Curzon was one of the greatest and most influential Governors-General of India. He was born in 1859 and he entered Parliament in 1886.[1] Before his appointment as Governor-General of India, he worked as Under-Secretary of State for India. He made a state-entry in Calcutta (now Kolkata) on 3rd January 1899. A young man of 40, he was full of vigour and energy. He had already visited India four times and possessed an intimate knowledge of the East. He had written three important books on Asian questions. He spent six eventful years in India and can be compared with only Lord Dalhousie. He worked hard not only himself but practically drove his subordinates to hard work.

CURZON'S FOREIGN POLICY

His Tribal Area Policy[2]
When Lord Curzon assumed office, the tribal area on the north-western frontier of India demanded his immediate attention. It has already been pointed out that in the time of Elgin II there arose trouble in Chitral and British forces were sent there to maintain law and order. Those forces were not withdrawn. There was also a Jehad against the British and the English sent two expeditions to meet the situation. In 1899, about 10,000 troops were still in Chitral, the Tochi Valley, Landi Kotal and Khyber Pass. Lord Curzon himself belonged to the *forward school* of thought and it might have been expected that he would follow a policy of further penetration into the tribal area. However, he followed neither the forward policy nor "back to the Indus" policy. He followed a

---

[1] Curzon from his Oxford days spoke and behaved with a superior air. This led to various rhymes by his contemporaries at Oxford and one of them was as under:

My name is George Nathaniel Curzon
I am a most superior person
My cheek is pink, my hair is sleek
I dine at Blenheim, once a week.

[2] "On the north-west frontier, the Government had to face two separate problems, one imperial and the other local".

middle-of-the-road policy. He was not prepared to evacuate Chitral, Quetta and the other frontier posts occupied by the British, but at the same time he was not prepared to carry the policy to its logical conclusion.

What Lord Curzon actually did was that he ordered the gradual withdrawal of the British troops from the tribal area. The place of those British troops was taken by the tribal levies which were trained and commanded by British officers. To give only one example, the Afridis of Khyber Rifles were put in charge of the Khyber Pass. Strategic railways were constructed up to Dargai, Jamrud and Thai Jamrud was at the entrance of the Khyber Pass and Thal was the gate of the Kurram Valley. The Government of India put a limit on the import of arms and ammunition into the tribal area. The people of the tribal areas were warned that while the Government of India would respect their independence, their outrage on the Indian soil would not be tolerated. The Government of India recruited a special police force for the purpose of protecting the people of India from the tribal raids. The members of the police were always to be on their guard to meet any attack at any time and to pursue the raiders into the tribal area. Roads were constructed in the tribal area so that there might be no difficulty if the raiders were to be pursued in the tribal territory. The tribal people were given a lot of work at the time of construction of these roads and their maintenance was also given to them so that they might be able to make some money. The Indian troops which were withdrawn from the tribal area were stationed at the cantonments which were established at the borders of the tribal area. These cantonments were linked up with roads. The object of all these measures was to enable the Government of India to rush reinforcements into the tribal area at the time of an emergency.

Previous to Lord Curzon, the north-west frontier districts were under the control of the Lieutenant-Governor of the Punjab and the Government of India had no direct control over them. The result was that everything had to be done through the Punjab Government. This resulted in a lot of delay. Moreover, on account of the preoccupation of the Lieutenant-Governor of the Punjab with the Punjab affairs, the problems of the north-west frontier were not given the attention that was due to them. That resulted in inefficiency. Lord Lytton had suggested the creation of a separate province under the direct control of the Government of India. However, his suggestion had not been accepted. In 1901, Lord Curzon was able to set up a separate North-Western Frontier Province under the control of a Chief Commissioner who was directly responsible to the Government of India. The new province had an area of 40,000 sq. miles. The move was opposed by some officials of the Punjab, but that had no effect.

The policy of Lord Curzon towards the tribal area was followed by his successors. Lord Curzon himself defended his policy in 1908 in these words: "If anybody had been disposed to doubt the success of the scheme of frontier policy which had now been in existence for 10 years, his doubt must have been dispelled, and I hope that we shall now hear no more of the wild-cat schemes of advancing into tribal territories, annexing up to the border, and driving routes through the tribal country".

According to Thompson and Garrat, "Lord Curzon did not solve the frontier problem. Many of its difficulties will remain as a legacy. But he introduced a system which has proved to be a sensible compromise between the conflicting views of experts". According to another writer, "The Curzon frontier policy has now been superseded by or perhaps it would be fairer to say has developed into...a new forward policy...not of military conquests but of civilisation".

Afghanistan

The relations of the Government of India with Afghanistan were not very cordial from the time of Lord Elgin II. Abdur Rahman, the Amir of Kabul, was in a very difficult position. He was accused by the British Government of creating trouble on his side of the frontier against the British. The Afghans accused him of a weak policy towards the Government of India. On the whole, he followed a policy of caution. He asked his countrymen to maintain peace and not to talk in terms of war. He declared that when the time for war would come, he would himself them against the British. Unfortunately, Abdur Rahman died in 1901. His son, Habib Ullah, came to the throne without any war of succession, but the relations of the Government of India with him were not cordial. That was due to the difference of opinion with regard to the interpretation of the treaty between Abdur Rahman and the Government of India. The point of view of the Government of India was that treaty was a personal one and consequently a new treaty had to be entered into with Habib Ullah. The contention of Habib Ullah was that the treaty was between the two countries and consequently there was no necessity of a revision or reaffirmation at the time of a new succession. This resulted in a deadlock. The new Amir did not draw the subsidy which his father was getting from the Government of India and there was practically no intercourse between Afghanistan and the Government of India for three years.

In 1904, Lord Curzon was away in England and in his absence Lord Ampthill acted as the Viceory. He sent Sir Louis Dane on a mission to Kabul. That mission remained in about three months and a half. It is true that certain concessions were made to the Amir of Kabul and his interpretation in the treaty was accepted, and his title "His Majesty" was recognised, but friendly relations were also established between the two countries. The Amir agreed to draw the arrears of his subsidy.

Persian Gulf

In the time of Lord Curzon, efforts were made by certain powers to establish their hold in one part or the other of Persia, but all those attempts were foiled by the vigilant Viceroy. In 1898, the Sultan of Oman gave to the French Government a coaling station with the right to fortify it. This place was near Muscat. When Lord Curzon came to know of it in 1899, he sent a naval squadron. The Sultan was threatened that if he did not withdraw the concession, strong action would be taken against him. The Sultan submitted and cancelled the concession.

In 1900, the Russians tried to establish a coaling station on the northern shore of the entrance to the Persian Gulf. That attempt was also foiled.

In 1899, the Government of India entered into an agreement with the ruler of Kaweit by which he bound himself not to make any concession to any foreign power. The result was that when Germany approached him for site for the terminus of the Berlin-Bagdad railway, he refused.

In 1903, Lord Lansdowne, the Foreign Minister of Great Britain, declared that Great Britain would regard the establishment of a naval base or fortified post in the Persian Gulf by any power "as a very grave menace to British interests which we should certainly resist with all the means at our disposal".

It is true that in certain cases Lord Curzon's policy towards the Persian Gulf was too provocative, but that helped to make the Persian Gulf secure for the British Government. No foreign power was allowed to have a footing from which it might challenge the British.

Tibet

As regards the relations of the Government of India, with Tibet, it was Warren Hastings who sent in 1774-75 Mr. George Bolgle to Lhasa. In 1783, Samual Turner was sent. In 1811-12, Manning went to Lhasa and met the Dalai Lama. In 1885-86, the Chinese Government gave permission for a British commercial mission to Tibet. In 1886, the Tibetans invaded Sikkim, but they were beaten back. In 1890, a convention settled the frontier between Sikkim and Tibet. In 1893, a trade mart was established at Yatung. In spite of all this, the Tibetans were not willing to have free intercourse with India "except through fear of something which they may regard as a greater calamity".

When Lord Curzon became the Governor-General, some new factors made their appearance. The people of Tibet began to show a strong desire to become independent of China. The new Dalai

Lama proved himself to be a strong ruler. He was influenced by Dorjieff who was a Russian subject by birth. Dorjieff had gone to Russia to collect money from the Buddhists in the territory of the Czar. In 1900 and 1901, Dorjieff was received by the Czar of Russia. The Russian press gave a lot of importance to the visit of Dorjieff to their country. No wonder there was a lot of uneasiness in the Government of India. Lord Curzon was not prepared to tolerate the increase of Russian influence at the capital of Tibet. It is true that the Russian Foreign Minister categorically stated that the visit of Dorjieff has absolutely no political importance, but that did not remove the suspicion of the Government of India. It could not be denied that new Dalai Lama was himself in favour of increasing the Russian influence in his country with a view to oust the Chinese influence.

Lord Curzon was in favour of sending a mission to Tibet. It was contended that the isolation of the Government of Tibet "is not compatible either with proximity to the territories of a great civilised power at whose hands the Tibetan Government enjoys the fullest opportunities both for intercourse and trade, or that due respect for the treaty stipulations into which the Chinese Government had entered on its behalf". The Home Government was not in favour of sending a mission to Tibet. It was thinking more in terms of establishing friendly relations with

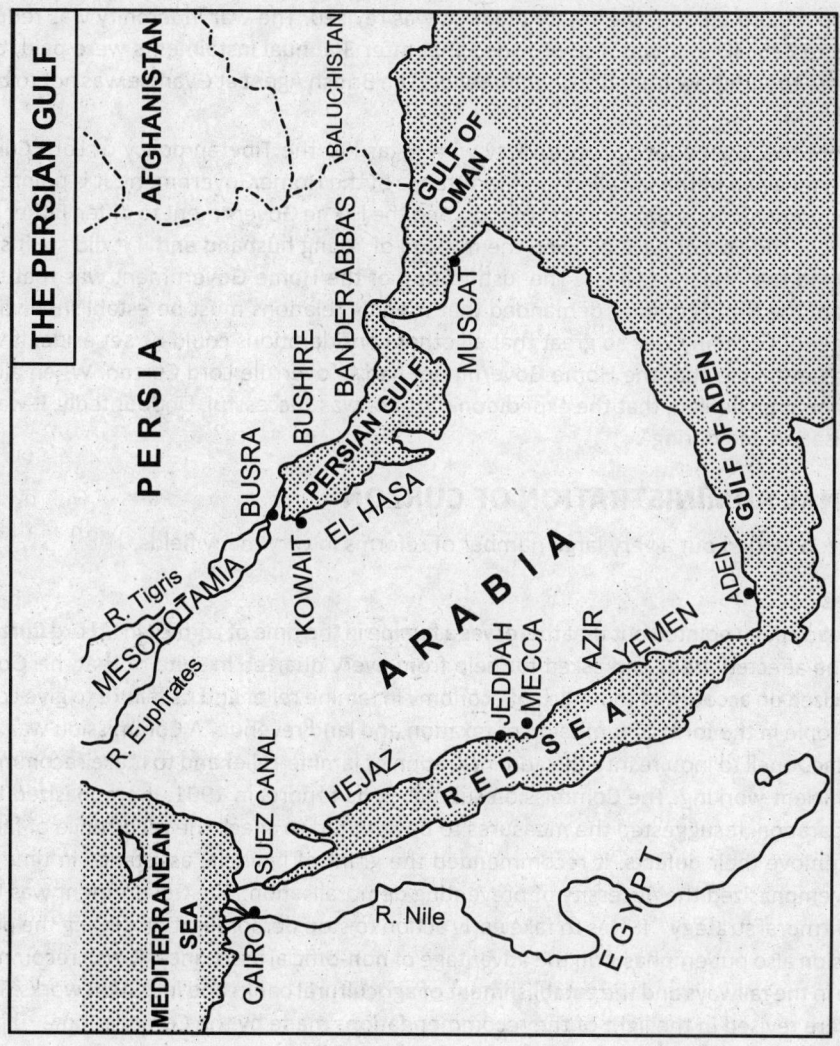

Russia than to antagonise her by sending a mission to Tibet. The Government of India pressed hard, but the Home Government followed delaying tactics. Ultimately, the Home Government agreed to the despatch of a mission under Younghusband. Once the mission started, it went on and on till it reached Lhasa itself. The resistance by the Tibetans was futile.

Younghusband entered into treaty with the Dalai Lama and that treaty is known as the Treaty of Lhasa (1904). According to this treaty, the Chumbi valley was to be occupied by the British troops till the whole of the war indemnity was paid. The amount of indemnity was fixed at ₹75 lakhs and it was to be paid in 75 equal instalments. Trade marts were to be established at Yatung, Gyantse and Gurtok. A British commercial agent was to be stationed at Gyantse but he was given the power to go to Lhasa if circumstances required. Great Britain was given complete control over the foreign policy of Tibet. No agent of any foreign power was to be allowed in Tibet. No part of Tibetan territory was to be given to any other country. No concessions were to be granted to any foreign power in the form of railways, roads, telegraphs, etc. If such concessions were given to any power, similar concessions had to be given to the British Government.

Young husband had gone beyond the powers given to him and no wonder the Home Government refused to accept the Treaty of Lhasa. The Russian Government protested. Ultimately, in spite of the opposition of Lord Curzon, the Treaty of Lhasa was revised. The war indemnity was reduced from ₹75 lakhs to ₹25 lakhs. It was also provided that after 3 annual instalments were paid, the British troops were to withdraw from the Chumbi Valley. The British Agent at Gyantse was not to be allowed to go to Lhasa.

There has been a lot of controversy with regard to the Tibetan policy of Lord Curzon. Lord Curzon complained of the uncalled for interference of the Home Government. It is pointed out that it was not proper for the Government of India and the Home Government to differ. Either the Home Government should not have allowed the mission of Young husband and if it did so, it should not have revised the Treaty of Lhasa. The justification of the Home Government was that the higher interests of the British empire demanded that friendly relations must be established with Russia. The danger of Germany was so great that all other considerations could be set aside. It was under these circumstances that the Home Government had to overrule Lord Curzon. When all has been said, it cannot be denied, that the expedition of Lhasa was successful. Undoubtedly, it was triumph of organisation and daring".

INTERNAL ADMINISTRATION OF CURZON

Lord Curzon carried out a very large number of reforms in very many fields.

Famines

It has already been pointed out that there was a famine in the time of Lord Elgin II. Lord Curzon himself toured the affected areas and asked for help from every quarter. In spite of that, his Government was criticized on account of too much of economy in famine relief and its failure to give concessions to the people in the form of remission of taxation and land revenue. A Commission was appointed under MacDonell to inquire into the administration of famine-relief and to make recommendations for its efficient working. The Commission submitted its reports in 1901. It emphasized the lack of real preparation. It suggested the measures to be adopted to check the recurrence of famines and also to remove their defects. It recommended the grant of financial assistance in time of famine and also emphasized the necessity of preventing demoralisation. The Government was to follow a policy of "moral strategy". It was to take early action to stop demoralisation among the people. The commission also put emphasis on the advantage of non-official assistance. It also recommended an increase in the railways and the establishment of agricultural banks and irrigation works. The famine codes were revised in the light of the recommendations made by the Commission.

Agriculture

Lord Curzon adopted many measures for the improvement of the lot of the agriculturists. The Punjab Land Alienation Act was passed in 1900. The result was that the lands of the statutory agriculturists could not be got by the non-agriculturists without the consent of the Government. Agricultural banks and co-operative societies were set up for the purpose of saving the agriculturists from the tyranny of the moneylenders. In 1904 was passed the co-operative Credit Societies Act. This Act provided for the formation of co-operative societies in urban and rural areas. The main object of the Act was to give relief to rural indebtedness. The Government was to render all necessary assistance.

Lord Curzon also tried to apply scientific methods to agriculture in India. To quote him, "Our real reform has been to endeavour for the first time to apply science on a large scale to the study and practice of Indian agriculture". In 1901, Lord Curzon appointed an Inspector-General of Agriculture. He also established an Agricultural Research Institute at Pusa in Bengal "to assist in the solution of the fundamental problems of tropical agriculture". The Government of India gave an annual grant of £130,000 for purposes of research and experimentation.

In 1901, a Commission was appointed to go into the question of irrigation in India. Sir Volvin Scott-Moncrieff was appointed its Chairman. The Commission submitted its report in 1903. It recommended an expenditure of ₹44 crores in 20 years. It was expected to increase the area under irrigation by 2½ million acres. Lord Curzon accepted many of the recommendations of the Commission. The result was that the Punjab canals were improved. The construction of the Upper Chenab Canal, the Upper Jhelum Canal and the Lower Bari Doab Canal was started.

Railways

Before Lord Curzon, there existed two systems of railway management. Some railways were managed by Companies and the others were managed by the Government of India through the Public Works Department. Lord Curzon appointed Sir Thomas Robertson to report on the railway system in India. The latter submitted his report in 1903. He recommended a complete overhauling of the whole system. His view was that railways should be worked "more as commercial enterprises than they have been in the past". Lord Curzon abolished the Railway Branch of the Public Works Department in 1905. The work of railways was given to a Railway Board of three members. New railway lines were opened. More than 28,150 miles of railway lines were completed and about 3,167 miles were under construction.

Police Reforms

The police system introduced in 1861 was not up to the expectations of the people and there was a lot of dissatisfaction when Curzon assumed office. In 1902, Curzon appointed the Fraser Commission to inquire into the working of police administration in the country. After a thorough investigation of the matter, the Commission submitted its report. It criticised in strongest terms the working of the police system. To quote, "The police force is far from satisfactory; it is defective in training and organisation; it is inadequately supervised; it is generally regarded as corrupt and oppressive; and it has utterly failed to secure the confidence and cordial cooperation of the people".

The recommendations of the Fraser Commission aimed at the utilisation of indigenous local institutions, employment of a better class of people with improved position and prospects, making arrangements for the better training of officers and rank and file, and closer supervision of the lower cadres in the police force.

(1) The Commission recommended the substitution of direct recruitment in place of promotion to higher ranks from lower ranks. (2) The minimum pay of a constable was to be such as to give

him a reasonable living wage and was not to be less than ₹8 p.m. in any case. (3) The Commission recommended an increase in provincial police force and the employment of existing village agencies available for police work. The system of beats of villages was to be abolished. The visits of the police constables to villages were to be restricted for the purpose of obtaining specific information. (4) The establishment of training schools for the training of constables and officers was also recommended. (5) The Commission recommended that the investigation of offences should be made on the spot. The detention of suspects without formal arrest was to be declared illegal. The practice of working for or relying on confessions was to be discouraged. The police work was not to be judged by statistics, but by local inspection and inquiry. (6) A Criminal Investigation Department was to be set up in every province and it was to work under the Central Government with its Director of Criminal Intelligence. The Government of India accepted the recommendations of the Commission. The implementation of the recommendations increased the police expenditure considerably. It was £28,91,344 in 1901-02 and it was £46,02,977 in 1911. However, there was no proportionate improvement in the working of the police system.

Military Reforms

Certain reforms were carried out in the military sphere. Between 1902 and 1904, Moplahs, Gurkhas and Punjabis replaced local recruits in infantry and cavalry to a large extent. In 1900, the native infantry was reorganised into four double Company battalions. Native officers remained in charge of each Company for internal administration, but British officers commanded them in parade and in the field.

Under Lord Kitchener, the native regiments were rearmed. Better guns were supplied to the artillery. The whole of the transport system was overhauled. In 1901, the Imperial Cadet Corps consisting of young men of princely and noble families was started. The services of the Indian army were utilised abroad. The Indians were employed against the Boxer insurgents in China and also in Somaliland. Indian troops in South Africa helped to save Natal Ladysmith.

In 1871, a Naval Defence Squadron had been set up for coastal defence. In 1903, the Indian defence was taken over by the Royal Navy and Internal Defence Squadron was abolished.

While Kitchener made useful reforms in the army, his influence in the matter of army control proved disastrous. He was determined to secure for himself complete authority over military affairs, whether executive or administrative. He wanted to reduce to impotence the military member of the Executive Council of the Viceroy. Lord Kitchener criticised the existing dual system in these words: "There is no doubt that if we had a big war on the frontier, there would be a frightful crash. A system under which transport, supply, remounts, ordnance are entirely divorced from the executive command of the army, and placed under an independent authority, is one which must cost an entire reorganisations as soon as the war is declared—rather late to begin". Lord Kitchener recommended the abolition of the dual control and the putting of the whole of the military administration under a single individual member known as "Commander-in-Chief and War Member of the Council".

The Home Government did not appreciate correctly the point involved in the controversy. Lord Roberts and Lord Lansdowne supported the compromise scheme for a member for military supply. Lord Curzon opposed the creation of a single army department of which the Commander-in-Chief was the head and to whom the whole business of military administration was to be transferred. A compromise was suggested. The Commander-in-Chief was to control exclusively the strictly military departments of all the administration and he alone was to possess the right to speak in the Executive Council of the Governor-General as an expert of military affairs. Other subsidiary departments, not purely military, were to be put in charge of a military supply member. Lord Curzon did not approve of the compromise formula and resigned. He was definitely of the opinion that the new arrangement was defective. His views was vindicated at the expense of the Indian soldier and British honour in the Mesopotamian fiasco when the Commander-in-Chief failed to perform his main duty of command.

Decentralisation of Finance (1904)

The Quinquennial Settlement made by Lord Ripon in 1882 was declared quasi-permanent.

Indian Universities Act, 1904

Lord Curzon tried to reform the education system in the country. He summoned a conference at Simla in 1901 and to this conference were invited the highest educational officers of the Government and the official representatives of the leading universities. The conference was followed by a Universities Commission. This Commission was presided over by Sir Thomas Raleigh who was the Law Member of the Government of India. Indian members were also associated with it. The Commission submitted its report and the Universities Bill was framed accordingly. The principal features of the Bill were explained by Lord Curzon in these words: "Its main principle is to raise the standard of education all round, and particularly, of higher education. What we want to do is to apply better and less fallacious tests than at present exist, to stop the sacrifice of everything in the colleges which constitute our university system, to cramming, to bring about better teaching by a superior class of teachers, to provide for close inspection of colleges and institutions which is now left practically alone, to place the government of the universities in competent, expert and enthusiastic hands, to reconstitute the Senates, to define and regulate the powers of the Syndicates, to give statutory recognition to the elected Fellows who are only appointed on sufferance. To show the way by which our universities, which are now merely examining bodies, can ultimately be converted into teaching institutions; in fact, to convert higher education in India into a reality instead of a sham".

Although the Indian Universities Bill was severely criticised by the people, it was passed in 1904. The provisions of the Act are given in another chapter on Education. Suffice it to say that this Act completely officialised the Indian universities.

Reform of the Bureaucratic Machinery

One of the difficulties that Lord Curzon found in carrying out his policy of centralisation was the unsatisfactory condition of the bureaucratic machine which had settled down in a well-worn groove and become "clogged and over-weighed in all its parts". The amount of noting and report-writing that was going on in the Government departments was so great that it took interminable time to wade through the file of a single case. According to Lord Curzon, "The system of working here is so radically vicious that a stage arises at which a question gets tied up in a tangle of manuscript and print in which the real issues are utterly obscured and from which no one seems able to extricate it". Curzon compared the system to a "gigantic quagmire or bog" into which every question that comes along sinks down. "Unless you stick a peg with a label over the spot at which it disappeared and from time to time go around and dig out the relics, you will never see anything of them again".

Lord Curzon had come across cases which had taken years to reach him. There was one case which was lingering on for full 61 years.

Lord Curzon's recommendations were embodied in the formation of regulations drawn up by a committee of departmental secretaries and put into force throughout the Central Secretariat. Copies of the regulations were sent to the Provincial Governments for enforcement in their respective secretariats. Lord Curzon tried to induce the departments to settle their business by personal consultation, avoid protracted controversies and reduce the practice of noting and prevent delay in arriving conclusions.

Lord Curzon also tried to effect considerable reduction in the printing of Government reports and statistics. According to Fraser, that was not a wise step. On account of their reduction in size, the reports of the Government became "a repellent collection of the driest bones imaginable". The Government failed to appreciate the importance of supplying statistics to the people.

The Calcutta Corporation

Lord Curzon got an opportunity to curtail the sphere of local self-government in India. A Bill to amend the Calcutta (now Kolkata) Corporation was before the Bengal Legislative Council. It was introduced as a result of the agitation carried on by the anti-Ripon organisation. The critics maintained that the Calcutta Corporation as then constituted was unfit to deal with the difficult problem of sanitation. The object of the new Bill was to decrease the powers of the Calcutta Corporation and to give more authority to the executive. The majority of elected representatives was retained in the Corporation, but "actual control over the affairs of the city" was transferred "to the executive committee largely British in character and composition".

Lord Curzon characterised this device as a clumsy and mischievous form of dualism. Ultimately, the Bill was changed according to his wishes and it became law in 1900. The new Act reduced the size of the Calcutta Corporation from 75 to 56. The 25 elected members of the Corporation who were the representatives of the rate-pavers were cut down. The British element was given a definite majority. The Corporation became an Anglo-Indian House. According to S.N. Banerjee, the Act of 1900 marked the extinction of local self-government in Calcutta.

Status of Presidency Governors

Lord Curzon believed in a policy of centralisation in every field. He wanted to gather all the leading strings into his own hands. He wished to know everything that was happening in all parts of India. He could not tolerate the least signs of independence on the part of officials, however high and dignified their position might be. This is illustrated by the unsuccessful attempt made by him to reduce the status and power of the Presidency Governors.

Lord Curzon did not approve of the attitude of aloofness assumed by the Governors of Bombay (now Mumbai) and Madras (now Chennai). In 1899, he wrote to the Secretary of State for India: "Decentralisation is all very well, but it appears to me in the case of Bombay and Madras to have been carried to a point in which the Supreme Government is nowhere, and in which the petty kings of those Governments are even conscious that responsibility attaches to anyone but themselves".

Lord Curzon complained of the silence of the Governors of Madras and Bombay and asked them to keep him informed of the events in their provinces. He suggested that the position of Presidency Governor should be reduced to that of the Governors of U.P., etc. His contention was that his proposal possessed the additional merit of reviving the popularity of the Indian Civil Service by adding two more attractive posts. However, his views were not accepted by the British Cabinet.

Policy of Officialisation

Lord Curzon believed that the Indians were lacking in all those qualities which made Englishmen good administrators. He had no faith in governing through the people or with their aid. He decided to reserve all higher posts for Englishmen. According to him, Englishmen possessed, partly by heredity, partly by upbringing and partly education, the knowledge of the principles of government, the habits of mind and the vigour of character which are essential for the task. The keynote of his government was that "the bureaucracy knows what is for the good of the people". He had no faith in the policy of educating Indians for self-government. He had no wish to sacrifice efficiency in the present for efficiency and freedom in the future. His faith was efficiency then and now.

The result was that share of the people in the administration of the country decreased during the Viceroyalty of Lord Curzon and the development of self-governing institutions received a set-back. According to Henry Cotton, "Lord Curzon had weakened and discouraged the schemes of self-government. He had officialised the universities and as far as possible the whole system of popular education; he had substituted a system of nomination to government service in place of competitive examination; and he had announced a practical declaration of race disqualification for the higher public offices. The end in view was to officialise the administration by every means in his power and this sinister aim was known to be underlying the partition of Bengal".

Lord Curzon held the Indians in contempt. In his Convocation Address to the Calcutta University in 1905, he declared thus: "I hope I am making no false arrogant claim when I say that the highest ideal of truth is to a large extent a Western conception... . Undoubtedly truth took a high place in the moral codes of the West, before it had been similarly honoured in the East where craftiness and diplomatic wile have always been held in much repute. We may prove it by the common innuendo that lurks in the words 'oriental diplomacy" by which is meant something rather tortuous and hypersubtle".

Reference may be made to a few other reforms carried out by Lord Curzon. The Mines Act and the Asian Labour Act were passed to give some protection to labour. The recommendations of the Currency Commission were given effect to in 1899 by establishing a 16 $d.$ rupee ratio and the gold exchange standard. Lord Curzon also levied countervailing duties upon bounty-fed sugar from Germany. He appointed a Director-General of Archaeology and passed in 1904 the Ancient Monuments Protection Act by which the Government took under protection the old historical buildings. Lord Curzon also provided for the appointments of the Chief Inspector of Mines, the Sanitary Inspector, Inspector-General of Agriculture, Inspector-General of Irrigation and Director-General of Intelligence.[3]

Partition of Bengal, 1905

The large size of the province of Bengal with its huge population of 78 million was considered to be too much for administration by a Lieutenant-Governor. Lord Curzon divided it into two parts. A new province of Eastern Bengal and Assam was created by amalgamating Assam and Chittagong with 15 districts of old Bengal. The new province was to have an area of about 106,000 sq. miles and a population of about 31 million.

The people of Bengal regarded the partition as a challenge to their nationalism and a strong agitation flared up. It was cleverly manipulated by the literary and legal classes whose vested interests were considered to be threatened by the new change. To the Government, the partition of Bengal was merely a readjustment of administrative boundaries. To the Indians, it meant the partition of a nation, an attempt to divide a homogeneous people, a deliberate and sinister attack upon the traditions, history and the language of the Bengalees. The partition split the Hindus of Bengal into two parts. In Eastern Bengal, they were outnumbered by the non-Bengalees. Lord Curzon refused to accept the proposal that Bengal, like Bombay and Madras, should be ruled by a Governor assisted by an Executive Council. He refused to submit to the agitation started by the people. The result was that the agitation went on growing in proportions with the lapse of time. It became a great national movement which agitated the minds of all the Indians. No wonder, the partition had to be cancelled in 1911.

Regarding the reaction of the people to the partition, Sir S.N. Banerjee writes thus: "The announcement fell like a bombshell. We felt that we had been insulted, humiliated and tricked. We felt that it was a deliberate blow aimed at the growing solidarity and self-consciousness of the Bengali-speaking population. Originally intended to meet administrative requirements, we felt that it had drawn to itself a political flavour and complexion, and, if allowed to be passed, it would be fatal to our political progress and to that close union between Hindus and Muslims upon which the prospects of Indian advancement so largely depended".

---

[3] "Lord Curzon's period of office was specially notable for a drastic overhauling of the whole machinery of administration".

ESTIMATE OF LORD CURZON

There is a lot of difference of opinion with regard to the achievements of Lord Curzon. It is probably true that much of the unrest in India was due to the restless energy of Lord Curzon. He condemned the people of India altogether. He had great contempt for them. He believed that Providence had appointed the Englishmen to carry on the administration of India and he would be going against the will of God if he gave any concessions to the people. To quote him, "If I felt that we were not working here for the good of India in obedience to a higher law and a noble aim, then I would see the link that holds England and India together severed without a sigh. But it is because I believe in the future of this country and the capacity of our race to guide it to goals that it has never hitherto attained that I keep courage and press forward". He refused to consider the public opinion in the country because, to quote him, "I searched my conscience and I asked myself who and what are the real Indian people". According to him, the Congress was "tottering to its fall, and one of my great ambitions while in India...is to assist it to peaceful demise". Lord Curzon declared in 1905: "That I have not offered political concessions is because I did not regard it as wisdom or statesmanship in the interests of India to do so. More places on this or that Council for a few active or eloquent men will not benefit the ryot".

According to Setalvad, "Lord Curzon was a very talented, efficient and hardworking Viceroy and he brought the whole administrative machine to a pitch of efficiency. He was, however, a great imperialist and always had visions of enlarging the extent and influence of the British empire. He looked upon India as a great asset for maintaining and extending the domination of Britain over large portions of the earth". Again, "He never thought or dreamt of independent India. In those days, it was said by people that Lord Curzon loved India as one loved his dog, a useful and obedient slave. His great strength of character as a stern administrator was illustrated by the action he took with regard to certain happenings in Burma. An offence of a most revolting character was perpetrated on a Burmese woman by a British soldier. Military authorities on the spot showed a culpable disposition to hush the matter up and were seconded in their apathy by local court officials. The prosecution of the soldiers concerned broke down on technical grounds although it was plain to everyone that acquittal involved a gross miscarriage of justice. With the concurrence of the Commander-in-Chief, Lord Curzon dismissed the culprit from the army high military officers were severely censured and in certain cases relieved of their command; the regiment was banished for two years to Aden and all leave and indulgence were stopped; the civil officers were severely censured and an Order-in-Council was issued in which the 'sense of profound horror and repugnance' with which the incident was viewed by Government was placed on record and 'the negligence and apathy that were displayed in responsible quarters' were reprobated".

Lord Curzon possessed great initiative, will power and eloquence. He was too much devoted to his duty. He worked hard in spite of his bad health, physical pain and domestic sorrow. He believed that Englishmen's justification in India lay in giving Indians a little more of "justice or happiness or prosperity, a sense of manliness or moral dignity, a spring of patriotism, a dawn of intellectual enlightenment, or a stirring of duty where it did not exist before". His view was that he had "worked for no other aim. Let India be my judge". He was a worshipper of efficiency and his false God made him commit many a blunder. According to Mr. Montagu, "Lord Curzon was like a motor-driver who spent all his energy and time in polishing the different parts of the machinery but he drove it without any destination. Like Dalhousie, he sowed the wind and left to his successor to reap the whirlwind. Although he was a great administrator, he was a failure as a statesman". According to Rash Behari Ghosh, "Lord Curzon left undone everything which he ought to have done and did everything which he ought not to have done".

According to Dr. Pattabhi Sitaramayya, "His curtailment of the powers of the Calcutta (now Kolkata) Corporation, his Official Secrets Act, his officialization of the Universities which made education costly...his Tibetan Expedition....and finally his Partition of Bengal, broke the back of loyal India and roused a new spirit in the nation. Even more galling to our sense of self-respect than his speech in Calcutta (now Kolkata) regarding our untruthfulness, was his sweeping charge that we Indians were, by our environment, our heritage and our upbringing, 'unequal to the responsibilities of high office under British rule'".

We may conclude with the following words of P.E. Roberts: "Whatever errors, whatever failures—and both error and failure are inseparable from human agency—critics may detect in his six years of office, it cannot be doubted that when the cloud belts of contemporary detraction have cleared away, Lord Curzon's name will stand amongst the foremost of those that make up the illustrious role of the Governor-General of India". (*British India*, p. 557).

REVIEW QUESTIONS

1. Analyse the foreign policy of Lord Curzon.
2. Write in brief about the tribal area of policy of Lord Curzon.
3. Discuss the salient features of the administrative system of Lord Curzon.
4. Elaborate on the reforms carried out by Lord Curzon.
5. Write a detailed note on decentralisation of finance.
6. Elucidate the policy of officialisation.
7. Bring out the main features of the Indian Universities Act, 1904.
8. Lord Curzon was one of the greatest and most influential Governors-General of India. Evaluate.
9. Throw light on the achievements of Lord Curzon.
10. Make an estimate of Lord Curzon.
11. Write short notes on the following:
    (a) Curzon's reform of the bureaucratic machinery
    (b) The Calcutta Corporation
    (c) Partition of Bengal, 1905

SUGGESTED READINGS

Arthur, Sir G.: *Life of Lord Kitchener*.
Curzon: *Leaves from a Viceroy's Note-book*.
Fraser: *India under Curzon and After*.
Raleigh, T. (Ed.): *Lord Curzon in India*.
Ronaldshay, Lord: *Life of Lord Curzon*.

18 India since Lord Minto

 LEARNING OBJECTIVES

- Discuss the policies and reforms of Lord Minto and his successors
- Bring out the main features of Minto-Morley reforms
- Throw light on the Gandhi-Irwin Pact and Mountbatten Plan

LORD MINTO II (1905-10)

Lord Minto, the successor of Lord Curzon was the great grandson of Lord Minto who was the Governor-General of India from 1807-13. He had a chequered career. He fought in the Second Afghan War and also worked as Governor-General of Canada from 1898 to 1904. Professor Dodwell has summed his character in these words: "The new Governor-General was no politician, but had enjoyed a wide and varied experience of men. He had always been a keen sportsman, he had served for many years in the army, and fought in the Second Afghan war, and in Egypt; he had taken an active part in the local administration according to the admirable tradition of English aristocracy, and he had occupied the high administrative post of the Governor-General of Canada. He had, therefore, seen men from many angles and his vision derived from his experience a solidity which is denied to those who only watch life from the study window, or confuse the problems of statesmanship with the fluctuations of party debate. In addition to these advantages, he has acquired in his entirely practical career the art of managing men, the knack of getting his own way or as much of it as circumstances permitted without domineering over or irritating those with whom he worked".

Lord Minto had to deal with a very difficult situation created by the partition of Bengal. As time passed on the agitation became stronger and stronger. No amount of repression on the part of the Government succeeded in crushing the movement. British goods were boycotted and violent speeches were made against the British Government. Many murders and dacoities were committed. The object of all these was to terrify the British imperialists in the country. Attempts were made on the lives of magistrates, police officials, collectors of revenue, etc. Even the informers of the Government were not spared. Their relatives also became the targets. The Government passed many severe laws such as the Acts of 1908 and 1910. Thousands of people were put behind the bars. Some of them were deported from the country.

Anglo-Russian Convention (1907)

Another important event of the Viceroyalty of Lord Minto was the Anglo-Russian Convention of 1907. By this, all the outstanding differences between Great Britain and Russia were settled, and the two countries came nearer to each other. As regards Afghanistan it was settled that Russia was to deal with Afghanistan through the Government of India. It is to be noted that Habib-Ullah, the Amir of Afghanistan, did not approve of the accord because he himself was not consulted. As regards Persia, its territorial integrity and independence were guaranteed both by Russia and Great Britain. It was also agreed that Northern Persia was to be under the sphere of influence of Russia and Southern Persia under the sphere of influence of Great Britain. Neither was to have any influence in Central Persia. As regards Tibet, both Great Britain and Russia agreed to accept the territorial integrity of Tibet and also abstain from interfering into its internal affairs. They both agreed to deal with Tibet through China and not to send any emissary to Tibet. Evidently, the object of preventing the spread of Russian influence in Tibet was achieved.

Trade with China

From the time of the English East India Company the Government of India used to export a lot of opium to China. This brought an annual revenue of ₹8 to 10 crores. The Chinese Government had raised objections to the trade of opium and had many a time requested the Government of India to stop it. In 1907, the Government of India agreed to reduce every year the export of opium. The export was to be stopped altogether after the lapse of some time. It is true that Government of India had to suffer the loss of a lot of revenue but it was undoubtedly a humanitarian step.

Minto-Morley Reforms

In 1909 was passed the Indian Councils Act which not only increased the number of non-official members of the Legislative Council but also increased their powers. This topic has been discussed at length in the chapter on Constitutional Development.

In 1910, King Edward VII died and George V succeeded him. Lord Minto left India in November 1910. He was succeeded by Lord Hardinge.

The Times of India wrote thus on the Viceroyalty of Lord Minto: "When the dust of controversy has subsided, when the political battleground has changed, India will always 'keep kindness' for the great gentleman who will remain in memory the Viceroy Charmeur. India will always remember with gratitude the Governor-General who, at a time of Storm and Drang, presented a calm, unruffled, courageous front to the storm and refused to be blown from the path he had marked out. India will always have a warm corner in her heart for the Viceroy who inspired a personal confidence in his rectitude at a time of stress and difficulty".

LORD HARDINGE (1910-16)

Lord Charles Hardinge was the grandson of Lord Henry Hardinge (1844-48) who fought the First Sikh War. Before coming out to India, he had no administrative experience, although he had some experience in the field of diplomacy. The new Governor-General was very sympathetic with the Indian aspirations. He identified himself so thoroughly with the cause of the Indians at home and abroad that he was probably the most popular Viceroy of India. We are told that he mixed freely with the Indians and sometimes visited the hostels and colleges of the Indian students. He won the confidence of the people of India by his sincerity of purpose.

The Delhi Durbar (1911)

After his accession to the throne in 1910, King George V paid a visit to India in 1911. A grand Durbar was held at Delhi near the present Radio Colony on 12th December 1811. A lot of money was distributed on that occasion. It was announced that the capital of India would be transferred from Calcutta to Delhi. The partition of Bengal was cancelled.[1] Assam was to be placed under a separate Chief Commissioner. According to Professor P.E. Roberts, "These changes were striking and dramatic. The transfer of the capital had no doubt many theoretical and logical advantages; it was defended by the Government on the ground that the consolidation of British Rule in India and development of the railway system made it no longer necessary for the Government to be upon the seaboard. The Viceroy hence forward would be increasingly concerned with matters of purely. Imperial interest, and the subordinate provincial Governorships would become more autonomous in their administration. Delhi, from its central position and its historical association, was obviously the best-fitted city in India for the capital of a quasi-federal empire. The re-union of Bengal was said to be not a reversal of the partition but a rearrangement after experience— a statement hardly consistent with facts".

Critics pointed out to the many concessions made at the time of the Coronation Durbar of Delhi. It was contended that the changes should have been brought about by an Act of Parliament and not by a declaration of the Government. That was not a proper procedure. It was also pointed out that the construction of new capital at Delhi would involve a lot of unnecessary expenditure.

---

[1] As regards the detail concerning the cancellation of the Partition of Bengal and the transfer of capital from Calcutta to Delhi, Lord Hardinge tells us that he received in January 1911 a proposal from Lord Crewe suggesting the possibility of modification of the partition of Bengal. His proposal was intended to satisfy that section of the Indian political community who regarded the partition as a mistake. His idea was to create a Governorship instead of Lieutenant-Governorship of Bengal with the capital of the province at Dacca, to form an imperial enclave of Calcutta directly under the Viceroy and to appoint Commissioners for the various divisions. The suggestion was that the rectification of the partition should be announced by King George at the Durbar to be held in India.

Lord Hardinge himself felt that if there was to be peace in the two Bengals, it was absolutely necessary to remove what was regarded by all Bengalis as an act of flagrant injustice without justification. It was realised that if nothing was done in that connection, there was every possibility of greater trouble in Bengal. The Government of Bengal was practically non-existent so far as the maintenance of peace and order was concerned. It was really the Viceroy who administered the province and it was to him and his Council that the Lieutenant-Governor and his officials looked for advice and support. The presence of the Legislative Assembly in Calcutta created an undue inevitable Bengali influence upon the members which was detrimental to legislative impartiality and presented a vast field for intrigue.

Sir John Jenkins, the Home Member of the Government of India, sent a memorandum to the Governor-General on 17th June 1911. He held very strong views on the urgency of the transfer of the capital from Calcutta to Delhi which he thought "would be bold stroke of statesmanship which would give universal satisfaction and mark a new era in the history of India". Sir John wanted the declaration to be made by the King in the Durbar to be held in Delhi. The change was intended to create a magical effect in the imagination on the masses of people. The idea of shifting the capital from Calcutta to Delhi was not entirely original. Lord Lawrence had considered the scheme and was in favour of it. Lord Curzon was in favour of shifting the capital to Agra.

Lord Hardinge approved of the plan of Sir John Jenkins and wrote a long letter to Lord Crewe on 19th July 1911. He emphasised the advantages to be derived from the new proposals. The Viceroy asked Lord Crewe to keep the whole thing sacred whether the same was accepted or not. On 7th August 1911, the Victory received a very satisfactory reply, Lord Crewe informed him that he had his "entire support and full authority to proceed".

Lord Crewe confided the substance of the scheme to the King who accepted it with great keenness. He was anxious to make the announcement himself at the Durbar and was very insistent as to the need of complete secrecy. Lord Crewe told the proposal to Lord Morley and Asquith and both of them were deeply impressed. Asquith was greatly struck by the bigness of the idea and considered that its merits and advantages far out-weighed any hostile arguments. The rest of the time before the holding of the Durbar was occupied in considering the legislative and statutory measures that were necessary to carry out the new policy. The secret was known to only 12 persons in India before the holding of the Durbar in December 1911.

That would also give a setback to the prosperity of Calcutta (now Kolkata). It was also maintained that the cancellation of the partition of Bengal in 1911 was not opportune because the agitation against it had become very weak by that time and such a step was absolutely unnecessary at that stage.

On 23rd December 1912, a bomb was thrown on Lord Hardinge when he was to make his state entry into Delhi. He himself was wounded and the person sitting behind him on the elephant was killed. In spite of this provocation, Lord Hardinge maintained his previous attitude of sympathy towards the Indians.

In 1912 it was rumoured that China would be conquering Tibet. The British Government gave a warning to the Chinese Government that the latter must desist from such a course. The result was that the fear of Chinese conquest of Tibet disappeared.

From the beginning of the 20th century, the Government of South Africa was following a policy of harassing the Indians in South Africa. Although the Indians were as much responsible for the prosperity of South Africa as the Europeans, the latter seemed to be determined to drive out the Indians from that territory. In 1913, a law was passed by which the immigration of Indians was limited and they were prohibited from trading, farming and holding property. Under the leadership of Mahatma Gandhi, the Indians of South Africa offered *satyagraha* against the unjust laws. Both Gandhi and his followers were arrested and put behind the bars. There was great resentment in India and Lord Hardinge shared the feelings of the people of the country. The result was that the Government of South Africa appointed a Commission and ultimately passed the Indian Relief Act of 1914. The new Act recognised as valid the monogamous marriages of the Indians. It also abolished the tax of £3 on every Indian labourer. It is true that the new Act did not remove all the grievances of the Indians in South Africa, but it was characterised by Mahatma Gandhi as the Magna Carta of Indian liberty in South Africa. As regards the system of indentured labour from India, the matter was taken up in 1910 by Gokhale and the system was ultimately abolished in 1917. The First World War started in September 1914. As Great Britain joined the war against Germany and Austria-Hungary, India also joined the war on the side of the British Government. The Indians gave unconditional help to the English in their hour of need and danger. Indian troops fought along with other Allied troops in the battlefield of France, Flanders, Egypt, Africa, Palestine, Mesopotamia and Macedonia.

LORD CHELMSFORD (1916-21)

Lord Chelmsford succeeded Lord Hardinge at a time when the First World War was going on. Before coming to India as Governor-General, he had worked in one of the States of Australia. In August 1917, the famous declaration was made by Edwin S. Montagu, Secretary of State for India, with regard to the goal of the British Government in India. That declaration runs thus: "The policy of His Majesty's Government with which the Government of India are in complete accord, is the increasing association of Indians in every branch administration and the gradual development of self-governing institutions with a view to the progressive realisation of responsible government in India as an integral part of the British empire. They have decided that substantial steps in this direction should be taken as soon as possible and that it is of the highest importance as a preliminary to considering what these steps should be that there should be a free and informal exchange of opinion between those in authority at home and in India. His Majesty's Government have decided, with His Majesty's approval, that I should accept the Viceroy's invitation to proceed to India to discuss these matters with the Viceroy and the Government of India, to consider with the Viceroy the views of Local Governments, and to receive with him the suggestions of representative bodies and others.

"I would add that progress in this policy can only be achieved by successive stages. The British Government and the Government of India on whom the responsibility lies for the welfare and advancement of Indian peoples, must be the judges of the time and measures of each advance, and they must be guided by the cooperation received from those upon whom new opportunities of service will be conferred and by the extent to which it is found that confidence can be reposed in their sense of responsibility".

After the declaration, Mr. Montagu came to India and toured the country in the company of Lord Chelmsford. Many deputations were interviewed and views were exchanged. Ultimately, the report was submitted and published. In 1919, the Government of India Act was passed. This Act introduced dyarchy in the provinces and added to the powers of the Central Legislature.

Reference may be made to the Third Afghan War of 1919. What actually happened was that the people of Afghanistan did not approve of the pro-British policy of Habib-Ullah. The result was that he was murdered. Aman-Ullah came on the throne of Kabul. There were disturbance in the Punjab in 1919 on account of the Rowlatt Act. The new King was able to occupy some parts of the North-Western Frontier. Ultimately, his advance was checked, and he was completely defeated. A treaty made in August 1921. By this treaty, the King of Afghanistan got the right to conduct his foreign affairs himself. The British control was abolished. The annual subsidy which the Government of India used to give to Afghanistan was also stopped.

Reference may be made to the non-cooperation movement started by Mahatma Gandhi. The object of the movement was to protest against the acts of high-handedness on the part of the British Government. Meetings were held all over the country and *hartals* were organised. The British Government imposed martial law. General Dyer was responsible for the tragedy of Jallianwala Bagh at Amritsar. In this non-cooperation movement both the Hindus and Muslims participated.

Reference may also be made to what is called the Khilafat movement. This movement was organised by the Muslims of India as a protest against shabby treatment meted out to Turkey by the Allies in spite of the repeated promises and assurances to the Indian Muslims. The Khilafat movement stood for the integrity of the Turkish empire. The Caliph to have his capital at Constantinople. They also demanded the establishment of a Muslim State of Palestine.

LORD READING (1921-26)

Lord Reading was born a humble Jew but rose to the high position of the Lord Chief Justice of England by sheer dint of hard work. There was a lot of opposition in the Government. There were strikes and riots in many places. There was a split in the Congress. One section of the Congress was in favour of entering the legislatures and thereby wrecking the constitution from within. These Congressmen were known as the Swarajists and were led by men like C.R. Das and Moti Lal Nehru. Ultimately, the Swarajists were allowed to enter the legislatures. On account of persistent demands of the Indians, the Muddiman Committee Report was published with regard to the working of dyarchy under the new Constitution.

LORD IRWIN (1926-31)

Lord Irwin had to deal with very serious problems during his term of Viceroyalty. In 1927 was appointed the famous Simon Commission. The Indians protested against its composition which was all White. No wonder, the Commission was boycotted by the people of India. There were *hartals* and boycotts all over the country. There were lathi-charges and shootings. In December 1928, the Congress at its Calcutta session passed a resolution asking from the British Government the grant of Dominion Status within a year. It is true that in October 1929, a statement was made in Parliament on behalf of the British Government that the goal of the British Government in India was to give Dominion Status to India, but such a declaration did not satisfy the Indian leaders and consequently at its Lahore session in December 1929, the Congress declared the achievement of full independence as its goal.

January 26, 1930 was declared as Independence Day for India and Civil Disobedience Movement started in the country. Mahatma Gandhi himself led the movement. Thousands of people were arrested and punished. Their properties were confiscated.

It was in this atmosphere that the Simon Commission submitted its report and the First Round Table Conference met in 1930 in London. Not much could be accomplished on account of the absence of the Congress. Through the efforts of Sapru and Jayakar, the Gandhi-Irwin Pact was made in 1931 and Gandhiji sailed for England as the sole representative of the Congress.

The work of Lord Irwin has been variously estimated. Some condemned him for his weakness and others condemned him for his repressive policy. There was a time when the Conservatives demanded a recall of Lord Irwin. Undoubtedly, he was a noble soul.

LORD WILLINGDON (1931-36)

Before his appointment as Governor-General in 1931, Lord Willingdon had acted as the Governor of Bombay and Madras from 1913 to 1924. He had also acted as the Governor-General of Canada from 1926 to 1930.

The Second Round Table Conference met in London during the period of his Viceroyalty. It failed to achieve its purpose on account of the attitude of Mr. Jinnah. As soon as Mahatma Gandhi came back from London, he was arrested. The reign of terror and repression started in the country. The more the movement was suppressed, the stronger it became. The ordinances passed by the Government were ineffective to crush the spirit of the people.

In August 1932 was announced the famous Communal Award by Ramsay MacDonald. Mahatma Gandhi strongly protested against it and threatened to go on fast unto death if the clauses relating to the Depressed Classes were not changed. Ultimately, the Poona Pact was signed and this pact altered the Communal Award so far as the representation of the Depressed Classes was concerned.

In 1932 was summoned the Third Round Table Conference in London. In March 1933 was issued the White Paper containing the proposals of the Government of England with regard to the new Constitution of India. In 1935 was passed the Government of India Act.

During the Viceroyalty of Lord Willingdon, earthquakes took place in Bihar and Quetta. There was a lot of loss of life and property.

Lord Willingdon was hated by the Indians on account of his policy of repression. Indian nationalism triumphed in spite of all the efforts of this great bureaucrat.

LORD LINLITHGOW (1936-44)

Before his appointment as Governor-General, Lord Linlithgow had a brilliant career. He was the Chairman of the Royal Commission on Indian Agriculture. He was also the Chairman of the Joint Select Committee of Indian Constitutional Reforms. He also had a hand in the drafting of the

Government of India Act, 1935. No wonder, he was sent to India to enforce the law which he had helped in making.

The Federal Part of the Act was not introduced at all. Only the Provincial Part was introduced. Elections were held in the beginning of 1937 and the Congress got a majority in many provinces. In spite of that, it refused to form Ministries unless an assurance was given that the Governors would not interfere in the day-to-day affairs of the departments under the control of the Indian Ministers. When such an assurance was given, Congress Ministries were formed and they continued to function till 1939 when they resigned after the declaration of the Second World War.

There was a split in the Congress during this period. Subhas Chandra Bose got himself elected as the Congress President in 1938 and 1939. There arose differences between him and Mahatma Gandhi and his followers. Ultimately Subhas Chandra Bose left the Congress and formed the Forward Block. In 1940, Lord Linlithgow made his famous August offer, but it was rejected by the Congress.

In March 1942, Sir Stafford Cripps came to India to arrive at some sort of an agreement with the Congress on the basis of the proposals brought by him with himself and approved by the British Cabinet. The Cripps Mission was also a failure.

In August 1942, the Congress passed the famous "Quit India" resolution. As a result to this, the Congress leaders were arrested and remained in jail throughout the World War II.

LORD WAVELL (1944-47)

During the period of Viceroyalty of Lord Wavell, the World War II came to a successful end. Germany was defeated and Japan surrendered in 1945.

Lord Wavell called in June 1945 a Conference at Simla with the object of coming to some sort of agreement with the major political parties in India. Unfortunately, the Simla Conference failed on account of the attitude of Muslim League.

When the Labour Party came to power in England, fresh elections were ordered in India for the provincial legislatures. A Cabinet-Mission consisting of Lord Pethick Lawrence, Sir Stafford Cripps and A.V. Alexander came to India in March 1946. After long negotiations, the Cabinet Mission issued its formula on 16th May 1946. The Cabinet Mission scheme provided for an Interim Government and also the procedure for the framing of a Constitution of India and also of the groups into which the provinces were to be combined. The Muslim League accepted the scheme and the Congress rejected it, on certain grounds. However, when the Congress accepted it, the Muslim League rejected it. There was the famous Calcutta Killing in August 1946. On 2nd September 1946, Pandit Jawaharlal Nehru formed the Interim Government. However, the Muslim League refused to join at the beginning, but later on did so.

The Constituent Assembly met in December 1946 at New Delhi. The Muslim League boycotted it. There was a controversy as to whether the grouping of provinces was compulsory or not and the British Government gave its verdict in favour of compulsory grouping.

LORD MOUNTBATTEN (MARCH 1947 TO JUNE 1948)

In March 1947, Lord Wavell was replaced by Lord Mountbatten. When he reached India, he found the situation very critical. The Muslim League was carrying on its wear and tear campaign all over the country especially in the Punjab. There were riots in March 1947. Lord Mountbatten felt that the only way to tackle the situation was to complete the work of transfer of power into the Indian hands within as short a period as possible. He held consultations with the Indian leaders for the same purpose. He went to London in May 1947 to discuss the matter with the British Government. On his return, he announced his famous June 3 Plan. By this Plan, it was proposed to divide India into two parts, viz., the Dominion of India and Dominion of Pakistan. Both the Dominions were to be given independence. The Plan was accepted by both the Muslim League and the Indian National Congress. The Indian Independence Act, 1947, was passed to give effect to the June 3 Plan. The division of the country took place on 15th August, 1947.

After the independence of India, Lord Mountbatten was again appointed as the Governor-General of India and he continued to occupy that position till June 1948. It was during this period that the invasion of Kashmir by the raiders took place. Kashmir acceded to India and the case of Kashmir was taken to the United Nations.

There was a lot of bloodshed both in India and Pakistan on account of communal riots. There was wholesale exodus of populations from India to Pakistan and *vice versa.*

Lord Mountbatten did a lot of useful work in connection with the Indian States. There was the possibility of a large number of independent states coming into existence in the country after the extinction of British paramountcy in India. It goes to the credit of Lord Mountbatten that he was able to persuade most of the Indian States to join one or the other Dominion. The result was that a lot of complications which otherwise would have given headache to the rulers of both India and Pakistan were avoided. When Lord and Lady Mountbatten left India in June 1948, there was a general feeling that one who belonged to them was going to depart from their country.

Shri C. Rajagopalachari was the Governor-General of India from June 1948 to January 1950. It was during his regime that police action was taken against the Nizam of Hyderabad. Kasim Razvi and his followers were defeated and Hyderabad became a part of the Indian Union. During this period, the Constituent Assembly passed the new Constitution of India which came into force on January 26, 1950. The relations between India and Pakistan were unsatisfactory. There was a lot of tension on account of the problem of Kashmir and evacuee property.

The Constitution of India provided for a President of India in place of the Governor-General of India and Dr. Rajendra Prasad was elected the First President and he continued to occupy that position up to 1962. He was a brilliant scholar. His nobility, devotion and sincerity were unequalled. He was succeeded by Dr. S. Radhakrishnan as President in 1962. Dr. Radhakrishnan was a remarkable personality in many ways. He was a great Sanskrit scholar. He was very near to Prime Minister Nehru. Before becoming President, he was the Vice-President of India and the Indian Ambassador in the Soviet Union.

On his retirement in 1967, Dr. Zakir Hussain became the President of India. He was not only a great nationalist but also an educationist. He lived a life of simplicity and dedication. He died in 1969. He was succeeded by V. V. Giri who continued to be President till 1974. He was succeeded by Fakhruddin Ali Ahmed. He died in harness and J. D. Jatti acted as President for some time. The next President was N. Sanjeeva Reddy who was the President from 1977 to 1982. Giani Zail Singh became the President in 1982.

Pandit Jawaharlal Nehru was the Prime Minister of India from 1947 to 1964. He was succeeded by Lal Bahadur Shastri who continued to be Prime Minister upto January 1966 when he died at Tashkent. The next Prime Minister was Mrs. Indira Gandhi. She were twice the Prime Minister of India, first from 1966 to 1977 and again from 1980 to 1984. When she was assassinated on 31 October 1984, she was succeeded by her son Rajiv Gandhi in October 1984.

When India became free, she had to face very big problems at the very beginning. Indian leaders like Jawaharlal Nehru, Sardar Patel and Dr. Rajendra Prasad, deserve credit for the manner in which they tackled the situation with the help of Lord Mountbatten. There was the problem of law and order. There were communal riots on a large scale. Caravans of refugees with horrible stories of murder, abductions and betrayals came to India and created innumerable problems. They clamoured for revenge. They were badly in need of shelter and food. For some time, everything seemed to have collapsed but credit goes to those who tackled the problem sympathetically and efficiently. Millions of refugees were rehabilitated. They also showed remarkable courage and qualities of self-help. Under the dynamic personality of Jawaharlal Nehru, three Five-Year Plans were prepared and executed. Canals were dug. Tube-wells were sunk in large numbers. Tractors were imported. Fertilisers were secured. Old industries were helped and new ones were set up, both in the public sector and private sector. There was a lot of industrial activity in the country and a big step was taken on the road to industrialisation. Big steel plants were set up in various states. Cement factories multiplied. The cooperative movement got great impetus. Cooperative societies were established for credit as well as marketing facilities. Thousands of primary health centres were established in the community development areas. An ambitious programme of rural electrification was implemented. Community Development Programmes were launched on Gandhiji's birthday on 2 October 1952. The need of social legislation was keenly felt and the Hindu Marriage Act, the Hindu Succession Act, the Hindu Minority and Guardianship Act and the Hindu Adoptions and Maintenance Act were passed by the Indian Parliament. The Untouchability (Offences) Act, 1955 was passed. It made untouchability a culpable offence. There was an all-round development in education.

The foreign policy of free India was formulated and elaborated by Jawaharlal Nehru. He believed in a policy of non-alignment. In the Cold War between the United States and the Soviet Union, he did not align himself with one side or the other. He was opposed to colonialism. He cooperated with Asian countries. He played an important part at the Bandung Conference of 1955. He condemned the policy to apartheid followed by the Union of South Africa. He had faith in the United Nations and its principles. It was in October 1947 that Pakistani tribesmen attacked Kashmir. After the accession of the State of Jammu and Kashmir to India, Indian forces were flown to Kashmir to drive out the invaders from the Kashmir valley. India took the Kashmir question to the United Nations but the same could not be resolved on account of the unhelpful attitude of Pakistan. Prime Minister Jawaharlal Nehru went to Pakistan to sign the Indus Water Treaty in 1960. In December 1961, police action was taken against Goa, Daman and Diu and they were annexed to India.

Nehru followed a vigorous foreign policy as a result of which the credit of India rose very high in the world. However, it was found even during his lifetime that his foreign policy was more idealistic than realistic. Nehru made a mistake in allowing China to occupy Tibet from where millions of Chinese soldiers could threaten the security of India. He signed a treaty to friendship with China in 1954 but failed to settle with China the question of Indo-China border at that time. China took advantage of the goodness of Nehru and not only attacked India in 1962 but also occupied large areas of Indian territory. It was the timely help from the United States which forced China to declare a unilateral cease-fire on 20 November 1962. In 1965, China helped Pakistan when the latter attacked India. Likewise, China supported Pakistan in 1971 when the latter attacked India. It is only in recent times that there is a little improvement in the relations between India and China.

Nehru established friendly relations with the Soviet Union and went on a state visit to that country. Bulganin and Khrushchev visited India in December 1955.

India also had friendly relations with the United States. Nehru himself visited the United States and India was given a lot of aid for her development. Nehru's relations with President Kennedy were particularly very cordial.

Nehru died on 27 May 1964. Through the efforts of Congress President Kamaraj, Lal Bahadur Shastri became the next Prime Minister. He was a Gandhian in thinking and way of life. He believed in honesty and hard life. The most important event of his time was the attack on Kashmir by Pakistan. To begin with, Pakistan made headway but her further advance was stopped when the Indian army opened the Lahore front. Ultimately, peace between the two countries was made at Tashkent through the good offices of Prime Minister Kosygin of the Soviet Union.

Shastri died on 10 January 1966. There was a struggle for power between Morarji Desai and Indira Gandhi and ultimately Indira Gandhi became Prime Minister. She was Prime Minister upto January 1977 when she had to resign on account of the victory of the Janata Party at the polls. She again became Prime Minister in January 1980 and was Prime Minister when she was assassinated on 31 October 1984.

There was a power struggle between Prime Minister Indira Gandhi and the organisational wing of the Indian National Congress. As a result of that, there was a split in the Congress in 1969. Mrs. Indira Gandhi came out successful in the struggle for power. Her rivals were completely defeated and she succeeded in establishing her control even over the Congress organisation.

In 1971, a large number of refugees entered India from East Pakistan where the Pakistan army was doing havoc. Prime Minister Indra Gandhi visited many countries to arouse public opinion against the treatment which was being meted out to the people of East Bengal. She also entered into Treaty of Friendship and Cooperation on 9 August 1971 with the Soviet Union. There was an assurance in the Treaty that in the event of an attack or threat thereof, India and the Soviet Union shall immediately enter into mutual consultations in order to remove that threat and take appropriate measures to ensure peace and security of their countries. Pakistan attacked India on 3 December 1971. India struck back on 4 December 1971. The war lasted exactly two weeks. The Pakistani forces in East Pakistan surrendered in Dacca on 16 December 1971. The Simla Conference was held in June 1972 between Mrs. Indira Gandhi and Mr. Bhutto, Prime Minister of Pakistan. The two countries agreed to withdraw their forces to their sides of the international border and accepted a step by step approach for the normalisation of relations. Later on, India returned Pakistani prisoners of war.

Mrs. Indira Gandhi nationalised fourteen big banks in the country. There was also take over of 106 General Insurance Companies by the Government. Coal industry was also nationalised. The Privy Purses and the privileges of the former rulers of India were abolished. The Constitution of India was amended to legalise the action of the Government.

On 18 May 1974 India carried out a nuclear test at Pokhran in Rajasthan. India refused to sign the Nuclear Non-Proliferation Treaty as she considered the same to be discriminatory.

On 12 June 1975, the election of Prime Minister Indira Gandhi to Lok Sabha was declared void. On 25 June 1975, an Emergency was declared in the country. All the leaders of the Opposition were arrested. Anybody who criticised the Government or the Prime Minister was put behind the bars. A strict censorship was imposed on the press and newspapers could not print any criticism of the Government. People suffered terribly during the period of Emergency. There was no rule of law in the country. The police and the bureaucracy played havoc. Even the Supreme Court of India held that persons arrested during the Emergency could not move the High Court for a writ of *habeas corpus*. The Constitution of India was radically amended in December 1976. Prime Minister Indira Gandhi was assured by her supporters that if she dissolved the Lok Sabha, she would certainly win a majority. She dissolved the Lok Sabha in January 1977 and elections were held in March 1977. However, Janata Party won a majority and formed the Government.

The Janata Government was in power from March 1977 to July 1979. During that period, a lot was done to remedy the wrongs done by Mrs. Indira Gandhi during the period of Emergency. The Constitution of India was amended twice. The Shah Commission was appointed to report on the atrocities committed during the Emergency. Provision was made for Special Courts to try Emergency cases. However, the Janata Government fell on 15 July 1979 on account of dissensions in the Janata Party.

Charan Singh became Prime Minister on 28 July 1979 and continued to be so till January 1980 although he did not face the Parliament even for a day. Elections were again held in January 1980 and Mrs. Indira Gandhi won. She was sworn as Prime Minister on 14 January 1980. In 1981 was held a meeting of the Non-Aligned Conference in New Delhi. In March 1983, the Non-Aligned Summit was held in New Delhi.

The Akali Dal started an agitation against the Government in Punjab. The Extremists/terrorists under the leadership of Jarnail Singh Bhinderwale took advantage of the situation in Punjab and entrenched themselves in the Golden Temple at Amritsar. There was a reign of terror in the Punjab. On 5 June 1984, the army entered the Golden Temple and cleared it. On 31 October 1984, Mrs. Indira Gandhi was assassinated and Rajiv Gandhi became Prime Minister.

Elections to Lok Sabha were held in December 1984 in which the Congress won an overwhelming majority. Elections to the States were held in January 1985. On 24 July 1985, there was Rajiv-Longowal Accord on Punjab. On 15 August 1985, there was an Accord on Assam. Elections were held in Punjab and Assam and the Akali Dal and the Asom Gana Parishad formed Ministries respectively.

REVIEW QUESTIONS

1. What was the important event of the Viceroyalty of Lord Minto? Discuss.
2. Explain the policies and reforms of Lord Chelmsford and Lord Linlithgow.
3. Write a detailed note on the events that took place during Lord Reading and Lord Irwin.
4. Discuss the features and importance of Gandhi-Irwin Pact.
5. Who was Lord Mountbatten? What was his plan in the history of India?
6. Critically examine the role played by Mountbatten in consolidating post-independent india.
7. Elaborate on the main features of Mountbatten Plan.
8. Was Lord Mountbatten good for India and Pakistan? Critically analyse.
9. Lord Mountbatten did a lot of useful work in connection with the Indian states. Examine.
10. Write short notes on the following:
    (a) Lord Willingdon
    (b) Lord Linlithgow
    (c) Gandhi-Irwin Pact
    (d) Minto-Morley Reforms
    (e) Mountbatten Plan

SUGGESTED READINGS

Durga Das: *From Curzon to Nehru and After.*
Edwardes Michael: *The Last Years of British India.*
Gupta, Hari Ram: *India-Pakistan War,* 1965.
Kulkarni, V.B.: *British Dominion in India and After.*
Mahajan, V.D.: *Fifty-five Years of Modern India,* 1975.
Mansergh, N.: *Transfer of Power (1942-47),* Vols. I, II & III.
Menon, K.P.S.: *The Indo-Soviet Treaty, Delhi,* 1971.
Menon, V.P.: *The Transfer of Power in India.*
Mellor, A.: *India since Partition.*
Moon, Penderel: *Gandhi and Modern India.*
Moraes, Frank: *Jawaharlal Nehru,* New York, 1956.
Morley, Lord: *Recollections.*
Nayar, Kuldip: *India: The Critical Years, Delhi,* 1971.
Pandey, B.N.: *The Break-up of British India.*
Prem Bhasin: *Riding the Wave.*
Spear, Percival: *India, Pakistan and the West* (1958).
Spear, Percival: India. *A Modern History,* 1961.
Strachy, John: *The End of Empire.*

19 Constitutional Development (1773-1950)

LEARNING OBJECTIVES

- Discuss the constitutional development of India from 1773 to 1950.
- Narrate the features and provisions of the various Acts passed in the constitutional history of India.
- Throw light on the events and reforms of the constitutional history of India.

THE REGULATING ACT, 1773

The Regulating Act was the first landmark in the constitutional development of India. It is well-known that Lord Clive got the Diwani of Bengal, Bihar and Orissa (now Odisha) from Shah Alam, the Moghul Emperor in 1765. The shareholders demanded larger dividends and the same was raised to 2½. The British Government also got annually a sum of £4 million from 1767 onwards. Edmund Burke condemned the British Government and maintained that the Government had "sanctified the bloodshed, this rapine, this villainy, this extortion—for the valuable consideration of £4,000,000. This crime tax being agreed to, we heard no more of malpractices".[1]

Although both the shareholders of the English East India Company and the British Government gained, the position of the people of Bengal became most unhappy. The people were the victims of famine and the corruption of the servants of the Company. According to Lecky, "Never before had natives experienced a tyranny which was at once so skilful, so searching and so strong. Whole districts which had been populous and flourishing were at last utterly depopulated, and it was noticed that on the appearance of a party of English merchants the villages were at once deserted and the shops shut, and the roads thronged with panic-stricken fugitives". According to Chatham,

---

[1] According to Ilbert, "The great events of 1765 produced immediate results in England. The eyes of the proprietors of the Company were dazzled by golden visions. On the dispatch bearing the grant of the Diwani being read to the Court of Proprietors they began to clamour for an increase of dividend, and, in spite of the Company's debt and the opposition of the Directors, they insisted on raising the dividend in 1766 from 6 to 10 per cent, and in 1767 to 12.5 per cent. At the same time the public mind was startled by the enormous fortunes which 'Nabobs' were bringing home, and the public conscience was disturbed by rumours of the unscrupulous modes in which those fortunes had been amassed. Constitutional questions were also raised as to the right of trading Company to acquire on its own account powers of territorial sovereignty. The intervention of Parliament was imperatively demanded". According to the Report on Indian Constitutional Reforms, "The Company's peril of bankruptcy was the immediate cause of Parliament's first intervention: but a more powerful motive was the growing feeling in England, to which the opulence and arrogance of officials-returning from India contributed, that the nation must assert its responsibility for seeing that the new and vast experiment of ruling a distant and alien race was properly conducted".

"India teems with inequities so rank as smell to earth and heaven. The things were so rotten that in April 1772 was appointed a Select Committee of 31 members to inquire into the affairs of the East India Company. In August of the same year, the English East India Company asked for a loan from the British Government. The Parliament appointed a Select Committee to examine the affairs of the Company and submit its report. The Committee submitted its final report in May 1773. It was then that the Parliament passed the Regulating Act of 1773.

There were other causes also which were responsible for the passing of the Regulating Act. Educated public opinion in England through the press and the floor of Parliament began to ask for control by the State over the political activities of the English East India Company. The factors which influenced public opinion were the abuses of the Company's rule in India and the attempts made by the 'Nabobs' to dominate English society. The British country-gentry not only hated the 'Nabobs' but also felt jealous of them. Moreover, there were rival parliamentary interests which clashed over the question of India. They were primarily interested in the rise and fall of ministries whose fate depended considerably on the support of the Directors of the English East India Company who had their interests in the House of Commons. Regulation and control by the State during the period 1773-1784 was due largely to the manipulation of the political machine.

Provisions of the Regulating Act

1. The Regulating Act gave the right of vote for the election of Directors of the Company to shareholders holding stock worth £1,000 for 12 months preceding the date of election. Formerly, Directors were elected for one year but the Act provided that in future they were to be elected for 4 years. However, one-fourth of them were to retire every year. The Directors were required to submit copies of letters and advices received from the Governor-General-in-Council. Copies of letters relating to revenue were to be sent to the Treasury and those relating to civil and military affairs were to be sent to one of the Secretaries of State. Governor-General of Bengal and the Governors of Bombay (now Mumbai) and Madras (now Chennai) were required to pay due obedience to the orders of the Directors and also keep them constantly informed of all the matters affecting of the interests of the Company.

2. Provision was made for a Governor-General of Bengal and his Council of 4 members. They were vested with "the whole civil and military Government of the said Presidency, and also the ordering, management and government of territorial acquisitions and revenues in the kingdom of Bihar, Bengal and Orissa (now Odisha)". Warren Hastings was appointed the first Governor-General of Bengal and Clavering, Monsan, Philip Francis and Barewell were appointed the members of his Council. Members of the Council were to hold office for 5 years and they could not be removed except by Crown on the representation of the Directors. Governor-General of Bengal was required to carry on the work according to the majority opinion of this Council. He could not overrule the majority view of this Council. However, he was given a casting vote in the case of a tie. Governor-General was also given the power of superintending and controlling the Presidencies of Madras and Bombay. However, in case of emergency and direct orders from the Directors in London, Presidencies of Madras and Bombay were not to act according to the orders of the Governor-General of Bengal.

3. Governors-in-Council of Bombay (now Mumbai) and Madras (now Chennai) were required to pay due obedience to the orders of Governor-General of Bengal. They were required to submit to the Governor-General-in-Council advice and intelligence on transactions and matters relating to the government, revenues and interests of the Company. They were required to forward all Rules and regulations framed by them to the Governor-General-in-Council. If they failed to carry out the orders of the Governor-General-in-Council or did not perform their duties properly, they could be suspended by the Governor-General-in-Council.

4. Governor-General-in-Council was given the power to make rules, ordinance and regulations for the good order and civil government of Company's settlement at Fort William and factories and places subordinate to it. These rules and regulations were not to be against the laws of England and were required to be registered with the Supreme Court. These could be disallowed by the King-in-Council within two years.

5. The Regulating Act provided for a Supreme Court with a Chief Justice and three puisne judges. Sir Elijah Impey was appointed the Chief Justice. The Supreme Court was given the power to try civil, criminal, admiralty and ecclesiastical cases. It was to be a Court of Record and Court of Oyer and Terminer and Gaol delivery in and for the town of Calcutta, Fort William and other factories subordinate to it. The jurisdiction of the Supreme Court was to extend to all the British subjects residing in Bengal, Bihar and Orissa. It was empowered to try all cases of complaints against any of His Majesty's subjects for crimes or oppressions. It was to try suits, complaints or actions against any person in the employment of the Company or His Majesty's subjects. It was given both original and appellate jurisdiction. Cases were to be tried by means of a jury.

6. The Regulating Act prohibited the receiving of presents and bribes by the servants of the Company. "No person holding or exercising any civil or military office under the Crown shall accept, receive or take directly or indirectly any present, gift, donation, gratuity or reward, pecuniary or otherwise". It was made clear that the offenders were to make double payment and were liable to be transported to England.

7. No British subject was to charge interest at a rate higher than 12 per cent. If the Governor-General, Governor, Member of the Council, a judge of Supreme Court or any other servant of the Company committed any offence he was liable to be tried and punished by the King's Bench in England. The Act also settled the salaries of the Governor-General, Governors, Chief Justice and other judges. Thus, Governor General was to get £25,000 annually. Every member of the Council was given £10,000 a year. The annual salary of the Chief Justice was fixed at £8,000 and that of an ordinary judge £6,000.

Criticism of the Regulating Act

It is universally admitted that the Regulating Act had many shortcomings.

1. A serious defect of the Regulating Act was that it did not define clearly the exact jurisdiction and powers of the Governor-General, the members of his Council and the Supreme Court. Whether the omission was deliberate or unintentional, there was a lot of conflict. The relations between the Governor-General and the Supreme Court were never happy. The result was that they always pulled in different directions.

2. The Supreme Court claimed to serve writs on the inhabitants of the country and make them appear before itself. Warren Hastings resisted this claim of the Supreme Court. In the case of Cassijurah, the Sheriff and the officers accompanying him were prevented by a company of Sepoys from executing a writ against the Raja. These Sepoys maintained that they were merely acting under the orders of the Governor-General.

    In the Patna Case (1777-79), a struggle for property rose between Bahadur Beg who was a farmer of revenue, a nephew of Shah Baz Khan who was dead and Nadirah Begum, widow of Shah Baz Khan. Bahadur Beg filed a suit against the Begum in the Diwani Adalat at Patna in 1777. The Qazi and the Mufti who were the Law Officers of the Company, recorded evidence in an irregular manner and came to the conclusion that the deeds produced by the Begum were all forged and so were declared invalid. The property was distributed according to Mohammedan Law. One-fourth of the property went to Begum and three-fourths to Shah Baz's brother, father of Bahadur Beg. The Begum appealed to the Sadar Diwani Adalat at Calcutta, but no action was taken by that Court. The Begum then brought the case to the Supreme Court not only against Bahadur Beg but the Qazi and Mufti also claiming damages of 6 lakhs of rupees. The Supreme Court ordered the arrest of all the 3 persons. They were arrested and brought to Calcutta from Patna. The Supreme Court held that the proceedings of the Law Officers were illegal as they had no power to hear the suit. The Supreme Court also found that the Begum had been treated harshly. The defendants were asked to pay ₹3 lakhs as damages and as they failed to do so, they were lodged in prison. The issue in the Patna case was whether judicial officers of the Company were subject to the jurisdiction of the Supreme Court or not. The action of the Supreme Court was criticised on the ground that it took cognisance of acts done by the judicial officers of the Company in the discharge of their public functions. The Supreme Court held that those judicial officers had been tried not for what they had done in the discharge of their regular functions but for something which was extraneous to their office for acting illegally. The Supreme Court claimed jurisdiction over the farmers of revenue as they were indirectly in the service of the Company. The whole question was decided by the Judicature Act of 1781.

3. Supreme Court claimed to have jurisdiction over the collectors of revenue of the Company for the wrongs done by them in their official capacity. It also claimed to try judicial officers of the Company for similar wrongs. It refused to recognise the jurisdiction of the provincial or country courts. It released a district treasurer who was imprisoned on a charge of embezzlement and remarked thus: "We know not what your Provincial Chief and the Council are: you might just as well have said that he was confined by the King of Fairies". Warren Hastings tried to remove this conflict by appointing Sir Elijah Impey as the judge of the Sadar Diwani Adalat. However, this arrangement did not last long because Impey was called back home. The Regulating Act did not specify as to which law was to be applied by the Supreme Court. It was a moot point as to whether the Hindu law, Mohammedan law, Christian law or the English law was to be applied. It was also not made clear as to whether the law of the defendant was to be applied or that of the plaintiff in case the two professed different religions. As a matter of fact, the judges of the Supreme Court knew only the English law and applied the same practically in every case. Evidently, this had very unfortunate results.

4. The Regulating Act did not contain any answer to many questions. It was not clearly defined as to who the servants of the English East India Company were and what actually constituted employment under the Company. A question could be asked as to whether farmers of revenue could be considered as servants of the Company.

5. The Regulating Art made the position of the Governor-General very weak. As a matter of fact he was merely at the mercy of the majority of the members of his Council. We are told that for 6 years there was a bitter struggle between the Governor-General and the members of his Council. He was outvoted and over-ruled and on many occasions had to follow a policy which he did not approve of It was only after the death of Monson and Clavering that Warren Hastings was able to manage his Council. Previous to this, his position was so hard that at one time he actually instructed his agent in London to tender his resignation to the Directors.

6. The raising of the qualifications of the voters from £500 to £1,000 converted the Court of Directors into an oligarchy. About 1.246 holders of stock were disfranchised. "The whole of the regulations, concerning the Court and Proprietors, relied upon two principles, which have proved fallacious, namely, that small numbers were a security against faction and disorder and that integrity of conduct would follow the greater property".

7. The control of Bengal over Madras (now Chennai) and Bombay (now Mumbai) was not effective.
8. According to Burke, the Regulating Act was "an infringement of national rights, national faith and national justice". According to Roberts, the Act was a half-measure and disastrously vague on many points. The titular authority of the Nawab of Bengal was left by implication intact and no assertion was made of the sovereignty of the Crown or Company in India. Principal Sri Ram Sharma has made the following observations: "In this way the Regulating Act made a bold attempt at securing good government in the Company's territory in India without the Crown's directly assuming the responsibility for the same. It was the first measure by which a European government assumed the responsibility for governing territories acquired by it outside Europe and inhabited by civilized people. No other European nation had so far made any such attempt. For the English as well, it was the first measure of its kind. The Act was passed at a time when controversy in colonial America was about to flare up into the War of American Independence. The British political philosophy at the time was dominated by Adam Smith's "Wealth of Nations" on the one hand and, the struggle between George III and the Whigs on the other. The Act bore the impress of all these stresses and strains. Its most praiseworthy feature was the setting up of the Supreme Court as a guarantor of good government in Bengal for all. It introduced the thin end of the wedge of direct administration by the Crown by insisting on securing timely information from the Company about its affairs in India. It recognised the Board of Directors for another 60 years in India; it translated the Directors' demand for honest administrators in India into a parliamentary mandate when it prohibited private trade and acceptance of gifts by the Company's public servants. Its principle of collegiate authority in the Governor-General and Council of Bengal remained substantially unmodified till 1861. It made an amateurish attempt at setting up one supreme authority for the Company's dominions in India.
9. According to P.E. Roberts, "The change in the constitution of the Court of Directors was made with the view of giving the members of the Court greater security of tenure, lessening the temptation to secure votes by corrupt dispensation of patronage, and encouraging a more continuous and consistent policy at home and abroad. Hitherto the twenty-four Directors were elected each year, and might have been completely changed at each election. As Clive once averred, they spent the first half of their year of office in discharging the obligations by which they had purchased their seats, and the other half in canvassing and preparing for a new election. At the first election after the bill was passed, six Directors were to be chosen for one year, six for two years, six for three years and six for the full term of four years. In practice, the six who retired each year were always re-elected for the following year and the effect therefore was, as Kaye notes 'to constitute a body of thirty Directors, of whom six forming a sort of non-effective list, go out every year by rotation'. It was of course possible for the proprietors at each election to have chosen six new members, but in practice they never did so". Again, the Regulating Act "had neither given the State a definite control over the Company, nor the Directors a definite control over their servants, nor the Governor-General a definite control over his Council, nor the Calcutta Presidency a definite control over Madras and Bombay".
10. According to Pouten Rouse, "The object of the Act was good, but the system that it established was imperfect".
11. According to the Report on Indian Constitutional Reforms of 1918, the Regulating Act "created a Governor-General who was powerless before his own Council and an executive that was powerless before a Supreme Court, itself immune from all responsibility for peace and welfare of the country—a system that was made workable by the genius and fortitude of one great man".
12. "The Regulating Act made a bold attempt at securing good Government in the Company's territory in India without the Crown's directly assuming the responsibility for the same".

The Regulating Act was the first of a long series of Acts passed by Parliament to change and regulate the Government of India. It made a beginning in the system of a written Constitution for British India. The right of the Parliament to interfere into the affairs of the Company, and to legislate for the possessions was recognised. It is a landmark in the transfer of power from the Company to Parliament. The Act established a collegiate rule in place of "one-man rule". It recognised the political functions of the Company. According to Lyall, "The system of administration set up by the Act of 1773 embodied the first attempt at giving some definite and recognizable form to the vague and arbitrary rulership that had developed upon the Company. From that time forward, the outline of Anglo-Indian Government was gradually filled in".

According to Herbert Cowell, "The essential character and object of that scheme were to weaken the power of the Government by vesting it in the hands of a majority, and to plant in its neighbourhood a Court, framed after the fashion of the existing Courts in England, with jurisdiction over all its executive acts and a veto on all its legislation. This tribunal vested with such extraordinary powers, and so ludicrously unsuited to the social and political condition of Bengal, was not merely to exercise a civil and criminal jurisdiction wholly strange and repugnant to the Indian people; it might sit one day on its common law side and give judgment to a suitor, and on the next day might sit on its equity side and restrain that suitor from proceeding to execution. It might on one side adjudge a man to be the absolute owner of property, and on the other side consign him to perpetual imprisonment if he did not, in his character of trustee, forthwith give it up to those beneficially entitled. In short, the whole system of English law and equity, with its rules and customs and process, handed down from feudal times, moulded during struggles between secular and ecclesiastical powers, between church and commonalty, between common law and civil jurisprudence, which time alone had rendered endurable to the people amongst whom it had grown up, a people widely different in habits, character, and form of civilization from any to be found in the East was introduced into India, not intentionally as a burden, but for its benefit and solution.

'The result was that the Court exercised large powers independently of Government often so as to obstruct it, and had a complete control over legislation. Political power was thus vested in Judges who had neither the responsibilities nor the machinery of government. Such a system could not endure under any circumstances. Although the Courts are independent of Government in England, both are absolutely subordinate to the Legislature, in which, however, the power of Government predominates. To make the Legislature subordinate to the Court, instead of Court subordinate to the Legislature, and at the same time, to direct it to enforce a system of law utterly inapplicable to India, independently of or in opposition to the Government, which was at the same time weakened by divisions purposely created appears to be the most destructive and pernicious policy that wit could devise. Although the judicial service should be independent of the executive, yet it must be subordinate to the Legislature, and legislation must be, if power and responsibility are to go together, the unfettered expression of sovereign authority, wherever that authority may reside, or from whatever source it be derived, whether from an electoral body or an absolute prince.

"The plan of controlling the Company's government by the King's Court entirely failed. The tribunal came to be regarded by the Natives, for whose protection it was established, with the utmost abhorrence. The policy which shaped the Regulating Act was, no doubt, well-intentioned, but it was rashly and ignorantly executed. None of the Parliaments of George III were remarkable for their wisdom; but it was reserved for the Parliament which sat in 1773 by its Colonial Customs Policy and its Regulating Act to throw the affairs of two hemispheres into confusion. It endeavoured to rule America on the principle of parliamentary taxation, and to control the Government of India by the operation of English Law Courts. The result was that British power in the West was subverted, and in the East was for a time seriously endangered. The anarchy which ensued continued till the policy of the Regulating Act was reversed, and Indian society assumed the form which it retained till the Company and Moghul Empire vanished".

JUDICATURE ACT OF 1781

It was admitted on all hands that there were many shortcomings in the Regulating Act and consequently an Act was passed in 1781 to remove them. The new Act provided that the public servants of the Company were not to be subject to the jurisdiction of the Supreme Court for things done by them in their official capacity. Revenue collectors and judicial officers of the Company's courts were also exempted from the jurisdiction of the Supreme Court for things done by them in their official capacity. Governor-General and the members of his Council were also exempted from the jurisdiction of the Supreme Court both individually and collectively "for anything counselled, ordered or done by them in their public capacity".

As regards the jurisdiction of the Supreme Court it was provided that it was to have jurisdiction over all the inhabitants of Calcutta (now Kolkata). It was to administer the personal law of the defendant. It was stated that "no person was to be subject to the jurisdiction of Supreme Court by reason of his being a land-owner or farmer of land or land-rent or for raising a payment or pension in lieu of any title to, or ancient possession of land or land-rent or for any compensation or share of profits for collecting rent...". Servants of the Company were to be subject to the jurisdiction of the Supreme Court for wrongs done by them or trespass. Cases could be brought before the Supreme Court by the agreement of both the parties. In cases relating to inheritance or succession to lands or goods, the jurisdiction of the Supreme Court was excluded. The Supreme Court was required to take into consideration and respect the religious and social customs and usages of the Indians while enforcing the decrees and processes. Government was also to keep them in view while making regulations.

Governor-General-in-Council was given the power to make regulations for the provincial courts and Councils. Formerly, the rules and regulations made by the Governor-General were required to be registered with the Supreme Court. This led to a lot of inconvenience. Consequently, the Act of 1781 provided that no such registration was required.

The Act provided that appeals were to be taken from the provincial courts to the Governor-General-in-Council. The latter was to be the final Court of Appeal except in those civil cases which involved £5,000 or more. In case the amount involved was more than £5,000, an appeal was to be taken to the King-in-Council.

According to Dr. Keith, the Act of 1781 "effected important changes in the system of 1778. The preamble showed clearly who had won the contest; it asserted the necessity of supporting the Government, the importance of the regular collection of the revenues and the maintenance of the people in their ancient laws".

According to Herbert Cowell, "The year 1781 marks a most important era in the history now under consideration. It terminated a period of fierce animosity and struggle between those who wished to see English law and Courts of Justice introduced at once into the country and rendered supreme over the Executive, and those who considered that such a policy was wholly impracticable, and that, circumstanced as the English then were, Government must for a long time to come control the authority of the Courts. It commenced the era of independent Indian legislation; of the authority of the Supreme Court, as it continued more or less to be exercised for eighty years; of the establishment of a Board of Revenue 'entrusted with the charge and administration of all the public revenues of the provinces, and invested in the fullest manner with all powers and authority, under the control of the Governor-General and Council'; of the recognition by Act of Parliament of the established Sudder and Provincial Courts; and of the recognition by Act of Parliament and in the revised Code of Bengal of the right of Hindus and Mohammedans to be governed by their own laws and usages. The plan of government, both as regards legislation and the Courts of Justice, in that year assumed a definite shape, and although many changes of course ensued in the long period (1781-1861) which separated the administration of Warren Hastings, the first Governor-General of India, from the close of that of Lord Canning, its first Viceroy, still they were changes of detail, often of great importance, but leaving unaltered the general character of the system then introduced.

"The year 1781 may therefore well be taken as the first dividing point of time at which the character of that history essentially changes, at which the boundaries of authority have at last become strongly defined".

DUNDAS'S BILL (1783)

The Amending Act of 1781 did not remove all defects of the Regulating Act and consequently many bills were introduced in Parliament to remedy them. In April, 1783, Dundas introduced his bill. According to it, the Crown was to have power to recall the principal servants of the Company. The control of Bengal Presidency over Bombay and Madras was to be increased. The Governor-General was to have the power of acting on his own responsibility in opposition to the opinions of his own Council. He was to be empowered to hold the office of Commander-in-Chief. Those Zamindars of Bengal who were displaced as a result of quinquennial settlements were to be restored. Obviously, the bill gave complete authority and control over British India into the hands of a person with the title of Governor-General and Captain-General. As Dundas was in the Opposition, the bill was dropped after introduction.

FOX INDIA BILL (1783)

In November 1783, Fox introduced his famous bill on India. The bill proposed to abolish the Court of Directors and the Court of Proprietors and set up two bodies. Seven Commissioners or Directors were to administer the revenues and territories of India. They were to appoint or dismiss all persons in the service of the Company. They were to be named in the Act and were to be irremovable except on an address from either House of Parliament. Vacancies were to be filled by the Crown. The Commissioners were to sit in London and Parliament was to have opportunity to inspect the minutes of their proceedings. Nine Assistant Directors were to be nominated in the Act from the Proprietors with the largest holding in the Company. They were to be appointed for five years and vacancies were to be filled by the Court of Proprietors.

According to Fox, his bill "was the only possible means of averting and preventing the final and complete destruction of the Company's interests". According to Malcolm, the seven Commissioners were "to act like trustees to a bankrupt house of commerce". Fox maintained that his Bill "was a child not of choice, but of necessity". The mixed system of Government was suited to the mixed complexion of British interests in India. He contended that "the Indian people in spite of every exertion, both of the legislature and Court of Directors, groan under the scourge, the extortion and the massacre of a cruel and desperate man whom, in my conscience and from my heart, I detest and execrate".

Burke gave a brilliant speech in support of the bill. He maintained that "Our Indian Government is in its best state a grievance". He described the Government of the Company as "one of the most corrupt and destructive tyrannies that probably ever existed in the world". There is not a single prince, state or potentate, great or small in India, with whom they have not come into contact, whom they have not sold... . There is not a single treaty they have ever made which has not been broken... . There is not a single prince or state, who ever put any trust in the Company who is not utterly ruined". According to him, the servants of the Company were "animated with all the avarice of age, and all the impetuosity of youth; they roll in one after another, wave after wave, and there is nothing before the eyes of the natives but endless, hopeless prospect of new flights of birds of prey and passage with appetites continually renewing for a food that is continually wasting. Their prey is lodged in England; and the cries of India are given to seas and winds to be blown about in every breaking up of the monsoon, over a remote and unhearing ocean".

It is to be noted that the Bill was passed by the House of Commons by 208 votes to 108 votes. However, it was defeated in the House of Lords on account of the interference of George III. George III made it clear in a letter that whoever voted for the Bill was "not only not his friend, but his enemy". Another cause of the defeat of the Bill was the tremendous unpopularity of Fox and North. Instead of discussing the merits of the bill, the opponents stressed the coalition of Fox and North. According to Pitt, the Bill was "one of the boldest, most unprecedented, most desperate and alarming attempts at the exercise of tyranny that ever disgraced the annals of this or any other country". According to Grenville, the object of the Bill was "no less than to erect a despotic system which might crush the free Constitution of England". According to Jenkinson, the bill was "setting up within the realm a species of executive Government, independent of the check or control of the Crown". Wilberforce compared the seven Directors and eight Assistant Directors to seven physicians and eight apothecaries who had come to put the patient to death. Fox answered his critics in these words: "I risk my all upon the excellence of this Bill; I risk upon it whatever is most dear to me, whatever men most value, the character, integrity, talents, honour, present reputation and future fame; these, and whatever else is precious to me. I stake upon the constitutional safety, the enlarged policy, the equality and the wisdom of this measure". Fox made a mistake in not consulting the English East India Company which was vitally interested in the measure and it is no wonder that the Company also opposed the Bill tooth and nail.

George III was not only responsible for the rejection of the Fox India Bill in the House of Lords, he also dismissed the Coalition Ministry on 18th December 1783. Having done so he invited Pitt, the Younger, to form the new Ministry. Pitt introduced his own Bill in January 1784. He did not command a majority in the House of Commons at the beginning and consequently got the Parliament dissolved at the appropriate moment and was able to secure a good majority. He reintroduced his Bill with certain modifications and was able to get the same passed in August 1784. The Bill is known as Pitt's India Bill. It is to be noted that Pitt took the precaution of neutralising the opposition of the English Company. The result was that the Bill was introduced in Parliament fortified and recommended by the consent of the Company. The Bill was essentially the same as that of Fox. However, he did not touch the patronage of the Company. Pitt himself pointed out that while the Fox India Bill ensured permanency of men, his Bill meant a permanency of the system.

PROVISIONS OF PITT'S INDIA ACT

1. Pitt's India Act provided for a Board of Control of six Privy Councillors. The Board was given comprehensive powers of supervision, direction and control over the Indian administration. All the dispatches from India were to be submitted to them and they were to have the right of modifying any instruction sent by the Directors to India. They were empowered to call the old files and thereby review the administration. Regarding the composition of the Board, it may be stated that real power fell into the hands of the President of the Board of Control from the very beginning. Two of its members, Chancellor of the Exchequer and Secretary of State, never attended its meetings. Out of the remaining four members, only the senior member attended and the other three members absented themselves. The President of the Board of Control managed to get the signatures of the Secretary of State and Chancellor of the Exchequer.

2. A Committee of Secrecy, consisting of three Directors, was appointed to take the place of the Court of Directors in political and military matters.

3. Directors were to retain the right of making appointments to different offices in India. They were also given the power of revising and reviewing the acts of the Indian administration.
4. The Court of Proprietors was deprived of its right of overriding decisions of the Court of Directors.
5. Governor-General-in-Council was given the power of superintending, controlling and directing the several Presidencies. Formerly the Executive Council of the Governor-General consisted of four members. Pitt's India Act provided that the Councils of Governor-General and Governors were to consist of 3 members and one of them was to be the local Commander-in-Chief.
6. It was declared that the official offenders were not to be pardoned if they were found guilty of having committed any offence. Better provision was made for the trial in England for offences committed in India. For the purpose of dealing with those cases, a Special Court of 3 Judges, 4 Peers and 6 members of the House of Commons was created.
7. The Act disapproved the policy of intervention as followed by the servants of the Company in India. The following clause was inserted into the Act: "Whereas to pursue schemes of conquest and extension of dominion in India are measures repugnant to the wish, the honour and the policy of this nation, the Governor-General and his Council were not without the express authority of the Court of Directors or of the Secrecy Committee, to declare war, commence hostilities, or enter into any treaty for making war, against any of the country, provinces or states in India...".
8. Governor-General was to be appointed by the Directors with the approval of the Crown. However, no such approval was required in the matter of the appointment of the Governors of the Presidencies and their Councils and also the members of the Governor-General's Council. The Crown could recall the Governor-General or the Governors.

The importance of the Pitt's India Act lies in the fact that it introduced what is known as the system of dual control from England. The President and the Board were destined to be the future Secretary of State for India and his Council. The Act helped the unification of India by making the Governor-General supreme over the Governors of the other Presidencies. The deletion of one member from the Executive Council of the Governor-General made his position stronger. He could act according to his judgment by using his casting vote. The same was the case with the Governors. The British Parliament claimed supremacy over the possessions of the Company in India. The new provision for trying per-sons of British descent committing offence in India was a novel one. The Proprietors lost their original importance and position. The Committee of Secrecy was given independent powers as apart from the Court of Directors.

Critics point out certain defects in the Pitt's India Act. The Government of India was vested in the majority of a constantly "changing Council". The result was that even a weaker member like Mr. Macpherson could become Governor-General. President of Board of Control could afford to be irresponsible as he was not required to submit his accounts to Parliament. The Director became meek and submissive before the President of Board of Control. Nothing was said with regard to the relationship between Board of Control and the Directors. According to Ilbert, "The double Government established by Pitt's Act of 1784, with its cumbrous and dilatory procedure and its elaborate system of checks and counterchecks, though modified in details, remained substantially in force until 1858. In practice the power vested in the Board was exercised by the Senior Commissioner other than the Chancellor of Exchequer or Secretary of State. He became known as the President of the Board of Control, and occupied a position in the Government of the day corresponding to some extent to that of the Secretary of State for India".

According to Lord Palmerston, 'The functions of Government and the responsibility have been divided between the Board of Control, the Court of Directors and the Governor-General in

India, and among these authorities it is obvious that despatch and unity of purpose can hardly by possibility exist. Before a dispatch upon the most important matter can go out to India, it has to oscillate between the Common Row and the India House".

ACT OF 1786

The Act of 1786 made Cornwallis the Commander-in-Chief of the Indian forces. He was also given the power to over-ride his Council on his own responsibility.

DECLARATORY ACT OF 1788

Dundas was the first President of Board of Control. He was a friend of Pitt, the Younger. He adopted an attitude which was not liked by the Directors and no wonder differences arose among them. The Board of Control sent four Royal Regiments of troops to India and charged their expenses to Indian Revenues. The Directors referred to the Act of 1781 and pointed out to the illegality of the procedure. The result was that the Declaratory Act of 1788 was passed by the British Parliament. It vested full power and supremacy in the Board of Control. This was a definite step in transferring the power of a Company to the Crown. It was also provided in a new Act that the Directors should place the annual accounts of the Company before Parliament. In matters of granting gratuity for services and increment in salaries, the Board of Control was required to take the approval of the Directors. About the new Act, Mill observed thus: "The Bill is an absurdity which resembled a contradiction in terms".

CHARTER ACT OF 1793

The English East India Company was given a new Charter in 1793. Act of 1793 is a very long one. It repealed many old laws and consolidated the existing ones. However, it did not make any alterations.

1. The Governor-General and the Governors were given the power to over-ride their Councils. The power had been given specially to Cornwallis in 1786.
2. The control of Governor-General over the Presidencies of Madras and Bombay was emphasised. It was laid down that when the Governor-General went to a Presidency, he superseded the Governor.
3. Governor-General was given the power to appoint a Vice-President of his Executive Council from the members of the Council. The Vice-President was to act in place of the Governor-General when the latter was absent from Bengal.
4. The Commander-in-Chief was not to be a member of the Council of the Governor-General unless he was specially appointed to be a member by the Court of Directors.
5. No leave of absence out of India was to be allowed to the Governor-General, Governors, the Commander-in-Chief and a few other high officials during their tenure of office.
6. The admiralty jurisdiction of the Calcutta, Supreme Court was extended to the high seas.
7. Power was given to appoint members of the civil service as Justices of the Peace to appoint scavengers for the Presidency towns, to levy a sanitary rate and to forbid the sale of liquor without a licence.
8. It was provided that the payment of the members and the staff of the Board of Control should be made out of the Indian revenues. This system continued up to 1919.
9. It was provided that the two junior members of the Board of Control need not be Privy Councillors.
10. The Act tried to regulate the finances of the Company. A particular amount was assumed to be the annual surplus of the Company. Out of the annual surplus, five lakhs of pounds were

to go to liquidation of the debts of the Company, and a similar amount was to be absorbed in increasing the dividend from 8 per cent to 10 per cent.

11. The Charter of the Company was renewed for 20 years. 3,000 tons were allowed for private trade but this right was never exercised.

CHARTER ACT OF 1813

The Charter Act of 1793 had renewed the Charter of the Company for 20 years. When the time for the renewal of the Charter arrived, there was a lot of agitation. The people demanded the ending of the commercial monopoly of the Company. They were determined to have a share in the trade with India. They pointed out four advantages which the abolition of monopoly would bring, viz., the extension of British commerce and industry, the prevention of the diversion of Indian trade to other countries of Europe or America, the reduction in the cost of trade, especially in transportation and warehousing charges, and the cheapening of the Indian raw imports into Britain. Stalwarts like Warren Hastings, Malcolm and Munro defended the monopoly of the Company. Ultimately, the Charter Act of 1813 was passed after many changes and compromises.

1. The Act of 1813 renewed, the Charter of the East India Company for 20 years. The Company was deprived of its monopoly trade with India, but she was to enjoy her monopoly of trade with China for 20 years. The Indian trade was thrown open to all British merchants, although they had to work under certain limitations. The Directors were to grant licences to those Englishmen who applied for permission to trade with India. Licences were also to be given to persons who wanted to come to India for the purpose of enlightening or reforming the Indians or for other lawful purposes. If the Directors refused to issue a licence, the Board of Control could be approached for the same purpose. The persons who tried to go to India without a licence were to be regarded as interlopers and were liable to punishment.

2. The Act laid down certain rules for the application of the Indian revenues. Maintenance of forces was to be the first charge on the revenues of the Company payment of interest was the second charge, and the maintenance of the civil and commercial establishment was the third charge. Provision was also made for the reduction of the debt of the Company. The Company was required to keep its commercial and territorial accounts separately.

3. It was provided that not more than 29 thousand troops were to be maintained out of the revenues of the Company.

4. The Company was authorised to make laws, regulations and articles of war for the Indian troops. It was also authorised to provide for the holding of Court-Martials.

5. The powers of superintendence and direction of the Board of Control were not only defined but also enlarged to a very great extent.

6. The local Governments in India were empowered to impose taxes on persons, and punish those who did not pay them. These powers were to be exercised by the local Governments subject to the jurisdiction of the Supreme Court.

7. The Act provided for the religious learning and education of the people of India. A sum of ₹100,000 a year was to be set "apart and applied to the revival and to the improvement of literature and the encouragement of the learned natives of India and for the introduction and promotion of a knowledge of the sciences among the inhabitants of the British 'Territories in India".

8. The Act also made provision for the training of the civil and military servants of the Company. The College at Haileybury and military school at Adiscombe were to be maintained and brought under the authority of the Board of Control. The colleges at Calcutta and Madras were also to work according to the regulations of the Board of Control.

9. The Act provided for the appointment of a bishop and three arch-deacons for the religious welfare of the Europeans in India.
10. The Act made special provisions for the administration of justice in cases in which the Britishers and Indians were involved. Special penalties were provided for theft, forgery and coinage offences.

CHARTER ACT OF 1833

1. The Charter of the Company was renewed in 1833. There was a lot of controversy before the Charter was actually renewed. The Englishmen were opposed to the continuance of the monopoly of the Company and consequently one of the provisions of the new Charter was that the monopoly of the Company was to be abolished. While the commercial functions of the Company ended, its political functions were to continue. The Government of India was to pay the debts of the Company. The shareholders of the Company were guaranteed a dividend of 10½ per cent per annum out of the Indian revenues for the next 40 years. The Indian possessions of the Company were declared to be held by the Company in trust for the British Crown.

2. The Charter Act restricted the patronage of the Directors. It was provided that nominations to seats in the Haileybury college were to be double the number of vacancies in the services. Nominated persons were to join the college and the top-most candidates among them were to be selected to fill the vacancies. This provision was amended in 1834 in favour of the Directors and continued up to 1853.

3. President of the Board of Control became the Minister for Indian affairs. His colleagues disappeared both in fact and in name. The minister was to have two Assistant Commissioners who were to be assistants and not colleagues. The Secretary of the Minister occupied a position of great importance on account of his presence in Parliament and he spoke for his chief when the latter sat in the House of Lords.

4. The Charter Act centralised the administration of the English Company in India. Governor-General in Bengal became the Governor-General of India. Governor-General-in-Council was given the power to control, superintend and direct the civil and military affairs of the Company in India. Presidencies of Bombay, Madras and Bengal and the other sessions were placed under the control, of the Governor-General-in-Council. All revenues were to be raised under the authority of the Central Government. The Central Government was to have complete control over expenditure. So far as the Presidencies were concerned, they were permitted to expand only that amount which was approved for them by the Central Government. The creation of any new office which carried a pension was to require the sanction of the Central Government. Governor-General-in-Council could suspend any member of the Governments Madras and Bombay who disobeyed him. If the provincial Government failed to carry out the orders of the Central Government it could be superseded. When the Governor-General went to a Presidency he was to supersede the Governor and exercise the right of over-riding the local Council.

5. The Charter Act also brought about the legislative centralisation of India. Formerly, the Presidencies could make their own laws and consequently there was a lot of confusion in the laws of the country. With a view to set up a uniform system of laws for the whole of the country, the Presidencies of Bombay and Madras were deprived of their law-making powers. In future, the Governor-General-in-Council alone was to make laws. He could make laws on all subjects. Those laws were to apply to all things and to all persons in British India. Those laws were enforceable by all the courts in the country and no one could refuse to enforce them.

Governor-General-in-Council was authorised to make Articles of War and Code of military discipline and provide for the administration of justice. The power of making laws included also the power of making, repealing, amending or altering any laws and regulations in force in India. However, there were certain limitations on the law-making power. Governor-General-in-Council could not alter the constitution of the Company or amend the Charter itself. It should not alter the Mutiny Act. It could not pass laws against the laws of England. The laws passed by the Government of India were to be called Acts. Before 1833, they were known as regulations.

6. The Charter Act added a new Member to the Executive Council of the Governor-General known as the Law Member. His work was purely legislative. He attended meetings of the Executive Council of the Governor-General by special invitation. He was not given any vote. Neither the presence nor the concurrence of the Law Member was necessary either for the consideration of the bill or for its passage. The quorum of the Executive Council was fixed at three for legislative work and two for administrative work.

7. The number of the members of the Councils of the Governors of Bombay (now Mumbai) and Madras (now Chennai) was reduced to two.

8. Bombay and Madras were to keep their separate armies under their Commanders-in-Chief, but they were to be under the control of the Central Government.

9. The Act provided for the codification of laws in India. Provision was made for the appointment of a Law Commission for that purpose. It was recognised that there was a lot of confusion and uncertainty in the laws in force in the country. The laws varied from Presidency to Presidency. What was legal at one place was illegal at another. What was considered to be a trivial offence at one place, was considered to be a serious one at another. To quote the Law Commission, "The British regulations having been made by three different legislatures, contained, as might be expected, very different provisions. Thus, in Bengal, serious forgeries were punishable with imprisonment for a term double of the term fixed for perjury. In the Bombay Presidency on the contrary perjury was punishable with imprisonment for a term double of the Madras Presidency. There were many more and equal glaring discrepancies. The result was utter chaos and confusion in administering the law of crimes". Referring to the confusion and uncertainty of the law, the judges of the Supreme Court of Calcutta stated that "no one could pronounce an opinion or form a judgment, however sound, upon any disputed right of persons respecting which doubt and confusion may not be raised by those who choose to call it in question; for very few of the public persons in office, at home not even the law officers, can be expected to have so comprehensive and clear a view of the present Indian system, as to know readily and familiarly the bearings of each part of it on the rest. There are English Acts of Parliament specially provided for India, and others of which it is doubtful whether they apply to India, wholly, or in part or not at all. There is the English common law and constitution of which the application, in many respects, is still more obscure and perplexed; Mohammedan law and usage, Hindu law, usage and scripture; Charters and Letters Patent of the Crown; Regulations of the Government, some made declaredly under Acts of Parliament particularly authorising them, and others which are founded, as some say, on the general power of Government entrusted to the Company by the Parliament and others assert on their rights as successors of the old native Government; some regulations require registry in the Supreme Court, others do not; some have effects generally throughout India, others are peculiar to one Presidency or two". According to Campbell, "Our criminal law is very much a patch-work...engrafted at all times and seasons on a ground nearly covered and oblitreated. The general result is that all the worst and most common crimes are satisfactorily provided for by special enactments; but that there is very great want of definition, accuracy

and uniformity as to the miscellaneous offences.... We have the main points of a tolerable system; but it wants remodeling, classification and codification". Regarding the condition of local system at that time, another writer has remarked thus: "At this time, each of the three Presidencies enjoyed equal legislative powers; though the Governor-General possessed the right of veto over the legislation of the subordinate Governments, it had in fact been little exercised. There had come into existence three series of regulations, as these, enactments were called frequently ill-drawn, for they had been provided by inexperienced persons with little skilled advice; frequently conflicting in some cases as a result of varying conditions but in others merely by extant; and in all cases enforceable only in the Company's Courts, because that had been submitted to and registered by the King's Court". (*Cambridge History of the British Empire,* Vol. V, p. 5.)

No wonder, Section 53 of the Charter Act, 1833 provided thus: "And whereas it is expedient... that such laws as may be applicable in common to all classes of the inhabitants of the said territories, due regards being had to the rights, feelings and peculiar usages of the people should be enacted and that all laws and customs having the force of law within the same territories should be ascertained and consolidated as occasion may require amended. Be it therefore enacted.... and the said Commission shall fully inquire into the jurisdiction, powers and rules of the existing courts of justice and police establishments in the said territories and all existing forms of judicial procedure and into nature and operation of all laws whether civil or criminal, written or customary, prevailing and in force in any part of the said territories and whereto any inhabitants of the said territories whether Europeans or others are now subject "and the said Commission shall from time to time make reports in which they fully set forth result of their said enquiries and shall from time to time suggest such alterations as may in their opinion be non-officially made in the said courts of justice and police establishments, forms judicial procedure and laws, due regard being had to the distinction of castes, difference of religion and the manners and opinions prevailing among different races and in different parts of the said territories".

10. Section 87 of the Act declared that no Indian subject of the Company in India was to be debarred from holding any office under the Company "by reason of his religion, place of birth, descent and colour". This was a declaration of very great importance. It is true its immediate effect was very little, but it was to have far-reaching effects in the long run.

11. Europeans were allowed to come to India and settle. However, they were "required to get themselves registered on their landing on the Indian soil. Governor General-in Council was empowered to take measures to protect Indians from insult and outrage with regard to their person, religion, and opinions at the hands of Europeans.

12. The Bishops of Bombay, Madras and Calcutta were to be appointed for the benefit of Christians in India.

13. The Government of India was required to take measures for the abolition of slavery and betterment of slaves.

14. The Act proposed to divide the Presidency of Bengal into two Presidencies, viz., Presidency of Agra and Presidency of Bengal. However, this provision was suspended by the Act of 1835 which authorised the appointment of a Lieutenant-Governor for the North Western Provinces. The Governor-General of India was to continue as the Governor of Bengal.

Critics point out that the Act of 1833 was passed before "empty benches and an uninterested audience" of the House of Commons. But the *Calcutta Gazette* of October, 1833, hailed the Charter's renewal by call for a general illumination and a display of fireworks, which were granted, and brought much satisfaction to a populace always agreeably avid for *Tamashas*". (*British Rule in India by Thompson and Garatt*, p. 302.)

According to Herbert Cowell, "Thus there was established in India one central legislative authority in place of the 'three Councils which had before existed. The new Council was armed with authority to pass Laws and Regulations for the whole of the British territories in India. It continued to exist with some changes and modifications till 1861, when it again gave way to the prevalent desire for local Legislative Councils. During that time, it passed a considerable number of Acts, some of general application throughout the empire, but the greater portion having a limited and partial operation. Local Legislatures had been tried and superseded by an Imperial Legislature, which in its turn was found inadequate to the political necessities of the country. An attempt was made to increase its usefulness and authority in 1853. But in 1861 a new system was introduced by which local Legislatures were re-established not to supersede, but to work in harmony with and to a certain extent in subordination to the Legislative Council of the Viceroy".

CHARTER ACT OF 1853

1. The Charter of the Company was renewed again in 1853. According to the new Act, the Law Member was made a full member of Executive Council of the Governor-General. Governor-General was given power to nominate a Vice-President of his Council. Discussion of measures which had already begun, was thrown open to public. Different legislative measures were entrusted to Select Committees for examination. Content of Governor General was made necessary for all legislative proposals.

2. Provinces were allowed to send one representative each to the Central Legislative Council. No measure concerning any province was to lie considered unless the representative from that province was present. The Chief Justice of the Supreme Court of Calcutta was to be an *ex officio* member of the Council and one more member was also to be appointed. Governor General was given the power of appointing two more civil servants as members of the Council. However, the power was never exercised.

   The Council in its legislative capacity was to consist of 12 members. There were the Governor-General, Commander-in-Chief, 4 members of the Council, and 6 legislative members. Out of these 6 members, 4 were the representatives from the provinces and the other two were the Chief Justice and a puisne judge. Representatives from the provinces were to be given £5,000 annually. "There was at least one member present with local knowledge and what may be called the English element in the Council was greatly increased".

3. Provision was made for the appointment of a separate Governor for the Presidency of Bengal, and until that was made, the Court of Directors might authorise the Governor-General of India in Council to appoint a. covenanted servant of ten years' standing as the Lieutenant-Governor of the Province. The latter appointment was made as it was the cheaper of the two.

4. Power was given to the Court of Directors to constitute a new Presidency. Power was also given to alter and regulate from time to time the limits of the various provinces. This power was used to create the Punjab into a Lieutenant-Governorship.

5. The patronage of the Court of Directors was taken away. In future, vacancies were to be filled up by competitive examination. A committee was appointed in 1854 with Lord Macaulay as President for that purpose.

6. The number of the Directors was reduced to 18 and 6 were to be nominated by the Crown.

7. The Act authorised the Crown to appoint a Law Commission in England. This Law Commission was required to examine and put into shape the mass of reports and drafts of the Act left by the Indian Law Commission and to recommend what legislation was necessary. The appointment of the English Law Commission was resented. It made the Home Government interfere in the details of the Indian legislative enactments and attempted to reduce the Indian Legislative

Council to the position of a mere registration office. Sir Charles Wood quarrelled with Lord Dalhousie on the question of the extent of the independence to be allowed to the council.

8. The Charter Act of 1853 renewed the powers of the Company and allowed it to retain possession of the Indian territories "in trust for Her Majesty, her heirs and successors" until Parliament shall otherwise provide.

Criticism. Observers point out that the Act of 1853 marks the beginning of a Parliamentary system in India. According to Cowell, "Discussion became oral instead of in writing; bills were referred to Select committees instead of to a single member; and legislative business was conducted in public instead of in secret".

The great defect of the Act of 1853 was that no Indian element was associated with the Legislative Council. Its knowledge of the local condition outside Bengal was not adequate for making laws for other provinces. "The terrible events of the Mutiny brought home to men's minds the dangers arising from the entire exclusion of Indians from association with the legislation of the country. According to Sir Syed Ahmed, this system deprived the people of India of the means of entering any protest against any unpopular measure. The government also got no opportunity of explaining their aims and intentions which were consequently misunderstood. In his Minute of 1860, Sir Bartle Frere advocated the need of including Indians in the Legislative Council in order to do away with "the perilous experiment of continuing to legislate for millions of people with few means of knowing except by rebellion, whether the laws suit them or not".

There were other difficulties which threatened to alter the whole structure of the Indian Government. "Contrary to the intentions of the framers of the Act of 1853, it (the Legislative Council) had developed into 'an Anglo-Indian House of Commons' questioning the Executive and its acts, and forcing it to lay even confidential papers before it. It had refused to submit legislative projects to the Secretary of State before their consideration in the Council, and had refused to pass any legislation required by the Secretary of State (or the Court of Directors before 1858); on the other hand it asserted its right of independent legislation".

The spirit of independence displayed by the Legislative Council from the very beginning disturbed its author, Sir Charles Wood, the President of the Board of Control. "I do not look upon it," said he, "as some of the young Indians do, as the nucleus and beginning of a constitutional parliament in India". Dalhousie pointed out that he had not "conceded to the Legislative Council any greater power than the law clearly confers upon it". It has been very aptly observed that Wood "was neither the first nor the last legislator to fail in limiting the consequences of Bill to his intentions:"

GOVERNMENT OF INDIA ACT, 1858

There was a lot of agitation in England against the continuation of the rule of the English East India Company. It was pointed out that a trading company whose main objective was profit could not be entrusted with the work of the administration of a sub-continent like India. The outbreak of the Mutiny and its suppression strengthened the hands of those who demanded the abolition of the rule of the Company. The Government of Great Britain decided to abolish the Company. Naturally, the Company protested. It challenged the most searching investigation into the causes of the Mutiny and maintained that the British Government was also responsible for errors of omission and commission of the Company because the British Government had the deciding voice in the affairs of the Company. The Company also took pride in its achievements in India. However, in spite of all this, Lord Palmerston introduced his Bill for the better Government of India in Parliament. While introducing the Bill, he declared thus: "The principle of our political system is that all administrative functions should be accompanied by ministerial responsibility, responsibility to Parliament, but in this case the chief functions in the Government of India are committed to a body not responsible to Parliament, not appointed by the Crown but elected by persons who have no more connection with India than consists in the simple possession of so much India stock". In spite of the opposition, the Act was passed by the Parliament in 1858.

Provisions of the Act

1. The Act of 1858 declared that hence forth "India shall be governed by and in the name of the Queen", and vested in the Queen all the territories and powers of the Company. However, the Government of India was to be carried on by the Viceroy on behalf of the Queen. The military and naval forces of the Company were transferred to the Crown.

2. The Board of Control and the Court of Directors were abolished and all the powers possessed by them were given to the Secretary of State for India and his Indian Council. The Secretary of State was given the power to superintend, control and direct the affairs of the Government of India. He was to sit in Parliament and was also to be assisted by a Parliamentary Under Secretary. Secretary of State was to be a member of the Cabinet, but his salary and allowances were made a charge on the revenues of India.

3. As regards the Indian Council of Secretary of State, it was to consist of 15 members. Out of the total, 7 were to be elected by the Court of Directors and the rest of the 8 members were to be appointed by the Crown. More than half the members of the Council were to be those persons who had lived in India for 10 years or more and had not left India for more than 10 years at the date of appointment. The members were to hold office during good behaviour. Each member was to get a remuneration of £1,200 annually from the revenues of India.

4. The Secretary of State was to preside over the meetings of the India Council. He was given not only a vote but also a casting vote. The Council was to meet twice a week. The members of the India Council could be divided into various committees for purposes of administrative convenience. Ordinarily, Secretary of State was given the power to over-rule even the majority decisions of the India Council. But in the case of grants or appropriation of Indian revenues, Secretary of State was not authorised to act against the majority view of his Council. The concurrence of a majority on members present at a meeting was required for division and distribution of patronage, for making contracts, sales and purchases on behalf of the Government of India and in all matters connected with the property of Government of India. The India Council was given control over civil and military servants of the Crown. Secretary of State was given the power of sending and receiving secret messages and dispatches from the Governor-General without the necessity of communicating them to the India Council. The India Council was a body of permanent civil servants who had expert knowledge about the affairs of India.

5. The Secretary of State for India was declared to be a corporate body which could sue and be sued in England and in India. Secretary of State was required to present every year in the British Parliament a report on the moral and material progress of India. Rules and regulations made in India or by the Secretary of State were to be placed before the House of Commons. The Governor-General and the Governors of the Presidencies were to be appointed by the Crown. The Lieutenant-Governors were to be appointed by the Governor-General subject to the approval of Her Majesty. Members of the various Councils were to be appointed by Secretary of State in Council.

6. It was laid down that except for the purposes of repelling invasion or for any other sudden or urgent necessity, Indian revenues were not to be employed for military operations outside India without the consent of Parliament.

7. The Act of 1858 divided the patronage between the Government of India and the Secretary of State in Council. All appointments and promotions "which by law or under any resolutions,

usage or custom are not made by any authority in India, shall continue to be made in India by the like authority". Appointments to the covenanted Civil Service were to be made by open competition in accordance with the rules made by the Secretary of State in Council with the help of the Civil Service Commissioners.

It may seem paradoxical but the fact remains that Parliament ceased to exercise control over India at the very moment it acquired it. The reason is that formerly power was in the hands of the Board of Control and Court of Directors and this made Parliament assert its authority. But when after the Mutiny, the Board of Control and Court of Directors were abolished and power came into the hands of the Secretary of State for India who was responsible to Parliament, the latter got satisfied. It was satisfied because it got what it wanted to get and having got it, it neglected to exercise the power of continuously controlling and criticising Indian administration. Another reason was that Secretaries of State for India were far abler men than the members of Board of Control. The quick means of communication between India and England made Indian news available in England much more swiftly than before. Parliament was content with leaving the Secretary of State alone to act as he pleased. The Secretaries of State managed the affairs of India in an efficient manner. Moreover, from 1857 to 1915, British politicians and parties were too much busy in other affairs of their own and had no inclination to study Indian problems. The intricacy and vastness of the Indian problems made it hardly worthwhile to pursue them even as a scientific hobby. As the most brilliant Englishmen had entered the Indian Civil Service and were carrying on the administration of India, it was thought ungenerous to criticise them. Thus, developed the theory of trusting the man on the spot and supporting him. The Secretary of State backed the Governor-General and the latter the Governors and so on. Members of Parliament found that nothing was to be gained by interfering with the Indian affairs. Thus, Parliamentary interest in India was neither continuous nor sustained.

According to Sir H.S. Cunningham, the assumption of the Government of India by the Crown was *"rather a formal than a substantial change"* All real power had passed into the hands of the President of the Board of Control and the Directors occupied the position of an advisory council, although they enjoyed considerable powers of initiative. The Act of 1853 had weakened the position of the Directors all the more. They were deprived of their patronage. Their number was reduced from 24 to 18. Out of these 18, six were appointed by the Crown. Unlike the previous occasions, the Act of 1853 did not renew the Charter of the Company for 20 years. It merely stated that the Indian territories were to remain under the administration of the Company in trust for the Crown until the Parliament decided otherwise. It was evident that the Act of 1853 was preparing the way for the assumption by the Crown of the Government of India in name as well as in fact. The Act of 1858 merely completed the process begun earlier. The Secretary of State for India took the place of President of the Board of Control and the India Council took the place of the Court of Directors. Out of the 15 members of the India Council, 7 were to be selected by the Court of Directors. It is true that some of the old powers of the Court of Directors passed to the Secretary of State, but its influence lingered on mainly in the Council.

It is pointed out that concentration of powers of the Court of Directors and Board of Control into the hands of the Secretary of State led to important consequences. To serve two masters may be a difficult business, but it had its advantages also. On account of the eternal rivalry between the Court of Directors and Board of Control, a shrewd and able Governor-General could, and often did, play one against the other and had his way. The same rivalry between the authorities stood in the way of formulating a strong and vigorous policy to which the Indian Government did not subscribe. Under the new set-up, the Secretary of State exercised his large powers practically without any control. He also exercised greater degree of influence. The Act of 1858 vested the India Council with large powers over the financial policy of the Government of India, but these powers also gradually fell into the hands of the Secretary of State and enabled him to exercise an effective control over the Viceroy and his Council.

According to a critic, "The double government of India was a system of hocus pocus which deluded public opinion, obscured responsibility and evaded parliamentary control".

QUEEN'S PROCLAMATION OF 1858

A Durbar was held by Lord Canning at Allahabad on November 1, 1858 to declare the assumption of the Government of India by the Crown. On that occasion, Lord Canning also read out the Queen's proclamation to the princes and people of India. We are told that the ministers were directed to frame the draft "bearing in mind that it is a female sovereign who speaks to more than a hundred millions of Eastern people, on assuming the direct government over them and after a bloody war, giving them pledges, which her future reign is to redeem and explaining the principles of her government. Such a document should breathe feelings of generosity, benevolence and religious toleration, and point out the privileges which the Indians will receive in being placed on an equality with the subjects of the British Crown, and the prosperity following in the train of civilization". It is a matter of fact that the Queen's Proclamation was worded in accordance with her sentiments.

The following is the text of the Queen's Proclamation—

"Victoria by the Grace of God, of the United Kingdom of Great Britain and Ireland and of the Colonies and dependencies thereof in Europe, Asia, Africa, America and Australia, Queen Defender of the faith.

"Whereas for diverse weighty reasons, we have resolved by and with the advice and consent of the Lords Spiritual and Temporal and Commons in Parliament assembled, to take upon ourselves the Government of the territories in India, heretofore administered in trust for us by the Honourable East India Company.

"Now, therefore, we do by these presents notify and declare that by the advice and consent aforesaid, we have taken upon ourselves the said Government; and we hereby call upon all our subjects within the said territories to be faithful, and to bear true allegiance to us, our heirs and successors, and to submit themselves to the authority of those whom we may hereafter, from time to time, see fit to appoint to administer the government of our said territories, in our name and on our behalf.

"And we reposing especial trust and confidence in the loyalty, ability and judgment of our right trusty and well-beloved cousin and Councillor Charles John Viscount Canning, do hereby constitute and appoint him, the said Viscount Canning to be our first Viceroy and Governor-General in and over our said territories and to administer the government thereof our name and generally to act in our name and on our behalf, subject to such orders and regulations as he shall, from time to time, receive from us through one of our principal Secretaries of State.

"We hereby announce to the Native Princes of India that all treaties and engagements with them by or under the authority of the Honourable East India Company are by us accepted, and will be scrupulously maintained, and we look for the like observance on their part.

"We desire no extension of our present territorial possession; and while we will permit no aggression upon our dominions or our rights to be attempted with impunity we shall sanction no encroachment on those of others. We shall respect the rights, dignity and honour of our Native Princes as our own; and we desire that they as well as our own subjects, should enjoy that prosperity and that social advancement which can only be secured by internal peace and good government.

"We hold ourselves bound to the Natives of our Indian territories by the same obligations of duty which bind us to all our other subjects, and those obligations by the blessing of Almighty God we shall faithfully and conscientiously fulfil.

"Firmly relying ourselves on the truth of Christianity and acknowledging with gratitude the solace of religion, *we disclaim alike the right and the desire to impose our convictions on any of our subjects*. We declare it to be our royal will and pleasure that *none be any wise favoured, none molested or disqualified by reason of their religious faith and observances;* but that *all shall alike enjoy the equal and impartial protection of the law,* and we do strictly charge and *enjoin all those who may be in authority under us that they abstain from all interference with the religious belief or worship of any of our subjects on pain of our highest displeasure.*

"And it is our further will that so far as may be, *our subjects of whatever race or creed be freely and impartially admitted to offices in our service,* the duties of which they may be qualified by their education, ability and integrity, duly to discharge.

"We know and respect the feelings of attachment with which the Natives of India regard the land inherited by them from their ancestors and we desire to protect them in all rights connected therewith subject to the equitable demands of the State and we will do that generally in framing and administering the law, due regard be paid to the ancient rights, usages and customs of India".

The proclamation went on to declare unconditional pardon, amnesty and oblivion for the past offences and ended by declaring that "When by the blessings of Providence internal tranquility shall be restored, it is our earnest desire to stimulate the peaceful industry, to promote works of public utility and improvement and to administer its government for the benefit of all our subjects resident therein. *In their prosperity will be our strength, in their contentment our security, and in their gratitude our best reward".*

To put in simple language, the Queen's Proclamation assured the Indian princes that their territories will not be annexed by the British Government and they shall be given the right of adoption. The British Government ordered its servants in India not to interfere in the religious affairs of the Indians. In framing and administering law in India, due regard was to be shown to the customs, ancient rites and usages of the Indians. Indian subjects of Her Majesty were declared equal with the British subjects in other parts of the Empire. Equal rights and opportunities were guaranteed to the Indians along with other British subjects. Pardon and amnesty were offered to all those Indians who were still in arms against the British Government and who were not guilty of murder of British subjects. Treaties of the English East India Company were declared to be in force.

The Queen's Proclamation of 1858 is a great landmark in the constitutional history of India. This declaration of policy remained the basis of Indian administration up to 1917 when a new declaration was made by the British Government with regard to India. The declaration tried to remove the fears of the Indian princes by guaranteeing to them their position. It also gave an assurance to the Indians that the Englishmen will not interfere in the religious affairs.

According to Mukerji, "It sealed the unity of Indian Government and opened a new era. This memorable Proclamation, justly called the Magna Carta of India, was published at every large town throughout the country and translated into the vernacular languages".

INDIAN COUNCILS ACT, 1861

According to Herbert Cowell, "The events which immediately led to the passing of the Indian Councils Act, 1861, were the differences which arose between the Supreme Government and the Government of Madras on the Income Tax Bill; the doubts which had been raised as to the validity of laws introduced into non-regulation Provinces without enactment by the Legislative Council; and the address of Legislative Council for the communication to it of certain correspondence between the Secretary of State and the Supreme Government of India".

While introducing the Bill in the House of Commons, Sir Charles Wood complained that, quite contrary to what was intended, the Legislative Council had become a sort of debating society or petty Parliament. He quoted with approval the criticism of Sir Lawrence Peel that the Legislative Council "has no jurisdiction in the nature of that of a grand inquest of the nation. Its functions are purely legislative, and are limited even in that respect. It is not an Anglo-Indian House of Commons for the redress of grievances, to refuse supplies, and so forth".

The view of the British Government with regard to the changes to be made was expressed by Sir Charles Wood in these words: "I propose that when the Council meets for the purpose of making laws, the Governor-General should summon in addition to the ordinary members of the Council, not less than six nor more than twelve additional members, of whom one-half at least shall not hold office under the Government. These additional members may be either Europeans, persons of European extraction, or Natives. Lord Canning strongly recommends that the Council should hold its meetings in different parts of India for the purpose of obtaining at times the assistance of those Native chiefs and nobles whose attendance at Calcutta would be impossible, or irksome to themselves. I do not propose that the Judges ex-officio shall have seats in the Legislature; but I do not preclude the Governor-General from summoning one of their number if he chooses. The Council of the Governor-General, with these additional members, will have power to pass laws and regulations affecting the whole of India, and will have a supreme and concurrent power with the minor legislative bodies which I propose to establish in the Presidencies and other parts of India". Again, "Lord Canning strongly feels that although great benefits have resulted from the introduction of members into his Council who possess a knowledge of localities, the interest of which differs widely in different parts of the country; yet change has not been sufficient in the first place to overcome the feeling which the other Presidencies entertain against being overridden, as they call it, by the Bengal Council; or, on the other hand, to overcome the disadvantages of having a body legislating for these Presidencies without acquaintance with local wants and necessities. This must obviously be possessed to a much greater extent by those residing on the spot. And, therefore, I propose to restore, I may say to the Presidencies of Madras and Bombay, the power of passing laws and enactments on local subject within their own territories; and that the Governor of the Presidency, in the same manner as the Governor-General, when his Council meets to make laws, shall summon a certain number of additional members, be as before, either European or Native, and one half of whom at least shall not be office-holders".

1. The new Act provided for the addition of a fifth member to the Executive Council of the Viceroy. He was required to be a gentleman of legal profession, a jurist rather than a technical lawyer.
2. The Act empowered the Governor-General to delegate special business to individual members of the Executive Council, and henceforward the various members of Council had their own portfolios and dealt on their own initiative with all but the most important matters. The most important matters were placed before the Governor-General and if any differences of opinion appeared, those were considered by the whole Council. Governor-General was authorised to nominate a President who was to preside over the meetings of the Executive Council in his absence. He was given the power of making rules and regulations for the conduct of the business of the Executive Council.
3. The Executive Council of the Governor-General was to be strengthened by the addition of not less than 6 and not more than 12 members nominated by the Governor-General for purposes of legislation.[2] Not less than half of the additional members were to be non-officials and they

---

[2] Sir Bartle Frere observed thus in 1860, "The addition of the native element has, I think, become necessary owing to our diminished opportunities of learning through indirect channels what the natives think of our measures, and how the native community will be affected by them.... No one will, I think, object to the only means of regaining in part the advantages which we have lost, unless he is prepared for the perilous experiment of continuing to legislate for millions of people, with few means of knowing, except by a rebellion, whether the laws suit them or not".

were to hold office for two years. The function of the Council was strictly limited to legislation and the Act expressly forbade the transaction of any other business. It was empowered "to make laws and regulations for all persons whether British or native, foreigners or others, and for all places and things whatever within the said territories, for all servants of the Government of India within the dominions of princes and states in alliance with Her Majesty". Certain restrictions were put on the legislative powers. The previous sanction of the Governor-General was required for introducing any legislation concerning certain specified subjects such as public debts, public revenues, Indian religious rites, military discipline and policy towards the Indian states. No law could be made which infringed the authority of the Home Government or violated the provisions of certain Acts made by the Parliament. Governor-General was given the power of vetoing any law passed by the Council. In case of emergency, he was also empowered to issue ordinances which possessed the same authority as law. These ordinances were to remain in force for six months unless they were disallowed or repealed by an ordinance or law. The cause of issuing an ordinance was to be notified to the Secretary of State for India at once. The approval of the Governor General was made necessary of every Act passed. The right to disallow Acts was reserved for the Crown and the general authority of the British Parliament and Crown were expressly reserved.

4. The Governments of Bombay and Madras were given the power of nominating the Advocate-General and not less than four and not more than 8 additional members at the Executive Council for purposes of legislation. These additional members were to hold office for two years. The business of the Council was to be strictly legislative. The consent of the Governor and the Governor-General was made necessary for all legislations passed or amended by the Governments of Madras and Bombay.

5. No distinction was made between the central and provincial subjects. However, measures concerning public debt, finances, currency, post-office, telegraph, religion, patents and copyrights were ordinarily put under the control of the Central Government.

6. The Governor-General was given the power to create new provinces. He was also given the power to appoint Lieutenant-Governors. He was also authorised to divide or alter the limits of any presidency, province or territory.

The Indian Councils' Act of 1861 marked an important step in the constitutional history of India. It made a beginning in representative institutions and legislative devolution. It helped the Governor-General to associate non-official Indians for purposes of legislation. The Central and Provincial Councils fulfilled the threefold purpose of publicity, discussion and information. The people got an opportunity to put forward their grievances and the Government got an opportunity to defend its policy. However, it is to be noted that the non-official members of the Council were nominated by the Viceroy and not elected by the people. These non-official members were either the Indian princes or their Diwans, big Zamindars or retired officials, and not the natural leaders of the people who could really reflect and mirror their views and aspirations. The non-official members did not show much interest in the meetings of the Council. As a matter of fact, they showed the utmost reluctance to come and utmost hurry to depart. That may be due to the fact that the powers of the Legislative Councils were very much restricted. The non-official members had practically no say in the matter. The Council merely registered the decrees of the executive. No doubt, the experiment was a failure, but it made the beginning of representative institutions.

The Act of 1861 had been considered to be a retrograde measure. The right of asking questions and the right to deliberate on matters of policy were not given to it. The position of the legislative councils has been described thus: "They are committees for the purpose of making law—committees by means of which the Executive Government obtains advice and assistance in their legislation, and the public derive the advantage of full publicity being ensured at every stage of the law-making process... . The Councils are no deliberative bodies with respect to any subject but that of immediate legislation before them. They cannot enquire into grievances, call for information or examine the conduct of the executive". (*Report on Constitutional - Reforms*, pp. 40-41.)

According to Principal G.N. Singh, the Indian Councils Act, 1861, is important in the constitutional history of India for two chief reasons. "Firstly, because it enabled the Governor General to associate the people of the land with work of legislation, and secondly by vesting legislative powers to the Governments of Bombay and Madras and by making provision for the institution of similar legislative Councils in other provinces it laid the foundations of the policy of legislative devolution which resulted in the grant of almost complete internal autonomy to the provinces in 1937".

The Act of 1861 made the Governor-General omnipotent, brought the whole of India under his control, vested powers of emergency in the Governor-General, put restrictions on the right of the people regarding free discussion and introduction of motions other than those of legislation, and tried to unify India by bringing both the Regulation and non-Regulation provinces under the supreme control of the Governor-General, who himself was to abide by the Crown, the authority of Parliament and its enactments. Thus the Act "modified the constitution of the Governor-General's executive council, and remodelled the Indian Legislatures".

According to Lord Macdonell, "The character of the Legislative Council established by the Act of 1861 is simply this, that they are Committees for the purpose of making laws—Committees by means of which the executive Government obtains advice and assistance in their legislation, and the public derive the advantage of full publicity being ensured at every stage of law-making process... . The Councils are not deliberative bodies with respect to any subject but of the immediate legislation before them. They cannot inquire into grievances, call for information, or examine the conduct of the executive. The acts of administration cannot be impugned, nor can they be properly defended in such assemblies, except with reference to the particular measure under discussion".

INDIAN COUNCILS ACT, 1892

1. For full 31 years, the British Government did not consider it necessary to give a further instalment of reforms to the people of India. Ultimately, Lord Dufferin suggested the grant of further reforms so that there may be no agitation. His detailed proposals, after notification, were carried through by Lord Cross as the Indian Councils' Act 1892. This Act enlarged the functions of the Legislative Councils. They were authorised to discuss the annual financial statement under certain conditions and restrictions. According to Lord Curzon: "It is not contemplated to vote the budget in India item by item in the manners in which we do it in this House. But it is proposed to give opportunities to the members of the Councils to indulge in a full, free and fair criticism of the financial policy of the Government". The great merit of the new provision was that "the Government will have an opportunity of explaining their financial policy, of removing misapprehension, of answering calumny and attack; and they will also profit by the criticism delivered in a public position, and with a due sense of responsibility by the most competent representatives of non-official India".

2. The members of the Councils were given the right of addressing questions to the Government on matters of public interest. A previous notice of 6 days was to be given to the Government for asking a question. The President might disallow any question without giving any reason. Questions on matters of public interest could be asked "subject to such conditions and restrictions as may be prescribed in the rules made by the Governor-General for the provincial Governors".

3. The number of additional members in the Council was increased. It was to be not less than 10 and not more than 16 in the case of the Supreme Council and not less than 8 and not more than 20 in the case of Madras and Bombay. The maximum number for Bengal was fixed at 20 and for North-Western Province and Oudh 15. Two-fifths of the additional members were to be non-officials.
4. As a result of the pressure brought by the Indian National Congress, the Government agreed to allow elections to be held in India under the rules, though the members so elected could take their seats only after being nominated by the Government. It was assured by the Government that "under this clause, it will be possible for the Governor-General to make arrangements by which certain persons may be presented to him, having been chosen by election, if the Governor-General should find that such a system can properly be established".

Defects in the Act

1. Although the Indian Councils' Act of 1892 was the outcome of a lot of agitation and patient waiting, it did not give anything substantial to the people of India. No wonder the critics point out many defects. The system of elections was a roundabout one. The people who got into the legislatures by this system did not represent the people in the real sense of the word. They could not sit in the legislatures as a matter of right of election.
2. The functions of the Legislative Councils were strictly circumscribed. The members could not ask supplementary questions. The President could refuse the asking of any question, and there was no remedy against his ruling. The Councils did not get any substantial control over the Budget.
3. The rules of election were unfair. Certain classes were over-represented and others did not find any representation at all. In the case of Bombay, out of the six seats two were given to the European merchants, but nothing was given to the Indian merchants. Two seats were given to Sind, but nothing was given to Poona and Satara.
4. The number of non-official members was very small. Out of 24 members at the Centre, 14 were officials, 4 were elected non-officials and 5 were nominated non-officials.
5. The Punjab was not given any representation in the Viceroy's Council.
6. According to Gokhale, "The actual working of the Act manifested its hollowness. Bombay Presidency was given 8 seats. Two seats were assigned by the Government of India in their rules to the University of Bombay and Bombay Municipal Corporation. The Bombay Government gave two seats to the European Mercantile community, one seat to the Sirdars of Deccan, one to the Zamindars of Sind, and only 2 seats to the general public". It is evident that public representation was almost negligible.
7. According to a critic, the Act of 1892 was "an attempt at compromise between the official view of the Councils as pocket legislatures, and the educated Indian view of them as embryo parliaments. It makes a definite parting of the ways, the first milestone on a road leading eventually to political deadlock and strangling of executive government. While no efforts were made to enlarge the boundaries of the educated class to provide them with any training in responsible government, or to lay the foundations of a future electorate to control them, the Act deliberately attempted to dally with the elective idea".
8. Sir Pherozeshah Mehta observed thus in 1890 when the bill was on the legislative anvil: "In framing it (the bill), the Prime Minister and the Indian Secretary of State seem to have been pervaded with a conception of the Indian people as a sort of Oliver Twist, always asking for more, to whom it would be, therefore, a piece of prudent policy to begin with offering as little as possible. The Government bill may be aptly described as a *most superb steam engine*

in which the necessary material to generate steam was carefully excluded, substituting in its place coloured shams to look like it".

9. Mr. Schwann, a member of Parliament described the increase in the number of additional members of the legislature "as a very paltry and miserable addition". In his presidential address at Poona in 1895, S.N. Banerjee observed thus: "If the Indian Council Act of 1892 is to be given effect to in the spirit in which it was conceived by the distinguished statesmen who took part in its enactment, if it is to give to the people of India a living representation of the whole community and not of a small section of people, the number of elected members must be sensibly increased".

10. The rights and privileges granted to the members of the legislative councils were strictly circumscribed. According to Smith, "The budget could be discussed but not until after the estimates had already been settled by the executive". As regards supplementary questions, Lord Lansdowne observed thus in 1892: "The questions must be so framed as to be merely requests for opinion and must not be in an argumentative or hypothetical form or in a defamatory language. No discussion will be permitted in respect of an answer given to a question". According to S.N. Banerjee, "They (the restrictions) seem to me to defeat the purpose of a beneficial legislation. In the House of Commons, sometimes when an answer has been given, further questions are addressed to the Minister on the same subject apparently with a view to offering an explanation or removing a misconception. In the House of Lords, even greater latitude is allowed in putting questions. One of the objects which the Government had in view in conferring the right of interpellation was to afford opportunities for clearing up misconceptions with regard to the measures of Government and the conduct of officials. Looking at the matter from this standpoint, the object which the Government had in view would be best served by adopting the practice of the House of Commons—a practice which has seen the wisdom of ages".

11. There was practically no chance for the non-official members to amend a bill introduced by the Government. The bill had to be passed in the form in which it had been previously approved of by the Government of India or the Secretary of State for India. Under the circumstances, debates in the legislatures were a mere formal ceremony. They were considered to be a farce by certain critics. To quote Sir Barnes Peacock, "He had always understood and still held that the office of a member of Council was a high and honourable one; but if he believed that the constitution of this Council was such that its members were bound to legislate in any manner that either the Board of Control or the Honourable Court of Directors might order, he should say that instead of being a high and honourable office, it was one which no man, who had a regard for his own honour and independence, could consent to hold, for his own part he could state freely and without hesitation that he would rather resign his office than hold it on that tenure. He believed that the trust and duty committed to every member of the Legislative Council was to act according to his own judgment and conscience".

12. In his Presidential address delivered in 1893 at the Lahore session of the Indian National Congress, Dadabhai Naoroji observed thus, "By the Act of 1892, no member shall have the power to submit or propose any resolution or divide the Council in respect of any such financial discussion, or in answer to any question asked under the authority of this Act or the rules made under this Act. Such is the poor character of the extent of the concession made to discuss finances or to put questions. Rules made under this Act shall not be subject to alteration or amendment at meetings for the purposes of making laws and regulations. Thus, we are to all intents and purposes under an arbitrary rule".

13. According to W.C. Banerjee, "The Act does not profess to give us much. We must go on with our agitation and not stop until we get what we all think and we all believe that what we

have a right to get". According to C.Y. Chintamani, "Strictly limited were the opportunities of members, not a few of them did make themselves useful.

14. According to Pandit Madan Mohan Malaviya, "The Act still left Indians without any real voice in the administration of their country. They found that the administration was not being conducted in the best interests of the people of the country, but it continued to be conducted on extravagantly costly lines. They found that level of taxation was maintained much higher than was necessary for the purpose of good administration; the military expenditure of the Government was far beyond the capacity of the country to bear; that an excessively large portion of the revenues raised from the people were being spent on what we may call imperial purposes". '

15. The Provincial Councils were too small in size to represent the people of the provinces. In the case of Bengal, 7 elected members represented 70 millions. There were certain parts of the provinces which were given practically no representation at all. In his Presidential address delivered at Lucknow, R.C. Dutt observed thus: "Half a dozen members elected under somewhat complicated rules can scarcely express the views of the people of a province with a population of 30 to 40 million or more. We do not wish for the absolute control of the administration of the country, but we do demand an adequate means of placing our views before the Government before it decides any question affecting our welfare".

However, one might conclude by saying that although the Act of 1892 fell far short of the demands made by the Indian National Congress, it was a great advance upon the existing state of things. By conceding the principle of election and giving the Legislative Councils some control over the Executive, it paved the way for future progress on those lines which were destined to place in the hands of the Indians a large measure of control over the administration of the country.

MINTO-MORLEY REFORMS (1909)

The period between 1892 and 1909 was one of storm and stress. The Viceroyalty of Lord Curzon witnessed a lot of agitation and discontentment in the country. The same could be said about Lord Minto. The agitation against the partition of Bengal was widespread. The Government of India had to resort to very harsh measures to put down the nationalist movement in the country. However, the Government thought of winning over the moderates and for their purpose passed the Indian Councils Act in 1909. It was Lord Morley who piloted the Bill through the British Parliament.

Provisions of the Act

1. The Act of 1909 increased the size of the legislative Councils. The additional members of the Governor-General's Council were increased up to a maximum of 60, those of Madras, Bengal, U.P., Bombay and Bihar Orissa to a maximum of 50 and those of the Punjab, Burma and Assam to 30.
2. Lord Morley insisted on retaining a substantial official majority in the Imperial Legislative Council and consequently it was provided that the Imperial Legislative Council shall consist of 37 officials and 23 non-officials. Out of the 37 officials, 28 were nominated by the Governor-General and the rest were to be *ex-officio*. The *ex-officio* members were to be the Governor-General, 6 ordinary members of the Council, and two extraordinary members. Out of the 32 non-official members, 5 were to be nominated by the Governor-General and the rest were to be elected.
3. The Act did not provide for any official majority in the Provincial Legislative Councils. The majority of the members were to be non-officials. However, this does not mean that there were to be non-official elected majorities in the Provincial Councils. Some of the non-officials were to be nominated by the Governor and the Government could always depend upon the unflinching loyalty of the nominated members. The Government could manage to have a

working majority in the Provincial Legislative Councils with the help of the officials and the nominated non-officials. To take one example, the Madras Legislative Council consisted of 21 officials and 25 non-officials. The *ex-officio* members were the Governor, 3 members of the Executive Council and the Advocate-General. The remaining 16 officials were nominated by the Governor. Out of the 26 non-officials, 5 were nominated and only 21 were elected. It is clear that there were 26 nominated members and only 21 elected members. Evidently, there was a nominated majority. The same applied to other Provinces.

4. According to the Government of India, territorial representation was not suited to the people of India. "Representation by classes and interests is the only practicable method of embodying the elective principle in the constitution of the Indian Legislative Councils". The Act provided for separate or special electorates for the due representation of the different communities, classes and interests. The remaining seats were allotted to the municipalities and district boards which were called "general electorates".

In the case of Madras, there were 21 elected members of the Legislative Council. Out of these, two were elected by the Mohammedans, 2 by Zamindars and 3 by landlords other than the Zamindars, one by the Corporation of Madras, one by the Madras Chamber of Commerce, one by the Madras Traders Association and one by the planting community. The rest of the 9 members were elected by the Municipal Councils, and District and Taluka Board. In the case of Imperial Legislative Council, the total number of the elected seat was 27. Out of these, 6 were allotted to the landlords, 5 to the Mohammedans and one to the Mohammedan landlords and one each to the Bengal and Bombay Chambers of Commerce. The remaining 13 seats were filled by the non-official members of the Provincial Legislative Councils.

5. The functions of the Legislative Councils were increased. Elaborate rules were made for the discussion of the budget in the Imperial Legislative Council. Every member was given the right to move any resolution relating to any alteration in taxation, any new loan or any additional grant to local Governments proposed or mentioned in the financial statement or explanatory memorandum. The Council was not permitted to discuss expenditure on interest on debt, ecclesiastical expenditure and State Railways, etc. It is to be noted that the financial statement was first referred to a Committee of the Council with the Finance Member as its Chairman. Half of its members were to be nominated by the head of the Government and the other half were elected by the non-official members of the Council.

6. The members were given the right of asking questions and supplementary questions for the purpose of further elucidating any point. But the Member in charge of department might refuse to answer the supplementary questions off-hand. He may demand some time for the same.

7. The members were given the power to move resolutions in the Councils. These resolutions were to be in the form of a definite recommendation to the Government. They must be clearly and precisely expressed and must raise definite issues. The resolutions were not to contain arguments, inferences, ironical expressions, etc. The President may disallow any resolution or part of a resolution without giving any reason for the same.

8. Rules were also framed under the Act for the discussion of matters of general public interest in the Legislative Councils. No discussion was permitted on any subject not within the legislative competence of the particular Legislature, any matter affecting the relations of the Government of India with a foreign Power or a native state, and any matter under adjudication by a court of law.

9. The Act raised the number of the members of the Executive Council in Bombay, Bengal and Madras to 4. It also empowered the Government to constitute an Executive Council for a Lieutenant-Governor's province also.

10. In the provinces, the University Senates, landlords, District Boards and Municipalities and Chambers of Commerce were to elect members. Muslims were given separate representation. Muslim members of the Legislatures were elected by the Muslims, themselves.
11. Disqualifications were imposed on political offenders. They could not offer themselves for election. However, the heads of the Governments were given the power to remove those disqualifications.

Criticism of the Act

1. The reforms of 1909 could not come up to the expectations of the Indians. What the people of India demanded was that there should be set up a responsible government in the country. But the sacred heart of the reforms of 1909 was "benevolent despotism". While introducing the Bill in the Parliament, Lord Morley had declared that he had no intention to give to the people of India responsible government. Under the circumstances, the reforms could not satisfy the people. It has been rightly pointed out that the people of India presented a cheque of £1,000 and they were given only £1. No wonder, the people were not satisfied. The reforms introduced a change not of kind but of degree. Minor additions were made in the powers of Legislatures and also in their size. But that was hardly substantial. The people were dissatisfied.

2. The reforms led to a lot of confusion. While parliamentary reforms were introduced, no responsibility was given. The result was thoughtless and irresponsible criticism of the Government. Indian leaders made legislatures the platforms for denunciation of the Government. The feeling that they would not have to shoulder responsibility made the members critical of the government.

3. The reforms introduced the system of elections. But the number of voters was very small. In some cases, the number of voters in a constituency did not exceed 9 or 10. Since the number was small, all the votes could be bought. Women were completely excluded.

4. The system of elections was indirect. The people elected members of local bodies. The latter elected members of an electoral college. The electoral college elected members of the provincial legislature and the members of the provincial legislature elected members of the Imperial Legislature. The result was that there was no connection between the people and the members sitting in the legislature. The members felt no responsibility towards the people.

   The representation of the people at large became in fact a process of infiltration through a series of sieves. The authors of the Montford Report of 1918 remarked thus: "There is absolutely no connection between the supposed primary voter and the man who sits as his representative in the Legislative Council, and the vote of the supposed primary voter has no effect upon the proceedings of the Legislative Council. In such circumstances, there can be no responsibility upon, and no political education for, the people who nominally exercise a vote. The work of calling into existence an electorate capable of bearing the weight of responsible government is still to be done".

5. The Act of 1909 introduced separate electorates for Muslims. The evil did not end here. In 1919, the Sikhs also got separate electorates. The Act of 1935 gave separate representation to Indian Christians, Anglo-Indians, Europeans and the Harijans. It cannot be denied that one of the effects of communal representation was the establishment of Pakistan in 1947.

6. The Act gave great importance to the vested interests by giving special representation to them, e.g., landholders, Chambers of Commerce, etc.

7. The Indians resented the maintenance of an official majority in the Imperial Council. Although the Government of India had expressed their willingness to allow the Indians to have a majority at the centre, Lord Morley did not agree to it on the ground that since the Indians were given

a non-official majority in the provincial councils, the Imperial Council should be maintained as their place of refuge in case they were defeated in the provinces.

8. Although non-official majority was given in the provincial councils, the practical result was nothing. The non-official majority was nullified by the fact that it included nominated members. There was no real majority of those who represented the people.

9. The Indians wanted the Government of England to make a clear indication as to what their goal was going to be in India. Was it to be the establishment of a responsible Government in India? If so, within how much time, and by what means? The Act of 1909 gave no answer to all these important questions.

10. The reforms were in the nature of a half-way House which could scarcely satisfy the expectations of the Indians who wanted the transfer of power.

11. The principle of responsible government was not allowed to germinate in the system. The responsibility still lay with the government. Parliamentary usages were adopted and generally followed; but the spirit of parliamentary government was absent. The result was friction. Influence without responsibility has always been disastrous in its operation. The debates lacked life because they would not affect the government. Whatever might be the opinion of the non-officials, the government always carried the day with the help of the official bloc. The authors of the Report on Indian Constitutional Reforms put the conditions created by the Reforms of 1909 in these words: "The Morley-Minto Reforms in our view are the final outcome of the old conception which made the government of India benevolent despotism (tempered by a remote and only occasionally vigilant democracy) which might as it saw fit for purposes of enlightenment consult the wishes of its subjects. To recur to Sir Bartle Frere's figure, the Government is still a monarch in durbar: but his councillors are uneasy, and not wholly content with his personal rule and the administration in consequence has become slow and timid in operation. Parliamentary usages have been initiated and adopted in the council up to the point where they cause the maximum of friction, but short of that at which by having a real sanction behind them they begin to do good: *We have at present in India neither the best of the old system, nor the best of the new. Responsibility is the savour of popular government and that savour, the present council wholly lack*".

Lionel Curtis has described the helpless situation thus created in these words: "The vital defect of Minto-Morley principle is that it leaves the whole responsibility for government on one set of men, while rapidly transferring power to another set of men. It operates to render electorates less fit for responsible government instead of more so. It creates a situation eminently calculated to exasperate the executive and legislature with each other and, therefore, to throw the British Government and the Indian community at large into a posture of mutual antagonism". "The elected members, untempered by any prospect having to conduct the Government themselves had everything to gain by harassing government and preventing it from passing the measures which it knows to be vital. In actual practice what happens is, not that government is defeated, but rather that it shrinks from proposing measures which it knows it cannot pass. The nerves of the state are slowly but surely paralysed. The elements of disorder grow and raise their heads. Every necessary measure for preserving order is denounced as an act of tyranny. The foundations of law decay, until suddenly, as in Ireland, the whole structure collapses, order has to be restored at the cost of bloodshed, and the growth of constitutional government is definitely postponed. No government suffering from creeping paralysis can maintain its prestige".

According to Shri K.M. Munshi, "Political changes known as Minto-Morley Reforms were brought in as a sop to the moderates. Legislative Councils established under it were not intended to bring Parliamentary Government as Viceroy Minto himself hastened to emphasise. Though they were merely consultative, special care was taken to see that 'class was set against class, community against community, each to cancel out the effect of the other'. Zamindars and commercial classes were given disproportionate representation at the expense of the politically minded classes, substituting those who cannot criticize for those who can, even going to the extent of creating special interests before such interests were organised or articulated. Morley, the Secretary of State, himself a radical in Britain, proved worse than a Tory so far as India was concerned".

According to Garrat and Thompson, "The Act made no theoretical change on the executive side, though the legislatures' right of criticism was increased. The changes in the legislatures were cautions and tentative. The King's Proclamation of November 28, 1908, had foreshadowed Reforms in which the principle of representative institutions would be prudently extended but Morley had no intention of introducing any democratic system of control in India... . For personal convictions, as well as for parliamentary convenience he intended to keep the legislature as *advisory bodies* and not as independent law-making ones... . Any hope of the Provincial Councils developing into autonomous units was defeated by the excessive decentralization which Morley encouraged, and Decentralization Commission did little to modify".

According to Dr. A.B. Keith, "The Reforms of 1909 failed in their object if that was to check the propaganda for self-government, and were clearly unlikely to satisfy the Extremists' demand. Inevitably the control of the Central Government over policy was reinforced by reminding the local governments that their officials must not adopt in the Legislatures, Central or Provincial, any attitude critical of the decisions of the Indian Government".

According to Pandit Bishen Narayan Dhar, "Reforms are incomplete in many respects and defective but our complaint is against Regulations which are extremely faulty, and in some aspects defeat the object of the Act". According to Surendra Nath Banerjee, "The Rules and Regulations framed for the implementation of the Reforms have practically wrecked the Reforms Scheme". He asked: "Is the bureaucracy having its revenge upon us for the part we have played for securing concessions?"

The Indian National Congress passed four resolutions dealing with the Reforms of 1919. In the words of Dr. Pattabhi Sitaramayya, "In the first it recorded the sense of disapproval of the creation of separate electorates on the basis of religion; it expressed dissatisfaction at (*a*) the excessive and unfairly preponderant share of representation given to the followers of one particular religion, (*b*) the unjust, invidious and humiliating distinctions made between Muslim and non-Muslim subjects of His Majesty in the matter of electorates, the franchise and the qualifications of the candidates, (*c*) the wide, arbitrary and unreasonable disqualifications and restrictions for candidates seeking elections to the Councils, (*d*) the general distrust of the educated classes running through the Regulations, and (*e*) the unsatisfactory composition of the non-official majorities in the Provincial Councils, rendering them ineffective and unreal". By the second resolution, it urged the creation of Executive Councils to assist the Lt. Governors of the United Provinces, the Punjab, Eastern Bengal and Assam and Burma. By the third resolution the Congress pointed out the unsatisfactory nature of the Reforms Regulations for the Punjab in (*a*) that the numerical strength of the Council was not sufficient to allow an adequate representation to all classes and interests, (*b*) that the elected element was unduly small and altogether insufficient, (*c*) that the principle of protection of minorities applied in the case of the Muslims in other provinces was not applied to non-Muslim minorities in the Punjab, and (*d*) that the Regulations tended to practically keep the non-Muslims of the Punjab from the Imperial Council. By a fourth resolution the Congress expressed dissatisfaction at the non-establishment of a Council for the Central Provinces and Berar and the exclusion of Berar from participation in the election of two members of the Imperial Legislative Council by the landholders and members of the District and Municipal Boards of Central Provinces".

Dr. Zacharia sums up his criticism of the Reforms of 1909 in the words: "The essence of these Reforms lay in conceding what at once was evacuated of all meaning. Thus, the elective principle of democracy was adopted; yet at the same time the anti-democratic communal representation was added. The official majority was done away with; but the elected members received in a minority. The membership was considerably enlarged; but an emphatic disclaimer was issued simultaneously that the new Councils in no way meant the introduction of a parliamentary system. The Council of India and even the Viceroy's Executive Council were opened to some very few select Indians but the liberal aspect of admitting Indians to the arena of government could in no way disguise the fact that real power remained safely in British hands".

The critics pointed out that Reforms of 1909 gave the people the shadow rather than the substance. "They granted *influence and not power*" and according to George Washington, "influence is not government". No wonder, Mazumdar described the reforms as "mere moonshine".

CIRCUMSTANCES LEADING TO MONTAGU-CHELMSFORD REFORMS (1919)

It goes without saying that the reforms of 1909 failed to satisfy the people of India. Even a moderate like Gokhale got convinced of the hollowness of the reforms. The reforms did not give any answer to the Indian demand that the British Government should declare as to what their goal in India was and what the British Government intended to do to achieve the same. The recommendations of the Decentralisation Commission of 1909 were utterly inadequate and disappointing. Lord Crewe, who became the Secretary of State after Lord Morley, appointed a Public Service Commission in 1912. This Commission spent two years in taking evidence but its report was not published until 1917. The way in which the machinery of the Government moved infuriated the people.

A critical study of the reforms of 1909 will show that the main object of the authors of the reforms of 1909 was to win over the Moderates. But that object was not realised as is evident from the contemporary utterances of the Moderate leaders. The discontentment and disappointment of the people resulted in revolutionary activities. The cult of the bomb became popular. The number of outrages committed by the terrorists was on the increase. Even a person like Lord Hardinge was not spared.

The Muslims were also getting restive. They had come to realise the importance of their position from their experience of separate electorates. They had found that the Government of India was only too glad to please them. This made them conscious of their position. The revision of the Partition of Bengal in 1911 did not satisfy the Hindus because they had got the thing done after a lot of suffering. This act of the Government annoyed the Muslims. The latter did not like the re-incorporation of the Muslim population of Eastern Bengal into the Hindu province of Bengal. The Muslims interpreted the action of the Government as a concession to the Hindus who had agitated and intimidated the Government. They emphasized "the connection between bombs and boons".

Moreover, the pre-war foreign policy of the British Government was a source of uneasiness to the Muslim population of India. The Muslim territories were being absorbed by the Christian Powers of Europe in the Balkans. The Muslims were annoyed over the acts of omission and commission of the British Government in the case of Morocco, Persia and Tripoli. The Balkan Wars were considered a part of a general attack on Islam. It is clear that the Muslims were as much annoyed as the Hindus although for different reasons.

The treatment of the Indians abroad was creating a lot of discontentment in India. Their cruel treatment in Natal and Transvaal especially aroused the Indians against the British Government and the latter was accused of neglect of the Indian interests. In 1913, Lord Hardinge voiced the unanimous opinion of the Indians when he stated "that the sympathy of India, deep and burning, and not only of India, but of all lovers of India like myself, goes for their compatriots in South Africa in their resistance to invidious and unjust laws". Mr. Gokhale went to South Africa to negotiate on behalf of the Government of India. However, nothing substantial was done to redress the grievances of the Indians. A Commission of Enquiry and Indian Relief Act were considered inadequate.

The Sikhs who had settled in Australia and Canada were badly treated. As regards the Western Coast of Canada, the position was complicated by the activities of a few Indian revolutionaries who had settled in U.S.A., and were responsible for the murder of anti-revolutionaries and of Mr. Hopkins who was working on behalf of the Government of India and the Dominion Governments. The dispute culminated in the dispatch of the Komagata Maru, a Japanese boat requisitioned to make a direct journey from India to Vancouver with the object of defeating the immigration restrictions. The Sikhs aboard the ship were not allowed to land. Returning after the commencement of the Great War in 1914 after great sufferings and privations, they formed the nucleus of a revolutionary movement in the Punjab.

It was in an atmosphere of discontentment that the Great War started in 1914. But in spite of all this, there was a generous response from the Indians. Mahatma Gandhi advised the Indians to render all possible help to the British Government. The Indian political parties made a sort of a truce, and allowed the Government to concentrate their attention on war effort. This attitude of the Indians facilitated the recruiting of some 8,00,000 combatants and 4,00,000 non-combatants on a voluntary basis. The Government of India contributed almost annually a sum ranging between £20 and 30 million. A free gift of £1,00,000,000 also was given to England. The Government of India met the normal charges of the Indian troops not employed in India or within her boundaries. Further responsibilities were taken in April 1918, although the war ended before these amounted to more than £12,000,000. Large contributions were given to the Red Cross Societies and a War Loan was started in India. The general goodwill was so great that the British Government was able to withdraw from the Indian soil a major part of their British troops. At one time the British troops in India were not more than 15,000.

However, by 1916, the things had changed. All hopes of a speedy and conclusive victory had disappeared and disillusionment had begun. The methods employed by the British Government in the matter of recruitment and collection of funds for the Red Cross, added insult to injury. Prices went up and added to the distress of the people. The Indians had been made to work under the august authority and supervision of some European officers. An idea began to gain ground that the people of India had nothing to do with the War. The Indian patriots were emboldened by the Irish rebellion and that apparent collapse of Western civilization. The commercial classes of India were at loggerheads with the Government on account of the war-time restrictions. They demanded a policy of protection. The Moderates were weakened by the death of Gokhale. Lord Sinha who had led the Congress to support the war efforts of Government, lost all his influence in the organisation. Mr. Asquith's declaration that "henceforth Indian questions would have to be approached from a different angle of vision," was not translated into action for full two years.

In 1915, Lord Sinha, the Congress President of the Bombay Session, advised the British Government to make a declaration of their goal in India with a view to pacifying the Indian youth who were "intoxicated with ideas of freedom, nationality and self-government".

Lord Chelmsford, who succeeded Lord Hardinge in 1915, at once came to the conclusion that the creation of British India "as an integral part of the British Empire with self-government was the goal of British rule". But it was difficult to define precisely the steps by which the Government hoped to realise that ideal. Sir Austen Chamberlain, the Secretary of State for India, was not prepared to be more explicit and precise in the matter of a formula "than to avow an intention to foster a gradual development of free institutions with a view to self-government". However, he had to resign on the Mesopotamian issue and was succeeded by Edwin S. Montagu.

AUGUST DECLARATION

Mr. Montagu was a great friend of India. He had sympathised with the aspirations of the people of India and as such can be compared with persons like Lord Pethick Lawrence and Sir Stafford Cripps. He brought a new outlook to his office. When the fortunes of the Allies were at their lowest ebb, he made the following declaration in August 1917: *"The policy of His Majesty's Government, with which the Government of India are in complete accord, is the increasing association of Indians in every branch of the administration and the gradual development of self-government institutions with a view to the progressive realisation of responsible Government in India as an integral part of the British Empire.* They have decided that substantial steps in this direction should be taken as soon as possible, and that it is of the highest importance as a preliminary to considering what these steps should be that there should be a free and informal exchange of opinion between those in authority at Home and in India. His Majesty's Government have accordingly decided, with His Majesty's approval, that I should accept the Viceroy's invitation to proceed to India to discuss these matters with the Viceroy and the Government of India to consider with the Viceroy the views of local Governments, and to receive with him the suggestion of representative bodies and others.

"I would add that *progress* in this policy *can only be achieved by successive stages. The British Government and the Government of India* on whom the responsibility lies for the welfare and advancement of Indian people, *must be judges of the time and measure of each advance* and they must be guided by the co-operation received from those upon whom new opportunities of service will be conferred and by the extent to which it is found that confidence can be reposed in the sense of responsibility".

The importance of the declaration lies in the fact that it started in categorical terms as to what exactly was going to be the goal of the British Government in India. It can be put on the same footing as the Queen's Proclamation of 1858. While the authors of the Report on the Indian Constitutional Reforms regarded it as "the most momentous utterance ever made in India's chequered history" which marked "the end of one epoch and the beginning of a new one". Pradhan declared that it was a "revolutionary pronouncement". To quote him again, "With the announcement of August 20, 1917, modern India has entered on a new era in her history".

According to G.N. Singh, the August Declaration created once again a division in the ranks of Indian Nationalists. The Moderates welcomed the declaration as the 'Magna Charta of India'. The Extremists, on the other hand, regarded the announcement as unsatisfactory both in language and substance and decided to continue agitation both for the release of the internees and for the better recognition of Indian claims and aspirations".

PROPOSALS FOR REFORMS

In 1916, the Government of India sent their Despatch to Chamberlain, Secretary of State for India, in which they made their suggestions regarding the concessions to be given to the Indians. The Despatch was never published but we have in Lord Zetland's biography of Curzon the nature and contents of the proposals. This is what Zetland says: "In their representations to the Secretary of State, the Government of India had been careful not to commit themselves to any specific form of self-government. The special circumstances of India, they pointed out, differed so widely from those of any other part of the Empire that they could scarcely expect an Indian Constitution to model itself on those of the British Dominions. All that they contemplated was a gradual progress towards a large measure of control by her own people which would ultimately result in a form of self-government, differing in many ways enjoyed by other parts of the Empire but evolved on lines which had taken into account India's past history and the special circumstances and traditions of her component peoples. Their proposals for assisting her towards this goal were, briefly, to confer greater powers and a more representative character upon existing local self-governing units such as District (rural) Boards and Municipal Councils; to increase the proportion of Indians in the higher administrative posts, and to have the way for an enlargement of the constitutional powers of the Provincial Legislatures by broadening the electorate and increasing the number of elected members".

The Secretary of State for India, Mr. Chamberlain, did not approve of the recommendations as they would merely "result in an embarrassing multiplication of irresponsible critics without affecting any real advance in the direction of self-government". He was in favour of appointing a small Commission to consider the ways and means by which some measure of authority and responsibility could be given to the Legislatures. "As to a formula for the purpose of making known the policy of the Government, he did not think it possible to be more precise than to avow on intention to foster the gradual development of free institutions with a view to self-government".

MEMORANDUM OF THE NINETEEN (1916)

When the imperial Legislature met at Simla in September 1916, its members resented the submission of the draft proposals by the Government of India to the Secretary of State without consulting them. The result was that the nineteen elected members of the Council including Jinnah, Surendra Nath Banerjee, Srinivasa Shastri, etc., submitted a Memorandum in which they put down their own views regarding the nature of the reforms that could satisfy the aspirations of the Indians.

The signatories of the Memorandum stated in the introductory was action as to how the Indians felt bitterly the treatment that was being meted out to them in the various parts of the British Empire. The Reforms of 1909 were utterly inadequate, for they transferred no real control into the hands of the Indians. They hoped that the Indian problem would be looked from "a new angle of vision" after the war. What India expected was not any reward for services rendered, but a change in her status in the British Empire where she should be recognised as a comrade in equal partnership. To quote, "What is wanted is not merely good government or efficient administration, but government that is acceptable to the people, because it is responsible to them".

As regards the changes to be effected, the Memorandum recommended that half the members of the Executive Councils should be Indians. The European half should be recruited from the ranks of men trained and educated in the public life of England so that "India may have the benefit of a wider outlook and larger experience outside the world". It was stated that a sufficient number of highly qualified Indians was available for employment in these posts. It was further recommended that the statutory provision which required three members of the Imperial Executive Council to belong to the public service in India, be deleted. The elected members of the legislature must have an effective control over the selection of the Indian Executive Councillors.

All the Legislative Councils in India should have substantial majority of elected members. Franchise should be broadened and extended directly to the people. Provision was to be made for an adequate representation of minorities, whether Hindu or Muslim.

The total membership of the Imperial Legislative Council should be increased. It should not be less than 150. The number might be 100 for major provinces and between 60 and 75 for minor ones. The budget should be passed in the form of money bills and fiscal autonomy be granted to India. The Imperial and Provincial Legislatures should have jurisdiction in matters concerning central and provincial spheres respectively. But the departments of Foreign Affairs and Military Affairs and the declaration of war or making of peace or treaty be reserved with the Government of India. Besides, the Governor-General-in-Council and the Governors-in-Council should have the right to veto but this power was to be exercised subject to certain conditions and limitations.

The Council of the Secretary of State should be abolished and the status of the Secretary of State for India be the same as that of the Minister-in-Charge of Colonies. His salary should be made a charge on the British revenues.

In case an Imperial Federation was established, India was to be placed on a footing of equality with other self-governing dominions.

Provincial Governments were to be granted the largest measure of autonomy. The United Provinces and other major provinces should have Governors recruited directly from England. They were to have Executive Councils also. Full independence in the matter of local self-government should be granted immediately. Indians were to be given arms on conditions analogous to those of the Europeans, and they be also allowed to offer themselves as volunteers in the army. Last but not least, it was prayed that Indians should be given commissions in the army on conditions similar to those of Europeans.

About the Memorandum, Pradhan writes, "The memorandum is an able and reasoned document and constitutes an important statement of the demands of the Indian people at the time".

CONGRESS-LEAGUE SCHEME (1916)

If the Memorandum was published in October 1916 the famous Congress-League Scheme was given to the world in December of the same year. The scheme was approved by the Congress on 29th December and the Muslim League on 31st December 1916. It resembled in many respects the Memorandum of October 1916 and it is remarkable to note that some of its recommendations were embodied in the Government of India Act, 1919.

The introductory portion of the Resolution states that the existing system of Government did not "satisfy the legitimate aspirations of the people" and consequently His Majesty the King Emperor should issue a proclamation announcing "that it is the aim and intention of British policy to confer self-government on India at an early date".

As regards the Scheme itself, the strength of the Provincial Legislature was to be not less than 125 members in the major provinces and from 50 to 75 in the minor ones. Of these, four-fifths were to be elected and one-fifth nominated. The members were to be elected directly by the people for five years with as broad a franchise as possible. Muslims were to be represented through special electorates in the proportion given in the scheme. It was laid down that no resolution or bill would be introduced by a non-official member if that affected a particular community and four-fifths of the members of that community in the provincial legislature opposed it. The Provincial head was not to preside over the Provincial Legislature. Its president was to be elected by the members of the Legislature. The right of asking supplementary questions was to be given to all and not only to the member who put the question. The divided heads of revenue were to be abolished and provinces were to make contributions to the Central Exchequer. Extensive powers of control should be given to Provincial Legislatures including the right to raise loans, impose and alter taxation, and vote on the Budget. The right of moving resolutions on all matters within the purview of the provincial administration should be allowed. Ordinarily, a resolution passed by the Legislature should be binding on the Government. But the Governor might veto the resolution. In case the resolution was passed once again within a year, it had to be carried out. The right of moving a motion for adjournment to discuss a definite matter of urgent public importance was granted in case not less than one-eighth of the members present asked for it. The consent of the Governor was not to be required for introducing a bill in the Provincial Legislature. Both the Governor and the Governor-General were given the power to veto the bills passed by a provincial legislature.

Governor was to be the head of every province and "ordinarily" he was not to belong to the Indian Civil Service. In every province there was to be an Executive Council, half of whose members were to be Indians elected by the elected members of the Provincial Legislatures. The recruitment of executive councillors from the I.C.S. was to be avoided as far as possible.

As regards the imperial Legislative Council, its membership was to be raised to 150. It resembled the provincial legislature in the matter of proportion of elected and nominated members and power of asking questions and supplementaries, introducing bills, passing resolutions and adjournment motions. One-third of the Indian elected members were to be Muslims. The elected members of the Imperial Legislative Council were to be elected by the elected members of the Provincial Legislature. The Budget was to be submitted for the vote of the legislature. Members were to hold office for five years. Military affairs and foreign and political relations of India including the right of declaration of war, making of peace and treaties, were to be excluded from the scope of the Imperial Legislature.

Half the members of the Executive Council of the Governor-General were to be those Indians who were elected by the elected members of the Imperial Legislature. Ordinarily, the members of the Indian Civil Service were not to be appointed to these posts. The right of making all appointments to the Imperial Civil Services should vest in the Government of India. Provinces should be given a large measure of autonomy in their own sphere and the Central Government should have the right of general supervision and superintendence over them. The Government of India was to be independent of the control of Secretary of State in legislative and administrative matters. A system of independent audit of account of the Government was to be established.

The India Council of the Secretary of State should be abolished and he be assisted by two permanent Under-Secretaries out of whom one should be an Indian. The salary of Secretary of State should be a charge on British revenues. His status should be the same as that of Secretary of State for Colonies. India should be given adequate and equal representation in any body that might be constituted to control Imperial affairs. "Indians should be placed on a footing of equality in respect of status and right of citizenship with other subjects of His Majesty the King throughout the empire". The military and naval services should be thrown open to Indians and adequate provision should be made for their selection, training and instruction in India. Indians should be allowed to enlist as volunteers. Judicial powers should be taken away from the Executive officers and the Judiciary be made independent.

The authors of the Report on Indian Constitutional Reforms regarded the Congress-League scheme as "the latest, most complete and most authoritative presentation of the claims of the leading Indian political organisations". But the scheme was full of defects.

It was demanded that European members of the Executive Councils of the Governors and the Governor-General should not be taken from the Indian Civil Service. But the difficulty was that the public men in England were not prepared to cut short their careers by accepting a post for five years, particularly when there was no pension attached to the post. Moreover, the system of election of Indian councillors did not commend itself. The necessity of having an executive which was sympathetic towards the people, could not be denied. But in the present case, the legislatures were not representative of the people because no electorates worth the name existed. "Election would deprive the Governors of all discretion in making recommendations as to his colleagues; and it would make it impossible to take steps to give all communities an opportunity for obtaining these appointments. Election is perhaps the best, though it is not the only method of securing representation; but when ability in administration ought generally speaking to be the test, nomination by those who are in the best position to judge must be more satisfactory than elections, success in which largely depends on other qualities". There was also the possibility of a deadlock between the two halves and in the event of divergence of views, there was no easy way to secure unity of action.

The scheme perpetuated the system of communal representation. It is interesting to note that the Muslims were to have separate representation even in those provinces where they were in majority. They were at the same time given weightage over and above their numerical strength in those provinces where they were in minority.

It can be doubted how the proposal requiring the withdrawal of any bill or resolution while four-fifths of the members of the interested community in the legislature objected, could work satisfactorily in actual practice. If the object of the clause was to safeguard the particular religious interests of any community, the remedy was bound to be ineffective.

The scheme started with the untenable proposition that provinces enjoy complete autonomy and consequently must have the power of raising loans, etc. Such a scheme is "compatible with parliamentary government but fundamentally incompatible with an executive which retains responsibility towards the Secretary of State and Parliament".

The proposal regarding the transfer of powers to the newly constituted legislatures without vesting them with responsibility, was bound to do more harm than good.

The scheme provided no connecting rod between the executive and legislative wheels of the machine which would enable them to work in collaboration with each other. This was bound to result in friction. "Parliamentary government avoids deadlocks by making the executive responsible to the legislature. Presidential government limits deadlocks, because all the organs of state must ultimately submit to a superior tribunal, the electorate of the nation. But a legislature elected by the people, coupled with a Governor appointed by distant power, is a contrivance for fomenting dissensions and making them perpetual".

The provision that the resolutions of the legislature should be binding on the executive, puts the latter in the awkward position of carrying out what it did not approve of. But the only other alternative was that the executive should remain in power so long as it enjoyed the confidence of the House. That implied the establishment of responsible government to which the British Government had not committed itself.

According to Dr. Lal Bahadur, "The fact was that in regard to communal adjustment, the Congress, generally speaking, suffered from self-delusion. Nothing could be done more head-strong than to hope for the disappearance of separate electorate after 10 years of its birth. The evil could easily be nipped in the bud, but it was allowed to grow till it served an easy steppingstone for the demand of Pakistan. A diplomatic blunder of high magnitude was committed in conceding the right of separate Muslim representation through members of the community themselves. It proved the British allegation of sharp division between the Hindus and Muslims and justified, for all intents and purposes, all earlier propaganda of the latter, regarding the exercise of the so-called high-handedness by the former. It was also an evidence of the tactful bankruptcy of the Congress leaders and their helpless lack of shrewdness. They ought to have understood that this concession to the Mussalmans would tear the nation for ever into two sharply divided communities and the breach would be widened by the foreign ruling power. The British Parliament recognised the Lucknow Pact as the only agreement between the Hindus and Muslims and it made assertive provision for separate electorate in the Government of India Act of 1919 and 1935. Once the basis of the division of the electorate was accepted, the recognition of the division of the country was inevitable. The Lucknow Pact demanded a heavy toll of the country's sacrifice and the price was paid in the formation of Pakistan". Dr. Lal Bahadur maintains that there was no pressing necessity to purchase Muslim support at an exorbitant cost. To quote him, "The Pact was bound to be transitory in character, for it was a child of circumstances. The Indian Mussalmans' consciousness of affinity with their co-religionists outside India was roused and an effective help for them a presupposed feeling of goodwill in the country and as soon as the danger was averted (or the fate was accepted) the incentive that sustained the agreement disappeared. Besides, a communal body that, from its very birth, had consistently advocated anti-patriotic dogmas and done all in its power to widen the gap between the Hindus and the Muslims, could be least expected to experience an overnight change in its fundamentals and pin its faith to the Congress ideology. Even war against Turkey would not shake the sense of loyalty which the Indian Muslims had developed for the British Government in the country. The Congress programme, on the other hand, demanded active opposition to the Government. The ideological differences between the two bodies made them ill-assorted mates that were ready to part company at the first opportunity. Looked at from whatever angle of vision the Lucknow Pact was foredoomed failure". (*The Muslim League*, p. 96.)

According to Coupland, "These were far more substantial concessions that the Muslims had been given by Morley and Minto to secure their acquiescence in the reforms of 1909... . The Pact concluded between the Congress and the League was the most striking expression of Indian nationalism so far achieved within the bounds of British India".

According to Kunte and Saletore, "The Congress brought about the communal unity at the sacrifice of an essential principle of national and democratic life. The Congress had always opposed the creation of separate electorates for the Muslims... .As against this the Lucknow Pact showed that the Congress had agreed to the system of communal representation, to the principle of weightage, and also to the communal veto in legislation. All these three concessions were wrong in principle and were opposed to the life-long convictions of many of the Congressmen and they formed decidedly the most objectionable feature of the Congress-League Scheme. And yet while the whole constitutional portion of the scheme was rejected by the Government, the communal agreement contained in it was accepted and was made a part and parcel of the reforms of 1919. This was, indeed, an irony of fate".

There is no denying the fact that the scheme suffered from many theoretical and practical defects. But the advocates of the scheme contended that their scheme gave them some substantial powers of control over the Government. They did not bother about the form of the Government or the inconveniences of the executive. What they cared for was that they should have some substantial powers in the working of the administrative machinery of the country and their scheme undoubtedly gave them that.

GOKHALE'S POLITICAL TESTAMENT

Before his death in 1915, Gokhale had prepared on the request of Lord Willingdon, a scheme of reforms to be given to India after the war. This so-called "Gokhale's Political Testament" was published in August 1917. Gokhale's main recommendation was the grant of provincial autonomy and the lessening of the control of the Government of India in the provincial sphere. He wanted the Executive Council or Cabinet of the Governor to consist of 6 members, three of whom were to be Indians. The Legislative Council was to consist of 75 to 100 members, of whom not less than four-fifths were to be elected. The relations between the Legislature and Executive were to be the same as those between the Reichstag and Executive in Germany before 1918. The Provincial Government was to work under the control of the Provincial Legislative Council, but otherwise, it was to have "complete charge of the internal administration of the Province". The Provinces were to have greater fiscal autonomy. They were to make contributions to the central revenues.

Since the provinces were to become "practically autonomous," the Executive Council was to consist of one instead of four existing members. His name was to be the Member of the Interior. Later on, he proposed the creation of five more members.

The Legislative Council of the Viceroy was to be known as the Legislative Assembly of India. It was to consist of about 100 members, the majority of whom were to be nominated members or officials. It was to have "increased opportunities of influencing the policy of Government by discussion, questions connected with the Army and Navy (to be now created) being placed on level with other questions".

The Government of India was to be made free in fiscal affairs from the control of the Secretary of State whose powers were to be curtailed in other matters also. His council was to be abolished and he himself put on the same footing as the Secretary of State for Colonies.

The Indians were to be admitted to the ranks of commissioned officers both in the army and navy and proper facilities were to be provided for their instruction.

If German East Africa was conquered from the Germans, it was to be handed over to the Government of India after the war and reserved for Indian colonisation.

THE ROUND TABLE GROUP

The Round Table Group was started by Lionel Curtis and his friends in South Africa after 1906 and it played a very significant part in bringing the various elements in the Union together. Encouraged by its results, the members thought of extending the scope of their studies and in that connection visited New Zealand, Australia and Canada. Not only were the centres of the groups started in the University towns of those countries, those were also opened at Oxford, Cambridge, London, etc. By means of discussion and criticism, the groups contributed to the study of the means by which the various parts of the British Empire could be brought together and the problems arising out of this huge combination of the states could be tackled satisfactorily. It is to be noted that the movement was not meant for propaganda, but for studying the problems which faced the Empire.

In the summer of 1915, the members of the Round Table Group, while preparing Vol. II of the Commonwealth of Nations, were faced with the problem of writing the chapters relating to India and the Dependencies. Curtis requested that a member of the group, who had expert knowledge about India, should present before the group his own views of the position of India in the British Commonwealth. Sir William Duke who had been the Lieutenant-Governor of Bengal, took up the task and placed before the group his famous Memorandum. His Scheme was printed and distributed among the members of the gathering who met at Oxford for three days to discuss its pros and cons. The draft was completely recast in the light of the discussions.

The Scheme as formulated in the Duke Memorandum was intended for circulation among the Round Table groups in the various parts of the British Empire for study and criticism. The results would have been used in the treatment of the Imperial problem on its Indian side. But certain circumstances did not allow that procedure to be followed.

Lord Chelmsford, who became the Governor-General of India in 1916, was formerly the Governor of New South Wales and had some knowledge of the Round Table group at Sydney. Before his departure for India, he was busy in discussing with experts, the Indian problem. When he came to know that the Round Table group in London was discussing the question of India, he requested them to show him their results. Thus, he was shown the Duke Memorandum. Since the meeting at Oxford thought that Lord Chelmsford might be embarrassed by the publication and circulation of so novel a scheme which came to be known by the name of dyarchy later on, it was decided not to circulate the Memorandum to the Round Table groups. The revised draft, however, was sent to Lord Chelmsford in India in May 1916.

Since Curtis had been "warned" by his friends "against the danger of attempting to study India at a distance" and they had advised him to "visit the country for the purpose of hearing what Indians, especially the Nationalists themselves, had to say on the subject", he left for India *via* Canada and Australia and reached Bombay towards the end of October 1916.

His visit to India and particularly his stay with big Englishmen and at the Government House and also his association with persons like Sir Valentine Chirol who was regarded by the patriotic

Indians as the greatest foe of their country, created misgivings in the minds of the public. A letter written by him to Mr. Kerr, the Secretary of the Round Table in London, fell into the hands of Indians and some extracts from it were published on the eve of the Congress session held in December 1916. Some extracts from the letter were quoted to show that Curtis was engaged in the work of vilification of the Indian nation. It was given out that a kind of conspiracy existed between Curtis and others against Indian nationalist aspirations.

This led to a lengthy controversy. Curtis had no intention to enter into duels but merely intended to study in a dispassionate manner the nature of the future constitutional advance for India. But the press campaign forced him to come forward to explain and justify his position and that of the Round Table groups on whose behalf he was carrying on all this work. In "A Letter to the People of India" issued from Delhi in March 1917, he explained the origin of the Round Table Movement, the nature of the work with which it was engaged, the stage at which the question of the status of India in the British Commonwealth came before the group, the drafting of the Duke Memorandum and the circumstances under which he had come to India. He emphasised the fact that his mission was purely academic and he belonged to no party. He declared that it was his sincere view that it was the duty of the British to do everything in their power to enable Indians to govern themselves as soon as possible and also share in the Government of the British Commonwealth as a whole. He further discussed as to how this could be achieved. His conclusion was that no further advance on the road to "responsible government" could be made on the basis of the Minto-Morley Reforms. If an attempt was made, that was bound to result in disaster. He said that he had been convinced that India must be represented in the Imperial Parliament, whose scheme the Round Table groups were preparing.

Curtis wrote another letter to Bhupendra Nath Basu on April 6, 1917 from Nainital, U.P. At the outset, he explained that the object of his visit was to study the question as to what place should India occupy in a reconstructed British Commonwealth after the war. He explained the causes responsible for the general indifference of the members of Parliament towards Indian problems. Because the British Parliament hardly found any time for Indian affairs and no further declaration of British policy had been made about India since 1858, there was bound to arise an uncomfortable situation. It was no fault of the civil servants who were still acting on the traditions and instructions of 1858.

As regards the nature of the future constitutional advance of India he stated in the same letter that more and more independence should be given to the provinces and Government of India should not touch those subjects that are handed over to the provinces. The system should be one which admits of each Province advancing at its own pace".

To achieve that goal, the first necessary step was to get rid of the official vote in the Provincial Legislative Councils. But this did not imply that there should be no official in the Councils. "Let members of the Government sit in the Council and speak. Let them be free to summon any other official they please to take part in the debates. But let voting be confined to members who are not officials". The great advantage of the system was that the time of the highly paid officials was not to be wasted merely for the purpose of recording their votes which the Government wanted them to do. The end to be achieved was that the councils should be made responsible in the true sense of the word for certain branches of administration and legislation.

The Governor of the Province was to summon that member of the Council who was most likely to command a majority of its members and entrust him with the task of forming a provincial government for the transferred parts of the administration. The leader was to select three colleagues who were to form the government along with the Leader. The Governor might help him with advice.

The ministers were to manage their own departments in their own way and were to be responsible for them also. They were to remain in power so long as they enjoyed the confidence of the Council. If they lost that, they were either to resign or ask the Governor to dissolve the Council.

He discussed the merits and demerits of the system of dyarchy propounded by him and came to the conclusion that that was the best alternative under the circumstances. He emphasised the fact that responsible government was to be first introduced in the provinces and later on in the Government of India.

Not only did Curtis propound his own views in the above letters, he profoundly influenced both Lord Chelmsford and Mr. Montagu. He also played an important part in the drafting of the Joint Address that was presented to the Viceroy and the Secretary of State for India by the Europeans and Indians in November 1917.

An attempt has been made to explain as to how the Round Table Movement and Lionel Curtis made a substantial contribution by suggesting in detail the lines on which the Government of India and the British Government could travel with a view to give India responsible government in the long run. It is true that when the London group started its discussion in 1915, there was no announcement of August 1917 before them. But it stands to their credit that they based their studies on the assumption that ultimately the establishment of responsible government was to be the goal of the British Government in India. In this, they anticipated both the Government of India and the Home Government. There is every likelihood of Lord Chelmsford having taken his clue from the Duke's Memorandum, and the Secretary of State getting his inspiration from the Government of India.

Lord Ampthill referred to the part played by Lionel Curtis in his speech in the House of Lords on December 16, 1919 thus: "The incredible fact is that, but for the chance visit to India of a globetrotting doctrinaire, with a positive mania for constitution-mongering, nobody in the world would even have thought of so peculiar a notion as that of 'Dyarchy'".

Instead of appointing a royal commission to make a report as to what should be given to the people of India, Mr. Montagu left London on October 18, 1917, as the head of a delegation and reached Bombay on November 10, 1917. After a study of about 5½ months in India, he left for London towards the end of April 1918. During his stay in India, only one idea had taken possession of his mind and that was the mission that had brought him to this country. According to Mr. Montagu himself, "I spent my whole time racking my brains as to how I am going to get something which India will accept and the House of Commons will allow me to do without whittling it down". He had to work so hard that he developed insomnia towards the end. Literally, he had worked himself to exhaustion. He not only toured the country but also met a large number of deputations. After prolonged thinking and study in conjunction with Lord Chelmsford, Montagu published his report in 1918. Montagu's Diary is both interesting and illuminating.

RECOMMENDATIONS OF 1918

The joint report of Montagu and Chelmsford analysed the meaning of the word "responsible government" and suggested that initial steps for the development of responsible Government should be taken in the provinces. The Government of India was to remain responsible through the Secretary of State to the British Parliament.

Full provincial autonomy was considered to be premature. However, the Governor was to have an Executive Council of two members of which one was to be an Indian. The Governor-in-Council was to deal with reserved subjects. The other subjects were to be transferred into the hands of the Indian ministers who were to be responsible to the Provincial Legislature. In his relations with the ministers, the Governor was not always to occupy the position of a constitution ruler. It was suggested that Local Self-Government, Education, Health and Sanitation, Agriculture, Public Works (except irrigation works), and Excise might be transferred to the ministers. The number of the non-official members was to be increased and direct elections were to be ordered wherever possible.

However, no substantial change was to be made in the Central Government. But the Council of the Governor-General was to have an Indian member. The control of the Secretary of State was to remain substantially the same as before.

The Report was published in July, 1918 and met with universal condemnation. Unfortunately, the whole atmosphere was poisoned by the publication of the Rowlatt Committee Report during the summer. The recommendations of the Rowlatt Committee were incorporated into two bills. According to them, judges were to have the power to try political cases without juries in the notified areas and Provincial Governments were given the powers of internment. The people forgot the recommendations of Montague and were furious at the reward given by the British Government in the form of Rowlatt Bill. Both Mahatma Gandhi and B.G. Tilak condemned the action of the Government in strongest possible terms.

At that time, there occurred the famous Jallianwala Bagh tragedy in 1919. Disturbances also took place in many other places in March and April, e.g., Delhi, Kasur, Lahore, etc. Martial law was imposed in certain parts of Punjab. The arrests of leaders also added fuel to the fire.

It was in this atmosphere of storm and stress that a Bill, embodying the recommendations made in the Report of 1918, was introduced in Parliament on June 2, 1919.

At the outset Mr. Montagu tried to explain the origin of the Reforms. He stated that much work had already been done when he became the Secretary of State. After the August announcement, he appointed a committee which sat at the India Office and this was presided over by Sir William Duke, the famous author of the *Duke Memorandum*. He also referred to other preliminaries before the introduction of the Bill in the House of Commons. Thus, it was clear that the Bill was the outcome of mature thinking and thorough consideration and not merely pushed through hastily.

He attributed the necessity of the Bill to 'legitimate' impatience of the Indians for reforms. He said that the August announcement had promised the grant of reforms as soon as possible. He did not want to be accused that since the war was over, the British were reluctant to fulfill the promise they had so solemnly made in 1917. Moreover, unreasonable delay was bound to be fatal to the object in view, i.e., the conciliation of the Indians.

He emphasised the fundamentally transitional character of the Reforms. They were not intended to endure for long. They were merely "a bridge between government by the agents of Parliament and government by representatives of the people of India". It is for this reason that he avoided making the Constitution a rigid one. That also explains why in a large number of cases, details were left to be filled in by means of rules. However, he assured the House that those Rules would be placed before it before the final passage of the Bill.

He said that the mere maintenance of law and order and peace and tranquility was meaningless, unless something substantial was conceded to the Indians. The grant of local self-government could not satisfy their aspirations, for that was already promised by Ripon.

He referred to three difficulties, viz., lack of education, caste system and religious differences, which stood in the way of the establishment of responsible government in India. But he believed that those could be overcome by the introduction of representative institutions. He confessed that the complete devolution of powers at once was not compatible with the maintenance of peace and order and hence undesirable. But there were certain matters that could be transferred into the hands of the Indians without suffering any irretrievable loss or injury. Other departments could still be kept in the reserve to be handed over on some later occasion. The ministers were to be given liberty in their departments and held responsible for them. Montagu definitely stated that he was not in favour of the establishment of two governments, "completely separate in the same area, with separate funds, separate finances, separate legislatures and separate executive staff". He advocated the creation of dyarchical form of Government in which the two parts had opportunities of "influence and consultation".

He stated that the time had not come for the grant of any concession at the centre. Only the legislature was to be made more representative.

He examined the Congress League Scheme, the Scheme put forward by the heads of the majority of provinces, the Indo-British Association Scheme, and still another one which proposed that in every province, one or two districts should be put completely under the control of the Indian officials and if successful, the process was to be continued in the division and ultimately in the whole province. His own conclusion was that the dyarchical system was the best as it left the scope for gradual progress in the future. He concluded his great peroration by an appeal to the members of the Commons to pass the Bill without delay.

In the discussion that followed, many members participated but prominent among them were Sir D. Maclean, Sir H. Craik, Colonel Wedgewood, Mr. Fisher (President of Board of Education), Mr. Spoor, Mr. Rees, Captain Ormsby-Gore and Brigadier-General Croft. Maclean said that term "dyarchy" suggested some connection with dacoity. Mr. Rees compared dyarchy to a man who had one head and two legs. One leg was the executive councillors and the second the ministers, and these two legs were to be directed by one head or brain of the Governor. About the Bill, Fisher said that it was "a measure, the effects of which...will be felt for generations and generations to come". Brigadier General Croft called it not only a revolutionary measure, but also, an instance of Liberalism gone mad. Fisher appealed to the British people to stand by their solemn pledge, and not fatally undermine their reputation for fair dealings and sense of justice. Mr. Spoor regarded the reforms as the "irreducible minimum", and gave a warning that no attempt should be made to whittle them down. While Wedgewood was prepared to accept dyarchy only as a transitional measure, he attached the system of indirect election for the legislatures.

On the motion of Mr. Montagu, it was decided to refer the Bill to a Joint Select Committee of the House of Lords and Commons. Lord Selborne was appointed its president. The committee included Montagu, Spoor, Lord Sinha, Lord Sydenham and others. It examined the reports of the Functions and Franchise Committees, Lord Crewe's Committee, and the Montford Report. It examined a large number of witnesses, Indians and English, and submitted a masterly Report to the House of Commons.

The Report of the Joint Select Committee contained recommendations regarding the changes that were necessary to be introduced in the Government of India Bill. The Committee proposed that a Standing Joint Committee of both the Houses should be set up for the purpose of keeping Parliament in closer contact with the Indian affairs. But the Committee was to have a purely consultative and advisory status.

The Committee proposed the inclusion of the whole of the announcement of August 20, 1917 in the Preamble to the Bill rather than only a part of it. It altered the Lists of the Central, Provincial and Transfer subjects included in the Functions Committee's Report. It disapproved of the separate purse for the Reserved Departments and recommended that the Governor should allocate a definite proportion of revenues for the reserved and transferred departments. If he wanted help in this work of division, he could refer the question to an authority appointed by the Governor-General.

The relations between the two halves of the provincial executive should be of such mutual sympathy that each helps and influences the work of the other. But one part was not to exercise control over the other. The ministers in charge of the transferred subjects were to be those elected members of the Legislative Council who enjoyed its confidence, and were capable of leading it. The ministers were to be expected from the very beginning to act together. Their status was to be similar to that of the members of the Executive Council, but their salaries were to be determined by the

Legislative Council. The Committee recommended that the habit of joint deliberations between the ministers and the councillors under the presidentship of the Governor should be encouraged. The Governor was directed to allow ministers to have their way and fix responsibility upon them, even if he had to use his veto power to negative any piece of legislation. The Committee recommended that the Governor should not preside over the meetings of the Provincial Legislative Council. Although for the first four years, the President was to be nominated by the Governor, subsequently he was to be elected by the Council. The Vice-President was to be elected by the Council from the very beginning. The Committee specifically laid down that they attached the "greatest importance to this question of the Presidency of the Legislative Council". It was proposed that the provincial budget should be submitted to the vote of the Legislative Council, subject to a few exemptions to be specified in the Bill. The Committee rejected the idea of instituting Grand Committees in the Provincial Legislatures.

The Committee made detailed recommendations regarding franchise. It proposed to increase the share of representation of the rural population and also the urban wage-earning classes. An effort was to be made to remove the disparity in the size of electorates in the different provinces. The Committee considered representation for the depressed classes to be inadequate. The non-Brahmins of the Madras Presidency and the Marathas of the Bombay Presidency were to be given separate representation by the reservation of seats. The question of representation of women was to be left to the option of the newly elected legislative councils which were empowered to allow that by means of resolutions. All graduates of over seven years' standing were to be given the right to vote for the University seats. The recommendations of the Franchise Committee in respect of the proportionate representation of Mohammedans, based on the Lucknow Pact, might be accepted. It was definitely laid down that no alterations were to be made in the franchise for the first ten years.

The Committee did not approve of the idea of keeping the Council of State as an organ for government legislation. It was to be constituted as a true second chamber from the very beginning. It was to consist of 60 members of whom not more than 20 were to be officials.

The Committee did not agree to accept the system of indirect election for the Legislative Assembly on a permanent basis. That may be allowed as a transitional measure for three years, but the Government of India was to devise means to remedy this defect at an early date. The Governor-General was to nominate the President of the Legislative Assembly for the first four years.

Although the Indian Budget was to be submitted to the vote of the Assembly, the Committee recommended the exemption of certain charges of a special or recurring nature from the voting. It was made clear that the Governor-General's power of certification was a real one and was "meant to be used if and when necessary".

The Committee recommended that the existing limitation on the number of the members of the Governor-General's Executive Council should be removed. Three of the Executive Councillors were to be public or ex-public servants who had been in the service of the Crown in India for 10 years. Not less than three members of the Council were to be Indians. One member should have definite legal qualifications.

The Committee recommended that all charges of the India Office, excluding "agency" charges, should be paid out of the British revenues. But it did not approve of the abolition of the Council of India which was to be reconstituted by the inclusion of more Indians into it.

In matters of fiscal policy, the Committee recommended that the Secretary of State for India should, so far as possible, avoid interference when the Government of India and its legislature were in agreement. Interference was to be limited to the safeguarding of the international obligations of the Empire or any fiscal arrangements within the Empire to which His Majesty's Government was a party.

The Committee recommended that every precaution should be taken to protect the interests of the public servants. If there occurred any friction between a minister and a public servant, it was to be one of the "most important duties" of the Governor to bring about a reconciliation. If that was not possible, the officer was to be provided with an equivalent career elsewhere or allowed to retire on a reasonable pension.

The Committee wanted it to be specifically laid down that the Statutory Commission was not to be appointed before ten years and no substantial change was to be made in the constitution during that interval.

After the Joint Select Committee had presented its Report, the Bill was introduced on December 5 1919 in the House of Commons for the third reading. On behalf of the Labour Party, Adamson supported the Bill and declared it to be a definite move in the right direction. But his complaint was that the Bill did not go far enough. He maintained that by not giving any control at the centre, the Government had lost the sympathetic co-operation of some of the best elements of the population of India. He thought it absurd to give the right of vote to only 5 millions out of 250 millions. Similarly, he regretted the exclusion of industrial workers and women from franchise. Maclean, Spoor and Ormsby-Gore also participated in the discussion. While winding up the debate in the Third Reading, Montagu expressed the hope that the future Parliament will take India on the road to responsible Government. He regarded the passage of the Bill as the ending of an era. He appealed to the feelings of mutual goodwill. He concluded with the remark. "Let us forget the past and start afresh".

When the Bill came up for discussion before the House of Lords on December 11 1919, Lord Sinha, Under Secretary of State for India, dealt at length with the history of the Reforms. Since the question of reform had been hanging since 1915, it could not be maintained with an amount of justice that the Bill before the House was a hasty measure. It was "the natural and inevitable sequel to the long chapter of previous legislation for the better Government of India". It was imperative to give reforms to India because not only her status in the British Empire had been raised during the war as a result of her participation in many imperial affairs on equal footing, but nationalism also had made great advance in the country. The aspirations of the natives had been pitcher high, but the existing administrative machinery in India was purely an official one. India might not be fully equipped for complete self-government, but she had to be given "some measure of control" at once if it was intended that she should fit herself for better things in the future.

Lord Sinha discussed at length the various alternative schemes that were put forward to suggest the line of advance to be followed in India. While criticising them all, he defended the Bill on many grounds. He also discussed the position of the Secretary of State, India Council, Civil Services in India, and the proposed Commissioners of Inquiry. He tried to emphasise the fact that the old system of Government which had worked in India in the nineteenth century could not be continued in the twentieth century. The Indians had reached the age of adolescence and if the British were to act as good guardians, it was their imperative duty to give Indians as much of liberty as was necessary for self-expression in their age of adolescence. Lord Sinha appealed to the members to discuss the Bill with earnestness, impartiality and fairness. He concluded by saying that "what is being given to India is like the grain of mustard seed which a man took and sowed in his field, which now is the least of all seeds, but when it was grown it was the greatest amongst the herbs and became tree so that the birds of the air came and lodged in the branches thereof".

Lord Carmichael said that he was happy that the Reforms would strengthen the hands of the Moderates in India. He did not share the view that the Indian ministers would not like the Civil Servants. On the other hand, the real danger was that they being new to the job, might not completely depend upon them. Of course, the position of the Governor would be a very difficult one.

Lord Crewe maintained that there was nothing "novel" in the Reforms and they could not be called "a leap in the dark". Their necessity arose because under the system set up in 1909, criticism was reaching dangerous limits. Moreover, Indians had given an unmistakable proof of their capacity by their splendid part in the war. While he approved of the creation of a High Commissioner for India, he was opposed to the appointment of a Parliamentary Committee of two Houses on the ground that that would lead to too much of interference into the affairs of India. He warned the Indians that it was not in their interest to start any agitation during the first few years of the inauguration of the Reforms.

Lord Sydenham, a great die-hard and an opponent of India's freedom, maintained that the Bill was "the most dangerous" piece of legislation. It did not arise out of "any desire on the part of the people of India". It was merely a concession to a small body of English-speaking Indians so that they may keep quiet. While he praised the services rendered by the Indian princes and the fighting classes of India, he criticised the Indian nationalists for having started the agitation when the Government was in trouble. Not only did they condemn the Government in the strongest terms by holding it responsible for all the miseries of India, they also stirred up class-hatred. He complained that the people who came to give evidence before the Joint Parliamentary Committee did not represent India. The real Indians were the masses who did not know English and consequently their case was lost by default. The result was that the Bill was going to establish an oligarchy in India. Lord Sydenham referred to the new danger to India arising from the spread of Bolshevism in the country and emphasised the imperative necessity of a strong government to meet the situation. But, unfortunately, the new Reforms were going to weaken the executive at the most critical juncture. He ridiculed the idea that the political institutions that had worked successfully in the West, would work similarly in the East. He criticised the hurry with which the Bill was being pushed through.

Lord Meston who had been deputed by the Government of India to present their point of view before Parliament, maintained that he could give firsthand information on the Indian affairs. He emphasised the fact that the Bill before Parliament was not the outcome of agitation or the noisy demands of the Indian politicians. It was the inevitable result of the work of the British in India. It is the British themselves who had created a national awakening in the country. He informed the House that revolution was out of the question in India and hence the Bill should not be held up on that score. He concluded by saying that the Bill was introduced at the request of Government officials who were engaged in carrying on the work of administration.

Lord Curzon, the leader of the House of Lords, supported the Bill in a reserved tone. He referred to the great work accomplished by the joint Parliamentary Committee. He also touched upon the fiscal policy of India and the India Council. He emphasised the need of mutual cooperation between the Government of India and the Home Government on the one hand, and the Indian Nationalist Press on the other.

Lord Ampthill condemned the Bill in the strongest possible terms. He held that the Bill was a "calamitous measure". While the situation in India was becoming critical everyday, the Bill was going to weaken the executive and impair its impartiality. He maintained that the Indian soil was not favourable for the growth of democratic institutions. The caste-system of the Hindus in itself was anti-democratic. The only effect of the Bill was going to be the establishment of the domination of the Brahmins in the country, and that was not at all welcome to the non-Brahmins. He accused the British statesmen for their mental bankruptcy and predicted that the whole of the future of India was going to be jeopardised by the passage of the Bill.

In spite of the stout opposition at the hands of men like Sydenham and Ampthill, the Bill was passed by the House of Lords on December 18, 1919 and it received the Royal Assent on December 23.

On the same day, a Royal Proclamation was issued by King George V to the Indian Princes and the people of India. It was hoped that the new Act "will take its place among the great historic measures passed by the Parliament of this Realm for the better government of India and for the greater contentment of her people". He declared that he was happy to watch the progress of democratic institutions in the country. He appealed to the leaders of the Indians and the ministers of the future to face responsibility, endure misrepresentation and make sacrifices for the common interests of the country. He hoped that the public servants would trust their new officers and work with them in harmony so that orderly advance towards free institutions by the Indians might become possible.

He expressed his earnest desire to remove all bitterness between the Indians and British officers. With that object in view, he directed the Viceroy to exercise on his behalf clemency to political offenders in the fullest measure which was consistent with public safety.

On the same occasion, he sent the happy news to the Princes of India that he had agreed to the establishment of a Chamber of Princes. He also assured them that their privileges, rights and dignity would be maintained in the future.

He announced his intention to send the Prince of Wales to India to inaugurate the New Chamber of Princes and the new Constitution in British India. He hoped that when the Prince of Wales visited the country mutual good-will and confidence would prevail among the Indians. He concluded with a prayer to "Almighty God that His Wisdom and under His guidance India may be led to greater prosperity and contentment and may grow to the fullness of political freedom".

Preamble of the Act of 1919. The Preamble to the Government of India Act of 1919 is very important and runs as follows: "Whereas it is the declared policy of the Parliament to provide for the increasing association of Indians in every branch of Indian administration, and for gradual development of self-governing institutions, with a view to the progressive realisation of responsible government in British India as an integral part of the Empire;

"And whereas, progress, in giving effect to this policy can only be achieved by successive stages and it is expedient that substantial steps in this direction should now be taken;

"And whereas the time and manner of each advance can be determined only by Parliament upon whom responsibility lies for the welfare and advancement of the Indian peoples;

"And whereas, the action of Parliament in such matters should be guided by the co-operation received from those on whom new opportunities of service will be conferred, and by the extent to which it is found that confidence can be reposed in their sense of responsibility;

"And whereas, concurrently with the development of self-governing institutions in the province of India, it is expedient to give to those provinces in provincial matters the highest measure of independence of the Government of India, which is compatible with the due discharge by the latter of its own responsibilities;

"Be it therefore enacted..as follows":

The following is an analysis of the Preamble as given by the late Sir Tej Bahadur Sapru:—

(1) British India is to remain an integral part of the British Empire.

(2) Responsible Government in British India is the objective of the declared policy of Parliament.

(3) Responsible Government is capable of progressive realisation only.

(4) In order to achieve responsible Government, it is necessary to provide for two things: the increasing association of the Indians in every branch of administration and the gradual development of self-governing institutions.

MAIN PROVISIONS OF THE ACT OF 1919

1. The Government of India Act, 1919 made many changes in the administration of India. Formerly, the Secretary of State for India used to be paid out of the Indian revenues. The new Act provided that in future he was to be paid out of the British revenues. However, some of the functions of the Secretary of State for India were taken away from him and given to a High Commissioner

for India who was to be appointed by the Government of India and paid by the Government of India. He acted as the agent of the Governor-General-in-Council. He was to be in-charge of the Stores Department, the Indian Student Department, etc. The control of the Secretary of State was reduced in the provincial sphere in so far as the transferred departments were concerned. But in the case of the Central Government of India, it remained as complete as before. The Secretary of State possessed and exercised the power of superintendence, direction and control over the affairs of India. It was the duty of the Governor-General to carry out the orders of the Secretary of State.

2. The Act of 1919 set up a bicameral legislature of the Centre in place of the Imperial Council consisting of one House. The names of the two Houses were the Central Legislative Assembly and the Council of State. The Council of State consisted of 60 members out of which 33 were elected and 27 were nominated by the Governor-General. The Central Legislative Assembly consisted of 145 members out of which 103 were elected and the rest were nominated. Out of the nominated members, 25 were officials and the rest non-officials. Out of the 103 elected members, 51 were elected by the general constituencies, 32 by communal constituencies (30 by Muslims and 2 by Sikhs), and 20 by special constituencies (7 by landholders, 9 by Europeans and 4 by Indian Commerce).

3. The life of the Central Legislative Assembly was 3 years and the Council of State 5 years but the same could be extended by the Governor-General. It is to be noted that the last Assembly sat for 11 years. The first Speaker of the Assembly was nominated by the Government, but the subsequent Speakers were elected by the members of the Assembly.

4. The Franchise Committee had recommended a system of indirect elections to the Central Assembly on the ground that direct elections though preferable were impracticable on account of the unwieldy character of the constituencies. Ultimately, the Government of India decided in favour of direct elections for both Houses of the Central Legislature.

5. As regards the franchise for both Houses of the Central Legislature, it was very much restricted. In the case of the Council of State, voters were assessed either to income tax on an annual income of not less than ₹10,000 to ₹20,000 or to land-revenue of ₹750 to ₹5,000. In addition, those who had previous experience in public work or who were recognised as men of high scholarship or academic worth were entitled to have their names enrolled on the election roll of general constituencies for the Council of State. As regards the qualifications of the voter for the Central Assembly, these were either the payment of municipal taxes amounting to not less than ₹15 to ₹20 per annum, or occupation or ownership of a house of the annual rental value of ₹180 or assessment to income tax on an annual income of not less than ₹2,000 to ₹5,000 or assessment to land revenue for ₹50 to ₹150 per annum, varying from province to province. It is to be noted that the total number of voters for the Council of State was about 17,364 and for the Central Assembly was about 909,874 in 1920.

6. The Governor-General was given the power to summon, prorogue and dissolve the chambers. He was also to have the right of addressing the members of the two Houses.

7. The Central Legislature was given very wide powers. It could make laws for the whole of British India, for the subjects of His Majesty and Services of the Crown in other parts of India, for the Indian subjects of His Majesty wherever they may happen to be and for all persons employed in His Majesty's defence forces. It could also repeal or amend laws for the time being in force in British India or applicable to the persons mentioned in the preceding sentence. However, the previous sanction of the Secretary of State-in-Council was required to pass any Legislation abolishing any High Court. The Indian Legislature had no power to amend or repeal

any Parliamentary statute relating to British India or do anything affecting the authority of Parliament or the unwritten laws or constitution of the United Kingdom.

The previous sanction of the Governor-General was required to introduce bills concerning the following subjects:—

(i) The public debt or public revenues of India.

(ii) Religion or religious rites and usages of the British subjects in India.

(iii) Discipline or maintenance of His Majesty's military, naval or air forces.

(iv) Relations of the Government of India with foreign States or Indian States.

(v) Any measure which repeals or amends any Act of a legislature or any ordinance made by the Governor-General, etc.

In addition to the above, the Governor-General was given the power of preventing the consideration, at any stage, of a bill or a part of a bill in either chamber of the Central Legislature if in his opinion it "affects the safety or tranquility of British India, or any part thereof". The Governor-General was empowered to enact laws which he considered essential for the safety, tranquility of interests of British India or any part thereof if either chamber refused or failed to pass them. Every Act so passed required the assent of His Majesty. The Governor-General possessed the power of making and promulgating ordinances for the peace and quiet Government of British India in cases of emergency. An ordinance issued by the Governor-General had the same force of law as a law passed by the Indian Legislature. It lasted for 6 months. The Governor-General had the power of returning any measure passed by the two Houses of the Central Legislature for re-consideration before signifying his assent or dissent. The assent of the Governor-General was essential for the enactment of a law by the Legislature. He had the power to give his assent or reserve the Bill for the signification of His Majesty's pleasure on the same. The Crown had the power of disallowing any Act made by the Indian Legislature or the Governor-General. The vetoing power of the Governor-General was real and was actually exercised on many occasions.

Members of both Houses of the Central Legislature were given the right of putting interpellations and supplementary questions, of moving resolutions and making motions of adjournment, and of introducing projects of legislation according to the rules. The members were given the right of freedom of speech in the two chambers.

8. As regards the Central Budget, the Government submitted proposals for the appropriation, in the form of demands for grant, to the vote of the Indian Legislative Assembly. However, there were certain non-voteable items in the Budget. These items were not open to discussion in either chamber, "unless the Governor-General otherwise directs". All other items of expenditure were submitted to the vote of Assembly which "may assent or refuse its assent to any demand or may reduce the amount referred to in any demand by a reduction of the whole grant". If the Governor-General was satisfied that any demand which had been refused by the Assembly was essential for the discharge of his responsibilities, he could restore the grant even if it was rejected by the Assembly. In cases of emergency, he was empowered "to authorise such expenditure as may in his opinion, be necessary for the safety or tranquility of British India or any part thereof".

It is evident that the Central Legislature was helpless before the Central Executive. The Executive was not only independent of the Legislature, but also had the power of over-riding the Legislature in almost all respects.

9. It has been rightly pointed out that the Act of 1919 introduced responsive and not responsible Government at the Centre. The members of the Executive Council of the Governor-General were nominated members. The people had neither any hand in their appointment nor in their

removal. No vote of no-confidence by the legislature could turn it. But it cannot be denied that the members of the Executive Council did respond to the wishes of the members of the Central Legislature and through them to the people of the country. Some of the members of the Legislature were the members of the Standing Committee such as Finance Committee and the Committee on Public Accounts. As such they got an opportunity to influence the Government. The members could not expose the Government by putting them questions, supplementary questions and moving motions of adjournment. They could also reject the Budget and move and pass resolutions against the Government. It is these factors which made the Government respond to the wishes of the members of the Legislature. Even the most irresponsible Executive Councillors could not afford to ignore the wishes of the members of the Legislature. Thus, it was that although the Executive was independent of the Legislature, the latter could influence its decisions. The large majority given to the elected members of the Central Assembly made things hot for the Government and the only way to improve the state of affairs was carry on the administration according to the wishes of the people.

10. The new Act provided for two lists of subjects: Central List and Provincial List. The principle underlying this division was that matters in regard to which uniformity in legislation was necessary or desirable for the whole of India or in more than one province should be regarded as central, while others in which only a particular province was interested, should be treated as provincial. The central subjects were; Defence, Foreign and Political Relation, Public Debt, Tariffs and Customs, Posts and Telegraphs, Patents and Copyright, Currency and Coinage, Communications, Commerce and Shipping, Civil and Criminal Law and Procedure, Major Ports, etc. The provincial subjects were: Local Self-Government, Public Health and Sanitation and Medical Administration, Education Public Works, Water Supplies and Irrigation, Land Revenue Administration, Famine Relief, Agriculture, Forests, Co-operative Societies, Low and Order, etc. As regards the residuary subjects, they were divided between the centre and the provinces on the same principle on which the lists were drawn up. It is to be noted that the division was not clear-cut or definite. There was a lot of overlapping. Critics point out that while subjects like commerce and law regarding property were placed in the Central List, important subjects like Excise and laws regarding Land Tenure were given to the provincial. Although all subjects in the Provinces List were provincial for purposes of administration, that was not the case for purposes of legislation. Certain parts of them in regard to which uniformity in legislation was considered taxing desirable, were made "subject to legislation by the Indian Legislature". These were borrowing and taxing powers of local self-governing bodies, infectious and contagious diseases of men, animals and plants, water supplies and irrigation, industrial matters including factories, electricity, settlement of labour disputes, control of newspapers, printing presses, etc.

The size of the Provincial Legislative Council was considerably enlarged. While about 70 per cent of the members of the Provincial Legislature were elected, about 30 per cent were nominated by the Governor. Some of these nominated members were officials and the others non-officials. The Legislative Council sat ordinarily for 3 years, but it could not be dissolved earlier by the Governor. The latter could also extend its life. The members were given the right of asking questions and supplementary questions. They could reject the budget, although the Governor could restore it, if necessary.

11. The Act of 1919 introduced dyarchy in the provinces. Under this system, the subjects to be dealt with by the Provincial Governments were divided into two parts: Transferred and Reserved subjects. The Reserved subjects were administered by the Governor with the help of the Executive Council and the Transferred subjects were dealt with by the Governor with the help of his ministers. While the members of the Executive Council were nominated by the Governor, the ministers were chosen by the Governor from the members of the legislature. The

following were the Reserved subjects: Administration of Justice, Police, Irrigation and Canals, Drainage and Embankments, Water Storage and Water Power, Land Revenue Administration, Land Improvement and Agricultural Loans, Famine Relief, Control of Newspapers, Books and Printing Presses, Prisons and Reformatories, Borrowing money on credit of the Province, Forests except in Bombay and Burma, Factory inspection, Settlement of Labour Disputes, Industrial Insurance and Housing. The following were the Transferred subjects: Local Self-Government including matters relating to Municipal Corporations and District Boards; Public Health, Sanitation and Medical Administration, including Hospitals and Asylums and provision for Medical Education; Education of Indians with some exceptions; Public Works, including Roads, Bridges and Municipal Tramways, but excluding Irrigation, Agriculture and Fisheries; Co-operative Societies; Excise; Forests in Bombay and Burma only; Development of Industries, including Industrial Research and Technical Education. The provincial Governor was not a constitutional head. He was given many special responsibilities. He was authorised to over-rule his ministers and the numbers of the Executive Council if that was considered necessary for the discharge of his responsibilities. The Governor was expected to encourage joint deliberation between the ministers and the members of the Executive Council. Provision was made for the temporary administration of Transferred subjects in the case of an emergency. If no minister was in charge of a Transferred subject, the Governor himself assumed temporary charge of it till a minister was appointed. The Governor-General-in-Council with the previous sanction of the Secretary of State-in-Council could revoke or suspend the transfer of all or any subjects in the province and in that case they would relapse into the position of Reserved subjects and be administered by the Governor-in-Council.

Working of Dyarchy. The system of Dyarchy worked in the Provinces from 1921 to 1937, but experience shows that the system did not work satisfactorily. Many factors were responsible for the failure of the system:

1. The very principle of dyarchy was faulty. The division of administration into two parts, each independent of the other, is opposed to political theory and the practice of Governments. The State is like an organism and the two parts cannot be separated completely. However, the actual division of subjects under the Act of 1919 was haphazard. There could not be a worse division than the one attempted in the Act of 1919. Sir K.V. Reddi, a minister of Madras, says: "I was a minister for Development without the forests. I was the minister for Agriculture minus irrigation. As minister of Agriculture, I had nothing to do with the administration of the Madras Agriculturists' Loans Act or the Madras Land Improvement Loans Act, Famine Relief, of course, could not be touched by the minister for Agriculture. Efficacy and efficiency of a minister for Agriculture without having anything to do with Irrigation, agricultural loans, land improvement loans, and famine relief is better imagined than described. Then again, I was a minister for Industries without factories, boilers, electricity and waterpower, mines or labour, all of which were reserved subjects". While the Education was a Transferred subject, the education of the Europeans and the Anglo-Indians was a Reserved subject.

   Shri C.Y. Chintamani, a minister of U.P., has given us some examples of the way in which dyarchy worked. In 1921, an inquiry was started in the Department of Agriculture on the question of the fragmentation of lands. When the report was submitted in 1922, it was felt that the question should have been dealt with by the Revenue Department and the case was transferred to that Department. In 1924, it was decided that the case should be sent to the Co-operative Department to which it related. Similar examples can be multiplied.

2. There was no love lost between the two halves of the Government. The ministers were the representatives of the people. The members of the Executive Council belonged to the

bureaucracy. They usually never pulled together. There was constant friction. Sometimes the ministers and the Executive Councillors condemned each other in the public. As a result of this, the work of administration suffered. As a rule, the Governor backed the members of the Executive Council because he himself belonged to the same service to which they belonged.

3. The position of the ministers was very weak. They had to serve two masters. Those were the Governor and the Legislative Council. A minister could be appointed by the Governor and dismissed at his will. He was responsible to the Legislature for the administration of his Department. He could be turned out by the Legislature by a vote of no-confidence. From the point of view of practical politics, the ministers cared more for the Governor than the Legislature. There were no strong parties in the provincial legislature. The result was that no minister had a majority to back him in office. He had always to depend upon the backing and support of the official bloc in the Legislature. While the elected members of the Provincial Legislature were divided into many groups on the basis of various religions, the support of the official bloc which always voted under the instruction of the Governor, was always available to a minister who cared for the Governor. No wonder, the ministers always looked up to the Governor and were dependent upon him. It is said that the Raja of Panagal openly used to say in the Madras Legislative Council that he was responsible only to the Governor, and no one else. In certain cases, the ministers hoped to become Executive Councillors after the expiry of their term of office as ministers. The result of all this was that the ministers sank to the position of glorified secretaries. C.Y. Chintamani rightly said that the ministers had no power. "The power is with the Governor and not with the ministers". The Governor could interfere in any matter under any minister. According to Kelkar, he was allowed to have his way in matters of policy, but was constantly over-ruled in matters of detail. "For instance, I could not picture myself how a Governor could support my policy of non-interference with a Municipal Committee who wanted to hoist a national flag on the municipal office and how the same Governor could ask me to uphold an order of a Deputy Commissioner who had suspended a Committee's resolution to the effect that its servants should put on Khaddar dress".

4. The Governors did not care to encourage the principle of joint responsibility amongst the ministers. The ministers never worked as a team. They were always quarrelling among themselves. In the case of the Calcutta Municipal Bill, the Nawab Sahib and Sir Surendranath Banerjee openly canvassed against each other in the Council. In 1928, Sir Feroz Khan Noon publicly criticized and condemned the action of the Hindu colleagues. It is to be noted that 'the dismissal or resignation of a minister did not affect his colleagues. The Governor dealt with every minister individually.

5. The position of the permanent services created many difficulties. The appointment, salary, suspension, dismissal and transfer of the members of All-India Services was under the control of the Secretary of State for India. These persons continued to be under the control of the Secretary of State for India even if they were appointed in the Transferred Departments. They did not care for the ministers. The ministers had no power to choose their own subordinates when vacancies occurred in their Departments. Most of the important jobs were reserved for the members of All-India Services. In the case of Madras, when the post of Surgeon-General fell vacant, the minister concerned could not get his nominee appointed. An I.M.S. officer was sent to fill the post. Although the minister desired to encourage the Indian system of medicine, the Surgeon-General did not care for his views. We are told that if there were certain superfluous jobs, the minister concerned had no right to abolish those job. In the case of U.P., a district officer refused to apply for appeal in an excise case as required by a minister. He was supported by a member of the Executive Council. As a general rule, the Governors could be expected to support the members of the civil services against the ministers.

6. According to the rules of executive business, case in which the minister differed from the opinion of the Permanent Secretary or the Head of the Department, or the Commissioner of a Division, had to be submitted to the Governor for the final orders. Both the Secretary and the Head of the Department had direct access to the Governor. The Secretary had a weekly interview with the Governor and could discuss everything about his department with the Governor. This must have weakened the position of the ministers. Sometimes the Governor knew things about a Department which the minister concerned did not know.

7. Another cause of the failure of dyarchy was the reservation of the Department of Finance in the hands of the Member of the Executive Council. All the nation-building departments were given to the ministers, but they were given no money for the same. The result was that the ministers had to depend upon the sweet will of the Finance Secretary. As a member of the Indian Civil Service, the Finance Secretary had no sympathy with the aspirations of the Indians as represented by ministers. He cared more for the needs of the Reserved Departments than for the Transferred Departments. According to C.Y. Chintamani, "The Finance Member was certainly more anxious to see that his Reserved Departments got all the money they required, before other departments got what they wanted". In certain cases, the Finance Department refused even to examine any scheme on the ground that no money was likely to be available. In the case of U.P., the Finance Department once upon a time issued a circular to all the Heads of the Departments directing them not to send proposals, involving expenditure. When actually money was found available, it was contended by the Finance Department that no money could be granted as proposals had not been put in for examination at the right time. Many a time, the reply of the Finance Department was that the proposals were not "'worth spending money on". We are told that even when schemes were approved, ways and means were found to defeat them or to delay them till the end of the financial year which compelled the minister to start from the very beginning once again. According to Chintamani, "I am prepared to state this without any exaggeration that it was from general experience of both the ministers in the United Provinces that they had to contend with great difficulties when they went to the Finance Department, that pretty frequently they had to go before the Governor, pretty frequently the Governor did not side with them and pretty frequently they could only gain their point in the end by placing their offices at the disposal of the Governor".

According to Punniah, "The department thus did not confine itself merely to an examination of the financial aspect of the proposals but often went into the policy underlying them. The Minister was responsible to the Legislature for policy while the Finance Member was not, and this, therefore, placed the Minister in a difficult position. Even when schemes were accepted by the Council, devices were found to defeat them or at last delay them till the end of the official year, which compelled the Minister to start at the very beginning once again. The veto of the Finance Department was final except when the Minister decided to take his case on appeal to the Governor, who pretty frequently sided with the Finance Department".

According to Sapru, "But the Devolution Rules seriously detracted from the advantages of the Joint purse by keeping the portfolio of finance in the hand of a member of the Executive Council. The Ministers thus had to look up to him and his Department for all schemes of expenditure. In the financial powerlessness of Ministers is to be found the chief cause of the failure of Dyarchy".

8. There was another hindrance in the way of the successful working of dyarchy. It was born under an unlucky star. The political atmosphere in the country was surcharged with suspicion and distrust on account of the happenings in the Punjab and the attitude of the British Government towards Turkey. The Monsoons failed in 1920 and added to the misery of the people. Slump also came in the market. The result of all this was that the finances of both the Central and

Provincial Governments were upset. The favourable balance of trade of India was upset. Under the Meston Award, the Provincial Governments were required to make certain annual contributions to the Government of India. On account of the financial crisis, the Government of India demanded the full contributions from the Provincial Governments which themselves were in a worse condition. Dyarchy could not be expected to work without finances.

9. The man in the street knew that the reforms of 1919 were in the nature of a half-way house. The Indians knew that they were going to get more in the future. The result was that the people of India were not in a mood to give the reforms a fair trial.

Regarding the working of dyarchy, Sir H. Butler says: "In India, it has almost become a term of abuse. I have heard one man shouting to another: 'You are a dyarchy'. 'I will beat you with a dyarchy' said one Indian boy to another and when questioned as to what dyarchy was, replied, a new kind of tennis racket'. I have been received in a Burma village by 'a dyarchy band braying against a Home Rule band with all the vigour of village faction, neither having the least idea of what Rule or dyarchy meant".

According to Roberts, "Dyarchy was the best transitional mechanism that appeared after a prolonged examination of alternatives. Herein, indeed, lurked the seeds of trouble. There have often, no doubt, been transitional periods in history, but they were only discovered to be such in the retrospective survey of historians. Successive stages in national development have generally been regarded as final by each generation in turn. The peculiarity about the decade 1919–29 is that it was a period required...by statutory enactment, to contemplate self-consciously its own ephemeral nature, with the inevitable result that it was always hastening despairingly to a long anticipated death bed". (*British India,* pp. 589-90.)

According to Dr. Appadorai, "Dyarchy was introduced with high hopes and it must be said that, on a theoretical analysis and if worked under ideal conditions, it is not without merits. It is the strictly logical solution of a situation in which it is desired to base the authority of Government in different matters on two different sources—a situation in which a complete transfer of responsibility is considered impossible by a ruling power. It is thus a bridge between autocracy and responsibility. It is educative in the sense that it gives men an opportunity to show what they can do, as it proceeds on the basis of proved results; it would put everybody on their mettle... . In practice largely because, I think, the conditions it postulates are too difficult to obtain, its achievements are much more modest. It is a trite remark that where it succeeded it succeeded only because the principle of dyarchy was largely ignored. But this much may be said: under dyarchy many persons have been brought in touch with problems of administration, and with the difficulties of a responsible form of government. This is a valuable asset, especially if the same people have an opportunity of working later under a system of full responsible government. And another good result is that the ideas of 'transferred subjects' and 'popular control' have brought about a concentration of public interest on certain beneficial activities of government—the nation building departments".

According to Palande, "Dyarchy was never intended to be an ideal in itself but as a stepping stone to a noble consummation, namely, a fully self-governing India. Indians were thoroughly dissatisfied with the whole project of dyarchy. The parliamentary appearances that it suggested were tantalizing. But those who had a personal knowledge of its inner working exposed its ridiculous contradictions and defects. The ideal manifestation of dyarchical government implied the complete self-effacement of an irresponsible bureaucracy, but unfortunately that quality was too superhuman to be a normal feature of the administration".

According to Punniah, "Dyarchy was a unique experiment which was tried in nine provinces for over a period of sixteen years. Its main object and purpose was to train the people of India in the art of responsible self-government. Its authors were, no doubt, aware of its defects and shortcomings, but thought that there was no better alternative to it under the circumstances".

According to Thompson and Garratt, the reforms were far from being a complete failure. Useful work was done in the provinces of the Indian ministers, and there was no breakdown during the first three years. The process of Indianisation within the Government was proceeding quickly if unostentatiously. (*British Rule in India,* p. 615.)

According to Coupland, "The Government of India Act, 1919 was by far the most important measure of Indian policy adopted by the British Parliament since the process of constitutional development began in 1861, for it crossed the line between legislative and executive authority. Previous measures had enabled Indians increasingly to control their legislatures but not their Governments. Some Indians, it is true, had been members of those Governments, but they had been officially appointed and were responsible, like their colleagues, to the Secretary of State and Parliament. Now Indians were to govern, so to speak, on their own. They were to take charge of great departments of Provincial administration, not as official nominees but as the leaders of the elected majorities in the Legislatures and responsible only to them. Limited and checked though it might be, this was a genuine transfer of power, and it was the appointment of these Ministers, more than anything else, that brought home the fact that the abdication of the British Raj had actually begun.

"Even more striking than the transfer of executive power was the constitutional method by which it was to be exercised, namely, responsible Government as understood and practised in Britain. The transferred field was to be governed under the British Parliamentary system. The reason for that was concisely stated at the outset of the Report. Englishmen believed in responsible government as the best form of government they know, and now in response to requests from India they have promised to extend it to India".

According to Professor Percival Spear, "The Montford reforms were attacked on all sides. Right-wing British opinion considered that they undermined the raj and gave authority to irresponsibility. Congressmen loudly proclaimed that they were a sham and not worth trying to work, and soon they were joined by some who had worked them for a time and acquired some grievance while so doing. Especially large targets were the reserved powers of the viceroy and governors, the lack of any ministerial responsibility at the centre, and the communal provisions. There is no doubt that the reforms were full of defects and difficulties. But now that they have passed into history we can see them in truer perspective. Time has dimmed many of the censures, while leaving others in sharper relief. The reserve powers, for example, are seen to have been perhaps only an excessive dose of a necessary medicine; many of them were retained by the critics themselves in the Constitution of 1949 on the plea of the necessity of a strong executive. Looking back after thirty years, we may pick out certain special points of weakness. One was the financial provisions. The central finances were flexible, but the provincial ones were not so that ministers often in fact found themselves without the means of carrying out cherished measures such as the extension of education. They tended, very naturally, to suspect the reserved half, who controlled the revenue, of starving them of funds. Then there was the question of responsibility. The more closely the ministers were identified with the governors and councillors, the more they were liable to lose the confidence of their supporters. Yet such co-operation was necessary if anything was to be done. On the British side, every assertion of authority in the interests of law and order increased their unpopularity while any constructive measure went to the credit of the minister. It has further to be noticed that the provincial reforms were on the parliamentary plan of ministerial responsibility toward elected councils. This system presupposes a party system to provide the ministers. In India the major Congress party would not play. Only in Madras and the Punjab were local parties strong enough to take office, and there the reforms worked better than anywhere else. Elsewhere there was a tendency for members to split into pressure and personal groups and for governors to construct *ad hoc* coalitions which did nothing but dissolve into fresh patterns. The reforms certainly suffered from lack of Congress cooperation as well as from excessive restriction and division of authority.

"When all this is said the fact remains that the reforms proved to be a solid and substantial achievement. They were an essential milestone on the road to self-government. Without them Indian political progress would have been belated, erratic, and probably revolutionary. They gave, by and large, enough inducement to enough people to work them, and enough scope to provide experience and incentives for the future. Whenever there were determined leaders backed by coherent parties, solid results could be achieved. Thus the Justice Party of Madras was able to reform the administration of the wealthy south-Indian temples; and the Unionist Party in the Punjab, led by Sir Fazhi-Husain and Chaudhri Chothu Ram, to extend education and protect the cultivator. Though tensions and frustrations could not be avoided, the new system went far enough and worked well enough to make further advance inevitable. This was its essential justification. It started a constitutional clock which would not stop. The present Indian government is the heir of Montagu as well as of Gandhi".

CONSTITUTIONAL DEVELOPMENT FROM 1919 TO 1935

The Reforms of 1919 were considered to be utterly inadequate by the Indians. The Indian National Congress at its annual session in 1919 condemned the Reforms as "inadequate, unsatisfactory and disappointing". While it asked the British Government to take early steps to establish full responsible Government in India in accordance with the principle of self-determination, it resolved to work the Reforms "so far as may be possible" with a view to bring about the early establishment of responsible government in India.

The Indians were not in an uncompromising mood, but certain events spoiled the political atmosphere in the country. On the Report of a Committee presided over by Justice Rowlatt, two bills were introduced in the Imperial Legislature in February 1919 and passed into law by the official majority in spite of the opposition of the people. Mahatma Gandhi appealed to the people of India to offer *Satyagraha* against the oppressive laws. *Hartals* were held all over the country. Disturbances took place at various places. Martial law was declared in the Punjab. On the Baisakhi day (13th April 1919), there occurred the Jallianwala Bagh tragedy. General Dyer ordered the opening of the fire on a peaceful crowd at Amritsar. 1,650 rounds were fired, about 400 people were killed and 1200 were wounded. The people were subjected to great humiliations. The crawling order was most resented. The people were required to pass through a street like four-footed animals. The Punjab leaders were jailed. At different places, bombs were thrown on innocent persons. All this resulted in resentment against the British Government.

Certain events brought the Congress and the Muslims together. The Muslims of India protested against the hard terms imposed on Turkey after the First World War. Mahatma Gandhi joined hands with the Muslims and started his non-violent non-co-operation movement for the redress of the Khilafat and the wrongs of the Punjab and the establishment of *Swarajya* in India. The Calcutta session of the Congress in September 1920 endorsed the policy of Mahatma Gandhi and called upon the people to give up their titles and honorary offices and also boycott schools, law courts, Legislative Councils, and British goods. The movement was very strong for two years. However, the events of the Chauri-Chaura in the U.P. where 22 policemen were burnt to death by a mob, made Mahatma Gandhi suspend the movement. The Mahatma was himself arrested in March 1922 and the movement collapsed.

Although the Moderates were '"prepared to do everything in their power to make the new constitution a success", they were themselves not satisfied with the Reforms. It was felt that the Reforms did not go far enough. On 3rd September 1921, a resolution was moved in the Assembly by Rai Jadunath Mozumdar Bahadur for the establishment of autonomy in the provinces and the introduction of responsibility in the Central Government. To that resolution, an amendment was moved by Mr. Jamnadas Dwarkadas in which he asked the Governor-General-in-Council "to appoint a committee consisting of officials and non-officials, including members of the Indian Legislature, to consider the best way of bringing about provincial autonomy in all the Governors' Provinces and of introducing responsibility in the Central Government and to make recommendations". Sir William Vincent, the Home Member, suggested the following formula which was adopted by the Assembly: "That this Assembly recommends to the Governor-General-in-Council that he should convey to the Secretary of State for India the view of this Assembly that the progress made by India on the path of responsible government warrants a re-examination and revision of the Constitution at an earlier date than 1929".

The Government of India submitted a report of this debate to the Secretary of State for India. The latter was of the opinion that the possibilities of the new constitution had not been exhausted. He maintained that progress was possible under the existing constitution. The merits and capabilities of the electorate had not been tested by time and experience. The new constitutional machinery had still to be tested in its working as a whole. The reply of the Secretary of State was followed by a resolution moved in the Assembly by Diwan Bahadur T. Rangachariar in February 1923 expressing extreme dissatisfaction with it. Another resolution was moved by Dr. Hari Singh Gour in July 1923 which recommended to the Governor-General to move the Secretary of State to carry out his suggestion with regard to further reforms possible under the constitution.

At this stage, the Swarajists appeared on the scene. So far the Congress had followed a policy of non-cooperation. However, certain of its leaders led by C.R. Das and Motilal Nehru turned to a new method of embarrassing the Government. That method was "of wrecking legislatures from within". The members of the Swarajist Party took the pledge of "uniform, continuous and sustained obstruction with a view to making the Government through the Assembly and the Council impossible", and they had a striking success in the elections.

In the new Assembly, Diwan Bahadur Rangachariar moved a resolution recommending "to the Governor-General-in-Council that he be pleased to take at a very early date the necessary steps (including, if necessary, appointment of a Royal Commission) for revising the Government of India Act so as to secure for India full Self-Governing Dominion Status within the British Empire and provincial autonomy in the provinces. "The Government opposed the resolution but proposed to make "a serious attempt to investigate justifiable complaints against the working of the scheme in practice, to assess the causes and to examine the remedies necessary". Neither the original resolution nor the proposal of the Government was acceptable to the Swarajist Party and consequently Pandit Motilal Nehru, leader of the Swarajist Party, moved the following amendment and the same was carried: This Assembly recommends to the Governor-General-in-Council to take steps to have the Government of India Act revised with a view to establish full responsible Government in India for the said purpose—

(a) "to summon at an early date a representative Round Table Conference to recommend with due regard to the protection of the rights and interests of important minorities the scheme of a Constitution for India; and

(b) "after dissolving the Central Legislature to place the said scheme for approval before a newly elected Indian Legislature for its approval and submit the same to the British Parliament to be embodied in a statute".

Muddiman Committee Report

The Government of India did not accept the resolution of the Assembly, but set up a Committee under the Chairmanship of Sir Alexander Muddiman:

1. "to enquire into the difficulties arising from, or defects inherent in the working of the Government of India Act and the Rules there under in regard to the Central Government and the Governments of Governors' Provinces; and
2. "to investigate the feasibility and desirability and of securing remedies for such difficulties or defects, consistent with the structure, policy and purpose of the Act,
    (a) by action taken under the act and the rules, or
    (b) by such amendments of the Act as appear necessary to rectify any administrative imperfections".

The Muddiman Committee did not submit a unanimous report. The majority view was that the existing constitution was working in most provinces and was affording valuable political experience. As the new constitution had been in existence only for a short period, it was not possible to say definitely as to whether it would succeed ultimately or not. However, detailed recommendations were made for improving machinery of the Government. The minority view was that dyarchy had absolutely failed and could not succeed at all in the future. It was only a fundamental change of the constitution which could bring about an improvement. To quote them, "It has been urged that an advance could be made by action under Section 19A of the Act and without any radical amendment of the Act itself. With all respect to those who maintain this view, we entirely differ from it:

"In the first place, it is obvious that under Section 19A the Secretary of State can only 'regulate and restrict' the exercise of the powers of superintendence, direction and control vested to him.

"In the second place, such regulation and restriction of powers must be with a view to give effect to the purposes of the Government of India Act. These purposes are defined in the preamble, and we think that even if the Secretary of State felt so disposed, he could not, by the mere exercise of his powers under this Section, abolish dyarchy.

"In the third place, reading the second and third parts of Section 19A with the first part, it seems to us that the relaxation of the control contemplated by Section 19A can only be with regard to Provincial Governments and cannot have any relation to the Central Government.... We also think that the relaxation of control provided by this section cannot mean the same thing as divestment".

In September 1925, the Report of the Muddiman Committee was discussed in the Central Assembly. The Government of India proposed to accept the principle underlying the majority report and proceed with the consideration of its recommendations. Motilal Nehru moved the following amendment which was carried in the Assembly in spite of the opposition of the Government: "That immediate steps should be taken to move His Majesty's Government to make a declaration in Parliament embodying such fundamental changes in the Constitution of India as would make government fully responsible; and that a Round Table Conference or Convention, representative of all interests, should be held to frame a detailed scheme which should be placed before the Legislative Assembly for approval and afterwards submitted to the British Parliament to be embodied in a statute".

Appointment of Simon Commission

In November 1927, was appointed the Simon Commission. Different views have been expressed as to why the Statutory Commission was appointed earlier than stipulated in the Act of 1919. According to some, the British Government was forced to appoint the Commission earlier on account of the agitation carried on in India. However, the real reason seems to have been different. In December 1925, Lord Birkenhead, Secretary of State for India in the Conservative Ministry, referred to the possibility of accelerating the Commission. The whole object of Lord Birkenhead and the Conservative Government was not to leave the Commission to be appointed by the Labour Government which, it was felt, would almost certainly come to power at the next general elections. Another object was to use the appointment of the Commission as a bargaining counter and to disintegrate the Swarajist Party.

The Statutory Commission consisted of seven members and was presided over by the late Sir John Simon. All of its members were Englishmen. The Commission was boycotted by the Indians on the ground that it had no Indian member. The excuse given for not appointing any Indian on the Commission was that the intention of the framers of the Act of 1919 was to confine the Commission to members of Parliament. However, the Act did not lay down any such restriction. But even if the British Government wanted to restrict the nomination to members of Parliament, there were two Indian members at that time. Lord Sinha was a member of the House of Lords and Mr. Shapurji Saklatwala was in the House of Commons. Lord Sinha had been closely associated with the various stages of constitutional reforms in India. His presence on the Commission would have been very valuable. The real reason seems to have been that the Conservative Government did not want any Indian to be on the Commission. According to Dr. A.B. Keith, an avoidable blunder was committed by the Indians by boycotting the Commission. Only a body external to India could properly decide whether the country was fit for a further step towards the goal of self-government or not. As India was not independent, she could not investigate her own case.

The Simon Commission was appointed "for the purpose of inquiring into the working of system of Government, the growth of education and development of representative institutions in British India and matters connected therewith" and reporting "as to whether and to what extent it is desirable to establish the principle of responsible Government, or to extend, modify, or restrict the degree of responsible Government then existing therein, including the question whether the establishment of second chambers of the local legislatures, is or is not desirable". As the inquiry was coming to a close, the Commissioners "were increasingly impressed by the impossibility of considering the constitutional problems of British India without taking into account the relations between British India and the Indian States". With the approval of the British Government, the Commission also considered the relations between British India and the Indian States.

The Simon Commission was boycotted not only by the Congress and other representative organisations, but also by other distinguished leaders of India. Resolutions were passed condemning the constitution of the Commission. To quote one, "We have come to a deliberate conclusion that the exclusion of Indians from the Commission is fundamentally wrong. The underlying principle of the scheme that Indians are to have no authoritative voice either in the collection of proper materials and evidence or in taking of decisions by way of recommendations of the Commission to Parliament is of such a character that India cannot, with any self-respect, acquiesce in it. Unless a Commission on which British and Indian statesmen are invited to sit on equal terms is set up, we cannot conscientiously take any part or share in work of Commission as at present constituted".

The day on which the Commission landed in India, there was a *hartal* all over the country. Wherever the members of the Commission went, they were greeted with black flags and cries of *"Simon go back"*. The Central Assembly was invited to form a committee to co-operate with the Commission, but it refused to do so. A large number of persons were arrested and prosecuted. However, prosecutions did not damp the enthusiasm of the people against the Commission.

The Nehru Report

The Indians condemned the appointment of an all-white Simon Commission and Lord Birkenhead, while justifying the exclusion of Indians from the Commission, challenged the latter to produce an agreed constitution and submit the same to the British Parliament for consideration. This challenge was accepted by the Indians and an All Parties Conference was held in Bombay on 19th May, 1928. This conference was presided over by Dr. M.A. Ansari. The conference appointed a Committee under the Chairmanship of Pandit Motilal Nehru to consider and determine the principles of a Constitution for India. Sir Tej Bahadur Sapru, Sir Ali Imam, Mr. M.S. Aney, Sardar Mangal Singh, Mr. Shuaib Quershi, G.R. Pradhan and Subhash Chandra Bose were its members. The Committee produced a report which has gone down in history as the Nehru Report. According to Dr. Zacharias, the report is "a masterly and statesman like report". According to another critic, "The Nehru Report deserves to be read and studied in all its details, as it sheds light on every subject it touches and displays a practical commonsense, which never loses itself in doctrinaire utopias, but which equally spurns to shelter itself behind the enunciation of mere platitudes. The recommendations of the report were unanimous except in regard to the basis of the constitution. While the majority favoured Dominion Status not merely as distant goal but as "the next immediate step," it, however, gave liberty of action to all those groups and parties which made complete independence their goal.

Although the Report envisaged a future linking up of the Indian States with the rest of India in a federal polity, it confined itself to British India. The Report laid down generally that all treaties made between the East India Company and the Indian States and all such subsequent treaties so far as they were enforced, would be binding on the Commonwealth of India and that the Commonwealth would exercise the same right in relation to and discharge the same obligations towards the Indian States as the Government of India exercised and discharged previously. In regard to matters of justifiable character, in case of differences between Commonwealth and Indian States on any matter arising out of treaties, engagements, *Sanads* or similar other documents, the Governor-General-in-Council may, with the consent of the State concerned, refer such matters to the Supreme Court for its decision.

As regards the communal question, the report made many wise recommendations. It proposed joint electorates with reservation of seats for minorities on population basis with the right to contest additional seats. No seats were to be reserved for any community in the Punjab and Bengal. Full protection was to be given to the religious and cultural interests of the Muslim community. New provinces on linguistic basis were to be created with a view to the "planning of Muslim-majority provinces against Hindu-majority provinces".

The Report enumerated 19 fundamental rights which were to be embodied in the statute. It was to be declared that all powers of the Government and all authority were derived from the people. No person shall be deprived of his liberty, nor shall his dwelling or property be entered, sequestered or confiscated, save in accordance with law. Freedom of conscience and free profession and practice of religion will be guaranteed to every person. The right of free expression of opinion and the right to assemble peacefully and without arms and to form associations or unions shall be guaranteed for purposes not opposed to public order or morality. All citizens shall have the right to free elementary education. All citizens shall be equal before law and possess equal civic rights. There shall be no penal law of a discriminatory nature. No person shall be punished for any act which is not punishable under the law at the time it is committed. No corporal punishment or other punishment involving torture of any kind shall be lawful. Every citizen shall have the right to a writ of *Habeas Corpus*. There shall be no State religion for the Commonwealth of India or for any province, nor shall any State endow any religion or give preference to any religion. No person attending any school receiving State-aid or other public money shall be compelled to attend religious instruction that may be given in the school. No person shall by reason of his religion, caste or creed be prejudiced in any way in regard to public employment, office of power or honour and the exercise of any trade or calling. All citizens shall have an equal right of access to, and use of, public roads, public wells and all other places of public resort. Freedom of combination and association for maintenance and improvement of labour and economic conditions shall be guaranteed to everyone and of all occupations. All agreements and measures tending to restrict or obstruct such freedom shall be illegal. No breach of contract of service or abetment shall be made a criminal offence. Parliament shall make suitable laws for the maintenance of health and fitness for work of all citizens, securing of a living wage for every worker, the protection of motherhood, welfare of children, and the economic consequences of old age, infirmity and unemployment. Every citizen shall have the right to keep and bear arms in accordance with the regulations made in that behalf. Man and woman shall have equal rights as citizens.

The Report provided for a Parliament of two Houses, viz., Senate and House of Representatives. Governor-General was to be appointed by the British Government. He was to be paid out of the Indian revenues and his salary was not to be altered during his continuance in office. Senate was to consist of 200 members elected by provincial councils. The House of Representatives was to consist of 500 members. It was to be elected on an adult franchise basis. The life of the Senate was to be seven years and that of the House of Representatives 5 years.

The Governor-General was to act on the advice of the Executive Council. Prime Minister was to be appointed by the Governor-General and other ministers were to be appointed on the advice of the Prime Minister. The Executive Government was to be collectively responsible to Parliament. Governor-General-in-Council was to appoint High Commissioners and other foreign representatives similar to those appointed by Canada and other Dominions. He was also to appoint Auditor-General of India.

The Governor of every province was to be appointed by the King of England. He was to be paid out of the provincial revenues. Provision was also to be made for a Legislative Council elected on an adult-franchise basis. The Provincial Council was to sit for 5 years. However, it could be dissolved earlier by the Governor. The latter could also extend its life under special circumstances. Provision was made for a President and Vice-President of the Legislative Council.

The Governor was to act on the advice of the Provincial Executive Council whose number was not to exceed 5. Governor-General was to select the Chief Minister and the other members of the Executive Council were to be appointed by him on the advice of the Chief Minister. Provision was to be made for a Supreme Court. It was to consist of Lord President and other Justices. The members of the Supreme Court were to be appointed by the Governor-General-in-Council, but were not to be removed from office except on an address from both Houses of Parliament praying for such removal on the ground of misbehaviour or incapacity. The Supreme Court was to have both original and appellate jurisdiction. Provision was also to be made for taking of appeals to the King-in-Council under certain circumstances.

Governor-General-in-Council was to appoint a Committee of Defence consisting of the Minister of Defence, Minister of Foreign Affairs, Commander-in-Chief, Commander of Air Forces, Commander of Naval Forces, Chief of the General Staff and two other experts. Prime Minister was to be the Chairman of the Committee. The functions of the Committee were to advise the Government and the various departments concerned on questions of defence and general policy.

As regards the civil services, all officers of public services at the time of the establishment of Commonwealth, were to become officers of that Commonwealth. The Governor-General was to appoint a Public Service Commission. All officers of the Army Services were to retain all their existing rights regarding their salaries, allowances and pensions. They were also to get compensation for any loss incurred by them.

The Nehru Report was submitted on 10th August 1928 and the All Parties Conference met at Calcutta on 22nd December, 1928 to consider the Report. As regards the communal question, Mr. Jinnah, on behalf of the All-India Muslim League, moved amendments to the Report. The first amendment was that one-third of the elected representatives of both the Houses of the Central Legislature should be Muslims, but the amendment was rejected. The second amendment was that in the event of an adult franchise not being established in the Punjab and Bengal, there should be reservation of seats for the Muslims on a population basis for 10 years subject to re-examination after the period, but the Muslims should have no right to contest additional seats. This amendment was also lost. The third amendment moved by Mr. Jinnah was that residuary powers should vest in the provinces. This was also not accepted. Another amendment moved by him was that no amendment of the constitution should be made unless it was first passed by both the Houses of Parliament separately by a majority of four-fifths and was approved by a similar majority of both the Houses in joint session. This amendment was unanimously accepted. It is to be noted that Sir Tej Bahadur Sapru pressed the Conference to accept the amendment of Mr. Jinnah with a view to secure a settlement. While doing so, he remarked thus: "The simple position is that for the sake of settlement, you are invited by Mr. Jinnah however illogical and unreasonable to agree to this proposition, which I consider not inconsistent with the Nehru Report. Speaking for myself I would like you to picture Mr. Jinnah whom I have known intimately for 15 years, as a spoilt child. If he is a spoilt child, naughty child, I am prepared to say, give him what he wants and be finished with it. I am not going to ask him to be reasonable, but we must, as practical statesmen, try to solve the problem and not be misled by arithmetical figures". However, it is to be noted that Mr. M.R. Jayakar, who represented the Hindu point of view, was opposed to the demands of Mr. Jinnah.

A session of the All-India Muslim League was convened in March 1929. The Subjects Committee of the League Session which met on March 31, approved of the Nehru report by a majority subject to certain specified safeguards which Jinnah had advocated at Calcutta Convention. At the opening session of the League, this resolution was adopted by a majority.

Jinnah's Fourteen Points (1929)

Mr. Jinnah summoned a meeting of the All-India Muslim League at Delhi in March 1929 and put forward his fourteen points as the minimum Muslim demands for any political settlement. While rejecting the Nehru Report, the resolution of the League laid down as under:

"That no scheme for the future constitution of the Government of India will be acceptable to the Mussalmans of India until and unless the following basic principles are given effect to and provisions are embodied therein to safeguard their rights and interests.

1. "The form of the future constitution should be federal with the residuary powers vested in the provinces.
2. "A uniform measure of autonomy shall be granted to all provinces.
3. "All legislatures in the country and other elected bodies shall be constituted on the definite principle of adequate and effective representation of minorities in every province without reducing the majority in any province to a minority or even equality.
4. "In Central Legislature Muslim representation shall be one-third.
5. "Representation of communal groups shall continue to be separate electorates as at present provided it shall be open to any community, at any time, to abandon its separate electorate in favour of joint electorates.
6. "Any territorial re-distribution that might at any time be necessary shall not in any way affect the Muslim majority in the Punjab, Bengal and North-West Frontier Province.

7. "Full religious liberty, i.e., liberty of belief, worship and observance, propaganda, association and education shall be guaranteed to all communities.
8. "No bill or resolution or any part thereof shall be passed in any legislature or any elected body if three-fourths of the members of any community in that particular body oppose such a bill, resolution or part thereof on the ground that it would be injurious to the interests of that community, or in the alternative such other method is devised as may be found possible and practicable to deal with such cases.
9. "Sind should be separated from the Bombay Presidency.
10. "Reforms should be introduced in the N.W.F. Province and Baluchistan on the same footing as in other provinces.
11. "Provision should be made in the constitution giving Muslims an adequate share along with other Indians in all the services of the State and in local self-government bodies having due regard to the requirements of efficiency.
12. "The constitution should embody adequate safeguards for the protection of Muslim culture and for the promotion of Muslim education, language, religion, personal laws and Muslim charitable institutions and for their due share in the grants-in-aid given by the State by the self-governing bodies.
13. "No Cabinet either central or provincial should be formed without there being a proportion of at least one-third Muslim Ministers.
14. "No change shall be made in the constitution of the Central Legislature except with the concurrence of the State constituting the Indian Federation".

There was a change of government in England. The Labour Party, headed by Ramsay MacDonald, came to power. High hopes were entertained regarding the future of India. While in the Opposition, Ramsay MacDonald had always sympathised with the Indian aspirations and advocated their cause. No wonder, the Indians were hopeful about the future.

Lord Irwin got convinced that it was not possible to maintain an irresponsible Central Government for long. He paid a hasty visit to England to confer with the new Labour Government and on his return issued the following statement on 31st October, 1929: "In view of the doubts which have been expressed both in Great Britain and India regarding the interpretation to be placed on the intentions of the British Government in enacting the Statute of 1919. I am authorised on behalf of His Majesty's Government to state clearly that in their judgment, it is implicit in the Declaration of 1917 that the natural issue of India's constitutional progress as there contemplated is the attainment of the Dominion Status". He also stated that the Simon Commission had suggested to His Majesty's Government and the latter had accepted the suggestion that after the publication of their Report and before its examination by the Joint Parliamentary Committee, they should call together a conference in which His Majesty's Government meet the representatives both of British India and of the States for the purpose of seeking the greatest possible measure of agreement for the final proposals which it would later be the duty of His Majesty's Government to submit to Parliament.

Critics point out that whatever may be thought about the statesmanship of this declaration, it should have not been made until the Commission had concluded its labours. It left that unfortunate body in the air, and at the same time stole its thunder. Moreover, the phrase "Dominion Status" was unhappily so ambiguous that it could be given various interpretations. The Government of India seem to have used the phrase in the sense in which it was employed in the Preamble to the Act of 1919 as applicable to the constitution of a dependency enjoying responsible Government. On the other hand, they gave to it the same meaning as was given to it by the Balfour Declaration of 1926. These Dominions were described as "autonomous communities within the British Empire equivalent in status, in no way subordinate to one another in any aspect, domestic or external affairs, though united by a common allegiance to the Crown and freely associated as members of the British Commonwealth of Nations". The Congress leaders also were not satisfied with the limited scope and purpose of the Round Table Conference. What the Indians demanded was the convening of a Constituent Assembly for the purpose of drafting a Constitution for India. It is evident that the views of the people of India and the British Government radically differed from each other. However, an interview was arranged between Mahatma Gandhi and Lord Irwin with a view to explore the possibilities of a compromise. The interview failed to achieve its purpose. The result was that when the Indian National Congress met at Lahore after a few days under the presidentship of Pandit Jawaharlal Nehru, it passed resolutions boycotting the Round Table Conference, declaring the object of the Indian National Congress as the attainment of *Swarajya* or complete independence for India and authorising the All India Congress Committee to start Civil Disobedience Movement. 26th January was observed as India's Independence Day and the Civil Disobedience Movement was started in March 1930. Mahatma Gandhi started his historic march to Dandi to violate the salt laws. Thousands of people all over the country deliberately violated certain laws of the country and courted arrest. There were lathi charges by the Police. Repression was in full swing. Ordinances were issued in quick succession by the Government to meet the situation. Editors and proprietors of newspapers and printing presses were arrested and fined. There seemed to be a complete breach between the Government and the nationalist movement in the country.

Simon Commission Report, 1930

The Report of the Simon Commission was published in May 1930. First of all, the Report considered as to what should be the ultimate constitutional framework of all India and what should be the place of provinces in that. The Report declared that the framework could not be of unitary type. It must be federal, not merely in response to the growth of provincial loyalties but primarily because it must embrace all India and it was only in a Federation that Indian States could be expected in course of time to unite with British India.

1. According to the Report, dyarchy should be abolished in the provinces and the whole field of provincial administration should be entrusted to ministers responsible to their legislatures. "Each province should as far as possible be the mistress in her own house". It was pointed out that the retention of reserved subjects implied the continuance of control over that part of the provincial administration by the Central Government and the Secretary of State for India. That was not a desirable thing. In the new provincial set up, the ministries were not to be formed entirely on the British model. The Governor was to be allowed to select those ministers who commanded a majority in the legislature. He was not to appoint a ministry on the advice of Prime Minister or Chief Minister. In all legislation and administration, ministers were to be free from interference by the Government or the Central Government except for such stated vital reasons as the maintenance of the safety of the province or the protection of minorities. It was recommended that franchise should be extended and the legislature be enlarged.

2. The Report recommended that the question of making Sind and Orissa as separate provinces should be given further expert examination. However, it should be decided forthwith to separate Burma from the Government of India. The North-West Frontier Province was considered to be ripe for the first step in constitutional advance. That province should be given a Legislative Council and its representation in the Central Legislature should be strengthened.

3. With regard to the Centre, the Report made recommendations which aimed at preparing the way for an All-India Federation The Central Legislature was to be refashioned on the federal principle. The members of the Federal Assembly or the Lower House were to be representatives

not of sections of the people of India at large but of the provinces. They were to be elected by the Provincial Councils. The elections and nominations to the Council of States were also to be on a provincial basis. The distribution of seats among the various provinces for the Assembly was to be roughly on population basis. Each province was to have three members in the Council of States.

4. So far as the Central Executive was concerned, there was a note of "gradualness" in the Report'. No substantial change was recommended. The whole Government was to continue as an official Government. There was to be no Government responsible to the Legislature. There was to be no dyarchy at the Centre. It was pointed out that there was the need of keeping the Centre strong and stable "while the Provincial Councils were learning by experience to bear the full weight of new and heavy responsibilities. The reason given for this was not the immediate need of the political situation in India, but the ultimate needs of the federation. It was started that the provinces must find themselves before the nature of their participation in a federal Government could be determined. It is necessary to take a long view of the development of Indian self-Government... . A premature endeavour to introduce forms of responsible Government at the Centre before the conditions for its actual practice have emerged would in the end result not in advance but in retrogression".

5. It was pointed out that an All-India Federation was to be set up in the distant future. The idea that "the federation of Greater India can be artificially hastened or that, when it comes, it will spring into being at a bound", was set aside. For the present, only one step was recommended. In order to "foster the sense of need for further developments and bring more nearly within the range of realisation other steps which are as yet too distant and too dim to be entered upon and described", a Council for Greater India should be set up, representing both British India and the States, discuss in a consultative capacity all matters of common concern, a list of which should be drawn up and scheduled. The Preamble of the new Act should record the desire to bring about a closer association between the two parts of India.

6. The Act of 1919 had provided for setting up of a commission after 10 years for inquiring into the working of the reforms and naming of recommendations for the future. The Report recommended that the method of periodical inquiry should be given up. The new constitution should be so elastically framed as to enable it to develop by itself. The provincial legislatures should have power to modify their own composition and procedure and self-government should grow not by making laws but by usages and conventions.

According to P.E. Roberts, the Simon Commission Report, "will always stand out as one of the greatest of India State papers. The impressive unanimity of the commissioners, who from their known party antecedents must clearly have sacrificed all but their deepest convictions to attain it, ought to have commended their sagacious and temperately worded conclusions to men of goodwill". (*British India,* p. 598). However, the Report was condemned by the Indians. The British Government itself had also partly forestalled it and ultimately side-tracked it, although some of its recommendations were ultimately embodied in the Act of 1935. According to Dr. A.B. Keith, "It was probably foolish of Indian opinion to repudiate the report out and out. If it had been accepted the British Government could hardly have failed to work on it, and responsible government could in the provinces have been achieved much earlier than it could be under any later scheme. Moreover, the pressure of such Governments on the Centre would doubtless have operated strongly in the direction of including the British Government to aim at federation and the States to come to terms with Indian political leaders. It is noteworthy that the Commission endeavoured to suggest that responsible government in India need not follow rigidly existing models, a fact which at once rendered it suspect in the eyes of Indian politicians, whose views on these topics have throughout shown a remarkable lack of ingenuity and a determination slavishly to copy Western models hardly compatible with the national spirit by which they are animated". (*Constitutional History of India*, pp. 293-94).

Round Table Conference (1930-31)

After the publication of the Simon Commission Report and its condemnation by the people of India the British Government called the First Round Table Conference in London. The Conference met in November 1930. As the Congress leaders were in jail, the Government appointed safe men belonging to other parties, communities and interests to represent India. Representatives from the Indian States were also invited to participate in the deliberations and included men like Sir Mirza Ismail, Sir Akbar Hydari and the Maharaja of Bikaner. There were lengthy discussions on the question of the future form of the Government of India. Ultimately, three basic principles were settled and accepted by the British Government. The form of the new Government of India was to be an All-India Federation in which the British Indian Provinces and the Indian States were to join. Subject to such reservations and safeguards as might be considered necessary for the transitional period, the Federal Government was to be made responsible to the Federal Legislature. Provinces were to be given autonomy in their own affairs. At the end of the First Round Table Conference, Ramsay Mac-Donald made the following important statement: "The view of His Majesty's Government is that responsibility for the Government of India should be placed upon Legislatures, Central and Provincial, with such provisions as may be considered necessary to guarantee, during a period of transition, the observance of certain obligations and to meet other special circumstances, and also with such guarantees as are required by minorities protect their political liberties and rights. In such statutory safeguards as may be made for meetings the needs of the transitional period, it will be a primary concern of His Majesty's Government to see that the reserved powers are so framed and exercised as not to prejudice the advance of India through the new Constitution to full responsibility for her own Government. Pledge after pledge had been given to India that British *Raj* was there not for perpetual domination. Why did we put facilities for education at your disposal? Why did we put in your hands textbooks from which we draw political inspiration? If we meant that the people of India should forever be silent and negative, subordinated to our rule, why have our queens and kings given you pledges? Why has our Parliament given you pledges? Finally, I hope, and trust, and I pray that by our labours together India will come to possess the only thing which she now lacks, to give her the status of a Dominion amongst the British Commonwealth of Nations—what she now lacks for that—the responsibilities and the cares, the burdens and difficulties, but the pride and the honour of responsible self-government".

As it was not considered advisable to proceed with the work of the final form of the future constitution of India in the absence of the representatives of the Indian National Congress, it was decided to call a Second Round Table Conference, and in the meanwhile efforts were to be made to bring about a reconciliation between the Congress and the Government. The efforts of Tej Bahadur Sapru and Sir M.R. Jayakar were crowned with success and the famous Gandhi-Irwin Pact was signed in March 1931. The Government released all the political prisoners. Mahatma Gandhi withdrew the Civil Disobedience Movement. An atmosphere of goodwill having been created Mahatma Gandhi left for London to attend the Second Round Table Conference as the sole representative of the Congress. In spite of the magnetic personality of Mahatma Gandhi and his devotion to the work in hand, the communal tangle could not be solved. Mahatma Gandhi gave a *Carte Blanche* to Mr. M.A. Jinnah but all efforts for a settlement failed on account of the uncompromising attitude of Mr. Jinnah and the part played by Sir Samuel Hoare, the Secretary of State for India. Realising the failure of his mission, Mahatma Gandhi left England in disgust and was arrested on his arrival in India.

If is true that as a result of the economic crisis in the world and especially in England, the Labour Government of Ramsay MacDonald had been replaced by a National Government, but somehow,

Ramsay MacDonald managed to follow his previous policy with regard to India at the Second Round Table Conference. Many problems were considered, but the members could not come to any definite conclusion. Consequently, the work was referred to various committees which were required to submit detailed reports. As regards the question of communal representation Ramsay MacDonald made it clear that if the various communities in India did not come to any definite settlement, the British Government would be forced to give its own Award regarding the same.

Communal Award (1932)

As the Indians could not arrive at any settlement, Ramsay MacDonald gave his famous "award" known as the Communal Award on 16th August 1932. The scope of this Award was purposely confined to the arrangements to be made for the representation of British Indian communities in the provincial legislatures, consideration of representation to the Central Legislature being deferred for the time being as that involved a question of the representation of the Indian States which needed further discussion. The hope was expressed that once a pronouncement was made upon questions of the method and proportions of representation, the communities themselves may find it possible to arrive at a *modus vivendi* on the communal problem. If before the passing of the new Government of India Act the Government was satisfied that the communities concerned were mutually agreed upon any alternative scheme they would be prepared to recommend to parliament the substitution of the alternative scheme for the Communal Award. "His Majesty's Government wish it to be most clearly understood that they themselves can be no parties to any negotiations which may be initiated with a view to revision of their decision and will not be prepared to give consideration to any representation aimed at securing modification of it which is not supported by all parties affected.... If before the new Government of India Act has passed into law they are satisfied that the communities who are concerned are mutually agreed upon a practical alternative scheme either in respect of any one or more of Governors' provinces or in respect of the whole of the British India, they will be prepared to recommend to Parliament that the alternative scheme should be adopted".

According to the Award, elections to the seats allotted to Muslim, European and Sikh constituencies were to be by voters voting for separate communal electorates covering between them the whole area of a province. Special provisions were made for excluded areas. Provision was to be made in the new Constitution of India to allow the revision of electoral arrangements after the lapse of 10 years with the assent of the communities affected, for the ascertainment of which suitable means were to be devised.

All qualified voters who were not voters in Muslim, Sikh, Indian-Christian, Anglo-Indian or European constituencies were entitled to vote in a general constituency.

Seven seats were reserved for the Marathas in certain selected plural member general constituencies in Bombay.

The members of the depressed classes who were qualified to vote, were to vote in a general constituency. However, special seats were to be reserved for them. Those seats were to be filled up by election from special constituencies in which only the members of the depressed classes electorally qualified were to be entitled to vote. Any person voting in such a special constituency was also to be entitled to vote in a general constituency. These constituencies were to be formed in those selected areas where the depressed classes were most numerous, and except in Madras, they were not to cover the whole of the area of a province. In the case of Bengal in some general constituencies, the majority of the voters belonged to the depressed classes. Consequently, no special number was to be fixed for their seats in that province. However, they were not to get less than 70 seats in Bengal. The maximum duration of the depressed classes constituencies was to be 20 years, provided they were not abolished earlier.

The election of the Indian Christians was to be by voters voting in separate communal constituencies. It was felt that practical difficulties would prevent the formation of the Indian Christian constituencies covering the whole area of a province and consequently special Indian Christian constituencies were to be formed in one or two selected areas in a province. The Indian Christian voters in those areas were not to vote in a general constituency. Outside those areas, they were to vote in a general constituency. Special arrangements were to be made in Bihar and Orissa where a large number of the Indian Christians belonged to the original tribes.

The Anglo-Indians were also to vote on communal lines. The intention was that the Anglo-Indian constituencies were to cover the whole area of a province and postal ballot was to be employed for that purpose.

Women were also given special representation on communal lines. The electors of a particular community were to elect their own quota.

Special seats were to be allotted to Commerce and Industry, Mining and Planting, to be filled up by election through the Chambers of Commerce and other associations. Their details were to be worked out later on.

Seats allotted to landholders were to be filled by the landholders' constituencies.

It was stated that the work of the determination of the constituencies was to begin soon. That Government reserved to itself the right of making slight variations in the number of seats given to the various communities with a view to facilitate the work of the delimitation of constituencies. However, the proportion was not to be materially changed. The composition of the second chambers in the provinces was not to disturb in any essential the balance between the communities resulting from the composition of the Lower House.

Poona Pact (1932)

Mahatma Gandhi in his letter written in March 1932 to Sir Samuel Hoare, Secretary of State for India, had warned him that he would resist with his life the grant of separate electorates to the depressed classes. When the Communal Award was published and it was found that the British Government was determined to give separate communal representation to the depressed classes Mahatma Gandhi wrote to Ramsay MacDonald that the matter was "one of pure religion" with him and he asked: "Do you realise that, if your decision stands and the constitution comes into being, you arrest the marvellous growth of the work of the Hindu reformers who have dedicated themselves to the uplift of their suppressed brethren in every walk of life?" Mahatma Gandhi's letter had no effect on the Prime Minister of England who took the matter light-heartedly and would not have bothered if the Mahatma had died. When the British Government refused to move in the matter and the condition of Mahatma Gandhi became serious on account of his fast unto death, the Indian leaders made up their minds to get the Award modified by mutual agreement. Negotiations took place with Dr. Ambedkar and Rajah and ultimately the Poona Pact was signed in September 1932 and was accepted by the Government.

The Poona Pact reserved seats for depressed classes out of the general electoral seats in provincial legislature as follows:—Madras 30, Bombay with Sind 15, Punjab 8, Bihar and Orissa 18, C.P. 20, Assam 7, Bengal 30, and U.P. 20. The total of the reserved seats for the depressed classes was 148.

As regards the procedure for elections to these seats by joint electorates, all members of the depressed classes registered in the general electoral roll in a constituency were to form an electoral college which was to elect a panel of 4 candidates belonging to the depressed classes for each of the reserved seats by the method of single vote. The four persons getting the highest number of votes in the primary election were to be candidates for election by the general electorate.

The depressed classes were to have representation in the Central Legislature on the principle of joint electorates and seats were to be reserved for them in the same way as in the case of the provinces. 18 per cent of the general seats for British India were to be reserved for the depressed classes.

The system of primary elections to a panel of candidates for election to Central and Provincial Legislatures was to be abolished after 10 years or earlier, if an agreement to that effect was made.

The depressed classes were to be given fair representation in the local bodies and the public services subject to educational qualifications.

In every educational grant in the provincial budget, an adequate sum was to be earmarked for the education of the depressed classes. The procedure to be adopted for election of the representatives of the depressed classes to the Central Legislature was postponed as that involved the whole system of representation at the Centre.

Third Round Table Conference

To take up the story of the Round Table Conferences, a Third Round Table Conference was called by the British Government rather reluctantly as it was of the opinion that the rest of the work could be done in India. The result was that the session of the Third Round Table Conference lasted from 17th November to 24th December 1932. The Labour Party did not co-operate in the deliberations and the Indian National Congress was unrepresented. The delegates to the Conference merely discussed the reports of the various committees appointed by the Second Round Table Conference and decided a few more points.

The White Paper (1933)

When the whole scheme regarding the future Constitution of India was thrashed out the British Government issued in March 1933, a small document known as the White Paper. It gave in detail the working basis of the new Indian Constitution with a dyarchy at the Centre and a responsible Government in the Provinces. As was to be expected the White Paper was condemned by the Indian public opinion. However, in spite of opposition and criticism, the British Government went on with its programme.

In April, 1933, a Joint Select Committee was appointed to examine and report on the Government proposals as contained in the White Paper. The Committee consisted of 16 members each from the House of Commons and House of Lords and its Chairman was Lord Linlithgow. The Committee invited representatives from British India and Indian States. After examining many witnesses and going through the Memoranda received from the Indian Association, the British Indian Delegations, Sir Tej Bahadur Sapru, M.R. Jayakar and other prominent individuals, the Joint Select Committee submitted its report on 22nd November 1934. Although it did not alter the fundamentals as given in the White Paper, it recommended many changes in the structure of the Provincial and Federal Legislatures and other matters also.

When the reforms scheme was thoroughly discussed and given final shape by the Joint Select Committee, a Bill was drafted on those lines and introduced in the House of Commons on 5th February 1935. Sir Samuel Hoare, Secretary of State for India, was in charge of the Bill which was severely criticised by the Labour Party for its limited scope. The Labour members tried to amend the Bill in such a way as to recognise explicitly India's right to Dominion Status. The diehards led by Winston Churchill tried to introduce reactionary elements into the Bill. However, the Government went on with its own scheme which was passed by the House of Commons on 4th June 1935. The Bill was introduced in the House of Lords on 6th June 1935, and was passed in July 1935. Here also the efforts of the Labour members to liberalise the Bill failed. As the Government had made some amendments in the Bill at this stage, the Bill had to be sent back to the House of Commons which accepted the proposed amendments. The Bill received the Royal Assent on 2nd August 1935 as Government of India Act, 1935.

Provisions of the Government of India Act, 1935

1. The Act provided for an All-India Federation. The question of Indian Federation presented peculiar problem on account of the disparity between the Indian States and Provinces of British India with regard to their legal status and their internal political structure. The Indian States were under the complete control of the Political Department of the Government of India. The Provinces on the other hand, had some sort of a democratic Government. According to the Act of 1935 all the provinces were to join the Indian Federation automatically. Entry into the Federation was to be a purely voluntary action on the part of each State, however small and insignificant that State may be. At the time of joining the Federation, the ruler of the State was to execute an Instrument of Accession in favour of the Crown. On acceptance of that Instrument, the State was to become a unit of the Federation. The Crown was forbidden to accept an Instrument of Accession if its terms appeared to be inconsistent with the scheme of the Federation. While the provinces were to be alike in respect of the position of the quantum of Legislative and Executive power in the Federation, the States were to differ regarding the extent of their powers in the Federation. The scope of the Federal jurisdiction in the States was to depend solely upon the transfers made by their respective rulers through their Instruments of Accession. The Instrument was to authorise the various Federal Authorities to exercise their respective functions under the Act in relation to that particular State. It was to be the duty of the ruler to see that due effect was given within his State to the provisions of the Act in so far as those provisions were made applicable by virtue of the Instrument. The ruler was authorised to extend the functions of the Federal authority in respect of his State by a subsidiary Instrument, but no subsequent Instrument could decrease the scope of the authority of the Federation as provided by the original Instrument of Accession.

    The Indian States were to send 125 members to the Federal Assembly and 104 members to the Council of States. The provinces were to send 250 members to the Federal Assembly and 156 members to the Council of States. The members from the Indian States were to be nominated by the rulers, but those from the provinces were to be elected on communal lines.

    The functions of the Crown with regard to the Indian Slates were to be performed in India by his representative who was the Viceroy himself.

    The Indian Federation as provided by the Act of 1935 was different from the other federal systems. There was no simple division of powers between the Centre and the units. The Act provided for three lists: Federal List, Provincial List, and the Concurrent List. The Federal Government was authorised to pass laws on the subjects given in the Federal List. The subjects given in the Provincial List were within the exclusive jurisdiction of the provincial Legislature. As regards the Concurrent List, both the Federal Legislatures and the Provincial Legislatures could pass laws on the subjects given in that List. However, if a law was passed by the Federal Legislature on any subject given in the Concurrent List, the Provincial Legislature could not make law on the same subject afterwards. As regards the residuary powers, the Governor-General in his discretion was given the power to decide as to which of the three Lists on particular subject was to be allotted.

2. The Act of 1935 also provided for dyarchy at the Centre. That dyarchy which was abolished in the provinces, was introduced at the Centre, Certain Ferderal subjects were reserved in the hands of the Governor-General to be administered by him with the assistance of not more

than 3 Councillors to be appointed by him. Those subjects were Defence, External Affairs, Ecclesiastical Affairs and the administration of Tribal Areas. In the administration of the other Federal subjects, the Governor-General was to be aided and advised by a Council of Ministers whose number was not to exceed 10. The Federal Ministry was to administer all the Federal Departments except the above-mentioned reserved Departments. The Federal Ministry was to be formed on the usual cabinet lines except that it was to include the representatives of the important minorities. It is true that the inclusion of these elements was not obligatory under the Act, but the Governor-General was instructed by means of an Instrument of Instructions to secure such representation to the best of his ability. In spite of the composite character of the Ministry, their responsibility was to be collective. The Ministry was to be responsible to the Federal Legislature.

Critics pointed out the weakness of the position of the Ministers on account of the large number of powers given to the Governor-General and to be exercised by him in his individual judgment and in his discretion. According to Professor K.T. Shah, "The position assigned under the new Constitution to the Council of Federal Ministers is ornamental, without being useful, onerous without ever being helpful to the people they are supposed to represent, responsibility without power, position without authority, name without any real influence". (*Federal Structure*, p. 223) To quote the same author, "It seems extremely doubtful if the popular ministers of the Federation of India will have any real opportunity to inaugurate constructive schemes of economic betterment or social reconstruction. The necessary funds are either unavailable because earmarked already for non-productive expenditure and lavish scale of over-head charges; or difficult to find in the absence of new taxation proposal which the Governor-General may not always view with favour. Additional burdens are especially difficult in a Federation to propose and particularly unwelcome in popular Governments... . If the communal curb upon ministerial enthusiasm does not prove quite effective, there are the enormous powers of the Governor-General, as protector and champion of the vested interests and imperialist, exploitation, which are bound to be employed to impede or frustrate to enthusiastic ministers. They are specific provisions in the constitution as any discrimination against British vested interests, which will hamper the work of the ministers in their work. The Ministers' own internal difficulties, want of solidarity, etc., may prevent them from achieving anything beneficial to the people". (*Ibid.*, pp. 249-50.)

3. The Federal Legislature was to be bicameral, consisting of the Federal Assembly and the Council of States. The Federal Assembly was to have a life of 5 years from the date of its first meeting. On the expiry of that period, it was to be automatically dissolved. However, the Governor-General was given the power to extend its life. The Council of State was to be a permanent body of which one-third members were to retire after every 3 years. The members from the States were to be nominated by the rulers. The representatives from British India were to be elected. The Hindu, Muslim and Sikh members were to be elected on communal lines.

While the members of Council of State were to be directly elected, those of Federal Assembly were to be indirectly elected. To quote Chintamani and Masani, "If indirect election to the popular house of the Federal Legislature is both unprecedented and objectionable what is to be said of direct election to the less important upper Chamber?... . The system of election devised for the Federal Assembly should have been adopted for the Council of State, minus the abomination of the separate communal device... . But no, the genius of the deciding authority thought to present India with a scheme which is a combination of the drawbacks of different systems, as a punishment for India's impudence in asking for responsible government instead of being content to sing Hallelujahs and TeDeums to the British bureaucracy and plutocracy.

According to Palande, "The Council of State was bound to be an assemblage of vested interests, reactionary oligarchs, and conservative politicians. The franchise for its election was to be exceptionally high: 40 per cent of its membership would be constituted by State nominees. Besides it was to be a permanent body and, therefore, was not to be subject to that wholesome cleansing which is periodically brought about by a dissolution and general election. The abnormally long term of nine years for its members was to breed irresponsibility and defiance and in the legislators. Upon this narrow based upper chamber the Act of 1935 conferred a power which in a democratic polity is an exclusive privilege of the lower chamber. The voting of grants of expenditure was denied to the Council of State by the Act of 1919. But the federal counterpart of that chamber was to be possessed of that privilege. In short, everything seems to have been conspired to make the upper chamber a strong instrument for checking the advance of democracy".

4. The powers of the Indian Legislatures were severely restricted. There were certain subjects on which neither the Federal Legislature nor the Provincial Legislatures could legislate. The Indian Legislatures were debarred from making any law affecting the Sovereign or the Royal Family or the succession to the throne or suzerainty of the Crown or any part of India, or the law of British nationality, or the Army Act, the Air Force Act, or the law of Prize Courts. The Indian Legislatures could not make any law amending any of the provisions of the Act of 1935, or any Order-in-Council made under it, or any rules made there under by the Secretary of State or by the Governor-General or a Governor in his discretion or in the exercise of his individual judgment. They could not make any law affecting the prerogative right of the Crown to grant special leave to appeal to the Privy Council except in so far as that was expressly permitted by the Act. They could not pass any legislation which discriminated against the British interests in commercial and other spheres. Moreover, there was a large number of subjects of vital importance on which initiation of legislation required previous sanction of the Governor-General in respect of Federal Legislation, of the Governor-General and the Governor in respect of Provincial legislation.

There were many non-voteable items in the budget over which the Federal Legislature was given absolutely no control. These non-voteable items constituted about 80 per cent of the Federal budget. If any item of the budget was rejected by the Federal Assembly, the same could be put before the Council of State if the Governor-General so directed. If the two Houses of the Federal Legislature differed with respect to any demand, the Governor-General was required to summon a joint sitting for voting on that demand and the decision of the majority was to prevail.

The Governor-General was empowered to summon a joint sitting of the two Houses of the Federal Legislature when a Bill passed by one Chamber was rejected by the other, or was amended in a form to which the first Chamber was not agreeable. After a Bill was passed by both the Chambers of the Federal Legislature, the Governor-General, in his discretion, might assent to it, or veto it or send it back for reconsideration or reserve it for His Majesty's consideration. The Act assented to by the Governor-General could be disallowed within a year by the King-in-Council.

5. The Act provided for the establishment of a Federal Court with jurisdiction over the States and the Provinces. The Court was to consist of a Chief Justice and two puisne judges. It was given both original and appellate powers. It was the duty of the Federal Court to interpret the constitution and to see that the provinces and the Federal Council acted only within those spheres which were reserved for them by the constitution. However, the last word in this matter was to be said by the Privy Council sitting in London.

6. The Act of 1935 abolished the India Council of the Secretary of State. The Secretary of State was given advisers who may or may not be consulted, or whose advice may or may not be followed, except in regard to their advice in respect of the services. This change was made because there was a lot of agitation in India against the continuation of India Council on account of its anti-Indian attitude.

7. In the exercise of powers in their individual judgment and in their discretion, the Governors, through the Governor-General, and the Governor-General himself, were made strictly responsible to the Secretary of State. However, it is to be noted that the control of the Home Government over Indian affairs was lessened. This was partly due to the introduction of provincial autonomy in the provinces and responsible government at the Centre. There was no control from London when the Governor-General and the Governors acted according to the advice and consent of their ministers.

8. Another important feature of the Act was the provision of elaborate safeguards. These safeguards were vital subtractions from the principle of responsible government as well as of self-government. These safeguards were of two kinds. In the first place, there was a denial of legislative powers to the Indian Legislatures in regard to a large number of subjects. Secondly, there was the grant of powers to the Governor-General or the Governors to override their ministers and legislators in certain circumstances including the assumption of absolute dictatorial powers in the event of the breakdown of the constitution. Critics pointed out that the provisions of the safeguards were against the territorial integrity of the country. In the words of Dr. Keith, "With the safeguarding of minorities, the essence of responsible Government is seriously, if not fully, compromised".

9. The constitution of 1935 was rigid. The British Government alone was given the authority to amend the constitution. According to S.M. Bose, "The Indian Legislatures have only been given powers to express by resolution to His Majesty's Government their intention of a constitutional change in respect of the matters specified in this section. But the actual powers of modifying the Act had been placed by the Act in the hands of His Majesty's Government by the Order-in-Council laid in draft before both Houses as provided in Section 309. In other words, no amending legislation by the Parliament will be required. In respect of those other matters specifically mentioned in the Act, variations may be made by Order-in-Council.

10. But the most important characteristic of the Act of 1935 was the provision of provincial autonomy. This was in accordance with the August Declaration of 1917. The Act of 1919 had given a little control in the provincial field into the hands of the Indian ministers. The Act of 1935 was a definite improvement on the Act of 1919 inasmuch as there were no reserved subjects with the Governor. However, this does not mean that the Act of 1935 established full-fledged responsible government in the provinces. That could not be so on account of the fact that the Governor was given many powers which he was to exercise in his discretion and in his individual judgment.

THE HOME GOVERNMENT

The Office of the Secretary of State for India was created by the Act of 1858 when the Board of Control and the Court of Directors were abolished after the Mutiny. The latter was a member of the British Parliament and also a member of the British Cabinet. Up to 1919, he was paid out of the Indian revenues but the Act of 1919 provided that in future he was to be paid from the British Treasury. He was assisted in his work by a Parliamentary Under Secretary, a Permanent Under Secretary, an Advisory Body and the India Office.

Under the Act of 1919, the Secretary of State enjoyed numerous powers. He was authorised to superintend direct and control the affairs of the Government of India. Both the Governor-General and Governors were required to pay due obedience to his orders. The Act of 1935 changed the position to a considerable extent. It granted what is known as provincial autonomy. As the Indian ministers came to have a lot of control over provincial administration, the control of the Secretary of State diminished over the provinces. Likewise, the establishment of dyarchy at the Centre by the Act of 1935 also lessened the control of the Secretary of State over the Government of India. The control of the Secretary of State came in only when the Governors or the Governor-General acted in their discretion. Similarly, when the Governors and the Governor General acted in their individual judgment and decided to do things against the advice of the ministers, the control of the Secretary of State appeared again. As the discretionary powers of the Governor-General and Governors were very large, the control of the Secretary of State also remained substantial. The Secretary of State exercised control over the Reserved Departments of Defence, External Affairs, Tribal Areas, the Ecclesiastical Affairs, and the Federal Railway Authority, and the Reserve Bank of India. He could control the whole administrative machinery of India by giving appropriate directions to the Central and provincial administrations.

He had many powers with regard to the services. He appointed officers belonging to the Indian Civil Service, Indian Police Service and the Irrigation Service. He determined the conditions of service of all such persons. He was the constitutional adviser of the Crown with regard to the Indian affairs. He advised the King in the exercise of all his powers of appointment and the vetoing of any Bill which may have been reserved by the Governor-General for the consideration of His Majesty or which may have been even assented to by the Governor-General.

The Secretary of State was required to submit all the draft Instrument of Instructions to be issued to the Governor-General and the Governors before Parliament for its approval. He was also to submit before Parliament all Orders-in-Council to be issued by His Majesty under the powers granted by the Act. He was the agent of Parliament and was also responsible to Parliament for the Indian affairs. It was his duty to supply the British Parliament with all information regarding Indian affairs and also to answer all questions regarding the same.

Professor K.T. Shah described the position of the Secretary of State in these words: "On a general review of all these varied and substantial powers the Secretary of State still stands out unmistakably as the most dominating authority in the Indian Constitution. His powers may not be so imposing in appearance as those of the Governor-General or the Provincial Governors. But these are merely his creatures, obedient to every nod from the Jupiter of Whitehall, amenable to every hint from this juggler of Charles Street. His powers extend not merely to matters of fundamental policy; to the protection of British vested interests; to the safeguarding of Britain's imperial domination. They comprise even matter of routine administration, the more important doings of the Indian Legislature, and even the appointments, payment or superannuation of certain officers in the various Indian Services or Governments. He has, in fact, all the powers and authority in the governance of India, with little or none of its responsibility".

Advisers. The Secretary of State was assisted by an Advisory Body. This Advisory Body was formerly known as the India Council and was set up by the Act of 1858 to assist the Secretary of State for India in the discharge of his duties. Under the Act of 1917, the India Council consisted of not less than 8 and not more than 12 members, appointed by the Secretary of State. The Secretary of State-in-Council was a corporate body which would sue and be sued and conducted business in the United Kingdom in relation to the Government of India. Ordinarily, the Secretary of State was not bound by the advice of the India Council, but in matters relating to grants from the revenues of India, making of contracts, and rules and regulations connected with the Civil Service he was bound by the majority view of the India Council.

The India Council was abolished by the Act of 1935. According to the new Act, the Secretary of State was to appoint not less than 3 and not more than 6 advisers. At least half of these persons were to be those who had held office in India for at least 10 years and who had not left India for more than 2 years at the time of their appointment. They were to hold office for 5 years only. They could not sit in Parliament. Their function was merely advisory and as a rule the Secretary was required to secure the concurrence of at least one-half of the advisers. The Act provided that "it shall be in the discretion of the Secretary of State whether or not he consults his advisers on any matter, and if so, whether he consults them individually and whether or not he acts in accordance with any advice given to him by them".

High Commissioner for India. The Government of India Act 1919 provided for the appointment of a High Commissioner for India in the United Kingdom. His pay, pension, powers, duties and conditions of employment were to be determined by an Order-in-Council. The office of the High Commissioner was created in 1920 by an Order-in-Council.

The Governor-General-in-Council was authorised to appoint from time to time a High Commissioner and also remove or suspend the same. He was to hold office for five years and was eligible for re-appointment. His salary of £3,000 was to be paid out of the Indian revenues, although he was not entitled to any pension. He was to enjoy "the same status as his Dominion colleagues". He was to be under the control and direction of the Governor-General-in-Council. His duties were to act as the agent of the Governor-General-in-Council in the United Kingdom, act on behalf of the local governments in India for such purposes, and in such cases as the Governor-General-in-Council may prescribe, and conduct such business relating to the Government of India hitherto conducted in the office of the Secretary of State-in-Council as may be assigned by the Secretary of State. He was empowered to make and sign contracts in the name and on behalf of the Secretary of State-in-Council. In 1920, the Stores Department, the Indian Students Department and certain other minor matters were transferred to the High Commissioner. He was to arrange for the probationary training of the officers of the All-India Services and their passage to India, payment of leave allowances and pensions. He was to make arrangements for civil officers sent to Europe for special study. He was to supervise the work of the Indians participating in Imperial International Exhibitions. The Act of 1935 did not make any substantial change in the office of the High Commissioner for India.

Federal Government. Under the Act of 1935, the Governor-General was the cornerstone of the entire Constitution of India. It was he who gave unity and direction to its various, diverse and often conflicting elements. It was he who was expected to keep the ship of the State on an even keel and to protect the British vested interests in India. It is desirable to discuss his position under the Act of 1935.

Appointed by the King on the advice of the British Prime Minister, the Governor-General acted in three different capacities. Ordinarily, he was to act according to the advice of the Council of Ministers. When he did that he acted as a constitutional head like the King of England or the Governor-General of Canada. But he did not always act according to the advice of the ministers. In certain cases, he acted *in his individual judgment*. While doing so, he was to consult his ministers, but may not act upon their advice. This he did when he performed the special responsibilities of the Governor-General. The following were the special responsibilities of the Governor-General:—

1. Safeguarding the financial stability and the credit of India.
2. The prevention of any grave menace to the peace or tranquility of India or any part of India.
3. Safeguarding of the legitimate interests of the minorities.
4. Safeguarding of the legitimate rights of the public servants and their dependents.
5. The prevention of commercial discrimination.

6. Prevention of discriminatory taxation against goods of British origin or Burmese origin.
7. Safeguarding of the interests of the Indian States and the dignity of their rulers.
8. The securing of the due discharge of his discretionary powers.

While acting *in his discretion,* the Governor-General did not even consult the ministers. He acted in his discretion in the following matters:—

1. He was in charge of the reserved departments of Defence, External Affairs, Ecclesiastical Affairs[3] and Tribal Areas and he appointed three Counsellors to help him in his work.
2. He could appoint and dismiss the Council of Ministers and also could preside over their meetings.
3. He could issue two kinds of ordinances. One type of ordinance he could issue at any time and that lasted for 6 months. The other kind of ordinance was issued when the legislature was not sitting. The Governor-General was also given the power to issue what were known as Governor-General's Acts. But these Acts had to be forwarded to the Secretary of State.
4. The previous sanction of the Governor-General was required for the introduction of certain bills in the Federal Legislature and the Provincial Legislatures. He was authorised to stop the discussion of any Bill at any time by the Legislature. He could withhold his assent to a Bill passed by the Legislature or send the same back for reconsideration or reserve the same for the consideration of His Majesty.
5. He was given control over about 80 per cent of the Federal Budget. The not-voteable items of the budget formed a major part of the budget.
6. The Governor-General could in his discretion send any instructions to the Governors and it was the special responsibility of the latter to carry them out.
7. The Governor-General could suspend the Constitution.
8. He was given the authority to summon, prorogue or dissolve the Federal Assembly. He could summon both Houses for a joint sitting. He could address the Legislature or send messages regarding a certain bill.

It is not possible to exhaust the discretionary powers given to the Governor-General under the Act of 1935.

Under the Act of 1935, the Governor-General was to be assisted by a Council of Ministers. The position has already been discussed above.

As regards the Federal Legislature, its composition and powers have been discussed above.

Government of the Provinces. The position of the Governor under the Act of 1935 resembled that of the Governor-General although it differed a little on account of the introduction of Provincial Autonomy. A Governor was appointed by the King by a Commission under the Royal Sign Manual. His office was constituted by Letters Patent. His salary was fixed by the Act. The job of a Governor was the prize post which usually went to those members of the Indian Civil Services who had brilliant record of service.

Like the Governor-General, the Governors also acted in three different capacities. Ordinarily, they were to act according to the advice of the ministers. When they did so, they acted as constitutional heads and their position could be compared to the Lt. Governor of a Canadian Province.

---

[3] According to C.Y. Chintamani, "The very existence of the Ecclesiastical Department is a source of genuine grievance to the Indian, both as citizen and tax-payer. In the first place there ought to be no such thing as an established church. In the second place, India is not a Christian country...".

They were also authorised to act in their *individual judgment*. While doing so, they had to listen to the advice of the ministers but they may or may not act upon their advice. The Governors acted in individual judgment while performing their special responsibilities which were as follows—

1. Prevention of any grave menace to the peace and tranquility of the Province or any part of the Province.
2. Safeguarding of the rights and legitimate interests of the public servants and their dependents.
3. Safeguarding of the rights and interests of the Indian States and the dignity of their rulers.
4. Safeguarding of the legitimate interests of the minorities.
5. Administration of partially excluded areas.
6. Prevention of commercial discrimination against Englishmen and their goods.
7. Execution of the orders and directions of the Governor-General issued by him in his discretion.
8. It was the duty of the Governor of C.P. to see that a reasonable share of the provincial revenues was spent for the benefit of the people of Berar.
9. It was the duty of the Governor of Sind to secure the proper administration of the Lloyd Barrage and Canal's Scheme.

The Governors acted *in their discretion* in the following cases:—

1. They could appoint and dismiss ministers. This power was very substantial. In the case of Bengal and the North-West Frontier Province, the power was used by the Governors to exclude a certain party and keep the other party in power.

   They presided over the meetings of the Council of Ministers. By doing so, they could influence the deliberations and conclusions of the ministers. Their great administrative experience must have been an asset to them.

2. They could issue two kinds of ordinances. One kind of ordinance could be issued by them at any time and that lasted for six months. The other type of ordinance was issued only when the Legislature was not sitting. They could issue what were known as Governor's Acts. In certain cases, their previous sanction was required for the introduction of certain bills in the Provincial Legislature. They could stop the discussion of any bill in the Legislature at any time. Even when the Bill was passed, the Governors could veto the same or send the same back for reconsideration by the Legislature. They could reserve the same bill for the assent of the Governor-General.

3. They appointed members of the Provincial Public Service Commission. They were given large powers regarding the Police Force and also the authority to suppress terrorists.

4. It is the Governors who decided what items of expenditure were to be regarded as "expenditure charged upon revenues of the province. These items were taken out of the control of the Legislature. The non-voteable items formed about 40 per cent of the budget. If the whole of the budget was rejected, Governors were authorised to restore the same.

5. Under Section 93 of the Act, the Governors were given the authority to suspend the Constitution and take over the administration in their own hands.

It is to be noted that under the Act of 1935, the Governors enjoyed substantial powers. The powers given to them were not merely kept in theory. They were intended to be exercised and were actually exercised. However, the extent to which these powers were exercised depended upon the character of the individual Governor and also the position and prestige enjoyed by the Provincial Ministry.

Provincial Ministers. The position of the Provincial ministers under the Act of 1935 was certainly superior to that of the ministers under the Act of 1919. There were no reserved departments.

All the departments were to be under the charge of the ministers. The Governor was expected to carry on the administration of the province according to the advice of the Ministers.

It was laid down in the Instrument of Instructions that the Governor was to summon that person to form the Ministry who could be expected to command a majority in the provincial Legislature. The other ministers were to be appointed by the Governor on the advice of the Chief Minister. It was the duty of the Governor to see that minorities were given representation in the Ministry. If a person was not a member of the Legislature at the time of his appointment, he was to get himself elected within six months of his appointment. The Governors were instructed to encourage collective responsibility amongst the ministers. They were allowed to preside over the meetings of the Council of Ministers.

However, it is to be noted that the powers of the minister were limited. They did not enjoy complete autonomy in the provincial field. The enormous powers of the Governor were responsible for the weakness of the position of the ministers. The Governor had many legislative powers and it is these powers which restricted the legislative control of the ministers. The Governor may not allow a particular bill to be introduced in the legislature. He may veto a bill which had been passed by the Legislature on the initiative of the ministry. He may stop the discussion of the bill at any time. The issuing of ordinances and the Governor's Acts also limited the legislative scope of the ministers. The same could be said about finance. The ministers were not given a free hand in the matter of proposing new taxes. The Governor may not give his sanction to a bill for that purpose. The ministers had not completed control over the budget, 40 per cent of which was non-voteable.

The Governors could dismiss their ministers and this was actually done in many cases. Fazl-ul-Haq, the Chief Minister of Bengal, was unceremoniously dismissed by the Governor in 1943. Alla Bux, the Chief Minister of Sind, was dismissed because he gave up the title of Khan Bahadur. The Governor of the Punjab dismissed Shaukat Hayat Khan.

Different views were expressed regarding the position of ministers under the Act of 1935. According to Lord Zetland, "Let it not be supposed that the field of government is to be divided into two parts, in which the Governor and the ministry operate separately at the risk of clashes between them. The essence of the new Constitution is that the initiative and responsibility for the whole of the government of province though in form vesting in the Governor, passes to the ministry as soon as it takes office". According to Sir Maurice Hallet, the Governor of U.P., "After all, the relations of a Governor with his Ministers were not those of a master and his servants; rather they are partners in a common enterprise—the good Government of the province". However, it is to be noted that the actual position of the Ministry depended upon its party strength in the Legislature and the personality of the members who constituted the Ministry. In the last analysis, much depended upon the personal equation.

Provincial Legislatures. The Government of India Act, 1935, did not set up provincial legislatures of a uniform pattern. The six provinces of Assam, Bengal, Bihar, U.P., Madras and Bombay were given two Chambers each while the legislatures of the Punjab, Sind, North-Western Frontier Province, Orissa and C.P. had only one Chamber. Where there were two Houses their names were the Provincial Legislative Assembly and the Provincial Legislative Council. Where there was only one House, it was merely the Provincial Legislative Assembly. While all the members of Assembly were elected, some of the members of the Council were nominated.

Legislative Assembly. The size of the Provincial Assemblies varied from province to province. It was 215 for Madras, 175 for Bombay and Punjab, 250 for Bengal, 228 for U.P., 152 for Bihar, 112 for C.P. and Berar, 108 for Assam, 50 for North-Western Province and 60 each for Orissa and Sind. The seats in the various provinces were distributed according to the Communal Award as amended by the Poona Pact. Some seats were known as general seats out of which some were reserved for the Scheduled Castes. Separate representation on communal lines was given to the Muslims, Sikhs, Anglo-Indians, Europeans and the Indian Christians. Some seats were reserved for commerce, industry, mining and planting, landholders, labour and universities. Out of the seats exclusively reserved for women, some were given to the Hindus and the others to the Muslims, Sikhs, Anglo-Indians and Indian Christians. In the case of the Punjab 42 were general seats, 31 seats were given to the Sikhs, 84 to the Muslims, one each to the Anglo-Indians and Europeans, 2 to Indian Christians, one to commerce, industry and planting, 5 to the land-holders, one to the Punjab University, 3 to labour, one each to Hindu and Sikh women and 2 to Muslim women. The Europeans in Bengal were given the highest representation, i.e., 11. The landholders both in U.P. and Madras got 6 seats each. 90 seats were given in Bengal to commerce, industry, mining and planting. In Bengal, out of a total representation of 78 seats given to the Hindus, 30 seats were reserved for the Scheduled Castes. The life of the Assembly was fixed at five years, but the same could be dissolved earlier. Its life could also be extended beyond the period of 5 years. The first general elections under the Act of 1935 were held in 1937 and the next elections were held not earlier than 1945.

Legislative Council. Legislative Councils were provided for only in six provinces. The maximum number of seats for a Provincial Legislative Council was 56 in Madras, 30 in Bombay, 65 in Bengal, 60 in U.P., 30 in Bihar and 22 in Assam. Out of a total of 56 seats in Madras, 10 seats were filled by the Governor through nomination. The general seats for Madras, Bombay, Bengal, U.P., Bihar and Assam were 35, 20, 10, 34, 9 and 10 respectively. Mohammedans had 17 seats each in Bihar and U.P 27 and 12 seats respectively in Bengal and Bihar Legislative Councils were filled by the Legislative Assemblies of those provinces. Some seats were reserved for Europeans and Indian Christians, e.g., three for Europeans in Bengal and three for Indian Christians in Madras.

The Provincial Legislative Council was a permanent body. The tenure of office of the members was nine years, but one-third of them had to retire after every three years.

The age qualification for membership of the Provincial Legislative Assembly was fixed at 25 and 30 for the Provincial Legislative Council. No person could become a member of both the Houses of the Legislature. Residence in the constituency for a certain number of days, usually, 180 or 120, was necessary for franchise. The voting qualifications varied from province to province. In the case of the Punjab, the right of voting was given to those who paid income tax or a direct municipal tax amounting to not less than ₹50 per year, those who paid land revenue amounting to not less than ₹5 per year, those who owned or occupied immovable property of the rental value of not less than ₹60 per year and those who possessed educational qualifications up to the primary standard. Right of voting was given to those women who possessed property qualifications in their own right, who were the wives or widows of persons with property qualifications, who were the wives of men with military service, who were the pensioned widows and mothers of those who served in the Indian Army or who had educational qualifications. The Joint Select Committee made the following observations about the new franchise. "We are satisfied on the information before us that the proposals taken as a whole are calculated to produce an electorate representative of the general mass of the population and one which will not deprive any important section of the community of the means of giving expression to its opinions and desires. The proposals will in the case of most provinces redress the balance between town and country, which is at the present time too heavily weighted in favour of urban areas; they will secure a representation for women, for the depressed classes, for industrial labour and for special interests and they will enfranchise the great bulk of the small land-holders, of the small cultivators, of the urban rate payers, as well as a substantial section of the poorer classes".

Powers of Provincial Legislatures. The Provincial Legislatures were authorised to pass laws on the subjects given in the Provincial List and Concurrent List. In the latter case, their powers were concurrent with that Federal Legislature. In case the Federal Legislature made a law on a subject included in the Concurrent List, the Federal Law had precedence over the Provincial Law. The powers of the Legislature also extended to those residuary subjects which were assigned to it by the Governor-General in his discretion. The Provincial Law included subjects, such as public order, the administration of justice, the constitution and organization of all courts except the Federal Court of India, preventive detention, police, prisons, reformatories, borstal institutions, public debt of the province, Provincial Public Services and Provincial Public Service Commissions, Provincial Pensions, compulsory acquisition of land, elections to the Provincial Legislature, salaries of Provincial Ministers, Speakers and Deputy Speakers, salaries, allowances and privileges of the members of the Provincial Legislature local self-government, public health and sanitation, hospitals and dispensaries, education, roads, bridges, ferries, water supply, irrigation and canals, agriculture, forests, fisheries, taxes on agricultural income, etc.

The Concurrent list included subjects like criminal law and criminal procedure, civil procedure, marriage and divorce, wills, intestacy and succession, registration and deeds and documents, trusts and trustees, contracts, bankruptcy and insolvency, legal, medical and other professions, newspapers, books and printing presses, boilers, criminal tribes, factories, welfare of labour, unemployment insurance, old age pensions, trade unions, industrial and labour disputes, electricity, etc.

It might appear from above that the powers of the Provincial Legislatures were very extensive. However, a critical study of the Government of India Act, 1935, shows that innumerable restrictions were put on them. Thus, the legislatures did not enjoy complete control over legislation. The previous sanction not only of the Governor but also of the Governor-General was required in certain cases even to introduce a bill in the Provincial Legislature. Even, if that hurdle was crossed, the Governor could stop the discussion on a bill at any stage. Even if the bill was passed by the Legislature, the Governor could veto it in his discretion or reserve the same for the approval of the Governor-General. The Governor was also given the power issuing ordinances and enacting what were known as the Governor's Acts. Even in the financial field, the powers of the Provincial Legislatures were limited. About 50 per cent of the provincial budget was not under their control. That was a charge on the revenues of the province. The British Parliament retained the right to make any law relating to any province. His Majesty's Government could set aside any law passed by any Provincial Legislature. It is obvious that the limitations imposed on the Provincial Legislatures impaired considerably the nature of provincial autonomy as established by the Government of India Act, 1935.

The Nature and Working of Provincial Autonomy. It cannot be denied that Provincial Autonomy as set up by the Act of 1935 was a definite improvement on the system set up by the Act of 1919. But it is wrong to suppose that Provincial Autonomy was intended to establish a full-fledged responsible government in the Provinces. Had that been the intention, the authors of the Act of 1935 would have stated the same in so many words. There was no necessity for coining a new term. The truth is that the British Government did not intend to give full responsible government in the provinces. It is clear from the large number of discretionary powers given to the Governors. The same intention becomes evident when we consider the nature and extent of the special responsibilities of the Governors. If the Governor was expected to play the role of the guardian of the British interests and the other vested interests that was bound to affect adversely the position of the Ministers. A study of the various statements made by the persons who were intimately connected with the framing and passing of the Act of 1935, shows that Provincial autonomy was expected to work under many restrictions.

According to Lord Zetland, who was the Secretary of State for India in 1937, "The Parliament of this country reserved to itself a potential measure of control in a certain limited and clearly defined sphere the special responsibilities of the Governors. Since the Governors, when acting in respect of special responsibilities, were responsible both for acts of commission and omission, to the Parliament of this country, he would naturally be prepared to answer any question bearing upon the discharge by the Governors of their duties within their sphere". This clearly points out to the limitations of Provincial autonomy.

On the occasion of the second Round Table Conference, Ramsay MacDonald remarked thus: "We are all agreed that the Governor's Provinces of the future are to be responsibly governed units, enjoying the greatest possible measure of control from outside interference and dictation in carrying out their policies in their own sphere".

According to the Report of the Joint Select Committee, Provincial autonomy is a scheme "whereby each of the Governors' Provinces will possess an Executive and Legislature...broadly free from control by the Central Government and a Legislature. This we conceive to be the essence of Provincial Autonomy, though no doubt there is room for wide differences of opinion with regard to the manner in which that exclusive authority is to be exercised...the Central Government and Legislature would, generally speaking, cease to possess in the Governors' Provinces any legal power or authority with respect to any matter falling within the exclusive provincial sphere, though, as we shall explain later, the Governor's authority to secure compliance in certain respects with directions which he may find it necessary to give".

It is rightly stated that there is a world of difference between the real significance of the word "Autonomy" and the so-called "Autonomy" as given by the British Parliament to India. "Provincial Autonomy is a mere farce and far from a living reality". "The Provincial Autonomy, according to the Government of India Act, is merely a sham".

According to Professor Percival Spear, "The years 1937-39 were notable for a great success, a great failure, and a great mistake. The success was the Congress ministries, for which both government and Congress must share the credit. The failure was the inability of the government to persuade the princes to join the Federation. The Viceroy was active and persuasive. But the princes had lost their enthusiasm of the First Round Table Conference. They were rent with jealousies among themselves; the more they saw of Congress with its democratic implications the less they liked it; they preferred dealing with the British direct (who were at least the devil they knew) to a Viceroy inevitably influenced by nationalist ministers at the Centre. The British seemed well established; they should be good for a number of years yet. So they held out for better terms either in the hope of being better placed in the eventual set up, or with the more purblind desire of enjoying their full prerogatives a little longer. The Viceroy, on his side, refrained from putting such pressure on the princes as would have compelled them to come in. There was in him a vein of scrupulosity which at times inhibited action. It appeared in 1943 when he failed to intervene in time in the Bengal famine for fear of wounding provincial susceptibilities. Thus, from the princes' point of view the last opportunity of saving their order by integrating it with a conservative federation was lost. Having let down the British over federation as they had previously let down the Congress over democracy and nationalism, they found themselves friendless after World War II. They had no popular backing, and they were snuffed out like so many candles. Great as this failure was, however, India may perhaps be grateful for the princes' folly. It was the princes' failure to co-operate which prevented the federal centre from coming into being. This fact enabled the Congress to take over complete power in 1947 and to set up a strong centre. Without a strong centre the development of modern India would not have been possible; with the princes there could not have been a strong centre". (*India, a Modern History,* pp. 393-94.)

Dejects of the Act

1. It seems desirable to refer to the important points of criticism levelled against the Act of 1935. According to Pandit Nehru, the new Indian Constitution was a "machine with strong brakes and

no engine". According to another critic, "The India Act of 1935 tests to the full Indian capacity for administration and government exactly as a man's capacity with hands and feet tied. To call the new Indian Constitution an edifice of self-government is a grim joke which the joker may enjoy, but not those at whose expense it is cracked". "Remember, the new Federal structure has got to be fought tooth and nail. It is difficult to find suitable language to characterise this. *It is disgusting, poisoning and offensive".* According to Pandit M.M. Malviya, "The new Act has been thrusted upon us. It has a somewhat democratic appearance outwardly, but it is absolutely hollow from inside". According to Sir Shanmukham Chetty, "It is indeed a far cry between the Government of India Act and Dominion Status". According to C. Rajagopalachari, "The new Constitution is worse than dyarchy". According to M.A. Jinnah, the scheme of 1935 was "thoroughly rotten, fundamentally bad and totally unacceptable". Dr. Keith denounced the proposed Federation as "bastard Federalism". According to C.Y. Chintamani, "I venture to describe the Government of India Act, 1935, as the anti-India Act.... . I feel with some bitterness that the Government of India at least in these matters may not incorrectly or unjustly be described as the Government 'against' India".

2. The Indians were not given control over the government of their country. They could not change or amend their constitution. The Whitehall framed the policy which was followed by the Government of India. The Indians detested the control from London.

3. The Indians detested the dyarchical form of Government at the Centre. It was pointed out that the evils of dyarchy which were found in the provinces under the Act of 1891 were bound to be repeated at the Centre also.

4. The inauguration of the All-India Federation depended upon the condition that a specified number of States joined the Federation. However, the Act gave the Indian States the choice to join or not to join the Federation. This was a serious drawback.

5. The Indian States were given a privileged position under the constitution. The representation given to them both in the Council of State and the Federal Assembly was more than what was due to them on the basis of their territory, population or the contributions to be made by them to the revenues of the Federal Government. While the members from British India were to be elected by the people, the Indian princes were allowed to nominate their quota. The critics pointed out that as the Indian princes were absolutely under the control of the Political Department of the Government of India and did what they were directed to do, the representative's from the Indian States were to be under the control of the British Government. They dare not vote against their masters. The nominees from the Indian States could be used by the British Government in India to serve their own interests and stop the progress of the country.

6. The Indians protested against the system of indirect elections to the Federal Assembly. It was contended that indirect elections were against the very canons of democracy. They were against the spirit of the times.

7. The Indians protested against the control which was to be exercised by the Secretary of State for India over the Indian Civil Service, the Indian Police Service and other All-India Services.

8. The Indian Army got the lion's share out of the Indian budget but the Indians were given absolutely no control over it as Defence was made a reserved subject. The Indians also protested against the pace at which the Indianisation of the Army was going on.

9. The seats in the Legislature were to be filled on the basis of the Communal Award. The result was that the constitution became communalism-ridden. The Communal Award cut at the very root of Indian nationalism and solidarity and was consequently the most dangerous. It was

pointed out that longer the period for which the Communal Award worked, the greater will be the difficulty in keeping the unity of the country.

10. According to Sir Shanmukham Chetty, "It is indeed a far cry between the Government Act and Dominion Status. The principle of Dominion Status asserts that the Dominion should have the right to the same measure of autonomy in external affairs as in internal matters and that it is the duty of the British Government to give effect to the doctrine accepted. But India has neither control in the internal nor the external affairs. The internal administration shall be under the guidance of the Governor-General and the Governors who are vested with tremendous powers; the external affairs shall be under the guidance of Parliament, the Crown and the Secretary of State. Indians shall not be able to work out their own destiny. The safeguard, reservations, special powers of the Governor-General and the Governors, the weakness of the Indian Legislatures, and the ministers in the Federal and the Provincial Governments with no Central responsibility and weak provincial autonomy, the Communal Award, the States' representation bought at the expense of British Indians, the financial and other economic drawbacks, half measures of the Indianisation of the Army with no control over the Defence—all these things show that Indians shall not be having Dominion Status".

11. According to Sir Shafat Ahmed Khan, "Though a number of important subjects have been transferred and placed in charge of ministers who are to be responsible to the Federal Legislature, they are elaborately fenced round by safeguards and other ingenious devices that it will be difficult for a minister to move freely and safely through this labyrinth and formulate a policy that will offer opportunities for the free and unhampered exercise of our national ability and energy. Ministers can be checked and controlled at almost every turn and their cherished plans might be thwarted by...a stubborn counsellor or a financial adviser steeped in theory and vanity. The special responsibility of the Governor-General will pervade every Department of Government and no subject will be free from it. It is not a special Department concerned exclusively with the legislation or administration of a specific subject, but a power or faculty whereby the Governor-General is empowered to put his fiat on any matter which trenches either directly or indirectly upon his authority as specified in the Act". Again, "the Legislature is so curiously composed and its procedure is so ingeniously contrived that it will find it difficult to function freely and independently. It will be destitute of organic unity, will let the momentum of a common allegiance and national solidarity, and may resolve itself into congeries of inconsistent and even destructive sections lacking the rudiments of leadership and team work, and exhibiting all the characteristic features of the Federal Parliament of Austria-Hungary before the war. It will not be a National Assembly but a Confederation of Indian States and Provinces, miniature League of Nations".

12. According to Fazl-ul-Haq, Premier of Bengal, under the Act of 1935, there was to be neither Hindu Raj nor Muslim Raj but the British Raj. (*The Indian Annual Register, 1937*, Vol. 2, p. 411.)

13. Commenting on the Government of India Bill, 1935, Mr. Attlee remarked thus: "The keynote of the Bill is mistrust". The Indian National Congress condemned the federal scheme on many grounds. It was pointed out that the scheme did not envisage any real transfer of power into the hands of the Indians. Moreover, the Federal Legislature was saddled with an element of conservatism in the form of the nominated representatives of the States. It was contended that the constitutional advancement of India would always be voted by the Indian States. According to Dr. Keith, "For the Federal scheme it is difficult to feel any satisfaction. The units of which it is composed are too disparate to be joined suitably together, and it is too obvious that on the British side the scheme is favoured in order to provide an element of pure conservatism in order to combat any dangerous elements of democracy contributed by British India.

On the side of the rulers it is patent that their essential preoccupation is with the effort to secure immunity from pressure in regard to the improvement of the internal administration of their States. Particularly unsatisfactory is the effort made to obtain a definition of paramountcy which would acknowledge the right of the ruler to misgovern his State, assured of British support to put down any resistance to his regime. It is difficult to deny the justice of the contention in India that *federation was largely cooked by the desire to evade the issue of extending responsible government to the Central Government of British India.* Moreover, the withholding of defence and external affairs from federal control, inevitable as the course is, renders the alleged concession of responsibility all but meaningless. Further, it is impossible to intervene in discussions of issues in which the provinces are alone concerned, their action will be justly resented by the representatives of British India, while, if they do not, there may arise the spectacle of government which when the States intervene has a majority, only to fall into a minority when they abstain. Whether a federation built on incoherent lines can separate successfully is wholly a matter of conjecture; if it does, it will probably be due to the virtual disappearance of responsibility and the assertion of the Governor-General backed by the conservative elements of the States of India".

14. The rulers of the Indian States criticised the federal scheme on the ground that it did not give them any power or authority to leave the federation if once they joined it. The federation had great power of coercing them. The representatives from British India were bound to dominate the Federal Legislature and Federal Executive and thereby influence the Viceroy to take steps which might impair their sovereignty.

15. The discretionary powers of the Governors reduced provincial autonomy to a farce. Those powers and responsibilities "combine, crib and confine" the powers of the provincial legislature and executive. Some of these powers and responsibilities were so vaguely defined that those could be interpreted to mean anything according to the exigencies of the movement. The Governor was made the sole judge to decide whether any particular matter fell within his discretionary scheme or affected any of his special responsibilities. The Governor could become a virtual dictator of the province within the letter of the law.

16. The powers of the Provincial legislature were very much restricted. The upper chambers were deliberately made reactionary bodies.

According to Professor Percival Spear, "Unlike the Montfort reforms of 1921 or anything that was done after World War II, the Government of India Act of 1935 was enacted from strength. It could be said that after both world wars Britain was too enfeebled to take an uncompromising stand. But in the thirties she had recovered from World War I, was emerging from the Great Depression and had just defeated the strongest frontal attack on the Indian government's authority since the Mutiny. There was no compelling force dictating concession or constitution advance. What was done was done through conviction and might be said to represent a minimum rather than a maximum. That was why there was an air of solidity about the Act, and why its major features proved to be so fruitful in the future. It was generally realized that there could be no going back on it.

"The Act was the constructive half of the dual policy of suppression of Congress defiance and advance toward self-government. It was meticulously drawn up and represented, in effect, a draft constitution for an Indian Dominion. It was made easy to fill in gaps later; old features which were left, such as the office of Secretary, could be lopped off without difficulty, and provision was made for a measure of change within the constitution. The London connection began to assume the appearance of a legal umbilical cord which could be snipped at the right moment,... .

"The view has been put forward that this Act was not only bulky in form but radical in nature and momentous in its consequences. This is not to say that it was without defects. They were important and had momentous consequences too. First among them was the nature of the federal tie between the princes and the Union. By the arrangements made, the six hundred princedoms were kept in being with all their anomalies of size, status, and institutions. Their direct relationship with the Crown was preserved, making change or amalgamation a matter of treaty rights, and the minimum of power was surrendered to the federal centre. At the centre itself they were given heavy weightage in both houses of the legislature, a weightage which was the heavier because the princes had the right of nominating all their representatives. These provisions would have made it difficult to develop the strong centre which India's development required. A major internal revolution would have been needed to assimilate "Indian India" into modern India, and it would have been almost impossible to carry through such a measure constitutionally in view of the position they were given in the central legislature. In the circumstances, India has cause for thankfulness that the princes were too stupid to see the advantages of the scheme from their point of view and failed in the event to join the federation. Apart from this major weakness, the federal structure was itself defective. The emphasis was on provincial autonomy, which would have made for a weak and perhaps divided India. The popular central legislature was elected indirectly by the provincial assemblies, which again tended to detract from its importance. By a curious anomaly, the British Indian members of the upper House were to be elected directly (on a restricted franchise), but the effect of this was nullified by the strangle hood possessed by the nominated princely representatives. We can sum up the position by saying that the federal structure was boldly conceived and skillfully worked out, but that the balance of political forces within it was such that the federal government would have been weak. It was calculated to maintain the *status quo* rather than to release dynamic and creative forces.

"A second weakness, though it was little noticed at the time by friend or foe, was the failure to recognize the plural nature of Indian society. There was communal representation, it is true, arid special measures for the 'Scheduled Castes. But there was no realization of the fact that India contained separate cultures a well as religions and communities, and that these cultures must find constitutional recognition if the state were to be healthy. It was not realized that the Muslim and Sikh held sectors of their communal life sacred, sectors in which they would accept no dictation from an outside authority. The attempt was made to fit the mantle of a unitary state upon the body of a plural society, and the result was stresses and strains. The allegiance of these lesser bodies was necessarily partial and conditional to a state claiming authority as complete as the Parliament in Britain. Herein lay one of the causes of Pakistan. It was this basic defect which underlay the arrangements for 'minorities'. They were all given safeguards of various kinds and special representation, but none of them was given a palpable share of power. Could a body of about ninety-million Muslims be seriously regarded as just a minority, even though the Caste Hindus were more than twice as numerous? The more the minorities were given treatment in relation to their numbers, the more conscious they became of the fact that they were minorities. And in democracies majorities rule".

CONSTITUTIONAL DEVELOPMENT FROM 1937 TO 1950

The whole of the Government of India Act, 1935 was not introduced. Only the part dealing with provincial autonomy came into force on 1st April 1937. The Congress took part in the elections and got a clear majority in six provinces. Later on, the number increased to 7. There was a deadlock to begin with but very soon the Congress ministries were formed. They remained in office till 1939 when the World War II broke out. The Congress ministries, resigned on account of differences with the British Government. Throughout the war, efforts were made by the British Government to win over the co-operation of the Indians. In 1940, the famous August Offer was made by Lord Linlithgow.

The August Offer was in the form of a statement made by the Viceroy on behalf of the British Government. The following is the summary of the so-called Offer:—

1. Though the differences which prevented national unity remained unbridged in India, the expansion of the Executive Council of the Governor-General and the establishment of an Advisory War Council should no longer be postponed.
2. In view of the doubts as to whether the position of minorities would be sufficiently safeguarded in any future constitutional change, the British Government reaffirmed its desire that full weight should be given to minority opinion. "It goes without saying that they could not contemplate transfer of their present responsibilities for the peace and welfare of India to any system of Government whose authority is directly denied by large and powerful elements of India's national life. Nor could they be parties to the coercion of such elements into submission to such a Government". This clearly indicated that the British Government was prepared to allow the Muslim League to have her own way in the matter of the partition of the country.
3. Subject to the fulfillment of their obligations—an allusion to such questions as defence, minority rights, the treaties with the States, and the position of the Secretary of State Services—the British Government concurred in the Indian desire that the framing of the new Constitution should be "primarily the responsibility of Indians themselves and should originate from Indian conceptions of the social, economic and political structure of the Indian, life".
4. Constitutional issues could not be decided at "a moment when the national life is engaged in a struggle for existence," but after the war a representative Indian body should be set up to formulate new Constitution, and in the meantime the British Government would welcome and assist any efforts to reach agreement as to the form and operation of this constitution-making body and as to the principles of the Constitution.
5. In the interval, the British Government hoped that all parties and communities in India would co-operate in India's war effort, and by thus working together pave the way for India's attainment of free and equal partnership in the British Commonwealth of Nations.

However, nothing came out of the August Offer on account of the attitude of the Congress. The offer was simply rejected.

Cripps Proposals (1942)

The deadlock in Indian politics continued. While the British Government refused to come to terms with the Congress, the latter refused to co-operate with the former. During this period, the Second World War was proceeding. The international situation began to deteriorate. In December 1941, Japan joined the war against the U.S.A. and Great Britain. The Japanese armies advanced swiftly all over the North-East Asian countries. The tide of their conquest rolled at a tremendous pace towards Burma and India. When Singapore fell in February 1942, the security of India was threatened. Rangoon fell on March 7. Colombo was bombarded. Some bombs fell on the eastern coast of India. Calcutta was threatened and refugees began to leave that great city.

But in spite of this threatening situation, the attitude of the Indian leaders did not change. The Congress was as hostile as ever. It was not prepared to help the British against anybody. It could help only if India was given independence. The Muslim League was more concerned with the partition of India than its immediate salvation from the Japanese conquest.

In March 1942, Sir Stafford Cripps,[4] the leader of the House of Commons, came to Delhi with proposals on behalf of the British Government. The following is the text of the Draft Declaration of the British Government brought by Cripps to India:—

---

[4] According to the *National Herald,* "The Cripps Mission was the result of American pressure. It was a stage-managed show to buy off world opinion and to foist preconceived failure on the people of India.

(a) "Immediately upon cessation of hostilities, steps shall be taken to set up in India, in the manner described hereafter, an elected body charged with the task of framing a new Constitution for India.

(b) "Provision shall be made, as set out below, for participation of Indian States in the constitution-making body.

(c) "His Majesty's Government undertake to accept and implement forthwith the constitution so framed subject only to;

  (i) "The right of any province of British India that is not prepared to accept the new Constitution to retain its present constitutional position, provision being made for its subsequent accession if it so decides.

  "With such non-acceding provinces, should they so desire, His Majesty's Government will be prepared to agree upon a new constitution giving them the same full status as the Indian Union and arrived at by a procedure analogous to that here laid down.

  (ii) The signing of a treaty which shall be negotiated between His Majesty's Government and the constitution-making body. This treaty will cover all necessary matters arising out of the complete transfer of responsibility from British to Indian hands; it will make provision, in accordance with undertakings given by His Majesty's Government, for the protection of the racial and religious minorities, but will not impose any restriction on the power of the Indian Union to decide in future its relationship to other member-States of the British Commonwealth.

  "Whether or not an Indian State elects to adhere to the constitution, it will be necessary to negotiate a revision of its treaty arrangements so far as this may be required in the new situation.

(d) "The constitution-making body shall be composed as follows unless the leaders of Indian opinion in the principal communities agree upon some other form before the end of hostilities:

"Immediately upon the result being known of provincial elections which will be necessary at the end of hostilities, the entire membership of the Lower Houses of Provincial Legislatures shall as a single electoral college proceed to the election of the constitution-making body by the system of proportional representation. This new body shall be in number about 1/10th of the number of the electoral college.

"Indian States shall be invited to appoint representatives in the same proportion to their total population as in the case of representatives of British India as a whole and with the same powers as British India members.

(e) "During the critical period which now faces India and until the new Constitution can be framed, His Majesty's Government must inevitably bear the responsibility for and retain the control and direction of the defence of India as part of their world war effort but the task of organising to the full the military, moral and material resources of India must be the responsibility of the Government of India with the co-operation of the people of India. His Majesty's Government desire and invite the immediate and effective participation of the leaders of the principal sections of the Indian people in the counsels of their country, of the Commonwealth and of the United Nations. Thus, they will be enabled to give their active and constructive help in the discharge of a task which is vital and essential for the future freedom of India".

Criticism

1. It is pointed out that the Draft Declaration was an advance on the August Offer in four respects. It conceded to the projected Indian Union the liberty to secede from the British Commonwealth;

Cripps emphasized this point at the press conference. The Indian Union was to be free to decide as to whether she was to remain within the British Commonwealth or to go out of it. (b) The framing of the new constitution was to rest not primarily, but solely in Indian hands. However, its acceptance was made subject to the fulfilment of British obligations. If the Indians could not become free as a single unit, they could become free as two or more units. Disagreement amongst the Indians was not to give the British Government an excuse to perpetuate their rule in India, (c) The August Offer had invited the Indian leaders to start discussing the principles of the new Constitution and the method of framing it. The Draft Declaration proposed a plan for a constitution-making body to be adopted if no Indian plan was agreed upon before the cessation of hostilities, (d) The Draft Declaration went farther than the August Offer as regards the character of the interim system of Government. The Offer had provided for the inclusion of a certain number of representative Indians into the Executive Council. The Declaration invited the leaders of the principal sections of the Indian people to participate in the counsels of India, the Commonwealth and the United Nations.

2. However, the Cripps Proposals were criticised by all the interested parties in India. Each party criticised the proposals from its own point of view. The objection of the Congress was not so much to the long-term arrangement as to interim arrangement. The Congress acted on the principle that one bird in hand was better than two in the bush. Cripps had given an understanding to the Congress that with the exception of the Defence Department, other departments would be completely in the hands of the Indians, and the Governor-General will act as a constitutional head. However, at a later stage, he withdrew that statement. This made the Congress suspicious regarding the honesty of the British Government. The Congress wanted the Executive Council of the Governor-General to work as a Cabinet. This the British Government was not prepared to concede.

3. It is pointed out that objections to the composition of the postwar Constituent Assembly, settlement on the question of Pakistan on the lines suggested in the Declaration, the division of powers under Defence, etc., were not pressed. The issue which proved fatal was the *veto of Viceroy*. There were obvious objections to the Executive Council being installed as an irremovable and irresponsible body with powers of a dictator and, therefore, the veto power could not be done away with altogether, but probably it would not have been difficult to set up a convention agreeing to act in an advisory capacity in the day-to-day administration but retaining the reserve of veto powers for special reasons only.

4. The Congress was opposed to the acceptance of the novel principle of non-accession of the provinces. To them it appeared that that implied the acceptance of the principle of Pakistan which would be a severe blow to Indian unity.

5. The Hindu Mahasabha opposed the Cripps Proposals on two grounds. It was opposed to the freedom given to the provinces to leave the Indian Union and set up separate governments of their own. The Sabha also objected to the elections on the basis of Communal Award which was anti-national and undemocratic.

6. According to Sir Tej Bahadur Sapru and Mr. M.R. Jayakar, "The creation of more than one Union howsoever consistent in theory with the principle of self-determination, will be disastrous to the lasting interests of the country and its integrity and security. An effort should be made to obtain before the end of the war an intercommunal agreement for the maintenance of Indian unity on a federal basis. If that failed, and provinces should manifest overwhelming wishes in partition, then the proposed experiment might be tried, provided that no decision for non-adherence should be valid without a 65 per cent majority in the Provincial Legislature concerned".

7. The Sikhs also opposed the provisions relating to the non-accession of the provinces. They stated that "we shall resist by all possible means the separation of the Punjab from all-India Union".

8. The Depressed Classes denounced the proposals on the ground that the necessary safeguards were not provided for their interests.

9. The Muslim League opposed the creation of a single Indian Union. It was feared that if one single Union was created the creation of another might become impossible. It also opposed the system of election by a single electoral college by proportional representation. This was not in accordance with the system of communal representation which enabled the Muslims to send their own representatives. The League also objected to the method and Procedure for the non-accession of Indian provinces. Their contention was that the provinces of India were created for administrative convenience and not on any logical basis. They demanded the redistribution of the provinces. They opposed the plebiscite by the whole of the adult population of India. They demanded the inherent right of self-determination for the Muslims alone. In short, the scheme was not acceptable to the League because Pakistan was not conceded unequivocally and the right of Muslim self-determination was denied, although the recognition given to the principle of partition was much appreciated.

10. The scheme failed because it was to be accepted or rejected as a whole. There was no scope for any negotiation or adjustment.

11. Critics pointed out two snags in the proposals: One was the repetition of the August Offer of 1940 and the addition of the explanation that "the present declaration is intended, not to supersede, but to clothe these general declarations with precision and to convince the people in India of the War Cabinet's sincere resolve". This created suspicion in the minds of the people. It indicated a necessity on the part of the British Government to safeguard its prestige. The second snag was that there was no indication in the proposals that the British Government was prepared to part with power.

12. Mahatma Gandhi was not at all impressed by the proposals brought by Cripps. He is stated to have told him thus: "Why did you come if this is what you have to offer? If this is your entire proposal to India, I would advise you to take the next plane home". Sir Stafford's reply was: "I will consider that".

13. A friend of Cripps remarked thus: "It is sad beyond measure that a man like Sir Stafford Cripps should allow himself to become the devil's advocate".

According to Professor Percival Spear, "Whatever the workings of the Mahatma's mind, there is no doubt that his was the decisive voice in rejection. There was anguish in the Congress camp as well as with the British. Rajaji left the Working Committee, and Nehru came near to the breaking point with Gandhi. It was his supreme test in discipleship, a test so severe that he welcomed his subsequent arrest as a release from intolerable tension. There seems no doubt that the decision was a mistake. It precipitated the Congress revolt, which only created bitterness. It kept the Congressmen out of government, in which they would almost certainly have occupied a key position. By the end of the war their situation would have been commanding. It left the field open to the Muslim League, which proceeded to occupy the key position which should have belonged to Congress".

The Cripps Mission was a failure as the Congress refused to accept the short-term arrangements contained in the proposals. After its failure, there was a lot of discontentment in the country. The Congress leaders got convinced that they could not expect anything from the British Government in the near future. It was under these circumstances that the Congress passed the famous 'Quit India' Resolution on 8th August 1942. In March 1944, Rajagopalachariar put forward his formula to resolve the political deadlock in India. However, his proposals were not accepted by Mr. Jinnah. In January 1945, the Desai-Liaquat formula saw the light of the day, but nothing came out of it. On 14th June 1945. Lord Wavell, Governor-General and Viceroy of India, gave a broadcast to the people of India. After that, he called a conference of the Indian leaders to end the deadlock. His proposals were not accepted and he made a public confession of his failure.

Cabinet Mission Scheme (1946)

When the Labour Party came to power in England in 1945, it ordered the holding of elections in the provinces in India. After that, the Labour Government sent the famous Cabinet Mission to India in March 1946. Prolonged discussions took place between the members of the Mission and the leaders of the Congress and the Muslim League. However, the two main parties could not come to any mutual understanding. The result was that the members of the Mission had to put forward their own formula for solving the constitutional deadlock. This formula was embodied in a joint statement issued by the Cabinet Mission and Lord Wavell on May 16, 1946.

After pointing out the impracticability of the Pakistan scheme, the statement of May 16 recommended that the new Constitution of India should take the following basic form:

1. There should be a Union of India, embracing both British India and the States which should deal with the following subjects: Foreign Affairs, Defence and Communications, and should have the powers necessary to raise the finances required for the above subjects.
2. The Union should have an Executive and a Legislature constituted from British India and States' representatives. Any question raising a major communal issue in the Legislature should require for its decision a majority of the representatives present and voting of each of the two major communities as well as a majority of all the members present and voting.
3. All subjects other than the Union subjects and all residuary powers should vest in the Provinces.
4. The States will retain all subjects and powers other than those ceded to the Union.
5. Provinces should be free to form Groups with executives and legislatures, and each Group could determine the provincial subjects to be taken in common.
6. The Constitutions of the Union and of the Groups should contain a provision whereby any Province could, by a majority vote of its Legislative Assembly, call for a reconsideration of the terms of the Constitution after an initial period of 10 years and at 10 yearly intervals thereafter".

As regards the constitution-making machinery, it was provided that the Legislative Assemblies of the provinces would elect the members of that body on the basis of one representative for one million of the population. The Sikh and Muslim legislators were to elect the quota of their communities, determined on the population basis. Others were to elect the representatives for the rest of the population. The representatives from the provinces were to divide themselves into three sections, A, B and C. Section C was to consist of the representatives of Bengal and Assam, Section B of the Punjab, Sind and North-West Frontier Province and Section A of the rest of the provinces of India. "These Sections shall proceed to settle the Provincial Constitution for the Provinces included in each Section, and shall also decide whether any Group Constitution shall be set up for these provinces and, if so, with what provincial subjects the Group should deal'. The representatives of the Sections of the Indian States were then to re-assemble and settle the Union Constitution.

TABLE OF REPRESENTATION

Section A

Province	General	Muslim	Total
Madras	45	4	49
Bombay	19	2	21
United Provinces	47	8	55
Bihar	31	5	36
Central Provinces	16	1	17
Orissa	9	0	9
Total	167	20	187

Section B

Province	General	Muslim	Sikh	Total
Punjab	8	16	4	28
North-West Frontier Province	0	3	0	3
Sind	1	3	0	4
Total	9	22	4	35

Section C

Province	General	Muslim	Total
Bengal	27	33	60
Assam	7	3	10
Total	34	36	70
Total for British India			292
Maximum for States			93
Total			385

The Provinces of India were given the power to opt out of the Groups by a decision of their Legislature after the general elections under the new Constitution.

The Resolutions of the Union Constituent were to require a majority of the representatives present and voting of each of the two major communities. The Chairman of the Constituent Assembly was to decide which resolution raised major communal issues and was to consult the Federal Court before giving his decision.

A plan for the interim Government was also envisaged in the Scheme of May 16, 1946.

The Cabinet Mission declared on May 12, 1946 that the British Government could not and would not in any circumstances transfer paramountcy to an Indian Government. However, it was made clear that when a new self-governing government or governments came into being in British India, it would not be possible for the British Government to carry out the obligations of paramountcy. In that case, all the rights surrendered by the States to the paramount power were to return to the Indian States. "Political arrangements between the States on the one side and the British Crown and British India on the other will thus is be brought to an end. The void will have to be filled either by the States entering into a federal relationship with the successor government or governments in British India, or, failing this, entering into particular political arrangements with it or them". This policy has been described as "a political scorched-earth policy".

Merits

The Cabinet Mission Scheme had both its merits and demerits. (1) Its greatest merit was that the Constituent Assembly was to be constituted on the democratic principle of population strength. The principle of weightage was discarded altogether. (2) The democratic method of the decision of issue by simple majority was adopted in the case of communal issues. However, safeguards were provided for minorities. (3) The proposals also provided for an Indian Union of Provinces and States, and rejected the idea of Pakistan completely. This was the last attempt made by British statesmen to save the country from division and disaster. Some of the anomalies of the Scheme were also due to the desire of the members of the Cabinet Mission to save Indian unity at any cost. (4) The Scheme required that all the members of the Constitution Assembly were to be Indians. Neither the British Government nor the non-official Europeans in India were to be given any representation in the Constituent Assembly. The European members of the Provincial Assemblies were to absent themselves from voting. (5) It was provided that there was to be no interference with the work of the Constituent Assembly either by the British Government or by its officials in India. Within the framework of the Scheme, the Constituent Assembly was to be its own master.

Demerits

However, there were also certain defects in the Cabinet Mission Scheme. (1) Although the rights of the Muslim minority were protected it was not done with regard to other minorities such as the Sikhs in the Punjab. (2) The proposals of the Cabinet Mission with regard to the grouping of the provinces were not clear. Both the Congress and the Muslim League interpreted the provisions differently. The Muslims regarded the *compulsory* grouping of the provinces as one of the cornerstones of the Cabinet Mission proposals and were not prepared to come to a compromise on that question. The Congress stand was that the making of groups was *optional* for the provinces. The latter were free to join or not to join any group. As a matter of fact, Mahatma Gandhi asked the people of Assam not to join the group if they did not approve of it. They were asked not to care for the consequences. To solve this difficulty, if was suggested that the provinces might join provisionally, but later on freedom might be given to them to leave it if they so desired. The Congress suggested that the matter might be referred to the Federal Court for decision. However, the British Government gave its verdict in favour of the compulsory grouping of the provinces. The Muslim League won and the Congress lost its point. (3) Another defect of the Scheme was the order in which the Union and Sectional Assemblies were to meet and work and draft their constitutions. It looked ridiculous first to form the constitutions of the groups and the provinces and then to frame the Constitution of the Union. It was like putting the cart before the horse. This practical difficulty would have been experienced if the whole scheme had been worked out in actual practice.

It is desirable to trace the events that followed the publication of the statement of May 19 1946. The All India Muslim League passed a resolution on June 6, 1946 by which it accepted the Scheme in its entirety. On the other hand, the Working Committee of the Congress passed a resolution on June 26, 1946 by which it accepted the Scheme partially. The Congress accepted only that part of the Scheme which dealt with constitution-making. The view of the Committee was that the grouping of the provinces was not to be compulsory. However, the Congress rejected the Interim Government scheme on the ground that the clarifications given to them on the subject were not acceptable. The resolution of the Working Committee of the Congress was ratified by the All-India Congress Committee.

The Sikhs rejected the Scheme completely on the ground that the compulsory grouping of the provinces as contemplated by the Scheme was suicidal to their interests.

Before the members of the Cabinet Mission left India they issued a statement along with Lord Wavell in which they expressed their satisfaction that the work of the making of the constitution would proceed with the consent of the major parties in India. They regretted that an Interim Government consisting of the various parties could not be formed on account of certain difficulties. It was hoped that after the elections to the Constituent Assembly were over, negotiations would be started for the formation of an interim Government consisting of the representatives of the various parties.

Jinnah who had accepted the Scheme in its entirety was annoyed at the British Government's decision to postpone the formation of the interim Government. He accused Lord Wavell of his having gone back on his promise. He was so very angry that the Muslim League under his leadership passed another resolution on July 29, 1946 by which it withdrew its former acceptance of the Cabinet Mission Plan. Jinnah was not contented with this negative action. The Muslim League also passed the famous *Direct Action* resolution by which both the Congress and the British Government were condemned for their breach of faith with the Muslims. It was declared that the time had come for the Muslim League to resort to direct action to achieve Pakistan. The resolution authorised the Working Committee of the League to prepare a programme of direct action at once. August 16, 1946 was fixed as the Direct Action Day. On that day, Hindu-Muslim riots took place in Calcutta on an unprecedented scale. There was a lot of bloodshed. There was an enormous loss of life and properly. The British Government did nothing to stop this wholesale massacre.

Lord Wavell invited Pandit Jawaharlal Nehru, the President of the Congress, to form the Interim Government. The Government formed by Pandit Nehru took office on September 2, 1946. The Muslim League refused to participate in the Interim Government. The members of this interim Government were Pandit Nehru, Sardar Patel, Dr. Rajendra Prasad, Mr. Rajagopalachari, Dr. John Matthai, Sardar Baldev Singh, Sir Shafat Ahmed Khan, Mr. Jagjivan Ram, Syed Ali Zaheer, Mr. Bhabha, Asaf Ali and Sarat Chandra Bose. On October 13, 1946, the Muslim League decided to join the Interim Government and on October 15, five members of the Muslim League were induced in the Interim Government. Some of the above members, therefore, resigned to make room for the five members of the Muslim League. The Government remained in office till the partition of India in August 1947.

Constituent Assembly

Elections to the Constituent Assembly took place in July 1946 and the Constitution Assembly met for the first time in New Delhi on December 9, 1946. The Muslim League refused to participate in its deliberations.

In February 1947, Mr. Attlee, Prime Minister of England, declared that the British Government would leave India before June 1948 even if no agreement was made between the Muslim League and the Congress. In March 1947, Lord Mountbatten was appointed Governor-General of India and after prolonged discussions both with the Congress and Muslim League leaders, he put forward his famous June 3 Plan in which he suggested the partition of the country into India and Pakistan. The scheme was accepted both by the Congress and the Muslim League. The proposals were put in the form of a bill which was passed by the British Parliament on 18th July 1947 as the Indian Independence Act, 1947.

The Indian Independence Act, 1947

The object of this Act was to give effect to June 3 Plan of Lord Mountbatten. It merely legalised what had already been promised to the people of India.
1. The Act provided for the partition of India and the establishment of two Dominions of India and Pakistan from the appointed day (15th August 1947). The Act also provided for the legislative supremacy of the two Dominions.
2. The Legislatures of the two Dominions were given full power to make laws having extra-territorial jurisdiction.

3. The British Government was to have no control over the affairs of the Dominions, Provinces or any part of the Dominions after 15th August 1947.
4. Until a new Constitution was framed for each Dominion, the Act made the existing Constituent Assemblies the Dominion Legislatures for the time being. The Assemblies were to exercise all the powers which were formerly exercised by the Central Legislature in addition to its power regarding the framing of a new Constitution.
5. Pending the framing of a new Constitution, each of the Dominions and all Provinces were to be governed in accordance with the Government of India Act, 1935. Each Dominion was authorised to make modifications in the Government of India Act, 1935 under the Indian Independence Act.
6. The Governor-General was given the power to modify or adapt the Government of India Act, 1935, as might be considered necessary till 31st March 1948. After that day, it was open to the Constituent Assembly to modify or adapt the old Government of India Act, 1935.
7. The right of the King to veto laws or to reserve laws for his pleasure was given up. This right was given to the Governor-General. He was given the full right to assent in the name of His Majesty to any law of the Dominion Legislature made in the ordinary legislative capacity.
8. The Act provided for the termination of the suzerainty of the Crown over the Indian States. All treaties, agreements and functions exercisable by His Majesty with regard to States and their rulers were to lapse from 15th August 1947. It was also provided that the existing arrangements between the Government of India and the Indian States were to continue pending the detailed negotiations between the Indian States and the new Dominions.
9. Agreements with the tribes of the North-Western Frontier Province of India were to be negotiated by the successor Dominion.
10. The office of the Secretary of State for India was to be abolished and his work was to be taken over by the Secretary of State for Commonwealth Affairs.
11. The title of "Emperor of India" was to be dropped from the royal style and titles of the King of England.
12. The Act terminated British authority over India, set up two independent Dominions, each with full authority to make any constitution it pleased. Both the Dominions were given full powers and rights to leave the British Commonwealth of Nations if they so pleased.

The Indian Independence Act of 1947 was a great landmark in the Anglo-Indian relations. It marked the ending of the British rule in India. It was a recognition of the right of the Indians to be free. But unfortunately, it divided India into two parts: India and Pakistan.

Partition of India

1. The Partition of India in 1947 was the outcome of many forces although the main cause was the isolationist policy of the Muslims in India. Under the influence of Sir Syed Ahmed Khan, the Muslims in India began to think and dream separately from the Hindus. They started feeling that their interests were different from those of the Hindus and they had nothing in common with them. They went to the extent of contending that their interests were opposed to those of the Hindus. If India was given a responsible government, the Hindu majority was bound to dominate the Muslims of India who were in a minority in the whole country. The Muslims also felt that they were educationally backward and consequently could not compete with the Hindus. With the passage of time, they drifted more and more away from the Hindus. The Muslim League ideology also estranged the Muslims from the Hindus. Sir Muhammed Iqbal and Mr. Jinnah also played their part in taking the Muslims away from the Hindus. Particularly after 1940, the Muslims insisted that they wanted a separate homeland. They were not prepared

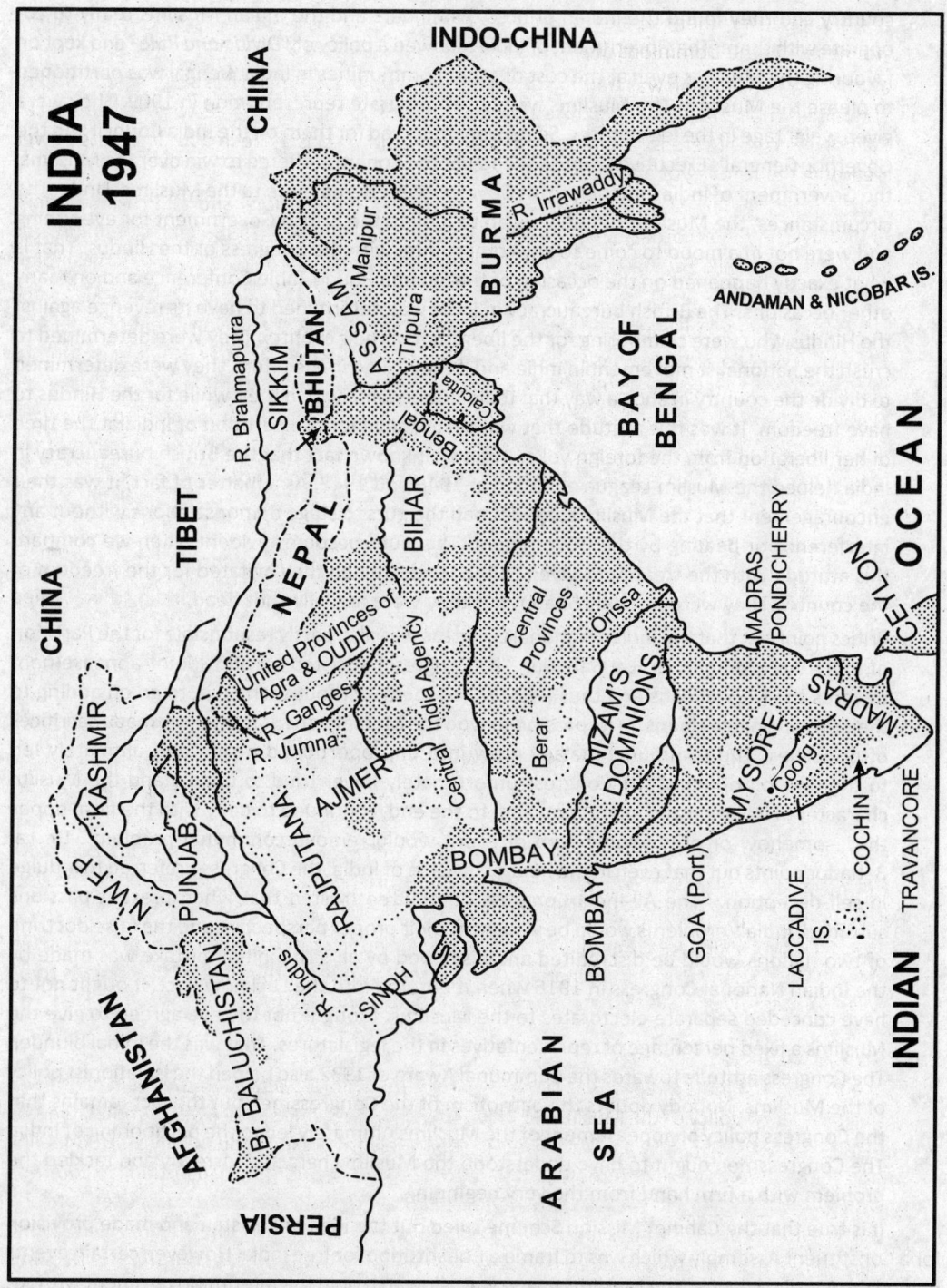

to come to any compromise on a permanent basis. This isolationist policy of the Muslims ultimately led to the partitioning of India.

2. However, it cannot be denied that the Muslims were helped immensely by the British Government in India. After the Mutiny of 1857, the Government of India wanted allies in the

country and they found the Indian princes, Zamindars and the Indian Muslims ready to co-operate with them. The Government of India followed a policy of *"Divide and Rule"* and kept on favouring the Muslims even at the cost of other communities in India. Bengal was partitioned to please the Muslims. The Muslims were given separate representation in 1909. They were given weightage in the legislatures. Seats were reserved for them on the India Council and the Governor-General's Executive Council. Whatever the Congress offered to win over the Muslims, the Government of India and the British Government offered more to the Muslims. Under the circumstances, the Muslims of India began to look to the British Government for everything and were not in a mood to come to any compromise with the Congress or the Hindus. That is what exactly happened on the occasion of the Second Round Table Conference and on many other occasions. The British bureaucracy in India was determined to have its revenge against the Hindus who were clamouring for the liberation of their country. They were determined to crush the nationalist movement in India and if they failed in the effort, they were determined to divide the country in such a way that it did not become worth their while for the Hindus to have freedom. It was this attitude that was responsible for the partition of India at the time of her liberation from the foreign yoke. It is a well-known fact that the British bureaucracy in India helped the Muslim League agitation in 1946 and 1947. As a matter of fact, it was their encouragement that the Muslim Leaguers had the guts to stage demonstrations without any interference or beating by the Government. The truth becomes evident when we compare this attitude with the treatment given to the Hindus when they agitated for the freedom of the country. They were not only beaten but they were actually shot dead.

3. Critics point out that the Indian National Congress was also partly responsible for the Partition of India. According to Dr. Lal Bahadur, "It (Congress) adopted an attitude of appeasement towards the Mussalmans and thus encouraged them, without wishing it, to go on adding to their unreasonable claims. In its passion to woo the Mussalmans, it frequently made sacrifices of principles. The communal malady grew into unproportioned height and ultimately led to the division of India. The Congress unfortunately never tried to understand the Muslim character of isolation and aggression and, to the end, continued to dally with the false hopes that, somehow or other, some turn of event would remove communal problem". Dr. Lal Bahadur points out that even in the hour of division of India, the Congress preferred to indulge in self-deception. "The All-India Congress Committee trusted that when present passions subsided. India's problems would be viewed in their proper perspective and the false doctrine of two nations would be discredited and discarded by all". The initial mistake was made by the Indian National Congress in 1916 when it entered into the Lucknow Pact. It ought not to have conceded separate electorates to the Muslims. It ought not to have agreed to give the Muslims a fixed percentage of representatives in the legislatures. That was the initial blunder. The Congress attitude towards the Communal Award of 1932 also helped the isolationist policy of the Muslims. Nobody doubts the patriotism of the Congressmen but the fact remains that the Congress policy of appeasement of the Muslims ultimately led to the partitioning of India. The Congressmen ought to have understood the Muslim character correctly and tackled the problem with a firm hand from the very beginning.

It is true that the Cabinet Mission Scheme ruled out the idea of Pakistan and made provision for a Constituent Assembly which was to frame a Constitution for free India. However, certain events helped the Muslim League. The Muslim League was allowed to join the Interim Government without agreeing to take part in the deliberations of the Constituent Assembly. Its members in the Interim Government refused to co-operate with the Congress members of the Interim Government of which Jawaharlal Nehru was the head. They proclaimed their loyalty to the Viceroy whose appointees and nominees they considered themselves to be. They openly talked of carving out a Pakistan. The division among the members of the Interim Government was reflected in the whole administrative machinery. According to the Report of General Secretaries of the Indian National Congress, "If the Civil Services, the police and the Army became divided in their loyalty and their members functioned on communal lines; nothing but mischief and chaos in the administration could result. And this was happening...for the League, this situation was in the nature of pressure tactics for its demand for Pakistan". The Muslim League members of the Interim Government removed the Hindu and Sikh officers from the key positions in their departments and put in their places Muslims who could be depended upon to help the cause of Pakistan.

It was during the period of the Interim Government that communal riots took place on a very large scale. The ever-increasing and ever-deepening chain of communal disturbances involving mass murder, arson or loot accompanied by unthinkable atrocities and horrors obliged the Working Committee (of the Indian National Congress) to consider the whole communal and political situation afresh. The only way out of the difficulty appeared to be the partitioning of India. Jawaharlal Nehru referred to this fact in these words on 3rd June 1947: "There has been violence, shameful, degrading and revolting violence, in various parts of the country. This must end". The Congress was not happy about the partitioning of India as it had consistently fought for the liberation of united India. The following words of Jawaharlal Nehru give an idea of the working of his inner mind: "For generations we have dreamt and struggled for a free and independent united India. The proposal to allow certain parts to secede, if they so will, is painful for any of us to contemplate".

The announcement of the British Government in February 1947 that it was determined to put power into the hands of the Indians at a very early date worsened the communal situation in the country and helped the cause of Pakistan. While making the declaration, "His Majesty's Government had hoped that it would be possible for the major parties to co-operate in the working out of the Cabinet Mission's Plan of May 1946, and evolve for India a Constitution acceptable to all concerned. However, that hope was not fulfilled as no pressure was put on the Muslim League to take part in the deliberations of the Constituent Assembly. The British Government also accepted the Muslim League's point of view that the grouping of the provinces under the Cabinet Mission Scheme was a compulsory one.

It appears that it was felt by the Congress leaders in the month of May 1947 that the partition of India was absolutely inevitable. "The Congress had to choose between partition and continuance of a state of affairs which was becoming more and more intolerable. According to Sardar Patel, "I felt that if we did not accept partition, India would be split into many bits and would be completely ruined.

"My experience of office for one year convinced me that the way we have been proceeding would lead us to disaster. We would not have had one Pakistan but several. We would have had Pakistan cells in every office". Again, "It was then that I was made fully conscious of the extent to which our interests were being prejudiced everywhere by the machination of the Political Department, and came to the conclusion that the best course was to hasten the departure of these foreigners even at the cost of the partition of the country. It was also then that I felt that there was the unification of the rest of India".

Prof. Percival Spear has observed thus: "Was partition inevitable? In my opinion it was so as soon as Jinnah resorted to direct action in 1946, for the only alternatives then were the frightful excesses of civil commotion and anarchy. But the die was probably cast much earlier, when the Congress failed to realize the new strength of the League in 1945 or to take office under the Cripps proposals of 1942. The Simla talks in 1945 were probably the last chance of getting the League to accept something short of full Pakistan; the Cripps offer of 1942 was the last chance for the Congress to smother the League before it became a formidable mass movement. But there is another point to remember before too much regret is felt for the lost unity of India. The federal provisions of the

Cripps and later proposals so reduced the powers of the central government that it is very doubtful if the great developments of Nehru's India would have been possible under them. It is probable that the centre would have been weak, and political energy spent by the communities in jostling for position instead of reorganizing the country. Industrial development would have waited on party tactics, and five-year plans on political polemics. Only a joint directorate of the two parties could have achieved the kind of development which has actually occurred, and of this there was never any sign. However, much partition may be regretted in principle, it was perhaps necessary, on this account, in the larger interests of the country".

According to Dr. Lal Bahadur, "The partition of India was an event of great importance. It ushered in an era of independence, though the enthusiasm for it was somewhat diminished due to division. But even the Partition is not without advantage. Had India remained a united whole, the Mussalmans would surely have dominated and would have shared in the amenities of life more than their due. Right traditions could never have developed as at every step special claims of the Mussalmans would have been advanced. They could have taken roots only if homage were not paid to Muslim appeasement. But seeing the history of the Indian National Congress this would have been impossible.... . But as it never understood Muslim mind and character, it also never adhered to principles in its dealing with Mussalmans. Expediency always came in operation in its treatment with the Muslims. The territorial integrity of India could be a benefit to the country only in the event of equal treatment to all and in the absence of Muslim appeasement policy. Since the Congress was incapable of doing it, the division of the country cannot be seriously lamented. It was choosing between the two evils—Muslim domination over the whole of the country and vivisection of Mother India—and in accepting the latter position, perhaps a better evil was chosen". (*The Muslim League,* p. 345).

On 15th August, 1947, India became free. The Constituent Assembly went on with its work and prepared a draft of the new Constitution of India in February 1948. The Constituent Assembly gave the Constitution its final shape on 26th November 1949. The same Constitution came into force on 26 January 1950.

The New Constitution of India

1. The Preamble of the Indian Constitution resolves to establish a Sovereign Democratic republic. It declares that sovereignty vests on the people of the country. The Preamble also refers to justice, liberty, equality and fraternity.

2. There were four kinds of States under the Constitution, viz., Part A States, Part B States, Part C States, and Part D-States. Part A States were previously the Governors' provinces. Part B States were previously ruled by Indian princes. Part C States were under Chief Commissioners and Lt.-Governors. However, as a result of the Seventh Amendment of the Constitution made in 1956, there were to be 14 States and six Union Territories. The old distinctions among States disappeared. The institution of Rajpramukhs was abolished. In 1960, the State of Bombay was divided into two States of Gujarat and Maharashtra. In July 1960, it was decided to set up a new State known as Nagaland.

3. As regards the citizenship of India, persons born or domiciled in India, refugees who have migrated to India from Pakistan and the Indians overseas who apply for Indian citizenship, are Indian citizens. The Constitution has adopted the principle of single citizenship for the whole of India. No person is entitled to claim that he is a citizen of two countries.

4. The Constitution provides for a large number of fundamental rights which are guaranteed to every citizen of India. Those rights are to be found in Articles 12 to 35 of the Constitution. The Supreme Court and the High Courts have been appointed the guardian of these fundamental

rights. Those rights are: right to equality before law, prohibition of discrimination on grounds of religion, race, caste, colour, sex or place of birth, equality of opportunity in matters of public employment, abolition of untouchability, right to freedom of speech and expression, right to assemble peacefully and without arms, the right to form associations and unions, the right to move freely throughout the territory of India, the right to reside and settle in any part of India, the right to secure, hold and dispose of property, the right to practice any profession or to carry on any occupation, trade or business, the right to life and personal liberty, the right to freedom from arrest and detention in certain cases, the prohibition of traffic in human beings and forced labour, the prohibition of employment of children in any factory or mine or in any other hazardous work, the right to freedom of conscience and free profession, the right to practise and propagate religion, the freedom to manage religious affairs cultural and educational rights, and the right to constitutional remedies.

5. The Constitution also contains what are known as the Directive Principles of the State Policy. These principles relate to those matters which the Government of India is to keep in view for the welfare of the people of the country. Accordingly, all the Indian citizens are entitled to adequate means of livelihood. There is to be equitable distribution of the material resources of the country. The economic freedom of the country demands the avoidance of the concentration of wealth and the mean of production. There is to be equal pay for equal work for both men and women. The wealth and strength of the workers are not to be abused. Children and young-men are to be protected against exploitation and moral and material abandonment. All workers are to get a living wage. There must be established just and humane conditions of work. All people have the right to work, to education and public assistance in case of unemployment, old age, sickness, etc. There is to be uniform civil code for all the people of the country. There is to be free and compulsory education for children. It is the duty of the State to raise the level of nutrition and the standard of living of the people. The State is to promote international peace and security, maintain just and honourable relations between nations, inculcate respect for international law and treaty obligations and encourage settlement of international disputes by arbitration. However, it is to be noted that Directive Principles of State Policy differ from fundamental rights inasmuch as they cannot be enforced by courts.

6. The Constitution provides for a President of the Indian Republic. He is elected indirectly by an electoral college consisting if the elected members of both Houses of Parliament and Legislatures of the States. The President must be a citizen of India. He must have completed the age of 35 and he must be qualified for election as a member of the House of the People. He is not eligible for election if he holds a job under the Government. He holds office for 5 years but can be re-elected. He gets a salary of ₹10,000 and allowances. He can be impeached for the violation of the Constitution. The Constitution provides a special procedure for the impeachment of the President. The President has been given a large number of powers in the legislative, executive and judicial spheres. He is also authorised to act in times of emergency. He is expected to act as a constitutional head like the King of England.

7. The Vice-President of India is the *ex-officio* Chairman of the Council of States. Any citizen of India who is 35 years of age or more and who is qualified for the membership of the Council of States can be elected to this office by both the Houses of Parliament. When the President is ill, or resigns, or dies, or is removed, or is absent for any other reason, the place is taken over by the Vice-President of India till such time as a new President of India is elected.

8. The Constitution provides for a Council of Ministers to assist the President. The President is to appoint the Prime Minister and the other Ministers are to be appointed by him on the advice of the Prime Minister. All the Ministers are collectively responsible to the House of the People.

It is the duty of the Prime Minister to communicate to the President all the decisions arrived at in the Cabinet. The Prime Minister is the link between the President and the Cabinet. His position is the same as that of the Prime Minister of England.

9. The Indian Parliament consists of two Houses, viz., the House of the People and the Council of States. The House of the People consists of 500 members who are directly elected by the voters in the several States. Every adult or grown-up citizen of India is given the right to vote. The life of the House of the People is 5 years. The House of the People has a Speaker and a Deputy Speaker. The Council of States is a permanent body of 250 members. Its members are elected indirectly. About one-third of its members retire after every two years. Twelve members of the Council of States are nominated by the President from men of learning and persons of experience. A member of the Council of States must be a citizen of India and must not be less than 30 years of age.

   It is to be noted that the House of the People is stronger than the Council of States. It has practically complete control over money bills. Even in the case of ordinary bills, the opinion of the House of the People prevails on account of its numerical majority in the joint session of the two Houses.

10. The Constitution provides for the Supreme Court of India consisting of a Chief Justice of India and not more than 7 other judges. However, the number can be increased by Parliament. All the judges of the Supreme Court are appointed by the President. Judges hold office during good behaviour till the age of 65. Provision is also made for *ad hoc* judges of the Supreme Court. Supreme Court has been given both original and appellate jurisdiction. As regards its original jurisdiction, it can try any dispute between the Government of India and one or more States, or between the Government of India and any State or States on one side and one or more other States on the other, or between two or more States if and in so far as the dispute involves any question, whether of law or fact, on which the existence or extent of a legal right depends. The Supreme Court has the power to issue directions or orders in the nature of writs of Habeas Corpus, Mandamus, Prohibition, Quo Warranto and Certiorari, or any of them for the enforcement of fundamental rights.

    The appellate jurisdiction of the Supreme court is of three kinds, viz., constitution, civil and criminal. An appeal can be taken from a High Court to the Supreme Court if a case involves a substantial question of law with regard to the interpretation of the Constitution. In civil cases, an appeal lies to the Supreme Court if the value of the subject matter of the dispute is not less than Rs. 20,000. In criminal cases, an appeal lies to the Supreme Court if the High Court on appeal reverses an order of acquittal of an accused person and sentences him to death. An appeal also lies if the High Court tries the accused and sentences him to death. Provision is made for the increase of its powers in criminal cases by Parliament.

    The Supreme Court also possesses advisory jurisdiction. It is to advise the President on questions of law and fact. It has also the power to grant special leave to appeal in certain cases. It has the power of review. It has been rightly said that the Supreme Court of India has more powers than any other Supreme Court in the world.

    The Constitution also provides for a High Court for every State. It is to consist of a Chief Justice and such other judges as the President of India may from time to time think fit. Every High Court has control over all courts subordinate to it throughout the territory under the court except any court constituted for the Armed Forces of India. Appointments, promotions and postings of district judges are to be made by the Governor in consultation with the High Court of the State.

11. The Constitution provides for a Union Public Service Commission and also State Public Service Commissions. Two or more States can have a joint Public Service Commission. The main functions of the Public Service Commissions are to recommend candidates for appointment and also to conduct examinations for recruitment to the Services.

12. The Constitution provides for a Comptroller and Auditor-General. He is to be appointed by the President to perform all duties and exercise powers relating to the accounts of the Union, and the States. His main duty is to keep a careful watch on the finances of the Union and the States and especially to see that the expenses voted by the Parliament or the Legislature of a State and laid down in Appropriation Act are not exceeded or varied.

13. The Constitution provides for the distribution of powers between the Union and the States. The Union List contains those subjects on which laws can be passed by the Indian Parliament. The State List contains those subjects on which laws can be made by a State Legislature. The Concurrent List contains those subjects on which laws can be passed both by the Union Parliament and the State Legislature. The residuary powers are given to the Union Parliament. The result of all this is that the Union Government is very strong under the new Constitution.

14. The Constitution provides for the freedom of trade, commerce and intercourse throughout the territory of India. However, certain restrictions can be placed in the interests of the public. According to the Constitution, no tax can be levied or collected except by authority of law. There are provisions for the creation of certain funds. The general fund is called the Consolidated Fund of India and into this fund goes all the income of the Government of India. There is also a Consolidated Fund for each State. In addition to these, there is a public account of India and public account for each State. Provision is also made for what is called a Contingency Fund of India and similar funds in every State. These funds are at the disposal of the President of India, or the Governor of a State. According to the Constitution, the superintendence, direction and control of elections to Parliament and Legislature of every State and of President and Vice-President including appointment of Election Tribunals are vested in the Election Commission. There will be only one general Electoral Roll for every territorial constituency. No person is ineligible for inclusion in that roll only on the ground of religion, race, caste, sex, or any of them. There are no property qualifications for the voters. Every person who is a citizen of India and who is not less than 21 years of age and who is not otherwise disqualified is entitled to vote at the elections of the House of the People and the Legislative Assemblies of States.

15. The Constitution provides that Hindi in Devanagari script shall be the official language of the Union. The English language shall continue for all official purposes of the Union for a period of 15 years, but the President may authorise the use of Hindi in addition to English language during the same period. If at the end of 15 years it is found that Hindi cannot replace English completely, Parliament may provide for the use of English for such purposes as may be specified by law. The Constitution recognizes the use of 14 Indian languages as regional languages for various States.

16. Provision is also made for the amendment of the Constitution. The Constitution is amended when the President gives assent to any bill after it is passed in each House of Parliament by a majority of not less than two-thirds of the members of the House present and voting. Exception is made in the case of amendments of certain particular provisions in which cases amendments require ratification by not less than one-half of the State legislatures.

Criticism of the Constitution

1. In the first place, the critics point out that there is nothing original in the new Constitution of India. Many sections have been taken word for word from the Government of India Act, 1935.

Similarly, many provisions have been borrowed from the Constitutions of other countries of the world. There is nothing indigenous about it. There is no mention of the Sabha or the Samiti of the Hindu period. There is also no reference to the political institutions of Medieval India. But it may be pointed out that there is nothing wrong in borrowing a political institution which otherwise works well. Moreover, it is difficult to fit in the ancient political institutions of India in a modern constitutional set-up.

2. The Indian Constitution is over-centralised and the Units have been reduced to the level of local bodies. It has already been pointed out that the Central Government has been made particularly strong with the object of maintaining the integrity and security of India. It was felt that there was no other way of checking the centrifugal tendencies which exist in the body-politic of India. The enormous powers of the Central Government are required to be used as a remedy for the disease.

3. The fundamental rights as provided in the Constitution are illusory and not real. They have been hedged in on all sides by so many limitations that the people are not materially benefited by their inclusion into the Constitution. But it must be conceded that the courts have acted enthusiastically in the matter of the enforcement of the fundamental rights. Moreover, the limitations have been imposed on the rights because absolute rights cannot be enjoyed by all. They are always the property of a few individuals only.

4. It is pointed out that the Directive Principles of State Policy were included into the Constitution without any purpose. Since they are not justiciable, they are ineffective. Every Government can afford to ignore them with impunity. They are merely moral precepts about which the politicians need not bother themselves. But it may be pointed out that these Directive Principles are bound to influence the course of legislation in the country. They are like a mandate from the people. No government which cares to retain public confidence will ever dare to act against these Principles.

5. It is true that the Constitution makes provision for those things which insure the independence of the Judges of the High Courts and the Supreme Court, the members of the Public Service Commissions and also the Comptroller and Auditor-General, but the members of the subordinate judiciary complain that there is nothing to insure their independence. The Constitution has simply ignored them. Likewise, the Government servants are not happy about their status under the new Constitution. In certain cases the officer concerned may not be given reasonable opportunity to prove his innocence. It rests with the authority empowered to dismiss or remove a public servant to decide as to whether it is reasonably practicable to give such opportunity or not, and his decision is final.

6. The Constitution provides for the promulgation of ordinances by the President of India or the Governor of a State. Critics point out that such a thing is not proper under a democratic set-up. There is no such provision in a free country like England and there is no reason why it should be retained in the new Constitution of India. There was some justification for such a power when India was ruled by a foreign country. It is improper to borrow one of the worst features of the old Constitution of India.

7. Critics condemn the emergency powers of the President. It is pointed out that these powers may be used by the President for the purpose of setting up a dictatorship in the country. The experience of Germany is pointed out as a warning.

8. The Constitution is unduly prolix and elaborate. It is probably the longest of its kind. It errs on the side of overelaboration with a view to avoiding obscurities. Our Constitution lacks the brevity of the American Constitution and is full of administrative details which are not to be found there. It would have been better if the framers of our Constitution had adopted

the American model and not followed the Government of India Act of 1935. The ambition of the framers of the Indian Constitution was to make it foolproof. They tried to avoid all those pitfalls which the working of the various constitutions had shown. The attempt to provide against all possible eventualities resulted in the length of the document.

9. As regards the provisions for suspension of State constitution there may be some justification for the interference of the President in the case of external aggression, but interference in the case of internal disturbance appears to be uncalled for. The existence of this power is a standing invitation and temptation to exercise it on the flimsiest grounds. This is bound to reduce the State autonomy to a farce. If the President of India in league with the Ministers commanding the confidence of Parliament takes it into his head to take over any State, so influenced to act on certain confidential but absolutely ungrounded complaints against the way a State Government is functioning, the Constitution does not provide any adequate safeguard or remedy. The way in which the Central Government took over the Government of PEPSU, Punjab and Kerala was not considered proper. The critics also point out that the Constitution does not provide any adequate remedy in the case of a breakdown at the Centre itself.

10. It is pointed out that the Indian Constitution does not invoke the blessings of God as is done in many other Constitutions. The omission is all the more surprising in a Constitution which is intended for a people who are known for their devotion of God. The framers of the Constitution have deliberately avoided any reference to religion so that the idea of a secular State may easily take root in the soil of the country. However, it can be argued that the expression "solemnly resolved" in the Preamble makes up for the omission of the name of God. The word "solemn" introduces into the Constitution a sufficient element of religiosity which can be considered to have given it a spiritual halo.

11. It is stated that the provision which allows the President to get the opinion of the Supreme Court on any question of public importance is a very objectionable one. It detracts from the dignity of the Supreme Court as the ultimate court of appeal in the country. It is bound to embarrass the Supreme Court when the same question on which it has already given its opinion to the President, comes up before it in the form of case between two parties. The question is whether the Supreme Court is bound by its previous opinion given to the President or not. It would have been better if such a provision had been avoided. The President of India can get the opinion of the Attorney-General who is expected to have the same qualifications as those of a judge of the Supreme Court.

12. It is argued that the Indian Constitution has been framed by lawyers and for lawyers. The Constitution has been designedly and deliberately so made as to bristle with difficulties in interpretation. Its object is to allow the legal profession to have a rich crop of litigation.

According to Dr. Jennings, the lawyer-politician has played a more important part in India politics than in the politics of any other country in the world. "As a lawyer, I cannot raise objections to this practice, though it must be confessed that there is danger in it, for the lawyer-politician is sometimes neither a good lawyer nor a good politician. Whether the dominance of the Constituent Assembly by the lawyer-politician has been good for India, must be left for history to say. What can at present be said is that it has added to the complexity of the Constitution".

13. Dr. Jennings points out that the Indian Constitution is far too large and therefore far too rigid. The rigidity of the Constitution is not determined solely by the nature of the amending process. It is also determined by the volume which has to be amended. The Indian Constitution is the longest Constitution and the process of amendment is also not simple.

14. The Socialists maintain that the Constituent Assembly was not a proper representative body and consequently it was not competent to frame a constitution for the people of India. On the

day of the enforcement of the new Constitution (26th January 1950), Shri Jai Prakash Narayan remarked thus: "Lastly, let us not forget that the Constitution that comes into force today and brings republic into being is in itself a source of greatest danger, to both individual freedom and social justice. Therefore, at the earliest opportunity a really representative Constituent Assembly must be convened to frame a new Constitution that may become a fit instrument of social democracy". It was suggested that to meet the objection, the new Constitution should be allowed to be amended by the ordinary process of a simple majority during the first five years. That had been actually done in the case of Ireland. Had this suggestion been acted upon, the representatives of the people in the new Parliament elected on the basis of adult franchise, would have got the opportunity to make the necessary changes in the light of the mandate of the people.

15. According to Laxmi Narain Sahu, "Democracy has been centred round Delhi just as holiness has been centred round Banaras". According to Prof. K. T. Shah, "The Constitution would make the Prime Minister a potential dictator". According to Shankar Rao Deo, General Secretary of the Congress in 1949-50, "As under the Constitution of Germany, our President has the potentiality of becoming a virtual dictator". According to A. C. Guha, "Power vested in the hands of the President was too much and smacked something like the power of the President of the Reich at the advent of Hitler". According to A. K. Ghosh, "Emergency powers vested in the President made him a potential dictator".

16. According to Dr. Jennings, the Indian Constitution is in a large measure a product of British rule. The Constitution of the United States was by reaction a product of George III and Lord North. The Indian Constitution is by reaction a production of the Governments of MacDonald (in his last and worst phase), Baldwin, Chamberlain and to a less degree Churchill. It is impregnated with the idea that law and Government are dangerous and ought to be kept in concentration camps. Possibly, these are implicit consequences of communal tensions and doubts whether democracy always throws up the ablest and most public-spirited representatives.

17. According to B. R. Misra, "The Indian Constitution is a centralised federal constitution. The financial character of the Constitution has made the Centre definitely stronger than it was even under the Act of 1935. Perhaps this was necessary under the new political setup of the country to check the working of separatist tendencies. The States, in view of their limited resources, must always look forward to the Centre for financial aid and thus will be following the dictation of the Union in all important financial and political matters". Again, "The success of the Constitution must depend upon the will of the people and the economic programmes of the political parties which will run the Government. Unless the economic condition of the masses is improved, the Directive Principles of State Policy will remain an idle dream". (*Economic Aspects of the Indian Constitution*, 1952, p. 71).

REVIEW QUESTIONS

1. Write the step-by-step constitutional history of India from 1773 to 1950.
2. Write an essay on the features and provisions of the various Acts passed in constitutional history of India.
3. Narrate the importance of the Act of 1961 in the constitutional history of India.
4. Throw light on the Montagu-Chelmsford Reforms.
5. Describe the Act of Morley-Minto Reforms.
6. Give an idea of the Dyarchy system.
7. Narrate the circumstances for the Act of 1935 of India.
8. Enumerate the constitutional importance of the Indian Independence Act, 1947.

9. Evaluate the composition and working of the Constitutional Assembly.
10. Review the Proclamation of Queen Victoria.
11. Elaborate on the features of the Constitution of India.
12. Write short notes on the following:
    (a) The Regulating Act, 1773
    (b) Pitt's India Act, 1784
    (c) The Government of India Act, 1858
    (d) August Declaration
    (e) Simon Commission
    (f) The Nehru Report
    (g) Round Table Conference (1930-31)
    (h) Communal Award, 1932
    (i) Poona Pact, 1932
    (j) The White Paper, 1933
    (k) The Government of India Act, 1935
    (l) Cripps Proposals, 1942
    (m) Cabinet Mission, 1946
    (n) Constituent Assembly
    (o) The Indian Independence Act, 1947
    (p) Partition of India
    (q) Features of the Constitution of India

SUGGESTED READINGS

Alexander, H.: *India since Cripps* (1944).
Alexandrowicz, C.H.: *Constitutional Developments in India* (1957).
Anand, C.L.: *The Government of India* (1936).
Appadorai, A.: *Dyarchy in Practice.*
Banerjee, A.C. (Ed.): *Indian Constitutional Documents.*
Campbell-Johnson: *Mission with Mountbatten* (1951).
Char, S.V. Desika: *Centralised Legislation* (1963).
Chatterji, A.: *The Constitutional Development of India* (1937-47).
Coupland, R.: *The Cripps Mission.*
Coupland, R: *The Indian Problem* (1805-1935).
Cowell, H.: *History and Constitution of the Courts and Legislative Authorities in India.*
Curtis L.: *Dyarchy.*
Keith, A.B.: *Constitutional History of India.*
Lumby, E.W.R.: *The Transfer of Power in India.*
Mahajan, V.D.: *Constitutional History of India.*
Masaldan, P.N.: *Evolution of Provincial Autonomy in India* (1953).
Menon, V.P.: *Story of the Wavell Plan.*
Menon, V.P.: *The Transfer of Power in India.*
Report of the Indian Statutory Commission.
Report on Indian Constitutional Reforms, 1918.

20 Growth of Central and Provincial Legislatures

  LEARNING OBJECTIVES

- Throw light on the evolution and development of the central and provincial legislatures
- Discuss the features of the various Acts culminating in the enforcement of Constitution in 1950

GROWTH OF THE CENTRAL LEGISLATURE

According to the Montagu-Chelmsford Report, "The germ of legislative power of the Government of India lies embedded in Elizabeth's Charter of 1600 which authorised the East India Company to make reasonable laws, constitutions, orders and ordinances not repugnant to English law for the good government of the Company and its officers". No copies of any laws, made under the early Charters are known to exist. The subsequent Charters changed the powers of the Company according to its needs. The Charter of 1726 empowered the Governor-in-Council and the three Presidencies to make laws, ordinances and regulations in their respective jurisdictions.

The Regulating Act of 1773 required that the Governments of Madras and Bombay must send copies of their laws and orders to the Government of Bengal. It is not clear as to whether the Governor-General of Bengal had any right to modify them or not. The Act of 1807 empowered the Governor-in-Council of Madras and Bombay to make regulations. In short, the power of legislation was exercised by the Executive Governments in the three Presidencies. Every President had its own system of laws which might be different from those existing in other Presidencies.

Charter Act of 1833

The Charter Act of 1833 is a great landmark in the field of legislation. It simplified the legislative machinery. It deprived the Presidencies of Madras and Bombay of their powers of legislation. The Governor-General-in-Council was given the powers to make laws on all the subjects for the whole of India. The Act also provided for the appointment of a Law Member in the Governor-General's Executive Council. His duties were purely legislative.

Charter Act of 1853

The Charter Act of 1853 made the Law Member a full member of the Executive Council of the Governor-General. The provinces were allowed to send one representative each to the Government of India. No measure concerning any province was to be considered unless the representative from that province was present. The Chief Justice of the Supreme Court of Calcutta was made an ex-officio member of the Council and one more member was appointed. The Governor-General was given the power of appointing two more civil servants as members of the Council. The Council in its legislative capacity consisted of 12 members. Those were the Governor-General,

Commander-in-Chief, 4 members of the Executive Council, and 6 legislative members. Out of these 6 members, 4 were the representatives from the provinces and the other two were the Chief Justice and puisne judge. The representatives from the Provinces were to be given £5,000 annually. It is clear that there was at least one member present with local knowledge.

Experience showed that the Council as constituted by the Act of 1853 "evinced an inconvenient tendency to interfere with the Executive". Sir Charles Wood complained in the House of Commons that the "Council had become a sort of debating society or petty Parliament". The Members of the Council asked all kinds of questions from the Government which put the latter in a very awkward position. It was pointed out that the Council had become an Anglo-Indian House of Commons.

Act of 1861

The Indian Councils Act of 1861 provided that the Executive Council of the Governor-General was to be strengthened by the addition of not less than 6 and not more than 12 members nominated by the Governor-General for the purpose of legislation. Not less than half of the additional members were to be non-officials. They were to hold office for two years. The function of the Council was strictly limited to legislation and the Act expressly forbade the transaction of any other business by the Council. It was empowered "to make laws and regulations for all persons whether British or native, foreigners or others, and for all places and things whatever within the said territories, for all servants of the Government of India within the Dominions of Princes and States in alliance with Her Majesty".

However, many restrictions were put on the powers of the Central Legislature. The previous sanction of the Governor-General was made necessary for introducing any legislation concerning certain specified subjects such as public debt or public revenue, religion, military or naval matters or the relations of the Government with foreign princes or States. No law could be made which infringed the authority of the Home Government or violated the provisions of certain Acts made by Parliament. Governor-General was given the power of veto. In cases of emergency, he was authorized to issue ordinances which had the same force as any other law. These ordinances were to remain in force for 6 months. However, they could be dissolved or repealed earlier. As soon as an ordinance was issued, it had to be intimated to the Secretary of State. The approval of the Governor-General was made necessary for every Act passed. The right to disallow Acts was reserved for the Crown and the general authority of Parliament and the Crown was expressed preserved.

Act of 1892

The Indian Councils Act of 1892 also changed the position and powers of the Central or Imperial Legislature. The number of the additional members was increased. It was not to be less than 10 and more than 16 in the case of the Imperial Legislative Council. Two-fifths of the additional members were to be non-officials. The Government agreed to allow elections to be held in India under the rules. However, the members so elected were to take their seats after they were nominated by the Government.

The powers of the Legislative Council were increased. The members were allowed to discuss the annual financial statement under certain conditions and restrictions. They were given the power of asking questions from the Government on matters of public interest. A previous notice of 6 days was to be given to the Government for asking a question. The President might disallow any question without giving any reason. Questions on matters of public interest could be asked "subject to such conditions and restrictions as may be prescribed in rules made by the Governor-General or the Provincial Governors".

Act of 1909

The Indian Councils Act of 1909 increased the additional members of the Governor-General's Council to a maximum of 60. Out of these 37 were officials and 23 non-officials. Out of the 37 officials,

28 were nominated by the Governor-General, and the rest were to be ex-officio. The ex-officio members were the Governor-General, 6 ordinary members of the Council and 2 extraordinary members. As regards the non-official members, 5 members were nominated by the Governor-General and the rest were elected.

The functions of the Legislative Council were increased. Elaborate rules were made for the discussion of budget by the Council. Every member was given the right to move any resolution relating to any alteration in taxation, any new loan or any additional grants to local Governments, etc. The Council was not allowed to discuss expenditure on interest, on debt, ecclesiastical expenditure, expenditure on State Railways, etc. The members of the Legislative council were given the right of asking questions and supplementary questions for the purpose of further elucidating any point. However, the Executive Councilor might refuse to answer the supplementary question off-hand. He may demand some time for the same. The members of the Council were also given the right of moving resolutions. These resolutions had to be clearly and precisely expressed in the form of definite issues. The resolutions were not to contain arguments, inferences, ironical expressions, etc. The President might disallow any resolution or part of a resolution without giving any reason for the same.

Rules were framed under the Act for the discussion of matters of general public interest. No discussion was permitted on any subject not within the competence of the Legislature, or any matter affecting the relations of the Government of India with a Foreign Power or a native State, or any matter under adjudication by a Court of Law.

An indirect system of elections to the Imperial Council was introduced. Its members were to be elected by the elected members of the Provincial Legislatures.

It is clear that the powers enjoyed by the Imperial Legislative Council were not substantial. It is true that all forms of a parliamentary system of government were introduced, but the substance was lacking. The members of the Governor-General's Executive Council, who were in-charge of the various Departments, were not responsible to the members of the Legislature. They could ignore them with contempt and they actually did the same. The discussions in the legislature lacked reality because the members of the Legislature knew that they would never be called upon to shoulder the responsibilities of the Government whatever their criticism of the Government might be.

Act of 1919

The Government of India Act, 1919 set up a bicameral legislature at the Centre. The names of the two Houses were the Central Legislative Assembly and the Council of State. The Council of State consisted of 59 members out of which 34 were elected and 25 were nominated by the Governor-General. The Central Legislative Assembly consisted of 143 members, out of which 103 were elected and the rest were nominated. Out of the nominated numbers, 25 were officials and the rest were non-officials. Out of the 103 elected members, 51 were elected by the general constituencies, 32 by communal constituencies (30 by Muslims and 2 by Sikhs), and 20 by special constituencies (7 by landholders, 9 by Europeans and 4 by Indian Commerce).

The life of the Central Legislative Assembly was 3 years and the Council of State 5-years, but the same could be extended by the Governor-General. It is to be noted that the last Legislative Assembly sat for 11 years. The first Speaker of the Assembly was nominated by the Government, but the subsequent Speakers were elected by the members of the Assembly.

The Governor-General was given the power to summon, prorogue and dissolve both Houses of the Central Legislature.

The Central Legislature was given specific powers. It could make laws for the whole of British India, for the subjects of His Majesty and Services of the Crown in other parts of India, for the Indian subjects of His Majesty wherever they might happen to be, and for all persons employed in His Majesty's Defence Forces in India. It could also repeal or amend laws for the time being in force in

British India. In certain cases, the previous sanction of the Secretary of State-in-Council was required for passing any legislation. Likewise, the previous sanction of the Governor-General was required to introduce certain bills in the Legislature.

The members of both Houses of the Central Legislature were given the right of putting questions and supplementary questions, moving resolutions and motions of adjournment. The Central Legislature was not given complete control over the budget. There were certain non-voteable items in the budget over which the Legislature had no control. As regards the voteable items, the Assembly could reject them, but the Governor-General was given the power to restore those items if he thought that expenditure on those subjects were necessary for the safety and tranquillity of India.

It can safely be stated that the Central Legislature under the Act of 1919 was helpless before the Central Executive. The latter was not only independent of the Legislature, but also had the power of over-riding the Legislature in almost all respects.

Act of 1935

Under the Government of India Act, 1935, provision was made for a Federal Legislature of two Houses, viz., Federal Assembly and the Council of State. The Federal Assembly was to have a life of 5 years from the date of its first meeting. On the expiry of that period, it was to be automatically dissolved. However, the Governor-General was given the power to extend its life. The Council of State was to be a permanent body of which one-third members were to retire after every 3 years. The Federal Assembly was to consist of 375 members and the Council of State 260 members. The members from the States were to be nominated by the rulers. The representatives from British India were to be elected on communal lines.

The powers of the Legislature were severely restricted. There were certain subjects on which it could not legislate. It could not make any law affecting the sovereign or the Royal Family or the succession to the Crown, or the law of British nationality, or the law of prize courts, or the Army, the Air Force Act, etc. The Federal Legislature could not make any law amending any provision of the Government of India Act, 1935, or any Order-in-Council made under it, or any rules made there under by the Secretary of State or by the Governor-General or a Governor. It could not pass any law which discriminated against the British interests in commerce and other spheres. In certain cases, the previous sanction of the Governor-General was required for introducing certain bills in the Federal Legislature.

The Federal Legislature had no control over the non-voteable items of the budget. These non-voteable items constituted about 80 per cent of the Federal budget. If any item of the budget was rejected by the Federal Assembly, the same could be put before the Council of State if the Governor-General so directed. If the two Houses of the Federal Legislature differed with regard to any demand, the Governor-General was required to summon a joint sitting for voting on the demand and the decision of the majority was to prevail.

The Governor-General was given the power to summon a joint sitting of the two Houses of the Federal Legislature when a bill passed by one chamber was rejected by the other or was amended in a form to which the first chamber was not agreeable. After a bill was passed by both the chambers of the Federal Legislature, the Governor-General, in his discretion, might assent to it or veto it or send it back for reconsideration or reserve it for His Majesty's consultation. The Act assented to by the Governor-General could be disallowed within a year by the King-in-Council.

Constitution of 1950

Under the new Constitution of India which came into force on 26th January 1950, the Union Parliament consists of two Houses, namely, the Council of States and the House of the People. The total strength of the Council of States is 250. Out of these, 12 are nominated by the President for their special knowledge and experience of literature, science, art and social service. The remaining

238 are elected from the various States. The House of the People consists of 500 members. All the members are elected by the electors in the various States. For purposes of election to the House of the People, the States are divided, grouped or formed into territorial constituencies.

The Council of States is a permanent House. It cannot be dissolved. Its members are elected for 6 years. One-third of them retire after every two years. The House of the People has a maximum duration of 5 years from the date appointed for its first meeting. After 5 years the House of the People is to be dissolved automatically. However, this period of 5 years may be extended by Parliament for a period not exceeding one year at a time.

The Union Parliament has the power to make laws relating to all subjects on the Union List and the Concurrent List. Any State may authorise the Government of India to legislate on certain matters and in that case Parliament can pass laws on those subjects also although they are given in the State List. In the case of the breakdown of the constitutional machinery in a State, the Union Parliament has the right to make laws for that State even on subjects that are included in the State List. The Union Parliament has the power to make laws on any subjects in the State List if the Council of States passes a resolution by a two-thirds majority declaring such matter or matters to be of national importance and interest. The Union Parliament can amend the Constitution by a two-thirds majority. The Supreme Court can declare any laws passed by the Union Parliament to be ultra vires if it in any way conflicts with the Constitution.

The Parliament controls the national finance. The Government cannot levy taxes, borrow money or spend any money without the permission and authority of Parliament. But this does not apply to those items of expenditure which are a charge on the national revenues.

The Union ministers are members of the Union Parliament and are also responsible to it. They must resign if they are out-voted in Parliament or a vote of no-confidence is passed against them.

Laws passed by Parliament are not valid unless they receive the assent of the President. No cabinet can dare to tender advice to the President to veto a bill passed by Parliament. The latter has the power to impeach the President on the ground that he has violated the Constitution. The proposal may be preferred by any House by a two-thirds majority and then the other House has to investigate the charge. If it is approved by a two-thirds majority in that House, then the President can be removed from his office.

On the request of the members of Parliament to the President, the Judges of the High Courts and the Supreme Court can be removed from office.

The two Houses of Parliament have equal powers except as regards the money bills, which can be introduced only in the House of the People. Then these money bills can be sent to the Council of States. If amendments made by the Council of States are accepted, it is good, otherwise the money bill will be taken to have been passed by Parliament on the expiry of 30 days. Bills, other than money bills, may be introduced in any chamber and in the case of disagreement over a bill, there may be a joint sitting of the two Houses. If that bill is passed by a majority at the joint sitting, it is to be deemed to have been approved by both Houses.

GROWTH OF PROVINCIAL LEGISLATURES

The history of the growth of the Provincial Legislatures is both interesting and instructive. While tracing the origin of the legislative powers of the provinces we find that in 1797 the Presidency of Bengal was authorised to issue independent regulations within its jurisdiction. Similar powers were given in 1807 to the Presidencies of Madras and Bombay. The result of this was that each Presidency developed its own system of laws. It was found that there were conflicting laws in the various Presidencies. Such a thing was not considered to be in the interests of the country. Consequently, the Charter Act of 1833 deprived the Presidencies of Madras and Bombay of their power of legislation. All legislation for the whole of India was to be made by the Central Government. This resulted in over-centralisation. The Government of India could not understand and appreciate the needs of the various Presidencies. Complaints were made against the abuses of the system.

Charter Act of 1853
The Charter Act of 1853 tried to remove some of the defects of the system. It was provided that each Presidency was to send one representative to the Central Government and no legislative measure for any Presidency was to be considered by the Governor-General-in-Council without the presence of the Member from the Presidency concerned. Even this innovation was not a remedy for the evils of the existing system. Lord Canning held the view that a partial return to the system which existed before 1833 "was advisable".

Act of 1861
The Indian Council Act of 1861 reserved the process started by the Charter Act of 1833. The Presidencies of Madras and Bombay were given the power of making laws. For legislative purposes, the Executive Council of the Governor was to be expanded by the addition of not less than 2 and not more than 4 additional members. No demarcation was made between the jurisdictions of the Central and the Provincial Legislatures. In certain cases, the previous sanction of the Governor-General was required for legislation by the local councils. All the Acts passed by the Provincial Governments required the assent of the Governor and the Governor-General. In exercise of the powers given to the Governor-General by the Act of 1861, Legislative Councils were established in Bengal in 1862, in U.P. in 1866, etc. It is to be noted that the function of these Councils was purely legislative and nothing else. Even those laws were in reality the orders of the Government. In spite of the defects of the system, no change was made till 1892.

Act of 1892
The Indian Councils Act of 1892 enlarged the Legislative Councils of the various Provinces. The number of additional members was fixed at 20 for Bengal and 15 for North-West Province and Oudh. In the case of Bombay and Madras it was to be not less than eight and not more than twenty. A system of indirect elections was also provided for. Certain corporate bodies were given the power of electing representatives and those persons were to be nominated by the Governor. The members of the Councils were given the power of asking questions and discussing the financial statement. However, no right of asking supplementary questions was given. The members also could not reject the budget. This was no doubt an advance on the Act of 1861, but that advance was not considered to be adequate by the people.

Act of 1909
The next step was taken by the Indian Councils Act of 1909. The Provincial Legislatures were enlarged up to a limit of 50 additional members in the larger provinces and 30 in the smaller provinces. The majority of the members were to be elected. The system of nomination after election was given up. It was provided that corporate bodies were to elect members of an electoral college and the latter were to elect members of the provincial legislature. The Mohammedans were given special representation by this Act. They were to vote in the special constituencies of the Muslims alone. The members of the Provincial Legislatures were given the right of asking questions and supplementary questions. But the supplementary questions could be put only by the person who put the original question. The members were given the right of discussing the budget and passing resolutions on it. It was the duty of the Government to take those resolutions into consideration. As a matter of fact, the Government completely ignored those resolutions. Under the Act of 1909, the Provincial Legislatures were "essentially consultative committees attached to the Executive". The voting qualifications were so high that the number of voters in any constituency was very small. As the system of elections was indirect, the sense of responsibility was lacking. The Legislative Councils

were given no control over the Government or legislation. Their members could merely criticise with the full knowledge that they would never be called upon to shoulder the responsibility. The result was that the members were reckless in their criticism of the Government. The Government also regarded these Councils with contempt.

Act of 1919

The Government of India Act of 1919 made great changes in the composition and functions of the provincial legislatures. Each Provincial Legislative Council was to consist of the members of the Executive Council of the Governor and the elected and nominated members. The size of these Provincial Legislatures was enlarged. Provision was made for general and special constituencies. Representation was given to various communities and interests. The Muslims and the Sikhs were given separate representation. Provision was also made for representation to the landholders, planters, mining interests, commerce and industries, universities, etc. The franchise for the Provincial Councils was lowered. The normal qualifications of a voter were passed on community, residence, occupation of a house, assessment of Income-tax, receipt of a military pension, holding of a piece of land, etc. Provision was made for representation of women also.

The Act of 1919 provided for a dyarchical system of Government in the provinces. The Indian Ministers were in charge of the transferred subjects, and reserved subjects remained with the Governor and the members of his Executive Council. The Ministers were chosen by the Governors from the members of the Legislature. Provision was made for the election of a Speaker of the Legislative Council.

The Act provided for two Lists, viz., Central List and Provincial List. The Provincial Legislature was given the power to make laws on matters given in the Provincial List. Its members were given the power of moving and passing resolutions on different subjects. They were also given the power of asking questions and supplementary questions.

They were also empowered to move votes of censure against the Government. They were also allowed to demand the adjournment of the House to discuss important matters of recent occurrence. The Legislative Council was given the power to discuss the provincial budget and reject the same. However, it had no control over the non-voteable items of the budget. If the budget was rejected, the Governor was authorized to restore the same.

There were certain limitations on the legislative powers of the Provincial Councils. In order to introduce certain bills, the previous sanction of the Government of India and the Governor was required. Even when a bill was passed by the Provincial Legislature, the Governor was empowered to certify, veto or reserve the same for the consideration of the Governor-General.

Act of 1935

Under Government of India Act, 1935, Provision was made for the establishment of two Houses of the Provincial Legislature in six provinces and only one House in the five provinces. The Upper House was known as the Provincial Legislative Council and the Lower House as the Provincial Legislative Assembly. The Upper House consisted of 21 to 65 members. Some of its members were elected and the others nominated by the Governor. The Legislative Council was a permanent body and one-third of its members retired after every 3 years. There was no change of the whole House at one time.

The Lower House consisted of 60 to 250 members. The life of the Lower House was 5 years but it could be dissolved earlier by the Governor. Its life also could be extended beyond 5 years by the Governor. It was provided that money bills were to be introduced only in the Lower House, although otherwise the powers of the two Houses were made equal. In the case of a conflict between the two Houses, provision was made for a joint sitting of two Houses.

It is to be noted that the powers of the Provincial Legislatures under the Act of 1935 were circumscribed. They were not given complete control over legislation. Even their control over the budget was not complete. About 50 per cent of the provincial budget was non-voteable. The Provincial Legislatures could not accomplish much.

New Constitution of 1950

Under the new Constitution of India which came into force on 26th January 1950, no distinction is made between the Indian States and the Provinces. They are all called States. In certain States, provision is made for two Houses of the State Legislature and in certain others, provision is made for a uni-cameral Legislature. Where there are two Houses, their names are Legislative Assembly and Legislative Council. Where there is only one House, it is called the Legislative Assembly. Article 169 of the Constitution provides for the abolition or creation of Legislative Councils in the States.

Provision is made for direct elections to the State Assemblies on the basis of adult suffrage. Approximately, one representative is elected for every 75,000 of the population. The total membership of a state Assembly is to vary from 60 to 500 according to its population. The life of the Assembly is 5 years, but it can be dissolved earlier by the Governor. Its life may be extended on the ground of an emergency.

The total number of the members of the Legislative Council is not to exceed one-fourth of the total number of members in the Legislative Assembly of that State. However, its membership is not to fall below 40. All the members of a Legislative Council are not elected. Some of them are nominated by the Governor. Others are elected by Municipalities, District Boards, Graduates, Teachers and members of the Legislative Assembly. It is a permanent House. One-third of its members retire after every two years.

As regards the powers of the State Legislature, they can make laws on the subjects given in the State List and the Concurrent List. However, if the Union Parliament passes a law on a subject included in the Concurrent List, the State Legislature cannot pass a law on that subject. The Constitution has provided for responsible Government in the States. The Government is in the hands of the Ministers who are not only the members of the Legislature but also responsible to it. The State Legislature has the right to pass a vote of no confidence against the Ministry, reject the budget or pass resolutions or adjournment motions against the Government. The Legislatures are given autonomy in their own sphere.

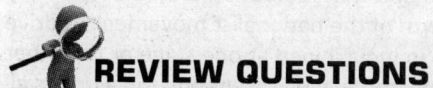

REVIEW QUESTIONS

1. Write an essay on the growth of the central legislature.
2. Discuss the history of the growth of the provincial legislatures.
3. Describe the provisions of the Charter Acts and the Government of India Acts.
4. The Government of India Act, 1919 made great changes in the composition and functions of the provincial legislatures. Discuss.
5. Write short notes on the following:
   (a) The Indian Councils Acts
   (b) The Government of India Acts
   (c) Constitution of India

SUGGESTED READING

Sharan, Parmatma: *The Imperial Legislative Council of India*, 1961.

21. The Nationalist Movement in India

LEARNING OBJECTIVES

- Discuss the nature and causes of the Nationalist Movement in India
- Trace the emergence of Indian National Congress and discuss the various stages of genesis of Indian National Congress
- Evaluate the part played by the moderates and extremists in the Indian National Movement
- Learn about the formation of Home Rule League and Ghadar Party

ITS NATURE

It is wrong to say that the Nationalist Movement in India was the result of a few agitators. Basically, nationalism in India arose to meet the challenge of foreign domination. The very existence of a foreign rule helped the growth of a national sentiment among the people. There was also a clash between the British interests in India and those of the Indian people. The British had conquered India to promote their own interests and they ruled over her primarily with that object in view. With the passage of time, there was a realisation in India and that realisation brought bitterness against foreign rule and that was responsible for the growth of the nationalist movement to drive out the foreigners from the country. All classes of people in India joined at one stage or the other the nationalist movement. The intelligentsia in India, the peasants, the artisans and the workers all played their part in the freedom struggle.

CAUSES

1. The nationalist movement in India was the outcome of a large number of factors and the most important among them was British imperialism. It was during the British rule that the whole of India was conquered and brought under one sovereign authority. This domination by one country over the whole of India enabled the people of India to think and act as one nation. Before the coming of the British to India, the people of the South were usually separated, from the rest of India except for short intervals. British imperialism helped the process of the unification of the country. Prof. Moon rightly says: "British imperialism in India gave her a political unity under a third party in spite of the many discordant elements in Indian society".

2. The improvements in the means of transport and communication also quickened the pace of the nationalist movement in the country. The Indian leaders found themselves in a position to carry on their propaganda in every nook and corner of the country. Without those means of communication and transport, such a thing would have been unthinkable. The frequent meetings of the leaders among themselves and their personal contact with the people in different parts of the country gave a momentum to the nationalist movement.

3. Many scholars, poets and religious reformers contributed towards the progress of the nationalist movement. The study and publication of the ancient Indian literature by the Asiatic Society of Bengal and scholars like Max Muller, Monier Williams, Colebrooke, Ranade, Hari Prasad Shastri, R.G. Bhandarkar, Rajendra Lal Mitra, etc., revealed to the people of India the majesty of the Sanskrit language and also inculcated among them a feeling of pride in their past and their faith in the future.

4. The religious and social reformers like Raja Ram Mohan Roy, Keshab Chandra Sen, Debendra Nath Tagore, Ishwar Chandra Vidyasagar, Swami Dayanand Saraswati, Ramakrishna Paramhans, Vivekanand and others exercised a tremendous influence on the people of India and they were responsible in different ways in putting the people of India on the road to progress. It is contended that political agitation in India began with Raja Ram Mohan Roy. His study of English literature, history and parliamentary institutions acquainted him with the western political ideas and he introduced the methods of political agitation by petitions, pamphlets, memorials, public meetings and the press. He was a great lover of liberty. To him, liberty was indivisible. The enslavement of one section of humanity was incompatible with the liberty of another section. He followed with intense interest the course of the French Revolution. He is said to have given a public dinner in the Town Hall of Calcutta as a mark of his joy at the establishment of constitutional government in Spain. Keshab Chandra Sen also made his contribution towards the cause of nationalism by helping the movement for social and religious reform. The missionaries of the Brahmo Samaj carried their message of new religious and social freedom far and wide all over the Indian continent.

Swami Dayanand Saraswati founded the Arya Samaj. He preached to the people of India the lesson of self-confidence and faith in their future; He reminded them of the glory and greatness of India's past and exhorted his audience to leave no stone unturned to make India great. He declared that good government was no substitute for self-government and the rule of India by the Indians was to be preferred in every way. It is well-known that many leaders of the Arya Samaj like Lala Lajpat Rai played a glorious part in the nationalist movement of the country. Col. Olcott has rightly pointed out that Swami Dayanand exercised "great nationalising influence upon his followers". The view of Annie Besant was: "It was Dayanand Saraswati who proclaimed India for the Indians.

Ramakrishna Paramhans exercised great influence on his followers. He has rightly been given the credit of assisting the growth of national consciousness among the people. The Ramakrishna Math and Mission have in many ways helped the cause of self-consciousness among the people of India. Swami Vivekanand was the pupil of Ramakrishna Paramhans and he in his own way helped the people of India in reviving their faith in themselves and also in the future of the country. About Swami Vivekanand, Niveditta says: "The queen of his adoration was the motherland". Like Swami Dayanand, Swami Vivekanand taught young India self-confidence and self-reliance. The founders of the Theosophical Society of India and Mrs. Annie Besant made their own contribution towards the cause of the national awakening. They asked the people of India to realise that they were not so bad as the Christian missionaries painted them to be. They were as good as many advanced people of the world were. They asked the people of India to look to their glorious past and try to bring back: the same. They taught people to have faith in themselves.

5. The Indian press and literature, both English and Vernacular, also aroused national consciousness. Great was the influence of newspapers like the Indian Mirror, the Bombay Samachar, the Hindu Patriot, The Amrita Bazar Patrika, The Hindu, The Kesari, The Bengalee, The Hurkura, The Bengal Public Opinion, The Reis and Rayet, the Somprokash, The Sulabh Samachar, The Sanjibam, The Sadharm, The Hitavadi, The Rast Goftar, The Indu Prakash, The Standard, The Swadeshmitran, The Herald of Bihar, The Advocate of Lucknow, etc., on the

political life of the country. The growth of the Indian press was phenomenal and by 1875; there were no less than 478 newspapers in the country. Without them, it would have been impossible to create an atmosphere in which the people of India could be made to think of their common problems and common grievances. Undoubtedly, the Indian Press played a meritorious role in not only creating a national awakening in the country but also guiding the people of India throughout their struggle for independence. It goes without saying that the Indian press also paid a part of the price for the freedom of the country. The Indian press was the target of the British Government from the very beginning, but it boldly and fearlessly faced the challenge.

The writings of Dinbandhu Hemchandra Banerjee, Navin Chandra Sen, R. C. Dutt, Rabindra Nath Tagore and Bankim Chandra Chatterjee affected the minds of the people of India. Through his writings, Rabindra Nath Tagore appealed to the higher sentiments of the people of India to work for the glory of their country. He tried to raise the moral tone of his countrymen. The Anand Math of Bankim Chandra Chatterji which embodied the patriotic song "Bande Mataram" (Hail to the Mother), has rightly been called "The Bible of Modern Bengalee patriotism".

6. It goes without saying that the concepts of nationality and patriotism were known to the Indians throughout their history. Ancient literature and religious texts testify to a well-defined image of Mother India and to a closer consciousness of national solidarity. The ancient Indians gave it the name of Bharatvarsha or simply Bharat. The Puranas expressly define the term Bharat as the country that lies north of the Indian Ocean and south of the snowy Himalayas. The Hindu consciousness of national frontiers is illustrated in their institution of pilgrimages which expects a Hindu to visit the various holy places, distributed throughout the length and breadth of the country.

7. There was a lot of discontentment in the country on account of many causes and that discontentment gave a stimulus to the growth of the nationalist movement in the country. The masses suffered from economic troubles. The middle classes suffered from the bugbear of unemployment. All the intelligent Indians felt and bewailed the economic exploitation of their country. The British officials working in India were a very heavy drain on the Indian resources. The economic system of India was adjusted to the needs of the people of England. The interests of the Indians were completely ignored. Blunt rightly points out that the vice of Indian finance was that the Finance Minister of India looked more to the interests of Great Britain than to those of India. All tariff duties were abolished in 1879 with a view to benefit Lancashire. In 1895, an excise duty of 5 per cent was imposed on Indian cotton goods with a view to countervail similar tariff on Lancashire goods imposed in the interests of revenue. The value of the Indian rupee in terms of the English pound was fixed in such a way as to help imports from England and discourage exports from India. Sir Henry Cotton condemned the economic exploitation of India and the consequent miseries of the people of the country. The Indians resented the attitude of the Englishmen towards them, The Europeans in India were arrogant. They had a very low opinion of the Indian character. They took pleasure in calling the Indians the creatures of an inferior breed, "half Gorilla, half Negro". They ridiculed the Indian black heathens "worshipping stocks and stones and swinging themselves on bamboo trees like bees". The European masters regarded the Indians as "the helots of the land, the hewers of wood and the drawers of water". The life of an Indian was estimated by most Europeans as no higher than that of a dog. In 1819, Sir Thomas Munro confessed that although the foreign conquerors have treated the natives with violence and cruelty, they had not treated them with so much scorn as the Englishmen had done. Seton Kerr, a Secretary to the Government of India, spoke of the "cherished conviction which was shared by every

Englishman in India, from, the highest to the lowest...the conviction in every man that he belongs to a race which God has destined to govern and subdue". Lord Roberts, who at one time was the Commander-in-Chief of India, did not regard even the bravest of the Indian soldiers as equal to a British officer.

There was a lopsided development of the Indian economy. While Indian handicrafts and industries were allowed to starve, Indian agriculture was encouraged with a purpose. Most of the raw materials were produced in the country so that those could be used to feed the industries in England. That policy made India dependent on England. The free trade policy helped the British manufacturers and sacrificed the interests of India. The public debt increased tremendously. After 1858, the Crown took over the entire debt of 70 millions from the English East India Company. Between 1858 and 1876, the public debt was practically doubled. Out of the additional debt, only about 24 millions were spent on the construction of railways and irrigation works. No proper use of the money was made while constructing the railways. Those who constructed them were given more than what was due to them.

Before the outbreak of the Mutiny in 1857, there were many Englishmen who honestly believed and worked for the good of India. However, during the Mutiny days a lot of blood was shed on both sides. The Europeans wreaked their vengeance on the helpless and innocent Indians after the Mutiny. It was this policy of oppression and repression, which added to the discontent of the country. The Indians were completely excluded from the legislatures in the country and also from the key-posts in the administration.

8. The English language played a very important part in the growth of nationalism in the country. It acted as the lingua franca of the intelligentsia of India. Without the common medium of the English language, it would have been out of the question for the Madrasis, Bengalees and the Punjabis to sit at one table and discuss the common problems facing the country. The English language also made the Indians inheritors of a great literature, which was full of great ideas and ideals.

9. The ground was ready and acts of omission and commission in the time of Lord Lytton accelerated the nationalist movement. The period from 1876 to 1884 has been called the seedtime of Indian nationalism. Lord Lytton held his famous Delhi Durbar in 1877 at a time when the people of South India were suffering terribly from the destruction brought about by famine. They wondered at the callousness of Lytton. An appropriate comment was made in these words: "Nero was fiddling while Rome was burning". The second Afghan War cost the Indian treasury a lot. No wonder, the Indians criticised Lytton mercilessly. In order to gag the Indian public opinion, Lytton passed the notorious Vernacular Press Act in 1878; The discriminatory provisions of this Act were universally condemned by the people belonging to all walks of life. Sir Erskine Perry points out that the Act was "a retrograde and ill-conceived measure injurious to the future progress of India". It was called the Gagging Act. Lytton passed the Arms Act in 1878 which made an invidious distinction between the Indians and the Europeans. While the Europeans were allowed to keep arms freely, the Indians could not do so without a licence. In the words of Surendra Nath Banerjee, the Arms Act "imposed upon us a badge of racial inferiority". Such a measure was derogatory to the self-respect of the people of India. Lord Lytton removed the import duty on cotton manufacturers with a view to help the British manufacturers and this was resented by the Indians. It is true Lord Ripon tried to remove some of the grievances of India but before he could do so, the Ilbert Bill controversy came to the fore.

10. The Ilbert Bill was a simple measure whose object was to put the Indian judges on the same footing as the European judges in dealing with all cases in Bengal Presidency. The necessity of this bill arose as the Indians who had joined the judicial service were rising in the ranks

and that involved the possible trial of Europeans by an Indian judge, without a jury. This was considered to be too much by the Europeans. A strong agitation was brought into existence by the Europeans who were not prepared to be tried by an Indian judge. Lord Ripon became the target of the agitation. He was boycotted by the European community. He was threatened to be kidnapped to England. Ultimately a compromise was arrived at which suited the Europeans. However, this set a wrong precedent. The flag of racialism was hoisted by the Europeans. The Indians realised that they could not expect any justice or fair play from the Englishmen when their own interests were involved. Surendranath Banerjee observes: "No self-respecting Indian could sit idle under the fierce light of that revelation. It was a call to high patriotic duty to those who understood its significance". Before the effect of the Ilbert Bill controversy was over, the Indians had already organised themselves into the Indian National Conference which was the forerunner of the Indian National Congress founded in 1885.

GENESIS OF INDIAN NATIONAL CONGRESS

There is no unanimity of opinion regarding the origin of the Indian National Congress. Dr. Pattabhi Sitaramayya says that the origins of the Congress are "shrouded in mystery". There are many accounts and theories about it.

1. The most widely accepted view is that Hume, under the protection of Lord Dufferin, organised the Congress with two main purposes and those were to provide a "safety-valve" to the anticipated or actual discontentment of the Indian intelligentsia and to form a quasi-constitutional party similar to her Majesty's Opposition in England. The view of W.C. Bonnerjee, the First Congress President, was that the Indian National Congress as it was originally started, was in reality the work of Lord Dufferin, Governor-General of India. According to him, when Hume in 1884 conceived the idea that it would be a great advantage to the country if leading Indian politicians could be brought together once a year to discuss social matters and be upon friendly footing with one another, he did not desire that politics should form part of their discussions. Hume was also of the view that the Governor of the province, where the politicians met, should be asked to preside and thereby cordiality should be established between the official classes and the non-official Indian politicians. With these ideas, Hume met Lord Dufferin at Simla early in 1885. The Viceroy showed keen interest in the matter and after considering it for some time, he sent for Hume and told him that in his opinion his project would not be of much use. He suggested to him that there was no body of persons in India who performed the functions which Her Majesty's Opposition did in England. Dufferin's view was that Indian politicians should meet every year and point out to the Government in what respects the administration was defective and how the same could be improved. The assembly proposed by him should not be presided over by the local Governor. It is contended that Hume was convinced of the argument of Dufferin and when he placed the two schemes, his own and that of Dufferin, before the leading politicians in Calcutta, Bombay, Madras and other parts of the country, the latter unanimously accepted Dufferin's scheme and proceeded to give effect to it.

2. Professor Sundar Raman has given a slightly different version of the same theory. According to him, Dufferin persuaded Hume to stay on and work in India rather than go back to England and work from there. The idea of Hume was to arouse the consciousness of the people of England by carrying on agitation in England. However, Dufferin convinced Hume that the latter could secure his own aims best by confining the agitation to India for the present and by helping the Indian public men all over the country to organise and develop a national organisation in India conducted by her own leaders with the help and sympathy of men like Hume.

   A similar view was expressed by Gokhale in 1913 in these words: "No Indian could have started the Indian National Congress. Apart from the fact that any one putting his hand to such a gigantic task had need to have Mr. Hume's commanding personality, even if an Indian had possessed such a personality and had come forward to start such a movement embracing all India, the officials would not have allowed it to come into existence. If the founder of the Congress had not been a great Englishman and a distinguished ex-official, such was the distrust of political agitation in those days that the authorities would have at once found some way or the other of suppressing the movement".

3. There is another theory, which attributes Hume's initiative to the fear of a rebellion of the peasants, especially in Northern India. There are two versions of the theory. One view is that Hume came to know of the impending calamity while still a member of the Indian Civil Service through the secret reports from the C.I.D. The other view is that Hume got the information not from official sources but from reports from Chelas and Gurus (disciples and masters). It was through them that Hume got access to 7 large volumes containing references to a general state of rebellion in Northern India. Critics point out that the theory of rebellion has no historical basis and it was merely for propaganda value.

4. Another view is that the Theosophical Society of India was the parent of the Indian National Congress. Olcott asserted in 1886 that the Theosophical Society had first shown the possibility of bringing men from different parts of India together into friendly relations which had never been known before. Raghunath Rao and N.N. Sen virtually accused Hume of having stolen their thunder. Their contention was that the real origin of the Congress should be traced back to the meeting held at Raghunath Rao's house in Madras late in December 1884. Rejecting this view, critics point out that the idea of holding annual conferences of representative men from different parts of the country in order to promote national objectives had been current in India long before the founders of the Theosophical Society landed in Bombay in February 1879.

5. The view of Dr. Nand Lal Chatterji is that the "Congress was founded in fact as a precautionary move against an apprehended Russian invasion of India". The relations between Russia and Afghanistan were very strained over the question of Punjdeh and there was a danger of Great Britain being involved in it. The fear of Russian advance in Central Asia worried the Government of India and the people of India gave a demonstration of their loyalty to the Crown by offering themselves as volunteers for the defence of their country. The Indian Press and the educated Indians demanded the organisation of a Volunteer Corps. The attitude of the Government was unsympathetic towards the movement which died out as the danger of Russian invasion receded. It is pointed out that Russophobia and the Volunteer Movement worked as a lever to political activity in India. The prevailing atmosphere in the country was conducive to the birth and growth of an all-India political organisation. It was in March 1885 that the Russian danger was at its highest and it was then that Hume met the Viceroy and explained to him his proposal to organise the Indian National Congress and succeeded in securing the neutrality, if not active support, of the Viceroy. Thus, Russophobia played its part in the creation of the Indian National Congress.

6. Another view gives the Congress an "impressive origin, a birth in substance, a spontaneous character". It is contended that "its roots are to be discovered in the separate political associations in various parts of India. It was watered by the controversies over the Vernacular Press Act, the Arms Act, the reduction of the age limit for entrance into the Indian Civil Service and the Ilbert Bill. Another view is that the Congress was "the first rich harvest of what had been sown long before by the wise and beneficent statesmen in the shape of schools and colleges". The view of Surendranath Banerjee is that the Congress was the "outcome of those civilising influences which Macaulay and his co-adjutors were instrumental in implanting in the Government of the country". Wedderburn regarded the Congress as "the direct result of the noblest efforts of the British statesmen, the

rational and healthy fruit of higher education and free institutions" granted to the people of India. The Congress was a visible embodiment of the national awakening in India as a result of the impact of Western civilisation on Indian thought.

FIRST SESSION OF CONGRESS

The first meeting of the Indian National Union which was subsequently renamed the Indian National Congress was to be held at Poona but its venue had to be shifted to Bombay. Originally it had been decided to request Lord Reay, Governor of Bombay, to be the first President of the Indian National Congress but the idea had to be dropped as the Governor was advised by the Viceroy not to accept the offer. In his place. W.C. Bonnerjee, a leading Barrister of Calcutta and a very safe and loyal person, was elected the first President. 72 delegates came from different parts, of the country and most important among them were Dadabhai Naoroji, Ranade, Pherozeshah Mehta, K.T. Telang, Dinshaw Wacha, etc. The meeting was truly a national gathering consisting of leading men from all parts of India.

SECOND SESSION OF CONGRESS

The second meeting of the Indian National Congress was held at Calcutta and was presided over by Dadabhai Naoroji. Dadabhai praised the blessings of the British rule in India and he was cheered by the members of the audience. Hume moved a resolution for three cheers for Her Most Gracious Majesty, the Queen Empress and a further resolution for the long life of the Queen. He also advised his colleagues to look upon Dufferin not as an enemy but as a friend and well-wisher. Dufferin invited the members of the Congress as "distinguished visitors" to a garden party at the Government House. A similar welcome was given by the Governor of Madras in 1887.

However, a change took place in the attitude of the Government. After the Madras session in 1887, an aggressive propaganda was started among the masses. Hume published a pamphlet entitled "An Old Man's Hope" in which he appealed to the people of England in these words: "Ah Men! well-fed and happy! Do you at all realise the dull misery of these countless myriads? From their births to their deaths, how many rays of sunshine think you chequer their gloom-shrouded paths? Toil Toil, Toil; hunger, hunger, hunger; sickness, suffering, sorrow; these alas, alas, alas are the key-notes of their short and sad existence".

In December 1889, the Congress Session was held at Bombay under the Chairmanship of Sir William wedderburne. It was attended by Charles Bradlaugh, a member of British Parliament. He addressed the Congress in these words: "For whom should I work if not for the people? Born of the people, trusted by the people, I will die for the people".

LAHORE SESSION

Dadabhai Naoroji was re-elected as the President of the Lahore Session of the Congress held in December 1893. His travel from Bombay to Lahore presented the spectacle of a procession. Citizens of the various places on the way presented him addresses. At the Sikh Golden Temple at Amritsar, he was given a robe of honour. He brought the following message from the Irish members of the British Parliament: "Don't forget to tell your colleagues at the Congress that every one of the Ireland's Home Rule members in Parliament is at your back in the cause of the Indian people". Addressing the audience at the Session, Dadabhai declared: "Let us always remember that we are children of our mother country. Indeed, I have never worked in any other spirit than that I am an Indian and owe duty to my work and all my countrymen. Whether I am a Hindu or a Mohammedan, a Parsi, a Christian, or of any other creed, I am above all an Indian. Our country is India, our nationality is Indian".

The next session of the Congress was held in Madras in 1894 under the Presidentship of Alfred Webb, an Irish member of the British Parliament. The next session was held at Poona in 1895 and was presided over by Surendranath Banerjee. Gokhale presided over the Banaras Session of the Congress in 1905. The next session was held at Calcutta in 1906 under the Presidentship of Dadabhai Naoroji. On that occasion, Dadabhai unfurled the flag of Swaraj for India and four resolutions on self-government, boycott, Swadeshi and national education were passed.

THE MODERATES (1885-1905)

The early Congressmen who dominated the affairs of the Indian National Congress from 1885 to 1905 were known as the Moderates. They belonged to a class, which was Indian in blood and colour but British in tastes, in opinions, in morals and in intellect. They were supporters of British institutions. They believed that what India needed was a balanced and lucid presentation of her needs before the Englishmen and their Parliament and their demands were bound to be satisfied. They had faith in the British sense of justice and fairplay. India's connection with the West through England was considered to be a boon and not a curse.

The Moderates believed in loyalty to the British Crown. This fact is clearly brought out by the statements made from time to time by the Moderate leaders. Dadabhai Naoroji is said to have observed thus: "Let us speak out like men and proclaim that we are loyal to the backbone; that we understand the benefits the English rule has conferred upon us". Surendranath Banerjee described his attitude towards England in these words: "Let us work...with unwavering loyalty to the British connection... . Then will the Congress have fulfilled its mission—justified the hopes of those who founded it, one who worked for it...not by the supersession of British rule in India, but by broadening its basis, liberalizing its spirit, ennobling its character, and placing it upon the unchangeable foundations of a nation's affections. It is not severance that we look forward to—but unification, permanent embodiment, as an integral part of that great Empire which has given the rest of the world the models of free institutions ... covered the world with free states". Again, "To England we look for guidance. To England we look for sympathy in the struggle. From England must come the crowning mandate which will enfranchise our peoples. England is our political guide and our moral preceptor in the exalted sphere of political duty. English history has taught those principles of freedom which we cherish with our lifeblood. We have been fed upon the strong food of English constitutional freedom".

The Moderates relied upon the solemn pledges given by the British Government to the people of India from time to time and the Queen's Proclamation of 1858 was one of them. Surendranath Banerjee called this proclamation as "The Magna Carta of our rights and liberties". He went to the extent of saying that "The Proclamation, the whole Proclamation and nothing but the Proclamation is our watchword, our battle cry and the ensign of victory. It is the gospel of our political redemption".

The Moderates believed in orderly progress and constitutional agitation. They believed in patience, steadiness, conciliation and union. To quote Surendranath Banerjee, "The triumphs of liberty are not to be won in a day. Liberty is a jealous goddess, exacting in her worship and claiming from her votaries prolonged and assiduous devotion". In 1887, Congress President Badruddin Tyabji observed: "Be moderate in your demands, just in your criticism, correct in your facts and logical in your conclusions". Dr. Rash Behari Ghosh is said to have observed: "You must have patience. You must learn to wait and everything will come to you in time".

The Moderates believed in constitutional agitation within the four corners of law. They believed that their main task was to educate the people, to arouse national political consciousness and to create a united public opinion on political questions. For this purpose they held meetings. They criticised the Government through the press. They drafted and submitted memorials and petitions to the Government, to the officials of the Government of India and also to the British Parliament. They also worked to influence the British Parliament and British public opinion. The object of the memorials and petitions was to enlighten the British public and political leaders about the conditions prevailing in India. Deputations of leading Indian leaders were sent to Britain in 1889. A British

Committee of the Indian National Congress was founded in 1906 and that Committee started a journal called "India". Dadabhai Naoroji spent a major part of his life and income in Britain doing propaganda among its people and politicians.

The object before the Moderates was "wider employment of India's in higher offices in the public service and the establishment of representative institutions". Surendranath Banerjee pointed out that "They lay at the root of all other Indian problems. If power were vested in us to legislate and to control the finances and to carry on the administration through and by our men, in accordance with the principles laid down by our representatives, we should have self-government in the true sense". This could be accomplished by the goodwill and cooperation of the British people. With their firm faith in the values of Western culture and the sense of justice of the Englishmen, no other attitude was possible. They believed in slow progress towards democracy which according to many of them was an exotic plant that would take time to get acclimatised to the Indian soil and involve long training for the people to get used to it.

The Moderates were fully aware of the fact that India was a nation in the making Indian nationhood was gradually coming into being and could not be taken for granted as an accomplished fact. They worked constantly for the development and consolidation of the feeling of national unity irrespective of region, caste or religion. They hoped to make a humble beginning in this direction by promoting close contacts and friendly relations among the people from different parts of the country. The economic and political demands of the Moderates were formulated with a view to unify the Indian people on the basis of a common political programme. They organised a powerful all-India agitation against the abandonment of tariff-duties on imports and against the imposition of cotton excise duties. This agitation aroused the feelings of the people and helped them to realise the real aims and purposes of British rule in India.

The Moderates carried on agitation for the reduction of heavy land revenue payments. They urged the Government to provide cheap credit to the peasantry through agricultural banks and to make available irrigation facilities on a large scale. They asked for improvement in the conditions of work of the plantation labourers. They demanded a radical change in the existing pattern of taxation and expenditure which put a heavy burden on the poor while leaving the rich, especially the foreigners, with a very light load. They demanded the abolition of salt tax which hit the poor and lower middle classes hard.

The Moderates complained of India's growing poverty and economic backwardness and put all the blame on the policies of the British Government. They blamed the Government for the destruction of the indigenous industries in the country. They demanded the rapid development of the modern industries and wanted the Government to give tariff protection to the Indian industries. They advocated the use of Swadeshi goods and the boycott of British goods. They demanded that the economic drain of India by England must stop.

The Moderates criticised the individual administrative measures and worked hard to reform the administrative system which was ridden with corruption, inefficiency and oppression. They demanded the Indianisation of the higher grades of the administrative services. The demand was put forward on economic, political and moral grounds. Economically, the high salaries paid to the Europeans put a heavy burden on Indian finance and contributed to the economic drain. The Europeans sent out of India a large part of their salaries and also got their pensions in England. That added to the drain of wealth from India. Politically, the European civil servant ignored the needs of the Indians and favoured the European capitalists at the cost of their Indian counterparts. It was hoped that the Indianisation of the services would make the administration more responsive to Indian needs, Morally, the existing system dwarfed the Indian character reducing the tallest Indian to permanent inferiority in his own country.

The Moderates demanded the separation of the judiciary from the executive. They were opposed to the policy of disarming the people of India by the Government. They wanted the

Government to spend more money on the spread of education in the country. They also took up the cause of the Indians who had migrated to the British colonies.

The Moderates opposed tooth and nail the restrictions imposed by the Government on the freedom of speech and the press. In 1897, Tilak and many other leaders were arrested and sentenced to long terms of imprisonment for spreading disaffection against the Government through their speeches and writings. The Natu brothers of Poona were deported without trial. The arrest of Tilak marked the beginning of a new phase of the Nationalist movement. The Amrita Bazar Patrika wrote: "There is scarcely a home in this vast country where Tilak is not now the subject of melancholy talk and where his imprisonment is not considered as a domestic calamity".

The Moderates demanded the expansion and reform of the existing Legislative Councils. They demanded the introduction of the system of direct elections and an increase in the number of members and powers of the Legislative Councils. It is true that their agitation forced the Government to pass the Indian Councils Act of 1892, but the Moderates were not satisfied with what was given to the people of India. No wonder, they declared the Act of 1892 as a "hoax". They demanded a larger share for the Indians in the Legislative Councils. Later on, the Moderates put forward the claim for Swarajya or self-government within the British empire on the model of the other self-governing colonies.

The basic weakness of the Moderates lay in their narrow social base Their movement did not have a wide appeal. The area of their influence was limited to the urban community. As they did not have the support of the masses, they declared that the time was not ripe for throwing out a challenge to the foreign rulers. That was likely to invite premature repression. To quote Gokhale, "You do not realise the enormous reserve of power behind the Government. If the Congress were to do anything such as you suggest, the Government would have no difficulty in throttling it in "five minutes". However, it must not be 'presumed that the Moderate leaders fought for their narrow interests. Their programmes and policies championed the cause of all sections of the Indian people and represented nation-wide interests against colonial exploitation.

ATTITUDE OF THE GOVERNMENT

As regards the attitude of the Government towards the Moderates, it became hostile soon after the inception of the Indian National Congress. Lord Dufferin looked upon the foundation of the Congress with suspicion in 1887, he attacked the Congress and ridiculed it as representing a "microscopic minority of the people". Hamilton, Secretary of State for India, accused the Congress leaders of possessing "seditious and double-sided character". He went to the extent of abusing Dadabhai Naoroji and declared that Dadabhai's residence and association with radical and socialist British leaders had "deteriorated whatever brains or presence of mind he may originally have possessed". The British officers publicly criticised and condemned the Indian National congress and its leaders. They were branded as "disloyal Babus," "seditious Brahmins" and "violent villains".

The Congress was described as a "factory of sedition" and the Congressmen as disappointed candidates for office and discontented lawyers who represented no one but themselves. Lord Curzon declared in 1900: "The Congress is tottering to its fall and one of my great ambitions, while in India, is to assist it to a peaceful demise". He described the Congress as an "unclean thing". Some Englishmen accused the Indian National Congress of receiving the Russian gold. Lord Elgin openly threatened the Indians in 1898 in these words: "India was conquered by the sword and by the sword it shall be held".

The British officials relied upon the policy of "divide and rule" to weaken the nationalist movement. They encouraged Sir Syed Ahmed Khan, Raja Shiv Prasad and other pro-British Indians to start an anti-Congress movement. They tried to drive a wedge between the Hindus and Muslims. They fanned communal rivalries among the educated Indians on the question of jobs in Government service.

ACHIEVEMENTS OF THE MODERATES

If we critically evaluate the work of the Moderates, it appears that they did not achieve much success. Very few of the reforms advocated by them were carried out. The foreign rulers treated them with contempt. To quote Lala Lajpat Rai, "After more than 20 years of more or less futile agitation for concessions and redress of grievances, they had received stones in place of bread". The Moderates failed to acquire any roots among the common people and even those who joined the Congress with high hopes, were feeling more and more disillusioned. The politics of the Moderates were described as "halting and half-hearted". Their methods were described as those of mendicancy or beggary through prayers and petitions.

The Moderates failed to keep pace with the yearnings and aspirations of the people. They failed to understand and appreciate the impatience of the people who were suffering under the foreign yoke. They did not realise that the political and economic interests of the Indians and the British clashed and consequently the British people could not be expected to give up their rights and privileges in India without a fight. Moreover, it was during this period that a movement started among the Muslims to keep away from the Congress and that ultimately resulted in the establishment of Pakistan. In spite of their best efforts, the Moderates were not able to win over the Muslims.

It is wrong to say that the political record of the Moderates was a barren one. Taking into consideration the difficulties they had to confront with at that time, the Moderates achieved a lot. It is their achievements in the wider sense that led later on to the more advanced stages of the nationalist movement. The Moderates represented the most aggressive forces of the time. They made possible a decisive shift in Indian politics. They succeeded in creating a wide political awakening and in arousing among the middle and lower middle-class Indians and the intelligentsia the feeling that they belonged to one common nation. They made the people of India conscious of the bonds of common political, economic and cultural interests and the existence of a common enemy and thus helped to weld them into a common nationality. They popularised among the people the ideas of democracy and civil liberty. They did pioneering work in mercilessly exposing the true character of British imperialism in India. Even though they were moderate in politics and political methods, they successfully brought to light the most important political and economic aspects of the Indian reality that India was being ruled by a foreign power for economic exploitation. The agitation of the Moderates in the economic field completely undermined the moral foundations of British rule in India.

This was the seedtime of Indian nationalism. The Moderates sowed the seeds well and deep. They evolved a common political and economic programme which united the different sections of the people. In spite of their many failures, they laid strong foundations for the national movement to grow upon and they deserve a high place among the makers of modern India. To quote Gokhale, "Let us not forget that we are at a stage of the country's progress when our achievements are bound to be small, and our disappointments frequent and trying. That is the place, which it has pleased Providence to assign to us in this struggle, and our responsibility is ended when we have done the work which belongs to that place. It will, no doubt, be given to our countrymen of future generations to serve India by their successes; we, of the present generation, must be content to serve her mainly by our failures. For, hard though it be out of those failures the strength will come which in the end will accomplish great tasks". Again, "The minds of the people have been familiarised with the idea of a united India working for her salvation; a national public opinion has been created; close bonds of sympathy now knit together the different provinces; castes and creeds hamper less and less the pursuit of common aims; the dignity of a consciousness of national existence has spread over the whole land. Above all, there is a general perception now of the goal towards which we have to strive and a wide recognition of the arduous character of the struggle and the immense sacrifices it requires".

THE SURAT SPLIT (1907)

In 1907, there was a split in the Congress and the Moderates parted company with the Extremists. That split was due to many causes. The Moderates had controlled the Congress from its very beginning and even now they were in control of it. They had their own ways of thinking and doing which were not acceptable to the younger generation who were impatient with the speed at which the Moderates were moving and leading the nation. Under the circumstances, a confrontation between the two was inevitable and that actually happened in 1907.

1. There were fundamental differences between the Moderates and the Extremists on the question of loyalty to the English throne and the continuance of British rule in India. The Moderates believed in loyalty to the English throne. They also believed that the continuance of the British rule was in the interests of the people of India. The view of the Extremists was that the British rule in India was a curse and the question of loyalty to the English throne did not arise at all.

2. Another difference between the two was regarding the emphasis on the ultimate goal as well as the actual form of ultimate goal. The Moderates believed in a policy of conciliation and compromise. They were satisfied with the small concessions given by the British Government from time to time. A little representation here and a few jobs there were enough to satisfy them. They stood for self-government for India in the same way as the position of the British dominions like Canada and Australia was. The Extremists did not bother about the petty concessions given by the British Government. They did not care for the petty reforms which they considered to be merely palliatives and not the final remedy. According to the Extremists, Swaraj alone was the final remedy. They considered installments of constitutional reforms as mere local applications.

3. The Moderates believed in adopting strictly constitutional methods for agitation and that also of the feeblest type, so that there was not the slightest chance of any violence. They believed in reasoned and emotional appeals, lucid presentation of the case, irresistible statements of facts, irrefutable arguments and presenting petitions. The view of Pherozeshah Mehta was: "We delegates meet together to present our Petition of Rights, our Grand Remonstrance, our appeal and our prayer". A,C. Mazumdar considered the right of petition to be the highest privilege of a nation. The Moderates were not prepared to resort to a policy of non-cooperation or passive resistance. They did not accept even the programme of Swadeshi wholeheartedly. They considered boycott as a vindictive act which was liable to create feeling of ill-will. On the other hand, the Extremists were convinced that constitutional agitation will lead them nowhere. They believed that constitutional methods could not cut ice against the autocratic rule of a foreign nation. They also believed that the Government of India would not allow even peaceful propaganda to go on and would intervene at every step to hinder and stop the progress of the nationalist movement. They believed that the national problems could not be solved by resorting to arguments, ethics and piety and only a vigorous agitation could meet the needs of the situation. They believed in a policy of passive resistance which could make the government of India impossible.

4. Another point of difference between the Moderates and the Extremists was with regard to their approach and strategy. Under the Moderates, the Congress movement was not a popular movement. It had no touch with the masses. As a matter of fact, the Moderates depended for their success on the goodwill and sympathy of the Englishmen. They worked on the hypothesis that if the grievances of the people of India were brought to the notice of the Englishmen, the same would be redressed. The Extremists rejected such an approach. They believed that the people of India were the masters of their own destiny and not any foreign power.

5. Another point of difference between the Moderates and the Extremists was regarding the fitness of Indians to rule themselves without depending upon the British Government. The Moderates believed that the people of India were still not fit for self-government. However, the Extremists believed that the people of India were fit to rule themselves and self-government could not be denied to them on the ground of their un-fitness.

6. Another point of difference between the Moderates and the Extremists was that while the Moderates believed that they would get what they asked for without any sufferings, the Extremists were of the definite view that the salvation of India was not possible without sufferings and self-sacrifice.

On account of these differences, there were clashes between the Moderates and the Extremists even during the 19th century. However, events during the Viceroyalty of Lord Curzon aggravated matters. There is no denying the fact that the Moderates were as much vehement in their denunciation of the partition of Bengal as the Extremists, but they had their own limitations and could not go beyond them. The Congress passed resolutions on boycott, Swadeshi and national education in 1906 but there was opposition from the Moderates. The result was that some of them were shouted down by the audience. The Moderates did not approve of all that happened at the Calcutta session in 1906 and tried to undo the same at the next session of the Congress in 1907 at Surat. This the Extremists were not prepared to allow them. Under the circumstances, an open clash between them was inevitable. When the Congress met on 27 December 1907, the atmosphere was surcharged and there were all kinds of rumours. The name of Dr. Rash Behari Ghose was proposed for the Presidentship. When Surendranath Banerjee got up to second the proposal, attempts were made to shout him down and pandemonium prevailed in the Pandal. The meeting had to be adjourned. On the next day, Dr. chose was elected the President, but when he got up to deliver his Presidential address, Tilak ascended the platform, stood in front of the president and demanded that he be allowed to address the audience. He refused to submit to the ruling of the Chair that he could not be allowed to address at that stage. While this tussle was going on, the rank and file of the Extremists created trouble and there were clashes. All efforts to persuade Tilak failed. He stood with folded hands and refused to go to his seat unless he was bodily removed. Some persons from Nagpur and Poona rushed to the platform with Lathis in their hands. A shoe was hurled from the audience and it struck Pherozeshah Mehta, Pandemonium prevailed. Chairs were thrown at the dais and sticks were freely used. The session had to be suspended.

On 28 December 1907, a Convention of the Moderates was held in the Congress Pandal from which the Extremists were excluded although some of them were willing to sign the necessary declaration. Those who did not wish to go back from the position taken at the Calcutta Congress met at a separate place to consider what steps were to be taken to continue the work of the Congress. It was in this way that the Surat Session of the Congress ended. After the Surat fiasco, it was clear that the Moderates were not prepared to yield to the Extremists. They knew that once the plant of extremism was planted, it was bound to grow. They were not prepared for any compromise. Tilak was ridiculed, abused and called a traitor. In spite of the attacks from the Moderates, Tilak was prepared to accommodate them. He wanted the Moderates and the Extremists to unite to carry on the work of the Indian National Congress.

The Moderates put the blame on the Extremists for the Surat split, their contention was that they had no intention to drop or alter the resolutions passed at the Calcutta Session of the Congress. What they intended to do was merely to modify or to use such words in those resolutions which would save them from chances of misconstruction, However, such a contention cannot be accepted. A critical study of the relevant record shows that what the Moderates intended to do was not only to save the Calcutta resolutions from misconstruction but also to reconstruct them with a view to watering them down. If that had not been so, the Moderates would have reaffirmed the Calcutta resolutions in their Madras Session held in 1908, but that was not done. At the Madras Session, the resolution on boycott was entirely dropped. Instead of national education, the Moderates merely talked about supplementing the existing institutions and the efforts of the Government. In 1906, the Congress had declared Swaraj or self-government, not only as their final goal but also demanded immediate steps leading to it. At the Madras Session, the Congress expressed deep and general satisfaction at the reform proposals formulated in Lord Morley's Despatch.

At the Calcutta Session in 1906, the Moderates had accepted the resolutions on Swaraj, national education, boycott and Swadeshi on account of the pressure brought on them from all quarters. In their hearts, they did not accept the new resolutions. Their fear was that the growing pace of the national struggle might lead to lawlessness and that would provide the British with an excuse to deny the reforms on the one hand and to crush all political activity on the other. They had no self-confidence. They did not believe that sustained and dignified national struggle was possible and desirable. They considered the Extremists irresponsible persons who were likely to put in danger the future of the country. The British Government also tried to win over the Moderates against the Extremists. There were frequent meetings between the Moderate leaders and the Viceroy before the Surat split. While the Extremists were roughly handled by the Government, the Moderates were shown all the favours. Lala Lajpat Rai, Sardar Ajit Singh, Tilak and many leaders of Bengal were deported. Public meetings were held all over the country to condemn the action of the Government. In Bombay the protesting crowd clashed with the military and police and many were killed. However, there was no word of condemnation by the Moderates. On the other hand, the Moderate Congress President observed thus in 1908 at the Madras Congress Session: "The clouds are now breaking. The time of the singing of the birds is come; and the voice of the turtle is heard in our land".

It cannot be denied that the Surat split not only weakened the Indian National Congress, but it virtually destroyed its effectiveness till the Lucknow Session in 1916. For the next 8 years, India's nationalist movement remained a house divided against itself, half constitutional and half revolutionary in aspirations.

RISE OF EXTREMISM OR MILITANT NATIONALISM

Many factors were responsible for the rise of extremism in the Congress. The Indian Council Act 1892 did not satisfy the aspirations of even the Moderates. It was contended that the policy of appeals and prayers had brought forth no result. The Government of India considered that policy as a sign of weakness. To quote Tilak, "Political rights will have to be fought for. The Moderates think that these can be won by persuasion. We think that they can only be obtained by strong pressure". The constant economic drain on the resources of the country due to foreign domination added to the discontentment in the country. The writings of men like Dinshaw Wacha, R.C. Dutt and Dadabhai Naoroji proved that the impoverishment of the people of India was due largely to the deliberate policy of the British Government. The policy of the Government of India sacrificed the industries of India in the interests of British manufacturers. There seemed to be no prospects for Indian industries.

Another cause was the discontent created by the outbreak of famine in 1897. It affected about 20 million people and 70,000 square miles of Indian territory. The attitude of the Government of India was rather unhappy. While the people were in the grip of famine, the Government was busy celebrating the Diamond Jubilee Celebrations of Queen Victoria. The money which was required for the relief of the people was being wasted on needless celebrations. This was interpreted as an attitude of callousness on the part of the Government.

The outbreak of the Bubonic Plague in Bombay Presidency also added to the discontentment among the people. It is true that the Government of India adopted certain measures to check the spread of the disease but the methods adopted by it were unfortunate. No consideration was shown for the sentiments of the people. Mr. Rand, the Plague Commissioner of Poona, was most ruthless in his operations. Such a state of affairs could not be tolerated by the people and no wonder the plague policy of the Government was attacked vigorously by the critics of the Government, particularly by Tilak. The resentment was so great that Mr. Rand and one of his associates were shot dead when they were returning from the Government House at Bombay after taking part in the Jubilee Celebrations of Queen Victoria.

The exclusion of the intelligentsia of India from all the big jobs in the country created bitterness. The anti-Indian policy of Lord Curzon added to the discontentment. The view of Lord Curzon was that "the highest ranks of civil employment must, as a general rule, be held by Englishmen". He emphasised that it was only the Englishmen who by their birth and training were fit to rule India, and not the Indians. According to him, Providence had selected the Englishmen to rule over India and to give freedom to India was against the will of God. Such a theory of divine right to rule could not be palatable to the Indians who were learning to demand the right to govern themselves. Lord Curzon was a bureaucrat par excellence and he put the greatest emphasis on efficiency. He had no sympathy with the aspirations of the people of India. As a matter of fact, he ignored them altogether. He acted unmindful of the reactions of the people. He regarded the administration as a machine and acted only in the interests of the efficiency of the machine, although the people were adversely affected by the machine. His reign was full of "missions, omissions and commissions". In 1899, he passed the famous Calcutta Corporation Act which completely officialised the Calcutta Corporation. The total number of the members of the Calcutta Corporation was reduced from 75 to 50. The 25 members who were eliminated were those persons who were the representatives of the people of Calcutta. The result of this measure was that there was a European majority in the Corporation. No wonder, the measure was vehemently condemned. In 1904 was passed the Indian Universities Act. This law reduced the size of the Syndicates, Senates and Faculties with a view to giving prominence to the Europeans. The result of this law was that the Indian Universities became the most officialised universities in the world. They were practically left with no autonomy. In 1904 was also passed the famous Official Secrets Act. The definition of the term "sedition" was widened. The Official Secrets Acts of 1889 and 1898 related to the disclosure of only military secrets. The Act of 1904 covered also the official secrets relating to the civil affairs and newspaper criticism which were likely to bring the government into contempt.

PARTITION OF BENGAL

His most controversial measure was the partition of Bengal in 1905 which led to widespread agitation not only in Bengal but also in other parts of India. The Government published its official scheme for the partition of Bengal on 20 July 1905. There was violent agitation against it. It was suggested that all Honorary Magistrates, Municipal Commissioners and members of District Boards should resign in protest. A national mourning for 12 months was also advocated. Seditious leaflets were printed and circulated among the people. When the agitation was at its height, Lord Curzon resigned as Viceroy on account of his differences with the British Government. However, the necessary legislation to give effect to the partition of Bengal was rushed through the Legislative Council in September 1905 in order to make sure that the partition became a settled fact before he left India. 16 October 1905 was the day fixed for the coming into force of the partition and after a month, Lord Curzon left India.

16 October 1905 was declared to be a day of national mourning throughout Bengal. It was observed as a day of fasting. There was a Hartal in Calcutta. People went to the Ganges barefooted in the early hours of the morning and took their bath. Rabindranath Tagore composed a national song for this occasion. The song was sung by huge crowds parading the streets. There were cries of Bande Mataram which became a national song of Bengal. The ceremony of Raksha Bandhan was observed on 16 October 1905.

The leaders of Bengal felt that mere demonstrations, public meetings and resolutions were not enough and something more concrete was needed and the answer was Swadeshi and boycott.

Mass meetings were held all over Bengal and big crowds took the oath of Swadeshi. Patients refused to take foreign medicines and were willing to take the consequences. People burnt foreign clothes and foreign cigarettes. Large sums were collected to help the Swadeshi movement. Many textile mills, soap and match factories, national banks and insurance companies were started. A prominent part was played by the students of Bengal in the Swadeshi agitation. They picketed the shops selling foreign cloth and other foreign goods. Women also joined processions and picketed the shops dealing in foreign goods. The programmes of Swadeshi and boycott went hand in hand.

The leaders of Bengal took up the work of national education in right earnest. National educational institutions were opened by them and literary, technical and physical education was given there. On 15 August 1906, National Council of Education was set up and Aurobindo Ghose was appointed the first Principal of the National College.

The Government of the new province tried to suppress the anti-partition agitation with a heavy hand. Meetings were broken and political leaders were insulted and threatened, Gorkha soldiers were let loose on the people. B. Fuller, Lieutenant-Governor of the new province, went out of his way to insult the people. Brutal repression took its heaviest toll at Barisal in East Bengal where the Provincial Council was disbanded on the strict orders of the Lieutenant-Governor. When the local leaders and the people protested, they were mercilessly battened on the chests and backs. Many were killed on the spot and hundreds of them were severely injured. The Lieutenant-Governor of the new province warned the Hindus that they would be thrown 500 years back and barred from Government service for 3 to 4 generations. Students were sent to jail for throwing away sweets made of foreign sugar. Gorkha soldiers were ordered to stop the singing of Bande Mataram by the people. Shopkeepers were ordered to supply the needs of the Gorkhas even if they did not pay for them. Orders were issued to stop the grants-in-aid to the educational institutions suspected of being against the Government. Disciplinary action against the teachers and professors was threatened. The Government also followed a policy of "divide and rule".

In its earlier stages, the anti-partition movement was led by the Moderates, but they were disheartened when Lord Morley, Secretary of State for India, declared that the partition was a settled fact which would not be changed. At this stage, the militant nationalists or the Extremists came to the fore and gave a call for passive resistance in addition to Swadeshi and boycott. They called upon the people to non-cooperate with the Government and boycott the Government schools and colleges, courts and Government offices. Their programme was "to make the administration under present conditions impossible by an organised refusal to do anything which shall help either the British commerce in the exploitation of the country or British officialdom in the administration of it...unless and until the conditions are changed in the manner and to the extent demanded by the people". The question of partition of Bengal got merged with the question of India's freedom. The Extremists called upon the people to offer sacrifices at the altar of the Motherland. In 1907, Lala Lajpat Rai and Ajit Singh were deported from the Punjab. In 1908, Tilak was arrested and sentenced to 6 years imprisonment. Chidambaram Pollai in Madras and Harisarvottan Rao and others in Andhra were put behind the bars. Aurobindo Ghose was arrested and prosecuted and although acquitted, he retired to Pondicherry. There was a lot of discontentment and bitterness in the country. This state of affair was allowed to continue.

Lord Minto was succeeded by Lord Hardinge and he and Marquis of Crew who was then Secretary of State for India, decided to take steps to pacify Indian resentment over the partition of Bengal. At the Delhi Durbar held in 1911 the King and Queen and the Secretary of State for India were present. The occasion was taken advantage of to announce the cancellation of the partition of Bengal.

The treatment of the Indians abroad also created resentment in the country. The Government of India had encouraged Indian labourers to go to British colonies and had given them big promises regarding their future. The Indians were responsible for the development of Kenya, Uganda, Fiji,

Mauritius, Trinidad and South Africa. In spite of their services, the Indians were despised, insulted and degraded. Their privileges were withdrawn. They were excluded from trade and were treated as intruders. They could not purchase property and could not vote. They were required to give their thumb impressions and carry identity cards. They were forced to travel in separate third-class railway compartments. They were driven out of tram cars and kept out of the hotels. They were not allowed to sit in public parks. They were required to walk only on the footpaths and live outside the towns in places set apart for them. They were required to put off lights and go to bed after 9 p.m. They were "spat upon, hissed, cursed, abused and subjected to a variety of other indignities".

Certain international events also had their repercussions in India. The rise of Japan after 1868 proved that even a backward Asian country could develop herself without Western control. The defeat of Italy by Abyssinia and Russia by Japan exploded the myth of European superiority. This was interpreted as a harbinger of the rise of the East. The Indians could take inspiration from those events. It was felt that if the European nations could be defeated by an Asiatic power, it was also possible for the Indians to drive away the Englishmen from their country.

The growth of education in India increased the influence of Western ideas of democracy, nationalism and radicalism. The educated Indians became the strongest advocates of militant nationalism. The treatment given to them by the foreigners added to their bitterness. They were low paid. Many of them were unemployed. They felt very strongly the foreign domination. There was a feeling in the country that self-government was necessary for the economic, political and cultural advancement of the country.

Leaders like Tilak and B.C. Pal preached the message of self-respect and asked the nationalists to rely on the character and capacities of the Indian people. They called upon the people to build their own future by their own efforts. They advocated agitation and mass action. They had no faith in the efficacy of constitutional methods. They believed that prayers, petitions and protests were not going to convince the British Government whose only object was to exploit the people of India with a view to add to their own prosperity. To quote Tilak, "Protests are of no avail. Mere protests not backed by self-reliance will not help the people. Days of protests and prayers have gone". Again, "Prepare your forces, organise your power and then go to work so that they cannot refuse you what you demand".

The methods of the Extremists were boycott, Swadeshi and national education. Boycott was directed primarily against the foreign goods but it also included the boycott of the Government services, honours and titles. About the methods of the Extremists, Lala Lajpat Rai wrote, "We desire to turn our faces away from the Government Houses and turn them to the huts of the people. We want to stop our mouth so far as an appeal to the Government is concerned and open our mouth with a new appeal to the masses of our people. This is the psychology, this is the ethics, this is the spiritual significance of the boycott movement". Both the boycott and Swadeshi movements were a great success.

In his whirlwind tour of the country, Tilak declared that the Moderates could not deliver the goods and the people should look up to the Extremists for the liberation of their Motherland. The repetition of the resolutions full of prayers to the Government could not bring any result. The remedy was not petitions, but boycott. After the Surat session, Tilak had no rest. Single-handed, he started a many-sided struggle and spread the fire of patriotism in every nook and corner of the Bombay Presidency. He went on tours and collected a lot of money for the various national causes. He asked his audiences to work for Swaraj and get ready for sufferings which alone could bring Swaraj. His slogan at the meetings was "Swarajya is my birth-right; I will have it".

The Government of India passed the Public Meetings Act, the Criminal Law (Amendment) Act, the Seditious Meetings Act, 1907, the Explosive Substances Act, 1908, the Newspaper (Incitement to Offences) Act, 1908 and the Indian Press Act, 1910 to take effective action against the Extremists. Several circulars and ordinances were issued which had the effect of abrogating the right of free speech and criticism. Processions, meetings and demonstrations were banned. Students and citizens were prohibited from taking part in politics. The students who defied the orders were rusticated from their schools and colleges. Many leaders were deported from Bengal alone. Tilak was arrested, sentenced to imprisonment for 6 years and kept in Burma in "virtual solitary confinement in a prison cell". Lala Lajpat Rai and Sardar Ajit Singh were arrested in the Punjab and sent to Burma. Aurobindo Ghose was kept in jail for a year awaiting his trial although he was acquitted by the court. Madan Lal Dhingra was hanged. Bhupendra Nath Datta, Editor of the Yugantar, was given a long sentence of imprisonment. The Yugantar, the 'Sandhya' and 'Bande-Mataram' were suppressed. Police raids, house searches, confiscations and espionage became the order of the day C.I.D. officers were let loose upon society. So great was the repression that Lord Morley had to ask Lord Minto to have more restraint.

As regards their achievements, the militant nationalists added a glorious chapter to the history of the nationalist movement. They clarified its objectives, taught people self-confidence and self-reliance and prepared the social base of the movement to include the lower middle classes, students, youth and women. New methods of political organisation and new modes of waging political struggles were introduced. However, the mass of the common people, the workers and the peasants, were still outside the mainstream of national politics. The Yugantar wrote thus on 22 April 1906 after the Barisal Conference: "The remedy lies with the people themselves. The thirty crores of people inhabiting India must raise their sixty crores of hands to stop this course of oppression. Force must be stopped by force".

THE HOME RULE MOVEMENT

When Great Britain was involved in the First World War, Indian leaders like Tilak and Annie Besant decided to put new life in the national movement in the country. As the Englishmen did not like the word Swaraj and considered the same to be "seditious and dangerous," Tilak decided to use the term "Home Rule" in place of Swaraj as the goal of his movement. In December 1915, he had deliberations with his colleagues and on 28 April 1916 the Indian Home Rule League was set up with its headquarters at Poona. The object of this League was to "attain Home Rule or self-government within the British Empire by all constitutional means and to educate and organise public opinion in the country towards the attainment of the same". A similar Home Rule League was founded by Annie Besant on 15 September 1916 with its headquarters at Adyar near Madras.

The advocates of the Home Rule Movement believed in constitutional methods and were opposed to violence and revolutionary agitation. They had no desire to embarrass the Government, which was fighting against Germany and Austria-Hungary. They were prepared to offer their cooperation to the British Government so that it could win the war. However, they believed that the grant of Home Rule to India was in the interests of the British Empire in its war against Germany and Austria as she could then fight with greater moral force.

In 1917, the two Home Rule Leagues of Tilak and Annie Besant worked in cooperation with each other. Tilak confined his activities to the Bombay Presidency and the Central Provinces and the rest of India was left to Annie Besant. The branches of the Home, Rule League were set up all over the country and there was a popular demand for Home Rule.

Tilak went on a whirlwind tour of the country in 1916 and appealed to the people to unite under the banner of the Home Rule League. His target was not the British Empire or the Emperor of India but the bureaucracy in India. In his public speeches, he declared emphatically that Home Rule was the only cure for India's political ills and grievances, that liberty was the birth-right of every man and that the aspiration to get one's liberty was the essence of human nature. A small minority from outside India could not be allowed to rule the country arbitrarily.

Annie Besant also toured the country and created a lot of enthusiasm among the people for the national cause. Her articles in the Commonweal and New India were very popular. C. Y. Chintamani says: "Annie Besant stirred the country by the spoken as well as the written word, as scarcely as anyone else could do". Annie Besant's work was particularly among the women of India who showed "uncalculating heroism, endurance and the selfless sacrifice of the feminine nature".

The British Government could not be expected to keep quiet in the face of a stir created by the Home Rule Leagues and their leaders and it decided to curb the activities of those leaders who were in the forefront of the movement. The existing statutes were tightened. There was already an ordinance to prevent the entry of undesirable aliens into India. The Defence of India Act 1915 superseded the ordinary criminal low of the country and action under it could be taken against agitators. The provisions of the Indian Press Act 1910 were strictly enforced to stop the propaganda of the Home Rule Leaguers. Circulars were issued by which the students of schools and colleges were forbidden from taking part in the Home Rule Movement. In July 1916, Tilak was prosecuted for delivering seditious speeches and was ordered to furnish a personal bond of ₹20,000. Externment orders were served on him and he was ordered not to enter Delhi and the Punjab. Similar action was taken against Annie Besant. She was ordered to furnish security for her press and the Commonweal and New India. In all, she deposited ₹20,000 and the whole of that amount was forfeited by the Government, The Government also took action against Annie Besant and her two associates; B.P. Wadia and G.S. Arundale. The Governor of Madras called Annie Besant for an interview and told her that she was to be interned. There was a lot of indignation all over the country against her internment: Protest meetings were held all over the country and the repression by the police was condemned.

REVOLUTIONARY AND TERRORIST MOVEMENT: CAUSES

Many factors were responsible for the rise and growth of the revolutionary and terrorist movement in the country. The rising of 1857 had its effect on the future generations of India. The sacrifices made by the Indians on that occasion gave inspiration to many, to follow their example. The spirit of revenge with which the rebel of 1857 was crushed and even the innocent Indians were massacred by the British soldiers even after the failure of the revolt inflamed the minds of many Indians. There was a general awakening in the country and the people started thinking in terms of ending the foreign rule at any cost even if the use of force was necessary for that purpose. The timidity of the Moderates exasperated the youth of India and they decided to take to violence to turn out the foreigners from the country. The Indian press was instrumental in putting the Indian case before the people and asked for action against British tyranny in the country. The minds of the Indians were also affected by the large number of political assassinations in Europe at the hands of the anarchists. The murderer of the Empress of Austria-Hungary is stated to have declared: "Long live anarchy! Let there be only 200 such brave men as myself and all the thrones of the world will be empty". All these murders took place a few years before the partition of Bengal in 1905 and naturally their effect on the youth was bound to be profound. The unification of Germany and Italy, the defeat of Italy by Abyssinia in 1896 and of Russia by Japan in 1904, the Nihilist Movement in Russia and the Young Turk Movement in Turkey had their effect on the revolutionaries in India. Many people in India were convinced that the British rule in India could not be ended by constitutional methods and force had to be employed for that purpose. These revolutionaries believed in the philosophy of bomb and pistol in one hand and the Gita in the other.

MAHARASHTRA

Tilak played an important part in furthering the cause of revolutionary movement in Maharashtra. In 1895, he inaugurated the Shivaji and Ganpati festivals. By doing so, he gave a religious sanction to the movement against the British Government. These festivals became the springboards of revolutionary enterprises. Fiery speeches were delivered on these occasions. At the Shivaji Coronation Festival held on 12 June 1897, Tilak called upon the people to "rise above the Penal Code into the rarified atmosphere of the sacred Bhagwat Gita". He justified the murder of Afzal Khan by Shivaji and observed, "If thieves enter our house and we have no strength to drive them out, should we not without hesitation shut them in and burn them alive? God has conferred on the Molechhas (foreigners) no grant of Hindustan inscribed on imperishable brass".

Towards the end of 1896, there was a severe famine in the Deccan and Tilak started a no-rent campaign. He called upon the peasants not to pay land-revenue to the Government. In 1897 occurred the plague and Mr. Rand was murdered. Tilak was arrested and sentenced to 18 months' rigorous imprisonment. There was a lot of political activity in Maharashtra. There were Shivaji clubs, anti-cow-killing societies, Ganpati choirs, national festivals, gymnastic clubs, etc. Poona, Nasik, Kolhapur and Bombay were the centres of these activities. The statue of Queen Victoria was mutilated at Bombay. An attempt was made to burn the Church Mission Hall, The Marathi press was revolutionary in tone. The editors of many newspapers and magazines were arrested and sentenced. Tilak himself was arrested in 1908, prosecuted and convicted and sentenced to 6 year's transportation.

Ganesh Damodar Savarkar, the younger brother of V.D, Savarkar, was the head of the revolutionary activities at Nasik. He was the founder of Abhinav Bharat Society. In April 1907 he printed 2,000 copies of the Marathi version of the autobiography of Mazzini. In 1909, he published a pamphlet, which contained many inflammatory verses. In one of the poems he said: "Take up the sword and destroy the Government because it is foreign and aggressive". The title of another poem was: "Who obtained independence without a battle?" He was prosecuted and sentenced to transportation for life with forfeiture of property.

V. D. Savarkar had sent a parcel containing 20 Browning automatic pistols with ammunition co Bombay concealed in the false bottom of a box forming part of the luggage of one Chaturbhuj Amin who was working as a cook in the India House. The pistols were to be used by the members of the Abhinav Bharat Society. Before the parcel reached India, Ganesh had already been arrested. The members of the Abhinav Bharat Society decided to murder Jackson, District Magistrate of Nasik, as he had convicted Ganesh Savarkar. Jackson was actually shot dead on 21 December 1909. The details of the Nasik conspiracy were divulged by one Ganu Vaidya who was a member of the Nasik Branch of Abhinav Bharat Society. Acting on the information supplied by him, the police rounded up 37 young men, 3 of whom were hanged, and the rest were sentenced to varying terms of imprisonment.

Mr. Jackson had arrested Ganesh Savarkar on the instigation of Sir Curzon Willie who had laid a ring of spies around the India House to watch the activities of the Indian students. He also dictated the British policies concerning India, He was shot dead on 1 July 1909 by Madan Lal Dhingra.

BENGAL

In addition to Maharashtra, the revolutionary movement was also strong in Bengal. The revolutionaries of Bengal came from the educated classes. The work done by Bankim Chandra Chatterji, Ram Krishna Paramhans, Swami Vivekananda, Raj Narain Bose and Nabagopal Mitra had its effect. Unemployment among the educated classes in Bengal made the situation intolerable. Things were made worse by the Anti-Bengalee attitude of the English officials who refused to recruit Bengalees in Government service. The Government advertisements contained the following words: "Bengalee Baboos need not apply". This was bound to have its repercussions. In order to reduce the influence of the Bengalees, lord Curzon partitioned Bengal in 1905. The people of Bengal who had fought against the European Indigo planters with their fish spears and bamboo clubs, were not going to be cowed down and they accepted the challenge.

On 23 December 1907, Mr. Allen, who was formerly the District Magistrate of Dacca, was shot in the back but the injury did not prove fatal. On 30 April 1908, Mrs. Kennedy and Miss Kennedy were killed by a bomb thrown by Khudi Ram which was actually meant for Mr. Kingsford, Presidency Magistrate. Khudi Ram was arrested, tried and hanged. He became a martyr and a hero. Schools were closed for 2 or 3 days as a tribute to his memory. His photographs had an immense sale. Youngmen began to wear Dhoties with the name of Khudi Ram woven into their borders.

In the Alipore conspiracy case searches were made by the police at Maniktala and other places. In May 1908, bombs, dynamite, cartridges, and correspondence were seized. Many persons were arrested, charged and convicted. Heavy punishments were inflicted on them. Narinder Gosain became an approver but he was shot dead by his companions in the jail. Nand Lal, the Sub-Inspector who had arrested Khudi Ram, was murdered. Asutosh Biswas who had acted as public prosecutor in the Gosain murder case and the Alipore conspiracy case was shot dead. Shams-ul Alam, Deputy Superintendent of Police who was connected with the Alipore case, was shot dead.

PUNJAB

The Punjab also played its part in the revolutionary movement. The Punjabis detested the policy of repression followed by the Government of India. They also protested against the treatment given to them in various parts of the British empire and the failure of the British Government to protect them. Sardar Ajit Singh, a revolutionary of the Bharat Mata Society of Lahore, took an active part against the Colonisation Act which deprived the peasants of Lyallpur and other districts of the fruits of the lands which they had converted from barren areas into rich fields. He addressed many meetings which began with the song of Banke Dayal known as "Pagri Sambhal Oh! Jatta," (Oh peasant! take care of the turban, i.e., self-respect). There were disturbances in Rawalpindi in May 1907 and many Arya Samaj leaders were attested and prosecuted.

On 23 December 1912, Lord Hardinge was taken in a procession on the back of an elephant in Delhi. When the people were showering flowers and coconuts on the procession in Chandni Chowk, a bomb exploded which injured the Viceroy and killed his A.D.C. The procession was turned into a funeral. The bomb was thrown by Rash Behari Bose. There was a lot of confusion and Rash Behari managed to escape. A reward of ₹7,500 was announced for the arrest of Rash Behari Bose. He was chased from place to place but every time he managed to escape. He went away to Japan under a fictitious name. He played an important role in organising the Indian National Army in Japan. He died in 1945.

The action taken by the Government in this connection is known as the Delhi conspiracy case. 13 persons were arrested in that connection and among them were Master Amir Chand, Dina Nath, Bhai Balmukand, Balraj Bhalla, Basant Kumar and Avadh Behari. Two of them were sentenced to 7 years imprisonment and 4 of them were hanged. Dina Nath became an approver. It is stated that when Avadh Behari was going to be hanged, an Englishman asked him what his last wish was and his reply was: "The end of the British rule". When the Englishman advised him to die peacefully, he replied, "Peace! I wish that a conflagration may break out in the country gutting the British rule. Let my country emerge out of this fire like pure gold".

THE GHADAR PARTY

The Ghadar Party was determined to wage war against the British in India and with that object in view decided to send arms and men to India to start a revolt with the help of soldiers and local revolutionaries. Several thousand men volunteered to go back to India. Millions of dollars were collected for that purpose. The Ghadarites contacted Indian soldiers in the Far East, South-East Asia and all over India and persuaded many regiments to revolt. 21 February 1915 was fixed for an all-India revolt and vigorous preparations were made for that purpose. Rash Behari Bose, Sachindra Sanyal, Ganesh Pingale and Baghi Kartar Singh prepared a master plan for that purpose. Some revolutionaries were killed and several others were arrested. They were also hanged. The all-India revolt failed because one Kirpal Singh passed on all the secret plans to the Government. Many places were raided and bombs were recovered. Secret papers were also captured by the Government. Most of the ring leaders of the Punjab fell into the hands of the police. The Ghadarites were tried in 9 batches in the Lahore Conspiracy Case and the supplementary cases. Out of 291 sent up for trial,

42 were sentenced to death and hanged and 114 were transported for life. 93 were imprisoned for varying terms and 42 were acquitted. Prominent leaders like Baghi Kartar Singh, Bhai Parmanand, Ganesh Pingale, Jagat Singh and Harnam Singh were also tried for conspiracy to overthrow the British Government. Kartar Singh and Pingale admitted that they were wholly responsible for the conspiracy.

The Tribunal announced its judgment on 13 September 1915. Bhai Parmanand was so indifferent to death that on that day, he slept till 8 in the morning. When he woke up, he found everybody around him laughing. One of them asked him, "Why? Are you going to your in-laws?" These blessed souls sang sweet songs for the Motherland and at last they prayed this together for the last time; "Oh Mother! We have not been able to snap your fetters. If any one of us remains alive he will strive for your honour and the liberty and equality of Indians". 24 of them including Kartar Singh, Pingale, Bhai Parmanand, Jagat Singh and others were awarded death sentence. On hearing that all of them began to dance. Those who were condemned to transportation for life cried out: "Give us death? Reward us with hanging!" Kartar Singh thanked the President. Pingale said this much; "So that's all!" The Viceroy commuted the death sentences of 17 to transportation for Life Pingale was hanged on 16 November 1915 and he was the last to be hanged. The Officer-in-charge told him, "I tried to give you as much time for life as I could. I kept your turn last". The reply of Pingale was: "Then you have made a mistake. I've been separated from my friends. They may lose their faith in me. Had you sent me earlier, I would have got the privilege of arranging for their reception and comforts there. Oh, you have deprived me of that good luck," He was questioned about his last desire and his reply was; "Kindly remove my chains so that I can offer prayers to my Mother with the palms of my hands joined". When the chains were taken off, he prayed aloud, "Lord, you know our heart's desire. Our only prayer is that you fulfil the mission for which we have so readily laid down our lives". It is stated that the Chief Justice was inclined to commute the death sentence of Kartar Singh but the latter replied, "I prefer gallows to life sentence. I wish I were born again to unfetter by Motherland. I shall be glad to be hanged every time I am reborn till my country achieved independence".

POST-WAR MOVEMENT

There was revival of the revolutionary and terrorist movement in the country when the people were suffering from a sense of frustration and pessimism after agitations and demonstrations against the Rowlatt Bills, the Non-cooperation movement and the Khilafat movement. The revolutionaries put before the young men of the country a new programme. They called upon them to start a revolutionary and uncompromising struggle for the independence of their country. They tried to impress upon the people of India the secret of the British character that they could be bullied, but not argued into justice and generosity. The terrorism of the Government was to be met by counter-terrorism. Such a policy alone could restore self-confidence among the people who were suffering from a sense of utter helplessness. The revolutionaries believed that the English masters and their hired lackeys should not be allowed to do whatever they liked, unhampered and unmolested and every possible difficulty and resistance must be thrown in their way. Terrorism had an international bearing and the attention of the enemies of England was drawn towards India through acts of terrorism and revolutionary demonstrations. The terrorists made it clear that they did not believe in terrorism for terrorism sake. They resorted to it as an effective means, of retaliation. The revolutionaries believed that the repressive measures of the Government had destroyed all hopes of political reform being gained without violence.

Moreover, armed resistance against something "Satanic and ignoble" was infinitely more befitting for any nation than the prevalence of "effortless and philosophical cowardice". The revolutionaries went to the villages not to get votes but to secure "co-martyrs" for the country who would die without anybody knowing where their corpses lay. They would like to go down in history unknown, unhonoured, unsung, unlamented and unwept. These "mad lovers" of the country were not actuated by avarice, rivalry, jealousy or enmity. They were inspired by divine motive of devotion and service. The revolutionaries were above sectarian and communal considerations. Unlike the former movements, religion was not allowed to have precedence over the secular and nationalistic outlook of its organisers who belonged to different religious groups in the country. The revolutionary brotherhood had reached a stage where there was no caste, no religion or even separate identity.

There was a fundamental difference between the pre-1919 phase and post-1919 phase of the revolutionary movement. The pre-1919 revolutionaries were inspired by Mazzini and Garibaldi of Italy and the Sinn Feinners of Ireland. The post-1919 revolutionaries derived their inspiration from the October Revolution of Russia and the socialistic principles of Soviet leaders like Lenin. The slogans and code words like "Bharat Mata Ki Jai, "Bande Mataram", "Om", "Ram Hari", "Allaho Akbar" and "Sat Sri Akal" were substituted by "Inqilab Zindabad", "Down with Imperialism", "Long Live the Proletariat" and "Long Live India". A leaflet issued by Naujawan Bharat Sabha discarded Buddha and Christ and described Karl Marx and Engels as the greatest men of the world. While the old revolutionaries got their inspiration from the Bhagwat Gita and the writing of Aurobindo, Vivekananda and Bankim Chandra Chatterjee, the new revolutionaries got their inspiration from the writings of Marx and Engels. While the revolutionaries like Lala Hardayal and his followers thought in terms of the past glory of ancient India, Sardar Bhagat Singh and his comrades relied upon the masterpieces of Lenin and such books as "Roos Ki Rajya Kranti".

The revolutionaries lived a life of sufferings, hardships, insults and humiliations at the hands of the agents of the foreign Government. They believed that no weapon could kill them and no fire could burn them. They were prepared in mind and body to pass through the severest ordeals. They were transported for life to the Andamans where life was extremely difficult. The jail authorities invented various devices to make the revolutionaries as miserable as they could. The prisoners were mishandled at the time of taking meals. Barbarous punishments were inflicted upon the revolutionaries to extort confessions or to convert them as approvers. Their hands were kept under the legs of the cots and the police constables sat on them. Sometimes they were wrapped in a blanket and then mercilessly beaten to avoid legal complications. Sometimes they were made to stand on their legs for days together with their hands tied with a chain nailed in the wall. Sometimes they had to wear cross bars which were worse than the bar fetters because the prisoners under this sentence could not bring their feet or legs close to each other and they had to walk, sit, work and sleep with stretched out feet and legs for weeks. Sometimes the revolutionaries resorted to hunger-strikes to remonstrate against the inhuman treatment meted out to them. They excited a lot of public sympathy. There were public hartals in support of their demands. A certain section of the press also sympathised with them. They published short stories, poems, plays and essays about them. Whenever an official was murdered, there was praise instead of condemnation. Whenever a revolutionary was hanged, he was praised as a courageous hero and a martyr.

KAKORI CASE

The revolutionaries were in great need of money for the manufacture of bombs and consequently a few revolutionaries boarded a train on 9 August 1925 on the Lucknow-Saharanpur line. They had with them revolvers and cartridges. After the departure of the train from the Kakori railway station, one of the revolutionaries pulled the alarm chain of the train. When the train stopped, the revolutionaries tried to take away money from the iron box, which was broken open with great effort by the hammer blows given by Ashfaq Ullah Khan. However, the revolutionaries were able to get Rs. 5,000 only. The Government took action and arrested about 40 persons. The trial in the Kakori case concluded on 7 April 1927. It was a mere farce. Pandit Ram Prasad Bismal, Roshan Singh and Rajendra Lahiri were given death sentence. Manmath Nath Gupta got 14 years and many others got death sentences. Ashfaq and Sachindra nath Bakshi were caught later on and given death sentence and transportation for life respectively.

The Simon Commission visited Lahore on 20 October 1928. The Hindustan Socialist Republican Party took out a huge procession against the Simon Commission, under the leadership of Lala Lajpat Rai. I.P. Saunders give blows on the head and chest of Lajpat Rai and theory caused grievous injuries on his person. As a result of those injuries, Lajpat Rai died on 17 November 1928. In order to have revenge. Sounders was murdered on 17 December 1928 by Raj Guru and Bhagat Singh. After the murder, Bhagat Singh and Raj Guru managed to escape.

On 8 April 1929, two bombs were thrown from the Visitor's gallery of the Central Assembly Hall in New Delhi by Bhagat Singh and B. K. Dutt. They could have run away but surrendered to the police. Their trial started on 7 May 1929 and on 12 June 1929, the Sessions Judge sentenced them to transportation for life.

In the Saunders murder case, the trial started at Lahore. Bhagat Singh was taken from Delhi to Lahore to stand his trial for murder, along with others. The tribunal which tried Bhagat Singh and his companions, gave its decision on 7 October 1930 and Bhagat Singh, Raj Guru and Sukh Dev were sentenced to death. They were hanged on 23 March 1931 at Lahore.

CONTRIBUTION OF REVOLUTIONARIES

It is true that the revolutionaries failed to bring about the independence of India. However, it cannot be denied that they had made their own contribution to the national cause. It is they who set an example before the Indians by sacrificing their own lives. They taught the people not by precept but by personal example. They taught them to face death and do everything for the sake of their country. By their sacrifices they created a new spirit which helped the Indians later on to win their freedom. It is they who revolted against the policy of the Moderates and thereby opened a new chapter in the history of the freedom movement in India. Their desperate deeds, daring plans, cool action and indifference to death won for them a lasting place in the memory of the nation. They succeeded in what they desired to do — evoking by the maximum sacrifices of the minimum chosen persons the spirit of minimum sacrifice on the part of the maximum number of people. The impression which the revolutionaries left on the minds of the people was very effective and great. They exhorted the people to live dedicated lives — self-sacrifice for national emancipation, a feeling of service for the needy and the oppressed and dislike for self-publicity. The revolutionaries were the heroes who left their footprints on the sands of time.

INDIA AND WORLD WAR I (1914-18)

When the war started, there was great enthusiasm in the country. The people of India were willing to serve the government in every possible way. After Marne, there was an increasing demand for Indian troops outside India. When Turkey joined the Central Powers in October 1914, Indian troops garrisoned the Suez Canal and repulsed a Turkish attack. Indian troops fought through the long campaigns of Macedonia and German East Africa. They played an important part in the Iraq campaign leading to the capture of Baghdad in 1917. In this way, they helped to find the present State of Iraq. They were in the Allied army which took Jerusalem in 1917. All this involved a great effort in India itself. Eight lakhs of men were recruited for the fighting forces, together with four lakhs of non-combatants. This resulted in a great expansion in the Military machine, a great mixture of classes and a stronger feeling of self-confidence all around. Indian self-confidence grew when the magnitude of their effort and the extent to which it depended upon Indians themselves, were realised.

In the administrative sphere, the British government made a mistake in allowing the British civilian officers to serve the forces during the war. Many of them never returned and those who returned found themselves in a strange new mental world to which it was difficult to adapt themselves. When times grew difficult towards the end of the war, the Government had only an ageing and tired cadre of officers to rely upon.

In the economic sphere, the first effect of the war was one of stimulus. The industrial development of modern India owes a good deal to the demands of World War I. However, increasing demands and expenditure led to rise in prices and ultimately enthusiasm was turned into discontent. Englishmen could be expected to put up with inconveniences because they felt that they were fighting for their very existence and their victory was likely to add to their glory. The same could not be said about the Indians for whom the War was merely an external affliction. No doubt, they became not only exhausted and war-weary but also sour, discontented and resentful.

The attitude of India towards Europeans and its people was altered radically and permanently. The Indians gave up the feeling that the Europeans were superior to them morally and technically. They were regarded merely as more powerful. The first War casualty in India was the image of Western superiority.

The Russian Revolution of 1917 also had a profound influence on the minds of the Indians. They felt that if the people of Russia could overthrow an imperialist regime, the same could be done by the Indians in their own country. The Fourteen points of President Wilson had great influence on the Indians. They also demanded the rights of national freedom and self-determination of peoples. No wonder, the Indians demanded self-government in the name of the fundamental principles accepted by the Allied Powers.

As regards the effect of war on Muslims, they were very unhappy. They did not approve of the dismemberment of Turkey, which was regarded as the sword of Islam. They also did not like the treatment given to the Arabs who were considered to be rebels against the Turkish Khalifa. Their princes were regarded as stooges of the infidel.

When the war started, the Congress was still a middle-class body of Westernised professionals with some commercial and industrial backing. It was firmly under the control of Gokhale and the Moderates. However, all this was changed during the war. Tilak came back from jail and became a leader of all-India importance. Tilak was opposed to the old policy of making prayers to the British Government. His contention was that every Indian had the birthright to be free. He laid the foundations for the great anti-government movement led by Gandhiji in the next few years.

JALLIANWALA BAGH TRAGEDY

Great atrocities were committed in the Punjab during the regime of Sir Michael O'Dwyer, Lieutenant-Governor of the Punjab. Sir Michael was known as the iron man of the Punjab. He had no faith in political reforms and consequently had no sympathy with the political agitators. He refused Tilak and B.C. Pal to enter the Punjab. The methods adopted by Sir Michael to raise war loans and to find recruits were very often unauthorised and oppressive. When the agitation against the Rowlatt Act started, Sir Michael gave on 7 April 1919 the following warning to the people of the Punjab: "The Government of this Province is and will remain determined that public order, which was maintained so successfully during the time of war, shall not be disturbed in times of peace. Action has therefore, already been taken under the Defence of India Act against certain individuals at Lahore and Amritsar. The recent puerile demonstrations against the Rowlatt Act in both Lahore and Amritsar indicate how easily the ignorant and the credulous people can be misled. Those who only want to mislead them incur a serious responsibility. Those who appeal to ignorance rather than, to reason have a day of reckoning in store for them". Amritsar observed Hartal peacefully both on 30 March and 6 April. However, on 9 April 1919, the Government of the Punjab passed orders for the deportation of Dr. Satyapal and Dr. Kitchlew and their internment at Dharmsala under the Defence of India Act. On 10 April 1919, they were removed by the police from Amritsar, When the people came to know of it, complete Hartal was declared in the city. The people marched in a procession to the residence of the Deputy Commissioner to demand the release of their leaders. They had no sticks or lathis with them. However, they were checked by the police at the railway level-crossing and there was firing. This infuriated the mob and there was wholesale burning of whatever fell in their way. Europeans were assaulted. Buildings were burnt and godowns were looted. When the troops appeared in the city, the mob disappeared. On 11 April 1919, the people were allowed to arrange for the funerals of the dead bodies.

On 12 April 1919, a proclamation was issued by General Dyer, who had taken charge of the troops the day before, that no meetings or gatherings of the people were to be held. However, no steps were taken to see that the proclamation was brought to the notice of the people living in the various localities of the city. The result was that it was announced on 12 April evening that there would be a public meeting on 13 April 1919 at 4-30 p.m. in the Jallianwala Bagh. Neither General Dyer nor other authorities took any action to stop the meeting. The meeting started at the right time and there were about 6,000 to 10,000 people present in the meeting. All of them were practically unarmed and defenceless. The Jallianwala Bagh is closed practically on all sides by walls except one entrance. General Dyer entered the Jallianwala Bagh with armoured cars and troops. Without giving any warning to the people to disperse, he ordered the troops to fire and he continued to do so till the whole of the ammunition at his disposal was exhausted. Hundreds of people were killed. The contention of General Dyer was that he wanted to teach the people a lesson so that they might not laugh at him. He would have fired and fired longer, he said, if he had the required ammunition. He had only fired 1,600 rounds because his ammunition had run out. The regime of Dyer imposed some unthinkable punishments. The water and electric supply of Amritsar were cut off. Public flogging was common. However, the "Crawling Order" was the worst of all.

NON-COOPERATION MOVEMENT

Under the leadership of Mahatma Gandhi, the Indian National Congress decided in 1920 to start the Non-Cooperation Movement. It was truly a revolutionary step. It was for the first time that the Congress decided to follow a policy of direct action. Many factors were responsible for this change. Mahatma Gandhi had so far believed in the justice and fair play of the British Government. He had given his full cooperation to the Government during the World War I in spite of opposition from men like Tilak. However, the tragedy of the Jallianwala Bagh, the Martial Law in the Punjab and the findings of the Hunter Committee destroyed his faith in the good sense of the Englishmen. He felt that the old methods must be given up. After the withdrawal of the Moderates, the Extremists were in complete control of the Congress and it was possible for the Congress to adopt a revolutionary programme. The terms of the Treaty of Sevres which was entered into between Turkey and the Allies were very severe and were resented by the Muslims of India. The Muslims tried to persuade the British Government to show leniency towards Turkey but they got a flat refusal. That resulted in resentment among them against the British Government. The Muslims started the Khilafat Movement and Mahatma Gandhi identified himself with them in that movement. The result was that Mahatma Gandhi was sure of Muslim support if the Congress started the Non-Cooperation Movement.

A special session of the Congress was held at Calcutta in September 1922 under the Presidentship of Lala Lajpat Rai and Mahatma Gandhi himself moved the non-cooperation resolution. There was a lot of opposition particularly from C.R. Das, B.C. Pal, Annie Besant, Jinnah and M.M. Malaviya but the resolution was carried by a majority of 1,855 against 873. The programme of the Non-Cooperation Movement was clearly stated in the non-cooperation resolution. It involved the surrender of titles and honorary offices and resignation from nominated posts in the local bodies. The non-cooperators were not to attend Government Levies, Darbars and other official and semi-official functions held by the Government officials or in their honour. They were to withdraw their children gradually from schools and colleges and establish national schools and colleges. They were to boycott gradually the British courts and establish private arbitration courts. They were not to join the army as recruits for service in Mesopotamia. They were not to stand for election to the

Legislatures and they were also not to vote. They were to use Swadeshi cloth. Hand-spinning and hand-weaving were to be encouraged. Untouchability was to be removed as there could be no Swaraj without this reform. Mahatma Gandhi promised Swaraj within one year if people followed his programme sincerely and whole-heartedly. Ahimsa or non-violence was to be strictly observed by the non-cooperators. They were not to give up Satya or truth under any circumstances.

The Non-Cooperation Movement captured the imagination of the people. Both the Hindus and Muslims participated in it. There was wholesale burning of foreign goods. Many students left schools and colleges and the Congress set up such national educational institutions as the Kashi Vidyapeeth, Banaras Vidyapeeth, Gujarat Vidyapeeth, Bihar Vidyapeeth, Bengal National University, National College of Lahore, Jamia Millia of Delhi and the National Muslim University of Aligarh. Seth Jamna Lal Bajaj declared that he would give ₹ 1,00,000 a year for the maintenance of non-practising lawyers. Forty lakh volunteers were enrolled by the Congress. Twenty thousand 'Charkhas' were manufactured. The people started deciding their disputes by means of arbitration. Mahatma Gandhi gave up the title of Kaiser-i-Hind and his example was followed by others.

Mahatma Gandhi was convinced that the only way to make the Government see reason was to start the civil disobedience movement and he decided to start the same in Bardoli (in Gujarat). The Congress Working Committee called upon the people of India to cooperate with the people of Bardoli "by refraining from mass or individual civil disobedience of an aggressive character, except upon the express consent of Mahatma Gandhi previously obtained". Mahatma Gandhi wrote to the Viceroy and gave 7 days to accept his demands. The Viceroy held the Congress responsible for all the lawlessness in the country, Mahatma Gandhi was left with no alternative but to launch the civil disobedience movement. Unfortunately, at this time, the tragedy of Chauri Chaura occurred which changed the course of Indian history. What actually happened was that a mob of 3,000 persons killed 25 policemen and one inspector. Similar tragic events had already occurred on 17 November 1921 in Bombay and on 13 January 1922 in Madras. This was too much for Mahatma Gandhi who stood for complete non-violence. The result was that Mahatma Gandhi gave orders for the suspension of the Non-Cooperation Movement at once. The Government was not satisfied with this action of Mahatma Gandhi and the Congress. It was feared that Mahatma Gandhi was out for a bigger trouble and consequently he was arrested on 13 March 1922. His trial began in Ahmedabad and he pleaded guilty. He took upon himself full responsibility for the occurrences in Madras, Bombay and Chauri Chaura and told Mr. Broom field, the British judge, that he would "do the same again" if he was set free. He was sentenced to 6 years' imprisonment.

The action of Mahatma Gandhi in suspending the movement was severely criticised from many quarters. According to Dr. Pattabhi Sita-ramayya, "Long letters were written from behind the bars by Pt. Motilal Nehru and Lala Lajpat Rai. They took Gandhi to task for punishing the whole country for the sins of a place".

Dr. R.C. Majumdar says that the most outstanding feature of the Non-Cooperation Movement was the willingness and ability of the people in general to endure hardships and punishments inflicted by the Government. It is true that the movement collapsed but the memory of its greatness survived and was destined to inspire the nation to launch a more arduous campaign. The movement served as a baptism of fire which initiated the people to a new faith and new hope and inspired them with a new confidence in their power to fight for freedom. As a result of this movement, the Congress movement for the first time became a really mass movement. The national awakening not only penetrated to the people at large but also made them active participants in the struggle for freedom. Moreover, the Indian National Congress was turned into a genuine revolutionary organisation. It was no longer a deliberative assembly but an organised fighting party pledged to revolution. (*History of the Freedom Movement in India*, Vol. III, p. 189.)

THE SWARAJIST PARTY

When C. R. Das and the other Bengal leaders were in Alipore Central Jail, they evolved a new programme of Non-Cooperation with the Government through legislatures. Their idea was to enter the legislatures in large numbers and "carry on a policy of uniform, continuous and consistent opposition to the Government". Moti Lal Nehru also shared the views of C.R. Das. In July 1922, C.R. Das came out of jail and began to carry on propaganda in favour of Council-entry.

When a meeting of the All-India Congress Committee was held at Calcutta in November 1922, there were differences of opinion among the Congress leaders on the question of Council-entry. While C.R. Das, Moti Lal Nehru and Hakim Ajmal Khan were in favour of it, C. Rajagopalachari, Dr. Ansari, etc., were opposed to it. In spite of lengthy debates, no decision was arrived at. At the annual session of the Congress held at Gaya in December 1922, the "No-changers" won a victory and the programme of Council-entry was rejected. C.R. Das who presided over the session resigned from the Congress and announced his decision to form the Swarajist Party. The object of the new party was to wreck the Government of India Act, 1919 from within the Councils. In March 1923, the first Conference of the Swarajist Party was held at the residence of Moti Lal Nehru at Allahabad and the future programme of the Party was decided. The keynote of the programme of the Party was obstructionism. Its members were to contest elections on the issue of the redress of the wrongs done by the British bureaucracy, to oppose every measure of the Government and to throw out all legislative enactments proposed by the British Government. The view of the Swarajists was that the seats in the legislatures must be captured so that they did not fall into the hands of undesirable persons who were tools in the hands of the bureaucracy in India. The leaders of the Swarajist Party declared that outside the Councils, they would cooperate with the constructive programme of the Congress under the leadership of Mahatma Gandhi and in case their methods failed, they would, without any hesitation, join Mahatma Gandhi's civil disobedience movement if and when launched by him.

The Swarajist Party fought the elections in 1923 and refused to come to any understanding with the Liberal Federation. The Swarajist Party won a majority in the Legislative Council of the Central Provinces. It was the dominant Party in Bengal. It also won good support in U.P. and Bombay. However, the Swarajist party was at its best in the central Assembly under the leadership of Moti Lal Nehru. By winning over the support of the Nationalist Party and a few other members, the Swarajist Party was able to command a working majority and was thus able to accomplish a lot. On 18 February 1924, the Swarajist Party was able to get a resolution passed by which the Government was requested to establish full responsible Government in India. A demand was also made that a Round Table Conference consisting of the representatives of India should be called at an early date to frame a Constitution for India. The appointment of the Muddiman Committee was the result of a resolution of the Swarajist Party. Moti Lal Nehru was requested to become a member of this Committee but he refused. Some of the demands in. the budget of 1924-25 were rejected by the Central Assembly as a result of the efforts of the Swarajist Party. The Assembly also refused to allow the Government to introduce the entire Finance Bill. In February 1925, V.J. Patel introduced a Bill asking for the repeal of, certain laws and with the exception of one, the Bill was passed. A resolution was passed with the help of the Swarajist Party demanding the release of certain political prisoners. The Swarajists resorted to walk-outs as a mark of protest against the policy of the Government. They boycotted all receptions, parties or functions organised by the Government. What was done in the Central Assembly was also done in those provincial legislatures where the Swarajists had some influence.

Dr. R.C. Majumdar says that the Swarajist Party rendered a signal service to the country. For the first time, the Legislative Assembly wore the appearance of a truly National Assembly where national grievances were fully voiced, national aims and aspirations expressed without any reservation and real character of the British rule exposed. The British autocracy and Indian bureaucracy stood exposed to the whole world.

THE CIVIL DISOBEDIENCE MOVEMENT

There was a lot of agitation in the country when the Simon Commission visited India. At the Calcutta Session of the Congress held in 1928, it was intended to pass a resolution declaring complete independence as the goal of India. However, Mahatma Gandhi intervened and Dominion Status was declared to be the goal of India. Mahatma Gandhi gave the assurance that he himself would lead the movement for independence if by the end of 1929 the British Government did not confer Dominion Status on India.

When the Congress leaders met on the banks of the river Ravi, near Lahore, in 1929 they were disappointed over the attitude of the British Government. Leaders like Jawaharlal Nehru, Subhash Chandra Bose and Srinivas Iyengar asked for bold action against the Government. In his presidential address, Jawaharlal Nehru condemned British imperialism, Kings and Princes and declared himself to be a socialist and a Republican. He called upon the leaders assembled there to take strong action in these words: "Talking of high stakes and going through great dangers were the only way to achieve great things". He declared that complete independence should be the goal of the Congress. Mahatma Gandhi also approved of that goal but he did not like to precipitate matters. A resolution was passed that the word Swaraj in the Congress Constitution means "complete independence". All Congressmen taking part in the National Movement were asked not to take part, directly or indirectly, in future elections and the sitting members were asked to resign their seats. The All-India Congress Committee was authorised to launch a programme of civil disobedience including the non-payment of taxes. At midnight of 31 December 1929, the Tricolour Flag of Independence was hoisted on the banks of the river Ravi by the Congress President, Jawaharlal Nehru.

26 January 1930 was declared Independence Day and a pledge was taken by the people of India on that date and the same was repeated year after year. From 14 to 16 February 1930, the Congress Working Committee met at Sabarmati Ashram and vested Mahatma Gandhi with full powers to launch the Civil Disobedience Movement "at a time and place of his choice". On 27 February, the plan of the agitation was announced and Mahatma Gandhi declared that he would first defy the Salt laws along with 78 chosen members of his Ashram. On 2 March 1930, Mahatma Gandhi wrote to the Viceroy in which he gave his own assessment of the situation in the country and put forward his programme to ease the situation. He made it clear that if his suggestion was not accepted, he would start the Civil Disobedience Movement. His threat was treated by the Government with amusement and contempt. On 12 March 1930, accompanied by 78 inmates of the Sabarmati Ashram, Mahatma Gandhi started on his march of 240 miles to the seacoast at Dandi. Huge crowds gathered at the Ashram to see him off. Gandhiji hoped that he would not return to the Ashram until Swaraj was won. His march assumed the character of a Padayatra with object of achieving Purna Swaraj for India. Moti Lal Nehru compared the Dandi march with the "historic march of Ramchandra to Lanka". Gandhiji described it as "the war against Salt Tax". Prayers were offered all over India for the success of Mahatma Gandhi's mission and the people watched with great interest the progress of the march. At every stage where Mahatma Gandhi halted on the way the people flocked in thousands to hear him and asked for his blessings. He addressed numerous meetings and urged the people to remain non-violent.

Gandhiji reached Dandi on 5 April and broke the salt laws on 6 April by picking up the salt lying on the beach. He called upon the people to celebrate the week from 6 April to 13 April as the national week and defy the salt laws and picket liquor shops, opium dens and foreign cloth-dealer shops. He also appealed to the people to leave the Government schools, colleges and services. There was a favourable response from the people. Public meetings were held all over the country. Hundreds of Government servants left their jobs. Many legislators resigned their seats and hundreds of people violated the salt laws. Liquor shops were boycotted. Peasants refused to pay taxes and debts. The country appeared to be in open revolt.

The Government followed a policy of repression to suppress the movement. Even before the movement was actually started, thousands of Congress workers were arrested and put in jails. Subhash Chandra Bose was sentenced to one year's rigorous imprisonment. On 16 April 1930, Jawaharlal Nehru was put in jail and his imprisonment was followed by thousands of others. Police firing, lathi-charges and arrests became the order of the day. Even women were not spared. From Delhi alone, about 1,600 women were arrested. On 23 April 1930, the Bengal ordinance was promulgated and the life of freedom, fighters was made very hard. The Press Act of 1910 was strictly enforced and many restrictions were put on the newspapers. Many newspapers and magazines stopped their publications. Civilian property was destroyed. Innocent men and women were beaten up. Prisoners were starved and suffocated. Hundreds of men and women were killed as a result of police firing.

Mahatma Gandhi was arrested on 5 May 1930 and his place was taken by Abbas Tyabji as a leader of the movement. When he was arrested, he was succeeded by Sarojini Naidu. Demonstrations were organised throughout India against Gandhiji's arrest. In Bombay, riots broke out. In Madras (now Chennai), police beating was indiscriminate. The boycott of British goods was the highest in Bengal, Bihar and Orissa (now Odisha). In U.P., the peasants and zamindars were called upon to withhold all payments of revenue. In the Central Provinces, Satyagraha was launched against forest taxes. In Karnataka a successful no-tax campaign was launched. In the Midnapur District of West Bengal, Gorkha troops and punitive police started a reign of terror which did not spare even the honour of women. The peasants cheerfully saw before their eyes the destruction of their huts and all the little possessions they had on earth but they refused to pay taxes. In Gujarat, the peasants began to migrate to the State of Baroda.

Regarding the results of the Civil Disobedience Movement of 1930, Louis Fischer wrote: "Gandhi did two things in 1950: he made the British people aware that they were cruelly subjugating India and he gave Indians the conviction that they would, by lifting their heads and straightening their spines, lift the yoke from their shoulders. The British beat the Indians with batons and rifle butts. The Indians neither cringed nor complained nor retreated. That made England powerless and India invincible".

The First Round Table Conference was held in London from 12 November 1930 to 19 January 1931. Not much was done at the Conference on account of the absence of any representative of the Congress. While winding up the deliberations of the Conference, Prime Minister Ramsay Macdonald declared that "steps would be taken to enlist the cooperation of those sections of public opinion which had held aloof from the Conference".

The Government seemed to be in a mood to come to terms with the Congress. It was felt that there was no prospect of the successful working of the new reforms unless the Congress was willing to work them. On 25 January 1931, Lord Irwin appealed to the people of India to consider the statement made by the British Prime Minister. He also declared that Mahatma Gandhi and all other members of the Congress Working Committee would be released at an early date to consider the matter "freely and fearlessly". In pursuance of this statement, the Congress leaders were released. Sir Tej Bahadur Sapru, M.R. Jayakar and V.S. Sastri were able to persuade Mahatma Gandhi to see the Viceroy and discuss the possibility of a compromise. The discussions between the Viceroy and Mahatma Gandhi continued for 15 days and on 5 March 1931 was signed the Gandhi Irwin Pact.

As regards the terms of the Pact, both the Congress and the Government were required to do certain things. The Government of India was to make concessions and the Congress was to withdraw the Civil Disobedience Movement. It was agreed that the Government would take steps for the participation of the representatives of the Congress in the Second Round Table Conference. It was specifically provided that if the Congress failed to give full effect to the obligations of the settlement, the Government was to be at liberty to take such action as might be considered necessary for the protection of the public and the individuals and due observance of law and order.

The spirit in which the Gandhi-Irwin Pact was signed did not last long. In spite of protests from all quarters, the Government carried out the execution of Sardar Bhagat Singh, Sukh Dev and Raj Guru on 23 March 1931. On 18 April 1931, Lord Irwin was succeeded by Lord Willingdon. The new Viceroy had no intention to abide by the terms of the Pact. In the United Provinces, the armed police and the magistracy terrorised and harassed the people. The houses of the Congress workers were raided. The Congress flag was burnt and women were insulted. The holding of public meetings was prohibited, and those who violated the law were prosecuted. The confiscated property of the peasants was restored with great difficulty in Gujarat. Congressmen were imprisoned without trial in Bengal. Legal practitioners were required to give undertakings. Prisoners were not released in Bombay. Peaceful picketing was not allowed. Many students were rusticated from schools and colleges. There were similar violations of the Pact in Madras and Delhi. Mahatma Gandhi brought those violations to the notice of the Government but there was no response. However, Mahatma Gandhi went to attend the Second Round Table Conference in London in 1931.

Mahatma Gandhi attended the conference as the sole representative of the Congress. He demanded control over defence and foreign affairs. There was a complete deadlock on the question of representation of minorities. M.A. Jinnah, H. H. the Agha Khan, and Dr. Ambedkar were not willing to come to a settlement with Mahatma Gandhi. Mahatma Gandhi was not satisfied with the statement of Prime Minister Ramsay MacDonald made on 1 December 1931, and declared that they had "come to the parting of ways" and their ways would hereafter "take different directions".

Mahatma Gandhi came back to India on 28 December 1931. On 29 December, he sent a telegram to the Viceroy in which he expressed his great concern over the happenings in the country. He particularly referred to the uncalled-for shootings in the country. In reply, the Government justified its stand. The Viceroy also refused to grant an interview to Mahatma Gandhi. On 4 January 1932, the Government of India issued 4 Ordinances, viz., the Emergency Power Ordinance, Unlawful Instigation Ordinances, Unlawful Association Ordinance and Prevention of Molestation and Boycott Ordinance. Within a short time, the number of Ordinances reached 13. The scope of these Ordinances was very comprehensive and they covered "almost every activity of Indian life".

By 10 January 1932, all leading Congressmen were behind the prison-bars. Not only the Congress was declared illegal, even those organisations which were in any way connected with it or were sympathetic towards it were declared illegal. Youth leagues, students' associations, national schools and institutions, Congress hospitals, Swadeshi concerns and libraries were all declared illegal. There were hundreds of names of this kind in each province.

Even before the civil disobedience movement was actually started by Gandhiji, he was arrested along with Vallabhbhai Patel who at that time was the President of the Congress. Thousands of Congressmen were arrested. The Government took forcible possession of the offices of the Congress. Lathi-charges were common to disperse the crowds. Even women and children were not spared. Every effort was made to break the spirit of the people. The cattle, household furniture, utensils, jewellery, etc., were either confiscated or destroyed. A deliberate policy was followed by the Government to make the lot of the political prisoners worse than that of convicts. A confidential circular was sent to all the prison authorities emphasising the fact that the prisoners of the civil disobedience movement must be dealt with severely. Whipping became a common punishment.

In spite of the pressure, the civil disobedience movement continued. Meetings and demonstrations were held in spite of the restrictions imposed by the Government. Liquor shops and foreign cloth shops were picketed. The people refused to pay taxes. Salt laws were broken. National flags were hoisted on the Government buildings. The boycott programme was very extensive affecting even banks, insurance companies and the bullion exchanges. The no-tax campaign was also continued. However, a stage came when the political enthusiasm of the people became less and less and feelings of frustration set in. The movement was suspended in May 1933 and completely withdrawn in May 1934. Gandhiji withdrew himself from active politics.

THE SECOND WORLD WAR AND THE CONGRESS

On 1 September 1939, the Second World War began. On 3 September 1939, the Viceroy of India declared war against Germany without consulting or taking into confidence the Indian leaders. Indian troops were sent to the various theatres of war for the defence of the British Empire. After having done all this, the Viceroy started consultations with the Indian leaders. The Working Committee of the Congress met at Wardha in September 1939 and after prolonged deliberations, a resolution was adopted in which it was declared that if the war was "to defend the status quo, imperialist possessions, colonies, vested interests and privileges then India can have nothing to do with it. If, however, the issue is democracy and a world based on democracy, then India is intensely interested in it. If Great Britain was fighting for the maintenance and extension of democracy, then she must necessarily end imperialism in her own possessions and establish full democracy in India". The British Government was called upon to declare its war aims "in regard to democracy and imperialism" and also to declare whether those aims were "going to apply to India and to be given effect to at present".

On 27 July 1940, a resolution was passed by the Congress in which an offer of cooperation in the war was made provided India's demand for independence was conceded and a provisional National Government responsible to the then Central Assembly was formed at the Centre. On 8 August 1940, the Viceroy issued a statement in which it was declared that the new Constitution of India would primarily be the responsibility of the Indians themselves. However, it was made clear that Great Britain "could not contemplate transfer of their present responsibilities for the peace and welfare of India to any system of Government whose authority is directly denied by large and powerful elements in India's national life, nor could they be parties to the coercion of such elements into submission of such a Government". It was also declared that after the war a "representative Indian constitution-making body would be set up and the Indian proposals as to its form and operation would at any time be welcome". The Congress was wholly disappointed with the August Offer.

It was in the month of March 1942 that Cripps was sent to India with certain proposals with a view to seek the cooperation of the Congress in the prosecution of the war. To begin with, the response to the Congressmen was favourable. Cripps is stated to have assured the Congress leaders that under the proposed scheme, the Governor-General would function as a constitutional head. It appears that the offer was made without consulting the Viceroy and consequently the Viceroy complained to Prime Minister Churchill and the latter informed Cripps that he would be repudiated if he 'went too far". Fresh instructions were sent to Cripps and the latter told the Congress President that the position of the Viceroy could not be changed without a change in the law. On 11 April 1942, a resolution was passed by the Congress Working Committee rejecting Cripps proposals. It was pointed out that only a free and independent India could undertake the defence of the country on a national basis.

"QUIT INDIA" MOVEMENT

After the failure of the Cripps Mission, there were differences of opinion among the Congress leaders regarding the future course of action to be adopted. The view of Maulana Azad who at that time was the Congress President, was that negotiations should be resumed with Great Britain and full cooperation should be extended to the United Nations if Great Britain made an absolute promise of Indian independence after the war and if the American President or the United Nations gave a guarantee that the promise will be fulfilled. Nehru's view was that the British Government must make a formal declaration of India's independence at once. The Provisional Government then formed should negotiate with Great Britain the terms of cooperation. The Commander-in-Chief of the Allied Forces was to be given full support in all decisions relating to military matters and the Japanese must be resisted by the Indians at all costs. Mahatma Gandhi advocated mass action to drive out the British out of India.

A meeting of the Congress Working Committee was held at Wardha and after a lot of discussion, a resolution was passed on 14 July 1942, which stated that the failure of the Cripps Mission and the attitude of the British Government towards India "has resulted in a rapid and widespread increase of ill-will against Britain and a growing satisfaction at the influence of Japanese arms". It was stated that the Congress desired "to build up resistance to any aggression on or invasion of India by the Japanese or any foreign power" and the Congress would change the ill-will against Great Britain into good-will "if India feels the glow of freedom". It was made clear that "in making the proposal for the withdrawal of the British rule from India, the Congress had no desire whatsoever to embarrass Great Britain or the Allied Powers in their prosecution of the war, or in any way to encourage aggression on India or increased pressure on China by the Japanese or any other power associated with the Axis Group". It was hoped that this "very reasonable and just proposal" would be accepted by Great Britain, "not only in the interests of India but also that of Britain and of the cause of freedom to which the United Nations proclaimed their adherence". It was made clear in the resolution that in case India's appeal was not accepted, the Congress would "then be reluctantly compelled to utilise all the non-violent strength it might have gathered since 1920, when it adopted non-violence as part of its policy, for the vindication of political rights and liberty". The final decision was to be taken by the All India Congress whose meeting was fixed for 7 August 1942 at Bombay (now Mumbai).

The Congress gave 24 days to the Government to make a favourable response. On 15 July 1942 Mahatma Gandhi told the foreign press that if the movement had to be launched it would be a non-violent one. On 25 July 1942, President Chiang Kai-shek wrote to President Roosevelt to intervene so that the Congress was not forced to launch the movement. The letter was forwarded to Churchill but nothing came out of it.

A meeting of the All India Congress Committee was held in Bombay on 7 August 1942 as scheduled. The general feeling was that an attempt be made to come to terms with the Government and for that purpose Mahatma Gandhi expressed the wish to meet the Viceroy. However, on 8 August 1942, the famous "Quit India" resolution was moved by Jawaharlal Nehru and passed by an overwhelming majority. It was declared in that resolution that the immediate ending of the British rule in India was an urgent necessity, both for the sake of India and for the success of the cause of the United Nations. India had become the crux of the question. Great Britain and the United Nations will be judged by the independence of India. Addressing the Congress delegates on the night of 8 August 1942, Gandhiji said, "I, therefore, want freedom immediately, this very night, before dawn, if it can be had. You may take it from me that I am not going to strike a bargain with the Viceroy for ministers and the like. I am not going to be satisfied with anything short of complete freedom. Here is a Mantra, a short one, that I give you. You may imprint it on your hearts and let every breath of yours give expression to it. The Mantra is: "Do or die.' We shall either free India or die in the attempt; we shall not live to see the perpetuation of our slavery".

When the resolution was passed, an appeal was made to Great Britain and the United Nations to respond to the "call of reason and justice". It was also decided that all efforts should be made to come to a settlement with the government and it was only when those efforts failed that the movement was to be started after Mahatma Gandhi had given his sanction. Mahatma Gandhi and Maulana Azad openly declared that they would approach the Viceroy again and the heads of the various Governments for an honourable settlement. It was also decided that Jawaharlal Nehru was to explain on 9 August 1942 to the United States the scope and contents of the 'Quit India' resolution.

It appears that the Government had already finalised their plans to arrest the Congress leaders and crush their movement and consequently, in the early hours of the morning of 9 August, Mahatma Gandhi, Jawaharlal Nehru, Maulana Azad, Sardar Patel, Rajendra Prasad, Acharya Kripalani, etc., were arrested. As many as 148 Congress leaders were arrested and interned along with their followers. The people were stunned, as their leaders were arrested all of a sudden, they did not know what to do. The result was that they carried on the movement in any way they could. All over the country, there were 'hartals' and strikes in factories, schools and colleges and public demonstrations. Angered by repeated firings and lathi-charges, the people took to violence at many places. They attacked the police stations, post offices, railway stations, etc. They cut off telegraph and telephone wires and railway lines. They burnt the Government buildings. Railway carriages were put on fire. Even the military vehicles were destroyed. Madras and Bengal were the most affected in this respect. In many places, the people got temporary control over towns, citizens and villages. British authority disappeared in parts of Uttar Pradesh, Bihar, Orissa, West Bengal, Maharashtra, Andhra and Madras. At some places, the people set up parallel Governments. To quote Jawaharlal Nehru, "For the first time since the great revolt of 1857, vast numbers of people rose to challenge by force (but a force without arms) the fabric of British rule in India".

The Government used all its machinery to suppress the movement. Hundreds of persons were arrested and imprisoned. A large number of them were killed chiefly by the firing of the military and the police. The people were insulted, assaulted and injured regardless of their position and status. Whipping was inflicted on many and heavy collective fines were imposed and recovered. K. C. Neogy called those fines as communal fines as those were realised only from the Hindus. There was machine-gunning of mobs from air at five places: Patna, Bhagalpur and Monghyr in Bihar, Nadia in Bengal and Talchar city. According to the official figures, the civilian casualties from August to December 1942 were 940 killed and many more injured. Nehru's view was that figures of the dead varied between 4,000 to 10,000. More than 60,000 persons were arrested up to the end of 1942, 26,000 persons were convicted and 18,000 were detained under the Defence of India Rules.

Many reasons have been given for starting the "Quit India" movement. The first was the growing threat of Japanese invasion of India. Mahatma Gandhi wanted to save India from that attack and his view was if the British Government withdrew from India, the Japanese might not attack India. Another reason was the defencelessness of the British position in India and their easy defeat in Singapore. The view of Mahatma Gandhi was that India would meet the same fate if the British did not withdraw from India. Another reason was the alarming growth of Axis propaganda which was having its effect on the minds of the people of India. This was particularly so on account of the broadcasts of Subhash Chandra Bose from Berlin in the Indian languages. Another cause was that the mind of Mahatma Gandhi was revolting against the racial discrimination shown in the process of evacuation from Burma. The British provided separate routes for the evacuation of Europeans and Indians. The White Road was meant for Europeans and the Black Road for Indians. The result was that the Indian evacuees had to undergo too many hardships on the way. There was a lot of resentment in the country when the people heard of the sufferings of the Indians and that contributed to the decision of Mahatma Gandhi to start the "Quit India" movement. Another cause was the sufferings of the people on account of the "scorched earth" policy followed by the British Government in India. The lands belonging to the people of India were taken for military purposes and they were not given adequate compensation. They were deprived of their means of livelihood. A lot of harshness was used by the Government while getting the houses of peasants evacuated for the military. The inefficient and ineffective controls and transportation muddles added to the sufferings of the people. Prices rose in those months and the people lost their faith in the paper currency issued by the Government. There was a lot of discontentment among the people and Mahatma Gandhi decided to take advantage of it.

The failure of the Quit India movement was due to many causes. The first was the tactical mistakes of organisation and planning. The arrest of Mahatma Gandhi and the Congress leaders left the people without any leadership or guidance. There was no co-ordination and no strategy. Those who led the movement were divided in their views on the course of action. Nobody knew what to do. The loyalty of the services and the superior physical strength of the Government succeeded in crushing the revolt. The movement did not have the support of the upper classes of India consisting of rich merchants, landlords and princes and also a part of labour. On the whole, the Muslims remained aloof from the movement. They were told by the Muslim League that the movement was directed to coerce the British Government to hand over to the Hindus the administration of the country.

As regards the gains of the revolt of 1942, Dr. Amba Prasad says that although the revolt failed it prepared the ground for independence in 1947. After the revolt, no doubt was left in the minds of the British rulers that the days of British domination of India were numbered. It was only a question of time. The revolt marked the culmination of the Indian freedom movement. It gave utterance to India's anger against imperialism and her determination to be free. It is true that there were many political developments and much parleying and bargaining between the revolt of August 1942 and the independence of India in August 1947, but there was no doubt about the fact that the freedom struggle was bound to win.

Two important events took place in 1945. One was that general elections took place in England and the Labour Party came to power. The other was the surrender of Japan on 14 August 1945 and the termination of hostilities in the Far East. Unlike Churchill, the new Labour Government was sympathetically inclined towards the Indian demand for freedom. As the pre-occupation with war was over, the Labour Government tried to solve the Indian problem. The Viceroy of India was summoned to London. After prolonged discussions, the Viceroy came back to India and declared on 19 September 1945 that the Government had decided to convene a constitution-making body in the near future. It was declared that elections to the Central Assembly and the Provincial Legislatures would be held "during the coming cold weather".

Elections to the Central Assembly were held in November and December 1945. In the first week of January 1946, the Parliamentary Delegation came to India to meet the Indian leaders. On 15th March 1946, Prime Minister Attlee declared in the House of Commons that India herself must decide her future Constitution and no minority in India would be allowed to place a veto on the advance of the majority. The Cabinet Mission reached Delhi on 24 March 1946 and on 16 May 1946, it gave its own solution of the problem known as the Cabinet Mission Scheme. On 2 September 1946, Jawaharlal Nehru formed the Interim Government. The Constituent Assembly met on 9 December 1946 but was boycotted by the Muslim League. On 20 February 1946, the British Government declared that it would transfer power into the hands of the Indians by a date not later than June 1948. Lord Mountbatten gave his 3 June Plan for the partition of India. The Indian Independence Act was passed in July 1947 and India became Independent on 15 August 1947.

WHY ENGLAND GAVE INDIA INDEPENDENCE?

1. There were many reasons which forced the British Government to grant independence to India and the most important was the strength of the nationalist movement. The movement under the leadership of Mahatma Gandhi had become so strong that the grant of independence could not be postponed for long. The "Quit India" Movement had shown that the people of India could go to any length to bring to an end the British Raj in the country. They made tremendous sacrifices to paralyse the administrative machinery. The British Government was fully aware of the slogans: "Do or Die" and "Now or Never". The organisation of the Indian National Army under Subhash Chandra Bose and the cry of "Delli Chalo" made the British Government realise the folly of resisting the demand of the people of India for independence.

2. Another cause was that the British Government lost faith in the loyalty of the armed forces in India, particularly the Navy. Throughout, Great Britain had relied upon force and military superiority for maintaining its hold over India. Force was always available to crush any revolt on the part of the Indians. However, circumstances changed to such an extent during the Second World War that the loyalty of the Indian forces could not be depended upon. Thousands of Indians from all over India joined the armed forces during the Second World War. They not only fought for the victory of the Allied Powers but also hoped that India would get independence after the war. No wonder when the war was over, these persons began to clamour for the

freedom of India. They were willing to give a helping hand to the nationalist movement in the country. Political consciousness was visible in the armed forces of the country. On 19 February 1946, the Ratings of the Royal Indian Navy stopped work and gave a notice to the Government that unless their demands were met by a particular date, they would resign en bloc. There were strikes at the Air Force bases. Signs of open revolt were visible in Bombay (now Mumbai), Calcutta (now Kolkata) and Karachi. It is true that the revolts were crushed but a feeling was created among the British that they could not keep India under their control with the help of the Indian forces. The British troops in the Indian Ocean could help in maintaining British control over India for some time, but that could not continue for long. It was under these circumstances that the British Government decided to withdraw from India.

3. After the end of the Second World War, the British authorities decided to try Col. Shah Nawaz, Captain Sehgal and Dhillon and other members of the Indian National Army for the crime of waging war against the King-Emperor before a Court Martial. There was a lot of agitation in the country against the decision of the Government. On 22 September 1945, the Congress Working Committee appointed a committee to defend the I.N.A. men. The trial started on 5 November 1945 in the Red Fort of Delhi and lasted up to 31 December. The decision was announced on 3 January 1946 and Shah Nawaz, Sehgal and Dhillon were found guilty and sentenced to transportation for life. Many more trials were held and the accused were found guilty. During the trial, the sufferings of the I.N.A. officers and men came to light. The arguments put forward by the defence counsel were published in the newspapers and read by millions of Indians. Shah Nawaz, Sehgal and Dhillon became popular heroes. There were mass demonstrations throughout the country for their release. On certain occasion, the police resorted to firing and many Indians lost their lives. The result was that Field Marshal Auchin-leck, Commander-in-Chief of India, granted clemency to Shah Nawaz, Sehgal and Dhillon. On 6 February 1946, the Government of India announced its decision not to proceed any further with the trials and consequently cases against the rest of the I.N.A. men were withdrawn. After their release, the I.N.A. officers and men toured all over the country and they were greeted with cries of "Jai Hind". So great was the enthusiasm among the people that the English began to feel that it was not possible for them to keep India in chains.

4. There had been a feeling in India that the British power was invincible. However, this impression was removed during the Second World War as a result of the military reverses suffered by the British troops at the hands of the Japanese. British troops were forced to evacuate Hong Kong, Singapore, Malaya and Burma. Their best ships, "The Repulse" and "Prince of Wales", were sunk. Great Britain was not in a position "to demonstrate in Asia the background of strength and influence which had for so long enabled her to rule a million people with one man on the spot".

5. Great Britain had to spend so much during the Second World War that she was completely exhausted. She was forced to borrow on an enormous scale. She had to depend upon other countries not only for foodstuffs but also for raw materials to run her factories. She depended upon American help in every field. The Englishmen had too many problems to tackle at home. It was felt that it was not wise to keep herself involved in India when all her energy was required at home. The American Government also put pressure on the British Government to grant India independence as the Allied Powers had been fighting for freedom and democracy. Even die-hards like Churchill began to feel that it was not of any advantage to keep India under bondage.

6. Mr. Attlee, Prime Minister of England at that time, had a lot to do with the grant of independence to India. He had always taken keen interest in the Indian affairs. When he became Prime Minister of England in 1945, he came to the conclusion that even if Great Britain was able to keep India in bondage with the help of force, that was not profitable to

her as by doing so, she was bound to lose the goodwill of the people of India and in that case, the Indo-British relations were bound to suffer in the long run. His view was that Great Britain was bound to gain if she was able to win the goodwill of the people of India by giving them independence. To begin with, he sent the Cabinet Mission to India, but when that failed, he sent Lord Mountbatten to complete the process of transfer of power in India.

7. Another reason why Great Britain decided to leave India was that she got involved in the cold war after the Second World War. Both the United States and the Soviet Union accused each other. The Russians had an advantage over the Americans in the cold war. They could always point out the fact that Great Britain was keeping India in chains. Great Britain could be in a better position if she granted India independence.

8. A large number of persons advocated the cause of India's freedom abroad. Among them were Louis Fischer, Pearl Buck, Lin Yu-tang, Norman. Thomas and J.J. Singh. The Indian viewpoint was put forward before the Conference at San Francisco which met to finalise the Charter of the United Nations. Great Britain was not only a signatory to the Charter but her delegates played an important part in framing it. This fact was bound to affect the attitude of the British Government towards India. She could not talk of freedom for all while keeping India in bondage.

9. Another factor which influenced the British decision to leave India was a change in the concept of the British Commonwealth. In July 1947, the Commonwealth Relations Office was set up. If the British could treat other Dominions in that manner, there was no reason why the same could not be done with regard to India. It was felt that even after India was given independence, she could be persuaded to be a part and parcel of the Commonwealth of Nations and hence no loss to Great Britain.

10. The view of Maulana Azad was that the British Government decided to leave India only after making sure that she could continue to have a foothold on the Indian sub-continent. The British decision to partition India and then to transfer power was the culmination of the policy of "divide and rule". The partition of India in which the Muslim majority provinces formed a separate and independent state would give Britain a foothold in India. A state dominated by the Muslim League would offer a permanent sphere of influence to Great Britain.

11. We are reliably informed by some respectable Indians who returned to India from England during the year immediately following the end of the Second World War that British soldiers who had first-hand knowledge of the poverty of the Indian masses spoke about it feelingly to their friends and relatives. That knowledge filtered down to the people. A feeling was created in England that perhaps with the independence, the Indians might be able to improve their economic condition. That explains the unanimous support given by the members of Parliament to the Indian Independence Bill in July 1947.

12. The view of Prime Minister Attlee was that the independence of India was the fulfillment of Britain's mission in India. The British were leaving India after fulfilling their mission in the country. They had taught the Indians to govern themselves and they were now leaving the reins of Government in their hands.

REVIEW QUESTIONS

1. Discuss the nature and causes of the Nationalist Movement in India.
2. Describe the origin of the Indian National Congress and throw light on its various sessions.
3. Explain the history of the Indian National Movement.
4. Assess the role of the moderates and extremists in the Indian National Movement.
5. What was the attitude of the government towards the moderates? Discuss.

6. Throw light on the achievements of the moderates and extremists in the Indian National Movement.
7. Write a detailed note on the Sural Split.
8. Many factors were responsible for the rise and growth of the revolutionary and terrorist movement in the country. Explain.
9. Write short notes on the following:
   (a) Sural Split, 1907
   (b) Militant Nationalism
   (c) Partition of Bengal
   (d) Home Rule Movement
   (e) Ghadar Party
   (f) Kakori Case
   (h) Quit India Movement
   (g) Jallianwala Bagh Tragedy
10. Write an essay on the Non-Cooperation and Civil Disobedience Movements.
11. Discuss the contribution of Gandhi in the Non-Cooperation and Civil Disobedience Movements.
12. Give an account of the Quit India Movement.

SUGGESTED READINGS

Agarwal, L.N.: *Indian Nationalist Movement.*
Ahluwalia, M.M.: *Freedom Struggle in India (1858-1909),* Delhi, 1965.
Amba Prasad: *The Indian Revolt of 1942.*
Argove, Daniel: *Moderates and Extremists in the Indian National Movement.*
Banerjee, S.N.: *A Nation in the Making,* London, 1925.
Bhartarya, S.C.: *The Indian Nationalist Movement,* Allahabad, 1958.
Bose, Subhash Chandra: *The Indian Struggle (1920-1934),* London, 1935.
Buch, M.A.: *Rise and Growth of Indian Militant Nationalism,* Baroda, 1941.
Chatterjee, Nand Lal: *India's Freedom Struggle,* Allahabad, 1958.
Datta, K.K.: *India's March to Freedom.*
Ghose, P.C.: *Indian National Congress,* Calcutta, 1960.
Girja, Mookerjee: *The Rise and Growth of the Congress in India,* London, 1938.
Hans, Kohn: *A History of Nationalism in the East.*
Heimsath, Charles H.: *Indian Nationalism and Hindu Social Reform,* Bombay, 1964.
Lovett, Sir Warney.: *A History of the Indian Nationalist Movement (1600-1919).*
Majumdar, B.B.: *Political Thought from Ram Mohan to Dayanand,* 1934.
Majumdar, R.C.: *History of the Freedom Movement in India.* Vols. I, II and III.
Mukherjee, Haridas & Uma: *The Growth of Nationalism in India (1857-1905),* Calcutta, 1957.
Raghuvanshi, V.P.S.: *Indian Nationalist Movement and Thought,* Agra, 1959.
Singh, Sita Ram: *Nationalism and Social Reform in India (1885-1920),* Delhi.
Singh, G.N.: *Landmarks in Indian Constitutional and National Development (1600-1919),* Banaras, 1930.
Sitaramayya, Pattabhi: *History of the Indian National Congress,* Vols. I and II.
Tara Chand: *History of Freedom Movement in India.*
Wolperi, S.A. Tilak and Gokhale: *Revolution and Reform in the Making of Modern India,* Berkeley, 1962.

22 Establishment of Pakistan

LEARNING OBJECTIVES

- Throw light on the condition of Muslims before 1871
- Know the history of the creation of Pakistan
- Evaluate the role of Sir Syed Ahmed Khan and Sir Mohammad Iqbal in the establishment of Pakistan

The English were the successors of the Muslim rulers in India and no wonder, on the eve of British expansion in this country, the Muslims occupied all places of profit, prestige, and influence. When that power was snatched away by the British, there was no love lost between the Muslims and the British. The latter also followed a policy of crushing completely the Muslims. According to Mohammad Norman, "The British people had decided that for the expansion of the new power and its continuance, the only course was to crush the Mussalmans and had deliberately adopted policies which had for their aim the economic ruin of Muslims and their intellectual stagnation and general degeneration." (*Muslim India.*)

CONDITION OF MUSLIMS BEFORE 1871

It is pointed out that the Permanent Settlement of Bengal "elevated the Hindu collectors who up to that time had held but unimportant posts, to the position of land-holders, gave them proprietary right in the soil and allowed them to accumulate wealth which would have gone to Mussalmans under their own rule." The Muslims were welcomed into the service of the English East India Company. It is stated that between 1852 and 1862, out of 240 natives admitted as pleaders of the High Court, there was only one Muslim. In certain cases, the British Government clearly stated that the jobs were only to be given to the Hindus and not to the Muslims. The educational policy of the British Government was responsible for the increase of unemployment and the closing of other avenues for the Muslims. The economic policy impoverished the Indian Muslims. In the Army, their recruitment was limited; in arts and crafts they were crippled and rendered helpless. The result of these policies was the catastrophe of 1857, which no human policy could have averted."

Even before the Mutiny of 1857, the Muslims had revolted against the British Government under the Wahabi leaders. It is true that the Wahabi Movement[1] in India was primarily a religious movement, but it was also a proletarian and revolutionary movement. The Wahabi leaders stirred

---

[1] The Wahabi Movement was started in Arabia towards the end of the 18th century. At the beginning, it was purely religious. It was brought to India by Syed Ahmed Brelvi. It acquired a popular and revolutionary character in India. It taught hatred against the foreign rulers. The Muslims who played an important part in the Mutiny were Wahabis.

the Muslims of India and a wave of enthusiasm swept over the whole country. The movement was ruthlessly suppressed by the British Government but it manifested itself in the form of the Mutiny. The prime movers in the Mutiny of 1857 were the Muslims and those Muslims were undoubtedly Wahabis. As the British considered the Muslims to be responsible for the Mutiny, they were treated very severely after 1858. In 1871, out of a total of 2,141 persons employed by the Bengal Government, there were only 92 Muslims, 711 Hindus and 1,338 Europeans. This state of affairs continued up to the 1870's. It was then that a change took place in the attitude of the British Government towards the Muslims. Sir William Hunter's book entitled *The Indian Mussalmans* which was published in 1871 marks the beginning of the change. It was contended that the Muslims were too weak for rebellion. "It was expedient now to take them into alliance rather than continue to antagonise them."

WORK OF SIR SYED AHMED KHAN

Principal Beck of the Mohammedan Anglo Oriental College, Aligarh, played a very important role in winning over the Muslims to the English side. He was able to convince Sir Syed Ahmed Khan, the great leader of the Muslims, that "while an Anglo-Muslim alliance would ameliorate the condition of the Muslim community, the nationalist alignment would lead them once again to sweat, toil and tears. He was further led to believe that supporting the Government was the surest who of making up the leeway for his community. As a result, his unique influence was used to keep the Muslims, particularly in Northern India, away from the Congress." Sir Syed had been known for his tolerant views. He had described the Hindus and Muslims as "two eyes of the beautiful bride that was India." He had declared in 1884 at Gurdaspur that the Hindus and Muslims should try to become of one heart and soul and act in unison. "If united, we can support each other. If not, the effect of one against the other would tend to the destruction and downfall of both." On another occasion, he had remarked thus: "In the word Nation, I include both Hindus and Mohammedans because it is the only meaning attached to it. With me it is not worth considering what is their religious faith' because we do not see anything of it. What we do see is that we inhabit the same land, are subject to the same rule of the same Governors, the fountains of benefit for all are the same, and pangs of famine also we suffer equally. These are the different grounds upon which I call both these races which inhabit India by one word, i.e., Hindus, meaning to say that they are inhabitants of Hindustan." The influence of Beck was so great on Sir Syed that the latter began to attack the Congress and the Hindus. He defined the Congress movement as "a civil war without arms." His contention was that if India was to be given an elective system based on worth or education or principles as demanded by the Congress, "the whole Council will consist of Babus so and so" and all Muslims "hated these fish-eating Babus of Bengal." He opposed the Congress demand for the holding of simultaneous competitive examinations for the civil service and prayed that "we are to be allowed to use the pen of our ancestors." Sir Syed's policy was based on fear of permanent domination of Muslims by Hindus educationally, economically and politically.

Sir Syed laid the foundation of the Indian Patriotic Association with a view "to publish and circulate pamphlets and other papers for information of members of Parliament, English journals and the people of Great Britain, in which those mis-statements will be pointed out by which the supporters of the Indian National Congress have wrongly attempted to convince the English people that all the nations of India and the Indian Chiefs and Rulers agree with the aims and objects of the National Congress to inform Members of Parliament and the newspapers of Great Britain and its people by the same means of the opinions of Mohammedans in general, all the Islamia Anjamans, and those Hindus and their societie which are opposed to the objects of the National Congress to strive to preserve peace in India and to strengthen the British ruler; and to remove those bad feelings from the hearts of the Indian people, which the supporters of the Congress are stirring up throughout the country and by which great dissatisfaction is being raised among the people against the British Government." Sir Syed also laid the foundation of the Annual Muslim Education

Conference in 1886, a year after the establishment of the National Congress. In 1893 was set up the Mohammedan Defence Association of Upper India. Sir Syed also saw that unless Mussalman religious ideas of the day could be freed from their superstitious accretions his educational scheme was not likely to succeed. But at a time when even to learn the mere rudiments of the English language was regarded by the gentle and the simple as the surest way of perdition and tantamount to a renunciation of Islam, his work was a very tedious one. Sir Syed did the work wholeheartedly and he was eminently successful.

WORK OF BECK

Beck organised the Muslim opposition in 1889 to Bradlaugh's Bill in the British Parliament for giving representative institutions to India. The memorial which was sent on behalf of the Muslims of India claimed that the introduction of democratic institutions was not suited to India because she was not one nation. In 1893 was organised the Mohammedans Defence Association with Beck as one of its Secretaries. The object of that association was to prevent the Muslims from joining the Congress. Beck wrote thus: "The objective of the Congress is to transfer the political control of the country from the British to the Hindus.... Muslims can have no sympathy with these demands. It is imperative for the Muslims and the British to unite with a view to fighting these agitators and prevent the introduction of democratic form of Government unsuited to the needs and genius of the country. We, therefore, advocate loyalty to the Government and Anglo-Muslim collaboration." Again, "The parliamentary system in India is most unsuited and the experiment would prove futile if representative institutions are introduced. The Muslims will be under the majority opinion of the Hindus, a thing which will be highly resented by Muslims and which, I am sure, they will not accept quietly." The important part played by Beck in alienating the Muslims from the Hindus was described in these words by Sir John Strachey in 1908: "An Englishman who was engaged in Empire building activities in far-off land has passed away. He died like a soldier at the post of his duty. The Muslims are a suspicious people. They opposed Mr. Beck in the beginning suspecting him to be a British spy, but his sincerity and selflessness soon succeeded in his gaining their confidence."

PARTITION OF BENGAL AND ITS EFFECTS

As regards the partition of Bengal, Lord Curzon was of the view that its boundaries were unscientific and required re-adjustment. According to Frases, "No other Provincial administrator in India had so large a charge and it was completed by the obstacles to rapid travel. A despatch written at the time stated that if the Lieutenant-Governor of Bengal spent the whole of the available season of the year in touring, he could only succeed during his term of office, in visiting a portion of his vast Province." According to the Calcutta Review, "Partition of the unwieldy Province of Bengal was long a crying administrative necessity admitted by all those who knew anything about the difficulty of officials." However, the real object of the partition of Bengal was the desire of the foreign rulers to strike a nail in Bengal nationalism by dividing its forces. According to G. N. Singh, "It was to drive a wedge between the two communities (Hindus and Muslims) and to create a new Mohammedan Province in which the Government was to be conducted on the basis of creedal differences. By setting up a separate Muslim Province of Eastern Bengal, the Government of India wanted to reward the Muslims for their loyalty and punish the Hindus for their defiance of British authority. The people of Bengal took up the challenge of Lord Curzon and started an agitation for the cancellation of the Partition, and the same was ultimately done in 1911.

The anti-partition movement had very significant results. "The wrongs of Bengal have done more towards strengthening the feeling of the nationality throughout India than any other cause during the last fifty years." According to Dr. Lal Bahadur, "The partition agitation was a demonstration on a large-scale of the capability of the nation to oppose the exercise of injustice by foreigners. It brought the whole of the dormant potentiality of the country to the fore and served as a period of trial to the patriots who stood the test of British rigours. The courage of our countrymen rose to unparalleled height and served as a valuable asset for all future struggle against foreign domination. It was further an inescapable indication that a determined and prolonged resistance would inevitably destroy the whole engine of tyranny and make the repression completely ineffective. The whole history of the Partition, the consequent agitation and the ultimate frustration of the original scheme taught our nation the value and importance of resistance against highhandedness and this lesson was never forgotten till independence was attained in 1947."

According to Sir Mancherjee Bhownaggree, "The modification of the Partition scheme is certainly a wise act of statesmanship and will go far to assuage the irritation cause by a policy whose object was believed by many to be the creation of disunion among the population of Bengal." According to Mrs. Annie Besant, "In closing the gulf between the two Bengals, the monarch has closed a gulf which yawned between two races and Lord Hardinge has won for himself a fame which will endure." According to Sir William Wedderburn. "This is glorious news; quite beyond not only what I expected but what I hoped for." According to Raja Peary Mohan Mukerjee, "The boon which has been conferred upon the people of Bengal by the re-union of our divided Province and by its elevation to the status of a presidency Government has stirred the hearts of our people and has filled them with the deepest of gratitude." According to Babu Ambica Charan Mazumdar, "What repressive laws, proscriptions, prosecutions and deportations have failed to achieve in six years, the kindly touch of the Royal Prerogative has accomplished in one minute."

However, the Muslims who had carried on agitation against the cancellation of the Partition were upset in 1911 and Nawab Mushtaq Hussain Viqar-ul-Mulk Bahadur observed thus on the occasion of the re-union of two Bengals: "So far as the Mussalmans are concerned, it may be understood to be the consensus of opinion that this re-union it generally disliked. In face of the assurances repeatedly given by successive Ministers of the Crown as to the Partition being a settled fact', the amalgamation betrays the weakness of the Government and will, in future, be regarded as one of the reasons for placing no trust in its utterances and actions."

When the Government of India made up their mind to give more concessions to India in the constitutional field about the year 1906 the Muslims put forward a demand for separate electorates for themselves. These demands were placed before Lord Minto by a Muslim deputation led by Sir, Agha Khan. But it must be noticed that everything was arranged by Archibold, the Principal of the Aligarh College. The deputation was a command affair. Mr. Archibold wrote thus: "Colonel Dun lop Smuth, Private Secretary of His Excellency, the Viceroy, informs me that His Excellency is agreeable to receive the Muslim deputation. He advises that a formal letter requesting permission to wait on His Excellency be sent to him. In this connection, I would like to make a few suggestions. The formal letters should be sent with the signatures of some representatives of Mussalmans. The deputation should consist of representatives of all the provinces. The third point to be considered is the text of the address. I would here suggest that we begin with a solemn assurance to loyalty. The Government's decision to take a step in this direction of self-government should be appreciated. But our apprehensions should be expressed that the principle of election, if introduced, would prove detrimental to the interests of the Muslim minority. It should respectfully be suggested that nomination or representation by religion be introduced to meet Muslim opinion. 'We should also say that in a country like India due weight must be given to the Zamindars. But in all these views, I must be in the background. They must come from you. I can prepare for you the draft of the address or revise it. If it is prepared in Bombay, I can go through it. As you are aware, I know how to phrase these things in proper language. Please remember that if we want to organise a powerful movement in the short time at our disposal, we must expedite matters."

Lord Minto received the deputation sympathetically and gave the following reply: "The pith of your address, as I understand it, is a claim that under any system of representation, whether it affects a municipality or a district board or a legislative council, in which it is proposed to introduce or increase an electoral organisation the Mohammedan community should be represented as a community. You point out that in many cases electoral bodies as now constituted cannot be expected to return a Mohammedan candidate, and if by chance they did so, it could only be at the sacrifice of such a candidate's views to those of a majority opposed to his community whom he would in no way represent; and you justly claim that your position should be estimated not only in your numerical strength, but in respect to the political importance of your community and the service it has rendered to the Empire. I am entirely in accord with you. Please do not misunderstand me. I make no attempt to indicate by what means the representation of communities can be obtained but I am as firmly convinced as I believe you to be that any electoral representation in India would be doomed to mischievous failure which aimed at granting a personal enfranchisement regardless of the beliefs and traditions of the communities composing the population of this continent." Lady Minto tells us in her Diary that Lord Minto described the day on which the Muslim deputation met him as "an epoch in Indian history."

Having committed himself to give separate electorates to the Muslims, Lord Minto took up the matter with Lord Morley, the Liberal Secretary of State for India. The latter was not in favour of the proposal of Lord Minto. But the Viceroy insisted that separate electorates alone, could satisfy the Muslims of India and nothing else. The result was that ultimately Lord Morley accepted the point of view of Lord Minto[2] and provision was made in the Act of 1909 for separate electorates for the Muslims. Lord Morley wrote to Lord Minto thus in December 1909: "I won't follow you again into our Mohammedan dispute. Only I respectfully remind you again that it was your early speech about their extra claims that started the (Muslim) hare. I am convinced my decision was best." It is clear that Lord Minto was the real father of communal electorates although the British officials also played their part.

In December 1906 was established the All-India Muslim League with a view to "support, whenever possible, all measures emanating from the Government, and to protect the cause and advance the interest of our co-religionists through the country to controvert the growing influence of the so-called Indian National Congress, which has a tendency to misinterpret and subvert British rule in India, or which might lead to that deplorable situation and to enable our young men of education, who for want of such an association have joined the Congress, to find scope, according to their fitness and ability, for public life."

It is to be observed that for a brief period the relations between the Hindus and Muslims were cordial[2] and the Congress and the Muslim League worked in collaboration. Many factors were responsible for this change. The most important cause was the treatment of Turkey by the European Powers before 1914. The Balkan Wars of 1912-13 weakened the power of Turkey in Europe. It appeared as if there was a kind of crusade against the Muslims in Europe. This was resented by the Indian Muslims who regarded the Sultan of Turkeys as the head of Islam. Turkey was considered to be the symbol of Islamic greatness. As the British Government did nothing to save Turkey, the Indians became bitter. As the Muslims were not consulted at the time of the cancellation of the partition of Bengal, they felt that they were betrayed by their British friends. Certain Muslim leaders also played their part. They captured the Muslim League under the leadership of M. A. Jinnah. As the constitution of the Muslim League was radically changed in 1913, Agha Khan was forced to resign from the presidentship of the Muslim League. The Sessions of the League and the Congress were held at the same place for some years. In 1916, both the Congress and the Muslim League held their

---

[2] Lord Morley wrote thus to Lord Minto: "Please remember in granting separate electorates, we are sowing dragon's teeth and the harvest will be bitter".

annual sessions at Lucknow. It was in that atmosphere of give and take that the famous Lucknow Pact was signed by the Muslim League and the Congress.[3]

LUCKNOW PACT, 1916

According to this Pact, the Provinces should be free as much as possible from the control of the Central Government in matters of finance and administration. Four-fifths of the Central and Provincial Legislative Councils should be elected and one-fifth nominated. The Central and Provincial Governments should be bound to act in accordance with the resolutions passed by their respective legislative councils, unless they were vetoed by the Governor-General-in-Council. The Central Legislative Council should have no power to interfere with the Government of India's direction of military affairs and the foreign and political relations of India including declaration of war and entering into treaties. The relations of the Secretary of State for India with the Government of India should be similar to those of the Colonial Secretary with the Governments of the Dominions. Although the Muslims were given many concessions to conciliate them, the British bureaucrats in India contended with the Muslims that they deserved more than what was given to them.

According to Dr. Lal Bahadur, "The fact was that in regard to communal adjustment, the Congress, generally speaking, suffered from self-delusion. Nothing could be done more headstrong than to hope for the disappearance of separate electorate after 10 years of its birth. The evil could easily be nipped in the bud, but it was allowed to grow till it served an easy stepping stone for the demand of Pakistan. A diplomatic blunder of high magnitude was committed in conceding the right of separate Muslim Representation through members of the community themselves. It proved the British allegation of sharp division between the Hindus and the Muslims and justified, for all intents and purposes, all earlier propaganda of the latter, regarding the exercise of the so-called high-handedness by the former. It was also an evidence of the tactful bankruptcy of the Congress leaders and their helpless lack of shrewdness. They ought to have understood that this concession to the Mussalmans would tear the nation for ever into two sharply divided communities and the breach would be widened by the foreign ruling power. The British Parliament recognised the Lucknow Pact as the only agreement between the Hindus and Muslims and it made, assertive provision for separate electorate in the Government of India Acts of 1919 and 1935. Once the basis of the division of the electorate was accepted the recognition of the division of the country was inevitable. The Lucknow Pact demanded a heavy toll of the country's sacrifice and the price was paid in the formation of Pakistan." Dr. Lal Bahadur maintains that there, was no pressing necessity to purchase Muslim support at an exorbitant cost. To quote him, "The Pact was bound to be transitory in character for it was a child of circumstances. The Indian Mussalmans' consciousness of affinity with their co-religionists outside India was roused and an effective help for them presupposed a feeling of goodwill in the country and as soon as the danger was averted (or the fate was accepted), the incentive that sustained the agreement disappeared. Besides, a communal body that, from its very birth, had consistently advocated anti-patriotic dogmas and done all in its power to widen the gap between the Hindus and the Muslims, could be least expected to experience an overnight change

---

[3] There were many circumstances, which drove the Muslim leaders to the side of the Congress. According to a writer in the Indian Review of October 1912, "For several months past, the Mohammedans of India have been passing through a state of discontent. The unblushing brutality with which Russia was treating Persia, the apparently unprovoked assault of Italy upon the Turkish position in Tripoli and lastly disappointment of the Indian Mohammedans over the Muslim University have all combined to create an atmosphere of restlessness among the Mohammedan subjects of the British Crown. And now, the long-dreaded trouble in the Balkans, a life and death struggle between the leading Islamic power and four minor kingdoms of Eastern Europe, has considerably excited the already exasperated followers of the Arabian prophet."

in its fundamentals and pin its faith to the Congress ideology. Even war against Turkey would not shake the sense of loyalty, which the Indian Muslims had developed for the British Government in the country. The Congress programme, on the other hand, demanded active opposition to the Government. The ideological differences between the two bodies made them ill-assorted-mates that was ready to part company at the first opportunity. Looked at from whatever angle of vision, the Lucknow Pact was foredoomed to failure." (*The Muslim League*, p. 96.)

It is to be noted that the Congress leaders like Mahatma Gandhi and Madan Mohan Malaviya attended the sessions of the Muslim League in 1915, 1916 and 1917 and spoke from its platform in support of several resolutions. The Raja of Mahmudabad who presided over the Calcutta session of the Muslim League spoke thus: "The interests of the country are paramount. We need not" try to argue whether we are Muslims first or Indians. The fact is we are both: to us the question of precedence has no meaning. The league has inculcated among the Muslims a spirit of sacrifice for their country as their own religion.'

It is on account of this friendly atmosphere that both the Hindus and Muslims participated in the Non-Cooperation Movement. As the Khilafat Committee and the Jamiat-ul-Ulema-i-Hind came to have their hold on the Muslim masses, the Muslim League suffered an eclipse after 1920. However, many members of the Muslim League were patronized by the British Government and occupied important offices in the Government.

When the Non-Cooperation Movement was withdrawn by Mahatma Gandhi, Hindu-Muslim riots broke out in various parts of the country. This created bad blood between the Hindus and the Muslims. The programme of Shudhi and Sangathan of the Hindus also made the Muslims anti-Hindu. M. A. Jinnah took advantage of the atmosphere and tried to put new life into the Muslim League. However, he did not achieve much success. When the Simon Commission was appointed, the members of the Muslim League were divided on the question of their attitude towards the Commission. One section led by Jinnah was in favour of boycotting the Commission, but the other section led by Sir Mohammad Shafi was in favour of cooperating with it. The result was that the two sections of the League held their sessions separately. The Nationalist Muslims like Hakim Ajmal Khan, Dr. Ansari, Dr. Kitchlew, Maulana Azad, Dr. Syed Mahmud and Asaf Ali formed themselves into a separate party. Jinnah found himself alone. According to Humayun Kabir, "He could not fit in with the Muslim moderates, for politically he was too much influenced by Congress ideology. Nor could he merge with the Progressive among the Muslims, for with his orthodox and conservative economic views, they seemed to him rank revolutionaries." He could not rejoin Congress whose programme of direct action he did not approve of. No wonder, he decided to retire from Indian politics and went away to England to practise law. However, within a few years, most of the Muslim leaders of all-India status such as Fazli Hussain, Ajmal Khan, Mohammad Shafi, Ansari and Mohammad Ali died and Jinnah found a golden opportunity to be the leader of the Muslims. He came back from England and took up the leadership of the League.

When the general elections were held in 1937, the Muslim League did not do well in the Muslim majority provinces. However, there were negotiations for cooperation between the Congress and the Muslim League. Jinnah proposed the establishment of coalition Governments between independent parties. To quote him, "There is really no substantial difference, now at any rate, between the League and the Congress. We shall always be glad to cooperate with the Congress in their constructive programme." The Congress invited the Muslim League to join ministries on certain terms were found to be unacceptable by the League. In the case of U.P. the terms required that the Muslim League group should cease to function as a separate group. The existing members of the Muslim League party in the U.P. Assembly were to become a part of the Congress party and were also to be subject to the control and discipline of the Congress party. "The Muslim League Parliamentary Board in the United Provinces will be dissolved and no candidates will thereafter be set up by the said Board at any by-election." The point of view of the Congress was that such terms were necessary for the purpose of maintaining discipline among the ministries. However, critics pointed out that the Congress was "drunk with victory." Jinnah considered the terms as "a direct rebuff" and declared that "the Muslims can expect neither justice not fair play under Congress Government." He attacked the Congress as a Fascist Hindu body which was out to crush all other parties in the country, particularly the Muslim League.

It is to be observed that the big Muslim landowners got afraid of the agrarian policy of the Congress. They feared that if everything was to be given to the peasantry, that could be done only at their cost and no wonder they joined hands with the Muslim League to strengthen their position.

The middle class among the Muslims also foresaw a bleak future for themselves. They felt that they could not compete with the Hindus in industry, in professions and in public services. The only way out of the difficulty was to set up a separate State for the Muslims where there would be no competition from the Hindus. They were also sensitive to the educational policy of the Congress. They condemned the Congress scheme of primary education through handicrafts. It was maintained that the Congress educational policy was essentially a Hindu one. The Muslims complained that their culture was being attacked by the Congress which was tantamount to an attack on the very existence of the Muslims. There were other causes for the denunciation of the Congress by the Muslim League. According to Brailsford, "On the eve of the elections of 1937 in the United Provinces, a leading Muslim politician who had hitherto belonged to the Congress Party deserted it, because he thought he would be defeated and went over to the Muslim League with his following. He was mistaken; the Congress was victorious and formed the Ministry. This man asked to be taken back to the fold and also to be rewarded with a cabinet post. Very naturally, but perhaps unwisely, the Congress refused — as any British party in a like case would have done. The consequences were unfortunate and to the English mind outstanding. The Muslim League redoubled its attacks on the Congress and on the strength of this and similar cases accused it of being a totalitarian party which sought to monopolise power." (*Subject India*, p. 83.)

Another factor which annoyed the Muslim League was the mass contact movement of the Congress under the leadership of Pandit Jawaharlal Nehru. Its object was to bring the Muslim masses into the fold of the Congress. Such a movement was considered to be a challenge to the very existence of the Muslim League. Jinnah declared that the Congress movement was "calculated to divide and weaken and break the Mussalmans and to detach them from their accredited leaders." No wonder, the Muslim League raised the cry of "Islam in danger." It was declared that under the despotism of the Congress rule, the Muslims were doomed to the fate of under-dogs." Asoka Mehta and Patwardhan pointed out in their book entitled *Communal Triangle* that the Muslim League had reached such a stage that it could not follow any other policy except that which was actually followed by it. It was a reactionary body and was controlled by the Muslim princes, landlords, industrialists and others who were the stooges of the British Government. The Muslim League had no constructive programme of its own and the only way it could become strong was by denouncing the Congress. It had asked for and got separate votes, separate electorates, and statutory safeguards. The next logical step was the demand for a separate State.

As time passed, the Muslim League shouted from the housetops the tyranny to which Muslims were being subjected in those provinces in which the Congress ministries existed. In March 1938, the Muslim League appointed a Special Committee under the Raja of Pirpur to enquire into the numerous complaints of oppression and ill-treatment meted out to Muslims in general and the workers of the League in particular." The Pirpur Report gave a list of the sufferings of the Muslims under the Congress regime and declared that "no tyranny could be so great as the tyranny of the majority." There was absolutely no substance in the charges of the Muslim League. According to Coupland, "The Congress Ministries had not lent themselves to a policy of communal injustice, still less of deliberate persecution." According to Sir Harry Haig, Governor of U.P., "The Congress Ministries dealt with the Muslims fairly and justly." The Congress President asked the Muslim League to submit the grievances of the Muslims under the Congress regime to an impartial tribunal, but the Muslim League refused to do so. It merely went on harping on the theme of persecution till the day the Congress Ministries resigned in 1939. During this period it looked to the Governor-General for the redress of its grievances and after that nothing was heard of them. The Muslim League observed the Deliverance Day when the Congress Ministries resigned. The Muslim League was not concerned with the truth or untruth of the myth of persecution. Its technique worked well. Jinnah came to be recognised as the champion of the Muslims in India. He became the leader of the Muslim community and the Muslim League became the representative Muslim body. Between 1937 and 1942, the Muslim League got 47 seats in 61 by-elections to the Muslim seats and the Congress got only four.

PAKISTAN

Sir Mohammad Iqbal is considered to be the father of the idea of Pakistan. At the Allahabad session of Muslim League held in 1930, he declared that the "formation of a consolidated North-West India Muslim State appears to me to be the final destiny of Muslims at least of North-West India." However, it is to be observed that Iqbal did not stand for a sovereign, independent State for the Muslims. According to Coupland, Iqbal stood for a loose federation of all-India, "the Central Federal Government only exercising those powers which are expressly vested in it by the free consent of the federal States." Iqbal is stated to have told Edward Thompson that "the Pakistan plan would be disastrous to the British Government, disastrous to the Hindu community and disastrous to the Muslim community."

In spite of this, some Muslim under-graduates at the Cambridge University were influenced by the ideas of Iqbal. Their leader was Rahmat Ali. In 1933, Rahmat Ali described the Indian Muslims as a nation and prepared a plan for the establishment of Pakistan which was to include the Punjab, Kashmir, Sind, Baluchistan and the N.W.F.P. He also referred to the establishment of Osmanistan of Hyderabad and Bang-i-Islam of Bengal and Assam. Rahmat Ali tried to propagate his ideas among the people. However, he did not meet with any encouragement. In August 1933, Sir Zafrullah Khan described the scheme as "chimerical and impracticable." Up to 1937 the Muslim League also did not approve of the idea of Pakistan. It was in 1938 that Jinnah demanded the division of India. In January 1940, he referred to the two nations of the Hindus and the Muslims in India.

Presiding over the Muslim League session in Lahore on 22nd March 1940, Jinnah declared that the Mussalmans were not in minority and they were a nation by any definition. To quote him, "If the British Government are really in earnest and sincere to secure peace and happiness of the people of this sub-continent, the only course open to us all is to allow the major nations separate homelands by dividing India into autonomous national States. There is no reason why the States should be antagonistic to each other. On the other hand, the rivalry and the natural desire and efforts on the part of one to dominate the social order and establish political supremacy over the other in the government of the country will disappear. It will lead more towards natural goodwill by international pacts between them, and they can live in complete harmony with their neighbours. This will lead further to a friendly settlement all the more easily with regard to minorities by reciprocal arrangements and adjustments between Muslim India and Hindu India which will far more adequately and effectively safeguard the rights and interests of Muslims and various other minorities.

"It is extremely difficult to appreciate why our Hindu friends fail to understand the real natures of Islam and Hinduism. They are not religions in the strict sense of the word, but are, in fact, quite different distinct social orders, and it is a dream that the Hindus and Muslims can ever evolve a common nationality, and this misconception of the Indian nation has gone far beyond the limits and is the cause of most of our troubles and will lead India to destruction if we fail to revise our notions in time. The Hindus and Muslims belong to two different religious philosophies, social customs and literatures. They neither inter-marry nor inter-dine and, indeed, they belong to two different civilisations which are based mainly on conflicting ideas and conceptions. Their aspects on life and of life are different. It is quite clear that Hindus and Mussalmans derive their inspirations from different sources of history. They have different epics their heroes are different, and different episodes. Very often the hero of one is foe of the other and, likewise, their victories and defeats overlap. To yoke together two such nations under a single State, one as a numerical minority and the other as a majority, must lead to growing discontent and final destruction of any fabric that may be so built up for the government of such a State."

PAKISTAN RESOLUTION (1940)

On 23rd March 1940, the Pakistan resolution was passed by the All-India Muslim League at its Lahore session. The resolution runs thus: "Resolved that it is the considered view of this session of the All-India Muslim League that no constitutional plan would be workable in this country or acceptable to Muslims unless it is designed on the following basic principles, namely, that geographically contiguous units are demarcated into regions which should be so constituted, with such territorial readjustment as may be necessary, that the areas in which the Muslims are numerically in a majority as in the North-Western and Eastern Zones of India should be grouped to constitute 'Independent States' in which the constituent units shall be autonomous and sovereign.

"This adequate, effective and mandatory safeguard should be specifically provided in the constitution for minorities in these units and in their regions for the protection of their religious, cultural, economic, political administrative and other rights and interests in consultation with them; and in other parts of India where the Mussalmans are in a minority, adequate, effective and mandatory safeguards shall be specially provided in the constitution for them and other minorities for the protection of their religious, cultural, economic, political, administrative and other rights and interests in consultation with them.

"This session further authorises the Working Committee to frame a scheme of constitution in accordance with these basic principles providing for the assumption finally by the respective regions of all powers such as defence, external affairs, communications, customs and such other matters AS may be necessary."

According to Dr. Lal Bahadur, "The Lahore Resolution was the highest culmination of Muslim aspirations roused by leaders from Sayid Ahmad's times. But it was never put so boldly as in 1940. It was vehemently criticised by organisations and individuals on several grounds and some believed it to be a practical impossibility but its authors knew that it would, one day, be a reality and those who had statesmanship and political imagination understood the danger lurking behind a demand of this character. It gave the League a new ambition and a new programme. A renewed stress was laid on the two-nation theory and communal differences were exaggerated with redoubled energy. It was, therefore, natural that the relations between the Congress and the League be marred in their highest degree." The Pakistan Resolution was also a personal triumph for Mr. Jinnah and it established his dictatorial leadership beyond all possibility of overthrow. On account of the Second World War, the British Government also began to rely more and more on the support of the Muslim League and Mr. Jinnah took full advantage of this fact. To quote Mr. Jinnah himself, "After the war was declared, the Viceroy naturally wanted help from the Muslim League. It was only then that he realised that the Muslim League was a power. For it will be remembered that up to the time of the declaration of war, the Viceroy never thought of meeting but of Gandhi and Gandhi alone. I believe that was the worst shock that the Congress High Command received, because it challenged their sole authority to speak on behalf of India." The Pakistan Resolution also endorsed the previous resolutions of the Muslim League repudiating federation at the centre. It was specifically declared that federation was altogether unacceptable to the Muslim League. To quote Jinnah himself, "Before the War was declared, the greatest danger to the Muslims of India was the possible inauguration of the federal scheme in the Central (Government... . I am sure that we have made no small contribution towards persuading the British Government to abandon the scheme of Central Federal Government." The Pakistan Resolution also received with satisfaction the Declaration of the Viceroy dated 18th October 1939 that the policy and plan of the Government of India Act, 1935, would be reconsidered. The Muslim League felt that it was strong enough to declare that no revised constitutional plan for India would be acceptable to Muslims if the same was framed without their approval and consent. The Pakistan Resolution insisted on the acceptance of the principle of division of the country. The Muslim majority areas were to be grouped into independent States which were to be autonomous and sovereign. The Resolution left the possibility of the extension of claim in some future favourable time. According to Dr. Rajendra Prasad, "When insisted to elaborate the scheme and furnish details as regards the territories to be included in the regions and other matters he has refused to do so, insisting that the principle should be first accepted and then and only then will he be prepared to work out or disclose details." The Resolution did not explain the nature of the sovereignty to be enjoyed by the Muslim States. The ambiguities left by the Resolution were pointed out in these words by Dr. Rajendra Prasad: "The questions that arise are (a) Who is to frame the constitution? (b) What is to be the nature of the constitution contemplated—theocratic, oligarchic, totalitarian, or any other? (c) What is the relation of these independent States going to be with the British Empire and the non-Muslim zones? (d) In case of breach of any of the mandatory safeguards for the protection of the minorities, how, by whom and under what sanction are these safeguards to be enforced? (e) What are the territories to be included in the Muslim State or States? (f)' What will be their resources and position? (g) What is the authority that will be in charge of defence, external affairs, etc.?"

Pakistan became the keystone of the ideological arch of the Muslim League after 1940. The idea met opposition from many quarters but the Muslim League asserted its determination to achieve the ideal of Pakistan at all costs. The Anglo-Indian bureaucracy encouraged Jinnah in his demand.

CAUSES OF PAKISTAN DEMAND

Reference may be made to some of the causes, which led to the demand for Pakistan.

1. It has already been pointed out that the refusal of the Congress to form Coalition Ministries with the Muslim League alienated it and it raised a lot of hue and cry in the country against the so-called atrocities of the Congress Ministries on the Muslim minority.
2. The Muslim League also objected to Mass Contact Movement of the Congress under the leadership of Jawaharlal Nehru. It considered the Muslims to be its exclusive sphere. About the Mass Contact Movement Sir Mohd. Iqbal wrote thus to Mr. M. A. Jinnah on 20th March 1937: "I suppose you have read Pt. Jawaharlal Nehru's address to the All-India National Convention and that you fully realize the policy underlying it in so far as Indian Muslims are concerned. I, therefore, suggest that an effective reply should be given to the All-India National Convention... . To this Convention you must re-state as clearly and as strongly as possible the political objective of the Indian Muslims, as a distinct political unit in the country." In the Lucknow session of the Muslim League held in October 1937, Mr. Jinnah observed thus: "I want the Mussalmans to ponder over the situation and decide their own fate by having one, single, definite, uniform policy which should be loyally followed throughout India."
3. It has also been pointed out that the middle-classes among the Muslims were not satisfied with their future in India. They felt that the Hindus were more than a match for them in practically

every sphere of life. There were no good prospects for them in a united India. It is these people who raised the cry of Pakistan where some very big jobs were sure to fall to their share.

4. The Muslims also did not approve of the Wardha Education Scheme and the Vidya Mandir Scheme as advocated by the Congress Ministries. They felt that their religion was likely to be affected by the Congress in various fields.

5. Some Muslims held the view that if a Muslim State was set up in India that could be taken as the first step towards the fulfilment of their dream of Pan-Islamism. Pakistan could become the centre where a movement could be started for the liberation of Muslims from foreign yoke.

6. The Muslims became very sensitive regarding the general attitude of the caste Hindus towards them. They felt that the touch-me-not attitude of the Hindus implied that the Hindus regarded the Muslims as inferiors. The Muslims considered themselves to be better than the Hindus and they could not tolerate the attitude of social boycott by the Hindus.

7. The utterances of some of the Hindu Mahasabha leaders in India also gave the Muslim Leaguers a handle. Shri V. D. Savarkar preached the gospel of Hindu Rashtra in 1937 and described the Congress as anti-Hindu and pro-Muslim. He appealed to the Hindus to repudiate the Congress and capture all the power in the country. Savarkar maintained that there were two separate nations in India and those were the Hindus and Muslims. The Muslims began to feel that in this atmosphere they were doomed to live under the superior authority of the Hindus who formed an overwhelming majority in the population of the country.

8. It is also pointed out that the Sudeten Movement in Czechoslovakia also influenced the Muslim League in putting forward its demand for Pakistan.

9. The British bureaucracy in India also played its part in goading on the Muslims to demand Pakistan for themselves.

It cannot be denied that the Cripps Proposals of March 1942 recognised the claim of the Muslim League for Pakistan. The proposals recognised "the right of any province of British India that is not prepared to accept the new constitution to retain its present position, provision being made for its accession if it so decides. With such non-acceding provinces, should they so desire, His Majesty's Government would be prepared to agree upon a new constitution, giving them the same full status as the Indian Union." No wonder, the Indian National Congress described the Cripps' proposals as "a severe blow to the conception of Indian unity."

The Congress Resolution laid down that "the acceptance beforehand of the novel principle of non-accession for a province is also a severe blow to the conception of Indian unity and an apple of discord likely to generate growing trouble in the provinces, and which may well lead to further difficulties in the way of the Indian States merging themselves in the Indian Union."

According to Mr. Jinnah, the Pakistan idea embodied in the Cripps' proposals was nebulous and serious obstacles were put in the way of its realisation. In his presidential address at the Allahabad session of the All-India Muslim League held on 4th April 1942, Mr. Jinnah observed thus: "The alleged power of the minority in the matter of secession suggested in the document is illusory, as Hindu' India will dominate the decision in favour of one All-India Union in all the provinces and the Muslims in Bengal and the Punjab will be at the mercy of Hindu minority in those provinces, who will exert themselves to the fullest extent and length for keeping the Mussalmans tied to the chariot-wheel of Hindustan." The Working Committee of the Muslim League passed the following resolution on 11th April 1942: "The Committee while expressing their gratification that the possibility of Pakistan is recognised by implication by providing for the establishment of two or more independent unions in India, regret that the proposals of His Majesty's Government, embodying the fundamentals, are not open to any modification and, therefore, no alternative proposals are invited." The history of the Muslim League after the return of the Cripps' Mission was one of ever-increasing demand of Pakistan. It was declared that "any scheme which seeks to torpedo the Pakistan demand of Muslim India will be resisted by the Muslim League and as such any political party which stands for the establishment of a democratic State in India can have no agreement with the Muslim League."

According to Dr. Shyama Prasad Mukerjee, the Cripps' proposals were likely to "sound the death-knell of Indian unity and freedom. India will then become a veritable chessboard on which not only Indian provinces (constituted mainly on a religious basis) may fight with each other but interested foreign nations may find ample scope for fateful intrigues and dissensions." According to Sir Bijoy Prasad Singh Roy, "The Cripps Mission led to (1) the stiffening of the attitude of Mahatma Gandhi and the Congress; (2) the insistence of the demand by Mr. Jinnah and the Muslim League for Pakistan; (3) the dissociation of Mr. C. Rajagopalachari from the Congress with a number of his disciples in Madras; (4) the growth of a sense of frustration in non-Congress political parties." According to Dr. Lal Bahadur, "The provision of non-accession provinces in Cripp's, proposals was undoubtedly disastrous in this connection. On the one hand, it whetted the demand for Pakistan and, on the other it raised dormant potentialities for its opposition. In Cripp's proposals, therefore, lay the germs of strained relations between the two communities of India." (*The Muslim League*, p. 296.)

DR. LATIF'S SCHEME

Dr. Latif prepared a scheme for dividing India into cultural zones and then confederating them. He was in favour of the transfer of populations on a large scale with a view to making the zones homogeneous. In addition to the North-Western and Eastern States for the Muslims, Dr. Latif advocated the creation of two more States for them. The Muslims living in the U.P. and Bihar were to be concentrated in "a block extending in a" line from the eastern border of Patiala to Lucknow, rounding up Rampur on the way." This State was to be known as the Delhi-Lucknow State. To quote him, "The Muslims below the Vindhyas and Satpuras are scattered all over the North in colonies of varying sizes and exceed 12 millions in number. For them a zone is to be carved. Such a zone the Dominions of Hyderabad and Berar may provide with a narrow strip of territory restored to them in the South, running down, viz., Kurnool and Cudappah to the city of Madras. There is a communal school of thought among the Muslims who prefer to have an opening to the western coast via Bijapur. Such a strip with an opening to the sea will be found necessary to settle the large Muslim mercantile and marine community living for ages on the Coromondel and Malabar coast." Dr. Latif was in favour of giving the ports of Calcutta (now Kolkata) and Madras (now Chennai) to the Muslim zone.

THE ALIGARH SCHEME

The Aligarh scheme was prepared by Professor Zafrul Hassan and Mohammad Afzal Hassan Qadri. According to the scheme, Berar and Karnatak were to be restored to Hyderabad. Moreover, all the towns of India with a population of 50,000 or more were to have the status of a borough with a large measure of autonomy. After the partition of India, the Muslims were to be recognised in Hindustan as a separate nation and allowed to have their separate organisation.

Edward Thompson had a conversation with Jinnah on the consequences of having two nations in one country. Thompson told Jinnah: "Two nations, Mr. Jinnah, confronting each other in every province, every town, every village." Jinnah's reply was: "Two Nations, confronting each other in every province, every town, every village, that is the only solution." Thompson replied: "That is a very terrible solution, Mr. Jinnah." The reply of Jinnah was: "It is a terrible solution. But it is the only one." (*Enlist India for Freedom*, p. 52.)

FORMULA OF RAJAGOPALACHARI

In 1944, Rajagopalachari put forward his formula with the consent of Mahatma Gandhi to satisfy the demands of the Muslims. The formula accepted the principle of Pakistan. According to this formula the Muslim League was to support the demand of the Congress for independence of India. During the transitional period the Muslim League was to join hands with the Congress in forming a provisional government. After the war, a commission was to be appointed to demarcate those contiguous areas in North-West and North-East India in which the Muslims were in an absolute majority. A plebiscite of all the inhabitants of those areas was to be taken to decide whether those areas wanted to be separated from Hindustan or not. If they decided to be separated, agreements were to be made for defence, communications, etc. These terms were binding on the parties only if the British Government transferred all control into the hands of Indians for the administration of the country. Jinnah rejected the formula of Rajaji. He condemned the offer of a "maimed, mutilated and moth-eaten" Pakistan. He declared that he would not accept anything less than the six provinces of Sind, Punjab, N.W.F.P., Baluchistan Bengal and Assam, subject only to the adjustment of their territories. Moreover, he was not prepared to allow the non-Muslims living in the Muslim-majority areas to vote along with the Muslims.

CABINET MISSION

After the end of the Second World War, elections were held in the provinces. The Muslim League was able to secure 446 seats out of a total of 495 Muslim seats. It was clear that the Muslim League had gained in strength and it had won success on the demand for Pakistan. Mr. Attlee, Prime Minister of England, declared that "the British Government recognised India's right to complete independence and to decide whether to remain within the British Commonwealth or not." He also declared that a "minority could not be allowed to veto the progress of the majority." He announced the decision of the Government to send a delegation of Cabinet Ministers to India to suggest a solution for the Indian problem. The Cabinet Mission reached India in March 1946. The members of the Mission met the leaders of the various parties. As they failed to persuade the political parties to come to an agreed settlement, they published their own proposals on 16th March 1946. After a careful examination of the demands of the Muslim League for Pakistan, the Mission came to the conclusion that it was not practicable to set up a solve reign Muslim State. Pakistan was not an acceptable solution for the communal problem. A proposal was made for a Federal Union of India. The Union Government was given very few powers. Provision was made for the grouping of provinces. Differences arose between the Congress and the Muslim League with regard to the clause relating to the grouping of provinces. The view of the Congress was that the grouping was to be a voluntary affair. The League maintained that it was to be compulsory. Ultimately, on 6th December 1946 the British Government gave its own interpretation in favour of the League.

Certain difficulties cropped up with regard to the formation of the Interim Government as provided for in the Cabinet Mission Scheme. On 16th June 1946, Lord Wavell issued invitations to six representatives of the Congress, five representatives of the Muslim League and three representatives of minorities. The Congress demanded the right to include one nationalist Muslim in its list of six members. As its claim was rejected the Congress refused to join the Interim Government. The Muslim League demanded that it should be allowed to form the Government even without the Congress. This view was not accepted by Lord Wavell and he appointed a 'caretaker' Government of officials. Jinnah attacked the British Government and on 29th July 1946, the Muslim League withdrew its acceptance of the Cabinet Mission Scheme. It decided to prepare a programme for Direct Action "to achieve Pakistan...and to get rid of the present slavery under the British and the contemplated future of Hindu domination."

On 6th August 1946 Lord Wavell invited the Congress to form the Interim Government at the Centre and the latter accepted the invitation. The Muslim League fixed 16th August 1946 as the Direct Action Day. To facilitate the action of the League, the League Ministry of Bengal declared 16th August a public holiday. On that day there was a lot of bloodshed in Calcutta and Sylhet. The great Calcutta Killing was followed by bloodshed in Noakhali and Tipperah. There were abductions, forced marriages, rapes, compulsory conversions to Islam and destitution of families.

On 2nd September 1946, Wavell administered the oath of allegiance to the members of the Interim Government in the Council Room of the Viceroy's House. When this was being done inside rival crowds outside were shouting: 'Victory to Hindustan; Long live Congress Committee" and "Death of Congress; Long live Pakistan."

The League was anxious to enter the Interim Government to play its own part. Although the Muslim League did not undertake to work in a spirit of cooperation with other members of the Interim Government and also did not agree to join the deliberations of the Constituent Assembly Lord Wavell took five nominees of the League into the Interim Government.

The first meeting of the Constituent Assembly was held on 9th December 1946. The Muslim League boycotted it and denounced the resolution of the Constituent Assembly as **ultra vires**, invalid and illegal.

Riots also took place in Bihar, Garhmukteswar, Lahore and Rawalpindi. The Muslims threatened to revive the days of Halaku and Chengiz Khan. Nothing was done to suppress the agitation of the League in the Punjab and law and order was allowed to collapse in that province. It was in that atmosphere of lawlessness that the Prime Minister of England declared on 20th February 1947 that the British Government would transfer power into the hands of the Indians by a date not later than June 1948. It was also declared that the British Government "would have to consider to whom the powers of the Central Government in British India should be handed over on the due date, whether as a whole to some form of Central Government for British India or in some areas to the existing Provincial Governments or in some such other way as may seem most reasonable and in the best interests of the, Indian people.

Lord Mountbatten's Plan of June 3, 1947 provided for the establishment of two separate dominions of India and Pakistan and the British Government was to withdraw from India on 15th August 1947. The provinces of Bengal and Punjab were to be partitioned. The Indian Independence Act was passed by the British Parliament in July 1947 and on 14th August M. A. Jinnah was declared the Governor-General of Pakistan and thus Pakistan became a reality.

REVIEW QUESTIONS

1. Analyse the condition of Pakistan before 1871.
2. What was the role of Sir Syed Ahmed Khan in the creation of Pakistan? Discuss.
3. Write a step-by-step history of the establishment of Pakistan.
4. Write a detailed note on the partition of Bengal. Discuss its role in the establishment of Pakistan.
5. Who for the first time gave the idea of the creation of Pakistan? Evaluate his role in the establishment of Pakistan.
6. Examine the causes which led to the demand for Pakistan.
7. Write short notes on the following:
    (a) Lucknow Pact, 1916
    (b) Pakistan Resolution, 1940
    (c) Formula of Rajgopalachari
    (d) Cabinet Mission

SUGGESTED READINGS

Ahmad, K.A.: *The Founder of Pakistan—Through Trial to Triumph.*
Alberuni, A.H.: *Makers of Pakistan* (1950).
Ambedkar, B.R.: *Thoughts on Pakistan.*
Beni Prasad: *Hindu-Muslim Questions.*
Bolitho, H.: *Jinnah* (1954).
El Hamza: *Pakistan — A Nation.*
Graham: *The Life of Sir Syed Ahmed Khan* (1909).
Ikram, S.M.: *Cultural Heritage of Pakistan* (1955).
Khaliquzzaman, Chaudhry: *Pathway to Pakistan.*
Khan, Syed Ahmed: *Causes of the Indian Revolt* (1873).
Mary, Countess of Minto: *India, Minto and Morley, 1905-1910* (1934).
Maulana Mohammad Ali: *My Life, a Fragment,* Ed. by Afzal Iqbal, Lahore, 1942.
Natesan, G.A. (Ed.): *Eminent Mussalmans.*
Norman, M.: *Muslim India* 1942.
Norman, M.: *Rise and Growth of All-India Muslim League.*
Rajendra Prasad: *Pakistan.*
Rajendra Prasad: *India Divided.*
Saiyed, M.H.: *M. A. Jinnah* (1945).
Smith, W.C.: *Modern Islam in India* (1946).
Spear, T.G.P.: *India, Pakistan and the West,* London, 1959.
Symonds, Richard: *The Making of Pakistan,* 1951.

23   Leaders of Modern India

LEARNING OBJECTIVES

- Study the lives and contribution of the leaders of modern India
- Distinguish between philosophies of Tilak and Gokhale
- Give an estimate of Mahatma Gandhi

In order to understand properly the development of nationalism in our country, it is desirable to study the lives and contributions of some of the greatest leaders of modern India and this chapter is devoted to that purpose.

DADABHAI NAOROJI (1825-1917)

Dadabhai Naoroji, affectionately known as the 'Grand Old Man of India', served India for 61 long years — 40 years before foundation of the Indian National Congress and 21 years after that. He was permanently settled in England and was elected a member of the House of Commons from an English Constituency. For some time, he was the Prime Minister of Baroda. He founded the British Indian Society in England to carry on propaganda in favour of India.

He was elected the President of the Congress thrice, viz., in 1886, 1893 and 1906. His election as the President of the Congress for the second time, 1893, was an appreciation of his election to the House of Commons, On that occasion, he took the opportunity to exhort the British "not to drive this force (the educated Indians) into opposition instead of drawing it to your own side." He contended that "this Congress represents the aristocracy of intellect." He hoped that "our faith in the instinctive love of justice and fair play of the United Kingdom is not misplaced." "The day, I hope, is not distant when the world will see the noblest spectacle of a great nation like the British holding out the hands of true fellow-citizenship and of justice."

He was elected the President of the Congress in 1906 as the Moderates felt that he was the only person who was not likely to be opposed by the Extremists. As that time, there was a lot of excitement in the country. The anti-Partition agitation was going on in Bengal. Swadeshi and Boycott were in the air. Even in 1906, Dadabhai Naoroji had not given up his faith in the justice of the Englishmen. In his presidential address in 1906, he observed thus: "Our faith and our future are in our hands. If we are true to ourselves and to our country and make all the necessary sacrifices for our elevation and amelioration, I for one have not a shadow of doubt that in dealing with such justice-loving, fair-minded people as the British, we may rest assured that we shall not work in vain. It is this conviction which has supported me against all difficulties," However, it cannot be denied that the credit of demanding Swaraj from the Congress platform for the first time belongs to Dadabhai Naoroji Swaraj was the key-note of his presidential address at the Calcutta (now Kolkata) session. To quote him, "We do not ask for favours. We want only justice. Instead of going into any further divisions or details of our rights as British citizens, the whole matter can be comprised in one word — self-government or Swaraj, like that of the United Kingdom or the Colonies."

It was under his President-ship in 1906 that four resolutions on self-government, boycott movement, Swadeshi and national education were passed by the Congress.

Dadabhai Naoroji was the first Indian politician to draw the attention of the people to the drain of India's wealth to Great Britain as a result of the British rule in India. He gave his views in the famous book entitled *Poverty and Un-British Rule in India*. Dadabhai Naoroji wrote thus to J. D. Sunderland in 1905: "The lot of India is a very sad one. Her condition is that of a master and slave; but it is worse; it is that of a plundered nation in the hands of constant plunderers with the plunder carried away clean out of the land. In the case of plundering raids occasionally made on India before the English came the invaders went away and there were long intervals of security during which the land could recoup and become again rich and prosperous. But nothing of the kind is true now. The British invasion is continuous and the plunder goes right on with no intermission and actually increases and the impoverished Indian nation has no opportunity whatever to recuperate." According to Dr. Pattabhi Sitaramayya, "Dadabhai Naoroji pointed out how since 1889-94 the population grew by 14 per cent but the net Government administrative expenditure by 16 per cent, while since 1884-85 the population grew by 18 per cent and the expenditure by 17 per cent. The military expenditure alone rose from ₹17 to 32 crores, 7 crores being spent in England. The recommendations of the Welby Commission in favour of an apportionment of the military expenditure between England and India were honoured in letter but disregarded in spirit for a contribution was made by England but the pay of the English soldiers was raised so as to take away thrice the contribution made."

According to Dr. Pattabhi Sitaramayya, the name of Dadabhai Naoroji comes first in the list of Indian patriarchs who "beginning his connection with the Congress from its very outset, continued to serve it till the evening of his life, and took it through the whole gamut of evolution, from the humble position of being a people's organ seeking redress of administrative grievances to that of a National Assembly working for the definite object of attaining Swaraj." Again, "it is impossible to recount within the short space of a few pages the services of one who lived and worked incessantly for India's uplift, whose pen knew no rest and whom Providence gave more than the proverbial three score years and ten. Dadabhai lived and laboured and has left behind him not only the noble example of a dedicated life but also in flesh and blood his grand daughters who are maintaining the noble traditions created by him." According to C. Y. Chintamani, "For 61 long years in England and India, by day and by night in circumstances favourable and adverse, in the face of discouragement which would have broken the heart of a smaller man, Dadabhai Naoroji served the Motherland with undeviating purpose, with complete selflessness and with vitality of faith which put to shame most young men. Withal, he was the greatest of souls and the most charitable in judgement and never made a personal enemy. In respect equally of the highest personal character and the greatest public services, Dadabhai Naoroji was the loftiest ideal his countrymen could set before themselves respectively to follow at a distance." Again, "The public life of India has been adorned by a galaxy of brilliant intellects and selfless patriots, but there has been in our time noncomparable with Dadabhai Naorji." According to Gokhale, "If ever there is the divine in man, it is in Dadabhai Naoroji."

GOPAL KRISHAN GOKHALE (1866-1915)

Gopal Krishan Gokhale was born at Kolhapur in 1866. He possessed remarkable qualities of head and heart and rose rapidly in life. He became a graduate at 18, a professor at 20, a member of the Bombay (now Mumbai) Legislative Council at 22 and President of the Indian National Congress at 39. He had an enormous capacity for hard work. His knowledge was vast, varied and exact. He was a master of direct expression and lucid exposition. According to Chintamani, who regarded Gokhale as his Guru, "He (Gokhale) was so intellectually honest that he would never utter an opinion except after cross-examining himself severely."

He started his life as a teacher, as a follower of Justice Ranade. Dr. Zacharias rightly points out that never had a Guru a more apt pupil than Ranade in Gokhale. He imbibed the spirit of the master and never wavered from the path of moderation and sweet-reasonableness as laid down by Ranade. He joined the Deccan Education Society and very soon he became the Principal of the Fergusson College. For about 20 years he worked on a nominal salary of ₹70 per month. He became the editor of the Quarterly Journal of the Poona Sarvajanik Sabha in 1887. Later on he became the Honorary Secretary of the Deccan Sabha. In 1897, he went to England to give evidence before the Welby Commission on Indian expenditure. He attacked Salt Tax as levied in India on account of the suffering which was caused to the poor people. He criticised the policy of the Government in excluding the Indians from the higher jobs in the country. He condemned the partition of Bengal and bitterly observed thus: "Then, all I can say is good-by to all hope of co-operating, in any way with bureaucracy, in the interests of the people." In 1905, he went to England to do propaganda on behalf of India. He went to South Africa and helped Mahatma Gandhi in his work and no wonder it was on his suggestion that Mahatma Gandhi decided to come to India to start his public life in this country. In 1905, Gokhale founded the Servants of India Society for the purpose of training "public workers pledged to work for the Motherland on a pittance and subject to rules of rigid discipline as well as loyalty to the Empire. In the preamble to the constitution of the Society, Gokhale wrote thus: "A sufficient number of our countrymen must now come forward to devote themselves to the cause in the spirit in which religious work is undertaken. Public life must be spiritualized. Love of the country must fill the heart that all else shall appear as of little moment by its side."

Gokhale had always a soft corner in his heart for the "starving, shrunken, shrivelled-up ryot toiling and moiling from dawn to dark to earn his scanty meal, patient, resigned, forbearing beyond measure, entirely voiceless in the Parliament of his Rulers and meekly prepared to bear whatever burdens God and man might be pleased to impose upon his back."

There are different views with regard to the place of Gokhale in the history of national development in India. While the Extremists in India dubbed him as a 'faint-hearted Moderate' who was prepared to be a willing tool in the hands of the British Government, the reactionaries described him as a "seditionist in disguise." As a matter of fact, he was neither a revolutionary nor a reactionary. He hated both the extremes. He was a constructive statesman who understood and fought for the rights and liberties of the people of India, but he was not prepared to ignore or belittle the difficulties of the Government of India. While he emphasized on the Government the necessity of understanding the point of view of the Indians, he requested the latter to move cautiously. It has rightly been pointed out that Gokhale "interpreted popular aspirations to the Viceroy and the Government's difficulties to the Congress." The people disparaged his moderation and the Government deprecated his extremism. His role was that of a unifier and reconciler. His view was that while both Britain and India stood to lose by mutual jealousies and hatred a lot could be gained by goodwill and healthy co-operation. To quote Gokhale, "The Englishman who imagines that India can be governed much longer on the same lines as in the past, and the Indian who thinks that he must seek a destiny for his country outside this Empire, of which now, for better or worse, we are a part—both alike show an inadequate appreciation of the realities of the present situation."

Gokhale attached great importance to the maintenance of law and order and was ready to grant the Government of India extraordinary powers to cope with the situation. Although the Indian Press Act, 1910, was a drastic step on the part of the Government of India, and was condemned by the public opinion in the country, he supported the bill in the Imperial Legislature in these words: "My Lord, in ordinary times I should have deemed it my duty to resist such proposals to the utmost of my power. The risks involved in them are grave and obvious. But in view of the situation that exists in several parts of the country today, I have reluctantly come, after a careful and anxious consideration, to the conclusion that I should not be justified in opposing the principle of this Bill. It is not merely the assassinations that have taken place, or the conspiracies that have come to light, or the political dacoities that are being committed that fill me with anxiety. The air in many places is still thick with ideas that are undoubtedly antagonistic to the unquestioned continuance of British rule, with which our hopes of a peaceful evolution are bound up; and this is a feature of the situation quite as serious as anything else. Several causes have contributed to produce this result of which the writings in a section of the press have been one. And to the extent to which a remedy can be applied to these writings by such executive action as is contemplated in the Bill, I am not prepared to say that the remedy should not be applied." He made a similar statement in 1911. Addressing the Council, he remarked: "Why, My Lord, even if I would defeat the Government today I would not do it. I would not do it for this reason: the prestige of the Government is an important asset at the present stage of the country and I would not lightly disturb it."

If he asked the people of India to move slowly, he impressed upon the Government the necessity of following the progressive policy towards India. No wonder, he moved Lord Morley to grant immediately an installment of reforms with a view to winning over a part of the people on the side of the Government. The part played by Gokhale in the passage of the Minto-Morley Reforms is well-known. He referred to the reforms at the Madras (now Chennai) session of the Indian National Congress as a "large and generous concession" by the Government to the people of India. He held the view that the people were never interested in disorder and chaos. If they were driven to that path, there was always some cause of discontent. The wise course to adopt was not one of repression, but to analyse the situation and remove the sources of trouble. To quote Gokhale: "There is only one way in which the wings of the disaffection can be clipped and that is by the Government pursuing a policy of steady and courageous conciliation." The words that he used to praise Lord Minto and Morley as the joint authors of the Reforms of 1909 follow the same line of argument. He said, "My Lord, I sincerely believe that Your Lordship and Lord Morley have between you saved India from drifting towards what cannot be described by any other name than chaos. For, however, strong a Government may be, repression never can put down the aspirations of a people and never will."

According to Hoyland, "He was a great master of the possible, a constructive statesman of the first rank, a bringer together of East and West in the common service of the needy: above all, an idealist, a foreseer, a prophet of new era of inter-racial goodwill and co-operation." According to Dr. V. H. Rutherford, Gokhale was "a diplomatist to his fingertips, who knew how to play on the national lyre without offending the official ear." According to Tilak, Gokhale was "the diamond of India, the jewel of Maharashtra and the prince of workers". According to Mahatma Gandhi, "Sir Pherozeshah had seemed to me like the Himalayas unscalable, the Lokmanya like the ocean one could not easily launch forth on the sea. But Gokhale was as the Ganges — it invited one to its bosom. In the sphere of politics, the place that Gokhale occupied in my heart, during his lifetime and occupies even now, has been and is unique." According to Lajpat Rai, Gokhale was the noblest and the best of Congress workers and his patriotism was of the highest and noblest type. According to Lord Curzon, "God has endowed you (Gokhale) with extraordinary abilities which you have placed unreservedly at the disposal of your country." According to Lord Morley, Gokhale had a "politician's head and a sense of executive responsibility."

LOKMANYA BAL GANGADHAR TILAK (1856-1920)

Bal Gangadhar Tilak was born on 23rd July 1856 and he died in August 1920. He was born in a Brahmin family in Maharashtra. He was a staunch Hindu and was well-versed in the Hindu scriptures. He took his law degree in 1879 and in collaboration with Agarkar, started a school for giving cheap education to the people. The Poona New English School founded by them made wonderful progress within a short time. In conjunction with other workers, the Kesari and the Maharatta were started. He was associated with the foundation of the Deccan Educational Society and the Fergusson College.

He started anti-cow killing societies, Akharas and Lathi Clubs with the object of creating among the people of Maharashtra a manly spirit so that they might be able to sacrifice themselves for the freedom of the country. He organised the Ganapati Festival and in doing so his purpose was to infuse among young men both religious and patriotic fervour. They were to learn to work together with courage, enthusiasm and discipline. The Ganapati Festival became more and more popular every year and it brought millions of Maharashtrians together on the same platform. It created in them the feeling of oneness. It awakened among them a new zeal. Tilak also started the Shivaji Movement in 1895. His object was to inspire the youth of India to follow the example of Shivaji and release

India from the political bondage of the foreigners. On the occasion of Shivaji Festival, there were lectures, fencing with Lathis, processions, Kathas and singing parties. About Afzal Khan's murder by Shivaji, Tilak observed thus: "With benevolent intentions Shivaji murdered Afzal Khan for the good of others. If thieves enter our house and we have not sufficient strength in our wrists to drive them out, we should, without hesitation, shut them up and burn them alive."

In 1897, Tilak was arrested for sedition and sentenced to 18 months' rigorous imprisonment by Judge Strachey. The Jury which tried him consisted of 6 Europeans and 3 Indians and all the Europeans found him guilty while all the Indians found him not guilty.

In 1908, he was tried for sedition and sentenced to 6 years' imprisonment. He was tried by a Jury consisting of 7 Europeans and 2 Indians. All the Europeans found him guilty and all the Indians found him not guilty. Tilak had to spend 6 years of imprisonment in the Mandalay Jail in Burma from 1908 to 1914.

Tilak brought a suit against Sir Valentine Chirol for libel and personally went to England to conduct that case. The Government of India and the British bureaucracy wholeheartedly helped Chirol and no wonder the suit was lost in 1919.

When the First World War started in 1914, he asked the people of India to help the British Government to the best of their ability. When he did so, he expected a reciprocal gesture from the British Government. He continued to follow this policy for two years. Instead of any reciprocal gesture on the part of the Government, the authorities in India put all kinds of obstacles in the Home Rule Movement started by him. The workers were not allowed to hold their public meetings. The result was that Tilak began to criticise the Government openly. His definite stand was that unless the people of India were assured of Home Rule, they must not help the British Government in war.

Views on National Language. Tilak was the first Congress Leader to suggest that Hindi, written in Devanagari script, should be the national language of India. At a Conference of the Nagari Pracharini Sabha held in December 1915 he declared that Devanagari should not only be the common script of the Aryan languages but also of the script of the national language.

Tilak was a research scholar of international fame. In spite of his being otherwise busy, he managed to produce works on the antiquity of the Vedas, The Orion and the Arctic Home of the Vedas. Dr. Bloomfield of John Hopkins University spoke of the Orion as "unquestionably the literary sensation of the year. History, the chronic re-adjuster, will have our hands uncommonly full to assimilate the results of Tilak's discovery and arrange her paraphernalia in the new perspective." Likewise, Tilak's Gita Rashasya which was written during his long imprisonment in Mandalay jail, is a monumental work and is rightly considered as his greatest contribution to philosophical thought. In this book, Tilak gave a new interpretation of the Gita. He demolished the old theory that a liberated soul had no obligation towards his fellow human-beings. Tilak gave the youth of India a new deal of work for, the ideal of selfless and disinterested service in humanity.

Philosophy of Defiance. The great contribution of Tilak was that he taught the philosophy of defiance to the people of India. He was born in an age which can be described as dark. The powerful impact of foreign rule had reduced the people to a state of utter helplessness. The failure of the Indian mutiny had broken the will of the people to resist the British Raj. It is true that the Indian National Congress was founded in 1885, but the British Government did not take it seriously. To begin with, it was regarded as something harmless and mildly liberal. It passed resolutions of loyalty to the throne and prayed for the safety and prosperity of the British Empire. There was not a word of hostile criticism in the resolutions passed by the Congress. Nobody can doubt the patriotism of men like Sir Pherozeshah Mehta, Justice Ranade and Gokhale, but their vision was limited. The Moderates pointed out the defects in the system of British administration in India but they were always afraid of challenging the British authority. The result was that their eloquent and fiery speeches left the British rulers cold. They knew that their fire did not burn and their flourishing swords had no edge to them.

Tilak believed that the policy of the Congress must be changed. The Congress must learn to defy authority. It must be ready to make sacrifice for the sake of winning freedom for the country. He did not want the people to be violent for the realisation of India's freedom but if India could not be free by peaceful means, there was no harm in using violence as well. He believed that the end justifies the means. He advocated the programme of Swadeshi and boycott of foreign goods and everything foreign. He did not want the Congress to fight for small gains. He wanted to fight for the ideal of the independence of the country. He started the National Party to change the programme of the Congress. It is true that the Moderates had their way up to 1914, particularly because from 1908 to 1914 he was shut up in the Mandalay jail, but when he came out, the Moderates could not stand against him. He carried the day. He converted the Congress from the admirers of the British Government into rebels against the British Empire. It has rightly been pointed out that Mahatma Gandhi and Jawaharlal Nehru were able to rear the grand edifice of Swaraj on the foundation laid by Lokmanya Tilak.

There was fire in the speeches of Tilak. He was fearless in what he said. He did not care for the consequences. He was regarded as the most dangerous man by the British Government. He has been called the father of Indian unrest. The Governor of Bombay (now Mumbai) wrote thus to the Secretary of State for India in 1908: "He (Tilak) is one of the chief conspirators, perhaps the chief conspirator, against the existence of the British Government in India, all the weak points of which he has made a careful study. "His Ganpati Festivals, Shivaji Celebrations; Paisa Fund and National Schools were all instituted for one purpose, the overthrow of British rule."

According to Ram Gopal, "He (Tilak) had forestalled Gandhi in all the movements that the Mahatma Gandhi launched after Tilak's death: no-rent campaign, boycott of government service, prohibition, Swadeshi were all preached and practised by him. "He talked of complete independence as back as 1897." Again, his was the life divine, and his countrymen elevated him not only to the position of Lokamanya, but adored him even as Tilak Bhagwan. In the encircling gloom, he appeared with a torch in his hand."

In 1908, the people shouted Tilak Maharaj ki Jai and Chhatrapati Tilak Maharaj ki Jai. He was regarded as great as Shivaji. During the disturbances in Bombay (now Mumbai) in 1908, a medal was struck having the effigy of Shivaji on one side and that of Tilak on the other. The names of Shivaji and Tilak were frequently coupled together and the latter came to be known as the man who is to expel the British from India. According to Swami Shradhanand, "Maharaj Tilak occupies an exalted position among the pioneers of political work who were the first to preach the doctrine of political unity. What other hero has suffered so much in the service of the motherland as this illustrious person has done? Will not the soldiers constituting the army for the service of the motherland bow down before the mandate of this weather-beaten General?"

In 1908, the Morning Leader wrote thus about Tilak: "There are very few people in England in a position to realise what the arrest of Mr. Bal Gangadhar Tilak, the National leader of Poona, actually means in India. His personal power is unapproached by any other politician in the country; he dominates the Deccan, his own country, and is adored with a kind of religious fervour by every Extremist from Bombay to the Bay of Bengal. The break-up of the National Congress at Surat was his doing; his the mind that conceived, his the pen that expressed, and his the force that has directed the extraordinary movement against which the bureaucracy is now calling up all its resources. He is a thinker and fighter in one."

Comparison of Tilak and Gokhale. Dr. Pattabhi Sitaramayya, the famous author of the History of the Indian National Congress, has attempted a comparison of Tilak and Gokhale in these words: "Tilak and Gokhale were both patriots of the first order. Both had made heavy sacrifices in life. But their temperaments were widely different from each other. Gokhale was a Moderate and Tilak was an Extremist if we may use the language in vogue at that time. Gokhale's aim was to improve the existing constitution; Tilak's was to reconstruct it. Gokhale had necessarily to fight it. Gokhale stood for co-operation wherever possible and opposition wherever necessary. Tilak inclined towards a policy of obstruction. Gokhale's primary concern was with the administration and its improvement; Tilak's supreme concern was the nation and its upbuilding. Gokhale's ideal was love and sacrifice; Tilak's was service and suffering. Gokhale's method sought to win the foreigner; Tilak's to replace him. Gokhale depended upon others' help; Tilak upon self-help. Gokhale looked to the classes and the intelligentsia; Tilak to the masses and the millions. Gokhale's arena was the Council Chamber; Tilak's forum was the village Mandap. Gokhale's objective was self-government for which the people had to fit themselves by answering the tests prescribed by the English; Tilak's object was Swaraj which is the birth-right of every Indian and which he shall have without let or hindrance from the foreigner. Gokhale was on a level with his age; Tilak was in advance of his times."

MAHATMA GANDHI (1869-1948)

Mahatma Gandhi, the Father of the Indian Nation, was born on 2nd October 1869 at Porbander in Kathiawar. At the age of 79, he was shot dead at Delhi. His father was a Dewan at Porbander and Rajkot. He was married at the age of 12. At the age of 19, he left for Great Britain to qualify for the Bar. Before leaving India, he made a promise to his mother that he would avoid three things, viz., meat, wine and women.

After qualifying himself for the Bar, Gandhi began to practise at Rajkot and from there he shifted to Bombay (now Mumbai). During his stay at Bombay Gandhiji came into intimate contact with Rajchandra Ravjibhai. The latter exercised a tremendous influence on him. As a matter of fact, Gandhiji got his first lessons of non-violence and truth from Rajchandra Ravjibhai.

Gandhiji went to South Africa in connection with a professional work on behalf of a Mohammedan firm. His stay in South Africa was the formative period of his political life. It was in South Africa that he put into practice his weapon of Satyagraha. He also developed self-confidence to lead a struggle. It was in that dark continent that he taught his countrymen to give up fear, resist evil by truth, and never to yield and strive to rise to the full stature of manhood.

Gandhi's opportunity came in 1906 when the Asiatic Registration Act was passed by the Government of South Africa. That Act required all Asiatic to register themselves and give their thumb impressions. This involved a measure of humiliation which was impossible for the Indians to put up with. Gandhiji not only protested against this enactment but also led a deputation to England. However, all that brought about no change. Under the leadership of Gandhiji, the Indians refused to get themselves registered or give their thumb impressions. The result was that thousands of them were sent to jail. Gandhi himself was awarded two months' imprisonment. As the movement was a novel one and the Government found itself helpless, a compromise was arrived at. The Indians agreed to get themselves registered voluntarily and Gandhiji was the first to offer himself for registration. However, the struggle had to be started once again as the Transvaal authorities refused to carry out their part of the contract. There was a lot of resentment in India against the treatment of the Indians. Then the invasion of Transvaal took place. Two thousand men marched into Transvaal under the leadership of Gandhiji. The march was a great landmark. It was the march of truth against untruth of justice against injustice and of non-violence against violence. A Commission of Inquiry was set up and ultimately the hated Asiatic Act was cancelled. The poll-tax was repealed. Marriages among the Indians were recognised.

Having won his laurels in South Africa, Mahatma Gandhi came to India in 1914. At that time he had complete faith in the love of justice of the Englishmen. No wonder, he appealed to the Indians to help the British Government unconditionally. It was after 1918 that doubts arose in his mind regarding the ideals of the British rule. The passing of the Rowlatt Bill in the teeth of opposition by the people, had profound influence on his mind. It became his firm faith that the British rule in India was Satanic.

In 1915, Gandhiji had said that "as a passive resister, I discovered that the British Empire had certain ideals with which I have fallen in love and one of those ideals is that every subject of the

British Empire has the freest scope for his energies and honour and whatever he thinks is due to his conscience.... And I have found that it is possible for me to be governed least under the British Empire. Hence my loyalty to the British Empire. To the Viceroy, he wrote thus in 1918: "If I could make my countrymen retrace their steps, I would make them withdraw all the Congress resolutions and not whisper 'home rule' or responsible government during the pendency of the war. I would make India offer all her able-bodied sons as a sacrifice to the Empire at this critical moment; and I know that India by this very act, would become the most favoured partner and racial distinctions would become a thing of the past." In the same strain was his advice to his countrymen in which he exhorted them "to fight unconditionally unto death with British for victory and agitate simultaneously also unto death if we must, for the reforms which we desire." The Rowlatt Act, the Punjab disorders and the Khilafat agitation, however, completely shattered his belief in the justice and good faith of England. In a letter to the Viceroy written in August 1920 he wrote thus: "Events that have happened during the past month have confirmed me in the opinion that the Imperial Government have acted in the Khilafat matter in an unscrupulous, immoral and unjust manner, and have been moving from wrong to wrong in order to defend their immorality. I can retain neither respect nor affection for such a government. Your Excellency's light-hearted treatment of official crime, your exoneration of Sir Michael O'Dwyer, Mr. Montagu's Despatch, and above all the shameful ignorance of the Punjab events and the callous disregard of the feelings of Indians betrayed by the House of Lords, have filled me with the gravest misgivings regarding the future of the Empire, have estranged me completely from the present government and have disabled me from rendering, as I have hitherto wholeheartedly rendered, my total co-operation."

A special session of the Congress was held at Calcutta in September 1920, and this session marks the beginning of the Gandhian era. Under Gandhiji, the Congress became more and more representative of the people, with a distinctive economic, moral, social and political programme and all flowing from the genius of one man. Gandhiji's resolution was carried by a majority of 1,866 votes against 884.

Mahatma Gandhi combined his Non-Co-operation Movement with the Khilafat Movement. He believed in the ideal of Hindu-Muslim unity. In spite of this outward co-operation for some time, it was found that there was no union of hearts. Differences arose between the Hindus and Muslims. The Moplah revolt in Malabar opened the eyes of the Hindus. Riots took place in Bombay on the day the Prince of Wales landed in that city. In February 1922, there took place serious rioting at Chauri-Chaura near Gorakhpur in Uttar Pradesh. At the place, 21 constables and one sub-inspector of police were shut up in a police station and burnt alive by a mob. The result was that Gandhiji withdrew his Non-Co-operation Movement. He was arrested by Government and sentenced to six years' simple imprisonment. At his trial, he pleaded guilty to the charge and made the following remark in his reply to the judge: "Non-violence is the first article of my faith. It is the last article of my faith. But I had to make my choice; I have either to submit to a system which I consider has done irreparable harm to my country, or incur the risk of the mad fury of my people bursting forth when they understood the truth from my lips. I know that my people have sometimes gone mad, I am deeply sorry for it; and I am therefore here to submit not to a light penalty but to the highest penalty. I do not ask for mercy. I do not plead any extenuating act. I am here therefore to invite and submit to the highest penalty that can be inflicted upon me for what in law is a deliberate crime and what appears to me to be the highest duty of a citizen."

There was a split within the Congress on the question of Council entry. Motilal Nehru and C. R. Dass were in favour of the Congress entering the legislatures and fighting the Government from within also. However, a compromise was arrived at after some time and the Swarajist party got its blessings.

From then onwards, Mahatma Gandhi continued to dominate not only the Congress but also the entire politics of the country. His position was absolutely unchallenged. In 1931, he went to London to attend the Second Round Table Conference, but came back empty-handed on account of the attitude of the British Government and Mr. Jinnah. On many occasions, he decided to fast unto death for various causes. India won her independence on 15th August 1947 under his leadership but he himself was murdered on 30th January 1948 by a fanatical Hindu.

Mahatma Gandhi has rightly been called the Father of the Nation. He was in every sense of the word the creator of modern India. It was under him that India won her independence. It is true that Tilak had anticipated him by advocating a policy of strong action against the British Government instead of a policy of mendicancy as followed by the Moderates in India, but it cannot be denied that it was under Gandhiji that the nationalist movement in India became a mass movement and not a movement of the mere intelligentsia of India. He followed various methods to achieve his ends. He started the Non-Co-operation Movement. He started the Civil Disobedience Movement. He violated the laws of the country. It was under him that the Congress passed the Quit India Resolution. He fasted. He courted arrest. He defied the might of the British Empire But he did all this with one object and that was the liberation of this country.

Nagendranath Gupta has summed up the contribution of Mahatma Gandhi to the nationalist movement in India in these words: "The movement led by Mahatma Gandhi has brought into prominence some of the greatest men that India has known in recent times, men who would be considered great in any country at any time. If Mahatma Gandhi is the Prophet, they are undoubtedly his apostles. The national movement in India may easily be divided into two phases, one before Mahatma Gandhi had joined the Indian National Congress and the other after he became the most conspicuous figure in it. In the earlier stage, Congressmen confined themselves to agitation and oratory, to ever-repeated assertion of then birth-right to Home Rule and severe criticism of Governmental action, to constitutionalism and reformism. Only the very greatest of them risked and sacrificed everything for achieving their goal. The rank and file was passive onlookers and onhearers, so to say. This might have gone on for any number of years without any prospect of freedom for India. Then came Mahatma Gandhi with his experience of the Transvaal, has spiritual outlook, his gentle nature and his inflexible will. There were willing hearts in India waiting for his call and they at once realised the- nature of the struggle that lay ahead of them. Since then the struggle for national freedom in India has grown ever wider and today it comprehends the entire nation, it has been a glorious record which is being added day after day, of sacrifice and suffering of women that vied with men in offering themselves as sacrifices at the altar of liberty. The old caution and timidity have disappeared for ever; the prison has lost its hardships and degradation, and there are no signs of hesitation or reluctance to suffer. Men or women are filled with the spirit of martyrdom and the determination to win by suffering what was hitherto accomplished by violence."

Mahatma Gandhi put great emphasis on communal unity. He believed that both the Hindus and Muslims must live as brothers and sisters in the country and in his efforts to do so he lost his life also. When after the Khilafat Movement in India, relations became bitter between the Hindus and Muslims on account of the atrocities committed by the Muslims over the Hindus in various parts of India, Mahatma Gandhi went on a 21 days' fast in September 1924 as a penance. The communal situation deteriorated in India in 1946 and 1947 as a result of the policy of Direct Action followed by the Muslim League. Then took place the Calcutta Killing in August 1946. Something worse than that happened in Noakhali. There were repercussions in Bihar and Garhmukteshwar (in U.P.). Then there were riots in Rawalpindi, Lahore etc. When the partition of India took place in August 1947, there was a wholesale killing of Hindus and Muslims by one another. All this was painful to Mahatma Gandhi. Instead of participating in the celebrations held in Delhi on 15th August 1947, at the time of transfer of power by the Englishmen into the hands of the Indians, Mahatma Gandhi decided to go to Noakhali in East Bengal. Bare-footed, he walked from village to village and tried to restore peace to that area. He did not care for his life which could be finished at any time by any Muslim. After restoring peace there, he came back to Bihar and persuaded the Hindus to take back the Muslims who had left their homes in fear. After that, he went to Calcutta and although he was mobbed by the Hindus, he was able to stop the fury of the people against the Muslims. It was the fast of Mahatma Gandhi for 72 hours that brought about the change of atmosphere in Calcutta. In the words of Lord Mountbatten, "What fifty thousand well-equipped soldiers could not do, the Mahatma has done —

he has brought peace. He is a one-man boundary force." After Calcutta, Mahatma Gandhi came to Delhi where the Hindus were determined to turn out the Muslims from the Capital of India. Lakhs of Hindu refugees had come to Delhi from West Pakistan and they clamoured for the turning out of the Muslims from Delhi to make room for them. They would have succeeded in their object if Mahatma Gandhi had not come to Delhi for the next few days. Mahatma Gandhi refused to allow the Hindus to turn put the Muslims. He went on a fast and demanded that the Hindus must allow the Muslims to live in Delhi. The mosques of the muslims were restored to them and the Muslims were allowed to live in peace.

Mahatmaji was a great social reformer. He took up the cause of the depressed classes in India and devoted the whole of his life to this noble mission. He asked the Hindus to give up their old prejudices against the depressed, classes. He asked them to open their temples for their worship. He himself lived in their quarters. Instead of calling them depressed classes, he gave them the name of Harijans or the people of God. He started a newspaper entitled The Harijan and himself edited the same during his lifetime. He regarded untouchability as a curse to Hindu society and the same was abolished in the Indian Constitution framed after the independence of India. He believed that one of the methods of improving the lot of the poor Indians was to stop the habit of drinking in the country and that is why he advocated the policy of prohibition. He was not ignorant of the fact that the policy of prohibition was bound to result in the loss of crores of rupees to the revenues of the Government but he was prepared to make that sacrifice in the higher interests of the country as a whole. He advocated the rights of women and stood for giving them equal status with men. Among his associates were not only men must also women and some of them are today occupying very high places in the country.

Gandhiji believed that the present system of education was not suitable to a poor country like India. He was in favour of a more utilitarian system of education. It was under his guidance that the Wardha Scheme of education was adopted. The children were to get not only the knowledge of three R's but also learn some art which was to help them while studying.

Mahatma Gandhi stood for Swadeshi. As a matter of fact, this was one of the weapons in his armoury against the British. He believed that he would be able to bring the Englishmen to their knees by persuading the Indians to boycott the foreign goods. The stopping of the Manchester and Lancashire mills was bound to hit the Englishmen economically. The adoption of Swdeshi was bound to save millions of rupees to the people of India. Mahatma Gandhi put the greatest emphasis on the use of Khadi as that was bound to add to the income of the poor people in this country.

Mahatmaji was not in favour of wholesale industrialization of the country on the lines of the West. As a matter of fact, he advocated the establishment of cottage industries. He rightly believed that cottage industries could go a long way in raising the standard of the poor people in the countryside. The setting up of more mills was bound to result in capitalism and great inequality of wealth. The lot of the poor was not going to improve thereby. Mahatmaji, a friend of the labourers, was always supporting their legitimate claims. However, he was opposed to the method of strikes as that was not in the interest of the country as a whole.

Estimate of Mahatma Gandhi

Mahatma Gandhi was known all over the world and no wonder tributes were paid to the greatness of the saint of Sabarmati. It is desirable to refer to some of them. According to Edward Thompson, "He is a superb judge of other men. His humanity is one of the profoundest things that history has seen. He has pity and love for every race, and most of all for the poor and oppressed." According to Remain Rolland, "Mahatma Gandhi has raised up three hundred millions of his fellowmen, shaken the British Empire and inaugurated in human politics the most powerful movement that the whole world has seen for nearly two thousand years". According to Louis Fischer, "The symbol of India's unanimous wish for freedom is Mahatma Gandhi. He does not represent all of India, but he does reflect the will of all India for national liberation. A great man is like good sculpture, made of one piece. A great man lives a single tracked life. Lincoln was great, he lived for the Union. Lenin was great, he lived in order to raise Russia out of the feudal mire. Churchill is great because all of his acts have been directed towards the preservation of England as a first-class power. And in the same way Gandhi is great because every single act that he performs is calculated to promote the one goal of his life — the liberation of India. He is not the man, he has no intention and never had, to rule India or administer India. His function ends when he frees India." Again, "Gandhi is the father of India's defiance and its symbol. Gandhi walks to sea to make salt in defiance of the British. It becomes a popular pilgrimage. The idealism of the youth spills into it. So does the leaderless nation's yearning for a leader. Gandhi has given his followers the elation of standing up to a foreigner who is the master in their house."

According to Lord Halifax, "I suppose there can be few men in all history who by their personal character and example have been able deeply to influence the thought of their generation." According to Sir Stafford Cripps, "There has been no greater spiritual leader in the world in our own times." According to Acharya Kriplani, "The Mahatma is more right when he is wrong than we are when we are right." Again, "Many of us are correct in our little correctness and are small in the process. But the Mahatma was incorrect in many things and yet correct in the sum-total and big in the very inconsistencies. In the end, he seldom or never came out at the wrong place." According to Nagendranath Gupta, "Is it not strange that although Mahatma Gandhi is the leader of a movement of political freedom, he has never been compared to such great national leaders as Rienze, Mirabeau, Washington, Hampden, Mazzini, Sun-Yat-Sen or Zaghlul Pasha? Yet he has been repeatedly and widely compared to great religious teachers like Zoroaster, Buddha and Christ, or a saint like St. Francis or Assisi. What political leader has observed fast for twenty-one days to do penance for his country and the warring factions of his countrymen?"

According to Dr. Rajendra Prasad, former President of India, "Mahatma Gandhi's contribution to Indian politics has been immense. The Indian National Congress had been in existence for thirty years when he returned to India finally from South Africa in 1915. The Congress had aroused and organised national consciousness to a certain extent; but the awakening was confined largely to the English educated middle classes and had not penetrated the masses. He carried it to the masses and made it a mass movement. Mahatma Gandhi's movement operated both horizontally and vertically. He took up causes which were not entirely political but which touched very intimately the life of large masses of people." Again, "Mahatma Gandhi's greatest contribution, however, does not consist in making the masses of India politically self-conscious and organising them on a scale they had never before been organised. To my mind his greatest contribution to Indian polices and perhaps to suffering humanity in the world at large lies in the unique method which he has prescribed and employed for fighting wrongs. He has taught us how it is possible for us to successfully fight the mighty British Empire without arms; he has given us and the world a moral substitute for war. He has lifted politics from the plane of sophistication and untruths where at its worst is generated into low intrigue and at its highest could not rise beyond diplomatic circumlocutions and secret diplomacy, to the pitch of a high idealism in which the end, however noble, can in no circumstances justify recourse to means which are not pure and immaculate. He has placed truth on its pedestal of glory even in politics, no matter how harmful its effect appears to be at the moment. His frankness and deliberate exposure of ugly or weak spots in ourselves to our so-called enemies has confounded both friends and opponents alike. But he considers our strength lies not in concealing our weakness but in knowing and combating it. The rigorous observance of non-violence, even where temporary advantages may apparently be gained by ignorance or mitigating it, has been recognised by experience to be not only the straightest course but also the wisest policy. It was the moral and spiritual fervour of his teaching which at once caught the imagination of the people, who saw and recognized that when all was dark around he showed us the way out of our misery and slavery. When we were feeling utterly helpless, he made us realise our own strength through Truth and Non-violence."

According to Prof. Percival Spear, "For nearly thirty years Congress was dominated by Gandhi, and India influenced more by him than by any other single man. It is not too much to say that the destiny of India was modified and the world itself influenced by this single personality. An unimpressive figure with a reedy voice, an ingratiating manner, and an astute expression concealed a character of great charm and baffling complexity. Gandhi was one of those men who concealed thought in the volume of his speech and meaning in the wealth of explanation. He was always explaining himself and was never understood. He convinced those whose attention was caught by one facet or other of his character in turn that he was a fanatic, a visionary, a consummate tactician, a saint, a prophet, or a trickster. To this day he remains an enigma; the only fact of which we can be quite certain is the magnitude of his 'influence upon the people and events of his time and afterwards."

REVIEW QUESTIONS

1. Dadabhai Naoroji is known as the 'Grand Old Man of India'. Elucidate.
2. What was the role of Dadabhai Naoroji in Indian Independence Movement? Elaborate.
3. Throw light on the contributions of Gopal Krishan Gokhale and Bal Gangadhar Tilak in Indian Independence Movement.
4. Discuss the views of Bal Gangadhar Tilak on national language. What was his philosophy of defiance to the people of India?
5. Compare and contrast the nationalism of Bal Gangadhar Tilak and Gopal Krishan Gokhale.
6. Analyse the main difference between approaches of Bal Gangadhar Tilak and Gopal Krishan Gokhale.
7. Gopal Krishan Gokhale was a mentor to both Mohamammad Jinnah and Mahatma Gandhi.
8. Evaluate the contribution of Mahatma Gandhi in Indian Independence Movement.
9. Mahatma Gandhi has rightly been called the 'Father of Nation'. Justify.
10. Mahatma Gandhi put great emphasis on communal community. Examine.

SUGGESTED READINGS

Athalye, D.V.: *The Life of Lokamanya Tilak*.
Gandhi, M.K.: *My Experience with Truth*.
Gandhi, M.K.: *Gokhale, My Political Guru* (1955).
Hoyland, J.S.: *Gopal Krishna Gokhale* (1947).
Karmarker, D.P.: *Bal Gangadhar Tilak* (1956).
Karandikar, S.L.: *Tilak* (1957).
Keer, D.: *Lokamanya Tilak* (1959).
Kelkar, N.C.: *Life and Time of Lokmanya Tilak* (1928).
Masani, R.P.: *Dadabhai Nauroji* (1939).
Parvate, T.V.: *Bal Gangadhar Tilak* (1958).
Parvate, T.V.: *Gopal Krishna*.
Prabhu, R.K.: *The Mind of Mahatma Gandhi* (1945).
Ram Gopal: *Lokamanya Tilak* (1956).
Saggi, P.D.: *Life and Work of Lal, Bal and Pal*, 1962.
Sastri, V.S.: *Srinivasa. Life of Gopal Krishna Gokhale* (1937)
Shahni, T.K.: *Gopal Krishan Gokhale*, Bombay, 1929.
Tahmankar, D.V.: *Lokamanya Tilak* (1956).

24. Decentralisation of Finance

LEARNING OBJECTIVES

- Discuss the history of financial decentralisation in India
- Throw light on financial relationship between the Central Government and the States, according to the Constitution

It is well known that up to the passing of the Charter Act of 1833 the princes enjoyed a lot of autonomy in matters of finance. It was the Act of 1833 that brought about financial centralisation. The Act provided that "no Government shall have power of granting of any new office or granting any new salary, gratuity or allowance without the previous sanction of the Governor-General." Indian finance remained centralized in the hands of the Government of India even after the passing of the Acts of 1853 and 1858. The Provinces were not given any right or authority on the Provincial revenues. They were merely the managing agents for the Government of India. The sources of taxation, the amount of taxation, the manner of collection and the authority for expenditure were all dictated from the headquarters. The provinces had absolutely no interest in the collection of the taxes. According to Sir William Hunter, "Towards the end of every year, each Local Government presented to the Governor-General-in-Council its estimates of expenditure during the coming 12 months. The Governor-General-in-Council, after comparing the aggregate estimates with the expected revenue from all India, granted to-each local Government such sums as could be spared for its local services." According to Strachey, "The whole of the revenues from all the provinces of British India were treated as belonging to a single fund, expenditure from which could be authorised by the Governor-General-in-Council alone. The Provincial Governments were allowed no discretion in sanctioning fresh charges. They could order without the approval of the Supreme' Government, and without its knowledge, the adoption of measures vitally affecting the interests of millions of people. They could make changes in the system of administration that might involve serious consequences to the State; they could for instance (and this is a case which actually occurred) alter the basis on which the assessment of the land revenue had been made, but they could carry out no improvement, great or small, for which actual expenditure of money was required. If it became necessary to spend £20 on a road between two local markets, to rebuild a stable that had tumbled down, or to entertain a menial servant on wages of 10 shillings a month, the matter had to be formally reported for the orders of the Government of India." A critic points out that "the distribution of public income degenerated into something like a scramble in which the most violent had the advantage, "with very little attention to reason. As local economy brought no local advantage, the stimulus to waste reduced to a minimum, and if no local growth of the income led to local means of improvement, the interest in developing the public revenues was also brought to the lowest level."

It was admitted on all hands that the system was faulty and required to be changed. The efforts of General Dickens and Mr. Laing did not improve matters. In 1867 a scheme was prepared by Strachey to revise that system. On the basis of that scheme, Lord Mayo took the first step on the road to decentralisation.

MAYO'S RESOLUTION (1870)

The Resolution of 1870 transferred to the control of the Provincial Governments the following heads of expenditure, with the revenue accruing from them, and in addition, a fixed annual Imperial Grant for the purpose: Jail, Registration, Police, Education, Medical Services, Printing, Roads, Miscellaneous Public Improvements, and Civil Buildings. The deficit, if any, was to be met either by local taxation or by the reduction of expenditure. Any portion that may be unspent by the end of the year was not to lapse to the Central Government, but was to remain at the disposal of the Provincial Government concerned. Provincial Governments were given powers, subject to certain conditions, to create appointments provided the salary in each case did not exceed ₹250 a month and the amounts could be met out of the assigned Grants. The Government of Lord Mayo hoped that the Resolution "will produce great care and economy; that it will import an element of certainty into fiscal system which has hitherto been absent; and that it will lead to more harmony in action and feeling between the Supreme and Provincial Governments than has hitherto prevailed." The operation of this Resolution, in its full meaning and integrity, will afford opportunities for the development of self-Government, for strengthening municipal institutions, and for the association of natives and Europeans to a greater extent than heretofore in the administration of affairs.

The chief defect of the system of 1870 was that Imperial Grants were made on the basis of expenditure in various provinces in 1870-71. No attempt was made to remove the existing inequalities, and to give Grants to provinces according to their actual needs. According to Dr. Gian Chand, "The province which had the low level of expenditure owing either to access to the Central Government or to its under-developed or backward state due to recent annexation was penalised for its economy, unassertiveness or worse still backwardness." The charge of R. C. Dutt was that the reform of Lord Mayo brought about an increase in the general burden of taxation. Each province, to augment its own revenues, imposed new taxes, mostly on land. The result was that the State-demand on the soil was increased. That was against the spirit of the Permanent Settlement in Bengal and as regards other provinces, it broke the rule adopted in 1855 and 1864 of limiting assessment to one-half the rental (*India in the Victorian Age*, p. 257). However, it has been pointed out that the practice of separating Central from Local taxation was almost universal in the modern States. Moreover, the system of Lord Mayo resulted in a lot of economy. According to Roberts, Lord Mayo "found serious deficit and left substantial surplus. He found estimates habitually untrustworthy, he left thoroughly worthy of confidence. He found accounts in arrears and statistics incomplete, he left them punctual and full." (*British India*, p. 417.)

LYTTON'S CHANGE

In 1877, the Government of Lord Lytton took the second step on the road to decentralisation. Several heads of expenditure such as Land Revenue, Excise, Stamps, General Administration, Stationery, Law and Justice were transferred to the Provincial Governments. It was also provided that any surplus above the estimated income was to be shared to the extent of one-half with the Government of India which also undertook to meet deficits to the same extent, if and when occurred.

RIPON (1882)

The next change was made in 1882 by Lord Cromer in the time of Lord Ripon. He introduced the system of Imperial, Divided and Provincial Heads of Revenue by which the revenues from all sources were divided into three categories. Income from Imperial Heads was to go to the Central Government. The provinces were to get all the income from the Departments under their control. Income from the Divided Heads was to be shared, mostly in equal portions, between the Imperial Government and the Provincial Governments. The deficit in the Provincial Budgets was to be made good by the Imperial Government by giving a fixed percentage of land revenue to the provinces. This settlement was made for five years and was renewed in 1887, 1892 and 1897.

According to Principal C. L. Anand, "The advantage of this system over the one which had hitherto generally prevailed, was that it gave the provincial Governments a direct interest not only in the provincialised revenue but also in the most important items of Imperial revenue, raised within their own province." The defects of this system were described in these words by Lieutenant-Governor of Bengal in 1896: "I must say I deprecate the way in which these quinquennial revisions have too frequently been carried out. The provincial sheep is summarily thrown on its back, close-clipped and shorn of its wool, and turned out to shiver till its fleece grows again. The normal history of a provincial contract is that — two years of screwing and sewing and postponement of works, two years of resumed energy on a normal scale, and one year of dissipation of balances in the fear that if not spent they will be annexed by the Supreme Government, directly or indirectly at the time of revision. Now all this is wrong, if not demoralising. I say the Supreme Government might not shear too closely each quinquennium. It would be an immense gain to Local Administration if the Government of India could see its way to each occasion. It is only in this that the element of fiscal certainty which was put forward in 1870 as one of its main objects, can be secured."

CURZON

In 1904, Lord Curzon tried to remove the defects of the settlement of 1882. Although the old division of revenues into the Imperial, Divided and Provincial Heads was continued, the shares of the Central Government and the Provincial Governments were revised. Expenditure on purely Imperial heads was to be incurred entirely by the Government of India. Expenditure incurred on the Divided Heads was to be divided between the Government of India and the Provincial Governments. The settlement was declared to be quasi-permanent and was to be revised only if found to be grossly unjust or in very extreme circumstances.

The object of quasi-permanent settlements was "to give the local government a more independent position and a more substantial and enduring interest in the management of their resources than had previously been possible." The Provincial Governments could count on the continuity of the financial policy and reap the benefits of their own economy. The Central Government also gained because as the quinquennial controversy ended, she was in a better position to calculate her own resources.

After some time, an important change was made with regard to famine expenditure. Formerly, the local governments were responsible for expenditure on famine and the Government of India came to their rescue only in case of shortage. What was done was that a new Famine Insurance Scheme was devised by means of which the Government of India put at the disposal of the local government concerned a fixed amount from which it could spend at the time of famine without drawing on its normal resources. When that amount was exhausted, further expenditure was to be shared equally by the Government of India and the focal government. In the last resort, the Government of India was to give further assistance from its own revenues.

DECENTRALISATION COMMISSION

The Decentralisation Commission was set up in 1907 by the British Government to enquire into the financial and administrative relations of the Government of India and the Provincial Governments and of authorities subordinate to them, and to report "whether by measure of decentralisation or otherwise," the system of government could be "simplified and improved." The Commission was presided over by Hobhouse, Under-Secretary of State for India. The other five members were senior I.C.S. officers. R.C. Dutt was the only Indian member. The Commission presented its report in 1909. It made the following important recommendations in the financial field:

(a) The Governor-General should not interfere with the revenues assigned to the provinces.
(b) Distributions should be fixed according to needs of the provinces.
(c) The residue should be taken in the shape of a fixed fractional share from a few of the main heads of revenue.

RESOLUTION OF 1912

The Government of India accepted generally the recommendations of the Decentralisation Commission and passed a Resolution on provincial finance on 18th May 1912. The Government of India was anxious to make their financial relations with the Provincial Governments as stable as possible. However, before declaring the provincial settlement permanent, they considered it necessary to examine certain alleged inequalities and adjustments. Regarding the inequality of treatment given to the various provinces, the view of the Government of India was that "if it exists at all, it is historical and inevitable...whilst its very existence is doubtful. The haggling of a quarter of a century has established a rough equality which should not be replaced by theoretical calculations'. According to Dr. Gian Chand: "There was no equity, rough or refined in the Settlement of 1911." But the Government of India proceeded on the assumption that there existed rough equality, between the various provinces. After making certain adjustments, the Government of India made the provincial settlement permanent. In certain provinces, fixed assignments had reached a high figure. The Government of India revised the provincial settlement and made some more heads wholly or partially provincial. The fixed assignments were proportionately reduced. The policy of giving lump sum grants to the provinces out of the surplus of the Government of India was revised in accordance with the recommendations of the Decentralisation Commission. The Commission had recommended the 'adoption of three principles with a view to removing the defects of "the policy of doles." Those principles were that regard should be made to the wishes of the Provincial Governments, the purpose for which grants are made may not be same in all provinces and the grants should not involve greater

Central interference. Moreover, new revised rules were issued by the Government of India in Connection with the control over provincial budgets. In future, the control was to be confined to Divided Heads and to the totals of revenue expenditure. The Provincial Governments were to be given authority to overdraw upon the balances with the Government of India and to budget for a deficit under certain conditions.

It is pointed out that in spite of the changes made by the Resolution of 1912, many defects remained in the system. Inequality in provincial expenditure was not removed. Independent powers of taxation and borrowing were not granted to the provinces. The old system of divided heads and giving of "doles" was allowed to continue. But in spite of these defects, it was declared that the provincial settlements with the provinces were "fixed in perpetuity."

MESTON SETTLEMENT

After the publication of the Report on Indian Constitutional Reforms in 1918, the new policy was inaugurated. The authors of the Report had recommended that the provinces should have their independent sources of revenue. This implied the abolition of the system of divided heads and the separation of Provincial finance from the Central finance. With the object of giving effect to the principle of bifurcation, the two lists were prepared in such a way that the Central and Provincial Governments were to have the least possibility of clash. If there was any doubt as to whether a particular matter was a provincial subject or a central subject, the final decision vested with the Governor-General-in-Council. "The principle of discrimination between Central and Provincial subjects is that where extra provincial interests predominate, the subject is treated as central; while, on the other hand, all subjects in which the interests of a particular province predominate, are provincial." Forty-seven subjects were declared to be Central subjects and the most important of them were Defence, External Affairs, Railways, Shipping and Navigation, Posts and Telegraphs, Customs, Income-tax Services, etc. Fifty-two subjects were included in the Provincial List and the most important were Education, Local Self-Government, Medical Administration, Public Health and Sanitation, Irrigation, Land Revenue, Famine Relief, Agriculture, Forests, Industries, Police, Justice, etc. As the distribution of subjects involved a deficit for the Central Government, a Committee known as the Provincial Relations Committee was set up with Lord Meston as its President to make recommendations as to how the deficit could be met. The Meston Committee recommended that the provinces should make contributions to the Government of India so that the budget might be balanced. It was estimated that the deficit was to be about ₹10 crores. The provinces were not required to pay equally, but according to their paying capacity. Different Provinces were to contribute different sums in different years. Another schedule gave the permanent and standard ratio at which each province was to be taxed in order to wipe out the Central deficit.

The following scale shows the contributions made by the provinces to the Central Government in 1921-22:

Provinces	Contribution in lakhs of rupees
Madras (now Chennai) ...	348
Bombay (now Mumbai) ...	56
Bengal ...	63
Punjab ...	175

United Provinces	...	240
Assam	...	15
Burma	...	64
C. P. and Berar	...	22

There was a general complaint against the Meston Settlement and both the officials and non-officials condemned in equal severity the unwisdom of the new system. The Inquiry Committee also wrote against the system. The revision, if not its complete abolition, was unanimously and persistently demanded. However, Sir Blackett, the Finance member of the Government of India, announced the complete and final remission of provincial contributions in his budget of 1928-29.

Although under the Reforms in 1919, the position of the Provincial Governments with regard to finance was considerably improved, there were still many restrictions on them. They had to maintain the All-India Services as directed by the Secretary of State for India. They were helpless with regard to their appointments and salaries. Their powers of taxation were very much restricted. They were not given the power to borrow on the security of their revenues. The Provincial Government resented those restrictions and desired an independent Provincial Department of Accounts and Auditing.

REFORMS OF 1935

The Government of India Act, 1935, introduced in the provinces what is known as provincial autonomy. The Act provided for a three-fold division of powers between the Federal Government and the Provinces. The Federal Government was given the power to pass laws on those matters, which were given in the Federal List. The Provincial Legislatures were given the power to make laws on those matters which were included in the provincial List. The Concurrent List contained those matters about which laws could be passed both by the Federal Legislature and the Provinces. However, many restrictions were allowed to be continued on the provincial finance. It is true that they were given the power of borrowing within certain limits, but their power to levy taxes was circumscribed. According to the Niemeyer Report, the provinces were given financial assistance by the Central Government to meet their deficits. The Report also recommended the distribution among the provinces of half of the income-tax receipts.

NEW CONSTITUTION

It is to be noted that even under the new Constitution of India which came into force in 1950, the various States of India do not enjoy complete autonomy in the sphere of finance.

The distribution of financial resources between the Union and the States follows the Government of India Act, 1935. Several taxes and duties have been exclusively given to the Union. Some are to be levied by the Union but collected and appropriated by the States. Certain taxes are to be levied as well as collected by the Union, but are assigned to the States within which they are leviable. Certain taxes are to be levied and collected by the Union but distributed between the Union and the States. Provision is also made for grants-in-aid by the Union to the States.

The taxes which belong exclusively to the Union are customs, corporation tax, taxes on capital value of assets of individuals and companies, surcharge on income-tax, fees in respect of matters in the Union List, excise duties on tobacco, and all other goods produced in India except alcoholic liquors for human use, opium and other drugs.

The taxes which belong exclusively to the States are land revenue, taxes on agricultural income, succession duties on agricultural land, taxes on land and buildings, taxes on mineral rights, opium and Indian hemp, taxes on consumption and sale of electricity, terminal tax, taxes on goods and passengers carried by road or inland waterways, taxes on vehicles, professions, trades and entertainments, sales tax, etc.

Stamp duties on Bills of exchange, Bills of lading, insurance policies, transfer of shares, etc., and excise duties on medicinal and toilet preparations containing alcohol are to be levied by the Union but are to be collected and appropriated by the States within whose jurisdiction they are levied.

The following taxes are to be levied as well as collected by the Union, but assigned to the States within which they are leviable: duties on succession to property other than agricultural land, estate duty in respect of property other than agricultural land, terminal taxes on goods or passengers carried by railway, air or sea, taxes on railway fares and freights, taxes on transactions in stock exchange and taxes on sale of and advertisements in newspapers.

The following taxes are levied and collected by the Union, but their proceeds are divided between the Union and the States in a certain proportion: taxes on income other than those on agricultural income and duties of excise as are included in the Union List, except medicinal and toilet preparations. President of Indian Union has to distribute the proceeds of income-tax between the Union and the States up to that time when it is fixed by the Finance Commission. The distribution of the Union excise duties is to be made by Parliament.

Article 275 provides that grants-in-aid shall be made every year by the Union Government to those States which are considered to be in need of help by Parliament. These grants are particularly for welfare of the Scheduled Tribes. Assam is to be given some special grant. In addition to this, temporary grants for a period of ten years shall be made to the States of West Bengal, Bihar, Assam and Orissa (now Odisha) in lieu of the shares of the export duty on their jute products as they used to receive before the commencement of the Constitution.

According to Professor B. R. Misra, "The rationale of the distribution of resources follows closely the principles adopted in the distribution of functions." Professor Seligman mentions three such principles: viz., the principles of efficiency, suitability and adequacy. Efficiency and suitability depend upon the nature of the tax and its administration. "No matter how well-intentioned a scheme may be or how completely it may harmonize with the abstract principles of justice, if the system does not work administratively, it is doomed to failure. The problems of efficiency and suitability really depend upon the choice between a wide or a narrow tax basis." Again, "To evolve a system of financial allocation in India, in conformity with the principles of efficiency, suitability and adequacy, is an extremely difficult task. Constitutional, natural and economic considerations place insurmountable difficulties in its way. A system which would obviously secure efficiency and suitability would break down on the principle of adequacy. Moreover, a system that might suggest itself as the most acceptable would not satisfy the conflicting claims and counterclaims of the various States. Hence financial allocation between the Government of India and the States has always been a matter of compromise. Such compromises are reflected in the system of 'doles' from the Centre to the States or 'contribution' from the States to the Centre or in the system of 'shared revenues'; or grants-in-aid from the Federation to the States."

REVIEW QUESTIONS

1. Who took the first step on the road of decentralisation of finance in India? Discuss.
2. Throw light on Mayo's Resolution, 1870.
3. Describe the contributions of Lord Lytton, Ripon and Curzon in decentralisation of finance.
4. Write a note on Decentralisation Commission.
5. What were the reforms of the Government of India Act, 1935 with regard to decentralisation of finance?
6. Discuss the economic aspect of Indian Constitution.
7. Write short notes on the following:
    (a) Resolution of 1912
    (b) Meston Settlement

SUGGESTED READINGS

Ambedkar, B.R.: *Evolution of Provincial Finance in British India.*
Bhargava, R. N.: *The Theory and Working of Union Finance in India.*
Kale: *Gokhale and Economic Reforms.*
Masaldan, P.N.: *Evolution of Provincial Autonomy in India,* Ch. VI.
Misra, B.R.: *Economic Aspects of Indian Constitution* (1958).
Pinto: *System of Financial Administration in India.*

25   Public Services in India

 LEARNING OBJECTIVES

- Discuss the history of Public Services in India
- Describe the reforms made in Public Services of India
- Throw light on the special provisions for the Public Services in India under the new Constitution

The history of Public Services in India dates back from the early days of the English East India Company. Even when political power fell into the hands of the Company, the actual administration was left in the hands of the Indian subordinates. The few servants employed by the Company had no training in their work. They were paid very low salaries. They made up the deficiency by indulging in private trade and accepting presents. Although their salaries were small they made fortunes within a short time. It is well-known that Lord Clive forced the servants of the Company to enter into new covenants with the Company by which they bound themselves not to engage in private trade or accept presents. It was for this reason that the services came to be known as the Covenanted Civil Services. In order to compensate the servants of the Company Lord Clive formulated a scheme, but it was rejected by the Directors.

REFORMS OF CORNWALLIS

Credit goes to Lord Cornwallis for making radical changes in the Civil Service of the Company. He reserved all the superior jobs for Englishmen and Europeans. He believed that only the Englishmen and Europeans by their birth and training were fit to rule the country. However, subordinate jobs were given to the Indians. He prohibited private trade for the servants of the Company and made it clear that those who violated this rule would be severely dealt with. On the positive side, he raised their salaries so that they could maintain a decent standard of living in India and also take something back home. For example, the salary of a Collector was fixed at ₹1,500 a month. His commission on revenue collection also brought him some money. The same was the case with other servants. The object of these reforms was to make the servants both efficient and honest. The Charter Act of 1793 put the reforms of Cornwallis on a permanent footing. It was declared that, "all vacancies happening in any of the offices, places or employments in the civil lines of the Company's service in India shall be from time to time filled up and supplied from amongst the Civil Servants of the Company belonging to the President wherein such vacancies shall respectively happen." No office carrying a salary of more than £500 a year was to be given to any servant who had not lived in India for at least three years as a covenanted servant. It was also provided that the seniority rule was to be strictly followed in matters of promotion.

LORD WELLESLEY

Students of history know how Lord Wellesley established the famous college at Calcutta for the training of the young Civil Servants. Those Englishmen who came to India as Civil Servants had to study for three years in the training college and study Indian languages, law and history. This college had to be closed down because the Directors refused to approve of it. However, the Directors themselves established in 1806 a college at Haileybury. The Charter Act of 1813 provided that no person was to be appointed a writer in India unless he had resided four terms at Haileybury and produced a certificate from the Principal of the college that he had followed all the rules and regulations of the college. Admission to this college was by means of nomination. The nomination was made by the directors who shared this patronage with the Board of Control. The College at Haileybury continued to function till 1858. The Charter Act of 1853 ended the patronage of the Directors of the Company and threw open the Covenanted Civil Service to a competition for all the natural born subjects of Her Majesty. According to Sir John Strachey, "The main object of the competition was declared to be this—to secure for the Indian Civil Service young men who had received the best, the most liberal, the most finished education that this country affords. The scheme for examination was accordingly made to embrace most of the subjects of honours school of the universities of Great Britain and Ireland."

It is true that Lord Cornwallis was prompted by honest motives in the matter of his reforms. But the natural result of his reforms was that the Indians were excluded completely from the higher jobs in the service of the company. This was the target of a lot of criticism. According to Sir Thomas Munro, "There is perhaps no example of any conquest in which the natives have been so completely excluded from all share of the Government of their country as in British India." According to Sir John Malcolm, "I regret as deeply as you or any man can, that there is no opening for natives. The system of depression becomes more alarming as our power extends. We must, or we cannot last, contrive to associate the natives in the task of ruling and in the benefits and gratifications that accrue from it." The Charter Act of 1833 tried to remove this defect and its 87th clause provided thus: "No native of the said territories, nor any natural born subject of His Majesty resident therein, shall by reason only of his religion, place of birth, descent, colour or any of them, be disabled from holding any place or employment under the said Company." However, this provision remained a dead letter. But with a similar object of removing the grievances of the Indians, Queen Victoria made the following Proclamation in 1858: "It is our further will that, so far as may be, our subjects, of whatever race or creed, be freely and impartially admitted to office in our service, the duties of which they may be qualified by their education, ability and integrity duly to discharge." A committee was appointed in 1860 by the Secretary of State for India to give effect to the pledge given in 1858. The Committee recommended that simultaneous examinations should be held both in England and in India to remove the injustice from which the Indians suffered. However, no action was taken on its recommendations.

INDIAN CIVIL SERVICE ACT

In 1861 was passed the Indian Civil Service Act. The object of this Act was to legalise certain appointments made in the past in contravention of the terms of the Charter Act of 1793 and to reserve almost all higher civil appointments for the members of the Covenanted Civil Service. In exceptional cases, the Government of India was given the power to appoint even those persons who were not members of the Covenanted Civil Service. However, the special reasons for those appointments were to be intimated to the Secretary of State for his sanction within 12 months.

For the recruitment of members to the Covenanted Civil Service open competitive examinations were held in London every year under the supervision of the Civil Service Commissioners. In 1860, the maximum age for candidates appearing at these examinations was lowered to 22. In 1866, it was lowered to 21. In 1878, it was further reduced to 19. The result was that it became practically impossible for any Indian to compete for these examinations. No wonder, up to 1870 only one native of India had successfully completed for the Covenanted Civil Service. The difficulty was not only of age, but other factors such as social, religious and financial difficulties made it difficult for the Indians to go to England to compete for the Service.

George Otto Trevelyan, a member of the Indian Civil Service, defended the policy of the Government in these words: "By choosing your civilians at an earlier age you will get hold of a class who now slip through your hands. A man of first-rate powers who has once tasted the sweets of University success will never be persuaded to give up his English hopes. At two and twenty, in the full view of a Trinity or Merton fellowship who would consent to exchange the Common Room in being, and Downing Street in prospect for the bungalow and the cutchery? Warren Hastings and Sir Charles Metcalfe were among the best scholars of their time at Eton and Westminster. If they had once worn the gown they would have been lost forever to India. Put the limit of age some three years earlier and you will have a fair chance of getting a Metcalfe every other year and a Hastinge once in a decade."

Lord Lawrence established nine scholarships of the value of £200 a year each, tenable for three years, to enable intelligent but poor Indians to go to England and study "for the various learned professions or for the civil or other services of India." This move of the Governor-General was disapproved by the Secretary of the State for India, the Duke of Argyll.

The Act of 1870 provided for the appointment of the natives of India, who had not passed the Civil Service examination, to posts reserved to the Covenanted Service "subject to such rules as may be prescribed from time to time by the Governor-General-in-Council and sanctioned by the Secretary-of-State-in-Council, with the concurrence of a majority of members present." However, it took nine years for the Government of India to make rules under this Act.

In 1878, Lord Lytton decided to close the Covenanted Civil Services to Indians and create "a close native service" to which were to be transferred some of the posts reserved for the Covenanted Service. However, the Secretary of State for India rejected the proposal.

When the rules were framed under the Act of 1870, they empowered the Governor-General-in-Council to appoint natives of India "of good family and social standing" to the posts reserved for the Covenanted service to the extent of one-sixth of the appointments made every year by the Secretary of State in England. Although the Statutory Civil Service was created, it did not succeed in actual practice. The Indians complained that greater importance was given to birth and social position than to intellectual capacity and moral fitness of the candidates.

When the Indian National Congress was established in 1885, it passed a resolution in the same year demanding the holding of simultaneous examinations both in India and England for recruitment to the Covenanted Civil Service.

AITCHISON COMMISSION

In order to study the position thoroughly, Lord Dufferin appointed a Commission in 1886 under the presidency of Sir Charles Aitchison "to devise a scheme which may be hoped to possess the necessary elements of finality and to do full justice to the claim of natives of India to higher and more extensive employment in the Public Service." The Aitchison Commission reported against the holding of simultaneous examinations in India and England. It was pointed out that the system of competition would benefit only a few classes and not the others. As the number of seats to be filled would be small and the number of candidates very large the rejected candidates might become centre of discontentment in the country. The Commission recommended the abolition of the terms Covenanted and Uncovenanted Services. It recommended the division of all the Services into three classes: Imperial Services, Provincial Service and Subordinate Service. All the important jobs were to be held by the Imperial and Provincial Civil Services. The Commission recommended the abolition of the Statutory Civil Service.

RESOLUTION OF 1893

In 1893, the House of Commons passed a resolution to the effect that "all competitive examinations heretofore held in England alone for appointment to the Civil Services of India, shall henceforth be held simultaneously both in India and England, such examinations in both the countries being identical in their nature, and all who compete being finally classified in one list according to merit." As the Government of India regarded the resolution to be dangerous, no action was taken on this resolution.

ISLINGTON COMMISSION

The position of the Civil Services in India was examined by the Royal Commission on Public Services in 1912. The Chairman of the Commission was Lord Islington. The Commission submitted its report in 1915, but it was published not till June 1917. But before the report could be considered on merits the situation in the country had changed completely. In August 1917, Montagu, Secretary of State for India, declared in the House of Commons that the policy of His Majesty's Government towards India was that of increasing association of Indians in every branch of administration. This announcement implied that the Indians were to be given a substantial share in the administration of the country.

RECOMMENDATIONS OF 1918 REPORT

The position of the Public Services was examined by the authors of the Report of 1918. According to them, it was a great weakness of public life in India that there were very few people who had opportunity for practical experience of the problems of administration. Their view was that more Indians should be employed in the administrative machinery of the country. They decided to remove those distinctions, which were based on race. They also recommended the holding of simultaneous examinations both in India and England. In the case of the Indian Civil Service, 33 per cent of the superior posts were to be recruited in India at the beginning and the percentage was to be increased by 1½ per cent annually. Similar percentages were to be fixed in other services. With a view to attracting the very best type of European and English officers to India, recommendations were made for better rates of pay, pension, leave and overseas allowances. Every public servant, wherever employed, was to be properly supported and protected in the exercise of his legitimate duties. The Government of India Act of 1919 gave effect to these recommendations.

When the British Government promised the establishment of responsible Government in India, the members of the Public Services were upset. Formerly, they used to rule the country. In the new set-up, they felt that they would be ruled and controlled by the Indian Ministers. They might be even insulted and humiliated by them. Consequently, they demanded safeguards. To meet their apprehensions, it was recommended that the members of the All-India Services, with a few exceptions, might be allowed to retire before they completed the service ordinarily required for earning pension, and were to be given a pension proportionate to their actual service. In spite of this, the relations between the services and the people of India went from bad to worse. They were persistently criticised in the legislatures. During the Non-Cooperation Movement the civil servants and their families were disrespected and even insulted. On account of the high prices, their economic position also caused them a lot of anxiety. Consequently, a scheme was adopted by which All-India officers selected for appointment before January 1, 1920, and not permanently employed under the Government of India, were allowed to retire before they had completed the normal full services on a pension proportionate to their length of service. Under this scheme, about 345 All-India service officers retired by 1924. Most of them had put in service varying from 10 to 25 years.

The Government of India was faced with the problem that an adequate number of Englishmen and Europeans was not coming forward for the All-India services. The Indians were critical on the ground that the rate of the Indianisation of services was not adequate. They also demanded that the Secretary of State should have nothing to do with the recruitment and control of services. The result was that a Royal Commission on Superior Civil Services in India was appointed in 1923. It is known as the Lee Commission because Lord Lee was its Chairman.

LEE COMMISSION (1923)

The Lee Commission made many recommendations. As regards the Indian Civil Service, the Indian Police Service, the Indian Forest Service and the Irrigation Branch of the Service of Engineers on which public security mainly depended, the Secretary of State was to be allowed to continue to recruit. His control with safeguards was to be maintained. As regards the Indian Educational Service, the Indian Veterinary Service, and the Indian Medical Service (Civil) which operated mostly in the Transferred field, it was recommended that the control of the ministers was to be made more complete by closing the recruitment on an All-India basis. The officers already in these services were to be allowed to retain their All-India status and privileges. However, new recruits to these services were to be appointed in future by the Provincial Government and were to form a part of the Provincial services. But this change was not to apply to the Indian Medical Service. Each province was to be required to employ in its Medical Department a certain number of officers lent from the Medical Department of the Army in India.

The Lee Commission recommended an increased rate of Indianisation. For the Indian Civil Service, 10 per cent of the superior posts were to be filled by appointment of provincial service officers to "listed" posts. Direct recruitment in future was to be on the basis of equal numbers between Europeans and Indians. It was estimated that within 15 years half the recruits to the Indian Civil Service would be Indians and half Europeans. As regards the Indian Police Service, recruitment was to be in the proportion of 5 Europeans to 3 Indians, allowing for promotion from provincial services to fill 20 per cent of vacancies. It was estimated that by 1949 the personnel of the Police Service would be half Europeans and half Indians. As regards the Indian Forest Service, the recruitment was to be in the ratio of 7 per cent Indians and 25 per cent Europeans. As regards the Irrigation Branch of the Indian Service of Engineers, there was to be direct recruitment of Indians and Europeans in equal numbers.

As regards the Central Services, the Lee Commission recommended the following proportions for recruitment:

1. On the Political Department 25 per cent of the total officers to be recruited annually were to be Indians.
2. In the Imperial Customs, not less than half the new entrants were to be statutory natives of India.
3. In the Superior Telegraph and Wireless Branch 25 per cent of the recruitment was to be done in England and 75 per cent in India.
4. In the case of State Railways, recruitment in India was to be increased as soon as possible up to 75 per cent. The remaining 25 per cent new entrants were to be recruited in England.

It is to be observed that in the case of Imperial Customs, Superior Telegraph and Wireless Branch and State Railways, recruitment was to be by open competition. In other cases, full discretion was given to the Government of India.

As regards the Provincial Services, the work of recruitment to the services employed in the Transferred field was handed over to the Provincial Governments. They were to be allowed to make their recruitment in their own way.

The Lee Commission also recommended an increase in emoluments and privileges of the members of the Civil Services. European members of all services were to be allowed to remit their overseas pay at the rate of 2s. for a rupee or to draw the same in London in sterling at the rate. The actual exchange rate at that time was 1s. 5d. Moreover, European members of the Superior Civil Services and their wives were to receive four return passages and one single passage for each child during the service. If any member of a Civil Service died while serving in India, his family was to be repatriated at the expense of the Government of India. The pensions of the members of the Indian Civil Service who attained ranks were considerably increased. Medical attendance by European officers was to be made available to them. Family pension funds were to be introduced. All future British recruits to the all-India services were to be given the option to retire on proportionate pension in case they did not want to serve. They could make claims for compensation.

The Government of India Act of 1919 had provided for the establishment of a Public Service Commission in India, but it had not been established so far. The Lee Commission recommended that the Public Service Commission should be immediately established.

GOVERNMENT OF INDIA ACT, 1935

1. When the Government of India Act, 1935, was on the legislative anvil, the members of the All-India services raised a lot of hue and cry for the safety of their position under the new set-up. The result of their agitation was that very many safeguards were provided in the Act of 1935. The Act secured more or less the existing conditions in future recruitment. The rights which were already enjoyed by the services were guaranteed to him. Special responsibility was imposed on the Governor-General and the Governors to secure "to members of the public services of any right provided for them by the Constitution Act and the safeguarding of their legitimate interests." It was provided that every civil servant in India was to hold office during the pleasure of His Majesty. If an office was prematurely abolished, the persons concerned were to be given compensation. Every servant was given right of action against the Crown for wrongful dismissal. No civil servant could the dismissed by an authority inferior to the appointing authority. No member was to be dismissed or reduced in rank unless he was given reasonable opportunity of showing cause against the action proposed to be taken in regard to him unless he was convicted of a criminal offence or was given reasonable opportunity to defend himself.

2. The Governor-General was authorised to make appointment to Civil Services in the Federal sphere except the Indian Civil Service, Indian Police Service and Indian Medical Service (Civil). He was also authorised to make rules for the conditions of those services.

3. In the Provincial sphere, the Governors were authorised to make appointment to Civil Services. They were also allowed to make rules for conditions to these services. The legislatures were also authorised to regulate the conditions of service. In the case of Railway Services, the power of making appointments was given by the Governor-General to the Federal Railway Authority. In the case of recruitments for higher posts in the Railway, the Federal Railway Authority was required to consult the Public Service Commission. The claims of Anglo-Indians were to be considered in the recruitment of the Central Services.

4. The Secretary of State, Governor-General and the Governors were given full discretion to deal equitably with any officer. These officers were allowed to address complaints to the Governor-General or the Governor and also to put in an appeal to the Secretary of State against any order

of punishment, censure or termination of service or alterations in the conditions of service. The Secretary of State was allowed to give compensation to any person who was adversely affected.

5. The salaries, emoluments and pension of the Civil Services were not to be subject to the vote of the legislatures. Pensions of retired officers and the pensions of their dependents were exempted from Indian taxation if they were residing permanently outside India.
6. The Indian Military Widows and Orphans Fund, the Superior Services (India) Family Pension Fund and funds to be formed out of the contributions under the Military Service Family Pension Regulations and the Indian Civil Service Family Pension Rules were vested in Commissioners who were appointed by the King-in-Council. These Commissioners were to hold and administer those funds. They were to pay the pensions.
7. Civil servants were indemnified against civil and criminal proceedings in respect of all actions done by them in good faith in the execution of their duty and the certificate of the Governor-General on the question of good faith was conclusive. Without the permission of the Governor-General or the Governor in his discretion no civil or criminal proceedings could be instituted against any officer in respect of acts done by him in his official capacity. The Governor-General or the Governor sanctioned prosecutions and also decided the courts in which the civil servants were to be tried.
8. The Act of 1935 also made provision for the establishment of a Federal Public Service Commission at the Centre and the Provincial Public Service Commissions in the various provinces. Provision was also made for a Joint Public Service Commission for two or more Provinces.
9. The strength of the Federal Public Service Commissions was fixed by the Governor-General and of the Provincial Commissions by the Governors concerned. Half the members of the Commission were to be those persons who had held office for at least ten years under the Crown in India. It was provided that the Chairman of the Federal Public Service Commission was not to have any appointment after his retirement.
10. The Federal Public Service Commission and the Provincial Commissions were required to conduct examinations to various services within their respective spheres. Generally, these Commissions were consulted on all matters relating to methods of recruitment, principles to be followed in making appointments, promotions, and transfers from one service to another, all disciplinary matters affecting a person serving in a civil capacity in India, and claims by a civil servant for the cost incurred in litigation for acts done in discharge of his duties or for the award of a pension for injuries sustained by him while on duty and the amount of such pensions. However, these Commissions were not consulted in the matter of the distribution of various jobs among the various communities. More duties could be given to their Commissions with the previous sanction of the Governor-General or the Governor.

In short, the position, emoluments and privileges of the members of the Civil Service were secured as much as it was humanly possible to do so.

SERVICES UNDER THE NEW CONSTITUTION OF INDIA

The new Constitution has also made special provisions for the Public Services of India:

1. Article 309 provides that Acts of the appropriate legislature may regulate the recruitment, and conditions of services of persons appointed to Public Services and posts in connection with the affairs of the Union or of any State. But it shall be competent for the President or the Governor to make rules regulating the recruitment and conditions of service of the public servants until provision is made by an Act of the appropriate legislature.

2. According to Article 310, every person who is a member of a defence service or of civil service of the Union or an All-India service or holds any post connected with defence or any civil post under the Union holds office during the pleasure of the President, and every person who is a member of a civil service of a State or holds a civil post under a State holds office during the pleasure of the Governor of the State. Notwithstanding that a person holding a civil post under the Union or a State holds office during the pleasure of the President or the Governor of the State, any contract under which a person not being a member of a defence service or of an All-India service or a Civil Service of the Union or a State, is appointed under this Constitution to hold such a post may, if the President or the Governor deems it necessary in order to secure the services of a person having special qualification, provide for the payment to him of compensation, if before expiration of an agreed period that post is abolished or his required to vacate that post.

3. According to Article 311, no person who is a member of the Civil Service of the Union or of an All-India Service or a Civil Service of a State or holds civil post under the Union or a State shall be dismissed or removed by an authority subordinate to that by which he was appointed. No such person shall be dismissed or removed or reduced in rank until he has been given a reasonable opportunity of showing cause against the action proposed to be taken in regard to him. This Article will not apply when a person is dismissed or removed or reduced in rank on the ground of conduct which had led to his conviction on a criminal charge, or where an authority empowered to dismiss or remove a person or to reduce him in rank is satisfied that for some reason, to be recorded by the authority in writing, it is not reasonably practicable to give that person an opportunity of showing cause, of where the President or Governor is satisfied that in the interest of the security of the State it is not expedient to give to that person such an opportunity. It the question arises whether it is reasonably practicable to give any person such an opportunity or not, the decision of the authority empowered to dismiss or remove such person or to reduce him in rank shall be final.

4. According to Article 312, if the Council of States has declared by a resolution supported by not less than two-thirds of the members present and voting that it is necessary or expedient in the national interest to do so, Parliament may by law provide for the creation of one or more All-India services common to the Union and the States and regulate the recruitment and conditions of service of persons appointed to any such service. The services known as the Indian Administrative Service and the Indian Police Service shall be deemed to be services created by Parliament under this Article.

5. Article 313 provides that until other provision is made under the Constitution, all the laws in force immediately before the commencement of the Constitution and applicable to any public service or any post which continues to exist after the commencement of the constitution, as an All-India Service or as service or post under the Union or a State, shall continue in force so far as consistent with the provisions of the Constitution.

PUBLIC SERVICE COMMISSIONS

According to Article 315, there shall be a Public Service Commission for the Union and a Public Service Commission for each State. Two or more States may agree that there shall be one Public Service Commission for that group of States, and if a resolution to that effect is passed by the legislatures of those States, Parliament may by law provide for the appointment of a Joint State Public Service Commission to serve the needs of those States. The Union Public Service Commission, if so requested by the Governor or Rajpramukh of a State, may with the approval of the President agree to serve all or any of the needs of the State.

According to Article 316, the Chairman and other members of a Public Service Commission shall be appointed, in the case of the Union Commission or a Joint Commission, by the President, and in the case of a State Commission, by the Governor of the State. As nearly as may be, one-half of the members of every Public Service Commission shall be persons who at the dates of their respective appointments have held office for at least 10 years either under the Government of India or under the Government of a State. A member of a Public Service Commission shall hold office for a term of 6 years from the date on which he enters upon his office or until he attains the age of 65 in the case of Union Commission and 60 years in the case of a State Commission or a Joint Commission. However, a member of a Public Service Commission may resign his office earlier. He may be even removed from his office. After retirement, a member of a Public Service Commission shall not be eligible for reappointment to that office.

According to Article 317, the Chairman or any member of a Public Service Commission shall only be removed from his office by an order of the President on the ground of misbehaviour after the Supreme Court, on reference being made to it by the President, has, on inquiry, reported that the Chairman or the member ought to be removed. The President or the Governor may suspend a member or a Chairman during the inquiry. The President may remove from office the Chairman or any other member of a Public Service Commission if the latter is adjudged insolvent or engaged during his term of office in any paid employment outside the duties of the office, or is in the opinion of the President, unfit to continue in office by reason of infirmity of mind or body. If the Chairman or any member of a Public Service Commission is or becomes in any way concerned or interested in any contract or agreement made by or on behalf of the Government of India or the Government of a State or participates in any way in the profit thereof or in any benefit or emolument arising therefrom, otherwise than as a member and in common with the other members of an incorporated company, he shall be deemed to be guilty of misbehaviour.

According to Article 318, the President or Governor may by regulations determine the number of the members of the Commissions and their conditions of service and make provisions with respect to the number of the members of the staff of the Commission and their conditions of service. However, the Conditions of service of a member shall not be varied to his disadvantage after his appointment.

Article 319 provides that on ceasing to hold office the Chairman of the Union Public Service Commission shall be ineligible for further appointment either under the Government of India or under the Government of a State. The Chairman of a State Public Service Commission shall be eligible for appointment as the Chairman or a member of the Union Public Service Commission or the Chairman of any State Public Service Commission. But he will not be eligible for any other employment either under the Government of India or under the Government of a State.

FUNCTIONS OF PUBLIC SERVICE COMMISSIONS

As regards the functions of Public Service Commissions, Article 320 provides that it shall be the duty of the Union Commission and the State Public Service Commission to conduct examinations for appointments to the services of the Union and the States. It shall also be the duty of the Union Public Service Commission, if so requested by any two or more States, to assist those States in framing and operating schemes of joint recruitment for any services for which candidates possessing special qualifications are required. The Union or State Public Service Commission shall be consulted—

1. On all matters relating to methods of recruitment to civil services and for civil posts.
2. On the principles to be followed in making appointments to civil services and posts and in making promotions and transfers from one service to another on the suitability of candidates for such appointments, promotions or transfers.

3. On all disciplinary matters affecting a person serving under the Government of India or the Government of a State in a civil capacity, including memorials or petitions relating to such matters.

4. On any claim by or in respect of a person who is serving or has served under the Government of a State or under the Crown in India or under the Government of an Indian State, in a civil capacity, that any costs incurred by him in defending legal proceedings instituted against him in respect of acts done or purporting to be done in the execution of his duty should be paid out of the Consolidated Fund of India, or as the case may be, out of the Consolidated Fund of the State.

5. On any claim for the award of a pension in respect of injuries sustained by a person while serving under the Government of India or the Government of a State or under the Crown in India or under the Government of an Indian State, in a civil capacity, and any question as to the amount of any such award.

Article 320 specifically provides that it shall be the duty of the Public Service Commission to advise on any matter referred to them and on any other matter which the President or the Governor may refer to them. The President as respects the All-India services and also as respects other services and posts in connection with affairs of the Union and the Governor as respects other services and posts in connection with the affairs of a State, may make regulations specifying the matter in which either generally or in any particular class of cases or in any particular circumstances, it shall not be necessary for the Public Service Commission to be consulted. These regulations shall be laid for not less than 14 days before each House of Parliament or each House of the Legislature of the State, as the case may be, as soon as possible after they are made. These regulations shall be subject to such modifications, whether by way of repeal or amendment, as both Houses of Parliament or State Legislature may make during the session in which they are so laid.

Nothing shall require a Public Service Commission to be consulted as respects the manner in which any provision referred in Article 16 (4) may be made or as respects the manner in which effect may be given to the provisions of Article 335. Article 16 (4) provides, that nothing shall prevent the State from making any provision for the reservation of appointments or posts in favour of any backward class of citizens, which, in the opinion of the State, is not adequately represented in the services under the State. Article 335 provides that the claims of the members of the Scheduled Castes and Scheduled Tribes shall be taken into consideration, consistently with the maintenance of efficiency of administration, in the making of appointments to services and posts in connection with the affairs of the Union or of a State.

According to Article 321, an Act made by Parliament or the Legislature of a State may provide for the exercise of additional functions by the Union Public Service Commission or the State Public Service Commission as respects the services of the Union or the State and also as respects the services of any local authority or other body corporate constituted by law or of any public institution.

Article 322 provides that the expenses of the Union or a State Public Service Commission, including salaries, allowances and pensions payable to members or staff of the Commission, shall be charged on the Consolidated Fund of India or the Consolidated Fund of a State.

Article 323 provides that it shall be the duty of the Union Public Service Commission to present annually to the President a report as to the work done by the Commission and on receipt of such report the President shall cause a copy of it to be laid before each House of Parliament. He is also to intimate on what parts of the report action has been taken. The same is the case with a State Public Service Commission or a Joint Commission. In their case, the report is to be placed before the State Legislature.

A perusal of the second and third reports of the Union Public Service Commission which covered the period from April 1951 to April 1954 shows that the Commission had to criticise the acts of omission and Commission of the Government of India. It was pointed out that in certain cases Government did not accept the recommendations of the Commission. That was considered to be an unfortunate precedent. The Commission stressed the necessity of putting a check on this tendency. The Government should be bound to accept the recommendations of the Commission. The Commission also recommended that a law should be passed by which no civil servant should be allowed to draw a pension unless he can produce a certificate that his appointment was made with the approval of the Commission. The Commission also criticised the delay caused by the Government in filling up vacancies for which candidates were recommended by the Commission. It was pointed out that in one case while results were declared in February 1951, the successful candidates were not appointed even in September 1951 when the next examination was held. The result was that the successful candidates at the previous examination had to take another examination to avoid the chances of being passed over. The Commission recommended that after the declaration of result the Government must not wait for filling the necessary vacancies.

The Commission criticised the making of temporary appointments in an undesirable manner. It was suggested that no temporary hand should be employed for more than a year and if that was done, the concurrence of the Commission must be taken. To quote the Commission, "These are really cases of improper use of the power to make temporary appointments about which there have been so much public complaints."

SHORTCOMINGS

It is desirable to refer to some of the shortcomings of the public services in India during the British regime.

1. The first thing to be noticed is that the Indians were excluded from all the big jobs in the country. Those were manned by Europeans and Englishmen. The Indians felt that their exclusion was derogatory to their self-respect and patriotic sentiment. They were made to feel that they were inferior to the foreigners and that particularly so in their own country.

2. The Congress pointed out that the members of the public service were paid on an extravagant scale. A poor country like India could not afford to pay huge sums of money to her administrators. The drain from this quarter was so great that practically very little was left for nation-building programmes. It was pointed out that the salary and emoluments of the Governor-General of India were more than those of the Prime Minister of England or the President of the U.S.A.

3. It was also contended that while India paid huge salaries to the civil servants, she was deprived of their experience after their retirement. The usual practice was that Englishmen who served in India left for their country after retirement. It was their country that took advantage of their administrative experience and not India which had paid them huge salaries and also given them opportunities to gain the experience.

4. According to Lord Morley, the bureaucracy in India was mechanical, lifeless and soulless. No administration could be progressive or beneficent which crushed the self-reliance of the people and gave them no scope for the realisation of their natural aspirations. But such was the case in India.

Even at present, a lot has to be done to make the public services in India efficient and honest. The Gorawal Report has made many suggestions in this connection. Let us hope that something is done immediately in these matters to make the public services of India suitable for the high responsibilities which await them under a welfare State.

REVIEW QUESTIONS

1. Write an essay on the history of public services in India.
2. Describe the changes made buy Lord Cornwallis in Civil services.
3. What was the role of lord Wellesley in public services in India? Explain.
4. Throw light on the provisions of the Indian Civil Service Act, 1861.
5. Discuss the recommendations of the various commissions for the public services of India.
6. Explain the functions of Public Service Commissions.
7. Discuss the defects of the public services in India during the British regime.
8. Elaborate on the provisions made by the New Constitution of India for the public services of india.
9. Write short notes on the following:
   (a) Union Public Service Commission
   (b) Resolution of 1893
   (c) Recommendation of 1918 Report

SUGGESTED READINGS

Appleby, Paul H.: *Public Administration in India, Report of a Survey.*
Barker, Ernest: *Future Government of India and Indian Civil Service,* London, 1919.
Blunt, Sir Edward: *The Indian Civil Service,* London, 1939.
Curry, J.C.: *The Indian Police,* 1932.
Dwarkadas, R.: *Role of Higher Civil Service in a Welfare State,* 1958.
O'Malley, L.S.S.: *The Indian Civil Service,* 1931.
Report of the Royal Commission on the Superior Civil Service in India (Lee Commission).

26. Growth of Local Self-Government in India

LEARNING OBJECTIVES

- Discuss the evolution of the local self-government in India
- Throw light on the step-by-step empowerment of the local self-government in India by various Commissions and Acts
- Analyse the defects in the present system

According to de Tocqueville, "Local institutions constitute the strength of free nations. A nation may establish a system of free government, but without municipal institutions it cannot have the spirit of liberty." The truth of this statement cannot be doubted and it is desirable to discuss as to how the system of Local Self-Government has grown in this country, what its present position is and how the same can be improved upon to serve the need of the country.

The earliest efforts in municipal Government in India were made in the Presidency towns of Madras (now Chennai), Calcutta (now Kolkata) and Bombay (now Mumbai). In 1687, an order of the Court of Directors directed the formation of a Corporation of Europeans and Indian members of the city of Madras (now Chennai). However, the Corporation did not survive.

Under the Regulating Act of 1773, the Governor-General nominated the servants of the Company and other British inhabitants, to be the Justice of Peace. They were empowered to appoint scavengers for the cleaning and repairing of the streets of Calcutta, Madras and Bombay, for making assessments for those purposes and for the grant of licences for the sale of spirituous liquors. The reason for such a provision lay in the insanitary state of affairs in the Presidency towns. We are told that the public drains were regarded as the natural receptacles for all refuse and filth. Carcasses were left to rot and putrefy in the streets. In one case, jackals preyed for two nights on a human corpse thrown near the gate of a building.

Between 1817 and 1830, spasmodic attempts were made in Madras and Calcutta to undertake works paid out of the lottery funds and much was done with this money in laying out these towns. On completion, the roads and drains were handed over to the Justices of Peace to be maintained by them out of their assessment. But even for maintenance work the funds never sufficed, and the Provincial Governments supplied the balances required. In the case of Bombay alone, a tax on carriages and carts was levied for the purpose of making roads. The Justices of Peace as a body did not take much interest in their work and their power was gradually concentrated in the hands of the Chief Magistrate who was helped in Calcutta (now Kolkata) by the Superintendent of Police to collect the taxes and supervise the work of conservancy. However, there was no trace of any popular Government.

In 1840, an Act was passed for Calcutta and in 1841 an Act was passed for Madras. These Acts widened the purposes for which the Municipal assessment was to be utilised. The inhabitants of the town were given control over the assessment and collection of taxes. However, much did not come out of these Acts. There was no response from the public. In 1845, an Act was passed for Bombay. This Act concentrated the administrative powers in the hands at a Conservancy Board on which were two European and three Indian Justices, with the Senior Magistrate of Police as Chairman.

PRESIDENCY TOWNS

A fresh attempt to grapple with the sanitation of the Presidency town was made in 1856 when Act XXIV and Act XXV were passed. The first Act dealt with the conservancy and improvement of the Presidency towns. The second Act provided for the better assessment and collection of rates. Special Acts were passed for the appointment of three commissioners in each town. In the Calcutta Act of 1856, special provisions were made for gaslighting and the construction of sewers. In the Bombay Act of 1858, power was given to levy dues. However, in spite of the above-mentioned legislation, the town remained filthy and the laws merely existed on paper.

We are told that there were quarrels between the Commissioner and the Justices of Peace at Calcutta but work was done in the field of sanitation. In the case of Bombay, the condition of sanitation was dreadful and the death rate rose very high. By the Act of 1855, the Justices were constituted as a body corporate, with control over the budget, but all executive power was concentrated in the hands of a highly paid Government official. A special Controller of Accounts was appointed to remedy the defects in accounts. With the appointment of Crawford as Municipal Commissioner and Dr. Hewlett as Health Officer, the work of sanitation was pushed on vigorously and the whole administration was tightened up. There was great agitation against the Commissioner. The Controller of Accounts failed to control the accounts on accounts of his being a subordinate of the Commissioner. After a lot of controversy the membership of the Bombay Corporation was reduced to 64. Out of these, 16 were nominated by the Government, 16 were elected by the resident Justices and 32 were elected directly by the ratepayers. The executive power was concentrated in the hands of the Commissioner. Provision was made for the weekly audit of the accounts by the Town Council. There was to be a monthly audit by paid auditors. Bombay could claim the credit of having a strong Executive Officer controlled rigidly in official matters by a Committee answerable to the Corporation, half of whose members were directly elected by the ratepayers. (For details see Bombay Municipal Act of 1872). In the case of Calcutta Corporation, the Government had to interfere in 1899 because the sanitary conditions became alarming. An Act was passed for the Calcutta Corporation in 1899. Under the new Act, only half the Commissioners were to be elected by the ratepayers, the remainder being appointed, 4 each by the Bengal Chamber of Commerce and the Calcutta Traders Association, 2 by the Port Commissioners and 15 by the Local Government. The powers of the Calcutta Corporation were confined to the fixing of the rates of taxation and to the performance of general functions. The executive power was vested in the Chairman. Provision was also made for a General Committee consisting of the Chairman and 12 Commissioners. The General Committee was given the power to decide matters which were too detailed for the decision of the Corporation but too important to be left simply to the decision of the Chairman.

In the case of Madras, the elective system was introduced in 1881. 16 out of 32 members were to be elected by the ratepayers. But the President and two Vice-Presidents were salaried officers who were appointed by the Government. The Madras Corporation was given the power to deal with the budget and the raising of loans, but the detailed scrutiny of accounts was left to two official auditors. Fresh taxes were levied for drainage and water supply. As Madras was not a great commercial centre, there was always a shortage of funds. In 1904, a new Municipal Act was passed on the lines of Calcutta. The number of Commissioners elected by the ratepayers was reduced. Special representation was given to the commercial interests in the town.

By 1918, all the Presidency towns had approximately a uniform system of Government. All the Corporations had a limited electorate, elaborate provisions for debt, full control over finance and a strong executive centred in a Government official.

NON-PRESIDENCY TOWNS

Outside the Presidency towns there was practically no attempt at municipal legislation before 1842. An Act was passed in that year in Bengal, but it practically remained a dead letter. Another Act was passed in 1850, which applied to the whole of British India. This Act was of permissive nature. The Government of any province was given the power to bring the Act into operation in any town only when it was satisfied that the inhabitants of that town wanted the same. In that case, the Government was authorised to appoint the magistrate and such number of inhabitants as may appear necessary to be Commissioners on whom large powers were conferred for making rules. It was under this power that octroi duties were levied. Under this Act and subsequent Provincial Acts, a large number of municipalities were set up in all provinces. In most provinces, the Commissioners were nominated and from the point of view of self-government, these Acts did not go far enough.

MAYO'S RESOLUTION OF 1870

It was only after 1870 that real progress was made in the direction of self-government. Lord Mayo's Government in their Resolution of 1870 dealing with decentralisation of finance, referred to the necessity of taking further steps to bring local interests and supervision to bear on the management of funds devoted to education, sanitation, public works, etc. New Municipal Acts were passed in the various provinces between 1871 and 1874. These Acts extended the elective principle. The results of the policy of 1870 were described in the Resolution of the Local Self-Government, 1882, thus: "Considerable progress had been made since 1870. A large income from local rates and cesses had been secured, and in some provinces the management of the income had been freely entrusted to local bodies. Municipalities had also increased in number and usefulness. But there was still a greater degree of progress in different parts of the country than varying local circumstances seemed to warrant. In many places, services admirably adapted for Local Government were reserved in the hands of the Central administration, while everywhere heavy changes were levied on municipalities in connection with the Police, over which they had necessarily no executive control."

RIPON'S RESOLUTION OF 1881

The next step was taken during the viceroyalty of Lord Ripon who has been rightly called the father of Local Self-Government in India. His resolution on Local Self-Government is a great landmark in the growth of Local Self Government in the country. After pointing out the beneficial effects on local finance of the Resolution of 1870, the Resolution of 1881 stated that the Governor-General of India thought that time had come when further steps should be taken to develop the idea of Lord

Mayo's Government. It was asserted that agreements with the Provincial Governments regarding finance should not ignore the question of Local Self-Government. The Provincial Governments were directed to transfer considerable revenues to the local bodies. The latter were also to be in charge of those matters, which were chiefly concerned with the localities.

The Government of India directed the Local Governments to undertake a careful survey of the provincial, local and municipal Acts. The object of the inquiry was to find out as to what sources of revenue could be transferred from the provincial to the local heads so that they could be administered by the Municipal Committees. Secondly, it has to be found out as to what items could safely be given away to the local bodies. Only those items were to be transferred which were understood and appreciated by the people. The third object of the inquiry was to devise steps that were "necessary to ensure more Local Self-Government."

In accordance with the Resolution of 1881, letters were addressed to the Provincial Governments by the Government of India. In these dispatches, the Government of India hinted at those items of expenditure that could conveniently be transferred to the local bodies for control. The Local Governments were directed to examine other items also that could be handed over to the local bodies. The Government of India recommended that the Magistrate or the Collector should be the President of the District Committees and Assistant or Deputy Magistrate, the President of the Subordinate Committees. In all these Committees, the number of the non-official members was to be not less than one-half and not more than two-thirds of the whole. The Local Governments were told that "it would be hopeless to expect any real development of self-government if the local bodies were subject to check or interference in matters of detail." It was also pointed out to them that the Governor-General-in-Council is anxious that the fullest possible liberty of action should be given to the local bodies.

The Provincial Governments not only approved of the policy contained in the Resolution of 1881 but also submitted their schemes to the Government of India. The latter decided to take the next step. Another resolution was issued in 1882.

RESOLUTION OF 1882

1. In this Resolution of 1882, Lord Ripon took special pains to make it clear that the expansion of the system of Local Self-Government would not bring about a change for the better from the point of view of efficiency in municipal administration. To quote him, "It is not primarily with a view to improvement in administration that this measure is put forward and supported. It is chiefly desirable as an instrument of political and popular education." The Governor-General was of the opinion that when after some time more local knowledge was acquired and more local interest was created, "improved efficiency will in fact follow." But there were bound to be initial failures in the new field. If the Government officials encouraged and supported the growth of local bodies, it was hoped that the period of failure would end very soon and substantial progress would be made.

2. The Governor-General of India refused to accept the general accusation that the people of India were indifferent to the principle of self-government. On the other hand, he was of the opinion that with the growth of education, the number of intelligent and public-spirited persons was bound to rise and their services could be profitably utilised for the management of local affairs. As regards the complaint that the previous experiments were not encouraging, the Governor-General held the view that the system was not satisfactorily tried. The previous

attempts at local self-government were over-ridden and practically crushed by direct official interference. It was hoped that if more trust was put in the non-official members, there was bound to be greater efficiency and improvement in the affairs of the local bodies.

3. Lord Ripon indicated the general lines on which further steps were to be taken so that some "real and substantial" progress might be made in the field of Local Self-Government. The first part of the recommendations was concerned with the fundamental principles. The Local Governments were directed to maintain and extent a network of Local Boards in every district. The area of jurisdiction of every Local Board was to be so small that both local knowledge and local interest on the part of the member of the Board could be secured. The number of non-official members was to be very large and the official element was not to exceed one-third of the whole.

4. Wherever practicable, the Local Governments were to introduce the system of election for the members of the Local Boards. Although Lord Ripon did not order the adoption of the system of elections for all the seats, he hoped that the system of elections would ultimately prevail. His own wish was that the system of elections should be introduced in as many places as the local circumstances might allow. But this was possible only if the Government officers accepted the principle ungrudgingly and set about to make it a success. In that case, each sub-divisional officer was to prepare a list of the candidates qualified to sit upon the Local Board and invite all those residing in any particular area to meet him on a day fixed at a convenient spot near their homes. He was to explain to them the objective of the Government and the nature of the duties they were required to perform. He was to ask them to elect the number of the representatives that had been fixed for the area in question. "In the course of a few years, when the members of the Board find that they have real powers and responsibilities entrusted to them, any Government interference will become unnecessary." The electors were to be left free in the matter of elections.

5. The second part of the recommendations of the Government of India was concerned with the degree of control to be retained by the Government over the Local Boards. It was the opinion of the Governor-General-in-Council that "the true principle" to be observed in this matter was that "the control should be exercised from without rather than from within." The Government should "revise and check the acts of local bodies but not dictate them."

6. The Government control should be exercised in two way. In the first place, the sanction of the Government should be made necessary to legalise certain actions of the Local Boards, e.g., raising or levying of taxes, etc. The number of the cases where sanction was required, was to be large at the beginning, but was to be reduced later on as the Local Boards got more experience. Secondly, the Local Government was authorised to interfere either to set aside altogether the proceedings of the Boards in particular cases or to suspend them temporarily in cases of crises and continued neglect of either duty. The power of absolute suppression was to be exercised only with the consent of the Government of India. A general principle for guidance was put in these words: "It should be the general function of the executive officers of Government to watch, especially at the outset, the proceedings of the Local Boards to point out to them matters calling for their consideration, to draw their attention to any neglect of duty on their part, and to check by official remonstrance any attempt to exceed their proper functions or to act illegally or in any arbitrary or unreasonable manner."

7. According to Lord Ripon, "It would be more convenient that they (executive officers) should supervise and control" the acts of the Local Boards rather than take actual part in the

proceedings. It appeared to him that "so long as the Chief Executive Officers are, as a matter of course, Chairmen of the Municipal and District Committees, there is little chance of these committees affording any effective training to their members in the management of local affairs, or of the non-official members taking any real interest in the local business. The non-official members must be allowed to feel that real power is placed in their hands, and that they have real responsibilities to discharge." Since that was lacking under the system of official Chairmen, the Governor-General wished "to see non-official persons acting wherever possible or practicable as Chairmen of the Local Boards." It was possible that a suitable non-official Chairman might not be available in a particular locality, but the policy of the Government should be to have as few official Chairmen as possible. An official Chairman was not to exercise the right of voting in the proceedings. Lord Ripon said that the natives "must not be overshadowed by the constant presence of the Burra Sahib."

8. The approval of the Local Government was made necessary to validate the election of a Chairman and the former could also disallow it.

9. The Local Governments were directed to hand over to the Local Boards complete control over the local rates and cesses, licences, tax assessments and collections, pounds and ferry-receipts, etc. The Local Boards were to be granted lump-sum grants from the provincial revenues.

10. The District Engineer was to help the local bodies in their work of supervision and maintenance of buildings. But the Engineer was to work as their servant and not as their master. The Local Boards were to be left free in the matter of initiative and direction of operations.

It is desirable to give the views of a few persons regarding the importance of Lord Ripon's Resolution of Local Self-Government. According to Prof. M. Venkatrangaiya, "It is a classic among the pronouncements made on the subject by the higher authorities and forms the basis of all subsequent developments in the history of Indian local institutions. It puts forward the case for the expansion of Local Self-Government in a most convincing manner and answers conclusively all the objections that might be raised in this connection. It points out clearly the nature of the obstacles to be faced in the practical application of the principle and suggested methods for overcoming them. Resolutions issued later on by the Government of India, and pronouncements made by the authorities in England on subsequent occasions, might have been lengthy but they have not added in any way to the arguments contained in this Resolution or affected their weight and strength. The Resolution is valuable above all as it gave a concrete and practical form to hopes and aspirations which uptill then were vague. It gave a definite lead and laid down a clear-cut path for all Provincial Governments really interested in the advance of Local Self-Government." (*Development of Local Boards in the Madras Presidency*, p. 47.)

According to D.E. Wacha, the Ripon Resolution "has forever made immemorable in the annals of India and Viceroyalty of the good liberal-minded Lord Ripon. That State paper conferred on the people, the genuine boon of Local Self-Government which they have since cherished with feelings of the warmest gratitude. It necessarily contemplated many unimportant fiscal and administrative changes in all parts of the Empire, and definitely laid down the broad principles upon which the decentralisation of provincial finance for Local Government could proceed." (*Rise and Growth of Bombay Municipal Government*, p. 292.)

Whatever be the importance of Ripon's Resolution, it cannot be denied that both the Provincial Government and the Government of India did not carry out the policy laid down in the Resolution. The result was that even after the lapse of 36 years when another Resolution was passed in 1918, no substantial progress had been made in the field of Local Self-Government. Men like Lord Curzon were the enemies of Local Self-Government. The British bureaucracy in India was determined to see that the local bodies did not succeed in their work. Thus, it was that all the good wishes and goodwill of Lord Ripon could not and did not improve the state of affairs in this country.

DECENTRALISATION COMMISSION REPORT (1909)

The Royal Commission on Decentralisation examined the whole question of Local Self-Government in India and made important recommendations. Particular reference was made to the lack of financial resources and their adverse effect on the working of local bodies. Sir Herbert Risley, Home Secretary to the Government of India, observed thus: "I think it must be admitted that the resources of district boards and district municipalities are not sufficient to enable them to work up to the modern standard of local administration. In municipalities, that is most conspicuously the case in respect of scheme of water supply and drainage, the advantages of which, especially of the former, are now pretty generally realised. Similarly, in some rural areas in Bengal the old sources of water supply have fallen into disrepair and the district boards are approached with demands far beyond their financial resources. In other parts of the same province the silting up of old channels and changes of levels are believed to cause malarial fever, and large schemes of drainage are advocated which the local bodies are unable to carry out."

The Commission put emphasis on the importance of village Panchayats and recommended the adoption of special measures for their revival and growth. A recommendation was made that village Panchayats should be given powers like summary jurisdiction in petty civil and criminal cases, incurring of expenditure on village scavenging and minor village works, construction, maintenance and management of village schools, management of small fuel and fodder reserves, etc. It was also recommended that village Panchayats should be given adequate sources of income and interference by district officers should be circumscribed. The Commission also recommended the establishment of a Sub-District Board in every *taluka* or *tehsil*. The Sub-District Boards were not to be completely under the control of a District Board for the whole district. Separate duties and separate sources of income were to be given to Sub-District Boards and District Boards.

As regards the municipalities, the Commission recommended the withdrawal of existing restrictions on their powers of taxation. The municipalities were to take over primarily education. Middle vernacular schools were also to be put under their control, if they so desired. Municipalities were to be relieved of expenditure on secondary education, hospitals, famine relief, police, veterinary works, etc.

The Resolution of 1915 passed by the Government of India contained official views on the recommendations of the Royal Commission on Decentralisation. A reference was made in the Resolution to "smallness and inelasticity of local revenue" and "the difficulty of devising further forms of taxation." However, no action was taken to give effect to the recommendations of the Commission and the situation remained as it was before.

RESOLUTION OF 1918

The British Government declared in August 1917 that the goal of British rule in India was to give responsible Government to the people of the country and the Government was to take steps for the progressive realisation of that same ideal. In 1918, the Government of India passed an important Resolution on Local Self-Government. The basic principle of that Resolution was that "responsible institution will not be stably rooted until they are broad-based and that the best school of political education is the intelligent exercise of the vote and the efficient use of administrative power in the field of Local Self-Government." According to the Resolution, the general policy should be one of gradually removing all the unnecessary control from the local bodies. The Government was to separate the spheres of action appropriate for local institutions from those appropriate for the Government. The Resolution formulated certain principles calculated to establish wherever possible complete popular control over local bodies. It suggested an elected majority in all the Local Boards, the replacement of the official chairman by the elected non-official chairman in the municipalities. The same was to be done in the case of rural bodies, wherever possible. The minorities were to be represented by nomination. The franchise was lowered to such an extent that the constituencies became really the representatives of the taxpayers. This resolution also put emphasis on the advisability of developing the corporate life of the village. The Government was to encourage the growth of village Panchayats. The only immediate action taken on this Resolution was that the District Officer was relieved of his duty as the Chairman of the District Board in all the provinces except the Punjab.

The Report on the Indian Constitutional Reforms of 1918 examined the existing system of Local Government in the country and came to the conclusion that throughout the educative principle had been subordinated to the desire for immediate results. It was stated that there should be as far as possible complete popular control in local bodies and the highest possible independence for them from outside control.

UNDER DYARCHY

Under the dyarchical system of Government set up by the Government of India Act of 1919, the Department of Local Self-Government was transferred into the hands of an Indian minister who was responsible to the Provincial Legislature for the same. It was but natural that the Indian ministers should do all that they could for the growth of Local Self-Government. It is true that they were handicapped on account of the lack of funds. As the Finance Department was under the charge of an Executive Councillor who had no sympathy for the nation-building schemes not much work was actually done in the provinces. In almost every province, the Legislature tried to make local bodies as effective training grounds for larger and wider political responsibilities. The general trend of these Acts was the same. Practically, all the Acts aimed at lowering the franchise, increasing the elected element to the extent of making it the immediate *arbiter* of policy in local affairs and at passing executive direction into the official hands. Laws were passed in every province for the growth of village Panchayats. On the whole, the effort was to lessen the official control and to make the local bodies representative of the people.

The Simon Commission Report contained certain references to Local Self-Government. It was pointed out that Village Panchayats had not made much progress except in Madras, Bengal and Uttar Pradesh. The Commission recommended the increase of the control of the Provincial Government over local bodies, so that more efficiency could be secured. A reference was made to England where "by numerous administrative devices, by inspection, by audit, by giving of grants-in-aid on conditions ensuring efficiency and by insisting on standards of competence in the municipal staff, the Local Government Board and its successor, the Ministry of Health, have steadily raised the standard of administration in local authorities." The Commission also referred to the unwillingness of the elected member to impose new taxes.

Provincial autonomy was introduced under the Government of India Act, 1935. The Department of Local Self-Government came under the control of a popular minister who could afford to put more money at the disposal of the local bodies. Laws were passed practically in every province to give more functions to local bodies. However, the sources of income of local bodies, instead of increasing, became less. Restrictions were placed on the powers of local bodies to levy or enhance terminal taxes on trades, callings and professions and municipal property. The net result was that not much progress was made in the field of Local Self-Government.

India became independent in 1947. Article 40 of the Constitution of India provides that village Panchayats should be reorganised and more powers should be given to them so that they can function successfully as units of self-government. Panchayat Raj Acts were passed in many States with a view to give more powers to village Panchayats. The Local Finance Enquiry Committee submitted its report in 1951. It referred to the hopeless financial conditions of local bodies and made recommendations to improve the same. The view of the Committee was that local bodies "can attain financial responsibility only by the exercise of such powers and having to bear consequences of their errors." The view of the Committee was that "with the grant of larger powers, will come an increased realisation of responsibility and the growth of improved public opinion will constitute a check which will prove more effective than official intervention."

DEFECTS IN THE PRESENT SYSTEM

Local bodies in India have to face many handicaps. There is an all-embracing control of the executive in every sphere of their activities. This undoubtedly destroys all initiative on the part of the members of the local bodies. Without initiative on the part of the people, we could never hope to put vigour into the lifeless bodies of local institutions. There is also a great handicap of finance. Local bodies do not have enough of resources to perform their duties in such a way that they can add to the fullness and richness of the lives of the people. New sources of revenues have to be found and the Government has to follow a liberal policy in the matter of grants-in-aid and the borrowing powers of the local bodies. There is also the lack of public interest in the work of local bodies. All means of modern propaganda must be employed to emphasize on the people the great importance of local bodies in the national life of the country and thereby induce them to take interest in them. There is also a great dearth of books on the subject. The result is complete ignorance on the part of the people with regard to local affairs. It is hoped that in the higher interests of the country as a whole, not only the people in general but also the powers that be, will take special interest in the work of local bodies. Let us not forget that without a vigorous system of Local Self-Government, the foundation of democracy becomes weak and shaky.

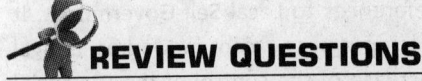

REVIEW QUESTIONS

1. Describe the evolution of the local self-government in India.
2. Write in detail about the Presidency Non-Presidency Towns.
3. Discuss the role of Mayo's Resolution in the growth of the local self-government in India.
4. Who is called the 'Father of Local Self-Government in India'? Evaluate his role in the expansion of the local self-government.

5. Write in brief about Ripon's Resolution.
6. Describe the role of the dyarchical system in the expansion of the local self-government.
7. Write short notes on the following:
    (a) The Royal Commission on Decentralisation
    (b) The Dyarchical System
    (c) Local bodies in India

SUGGESTED READINGS

Cross: *Development of Self-Government India (1858-1914)*.
Gopal, S.: *The Viceroyalty of Lord Ripon*, 1958.
Jha and Rendel: *Indian Local Self-Government*.
Tinker, Hugh: *The Foundations of Local Self-Government in India, Pakistan and Burma*, 1954.
Wolfe, Lucien: *Life of Lord Ripon*.

27 History of the Press in India

LEARNING OBJECTIVES

- Discuss the early history of the Press in India
- Describe the history and development of Indian Press and various Press Acts
- Know about the establishment of Press Trust of India and freedom of expression as given in the new Constitution.

EARLY HISTORY OF THE PRESS UP TO 1822

The history of the Press in India starts with the Englishmen in the days of the East India Company. It was in the second half of the eighteenth century that the Anglo-Indians and Europeans started their journals. The object of those journals was twofold: information and amusement. Those journals contained lengthy extracts from newspapers and journals published in England or Europe.

Warren Hastings and Hicky. The Bengal Gazette was started as a weekly in 1780 by Hicky. From the very outset, the management of the journal came into conflict with Warren Hastings who was the Governor-General of Bengal at that time. The journal criticised Mr. Hastings and the general policy of Warren Hastings took strong action against Mr. Hicky. The latter was arrested and imprisoned and the journal had to be stopped in 1782. It is a matter of history that Mr. Hicky was a very bold man and a great upholder of the liberty of the press. He was a pioneer in the history of journalism in India. The following words give an idea of the man Hicky was: "Mr. Hicky considers the liberty of the press to be essential to the very existence of an Englishman and a free Government. The subjects should have liberty to declare their principles and opinions, and every act which tends to coerce that principle is tyrannical and injurious to the community."

Cornwallis and Duane. Like his predecessor, Lord Cornwallis had his own difficulties with the press. Mr. Duane, the editor of the Indian World, wrote the stuff which could not be tolerated by Cornwallis. Consequently, Duane was arrested and humiliated. The tussle between Mr. Duane and the Governor-General continued for many years and ultimately Duane was deported to Europe.

In 1796, Mckenly, the editor of the Telegraph, displaced the authorities by publishing the article in which he made certain allegations against certain Government servants. In the same year the editor of the Calcutta Gazette was censured for having referred to certain communications which had passed between the Court of Directors and the French Republic.

Lord Wellesley (1798-1805). When Lord Wellesley assumed the reins of Government the situation was critical. The danger of a French invasion was occupying the mind of everyone. Sultan Tipoo was negotiating with the French with a view to turning out the Englishmen from India. The Marathas who had won their victory over the Nizam, were entertaining ambitious dreams regarding their future. It was felt that a strict supervision over the press would be necessary in the interests of the safety of the Englishmen in India. No wonder, censorship was established in 1799 over all the newspapers that were published in the country. It was laid down that the names of the editors and proprietors should be published in the newspapers. The Government took action against Charles Maclean, the editor of the Bengal Kirkaru. Ultimately, the editor was deported to England. The government view was that Mr. Maclean had "assumed a privilege of animadverting, through the medium of a public print upon the proceedings of a court of justice, and of censuring the conduct of a public officer for acts done in his official capacity." Maclean also hit back. While in England, he took an active part in the agitation that ultimately led to the resignation of Lord Wellesley. No change was made in the time of Lord Minto (1808-1813).

Lord Hastings (1813-23). Lord Hastings or Earl of Moira appreciated the important part played by an independent press and consequently encouraged the pressmen to perform their legitimate functions. To begin with, he slightly modified the regulations regarding censorship in 1813. Five years after (1818) he abolished the post of Censor on the receipt of certain complaints. However, this does not mean that the press in India became absolutely free. Fresh regulations were issued in the same year. According to those regulations, the editors were required to desist from "publishing animadversions on the proceedings of the Indian authorities in England, disquisitions on the political transactions of the local administrations, or offensive remarks on the public conduct in the press of the Council, the judges or the Bishop of Calcutta (now Kolkata), discussion having a tendency to create alarm or suspicion among the natives as to any intended interference with their religion, the re-publication from English or other newspapers of passages giving under the preceding heads or otherwise calculated to affect the British power or reputation in India and private scandal or personal remarks on individuals tending to excite dissensions in society."

Buckingham. One of the results of the abolition of censorship in 1818 was that new journals came into existence. J. S. Buckingham started the Calcutta Journal in 1818. He was a very bold and fearless man. He did not spare even the Chief Justice of the Supreme Court, the Governor of Madras (now Chennai) and the Lord Bishop of Calcutta. Like Hicky and Duane, he was deported from the country; This great Soul made a name for himself in England.

MUNRO'S RECOMMENDATIONS

The Government of India deputed Sir Thomas Munro to examine and report on problem of press in India. The latter studied the whole question and made his recommendations to the Government. His view was that the problem of the European press was not a serious one. According to him, "As far as the Europeans only, whether in or out of service, the freedom or restriction of the press could do little good or harm, and would hardly deserve any serious attention." However, he recommended the maintenance of censorship in their case and also the retention of the power to deport editors and pressmen out of the country. In the case of the Indian press, Munro expressed both his anxiety and fears. According to him, "But though the danger be distant, it is nevertheless there. It could corrupt and disaffect the Indian army and work for the overthrow of the British power. It might spread among the people the principles of liberty and stimulate them to expel the strangers who rule over them and to establish a national government.... A free press and domination of strangers are things, which are quite incompatible and cannot long exist together."

Regulations of 1823. The Government of India accepted the recommendations of Munro and placed new regulations before the Supreme Court in March 1823 for registration. These regulations provided that no press was to be established nor any paper or book was to be printed without obtaining a licence for that purpose from the Government. All the papers and books printed under the system of licences were to be submitted to the Government for inspection. The latter was authorised to stop the circulation of any book or paper by a mere notice in the Government gazette. Although men like Raja Ram Mohan Roy and Dwarka Nath Tagore protested against those regulations, the same were registered and came into force on 15th April, 1823.

"Liberators of the Indian Press." The regulations that were made in 1823 continued to remain in force up to 1835 when they were cancelled by Sir Charles Metcalfe. The latter took this step when he was acting as the Governor-General. He was assisted in this work by Lord Macaulay who was the Law Member with the Government of India at that time. The result was that the Indian press became as free as its counterpart in England. One of the effects of this action was that the English Company recalled Sir Charles Metcalfe from India. However, the people of Calcutta built a Hall in his honour.

LICENSING ACT OF 1857

The Indian Press continued to be free from 1835 to 1857. When the Mutiny broke out in 1857, it was found necessary to put restrictions on the press in the country. Accordingly, Act XV of 1857 was enacted to regulate the establishment of printing presses and to restrain in certain cases the circulation of printed books and papers. These restrictions were of a temporary nature and were withdrawn soon after the Mutiny.

During the 1860's the Bengalee and the Amrit Bazar Patrika in Bengal and the Akhbar-e-Am at Lahore where started as weeklies.

ACT OF 1867

Act XI of 1835 which was enacted by Sir Charles Metcalfe was replaced by Act XXV of 1867. The object of the new Act was to regulate the printing presses and newspapers and also to preserve copies of books printed in British India and also the restriction on those books. The Act of 1867 is still in force although certain amendments were made in 1893 and 1940.

VERNACULAR PRESS ACT, 1878

Lord Lytton was a great imperialist and his forward policy was responsible for the tragedy of the Second Afghan War. No wonder, he was universally condemned by the Indians. Lord Lytton also hit back. On 13th March 1878, he sent a telegram to the Secretary of State for India requesting his consent by telegram to a Press Law on the lines of the Irish Coercion Act of 1870. His justification was "the increasing violence of the native press, directly provocative of rebellion." He got the sanction for that bill within a day. As soon as the sanction was received, the bill was enacted into law within a couple of hours. The law was known as the Vernacular Press Act although it was nicknamed as "The Gagging Act."

The Vernacular Press Act empowered a magistrate, with the previous sanction of the Provincial Government to require a printer or publisher to deposit a security or enter into a bond binding himself not to print or publish anything likely to incite feelings of disaffection towards the Government or hatred between the different races of India. The Government was authorised to warn as well as to confiscate the plant, the deposit, etc., in the event of the publication of some undesirable matter. The printer was given the option of submitting proofs to the official censor and dropping all rejected matter and thus escape from the clutches of law.

Divergent views were held with regards to the Vernacular Press Act. While Englishmen in general and the Government of India in particular justified its enactment, the Indians condemned it in the strongest possible terms. The view of Sir A. Arbuthnot was that as a result of this legislation, seditious and disloyal writings stopped completely and there was no interference with the legitimate expression of opinion. According to S. N. Banerjee, "Within less than fifteen months, the vernacular press all over India, save that of Madras (now Chennai), was muzzled." A big meeting was held in the Town hall at Calcutta. "It was one of the most successful meetings ever held in India. It sounded the death-knell of the Vernacular Press Act." In an article in the Times of India, Sir Pherozeshah Mehta also criticised the Act. He pointed out that the Vernacular Press was not guilty of disloyalty to the British rule. "The worst that could be said of it was that on occasions it was guilty of angry recriminations, exaggerated generalisation and vulgar personalities. But such effusions conveyed no treasonable ideas to a native reading them with his national knowledge of native modes of thought and expression. It was at all times difficult to draw the line between severe, though just, criticism of Government and its measures, and the licentious abuse of them, bordering on the preaching of sedition and the propagation of disaffection. If the judges of distinction were to be the very men who were the objects of criticism, they would be more than human if in course of time and by gradual stages all hostile criticism was not brought within the pale of proscription. If the Vernacular Press was licentious, the system of licensing would but aggravate and intensify its mischievous tendencies and annihilate nothing but honest and useful criticism, particularly in the case of a press in its infancy.

"Moderate and respectable men, their functions not yet hardened into habits, would retire from the field without a struggle. Violent and unprincipled agitators would thrive on the persecution which would furnish the very nourishment necessary for their existence. And while the sound and healthy political growth of the people would be indefinitely retarded, the government would be deprived of all trustworthy sources of keeping itself well-informed of the real inner feelings and thoughts of the people towards them. Deprived of free and sincere criticism, it would hardly know to steer its way through servile adulation or scurrilous abuse."

According to Mody, "The Act was utterly uncalled for, unduly repressive in character and inspired by sinister motives. It was a Draconian piece of legislation based for the most part on the Irish Coercion Act of 1870 and in some respects more stringent than the latter, which was a special measure brought into existence to deal with a special emergency." Again, "Perhaps, the worst feature of the Act was that it exempted from its operation all English newspapers, though in many cases they were the greatest sinners. As Mr. (afterwards Sir) Arthur Hobhouse, one of the most distinguished lawyers of the time, observed, it was Englishmen who said the worst things of the government and said them most continually; and he condemned the distinction as "class legislation of the most striking and invidious description, at variance with the whole tenor of our policy, and only to be justified by the most cogent proofs of danger from maltreated class."

According to Sir Erskine Perry, a member of India Council of the Secretary of State for India, "No imperial legislature could forge a more powerful weapon for extirpating an obnoxious press." Again, the Act was "a retrograde and ill-conceived measure injurious to the future progress of India."

There was a change of Ministry in England in 1880 when the Conservative Government of Disraeli was defeated in the General Elections and Gladstone came to power at the head of a great liberal majority.

One of the results of the change in the Government at home was that Lord Lytton was called from India and Lord Ripon was appointed his successor. In spite of the sympathetic attitude of Lord Ripon, it was not possible to repeal the Vernacular Press Act at once. However, this was done in 1882. Although the Indians praised Lord Ripon for this gesture of goodwill on his part, Englishmen were not happy. According to Prof. Dodwell, the freedom of the Indian press was bound to be injurious to the interests of the British Government in India. A free Indian press was bound to criticise the acts of omission and commission of the Government, and thereby bring it into disrepute.

THE NEWSPAPERS (INCITEMENT TO OFFENCES) ACT, 1908

It is well-known that the partition of Bengal by Lord Curzon and his anti-Indian policy resulted in a lot of agitation throughout the length and breadth of the country. A movement was set on foot to drive out the Englishmen bag and baggage from the country. As time passed on the situation became critical. Consequently, Newspapers (Incitement to Offences) Act was passed in June 1908. In the words of the Law Member of the Government of India, the object of the Act was to put an end to the existence of those newspapers which contained any incitement to murder or any offence under the Explosive Substances Act, 1908, or any act of violence.

According to this Act, a district magistrate was empowered to confiscate the printing press where a newspaper containing an incitement to violence was printed. He was to call upon the members to show cause as to why the orders should not be made absolute. If on hearing the evidence the magistrate was satisfied that the newspaper had committed the offence, the conditional order was to be made absolute and the police was directed to attach the press and other property mentioned in the order. In the case of emergency, the magistrate was to issue warrants for attachment and even before making the order absolute. Provision was made for the taking of appeals to the High Court within 13 days of the date of the order being made absolute. The Government was also authorised to annul the declaration of the printer or publisher of the newspaper under the Act of 1877.

On account of the stringent provisions of the Act of 1908, the Yugantar, the Sandhya and the Bandematram stopped their publication. Although the Government had vast powers under the Act of 1908, it was contended by the Government that those powers were not sufficient to stop the dissemination of seditious literature through the press. Consequently, the Indian Press Act was passed in 1910 to meet the situation.

THE INDIAN PRESS ACT, 1910

The Act of 1910 empowered a magistrate to require a deposit of not less than ₹500 and not more than ₹2,000 from the keepers of news printing presses and publishers of newspapers. The Local Government was empowered to require the existing presses and publishers of newspapers to deposit not less than ₹500 and not more than ₹5,000 as security. A magistrate was authorised to dispense with the deposit of any security or cancel or vary any order already issued in this connection if he had any special reasons for doing so.

The Act of 1910 defined the term "objectionable matter" whose publication was to entitle the Government to declare security forfeited to His Majesty. All attempts, direct or indirect, to seduce persons as employed in His Majesty's defence forces or to intimidate the people to give money for revolutionary work or to prevent them from giving help in discovering and punishing revolutionary crime, were included in the definition of objectionable matter. The definition of seditious publication was widened to include writings against the Indian princes, judges, executive officers and public servants. Section IV was so worded as to leave little scope for independent criticism of Government action by the press. The power of deciding whether any particular publication did or did not offend against Section IV was given to the Provincial Government and not to the ordinary courts.

Further, if the security of a printing press or newspaper was confiscated and the keeper of the press or the publisher of a newspaper wanted to make a fresh declaration under the Act of 1867, each of them had to deposit with the magistrate, a security of not less than ₹1,000 and not more than ₹10,000. If, in the opinion of the Government, the printing press of the newspaper offended against Section IV of the Act, the security was to be forfeited to His Majesty.

The Act also authorised the customs officers and officers of post offices to detain any packet or parcel or consignment suspected to contain any objectionable matter and deliver the same to the Provincial Government. Provision was made for an appeal to the High Court. It was to be heard by a Special Bench of three judges. The appeal was to be filed within two months of the date of order of forfeiture by the Provincial Government.

CRITICISM OF THE ACT OF 1910

The Indian Press Act of 1910 muzzled the Indian Press. There was a lot of hue and cry throughout the length and breadth of the country. The Press Association of India exposed the shortcomings of the new legislation and tried to save the newspapers and presses from the arbitrary orders of the Government. The Act was vigorously applied during the World War I. It was pointed out in 1919 that the Act of 1910 had penalised over 350 presses. Securities amounting to over £40,000 were demanded from 300 newspapers. Over 400 publications were penalised. Owing to the demand of security, more than 200 printing presses and 130 newspapers were not started. Newspapers like the Amrit Bazar Patrika, Bombay Chronicle, The Hindu, The Tribune, The Punjabee, Hindvasi, etc., were subjected to the rigours of the Act. Although the public demanded an impartial inquiry into the allegations, their demand was not conceded.

A Special Bench of the Calcutta High Court tried the case entitled Mohammed Ali versus Emperor and Chief Justice Jenkins and Justice Stephen passed certain strictures in their judgments. According to the Chief Justice, "The provisions of Section 4 are very comprehensive and its language is as wide as human ingenuity could make it. Indeed, it appears to me to embrace the whole range of varying degrees of assurance from certainty on the one side to the very limits of impossibility on the other. It is difficult to see to what lengths the operation of this section might not be plausibly extended by an ingenious mind. They would certainly extend to writings that may even command approval. An attack on the degraded section of the public which lives on misery and shame of others would come within this widespread net, the praise of a class might not be free from risk. Much that is regarded as standard literature might undoubtedly be caught." Again, "The Advocate-General has admitted, and as I think, very properly, that the pamphlet is not seditious and does not offend against any provision of the criminal law of India. But he has contended and rightly, in my opinion, that the provisions of the Press Act extend far beyond the criminal law; and he has argued that the burden of proof is cast on the applicant so that however meritorious the pamphlet may be, still, if the applicant cannot establish the negative the Act requires, his application must fail. And what is this negative?

It is not enough for the applicant to show that the words of the pamphlet are not likely to bring into hatred or contempt any class or section of His Majesty's subjects in British India or that they have not a tendency in fact to bring about that result. But he must go further and show that it is impossible for them to have that tendency either directly or indirectly and whether by way of inference, suggestion, allusion, metaphor implication. Nor is that all, for we find that the legislature has added to this the all embracing phrase or otherwise." He concluded with the following words: "Mr. Mohammed Ali then has lost his book but he has retained his character, and he is free from the stigma that he apprehended. And, this doubtless, will be some consolation to him when we dismiss, as we must, his present application."

In the matter of New India Printing Works, Justice Abdul Rahim made the following observations on the scope of Section 4 and the discretionary powers of the Government: "That, generally speaking, the terms of the section are extremely wide and comprehensive, cannot be doubted. They vest the Local Government with a discretion so large and unfettered that the keeping of printing press and the publication of newspapers become an extremely hazardous undertaking in the country. A press may be devoted to the printing of most useful and meritorious literature, or often publications of an entirely innocent and non-controversial nature, yet it will be liable to forfeiture if any matters printed in such press are considered by the Government to be objectionable within the meaning of the Act. It may be doubted if it is possible for the keeper of any printing press in the country to maintain such an efficient expert supervision over matters that are printed as to delete everything that might be regarded to fall within the widespread net of Section 4.

"Similarly, newspaper may be consistently staunch in its loyalty to the Government, its general policy may be above all reproach, the sincerity and bona fides of the intentions of the editor may not be liable to question, but if any 'letters or other writings were let in, may be through carelessness, which come within the scope of any of the clauses of Section 4, the Government may at once, without any trial or even a warning, forfeit the security, and in this way ultimately put an end to the newspaper itself. That the influence of a periodical on public life in the country is on the whole decidedly beneficial need not be a bar to the Government's action. The Local Government, it may be assumed, will not indiscriminately exercise the powers which it possesses under his enactment but the vesting of such unlimited power in the Executive Government is undoubtedly a serious encroachment on the freedom which the press in India enjoyed before the passing of the Act."

In Farooq Ali v. the Crown, Sir Alfred Kensington, the Chief Justice of the Punjab Chief Court, remarked thus: "In estimating the results of the writing of the King before us, we are necessarily guided, to so large an extent, by the conclusion arrived at by Government under its wider knowledge of all that may be going on beneath the surface in India that we could hardly interfere with propriety unless it was obvious that there had been some palpable misunderstanding of the writing called in question." In the case of Ghulam Qadir Khan v. the Crown, the same judge remarked thus: "We are by the Act given certain extraordinary powers of interference, but these powers are strictly limited. We are authorised by statute to set aside an order of forfeiture, but not to make any other change. In this construction of our powers, it is not open to us, even if we should desire to do so, to do anything more than either reject the application or set aside the order of forfeiture as a whole."

According to Justice T.V. Seshagiri Ayyar, "The first obnoxious feature was that it substituted the discretion of the executive for the rights of publicity, audience and appeal. Secondly, it specifically violated the first principle of jurisprudence by directing the accused to prove that he was innocent. Thirdly, though an appeal was provided for it has been pointed out in both the Calcutta and the Madras High Courts that the High Court had no power to question the discretion of the executive. Furthermore, the provision had the effect of humiliating the intelligentsia since the journalists were asked to furnish security, at the discretion of the Executive, before they could publish a newspaper. This humiliation no intelligent man would like to be subjected to and consequently the Act had been the cause of considerable disaffection in the country."

In the Comrade case, the Advocate-General argued thus: "I admit the pamphlet is not seditious in its nature and is quite outside the scope of the Penal Code, and I am willing to concede that the petitioner was actuated by the best motives. But the scope of the Indian Press Act is far wider than that of the Penal Code. The provisions of Section 4 are extremely comprehensive, and the onus is cast on the petitioner to establish the negative that it is impossible for the pamphlet under any circumstances to come within the purview of the section."

After the passing of the Government of India Act, 1919, and the inauguration of the reforms, Sir Tej Bahadur Sapru was appointed the First Indian Law Member. A committee was appointed under him to examine the working of the Act of 1910. The report of the Committee was that the Act should be repealed. The recommendation of the Committee was accepted by the Government.

THE INDIAN PRESS (EMERGENCY POWERS) ACT, 1931

During the 1920's nothing significant happened in the field of the Indian Press. However, the Indian National Congress decided at its Lahore session in 1929 to start a vigorous campaign against the Government, for the emancipation of the country. In pursuance of that resolution 26th January was declared as the Independence Day and the civil disobedience movement started in full swing in 1930. The Indian Press also played a very important part in the freedom movement. It exposed the acts of omission and commission of the British Government. Prominent place was given to the arrests of the leaders and the *lathi* charging of the people. It was in this atmosphere that the Indian Press (Emergency Powers) Act was passed in 1931. The object of that Act was to provide against the publication of the matter which incited or encouraged murder or violence. Provision was made for the deposit of security by the keepers of printing presses. The Provincial Government was given the power to declare the security of the press forfeited in certain cases. If a printer applied for a fresh declaration, he would be required by a magistrate to deposit a security of the value of not less than ₹1,000 and not more than ₹10,000 as the magistrate might think fit. If even after the forfeiture of the security and the deposit of a new security, the newspaper published objectionable matter, the Provincial Government could forfeit the new security also. Provisions which applied to keepers of printing presses equally applied to the publishers of the newspapers.

Section XI penalised keeping of presses or publishing of newspapers without making the deposit as required by the Provincial Government or the magistrate. If a press did not deposit the security but when on doing its work, it could be forfeited to His Majesty and the declaration of the publisher was liable to be cancelled.

A magistrate may authorise any person to publish a news-sheet or news-sheets from time to time. Any police officer empowered for the purpose by the Provincial Government could seize any unauthorised news-sheet or unauthorised newspaper wherever found. The unauthorised news-sheets or newspapers were to be produced before the magistrate and could be ordered to be destroyed. The Government was given the power to seize and forfeit undeclared presses producing unauthorised news-sheets and newspapers. The penalty for disseminating unauthorised news-sheets and newspapers was imprisonment up to 6 months, with or without fine. The Provincial Government was given the power to declare certain publications forfeited to His Majesty and also issue search warrants for the same. The Customs officers were authorised to detain packages containing certain publications when imported into British India. No unauthorised news-sheet or unauthorised newspaper could be transmitted by the post and the Government was given the power to detain those articles while being transmitted by post. Provision was made for applications being made to the High Court to set aside the order of forfeiture. Those applications were to be heard by a Special Bench of the High Court consisting of three judges.

It is obvious that the powers conferred by the Indian Press (Emergency Powers) Act of 1931 were sweeping in their nature and scope. The powers were used by the Provincial Governments to prohibit the publication of the names and portraits of well-known leaders of the civil disobedience movement as "the publication of such pictures tends to encourage the movement." Other restraints included the prohibition of the publication of Congress propaganda of any kind including messages from the persons arrested, messages issued or purported to be issued from person in jail, exaggerated reports of political events, notices and advertisements of meetings, processions and other activities tending to promote civil disobedience movement or any other matter in furtherance of the same. Under the Act of 1931, the British Government took action against many newspapers. The printers and publishers of the Bombay Chronicle were called upon to deposit ₹3,000 each for the publishing an article by Horniman. The printer and publisher of the Anand Bazar Patrika each received demand for ₹1,000. A security of ₹6,000 was demanded from the Amrit Bazar Patrika. ₹6,000 were deposited by The Liberty of Calcutta. A security of ₹6,000 was deposited by the Free Press Journal and was later on forfeited by the Bombay Government. Similar actions were taken against other journals also. Virtually, there was a reign of terror in the country.

FOREIGN RELATIONS ACT, 1932

The Foreign Relations Act of 1932 replaced an Ordinance of 1931. Its object was to penalise publications calculated to interfere with the maintenance of good relations between His Majesty's Government and friendly foreign States. The necessity of this law arose when the newspapers criticised the administration in certain States adjoining the frontiers of India. The Act provided that where an offence under Chapter XXI of the Indian Penal Code was committed against the ruler of a State outside but adjoining India, or against the consort or son of Principal Minister of such a ruler, the Governor-General-in-Council might make, or authorise any person to make, a complaint in writing of such an offence and any court competent in other respects to take cognizance of such offence might take cognizance of such a complaint. Any book, newspaper or other document containing such specified defamatory matter, which tended to prejudice the maintenance of friendly relations between His Majesty's Government and the Government of such State, could be retained in the same manner as seditious literature.

In January 1933, four ordinances were promulgated which conferred certain powers for the maintenance of law and order and particularly widened the operative section of the Press Act so as to permit action against the publication of matter calculated to encourage the civil disobedience movement.

INDIAN STATES (PROTECTION) ACT, 1934

The object of this Act was to prevent unreasonable attacks on the administration of Indian States in the newspapers of British India and provide authorities in British India with powers to deal with bands or demonstrators organised on semi-military lines, for the purpose of entering and spreading disaffection in the territories of the Indian States.

The above laws continued to remain in force up to 1939 when the World War II broke out. In order to meet the difficult situation, the Government of India was forced to pass the Defence of India Act. The Government also framed rules known as the Defence of India Rules. These rules enabled the Government to control the Indian Press for six long years. Action was taken against those newspapers which dared to violate the above rules and laws. However, the Act and the Rules lapsed after the ending of the World War II.

PRESS TRUST OF INDIA LTD.

The most notable event in Indian journalism in 1948 was the formation of the Press Trust of India Ltd. This organisation took over the supply of news to and from India. This was done on the basis of an agreement with the Reuters. This agreement enabled the Indian Press to get complete control over its own internal news supply. The Press Trust is a non-profit-making concern and membership is open to all newspapers of India. The P.T.I. has now become independent of the Reuters.

PRESS LAWS INQUIRY COMMITTEE, 1948

The Government of India set up a Press Law Inquiry Committee under the Chairmanship of Shree Ganganath Jha. The Committee was required to gather all the existing press laws of India and make recommendations as to what directions in which the law required to be modified. The Central Legislature nominated some members to the Committee. Three editors were also recommended by the Indian Newspaper Editors' Conference. The Committee made the following recommendations:

1. An explanation should be added to Section 153-A I.P.C. (promoting enmity between classes) to the effect that it does not amount to an offence under that Section to advocate a change in the social or economic order provided such advocacy does not involve violence.
2. Repeal of the Indian States (Protection) Act of 1934.
3. Repeal of the Foreign Relations Act of 1932.
4. Before taking action against the Press under emergency legislation, Provincial Governments should invariably consult the Press Advisory Committee or a similar body.

5. Repeal of the Indian Press (Emergency Powers) Act of 1932 was recommended but it was also suggested that certain provisions of that Act which did not find a place in the ordinary law of the country, should be incorporated into that law at suitable places.
6. Section 124-A I.P.C. relating to sedition should be amended so as to apply only to acts or words which either incite disorder or are intended or tend to incite disorder.
7. Section 144, Cr. P.C., should not applied to the press and separate provision should be made, if necessary, for dealing with the press, in urgent cases of apprehended danger.
8. Necessary provision should be made in the Law to empower courts to order the closing down of a press for a special period in case of repeated violations of law.

THE INDIAN CONSTITUTION

Article 19 of the new Constitution of India which came into force on 26th January 1950, provided for the freedom to expression. However, it was found from experience that the right freedom of expression was held by some courts to be so comprehensive that no action could be taken against any individual who advocated murder and other violent crimes. Consequently, the Constitution (First Amendment) Act was passed in June 1951. It was provided that the right to freedom of speech was to be subject to all laws imposing restrictions with regard to the security of the State, friendly relations with foreign States, public order, decency or morality, contempt of court, defamation and incitement of offences.

PRESS (OBJECTIONABLE MATTER) ACT, 1951

In the course of the debate in Parliament on the Constitution (First Amendment) Bill, the Government of India promised to introduce a Press Bill which was free from the objectionable features of the Indian Press (Emergency Powers) Act of 1931 and which was in accordance with the new Constitution of India. Such a bill was introduced in Parliament on 21st August 1951, and was named as the Press (Incitement to Crimes) Bill. However, its name was changed later on with a view to dissociating this Bill from the Act of 1908, which had a similar title. The amended Bill was passed by the Parliament and received the assent of the President in October 1951.

According to the Objects and Reasons of the Act, the new law was directed against the encouragement of violence or sabotage of certain other very grave offences and the publication of scurrilous matter. No precensorship was imposed on any newspaper. No action was to be taken against any newspaper unless it actually abused its freedom by the publication of some objectionable matter. Security could not be demanded arbitrarily. That could be done only after proof of the actual abuse of the freedom of the press by the publication of objectionable matter. Even in their case, the demand of security or its forfeiture was not to be provided by the executive, but by the Sessions Judge. The Sessions Judge was to pass orders only after a full trial. He was to hear both the Government and the keeper of the press or the publisher of the newspaper. The publisher or the keeper could claim the right to be tried by a special jury composed of persons particularly qualified to sit in judgment over cases of the abuse of the freedom of the press by journalistic experience or by an association with public affairs. A right of appeal was provided to the High Court on all points involved in every case. The amount of security was not to be excessive and in no case more than the amount specified in the complaint made by the competent authority was to be ordered. Provision was made for the return of the security if no further action was taken in respect of the press or the newspaper or news-sheet for a period of two years from the date of deposit. Provision was made against double penalty. Any offence punishable under the Act and any abetment of such offence was made cognisable and bailable. This Act repealed all other laws relating to the press.

It seems desirable to define the term "objectionable matter" as this term is very prominent in the Act itself. According to Section 3 of the Act, the expression "objectionable matter", means any words, signs or visible representations which are likely to incite or encourage any person to resort to violence or sabotage for the purpose of overthrowing or undermining the Government established by law in India or in any State thereof or its authority in any area; or incite or encourage any person to commit murder, sabotage or any offence involving violence; or incite or encourage any person to interfere with the supply and distribution of food or other essential commodities or with essential services; or seduce any member of any of the armed forces of the Union or of the police forces from his allegiance to his duty, or prejudice the recruiting of persons to serve in any such force or prejudice the discipline of any such force; or promote feelings of enmity or hatred between different sections of the people of India; or which are grossly indecent or scurrilous or obscene or intended for blackmail. It is well-known that when the above Bill was on the legislative anvil, a lot of hue and cry was raised by the press. However, the Government gave an assurance to the press that it would not abuse these powers and that the matter would be discussed once again after the lapse of two years. The life of the Act was extended for two years in 1954 and the same has been allowed to lapse now.

PRESS COMMISSION

The Government of India appointed on 23rd September 1952, a Press Commission consisting of 11 members. The chairman of the Commission was Justice G. S. Rajadhyaksha. The Commission submitted its report in August 1954.

The Commission recommended the establishment of an all-India Press Council. The Council was to consist of 25 members of whom 13 or more were to be working journalists of standing in the profession, including working editors. It was to have in addition a chairman who should be either sitting or a retired judge of a High Court. He was to be nominated by the Chief Justice of India. The following were to be the objectives, of the Press Council:

1. To safeguard the freedom of the press and to help the press to maintain its independence.
2. By censuring objectionable types of journalistic conduct and by all other possible means to build up a code in accordance with the highest professional standards.
3. To keep under review any development likely to restrict the supply and dissemination of news of public interest and importance.
4. To encourage the growth of the sense of responsibility and public service among all those engaged in the profession of journalism.
5. To study development in the press which may tend towards concentration or monopoly and if necessary to suggest remedies thereof.
6. To publish reports, at least once a year, regarding its work and reviewing the performance of the press, its development and the factors affecting them.
7. To improve methods of recruitment, education and training for the profession, by the creation of suitable agencies for the purpose such as a Press Institute.

The Press Registrar is to keep a close watch on the circulation of newspapers. If he comes to the conclusion that in a particular area or in a language, a monopoly has developed, he is to bring it to the notice of the Press Council who will conduct an investigation into the existence of the monopoly, whether that had acted against public interest, whether undesirable practices had been resorted for eliminating competition and what measures, if any, were necessary to deal with the situation. The State Trading Corporation for Newsprint was to be entrusted with a monopoly of imports and could take over the entire output of Indian mills on a fair basis and sell the same along with imported newsprint at equated prices.

The Commission recommended that the publication of newspapers and periodicals should be made a central responsibility and suggested the banning of crossword puzzle competition forms. It recommended the introduction of price-page schedule for newspapers and suggested that advertisements should not cover more than 40 per cent of the total space. The Commission favoured single unit papers and recommended that in case of multiple editions, each unit should be separated from the others in the matter of accounts. Where a chain consisted of a number of groups, each group was to be separated from the other. The adoption of a strict code of advertising by an association of publishers was recommended. The Commission recommended the enactment of legislation to regulate the newspaper industry which should make it punishable with fine or imprisonment to give fraudulent advertisement.

The Commission found considerable degree of concentration in the ownership of Indian newspapers and felt that there was danger that the tendency might develop in the future. The proposed Press Council was to review at the end of 5 years all the consequences of newspaper ownership in the light of circumstances then existing to make appropriate recommendations.

The news agencies should not be owned or controlled by the State and any assistance from the State to the news agencies should be without strings attached. The State should have no voice in the control of the agency either editorially or administratively.

The Commission recommended that a public corporation based on the existing organisation but controlled by a Board of Trustees under a chairman to be appointed by the Chief Justice of India should take up the management of the Press Trust of India. No organisational changes were prescribed for the United Press of India. The employees should have representation on the Board of Trustees.

In recent years, the Indian Parliament has passed a few laws concerning the Press in India. The names of some of them are the Delivery of Books and Newspapers (Public Libraries) Act, 1954, the Working Journalists' (Conditions of Service) and Miscellaneous Provisions Act, 1955, the Newspaper (Price and Page) Act, 1956, Parliamentary Proceedings (Protection of Publication) Act, 1960, etc.

REVIEW QUESTIONS

1. Give an account of the early history of the press during the British period.
2. Explain the recommendations of the Sir Thomas Munro report.
3. Write an essay on the history and development of Indian press and Press Acts.
4. Elaborate on the provisions of the various Acts regarding the history of the press in India.
5. What does the Constitution of India say about freedom of the press? Elaborate.
6. Write short notes on the following:
    (a) Munro's recommendations
    (b) The Indian Press Act, 1910
    (c) Press Trust of India
    (d) Press Commission

SUGGESTED READINGS

Barns, H.: *The Indian Press*, 1946.
Ghosh: *Press and Press Laws in India*.
Sen, Sachin: *The Press and Democracy*, Calcutta, 1957.

28 History of Education

 LEARNING OBJECTIVES

- Throw light on the early history of education and educational institutions in India
- Discuss the development of modern education in India in British era
- Know about the development of education in post-independence

EARLY HISTORY OF EDUCATION

When the English East India Company acquired territories in various parts of India, it found that both the Hindus and the Muslims had their educational institutions which were linked up with their religion. The Pandits taught Sanskrit to the Hindus in their *Pathshalas* and the Maulvis taught the Muslims in the mosques. To begin with, the Company left the Indian system undisturbed and respected the endowments made by the Indian rulers. However, Warren Hastings established the Calcutta (now Kolkata) Madrassah "to qualify the sons of Mohammedan gentlemen for responsible and lucrative offices in the State." The subjects taught were theology, logic, rhetoric, grammar, law, natural philosophy, astronomy, geometry, and arithmetic. A few years later, John Owen, Chaplain to the Bengal Presidency, requested the Government to establish schools for the purpose of teaching English "to the natives of these provinces." Nobody cared for his request. However, after a few years, another educational institution was set up at Banaras "for the preservation and cultivation of the Laws, Literature and Religion of the nation; to accomplish the same purpose for the Hindus as the Madrassah for the Mohammedans and specially to supply qualified Hindu Assistants to European Judges."

In 1792-93, when the House of Commons debated the renewal of the Charter of the East India Company, Wilberforce carried a resolution emphasising the adoption of such steps as it would lead to the advancement in useful knowledge of the people of India. He suggested the sending of school masters and missionaries to India. The move of Wilberforce was opposed and it was maintained that the Hindus had "as good a system of faith and morals as most people." It was pointed out that it would be madness to give them any kind of learning other than what they possessed.

After a few years, Charles Grant, one of the Directors of the Company, submitted a memorandum in which he lamented the low moral condition of the people of India. He asked the Company to improve their condition by imparting to them a knowledge of the English language which was to serve as "a key which will open to them, a world of new ideas". As the Muslim rulers had taught Persian to the Indians, in the same way the Englishmen should teach English to the people of India. To quote him, "It would be extremely easy for Government to establish, at moderate expense, in various parts of provinces, places of gratuitous instruction in reading and writing English;

multitudes, especially of the young, would flock to them; and the essay books used in teaching might, at the same time, convey obvious truths on different subjects. The Hindus would, in time become teachers of English themselves; and the employment of our language in public business, for which every political reason remains in full force, would, in the course of another generation, make it very general throughout the country. There is nothing wanting to the success of this plan, but the hearty patronage of Government."

In 1811, Lord Minto regretted the neglect of literature and science in India and suggested improvements in existing colleges in addition to the establishment of new ones. A clause was inserted in the Charter Act of 1813 stipulating that "a sum of not less than one lakh of rupees in each year shall be set apart and applied to the revival and improvement of literature and for the introduction and promotion of knowledge of the sciences among the inhabitants of the British territories in India."

Raja Ram Mohan Roy formed an association for founding an institution where the Hindus were to receive instructions in European languages and sciences. The Hindu College was founded in 1817. In 1818, the Bishop of Calcutta (now Kolkata) opened an institution which was to serve the double purpose of training young Christians as preachers and of imparting a knowledge of the English language to Hindus and Muslims. Raja Ram Mohan Roy opposed the establishment of a Sanskrit College at Calcutta. However, nobody bothered about this protest. The Court of Directors of the Company were happy at the prospect of having qualified Indians to help them in the administration. To quote them, "As the means of bringing about this most desirable object, we rely chiefly on their becoming thorough a familiarity with the European literature and science, imbued with the ideas and feelings of civilized Europe — on the ample cultivation of their understanding, and specifically on their instruction in the principles of moral and general jurisprudence."

Elphinstone in his Minute of 1823 urged the establishment of schools for teaching English and European sciences. In a communication to the Commissioners for Indian Affairs, Elphinstone wrote thus: "I conceive it is more important to impart a high degree of education to the upper classes than to diffuse a much lower sort of it among the common people. The most important branch of education is that designed to prepare natives for public employment. If English could be at all diffused among persons who had the least time for reflection, the progress of knowledge by means of it would be accelerated in a ten-fold ratio since every man who made himself acquainted with a science through English would be able to communicate it in his own language to his countrymen." He proposed the establishment of a school at Bombay where English might be taught "classically" and where instruction might also be given in that language on history, geography and science. In 1833, he set up a similar school at Poona. In 1834 the Elphinstone College at Bombay. It was expected to train "a class of persons qualified by their intelligence and morality for high employment in the civil administration of India."

By this time, demand for the study of English had increased tremendously. English books were being sold by thousands. There was practically no demand for Sanskrit and Arabic books. In order to satisfy the popular demand, English classes were attached to the Calcutta Madrassah and the Sanskrit College at Calcutta (now Kolkata). The same was done in the Agra College which was established in 1811. In spite of that, the Oriental Colleges were not popular. There started a controversy as to whether instructions should be given through English or through Arabic or Persian. The Anglicists maintained that all instruction should be given through English. The Orientalists insisted on teaching through the oriental languages. To settle the controversy, the Government appointed a Committee. Among the Orientalists were many distinguished officers of the Government and their view prevailed for some time. When Lord Macaulay was appointed the Chairman of the Committee in 1835, the parties were so evenly balanced that things had come to a deadlock. Lord Macaulay wrote a Minute which turned the scales against the Orientalists. He discussed the Charter Act of 1813 which provided a sum of money for the revival and promotion of literature and for the introduction of the knowledge of sciences among the inhabitants of India. He disputed the view that by literature Parliament could have meant only Arabic and Sanskrit literature as he had not yet found an Orientalist "who could deny that a single shell of a good European library was worth the whole native literature of India and Arabia." His argument was that English was the language spoken by the ruling class. It was likely to become the language of commerce "throughout the seats of East." He came to the conclusion that the Government was free to employ its funds in teaching what was better worth knowing than Sanskrit or Arabic. "Neither as the languages of law nor as the languages of religions have Sanskrit or Arabic any peculiar claim to our encouragement,' and "it is possible to make natives of the country thoroughly good English scholars" to which end efforts should be directed. Lord Macaulay had expressed similar views in the House of Commons before he came to India. To quote him, "Are we to keep the people of India ignorant in order that we may keep them submissive ? Or do we think that we can give knowledge without awakening ambition? Or do we mean to awaken ambition and provide it with no legitimate vent .... It may be that the public mind of India may expand under our system until it has outgrown that system, that by good Government we may educate our subjects into a capacity for better government, that having become instructed in European knowledge, they may, in some future age, demand European institutions. Whether such a day will ever come, I know not. Whenever it comes, it will be the proudest day in English history. The sceptre may pass away from us. Victory may be inconstant to our arms. But there are triumphs which are followed by no reverse. There is no empire exempt from all natural causes of decay. There triumphs are the pacific triumphs of reason over barbarism; the empire is the imperishable empire of our arts and our morals, our literature and ours laws." Again, "The question before us is simply whether, when it is in our power to teach this language—English—we shall teach languages in which, by universal confession, there are no books on any subjects which deserve to be compared to our own; whether, when we can teach European science, we shall teach systems which, by universal confession, wherever they differ from those of Europe, differ for the worse; and whether, when we patronise sound philosophy and true history, we shall countenance, at the public expense, medical doctrines which would disgrace an English farrier, astronomy which would move laughter in the girls at an English boarding school, history abounding with kings thirty feet high and reigns thirty thousand years long, and geography made up to seas of treacle and seas of butter."

Lord William Bentinck, the Governor-General, approved of the Minute of Lord Macaulay. A resolution was passed on 7th March, 1835, and the following points were emphasised in that resolution:

1. That "the great object of the British Government ought to be the promotion of European literature and science amongst the natives of India and that all funds appropriated for the purposes of education would be best employed on English education alone;
2. "that while the colleges of oriental learning were not to be abolished, the practice of supporting their students during their period of education was to be discontinued;
3. "that Government Funds were not to be spent on the printing of Oriental works; and
4. "that all the funds at the disposal of the Government would hence forth be spent in imparting to the Indians, a knowledge of English literature and science."

According to H.H. Wilson, "Upon the proposal to appropriate all the funds to English education, there was a petition from the Mohammedans of Calcutta, signed by about 8,000 people, including all the most respectable Maulvis and native gentlemen of the city. After objecting to it upon general principles, they said that the evident object of the Government was the conversion of the natives; and they encouraged English exclusively and discouraged Mohammedan and Hindu studies because they wanted to induce the people to become Christians." With a view to removing the misgivings of the Muslims, Lord William Bentinck declared a policy of strict neutrality. "In all schools and colleges, interference and injudicious tampering with the religious belief of the students, mingling direct or indirect teaching of Christianity with the system of instruction, ought to be positively forbidden."

A reference may be made to the work done by the Christian Missions in the field of education. In 1716, the Danish missionaries opened an institution for the training of teachers. In 1717, they opened two charity schools at Madras (now Chennai). They were also instrumental in opening English schools at other places. Missionaries like Carey, Marshman and Ward started their work at Serampore in 1793. By 1820, the Missionary societies were doing a lot of work in this field, but their primary object was not to educate the people, but to preach Christianity. The Missionaries realised that the spread of English language would help the spread of Christianity in the country. In Bombay (now Mumbai) the Wilson College was started and in Madras the Christian College. In 1853, the Saint John's College was founded at Agra. Missionary colleges were also founded at Masulipatam and Nagpur. The Bible Classes were made compulsory in these institutions. According to Dr. Duff, "One great object was to convey, as largely as possible, a knowledge of our ordinary improved literature and science to the young persons; but another, and a more vital object was to convey a thorough knowledge of Christianity with its evidences and doctrines. Our purpose was, therefore, to combine in close, inseparable and harmonious union, what has been called a useful secular with a decidedly religious education."

A Government Resolution of 1844 provided that for public employment in every case, preference would be given to those who had been educated in Western science and were familiar with the English language. According to Lord Auckland, "I would make it my principal aim to communicate through the means of the English language, a complete education in European literature, philosophy and science to the greatest number of students who may be ready to accept it."

WOOD'S DESPATCH OF 1854

Sir Charles Wood's Despatch to the Court of Directors has been described as, "The Magna Carta of English Education in India." It set forth a scheme of education far wider and more comprehensive than any one which had been suggested so far. It enunciated the aim of education as the diffusion of Arts, Science, Philosophy and the literature of Europe. The study of Indian languages was to be encouraged. The English language was to be taught wherever there was a demand for it. Both the English language and the Indian languages were to be regarded as the media for the diffusion of European knowledge. It was felt that the time had come for the establishment of universities in India which might encourage a regular and liberal course of education by conferring academic degrees as evidence of attainment in the different branches of Science and Art. It was decided to establish universities on the model of the London University. Each university was to consist of a Chancellor, Vice-Chancellor and a Senate. The Senate was to manage the university funds and frame regulations for the holding of examinations. Professorships were to be instituted in various branches of learning among which were law, civil engineering and classical oriental languages. Calcutta and Bombay were to have the first universities. A university might be created at Madras also or at any other place in India where a sufficient number of institutions existed from which properly qualified candidates for degrees could be supplied. It was laid down that the affiliated institutions would be periodically visited by Government Inspectors. It was hoped that a spirit of healthy rivalry could grow among the educational institutions, and the division of university degrees and distinctions into different branches would direct the efforts of highly educated men to the studies which were necessary to success in the various active professions of life.

The Despatch also recommended the establishment of institutions for training teachers for all classes of schools. The existing Government Schools and Colleges were to be maintained and their number was to be increased if and when necessary. New Middle Schools were to be established. More attention was to be given to elementary education. The system of grants-in-aid was to be started by the Government to help the private enterprise. However, these grants were to be given on the principle of religious neutrality. A comprehensive system of scholarship was to be started. Female education was to be encouraged by the Government. A Director of Public Instruction was to be appointed in every province. He was to be assisted by Inspectors and Assistants or Deputy Inspectors. According to Prof. Dodwell. the men in charge of the Department were primarily administrators and consequently, education tended to become a matter of routine administration.

THE HUNTER COMMISSION, 1882

In 1882, Lord Ripon appointed a Commission "to enquire into the manner in which effect had been given to the principles of the Dispatches of 1854 and the suggest such measures as it may think desirable in order to the further carrying out of the policy therein laid down." The Hunter Commission collected a lot of useful information and made the following recommendations:

1. While advocating the gradual withdrawal of the State from direct support and management of institutions of higher education, the Commission felt that this withdrawal could only be by slow and cautious steps. A College or a Secondary School was to be handed over to the Indians provided there was a reasonable prospect that the cause of education would not suffer through the transfer.
2. Provision was to be made for ordinary and special grants to colleges.
3. There were to be alternative courses in the large colleges.
4. Certain general principles were to be followed as regards college fees and exemption from them.
5. New regulations regarding scholarships were to be framed.
6. An attempt was to be made to prepare a model textbook based upon the fundamental principles of natural religion such as may be taught in all Government and non-government colleges.
7. "The principal of one of the professors in each Government and aided college, was to deliver to each of the college classes, in every session, a series of lectures on the duties of a man and a citizen."
8. Special measures were to be adopted for the encouragement of education among the Mohammedans.
9. All elementary schools were to be inspected and supervised by the Educational Officers of the Government.
10. The Commission put emphasis on physical and mental education of the students.
11. According to the Commission, primary education needed strongest encouragement. A part of the provincial revenues should be exclusively reserved for primary education. Primary education should be given by the State, district boards, and municipalities. Secondary education should be encouraged through local or private bodies. All secondary schools should be made over to private management wherever that is possible.

The Government of India accepted the recommendations of the Commission and directed the preparation of an annual report reviewing the progress of education in the country. Higher education progressed at great speed during the next few decades.

In January 1902, Lord Curzon appointed a Commission to "enquire into the conditions and prospects of the universities established in British India; to consider and report upon any proposals which may have been or may be made for approving their construction and working, and to recommend such measures as may tend to elevate the standard of university teaching, and to promote the advancement of learning. The Commission made the following recommendations:

1. The legal powers of the older universities should be enlarged and all the universities be recognised as teaching bodies. The local limits of each university should be more accurately defined and steps taken to remove from the Calcutta, list, the affiliated colleges in C.P., U.P., etc.
2. The Senate, the Syndicate and the Faculties should be reorganised and made more representative than before.
3. The affiliation rules should be framed in such a way as to secure that no institution shall be admitted to affiliation unless on the fullest information, and that no institution once admitted be allowed to fall below the standards of efficiency required for affiliation and the Syndicate should satisfy itself from time to time on this point.
4. There should be a properly constituted governing body for each college.
5. Attention should be paid to the residence and discipline of students.
6. The courses and methods of examination in all subjects should be changed according to the suggestions made in the Report.

UNIVERSITIES ACT OF 1904

The Government of Lord Curzon accepted the recommendations of the Raleigh Commission and embodied them in the Universities Act of 1904. The Act reconstituted the governing bodies of the universities. The Senate of the university was to have not less than 50 and not more than 100 members. The number of elected fellows was fixed at 20 for Universities of Calcutta, Bombay and Madras and 15 for the other two. Statutory recognition was given to the Syndicates with adequate representation of university teachers on them. Conditions for affiliation to the university were clearly laid down and were intended to be rigorously observed. The university was given the power of making provision for the instruction of students through the appointment of university professors and lecturers and to do all acts which tend to the promotion of study and research. The Government was vested with certain powers regarding the regulations to be framed by the Senates and the Governor-General-in-Council was empowered to define the territorial limits of the universities.

According to Chirol, "As was to be expected under a Viceroy who was a great autocrat with an overwhelming faith in the efficiency of Government machinery, the chief purpose of the Act of 1904 was to tighten the hold of the Government on the Universities, and in the first place, on their Senates, which were still retained as the ruling bodies, by reducing their total number whilst increasing to an overwhelming majority, the proportion of those nominated by the Chancellor and giving ex-officio seats on them to Provincial Directors of Public Instruction. In the Syndicates, which were the executive bodies, provision, at first sight effective, was made for a large number of college teachers, but none was eligible who was not already a member of the Senate. Increased powers of supervision over existing colleges and the imposition of more stringent conditions for the affiliation of new ones, were steps in the right direction, but they came too late and made no attempt to deal with the fungus growths which, in so many schools, were rotting the foundations on which a sound college education could be built up. New faculties were created to deal with the university curricula and with the methods of university examinations, but these were also to be mere examinations from the Senate. Practically nothing was henceforth to be done without the approval of Government."

The public opinion in India was very critical of this Act as the number of seats in the Senate thrown open to elections was very small and the restriction of numbers was supposed to create a majority for Europeans. The provisions for the exercise of teaching functions by the University were not considered very important as such provisions in the previous Acts had not been utilised. The new regulations for affiliation of colleges were registered as a means to hamper India's private effort in the field of education.

Although Lord Curzon disallowed all intentions of turning the universities into State departments or to "fetter the colleges and schools with bureaucratic handcuffs," yet the main result of the passing of the Act was to Europeanise the Senates and Syndicates of the universities and to turn them into some of "the most completely Governmental Universities of the world." This was recognised by the Calcutta University Commission. What Lord Curzon intended to do was to assert the doctrine of State responsibility and control in matters of university education. The Indian opposition was based on the growing conviction that Lord Curzon was bent upon restricting the opportunities for higher education open to young Indians. According to Frazer, "Educated Indians sincerely thought that the Viceroy meant to deal a blow at the university system." According to the same author, the source of the greatest controversy of Lord Curzon's Viceroyalty which produced bitterness among the leaders of Indian opinion and which was responsible for making the Viceroy most unpopular with the educated classes in India, was the Act of 1904.

RESOLUTION OF 1913

A Government Resolution was issued in 1913 and this clarified the policy with regard to higher education. As India would not be able to dispense altogether with the affiliating universities for a long time, it was necessary to restrict the area over which such universities would have control. New teaching and residential universities were to be established within every province. Teaching universities were to be established at Dacca, Aligarh and Banaras. New affiliating universities were to be established at Rangoon, Patna and Nagpur. The outbreak of the World War delayed the implementation of the Resolution, but universities were started at Banaras and Patna in 1916 and 1917.

CALCUTTA UNIVERSITY COMMISSION

The Government of India in the time of Lord Chelmsford appointed the Sadler Commission for the purpose of holding an inquiry of a very comprehensive and searching character into the problems of the Calcutta University. The terms of reference included all aspects of collegiate and university education. Problems of secondary education were not excluded from the scope of inquiry. The Commission was expected to study the organisation and working of other Indian Universities with a view to helping it to formulate the policy of the Calcutta University. The Commission submitted a voluminous Report in 1919 dealing practically with every problem of secondary and university education. The main recommendations of the Sadler Commission were as follows:

1. The intermediate classes of the university were to be transferred to secondary institutions and the stage of admission to the university was to be that of the existing Intermediate Examination.
2. Secondary and Intermediate education was to be controlled by a Board of Secondary Education and not by university.
3. The Government of India should cease to have any special relationship to the University of Calcutta and the Government of Bengal should take its place.
4. The duration of the Degree Course should be three years after the Intermediate stage, the provisions being applied immediately in regard to Honours Courses and soon after to Pass Courses.
5. The teaching resources of the City of Calcutta were to be organised to create a real teaching university and the project of a university at Dacca was to be carried into effect at the earliest possible moment. The mofussil colleges were to be organised in such a way as would encourage the gradual rise of new university centres by the concentration of higher teaching at a few point:

6. Special attention was to be paid to the education of women and a Board was to be created for that purpose.
7. The Government service system being unsuitable for universities, a new organisation of the teaching service in universities was necessary.
8. Problems of vocational and professional training including that of teachers, lawyers, medical men, engineers, architects and agriculturists were to be seriously taken in hand by the university and numerous reforms were suggested for that purpose.
9. The medium of instruction for most subjects up to High School stage was to be the vernacular, but for later stages, it was to be English.
10. The method of examinations required complete overhauling. The Government of India drafted a Bill to enforce the recommendations of the Commission. However, financial difficulties stood in the way. In 1920, the recommendations of the Commission were forwarded to the Provincial Governments by the Government of India. The Dacca University and Lucknow University were started in 1920 on unitary teaching lines. The Allahabad University was started in 1921 and Delhi University was started in 1922 on the same lines.

Under the Government of India Act, 1919, the department of education was transferred into the hands of the Indian Ministers responsible to the Provincial Legislatures. However, the Government of India controlled and guided the general policy of higher education. Under the Government of India Act, 1935, entire university education was placed under the control of the Provincial Governments. The only exception was in the case of a university which functioned in two provinces.

SERGEANT SCHEME FOR EDUCATION

This scheme was prepared by Sir John Sergeant, the Educational Adviser to the Government of India. It sought to introduce universal, free and compulsory education for boys and girls between the ages of 6 and 14. The scheme was estimated to cost ₹200 crores a year. This basic education was to consist of two stages, the junior stage covering 5 years and the senior stage covering 3 years. After the primary stage, all the boys and girls were not to be allowed to go to the High Schools. Only those were to be allowed to proceed who were expected to profit from higher education. Approximately, one out of every five was expected to join the High Schools. Schools were to be maintained out of public funds as far as possible. Restrictions were also to be placed on the admission of students into colleges. Intermediate Course was to be included in the High School Course, and the college teaching was to last for three years. A national youth movement was to be started throughout the country. The movement was to teach the young men to build their bodies and serve their country.

RADHAKRISHNAN COMMISSION

The Government of India appointed in 1948, a University Commission under the Chairmanship of Sir S. Radhakrishnan. The Commission submitted its report in 1949. The Commission made detailed recommendations regarding the teaching staff and their service conditions, the standard of teaching, research, professional education and examinations. It recommended higher salaries and better service conditions. It also recommended the opening of occupational institutions, refresher courses, increase in working hours, the prescribing of good textbooks, improving of library facilities and setting up of laboratories. It put emphasis on acquaintance with one's physical environment, introduction of basic ideas of science, effective use of language, appreciation of higher values and social cooperation. It laid stress on increased facilities for post-graduate research and teaching. It advocated more facilities for the study of professional courses like agriculture, commerce, etc.

The Commission recommended that pre-University education should be of 12 years' duration. More funds should be allocated by the Government for education. More scholarships and stipends should be given to students. No college should admit more than 1000 students. There should be no hasty replacement of English as the medium of instruction for higher education. Examination standards should be raised and made uniform in all the universities. University education should be put in the Concurrent List in the Constitution of India. To look after university education in the country, a University Grants Commission should be set up. Rural Universities should be established on the model of Shantiniketan and Jamia Millia.

UNIVERSITY GRANTS COMMISSION

Most of the recommendations of the Radhakrishnan Report were accepted by the Government of India. In 1956, the parliament of India passed the University Grants Commission Act, which provided for the appointment of a University Grants Commission by the Central Government. Nine members of the Commission are appointed by the Central Government. Every member holds office for a period of six years. It is the duty of the Commission to take all such steps as it may think fit for the promotion and coordination of University education and for the determination and maintenance of standards of teaching, examination and research in the Universities. For the purpose of ascertaining the financial needs of a university or its standards of teaching, examination and research, the Commission can cause an inspection of any Department or Departments. If a university does not comply with a recommendation of the commission, the latter can withdraw its grant to that University.

SECONDARY EDUCATION COMMISSION

In 1952, the Union Government appointed the Secondary Education Commission under the Chairmanship of Dr. A. Lakshmanaswami Mudaliar, Vice-Chancellor of Madras University. The Commission submitted its report in August 1953. The major recommendations of the Commission were the installation of higher secondary system with diversified courses, the three language formula, the emphasis on educational and vocational guidance, improvement in the system of education, in the teaching staff and in the methods of teaching. Those recommendations were discussed by the Central Advisory Board of Education and accepted with certain modifications. A scheme of higher secondary education was launched all over India. An All-India Council of Secondary Education was set up at the Centre. The National Council of Educational Research and Training was established at the Centre for guiding education at its various levels, developing special aspects of education and providing educational guidance and facilities to the States.

KOTHARI COMMISSION

An Education Commission was appointed by the Government of India in July 1964 to "advise the Government on the national pattern of education and on the general principles and policies for the development of education in all states and in all aspects." Dr. D.S. Kothari was appointed its Chairman. Distinguished educationists and scientists from the United Kingdom, the United States, and the Soviet Union were associated with it. The UNESCO Secretariat made available the services of J. F. McDougall who served as Associate Secretary of the Commission. The Commission submitted its report on 30 June 1966.

The Commission recommended that tuition fee at the primary stage should be abolished in all Government, local authority and private schools as early as possible. Free textbooks and writing material should be provided at the primary stage. Steps should be taken to ensure at the end of the lower primary stage that no promising child is prevented from continuing his studies further and to "this end, a scholarship of an adequate amount should be provided to every child who may need it. Special attention should be paid to the education of women, handicapped children, backward classes, backward tribes, tribal people and scheduled castes. Allocations for the construction of school buildings would be increased in Central and State budgets.

The Commission emphasised the need for an urgent reform in education to relate it to the life, needs and aspirations of the people and thereby make it a powerful instrument of social, economic and cultural transformation. Education should be so developed as to increase productivity, achieve social and national integration, accelerate the process of modernisation and cultivate social, moral and spiritual values. Guidance and counselling should be regarded as an integral part of education. Guidance should begin from the lowest class in the primary school. Teachers should be oriented to the special techniques of dealing with talented children, especially for providing an atmosphere for free expression and creative work.

The Commission made certain recommendations regarding university education and education of the handicapped. The Government accepted most of the recommendations of the Commission.

Largely based on the recommendations of the Kothari Commission, the Government of India adopted a resolution on education which put emphasis on free and compulsory education upto the age of 14, improved status and emoluments of teachers, adoption of three-language formula, education for agriculture and industry, etc.

In 1985, there was an examination of the existing system of education and a national debate is going on.

REVIEW QUESTIONS

1. Write in detail about the history of education during the British period.
2. Discuss the development of education in modern India.
3. Describe the recommendations of the Hunter Commission, 1882.
4. Give an account of the provisions of the Universities Act, 1904.
6. Elaborate on the recommendations of the various Education Commissions in the history of modern India.
7. Write short notes on the following:
    (a) Hunter Commission, 1882
    (b) University Grants Commission
    (c) Secondary Education Commission
    (d) Kothari Commission
8. Throw light on the development of modern Indian education.

SUGGESTED READINGS

Basu, Aparna: *Growth of Education and Political Development in India (1898-1920)*.
Dayal, B.: *The Development of Modern Indian Education*, 1953.
Mathew, Arthur: *The Education in India*, 1926.
Mukerjee, S. N.: *History of Education in India*, 1957.
Nurullah and Naik: *History of Education in India during the British Period*, 1956.
Reports of Radhakrishnan and Kothari Commissions.

29 Religious and Social Development

LEARNING OBJECTIVES

- Throw light on the religious and social reforms of modern India
- Know about social reformers in India during the 19th Century and later
- Give an account of religions and social reforms within Islam, Sikhs, Parsees and Christians

India made a tremendous progress both in the religious and the social fields during the 19th century and after. It was a period of transition from medievalism to the modern age. The Indian mind was stirred as a result of its contact with the forces from the West and no wonder progress was registered in many fields.

RAJA RAM MOHAN ROY (1774-1833)

The name of Raja Ram Mohan Roy stands foremost in the field of religious and social development. He was born in 1774 in an old-fashioned and well-to-do Brahmin family in Bengal. When he was hardly 15, he wrote a pamphlet in Bengali in which he denounced idol-worship which, he asserted, was not recognised in the Vedas. Young Ram Mohan Roy had to pay very heavily for it. He was turned out from his orthodox family and he had to live in exile. However, he made the best of the opportunity offered to him by Providence. He travelled far and wide and thus was able to gather a lot of experience and learning. He already knew Arabic and Persian and now he was able to master Sanskrit. He also picked up some knowledge of English, French, Latin, Hebrew and Greek. As he was able to study in original the scriptures of the important religions of the world, he was in a position to have a comparative idea of religion as such. No wonder, his concept of universal religion was not based on any abstract principles but on a profound knowledge of the various religions.

In 1805, Ram Mohan Roy joined the service of the English East India Company in Bengal, and continued to work there up to 1814. After his retirement, he settled in Calcutta (now Kolkata) and devoted himself entirely to the service of the people. In 1814, he started the Atmiya Sabha. In 1828, he founded the Brahmo Samaj. He went to England in 1831 on a special mission to plead the cause of the Mughal Emperor of Delhi. While he was still busy in that work, he died at Bristol on 27th September 1833. He was given the title of Raja by the Mughal Emperor.

In all his activities, Raja Ram Mohan Roy was actuated by a deep love of his motherland and an intense sympathy for the ignorant and the poor. As it was not possible to have an armed rebellion against the Englishmen, he continued to educate the public opinion and thereby encouraged political consciousness among his countrymen. He adopted all possible means to raise the morale of the people.

Although he himself was one of the foremost Orientalists of the age, his conviction was that India could progress only through liberal education covering all the branches of Western learning.

No wonder, he gave all his support to those who stood for the introduction of the study of English language and Western sciences in India and he was ultimately successful in his efforts. He helped in the foundation of the Hindu College, which was the best modern institution of its time in those days.

The Raja fought for the freedom of the Press. He himself founded and edited a Bengali journal called the Samvad Kaumudi which was among the earliest Indian-edited newspapers. He carried on a vigorous agitation against the Press Regulations of 1823. He submitted a memorial to the Supreme Court in which he dwelt on the benefits of a free press. His agitation for the freedom of the Press must have paved the way for the final emancipation of the press in 1835.

The Raja stood for the abolition of 'sati'. He carried on ceaseless propaganda against this inhuman custom both in the press and on the platform. The opposition was so great that there was a time when his very life was in danger. However, he was not intimidated by the attacks of his enemies. It was his consistent support which enabled Lord William Bentinck to ban 'sati' in 1829. When the orthodox people put in a petition before the Privy Council in England he put in a counter-petition before the British Parliament on behalf of his progressive friends and co-workers. He was happy when the Privy Council rejected the petition. The abolition of 'sati' put the Raja in the front rank of the world's humanitarian reformers.

During his stay in England from 1831 to 1833, the Raja agitated for reform in the administrative system of British India. He was the first Indian to be consulted on Indian affairs by the British Parliament. While giving his evidence before a Select Committee of House of Commons, he suggested reforms in practically all branches of Indian administration. The political ideas of the Raja were influenced by European philosophers and jurists like Bacon, Hume, Bentham, Blackstone and Montesquieu. He advocated the peaceful settlement of international disputes through the mediation of a congress composed of an equal number of members from the Parliaments of the countries concerned.

Before everything else, Raja Ram Mohan Roy was a religious reformer and seeker after truth. His study of Christianity, Islam and Hinduism brought him to the conclusion that there was the prevalence of, the monotheistic principle in all religions. This helped him to create, house and endow the first theistic church at Calcutta. The Raja was friendly to all religions. He was stirred by the monotheism of Islam and ethical and moral principles of Christianity. No wonder, the Muslims regarded him as a Muslim, Christians as a Christian, Unitarians as a Unitarian and Hindus as a Vedantist. As a matter of fact, he was none of these in a conventional sense. He believed in the fundamental truth and unity of all religions. He was not prepared to allow any form of worship to be criticised. Worship in the Brahmo Samaj was conducted in such a way as to strengthen the bonds of union between men of all faiths, persuasions and creeds. The Raja was not a prophet but a reformer who tried to preserve all that was true and pure and removed all that was false and superstitious. His ideas were welcomed by the Unitarian and theistic circles in the West.

The Raja made his contribution to literature also. He was a prolific writer in many languages. He was one of the greatest savants of his age. He was a great linguist and master of style. He is known as one of the creators of modern Bengali prose.

The Raja has been rightly called "the herald of a new age." According to Monier-Williams, the Raja was "perhaps the first earnest-minded investigator of the science or comparative religions that the world has produced." According to Seal, the Raja was "the harbinger of the idea of universal humanism, the humanist, pure and simple, watching from his conning tower, the procession of universal humanity in universal history." According to Miss Colet, "Ram Mohan stands in history as the living bridge over which India marches from her unmeasured past to her incalculable future. He was the arch, which spanned the gulf between ancient caste and modern humanity, between superstition and science, between despotism and democracy, between immobile custom and conservative progress, between a bewildering polytheism and a pure, if vague, theism." According to Nandlal Chatterjee, Raja Ram Mohan Roy "was the human link between the unfading past and the dawning future, between vested conservatism and radical reform, between superstitious isolationism and progressive synthesis, in short, between reaction and progress."

According to Rabindranath Tagore, Raja Ram Mohan Roy "inaugurated the modern age in India." He has also been described as the Father of Indian Renaissance and the Prophet of Indian Nationalism. Behind all of his ideas of social and religious reforms, there lay the thought of bringing about the political regeneration of his countrymen. To quote him, "I regret to say the system adhered to by the Hindus is not well-calculated to promote their political interest. The distinction of castes, introducing division and sub-divisions among them, has entirely deprived them of political feeling, multitude of religious rites and ceremonies and the laws of purification have totally disqualified them from undertaking any difficult enterprise. It is, I think, necessary that some change should take place in their religion at least for the sake of their political advantage and social comfort."

Like the Moderates of the latter half of the 19th century and the beginning of the 20th century, Raja Ram Mohan Roy believed that the British rule in India was a divine dispensation. It was all for the good of the people of this country. He did not stand for the full independence of the country. He believed that Indians should be given more and more share in the administration of the country by gradual stages. He was in favour of only those political demands for which his countrymen were already competent. He stood for civil liberty for all with all its implications.

The work of Raja Ram Mohan Roy was in the nature of the preparation of this country for political advancement in the future. By removing the social and religious evils, he prepared the Indians for political consciousness. He was undoubtedly the pioneer in this field and no wonder he has been rightly called the father of Indian Nationalism.

BRAHMO SAMAJ

The Brahmo Samaj was founded in 1828 by Raja Ram Mohan Roy. It was the culmination of his earlier Atmiya Sabha of 1814. In the Trust Deed of the Brahmo Samaj, drawn up in 1830, Raja Ram Mohan Roy made it clear that he aspired only to establish a strict monolatrous worship of the Supreme Being, a worship of the heart and not of the hand, a sacrifice of self and not of the possessions of the self. The Brahmo Samaj advocated the worship of one God and the brotherhood of man. It also stood for respect for all religions and their scriptures. Followers of all religions were invited to come and worship in the same temple in the spirit of brotherhood.

In the words of Ramsay MacDonald, "The Brahmo Samaj was unwilling to desert Hinduism, but was willing to become liberal and respond to the impact of western faiths."

After the premature death of Raja Ram Mohan Roy, the Brahmo Samaj was left without any organisation, constitution, membership, covenant or pledge. There was a period of depression, but it was revived by the efforts of Maharishi Devendra Nath Tagore (1817-1905). Within five years of his joining the Samaj in 1843, the Maharishi put new life into the organisation and introduced a regular form of church service, including thanksgiving, praise and prayer.

Keshav Chandra Sen was also an important member of the Brahmo Samaj. However, he put more emphasis on Christian and Vaishnava teachings. This led to a breach in the Brahmo Samaj. The two parts of the Brahmo Samaj came to be known as the Sadharan Brahmo Samaj and the Adi Brahmo Samaj. Keshav Chandra also organised a new church known as Navavidhan Samaj in which he was regarded as the prophet. As regards the work of Keshav, he played an important part in the passing of the Marriage Act of 1872. The Cooch-Behar Marriage case of 1878 was a turning point in his life. His daughter was less than 14 and she was married to the Maharaja of Cooch-Behar who was less than 16. People protested against this action of Keshav and public meetings were held to turn him out from the Brahmo Samaj.

It goes without saying that the Brahmo Samaj was responsible for changing the outlook of the Hindus towards Western ideas. If influenced the life of the people in very many ways. Even now the Brahmo Samaj has its followers and institutions in various parts of India.

PRARTHANA SAMAJ

In 1849, the year of the annexation of the Punjab, a society called Paramhans Sabha was started in Maharashtra. Its influence was restricted and it broke up very soon. Another organisation was started by Dr. Atma Ram Pandurang with the object of rational worship and social reform. The name of the society was the Prarthana Samaj. This society conducted night schools for working people, and associations of women for education of girls. It also ran an orphanage and an asylum at Pandarpur. It also set up a Depressed Classes Mission for improving the condition of the depressed classes. Two great members of this Samaj were Sir R. G. Bhandarkar and Justice Ranade. Ranade was responsible for the Deccan Education Society. He did a lot for the education of the people. Gokhale started the Servants of India Society and N. M. Joshi started the Social Service League to collect and study social facts and discuss social problems with a view to forming public opinion on questions of social service and secure for the masses better and reasonable conditions of life and work.

THE THEOSOPHICAL SOCIETY

The society was founded by Madame Blavatsky and Col. Olcott in 1875 in the United States. In 1879, both of them came to India and established the headquarters of the Society at Adyar near Madras (Chennai). The Theosophical Society became prominent in the time of Mrs. Annie Besant. She joined the society in 1889 and came to India in 1893. On her arrival in India she dedicated her whole life to the cause of the society. She explained her mission in these words: "The Indian work is, first of all, the revival, strengthening and uplifting of ancient religions — Hinduism, Zoroastrianism and in Ceylon and Burma, Buddhism. This brought with it a new self-respect, a pride in the past, a belief in the future and as an inevitable result, a great wave of patriotic life, the beginning of the rebuilding of a nation." She was responsible for the founding of the Central Hindu School at Banaras which later on grew into the Banaras Hindu University.

RAMAKRISHNA MISSION

The Mission was started in 1896 by Swami Vivekananda in the memory of Ramakrishna Paramhansa. The Mission has branches all over India and has done a lot of humanitarian work in the country. "The disciples of Ramakrishna do not accept the full programme of Brahmo Samaj but they are all liberal thinkers and do not stick to the orthodox principles. His disciples are divided into two groups: first the ascetics who do not marry and dedicate their lives to God and the service of men. The followers of the second group live in the world and earn their livelihood, but try to regulate their lives According to the teaching of Ramakrishna. They are not social reformers in the literal sense of the word, but they are helping in the reconstruction of society in several ways." The Ramakrishna Mission has set up a large number of schools, orphanages and dispensaries.

According to Dr. Radhakrishnan, "Swami Vivekanand was a saintly personality who was not content merely with preaching and practising the highest ideals of Hindu religion and philosophy. His motto was worship of God through the service of the poor and lowly and he called upon his countrymen and women to shake off the age-old lethargy, remove the abuses which had crept into their society and work for the freedom of their motherland.

Vivekanand was not merely an idealist dreamer. He insisted on character-building, on discipline, and on strength of mind, physical and spiritual. To him love for the Motherland was the first commandment and religion came next. The burden of his message to the youth of India was "Be strong and the fearless." To quote Vivekanand, "Above all, be strong, be manly. I have respect even for one who is wicked so long as he is manly and strong, for his strength will make him some day give up lies, wickedness or even give up all work for selfish ends, and will then eventually bring him into the his." According to Jawaharlal Nehru, "Vivekanand spoke of many things but one constant refrain of his speech and writing was *Abhaya* — be fearless, be strong."

According to Romain Rolland, "He (Vivekanand) was energy personified, and action was his message to men."

In her great book "The Master as I saw Him," regarded by Sri Aurobindo as "the best study of Vivekanand," sister Nivedita says: "Throughout those years in which I saw him almost daily, the thought of India was to him like the air he breathed. True, he was a worker at foundations. He never used the word 'nationality' nor proclaimed an era of 'nation-making'. 'Man-making' he said, was his own task. But he was born a lover, and the queen of his adoration was his Motherland.... He was hard on her sins, unsparing of her want of worldly wisdom, but only because he felt these faults to be his own. And none, on the contrary, has ever so possessed by the vision of her greatness."

DEV SAMAJ

The Dev Samaj was founded by Satyanand Agnihotri in 1887. This movement had its headquarter at Lahore. It set up schools and colleges for the people. An important feature of this organisation is that it is militantly atheistic.

ARYA SAMAJ

Swami Dayanand was the founder of the Arya Samaj. The son of a well-to-do Brahmin in Gujarat, he left his family in search of truth. He wandered all over India and studied at many places. However, he got his real learning at the feet of Swami Virjanand. After completing his education, he devoted the rest of his life in the propagation of Vedic religion and the reform of Hindu society. In 1875, he founded the Arya Samaj which ultimately became a great religious, social and educational movement. Later on, a large number of schools and colleges were set up all over the country and they became the centres of aggressive and militant nationalism in the country. The Arya Samaj gave India such great leaders as Lala Lajpat Rai and Swami Shradhanand. The British Government regarded the D.A.V. Colleges and Schools and Gurukula as the centres of sedition and breeding grounds of patriots and revolutionaries. The Arya Samaj did a lot of work in the field of untouchability, education of women, weakening of the bonds of castes, the remarriage of widows and the discouragement of early marriages of children. The Arya Samaj made the Hindus militant and aggressive. The policy of Shuddhi brought many converts to Hinduism.

Swami Dayanand helped the cause of nationalism in an indirect manner. He put faith in the people in their future. By removing the evil customs from the Hindus, he prepared them for the battle of freedom. In this way, he did the same work as was done by Raja Ram Mohan Roy. He was perhaps the first Indian to preach the gospel of Swadeshi and 'India for the Indians'. He declared that good government was no substitute for self-government. He depicted the glory of India's past and called upon the Indians to take pride in their past and also build up a similar future. The movement started by him became a mass movement and created a new spirit and new life among his followers. Swami Dayanand was fearless. He believed in truth. His motto was *Satyam Eva Jayate Na Anritam* (Truth alone triumphs and not untruth). He anticipated Mahatma Gandhi in his constructive programme.

According to Dr. S. Radhakrishnan, the President of India, among the makers of modern India who had played an important role in the spiritual uplift of people and kindled the fire of patriotism among them, Swami Dayanand occupied the chief place. He was a great social reformer and he worked to eliminate all those distinctions which have divided the people of our country. He preached social equality between men and women. All modern social legislation had been inspired by his teachings. He fought against superstition and restrictions which forbade women and a certain section of Hindu society, the study of the Vedas. He believed in God alone and did not want the people to mistake shadows for the substance. Men like Swami Dayanand were the manifestation of the Supreme being. His teachings were based on reason. He advised the people against blind faith and asked them to examine everything and formulate their own opinions about the merits and demerits of religious beliefs and social customs.

According to Sri Aurobindo, "Among the great galaxy of remarkable figures that will appear to the eye of posterity at the head of the Indian Renaissance, one stands out by himself with the peculiar and solitary distinctness, one unique in this type, as he is unique in his work. It is as if one were to walk for a long time amid a range of hills rising to a greater or lesser altitude, but all with sweeping contours, green-clad, flattering the eye even in their stands apart, piled up in sheer strength, a mass of bare and puissant granite, with verdure on its summit, a solitary pine jutting out into the blue, a great cascade of pure, vigorous and fertilising water gushing out from its strength as a very fountain of life and health to the valley. Such is the impression created on my mind by Dayanand. He was "a great soldier of Light, a warrior in God's world, a sculptor of men and institutions, a bold and rugged victory of the difficulties which matter presents to spirit." He brought back an old Aryan element into the national character. "He was not only plastic to the great hand of Nature, but asserted his own right and power to use life and Nature as plastic material. We can imagine his soul crying still to us with our insufficient spring of manhood and action, 'Be not content, O Indian, only to be infinitely and grow vaguely, but see what God intended these to be, determine in the light of His inspiration to what thou shalt grow. Seeing, hew that out of thyself; hew that out of Life. Be a thinker, but be also a doer; be a soul, but be also a man; be a servant of God but be also a master of Nature. For this was what he himself was; a man with God in his soul, vision in his eyes and power in his hands to hew out of life, an image according to his vision. Hew is the right word. Granite himself, he smote out a shape of things with great blows as in granite."

The Arya Samaj was founded in 1875. Although the life of its founder was cut short in 1883, its followers carried out the work started by the founder. Very soon, it came to the forefront in the reform of Hindu society. It started the work of Shuddhi or conversion or reconversion of persons to Hinduism. It started a large number of schools and colleges. It played an important part in the national life of the country. Mahatma Hans Raj, Guru Datt Vidyarthi and Lala Lajpat Rai were great followers of the Arya Samaj. Mahatma Hans Raj was the founder-principal of the D.A.V. College, Lahore, which was one of the biggest educational institutions in Northern India. In addition to the D.A.V. College, Lahore, very many schools and colleges were started by the D.A.V. College Managing Committee. In 1892, the Arya Samaj was split up into two parts, viz., the D.A.V. College Section and the Gurukul Section. Mahatma Hans Raj was the leader of the first Section and Swami Shradhanand was the leader of the other Section. The Gurukul Party started the famous Gurukul Kangri in 1902 which has grown into a university. It goes without saying that the Arya Samaj has played and is even now playing an important role in the educational field. It has been responsible for moulding the lives of crores of young men and women of this country.

ISLAM

For a long time, the Muslims refused to reconcile themselves with the changes brought about by the advent of the English in India. The result was that they remained unaffected by the new changes in society. Sir Syed Ahmed Khan (1817-98) was responsible for bringing about a change in the outlook of the Muslims. He asked the Muslims to change their political, religious, educational and social ideas and bring about a working harmony between East and West. He went to England and on his return started the M.A.O. College at Aligarh in 1875. It is true that there was a lot of opposition to begin with but ultimately this grew into the Aligarh Muslim University in 1920. Sir Syed also tried to prepare the Urdu translations of books on English literature and scientific works. He was also in favour of the abolition of *Purdah* and education of women. He propagated his views through his magazine called "Tahzil-ul-Akhlaq (Reform of Morals)." It goes without saying that his lifework brought about revolution among the Muslims. A large number of societies or Anjumans were started by the Muslims for the service of their community. A powerful Muslim press also came into existence. The origin, growth and development of the All-India Muslim League and the help given to it by the British Government made the Muslims stronger and stronger.

Reference may also be made to the **Ahmediya** movement which was started by Mirza Ghulam Ahmed. The Mirza was born at Qadian in District Gurdaspur of the Punjab. He was conservative and reactionary in his outlook. He was opposed to the abolition of Purdah. He defended the Islamic law of divorce and polygamy. After the death of the Mirza in 1908, the movement was managed by a Khalifa. However, a split took place in 1914, One group came to be known as the Lahori Party and the other group came to be known as the Qadiani Party. The Qadiani Party considered the founder as a Prophet (Nabi). The Lahori Party considered the founder merely as a reformer in Islam (Mujadhid).

SIKHS

Sikhs were also influenced by the prevailing atmosphere in the country. They started the Chief Khalsa Diwan and set up the Khalsa College at Amritsar. The Shiromani Gurdwara Prabandhak Committee was started by the Sikhs to get rid of corrupt Mahants and reform the Gurdwaras. The Sikhs succeeded in their objective. They have been successful in starting a large number of schools and colleges in various parts of the country.

PARSEES

Parsees started the Rahnumai Mazdayasnan Sabha or Religious Reform Association for the "regeneration of the social condition of the Parsees and the restoration of Zoroastrian religion to its pristine purity," K. R. Cama did a lot for the spread of education among the Parsees. B. M. Malabari also rendered great service to the community. In 1910, a Zoroastrian Conference was also held.

CHRISTIANITY

During the 19th century, the Christians did a lot in spreading education and converting the Indians to Christianity. It was laid down in the Charter Act of 1813 that "it is the duty of this country to promote the introduction of useful knowledge and of religion and moral improvement in India and that facilities be offered by law to persons desirous of going to and remaining in India to accomplish this benevolent design." Consequently, Bishops were appointed in the Presidencies. A large number of high caste educated Hindus were converted to Christianity. Missionaries like Carey, Duff, Grant, Marshman and Dr. Forman did a lot in converting people to Christianity. Although their main work was the conversion of the Indians, they were also responsible for spreading education in the country. Another effect of Christianity was that the Indian religions tried to reform themselves in order that they might be saved from its attacks. The caste Hindus also changed their attitude towards the depressed classes.

SOCIAL DEVELOPMENT

Sati. The most important social reform of the 19th century was the abolition of 'sati' or the practice of burning Hindu widows on the funeral pyres of their husbands. The practice of 'sati' was a very ancient one and although it did not become equally common throughout India, Bengal, Rajputana and the South Indian kingdom of Vijayanagar were its main medieval strongholds. 'Sati' was never in theory a religious obligation, but merely a highly meritorious act, which was intended to bring reward in the next life. It was believed that by burning herself on the funeral pyre, a widow sanctified her ancestors, removed the sins of her husband and got rest for herself for ages to come. She was believed to live in heaven after death.

With all the force of high precedents and romantic stories behind it, 'sati' for a woman of high character and was transferred from a pious act into almost an obligation. Strong social pressure was brought on a widow to induce her to burn herself along with her husband. The position of widows among the Hindus was also a factor which helped the growth of this custom. The life of a Hindu widow was full of misery. She was expected to eat only one meal a day. "She was not to sleep on a bed. She was never to put on good clothes. She was to live a life of renunciation. In some cases, her head was clean-shaved. To quote Abbe Dubois, "Doomed to perpetual widowhood, cast out of society, stamped with the seal of contumely, she has no consolation whatever except may be the recollections of hardships she has had to endure during her married life."

It is very difficult to say how far sati was voluntary. It is true that there must have been cases when women out of family pride went happily to the funeral pyres and the history of Rajputana is full of such examples, but in most cases, widows were practically left with no choice. They were forced to sacrifice themselves by the Brahmins and their relatives. There were also women who wanted to be sati but who found themselves too weak to do so. In such cases, once a woman announced her intention of becoming 'sati' she was not allowed to retract. Reference may be made to some examples to show the nature of sati.

The following is the report by a Superintendent of Police, Ewert: "It is generally supposed that a sati takes place with the free will and consent of the widow, and that she frequently persists in her intention to burn, in spite of the arguments and entreaties of her relations. But there are many reasons for thinking that such an event as a voluntary 'sati' very rarely occurs; few widows would think of sacrificing themselves unless overpowered by force or persuasion, very little of either being sufficient to overcome the physical or mental powers of the majority of Hindu females. A widow, who would turn with natural instinctive horror from the first hint of sharing her husband's pile, will be at length gradually brought to pronounce a reluctant consent, because distracted with grief at the event, without one friend to advise or protect her, she is little prepared to oppose the surrounding crowd of hungry Brahmins and interested relations, either by argument or force.... In this state of confusion a few hours quickly pass and the widow is burnt before she has had time even to think on the subject. Should utter indifference for her husband, and superior sense, enable her to preserve her judgment, and to resist the arguments of those about her, it will avail her little — the people will not be disappointed of their show; and the entire population of a village will turn out to assist in dragging her to the bank of the river and in keeping her down on the pile. Under these circumstances nine out of ten widows are burnt to death."

The following is a dramatic account of sati as given by Abbe Dubois: "In (1874), in a village of the Tanjore district called Pudupettah, there died a man of some importance belonging to the Komatty (Vaisya) caste. His wife, aged about 30 years, announced her intention of accompanying her deceased husband to the funeral pyre. The news having rapidly spread abroad, a large concourse of people flocked together from all quarters to witness the spectacle. When everything was ready for the ceremony, and the widow had been richly clothed and adorned, the bearers stepped forward to remove the body of the deceased, which was placed in a sort of shrine.... Immediately after the funeral car followed the widow, borne in a richly decorated palanquin. On the way to the burning ground she was escorted by immense crowd of eager sightseers lifting their hands towards her in token of admiration and rending the air with cries of joy. She was looked upon as already translated to the paradise of Indra, and they seemed to envy her happy lot.

"While the funeral procession moved slowly along, the spectators, especially the women, tried to draw near her to congratulate her on her good fortune, at the same time expecting that, in virtue of the gift of prescience such a meritorious attachment must confer upon her, she would be pleased to predict the happy things that might befall them here below. With gracious and amiable mien she declared to one that she would long enjoy the favours of fortune; to another that she would be the mother of numerous children who would prosper in the world; to the third that she would live long and happily with a husband who would love and cherish her; to a fourth that her family was destined to attain much honour and dignity forth....

"During the whole procession, which was a very long one, the widow maintained a calm demeanour. Her looks were serene, even smiling; but when she reached the fatal place where she was to yield up her life in so ghastly a manner, it was observed that her firmness suddenly gave way.... Her looks became wildly fixed upon the pile. Her face grew deadly pale. Her very limbs were shaking in a convulsive tremor.... The Brahmins who conducted the ceremony, and also her near relatives, ran quickly to her, endeavouring to keep up her courage and revive her drooping spirits. All with no effect. The unfortunate woman bewildered and distracted, turned a deaf ear to all their exhortations and preserved a deep silence.

"She was then made to leave the palanquin, and as she scarcely able to walk, her people helped her to drag herself to a pond near the pyre. She plunged into the water with all her clothes and ornaments on, and was immediately afterwards led to the pyre, on which the body of her husband was already laid. The pyre was surrounded by Brahmins, each with a lighted torch in one hand and a bowl of ghee in the other. Her relatives and friends, several of whom were armed with muskets, swords, and other weapons, stood closely round in a double line, and seemed to wait impatiently for the end of this shocking tragedy. This armed force, they told me, was intended not only to intimidate the unhappy victim in case the terror of her approaching death would induce her to run away, but also to overpower any persons who might be moved by a natural feeling of compassion and sympathy, and so tempted to prevent the accomplishment of the homicidal sacrifice.... The poor widow was instantly divested of all her jewels, and dragged more dead than alive, to the pyre. There she was obliged, according to custom, to walk three times round the pile...during the second (round) her strength wholly forsook her, and she fainted away.... Then, at last, senseless and unconscious, she was cast upon the corpse of her husband. At that moment the air resounded with noisy acclamations. The Brahmins, emptying the contents of their vessels on the dry wood, applied their torches, and in the twinkling of an eye the whole pile was ablaze."

Here is another account given by Captain Sleeman in his "Rambles and Recollections": "After bathing, she called for a pan (betel leaf) and ate it, then rose up, and with one arm on the shoulder of her eldest son, and the other on that of her nephew, approached the fire. I had sentries placed all round, and no other person was allowed to approach within five paces. As she rose up fire was set to the pile and, it was instantly in a blaze. The distance was about 150 yards. She came on with a calm and cheerful countenance, stopped once, and casting her eyes upward, said, 'Why have they kept me five days from thee, my husband? On coming to the sentries her supporters stopped — she walked once round the pit, paused a moment, and, while muttering a prayer, threw some flowers into the fire. She then walked up deliberately and steadily to the brink, stepped into the centre of the flame, sat down, and leaning back in the midst as if reposing on a couch, was consumed without uttering a shriek or betraying one sign of agony."

Whether sati was voluntary or under compulsion, it cannot be denied that the custom was a horrible one. Even before the British regime, efforts had been made to stop it. Albuquerque, the Portuguese Viceroy, prohibited sati in Goa in 1510. Some Mughal Emperors also issued orders against this practice. Baji Rao, the last Peshwa, also discouraged sati. The Dutch, the French and the Danes were also against it. However, the problem of the English East India Company was a very serious one. The Company had declared its intention of respecting the beliefs of the Hindus and the Muslims. No wonder, Warren Hastings refused to interfere in the matter of sati. In the time of Cornwallis, a British magistrate, on his own initiative, stopped sati from taking place. When he referred the general question for orders to the Government, he was told that he must in future confine himself to dissuasion. Lord Wellesley referred the question to the Nizamat Adalat, but the judges did not advise the abolition of sati. However, they recommended strict enforcement of the limitation placed on it by Hindu law. Lord Minto did not tackle the problem. In 1812, the question was raised by another magistrate and he was asked to follow the view of the judges of the Nizamat Adalat. This created a very unfortunate position which has been described in these words: "Previous to 1813 no interference on the part of the police was authorised, and widows were sacrificed legally or illegally as it might happen; but the Hindus were then aware that the Government regarded the custom with natural horror, and would do anything short of direct prohibition to discourage and gradually to abolish it. The case is now altered. The police officers are ordered to interfere, for the purpose of ascertaining that the ceremony is performed in conformity with the rules of the Shastras, and in that event to allow its completion. This is granting the authority of Government for the burning of widows; and it can scarcely be a matter of astonishment that the number of sacrifices should be doubled when the sanction of the ruling power is added to the recommendations of the Shastras."

Many officials urged the prohibition of 'sati' but the Government hesitated on account of the fear of resistance from the people. Men like Raja Ram Mohan Roy were in favour of educating the public opinion against the practice of sati. In a prepared petition, he gave his views in these words: "Cases have frequently occurred when women have been induced by the persuasion of their next of heirs, interested in their destruction, to burn themselves at the funeral pile of their husbands. That others, who have been induced by fear, to retract a resolution rashly expressed in the first moments of grief, of burning with the deceased husband have been forced down upon the pile and then bound with ropes and green bamboos until consumed with the flames; that some, after flying from the flames, have been carried back by their relatives and burnt to death."

In 1823, the Home Government asked the Government of India to tackle the problem afresh but nothing was done for some time. When Lord William Bentinck became Governor-General, he had consultations with his officials and public men of the country and ultimately came to the conclusion that the evil must be stopped. On 4th December 1829, sati was made illegal in Bengal. It was laid down that persons assisting, even in a voluntary sati, were to be held guilty of culpable homicide. Similar legislation was passed in the presidencies of Madras (now Chennai) and Bombay (now Mumbai).

The fear of rebellion proved to be groundless. The opponents of the Governor-General had not the courage to accept the challenge. A large number of Bengali gentlemen sent a petition to the Privy Council against the interference of the Government in their rights and liberties. However, that petition was rejected and the matter ended. Some writers have condemned the British Government for not taking action earlier. However, it must not be forgotten that the Government was bound to follow a policy of caution in delicate matters of religion. It was only when the policy of educating the people against sati failed that it was decided to take coercive action. Moreover, before the time of Bentinck, the position of the English company itself was not very strong in this country.

The British Government did not rest content with the abolition of 'sati' in British India alone[1]. Efforts were made to stop 'sati' even in the Indian States and those were ultimately successful. In some cases, mere pressure was enough to stop the practice. In some cases, the practice was stopped when a State came under the British control for a temporary period on account of the minority of an Indian prince. In other cases, States were annexed to British India and then the practice was stopped. In some cases, when a Raja desired to enter into a treaty with the English Company, the abolition of the practice of 'sati' was made a precedent condition. The practice was also stopped in the Rajput States. One by one, the Rajput States surrendered to British pressure. The last 'sati' at the death of an Indian ruler took place in 1861. However, the battle was won by 1850 and the 'sati' in 1861 was merely its last shot.

Abolition of Infanticide. The custom of infanticide was particularly prominent among the Rajputs who considered an unmarried daughter as a disgrace to their family and who also found it difficult to find suitable husbands for their daughters. According to Tod, "Although religion nowhere

---

[1] In the Regulation provinces 'sati' had been prohibited by a Regulation passed in 1829. In Sind the Regulation was not operative and the evil was left to be dealt with according to individual predilection. When it was represented by the Brahmans that it was a practice sanctioned by religion and one which should be respected, Sir Charles Napier replied: "Be it so. This burning of widows is your custom. Prepare the funeral pile. But my nation has also a custom. When men burn women alive we hang them and confiscate all their property. My carpenters shall, therefore, erect gibbets on which to hang all concerned when the widow is consumed. Let us all act according to national customs." Tiamus quamus molutasit et fugit fuga. Rum sit porem acepti omnis nihillat.

authorises this barbarity, the laws which regulate marriage among the Rajputs powerfully promote infanticide. Not only is intermarriage prohibited between families of the same clan but between those of the same tribe." The difficulty was magnified by the extravagant expenditure which Rajput conventions demanded on the occasion of a daughter's marriage. Chieftains and landholders were constantly reminded by the priests, and bards of the munificence of their ancestors at marriage feasts. The birth of a daughter was a liability and thus the custom of female infanticide sprang up.

In 1795, infanticide was declared to be murder by Bengal Regulation XXI. In spite of this, the custom continued. Daughters were killed by the administration of opium or by suffocation immediately after birth. Sometimes, the mother was forced to starve the child.

The evil of female infanticide was ended by propaganda and the forceful action on the part of the British Government. The offenders were warned that very strong action would be taken against them if they committed the offence.

Raja Ram Mohan Roy also raised his voice against the evils of polygamy and Kulinism. Through the efforts of Keshav Chandra Sen, the Native Marriage Act of 1872 was passed. This Act abolished early marriage, made polygamy penal, sanctioned widow remarriages and inter caste marriages for those who chose to come under the Act. The Arya Samaj also carried on a vigorous agitation for reform in this field. M. B. Malabari, the Parsi reformer carried on agitation against the child marriage. In 1891, the famous Age of Consent Act was passed which raised the age of consummation from 10 to 12 in the teeth of opposition. The critics maintained that the Act "was an infringement of the Queen's Proclamation of 1858 by which she pledged her government to a policy of non-interference with the religions of her Indian subjects." In 1901, the Government of Baroda passed the Infant Marriage Prevention Act. This Act fixed the minimum age of marriage for girls at 12 and for boys at 16. In 1930 the famous Sharda Act was passed. The object of the Act was to discourage the solemnisation of marriages between boys under 18 and girls under 14 years The Act has remained a dead letter on account of the opposition of the Hindus and the apathy of the Government.

Widow Remarriage. A movement was started for the remarriage of Hindu widows. This movement got a momentum during the period of the agitation for and against sati. The daughter of Babu Shyam Chandra Dass became a widow and he circulated among the Pandits of India the question "whether the widowed daughter of a Sudra who had not known her husband and who was unable to practise the higher virtue of concremation with her husband's corpse, or endurance of the hardships of life of widowhood, can be remarried agreeably to the Shastras." Pandits met and gave a certificate of permission. However, it was pointed out that the permission applied only to Sudras and not to the caste Hindus.

Pandit Ishwar Chandra Vidyasagar, the great Sanskrit scholar, was responsible for carrying on a vigorous agitation for the remarriage of widows. He quoted chapter and verse from the Shastras to prove that widow remarriage was not banned by the Hindu scriptures. A large number of signatures were collected and petitions were sent to the Government. Ultimately, a law was passed in 1856 by which the remarriage of widows was legalised. It was declared that the issues of the remarried widows were to be legitimate. After the passing of the law, a large number of widows were remarried. The Brahmo Samaj also advocated the remarriage of widows. The Arya Samaj did not lag behind in this connection. In Maharashtra, Pandit Vishnu Sastri did a lot of work for the cause of Hindu widows. Ranade also gave his helping hands. Sir R. G. Bhandarkar, Agarkar, and D. K. Karve have also done a lot in the same connection. Karve himself remarried a Brahman widow in 1899. He opened at Poona a Hindu Widow's Home. The All-India Women's Conference has also done a lot of work in this connection.

Medical colleges have been set up for the education of women. The Lady Dufferin Fund provided for the training of women as doctors, hospital assistants nurses and midwives. Women of India have also got the right of vote. Their cause was facilitated by the attitude of the Indian National Congress and its leaders like Mahatma Gandhi and Pandit Nehru.

With a view to saving the Indians from the attacks of Christian missionaries, the Arya Samaj, the Ramakrishna Mission, and other associations did much for the improvement of the lot of the depressed classes. In 1906, the Depressed Classes Mission Society of India was founded with the object of improving "the social as well as the spiritual conditions of the depressed classes viz., the Mahars, the Chambers, Parhais, Namasudras, Dhedes, and other classes considered as untouchables in India by promoting education, providing work, remedying their social disabilities, preaching to them, principles of liberal religion, personal character and good citizenship." Mahatma Gandhi spent a lot of his time in improving the condition of the Harijans. His weekly paper The Harijan was devoted to this cause. The new Constitution of India has made untouchability, an offence. The Government is also doing a lot for the backward classes by giving them special scholarships and other facilities.

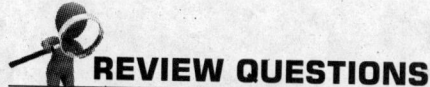

REVIEW QUESTIONS

1. Write an essay on the religious and social development of modern India.
2. Evaluate the role of Raja Ram Mohan Roy in religious and social development.
3. State the principles of Brahmo Samaj.
4. Sketch the role of Raja Ram Mohan Roy in the socio-religious movement of the 19th century.
5. Assess the role of religion in social development.
6. Describe the role of religious institutions in promoting social development.
7. Can religion contribute to social development? Explain.
8. Write short notes on the following:
   (a) Prarthana Samaj
   (b) Theosophical Society
   (c) Ramakrishna Mission
   (d) Arya Samaj
   (e) Sati

SUGGESTED READINGS

Chatterjee, Ramanand: *Ram Mohan Roy and Modern India*.
Farquhar, J.N.: *Modern Religious Movements in India*.
Parekh, Manilal: *The Brahmo Samaj* (1929).
Ranade, M.G.: *Religious and Social Reform* (1902).
Rolland, Romain: *The Life of Vivekananda*.
Sastri, Sivanath: *History of the Brahmo Samaj*.
Walter, H.A.: *The Ahmediya, Movement* (1918).
Parekh, Radhey Shyam: *Contribution of Arya Samaj in the Making of Modern India* (1875-1947).
Pandey, Dhanpati: *The Arya Samaj and Indian Nationalism*.

30 Anglo-Afghan Relations

LEARNING OBJECTIVES

- Comment on Anglo-Afghan relations during the 19th century
- Explain the causes and effects of the Afghan Wars

Referring the basis of British policy towards Afghanistan during the 19th century, Dr. Bisheshwar Prasad observes thus "Controversy has raged on the possibility of a Russian invasion of India and opinion has been divided on the practicability of these routes for a modern army as well as on the military resources of Russia in Central Asia which she could hurl against India. Optimism has alternated with pessimism and sentiment and dogmas have affected dispassionate and factual analysis of this question. Some have magnified the difficulties of the lines of communication and taken shelter behind the illusionary complacence that Russian forces even if they succeeded in traversing the desolate gap between the two Empires by way of Herat, Farah and Kandhar, would have been so completely decimated by terrain and the hounding tribesmen that no more than a small rabble would be left to counter the mighty arm of the British on the Khyber Bolan line or the Indus river. Others have taken pain to show that the Herat-Kandhar-Bolan route is easily negotiable for wheeled traffic; the terrain is capable of railway construction and the Helmand Valley is a granary which can maintain a large force. They consider Herat as the main gate which once pierced, the flood of invasion would sweep unhindered and deluge the defences of India. With the construction of the Caspian railway from Krasnovodsk to Mery and extension of Kushk Post, and its connection with the Central Asian railway connecting Termez, the distance which divided the Afghan frontier from the Russian bases was eliminated. The danger to Herat on one side and possibility of an approach on the Hindu-Kush on the other, whether towards Kabul or through Faizabad to Chitral came to be practical realities. In later years, with the advance of science, the desert and the mountain could not remain impassable barriers as they were in early days. Thus, a group of publicists and strategists have not without reason believed in the in pregnability of the Indian frontiers through Afghanistan, more particularly by the Herat-Kandhar route. Similarly, with regards to the Russian military potential, there have been conflicting views. Bougler in 1879 pointed out that while Russia could not release more than thirty thousand men from her bases in Tashkant-Feghana area, she could easily assemble a force of one hundred fifty thousand in her Trans-Caspian regions and maintain it on the Herat line. The problem was not so much of manpower as of maintenance of the forces on a long, inhospitable and possibly hostile line of communications. With the development of railways and roads and the exploitation of water transport, the difficulties were greatly resolved in the area up to the Oxus. Yet the problems of administration remained no less acute in Afghanistan, if she did not align herself with the invader

Thus, among the militarists in the nineteenth century two groups were formed, one exaggerating the difficulties of the route and thereby discounting the prospects of invasion, the other conveniently making light of them and for ulterior motives raising the ghost of Russian invasion. While the one, therefore, was prepared to make a stand on the Indus or the mountain ridge that divided India from Afghanistan on this side of the mighty passes, the other would advance to meet the enemy at the gate of Herat or beyond the Hindu-Kush in the plains of the Oxus. For one, the defensible frontier was the Indus, while for the other, the scientific frontier was the Hindu-Kush. This diversity of opinion arising out of the difference in their strategic outlook affected the whole course of diplomacy towards Afghanistan and influenced the policy of defence which hinged on the attitude of the Afghan rulers towards India. The practicability or otherwise of the rampart of the Hindu Kush and the necessity of offering resistance to hostile forces at Herat have made Afghanistan an important factor in the defence of India.

"Whatever be the strategic line of resistance, it was essential that no hostile influence should preponderate in Kabul, for once the Russians were established there the base of operations would shift from beyond the Oxus to the neighbourhood of the frontier of India. Britain would then be compelled to maintain considerable forces in the North-Western Frontier, financially, a serious drain. Close vicinity of Russia was also dangerous for political stability of their rule. All these considerations prompted the policy that the Afghan ruler should be friendly and amenable to British influence. From Bentinck to Curzon, every Governor-General cherished the same policy but difference arose in the method of achieving it or in the extent of control to be exercised. Essential motive was the protection of Herat-Hindu-Kush frontier which one group desired to secure by leaving the Amir to himself while the other was prepared, if possible, to locate British military outposts, and construct roads, railways and telegraphs either by coaxing and subsidising the Amir or break him into submission. Two wars and considerable diplomacy were employed to secure this end." (*Mahamahopadhyay Prof. D. V. Potdar, Commemoration Volume*, pp. 65-67.)

As regards the relations of the Afghans with the Government of India, we may start with the successors of Ahmed Shah Abdali. His son Timur Mirza was a weak ruler. On his death in 1793, he was succeeded by his brother, Zaman Shah. Within 5 years, he was able to consolidate his position and reached the height of his power. From Lahore, he thought of repeating the exploits of his forefathers and penetrating into the heart of India. Although he had not much chance of success, the prospect of an invasion by Zaman Shah "kept the British Indian Empire in a chronic state of unrest." It is a matter of common knowledge that all the disgruntled elements in India invited Zaman Shah to attack India. No wonder, Lord Wallesley was asked "to keep a very watchful eye upon the motions of that Prince, whose talents, military force, and pecuniary resources, afford him the means of being a formidable opponent." Lord Wallesley had to assemble a large army for the purpose of meeting a possible attack by King Zaman Shah. However, trouble arose between Afghanistan and Persia and consequently the attention of Zaman Shah was diverted to that side. Ultimately, King Zaman Shah was overthrown, captured and blinded. Later, he managed to escape to Bokhara, Herat and finally to Ludhiana in the Punjab. He spent the rest of his life as a pensioner of the East India Company."

After Zaman Shah, Mahmud became the ruler of Afghanistan. He was merely a puppet in the hands of Fateh Khan. There was lawlessness in the country and after three years of rule, Mahmud was ousted by Shah Shuja.

Shah Shuja ruled from 1803 to 1809. He too had not a very comfortable time. According to Kaye, the resources of Shah Shuja "were limited, and his qualities were of too negative a character to render him equal to the demands of such stirring times. He wanted vigour; he wanted activity; he wanted judgment; and above all he wanted money." He committed the folly of annoying Fateh Khan and other Sardars. Sind was conquered in 1805 but trouble arose in his own country. Ultimately, he was defeated by Fateh Khan at a place near Gandmark. In 1809, Mahmud Shah was put on the throne once again. Shah Shuja retired to Ludhiana where he became a pensioner of the East India Company.

Although Mahmud Shah was put on the throne once again and he remained in power for 7 years (1809-16), he was a very weak ruler. He was merely a tool in the hands of Fateh Khan. He wished for power with reference only to the "sweats of life and the pleasures which it procured, leaving to others, the cares of Government." Unfortunately, Mahmud Shah got Fateh Khan arrested, blinded and cut to pieces. This led to lawlessness in the country and it continued from 1818 to 1826.

In 1826, Dost Mohammad was able to seat himself on the throne of Kabul. He was a brave, religious-minded and enterprising king. For 12 years (1826-1838), he ruled the country successfully. Shah Shuja tried to get back the throne in 1834 but Dost Mohammad was more than a match for him. Dost Mohammad lost Peshawar to the Sikhs, and in spite of his best efforts failed to get back the same.

The position of Dost Mohammad was not very strong. On the north, there were revolts in Balkh; on the south, one of his brothers was holding out against him at Kandhar; on the east, he was harassed by Ranjit Singh at Peshawar, with Shah Shuja and the British Government in the background; on the west there was Mahmud Shah and Kamran at Herat with Persia plotting behind and Russia looking in the distance. Dost Mohammad was willing to enter into an alliance with the English East India Company only if the British Government promised to recover for him Peshawar from Ranjit Singh and also not to help Shah Shuja against him.

AFGHAN WAR I

At this time, a new development took place. Russia was trying to increase her influence in Central Asia. She commanded great influence on the King of Persia. Lord Palmerstone, the British Foreign Secretary, suffered from 'Russophobia'. He was determined to check the spread of the power of Russia at any cost. Mohammad Mirza became the King of Persia. He was a great friend of the Russian Government. Consequently, the control of Russia over Persia was enormous. On the instigation of the Russia Government, the Shah of Persia actually besieged Herat. However, through the efforts of Pottinger, the siege of Herat was lifted.

In 1836, Dost Mohammad sent a letter of congratulations to Lord Auckland when he came to India as Governor-General. He also asked for British help against Ranjit Singh. The straight reply of Auckland was that it was "not the practice of the British Government to interfere with the affairs of other independent States." Lord Palmerstone, the British Foreign Secretary, directed the Government of India to take all the necessary steps to check the growing strength of Russia. In June 1836, a Secret Committee of the Directors of the Company asked Lord Auckland "to judge as to what steps it may be proper and desirable for you to take to watch, more closely than as hitherto been attempted, the progress of events in Afghanistan and counteract the progress of Russian influence in a quarter which, from its proximity to our Indian possession could not fail, if it were once established, to act injuriously on the system of our Indian alliances, and possibly to interfere even with the tranquillity of our own territory. The mode of dealing with this very important question, whether by dispatching a confidential agent to Dost Mohammad of Kabul merely to watch the progress of events, or to enter into relations with this chief, either of a political or merely, in the first instance, of a commercial character, we confide to your discretion, as well as the adoption of any other measures that may appear to you desirable in order to counteract Russian adventures in that quarter, should you be satisfied from the information received from your agents on the frontier, or hereafter from McNeil on his arrival in Persia, that the time has arrived at which it would be right for you to interfere decidedly in the affairs of Afghanistan. Such an interference would, doubtless be requisite, either to prevent the extension of Persian domination in that quarter, or to raise a timely barrier against the impending encroachment of Russian influence."

Alexander Burnes, a great traveller and adventurer, was chosen by Lord Auckland to be sent to Kabul. Outwardly, it was declared that he was to start from the delta of the Indus and find out the potentialities of that river for purposes of navigation. He was directed to measure the breadth and depth of the river on the way. Burnes passed through Punjab and Peshawar. When he reached Kabul,

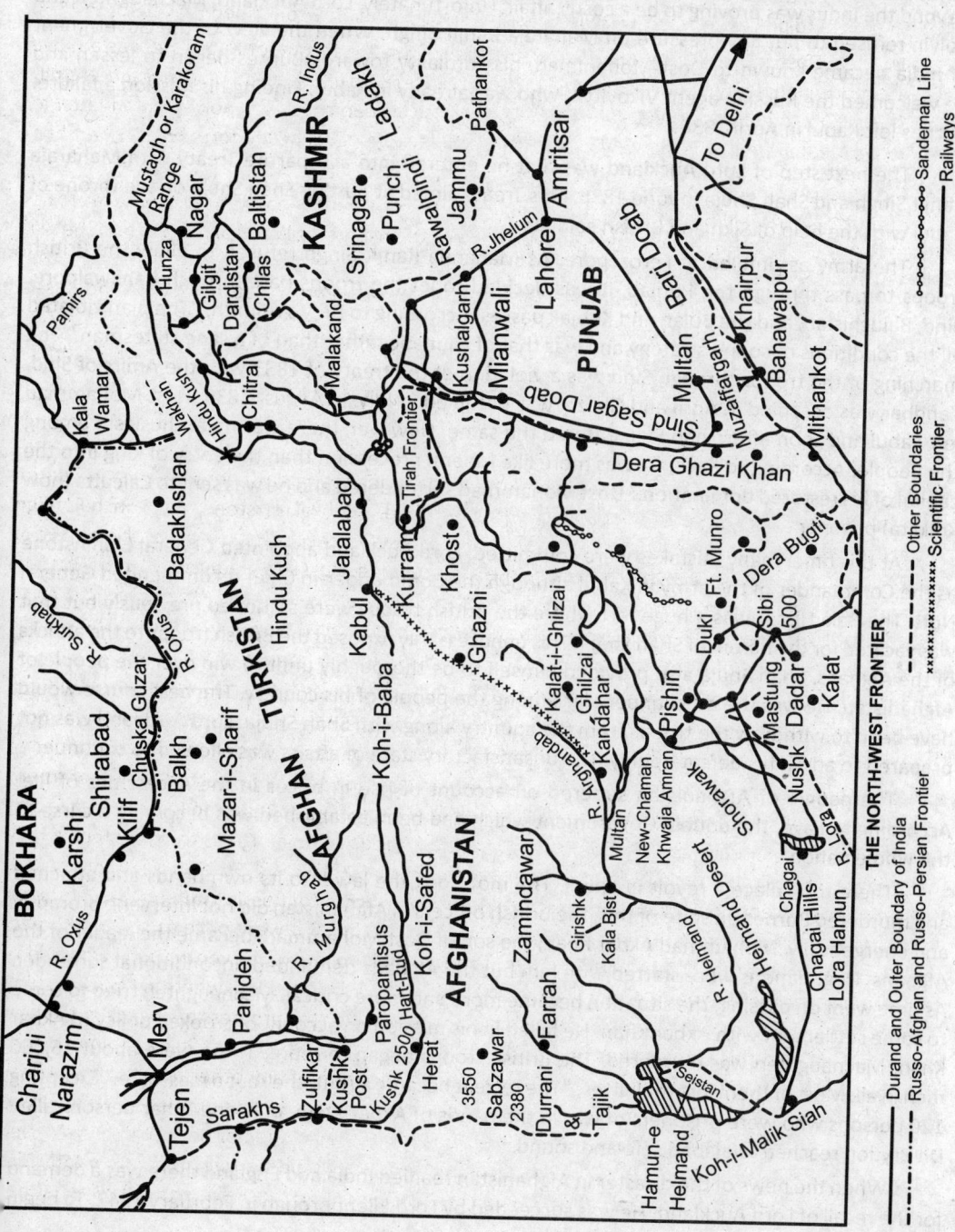

he was well received by Dost Mohammad. The latter asked him to recommend to his Government to help him in getting Peshawar from Maharaja Ranjit Singh. He also offered to enter into an agreement with the British Government, if his wish regarding Peshawar was granted. Burnes communicated the views of Dost Mohammad to Lord Auckland and asked him to put pressure on Ranjit Singh to give up Peshawar to the Afghans. Burnes own view was that Maharaja Ranjit Singh would not raise any serious objection to his surrender of Peshawar because the retention of the territory by Ranjit Singh beyond the Indus was proving to be a costly affair. Unfortunately, Lord Auckland, Macnaughten and Colvin refused to put any pressure on Maharaja Ranjit Singh. When the view of the Government of India became known to Dost Mohammad, his cordiality towards Burnes began to lessen and he welcomed the Russian agent Vikovitch, who was already in Kabul. Finding his mission a failure, Burnes left Kabul in April 1838.

The next step of Lord Auckland was that he entered into a Tripartite Treaty with Maharaja Ranjit Singh and Shah Shuja in June 1838. This Treaty aimed at putting Shah Shuja on the throne of Kabul with the help of Sikh and British soldiers.

The army assembled at Ferozepore. As Maharaja Ranjit Singh refused to allow the British troops to pass through the Punjab, it was decided to let the troops pass through Bahawalpore, Sind, Baluchistan, and the Bolan and Khojak passes. According to Dr. V. A. Smith, "The plan violated all the conditions of sound strategy and was that of a lunatic rather than of a sane statesman." The marching of the troops through Sind was a violation of the treaty of 1832 with the Amirs of Sind. Kandhar was occupied in April and Ghazni was occupied in July. In August 1839, Dost Mohammad left Kabul and soon after Shah Suja entered the same. However, there was no enthusiasm among the people. According to Kaye, "It was more like funeral procession than the entry of king into the capital of his restored domination." Dost Mohammad surrendered and he was sent to Calcutta (now Kolkata) prisoner.

At this time, many mistakes were committed. Lord Auckland appointed General Elphinstone as the Commander of the army in Kabul although the Commander-in Chief recommended General Nott. The Bala Hissar was a huge fort where the British troops were stationed previously but that was vacated for the harem of Shah Shuja. This unnecessarily exposed the British troops to the attacks of the Afghans. Shah Shuja also provided himself to be thoroughly unfit to win over the people of Afghanistan. He was the most unpopular among the people of his country. The best course would have been to withdraw the troops from the country along with Shah Shuja. Lord Auckland was not prepared to admit his defeat openly. The unsatisfactory state of affairs was allowed to continue.

The people of Afghanistan suffered on account of rise in prices in the necessities of life. According to Kaye, the double Government which had been established was becoming a curse to the whole nation.

There took place a revolt in Kabul. The mob took the law into its own hands and attached and murdered Burnes. In spite of this, the British officers in Afghanistan did not intervene promptly and energetically. Mohammad Akbar Khan, the son of Dost Mohammad, became the leader of the Afghans. Negotiations were started with him but the Afghans demanded unconditional surrender. As time went on passing, the situation became more and more critical. Macnaughten tried to come to some settlement with Akbar Khan. He failed in his mission on account of crooked policy of Akbar Khan. Macnaughten was murdered. The British troops began to retire. These were about 16,000 men in all. Most of them lost their lives. "The retreat became a rout, the rout a massacre." Excepting 120 persons who were prisoners of war in the hands of Akbar Khan, only one other person called Dr. Brydon reached Jalalabad safe and sound.

When the news of the disaster in Afghanistan readied India and England there was a demand for the recall of Lord Auckland. He was succeeded by Lord Ellenborough in February 1842. To begin with, he declared that the British Government would not endanger its armies and the Empire for the purpose of supporting the Tripartite Treaty. Only that course would be adopted which was dictated by military considerations. The reputation of the British army was to be re-established by the infliction of some signal and decisive blow upon the Afghans. When he got the news of the defeat of General Elphinstone and the surrender of Ghazni by Palmer, he issued orders for the evacuation of Kabul and Kandhar. Many military officers protested against the orders of Lord Ellenborough. The latter was able to maintain an empty show of consistency and also satisfy the universal demand for the decisive reconquest of Kabul and the recovery of the prisoners as a preliminary to withdrawal.

Pollock won a decisive victory over Akbar Khan near the Pass of Khurd Kabul. He entered Kabul and hoisted the British Flag at the Fort of Bala Hissar. Nott also joined him. In order to avenge the wrongs done to the Englishmen, the British army blew up the great Bazar of Kabul with the help of gunpowder. After that, the British forces left Afghanistan.

In October 1842, Lord Ellenborough made the following declaration: "The Governor-General will willingly recognise any Government approved by the Afghans themselves which shall appear desirous and capable of maintaining friendly relations with neighbouring States. Content with the limits nature appears to have assigned to its Empire, the Government of India will devote all its efforts to the establishment and maintenance of general peace, to the protection of the sovereigns, and chiefs, its allies and the prosperity and happiness of its own faithful subjects."

Dost Mohammad was released from Calcutta (now Kolkata) and allowed to go to Kabul. He remained on the throne of Kabul till 1863.

CRITICISM OF THE AFGHAN WAR I

1. The first Afghan War was a complete failure. Although 20,000 lives were sacrificed and 15 million sterling were spent, neither the Government of India nor the British Government gained anything. The same Dost Mohammad was restored to the throne of Kabul after the war. It was felt that there was no alternative to that. The Government of India did not maintain its control on any part of the territory of Afghanistan. The boast of Lord Ellenborough was that the victorious English army brought to India from Ghazni those gates of Somnath which were taken away by Mahmud of Ghazni during the 11th century. He claimed that "the insult of 800 years is at last avenged." According to Kaye, the proclamation "was past all denial. It was a folly too if the most senseless kind, for it was calculated to please none and to offend many." While the Hindus did not care for the gates which were found not to be genuine, the feelings of the Muslims of India were injured.

2. Kaye has made the following observations on the failure of the First Afghan War: "No failure, so total and so overwhelming as this is recorded in the pages of history. No lesson, so grand and impressive is to be found in all the annals of the world. It is upon record that this calamitous war cost natives of India whose stewards we are, some 15 millions of money. All this enormous burden fell upon the revenue of India, and the country for long years afterwards groaned under the weight." The British Government failed to have a friendly power on its borders. After an enormous waste of money and loss of human blood, the Englishmen left "every town and village of Afghanistan bristling with their enemies."

3. According to Trotter, the utter collapse of Auckland's "policy baneful, lawless and blundering as it was sprung mainly from the choice of generals ill-fitted for their work. Macnaughten's cheery trustfulness, Elphinstone's bodily and mental decay. Shelton's stupid willfulness, chronic dissensions between civil and military powers, Sale's withholding of timely succour; all conspired with Lord Auckland's half-measures and ill-timed economies to work out the dramatic nemesis of an enterprise begun in folly and wrongdoing." According to Kaye, the English policy

in Afghanistan was unrighteous and "the wisdom of our statesmen is but foolishness, and the might of our armies is but weakness, sitting heavily upon an unholy cause."

4. Critics point out that there was no justification for Lord Auckland to send the British armies to Afghanistan in November 1838. The British objection was to the siege of Herat by the Persians aided by the Russians. However, the siege was raised in September 1838. After the withdrawal of the Persian troops from Herat, there was absolutely no justification for British intervention in Afghanistan.

5. It is also pointed out that as an independent ruler of Afghans, Dost Mohammad had every right to enter into an alliance with Russia. The British Government had no right to protest against it. Moreover, the Russian agent was recalled from Kabul under pressure from the British Government. When all this was accomplished before the beginning of war, Lord Auckland must explain as to why he started it.

6. We have it on the authority of Alexander Burnes and others that Dost Mohammad was a capable ruler. Shah Shuja did not stand any comparison with him. It was folly on the part of Lord Auckland to decide to put Shah Shuja on the throne of Kabul in place of Dost Mohammad.

7. According to Kaye, Lord Auckland sent his troops to Afghanistan "in defence of every consideration of political and military expediency; and there were those who, arguing the matter on higher grounds than those of mere expediency, pronounced the certainty of its failure because there was a canker of injustice at the core. It was, indeed, an experiment on the forbearance alike of God and of man; and, therefore, though it might dawn in success it was sure to set in failure and disgrace. Great men like Duke of Wellington, Lord Wellesley, Sir Charles Metcalfe and others predicted the failure of the policy of Lord Auckland." According to the Duke of Wellington, "The consequence of crossing the Indus, once to settle a Government in Afghanistan, will be a perennial march into that country." According to Innes, the First Afghan War was probably "the most unqualified blunder committed in the whole history of the British in India."

8. According to Dr. V. A. Smith, "Lord Auckland had not the sense to see the truth and was led away by ill-chosen and unwise advisers to break treaties only six-years old, to bully the weak; to pursue a fantastic policy; to persist in that policy when the reasons for it, such as they were, had ceased to exist; to violate the principle of strategy; to throw thousands of lives by entrusting them to an incapable commander; and finally at last to acquiesce silently in the grabling of the documents submitted for the information of Parliament."

9. It is pointed out that the British Government had no right to pass their troops through Sind. Not only the British troops passed through Sind, that territory was also made the base of operations. It was this act which facilitated the annexation of Sind in the time of Lord Ellenborough.

LORD LAWRENCE'S POLICY OF MASTERLY INACTIVITY

The Government of India maintained friendly relation with Dost Mohammad from the time of his restoration to that of his death in 1863. When he died, he left 16 sons and as usual, a war of succession started among them and there was anarchy in the country. Sher Ali had been chosen by Dost Mohammad as his successor and he asked the Government of India to help him against the other rivals particularly Mohammad Afzal and Mohammad Azim Khan. It is true that Lawrence recognised Sher Ali as the ruler of Kabul, but he refused to meddle with the internal affairs of his Afghan neighbours. Lawrence remembered how earnestly in 1857, Dost Mohammad had requested him never to take part in the strife which would certainly break out among his sons, and let them fight it out by themselves and then acknowledge the winner as king.

The sympathies of the Viceroy were with Sher Ali, but to support him with arms and money would have been a costly and perilous mistake. It would have turned against Sher Ali the bulk of his best followers. It would have drawn the British into entanglements fatal to the financial well-being of India. It would have given Russia a decent pretext for meddling into Afghan affairs. John Lawrence knew the Afghans better than most men and better indeed, than any other Englishman of his day. He saw that strict neutrality was the best way to secure the confidence and good will of the Afghan nation. He respected the treaty of 1855 which bounded the Englishmen to respect the Afghan territories and never to interfere into them. Lawrence rebuked his Vakil at Kabul for making overtures of friendship with Azim Khan. When Afzal Khan became the master of Kabul, Lawrence refused to acknowledge him as the ruler of Herat and Kandhar. Lawrence wrote thus to Afzal Khan: "If your Highness is able to consolidate your Highness's power in Kabul, and is sincerely desirous of being a friend and ally of the British Government, I shall be ready to accept your Highness as such: but I cannot break the existing engagements with Amir Sher Ali Khan."

In his letters to the Home Government, Lawrence wrote again and again that he was determined to follow the policy explained above. His policy was that of "friendship towards the actual rulers combined with rigid abstention from interference in domestic feuds. By these means, we shall be enabled to maintain our influence in Afghanistan far more effectually than any advance of our troops — a contingency which could only be contemplated in the last resort, which would unite as one man the Afghan tribes against us, and which would paralyse our finances."

The fortunes of Sher Ali changed by 1868. Afzal Khan died in 1867 and Azim Khan, his successor, became a fugitive. In the eyes of the people of Afghanistan, Sher Ali became the rightful sovereign on account of his victories. Lawrence also changed his attitude towards him. He not only congratulated him on his victory, but also offered to help him to maintain the bonds of amity and goodwill. As far as possible, those bonds were also to be strengthened. A large number of muskets were handed over to Sher Ali. Lawrence informed Sher Ali that another sum of ₹6 lakhs would be offered to him as a token of the British desire to see "a strong, just and a merciful Government established throughout Afghanistan" Lawrence merely wanted "abiding confidence, sincerity and goodwill." He secured the permission of the Home Government to meet Sher Ali in person. However, Sher Ali and Lawrence could not meet as the latter left India a few months earlier than the arrival of the former in India.

According to Lawrence, "The Afghan is courageous, hardy, and independent, the country he lives in, is strong and sterile in a remarkable degree, extraordinarily adapted for guerrilla warfare; these people will never cease to resist so long as they have a hope of success and, when beaten down they have that kind of elasticity which will ever lead them to renew the struggle whenever opportunity of so doing may occur. If we enter Afghanistan, whether it be to punish the people for the alleged faults of their chiefs or to rectify our frontier, they will assuredly do all in their power to resist us. We want them as friends and not as enemies. In the latter category, they are extremely dangerous to us." Again, "So far as diplomacy and diplomacy alone is concerned, we should do all in our power to induce the Afghans to side with us. We ought not, in my mind, to make an offensive and defensive treaty with them — this had been for many years their desire; but the argument against it is that if we made such a treaty, we should be bound to restrain them from any attacks on their neighbours and to prevent such assaults on them, while it would be next to impossible for us to ascertain the merits of such complaints. We should thus constantly find ourselves in a position to please neither party and even bound to defend causes for which the Afghans were to blame."

Under the strong sway of Lawrence, the Firebrand Party had no chances of success. They might cry aloud, but no heed was given to them. Some of these important persons were Sir Bartle Frere and Sir Henry Rawlinson. Lawrence put aside all proposals for a forward policy in Kilat or Afghanistan as useless for the purpose of counteracting Russia and dangerous to the well-being of India herself. With the strongest natural frontier in the world, bordered by deserts and rugged hills, with the sea at Bombay (now Mumbai) and Karachi for bases, with a powerful army well-equipped in every way and ready to move by rail or road to any place, with a people well-governed, lightly taxed and generally contented, Lawrence knew that the Englishmen could afford to wait before the danger appeared from the north-west.

As regards the advance to Quetta Lawrence regarded it as a gross military blunder no less than a wanton menace to Afghanistan. When the Russians occupied Bokhara and other places in Central Asia, Lawrence kept his head cool and refused to find any danger in the latest advance to Russia. His view was that the true danger to the British rule in India lay nowhere across the frontier, but in India itself. According to him, a Russian invasion of India was not more likely and a good deal less feasible than a French invasion of England.

In January 1869, Lawrence wrote thus: "We object to any active, interference in the affairs of Afghanistan by the deputation of a high British officer with or without a contingent or by the forcible or amicable occupation of any post or tract in that country beyond our own frontier, inasmuch as we think such a measure would under present circumstances, engender irritation, defiance, and hatred in the minds of the Afghans, without in the least strengthening our power either for attack or defence. We think it impolitic and unwise to decrease any of the difficulties which would be entailed on Russia, if that power seriously thought of invading India as we should certainly decrease them if we left our own frontier and met her halfway in a different country, and possibly in the midst of a hostile or exasperated population. We foresee no limits to the extent which such a move might require, and protest against the necessity of having to impose additional taxation on the people of India, who are unwilling, as it is, to bear such pressure for measures which they can both understand and appreciate. And we think that the objects which we have at heart may be attained by an attitude of readiness and firmness on our frontier, and by giving her all our care and expanding; all our resources for the attainment of practical and sound ends, over which we can exercise an effective and immediate control."

Lawrence also made suggestions for the adoption of certain positive measures for the defence of the British Empire in India. He advocated a careful husbanding of all those resources, both moral and material, which would enable the Englishmen to meet a storm from within or without. He was also in favour of arriving at a clear and friendly understanding with Russia for the purpose of counteracting rumours and preventing the unnecessary alarms. He wanted the Russian Government to be told in firm but courteous language that it must not interfere into the affairs of Afghanistan or any other State on the frontier of India.

Lawrence was thoroughly convinced that the Afghans would be the enemies of those who interfered and friends of those who would not interfere except when they were attacked by an outsider. If such a policy were followed, the Afghans would offer a deadly opposition to a Russian advance. They might be tempted to join the Russians on the promise of sharing in the plunder of India. He believed the Afghans to be unwilling recipients of Russian messages. He would remonstrate directly with Russia himself and would like her to see that behind the remonstrance were iron clads and battalions.

If the general war were to break out and if Russia not having been stopped by British counter-operations in Europe, were to advance towards India, then on no account would he meet her in Afghanistan. That would be tantamount to wasting their resources in men and playing into the hands of the enemy. The Afghans would be bitterly hostile to such advance even though cowed with momentary submission. In that case, he would help them with money and material not men. Thus strengthened, they might hamper movements or retard the advance of the Russians. If the God of battles steels the hearts of British soldiers, the Russian invasion is to be repelled decisively. Such was the substance of Lawrence's Afghan policy. His policy was once described by Willie in the "Edinborough Review" as that of "masterly inactivity." This expression has both truth and untruth in it.

As regards the Russo-Afghan question, Lawrence wrote thus in January 1869: "Should a foreign power, such as Russia, ever seriously think of invading India from without, or what is more probable of stirring up the elements of disaffection or anarchy within it, our true policy, our strongest security, would then, we conceive, be found to lie in previous absence from entanglements at either Kabul, Kandhar, or any similar outpost; in full reliance on a compact, highly equipped and disciplined army stationed within our own territories, or on our own border, in the contentment if not in the attachment of the masses; in the contentment, if not in the sense of security of title of possession with which our whole policy is gradually imbuing the mind of the principal chiefs and the native aristocracy; in the construction of material works within British India which enhance the comfort of the people while they add to our political and military strength; in husbanding our finances and consolidating and multiplying our resources, in quiet preparation for all contingencies which no honest Indian statesman should disregard."

The question as to when it is right or prudent to recognise a de facto Government must depend upon the circumstances of each case. Moral recognition with a denial of material support can be of little value in the contest for a throne like that of Afghanistan. British recognition of Sher Ali did not prevent him from losing his kingdom. Although the Government of India recognised Azim Khan, that could not keep him on the throne of Kabul. To have intervened with material help, to maintain upon the throne a ruler not acknowledged by his people, was a dangerous policy forbidden by the provisions of the existing treaties.

It is to be noted that Lawrence's policy towards Afghanistan was continued by his successors, Lord Mayo and Lord Northbrook. When the same was reversed by Lord Lytton, disastrous consequences followed. Lord Mayo wrote to Lawrence in these words: "I believe that when you sent Sher Ali the money and arms last December, you laid the foundation of a policy which will be of the greatest use to us hereafter. I wish to continue it." Lord Northbrook preferred to resign rather than follow a different policy towards Afghanistan.

LORD MAYO (1869-72)

It has already been pointed out that Lord Lawrence had got the permission of the Home Government to have a meeting with Sher Ali. However, he could not meet the Amir because he left India earlier than the Amir could manage to visit this country. The meeting planned by Lawrence took place at Ambala in March 1869 when Sher Ali and Lord Mayo met together. At the meeting, Sher Ali asked for a definite treaty between the countries. He asked for a fixed annual subsidy, assistance in arms, recognition of his younger son, Abdullah Jan as heir to the throne in place of Yakub Khan and an assurance that the British Government would support him and his family on the Kabul throne. Lord Mayo found that it was not possible for him to oblige the Amir. He was determined to adhere to the policy of Lawrence regarding Afghanistan. Lord Mayo made it clear to Sher Ali that "under no circumstances would a British soldier ever cross his frontier to assist in coercing his rebellious subjects; that no European officers would be placed as residents in his cities; that no fixed subsidy or money allowance would be given for any named period; and that no treaty would be entered into obliging us under any circumstances to recognise him and his descendant rulers of Afghanistan." However, Lord Mayo promised to render Sher Ali "all the moral support in his power, to supply him at need with money, arms, ammunition and native workmen, and to correspond freely with him through the Commissioner of Peshwar and their native agents in Afghanistan". On his part, Sher Ali undertook to do what he could do to comply with wishes of the British Government on matters connected with trade. In spite of this, Sher Ali returned to Kabul with the conviction that he had nothing to fear and much to gain from the moral support of his English friends.

LORD NORTHBROOK (1872-76)

It is pointed out that the Afghan policy of Lord Northbrook was more masterly than that of Lawrence. In March 1874, Disraeli became the Prime Minister of England and Salisbury the Secretary of State for India. Both were in favour of having a British resident at Kabul. Lord Northbrook preferred to resign than submit to that. Lord Northbrook also maintained friendly relations with the Amir. He asked the permission of the Secretary of State for India to give help to Sher Ali in the form of money and war materials.

LORD LYTTON

When Lord Lytton was sent to India by the Conservative Government at home, he brought instructions for a more definite, equilateral and practical alliance with Sher Ali. He was given the authority to offer the Amir most of the terms he had asked for before. His younger son was to be recognised. Lytton was also allowed to give a written pledge by way of treaty or otherwise of British support in case of a foreign aggression. However, those terms were to be granted to Sher Ali only if he agreed to keep a British resident at Herat.

The Amir was asked to receive a mission, which was to announce the title of "Empress of India." Sher Ali refused to do so. Moreover, Sher Ali could not give any assurance.

Lytton held the view that between Great Britain and Russia, Afghanistan was like "an earthen pipkin between two iron pots." If the Amir remained a friend of Great Britain, by military strength of the latter "could be spread around him as a ring of iron, and if he became our enemy, it could break him as a reed." Lord Lytton was also in favour of the disintegration of Afghanistan so that that country might never become a stronger power.

Disraeli was a great imperialist and Lord Lytton carried out his policy with regard to Afghanistan. In June 1878 when the Congress of Berlin met, General Stoletoff started for Kabul. Sher Ali tried to stop him. He appealed and protested but both of them were ignored. The Czar of Russia threatened to make Sher Ali responsible if anything wrong went with the General. Sher Ali had to submit much against his own wishes. He was forced to enter into a treaty with Russia by which he agreed to maintain permanent and perpetual friendship between the two countries. When Lord Lytton came to know of the arrival of a Russian mission in Kabul, he asked Sher Ali to accept a British Envoy also, but Sher Ali refused to accept that demand. Although the Russian Envoy retired from Kabul under orders from his own Government, Lord Lytton failed to take advantage of the change in the situation. Both Lytton and Salisbury insisted that Sher Ali must have a British resident. According to Lord Lytton, "A tool in the hands of Russia, I will never allow him to become. Such a tool it would be my duty to break before it could be used."

If we examine the matter critically, it has to be admitted that Sher Ali was the ruler of an independent country and, therefore, he was not bound to accept a British resident. The British Government had no justification to insist on such a course. In spite of all this, Lytton insisted that Sher Ali must receive a British Envoy. The letter of Lord Lytton reached Kabul on 17th August 1878, when Abdullah Jan died. Sher Ali was so very unhappy that the reply to Lord Lytton's letter was delayed. Moreover, the Amir consulted the Russian Envoy who was at that time in Kabul. All this annoyed Lytton. He sent Sir Neville Chamberlain on a mission to Peshawar but the latter was not allowed to go beyond Ali Masjid. This was too much for the Government of Lord Lytton. An ultimatum was sent to the Amir in November 1878 demanding from him a full and suitable apology and his approval to accept a British Envoy. As no reply came the British forces were ordered to enter the territory of Afghanistan after the expiry of the ultimatum.

When his country was attacked, Sher Ali asked the Russian Government to help him. Unfortunately, he was betrayed by the Russian Government at that time. Finding himself helpless

Sher Ali ran away and died in February 1879. His son started negotiations with the British Government and concluded the famous Treaty of Gandmak in May 1879. Yakub Khan agreed to conduct his foreign relations with other States in accordance with the advice and wishes of the British Government. He was to accept a permanent resident at Kabul. He was to assign the Kurram Pass to the British Government. On their part, the British Government promised to support him on the throne and also help him with men, money and materials. The British troops were to be withdrawn from Afghanistan. According to P. E. Roberts, this treaty marked the apogee of Lytton's Afghan policy. According to Disraeli, the treaty gave a scientific and adequate frontier to the Government of India. However, this success was short-lived.

The people of Afghanistan could not tolerate the presence of a British resident at Kabul and an agent at Herat. Yakub's dependence on the British Government lowered him in the estimation of his countrymen. The new Amir was shifty, unstable and lacking in character. Major Cavagnari was not fit for the job given to him as the British resident. He was not the person who could handle a delicate situation. The result was that within less than a month and a half of his arrival in Kabul, Major Cavagnari was murdered by the Afghan troops. It is not possible to say as to how much Yakub was implicated in this matter but with the murder of Cavagnari the Treaty of Gandmak was ended. British forces were rushed into Afghanistan. The Afghans were defeated at Charasiab in October 1879. Yakub was sent to India as a State prisoner. The British Government decided to disintegrate Afghanistan.

However, at this stage Abdur Rahman appeared on the scene. He was one of the grandsons of Dost Mohammad, and had lived for many years as a pensioner of the Russian Government. In 1880 he thought of trying his luck and left for Afghanistan. Without wasting any time, Lytton decided to recognise Abdur Rahman as the Amir of Afghanistan, but before he could do that he was called back in 1880 on account of a change of Government at home.

Lord Ripon recognised Abdur Rahman as the Amir of Afghanistan on the condition that he was to have no political relations with any foreign power except England, and that the districts of Pishin and Sibi were to be retained by the British Government. The Amir was to get an annual subsidy from the Government of India. As the foreign affairs of Afghanistan were to be in the hands of the Government of India, it was not found necessary to insist on establishing a British resident at Kabul. This settlement lasted for a long time. The British Government maintained happiest relations with Afghanistan throughout the long reign of Abdur Rahman. When Ayyub Khan challenged the authority of Abdur Rahman, he was defeated at Maiwand and Kandhar. All British troops were withdrawn from Afghanistan by Lord Ripon.

CRITICISM OF THE SECOND AFGHAN WAR

Lord Lytton has been condemned for his policy towards Afghanistan which resulted in the disasters of the second Afghan War. According to some, it was a war of aggression which failed to achieve its object. According to Lord Hartington, Lytton was "The incarnation and embodiment of an Indian policy which is everything an Indian should not be." Gladstone condemned Lord Lytton's policy in these words: "We made war in error upon Afghanistan in 1838. To err is human and pardonable. But we have erred a second time on the same ground and with no better justification. This error has been repeated in the face of every warning conceivable and imaginable and in the face of an unequalled mass of authorities. It is proverbially said that history repeats itself, and there has rarely been an occasion in which there has been a nearer approach to identity than in the case of the present and former war. May Heaven avert the omen. May Heaven avert repetition of the calamity which befell our country in 1814."

Although Disraeli and Salisbury supported Lord Lytton in public, they did not approve of his sending Chamberlain. According to Disraeli, Lytton's policy, "is perfectly fitted to a state of affairs in which Russia was our assailant; but Russia is not our assailant. She has sneaked out of her hostile position with sincerity in my mind but scarcely with dignity, and if Lytton had only been quiet and obeyed my orders, I have no doubt that under the advice of Russia, Sher Ali would have been equally prudent."

According to Lord Salisbury, Lytton forced the hands of the Home Government from the very beginning. He thought only of India and dictated the foreign policy of the British Government in Europe and Turkey. He twice disobeyed orders, once in acting on the Khyber Pass and secondly in sending the mission contrary to the most express and repeated orders that he was not to do so till the British Government got an expected dispatch from Russia. Salisbury bitterly complained of the conduct of Lytton. According to Disraeli, Lytton was "told to wait until we had received an answer from Russia to our remonstrance. I was very strong on this, having good reasons for my opinion. He disobeyed us. I was assured by Lord Salisbury that under no circumstances was the Khyber Pass to be attempted. Nothing would have induced me to consent to such a step. He was told to send the mission by Kandhar. He has sent it by the Khyber."

Whatever the criticism of the Second Afghan War it cannot be maintained that the war was absolutely without any result. Sher Ali who was inclined towards Russia was turned out and in his place was seated Abdur Rahman who was friendly inclined towards the Government of India. The influence of Russia at Kabul was checked. The Khan of Kelat came under the control of the British Government. The Province of Baluchistan was created. Quetta also remained in the hands of the British Government.

In 1884, the Russians occupied Merv. This was not liked by the British Government. In March 1885, there took place the famous Panjdeh incident. There was a clash between Russian and Afghan troops. There was an immediate danger of war. However, the situation was saved by the efforts of Lord Dufferin, the Viceroy of India. Abdur Rahman also behaved in a restrained manner. To begin with, Gladstone described the Russian attack on Panjdeh as an unprovoked aggression. He called up the reserves and ordered military preparation. However, he agreed to refer the matter to the arbitration of King of Denmark. The result was that the war was averted. The Russians retained Panjdeh but Amir Abdur Rahman got Sul Faqir pass. The boundary line between Russia and Afghanistan was settled later on and ratified in July 1887.

In 1901, Abdur Rahman died and he was succeeded by Habib Ullah. For some time, the relations between the Government of India and the new Amir were not cordial. However, in March 1905, the misunderstanding was removed and the Amir began to draw his subsidy. The Amir was suspected of leanings towards Russia. In 1907, the famous Anglo-Russian Convention was held in which Russia recognised that Afghanistan was not within the sphere of her influence. Russia also agreed to conduct her relations with Afghanistan through the Government of India. However, these provisions were not satisfied by the Amir. In 1910, Habib Ullah was murdered. His people did not approve of his policy in westernising his countrymen.

His son Aman Ullah was not friendly inclined towards the British Government. This led to the third Afghan War. Aman Ullah entered the British territory and his troops began to destroy whatever came in their way. Although there were defeats in the beginning, the Indian army succeeded in beating back the invaders. With the treaty of Rawalpindi ended the Third Afghan War. This treaty was signed in August 1919. Another treaty was made in, November 1921. The net result of these two treaties was that Afghanistan became completely free in her foreign affairs. The British Government was not to pay any subsidy to Afghanistan. In 1922, an Afghanistan Minister was appointed in London and a British Minister at Kabul.

The people of Afghanistan resented the reforms of Aman Ullah and consequently he was forced to abdicate. Power fell into the hands of Bachha Sakka for some time. However, order was restored by Mohammad Nadir Shah who became the King of Afghanistan. The Government of India did not interfere into the internal affairs of Afghanistan whenever there was trouble in that country.

REVIEW QUESTIONS

1. Write an essay on Anglo-Afghan relations.
2. Bring out the relations of the Afghans with the Government of India.
3. Discuss the causes and effects of the Afghan Wars.
4. How did the Afghan Wars start? Provide critical comments on the Afghan Wars.
5. Sketch the policy of masterly inactivity of Lord Lawrence.
6. Evaluate the roles of Lord Mayo, Lord Northbrook and Lord Litton with regard to Anglo-Afghan relations.
7. What was the British policy towards Afghanistan? Explain.

SUGGESTED READINGS

Adye, J.M.: *Indian Frontier Policy* (1897).
Amir Abdur Rahman: *Autobiography*.
Andrews, C.F.: *Our Scientific Frontier*.
Bellow, H. W.: *North-West Frontier and Afghanistan*.
Bruge, R.I.: *The Forward Policy and its Results* (1900).
Durand: *The First Afghan War and its Causes* (1879).
Hanna, H.B.: *The Second Afghan War*.
Havelock, H.: *Narrative of the War in Afghanistan* (1840).
Kaye, J.W.: *History of the War in Afghanistan*.
Wheeler, S.: *The Ameer Abdul Rahman* (1895).
Woodruff, Philip: *The Man Who Ruled India*.
Wyllie, J.W.S.: *Essays on the External Policy of India* (1875).

31 The North-Western Frontier Policy

LEARNING OBJECTIVES

- Discuss the North-Western Frontier Policy of the British
- Know the effects of the North-Western Frontier Policy on India

It is a matter of history that the North-Western Frontier has given a lot of trouble to the people of India. The Sakas, Hunas, the Kushans, the Pathans and the Mughals entered India through the North-Western Frontier. To begin with, the British Government was not directly concerned with the North-Western Frontier because Punjab was controlled by the Sikhs and Sind by the Amirs. However, after the annexation of Sind in 1843 and the Punjab in 1849, the problem really came to the forefront. The Russian advances in Central Asia and their attempts to woo Afghanistan made the British Government nervous about the safety of India. The British Government was not prepared to allow Russia to secure any influence in that region. It was also interested in maintaining law and order in the areas adjacent to the North-Western Frontier. The Sind frontier extending for about 150 miles from Kasmore to the Hala mountains, was exposed to the attacks of the Bugtis, Dombkis and Jakranis from the Kachchi region. The Punjab frontier was ill-defined and unscientific. There was a vast tribal area in between the administrative frontier of India and Afghanistan over which no one had any real control. There was no law as such. Might was right and the rifle settled most of the disputes.

The problem of the North-Western Frontier was a difficult one and the British were not able to evolve any definite policy. Whatever was done was mostly ad hoc in nature and kept on changing from time to time. It was found that social, political and geographical factors were not the same all along the North-Western Frontier and hence it was not possible to have one policy for the entire frontier. The Sind frontier was much more accessible, politically much more integrated and under the effective control of their Maliks and hence posed a lesser problem than the Punjab frontier which was long, mountainous and ill-defined. The Pathan tribes living there were too intractable and freedom loving to accept the authority of the Maliks. No wonder, there came into existence two schools of frontier administration known as the "Sandeman System" and the "Close Border System." The Sandeman System applied to Baluchistan and the Close Border System to the Punjab Frontier.

SIND FRONTIER

Experience showed that the policy of Sir Charles Napier in suppressing the Baluchi tribes by ruthless force was not a success. His building of forts along the Sind frontier and the posting of detachments of the troops at certain vulnerable points did not prove to be very effective. No wonder, his policy was reversed by Major John Jacob who succeeded him in Sind. The view of Jacob was that the Baluchi tribes could be softened if the benefits of Western civilisation could be extended to them. With that object in view, he started a vigorous campaign for "pushing back the desert" by providing facilities for widespread cultivation of land and extensive irrigation. Jacob also introduced the system of constant patrolling of the frontier instead of keeping the troops stationary at certain points. The Baluchi tribes had an aristocratic and oligarchical form of Government, and hence the Government

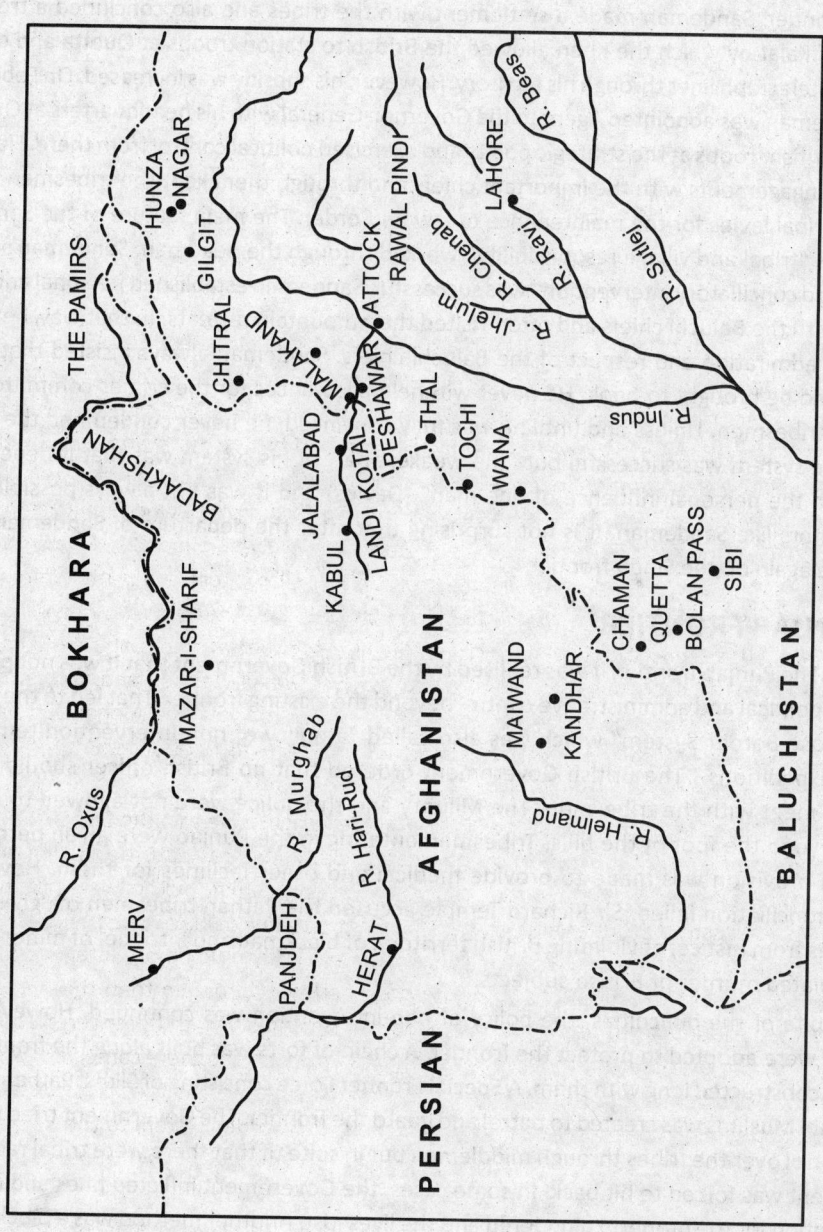

of India did not find much difficulty in controlling them through their chiefs. As the Khan of Kalat exercised a substantial amount of control over those tribes, the British Government followed a policy of strengthening his influence. By the treaty of 1854, the Khan of Kalat was given an annual subsidy of ₹50,000 to control the tribes and maintain law and order. In return, the Khan was required not to negotiate with any other power without the consent of the British Government. The Khan of Kalat managed to raise an army of his own which was not liked by the other Chiefs. That led to a civil war. The result was that the British border became unsafe once again.

It was at this time that the Government of India sent Sandeman to restore law and order on the Sind frontier. Sandeman made a settlement with the tribes and also concluded a treaty with the Khan of Kalat by which the Khan allowed the British to station troops at Quetta and construct railway and telegraph lines through his territory. However, his subsidy was increased. On February 21, 1877, Sandeman was appointed Agent to the Governor-General with his headquarters at Quetta. He stationed British troops at the strategic points and exercised political control from there. He entered into close engagements with the important chiefs and through them kept the tribesmen in check. He raised tribal levies for the maintenance of law and order. The main feature of the Sandeman's System was "tribal and village responsibility" worked through the headman. Sandeman's policy of "friendly and conciliatory intervention" was successful. Sandeman established personal and friendly relations with the Baluchi chiefs and often visited their mountain retreats. In that way, he was able to win the admiration and respect of the Baluchi chiefs. Sandeman always insisted that only the guilty should be brought to book. He never withheld allowances for the crimes committed by the individual tribesmen. Unless and until he was fully convinced, he never condemned the action of a tribe. The system was successful but "the weakest part of his system was that it depended too much upon the personal influence of one man" (Davies) and it was not always possible to have administrators like Sandeman. It is not surprising that after the departure of Sandeman, trouble arose once again on the Sindh frontier.

THE PUNJAB FRONTIER

As regards the Punjab frontier, it was realised by the British Government that it was not possible to extend its political and administrative control beyond the existing frontier. That led to the evolution of the "Close Border System" which was also called "a policy of non-intervention tempered by punitive expeditions." The British Government ordered that no British officer should cross the border or meet with the tribesmen. The Military and the police were not allowed to chase the raiders beyond the foot of the hills. Tribesmen entering in the Punjab were given permission to trade and provision was made to provide medical and other facilities for them. However, the policy of conciliation failed. Sir Richard Temple accused the Pathan tribesmen of "giving asylum to fugitives from justice, of violating British territory, of blackmail and intrigue, of minor robberies and of isolated murder of British subjects."

In spite of the difficulties, the policy of non-intervention was continued. However, certain measures were adopted to protect the frontier. A chain of forts was built along the frontier. Roads were also constructed long with them. A Special Frontier Force consisting of Sikhs, Pathans, Gorkhas and Punjabi Muslims was created to patrol and guard the frontier. The Government tried to exercise some control over the tribes through middlemen but in spite of that there were tribal raids and the Government was forced to hit back. In some cases, the Government inflicted fines and demanded compensation for the property plundered and the lives lost. Another method was a blockade of the tribes. Sometimes, military expeditions were sent to destroy shops and houses of the tribesmen and extract fines from them. However, it cannot be denied that this policy of "butcher and bolt" was not successful. It left behind "a legacy of hatred and contempt."

THE FORWARD POLICY

The Government of India followed what is known as the Forward Policy in the time of Lord Lytton. That resulted in the Second Afghan War. The failure of the second Afghan War discredited the Forward Policy for some time, but the same was revived during the Viceroyalty of Lord Lansdowne (1888-94). A strategic railway was completed up to the Bolan Pass. A general activity was evident along the frontier line from Quetta to Kashmir. In 1889, certain charges were brought against the Maharaja of Kashmir and the Government of India took over the administration of that State. A British officer was sent to Gilgit in 1889. In 1892, the Chief of Chitral died, and he was succeeded by his son. The Government of India sent Dr. Robertson to Chitral in 1893 as its envoy. The Government of India also sent Sir Mortimer Durand to Afghanistan, and a satisfactory settlement was arrived at between the two countries. Abdur Rahman, the Amir of Afghanistan, agreed not to interfere with the Afridis, Waziris and other frontier tribes. The boundary line was to be demarcated by the Afghan and British Commissioners. Some districts were ceded to Abdul Rahman and he agreed not to interfere in Swat, Bajur, Dir and Chitral. He also gave up his claims to the railway station at Chaman. The Government of India agreed not to raise any objection to the purchase and import of ammunitions of war by the Amir of Afghanistan. The annual subsidy was raised from 12 lakhs to 18 lakhs. It cannot be denied that the Durand Agreement of 1893 led to the extension of British influence in the tribal area.

The Forward Policy of Lord Lansdowne was continued by Lord Elgin (1894-1899). A British agency had been established at Gilgit with an outpost in Chitral at Mastuj. In January 1895, the ruler of Chitral was assassinated. When Dr. Robertson, the British Agent at Gilgit, went to Chitral, he and his small force were besieged by the rebellious chiefs. A British force was sent from Gilgit to give relief and it succeeded in doing so. Lord Elgin wanted to retain Chitral but he was overruled by the Home Government. However, under the Unionist Government of Lord Salisbury, the British Government decided not only to retain Chitral but also ordered the construction of a military road from Chitral to the frontier with garrisons to protect it.

The outbreak of frontier war of 1897-98 was due to many causes. The tribesmen did not like the intervention of the British Government in Chitral. They also did not like the demarcation of the Durand Line and the extension of British influence over the Sherani country, the Samana, the Kurrum valley, Waziristan and Chitral. The preaching of the Mullahs and the rumours of the British intention to annex the tribal territory also added to the trouble. The people of Swat attacked the fortified posts at Chakdara and Malakand. The Afridis attacked the posts on the Samana Ridge. However, the Malakand Field Force, commanded by Sir Bindon Blood relieved Chakdara and pushed on the campaign vigorously, compelling the Mohmands to submit in January 1898. Sir William Lockhart commanded the force against the Afridis and they submitted in 1898.

Lord Curzon gave up the forward policy and evolved a new policy of his own. He gradually withdrew a large number of troops from the forward areas such as the Khyber Pass, the Kurram Valley, Waziristan and the trible country generally. Only in exceptional cases isolated posts such as Malakand and Dargai were retained and fortified. He replaced regular troops by tribal levies which were trained and commanded by British officers. The 4,000 regular troops stationed at the Khyber Pass were withdrawn and were replaced by the Khyber Rifles consisting of Afridis and other tribes. The regulars were replaced in the Samana range and the Kurram Valley by Samana

Rifles, and the Kurram militia. The Tochi Valley was placed in charge of the North Waziristan Militia. The Gomal Pass was put under the charge of South Waziristan Militia. While making these arrangements, Lord Curzon acted on the principle of making the tribesmen themselves responsible for the maintenance of order. Lord Curzon also concentrated a large number of troops at strategic points in British territory so that they could be easily available for crushing any tribal rising. Curzon also started the construction of roads, bridges and railroads connecting the tribal area with the settled districts. Strategic railways were built up to Dargai, Jamrud, at the entrance of the Khyber Pass and Thal, the gate of the Kurrum Valley. Lord Curzon tried to impress upon the tribesmen that while their independence would be respected, their raids into British territory would not be tolerated. It is admitted that the policy of Curzon was successful on the whole. It is clear from the fact that "with the exception of the blockade of the Mahsud Waziris, in 1901, the fierce conflicts of 1897-8 were followed by ten years of peace." It may also be remembered that Lord Curzon was responsible for the creation of the new province known as the North-West Frontier Province. This he did by joining the trans-Indus districts of the Punjab with the political charges of the Malakand, the Khyber, the Kurram, Tochi and Wana. It is pointed out that by his new policy, Curzon was able to cut down expenditure on the defence of the North-Western Frontier. "In seven years, he only spent £248,000 on military movements on the North-West Frontier as against 4,584,000 during the years 1894-98.

It is pointed out that the policy of Curzon failed during the Afghan War of 1919. The Tribal Militia failed to check the tribesmen. The Khyber Militia disappeared. The Waziri Militia either mutinied or deserted. However, the occupation of Dakka by British troops and the defeat of General Nadir Khan compelled the ruler of Afghanistan to sue for peace. Operations were vigorously conducted against the Waziris and Mahsuds. The British forces entered into the heart of Mahsud territory and established a camp at Ladha. The occupation of the Mahsud territory continued up to 1923-24.

A new frontier policy was tried in Waziristan. The tribal levies were replaced by Khassadars and scouts. The Khassadars had no British officers and no uniforms. They were also required to provide their own rifles. The difference between the tribal levies and Khassadars was that while the tribal levies were officered and trained by British officers and provided with rifles, the Khassadars had no British officers and had to provide their own rifles. The advantage of the system was that the Khassadars were paid only if they protected the caravans and performed other police duties and if they deserted, they lost their pay but the Government did not lose their rifles or the lives of their officers, whether Indian or British. The result was that while regular troops garrisoned Razmak, the Khassadars and irregulars maintained law and order. This policy was continued during the rest of the period of British Rule in India. It cannot be denied that it was no solution of the problem. There was practically no peace on the frontier. There was sometimes peace and sometimes war. Probably, the whole approach to the problem was wrong.

REVIEW QUESTIONS

1. Write an essay on the North-Western Frontier Policy.
2. The North-Western Frontier has given a lot of trouble to the people of India. Comment.
3. Write in brief about the Sind Frontier Policy.
4. Discuss the features of the Forward Policy of the North-Western Frontier. What was its impact on the people of India?

5. Write short notes on the following:
   (a) Sind Frontier Policy
   (b) Punjab Frontier Policy
   (c) Forward Policy
6. Lord Curzon gave up the Forward policy and evolved a new policy of his own. Comment.

SUGGESTED READINGS

Adye, J.M.: *Indian Frontier Policy,* 1897.
Andrews, C.F.: *Our Scientific Frontier.*
Bellow: *North-West Frontier and Afghanistan.*
Bruge, R.I.: *The Forward Policy and its Results.*
Davies: *The Problem of the North-West Frontier,* 1932.
Holdich, Sir T.: *The Gates of India.*
Report of the North-West Frontier Committee (Bray Committee), 1921.

32   The Indian States

LEARNING OBJECTIVES

- Describe the three stages of the British relations with the Indian states till the introduction of the reforms of 1919
- Discuss the British policies towards the development of Indian states
- Give an account of accession of India states in Indian Union
- Know about integration, democratisation and reorganisation of the states

Sir William Lee-Warner, in his famous book called *The Native States of India*, pointed out three epochs in British relations with the Indian States till the introduction of the Reforms of 1919. During the first period, the English East India Company followed the "policy of the ring-fence" and this period lasted from 1757 to 1813. The second period lasted from 1813 to 1858 and was called by him by the name of "Subordinate Isolation". The third period extended from 1858 to 1919 and was designated by him as the period of "Subordinate Union".

RING-FENCE POLICY (1757-1813)

According to Lee-Warner during this period, "The British endeavoured as far as possible to live within a Ring-Fence, and beyond that they avoided intercourse with the chiefs." The English East India Company at that time was not very strong. It was not in a position to interfere into the internal affairs of the Indian States. The Company had neither the strength nor the resources to defeat the Indian States. It was only one of the important powers in India. The other powers were the Marathas, the French, the Nizam, and the Sultan of Mysore. The result of this situation was that whenever the Company entered into any treaty with an Indian State, it did so on the basis of equality and reciprocity.

On the whole, the Company followed a policy of non-intervention in the affairs of the States. It was laid down in Pitt's India Act of 1784 that the Home Government did not approve of the intervention of her officers in India into the internal affairs of the Indian States. However, it cannot be denied that on certain occasions the Company had to interfere in the affairs of the Indian States. Thus, Warren Hastings fought the First Maratha War and the Second Mysore War. Likewise, Lord Cornwallis fought the Third Mysore War and annexed half of its territory. Lord Wellesley had to fight the Fourth Mysore War, and the Second Maratha War. He also made Hyderabad and Oudh enter into subsidiary alliances with the Company. Lord Minto made the treaty of Amritsar in 1809 with Maharaja Ranjit Singh, and granted protection to the Cis-Sutlej States whose very existence was being threatened by Ranjit Singh.

About this period, Lee-Warner says: "When the events of these 56 busy years are called to mind, the palpable anxiety of the Company to end both annexation and alliances stands out in the dealest relief. There is the battle of Buxar in 1764 when Oudh lay at the feet of Major Munro, but was not annexed; the Rohilla War after which Warren Hastings conquered and conferred territories on the Wazir of Oudh; the First Maratha War which closed in the restitution of Bassein and the restoration of the status quo by the treaty of Salbai (1782); and finally four Mysore Wars...from which the Allies of the British derived the main advantage whilst the former Hindu dynasty of Mysore was gratuitously raised from the ashes of Hyder Ali's and Tippo's dominions."

About this period, Panikkar points out two things in particular regarding the relations of the English Company with the Indian States. In the first place, "all the treaties, except that with Mysore, are negotiated on a basis of equality. The Company did not claim any paramountcy or imperial authority and the treaties themselves merely show that at least in the case of those States which were not conquered, there was a spirit of reciprocity." Secondly, "each of these treaties guarantees in a most solemn manner the absolute authority of the ruler over his subjects and most unequivocally repudiates any claim to intervene in the affairs of the State." (*The Evolution of British Policy towards Indian States*, 1774-1858.)

POLICY OF SUBORDINATE ISOLATION (1813-58)

During this period, the Company made all the Indian States subordinate to itself by making them enter into subsidiary alliances with itself. The Indian States were made to accept the Company as the paramount power in the country. They were to give either money or enough of territory so that the Company might be able to keep a contingent force either in the State itself or outside the State for its protection. The State joining the subsidiary alliance had to turn out all the non-English and European employees from its service. It was not to conduct any foreign relations except through the British Government. In all its disputes with other powers, the State was to recognise the British Government as the arbitrator. The British Government, in return for the above, was to guarantee the territorial integrity of the State.

Writing about the subsidiary system, Sir Thomas Munro remarked that "it is the natural tendency to render the Government of every country in which it exists weak and oppressive, to extinguish all honourable spirits among the higher grades of society, to degrade and impoverish the whole people." The London Times wrote thus in 1853. "It has been said that we give these Princes without responsibility. Our hand of iron maintains them on the throne despite their imbecility, their vices and their crimes. The result is chronic anarchy under which the revenues of the court are dissipated between mercenaries of the camp and the minions of the court. The theory seems in fact admitted that the Government is not for the people, but the people for the King and that so long as we secure from the King his sinecure loyalty, we discharge all the duty that we as sovereigns of India owe to his subjects who are virtually ours."

Lord Hastings brought into the subsidiary system, 145 States in Central India, 145 States in Kathiawar and 20 in Rajputana. He enunciated a policy of complete subordination and isolation, but he was against the annexation of the Indian States. His successors did not share his views and annexed Sind, the Punjab, Oudh, and other minor States. The opinion of Lord Dalhousie was that Lord Hastings was wrong in propping up minor principalities and the only way of preventing misrule in the States was to annex them. He evolved the theory of constructive feudalism and enunciated the doctrine of lapse and escheat by which he annexed Satara, Nagpur, Tanjore, Jaipur and Jhansi.

The doctrine of lapse implied that on the failure of the natural heirs, the sovereignty of the independent States, of those created by the British Government or held on a subordinate tenure, lapsed to the Paramount Power. The British Government did not acknowledge the right of those States to adopt heirs, although such a practice had existed for a long time. However, the doctrine of lapse did not apply to "protected allies." Referring to the abuses in the administration of some of the Indian States, Lord Dalhousie declared that "the British Government in the exercise of a wise and sound policy is bound not to put aside or neglect such rightful opportunities of acquiring territory or revenue as may from time to time present themselves whether they arise from the lapse of subordinate States by the failure of all heirs of every description whatsoever, or from the failure of natural heirs where succession can be sustained only by the sanction of the Government being given to the ceremony of adoption, according to Hindu law. The Government is bound, in duty as well as policy, to act on every such occasion with the purest integrity, and in the most scrupulous observance of good faith. Whenever even a shadow of doubt can be shown, the claims should at once be abandoned."

According to G. N. Singh, the two policies of annexation and subsidiary alliances must share the blame to a large extent for the Mutiny of 1857.

Regarding the second period, Colonel Luard says: "This period is by far the most important in the history of the relationship of the States to the British Government. It witnessed their metamorphosis from, a congeries of quasi-independent units, some openly hostile, most at heart antagonistic, and all doubtful and resentful...step by step sorely against its will the Company had been driven by inexorable fate, to abandon its policy of Ring-Fence and non-interference, and so pass through the system of subordinate alliance to the wise and generous policy of co-operative partnership which holds at the present day." (*Cambridge History of India*, Vol. V.)

POLICY OF SUBORDINATE UNION

The Mutiny was a turning point in the history of relations of the Government of India with the Indian States. It was admitted on all hands that one of the important causes of the Mutiny was Dalhousie's policy of wholesale annexation of the Indian States on one pretext or the other. In order to remedy the state of affairs, it was considered necessary to make a change in the policy of the Government of India with regard to the Indian States. Consequently, it was declared in the Queen's Proclamation of 1858 that the British Government in future would not annex the Indian States. "We hereby announce to the Native Princes of India that all treaties and engagements made with them by or under the authority of the Honourable East India Company are by us accepted and will be scrupulously maintained, and we look for the like observance on their part. We desire no extension of our present territorial possessions. We shall respect the Rights, Dignity and Honour of the Native Princes as our own. The Indian rulers were to be given the right of adoption in case they had no son to succeed them. No State was to be annexed on the ground that the ruler had no son. The Indian States were to be given Sanads and we are told that 160 Sanads were issued to the Indian rulers. They were assured that no harm would be done to them "so long as your House is loyal to the Crown and faithful to the conditions of the treaties, grants and engagements which record its application to the British Government." But before granting Sanads, Lord Canning made it clear that the Sanads "will not debar the Government of India from stepping in to set right such serious abuses in a native Government as may threaten any part of the country with anarchy or disturbance, nor from reason to do so ... Neither will this assurance diminish our right to visit a State with the highest penalties, even confiscation, in the even disloyalty, or flagrant breach of engagement." In the words of Prof. Dodwell, "The significance of these Sanads was that the States were to be perpetuated as an integral part of the Indian system. They were no longer mere transitory Governments awaiting political changes which would permit and justify their gradual extinction. The princes were no longer looked upon as rulers driven by force into an unequal alliance. They had become members of the Empire, and the new position was accepted not unwillingly." (*Cambridge History of India*, Vol. VI.) It was declared that the treaties which had been made by the Company with the Indian States were to continue.

The Mutiny had embittered the relations of the Government of India with the people of India. The Britishers were not prepared to forget the cold-blooded murders of the Europeans during the Mutiny days and the same was equally true of the Indians. Under the circumstances, the British Government in India looked to some allies in the country against the people of India. This they could find among the Indian princes. No wonder, the old policy of jealousy and suspicion against the Indian States was given up. Instead of keeping them separate, the British Government tried to bring them together. But this does not mean that the Indian States were given more independence of action than they enjoyed before. It is to be noted that on many occasions the British Government made declarations of their paramountcy over the Indian States.

BRITISH PARAMOUNTCY IN INDIA

Lord Canning declared in 1858: "The Crown of England stands forth the unquestioned ruler and paramount power in all India. There is a reality in the sovereignty of England which has never existed before and which is not felt but eagerly acknowledged by the chiefs." Similar statements were made by Lord Mayo, Lord Lytton, Lord Lansdowne, Lord Minto and Lord Reading. In 1909, Lord Minto said: "Our policy is with rare exceptions one of non-interference in the internal affairs of native States. But in guaranteeing their internal independence and in undertaking their protection against external aggression, it naturally follows that the Imperial Council had assumed a certain degree of responsibility for the general soundness of their administration and would not consent to incur the reproach of being indirect instrument of misrule. There are also certain matters in which it is necessary for the Government of India to safeguard the interests of the community as a whole as well as those of the Paramount Power, such as railways, telegraphs and other Services of an imperial character. But the relationship of the Supreme Government to the States is one of sovereignty."

Lord Reading wrote thus to the Nizam of Hyderabad in March 1926: "The sovereignty of the British Crown is supreme in India and therefore no ruler of an Indian State can justifiably claim to negotiate with the British Government on an equal footing. Its supremacy is not based only on treaties and engagements but exists independently of them and quite apart from its prerogative in matters relating to foreign power and policies. It is the right and duty of the British Government, while scrupulously respecting all treaties and engagements with the Indian States, to preserve peace and good order. I remind your Exalted Highness that the ruler of Hyderabad along with other rulers received in 1868, a Sanad declaratory of the British Government's desire for perpetuation of His House and Government subject to the continued loyalty to the Crown; and no succession to the Masand of Hyderabad is valid unless it is recognised by His Majesty King Emperor; and that the British Government is the only arbitrator in a disputed succession... . The varying degrees of internal sovereignty which the rulers enjoy are, all subject to the due exercise by the paramountcy of this responsibility."

THE GAZETTE NOTIFICATION NUMBER

1700-E dated August 21 1891, described the position of the Indian States in these words; "The principles of international law have no bearing upon the relations between the Government of India as representing the Queen Empress on the one hand and the native States under the sovereignty of Her Majesty on the other. The paramount Supremacy of the former presupposes and implies the subordination of the other." A resolution of the Government in 1920 ran thus: "When in the opinion of the Governor General, the question arises of depriving a ruler of an important State temporarily or permanently of any of the rights, dignities, powers or privileges to which he, as a ruler, is entitled, or debarring a successor, heir apparent or any other member of the family of such a ruler, who according to law and custom of his State is entitled to succeed, the Governor General will appoint a

Commission of inquiry to investigate the facts of the case and offer advice unless such ruler desires that a Commission shall not be appointed. In case the ruler did not agree to the appointment of a Commission, his fate was doomed."

Regarding the nature of the relationship between the Paramount Power and the Indian States, the Butler Committee stated that that was "a living, growing relationship shaped by circumstances and policy, which is the mixture of history, theory and modern fact," An official announcement of 1877 stated that "Paramountcy is a thing of gradual growth...shaped partly by conquest, partly by treaty and partly by usage...".

The Government of India emphasised their supremacy on many other occasions. In 1876, Queen Victoria assumed the title of Kaiser-i-Hind after the death of the last Mughal Emperor, Bahadur Shah II. On this occasion, Lord Lytton held a Durbar at Delhi and the rulers of all the Indian States were made to attend this Durbar. It is stated that the rulers of the big States protested against the lowering of their status and dignity but they were made to swear a perpetual allegiance to the British Crown and forego their claim to be treated according to the treaties and engagements entered into by them with the Company.

It is to be noted that the British Government emphasised the subordinate position of the Indian States, although the latter were guaranteed their perpetual existence. During this period, the Governor-General-in-Council through the Political Department of the Government of India, exercised complete control over the Indian States. As a matter of fact, the Indian princes had absolutely no independence of action. They were under the control of the Residents. The resident *watched* the British interests in the State and offered friendly advice to the prince. He acted as the channel of communication between the State and the Paramount Power. As a matter of fact, he was the real ruler and master of the prince. According to Panikkar, "All those who have direct experience of Indian States know that the whisper of the Residency is the thunder of the State and there is not matter on which the resident does not feel qualified to give his advice." His advice was usually an order or a command.

The British Government claimed right to control the use and grant of all titles, honour, salutes and matters of precedent. The ruler could not accept foreign title without the consent of the British Government. He could not confer any titles. The number of salutes to which a prince was entitled was fixed by the British Government.

The Paramount Power asserted and exercised the right of deposing princes or forcing them to abdicate in certain circumstances as in the case of Baroda and Manipur. It is desirable to say a few words about these two cases.

In the case of Baroda, on the death of his brother in 1870, Mulhar Rao Gaikwar succeeded to the throne of Baroda. The administration of the State deteriorated. In 1874, the Government of India appointed a Commission of Inquiry to investigate into the matter and suggested reforms. The ruler protested. The reply of the Government of India was given in these words:

"This intervention although amply justified by the language of treaties, rests also on other foundations. Your Highness has justly observed that 'the British Government is undoubtedly the Paramount Power in India, and the existence and prosperity of the Native States depends upon its fostering favour and benign protection.' This is especially true of the Baroda State, both because of its geographical position intermixed with British territory, and also because a subsidiary force of British troops is maintained for the defence of the State, the protection of the person of its ruler, and the enforcement of his legitimate authority.

"My friend, I cannot consent to employ British troops to protect anyone in a course of wrong-doing, misrule on the part of a government which is upheld by the British power is misrule in the responsibility for which the British Government becomes in measure involved. It becomes therefore not only the right but the positive duty of the British Government to see that the administration of a State in such a condition is reformed, and that gross abuses are removed.

"It has never been the wish of the British Government to interfere in the details of the Baroda administration, nor is it my desire to do so now. The immediate responsibility for the Government of the State rests, and must continue to rest upon the Gaikwar for the time being. He has been acknowledged as the sovereign of Baroda, and he is responsible for exercising his sovereign powers with proper regard to his duties and obligations alike to the British Government and to his subjects. If these obligations be not fulfilled, if gross misgovernment be permitted, if substantial justice be not done to the subject of the Baroda State, if life and property be not protected, or if the general welfare of the country and people be persistently neglected, the British Government will assuredly intervene in the manner which in its judgment may be best calculated to remove these evils and to secure good Government. Such timely intervention, indeed, to prevent misgovernment culminating in the ruin of the State is no less an act of friendship to the Gaikwar himself than a duty to his subjects."

The Commission came to the conclusion that there were many abuses in the administration of the country. The Government of India gave a warning to the ruler to introduce certain reforms within 18 months, failing which he would be removed from his throne. At this time, the Viceroy got the information that the ruler had tried to poison the Resident. He was tried by a Commission, but there was no unanimous decision. In spite of this, the Government of India deposed him. Another young member of the Gaikwar family was put on the throne.

In the case of Manipur (1891), the Raja of Manipur was driven out of his State by the rebellion whose leader was his brother called Senapati. The Yuvraj was absent from the States but soon returned and took charge of the Government. The Government of India was not willing to restore the Raja of Manipur as he appeared to be unfit for ruling.

While the Government of India recognised the succession of the Yuvraj, it wanted to remove the Senapati from the State. For that purpose, the Chief Commissioner of Assam went to Manipur, but was captured and beheaded. This could not be tolerated by the Government of India. Armies were rushed into the State. The Yuvraj and the Senapati were arrested, tried for murder and rebellion and executed. The Government of India declared in 1891 that "every succession must be recognised by the British Government and no succession is valid until recognition has been given." The following principles were laid down in the Manipur case:—

1. The Government of India have the undoubted right to settle the succession and intervene in the case of rebellion against the chief.
2. Principles of international law would not apply to the Indian States.
3. Resistance to the Imperial orders constitutes rebellion.
4. The Paramount Power has the right to inflict punishments to those who put to death its agents while discharging their lawful duties imposed on them.

The rulers were required to pay succession duties which could be exempted by the British Government only on special grounds. The subjects of the Indian States had to apply to the Government of India for passports to go out of India. On account of double allegiance, it was provided that in the case of a conflict, the allegiance to Crown was to prevail.

The Government of India had complete control over the issue of all licences for arms and ammunition. The case of Patiala shows the helplessness of the States. In 1926, the Government of Patiala requested the Government of India to allow the issue of 25 pistols. The reply was that the State authorities should explain as to why they wanted 25 pistols more when they already had 48.

The appointment of the Diwans, the chief ministers and other important officers of the State had to be approved by the Political Department of the Government of India.

The British Government exercised the right of establishing a regency whenever the prince was a minor or the ruler of a State was temporarily suspended or permanently separated from the State.

The British Government asserted the right of wardship over minor princes including the right to control their education. Lord Curzon insisted, that it was the duty of the British Government to satisfy itself "that the young chief has received the education and training that will qualify him to rule before he is invested with powers to govern the State."

Important legislation in the State required the previous sanction of the Government of India. At the time of a regency, the Paramount Power got many rights and concessions. It was during this period that new precedents were established. States were deprived of the right of having their own coins. Such a thing was done in the case of Baroda, Mysore, Travancore, Alwar, Jaipur, etc. But this was resented by the Indian princes.

The Paramount Power also had the right to entertain petitions from the subjects of the Indian States against the State administration. Usually, the Paramount Power interfered only when the things reached a critical stage.

The rulers were not allowed to deal directly with any foreign State or with the subjects of any foreign State. They could not receive consular agents in their territories. They could not employ Europeans without the consent of the British Government. All forcing interests of the State were secured through the Government of India.

MINTO'S UDAIPUR SPEECH (NOVEMBER 1909)

Reference may be made to the following speech of Lord Minto in which he outlined the history of the policy of the British Government towards Indian States: "It is sometimes asked by ruling chiefs, as well as by the public in India and in Europe, what our policy towards Native States is. I can only tell you that the basis of the policy was laid down in Queen Victoria's Proclamation of 1858 and repeated in the Coronation message of His Majesty the King Emperor. In 1858, Queen Victoria addressed the Princes of India as follows: 'We hereby announce to the Native Princes of India that all treaties and engagements made with them by, or under the authority of the Hon'ble East India Company are by us accepted and will be scrupulously observed, and we look for the like observance on their part. We desire no extension of our present territorial possessions, and while we will admit no aggression upon our dominions or our rights to be attempted with impunity, we shall sanction no encroachment on those of others...and 44 years later the King Emperor wrote: 'To all my feudatories and subjects throughout India, I renew the assurance of my regard for their liberties, of respect for their dignities and rights, of interest in their advancement, and of devotion to their welfare, which are the supreme aim and object of my rule, and which, under the blessing of Almighty God, will lead to the increasing prosperity of my Indian Empire and the greater happiness of its people.'

"In pursuance of these pledges our policy is with rare exceptions, one of non-interference in the internal affairs of Native States. But in guaranteeing their internal independence and in undertaking their protection against external aggression it naturally follows that the Imperial Government has assumed a certain degree of responsibility for the general soundness of their administration and could not consent to incur the reproach of being an indirect instrument of misrule. There are also certain matters in which it is necessary for the Government of India to safeguard the interests of the community as a whole, as well as those of the Paramount power, such as railways, telegraphs and other services of an imperial character. But the relationship of the Supreme Government to the States is one of Sovereignty. Your Highness will, I know, recognise the difficulty that must exist in adhering to a uniform policy owing to the varying conditions of different States. It is this diversity of conditions which renders too dangerous any attempt at complete subservience to uniformity. I have, therefore, made it a rule to avoid as far as possible the issue of general instructions and have endeavoured to deal with questions as they arose with reference to existing treaties, the merits of each case, local conditions, antecedent circumstances, and the particular stage of development, feudal and constitutional of undivided principalities.

"The foundation-stone of the whole system is the recognition of identity of interests between the Imperial Government and the Durbars and the minimum interference with the latter in their own affairs. I have always been opposed to anything like pressure on Durbars with a view to introducing British methods of administration. I have preferred that reforms should emanate from Durbars themselves and grow up in harmony with the traditions of the State. It is easy to overestimate the value of administrative efficiency. It is not the only object to aim at, though the encouragement of it must be attractive to keen and able political officers and it is not unnatural that the temptation to further it, should, for example, appeal strongly to those who are temporarily in charge of the administration of the State during a minority. Whether they are in sole charge or associated with a State Council, their position is a difficult one. It is one of peculiar trust and through abuses and corruption must, of course, as far as possible, be corrected, I cannot but think that political officers will do wisely to accept the general system of administration to which the Chief and his people have been accustomed. The methods sanctioned by tradition in States are usually well adapted to the needs and relations of the ruler and his people. The loyalty of the latter to the former is generally a personal loyalty which administered efficiently, if carried out on lines unsuited to local conditions, would lessen or impair. "I can assure political officers, I am speaking in no spirit of criticism. No one has a greater administration of their services than I have. My aim and object will be, as it has always been, to assist them, but I would impress upon them that they are not only the mouth-piece of Government and the custodians of Imperial policy, but that I look to them also to interpret the sentiments and aspirations of the Durbars. It is upon the tactful fulfilment of their dual functions that the Supreme Government and the Chiefs must mutually rely. It is upon the harmonious co-operation of Indian Princes and Political Officers that so much depends on co-operation which must increase in value as communications develop and new ideas gain ground."

Minto's speech was well received by the press in India, as the following extract shows: "The speech which the Viceroy delivered on Wednesday evening at Udaipur, spoken to his Rajput host and a dinner table audience, was evidently, in fact, addressed to that whole two-fifths of the Indian Empire which is represented by the aggregate of the Native States.... Perhaps no utterance of the kind of so much significance has been heard since Lord Curzon's speech at Gwalior in November 1899. As that well-remembered manifesto was the indication of a policy, so too was Lord Minto's speech at Udaipur."

CHAMBER OF PRINCES

The authors of the Montagu-Chelmsford Report were of the view that time had come to end the isolation of the Indian rulers and something should be done to provide for joint consultations and discussions by them for the furtherance of their common interests. It is true that Lord Lytton had, at one time, suggested the formation of an Imperial Privy Council consisting of the rulers of Indian States but his suggestion had not been accepted. The same was true of the suggestion of Lord Curzon for the formation of a Council of ruling Princes. The proposal of Lord Minto to set up an Advisory Council of Indian rulers and big landlords to combat the nationalist movement in the country had not been accepted. During the regimes of Lord Hardinge and Lord Chelmsford, conferences of Indian rulers were pretty regular and the Montagu-Chelmsford Report recommended that those conferences should be replaced by a permanent body known as the Council of Princes which would give the Indian rulers "the opportunity of informing the Government as to their sentiments and wishes, of broadening their outlook and of conferring with one another and with the Government of India."

Another recommendation was that the Council of Princes should annually appoint a Small Standing Committee to advise the Political Department on matters affecting the States. The Government of India consulted the Indian rulers with regard to the above recommendations and ultimately the Chamber of Princes was set up on 8 February 1921 by a Royal proclamation. The ceremony of its inauguration was performed by the Duke of Connaught on behalf of the King Emperor in the Diwan-i-Aam of the Red Fort in Delhi. A passage in the proclamation was in these words.

"My Viceroy will take its counsel freely in matters relating to the territories of Indian States generally and in matters that affect these territories jointly with British India or with the rest of my Empire. It will have no concern with the internal affairs of individual States or their rulers or with the relations of individual States with my Government, while the existing rights of these States and their freedom of action will in no way by prejudiced or impaired."

The Chamber of Princes consisted of 120 princes in all. Out of those, 12 members represented 127 States and the remaining 108 were members in their own right. About 327 States were given no representation at all. Some important Indian rulers did not join it. Ordinarily, the Chamber of Princes met once a year and was presided over by the Viceroy. It elected its own Chancellor who presided over its meeting in the absence of the Viceroy. The Chancellor was the President of the Standing Committee of the Chamber of Princes. The Standing Committee met twice or thrice a year at Delhi to discuss the important questions facing the Indian States. Every year, the Standing Committee submitted its report to the Chamber of Princes. The princes also had informal conferences among themselves when they went to Delhi to attend the session.

The Chamber of Princes was a deliberative, consultative and advisory body. Its importance has been stated by the Simon Commission Report in these words: "The establishment of the Chamber of Princes marks an important stage in the development of relations between the Crown and the States, for it involves a definite breach in an earlier policy, according to which it was rather the aim of the Crown to discourage joint action and joint consultation between the Indian States and to treat each State as an isolated unit apart from its neighbours. That principle, indeed, has already been giving place to the idea of conference and co-operation amongst the ruling princes of India, but this latter conception was not embodied in permanent shape until the Chamber of Princes was established. The Chamber has enabled thorough interchange of views to take place on weighty matters concerning relationship of the States with the Crown and concerning other points of contact with British India."

THE BUTLER COMMITTEE

On 16th December 1927, Lord Birkenhead, Secretary of State for India, appointed a Committee of 3 members, viz, Sir Harcourt Butler, Prof. W. S. Holdsworth and the Hon'ble S. C. Peel to enquire into the relationship between the Indian States and the paramount power and to make suggestions for the more satisfactory adjustment of the existing economic relations between the Indian States and British India. Sir Harcourt was the Chairman of the Committee. He and his colleagues came to India in January 1928 and visited 16 States. The proceedings of the Committee were held in camera. The Committee did not examine the representatives of the people of the Indian States on the ground that that was not within their terms of reference. However, they accepted a written statement from the All-India States People's Conference. However, most of the work of the Committee was done in England, where the Indian rulers did their level best to put forward their point of view before the Committee.

According to the recommendations of the Butler Committee, the Viceroy and not the Governor-General-in-Council should be the agent of the Crown in dealing with the States. The relations between the Crown and the Princes should not be transferred without the consent of the princes to a new Government in British India responsible to the legislature. The scheme regarding the creation of a

State Council should be rejected. Intervention in the administration of a State should be left to the decision of the Viceroy. Special Committees should be appointed to enquire into disputes that may arise between the States and British India. A Committee should be appointed to enquire into the financial relations between the Indian States and British India. There should be separate recruitment and training of political officers drawn from the Universities of England.

The authors of the Butler Committee Report enunciated the theory of direct relationship between the Indian States and the British Crown. It was contended that the relationship of the Indian States was not with the Government of India but with the British Crown. This theory was put forward with a view to setting up a "Chinese Wall" between British India and the Indian States. As a matter of fact, the theory of direct relationship was being gradually evolved from 1917 when the famous August Declaration was made to give India responsible Government by stages. Its first sign was to be seen in the transfer of the relationship of Indian States from the provinces to the Central Government. In an inspired letter, the Maharaja of Indore wrote that "His Highness's treaty relations are with the Viceroy as a representative of His Majesty, the King Emperor." With "autonomous Government, British India can but occupy with regard to Indore the position of a sister State like Gwalior or Hyderabad, each absolutely independent of the other and having His Majesty's Government as the connecting link between the two." The theory of direct relationship was also advocated by Dr. A. B. Keith and Sir Leslie Scott. According to Dr. Keith, "It is important to note that the relations of the Indian States, however conducted, are essentially relations with the Crown and not with the Indian Government and that this fact presents an essential complication as regards the establishment of responsible Government in India. It is clear that it is not possible for the Crown to transfer its rights under a treaty without the assent of the Native States to the Government of India under responsible Government."

Sir Leslie Scott was an eminent lawyer and he was engaged by the Standing Committee of the Chamber of Princes to represent them before the Butler Committee. In an article contributed to the Law Quarterly Review, Sir Leslie laid down five propositions, some of which might be accepted as true, others palpably false and advanced to perpetuate British strange hold of India and to keep the States out of a united constitution forever. Two of these were that the contracts or treaties between the Princes and the Crown were between two sovereigns and not between the Company and the Government of British India, and that the Princes in making those contracts or treaties gave their confidence to the British and the Crown could not assign the contracts or treaties to any concerned party. The British Government, as Paramount Power, had undertaken the defence of all States and to remain in India with whatever military and naval forces might be requisite to enable it to discharge that obligation. The British Government could not hand over those forces to any other Government, to a foreign power such as France or Japan, or even to British India. The Indian Princes were very much pleased with the theory which was intended to help them to exclude themselves from the control of the Government of India when it came into the hands of the Indians.

The recommendations of the Butler Committee were criticised by the Indians from all walks of public life. The view of C. Y. Chintamani was: "The Butler Committee was bad in its origin, bad in the time chosen for its appointment, bad in its terms of reference, bad in its personnel and bad in its line of inquiry, while its report is bad in reasoning and bad in its conclusions." The view of Sir M. Visvesaryya was: "In the Butler Committee Report, there is no hint of a future for the Indian States' people. Their proposals are unsympathetic, unhistorical, hardly constitutional or legal... . There is no modern conception in their outlook. Certainly nothing to inspire trust or hope."

Criticising the Butler Committee Report, the Nehru Committee pointed out that "an attempt is being made to convert the Indian' States into an Indian Ulster by pressing constitutional theories into service" and gave the following warning: "It is inconceivable that the people of the States who are fired by the same ambitions and aspirations as the people of British India would quietly submit to existing conditions for ever, or that the people of British India bound by the closest ties of family, race and religion to their brethren on the other side of an imaginary line will never make common cause with them."

The rulers of the Indian States were also disappointed with the findings of the Butler Committee with regard to the unfettered discretion of the political department in its relations with Indian States. They had been hoping that they would be given more independence from the Political Department.

On the occasion of the First Round Table Conference held in London in 1930, the Indian Princes accepted the proposal for the creation of an All-India Federation in which both British Indian Provinces and the Indian States were to be brought together. On the first day of the plenary session of the Conference, Sir Tej Bahadur Sapru declared himself decisively for a federal system of Government at the Centre and he invited the Indian rulers to agree to the creation of an All-India Federation. His contention was that the Indian rulers would be a stabilising factor in the federal set-up and their adherence would enable the process of national unification to begin without delay. British India would benefit from their experience in the matter of defence. Sir Mohd. Shafi and M.A. Jinnah welcomed the idea of an All-India Federation. The Maharaja of Bikaner identified himself with the aspirations of British India "with passion for an equal status in the eyes of the world, expressed in the desire for dominion status which is the dominant force amongst all thinking Indians today." He gave an assurance that the Indian rulers would come in provided their rights were guaranteed. The Nawab of Bhopal declared: "We can only federate with a self-governing and federal British India."

The Indian National Congress had not been represented in the First Round Table Conference and consequently, an attempt was made soon after the First Round Table Conference to come to a compromise with the Congress which was carrying on the Civil Disobedience Movement. The Gandhi-Irwin Pact was signed in March 1931 and Gandhiji attended the Second Round Table Conference on behalf of the Congress. Gandhiji was not opposed to the federal idea but he was against dyarchy at the centre even for the transitional period. He asked for complete control over defence and external affairs. He stood for full responsible Government at the centre. That demand was not accepted by the British Government. At the end of the Second Round Table Conference, Prime Minister Ramsay Macdonald declared: "The great idea of an all-India federation still holds the field. The principle of a responsible federal government, subject to certain reservations and safeguards through a transition period, remains unchanged. And we are all agreed that the Governor's provinces of the future are to be responsibly governed units, enjoying the greatest possible measure of freedom from outside interference and dictation in carrying out their own policies in their own sphere."

The Third Round Table Conference met in 1932, but it was not attended by any important Indian ruler. The Viceroy was asked to explain to the individual rulers the federal scheme and secure some indication of their views in order to prepare a favourable atmosphere for the reception of the White Paper which the British Government intended to publish concerning the constitutional proposals. In March 1933, the White Paper containing the proposals of the British Government with regard to India was published and in April 1933, a Joint Select Committee of both Houses of Parliament was appointed to consider the future Government of India with special reference to the White Paper proposals. The Committee was given the authority to consult delegates from British India and Indian States. The Joint Select Committee submitted its Report in October 1934. In December 1934, a Bill based on the Joint Select Committee's Report was introduced, The Chamber of Princes appointed a Committee to examine the Government of India Bill. The Committee suggested a number of amendments and alterations. Those suggestions were thoroughly examined by the Secretary of State for India. On 4th August, 1935, the Government of India Bill received the Royal assent.

GOVERNMENT OF INDIA ACT, 1935

The Government of India Act, 1935, provided for a federal form of Government for the whole of India. Under that Act, the Indian States were given more representation in the federal legislature than was due to them on the basis of their population and area. While 250 seats were allotted to British India, the Indian States got 125 seats. In the Council of State, the Indian States were given the right to send 104 members out of a total of 260 members. While the representatives from the provinces were to be elected, those from the States were to be nominated by the rulers of the States concerned. While the inclusion of the provinces into the federation was to be automatic or compulsory, the Indian States were given the option to join the federation or not. While the control of the federal Government over the provinces was to be uniform, it was to vary in the case of Indian States according to the terms of the Instrument of Accession signed by the particular ruler at the time of joining the federation and accepted by the Crown.

A critical examination shows that the Indian States were given more representation than was due to them on the basis of their area, population or resources. Moreover, they were given the option to join or not to join the federation. The Joint Select Committee's Report gave the following reasons for treating the provinces and the Indian States differently: "The main difficulties are two: that the Indian States are wholly different in status and character from the Provinces of British India, and that they are not prepared to federate on the same terms as it is proposed to apply to the Provinces. On the first point, the Indian States, unlike the British Indian Provinces, possess sovereignty in various degrees and they are, broadly speaking, under a system of personal government. Their accession to a Federation cannot, therefore, take place otherwise than by the voluntary act of the ruler of each State, and after accession, the representatives of the acceding State in the Federal Legislature will be nominated by the ruler and its subjects will continue to owe allegiance to him. On the second point, the rulers have made it clear that while they are willing to consider Federation now with the Provinces of British India on certain terms, they could not, as sovereign States, agree to the exercise by a Federal Government in relation to them of a range of powers identical to the Provinces on whom autonomy has yet to be conferred."

Lord Linlithgow succeeded Lord Willingdon in 1936. He came to India with the determination to inaugurate the Federation during his tenure of office. His view was that a direct personal approach to the Indian rulers would help him to persuade most of them to join the Federation. It was with that object in view that he sent his emissaries to the rulers of the Indian States. These emissaries were provided with draft copies of Instrument of Accession and written instructions from the Viceroy. The three emissaries to the various States met the Indian Rulers and their Advisers. As a result of the talks, it became clear that what was worrying the Indian rulers was not whether the proposed Federation would enable them to contribute to the glory of India as a whole but whether their own position would be better and safer inside the Federation than outside it. Their attitude could be summed up in these words: "We are being given the opportunity of entering a federation from which when once we are in, there is no escape. Nor, since the ultimate interpreter of the federal constitution is the Federal Court, can the Government of India or anyone else predict the course of future events or anticipate the use which federation will make of its powers. We owe it, therefore, to ourselves and to our successors to safeguard to the utmost our own position inside the federation. That is the light in which you must regard the limitations which we have proposed, and if they seem unduly numerous and too widely drawn, remember that we have good reason for making them so."

It is true that Lord Linlithgow was very serious about his work, but the Political Department of the Government of India was creating hurdles in the way by putting emphasis on the loss which the rulers were to incur as a result of joining the Federation. Although many concessions were offered to the Indian rulers, they could not be persuaded to join the federation. While all this was happening, the Second World War broke out in September 1939. On llth September, 1939, Lord Linlithgow declared that while Federation remained, as before, the objective of His Majesty's Government, "the compulsion of the present international situation and the fact that, given the necessity for concentrating on the emergency that confronts us, we have no choice but to hold in suspense the work in connection with preparations for Federation."

In August 1940, Lord Linlithgow put forward certain proposals on behalf of His Majesty's Government with a view to securing the co-operation of the people of India. One of the proposals was to set up a War Advisory Council containing the representatives of British India and the Indian States. However, the so-called August offer was rejected by the Congress.

In March 1942, Sir Stafford Cripps came to India with certain proposals on behalf of His Majesty's Government with regard to the future set-up in the country. In one of his interviews, Sir Stafford stated that it was the intention of the British Government to give full freedom to all provincial units and the Indian States to come into the new Union or to stay out. Moreover, the British Government did not intend to stay in India unless the Indian people wanted them in their own interest to stay and except to the extent that it might be unavoidable for the fulfilment of the British a Government's treaty obligations to the non-adhering States. On 10th April, 1942, the Indian States' delegation met and adopted the following resolution which was conveyed to Sir Stafford: "The Indian States will be glad as always, in the interest of their motherland, to make their contribution in every reasonable manner compatible with the sovereignty and integrity of the States, toward the framing of a Constitution for India. The States should be assured, however, that in the event of a number of States not finding it feasible to adhere, the non-adhering States or groups of States, so desiring, would have the right to form a union of their own, with full sovereign status in accordance with a suitable and agreed procedure devised for the purpose."

The Cripps mission was a failure but the rulers of the Indian States realised after the departure of the mission that their future was not safe. It was found that if the interests of the Indian States came into conflict with those of British India, the British Government was going to care for British India and not for them. It was at this time that Jawaharlal Nehru declared that treaties with the Indian States must be scrapped and those who talked of those treaties were "lunatics, knaves or fools." It was in this atmosphere that the rulers of the Indian States started devising plans to safeguard their own interests in the future. The Nawab of Bhopal urged upon the political department to take all those measures which were necessary to safeguard their position in the event of changes taking place in the constitutional set-up in the country. In his address to a meeting of the Chamber of Princes held on 17th January 1946, Lord Wavell assured the Indian Princes that no changes in their relationship with the Crown or the rights guaranteed to them by treaties and engagements would be initiated without their consent. However, he impressed upon the rulers the necessity of placing their administration on modern lines for the welfare of their subjects which could be done only by ensuring that all States fulfilled the three fundamental criteria of good Government: political stability, adequate financial resources, and effective association of the people with the administration. The Viceroy asked the rulers of the smaller States to pool their resources and form political entities of a sufficient size.

On 19th February 1946, Prime Minister Attlee announced the decision of the British Cabinet to send three Cabinet Ministers to India. On 15th March 1946, he referred to the Indian States in the British Parliament in these words: "I hope that the statesmen of British India and of Princely India will be able to work out a solution of the problem of bringing together, in one great polity, these disparate constituent parts. There again, we must see that the Indian States find their due place; there can be no positive veto in advance and I do not believe for a moment that the Indian Princes would desire to be a bar to the forward march of India. But, as in the case of many other problems, this is a matter that Indians will settle themselves."

In his interview with the Cabinet Mission and the Viceroy held on 2nd April 1946 the Nawab of Bhopal pointed out that the Indian States wanted to continue their existence with the maximum degree of sovereignty. They desired no interference in their internal affairs by British India. He suggested the formation of a Privy Council of the Indian States of British India. The Nawab urged that paramountcy should not be transferred to an Indian Government in the event of India becoming independent. In the same afternoon, Lord Pethick-Lawrence and the other members of the Cabinet Mission met the Standing Committee of the Chamber of Princes. The rulers were told that if British India became independent, paramountcy would end. The British Government did not contemplate keeping any troops in India for the maintenance of internal order. The Crown would not be in a position to carry out its treaty obligations and hence the Indian States would also be released from their obligations under their treaties.

On 16th May 1946, the Cabinet Mission announced its proposals with regard to the future set-up of India. About the States, it was declared that with the attainment of independence by British India, whether within or without the British Commonwealth, the relationship which had hitherto existed between the Indian States and the British Crown would come to an end. Paramountcy could neither be retained by the British nor transferred to the new Government. It was pointed out that the rulers had given an assurance to the mission that they were ready and willing to co-operate in the new development of India. The form of co-operation was to depend upon the result of negotiations between the Indian States and the future Government of India. In their broadcast on 16th May 1946, both the Secretary of State for India and Sir Stafford Cripps made only casual references to the States. They asserted that paramountcy could not be handed over to anyone and hence it must cease. They left the future relationship between the States and British India for negotiations.

On 22nd May 1946, the Cabinet Mission published a Memorandum on States' Treaties and Paramountcy. It was pointed out in that Memorandum that when a new, fully self-governing or independent government or governments came into being in British India, the influence of His Majesty's Government with these Governments would not be such as to enable them to carry out the obligations of paramountcy. The British Government had no intention of keeping British troops in India for that purpose. The result was that paramountcy would come to an end. The existing political arrangements between the States on the one hand, and the British Crown and British India on the other were to come to an end. The void was to be filled up by the States entering into a federal relationship with the successor Government or Governments in British India. The Memorandum referred to the desirability of the States forming or joining administrative units large enough to enable them to be fitted into the constitutional structure.

On 17th May 1946, the Nawab of Bhopal asked for certain clarifications from Lord Wavell, particularly regarding the independence of the Indian States. The reply of Lord Wavell was that the settlement of most of the matters raised by the Nawab did not rest with him or the Cabinet Mission as they related to the terms which the States were free to negotiate for their own association with the new constitutional structure. To the Nawab, the letter of Lord Wavell was disappointing and he wrote to him again asserting that the States were entitled to claim that the Crown should not leave them at the mercy of British India. He pointed out that it could never be the intention of His Majesty's Government to leave the States as "a sort of no man's child" without any effort on the part of the crown to protect their legitimate and reasonable rights and claims. The reply of Lord Wavell was that he appreciated the anxiety of the Nawab but he could not help him in the matter and he asked him to discuss the matter with Sir Conrad Corfield, the Political Adviser to the Government of India. The view of Sir Conrad was that the decision regarding the lapse of paramountcy at the end of the interim period placed the Indian States in the best bargaining position possible for the purpose of fitting themselves in the future constitutional structure. He advised the States to set up a Negotiating Committee to settle the terms on which they would be prepared to participate in the discussions of the Constituent Assembly. He gave a promise of help to the Indian States by the Political Department during the interim period.

It was under these circumstances that the Standing Committee of the Chamber of Princes set up a Negotiating Committee and authorised the Chancellor of the Chamber of Princes to arrange discussions with the corresponding body of the British Indian Constituent Assembly as contemplated by the Cabinet Mission. It was on 21st December 1946, that the Constituent Assembly passed a resolution appointing a Negotiating Committee to negotiate with the Negotiating Committee set up by the Indian States. Speaking on the resolution, Jawaharlal Nehru declared: "I regret, I say frankly, that we have to meet the Rulers' Negotiating Committee. I think that, on the part of the States, there should have been on the Negotiating Committee representatives of the people of the States. I think even now that the Negotiating Committee, if it wants to do the right thing, should include some such representatives but I feel that we cannot insist upon this at this stage." However, this had no effect on the Indian Princes.

On 20th February 1947, Prime Minister Attlee declared in the House of Commons that the British Government would transfer power to responsible Indian hands not later than June 1948. With regard to the States, he observed: "As was explicitly stated by the Cabinet Mission, His Majesty's Government do not intend to hand over their powers and obligations under paramountcy to any Government of British India. It is not intended to bring paramountcy, as a system, to a conclusion earlier than the date of the final transfer of power, but it is contemplated that for the intervening period, the relations of the Crown with individual States may be adjusted by agreement."

This announcement introduced an element of urgency and Jawaharlal Nehru contended that it would be to the advantage of the States if their representatives joined the Constituent Assembly during the April Session. The Nawab of Bhopal who was the Chancellor of the Chamber of Princes, pointed out the difficulty to do so without a meeting of the Indian rulers for that purpose. It was, however, decided that 50 per cent of the States' representatives should be elected and efforts should be made to increase the elected quota as far as possible. Jawaharlal Nehru also invited the representatives of the States to function forthwith on some of the Committees set up by the Constituent Assembly, particularly the Union Powers Committee and the Fundamental Rights Committee. However, the attitude of the Chancellor was that he could not arrive at any decision without consulting the General Conference of the rulers.

There arose differences between the Chancellor of the Chamber of Princes and the Maharaja of Bikaner. The Maharaja did not approve of the policy of "Wait-and-see" adopted by the Chancellor. He was in favour of the Indian States joining the Constituent Assembly at once. The lead of the Maharaja of Bikaner was followed by the Maharaja of Patiala who issued a public statement criticising the policy of sitting on the fence. The Chancellor, Nawab of Bhopal, tried to dissuade the rulers from entering the Constituent Assembly and even his personal appeal to the rulers had no effect. On 18 April 1947, Jawaharlal Nehru declared that any State which did not come into the Constituent Assembly, would be treated as hostile State. Such a State would have to bear the consequences of being so treated. Liaquat Ali Khan, the leader of the Muslim League in the Central Legislature and the Cabinet, criticised the statement of Nehru and observed that the Congress had no right to coerce the States. According to him, "The States were perfectly within their right in refusing to join the Constituent Assembly." He appealed to the States to "disregard the idle threat." In spite of this, on 28 April 1947, the representatives of the States of Baroda, Bikaner, Patiala, Jaipur, Cochin and

Rewa took their seats in the Constituent Assembly. After that, one by one, the other States also started sending their representatives to the Constituent Assembly.

On 3 June 1947, Lord Mountbatten announced his plan by which power was to be transferred into the hands of the Indians much earlier than June 1948. However, the policy towards the Indian States was to be governed by the Cabinet Mission Memorandum of 12th May 1946. The Nawab of Bhopal resigned his Chancellorship of the Chamber of Princes and stated thus in his letter of resignation. "Now that Your Excellency has indicated to us the policy of His Majesty's Government in regard to the future of the Indian States, and Bhopal State would, as soon as paramountcy is withdrawn, be assuming an independent status, I consider it desirable that I should tender my resignation of the office of Chancellor of the Chamber of Princes with effect from today. Another reason for my resignation is that the Chamber, as now constituted, formed part of a constitutional machinery which, in my opinion, will now become functus officio." In another letter addressed to the Viceroy, the Nawab observed that, "the State of Bhopal does not wish to remain associated in any manner whatsoever with the Chamber of Princes or any of its subordinate organizations. It cannot therefore be represented by the Standing Committee of that body and will negotiate direct with the successor Governments of British India in regard to its interests, and its future political relationship with Pakistan and Hindustan." On the resignation of Nawab of Bhopal as Chancellor, the Maharaja of Patiala became the Chancellor and it must be said to his credit that he played a very glorious role so far as the higher interests of India as a whole were concerned and it will be the height of ingratitude for the people of India to forget the services tendered by him to his country at that critical moment. There was every possibility of the division of India into a very large number of independent States. The rulers had their own armies and the danger was a very real one. The Maharaja of Patiala threw in his lot with the Indian Government and all the intrigues of the political department ultimately came to nothing.

On 11th June 1947, Sir C. P. Ramaswami Aiyar declared that the State of Travancore had decided to become an independent Sovereign State. On 12 June 1947, a similar announcement was made by the Nizam of Hyderabad. On 15 June 1947, the All-India Congress Committee laid down its policy towards the Indian States. The Princes who had not joined the Indian Constituent Assembly were invited to do the same and "co-operate in the building of the constitutional structure of free India in which the States will be equal and autonomous sharers with other units of the Federation." The Congress also urged the States to hasten progress towards responsible Government "so as to keep in line with the fast changing situation in India and at the same time to produce contentment and self-reliance in their people." The Congress rejected the claim of the Princes to become independent. It claimed for the people of the States the dominant voice in decisions concerning them. The Congress Resolution declared that the All-India Congress Committee did not admit the right of any State in India to declare its independence and to live in isolation from the rest of India. That would be a denial of the course of Indian history and of the objectives of the Indian people today. Jawaharlal Nehru also declared that the claim of the States to independence could not be sustained as independence did not depend on a mere declaration by a State but rested fundamentally on recognition by other States. The lapse of paramountcy of the British Crown did not make the Indian States independent. To quote him, "I should like to say and other countries to know that we shall not recognise the independence of any State in India, further that, any recognition of any such independence by any Foreign Power will be considered an unfriendly act."

The Indian Independence Act, 1947, provided that the sovereignty of His Majesty over the Indian States lapses, and with it all treaties and agreements in force on that date. As a result of this provision, the Indian States became completely independent and the Governments of India and Pakistan did not inherit the rights or authority of the former Government of India. The Act did not attempt a solution of the problem of the States, and left the same to be tackled by the new dominions. However, the authors of the Act did not contemplate that the Indian States would become independent States as such and thereby disrupt the unity of India. Sir Hartley Shawcross, Attorney-General of England, observed thus in Parliament: "We do not propose to recognise the States as separate international entities on August 15." Mr. Attlee, Prime Minister of England, also observed thus: "A feature running through our relations is that they (the States) have received no international recognition of independence of India as a whole. With the ending of these treaties and agreements, the states regain their independence. But they are part of geographical India and their rulers and people are imbued with a patriotism no less great than that of their fellow Indians in British India. It would be, I think, unfortunate if owing to the severance of their paramountcy relations with the Crown they were to become islands cut off from the rest of India. The termination of their existing relationship need have no such consequences. In fact, already a number of States have declared their willingness to enter into relationship with the new Dominions and some have been represented in the Constituent Assembly of India. It is the hope of His Majesty's Government that all the States will in due course find their appropriate place with one or the other Dominion within the British Commonwealth."

Before we discuss the manner in which the problem of the States was tackled by the Congress after the June 3 Plan, it is desirable to refer to the policy of the Congress before 1947. At the Haripura session of the Congress in 1938, the following resolution was passed: "The Congress stands for the same political, social and economic freedom in the States as in the rest of India and considers the States as integral parts of India which cannot be separated. The Purna Swaraj or Complete Independence, which is the objective of the Congress, is for the whole of India inclusive of the States for the integrity and unity of India must be maintained in freedom as it has been maintained in subjection. The only kind of Federation that can be acceptable to the Congress is one in which the States participate as free units enjoying the same measure of democratic freedom as the rest of India. The Congress, therefore, stands for full responsible Government and the guarantee of civil liberty in the States and deplores the present backward conditions and utter lack of freedom and suppression of civil liberties in many of these States."

The result of the new policy was the fusion of the freedom movement in the States and Provinces.

On 15 June 1947 all-India Congress Committee laid down its policy towards the Indian States. The Princes who had not already joined the Constituent Assembly were invited to do the same and "co-operate in the building of the constitutional structure of free India in which the States will be equal and autonomous sharers with other units of the Federation." The Congress also urged the States to hasten progress towards responsible Government "so as to keep in line with the fast changing situation in India and at the same time to produce contentment and self-reliance in their people. The Congress rejected the claim of the Princes to become independent. It claimed for the people of States the dominant voice in decisions concerning them. The Congress Resolution stated thus: "The A.I.C.C. cannot admit the right of any State in India to declare its independence and to live in isolation from the rest of India. That would be a denial of the course of Indian history and the objectives of the Indian people today.

"The A.I.C.C. trusts that the rulers of the States will appreciate fully the situation as it exists today and will in full co-operation with their people enter as democratic units in the Indian Union, thereby serving the cause of their own people as well as of India as a whole.

"The Committee does not agree with the theory of paramountcy as enunciated and interpreted by the British Government, but even if that is accepted the consequences that follow from the lapse of that paramountcy are limited in extent. The privileges and obligations as well as the subsisting rights as between the States and the Government of India cannot be adversely affected by the lapse of paramountcy. The rights and obligations have to be considered separately and renewed or changed by mutual agreement. The relationship between the Government of India and the States would not be exhausted by the lapse of paramountcy. The lapse does not lead to the independence of the States. Both from the point of view of the spirit underlying the Memorandum of May 12, and the Statement of 16 May, 1946, as well as the acknowledged rights of the people all over the world today, it is clear that the people of the States must have a dominating voice in any decision regarding them. Sovereignty, it is admitted, resides with the people and if paramountcy lapses resulting in the ending of the relationship of the States to the Crown, the inherent rights of the people are not affected thereby for the worse."

On that occasion Pt. Nehru pointed out that the claim of the States to independence could not be sustained as independence did not depend on a mere declaring by a State but rested fundamentally on recognition by other States. The lapse of paramountcy of the British Crown did not make the Indian States independent. To quote him, "There is certain inherent paramountcy in the Government of India, which cannot lapse – inherent paramountcy in the dominant State in India must remain because of the very reasons of geography, history, defence, etc., which gave rise to it when the British became the dominant power in India. Pt. Nehru pointed out that there were only two alternatives before the States. Either they were to join the Indian Union and become equal and autonomous partners in it or accept the paramountcy of the Indian Union as they could not live in a void. "There was no third way out of the situation — third way meaning independence or social relation to a Foreign Power." Pt. Nehru made it clear that the Indian Union did not desire any paramountcy or sovereignty but it was not prepared to allow the Indian States to have their agreements with any Foreign Power. "We cannot permit anything to happen in India in any State which affects fundamentally, the security of India either in relation to defence arrangements or in relation "to contact with Foreign Powers." Pt. Nehru concluded with the following warning: "I should like to say and other countries to know that we shall not recognise the independence of any State in India, further that any recognition of any such independence by any foreign power will be considered an unfriendly act."

ACCESSION OF STATES

The Congress was able to tackle the problem of the Indian States successfully and the credit goes to Sardar Patel, Lord Mountbatten and Mr. V. P. Menon. On the suggestion of Sardar Patel, the States Ministry was acceptable to the princes. They were set up and he himself became its head. An Instrument of Accession was drawn up which was required the Princes to hand over to the Indian Union only the subjects of defence, foreign relations and communications. In other matters, their autonomy was to be scrupulously respected. Sardar Patel made it clear to the Princes that it was not the desire of the Congress "to interfere in any manner in the domestic affairs of the States." He also appealed to the patriotism of Indian Princes thus: "We are at a momentous 'stage in the history of India. By common endeavour we can raise the country to a new greatness while lack of unity will expose us to fresh calamities. I hope the Indian States will bear in mind that the alternative to cooperation in the general interest is anarchy and chaos which will overwhelm great and small alike in common ruin if we are unable to act together in the minimum of common tasks. Let not the future generations curse us for having had the opportunity but failed to turn it to our mutual advantage. Instead let it be our proud privilege to leave a legacy of mutually beneficial relationship which would raise this Sacred Land to its proper place among the nations of the world and turn it into an abode of peace and prosperity." Addressing the Chamber of Princes on 20th July, 1947, Lord Mountbatten also endorsed the appeal of Sardar Patel and advised the Indian States to accede to one or the other of the dominions before August 15, 1947. He pointed out that if nothing was put in the place of coordinated administration that had grown up under the British rule, only chaos would result and that was bound to hurt the State most. No State could live in isolation. The subjects which were proposed to be vested in the Federation were the subjects which the States could not handle themselves. The States had not administered their external relations or their defence and were not in a position to handle them in the future. Communications were a means of maintaining the life-blood of the whole sub-continent. The three subjects were such which could be left to be handled on their behalf "for their convenience and advantage by a large organization." Lord Mountbatten also stressed the factors that were to be taken into consideration by the States while acceding to any dominion. "There are certain geographical compulsions which cannot be evaded." "The vast majority of States were irretrievably linked up with India." He concluded his address thus: "I am not asking any State to make intolerable sacrifice of either its internal autonomy or independence. My scheme leaves you with all the practical independence that you cannot possibly use and makes you free of all those subjects which you cannot possibly manage of your own. You cannot run away from the Dominion Government which is your neighbour any more than you can run away from the subjects for whose welfare you are responsible."

The net result of all the efforts was that by 15th August 1947, with the exception of Junagadh, Hyderabad and Kashmir, as many as 136 salute and fully jurisdictional States acceded to the Indian Union. On 15th August, Lord Mountbatten paid the following tribute to Sardar Patel: "Thanks to that far-sighted statesman, Sardar Vallabhbhai Patel, Minister in charge of the States Department, a scheme was produced which appeared to me to be equally in the interests of the States as of the Dominion of India. It is a great triumph for the realism and sense of responsibility of the rulers and the governments of the States as well as for the Government of India that it was possible to produce an Instrument of Accession, which was equally acceptable to both sides, and one moreover so simple and straightforward that within less than 3 weeks, practically all the States concerned had signed the Instrument of Accession."

Junagadh

Junagadh was an important State in the group of the Kathiawar States. It was bounded by other Indian States except the South and South-west where the Arabian Sea lies. This State had no geographical contiguity with Pakistan. The distance between Port Veraval of Junagadh and Karachi is about 300 miles. The area of the State was 3,337 square miles and its population according to the census of 1941 was 6,70,719. More than 80 per cent of the people were Hindus. There were many islands of the Junagadh State in the States of Gondal, Bhavnagar and Navanagar. Parts of the States which had acceded to India were interspersed with Junagadh territory and access to them was possible only through Junagadh. The railways and posts and telegraphs of the State were an integral part of the Indian system. The railway police, telegraphs and telephones were administered by the Government of India. The Nawab of the State lived a life of luxury and his chief pre-occupation in life was dogs of which he had hundreds.

There was speculation that Junagadh was going to join Pakistan and the Nawab took pains to contradict it. The following press note was issued by the Government of Junagadh on April 11, 1947: "What Junagadh pre-eminently stands for is the solidarity of Kathiawar and would welcome the formation of a self-contained group of Kathiawar States. Such a group while providing for the autonomy and entity of individual States and their subjects would be a suitable basis for co-operation in matters of common concern generally and co-ordination where necessary." A similar repudiation was issued on April 22, 1947.

Sir. Shah Nawaz Bhutto, a Muslim League politician of Karachi, was appointed a member of the State Council of Ministers of Junagadh. In May 1947, he was appointed the Dewan of the State. The Nawab of Junagadh came under the influence of the Muslim League.

The Government of India sent an Instrument of Accession to the Nawab of Junagadh for his signatures. On August 13, 1947, Sir Nawaz sent the reply that the matter was under consideration. In spite of it, the Government of Junagadh issued the following communique on August 15, 1947, announcing her accession to Pakistan: "The Government of Junagadh has during the past few weeks been faced with the problem of making its choice between accession to the Dominion of India and accession to the Dominion of Pakistan. It has had to take into very careful consideration every aspect of this problem. Its main pre-occupation has been to adopt a course that would, in the long run, make the largest contribution towards the permanent welfare and prosperity of the people of Junagadh and help to preserve the integrity of the State and to safeguard its independence and autonomy over the largest possible field. After anxious consideration and the careful balancing of all factors the Government of the State has decided to accede to Pakistan and hereby announces its decision to that effect. The State is confident that its decision will be welcomed by all loyal subjects of the State who have its real welfare and prosperity at heart."

The Government of Junagadh did not communicate to the Government of India the fact of its accession to Pakistan. There was a lot of correspondence between the Governments of India and Pakistan about Junagadh and ultimately on September 13, 1947, the Government of Pakistan informed the Government of India that she had accepted the accession of Junagadh to Pakistan and also signed a Standstill Agreement. There is no doubt about the fact that there were prolonged secret negotiations between the Nawab and the Dewan on the one hand and the Government of Pakistan and Mr. M. A. Jinnah on the other. When the Nawab and the Dewan ran away from the State, many letters fell into the hands of the Government of India and in one of those letters it was stated that Sir Shah Nawaz Bhutto had written to Mr. Jinnah about the interview he granted him on 16 July, 1947, in which Mr. Jinnah had advised the Nawab to keep out under any circumstances until 15 August. There was also a reference to the assurances of Mr. Jinnah that he would not allow Junagadh to starve as "Veraval is not far from Karachi." There was also the following passage in one of those letters: "Junagadh stands all alone surrounded by Hindu rulers' territories and British Indian Congress provinces. We are of course connected by sea with Pakistan. If geographical position by land was fairly considered, Kutch, Jamnagar and other territories adjoining Junagadh geographically should be considered connected with Pakistan as they once in the past actually formed part of Sind. Though the Muslim population of Junagadh is nearly 20 per cent and non-Muslims form 80 per cent, 7 lakh Muslims of Kathiawar survived because of Junagadh. I consider that no sacrifice is too great to preserve the prestige, honour and rule of His Highness and to protect Islam and the Muslims of Kathiawar."

The accession of Junagadh to Pakistan was condemned by the rulers of the other States of Kathiawar. Jam Saheb of Nawanagar and the rulers of Bhavnagar, Dhrangadhra, Morvi, Porbandar, Gondal and Wankaner sent their protests. The reply of the Nawab was in these words: "The Indian Independence Act did not and does not require a ruler to consult his people before deciding on accession. I think we are making an unnecessary fetish of the argument of geographical contiguity. Even then this is sufficiently provided by Junagadh's seacoast with several ports which can keep connection with Pakistan."

The Jam Saheb of Nawanagar told the Government of India that if the latter did not take immediate and effective steps to protect the other Kathiawar States, the people would lose all faith in the Government of India. There were also rumours that Pakistan had offered to give military assistance to Junagadh. On 17 September 1947, the Government of India decided to disperse around Junagadh troops of the acceding States. However, there were strict orders that the State of Junagadh was not to be occupied. On 24 September 1947, the Government of India decided that a brigade should be suitably dispersed in Kathiawar to protect the States which had acceded to the Indian Union. It was also decided to send troops to the states of Mangrol and Babariawad. On September 25, 1947, the Prime Minister of Pakistan sent a telegram to the Government of India in which it was asserted that the Nawab of Junagadh had every right to accede to Pakistan regardless of the territorial location of his State.

The situation in Junagadh was deteriorating day by day. More than a lakh of Hindus ran away from the state of Junagadh. Law and order in the whole of Kathiawar practically collapsed. It was at this stage that the Congress leaders of Kathiawar announced in Bombay (now Mumbai) on 25 September 1947, the establishment of a provisional Government (Arzi Hakumat) of Junagadh. The provisional Government consisted of 6 members with Samaldas Gandhi as President "with all power, authority and jurisdiction heretofore vested in and exercised by the Nawab of Junagadh prior to 15 September 1947." When Samaldas Gandhi and his colleagues journeyed from Bombay to Rajkot, they were greeted by large crowds at the wayside railway stations. They set up their headquarters at Rajkot and enrolled a large number of volunteers. Junagadh troops entered the State of Mangrol which had acceded to the Dominion of India. It was then decided to send Indian troops to occupy the State of Mangrol. It was found that the Khan of Manavadar was arresting local leaders and harassing the people. In order to prevent a flare up in the State, that Stare was also taken over on 22 October 1947.

When the Nawab of Junagadh found that help from Pakistan was not enough to keep him on the throne, he ran away from the state towards the end of October 1947. He took with him to Karachi not only the members of his family but also all his jewellery and all the available cash in the State treasury. Although the Nawab ran away, Sir Shah Nawaz continued as Dewan of the state of Junagadh. On 27 October 1947, Sir Shah Nawaz wrote the following letter to Mr. Jinnah. "Our principal sources of revenue, railways and customs have gone to the bottom. Food situation is terribly embarrassing though Pakistan has come to our rescue with a generous allotment of foodgrains. There has been a harsh treatment of Muslims travelling on Kathiawar railway lines who have been subjected to several kinds of hardships and humiliations. Added to this, His Highness and the royal family have had to leave because our secret service gave us information in advance of serious consequences to their presence and safety. Though immediately, after accession, His Highness and myself received hundreds of messages chiefly from Muslims congratulating us on the decision, today our brethren are indifferent and cold. Muslims of Kathiawar seem to have lost all enthusiasm for Pakistan." Again, "No doubt Your Excellency's Government offered us seven companies of Crown Police but we felt that if they were to come and be confronted by the vast enemy forces arrayed against us it would be sheer wastage of human material and equipment. The situation has therefore so worsened that responsible Muslims and others have come to press me to seek a solution of the impasse. I do not wish to say much more. My Senior Member of Council, Capt. Harvey Jones, must have apprised you of the serious state of things. The question is delicate but I feel it must be settled honourably to the satisfaction of all. It is impossible for me to court any further bloodshed, hardship and persecution of loyal people. Myself I do not mind what suffering is imposed on me but I do not wish to take the responsibility any further if it can be avoided for thousands of His Highness' subjects. I should therefore suggest that you immediately arrange for a conference of the representatives of the two Dominions to decide the Junagadh issue."

Finding his position precarious, Sir Shah Nawaz opened negotiations with Samaldas Gandhi on 7 November 1947 through Captain Harvey Jones, Senior Member of the Junagadh State Council, requesting Samaldas Gandhi to take over the reins of Government and restore law and order in the

State. However, the Muslims of Junagdh prevailed upon Shah Nawaz to hand over the Government not to Samaldas Gandhi but to Mr. Buch who at that time was the Regional Commissioner, Western India and Gujarat States. It was under these circumstances that Mr. Buch took over the administration of Junagadh on 9 November 1947. Sir Shah Nawaz had already left for Karachi a day earlier.

As soon as normal conditions were restored, the Government of India arranged a referendum of the people of Junagadh with regard to the question of accession. Shri C. B. Nagarkar, I.C.S., supervised the referendum which took place on 20 February 1948. Out of a total of 2,01,457 registered voters, 1,90,870 exercised their right of vote. Only 91 voters voted for accession to Pakistan. A referendum was also held in the States of Mangrol, Manavadar, Babariawad, Bantwa, and Sardargarh. Out of 31,434 votes cast for all these States, only 39 voted for accession to Pakistan. It was in this way that the problem of Junagadh was solved.

Hyderabad

Geographically, Hyderabad occupied a pivotal position in the heart of India. This State was surrounded by the Central Provinces in the North, Bombay in the West and Madras on the East and South. Its population was nearly 60 million and the annual revenue was ₹26 crores. Its area was more than 82,000 square miles. It had its own coinage, paper currency and stamps. Although the Hindus formed more than 85 per cent of the total population of Hyderabad, their representation in the Civil Services and the army was practically nil and the Government machinery was a monopoly of the Muslims. Although it was a very important State, it was not given any privileged position by the British Government. The latter asserted its right to intervene in its affairs whenever it considered to be necessary. After the announcement of 3rd June 1947 plan by the British Government, the Nizam of Hyderabad issued a **firman** declaring his intention not to send his representatives to the Constituent Assembly of either India or Pakistan. He made it clear that after 15 August 1947, he would be a completely independent sovereign ruler. The intention of the Nizam was to make Hyderabad a Dominion of the Commonwealth of Nations.

On July 11 1947, the Nizam sent a delegation to Delhi to meet Lord Mountbatten. One of the members of the delegation was Sir Walter Monckton. The discussions centred round three points: the retrocession of Berar to the Nizam, the grant of Dominion Status to Hyderabad and the accession of the State of Hyderabad to the Indian Union. The delegation was told that it was not possible to hand over Berar to the Nizam. The delegation was also told that it was not possible to grant Dominion Status to Hyderabad. The members of the delegation went to the extent of saying that if the Nizam was pressed hard, he might join Pakistan. The delegation was told that the Government would not enter into a Standstill Agreement without the State of Hyderabad acceding to India. The Nizam asked for two months to consider his position and that time was allowed to him. Lord Mountbatten was hopeful that ultimately Hyderabad would accede to India.

On 8 August 1947, the Nizam wrote to Lord Mountbatten that he could not think of bringing Hyderabad into an organic Union with either India or Pakistan. He was, however, prepared to enter into a treaty with India which would conform to all-India standards so far as railway communications were concerned. Hyderabad would also contribute an agreed number of troops for the defence of India. He was prepared to conduct the foreign policy of his State in general conformity with the foreign policy of India. All this was to be done on the condition that in event of a war between India and Pakistan, Hyderabad would remain neutral. Hyderabad was also to have the right to appoint Agents-General wherever it thought fit. There was also to be a provision in the treaty that if India seceded from the British Commonwealth, Hyderabad was free to review the situation de novo. Sir Walter Monckton resigned as Constitutional Adviser to the Nizam as there was a violent attack upon him in the Hyderabad press but he was persuaded to continue by Lord Mountbatten.

The suggestion of Sir Walter Monckton was that the Nizam could be persuaded to enter into a treaty provided the term "Instrument of Accession" was substituted by the term "Articles of Association." However, this was not acceptable to Sardar Patel who insisted on the Nizam acceding to the Dominion of India. His view was that if the Nizam was given a special treatment that would be misinterpreted by the rulers of the Indian States who had already acceded to the Dominion of India. The view of Sardar Patel was that the Nizam must refer the question of accession to the people of his State and act according to their decision. Lord Mountbatten offered to the Nizam to have the referendum under the supervision of British Officers. However, that offer was rejected by the Nizam. On 18 September 1947, the Nizam wrote that short of accession, Hyderabad was ready and willing to enter into a treaty of association with India. At the same time, the Nizam contacted Mr. M. A. Jinnah with a view to secure the services of Sir Zafrullah Khan as the President of his Executive Council. However, he was not successful in that. The Nizam pointed out to the Government of India that if Hyderabad acceded to the Dominion of India, the Muslims who formed about half the population of Hyderabad city would not tolerate it and they would create such a trouble as would not be possible to control. Sir Walter Monckton wrote to Lord Mountbatten that the attitude of the Nizam had stiffened and he was not prepared to reconsider the question of accession. He would prefer the negotiations to break down rather than accept accession. That was due to the influence of Pakistan on the Nizam and the latter wanted him to go to Karachi to have an interview with Mr. Jinnah.

There were protracted negotiations in which Sir Walter Monckton and Sir Sultan Ahmed, besides others, participated. Ultimately, drafts were prepared which were acceptable to the Government of India and the delegation sent by the Nizam. Those drafts were taken by the delegation to Hyderabad on 22 October 1947, for the approval of the Nizam with the promise that they would come back on 26 October 1947. The Nizam referred the matter to his Executive Council for advice and the Executive Council advised the Nizam to accept those drafts. The Nizam approved the decision of the Executive Council but postponed the signing of the agreement till 26 October 1947. At about 3 o'clock in the morning of 26 October 1947, a crowd estimated at about 25,000 to 30,000 surrounded the houses of Sir Walter Monckton, Nawab of Chhattari and Sir Sultan Ahmed. They shouted that the delegation would not go to Delhi. The result was that the Nizam ordered that the delegation should not go to Delhi. The advice of Kasim Razvi to the Nizam was that as the hands of the Indian Union were full with other problems, they would not be able to take action against Hyderabad and the Nizam could afford not to accede to the Indian Union. Although Sir Walter Monckton, Sir Sultan Ahmed and the Nawab of Chhattari suggested to the Nizam that the advice of Kasim Razvi was likely to lead to disaster, the Nizam was inclined to listen to Kasim Razvi and hence all of them tendered their resignations. The Nizam sent a letter to Lord Mountbatten in which he said that if negotiations with the Government of India broke down he would immediately negotiate and conclude an agreement with Pakistan. As a matter of fact, the Nizam had already sent two persons to Karachi and they had come back with a reply from Pakistan. Lord Mountbatten was very unhappy about the change in the attitude of the Nizam. He did not like the replacement of the old delegation by a new one. He told the members of the new delegation that it was not wise on the part of the Nizam to threaten to conclude a Standstill Agreement with Pakistan if he failed to sign one with India. He expressed the view that the time had come for the Nizam to take a final decision one way or the other India would be put to some inconvenience if no Standstill Agreement was signed but that would ultimately prove to be disastrous for the Nizam. Lord Mountbatten tried to remove the impression that India was weak and hence could not give full attention to the problem of Hyderabad.

Kasim Razvi also visited Delhi and met Sardar Patel. In his interviews, he declared that Hyderabad would never surrender her independence and if the Government of India insisted on a plebiscite, the sword would be the final arbiter.

In spite of the difficulties in the way, a Standstill Agreement was signed between the Government of India and the Nizam on November 29 1947. It was provided that until new arrangements were made all the agreements and administrative arrangements on matters of common concern, including defence, external affairs and communications which had existed between the Crown Representative and the Nizam before the transfer of power, would be continued as between the Government of India and the Nizam. The Government of India and the Nizam also agreed to appoint their agents in Hyderabad and Delhi respectively and give them every facility for the discharge of their functions. The Government of India was not to exercise any paramountcy function in their relations with Hyderabad. Nothing in the Agreement was to create, in favour of either party, any right continuing after its termination, or derogate from any right which, but for the Agreement, would have been exercisable by either party after the date of its termination. Any dispute arising out of the Agreement was to be referred to two arbitrators, one to be appointed by each of the parties and an umpire to be selected by those arbitrators. The Agreement was to come into force immediately and was to remain in force for a period of one year.

The Standstill Agreement was taken in different lights. Lord Mount-batten hoped that the Agreement would provide a basis for a satisfactory long-term solution. He hoped that before the Standstill Agreement expired, it would be possible for Hyderabad to accede to India. The view of Jawaharlal Nehru was that the Agreement would purchase communal peace in the south for at least one year. Sardar Patel was doubtful about the bona fides of the Government of Hyderabad. The Nizam and his advisers took the Agreement as something which gave them breathing space in which they were to secure the withdrawal of the Indian troops from Hyderabad and ultimately become independent.

Shri K. M. Munshi was appointed as India's Agent-General in Hyderabad. Unfortunately, the attitude of the Nizam Government towards him was positively hostile from the very beginning. He was not given even a building for his residence or office. Ultimately, two of the buildings belonging to the Indian army were put at his disposal.

The Nizam began to press for the speedy withdrawal of the Indian troops and the supply of arms and ammunition for the Hyderabad army and police. The Nizam also issued two Ordinances by which he put restrictions on the export of all precious metals from Hyderabad to India and also made Indian currency as not legal tender in the Hyderabad State. The Government of Hyderabad also advanced a loan of ₹20 crores to Pakistan in the form of Government of India's securities. The Government of India protested against these developments but nothing was done to remove the objection. At this time, the activities of the Razakars increased tremendously. Kasim Razvi and his followers made all kinds of objectionable speeches with the object of inflaming communal passions inside and outside of Hyderabad. Razvi declared that the Razakars were the liberators of the Muslims of India. The Razakars began to attack the neighbouring provinces like Madras, Bombay and the Central Provinces. The situation became so serious that the common saying was that the Razakars ruled by day and the Communists ruled by night. The Government of Madras asked for military help to save its people from the raids of Razakars. This state of affairs continued for many months. Shri K. M. Munshi was practically a prisoner in his house in Hyderabad. El Edroos, the Commander-in-Chief for the Hyderabad forces, called upon the people in a radio talk to be ready for any emergency. In his speech delivered on March 31 1948, on the occasion of the inauguration of the Hyderabad Weapons Week, Kasim Razvi urged the Muslims of Hyderabad not to sheathe their sword until their objective for Islamic supremacy was achieved. He asked them to march forward with the Koran in one hand and the sword in the other to hound out the enemy. He also declared that "the forty-five million Muslims in the Indian Union would be our fifth columnists in any showdown." On April 12 1948, Kasim Razvi declared, "The day is not far off when the waves of the Bay of Bengal will be washing the feet of our

Sovereign." He went to the extent of saying that he would plant the Asaf Jahi Flag on the Red Fort in Delhi. When Laik Ali, the new Prime Minister of Hyderabad, met Sardar Patel, the latter referred to the speech of Kasim Razvi and asserted that such things could not be tolerated. To quote Sardar Patel, "You know as well as I do where power resides and with whom the fate of the negotiations must finally lie in Hyderabad. The gentleman (Kasim Razvi) who seems to dominate Hyderabad has given his answer. He has categorically stated that if the Indian Dominion comes to Hyderabad it will find nothing but the bones and ashes of one and a half crores of Hindus. If that is the position, then it seriously undermines the whole future of the Nizam and his dynasty. I am speaking to you plainly because I do not want you to be under any misapprehension. The Hyderabad problem will have to be settled as has been done in the case of other States. No other way is possible. We cannot agree to the continuance of an isolated spot which would destroy the very Union which we have built up with our blood and toil. At the same time, we do wish to maintain friendly relations and to seek a friendly solution. That does not mean that we shall ever agree to Hyderabad's independence. If its demand to maintain an independent status is persisted in, it is bound to fail."

The view of Lord Mountbatten was that if he could persuade the Nizam to visit Delhi, it would be possible to bring him round and with that object in view, he sent him an invitation to visit Delhi. However, that invitation was refused by the Nizam. Lord Mountbatten sent his Press Attache to Hyderabad to meet the Nizam, study the situation and make a report to him. The report submitted by the Press Attache was that the Nizam was the keyman in the situation and nothing was being done without his approval. He also reported that the Nizam was in a mood of aggressive fatalism.

The situation on the border began to worsen. On the evening of May 22 1948, the mail train from Madras to Bombay was attacked at Gangapur Station inside the Hyderabad State. The attack was made by a party of men equipped with daggers, hockey sticks and lathis. The Government of India took a very serious view of the matter.

Lord Mountbatten made very serious efforts to settle the matter before his departure in June 1948. He put personal pressure on Sardar Patel to agree to the four changes suggested by the Hyderabad delegation. In spite of that, the Nizam put forward other demands which were not acceptable to the Government of India and the result was that in spite of his best efforts, Lord Mountbatten left India on June 21 1948 without solving the Hyderabad problem.

After the departure of Lord Mountbatten, the relations between India and Hyderabad began to worsen. Charges of border raids and breaches of the Standstill Agreement were made on both sides. Sidney Cotton, an Australian, was employed by the Hyderabad Government to smuggle arms and ammunition into Hyderabad. The Government of Pakistan began to cash a portion of the ₹20 crores of the Government of India Securities which the Government of Hyderabad had offered to the Government of Pakistan as a loan. There was a reign of terror. People were being killed and their eyes were being taken out. Women were being raped and houses were being burnt down in large numbers.

The situation was becoming intolerable. Both the press and the public opinion in India accused the Government of India of inaction in the face of repeated violations of Indian Territory. The stories brought by the evacuees from Hyderabad made the people indignant. Attacks on the through trains created panic. It was under these circumstances that the Government of India decided to take action.

In the early hours of 13 September 1948, Indian forces commanded by Major-General J. N. Chaudhuri under the direction of Lieut.-General Maharaj Shri Rajendra Sinhji who was then the General Officer Commanding-in-Chief, Southern Command, entered the Hyderabad State. There was some stiff resistance on the first and second day and after that the same collapsed. On the evening of 17 September 1948 the Hyderabad Army surrendered. On 18 September 1948, the Indian troops entered Hyderabad city. The police action lasted for 108 hours. It was learnt that if action had not been taken on 13 September 1948, Lt. T. T. More who was captured with his jeep full of explosives, would have destroyed all the important bridges in the State and it would have been very difficult for the Indian army to move forward.

On 18 September 1948, Major-General Chaudhuri took charge as Military Governor. On 19 September, Kasim Razvi was arrested. The Razakars were disbanded and many of them were detained under the Public Safety Regulations. Strong action was taken against the Communists and their resistance was crushed.

The administration under Major-General Chaudhuri lasted up to December 1949 when Shri M. K. Vellodi, I.C.S., took over as Chief Minister. In 1950, four representatives of the Hyderabad State Congress were appointed as Ministers. In March 1952, general elections were held and a Congress Ministry was installed with the Nizam as a constitutional head. In 1956 was passed the States Reorganisation Act by which the State of Hyderabad was split up and it ceased to exist. Most of its territories went to the State of Andhra Pradesh.

Jammu and Kashmir

The State of Jammu and Kashmir had strategic importance on account of its international boundaries. To the East was Tibet, to the North-East was the Sinkiang province of China and to the North-West was Afghanistan. Gilgit was a part of the territory of the State of Jammu and Kashmir. The majority of the population of the State of Jammu and Kashmir consisted of Muslims although the Buddhists were in majority in Ladakh. At the beginning of 1947, Maharaja Hari Singh was the ruler of the State and Pt. Ram Chandra Kak was its Prime Minister.

After the announcement of June 3 Plan, Lord Mountbatten visited Kashmir and for four days discussed the question of accession of the State of Jammu and Kashmir with Maharaja Hari Singh. He told him that independence was not practicable and the State would not be recognised as a Dominion by the British Government. He gave an assurance to the Maharaja that up to 15 August 1947, he could join any Dominion and there would be no difficulty. Even if he acceded to Pakistan, India would not raise any objection. However, it was desirable to ascertain the wishes of the people before acceding to any Dominion as the majority of its people were Muslims. Lord Mountbatten failed in his mission as the Maharaja refused to commit himself. After 15 August 1947, Lord Ismay went to Srinagar and tried to persuade the Maharaja to join one Dominion or the other but his mission also failed.

It cannot be denied that it was not easy for the Maharaja to make a decision. He was himself a Hindu and he would not like to join Pakistan at once. Moreover, he was not sure of the fate of his Hindu subjects in the event of his joining Pakistan. There was also the possibility of the opposition from the National Conference, which was the most powerful and vocal organisation in the State. If he acceded to India, there was also the possibility of adverse reactions in Gilgit and certain other areas which were contiguous to Pakistan. Moreover, the road communications were with Pakistan. Till the declaration of the Radcliffe Award there was no land communication between India and the State of Jammu and Kashmir. Moreover, Maharaja Hari Singh was thinking in terms of becoming an independent ruler.

Shortly before 15th August 1947, Pt. Ram Chandra Kak was replaced by Major-General Janak Singh as Prime Minister. The Government of Jammu and Kashmir announced its intention of entering into Standstill Agreements both with India and Pakistan. India was not enthusiastic about it even after the announcement of the Radcliffe Award which connected India with the State by Road. Pakistan signed a Standstill Agreement but with an ulterior motive. In spite of the Agreement, the Pakistan authorities cut off the supply of food, petrol and other essential commodities. Restrictions were put on the transit of travel between Kashmir and Pakistan. Goods belonging to the State lying in the towns of Pakistan were not allowed to be transported to the State of Jammu and Kashmir. The State had practically no petrol for its transport organisation. Military pressure was put on Jammu and Kashmir to accede to Pakistan. Mr. M. A. Jinnah sent his British Military Secretary thrice to Srinagar to bring about Kashmir's accession to Pakistan. Mr. Jinnah also wrote to Maharaja to allow him to spend the summer in Kashmir on account of his bad health and offered to make his own arrangements. Major Shah was sent to Kashmir to arouse the people in favour of Pakistan and also to intimidate the Maharaja to accede to Pakistan. There were hit and run border raids on the State. It was under these circumstances that Mr. Justice Mehr Chand Mahajan took over as the Prime Minister of the State.

On 15 October 1947, the new Prime Minister complained to the British Prime Minister that the Government of Pakistan had broken the Standstill Agreement by discontinuing the supply of essential articles and by stopping, without any reason, the railway service from Sialkot to Jammu. He also pointed out that the whole of the State border from Gurdaspur to Gilgit was threatened with invasion and the same had already started in Poonch. He requested the British Prime Minister to advise the Government of Pakistan to deal fairly with the State of Jammu and Kashmir. However, he got no reply. On 18 October 1947, a protest was sent to the Governor-General and the Prime Minister of Pakistan against the breaches of the Standstill Agreement and the raids on the State. Mr. M. A. Jinnah. Governor-General of Pakistan sent a reply on 20th October 1947 in which he protested against the tone and language of the communication.

The all-out invasion of Kashmir started on 22nd October 1947. The raiders included Afridis, Wazirs, Mahsuds, Swathis and the soldiers of the Pakistan Army on leave. They were led by regular officers who knew Kashmir well. They advanced from Abbottabad in North-Western Frontier Province along the Jhelum Valley Road. They captured Garhi and Domel and arrived at the gates of Muzaffarabad. All the Muslims in the State Battalion at Muzaffarabad deserted and acted as advance guard to the raiders' column. They marched towards Baramula, along the road leading to Srinagar. All the Muslims in the State Forces deserted and joined the raiders. Brigadier Rajinder Singh, Chief of Staff of the State Forces, gathered together about 150 men and proceeded towards Uri. He engaged the raiders for two days and in the rearguard action destroyed the Uri Bridge. Not only the Brigadier himself but all his men were cut to pieces in the battle. On 24th October 1947, the raiders captured the Mahura Power House which supplied electricity to Srinagar, and that plunged Srinagar in darkness. The raiders declared that they would reach Srinagar on 26 October 1947 and celebrate the Id celebrations in the Srinagar mosque.

Such was the critical situation when the Government of India received an appeal for help from the Maharaja of Jammu and Kashmir on 24 October 1947. Even earlier than that, Field-Marshal Auchinleck, the Supreme Commander, had received a message from Pakistan Army Headquarters giving information about the advance of the raiders and their probable destination. Although the information was passed on to the Government of India, no action was taken on it. Even when the appeal came from the Maharaja on 24 October no immediate action was taken. On the morning of 25 October 1947, a meeting of the Defence Committee was held under the presidentship of Lord Mountbatten. It was decided that no immediate action be taken by the Government of India and Shri V. P. Menon be sent to Srinagar immediately to study the situation on the spot and report to the Government of India. Shri V. P. Menon immediately left by plane and reached Srinagar. From the aerodrome, he went straight to the residence of Prime Minister Mehr Chand Mahajan. The latter put all the facts before Shri V. P. Menon about the situation at that time. It was decided to send immediately the Maharaja from Srinagar to Jammu. There were rumours at night that the raiders had infiltrated into Srinagar and hence it was not considered safe to remain in the city for the night and hence, Shri V. P. Menon and Prime Minister Mehr Chand Mahajan immediately went to the aerodrome and early in the morning of 26 October the plane left Srinagar and reached Delhi. Prime

Minister Mehr Chand Mahajan met Prime Minister Jawaharlal Nehru and Deputy Prime Minister Sardar Patel and apprised them of the serious and dangerous situation in the State. He solicited army help and made it clear that the army must be flown at once, otherwise the whole town of Srinagar would be completely destroyed. He was told that it was not possible to send the army at a moment's notice but that did not impress him. Prime Minister Mahajan put his case in these words to the Indian leaders: "Give army, take accession and give whatever powers you want to the popular party, but the army must fly to Srinagar this evening, otherwise I will go and negotiate terms with Mr. Jinnah, as the city must be saved." On this Prime Minister Nehru flew into a rage and asked Prime Minister Mahajan to go away. It was at this moment that Sheikh Abdullah who was staying in the Prime Minister's house and was over-hearing the talks, sent a slip of paper to Prime Minister Nehru. Prime Minister Nehru read that slip of paper and his attitude was completely changed. Sheikh Abdullah was against the accession of Kashmir to Pakistan and there was no love lost between him and Mr. Jinnah. He wanted, as desired by his party, the accession of the State to India, but he was also keen that power should go in his hands and the Maharaja should become a constitutional head. The result of the negotiations on the morning of 26 October 1947 was that at the persistent request of Prime Minister Mahajan, the Indian Cabinet agreed to accept the accession of the State and send its army to Srinagar on the morning of 27 October 1947 to defend the State. Shri V. P. Menon again went to Jammu accompanied by the Prime Minister Mahajan and after getting the Instrument of Accession from the Maharaja, he flew back to Delhi. Sardar Patel was waiting at the aerodrome and both of them went straight to a meeting of the Defence Committee which was arranged for that evening. There was a long discussion and ultimately it was decided that the Accession of Jammu and Kashmir should be accepted subject to the proviso that a plebiscite would be held in the State when the law and order situation allowed. It was also decided that an infantry battalion should be flown to Srinagar the next day. This decision had the fullest support of Sheikh Abdullah. It must be pointed out that Lord Mountbatten and the 3 British Chiefs of Staff of the Indian Army, Navy and Air Force pointed out the risks involved in the operation for which there was hardly any preparation.

In the early hours of the morning of 27 October 1947, more than 100 civilian aircraft and Royal Indian Air Force planes were mobilised to fly troops, equipment and supplies to Srinagar. It must be admitted that it was the heroism and enthusiasm shown by the civilian and Royal Indian Air Force pilots and the ground crews that made the air-lift a success. Some of the pilots did several sorties in the course of the day. It was in this way that the timely arrival of the Indian forces in the morning of 27 October 1947 saved Srinagar.

Mr. M. A. Jinnah was impatient with what was happening in Kashmir. His Private Secretary, Khurshid Ahmed, was already in Srinagar but alter the arrival of the Indian troops, he was arrested and sent back to Pakistan. When M. A. Jinnah heard about the acceptance of the accession ol Jammu and Kashmir by India and the arrival of the Indian troops in Srinagar, he gave orders to General Gracey, the Acting Commanding-in-Chief of the Pakistan Army, to send Pak troops to Kashmir but the General refused to do so without the approval of Field Marshal Auchinleck. The Field Marshal also flew to Lahore on the morning of 28 October 1947 and explained to Mr. Jinnah that the State of Jammu and Kashmir had acceded to India and if Pak troops entered Kashmir, there was every likelihood of a war between the two countries and if that happened, all British Officers serving in the Pakistan Army would be automatically and immediately withdrawn. It was under these circumstances that Mr. Jinnah cancelled his previous orders for Pakistan troops to march into Kashmir.

On 30 October 1947, a statement was issued by the Government of Pakistan in which it was stated that accession of Kashmir to India was "based on fraud and violence and as such cannot be recognised." It was also stated therein that the State troops were the first to attack the Muslims in the State and the Muslim villages on the Pakistan border and that provoked the raiders to attack the State. It was also at this time that Pakistan established her control over Gilgit which was a part of the State of Jammu and Kashmir.

On 1st November 1947, Lord Mountbatten and Lord Ismay flew to Lahore and had a long conference with Mr. M. A. Jinnah. The latter contended that the accession of Kashmir to India was brought about by violence and the reply of Lord Mountbatten was that the violence had come from the tribal raiders. Lord Mountbatten suggested a plebiscite under the auspices of the United Nations but Mr. Jinnah pressed for a plebiscite under the joint control and supervision of the Governors-General of India and Pakistan. Many other things were discussed at the meeting but nothing came out of it and Lord Mountbatten came back to Delhi. On 4 November 1947, Prime Minister Liaquat Ali Khan broadcast from Lahore in which he said that the accession of Kashmir to India was a fraud perpetrated on its people by its cowardly ruler with the aggressive help of the Government of India.

Major-General Kalwant Singh was put in charge of the Military operations in Kashmir. On 8 November 1947, his forces occupied Baramula. When the Indian troops entered the city, it was found that the tribesmen had taken away all its wealth and women. Out of the female population of 14,000, only about 1,000 were left. The destruction of Baramula could be compared with the sacking of Delhi by Nadir Shah in 1739. By 11 November 1947, Indian troops reached the heights of Uri and the tribesmen were in so great hurry that they gave up Tangmarg and Gulmarg without firing a shot. One cannot help admiring the courage with which Air Commodore Mehar Singh flew Major-General Thimayya over an unchartered mountainous route more than 23,000 feet above the sea level and landed him safely at Leh on an improvised air strip. It was in this way that Leh and Ladakh valleys were cleared from the raiders by Major-General Thimayya. The credit of recovering Poonch goes to Major-General Atma Singh.

It was on the persuasion of Lord Mountbatten that the Government of India took their complaint to the United Nations against the Pak invasion of Jammu and Kashmir. A cease-fire was ordered with effect from 1st January 1949. Many efforts were made by the United Nations to resolve the dispute between India and Pakistan but they have not succeeded.

In 1965, Pakistan sent her infiltrators into the Kashmir Valley and then attacked the Chhamb area. That resulted in a war between India and Pakistan not only in the State of Jammu and Kashmir but also in East Punjab. As a result of the good offices of the Soviet Union, the war was brought to an end and the famous Tashkent Declaration was issued in January 1966, but in spite of this the relations between the two countries are bitter on account of the question of Kashmir.

The accession of the State of Jammu and Kashmir has been criticised by Pakistan on many grounds. It is pointed out that the State of Jammu and Kashmir had an overwhelming population of Muslims and hence the State ought to have acceded to Pakistan. However, the fact must not be ignored that the partition of the country had not taken place on the two-nation theory. If that had been so, there was no necessity of holding a plebiscite in the North-West Frontier Province with its 90 per cent Muslim population. There was also no necessity of consulting the legislatures in Bengal and the Punjab. The separation of the predominantly Muslim areas from the rest of India was in the nature of a political division. Moreover, it must not be forgotten that Muslims are even today the citizens of India and occupy the highest positions in the country and that also proves that the partition of the country did not take place on the basis of the two-nation theory.

It is well known that Mr. M. A. Jinnah did his level best to secure the accession of the predominantly Hindu State of Jodhpur and Jaisalmer to Pakistan and offered tempting terms for that purpose. It is a different matter that he failed but it could not be denied that Mr. Jinnah did his best to secure their accession to Pakistan. Moreover, the Muslim ruler of the State of Junagadh actually acceded to Pakistan and the Government of Pakistan, accepted it. That also contradicts the two-nation theory as the population of Junagadh was over 85 per cent Hindu.

It must be observed that the Government of India was not enthusiastic about the accession of the State of Jammu and Kashmir to India. Nothing was done by the Government of India to force the hands of the Maharaja. As a matter of fact her attitude was one of indifference. It is possible that if the raiders had not attacked the State of Jammu and Kashmir, the Government of India which had her hands otherwise full would not have bothered about the State of Jammu and Kashmir. It was only when the raiders attacked the State of Jammu and Kashmir and there was the immediate danger of the fall of Srinagar into their hands that the Maharaja of Jammu and Kashmir requested the Government of India to come to his help and as that help could be given only if that State acceded to India, the Government of India was forced to send her troops into the State of Jammu and Kashmir. If the attitude of India was one of indifference, it is well known that Pakistan adopted all kinds of tactics to put pressure on the Maharaja to accede to Pakistan. It is also known that the leader of the raiders was one General Tariq who was later on identified as Major-General Akbar Khan of the Pakistan Army. It is this Akbar Khan who later on became the Commanding-in-Chief of Pakistan.

INTEGRATION AND DEMOCRATISATION OF STATES

The accession of States was only a partial solution of the problem of the States. The people of the States were restive and wanted to have a share in the administration. The Government of India was also favourably inclined towards their aspirations. The administration of the Indian States required to be modernised. The work of integration, democratisation and modernisation of the Indian States was done simultaneously. Integration involved the elimination of the small States by their merger with the neighbouring Provinces or States, or their consolidation into larger political units by means of the Unions of the States. By those means a few viable and sizeable units were to be created. Integration also involved the establishment of "a common Centre in the whole of India, able to function efficiently in the Provinces and States alike in matters requiring all-India action." In the words of the White Paper on the States, "The aim was the integration of all elements in the country in a free, united and democratic India."

1. As regards the merger of the smallest States into the neighbouring States or Provinces, the Orissa (now Odisha) and Chattisgarh States were the first to be merged. Those States were 39 in number and had a population of 70 lakhs and an area of 56,000 sq. miles. Individually those States were too small for a modern system of administration. Their mergers were negotiated by Sardar Patel on 14 and 15 December 1947. According to the Merger Agreements, the ruling Princes surrendered to the Dominion Government "full and exclusive authority, jurisdiction and power for and in relation to governance" of their States and agreed to transfer their administration on 1st January 1948. On 1st January 1948, these States became parts of Orissa and Central Provinces. On December 16 1947, Sardar Patel observed thus: "It should be obvious to everyone, however, that even democracy and democratic institutions can function efficiently only where the units to which these are applied can subsist in a fairly autonomous existence. Where, on account of smallness of its size, isolation of its situation the inseparable link with a neighbouring autonomous territory, be it a Province or a bigger State, in practically all economic matters of everyday life, the adequacy of the resources to open up its economic potentialities, the backwardness of its people and sheer incapacity to shoulder a self-contained administration, a State is unable to afford a modern system of Government, both democratisation and integration are clearly and unmistakably indicated."

The next merger was that of the Deccan States numbering 17. They were merged with Bombay in March 1948. Kolhapur was merged later on. In this way, an area of 10,860 sq. miles and a population of 27 lakhs was merged in the Bombay Presidency. In June 1948, the Gujarat States numbering 289 were merged in Bombay Presidency. These States covered an area of 17,

680 sq. miles and had a population of 27 lakhs. In May 1949, Baroda was merged in Bombay Presidency. It has an area of 8,236 sq. miles and a population of 30 lakhs. A few small States in the Punjab, the States of Banganapalli, Pudukotto and Sandur in Madras, Cooch-Behar in West Bengal, the Khasi Hills States in Assam and Tehri-Grahwal, Banaras and Rampur in U.P. were merged in the surrounding Provinces in 1948 and 1949.

The Merger Agreements of practically all the States were in identical terms. The merged States became parts and parcel of the Provinces into which they were included. The people of the merged States were given representation in the Provincial Legislatures. The Government of India Act, 1935, as amended was applied to them in the same way as was done to other Provinces of India.

2. Another form of integration of States was the consolidation of States into Centrally administered areas. This was done in the case of Himachal Pradesh, Vindhya Pradesh, Kutch, Bilaspur, Bhopal, Tripura and Manipur. 21 States in East Punjab covering an area of 10,600 sq. miles with a population of about 10 lakhs were consolidated into the Union of Himachal Pradesh This Union was inaugurated on April 15 1948. Vindhya Pradesh was created by consolidating the Bundelkhand and Baghelkhand States numbering 35 with an are of 24,600 sq. miles and a population of 36 lakhs. Vindhya Pradesh was created into a States Union in April 1948 with a responsible ministry but later on its Government was taken over by the Government of India on 1st January 1950. Kutch with an area of 17,249 sq. miles and a population of 5 lakhs was made a Chief Commissioner's Province in May 1948. The State of Bilaspur in the Punjab was taken over by the Government of India on October 12 1948. The State of Bhopal was taken over by the Government of India on 1st June 1949. The State of Tripura was taken over by the Government of India on October 15 1949.

3. Another form of integration of States was the formation of the States Unions. These Unions were created "with due regard to geographical, linguistic, social and cultural affinities" of the people living in the States. Their rulers came to be known as Rajpramukhs.

On February 15 1948, the United States of Kathiawar (Saurashtra) was inaugurated. This Union had 222 States, estates and talukas. Its area was 21,451 sq. miles and its population was 41 lakhs. The important States of the Union were Nawanagar and Bhavanagar. According to the terms of the covenant, the States agreed to unite and integrate their territories into one State with a common executive, legislature and judiciary. There was to be a Council of Rulers with a Presidium of five members. The rulers were to elect the President and Vice-President of the Presidium. The President was to be the Rajpramukh of the Union. All the executive powers were put in the hands of the Rajpramukh but he was to be aided and advised by a Council of Ministers. In other words, he was to act as a constitutional head. That covenant fixed the privy purses of the rulers and guaranteed their private property, personal privileges and the right of succession.

On March 18, 1948 was created the United States of Matsya consisting of Alwar, Bharatpur, etc. The Union of Vindhya Pradesh was created on April 1948. The United States of Gwalior, Indore and Malwa or Madhya Bharat was inaugurated on May 28, 1948. It had an area of 46,710 sq. miles and a population of 80 lakhs. The Patiala and East Punjab States Union (PEPSU) consisting of 7 big States such as Patiala, Nabha, Kapurthala, etc. was inaugurated on August 20 1948. It had an area of 10,999 sq. miles and a population of 35 lakhs. The United States of Rajasthan was created in three stages. The first United States of Rajasthan consisting of Mewar and nine other small Rajputana States was inaugurated on April 13 1948. The State was reconstituted to include Jaipur, Jodhpur, Jaisalmer and Bikaner. On May 15 1949, the United States of Matsya was incorporated into Rajasthan. The United State of Travancore-Cochin came into being on 1st July 1949. Its total area was 9,155 sq. miles and its population was 93 lakhs.

Under the Indian Princes, the States had autocratic governments. The people had absolutely no voice in the administration of the States. The Princes did whatever they pleased. There was practically no distinction between the public revenues and the private revenues of the ruling Princes.

However, such a state of things could not exist after the independence of India and the integration of the States. The people of the States were demanding a share in the administration and the Government of India had full sympathy with them. No wonder, when the Indian States were merged into the Provinces, the people of those States were put on the same footing as the people of the provinces concerned. When the Government of India created Centrally administered areas, the people of those States were also associated with the administration. When the Unions of the States were created, full-fledged responsible government was established in them. It is true that the people living within the centrally administered areas were not given full control over their administration, but the people of other Indian States were given responsible government. Legislatures were set up in the States and the Ministries were made responsible to them. The Rajpramukhs were made constitutional heads.

THE STATES REORGANISATION COMMISSION

For a long time, there was a demand for the reorganisation of the provinces of India on linguistic lines. It was contended that the existing provinces were not created by the British Government on any scientific principle. Those were set up from time to time on grounds of expediency. In 1948, the Linguistic Provinces Committee known as the Dar Committee was set up to go into the matter. The Committee reported against the proposition. Its view was that nationalism and sub-nationalism were two emotional experiences which grew at the expense of each other. A Committee consisting of Prime Minister Jawaharlal Nehru, Sardar Patel and Dr. Pattabhi Sitaramayya was set up to examine the findings of the Dar Committee. As a result of the death of Sriramulu, the situation in Andhra became very tense and the Government of India appointed Mr. Justice Wanchoo (as he then was) to report on the matter. It was under these circumstances that the first linguistic State was set up in Andhra. This gave an impetus to the supporters of the idea of linguistic States and ultimately Prime Minister Nehru made a statement in Parliament on 22 December, 1953, to the effect that a Commission would be appointed to examine "objectively and dispassionately" the question of the reorganisation of the States of Indian Union "so that the welfare of the people of each constitutent unit as well as the nation as a whole is promoted." The Commission was appointed under a resolution of the Government of India in the Ministry of Home Affairs. Mr. Fazl Ali was appointed the Chairman of the Commission and its two other members were Pandit Hridayanath Kunzru and Sardar K. M. Panikkar.

Para 7 of the resolution mentioned above runs thus: "The commission will investigate the conditions of the problem, the historical background, the existing situation and the bearing of all important and relevant factors thereon. They will be free to consider any proposal relating to such reorganisation. The Government expects that the Commission would, in the first instance, not go into the details, but make recommendations in regard to the broad principles which should govern the solution of this problem. The language and culture of an area have an undoubted importance as they represent a pattern of living which is common in that area. In considering a reorganisation of States, however, there are other important factors which have also to be borne in mind. The first essential consideration is the preservation and strengthening of the unity and security of India. Financial, economic and administrative considerations are almost equally important, not only from the point of view of each State, but for the whole nation. India is embarked upon a great ordered plan for the economic, cultural and moral progress. Changes which interfere with the successful prosecution of such a national plan would be harmful to the national interest."

The Commission submitted its report to the Government of India on 30 September 1955 and it was released to the public on 10 October 1955. According to the recommendations of the Commission, the Indian Union was to consist of 16 States as against the existing 27 and three Centrally-administered territories. The States that were to disappear were those of Travancore-Cochin, Mysore, Coorg, Saurashtra, Kutch, Madhya Bharat, Bhopal, Vindhya Pradesh, PEPSU, Himachal Pradesh, Ajmer and Tripura. In certain cases, the whole of the State and in certain others only a part was to be merged in a neighbouring State or States. PEPSU and Himachal Pradesh were to form part of the Punjab. All the Part 'C' States were to be abolished. The distinction between Part 'A' and Part 'B' States was to be done away with.

The Commission recommended the abolition of the institution of Rajpramukhs. Special safeguards were recommended for linguistic minorities. The minorities were given the right to have instruction in their mother-tongue at the primary school stage. In the interests of national unity and good administration, the Commission recommended the reconstitution of certain All-India Services, viz., the Indian Medical and Health Services. With the same object in view, the Commission recommended that as a general rule, 50 per cent of the new entrants in the All-India Services should be from outside the State concerned and regular transfers to and from the Centre and the States should be arranged. At least one-third of the number of judges in a High Court should consist of persons recruited from outside that State so that the administration might inspire confidence and help in arresting parochial trends. The Commission put emphasis on the need for encouraging the study of Indian languages other than Hindi. It also recommended that for some time to come, English should continue to occupy an important place in universities and institutions of higher learning, even after the adoption of Hindi and the regional languages for official and educational purposes.

According to the Commission, the linguistic complexion and the communicational needs of the Punjab did not justify the creation of a Punjabi-speaking State. The creation of such a State was likely to disrupt the economic life of the area. There was no case for a Punjabi-speaking State because it lacked the general support of the people inhabiting the area, and because it was not to eliminate any of the causes of friction from which the demand for a separate Punjabi-speaking State had arisen. The Punjabi Suba was to solve neither the language nor the communal problem. On the other hand, it might further exacerbate the existing feelings. PEPSU and Himachal Pradesh were too small to continue by themselves. Having regard to the economic and administrative links between PEPSU and the Himachal Pradesh on the one hand and the present Punjab State on the other, the merger of these two States in the Punjab was justified.

During its inquiry the Commission received 152,250 memoranda, petitions and communications, travelled 38,000 miles and interviewed over 9,000 persons in an effort to get a complete cross-section of public opinion. The report of the Commission comprised 267 printed pages, including two minutes of dissent by Sir Fazl Ali and Sardar K. M. Panikkar. The first opposed the merger of Himachal Pradesh in the new Punjab and the second objected to the retention of U.P. in undivided form.

There was a lot of agitation against the recommendations of the Commission. The interested parties tried to create a sort of chaos in the country. The Maharashtrians raised a lot of hue and cry over the city of Bombay. The Congress High Command declared that it was willing to make alterations in the recommendations of the Commission if all the interested parties agreed upon any alternative. Prolonged negotiations were held and many changes were made in the recommendations of the Commission but the problem of Bombay City gave headache to all. Even when the States Reorganisation Bill was sent to Parliament, the Maharashtrians were absolutely dissatisfied. However, when the Bill was being discussed in Lok Sabha, better sense prevailed and it was decided to create the bilingual State of Bombay containing all the territories of Maharashtra and Saurashtra with Bombay as capital. The Bill was passed by the Lok Sabha and Rajya Sabha and received the assent of President on August 31, 1956.

THE STATES REORGANISATION ACT, 1956

The States Reorganisation Act provided for the creation of the new State of Andhra Pradesh by adding certain territories to the existing State of Andhra. Most of the territories were to be taken from the State of Hyderabad. Certain territories were added to the State of Madras. Provision was made for the creation of the new State of Kerala comprising the territories of the existing State of Travancore-Cochin. A new part 'C' State known as Laccadive, Minicoy and Aminidivi Islands was created. To the existing State of Mysore, certain territories taken from Hyderabad, Madras, Bombay and Coorg were added. A new State of Bombay consisting of certain territories taken from the States of Hyderabad and Madhya Pradesh and the territories of the existing States of Bombay, Saurashtra and Kutch was to be created. A new State of Madhya Pradesh comprising the territories of the existing State of Madhya Pradesh; Vindhya Pradesh, Bhopal and certain territories taken from Rajasthan was to be created. Ajmer was added to the State of Rajasthan. Patiala and East Punjab States Union was added to the State of Punjab. The first Schedule to the Constitution of India was amended. There were to be 13 Part 'A' States of Andhra Pradesh, Assam, Bihar, Bombay, Kerala, Madhya Pradesh, Madras, Mysore, Orissa, Punjab, Rajasthan, Uttar Pradesh and West Bengal, one Part 'B' State and five Union Territories of Delhi, Himachal Pradesh, Manipur, Tripura, and the Laccadive, Minicoy and Amindivi Islands.

India was to be divided into five zones. Each zone was to have a Zonal Council. The Northern Zone was to consist of the States of Punjab, Rajasthan, Delhi, Himachal Pradesh, etc. The Central Zone was to consist of the States of Uttar Pradesh and Madhya Pradesh. The Eastern Zone was to consist of Bihar, West Bengal, Orissa, Assam, Manipur and Tripura. The Western Zone was to consist of the States of Bombay and Mysore. The Southern Zone was to consist of Andhra Pradesh, Madras and Kerala. Each Zonal Council was to consist of a Union Minister to be nominated by the President, Chief Ministers of each of the States included in the zone and two other Ministers of each State. The Union Minister was to be the Chairman. The Chief Ministers of the States included in each zone were to act as Vice-Chairmen of the Zonal Councils by rotation, each holding office for a period of one year at a time. Each Zonal Council was to have certain advisers to help her in the performance of its duties. It was to meet at such time as the Chairman of the Council fixed. It was to meet in the States included in the Zone by rotation. All questions were to be decided by a majority vote. However, the Chairman was to have a casting vote in case of a tie. The proceedings of every meetings of the Zonal Council were to be forwarded to the Central Government and also to each State Government concerned. Each Zonal Council was to have a Secretariat staff consisting of a Secretary and such other officers as the Chairman may consider necessary. The Chief Secretaries of the States represented in each Council were to be the Secretary of the Council by rotation. They were to hold office for a period of one year at a time. The office of the Zonal Council was to be located at such a place within the zone as may be determined by the Council. The Central Government was to bear all the expenses of the office. The Zonal Council was to act as an Advisory Body and was to discuss those matters in which some or all the States represented in the Council had a common interest. The Council was to advise the Central Government and the government of each State concerned regarding the action to be taken on any such matter. It was to discuss and make recommendations with regard to any matter of common interest in the field of economic and social planning, any matter concerning border disputes, linguistic minorities or inter-state transport and any matter connected with or arising out of the reorganisation of the States. Provision was made for joint meeting of the Zonal Councils. Changes were made in the number of seats allotted to each state in the Council of States.

The Central Government was to set up a Delimitation Commission consisting of three members. The Chief Election Commissioner was to be its ex-officio member and the other two members were to be appointed by the Central Government. The Chairman of the Commission was to be appointed by the Central Government from the members. The Commission was to determine on the basis of population figures the number of seats to be reserved for the Scheduled Castes and Scheduled Tribes of each of the States of Andhra Pradesh, Bombay, Kerala, Madhya Pradesh, Madras, Mysore, Punjab and Rajasthan in the House of the People and the Legislative Assemblies of the States. It was to determine the Parliamentary and Assembly constituencies into which each new State was to be divided, extent of and the number of seats, to be allotted to each constituency and number of seats to be reserved for the Scheduled Castes and Scheduled Tribes of the State in each constituency. Provision was made for the creation for each of the new States a State Cadre of the Indian Administrative Service and a State Cadre of the Indian Police Service. The initial strength and composition of each of the Cadres was to be fixed by the Central Government.

The Government of Part 'C' States Act, 1951 was repealed with effect from 1st November 1956. The Third Schedule to the States Reorganization Act, 1956 gave details regarding the number of seats allotted to each State in the House of the People and the Legislative Assembly.

With effect from January 20 1957, the State of Jammu and Kashmir was declared to be an integral part of India, The Constituent Assembly dissolved itself after framing a new Constitution for the State.

After the establishment of the composite State of Bombay under the States Reorganisation Act, 1956, there was a lot of agitation for the separation of Maharashtra from Gujarat. For a long time the Government of India resisted the demand. That led to riots on a large scale and ultimately the Government of India was forced to enact the Bombay Reorganisation Act, 1960. It received the assent of the President on April 25 1960. It provided for the creation of two separate States of Maharashtra and Gujarat. The capital of Maharashtra was to be Bombay and that of Gujarat was to be at some other place. While Maharashtra was to have Bombay High Court, Gujarat was to have its separate High Court at some other place. Separate representation was given to Maharashtra and Gujarat in Lok Sabha and Rajya Sabha. Gujarat was to send 22 and Maharashtra 44 members to Lok Sabha. They were also to send 11 and 19 members to Rajya Sabha respectively. The Legislative Assembly of Gujarat was to consist of 132 and that of Maharashtra 264 members. There was to be no Legislative Council for Gujarat, but the Legislative Council of Maharashtra was to consist of 78 members. Provision was also made for the division of the assets of the former State of Bombay between Maharashtra and Gujarat.

In July 1960, the Government of India decided to set up the new State of Nagaland with Kohima as its capital. This was done to satisfy the discontented elements in that region. An Act was passed in 1962 to implement that decision. In April 1970 was created the new state of Meghalaya.

There was some trouble in Punjab. There was an agitation for the creation of a Punjabi Suba. When it assumed alarming proportions, the Government of India appointed a Boundary Commission which was presided over by Mr. Justice Shah of the Supreme Court of India. The direction given to the Commission was: "The Commission shall examine the existing boundary of the Hindi and Punjabi Regions of the present State of Punjab and recommend what adjustments, if any, are necessary in that boundary to secure the linguistic homogeneity of the proposed Punjab and Haryana States. The Commission shall also indicate the boundaries of the hill areas of the present State of Punjab which are contiguous to Himachal Pradesh and have linguistic and cultural affinity with that territory. The Commission shall apply the linguistic principle with due regard to the census figures of 1961 and other relevant considerations. The Commission may also take into account such other factors as administrative convenience and economic well-being, geographic contiguity and facility of communication and will ordinarily ensure that the adjustments that they may recommend do not involve breaking up of existing tehsils."

The Commission submitted its report in May 1966. Some areas which formerly belonged to Punjab were given to Himachal Pradesh and the rest of the Punjab was divided into the States of Punjab and Haryana. The majority of the members of the Commission recommended that Chandigarh be given to Haryana. The Report was not accepted in full by the Government of India. The Punjab Reorganisation Act, 1966. was passed by the Indian Parliament and it received the assent of the President on September 18, 1966. It was provided that a new State known as Haryana shall be set up and it was to have Hissar, Rohtak, Gurgaon, Karnal and Mahendragarh districts, Narwana and Jind Tehsils of Sangrur district, Ambala, Jagadhri and Naraingarh districts. Pirjore Kanungo circle of Kharar tehsil of Ambala District and the territories in Manimajra Kanungo circle of Kharar tehsil of Ambala District specified in the First Schedule. Provision was made for the establishment of the Union Territory of Chandigarh. It was also provided that to the Union Territory of Himachal Pradesh, Simla, Kangra, Kulu and Lahaul and Spiti Districts, Nalagarh Tehsil of Ambala district, Loharu, Amb, and Una Kanungo circles of Una Tehsil of Hoshiarpur District, the territories in Santokhgarh Kanungo circle of Una Tehsil of Hoshiarpur District, etc., would be added. The rest of the territory of Punjab was to belong to Punjab. Provision was made for the allocation of seats in the Council of States, House of the People, and Legislative Assemblies. There was to be a common High Court for the States of Punjab and Haryana and the Union Territory of Chandigarh. Provision was also made for the distribution of assets, etc., among the States.

The Punjab Reorganisation Act, 1960 did not satisfy the aspirations of the Sikhs and they were particularly sore about Chandigarh. No wonder, the Sikhs started agitation once again and Sant Fateh Singh went on fast unto death and fixed a date for burning himself alive unless Chandigarh was given to Punjab. There were negotiations at the eleventh hour and ultimately it was agreed to refer the disputes between the States of Punjab and Haryana to the arbitration of Mrs. Indira Gandhi, Prime Minister of India.

Due to certain circumstances, the decision was not given by Indira Gandhi. The result was that tension began to grow between the two states. Shri Pheruman went on fast unto death to get Chandigarh for Punjab, but even his death did not move the Prime Minister to give her decision. Ultimately, Sant Fateh Singh once again did the miracle. He declared that he would go on fast on 26 January 1970, and immolate himself on 1 February 1970, if Chandigarh was not given to Punjab. He actually went on fast on 26 January. The situation became tense. It was under these circumstances that Indira Gandhi announced on 29 January 1970 that Chandigarh will be merged in Punjab and Haryana will be compensated by the transfer of 114-Hindi-speaking villages of Fazilka Tehsil, including Fazilka and Abohar towns in Punjab and 6 villages from the Chandigarh Union Territory. In addition, Haryana was to get from the Government of India ₹20 crores, half of which was to be in the form of a grant and the rest as loan to build a new capital. Chandigarh was to remain a Union Territory for the maximum period of five years as joint capital of both Punjab and Haryana, after which it was to be transferred to Punjab. It was also announced that the remaining territorial disputes between the two states will be referred to a Commission which was to submit its report within a short time. The terms of references of the Commission will be settled in consultation with the Governments of Punjab, Haryana and Himachal Pradesh. The Hindi speaking villages in Fazilka and the six villages in the Union Territory, which were to be transferred to Haryana, will be outside the purview of the proposed Commission.

BORDER DISPUTES BETWEEN MAHARASHTRA AND MYSORE

It was in the year 1957 that the Government of Bombay submitted a memorandum to the Ministry of Home Affairs suggesting the readjustment of border areas between Bombay and Mysore States. It was stated in that memorandum that while, the States Reorganisation Act had settled of the main framework of the reorganisation of states on a linguistic basis, a large number of marginal territorial adjustments had still to be made. The Government of Mysore reacted adversely to the claim made by the Government of Bombay. The Government of Bombay requested that its proposal be placed before the Zonal Council at an early date. The Zonal Council was unable to decide the matter before the two States of Maharashtra and Gujarat were formed, and a new Western Zone came into existence and the Mysore State was taken out of the Western Zone and included in the Southern Zone. On the suggestion of the Home Minister of India, it was agreed to refer the boundary dispute to a Four-Man Committee. Each State nominated two representatives. Nothing came out of this Four-Man Committee in spite of the waste of two years.

Agitation started once again and continued for about 4 years. The Chief Ministers of the two States met from time to time but they failed to come to any compromise. A high-power delegation of Congressmen from Maharashtra and Bombay met the Prime Minister, the Congress President and the Home Minister and urged upon them the necessity of appointing a Commission at once. They made it clear that if that was not done at once, there was the possibility of the Congress losing heavily in the forthcoming general elections. A delegation arrived from Kasaragod with a mass petition demanding that the Working Committee should decided in favour of the merger of Kasaragod in the Mysore State. It was under these circumstances that Dr. Mehr Chand Mahajan former Chief Justice of India, was appointed on October 25 1966, as One-Man Commission to resolve the boundary disputes between the States of Maharashtra, Mysore and Kerala. The Commission had to do a lot of touring and ultimately it submitted its Report on August 25 1967 and the same was released to the public on November 4 1967. In this Report, Dr. Mehr Chand Mahajan recommended the transfer of certain villages from Mysore to Maharashtra and vice versa. He also recommended the incorporation of Kasaragod in the State of Mysore. Dr. Mahajan favoured neither one party nor the other. He accepted neither all the claims of Maharashtra nor those of Mysore.

In April 1970 was created the new state of Meghalaya. In the beginning of 1971, the Union Territory of Himachal Pradesh was created as a State. The North-Eastern Areas (Reorganisation) Act, 1971 gave Manipur, Tripura and Meghalaya the status of States. Union Territories were created out of Mizoram and Arunachal Pradesh by reorganising the State of Assam.

When the Indian states were merged into the Union of India, their rulers were left with their Privy Purses and a few personal privileges. In 1967, the All India Congress Committee passed a resolution demanding their abolition. A bill was introduced in Parliament. It was passed by Lok Sabha but it failed to secure the requisite majority in Rajya Sabha on 5 September 1970. That very night, the President of India signed an instrument by which he withdrew recognition of the rulers. The order of the President was challenged in the Supreme Court of India. The Supreme Court quashed that order and held that the Indian rulers were entitled to all their pre-existing rights and privileges, including the right to Privy Purses. General elections were held in the beginning of 1971 and the new Parliament approved of the 26th Constitution Amendment Bill in December 1971 and the President gave his assent on 31 December 1971 and thereby terminated the Privy Purses and the titles and privileges of the Indian rulers. In 1975, Sikkim was added as a State of the Union of India.

REVIEW QUESTIONS

1. Give a detailed description of the relationship between the English and Indian states in different epochs.
2. Give an account of the British government policies towards the development of the Indian States.
3. Discuss in detail the policies of the British towards the growth and development of the Indian states in different periods.
4. Throw light on the recommendations of the Butler Committee.
5. Explain the salient features of the Government of India Act, 1935.
6. Write a detailed note on the integration and democratisation of states.
7. Discuss the recommendations of the States Reorganisation Commission.
8. Bring out the main features of the States Reorganisation Act, 1956.
9. Write short notes on the following:
   (a) Ring-Fence Policy
   (b) Policy of Subordinate Isolation
   (c) Policy of Subordinate Union
   (d) Reorganisation of Indian states

SUGGESTED READINGS

Ambedkar, B.R.: *Thoughts on Linguistic States*, 1955.
Menon, V.P.: *The Story of the Integration of the Indian States*, 1956.
Mukherjee and Ramaswamy: *Reorganisation of Indian States*.
Panikkar, K.M.: *The Evolution of British Policy towards Indian States (1774-1858)*, 1929.
Phadnis, Urmila: *Towards the Integration of Indian States*.
Rao, V. Venkata: "The Political Map of India", *The Indian Journal of Political Science*, 1956, pp. 176-204.
Report of the States Reorganisation Commission, 1955.
Sharma, P.K.: *Political Aspects of States Reorganisation in India*, 1969.
Singh, G.N.: *Indian States and British India*.
Varadachariar: *Indian States in the Federation*.
White Paper on Indian States, 1950.
Warner, Lee: *The Native States of India*, 1910.

33 Legacy of British Rule in India

LEARNING OBJECTIVES

- Throw light on the legacy of the British rule in India
- Assess the views of various historians on the impact of the British legacy on India

British rule in India lasted for about 200 years and the British left India in 1947 after transferring power into the hands of the Indians in a peaceful manner. Such a long rule was bound to leave behind a rich legacy.

1. The most important legacy of British rule in India is the unification of India. Undoubtedly, it was British imperialism which brought about the unification of the country and enabled the people of India to think as one nation. Before the coming of the English to India, the people of the South were usually separated from the rest of India except for some short intervals. Prof. Moon rightly says that "British Imperialism in India gave her a political unity under a third party in spite of the many discordant elements in Indian society." The whole of India came to be governed from one Central Government. It is true that there were provincial Governments but those were merely the agents of the Central Government and it was their duty to carry out its orders.

   It is rightly pointed out that the unity given to India by the British was not a complete one. During the British rule, India was divided into British India and non-British India and the latter was ruled by the Indian Princes, Chiefs and estate-holders. In spite of the emergence of a strong nationalist movement in the country, the people in the States were separate and it required a lot of effort on the part of men like Sardar Patel to make them a part and parcel of the Union of India. Moreover, the British created many invidious distinctions which were liable to create a split in Indian society. They recruited in the Indian army soldiers only from the so-called martial races. The object was to recruit only those who were loyal to the British rule in India. In public services also, preference was shown to the Muslims, Anglo-Indians, Europeans and certain castes or sub-castes among the Hindus. From 1909 onwards, separate representation was given to the Muslims, Sikhs, Anglo-Indians, Indian Christians and Europeans. They were given not only separate representation but even weightage in their representation in order to keep them away from the mainstream of national life. The net result was that the unity given to India by the British was not a solid one and ultimately it led to the partition of the country in 1947.

2. Another legacy of British rule was the emergence of a sense of national consciousness in India. British rule in India brought the Indians into intimate contact with the European countries and they were very much influenced by them. The 19th century in Europe was the century of nationalism and liberalism and the Indians learnt their lessons in nationalism and liberalism

from the Europeans. It was rightly felt by the people of India that if Germany and Italy could achieve their independence and unity, they also could do the same. The practical examples of those countries created a new spirit among the Indians to fight for the liberation of their country. National consciousness was also aroused by the Indian press and literature, both in English and in vernacular. The discontentment of the people with many acts of omission and commission of the British in India also simulated the nationalist movement in the country. The English language also played its part in the growth of nationalism. It acted as the **lingua franca** for the intelligentsia of India. Without the common medium of the English language, it would have been impossible for the people of India coming from various parts of the country to discuss at one place the common problems facing the country. The English language also put the English literature into the hands of the Indians and that also had its effect on the growth of national consciousness in the country. It cannot be denied that national consciousness in India arose as a direct result of her connection with England. It is men like Hume who played an important part in the creation of the Indian National Congress which played a glorious role in the awakening of the national consciousness in the country.

It is rightly pointed out that the idols of the early Indian nationalists were the European patriots. During the 1870's, Surendra Nath Banerjee often put the following question to the members of his audience: "Who among you will be a Mazzini, a Garibaldi? The reply used to be: "All, all." The Irish movement for home-rule was closely watched by the Indians and that also provided them with inspiration. Bradlaugh, an Irish statesman-politician, visited India and addressed the annual session of the Indian National Congress. It cannot be denied that the concept of human rights and human equality is taken from the West.

3. Another legacy of British rule in India was the adoption of a democratic form of Government in the country. The present Constitution of India provides for a democratic form of Government for the country and the credit must go to the British for evolving the same. The beginnings were made in the year 1853 and the process was continued in 1861, 1892, 1909, 1919 and 1935. By stages, British Government transferred to Indians larger and larger share in the administration of the country. The result was that partly by this process and partly as a result of the experience gained from other sources, the leaders of India were able to take over the responsibility of running the administration of the country in 1947. What was given to the people of India by the British in 1947 was a democratic Government and the same was continued after that. This very process was applied to the Indian States after 1947. The result was that a democratic form of Government was set up in the whole of India. It is not possible to forget or ignore the meritorious services of men like Lord Ripon who set up municipalities and District Boards for the purpose of giving political and popular education to the people of India.

4. Another legacy of British rule in India is the Parliamentary form of Government in the country. British Parliament is rightly called the mother of Parliaments. The British introduced in India what they had in their own country. It was slowly and slowly that in 1861, 1892, 1909, 1919 and 1935, Parliamentary institutions and practices, were introduced in the country. The Indians were allowed to put questions and supplementary questions to the Government of the day. They were allowed to discuss and criticise the budget of the country and also reject the same. Dyarchy was introduced in the provinces in 1919 and this Indian Ministers were put in charge of certain Departments in the provinces. A further step was taken in 1935 when provincial autonomy was introduced and the responsibility for the administration of most of the Departments in provinces was put in the hands of the Indians. The Government of India Act, 1935 also provided for a large measure of parliamentary form of Government at the Centre with many reservations. But the Federation never came into being. The net result of all this was that when the British left India in 1947, India had a parliamentary set-up in the country. Even when the Constituent Assembly laboured hard to frame a Constitution of India, it was decided to retain the parliamentary form of Government for the country and the same is embodied in the new Constitution of India, both at the centre and the States. Even in the Union Territories,

a parliamentary form of Government prevails and all this is a legacy of the British rule in India. It is true that men like Chief Justice Mehr Chand Mahajan and Chief Justice M. C. Chagla have advocated a presidential form of Government for the country with a view to remedy some of the ills which have come in the country as a result of the working of the parliamentary institutions during the last few years but in spite of that the parliamentary form of Government is being maintained in the country as a whole. We find every day parliamentary practices and usages from England being quoted and followed both in the Indian Parliament and the State Assemblies.

5. Another legacy of the British rule is the rule of law. One of the greatest achievements of the British in their own country was the establishment of the rule of law. This they did after a long struggle. When British institutions were introduced, the rule of law was also introduced in the country. No man was to be punished except according to law. All were equal before the law. Public servants were not to enjoy any special privileges. If any person violated the law of the country, he was to be punished irrespective of his status. The same law was to apply to all. The Code of Civil Procedure, the Code of Criminal Procedure, the Indian Evidence Act, the Indian Penal Code, the Indian Contract Act, the Sale of Goods Act, the Partnership Act, etc, applied equally to all whether an individual was a Hindu, Muslim or a Christian.

The rule of law was applied impartially by the British in India so far as the relations between the Indians were concerned. However, a departure was made in the case of Europeans who were entitled to a special procedure in criminal cases against them. That led to a lot of agitation on the occasion of the Ilbert Bill but the distinction was continued. Moreover, public servants could not be prosecuted without the permission of the Government in certain cases. In spite of these exceptions, the rule of law was enforced in the country by an independent judiciary. This rule of law has also been adopted by the people of India even after the departure of the British from the country. The Indian Constitution embodies the rule of law and with a few exceptions, every effort is made to stick to the principles of rule of law in the country.

6. Another legacy of the British rule is the present legal system in the country. The more critically we study the present legal set-up in the country, the more it becomes clear that the present legal system in the country is a legacy of the British rule. We teach the same textbooks on law as they do in England. Jurisprudence by Salmond is as much taught in India as in England. We follow the analytical system as they do in England. The method of Case Law is now being introduced after the independence of the country but the old basis still continues. The Code of Civil Procedure, the Code of Criminal Procedure, the Indian Evidence Act, the Indian Penal Code, the Indian Contract Act, the Sale of Goods Act, the Partnership Act, etc., are a legacy of the British rule in India. As a matter of fact, whatever law was found useful in England was introduced into India. A comparison of the Statutes of India up to 1947 with the Statutes in England on the same subject is both instructive and profitable. It clearly shows how much our past legislation was based on the legalisation in England in the same field. Even today, we quote everyday decisions from the courts in England. Lord Denning is more popular in India than any other judge of any other court in the world. The Supreme Court is merely a continuation of the Federal Court of India and the Privy Council. We cannot forget the excellent work done by the Indian Law Commissions during the 19th century. All this is a legacy of the British rule in India and this has become a part and parcel of our national life.

However, the legal system inherited from the British is very expensive and beyond the reach of the man in the street. It is also time-consuming. It takes years to dispose of a case and there is truth in the contention that justice delayed is justice denied. The legal system is very complicated and beyond the comprehension of the common man. One takes a very serious risk if one appears in a court of law without a lawyer, although the court is always presided over by a judge. The latter is in a way useless to the litigant. He can decide a matter but cannot advise him as to what he should do.

7. Another legacy is the present system of administration in the country. Before the beginning of British rule in India, the working of the Government depended very much upon the sweet will

of the ruler concerned. If he was able, everything was all right. Under an inefficient or weak ruler, the whole thing collapsed. It goes to the credit of the British Government that they set up a systematic framework which continued the work in a routine manner. Administrative Manuals were prepared in every Department containing detailed instructions regarding its working. There was to be no ambiguity about the same and hence the chances of arbitrary action or the failure of administrative machinery were very much lessened. A system of competitive examinations was introduced and the result was that the best talent in the country was attracted. This does not mean that everybody was appointed on the basis of merit alone. It is well-known that in many cases, even nominations were made. However, the administrative set-up was pretty efficient. The Indian Civil Service did a marvelous job and some of the officers brought with them a standard of efficiency which was rarely equalled but never surpassed. As the officers were trained and came to have a lot of experience in due course of time, the administrative machinery was able to shoulder the responsibilities of the government of a big country like India. Bureaucracy had its advantages and disadvantages but it goes to its credit that India enjoyed such an efficient administration which she had never seen before. It is true that the Indians hated the Civil Servants on account of their bias against them, but these very men were found to be useful when the British left India in 1947 and the responsibility of running the administration fell on the Indians themselves. The manner in which they faced the problems after the independence of India does them credit and that was undoubtedly a legacy of the British rule in India. The example set by the Indian Civil Service in the matter of efficiency deserves to be followed by the present and future generations of India.

8. Another legacy of the British rule in India is the industrialization of the country. It cannot be denied that there was practically no money which was required for the industrialization of the country. It is the Englishmen who invested their money in the railways which were constructed in every nook and corner of the country. It is their spirit of the enterprise that did the trick. Railways were constructed both for commercial and military purposes. Without the British lead, it would have been difficult to accomplish the same. It is the Englishmen who set up jute mills and cotton textile mills in the country. They were responsible for the growth of indigo and tea. They took the lead and the same was followed by others. The Tatas and the Birlas came later on in the field. The system of joint stock companies was introduced in the country by the British. India moved from the cottage industries to the factories and that is very much a legacy of British rule in India.

9. The urbanisation of India is also a legacy of the British rule. Formerly, most of the Indians lived in the villages. It is the Englishmen who set up factories where millions of Indians assembled from the villages. The old towns were replaced by large towns like Bombay (now Mumbai), Madras (now Chennai) and Calcutta (now Kolkata). Industrial towns like Ahmedabad also came into prominence. Urbanisation brought to the fore the problem of slums. The joint family ties were weakened. The very face of society underwent a revolution.

10. Another legacy is the present educational system in the country. It is true that before the coming of the British in India, we had our Pathshalas and Madrassas but not much could be expected from them in the field of higher learning. Credit must go to the Englishmen for setting up universities, colleges, high schools and other schools in the country. It is true that to begin with the Indian Universities were merely examining bodies and practically no teaching work was done in them. However, that stage has passed away and there are many universities in the country which are doing teaching work as well. Indian Universities have become the centres of higher education and research. It would have been difficult to secure the millions of officers and clerks required for running the present administrative machinery without the Universities set up by the Englishmen. It is not denied that a lot was accomplished as a result of co-operation received from the Indians but the credit for giving the initiative must go to them. They introduced in India what they had in their own country and it goes without saying that we have benefited immensely. Critics may find many shortcomings in the present

educational system in our country, but it will be practically impossible to replace the same by another system of education.

11. It is the Englishmen who helped India to discover her past. It is them who led the way which was followed later on by the Indian scholars. It was the efforts of Englishmen that helped us to decipher the Brahmi script. Without it, it would have been impossible to decipher the various inscriptions that were discovered from the various parts of the country. The glory and grandeur of Asoka would have remained hidden from without the labours and efforts of English scholars. It would have been difficult to decipher the inscriptions of Asoka. It is the Englishmen, who translated into English the whole of the Buddhist literature and made it available to the Indians. It is they who translated the Ceylonese chronicles, viz., Dipavamsa and Mahavamsa. The Sacred Books of the East series did a lot to reveal to India the glory of her past and the knowledge of the ancient saints of India. We cannot forget the debt that we owe to scholars like Max Muller, Weber, Macdonnell, Monier Williams, Barnett, Winternitz, A. B. Keith, Rhys Davids, H.H. Wilson, Allen, Fleet, Sir Mortimer Wheeler, Sir John Marshall, etc. It was Dr. V. A. Smith who did the pioneer work in the History of Ancient India. Cunningham's work in the field of archaeology is well-known. The work of Pargiter on the Puranas is remarkable. The 5 volumes of the Cambridge History of India are a true legacy of British rule in India. We cannot forget the work done by the British scholars on Sanskrit in general and the Vedas in particular. Mcrindle did an immense work in collecting and editing all references about India by Megasthenes and others. It is the Englishmen who edited and translated the accounts of Fahein, Hiuen Tsang and Itsing. The lead was given by the Englishmen to hunt out old manuscripts and later on those manuscripts were collated and translated. *The History of India as Told by Her Own Historians* by Elliot and Dawson was also due to the industry of Englishmen. Akbarnama, Ain-i-Akbari, Humayun Nama, Tuzk-i-Jahangiri. Tuzk-i-Babari, ets., were all edited and translated into English by the Englishmen and all that helped the growth of learning in the country. All this is a legacy of the British rule in India.

12. Indian literature was also influenced by the British rule in India. It is true that the Englishmen, to begin with, used Persian and Urdu for their administrative work, later on English was introduced in every sphere of the government. English education spread slowly but steadily and ultimately that had a tremendous influence on the people of India. The knowledge of English brought with it the knowledge of the English literature and all that it contained. The result was that the Indians were very much influenced by the Western learning. We had no such thing as newspapers in the modern sense of the term in the past. It is the Englishmen who started newspapers for themselves and slowly and slowly Indian newspapers appeared both in English and the various vernacular languages of India. Indian drama was very much influenced by the English drama. The technique of writing novels in India was very much influenced by what was there in England. Even Indian poetry was affected by English contact. The Indians learnt to write short stories, satires, One-Act plays, etc., on the model of English example. The English principles of literary criticism were copied in this country. Western influence on Indian art is total. Modern Indian art has become experimental like that of Europe and America. It has gone through all the European historical styles. Recently Indian art has taken a new turn under the inspiration of some Englishmen and Indians such as Havell, Abanindranath Tagore and others.

13. It is well known that the English East India Company was opposed to missionary activity in its territorial possessions in India. It was under pressure that it allowed in 1813 missionaries to travel on its ships and admitted to British Bishop at Calcutta. British Prime Minister Spencer Percival was a friend of the Evangelicals and he helped the missionaries to overcome in 1808 the opposition of the English Company to allow missionaries in its territories. These missionaries did a tremendous job and were able to convert lakhs of Indians to Christianity.

The propaganda of the Christian missionaries had its repercussions on Indian society. Under Christian criticism, the Hindus learnt to re-examine the tenets of their religion and were in turn influenced by Western concepts. Raja Ram Mohan Roy, who is described by Nicol Macnicol as "India's Columbus in the discovery of a new continent of truth", made the first organised effort to adopt Hinduism to the new conditions. He was a scholar of Sanskrit, Hebrew, Greek, 'Persian, Arabic and English. He was a follower of Vedantic philosophy but admirer of Christianity. He was ready and willing to borrow everything that was good in Christianity. He stood for western learning for the Indians. He demanded the abolition of **Sati**. He founded the Brahmo Samaj which has been described by Mayhew as "doctrinally similar to Victorian utilitarianism. He stood for the synthesis of Eastern" and Western cultures.

The propaganda of the Christian missionaries also provoked Swami Dayanand, founder of the Arya Samaj. He called upon the Hindus to remove the evils that had crept into Hindu society. He gave the Hindus self-confidence and determination to fight for their existence and progress. He assured them that their religion was better than Christianity or Islam.

His propaganda made the Christians and Muslims uneasy. A large number of D.A.V. Schools and Colleges were set up in the country and those were instrumental in spreading western knowledge in India in addition to Indian culture.

Swami Vivekananda preached "oneness of all religions." He asked the Hindus to become better Hindus, Muslims to become better Muslims and the Christians to become better Christians. He interpreted Indian thought to Western people and provided a bridge between the East and the West. He was not apologetic in his speeches or writings. He spoke and wrote with self-confidence and righteous pride.

Mahatma Gandhi, Maharishi Aurobindo, Tagore, Nehru and Dr. Radhakrishnan were influenced by the West. It is well-known that Gandhiji admired Christianity. He often admitted that his concept of nonviolence was influenced by the Sermon on the Mount. In his daily prayer meetings, the popular hymns were: "When I survey the wonderous Cross" and "Lead kindly Light amid the encircling gloom." About Maharishi Aurobindo. the greatest modern Indian philosopher, thinker, saint and mystic, Hakim says: Sri Aurobindo has by a great spiritual vision comprehended into one organised whole the heritage of the East the West, the old and the new." It cannot be denied that Marx has also influenced modern Indian thought and life.

14. The biggest legacy of the British rule in India is that very many Indians learnt not only to dress like Englishmen but also to think, speak, write and act as Englishmen. The result is that although the Englishmen went away in the year 1947, their thoughts, their dress and their institutions have become a part and parcel of our lives. Not only our leaders but even the common people copy the west in the matter of dress. Even to-day, many people in India take pride in speaking English and writing in English. Most of the work of the Government is also done in the English language. Even to-day, English literature inspires many of us and moulds our way of thinking and acting.

The view of Dr. Tara Chand is that the British impact was like the application of hoe and shears to prune to rotten roots and dead branches. It was like the advent of the spring tide after a formidable winter. The changes brought about by British rulers in polity and economy of India, though in some cases, quite radical, failed to affect a social revolution which could only take place if Indian economy had grown out of its medieval agrarian system into a modern industrial regime. Whatever degree of modernisation was achieved was more or less confined to the cities and affected the villages only indirectly and superficial. The change of mind was largely a bourgeois phenomenon, a change of the middle-class intelligentsia. This was natural and inevitable. The educated class alone had the opportunity to assimilate. Western knowledge, to study close Western sciences, philosophy and literature and to learn by actual participation in Western type activities, the values and modes of Western life. Their reaction to the ideology from the West took several forms. Some Indians were swept off their feet completely. They rejected their Indian traditions root and branch. A second school of thought took the opposite extreme and justified the whole of this tradition. In the middle was a group of thinkers who endeavoured to shift the wheat from the chaff, the national and the pure and the high-minded from the fatuous, degrading and false.

R. P. Dutt says. "In the earlier period of British Rule, in the first half of the nineteenth century, the British rulers—in the midst of, and actually through all the misery and industrial devastation— were performing an actively progressive role, were in many spheres actively combating the conservative and feudal forces of Indian society... . This was the period of courageous reforms, of such measures as the abolition of suttee (carried out with the wholehearted co-operation of the progressive elements of Indian society), the abolition of slavery (a more formal measure in practice), the war on infanticide and thuggism, the introduction of western education and the freeing of the Press. Rigid in their outlook, unsympathetic to all that was backward in Indian traditions, convinced that the nineteenth century bourgeois and Christian conception was the norm for humanity, these early administrators nevertheless carried on a powerful work of innovation representing the spirit of the early ascendant bourgeoisie of the period; and the best of them like Sir Henry Lawrence, won the respect and affection of those with whom they had to deal... . The deepest enemies of the British were the old reactionary rulers who saw in them their supplanters. The most progressive elements in Indian society, at that time represented by Ram Mohan Roy and the reform movement of the Brahmo Samaj, looked with unconcealed admiration to the British as the champions of progress, gave unhesitating support to their reforms, and saw in them the vanguard of a new civilization." (*India Today*, pp. 273-74.)

About the legacy of the British rule in India, K. Santhanam says that by extinguishing and suppressing many medieval vested interests, British imperialism did clear the way for the emergence of modern India. It established peace and the rule of law. It evolved the Indian Penal Code, the Code of Civil Procedure and the Code of Criminal Procedure and civil laws except those regarding marriage, adoption, inheritance and succession, which were common to the whole country. The English education infused the people with the ideas of freedom and democracy and that provided a valuable climate for the birth of Indian nationalism. It built up railways and promoted plantation industries of tea and coffee which became valuable assets of Indian economy. In the beginning of this century, it permitted and occasionally encouraged the development of modern industries of jute, cotton and sugar. Though it was done under pressure, the introduction of the principle of representative Government in 1909 provided valuable introduction to the principle and procedure of parliamentary democracy.

As regards the debit side of the British rule, a tremendous blow was given to Indian economy by the destruction of cottage industries of India and the premature and forcible introduction of machine-made foreign goods. Millions of persons engaged in cottage industries were forced to fall back upon agriculture which has already over-crowded. By discouragement of the growth of modern industry, the Indian economy was kept at least 100 years behind the economy of Europe and America. The country was systematically drained of capital resources and the people reduced to poverty. The policy of divide and rule made the Hindus and Muslims enemies of each other and ultimately resulted in the Partition of India. British imperialism resulted in social, economic and moral stagnation which still persist in spite of the struggle for freedom and decades of independence. (*British Imperialism and Indian Nationalism*, pp. 60-61.)

However, there are some writers who have written critically about the British rule in India. Dadabhai Naoroji, the grand old Man of Indian nationalism and a Liberal member of the House of Commons, who was elected and re-elected President of the Indian National Congress many a time like Jawaharlal Nehru later on, while praising the many blessings of law and order which was given by the British to India, characterised the British rule in India as "un-British" as the despotic system of Government in British India was destructive to India as well as to British ideals and honour. There are many others who hold the view that the British could have done more than what they actually did in India. We may conclude with the following observation of Edward Thompson and G. T. Garratt:

"Whatever the future may hold, the direct influence of the West upon India is likely to decrease. But it would be absurd to imagine that the British connection will not leave a permanent mark upon Indian life. On the merely material side the new Federal Government will take over the largest irrigation system in the world with thousands of miles of canals and watercuts fertilising between thirty and forty million acres; some 60,000 miles of metalled roads; over 42,000 miles of railway of which three-quarters are State-owned; 230,000 scholastic institutions with over twelve million scholars; and a great number of buildings, including government/offices, inspection bungalows, provincial and central legislatures. The vast area of India has been completely surveyed, most of its land assessed and a regular census taken of its population and its productivity. An effective defensive system has been built up on its vulnerable North-West frontier, it has an Indian army with century-old traditions, and a police force which compares favourably with any outside a few Western countries. The postal department handles nearly 1,550 million articles yearly. The Forestry Department not only prevents the denudation of immense areas, but makes a net profit of between two and three crores. These great State activities are managed by a trained bureaucracy which is today almost entirely Indian.

"The spiritual heritage is far more difficult to estimate and for many years most people will have their judgment warped by the racial animosities of the last half-century. How much of the common language and common culture which we have introduced will survive under the new constitution? Will the three per cent of 'English educated' Indians cling to their knowledge when the present racial animosity has become less acute, and will a happier relationship begin when English administrators go East only at Indian invitation? Many special virtues, as well as failings, went to the building up of the British Empire and its retention by a minute force. A high sense of duty, incorruptibility, a passion for improving, a recognition of social responsibility, these may be remembered and be better appreciated when the friction due to disputed authority, economic grievances, and social differences has been forgotten." (*Rise and Fulfilment of British Rule in India*, pp. 654-55.)

REVIEW QUESTIONS

1. Critically examine the legacy of the British rule in India.
2. What do you know about British imperialism and Indian nationalism? Explain.
3. The unification of India is the most important legacy of the British rule. Examine.
4. The emergence of a sense of national consciousness in India is also a legacy of the British rule. Evaluate.
5. Analyse the impact of the British legacy on post-independent India.
6. The legal system of our country is inherited from the British. Comment.
7. The most important enduring legacy of Britishers is 'Colonial Mentality', which has continued to impede India's development and identity. Examine.
8. Elaborate on the contribution and impact of the British rule on India.

SUGGESTED READINGS

Banerjee, S.N.: *Speeches and Writings* (Madras).
Chimamani, C.Y.: *India and Lord Curzon*, Hindustan Review and Kayastha Samachar, June, 1901.
Dutt, R.C.: *Economic History of India—Early British Rule*, (London, 1956),
Dutt, R.P.: *India Today*.
Joshi, G.V.: *Writings and Speeches* (Poona, 1912).
Mudhokar, R.N.: *The Economic Condition of the People of India* (Madras, 1898).
Naoroji, Dadabhai: *Essays, Speeches and Writings*, edited by C. L. Parekli (Bombay, 1887).
Nundy, Alfred: *The Poverty of India* (Madras, 1898).
Santhanam, K.: *British Imperialism and Indian Nationalism*.
Thompson, Edward and G. T. Garratt: *Rise and Fulfilment of British Rule in India*.

34

Economic Impact of British Rule in India

LEARNING OBJECTIVES

- Assess the economic impact of the British rule on peasantry, agriculture and industries in India
- Throw light on the agrarian policy of the British government in India
- Know about the theory of 'Economic Drain' by Dadabhai Naoroji

INTRODUCTION

India had been conquered many times prior to the coming of the British but those conquests had resulted in changes in political regimes only. So far as the basic economic structure of India was concerned, those conquests did not affect it. The self-sufficient Indian village based on communal possession of land, unity of village industry and agriculture, the village as the unit of revenue settlement and the village production almost exclusively for village use, survived for centuries. The British conquest of India was of a different type. It was the conquest of India by a modern nation which had abolished feudalism in its own country and created a modern bourgeois society. It was the rule of a people who had already partly overcome feudal disunity of their country and integrated themselves into a modern nation through the rise and expansion of capitalism which had made the social, political and economic unification of a country possible. The British brought about an agrarian revolution. They introduced individual ownership of land. They undermined both the agrarian economy and autarchic village of India of the pre-British period. The destruction of the autarchic village and the collective life of the people was historically necessary for the economic and social unification of the Indian people. The Indian villages had been the strongholds of social passivity and intellectual inertia reproducing the same types of existence for ages-A radical change was made in that direction.

PEASANTRY

As a result of the British rule, the peasantry in India became very poor. The share claimed by the Government as land revenue was so high that even Lord Cornwallis had to say that one-third of Bengal had been transformed into a jungle inhabited only by wild beasts. Even after the British rule was firmly established in the country, the things did not improve. The Government took the place of the Zamindars and levied excessive land revenue which was fixed as high as one-third to one-half of the produce. Bishop Heber wrote in 1826, "Neither native nor European agriculturist, I think, can thrive at the present rate of taxation. Half of the gross produce of the soil is demanded by government. In Hindustan (Northern India) I found a general feeling among the King's officers... that the peasantry in the Company's provinces are on the whole worse off, poorer and more dispirited than the subjects of the native provinces; and here in Madras (now Chennai) where the soil is, generally speaking, poor, the difference is said to be still more marked. The fact is, no native prince demands the rent which we do" Mr. J. O Miller a member of the Viceroy's Executive Council, admitted this fact in those words, "Excessive enhancements are the most serious blot now left in our revenue settlement. It is very easy to justify them by arithmetical calculations but their effect on the people is apt to be left out of sight. The most recent case in which we know of the expression of the discontentment is Rawalpindi." The same point was emphasized by Mr. Gokhale in these words, "The peasantry were in debt to an extent which was experienced in no other part of the world... largely due to the system of land administration which imposed a burden far beyond what the land could bear." The Famine Commission of 1901 observed, "It is probable that at least one-fourth of the cultivators in the Bombay (now Mumbai) Presidency had lost possession of their lands and only less than one-fifth of them were free from debt."

ZAMINDARS

A large number of old Zamindars were ruined in Bengal and Madras on account of the policy of Warren Hastings to auction the right of revenue collection to the highest bidders. The Permanent Settlement of Bengal of 1793 had a similar effect at the beginning. The heaviness of land revenue and the rigid law of collection under which the Zamindari estates were sold in case there was delay in the payment of revenue, worked havoc to begin with. By 1815, nearly half of the landed property of Bengal had been transferred from the old Zamindars to merchants and other moneyed classes who usually lived in towns and were very particular in collecting their share unmindful of the consequences so far as the peasants were concerned. These absentee landlords had no sympathy for the tenants and increased the rent as much as they possibly could and ejected those tenants who refused to pay them. The result was that pressure on agriculture increased. That led to the lowering of income from land which had to be shared by many persons. That further led to the poverty of the peasants. A large number of intermediaries came into existence. They received the land from the landlord and passed on the same to others for cultivation and the latter also did likewise. In some cases in Bengal the number of rent-receiving intermediaries between the actual cultivator and the Government was so high as 50. No wonder, the condition of the actual cultivators who had ultimately to bear the burden of maintaining a large number of superior landlords, was very bad. They were left with practically nothing. Many of them were little more than slaves.

AGRICULTURE

There was stagnation and deterioration in agriculture. The Zamindars did not invest any money in their lands and the actual cultivators had practically no means to do so. Under the circumstances, the yield from land became less and less. Sub-division and fragmentation of land was also responsible for poor yield.

INDUSTRIES

The economic policy of the British Government in India proved disastrous for the Indian people. The Indian shipping industry was adversely affected by the decision of the Court of Directors of the English East India Company to use only British ships and prohibit Indian ships for the purpose of trade. Indian paper industry was undermined by the British policy to purchase only British-made paper for use in India. The industry dealing with the damascening and inlaying of arms, weapons and shields which were common in Kutch and Sind. suffered by removing the necessity for it and the prohibition of the use and possession of arms by Indians. Iron-smelting industries in India also suffered. The village industries in India collapsed and India became "an economic appendage of another country." Most of the handicraftsmen lost their means of livelihood and were reduced to the level of starvation. Industrial development in India was slow and stunted and did not represent at all an industrial revolution. Even the limited development was not independent but was under the control of foreign capital. The structure of industry was such as to mark its further development dependent on Britain. There was almost a complete absence of heavy capital goods and chemical industries without which rapid and autonomous industrial development could not take place. Machine tools and engineering and metallurgical industries were virtually non-existent. India was entirely dependent on England in the field of technology. No technological research was carried on in the country. India underwent a commercial transformation and not an industrial revolution. The trend was not towards an Indian industrial capitalist economy but towards a dependent and under-developed colonial economy. The distribution of industry was extremely lopsided and concentrated in a few regions and cities of the country. Even irrigation and electrical power facilities were unevenly distributed.

The British Government controlled trade and industry purely with a view to foster British interests. The growth of foreign trade did not contribute to the welfare of the Indian people because the balance of trade was merely to pay off the Home Charges etc. The growth of foreign trade was neither natural nor normal. The country was flooded with manufactured goods from Britain and forced to produce and export the raw materials which Britain and other foreign countries needed.

INDIA A COLONY

As a result of the British rule, India was transformed into a colony. It was a major market for British manufactures, the big source of raw materials and foodstuffs and an important field for the investment of British capital. Its agriculture was highly taxed for the benefit of imperial interests. The bulk of the transport system, modem mines and industries, foreign trade, coastal and international shipping and banks and insurance companies were all under foreign control. India provided employment to thousands of middle-class Englishmen and nearly one-third of its revenue was spent in paying salaries to Englishmen. The Indian army acted as the chief instrument for maintaining the far-flung empire and protecting and promoting British imperial interests in various parts of the world. Above all, Indian economic and social development was completely subordinated to British economy and social development. During the very years when Britain was developing into a leading developed capitalist country of the world, India was being under-developed into a backward colonial country. Dr. Tara Chand says, "Imperial Britain treated dependent India as a satellite whose main function was to sweat and labour for the master to subserve its economy and to enhance the glory and prestige of the empire."

ECONOMIC CONDITION

The economic condition of India in the last half of the 19th century was miserable in the extreme. Detailed accounts of it were given by William Digby in his book entitled "Prosperous British India," by Dadabhai Naoroji in "Poverty and Un-British Rule in India" and by R. C. Dutt in his "Economic History of India." After observing that there were only four famines between 1800 and 1825 and 22 famines between 1875 and 1900, Digby wrote. "To me it appears that the twenty-two as contrasted with the four are the product of our system of rule, of what we have done, of what we have not done. And, without malice towards any, with a heart very full of sympathy and very sore for those who have become so degraded and so full of suffering and who are wholly blameless, I tell the tale of India as I know it—I cannot, if I am to retain any sense of duty, refrain from so telling." He ridiculed the British claim of having become a trustee of India through a decree of Providence and observed, "We have become so accustomed to regarding India as a milch cow, though we never shock the effects or our sensibilities by using such an inelegant and indelicate expression, that anything which in the slightest degree appears to interfere with the continuance of this state of things seems to us to be contrary to what Divine Providence has designed on our behalf, the British nation, as everyone knows, being God's own, incapable of wrong doing. India is our wash pot and over the islands of the Sea have we cast our shoe". While India was becoming poorer, British economy developed to such an extent that besides exporting manufactured goods, there was surplus capital seeking investment. In 1852, the total foreign investment of the United Kingdom was £ 218 million but by 1892 it increased to more than £ 2,000 million. It is true that India's exports increased from ₹33 crores in 1860-61 to ₹177 crores in 1907 and the imports rose during the same period from ₹22 crores to ₹127 crores, but that brought no prosperity to India because the balance was used for paying the Home Charges.

ECONOMIC DRAIN

There was the drain of India's wealth to England. Every year India had to pay about £ 16 million on account of Home Charges which was due from India to England on account of interest on debt, charges for civil administration, army, stores, guaranteed railways and Madras Irrigation Works. It is calculated that India remitted more than ₹50 crores in the years ending 1895-6. In addition to this amount, there were other charges of the army such as rewards, pensions and gratuities which had to be paid every year and those were ₹26 crores in the 10 years ending 1887 and more than ₹35 crores in the 10 years ending 1900-1. It is stated that the pensions payable to the retired military officers in the United Kingdom consumed almost half the salt tax gathered from the whole of India. A colonel of Indian army retired on a pension of £1,100 to £1,200. India lost a lot of money on account of the exchange ratio fixed by the British Government for India. A part of the salaries received by the British and European officers in India were also sent by them out of India. There were also European and English traders, capitalists, planters, shipowners, gold-miners, etc. who remitted every year huge amounts. The view of William Digby was that the total drain amounted to £60,080 millions up to the end of the 19th century. The estimate of Hyndman was that the actual drain was £30 million. Later on, he increased the figure to £40 million. The view of A. J. Wilson was that the annual drain was £35 million. Mr Maclean observed. "A sum of something like £ 300,000,000 a year comes to England and for which India gets no return whatever." There were loud protests against this colossal drain of wealth from India. Mr. W. T. Thornton wrote in 1880, "Neither did it occur to any practical administrator to enquire, nor did any theoretical economist volunteer to point out how greatly the investment of English capital on Indian public works must, by necessitating the remittances to England of annual interest or profit on investment, derange the Indian exchange, nor how grievous would be the effects of the derangement. Railways are good, irrigation is good, but neither one nor the other good enough to compensate for opening and continually widening a drain which has tapped India's very heart-blood and has dried up the mainspring of her industrial energy. There is for India just now no other public work half so urgent as the restoration of equilibrium between income and expenditure." An Indian newspaper wrote in 1896, "Like locusts, they come in swarms and drain the country of its riches, which they spend not in India but in their own country. The Musalman rulers were more avaricious and grasping, but they had made India their home and what they took from the people went back to the people: even their wasteful expenditure benefited the people."

Dadabhai was the high priest of the drain theory and for years he carried on propaganda against the economic drain of India. The best exposition of his thesis is to be found in his book entitled "Poverty and Un-British Rule in India." The view of Dadabhai was that economic drain was the real, the principal and even the sole cause of the loss, sufferings and poverty of India, all other reasons and causes being "only red-herrings drawn across the path." Dadabhai maintained that the drain facilitated penetration and exploitation of India by foreign capital. By preventing the accumulation of capital within India and by thus prostrating internal capital, the drain permitted foreign capitalists to come to country without having to face any indigenous competition and thereby to monopolise and to reap all the advantages of India's material resources. The drain also acted as the chief source of the accumulation of foreign capital invested in India because a large part of the drain was brought back to India as foreign capital. Dadabhai went to the extent of declaring that the entire evil of the drain was due to the excessive employment of Englishmen in Indian administration. To quote him, "The sole cause of this extreme poverty and wretchedness of the mass of the people is the inordinate employment of foreign agency, the Government of the country and the consequent material loss to and drain from the country." Again, "It is a question of life and death to the country. Remove this one evil and India will be blessed in every way."

Dadabhai made a comparison between the British rule in India and the previous rulers of this country. He pointed out that although the Mughals and the Marathas plundered the people of India, their wealth remained within the country and was spent inside it. Individual citizens might suffer or be oppressed and deprived of their wealth, but the country as a whole did not lose, the loss of one citizen being the gain of the other. As regards the British rule, Englishmen took wealth out of the country and spent it abroad. Under the old rulers, even if the burden of taxation was very heavy, the economic effects were not as disastrous for the people as the effects of taxation under the British because then all money realised from taxes was spent in India. In the case of the British Government the same was sent out of India. Even when invaders like Nadir Shah came, they looted the country and went back immediately and the loss of wealth was temporary. In the case of British rule, the drain was a part of the existing system of government and was therefore ceaseless and continuous increasing from year to year. The wounds were kept perpetually open and the drain was like a running sore. The former rulers of India were like "butchers" chopping irregularly here and there but the mechanised efficiency of England was cutting the very heart of the country almost with sharp surgical knives. To quote Dadabhai, "The lot of India is a very sad one. Here condition is that of a master and a slave: but it is worse; it is that of a plundered nation in the hands of constant plunderers with the plunder carried away clean out of the land. In the case of the plundering raids occasionally made on India before the English came, the invaders went away and there were long intervals and security during which the land could recuperate and become again rich and prosperous. But nothing of the kind is true now. The British invasion is continuous and the plunder goes right on with no intermission and actually increases and the impoverished Indian nation has no opportunity whatever to recuperate."

FAVOURS TO BRITISH INDUSTRIES

The Indians protested against the favours shown to British industry in India unmindful of the adverse effects on Indian industries. The British capitalists were the favoured children of the state. All the coalfields, gold mines, jute and hemp mills, breweries, coffee and tea plantations and indigo factories were exclusively in the hands of the Europeans. Three-fourths of the woollen and paper mills, jute press, oil mills, timber mills, cotton ginning and pressing factories, etc. were owned by Europeans. All the shipping trade, railways and banks were in their hands. Mr. Maclean declared in the House of Commons in 1900, "All the resources of India may be said to be mortgaged to this country." Cotton duties on the import of British cotton goods were abolished although that meant an annual loss of crores of rupees to the Indian exchequer. Later on, when 5% import duties were levied on cotton manufactures from England, a similar duty was imposed on the cotton-manufactured goods in India. That was done in spite of opposition from the members of the Executive Council of the Governor-General and the members of the India Council of the Secretary of State for India. It was pointed out that India was held and governed in the interests of the British merchants. It had to be conceded that India was defenseless in matters where the English and Indian interests clashed. The people of India condemned the free trade policy followed by the Government of India with regard to the import of British goods. Dadabhai Naoroji stated that free trade between India and England was something like a race between a starving and exhausting invalid and a strong man with a horse to ride on. The free trade policy imposed on India was one-sided. Indian products that could still compete with British or British-controlled colonial producers were subjected to heavy import duties in Britain. In 1824, Indian textiles paid duties ranging from 30% to 70%. Indian sugar paid a duty that was 3 times its cost price. In some cases, duties in Britain were as high as 400%. Import duties on such products were removed only after their export to Britain had ceased altogether. Indian producers were prevented from taking advantage of the emergence of an all-India market by the Government decision to erect and maintain a vast structure of internal customs duties. India was placed in the position of taxing the movements of its own products while letting foreign goods move freely. These internal duties were abolished only in the 1840's by which time the British manufacturers had acquired a decisive edge over Indian handicrafts even within the Indian markets. The free trade policy of the Government of India stood in the way of the development of the country. Lala Murlidhar of the Panjab observed in 1891. "Free trade fairplay between nations, how I hate the sham." What fairplay in trade can there be between India and the bloated capitalist England?" Again, "What are all these deliers and lamps and European-made chairs and tables and smart clothes and hats, English coats and bonnets and frocks and silver mounted canes and all the luxurious fittings of your houses but trophies of India's misery, mementoes of India's starvation?"

RAILWAYS

The people resented the enormous waste of money in the construction of railways in India. Most of the railways were constructed for strategic purposes with no regard for economy. As a matter of fact, money was recklessly wasted. Huge amounts were borrowed and squandered in India. William Massey, a Finance Member of the Government of India, observed, "The East India Railway cost far more if not twice as much as it ought to have cost; enormous sums were lavished and the contractors had no motive whatsoever for economy. All the money came from the English capitalist, and so long as he was guaranteed 5% on the revenues of India, it was immaterial to him as to whether the funds that he lent were thrown into the Hoogly or converted to brick and mortar." A similar observation was made by Lord Lawrence in these words, "I think it is notorious in India among almost every class that the railways have been extravagantly made; that they have cost a great deal more than their worth, or ought to have cost." Critics maintain that railways "resulted in the exploitation of our resources by the Indigo, tea, coffee and other planters." The construction of military railways on a large scale brought no gain to the people. As almost all the capital was subscribed by the English capitalists, the entire profits were also carried away by them. About £5,750,000 were taken away in 1894-5 alone. Railways constituted a drain on India in the form of interest on capital, purchase of stock in England and excessive salaries paid to Europeans. In 1897, 4,692 Europeans employed on the railways drew salaries amounting to more than ₹80 lakhs, whereas 207,047 Indian employees drew not even one-fifth of the above amount.

THE CIVIL SERVICES

The people resented the heavy cost of civil services in the country. The salaries and expenses of the Civil departments of the Government of India exceeded ₹112 crores in the ten years ending 1887 and ₹151½ crores in the 10 years ending 1900-1. The salaries of British officials in India and England were excessive and exorbitant. In India, the Viceroy was paid ₹2,40,000 a year in addition to other allowances. In Ceylon, the highest paid authority got ₹80,000 a year and Secretaries to the Government got ₹24,000 annually, but in India they were paid ₹40,000 to ₹50,000. The annual salary of Bismarck, Chancellor of Germany, was ₹42,000, that of the Prime Minister of England ₹50,000 but the Lieutenant-Governors in India got ₹1,00,000 and the Governors ₹1,28,000. A newspaper wrote thus in this connection, "The Viceroy obtains three lakhs and 70 thousands of rupees every year as salary and allowance; in other words, he obtains eight times the monthly income of the Prime Minister of England. If in England, the salaries of the highest officers had been fixed at such high sums, the people would have rebelled."

FAMINES

It is true that there used to be famines in India before the British rule, but their frequency increased during the British regime. While previously there were on the average only three famines in a century or one famine in 33 years but during the British rule there was one famine in every 3 years and each famine affected vast regions of British India. While the people suffered from famines, the Government of India refused to stop the export of food grains from India to England. There was a terrible loss of life as a result of famines. During the famine of 1860, as many as 5 lakhs of people died. The number of deaths in the famine of 1866 was 13 lakhs. More than 14 lakhs died in the famine of 1868-70 in Western U.P., Bombay and the Punjab. Many states in Rajputana lost one-fourth to one-third of their population. Perhaps the worst famine in Indian history occurred in 1876-8 in Madras, Mysore, Hyderabad, Maharashtra. Western U.P. and the Punjab. Maharashtra lost 8 lakhs people, Madras nearly 35 lakhs, Mysore nearly 20% of its population and Uttar Pradesh over 12 lakhs. Drought led to a country-wide famine in 1896-7 and then again in 1899-1900. The famine of 1896-7 affected over 9.5 crore people of whom nearly 45 lakhs died. The famine of 1899-1900 caused widespread distress. In spite of official efforts to save lives more than 25 lakhs people died. Another famine in 1943 carried away nearly 3 million people in Bengal.

REVIEW QUESTIONS

1. Critically analyse the economic impact of the British rule in India.
2. As a result of the British rule, the peasantry in India became very poor. Examine.
3. Throw light on the economic policy of the British government in India.
4. Write a detailed note on economic drain.
5. During the British rule, India was transformed into a colony. Comment.
6. Discuss the economic condition of the people of India during the British rule.
7. Write short notes on the following:
   (a) Famines in India before the British rule
   (b) Agrarian revolution

SUGGESTED READINGS

Banerjee, P.N.: *Fiscal Policy in India,* Calcutta, 1922.
Basu, B.D.: *Ruin of Indian Trade and Industries,* Calcutta, 1935.
Bhatia, B.M.: *Famines in India,* London, 1963.
Bipan Chandra: *The Rise and Growth of Economic Nationalism in India (1880-1905),* New Delhi, 1966.
Das, M.N.: *Studies on Economic and Social Development of Modern India (1848-56),* Calcutta, 1959.
Digby, William: *Prosperous British India,* London, 1901.
Dutt, R.C.: *Famines and Land Assessments in India.*
Dutt, R.C.: *The Economic History of India.*
Dutt, R.C.: *The Peasantry of Bengal,* Calcutta, 1874.
Hutchins, F.G.: *The Illusion of Permanence. British Imperialism in India,* Princeton, 1967.
Kling, B.B.: *The Blue Mutiny: The Indigo Disturbances in Bengal, 1859-62,* Philadelphia, 1966.
Loveday, A.: *History of Indian Famines.* London, 1914.
Rai, Lala Lajpat: *England's Debt* to India.
Rai, Lala Lajpat: *Unhappy India,* Calcutta, 1928.
Ray, P. C.: *Indian Famines-Their Causes* and Remedies, Calcutta, 1901.
Ray, P. C.: *Poverty Problem in India,* Calcutta, 1895.
Sanyal, N.: *Development of Indian Railways,* Calcutta, 1930.
Telang, K.T.: *Free Trade and Protection from an Indian Point of View,* Bombay, 1877.
Thorner, D.A.: *Investment in Empire,* Philadelphia, 1950.
Thorner, D.A.: *Land and Labour in India,* London, 1962.
Vicajee, F.R.: *Political and Social Effects of Railways in India,* London, 1875.

35 Famines in India and Development of Famine Policy

LEARNING OBJECTIVES

- Know about the major famines of India during British rule
- Throw light on the various Commissions appointed in British India to study the causes of famines and offer relief
- Give an account of the Bengal famine of 1943

INTRODUCTION

India has suffered from famines since time immemorial. It appears that in earlier times, a major famine occurred once in every 50 years. From the beginning of the 11th century to the end of the 17th century, there were 14 famines almost all of which were confined to small local areas.

The frequency of famines increased during the 19th century. In a period of about 90 years from 1765 to 1858, the country experienced 12 famines and four "severe scarcities". Between 1860 and 1908, famine or scarcity prevailed in one part of the country or the other in 20 out of a total of 49 years. There was not only an increase in the frequency of famines, there was also a change in their nature. The nature of famines in the latter half of the 19th century changed from a shortage of food supply as in the past, to a lack of purchasing power with those who suffered from starvation. In reality, it was both. The abnormal rise in food prices during the years of drought was itself a measure of the shortage of food grains in the country as a whole. The railways only helped in the distribution of the available supplies throughout the country. Instead of an extreme scarcity in one region, one could expect more even shortage over the country as a whole and consequently a mild rise in prices. The emergence of "destructive" instead of "constructive" speculation in food-grains which accentuated price fluctuation through stock-holding in the face of rising prices and disholding of stock on a falling market, the disappearance of domestic stocks which people were accustomed to keep in the past and the development of a large export trade in grain were factors which contributed to the rise in prices of food grains during the period of famine. As a result of these developments, the rise in prices and the consequent suffering of the people were out of all proportion to the natural scarcity. The human and institutional factors were becoming more important than the natural calamity in causing distress and starvation.

BENGAL FAMINE OF 1769-70

There was a dreadful famine in Bengal in 1769-70 which claimed a third of the population of the province. Practically no relief measures were undertaken by the English East India Company. As a matter of fact, the servants of the Company made huge profits by buying up rice and selling the same at high prices. There was scarcity in Madras in 1781 and 1782. There was a severe famine in the whole of Northern India in 1784. There was the repetition of a famine in Madras in 1792. There was a famine in North-Western Provinces and Oudh in 1803. The Guntur famine of 1833 took away a heavy toll of life. Two lakhs of people out of a total population of 5 lakhs, died of starvation. When in 1837, famine visited the upper reaches of the Ganges and the Jumna, the local Government laid down the principle that while the state found work for the able bodies, the whole community must look after the helpless and infirm. The measures adopted were wholly insufficient. Heavy mortality resulted and violent riots broke out.

FAMINE OF 1860-61

There was a famine in North-Western Provinces in 1860-61. The genesis of this famine lay in the disturbances of 1857 in the course of which villages in North-Western Provinces were plundered and burnt so that the local stores of grains were destroyed. Moreover, cultivation was interrupted during the next two years due to the punishments meted out to the villages and heavy fines imposed on them for their alleged complicity in the crimes of 1857. During the two years preceding the famine, rainfall was deficient. The result was that the people of North-Western Provinces were completely unprepared to face the drought of 1860. However, the drought was not widespread, but no attempt was made by the state to control the prices of food grains and activities of the speculators or guarantee a minimum wage and employment to labour. The poorer classes deserted their famine-stricken villages to find work in the neighbourhood. In spite of that, there were "a minimum of two lakh deaths". It was for the first time that a special enquiry was held into the causes, area and intensity of the famine. Colonel Baird Smith was deputed to examine those matters but his report did not lead to the formulation of general principles of famine relief.

FAMINE OF 1865-66

The scarcity in the Deccan districts of Bombay in 1862 was local and mild in character. The famine of 1865-6 covered a vast area. The districts of Bihar bordering on either bank of the Ganges, North Bengal, Orissa and districts in Madras Presidency lying along the Bay of Bengal were affected. The blackest portion of the tract comprised the three districts of Orissa division. There was a terrible loss of 1.3 million lives in Orissa. There was also a famine in Bengal and Bihar at the same time. The relief given by the Government was extremely belated, inadequate and ill organised. The wages paid to the labourers varied from 6 pice in Champaran and Monghyr for an adult and 3 pice for a child to 9 pice for an adult and 3 pice for a child in Shahabad.

CAMPBELL COMMITTEE

This calamity proved a turning point in the history of Indian famines as it was followed by the investigations and report of a Committee presided over by Sir George Campbell which laid the foundations of a definite famine policy. The Campbell Committee made recommendations which in certain respects anticipated those of the Royal Commission of 1880. The report of the Committee produced a change of outlook. Sir John Lawrence who was the Governor-General at that time, blamed himself bitterly for having accepted the facile assurances of the Bengal Government and when famine again appeared elsewhere in 1868, declared that his object was "to save every life" and that district officers would be held responsible if preventable deaths occurred. The old doctrine that the public would be responsible for the relief of the helpless and infirm was entirely abandoned. Money was borrowed in order to finance additional railways and canals.

FAMINE OF 1868-70

A famine of great severity overtook Northern India in 1868—70. The drought in 1868 covered parts of the Punjab, North-Western Provinces, Central India and Central Provinces, but the main fury of the famine fell on Rajputana. It was during this famine in North-Western Provinces that a clear departure was made from the previous policy and the Lieutenant-Governor instructed the local officers that "every district officer would be held personally responsible that no deaths occurred from starvation which could have been avoided by any exertion or arrangement on his part or that of his subordinates."

FAMINE OF 1873-74

The famine of 1873-74 in Bengal and Bihar occupies a unique position in the history of famines in India. The famine was actually very severe but the tragedy was avoided on account of a new food policy adopted by the local Government and administration of relief on a more liberal scale. The timely arrival of imports helped to keep down the prices of food-grains and saved the people from the rigours of famine. The relief policy of the Bengal Government during this famine differed from its earlier policy in the matter of liberality of wage scales on relief works and measures of indirect relief in the form of advances of grains and cash to Zamindars for the relief of their tenants. The policy on relief works was to offer employment to anyone who sought it at the normal rate of wages and get full normal work from him. However, later on the wages were reduced and the work was increased.

FAMINE OF 1876-78

The great famine of 1876-8 ravaged the country for 3 years and was a great calamity of its kind in respect of the area and the population affected and the duration and intensity of the distress. In all, a total area of 2,05,600 sq. miles covering a population of 36.4 million was affected. The Government of India felt that famine relief would involve a great financial strain and sent Sir Richard Temple to Bombay and Madras "to consult with the Government of the two Presidencies" and impress upon them the need for economy in relief expenditure. It was pointed out that "while it is the desire of the Government of India that every effort should be made, so far as the resources of the state admit, for the prevention of deaths from famine, it is essential in the present state of finances that the most severe economy should be practiced." It was said that the Government held that "the task of saving life, irrespective of the cost, is one which is beyond our power to undertake." However, "from the history of past famines, rules of action may be learnt which will enable them in future to provide efficient assistance for the suffering people without incurring disastrous expenditure." The financial considerations began to weigh so heavily with the Government that the earlier policy of "saving every life whatever the cost" was completely given up. That added to the gravity of the natural calamity and made this famine one of the most disastrous in the annals of Indian famines.

STRACHEY COMMISSION

The Government of India appointed a strong Commission under General Sir Richard Strachey which reported in 1880, formulating general principles and suggesting particular measures of a preventive or protective character. It recognized to the full the duty of the state to give relief in times of famine, but held that this relief should not be so administered "as not to check the growth of thrift and self-reliance among the people, or to impair the structure of society which, resting as it does in India upon the moral obligation of mutual assistance, is admirably adapted for common effort against a common misfortune." The Commission insisted on the urgent need of proper statistical collection of facts relating to the condition of agricultural community. Relief should elsewhere be administered on the following basic principles:

1. Employment on works must be offered before the physical efficiency of applicants had been impaired by privation. All applicants must be received but efforts should be made to prevent the abuse of relief by those who were not really in want. The work should be of permanent utility and capable of employing a considerable number of persons for a considerable period. Wages should be adjusted from time to time in order to provide sufficient food for a labourer's support, allowing him a day's rest in the week. Separate rates should be prescribed for different ages, sexes and classes and allowances' must be made for dependent children of labourers.

2. The Government recognized that the grant of relief was the duty of the state and not of the general public. Raw grain or money might be distributed in villages and cooked food might be given at centres. Relief in villages required very careful organization and control and for this purpose, distressed tracts must be divided into circles and each circle must be placed under a competent officer. Non-officials might be asked to volunteer assistance.

3. As a general rule, the Government should trust private trade to supply and distribute food, giving it every possible facility. It should prohibit the export of grain only if reasonably certain

that such action was necessary to conserve the resources of India as a whole. Supplies of food in distressed areas should be carefully watched.

4. As regards suspensions and remissions of land revenue and rents, the Commission recommended that in times of famine landlords should be encouraged and assisted by loans on easy terms to open works on their estates which would offer employment to labourers and poorer tenants. Loans should also be given for purchases of seed grain and bullocks.

5. The cost of relief must be so localised as to bring home to its administrators a sense of personal responsibility for expenditure. This could be done by throwing the burden of famine expenditure on local taxation and administering relief through representative members of the tax-paying body, themselves responsible for providing all needful funds. There was always a limit beyond which provincial revenues could not supply famine relief and must be assisted from Imperial funds. In ordinary times also, the Central Government should assist local Governments to undertake water storage and other protective works.

6. In times of excessive drought, facilities should be given for the migration of cattle to grassy forest areas where abundant pasturage was procurable.

The recommendations of the Commission were generally accepted and steps were taken to create new resources by which in normal times a surplus of revenue could be secured to meet the extra-ordinary charges thrown on the state by famine. It was finally decided that ₹15 million should always be entered in the budget under the head "Famine Relief and Insurance". In 1883, the provisional Famine Code was promulgated. It formed a guide and a basis for the various provincial famine codes which were subsequently prepared, approved by the Central Government and revised again and again as experience widened. Between 1880 and 1896, minor droughts in different provinces afforded opportunities of testing the revising of provincial codes.

As a result of scanty 'rainfall, the rabi crop of 1884 was deficient in 5 districts of the Southern and South-Eastern parts of the Punjab. In 1884 - 85, there was scarcity in some parts of Madras. In 1886-87, there was scarcity in Central Provinces on account of a long break of rains in August and September. In 1888-89 there was a famine in North Bihar, in the tributary States of Orissa and in Ganjam district in the Madras Presidency. There was scarcity in Kumaon and Garhwal in 1890. In 1890-92, there were scarcities in Madras, Bombay and Bengal.

The great famine of 1896-97 affected almost every province, though in varying degrees of intensity. The total population affected was estimated at 34 millions. Extensive relief measures were undertaken and in many parts of the country the people were 'relieved in their own homes. The total cost of relief was estimated at ₹7.27 crores.

LYALL COMMISSION

The famine was followed by the appointment of a Commission presided over by Sir James Lyall, ex-Lieutenant-Governor of the Punjab, who found it most difficult to compare degrees of distress with those observed in previous famines as conditions had largely changed with the expansion of railways. The Commission largely adhered to the views expressed by the Strachey Commission, suggesting alterations which were designed to impart greater flexibility. The Commission observed, "It may be said of India as a whole that of late years, and owing to high prices, there has been a considerable increase in the incomes of the land-holding and cultivating classes and their standard of comfort and expenditure has also risen. With the rise in transfer-value of their holdings, their credit also has expanded. During recent famines they have shown greater powers of resistance. The poorer professional classes suffer severely from rise of prices but do not come on relief. The wages of day labourers and skilled artisans have not risen. The rise in prices of food has not been accompanied by a rise in the wages of labour. On the contrary, as competition falls off, the rate of wages offered falls frequently below the customary rate."

FAMINE OF 1900

Before the proposals of the Lyall Commission were fully considered by the Government, India was visited in 1900 by a drought the greatest in extent and intensity which had been experienced for

200 years. The area affected amounted to more than 400,000 sq. miles with a population of about 60 millions. It embraced the greater part of the Bombay Presidency, the Central Provinces, Berar and much of the Punjab, the States of Kathiawar and Rajputana, the Nizam's dominions, Baroda and the Central Indian principalities. The loss in crops alone amounted to £50 millions in British India and £30 millions in the Indian Stages. The fodder famine destroyed all kinds of cattle. In the matter of saving human lives and relieving distress, the results achieved were not very flattering. The Famine Commission estimated that the excess of mortality over the normal death rate in the year 1900 was 1.25 millions of which 1 million were British subjects and the rest were immigrants into British territory from the Indian States. The highest number of deaths, viz., 7,45,376 was recorded in Bombay, followed by 1,87,686 in the Central Provinces, 1,27,409 in the Punjab and 1,25,926 in Berar. William Digby put the mortality due to famine and famine diseases at 3.25 million. This was in spite of the fact that ₹16.5 crores were spent on relief work.

MACDONNEL COMMISSION

The Government appointed a Commission under the Presidency of Sir Anthony MacDonnel. Their report was published in 1901. It summarised the accepted principles of relief and suggested variations. It emphasized the benefits of a policy of "moral strategy", early ascertainment and publication of suspensions of revenue and rents, early distribution of advances for purchase of seed and cattle and the sinking of temporary wells. It recommended the appointment of a Famine Commissioner in a province where relief operations were expected to be extensive. It recommended stricter regulation of famine relief in certain respects, exports to enlist non-official assistance on a larger scale and preference in particular circumstances of village works to the large public works. It also recommended considerable increase in the rolling stock.

There was a famine in Deccan Districts of Bombay Presidency in 1905-06. It affected 23,000 sq. miles and 3 million people out of a total area of 24,000 sq. miles and a total population of 7 millions in those districts. A famine of considerable severity was experienced in the United Provinces of Agra and Oudh in 1907-08 as a result of failure of rains.

On account of various factors, there was a rise of prices in food grains in 1918 and there was also a failure of rains. An extremely severe, widespread and deadly epidemic of influenza added to the general distress. Relief measures were taken by the Government and the distress ended with the abundant rains of 1919.

BENGAL FAMINE (1943)

There was a famine in Bengal in 1943. It has been called a tragedy in unpreparedness. Due to neglect, the food situation in India had been allowed to grow from bad to worse. In spite of the low standard of living of the people of India, the country was unable to the population from domestic production of cereals. No steps were taken in India at the beginning of the World War II to meet any dislocation in production, supply and distribution of food that War might cause. When imports of rice from Burma stopped due to its occupation by the Japanese and the system of distribution of domestic supplies broke down on account of the "Denial policy" of the Government and activities of traders, a tragedy of great magnitude overtook Bengal. The country, the people and the administration, both at the Centre and in the provinces, were found unprepared to meet the challenge. The result was chaos which gave antisocial elements an opportunity to make individual fortunes and hold their countrymen to ransom while a million and a half poor, helpless and innocent people died due to sheer hunger. The Famine Enquiry Commission observed, "It has been for us a sad task to enquire into the course and causes of the Bengal famine. We have been haunted by a deep sense of tragedy. A million and a half of the poor of Bengal fell victims to circumstances for which they themselves were not responsible. Society, together with its organs, failed to protect its weaker members. Indeed, there was a moral and social breakdown, as well as administrative breakdown."

It has been rightly said that both man and God joined hands to produce the tragedy in Bengal. The famine might be called "more man-made, than an act of God." Man merely exploited the situation created by nature and World War II. The root cause of the famine is to be found in the series of crop famines that Bengal experienced beginning from 1938 and in the conditions created by the War. There was the stoppage of normal imports from Burma, dislocation of trade and movements of food-grains on account of controls and the nearness of Bengal to the theatre of War in the East, the building up of provincial and even district barriers against the movement of grains and other essential supplies, the increase in the demand for food on account of the demand from the army and refugees from Burma and the rise in prices. None of these was a man-made factor. The fault was with the Government which did not take into consideration the change in circumstances in Bengal and did nothing to control the situation so long as Lord Linlithgow was the Governor-General and Viceroy of India. It was only when Lord Wavell took over from him as Governor-General that the situation was tackled on a war footing. However, the famine took a heavy toll of life in Bengal. From July to December 1943, the death rate rose by 108.3 per cent. The view of Prof. K. P. Chattopadhyaya of Calcutta University is that as many as 3.5 million people died during the famine. The estimate of the Famine Enquiry Commission was 1.5 million deaths. Almost the whole of Bengal, in greater or less degree, was affected by the famine and suffered loss of life.

REVIEW QUESTIONS

1. Write an essay on the major famines of India occurred during the British rule.
2. Discuss the nature of the famines occurred in India during the period of the British rule.
3. The frequency of famines increased during the 19th century. Discuss.
4. Describe the causes of the Bengal famine of 1769-60.
5. Discuss the development of famine policy.
6. Write a detailed note on the Famine Commissions of British India.
7. Discuss the history and economics of the famines of India.
8. Write short notes on the following:
    (a) Bengal famine
    (b) Strachey Commission
    (c) Lyall Commission
    (d) Indian famines

SUGGESTED READINGS

Anstey, Vera: *Economic Development of India.*
Bhatia, B.M.: *Famine in India, New Delhi,* (1963).
Brooke: Report on Famine in Rajputana (1871).
Digby, William: *Prosperous British India.*
Dutt, R.C.: *Economic History of India.*
Dutt, R.C.: *Famines in India.*
Famine Enquiry Commission Report on Bengal (1945).
Henvey, Frederick: *Narrative of Famine in NWP and Punjab* (1869).
Loveday, A.: *History and Economics of Famines in India* (1914).
Nash, V.: *The Great Famine* (1900).
Orissa Famine Commission Report (1867).
Ray, S.C.: *Papers Dealing with Indebtedness in India* (1915).
Ray, S.C.: *Economic Causes of Indian Famines.*
Report of the Indian Famine Commission (1901).

36. Peasants' Movement and Uprisings

 LEARNING OBJECTIVES

- Discuss the nature and results of the peasant movements and uprisings during the 19th and 20th centuries
- Throw light on the revolts under Communists in India

INTRODUCTION

The British rule in India brought about many changes in the agrarian system in the country. The old agrarian system collapsed and under the new system, the ownership of land was conferred on the Zamindars who tried to extort as much as they could from the cultivators of land. Very little was left to the peasants after paying to the Zamindar. The income of the peasants was so little that they were always at the mercy of the moneylenders who tried to exploit them as much as they possibly could. The courts set up by the British Government also favoured the moneylenders against the peasants and the result was that the moneylenders were able to take away practically all that the peasants possessed. The moneylenders manipulated their accounts in such a manner that even after getting many times the amount given to a peasant as loan, the loan remained unsatisfied. The lot of the peasants was extremely miserable. The various peasant movements and uprisings during the 19th and 20th centuries were in the nature of a protest against the existing conditions under which their exploitation knew no limits.

THE SANTHALS' REBELLION (1855-73)

Originally, the Santhals belonged to Manbhum, Barabhum, Hazaribagh, Birbhum, Midnapur and Bankura areas. They left their ancestral home on account of the oppressive demands of the Zamindars after the Permanent Settlement of Bengal in 1793 and they settled in the plains skirting the Rajmahal hills. When the Santhals cleared the lands and raised crops on them, the Zamindars from the adjoining areas claimed those lands and started extorting money from the Santhal peasants. The moneylenders also appeared on the scene and oppressed them. The police and revenue and court officials also helped, the Zamindars and moneylenders against the peasants. Instead of helping the peasants, the Government seemed to be a party to their oppression. The pitiable condition of the Santhal peasant is described in these words: "The Santhal saw his crops, his cattle, even himself and family appropriated for a debt which ten times paid remained an incubus upon him still." The Zamindars were invested with the powers of ownership of lands which peasants had customarily considered and cultivated as their own. The moneylenders were given powers to get peasants imprisoned for failure to repay their debts. The Santhals never thought that they could be evicted from their ancestral homesteads, holdings and forests for failure to pay taxes and debts. The self-respecting Santhal peasants could not reconcile themselves to the preposterous rights conferred by the British Government on the Zamindars to distrain their properties, including their draught cattle and grain crops. The Santhal peasants revolted against the unjust order of, the day imposed on them by the British Government, Indian Zamindars and moneylenders.

The peasants "banded themselves (especially in Patna District) to resist short measures; illegal cesses and forced deliveries of agreement (one sided) to pay enhanced rents". There were also comb nations of peasants in East Bengal refusing to pay except what they considered just. They found their leaders in two brothers, Sidhu and Kanhu, who claimed to have received some occult blessings from the gods to put an end to the atrocities of officers and deceit of merchants. As many as 35,000 Santhals formed their bodyguard. They armed themselves with their traditional weapons of bows, arrows, axes and swords. They began to march to Calcutta to place their petition before the Governor to free them from their oppressors. However, one Government Inspector obstructed their march and provoked them on 7 July 1855 into violence. Thus, began their rebellion and their resultant massacre at the hands of the British. The British officers confessed later on that "it was not war, it was execution; we had orders to go out whenever we saw the smoke of a village rising about the jungle. The Magistrate used to go with us. I surrounded the village with my sepoys and the Magistrate called upon the rebels to surrender." The Santhal peasants defied the orders of the Government and they were brutally fired upon and butchered **en masse.** They displayed exceptional courage and military discipline. They faced successive volleys of British bullets with 'reckless heroism. Ultimately, the Government had to yield to their demands and pass the Bengal Tenancy Act which re-established the lost permanency of tenure and fixity of feudal exactions. Moreover, the Santhal area which had been administratively broken up and merged into the neighbouring districts, was reorganised into a separate entity known as the Santhal Parganas. Thus, the Santhals succeeded in forcing recognition of their special status as a national minority. The Santhal revolt also had its repercussions in other parts of the country at the time of the indigo strike of 1860, the Pabna and Bogra Uprising of 1872 and the Maratha peasant rising in Pabna and Ahmednagar in 1875-76.

THE REVOLT OF 1857-58

During the Revolt of 1857, the peasants of most of Oudh and Western U.P. forgot their oppressions by the local Zamindars and joined hands with them against the British Government. They played a heroic part, displayed great military skill, prowess and achieved victories. However, they had to pay very bitterly for their display of patriotism. After the Revolt was crushed, the lands of the peasants were treated as the property of the Zamindars and they were reduce from the status of proprietors to that of tenants-at will of their own former lands. The peasants of the Meerut Division were made to pay some additional cesses as a punitive impost for participation in the Revolt.

STRIKE OF BENGAL INDIGO CULTIVATORS

One of the greatest peasant movements of modern era was the indigo agitation that engulfed Bengal in 1859-60. The cultivation of indigo was a monopoly of the Europeans. The European planters compelled the peasants to cultivate indigo and subjected them to untold oppression. In order to force the peasants to produce indigo at uneconomic rates, the planters resorted to illegal beatings and detentions. This oppression was described in detail by Dinbandhu Mitra in his Bengali play called Nil Darpan published in 1860. Rev. James Long also published a widely circulated pamphlet in Bengali called "The Oppression of the Indigo Planters" and supported the demand of the peasantry. The anger of the peasants burst out in 1859. Hundreds of thousands of peasants refused to cultivate indigo and resisted the physical brutality and violence of the planters and their armed retainers. They assembled with staffs, swords, bows and arrows and matchlocks to defend their settlements. In Pabna an army of 2,000 peasants appeared and wounded the horse of a Magistrate. Otherwise, there was little violence. Harishchandra Mukhopadhyaya, Girish Chandra Basu, Dinabandhu Mitra, Sisir Kumar Ghosh and many other well-known intellectuals supported the cause of the peasants. The Government was forced to appoint the Indigo Commission. The strength and determination of the indigo cultivators was described in these words in the report of the Commission. The dislike to this particular kind of cultivation was so strongly manifested and appeared to be so deeply seated that we could not mistake the reality of the feeling. It is not easy to possess those who have not witnessed the demeanour and heard the language of the ryot, as we have done, with a just appreciation of this intense dislike. Ryots of different concerns, at miles distance from each other, have expressed to us the same idea in language clear, emphatic and pointed and striking as coming from the mouths of persons in their rank of life, namely, that indigo and its attendant evils had been the 'bane of their lives." Witness after witness appeared before the Indigo Commission and testified to their intense hatred of the system of indigo cultivation. Repeatedly, the Commission asked them about the terms on which they were willing to sow indigo in future. A typical reply was: "Let there be profit or let there be loss, I will die sooner than cultivate indigo". The Government learnt a lesson from the Santhal revolt and took steps to remove the grievances of the peasants by passing a law in 1862. Gradually, the indigo planters of Bengal moved to Bihar and Uttar Pradesh. The indigo peasants of Bihar revolted on a large scale in Darbhanga and Champaran in 1866-68. Likewise, the peasants of Jessore in Bengal revolted in 1883 and 1889-90.

EAST BENGAL (1872-76)

Agrarian unrest broke out in East Bengal during the 1870's. The powerful Zamindars of Bengal were notorious for the oppression of their tenants and they freely resorted to ejectment, harassment, illegal seizure of property, including crops and chattel and extortions and large-scale use of force to increase rents and to prevent the peasants from acquiring occupancy rights. The Bengal peasants had a long tradition of resistance going back to 1782 when the peasants of North Bengal had rebelled against Debi Singh, the revenue farmer of the English East India Company. From 1872 to 1876, they united in no-rent unions and attacked Zamindars and their agents in different parts of East Bengal. Peasant resistance collapsed only when the Government intervened and took strong action against them. However, peasant unrest broke out from time to time in the succeeding years. Ultimately, the Government had to undertake legislation to protect the peasants from the worst aspects of the Zamindari system.

MAHARASHTRA (1875)

A major agrarian revolt occurred in the Poona and Ahmednagar Districts of Maharashtra in 1875. In Maharashtra, the Government had settled the land revenue directly with the peasants. However, the Government demand was fixed at such a high level that most of the peasants found it impossible to pay without borrowing from the moneylenders who charged very high rates of interest. The result was that more and more land was mortgaged or sold to the moneylenders who resorted to every possible legal or illegal trick and chicanery to strengthen their hold over the cultivator and his land. The patience of the peasants was exhausted by the end of 1874. The trouble started in village Kardeh in Sirur Taluka in December 1874 when a Marwari moneylender, Kaloo Ram by name, obtained a decree of eviction against Baba Saheb Deshmukh, a cultivator in debt to him for Rs. 150. The moneylender pulled down the house of Deshmukh and that led to trouble. The peasants of Poona and Ahmednagar Districts organised a social boycott of the moneylender which was transformed into agrarian riots. Everywhere they took forcible possession of their debt bonds, decrees and other documents dealing with their debts and burnt them in-public. The police failed to meet the fury of the peasant resistance. It was suppressed only when the whole military force at Poona, horse, foot and artillery, took the field against them. The intelligentsia of Maharashtra supported the demands of the peasants. It was pointed out that the real source of the misery of the peasants lay in the high land revenue demanded by the Government and its failure to provide credit at low rate of interest to the peasants.

The Government appointed the Deccan Riots Commission to investigate into the causes of the uprising. The Deccan Agriculturists Relief Act was passed in 1879 and it empowered the Government to appoint village registrars before whom the agriculturalist were to execute all instruments relating to obligations for payment of money and all charges on property and all conveyances and leases. Thus, a deed not registered and attested in that manner was not to be deemed to be valid. The right of the debtor to demand receipts for all payments made by him was formally recognised and provides on was made for furnishing to him by his creditor an annual statement of his accounts. The Act made provision for declaring insolvent any debtor found to be hopelessly involved. The Act abolished imprisonment for non-payment of debt, allowed the courts to go behind the contract and modify it in favour of the agriculturalist in order to reduce an impressive rate of interest, to prevent sale of land unless specifically pledged and to restore the land to the cultivator even when there was a sale deed. The period of limitation was raised from 3 years to 12 years in the case of suits based on registered deeds and 6 years in the case of other suits. The importance of this Act lies in the fact that it gave an indication of the direction in which the state policy was to move in future. The Act was designed to be an interim measure of relief from special distress in which the Deccan peasantry found itself at that time. More permanent remedies like restrictions on the transfer of land and the creation of institutional agencies of rural credit were to come later.

MOPLAH PEASANTS

Goaded by oppression from the landlords (Genmis), the Moplah peasants of Malabar (North Kerala) organised 22 rebellions from 1836 to 1854. Their discontent found renewed expression into major outbreaks from 1873 to 1880.

RIOTS IN ASSAM

High land revenue assessment led to a series of peasant riots in the plains of Assam during 1893-94. The peasants removed to pay the enhanced revenue demand, unitedly resisted official attempts to seize their fields and fought back the revenue collectors. The Government mobilised a large number of soldiers and armed policemen to suppress the peasant movement. A large number of peasants were killed in firings and bayonet charges.

THE PUNJAB LAND ALIENATION ACT, 1900

The peasants of the Punjab agitated and threatened to revolt to prevent the rapid alienation of their lands to the urban moneylenders for failure to pay debts. The Government of India did not want any revolt in that province which provided a large number of soldiers to the British army in

India. In order to protect the peasants of the Punjab, the Punjab Land Alienation Act was passed in 1900 "as an experimental measure" to be extended to the rest of India if it worked successfully in the Punjab. The Act divided the population of the Punjab into three categories viz. the agricultural classes, the statutory agriculturist class and the rest of the population including the moneylenders. Restrictions were imposed on the sale and mortgage of the land from the first category to the other two categories.

SOUTH INDIA IN FERMENT

The peasants of the Krishna and Godavari Deltas and those of Karnataka and Rayalaseema revolted several times from the beginning of the 19th century to protest against the exorbitant land revenue exactions, the neglect of irrigation facilities and the extortionate methods of tax-collection. G. Lakshminarasu Chetti organised a grand constitutional agitation against the Madras Tortures Act and succeeded in getting it repealed. This saved them from being put to several cruel and inhuman tortures for failure to pay taxes. The peasants of South India abandoned their lands and villages and migrated to the neighbouring states or even British Districts. The solidarity of the peasants was so great that the Government had to climb down and agree to a reduction of their tax burdens in order to persuade, them to come back to their lands and villages.

Natarajan writes that a study of the peasant uprising during the second half of the 19th century shows that the Indian peasants have a proud heritage. Each new uprising focussed attention on the foremost demands of the Indian peasantry, particularly the end of Zamindari and money-lending oppression. Each struggle enriched the consciousness of the peasants and raised it to a higher and more mature level. The courage and heroism with which the peasants raised the banner of revolt testified to the reality of their grievances and their determination to put an end to their oppression. As a result of the Sahthal Insurrection, the Santhal Parganas were organised as a separate entity and the Santhals were recognized as a national minority. The strike of the indigo cultivators succeeded in re-asserting the right of the peasant to sow the crops he chose and in forcing the indigo planters to move from Pabna, Bogra and Barasat to Champaran and other parts of India. The Maratha Peasant Uprising forced the Government to pass the Deccan Agriculturists Relief Act of 1879. The massive fights put up by the peasantry shook the confidence of the British in their ability to hold on to their dominion in India.

CHAMPARAN (1917-18)

The European planters of Champaran in Bihar resorted to illegal and inhuman methods of indigo cultivation at a cost which was wholly unjust. Under the Tinkathia system in Champaran, the peasants were bound by law to grow indigo on 3/20 part of their land and send the same to the British planters at prices fixed by them. They were liable to unlawful extortion and oppression by the planters. Mahatma Gandhi took up their cause. The Government appointed an Enquiry Commission of which Mahatma Gandhi was a member. The grievances of the peasants were enquired into and ultimately the Champaran Agrarian Act was passed in May 1918. About the Champaran Satyagraha, Dr. Rajendra Prasad writes, "At that time the Home Rule agitation was at its height in India. When we used to ask Mahatmaji to let Champaran also join that movement, he used to tell us that the work that was being done in Champaran was the work which will be able to establish Home Rule. At that time the country did not perhaps realise the importance of the work, nor did we, who were there to do. But today when we look back upon the methods of work pursued there and consider the history of the national struggle, then we can see that the great movement of today is only an edition of the work in Champaran on an immensely vaster scale." About the contribution of the Champaran struggle to the development of the nationalism, E.M.S. Namboodiripad observes, "Despite stiff opposition by the European planters and their protectors in the bureaucracy, Gandhiji and his comrades were able to bring the struggle to a successful conclusion. This, therefore, may be said to be the first dress-rehearsal of that type of national struggle which Gandhiji was subsequently to lead on more than one occasion. Here was a movement in which a band of selfless individuals from the middle and upper classes identified themselves with and roused the common people against the powers that be in order to secure some well-defined demands."

SATYAGRAHA OF KAIRA (1918)

In the Kaira District the crops failed in 1918, but the officers insisted on collection of full land revenue. Gandhiji organised the peasants to offer Satyagraha. They refused to pay land revenue and were prepared to suffer. Even those who could afford to pay, refused to pay. They suffered imprisonment for defying unjust laws. The Satyagraha lasted till June 1918. The Government was ultimately forced to surrender and a settlement was made with the peasants and their just demands were conceded.

MOPLAH REBELLION (1921)

The Moplah formed a majority of the population in the Earnad and Walluvanad Talukas and followed the Khilafat leaders. Both the Congress and Khilafat Parties had begun to organise a movement for tenancy reforms which was strongly opposed by the big landlords of Malabar. The manager of a large Hindu princely estate persuaded the police to search the house of the local Khilafat Secretary for a gun that was alleged to have been stolen from the palace. Thousands of Moplahs were summoned by drumbeats to prevent the arrest of their leader. When the police broke into a mosque in search of the fugitive, the Moplahs throughout the two Talukas rose in revolt, sacked the police stations, looted Government treasuries and destroyed the records of debts and mortgages in the courts and registries. For 6 months, there was no British rule throughout that region. A leader emerged to govern it. He administered the territory, supervised the execution of the police who had committed atrocities and of traitors who helped the British forces, put an end to the looting and announced the suspension of land revenue and rent for one year. He commanded the poor peasants to harvest the crops of their landlords and used the surplus to feed his army.

When the Moplahs resorted to violence the Congress Party under Mahatma Gandhi withdrew its support. When the British troops attacked, the movement acquired a communal colour. The rebels killed about 500 Hindus, sacked about 100 temples and forcibly converted 2,500 Hindus to Islam. There was a fierce struggle between British and Gorkha troops on one hand and the rebels on the other. It is said that about 10,000 rebels died in the prolonged guerrilla warfare. The leaders of the rebels were shot, hundreds of their followers were hanged or deported to the Andamans and 61 prisoners died of suffocation.

CHAURI CHAURA (1922)

Chauri Chaura is situated in Gorakhpur District of Utttar Pradesh. There was vigorous picketing of foreign cloth and liquor shops in the Bazar. The local landlord who was the owner of the Bazar, resisted picketing. On 1 February 1922, the local police officer visited the Bazar with a police force and beat some of the volunteers and peasants engaged in the picketing of the shops. The result was that a large number of people from the surrounding villages came to Chauri Chaura on 4 February, 1922 and marched in a big crowd to the Police Station. There the volunteers and peasants asked the local police officer why he had beaten them and challenged the police to prevent them from picketing. There was a scuffle and the police constables opened fire and killed a few persons. All the 21 constables at the Police state along with the young son of the Sub-Inspector, were overpowered and both the Police Station and the Policemen in it were set on fire. All of them died. Those who tried to run out of the Station were caught, beaten, soaked in kerosene and hacked to pieces and then thrown into the fire. It is said that the peasants were forced to express their resentment against the oppression of the Government.

VIZAG REVOLUTION (1923)

The Vizag Agency Tribes waged a two-year war against the British Government under their leader, Sitarama Raju. They made the fullest military use of the strategic advantages of the hills and valleys and their traditional weapons. To begin with, they asked for free use of forest lands and produce but ultimately they demanded the establishment of Swaraj for the whole of the Agency area. The British Government took strong action against the rebels and killed thousands of them. Sitaram Raju was killed along with other leaders. Strong action was taken against the people who had joined the rebels. In August 1942, these people gave a fine account of their anti-imperialist spirit.

SATYAGRAHA STRUGGLE BETWEEN 1921-30

During this period, a number of Satyagraha campaigns were organised against unjust laws and imposts. The struggles were those of Bardoli and Pedanadipadu and Duddukuru in 1921 against the land tax, the struggles against Karnataka Forest laws in 1921 and 1931-34, the rent exactions in Uttar Pradesh and Bihar in 1921 and 1931-33, the anti-resettlement campaigns of Godavari and Krishna Deltas and a number of peasant struggles against the landlords of Venkatagiri (1931), Tsadumu and Munagala (1939) were organised in the South. There were also the land Satyagraha in Bihar (1939), the anti-zamindari fight in Bengal and Andhra, canal duties struggle of the Punjab and Bengal (1939), the jute prices struggle of 1937-42 and the debt relief agitation of Bengal.

BARDOLI SATYAGRAHA (1929-30)

With the blessings of Mahatma Gandhi, Sardar Patel organised and led the Bardoli peasants against the resettlement enhancements proposed by the Government. Under the guidance of Sardar Patel, the peasants braved all risks, faced with courage the loss of their beloved cattle and ancestral lands and even risked eviction from their villages. Ultimately, they won. That was in 1929.

In 1930, the peasants of Bardoli rose to a man, refused to pay taxes, faced the auction sales and the eventual loss of almost all of their lands but refused to submit to the Government. However, all their lands were returned to them when the Congress came to power in 1937-39.

REVOLTS OF PEASANTS IN INDIAN STATES

The condition of the peasants in the Indian States was even worse than that of the peasants in British India. They were required to pay a large number of illegal Abwabs or imposts. As was to be expected, the peasants began to protest. To begin with, the Loharu, Patiala and Nabha peasants revolted. They organised a "farm strike", abandoned their villages and ran into the neighbouring forests. They were pursued by the armed police and the military on horseback. After some fight, they gave up their Satyagraha. The Satyagraha of the peasants of Mansa for rent reductions met with some success after a struggle of 3 months. The people of Mysore and Travancore State struggled for responsible government. Hundreds of peasants and workers were killed. Only a few political concessions were made and feudal dues were reduced. In the case of Orissa States, some of the princes ran away from states for-some time due to the fury of the revolts by the peasants. They promised to abolish a number of feudal dues such as forest fees, free supply of fuel wood, grass, forced labour and supply of animals. They also promised to reduce rents. However, those concessions were withdrawn as soon as British forces came to help them. The peasants rebelled again and marched on the capital of the princes and demanded many economic and political concessions. The British military fired on them, killed a large number of the rebels and suppressed their revolts. More than 30,000 peasants left their villages in a number of states including Nilgiris, Dhenkenal and marched into the neighbouring forests of Orissa. They built small huts out of forest leaves and branches and lived in those improvised camps for many months. Ultimately, they came back on the assurance that no action will be taken against them.

The peasants of a number of Maharashtra and Karnataka States revolted and got a number of concessions. The peasants of Jaipur, Gawalior and Udaipur rose against their local Thakurs and other feudal lords. They were led by Jamnalal Bajaj, a follower of Mahatma Gandhi. They achieved victory on their economic front. All over the Rajasthan States, the peasants had to struggle hard for months after August 1947 to get rid of forced labour, Abwabs and eventually Jagirdari or Thakurdari systems.

REVOLTS UNDER COMMUNISTS

The most successful Communist-led peasant revolts were those of Tebhaga in 1946, Telengana in 1946-48, Naxalbari in 1967 and Andhra Pradesh in 1969-71. All of these revolts started as strikes or some other form of popular action initiated by the peasants for the redress of specific grievances. The Tebhaga revolt began with a demand for the reduction of the rights of the occupying tenants (Jotedars) in the crop from half to one-third and a corresponding increase in the rights of poor peasant sharecroppers (Adhiars or Bargadars). In Telengana, the demands were for the abolition of illegal exactions by the Deshmukhs and Nawabs or feudal lords and later on for the cancellation of the debts of the peasants. In Thangavur, the demands were for halving the rents paid by cultivating tenants and doubling the wages of landless labourers. In Naxalbari, the peasant unions began by taking over land which the Communist led West Bengal Government had already decreed should be removed from the Jotedars, the former occupancy tenants who had become the owners of the land with the abolition of the Zamindari rights. Although the law provided for the distribution of the land among the landless, the proprietors refused to surrender. The peasant unions turned out the landlords and distributed the land among the peasants. In 1969 in Warangal, Khammam and Karimnagar Districts of Andhra Pradesh, the Communist peasant unions began their armed struggle which had been taken from them by the neighbouring landlords and re-distributing the same among the tribal peasants.

The CPI(M) developed the policy of "annihilation" of landlords, police, moneylenders, oppressive bureaucrats and enemies of other political parties by secret squads recruited from young party members and their associates in the cities and poor peasants and land labourers in the countryside. A large number of landlords in Eastern India were assassinated within a period of 3 years. There was criticism of the annihilation policy and after the death of Charu Mazumdar, the policy of annihilation was given up.

REVOLT OF VEERA GUNNAMMA (1940)

On 31 March 1940, the local police and the Magistrate arrested 7 of the local peasant leaders of Mandasa on very flimsy grounds. The women protested against the unjust arrests and police insulted them. Veera Gunnamma abused them for their behaviour. They fired on her six times and killed her.

AUGUST REVOLUTION AND PEASANTS

During the Quit India Movement, the Indian peasants played a heroic, dynamic and effective role. It is true that the students and the middle classes also did a lot but the peasants are said to have excelled all. They rose spontaneously and simultaneously and upset the means of transport of the British war machine. Police stations and other local officers of Government were captured. Wherever they succeeded in overcoming the local forces of the Government, they established their Panchayats. In several areas in Uttar Pradesh, Bihar, Bengal, Maharashtra and Tamil Nadu, they established their rival Governments. In Midnapore and Satara Districts, the British Government was not able to regain control over the whole regions consisting of the masses of peasants for years.

REVOLT OF TELENGANA

The revolt in Telengana and the adjoining Districts was one of the post-war insurrectionary struggles of peasants in India. It was launched by the Communist Party of India. It began in the middle of 1946 and lasted over 5 years till it was called off on 21 October 1951. This struggle developed in the Nizam-governed feudal state of Hyderabad into a peasants' and people's armed revolt. During the course of the struggle, the peasantry in about 3,000 villages succeeded in setting up Gram Raj on the basis of fighting village Panchayats. In those villages, the landlords were driven away from their lands which were seized by the peasants. One million acres of land was redistributed among the peasantry under the guidance of the people's committees. All evictions were stopped and forced labour was abolished. The high rates of interest were cut down or altogether forbidden. The daily wages of the agricultural labourers were increased and a minimum wage was enforced. The forest officialdom was forced to abandon the entire forest belt. For a period of 12 to 18 months, the entire administration of these areas was conducted by the village peasant committees. A powerful militia consisting of peasants and other workers was built up.

After the police action in September 1948, the Government of India had to deal with the Telengana revolt and it took about 3 years to liquidate the rebels. It is said that as many as 4000 Communists and peasant militants were killed. More than 10,000 Communist cadres and people's fighters were put into detention camps and jails for a period of 3 to 4 years. It was with great difficulty that the authority of the Government of India and the State of Hyderabad was restored.

REVIEW QUESTIONS

1. Write an essay on the various peasant movements and uprisings during the 19th and 20th centuries.
2. What was the Champaran Satyagraha? Who led it and why was it started?
3. Discuss the causes and results of the Chauri Chaura incident (1922) and Bardoli Satyagraha (1929-1930).
4. What was the August Revolution? Discuss its causes and results.
5. A number of Satyagraha campaigns were organised against unjust laws and imposts during the period 1921-1930. Explain.
6. Write short notes on the following:
   (a) The Punjab Land Alienation Act, 1900
   (b) Chauri Chaura incident
   (c) Bardoli Satyagraha

SUGGESTED READINGS

Datta, K.K.: *The Santhal Inssurection of 1955–57,* Calcutta, 1940.
Desai, A.R. (Ed.): *Peasant Struggles in India,* New Delhi, 1979.
Dhanagare, D.N.: *Agrarian Movements in Gandhian Politics.*
Natrajan, L.: *Peasant Uprising in India.*
Pavier, Barry: *The Telengana Movement, 1944-51,* Vikas, 1981.
Sen, S.: *Agrarian Relations in India.*
Report of the Indigo Commission.
Report of the Deccan Riots Commission.

37 The Left Movements in India

LEARNING OBJECTIVES

- Provide a comprehensive account of the left movements in India
- Describe the role of the Communist Party of India in Indian independence
- Give an account of performance of Communists in first General Elections and developments thereafter
- Know about the Congress Socialist Party and Forward Bloc

INTRODUCTION

The terms 'Left' and 'Right' are used in a particular sense. Those who stand for revolutionary changes come within the compass of the left movements and those who stand for *status quo* are said to belong to the right. While dealing with the left movements, we are mainly concerned with the Communist Party of India.

There were many circumstances which favoured the growth of the left movements in India. The result of the World War I was that the prices of necessities of life rose. There were famine conditions in many parts of the country. There were crippling financial burdens on the people. The success of the Russian Revolution in 1917 fired the imagination of the Indian intellectuals, political leaders, the terrorists and even the workers and made them aware of a new ideology. The slogans of Swaraj and Swadesi by Mahatma Gandhi and his efforts to carry the message to the people gave a new orientation to the nationalist movement in the country. Even the workers and peasants were drawn into the mainstream of national life. Those developments helped the growth of the socialist movement. The growing unemployment among the educated people made them lose faith in the Liberalism of the 19th century and they were attracted towards terrorism and revolutionary ideology. Many radicals were not satisfied with the weak policy of Mahatma Gandhi. It was felt by them that policy of non-violence stood in the way of the development of a revolutionary mass struggle against the British Government.

Lala Lajpat Rai was possibly the first Indian writer to write about socialism and Bolshevism but his attitude towards the latter was not sympathetic. He presided over the first Indian Trade Union Congress held in 1920. In 1920-23, M. N. Roy wrote two books in which he criticised the bourgeois domination of the Indian National Congress. M. N. Roy and Virendra Chattopadhyaya were the two Indian leaders who were deeply interested in Communism in the early twenties. In 1926, Moti Lal and Jawaharlal Nehru visited the Soviet Union. In 1918, a Kisan Sabha was organised at Allahabad but it was not influenced by socialist ideology. In 1924, the Central Kisan Sangh was established at Allahabad. In April 1936, the All India Kisan Sabha was established.

THE COMMUNIST PARTY OF INDIA

The World War II came as a shock in India as elsewhere to many people who began to find out some solution of the social and economic ills which were responsible for the World War. When this was going on, the Russian Revolution led by Lenin and Trotsky broke out. The leaders of the Asian Revolution promised to the people of the world a better future based on peace, equality and social justice. It was on this wave of idealism that communism came to India. India at that time was preparing herself to launch its mass struggle against British rule under the leadership of Mahatma Gandhi. In this atmosphere, the Russian Revolution was received favourably in India and was considered as a great liberating force. The intellectual and emotional climate in India in the early twenties was receptive to the ideas of communism.

The Soviet leaders tried to establish a section of Communist International in the heart of India itself. Organisationally M. N. Roy was perhaps the first link between the Communist International and the newly born communism in India which wars throughout the greater part of the twenties still at the level of ideas. M. N. Roy made his first appearance in Russia in 1920. Roundabout 1921-22, he began to publish from various places in Europe an English periodical first entitled "Vanguard" and later "The Masses of India". A large number of copies of this journal were sent to individual nationalists, trade unionists and intellectuals in India. In 1923, S. A. Dange started the publication of an English Weekly entitled "Socialist". At about the same time, Janavani, a Bengali Weekly, was started from Calcutta. In July 1924, the Comintern decided to accept the advice of M. N. Roy that the Communist Party of India should be established as a branch of the Communist International.

Organised communism came to India when the followers of M. N. Roy came to this country. Nalini Gupta returned to India in 1921 on behalf of M. N. Roy. Abani Mukherji came to India in 1923 on behalf of Virendranath Chattopadhyaya. Both of them had been members of terrorist organisations in Bengal before they went outside India. Their activities resulted in the Kanpur conspiracy case in 1924. The charge against the communist leaders was that they were organising a conspiracy to over-throw the Government of India by violent means. The accused, in that case were S. A. Dange, Muzaffar Ahmad, Shaukat Usmani and Nalini Gupta.

Roundabout 1924, the Communist International developed some doubt about the ability of M.N. Roy to deliver the goods. It was decided to adopt new tactics to strengthen communist movement in India. It was agreed to adopt a scheme of direct contact between the Comintern and the communist organisation and groups in British India. However, the Communist organisations in India were directed through the Communist Party of Great Britain and R. Palme Dutt became an important figure in this connection. He was throughout in closer touch with Moscow than most of his colleagues in the Communist Party of Great Britain.

A series of British communists were sent to India to help the communists in this country. Percy E. Glading was the first to come to India. He was followed by George Allison who arrived in Bombay in April 1926. He was sent to India to develop the left-wing inside the Trade Union Congress but to keep out of party politics except in an advisory capacity. However, he took a prominent part in labour troubles in Bombay and Bengal as a result of which he was apprehended in 1926, prosecuted and convicted on a charge of using forged documents and-having counterfeited the seal and stamp of the British Foreign Office on his passport. He was sentenced to 18 months' rigorous imprisonment and was deported on the expiry of his sentence.

The place of George Allison was taken by Phillip Spratt who arrived in India in December 1926 to open in India a Labour Research Organisation through which Soviet money could be received and distributed in India. When Spratt came to India, the Communist Party of India had barely a dozen nominal members and not much activity. Spratt devoted all his energy to the development of Communist Party in India. He was joined in September 1927 by Benjamin. Francis Bradley who also took an active part in the organisation of the Workers' and Peasants' Party and of the employees of cotton mills and railways. H. L. Hutchison came to Bombay in September 1928 but his mission was not a success.

It is worthy of notice that during those early days, the hand of Spratt was everywhere. He planted the seeds of revolt in the Punjab. He set up a Workers and Peasants Party in the United Provinces which held its inaugural conference at Meerut in October 1928. Within a month, branches were set up in Delhi, Allahabad, Meerut, Gorakhpur and Jhansi. During all this time, Spratt was carrying on correspondence with his counterparts on the European Continent and in England informing them of the progress achieved, the difficulties experienced and the necessary instructions in that connection. There was a steady and expensive stream of communist literature into India and different methods were employed to smuggle communist literature without the same being captured by the Government of India.

Soon after the Comintern Resolution of September 1928 was passed, the Communist Party met at Calcutta in December 1928. It was at this meeting that the swing to the left was applied to India. A new Central Executive was first elected. The main decisions were to make the party active and to do propaganda in the name of the Communist Party of India, to affiliate to the Communist International and send Muzaffar Ahmed to Moscow as a delegate to the Executive Committee of the Communist International.

Perhaps the greatest success of the communists during this period was the influence they managed to acquire in trade unions in India and their success in disrupting and splitting them to their advantage. As a result of industrialisation of India, a sizeable labour force had been created. Rising prices and the consequent unrest encouraged the birth of trade unions. The Madras Union, was established by B. P. Wadia in 1918. In 1920, the All India Trade Union Congress was established for purposes of coordination. In 1925 was formed the All India Railwaymen's Federation. By 1925-26, labour organisations acquired a certain measure of strength and stability and their spokesman in the Legislatures succeeded in giving expression to some of the needs of the workers. The Communists appeared on the scene and their sole objective was to capture the key trade unions with a view to utilizing them for the political ends of their party. From 1926 to 1928, the influence of the communists increased immensely. They started several weekly journals like Kranti in the Marathi language.

MEERUT CONSPIRACY CASE

Communist activity was abruptly cut short by the arrest of 31 of its most important leaders from different parts of India on 20 March 1929, including Spratt, Bradley, Muzaffar Ahmed, Shaukat Usmani and S. A. Dange. Hutchison was arrested a few weeks later. There were comprehensive searches throughout the country and a large amount of information was collected about the working of the communists in the country. The lower court made a preliminary enquiry into the case and finalised its hearing of the case on 14 January 1930. The Court found that it had been definitely proved that Communist International was founded in 1919 with its headquarters at Moscow and its chief aim was to establish Workers, republics in every country. For that purpose, it excited violent revolutions in all countries. It was determined to bring about a revolution in India with the object of overthrowing the sovereignty of the King Emperor in British India. With that object, it formed a conspiracy with persons and bodies in Europe and India and elsewhere to excite the Indian workers and peasants to revolution. The conspirators laid down a general plan of campaign under the direction of the Communist International. That plan included the formation of such bodies as a Communist Party of India and Workers, and Peasants parties. The immediate work of those parties was to gain control of the working classes by organising them in unions, teaching them the principles of communism, inciting them to strikes in order to educate them and teach them solidarity and to use every possible method of propaganda and instruction. The workers were taught mass organisation with a view to the declaration of a general strike followed by revolution. The peasants were also organised to form an effective reserve force for the proletarian masses and to affect an agrarian revolution. In pursuance of those aims, a Communist Party in India and four Workers' and Peasants' Parties in Bombay, Bengal, the Punjab and the United Provinces were formed. Those bodies were given financial aid from Moscow and their policy was dictated from Moscow, directly and via England and the Continent, through communications conducted in a secret and conspiratorial manner. In addition to this, Allison, Spratt and Bradley were sent to India for the express purpose of organising the work and fomenting revolution. In pursuance of those directions and with financial help thus obtained, those bodies organised unions, conducted demonstrations, edited papers, instituted youth movements, initiated and conducted strikes and used all possible methods of propaganda. In all those activities, the accused had taken part with full knowledge and approval of their aims and objects and directly or indirectly in league with the conspirators outside India.

The Additional Sessions Judge who took up the actual trial of the case, pronounced judgment on 16 January 1933, sentencing all but four of the 31 accused persons to varying terms of imprisonment. Muzaffar Ahmed was sentenced to life imprisonment. S. A. Dange, S. V. Ghate, K. N. Jogkelar, R. S. Nimbkar and Spratt were given 12 years. Bradley, Mirajkar and Usmani were given 10 years' transportation. The lightest sentence was 3 years' imprisonment. The Allahabad High Court confirmed all the findings but reduced the sentences of imprisonment of the various accused. Some of them were immediately released in September 1934 and the rest in the autumn of 1935.

It is worthy of notice that there was widespread nationalist sympathy for the accused at Meerut. The communists were able to enlist for their legal advice and defence the services of younger nationalist spokesmen. Among them were Pandit Jawaharlal Nehru, Farid-ul-Huq Ansari and Dr. Kailash Nath Katju. The trial lasted for many years and the accused took full advantage of it to make propaganda in favour of communism. However, the removal of the leading communists in March 1929 dealt a heavy blow to the Communist Party of India. The industrial situation improved considerably. There, was a cessation of strikes in general. Rivalries and petty squabbles grew within the Communist Party.

The period from 1930 to 1935 was one of wilderness for the Communist Party in India. The Communists not only held aloof from the freedom struggle led by the Indian National Congress during this period but also did everything they could to weaken and sabotage it. While the patriotic Indians were boycotting foreign cloth, the Communists advocated the use of foreign cloth as a gesture of solidarity with the British workers in Lancashire. While Mahatma Gandhi advocated the methods of non-violent resistance, the Communists asserted the right to use violence. The Indian Communists insulted the national flag of India on the sands of Chowpatty in Bombay. To the Communists in India, the struggle for national independence was not so much a struggle for national liberation as one for strengthening a sector of world capitalism and imperialism. A new constitution was adopted by the Communist Party of India in 1934. The Communists gave a call for a countrywide strike of all textile workers with effect from 23 April 1934 and the strike was actually started. The Government took immediate action and arrested the Communist leaders. The Communist Party was declared illegal in July 1934 along with some dozen trade unions under Communist control and the Young Workers League. The workers of the Communist Party completely went underground.

R. Palme Dutt and Bradley published their thesis entitled "The Anti-Imperialist People's Front" in India in March 1936. They described the Indian National Congress as merely the united front of the Indian people in the nationalist struggle. They advised the Communists to join the Indian National Congress and utilise the Congress organisation to strengthen the left wing within the Congress called the Congress Socialist Party and oust the reactionary right-wing elements in the Congress. The Communists, the Congress Socialist Party and the Trade Unionists planned to organise a popular front on the basis of a common minimum programme. However, the Communists did not meet with much success as they did not work with the Congress in the spirit of cooperation. Their object was merely to isolate the Congress leadership from the rank and file and capture the larger organisation for the party ends. Everything was done to belittle the role and inspiration of the nationalist movement led by the Congress. In order to implement the "Trojan horse" strategy, a minimum programme was decided upon and instructions were issued to individual Communists to push it through. The

Politbureau declared that "individual enrolment is not a substitute for collective affiliation but only one of the means to intensify the agitation and strengthen the demands for collective affiliation, from inside the Indian National Congress platform in alliance with the Indian National Congress rank and file and by mobilising them under our leadership on this and other allied immediate issues." The agitation was not to be carried on from inside alone but was to be supported by agitation from outside. After infiltrating into the Congress, a programme of appeal to the rank and file of the Congress was started. The Communists complained that the failures of Mahatma Gandhi in the Congress watered down the anti-imperialist content in the Lahore Resolution of 1929 on complete independence. The Communists failed in their objective. They could neither capture the Congress leadership nor make it accept their programme nor adopt their slogans. It was clear that so long as Mahatma Gandhi's personality dominated the national scene, the Communists could not succeed so far as the Congress was concerned. Efforts were made to influence the Congress through Pandit Jawaharlal Nehru, Subhas Chandra Bose and the Congress Socialist Party under the leadership of Jayaprakash Narayan. The Congress Socialist Party opened its doors to the Communists and through that party the Communists came to occupy important positions in the Indian National Congress.

THE COMMUNISTS AND GOVERNMENT OF INDIA

Up to August 1939, the Communists in India were praising the Soviet Union under Stalin and condemning Hitler. However, they found them-selves in an awkward position after Stalin entered into a Non-Aggression Pact with Hitler. Overnight, Hitler became a friend of peace and England and France became the imperialist warmongers. The Communists condemned England for dragging India into an imperialist war against her will. Mahatma Gandhi and Nehru were denounced as saboteurs of Indian independence and agents of imperialism. The Congress Socialists were described as henchmen of Mahatma Gandhi. A virulent attack was started against the leaders of the Congress and the Socialist Party. The Communists did not succeed entirely because the rank and file of both the parties were loyal to their leaders. However, the Communists did succeed in causing a split in the All-India Students' Federation and the All-India Kisan Sabha which had been built by the Socialists. The All-India Trade Union Congress gradually became the preserve of the Communists. The Congress Socialist Party which had been working very hard for a united front saw the futility and danger of trying to work with the Communists and decided to break the alliance. The result was that all the Communists were expelled from the Congress Socialist Party. It is pointed out that this decision was taken in the nick of time and a little delay would have broken the Congress Socialist Party entirely. However, while parting, the Communists carried with them almost intact three of the best organised state branches of the Congress Socialist Party in Andhra, Tamil Nadu and Kerala.

The Communists induced the workers to go on strike to impair war production. On 2 October 1939, the Communists organised a strike in Bombay in which 90,000 workers were stated to have participated. The Government of India took action against the Communists by arresting their leaders. The Communists continued to be arrested in 1940.

However, everything changed for the Communist Party of India after Hitler attacked Russia on 22 June 1941. The imperialist war became a "people's war". The Communists in India decided to support the Government of India in every way in their war-effort as England and Russia were to fight together against Hitler. The Government of India released the Communist leaders from detention. The ban on the Communist Party was lifted and it could now work as a legal party. The Communist Party recommended that the Cripps proposals be accepted and it attacked the Congress for rejecting them. After the Quit India Resolution was passed by the Congress on 8 August 1942 and the arrest of its leaders, the Communist Party, fought on the side of the British Government. The underground resistance leaders of the Congress and the Socialist Party were condemned as fifth columnists. The Communists considered it as their duty to spy on the Indian patriots and get them arrested wherever possible. They became police informers. There was complete cooperation between the officials of the Government of India and the members of the Communist Party. The

Communist Party placed its services at the disposal of the Government of India against all those who took part in the Quit India Movement and the Azad Hind Fauj of Subhas Chandra Bose. They struggled hard to get them arrested. On the industrial front, the Communists did their utmost to keep the workers out of the national unrest. There were to be no strikes but more and more work for the Government. The workers were asked to forget the class struggle and not to strike but to work for increased production. The peasants were asked to forget their grievances and grow more food and surrender it to the Government to feed the armies.

The Communists did their utmost to sabotage the national movement for India's freedom. They also tried to sabotage the efforts aimed at bringing about a compromise between the Indian National Congress and the Muslim League. They whole-heartedly supported the demand for Pakistan. They went a step further by saying that every linguistic group in India had a distinct nationality and was, therefore, entitled to the right to secede. That would have resulted in the dismemberment of the, country and its Balkanisation into a large number of independent states.

For practically 3 years from 1942 to 1945, every active Indian patriot and political worker was either in jail or underground. This gave an opportunity to the Communists to capture the labour, students, peasants and women organisations in the country. The All-India Trade Union Congress became a purely Communist front. The Communists infiltrated into the All-India Women's Conference.

In spite of all this, the Communists were isolated and discredited by 1945. Their efforts to destroy the influence of Mahatma Gandhi and the Congress leaders failed completely. Their efforts to approach Mr. Jinnah and the Muslim League also failed. They lost support both among the peasants and the industrial workers. Their only influence was among the upper-class intellectuals with whom it was fashionable to be Communists. When Mahatma Gandhi was released in 1944, the Communists tried to approach him but he refused to have anything to do with them. When the members of the Congress Working Committee were released in June 1945, the Congress resumed normal, functioning and the Communists were expelled from the Congress.

TELENGANA

When India became independent in August 1947, the Communist Party decided to give support to the Nehru Government. Their underlying motive was to support Prime Minister Nehru against Sardar Patel. The idea was to create a schism or split in the Congress ranks. The Communist support to Nehru, did not last long on account of a change in the Russian policy and world alignments. Communist agitation was very strong in the rural districts of Telengana in Hyderabad. The Communists had entrenched themselves in that area before the police action against Hyderabad in 1948. It was found that there was no law and order in that area and the Communists practically ruled that area. The Government of India decided to take strong action against the Communists. Between October and December 1950, there were no less than 344 serious incidents, including 96 murders, 151 attacks on the police and military and 82 attacks on the home guards and village officials. During this period, the police killed 223 Communists and arrested 143 of them. They recovered from them guns and rifles along with ammunition and explosives. Towards the end of 1951, there was a decrease in terrorism.

Attempts were made by the Communists to persuade the police and the troops to desert their offices, murder their officers and join the Communist Party.

On 17 September 1951, the Communist Party issued a statement from Bombay in which they challenged the Government of India to withdraw the Preventive Detention Act and stop the policy of repression against the Communists. In return, the Communist Party promised to give up terrorism and act in at legal manner through constitutional means.

FIRST GENERAL ELECTIONS AND COMMUNISTS

When the General Elections were held in India in 1952, the Communists were able to capture as many as 23 seats in Parliament and the Communist Party came second only to the Congress Party.

In many State Assemblies also, the Communist Party emerged as the second largest party and was leading the Opposition group. Critics point out that the Communists were able to achieve this success by concentrating on certain selected constituencies. Although the Socialist Party got 10.50 per cent votes and the Communist 5.81 per cent votes, the Communists were able to show better results. The General Elections gave an excellent opportunity to the Communist Party to enlist sympathisers, restore mass contact and revitalise the Communist Party. On 4 September 1953, P. Sundarayya, the Communist leader in Rajya Sabha, declared that the members of his party were in Parliament to see that the Indian Constitution was wrecked and replaced by a new Constitution.

PEPSU

In the beginning of 1952, efforts at reorganising the peasant front by the Communists became noticeable and reports of peasant discontent fostered by the Communists began to appear from various corners of India, including Assam and Nepal. However, the situation was the worst in the State of PEPSU where the Communists were able to set up zones of parallel Government. Self-constituted Panchayats started dispossessing the farmers of their lands and distributing them among the landless labourers. Neither the farmers nor the police were able to counter the mass intimidation practiced by the Communist Panchayats. By March 1953, there was complete chaos in the Starte of PEPSU. Ultimately, the Constitution was suspended in the State of PEPSU and the Government of India was able to crush the Communist agitation. At that time the Communists revived their old front of All-India Kisan Federation. They also decided to hold in New Delhi by the end of 1953 an Asian Peasant Convention in order to help cement "fraternal bonds of mutual understanding between peasants of all Asiatic countries and strengthen the forces of peace and dissipate the clouds of imperialist war from our fair Continent."

SPLIT IN COMMUNIST PARTY

There was a split in the Communist Party of India after the Vijayawada Congress of 1961 and another Communist Party of India called CPI (Marxist) came into existence. The old Communist Party continued under the leadership of S. A. Dange. The claim of the CPI-M is that it is the only party, which stands firmly consistently for socialism and rejects the "parliamentary road to socialism". It also aims at socialisation of means of production.

The Communist Party of India supported Prime Minister Indira Gandhi during the Emergency (1975-77) but it was opposed by CPI-M. At present, the Communist Party of India is weaker than CPI-M. Formerly the CPI-M had its Government in Kerala and West Bengal but now it rules in West Bengal alone.

THE CONGRESS SOCIALIST PARTY

The foundation of the Congress Socialist Party in May 1934 was an important step in the development of socialism in India. The Bihar Socialist Party was founded in 1931 and the Bombay Socialist group was organised in 1934. The Congress Socialist Party was founded by those younger Congressmen who during their long terms of imprisonment in the Civil Disobedience Movement came into contact with Marxist ideas. They were not satisfied with the conservative leadership of the Congress Party after 1933. They had their reservations about Mahatma Gandhi's constructive programme. They felt that it was necessary to organise the workers and peasants on class lines and bring them into the freedom movement. Those who thought alike met together at Patna and Bombay in 1934 and thus the Congress Socialist Party was launched with Jayaprakash Narayan as its General Secretary. Acharya Narendra Deva, Dr. Ram Manohar Lohia, Kamala Devi Chattopadhyaya, Yusuf Meherally, Minoo Masani, S. M. Joshi and other comrades were his colleagues. There were also young people like E.M.S. Namboodiripad, P. Ramamurthy, Sundarayya and others. They later on left the Congress

Socialist Party and joined the Communist Party. However, Jayaprakash Narayan continued to have excellent relations with them.

At its first Conference in Bombay in 1934, the Congress Socialist Party adopted a 15-Point programme which included the repudiation of the public debt of India, transfer of all power to producing masses, planned development of the economic life of the country by the state, socialisation of the key industries, state monopoly of foreign trade, cooperative and collective farming, organisation of cooperatives for production, distribution and credit and elimination of princes and landlords without compensation. The members of the Congress Socialist Party criticised the leadership of the Congress but professed loyalty to the organisation. In the words of Acharya Narendra Deva, their object was "to resuscitate and reinvigorate the Congress" and to draw into it the mass of workers and peasants in order to widen the base of the anti-imperialist front. They criticised Mahatma Gandhi and his non-violence, his ethical approach to politics and his theory of trusteeship.

There was bound to be a clash between the members of the Congress Socialist Party and the old members of the Congress. They differed on the question of the Government of India Act, 1935, the formation of ministries in 1937, the organisation of Kisan Sabhas and agitation for agrarian reforms, the release of political detenus and agitation in the Indian States. There were bitter controversies in which the Congress leadership was severely criticised. Jayaprakash Narayan went to the extent of saying that "Gandhism has played its part. It cannot carry us further and hence we must march and be guided by the ideology of socialism." The leaders of the Congress Socialist Party did not realise the difficulties of the Congress Party which had to fight both against the British Government and the Muslim League and that could not be done without discipline in the Congress Party itself.

It is true that Jawaharlal Nehru was ideologically the closest to the Congress Socialist Party. He was in jail when the new party was formed and when he became the Congress President, he included Jayaprakash Narayan, Narendra Deva and Achyut Patwardhan in the Congress Working Committee. Mahatma Gandhi was against the Congress Socialist Party and he made it clear that if the Congress Socialist Party gained ascendancy in the Congress, he would not remain in the Congress. He did not approve of class war, expropriation and violence. Subhas Chandra Bose asked Nehru to be firm with the Congress establishment but Nehru was not prepared to defy Gandhi or break away from the Congress. Mahatma Gandhi offered again and again to step down if his ideas were not acceptable to the Working Committee or the All-India Congress Committee. In October 1939, Mahatma Gandhi wrote to Nehru, "I must not lead it I cannot carry all with me. There should be no divided counsels among the members of the Working Committee. I feel you should take full charge and lead the country leaving me free to voice my opinion." Nehru was not prepared to allow Mahatma Gandhi to give up the leadership of the Congress. He was not unaware of his own limitations. He could rouse the masses and inspire the intelligentsia but he was not an expert in party management.

Whatever the differences between the Congress Socialist Party and the leadership of the Indian National Congress, there was no intention to carry the opposition to the breaking point. The Congress Socialists knew well that they could not realise their programme unless the British were ousted from India and that could be done only by the Indian National Congress. The Congress Socialist Party got a lot of support from the youth, the industrial labour and the peasantry, but it was still at minority. It was not a homogeneous group. It consisted of Marxists like J.P. Narayan and Narendra Deva, Socialist Democrats like Asoka Mehta and M. R. Masani, Gandhians like Patwardhan and populists like Dr. Ram Manohar Lohia. It is true that the Congress Socialist Party was not able to have its own way on many important issues but it certainly succeeded in giving radical orientation to the Congress policies in certain respects. The Second World War and the breach with the Government brought the Congress Socialists nearer to Mahatma Gandhi and the Congress leadership. Both the Congress leadership and the Congress Socialists worked against the Government during the Quit India Movement. During that movement, J. P. Narayan who was already in jail since 1940, made a daring escape from Hazaribagh jail with colleagues like Ram

Nandan Misra and joined the ranks of the freedom fighters. Achyut Patwardhan, Aruna Asaf Ali, Dr. Lohia, Sucheta Kriplani and others were operating under the name of the underground All-India Congress Committee and trying to widen the scope of the mass struggle. When J. P. Narayan came out of jail, he declared that only armed resistance could achieve the objectives. He organised squads which operated in Bihar. Nepal was used as a base of operations. Ultimately, J. P. Narain and Dr. Lohia were arrested.

The Congress Socialists were always keen to consolidate all leftist forces in the country. The Congress Socialist Party opened its doors to the Communists in 1936. The Communist Party was an illegal party at that time and its leaders were happy to get a chance of functioning openly through the Congress Socialist Party and the Indian National Congress. The Communists created trouble for the leaders of the Congress Socialist Party and hence were expelled from it in 1940. However, they took away with them the Southern branches of the Congress Socialist Party. If the Communists had not been expelled in 1940, they would have created more trouble.

About the Congress Socialist Party, Shri P. L. Lakhanpal wrote the following in 1946, "The role played by the C.S P. within the Congress as well as without it was magnificent indeed. Within it, it served as a rallying point for all the radical elements; without it, it organised peasant movements, brought about a union between the various T. U. Congress and Federations, won the sympathy and support of the other radical organisations and put socialism till then a subject for academic discussion on the political map of India". (*History of the Congress Socialist Party, Lahore,* p. 46, 1946.)

In March 1948, at the Nasik Convention, the Socialists decided to leave the Congress because the leadership of the Congress forbade all inner groupings within that organisation. The Socialists left the Congress in 1948 and formed a separate party known as the Socialist Party of India. After the General Elections of 1952, the Socialist Party and Krishak Mazdoor Praja Party led by J. B. Kriplani decided to merge. The decision for merger was taken on 25 August 1952 at Lucknow and the merger actually took place at a meeting in Bombay on 26 and 27 September 1952.

The National Executive of the Praja Socialist Party at its meeting in Bombay on 16 October 1959 outlined a 12-point programme for India. It stood for intensification of agricultural and industrial production, equitable distribution and democratic decentralisation. Its basic political and economic philosophy was to bring about a reconciliation and synthesis of nationalism, secularism and democratic decentralisation.

The Socialist Party was merged in the Janata Party in 1977 and also joined the Janata Government. After the fall of the Janata Government in 1979, some of the Socialist members remained in the Janata Party and some joined the Lok Dal.

FORWARD BLOC

A reference may be made to some other minor leftist parties in India. The Forward Bloc was formed by Subhas Chandra Bose after his quarrel with Mahatma Gandhi. The Forward Bloc accepted the creed, policy and programme of the Congress but was not bound to have confidence in the Congress High Command. When India became free in 1947, the Forward Bloc described the transfer of power as a bogus one. Its view was that the bourgeois leadership of the Congress had entered into a partnership with British imperialism to defeat the mass struggle.

The Revolutionary Socialist Party was started in 1940. In the tussle between Mahatma Gandhi and Subhas Chandra Bose, it supported Subhas Chandra Bose. It did not support the Government of India even after the Soviet Union joined World War II. The Bolshevik Party of India was started in 1939 by N. Dutt Mazumdar. The Revolutionary Communist Party was started in 1942. The Bolshevik-Leninist Party was started in 1941. Shri M. N. Roy started the Radical Democratic Party in 1940.

REVIEW QUESTIONS

1. Discuss the circumstances which favoured the growth of the left movements in India.
2. Write a detailed note on the emergence and growth of the left movements in India.
3. Discuss in detail the history of the Communist Party of India.
4. Discuss the role of the Congress Socialist Party in the development of socialism in India.
5. Assess the role of the Communist Party of India in Indian independence.
6. When did Communism start in India?
7. Write short notes on the following:
   (a) Communism
   (b) Meerut Conspiracy Case
   (c) Split in Communist Party
   (d) The Congress Socialist party

SUGGESTED READINGS

Abid Ali: *The Indian Communists,* 1965.
Adhikari, G. (Ed.): *Documents of the History of the Communist Party of India,* New Delhi, 1974.
Arumugam, M.: *Socialist Thought in India,* New Delhi, 1978.
Balram, N. E.: *A Short History of Communist Party of India,* 1967.
Bhargava, G. S.: *Leaders of the Left,* Bombay, 1951.
Chowdhry, S. R.: *Leftist Movements in India.*
Desai, A. R. (Ed.): *Peasant Struggles in India,* New Delhi, 1979.
Gadre, Kamala: *Indian Way to Socialism,* New Delhi, 1966.
Ghosh, Ajoy: *Theories and Practices of the Socialist Party of India,* Bombay, 1952.
Ghose, Sankar: *Socialism and Communism in India,* Bombay, 1971.
Gupta, Ram Chandra: *J.P. from Marxism to Total Revolution,* New Delhi, 1981.
Haithcox, J.P.: *Communism and Nationalism in India,* Bombay, 1971.
Kautsky, John H.: *Moscow and The Communist Party of India,* 1956.
Lakhanpal, P.L.: *History of the Congress Socialist Party,* Lahore, 1946.
Limaye, Madhu: *Communist Party: Facts and Fiction,* Hyderabad, 1951.
Limaye, Madhu: *Evolution of Socialist Party,* Hyderabad, 1952.
Masani, M.R.: *The Communist Party of India*, London, 1954.
Mehrotra, Nanakchand: *Lohia: A Study,* 1978.
Nanda, B.R. (Ed.): *Socialism in India,* Delhi, 1972.
Overstreet, G.D. and Marshall Windmiller: *Communism in India,* 1959.
Petrie, David: *Communism in India (1924-27).*
Prem Bhasin: *Socialism in India.*
Sengupta, Bhabani: *Communism in Indian Politics,* 1978.
Sinha, L.P.: *The Left Wing in India (1919-47),* 1965.
Singh, Hari Kishore: *A History of the Praja Socialist Party (1934-59),* Lucknow, 1959.
Weiner, Myron: *Political Parties in India.*

38 Role of Mahatma Gandhi in the Nationalist Movement

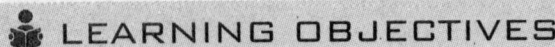

LEARNING OBJECTIVES

- Examine the role of Mahatma Gandhi in the nationalist movement
- Know about the views of various scholars and historians on Mahatma Gandhi's contribution to Indian National Movement

INTRODUCTION

It is true that Mahatma Gandhi alone was not responsible for the independence of India. It has to be conceded that a lot of work had already been done in that direction by the Indian leaders who preceded him. Undoubtedly, the Moderates played their part in laying the foundations of the nationalist movement in the country. It was under their leadership that the leaders of public opinion in India met every year at one place and deliberated upon the problems facing the country. They passed resolutions in which they asked the Government to remove certain grievances of the people. They also demanded the introduction of representative institutions in the country. They worked through the Councils in which they exposed the evils of the foreign Government in the country. They criticised the various measures passed by the Government. They brought to the notice of the public of India and the British Government the sufferings of the people of India as a result of the continuous economic drain of the country. They did what was possible to be done by following the constitutional methods.

The nationalist movement was taken a step further by the Extremist leaders like Tilak, B. C. Pal, Lala Lajpat Rai and Aurobindo Ghose. They employed both constitutional and unconstitutional methods to criticize the working of the British administration in India and called upon the people to demand from the Government that they must be given a share in the administration of the country. Tilak declared in his speeches "Swaraj is my birth-right and I will have it". He even advocated violence against the Government to achieve independence for the country. He asked the people to take action against those Englishmen who were oppressing the people in India. He wrote articles and gave speeches in which he asked the people to demand their rights and fight for them and make sacrifices for the achievement of those rights. Lala Lajpat Rai asked the people to depend upon their own efforts and not to beg for favours from the Government. He was beaten while leading a demonstration against the Simon Commission and actually died as a result of the injuries received by him on that occasion. The new ideas of militant nationalism advocated by Aurobindo Ghose played their part in the national awakening.

The same can be said about the part played by Pandit Jawaharlal Nehru, Sardar Patel, Rajendra Prasad, Maulana Azad and many others who spent their whole lives fighting against the British Government. They were imprisoned on many occasions. They suffered at the hands of British bureaucracy, but they continued the struggle.

The Revolutionaries also played their part in India's struggle for freedom. They not only suffered for the cause of India but also sacrificed their lives while doing so. They were hanged. They were sent to the Andamans where inhuman conditions prevailed and were subjected to all kinds of atrocities, unknown to the world. They were beaten. They were tortured. They suffered in the cause of India's freedom without any complaint. Many of them preferred to die unknown and unsung.

However, the part played by Mahatma Gandhi in India's struggle for independence was unique. He is rightly called the "Father of the Indian Nation". He was really the Generalissimo of the Congress. Before Mahatma Gandhi appeared on the political horizon of India, the nationalist movement in the country was confined to cities and towns and the intellectuals of the country who had no touch with the masses of India. Mahatma Gandhi brought about a revolution in the nature of the nationalist movement in the country. Whatever he did, his one object was to involve the masses of India in the national movement. He worked among the peasants and he appealed to them for support. He appealed to the workers and got their support.

It was Mahatma Gandhi who was responsible for starting the Non-Cooperation Movement in 1920. It was under his leadership that massive preparations were made all over the country. The movement was not confined to the cities or the middle classes or the upper middle classes of India. It is the masses that participated in it. Mahatma Gandhi alone had the courage to suspend the movement when it was at its height. No other leader would have survived such an action. Mahatma Gandhi was the leader of the Civil Disobedience Movement from 1930 to 1934. It was he who started the movement in 1930 by his march to Dandi to violate the salt laws. He was the unquestioned and unrivalled leader of the movement. It was he who negotiated the Gandhi-Irwin Pact of 1931 on behalf of the Congress. It was he who alone went to the Second Round Table Conference as the only representative of the Congress. He alone could deliver the goods on behalf of the Congress. It was Mahatma Gandhi who first suspended the Civil Disobedience Movement in 1933 and then withdrew it in 1934 Nobody can deny the part played by Mahatma Gandhi in the Quit India Movement. During the deliberations of the Congress at Bombay on 7 and 8 August 1942, everybody looked up to him for guidance and leadership. His was the last word. It was he who asked the people to either get freedom for their country or die fighting for the national cause. He remained the leader of the Congress till India won independence.

It is true that there were many other nationalist leaders of India who had spoken at length about the poverty of the masses of India and Britain's exploitation of India, but hardly anything had been done by them for improving the lot of the poor masses. It was Gandhiji who made it clear that the Congress represented the dumb, semi-starved millions scattered over the length and breadth of India and initiated, practical steps to improve their social and economic condition. He put emphasis on the abolition of untouchability which he called a great curse. He set up the Village Industries Association, the Cow Protection Association and the Basic Education Society. He advocated the use of Khadi by all Indians as that alone could improve the lot of the poor masses living in the villages.

As a fighter for India's freedom, Mahatma Gandhi had no peer. He was not only a saint but also a politician. He employed moral means for the attainment of political ends. He used soul force against brute force. He advocated legal and extra-legal methods but not immoral or dishonest methods. He was the unique national figure. He was a social reformer, a religious reformer, a prophet and a nationalist fighting for India's freedom. The effect of the nationalist movement led by him was that even the British politicians began to realise that India could, not be kept in bondage for long. This is clear from the following passage from the diary of the King George VI dated 28 July, 1942. "He (Sir Winston Churchill) amazed me by saying that his colleagues and both, or all three parties in Parliament were quite prepared to give up India to the Indians after the war. He felt they had already been talked in to giving up India. Crips, the Press and the US public opinion have all contributed to make their minds up that our rule in India is wrong and has always been wrong for India."

Mahatma Gandhi was a nationalist par excellence. His greatest contribution to the Indian nationalist movement lays in the fact that he created a mass basis for that movement. He was the pioneer of the first mass national liberation struggle of the Indian people after 1857. He exploded the illusion lovingly cherished by the Moderates that freedom could be obtained only with the assistance and cooperation of foreign "democracy". He was the first to gauge the importance of the role of the masses and the extra-constitutional mass action in the national liberation struggle in sharp contrast to his predecessors like Tilak and other militant nationalist leaders who did not properly appreciate their decisive importance for making the national struggle for independence effective. As a matter of fact, the requisite political imagination to evolve a suitable programme for drawing the mass of people into the orbit of that movement such as Mahatma Gandhi accomplished, was conspicuous by its absence.

Under the leadership of Mahatma Gandhi, the people of India became heroic, audacious fighters for national freedom, courters of jails and receivers of hailstorms of bullets of the imperialist enemy. Mahatma Gandhi injected the people with deep hatred for the "Satanic" British Government and with an unquenchable thirst for national freedom. He was the highest expression of nationalism. Subjectively, he incarnated the very spirit of nationalism, its profound hatred of foreign enslavement and heroic will and determination to end that enslavement.

According to Romain Holland "Mahatma Gandhi has raised up 300 millions of his fellowmen, shaken the British Empire and inaugurated in human politics the most powerful movement that the whole world has seen for nearly 2000 years." Louis Fischer wrote: "The symbol of India's unanimous wish for freedom is Mahatma Gandhi. He does not represent all of India, but he does reflect the will of all India for national liberation. Gandhi is great because every single act that he performs is calculated to promote the one goal of his life — the liberation of India. He is not the man, he has no intention and never had to rule India or administer India. His function ends when he frees India." Again, "Gandhi is the father of India's defiance and its symbol. Gandhi walks to sea to make salt in defiance of the British. It becomes a popular pilgrimage. The idealism of the youth spills into it. So does the leaderless nation's yearning for a leader. Gandhi had given his followers the elation of standing up to a foreigner who is the master in his house."

Percival Spear writes, "For nearly thirty years Congress was dominated by Gandhi and India was influenced more by him than by any other single man. It is not too much to say that the destiny of India was modified and the world itself influenced by this single personality." The same writer says that Gandhi made the Congress a truly national instrument, a political microcosm of the national life. As a result of his tactics and attitudes at various times, it became identified with most of the progressive movements in the country. By means of its anti-Government campaigns and by admittance to leadership of people like Mrs. Sarojini Naidu, it became closely identified with the movement for women's liberation. Gandhi's crusade for the Harijans was in the Congress sense unofficial but the Mahatma's prestige effectively linked it with Congress in the public mind. Gandhi introduced moral values into politics. The early Congressmen were high-minded and earnest men but their creeds were unknown to the masses and if they could have been communicated, would have been unintelligible. In this sphere, Gandhi provided the necessary hyphen. He translated his moral ideals into popular terms and so made the whole political movement seem more of a pilgrimage than a war. He attracted high-minded followers to himself and thereby raised the whole tone of public life. The influence of Gandhi is one of the factors which distinguishes Indian public life from that of the other Asian countries and has given India a unique position in the present international community. Gandhi could secure acquiescence from men like Nehru even when he could not convince them. Gandhi died for his faith and in dying he created a nation. It was the influence of Gandhi which primarily kept India peaceful during those years of unavoidable tension. Under other leaders, India might have slipped into a large-scale terrorist movement or exploded in a violent outbreak which could have led to widespread repression, delayed independence and left the legacy of bitterness. The whole relationship of India with the West would have been placed in jeopardy.

Gandhi evolved a method of non-violent revolution which in fact largely succeeded in maintaining the goodwill between the combatants. Gandhi's influence in restraining his more ardent followers and keeping the party clear of the real terrorists was as important as the skill and ingenuity with which he perplexed the British.

The view of Sir Penderel Moon is that Gandhi basically changed the character of the Congress in the years 1920-21. From a small, upper middle class Westernised institution, he converted the Congress into extensive political organisation of an essentially Indian character with a strong appeal to the lower middle classes. It became the spearhead of a mass movement in so far as under his leadership, it attracted the support or at least the sympathy of a majority of literate Hindus throughout the country and in urban areas of many of the illiterates also. Centuries of autocratic rule, mostly the rule of foreigners had demoralised much of the population of India and fostered timidity and submissiveness. One of the virtues that Gandhi preached and practiced in his own life was fearlessness. "By his exhortations, by his own example and by organising disciplined movements of defiance of the Government, he did more than any one man to instill in the Hindus self-confidence, self-respect and a readiness to stand up for themselves. For this as much as for the actual attainment of independence, he deserves the title of Father of the Nation." (*Gandhi and Modern India*, p. 288.)

About Mahatma Gandhi, Rajni Palme Dutt wrote in 1927, "The achievement of Gandhi consisted in that he almost above all the leaders sensed and reached out of the masses. This was the first great achievement of Gandhi. And this positive achievement of Gandhi is bigger than all the idiosyncrasies and weaknesses which are brought against him and constitute his real contribution to India Nationalism." His second achievement was the policy of action of action of the masses, non-cooperation to win Swaraj and at the height of his agitation, mass Civil Disobedience Movement. (*Modern India*, pp. 72-73.)

About the work of Mahatma Gandhi, Jawaharlal Nehru wrote, Reactionary or revolutionary, he has changed the face of India, given pride and character to a cringing and demoralised people, built up strength and consciousness in the masses and made the Indian problem a world problem." Commenting upon the impact of Mahatma Gandhi on Indian politics, he further observed, "And then Gandhi came. He was like a powerful current of fresh air that made us stretch ourselves and take deep breaths, like a beam of light that pierced the darkness and removed the scales from our eyes, like a whirlwind that upset many things but most of all the working of people's minds. He did not descend from the top; he seemed to emerge from the millions of India, speaking their language and incessantly drawing attention to them and their appalling condition. Get off the backs of these peasants and workers, he told us, all you who lived by their exploitation, get rid of the system that produces this poverty and misery." Again. "Gandhiji's influence is not limited to those who agree with him or accept him as a National Leader, it extends to those also who disagree with him and criticise him. To the vast majority of India's people, he is the symbol of India determined to be free, of militant nationalism, of a refusal to submit to arrogant might, of never agreeing to anything involving national dishonour. Though many people in India may disagree with him on a hundred matters, though they may criticize him or even part company from him on some particular issue, at a time of action and struggle when India's freedom is at stake, they flock to him and look up to him as their inevitable leader."

Dr. Rajendra Prasad, India's first President of India after Independence, wrote, "Mahatma's contribution to Indian politics has been immense. The Indian National Congress had been in existence for thirty years when he returned to India from South Africa in 1915. The Congress had aroused national consciousness to a certain extent, but the awakening was confined largely to the English educated middle classes and had not perpetrated the masses. He carried it to the masses and made it a mass movement. Mahatma Gandhi's movement operated both horizontally and vertically. He took up causes which were not entirely political, but which touched very intimately the life of large masses of people".

The view of Dr. S.R. Mehrotra is that Mahatma Gandhi made the Indian National movement more truly Indian and national than it had been so far. He provided it with a firmer and larger indigenous base. He emphasized the fact that national freedom meant something wider and deeper than emancipation from a foreign yoke. It was a matter of preserving national culture and building up a national character, developing internal strength and renewing all departments of life. His contention was that India would gain little if she only shook off the alien Government and did not get back her soul. Every nation represents an ideal, principle, a spirit and India must discover herself. Mahatma Gandhi converted the Indian national movement into a genuine mass movement. He carried politics, from the drawing rooms and Council Chambers to the streets and fields. He was a great mobilizer. By, his personal charisma, by his capacity for mediating between various groups and forces, by his skilful use of popular myths and symbols and his interpretation of tradition for modern purposes, he drew into the national movement the peasants, workers, untouchables and women who had hitherto remained virtually untouched by it. Gandhi was a great organizer and builder. He transformed the character of the Congress by giving it a new direction, a new constitution, a new organisational structure, a new technique of agitation, a new leadership and a new programme of action. He broke the hypnotic spell of the British Raj in India. He removed the fear of the people and taught them to say "No" to their oppressors. He uplifted the spirit and exalted the dignity of a vast people by teaching them to straighten their backs, to raise their eyes and to face circumstances with steady gaze. (*Towards India's Freedom and Partition*, pp. 153-54, pp. 156-57.)

Rajni Kothari writes about Gandhi, "He realised clearly what few before him did, that the urbanised middle class alone did not provide a sufficient basis for national awakening. The task was to penetrate the masses, to arouse them from their state of apathy and isolation, to provide them with self-confidence and a positive clan in place of both the defensive postures of Moderates and the inferiority complex of the anti-Western radicals, and to confront the authorities with proof that they were dealing riot with a small group of agitators, but with tens of thousands of people organised and disciplined into a great movement, drawn from all over the country." (*Politics in India*, p. 51).

The contention of Sir Penderal Moon is that Gandhi was a Hindu and he imparted to the Congress his own Hindu bias. This Hinduising of the national movement was injurious and ultimately fatal to Hindu-Muslim unity. Gandhi was blind to the adverse effects on Muslim opinion of his Hinduism. In his writings and speeches, Gandhi constantly employed language, imagery and symbolism derived from Hindu sources. The result was that the Muslims were alienated. It is true that the Muslim politicians and the British were also responsible for not bringing the Hindus and Muslims together, but the main responsibility for failure falls on Gandhi and the Congress. However, the fact is that Mahatma Gandhi cannot be held responsible for the alienation of Muslims. The responsibility for that was that of the Government of India which from the very inception of the Indian National Congress left no stone unturned to wean away the Muslims from the Congress. This is clear from all the favours shown to Sir Syed Ahmed Khan by the Government of India and the British Government. The Government of India had a hand in the creation of the Muslim League with a view to fight against the Congress leaders who were agitating for India's freedom. At every stage, the Government helped the Muslim League against the Congress. No student of recent Indian history can deny the support given by the Government of India and the British Government to the demand put forward by Mr. M. A. Jinnah for Pakistan. Mahatma Gandhi and the other Congress leaders did everything in their power to win over the Muslims by offering them all kinds of concessions but they failed because the British Government was always ready to give them more. It is not correct to say that Mahatma Gandhi was in any way communalist. This is clear from the fact that he tried his best to check the communal riots in the country in 1947. When India became free on 15 August 1947, Mahatma Gandhi was not in New Delhi but in Bengal with the Muslims. As a matter of fact, he was shot on account of his efforts to help the Muslims of Delhi and his attitude towards Pakistan. It has rightly been said that more than any other single individual, Mahatma Gandhi placed before the people a picture of secular India and communal harmony. India chose to remain a secular republic in spite of what was happening in Pakistan. Mahatma Gandhi was no friend of the Hindu communalists. His outlook was thoroughly nationalist.

We may conclude by quoting the following tribute paid by the Indian Parliament through a resolution passed by it on 25 December 1969: "That this House, on the occasion of the centenary year of Mahatma Gandhi, pays its respectful tribute to the memory of the Father of the Nation, who led the country to Swarajya by non-violent means, who infused a new spirit into the masses, who uplifted the teeming millions of the oppressed and the down-trodden, who awakened the national conscience of the people, and who inspired the people with a spirit of dedication and service, places on record its deep gratitude to that Apostle of Ahimsa who crusaded for peace, justice and equality and gave the strife-ridden world the message of universal brotherhood and humanism; and rededicates itself to promote the high ideals of Truth, non-violence and service to the nation and to humanity, for which the Mahatma lived and sacrificed his life."

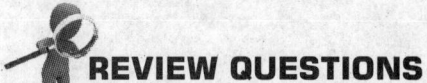

REVIEW QUESTIONS

1. What is the nationalist movement? Who started Indian independence movement?
2. What was Gandhi's role in the Indian independence movement? Explain.
3. Discuss the role of various leaders in the nationalist movement.
4. Throw light on the achievements of Mahatma Gandhi.
5. Write short notes on the following:
    (a) Mahatma Gandhi and his non-violent ways
    (b) Mahatma Gandhi and Indian national movement
6. Examine the role of extremists in the Indian national movement.

SUGGESTED READINGS

Ashe, Geoffrey: *Gandhi — A Study of Revolution.*
Bose, N.K.: *Gandhism and Modern India,* Gauhati, 1970.
Dutt, Rajni Palme: *Modern India.*
Fischer, Louis: *Life of Mahatma Gandhi,* New York, 1950.
Holmes, J.H.: *Mr. Gandhi,* New York, 1950.
Keer, Dhannjaya: *Mahatma Gandhi—Political Saint and Unarmed Prophet,* Bombay, 1973.
Kothari, Rajni: *Politics in India.*
Kripalani, J.B.: *Gandhiji—His Life and Thought.*
Mehrotra, S.R.: *Towards India's Freedom and Partition,* New Delhi, 1979.
Moon, Sir Penderel: *Gandhi and Modern India,* London, 1968.
Nanda, B.R.: *Mahatma Gandhi: A Biography,* London, 1968.
Rolland, Romain: *Prophets of New India,* New York, 1930.
Shriman Narayan: *Gandhi: The Man and His Thought.*
Tendulkar, D.G.: *Mahatma: Life of Mohandas Karamchand Gandhi,* 8 Vols.
Watson, Francis: *Gandhi.*

39   The Renaissance in India

 LEARNING OBJECTIVES

- Know the meaning of Renaissance in Indian
- Explain the condition of India before Renaissance
- Examine the Western impact on the Indian Renaissance
- Throw light on the various aspects of Indian Renaissance
- Give an account of the contribution of Indologists, Indian writers and social reformers towards Renaissance in India

MEANING OF RENAISSANCE IN INDIA

Webster's 'Dictionary defines Renaissance as a revival or rebirth. It refers to the "revival of art, literature and learning in Europe in the fourteenth, fifteenth and sixteenth centuries". Etymologically, the term Renaissance consists of the Latin *re* plus *nasci* meaning "again" and "to be born." A renaissance is a revitalizing or a resurgence of past forces, views and traditions. It involves a digging down to the old and bringing it to the surface again. Such a definition is very narrow when applied to the conditions in India. The reason is that the Renaissance in India was not merely a revivification of India's past but a response to the intrusion of external forces as well. The leaders in India had also to deal with the new conditions created by modern science and technology. The Renaissance in India was a movement which confronted the threefold challenge of the past, the modern and the alien.

The Renaissance in India was not like the Renaissance in Europe. It was not a return to India of the past. It was essentially a matter of spirit which produced striking changes in the realm of religion, society and culture along with a demand for national regeneration. There arose a new self-consciousness among the people of India. The soul of India began to unfold itself and break the shackles of the past. It is maintained that the Renaissance stirred the Indian soul to its very depths and Modern India owes everything to the Renaissance which was followed by reformation movements all over India. It also paved the way to national regeneration. The spirit of Renaissance and the subsequent reform movements affected almost all the aspects of national life. There were new developments in religious, social and political life. There were new trends in the fields of education, literature, fine arts and science.

The view of Sir Jadunath Sarkar is that the Indian Renaissance was at first an intellectual awakening, which profoundly affected our literature, education, thought and art. In the next succeeding generation, it became a moral force and reformed the Indian society and religion. In the third generation, it brought about the economic modernisation of India and ultimately the political emancipation.

In his book entitled "The Renaissance in India", Sri Aurobindo has attempted an analysis of the Renaissance in India. He points out that the eighteenth and early nineteenth centuries in India were periods of political decline, defeat and anarchy which practically killed the creative spirit in religion and art. India began to imitate Europe and forgot her own achievements in the past. However, the life-breath of the nation moved as a subordinate under-current in the religious movements of Bengal and Punjab, in the political aspirations of Maharashtra and the literary activity of Bengal.

SRI AUROBINDO ON THE RENAISSANCE IN INDIA

Sri Aurobindo points out the Renaissance in India in the nineteenth century had three aspects. In the first place, it aimed at a recovery of the old spiritual gospel contained in the scared books of the country. The researches of European Indologists helped the people in the West and in India to understand and appreciate the achievements of the Indians in the past. Philosophers and thinkers like Schopenhauer, Emerson, Thoreau and Royce highly praised India's wisdom in the past. Indian saints and mystic leaders in India also helped the same process. Secondly, this re-invigorated spirituality inspired fresh activity in the fields of philosophy, literature art, etc. Thirdly, an attempt was made to deal in the original way with modern problems in the light of the new inspiration.

Sri Aurobindo did not compare the Indian Renaissance with the European Renaissance of the fifteenth century. He compared it to the Celtic Renaissance when Ireland wanted to go back to the older culture after a long period of British domination. In his analysis of the Indian Renaissance, Sri Aurobindo put great emphasis on the recovery of the spiritual traditions and heritage of the past. According to him, the establishment of new religious sects in India was a central event in the Indian Renaissance. The Brahmo Samaj, the Arya Samaj, Ramakrishna Paramhans and Vivekananda, the neo-Vaishnavism of Bengal and the Renaissance in Islam tried to go back to the past and recover the light of old wisdom. Sri Aurobindo referred to the cosmopolitanism, eclecticism, religious rationalism and logic of the Brahmo Samaj. Of all the leaders of the Renaissance in India, Dayananda appealed most to Sri Aurobindo. He considered him as a unique personality which created a vigorous Aryan manhood in India. Aurobindo found a national instinct in the reliance of Dayananda on Vedic wisdom. To quote Aurobindo, Dayananda "brings back an old Aryan element into the national character." Aurobindo gave credit to the Theosophical Society for getting some recognition in the West for some of the psychic, occult and esoteric achievements of the old Hindus. According to Aurobindo, Ramakrishna Paramhans was "the man who had the greatest influence and has done the most to regenerate Bengal." Vivekananda proclaimed to the world that India was awake not only to exist but also to conquer. In India itself, Vivekananda was a leader who wanted "preservation by reconstruction." Aurobindo also referred to the achievements of J.C. Bose and Rabindranath Tagore in the field of Indian Renaissance. Aurobindo believed that the spiritual and intellectual advance of India was bound to come. To quote him, "The Renaissance in India is as inevitable as the rising of tomorrow's Sun and the Renaissance of a great nation of three hundred millions with so peculiar a temperament, such unique traditions and ideas of life, so powerful an intelligence and so great a mass of potential energies cannot but be one of the most formidable phenomena of the modern world."

CONDITION OF INDIA BEFORE RENAISSANCE

Before the Renaissance in India in the nineteenth century, the condition of India was very bad. In the words of H.G. Rawlinson, "General condition of India in the eighteenth century was perhaps the unhappiest in the chequered history of the country." Particularly after the death of Aurangeb, the Mughal Empire disintegrated rapidly. There was anarchy and chaos in the country. The Marathas spread their power in the North and carried fire and sword in the countryside. The Pindaries carried on their raids and destruction. The prestige of the Mughal Empire was completely gone after the sack of Delhi by Nadir Shah in 1739. There was anarchy in the Punjab and the Sikh Misls were fighting for-supremacy with one another. There was no law and order in the Punjab, till Maharaja Ranjit Singh established his authority in the beginning of the nineteenth century. The invasions of Ahmed Shah

Abdali further added to the confusion in the country. Ahmad Shah Abdali defeated the Marathas in the third battle of Panipat in 1761. Ali Vardi Khan set up an independent state in Bengal but the same was brought under their control by the English East India Company in the second half of the eighteenth century. The Nizam, Hyder Ali and Sultan Tipu were fighting among themselves and also against the British. Towards the end of the eighteenth century, the English East India Company started establishing its authority in Bengal and the Deccan but still their position was shaky. There was no settled Government or a regular system of administration.

As a result of lawlessness and anarchy, the material prosperity of the people was destroyed. Trade and communications were interrupted. The fine arts declined. The condition of the common man was miserable. To quote, "In social usage, in politics, in the realm of religion and art, we had entered the zone of uncreative habit of decadent traditions and ceased to exercise our humanity". It was indeed a dark age in every way and nothing of great importance was produced at that time. All indigenous arts and crafts declined. There was no place for reason in religion which was hooded by meaningless ceremonies and rites. Superstitions and dogmas were all powerful. The people were pessimistic and found no hope in the future. They became fatalists. Their vision became narrow. Their lives were miserable.

There was no safety of life and property. There were mercenaries and soldiers of fortune who roamed about in the country and murdered and plundered at will. Agriculture, industry and trade were utterly ruined. There was no strong political power in the country to defend her against the foreign invaders. In a way, the old order was dead and there was nothing in sight to take its place.

BRITISH IMPACT

It was at this time that India came into contact with the West and that completely changed her. British imperialism helped the process of the unification of the country. The British brought the entire country under the control of a single administration. They unified the country by introducing a uniform system of laws and Government. The introduction of the modern methods of communication and transport produced a unifying effect. The new industries were all-India in their scope for the sources of their raw materials and their markets. Even their labour force was recruited on a wide inter-regional basis. The economic life and lot of the Indian people got interlinked and their economic life became a single whole. The two new classes born in India at that time were the capitalist class and the working class and they were all-India in character and stood above the traditional divisions of caste, region and religion.

The highly centralised character of British rule in India promoted the growth of Indian nationalism. Centralisation meant not only the subordination of the Governments of various provinces and the Indian states to the Central Government; it also involved uniform and sometimes even common laws, institutions and taxes for the whole country. The Government of India was "one and indivisible" and its actions often had the effect of encouraging the people of India to feel that they too were or should be one and indivisible.

The introduction of the English language was an event of great importance in the history of India. It went a long way in transforming the ideas and mentality of the people of India. English education broke the intellectual isolation of the Indian mind and brought it into close contact with literature, philosophy, economics, politics, history and science of the West. It broadened the outlook of the Indians who got new progressive, social and political ideas of the West in place of mythical geography, superstitions and rituals, legendary history, tyrannical monarchy and pseudo-science.

The English language made the Indians the inheritors of a great literature which was full of great ideas and ideals. Tagore writes, "We had come to know England through her glorious literature which had brought new inspiration into our young lives. The English authors whose books and poems we studied were full of love for humanity, justice and freedom. This great literary tradition had come down to us from the revolutionary period. We felt its power in Wordsworth's sonnets about human liberty. We glorified in it even in the immature production of Shelley written in the enthusiasm of his youth when he declared against the tyranny of priest craft and preached the overthrow of all despotisms through the power of suffering bravely endured. All this fired our youthful imaginations. We believed with all our simple faith that even if we rebelled against foreign rule, we should have the sympathy of the West. We felt that England was on our side in wishing to gain our freedom." Again, "It was chivalrous West which trained the enthusiasm of knight errants ready to take upon themselves the cause of the oppressed of those who suffered from the miserliness of their fate and we felt certain that the special mission of Western civilization was to bring emancipation of all kinds to all races of the world. Though the West came to our shores as cunning tradesmen, it brought with it also the voice and a literature which claimed justice for all humanity."

The view of K. M. Panikkar is that the introduction of English language helped the cause of unity in the country and without it, India would have been split into as many different units as there are languages in India. According to Dadabhai Naoroji, "The introduction of English education with its great, noble, elevating and civilising literature and advanced science, will for ever remain a monument of good work done in India and a claim to gratitude upon the Indian people." The view of Surendranath Banerjee is that English language was the means of uniting the varied races and religions, the peoples and complexities of our multiform civilisation in the golden chains of indissoluble union. It was our common means of communication North, South, East and West. According to Sir Henry Cotton, the English language served to unite the varying forces among the Indian people. No other bond of unity was possible. The view of C. Sankaran Nair is that the teaching of English in India helped the Indians to acquire English conceptions of duty, rights and brotherhood. To quote M. Shyama Shankar, "Let the manifold blessings that English education has conferred on India be written in letters of gold and preserved in the shrines of grateful Indian hearts for all ages to come. It is English education that has arrested the course of degeneracy in India. It is English language that has awakened her from her slumber under her fast gathering ignorance and inertia. She is knowing herself, knowing her glorious past and the grand destiny that awaits her in the future." Dr. A. R. Desai points out that the study of the English language unfolded the treasures of democratic and nationalist thought crystallized in precious scientific works. Their study clarified, made more vivid and even fanned into fire the nascent nationalism of the educated Indians. Knowledge of the English language also brought within the reach of an educated, Indian the most vital portion of the scientific, philosophical, sociological and literary achievements of the non-English speaking peoples. Through English translations, he could study Plato, Aristotle, Spinoza, Kant, Auguste Comte, Nietzsche, Hegel, Benedetto Croce, Spengler, Karl Marx, Machiavelli St. Simon, Bakunin, Proudhon, etc. and was bound to be influenced by them. This widened his outlook and enabled him to think and dream of India as a part of world community. Dr. S. R. Mehrotra writes that English education not only enabled the Indians to absorb European ideas but also provided them with new and powerful means of interregional solidarity. English replaced Sanskrit, Persian or Hindustani as the lingua franca of the educated classes in India.

Another factor which helped the Renaissance was the coming of the Christian missionaries in India from the beginning of the nineteenth century. They spread not only Christianity but also education in the country. They opened schools and colleges and set up printing presses in the country. They opened hospitals and started other works of public charity. As a result of their activities, there spread a lot of scepticism among the Indians some of whom were converted to Christianity. However, in the long run, the activities of the missionaries and their condemnation of Hindu religion resulted in a strong reaction among the Hindus and that led to the establishment of the Brahmo Samaj, Arya Samaj, Ramkrishna Mission, etc.

Another factor that helped the Renaissance was the press in India. The printing presses helped the publication of a large number of books which facilitated the task of education among the people. Newspapers and periodicals were also started, and they played their part in awakening the people.

The establishment of the All-India services like the Indian Civil Service, etc. and the provincial services like the Revenue and Judicial Services, bound together the various units of India in a manner never attempted before and created the steel-frame within which the administrative unification of India became a reality. The creation of the Indian Army by the British, though recruited and officered by them mainly in their own interest, also proved to be an integrating force. Recruited as it was from the various parts of the country and organised on a non-political basis, the Indian Army built up a glorious reputation on three Continents and provided free India with the basis of a national defence force.

The British in India constructed a large number of railways and roads which opened the interior and linked up various parts of the country. But for the railways, motor buses and other modern means of communication, political and cultural life on a national scale in India would not have been possible. They played an important part in organising the political movement of the Indian people on a national scale. To quote Dr. A. R. Desai, "Modern means of transport were a formidable force in unifying the Indian people socially. The locomotive, triumphantly traversing a big physical distance, also helped to annihilate the social distance dividing the people living in different parts." The roads built by the British in India included a number of trunk roads stretching diagonally across the country. Their measurement went into thousands of miles. They formed a framework linking most of the important centres of population, industries, trade and strategic points and subsidiary roads. This medium of transport became an important factor in the growth of a unified national economy. It created a national consciousness in the mercantile classes of India. Traders and craftsmen frequently journeyed from place to place and began to take interest in the emotional integration of India. Besides the upper classes, the mass of lower classes were also mobilised. Like the railways, the road transport made possible the mass migration of people from one place to another. To get new employment or to improve their prospects, the poor people often used road transport from North to South and East to West. That resulted in social and cultural cohesion.

The changes brought about by the British in the field of law also helped the cause of the Renaissance. K. M. Panikkar writes, "The establishment of the great principle of equality of all before law, in a country where under the Hindu doctrines a Brahman could not be punished on the evidence of Sudras and even punishments varied according to caste and where according to Muslim law an unbeliever's testimony could not be accepted against a Muslim, was itself a legal revolution of the first importance."

The view of B.C. Pal is that "The Penal Code and the Criminal Procedure Code have set up a standard of personal freedom that was unknown, truth to say, both to Hindu and Muslim criminal law and administration. The Criminal Procedure Code secures special privileges for European British-born subjects in India. But so far as the natives of the country are concerned, it has no room for any differential treatment as between one man and another. In the eyes of the British law, the Zamindar and the Ryot, the Brahmin and the Pariah, the prince and the peasant are equal. The stupendous mass upheaval which we see about us today could never have happened but for the levelling down process of the British law and administration which paid no regard to distinction of caste or rank or wealth among the people."

The result was that there developed among the people a critical outlook on the past and new aspirations for the future. Reason and judgement took the place of faith and belief. Superstition wielded to science. Immobility was replaced by progress. The old apathy and inertia on the part of the people was replaced by optimism and a determination to go ahead. They were ready to remove the abuses from society and open a new chapter in the history of the country.

INDOLOGISTS

It is true that English education had an adverse effect on some sections of the Indians, but by and large it led to a better appreciation by Indians of their past glory and attainments. The great Orientalists who established the Asiatic Society of Bengal in 1783, have earned from all Indians a lasting debt of gratitude for their pioneering work in the field of re-discovering India's great intellectual heritage. "Although the Orientalists were defeated on the question of educational policy, their high evaluation of India's classical heritage helped eventually to foster in English-educated Indians a pride in their own past which was of cardinal importance in the nineteenth century Renaissance of Hinduism and the rise of Hindu nationalism."

Sir William Jones (1746-1794) translated Kalidasa's Shakuntala (1789) tile Gita Govinda and the Manusmriti (1794). Charles Wilkins (c. 1750-1836) brought out a translation of the Gita in 1785 and of the Hitopadesha in 1787. H.H. Wilson (1786-1860) translated the Vishnu Purana and the Rigveda. H.T. Colebrooke (1765-1836) also made his contribution in the same field. After a study of the Upanishads, Schopenhauer declared that their study was the most beneficial and the most elevating study in the whole world and solace both of his life and his Death. Christian Lessen (1800-1876), E. Burnouf (1801-1852), August Schlegel, Bohtlingk (1815-1904), Rudolf Roth (1821-1895) and Max Mueller (1823-1900) were the founders of Sanskrit studies in Europe. The first printed editions of the four Vedas were brought out for the first time in the world by German scholars. In 1848, Theodor Benfey published the Samaveda. In 1849-74, Max Mueller printed the Rigveda. In 1852, Altharvaveds Weber (1825-1901) published the Vajasanevi Samhita. In 1856, Rudolf Roth published the Atharvaveds with the help of W.D. Whitney (1827-1894). In 1846, Rudolf Roth published "The Literature and the History of the Vedas".

In 1834, James Prinsep (1790-1840) discovered the clue to the Asokan inscriptions Alexander Cunningham and Fergusson (1808-1836) did pioneering work in the study of Indian architecture and archaeology. Grierson (1847-1941), Burgess, Fleet and Hultzsch were leaders in the foundation of new disciplines of Indian philology, ethnology and epigraphy, Monier-Williams (1819-1900), Muir, Griffith (1826-1906), E.B. Cowell (1826-1903), George Buhler (1837-1893), E. Senart (1847-1928), Dr. H. Jacobi (1850-1937), Lanman (1850-1941), Wackernagel (1853-1940), Garbe (1857-1927), Kielhorn, Hopkins (1857-1932), Sylvan Levi (1863-1926), Alfred Ludwig, A. Hillebrandt (1853-1927), Oldenberg (1854-1920), Karl Geldner (1854-1929), A.A. Macdonell (1854-1925), M. Bloomfield, Franz Bobb (1791-1867), Deussen (1845-1919) and Dr. A.B. Keith (1879-1945) were great Sanskrit scholars. G. Tumour, T.W. Rhysdavids, C.A.F. Rhysdavids, Oldenberg, Stcherbatsky (1866-1942), Poussin (1869-1938), Paul Dahlke and others made their contributions to the study of Buddhist history. M. Elphinstone (1779 1859) and V.A. Smith (1848-1920) were pioneers in the writing of the history of India. The works of the above-mentioned foreign scholars revealed the glory and greatness of India's past.

INDIAN WRITERS

The writings of Dinabandhu Mitra, Hem Chandra Banerjee, Navin Chandra Sen (1849-1909), Rabindranath Tagore, D.L. Roy, Bankim Chandra Chatterjee, Bharatendu Harishchandra, Vishnu Shastri Chiplunkar, Rammohan Roy, Rajendra Lal Mitra (1824-1891), Sir R.G. Bhandarkar, Hara Prasad Sastri, R.C. Dutt, Tilak, etc. affected the minds of the people of India. In 1860, Dinabandhu Mitra produced in his book entitled "Nila Darpan" (Mirror of Indigo) a scathing satire on the indigo planters of Bengali Hem Chandra Banerjee (1838-1903) "voiced in his national lyrics the sense of impotence of his people to assert their legitimate rights and self-respect against their British masters." B. C. Pal writes, "Hem Chandra, however, was our special favourite. The intense patriotic passion that breathed through his poems captured our youthful mind in a way that no other Bengali poems had done. The new generation of English-educated Bengalees had already commenced to advance themselves to positions of trust and responsibility in the new administration. In the learned professions of law and medicine also, they were gradually asserting themselves as against the British members. A new spirit of independence and self-assertion was increasingly manifesting itself in the conduct and conversations of the English-educated Bengalees. All these had already commenced to provoke a racial conflict in the country. Hem Chandra was in a special sense the poet of this new conflict and of the racial respect and sensitive patriotism born of it." Govinda Chandra Roy gave expression to his feelings of patriotism in some of his most touching songs.

Through his writings, Rabindranath Tagore (1861-1941) appealed to the higher sentiments of the people of India to work for the glory of their country. He tried to raise the moral tone of his countrymen. He interpreted in a unique way the true Spirit of Indian culture and civilisation. To quote Ramsay MacDonald, "Tagore's poetry is India. It is the product of his devotion to Indian culture. It is the soul of a people, not merely the emotion of a man; a systematic view of life, not merely a poetic mood; a culture, not merely a tune". (*Government of India*, p. 245.)

The greatest contribution of Bankim Chandra Chatterjee (1838-1894) was that he raised nationalism to the dignity of a religion. He was convinced that nothing could move the hearts of the Indians more than religion and therefore he pleaded patriotism as the highest religion. He identified the Motherland with Durga, Laxmi and Saraswati. As a matter of fact, he gave a new orientation to image worship by symbolising the goddesses as the Motherland. To quote Bankim Chandra, "It is Thy image we raise in every temple". In his Anand Math, Bankim Chandra gave a new image of the Goddess Kali. To quote him, "Kali is the symbol of degradation of India. She is black in colour because of the intense misery of the country. She is naked because India had been denuded of all her wealth. She wears the garland of human skulls because the whole country has become a vast burial ground. She has Siva under her feet to show that Indians are trampling down their own welfare." Bankim Chandra was the inspired sage.

The **Anand Math** of Bankim Chandra which embodies the patriotic song "Bande Mataram" (Hail to the Mother!) has rightly been called "the Bible of modern Bengalee patriotism." The view of B.C. Pal is that Bankim Chandra was a prophet of Indian cultural Renaissance. Aurobindo Ghose wrote thus: "As a poet and a stylist, Bankim did a work of supreme national importance not for the whole of India but for Bengal which was destined to lead India and be the vanguard of national development." Bankim was a "seer and a nation-builder" and "one of the makers of modern India."

The literary and cultural heritage of Bengal was also enriched by Madhusudan Dutt (1828-73), Manmohan Bose and Girish Chandra. Madhusudan Dutt wrote Sarmishta, Tilottma and Meghnad Vadh Kavya.

Vishnu Krishna Chiplunkar (1850-1882) was a great writer and he called himself "The Shivaji of the Marathi language." He wrote bitter criticisms of Mahadev Govinda Ranade, Gopal Hari Deshmukh and Swami Dayananda. He made his literary contributions through the Kavyetihasasam-graha and the Nibandhamala. He was regarded as the Brihaspati of the Marathi literature; He compared Western education to "the milk of the tigress" because it inspired sentiments of virility and liberty. However, he was opposed to wholesale imitation of the West as he had a deep love for the institutions, traditions and culture of Maharashtra. He stood for "education for the masses and took an active part in founding the Kesari and the Mahratta, the two Weeklies of Maharashtra. As a writer, journalist, educator and a founder of the two presses, Chiplunkar was a very important figure in Maharashtra and he tried to arouse the latent patriotic sentiments of the people of Maharashtra. He was a selfless patriot and his place in Maharashtra can be compared to that of Bankim Chandra in Bengal.

Sir R. G. Bhandarkar (1837-1927) obtained recognition throughout India as a great Indologist and a Sanskrit scholar. He attained world-wide fame. He was keenly interested in social reform.

RAMMOHAN ROY AND BRAHMO SAMAJ

A very important effect of the contact of Western culture in India was that it instilled into the minds of the Indians a spirit of rational enquiry into the basis of their religion and society. That spirit was typified by the personality of Raja Rammohan Roy (1772-1833). The Raja was a man of unusual intellectual ability. He was a profound scholar of Sanskrit and Persian and a great admirer of British culture. He was one of those who felt that India had everything to gain from contact with the West and he tried to imbibe the best that West could offer. He took a leading part in starting the English-medium schools in Bengal through which the youth could acquire the most modern Indian education. He introduced rationalistic principles in social and religious ideas. He was the founder of the Brahma Sabha which developed into the Brahmo Samaj. This organisation was the first deliberate attempt in modern India to reform Hinduism and restore it to its pristine glory. The main emphasis of the Raja was on social reform in order to purge Hindu society of the evils prevailing in it. He attacked the strongest part of the citadel of Hindu religion and society. He opposed the worship of images of gods and goddesses, denounced Sati, polygamy and abuses of the caste system. He favoured the remarriage of Hindu widows. He repudiated the prohibition of crossing the sea by his voyage to England. By these successive shocks, he tried to reform Hindu society.

He was the pioneer of political reform in modern India. It is contended that the liberal movements for religious and social reform were closely connected with the movement for political emancipation.

Debendranath Tagore (1817-1905) was an associate of Raja Rammohan Roy and after his death, he took up the leadership of the reform movement. He was a man of deep learning and spiritual poise. He wielded great intellectual authority in the Brahmo Samaj. He "proclaimed the supremacy of human reason which was in its original institutions really the Eternal Light of God reflected through the mind of man over all scriptures and hallowed injunctions."

Another leader of the Brahmo Samaj was Keshab Chandra Sen. He was deeply influenced by Christianity. He gathered around himself a group of younger men who were zealous not only in propagating the reform of Hinduism but also in social service such as famine relief. Gradually, a rift developed between the old conservative group and the Brahmo Samaj and the young reformers led by Keshab Chandra Sen. Ultimately, there was a split. The old party led by Debendranath Tagore came to be known as the Adi Brahmo Samaj. In 1868, Keshab Chandra Sen founded the Brahmo Samaj of India. In 1871, he died. In 1878, the Sadharan Brahmo Samaj was founded by some of his followers.

Although the Brahmo Samaj was the visible embodiment of the new spirit, it never became a powerful movement. It began to lose its importance in less than half a century after its foundation. However, it effectively helped the progress of Hindu society by stemming the tide of conversion to Christianity by holding a living example of society based on progressive and liberal views and by supplying eminent persons who advanced liberal ideas in other spheres of life such as politics.

PRARTHANA SAMAJ

In 1849 was started in Maharashtra a society called the Paramhans Samaj. Its influence was restricted and it broke up very soon. Another organisation was started by Dr. Atmaram Pandurang (1823-1898) in 1867 with the object of rational worship and social reform. The name of the society was the Prarthana Samaj. In 1870, R.G. Bhandarkar and M.G. Ranade joined the Prarthana Samaj and strengthened it. The two main planks of the Samaj were theistic worship and social reform. Its greatest service was the organisation of social reform movement. It laid emphasis on the abandonment of caste, introduction of widow-remarriage, encouragement of female education and the abolition of Purdah and child marriage. In the words of Miss Collet, the Prarthana Samaj "never detached itself so far from the Hindu element of Brahmanism as many of the Bengalee Samajes and both in religious observances and social customs, it clings far more closely to the old models." Another writer describes the Prarthana Samaj as composed of men paving allegiance to Hinduism and to he Hindu society with a protest.

ARYA SAMAJ

Unlike the Brahmo Samaj with its leanings towards Christianity, the Arya Samaj founded in 1875 by Swami Dayananda (1824-1883) who is considered by Sri Aurobindo as one of its great and formative spirits," was a true Hindu Protestant Reformation. The slogan of Davananda was: "Back to the Vedas." He stood for the pristine purity of Vedic Hinduism. He announced all post-Vedic Hindu scriptures such as the Puranas, the Brahmanas and even the Upnishadas. He attacked Vedantism. Trantricism and popular Pauranic Hinduism. He condemned caste distinctions and advocated full equality for women with men. He started a violent campaign against untouchability.

Swami Dayananda was a remarkable human dynamo endowed with extra-ordinary power and energy. His Arya Samaj succeeded in shaking the whole structure of Hinduism in the Punjab. The view of Sir S. Radhakrishnan is that Swami Dayananda played an important role in the spiritual uplift of the people and kindled the fire of patriotism among them. He was a great social reformer. He preached social equality between man and woman. All modern social legislation had been inspired by his teachings. His teachings were based on reason. He advised the people against blind faith and asked them to examine everything and formulate their own opinions about the merits and demerits of religious beliefs and social customs. He was perhaps the first Indian to preach the gospel of Swadeshi and "India for the Indians". He anticipated Mahatma Gandhi in his constructive work.

The view of de Reincourt is that "there is little doubt today that the great revolt in Bengal in 1905 was largely the indirect result of the Arya Samaj's religious nationalism and that Dayananda's organisation was the first real concrete nucleus of political nationalism. The Arya Samaj showed that Hinduism, long hibernating in a self-enclosed world of its own, was beginning rapidly to awake and face the realities of the nineteenth century. It also revealed that there was fire within the great body of Hinduism which, if struck by a competent hand, could be coaxed into a blaze of life and energy. The concept of the gentle and often servile Hindu began to disappear."

THEOSOPHICAL SOCIETY

The Theosophical Society was founded in the United States of America in 1875 by Madame H.P. Blavatsky (1831-91) and Colonel H.S. Olcott along-with others. In 1879, Blavatsky and Oltcott came to India and established the headquarters of their Society at Adyar near Madras. The Theosophical Society became prominent in the time of Mrs. Annie Besant who joined the Society in 1889 and came to India in 1893. She dedicated her whole life to the cause of the Society. She explained her mission in these worlds: "The Indian work is, first of all, the revival, strengthening and uplifting of ancient religions — Hinduism, Zoroastrianism and in Ceylon and Burma, Buddhism. This brought with it a new self-respect, a pride in the past, a belief in the future, and, as an inevitable result, a great wave of patriotic life, the beginning of the rebuilding of a nation." She started the Central Hindu School at Banaras which later on developed into the Banaras Hindu University.

The fundamental philosophical doctrines of the Theosophical Society, such as Karma and Nirvana, were common to both Buddhism and Brahmanism and hence the Indians were attracted towards it. The English educated Indians had a special reason to welcome Theosophy. Most of them had no faith in the many current religious and social doctrines, customs and traditions, but had not the courage to openly repudiate them for fear of social cstracism. They were "condemned to live in an agonising mental and moral conflict" They found in Theosophy a "veritable gospel of peace and salvation." By subtle philosophical theories of graded, elevation of man by stages, Theosophy defended the current practices of Hinduism. It reconciled the ideal of universal brotherhood with the caste system and the fundamental unity of the Supreme. Being with the worship of numerous gods and goddesses of Hinduism. By these means, Theosophy helped very materially to remove the "inferiority complex" from the minds of educated Indians. The great work of Theosophy was "in the moral reclamation of many of these educated Hindus who readily accepted the somewhat rigid disciplines of the new cult that demanded of its votaries complete abstinence from intoxicating drinks and absolute social purity for the attainment of that high level of psychic and spiritual power which it promised."

RAMAKRISHNA PARAMHANS

The life and teachings of Ramakrishna Paramhans and Swami Vivekananda—two spiritual giants—constitute a fascinating and inspiring chapter in the history of modern Indian thought. Ramkrishna (1836-1886) whose original name was Gadadhar Chattopadhaya, was born in the village of Kamarpukur in the Hoogly District of West Bengal. At an early age, he began showing unusual signs of religious ecstasy. At the age of 19, he came to Calcutta to live with his brother who had been appointed the priest of a newly erected temple at Dakshineshwar on the banks of the Ganges. Ramakrishna started his carrier of spiritual disciplines and attainments as a devotee of the great Goddess Kali.

During his stay at Dakshineshwar, Ramakrishna experienced profound spiritual developments. He had visions, trances and ecstasies. Most of his time was spent in spiritual rhapsodies. He had a carving to see God face to face and he was successful in his mission. He adopted the spiritual practices of Islam and Christianity and he had fruitful spiritual experiences. The cumulative effect of these experiences was that he came to the conclusion that all spiritual paths within and without Hinduism, if correctly followed, lead to the same goal. His fame began to spread far and wide and all kinds of people came to see him. The rich and the poor, the educated and the illiterate, the villager and the Calcutta city-dweller, all were drawn to his place. The secret of his attraction was that he was a spiritually realised saint.

Among those who came to see him were the great literary and cultural figures of contemporary Bengal — men like Michael Madhu Sudan Dutt, Ishwar Chandra Vidyasagar, Debendranath Tagore and Keshab Chandra Sen. All those who came to see him were given the same message. They were asked not to waste their time in partisan squabbles over the superiority of this or that creed, or this or that religion. They were advised to seek God with a pure and dedicated heart. Ramakrishna showed by his practical example that Hinduism was not an archaic and dying religion. Acting as a mighty spiritual beacon, he generated a powerful current of fresh life into Hindu society. He was not concerned with caste or creed, with empty ceremonies or shallow rituals. He was the apostle of divine realisation. He created a spiritual revolution.

SWAMI VIVEKANANDA (1863-1902)

The greatest disciple of Ramakrishna Paramhans was Swami Vivekananda who carried the message of his Master all over India, Europe and America. In 1893, he attended the Parliament of Religions held in Chicago. He created a sensation in the great assembly by his brilliance and nobility. He came back to India in 1897 and was given a hero's welcome.

On his return to India, he undertook a tour from Kanyakumari to Kashmir and delivered lectures wherever he went. In those lectures, he thundered against the evil practices in Hindu society and called upon the people to leave no stone unturned to make their future bright. He made them realise the greatness of India in the past and gave them fresh hopes for the future. He insisted on character-building, discipline and strength of mind. He brought about a new life among the people. He inspired them to work for the glory of their country.

It is clear from above that the nineteenth century witnessed a profound Renaissance in India which was brought about mainly as a result of the British impact. The great social reform leaders and movements all combined to bring about an intellectual, social, cultural and spiritual ferment which shook Hindu society to its depths and gave birth to the national movement in the country.

There was a spiritual movement in India led by Sri Aurobindo in the beginning of the twentieth century. It interpreted Indian Renaissance as the rebirth of the soul of India into a new body of enthusiasm and energy, a new form of its innate and ancient spirit. It put emphasis on the greater and nobler action of the spiritual motive in every sphere of Indian life. It aimed at magnanimous achievements and higher activity which ends in the discovery, expression and manifestation of the Divine Self in human being. The mental, emotional and aesthetic parts and inborn potentiality of human being were to be unfolded and developed fully for their greater satisfaction and finer nature of human beings. The movement found "in all-round spirituality the master-key not only to unlock the treasures of the past but also to remould the present on the basis of true appraisal both of the East and the West."

It is worthy of notice that "at first, the revived Hinduism was on its defence, rather cautions and timid in maintaining its position and inclined to compromise with the enemy. But soon it took the offensive, marched forward and even entered the hostile camp and asserted in ringing tones its right to live as one of the civilising influences of mankind."

As a result of these religious movements, there arose in this period a number of reformers, teachers, saints and scholars who purified Hinduism by denouncing some of its later accretions, separated its essentials from non-essentials, confirmed its ancient truths by their own experience and even carried its message to Europe and America. They were able to view their religion apart from the mythological, ritualistic and sociological forms in which it was embedded. They successfully interpreted Hinduism and its religious philosophy and main principles independent of Indian caste system, mythology, external rites and ceremonies. It was due to all this that today Hinduism is as fresh, vitalizing and vigorous as it was in any of the periods previously. The old fear that Hinduism might be overshadowed by Christianity or eclipsed by western civilisation and culture exists no longer. It has successfully outlived the Christian missionary propaganda of modern age as it survived the Muslim religious persecution of the Medieval period and the religious schism caused by Buddhism and Jainism in ancient times. It is now capable enough to meet any of the modern religions of the world on equal footing as their friend and ally in a common cause. "If the world in its present distracted state needs spiritual message and looks for a light to guide its footsteps in the darkness that has enveloped its path, renascent India is in a position to give it through the greatest of her prophets."

As a result of the efforts of the Brahmo Samaj and Raja Rammohan Roy the Arya Samaj and Dayanand, the Prarthna Samaj and Ranade, the Ramakrishna Mission and Vivekananda, Sri Aurobindo, Maharishi Raman and Mahatma Gandhi, many social reforms were carried out in Hindu society. The Sati system was abolished. Infanticide disappeared. Women were given education and freedom. Child marriage has been declared illegal. Widow re-marriage has been made legal. Monogamy has become the order of the day. Polygamy has become rare. Purdah system has disappeared. Inter-caste marriages are being performed. The ban on inter-dining has been lifted. Every effort is being made to remove untouchability from Hindu society. The Renaissance has enabled the Indians to pay more attention to life on earth and promote the general material and moral prosperity of the people.

VERNACULAR LITERATURE

A significant feature of the Renaissance was the rapid growth of Vernacular literature in India. Bengal took the lead in this matter. The names of the distinguished writers in Bengali are Rammohan Roy,

Akshay Kumar Dutta, Iswarchandra Vidyasagar, Devendranath Tagore, Madhusudan Dutta, Rajnarain Bose, Dwijendralal Roy and Bankim Chandra Chatterjee. These writers were a prelude to the rise of Rabindranath Tagore who contributed to all aspects of culture and literature viz., prose, poetry, drama, novel, essay, short story, music, painting, dancing, etc. Dr. Mohammad Iqbal wrote in Urdu and Persian. Munshi Prem Chand wrote in Hindi and Urdu. Sarat Chandra Chatterjee wrote in Bengali. Bharatendu Harish Chandra and Maithili Sharan Gupta wrote in Hindi. Likewise, a lot of writing was done in Gujarati, Marathi, Telugu, Tamil, Malayalam, Kanarese, Urdu and Punjabi.

The prose literature in Indian vernaculars began with the translation of English prose works. Indian writers wrote essays in the light of Western ideology. They imitated Western style and theme in their writings. They applied Western methods of study to oriental literature. Indian drama was considerably influenced by Western drama. The style, technique and theme of the Western playwriters like Ibson, Galsworthy and Bernard Shaw were imitated by Indian writers. The growth of One Act Play in Indian literature was the result of Western literary influence. The works of writers like Laxminarain Mishra, Govinda Pant, Ashka, Premi, Udai Shanker Bhatt, Kailashnath Bhatnagar, Seth Govind Das, etc. show the influence of Western drama. Indian story and novel were profoundly influenced by Western literature. Poetry was also influenced. English sonnet, ode and blank verse were imitated. Madhusudan Dutta in Bengali and Ayodhya Singh Upadhyaya in Hindi achieved marvellous success in blank verse. English lyrics were followed. English thought and style were imitated in poems on love and mysticism.

SPIRIT OF RESEARCH AND DISCOVERY

Another striking feature of the Indian Renaissance manifested itself in the scientific spirit of research and discovery. The Preservation of Ancient Monuments Act was passed in the time of Lord Curzon. Under the guidance of the Archaeological Department of the Government of India and other research institutions and organisations, a large number of excavations have been undertaken on the pre-historic sites like Mohenjodaro, Harappa, Nalanda, Kausambi, Hastinapur, Rupar, Kalibangan and Lothal. A lot of material of historical importance is now available as result of these excavations and the reading and decipherment of ancient inscriptions.

The discoveries of Shri Ramanujam in the field of pure Mathematics and of Sir Jadgish Chandra Bose in the field of Botany, are real and substantial contributions of new India to the knowledge of the world. Sir C.V. Raman and Dr. Meghnad Saha have made outstanding contributions in Physics. Shri P. C. Ray, J. C. Ghose and Dr. S. S. Bhatnagar made their contribution in the field of chemical science. S. Chandrasekhar has made his contribution in the field of astronomy. S.C. Roy and Birbal Sahni have made their contributions to scientific knowledge.

FINE ARTS

The spirit of the Renaissance had also its influence on fine arts in India. The first efforts at original production were to import Western models wholesale for presenting Indian motifs. The lead came from Travancore and Poona. This was resented by Bengal which made a bold bid for the conventions of the Buddhist school. This stimulated the study of old Indian art as practiced through different periods and in different areas. The discovery of the Gandhara art and the Gupta art created a sense of pride among the people. In this connection, Annie Besant says that India rediscovered herself and got once again what "is the admiration of the world for its sublime spirituality, its intense devotion and its depth of intellectual insight, a culture which had endured for unknown millennia and its civilisation so magnificent that the world has not yet seen its equal."

To begin with, Indian art was merely imitative and not genuinely creative. However, as a result of the work of E. B. Havell, Principal of the Calcutta School of Art and of Abanindranath Tagore, the painter, there came into existence a new school of art known as the Bengal School of Painting which derived its inspiration from Indian sources, from the paintings in the caves of Ajanta and from Rajput and Mughal paintings. As it derived its inspiration from traditional Indian sources, it produced art that was real and creative.

Abanindranath Tagore and his faithful disciples Surendra Gangoli, Nandlal Bose and Asit Kumar Haldar furthered the cause of reawakening in painting. The other artists of this period who earned international fame were Abdur Rehman Chaghatai and Amrit Sher Gill. Dr. A.K Coomarswami has done a lot to emphasize the majesty, splendour and glory of Indian art. He completely revolutionised the Western attitude towards Indian art. The Schools of Arts in Bombay, Calcutta, Lucknow and Indore have made their contribution towards the revival of painting. The names of Fergusson, Percy Brown and Sir John Marshal are also important in this connection.

Music and dancing have also been influenced by the Renaissance in India. The Sangit Samaj of Calcutta and Jnanottejak Mandir of Bombay have created awakening in the field of music. Pandit P.N. Bhatkhande inaugurated new education in music and infused a new spirit for music among people. Vishnu Digambar also tried to revive music. His disciples were spread all over Northern India and Bombay. Rabindranath Tagore also revived Indian music. Many 'other institutions have been set up at different places like Delhi, Lucknow, Gwalior, Calcutta, Madras, Poona, etc. for the promotion of music. By his brilliant exposition and masterly demonstration of Indian music, Dilip Kumar Roy won admirers in Western countries. By his charming and scientific dances, Uday Shanker revived keen interest in Indian dances. The other prominent exponents of Indian dances are Rukmani Devi, Ramgopal, Radha, Shriram and Damyanti Joshi.

The Renaissance in India revitalized all spheres of life and reawakened the people of India from their lethargy. The new spirit found its manifestation in the realms of religion, politics, literature, philosophy and industry. The reawakening in the field of politics caused widespread nationalism and the freedom struggle. Under the leadership of Dadabhai Naoroji, Pherozeshah Mehta. Surendranath Banerjea, Gokhale, Tilak, Lajpat Rai, Mahatma Gandhi, Sardar Patel, Jawaharlal M Nehru and Subhas Chandra Bose, India won her freedom after a long struggle. The reawakening in the social field entirely changed the social life of the country. The various social evils were removed. A new feeling of unity has dawned in the country. The study of Sanskrit has been revived. Vernacular languages in India have become rich. Fine arts have made progress. Progress has been made in the field of science. There is an atmosphere of progress all around.

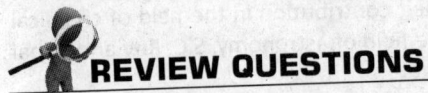

REVIEW QUESTIONS

1. What do you mean by renaissance in India? Discuss its various aspects.
2. Give a historical analysis of Indian renaissance.
3. Discuss the condition of India before renaissance.
4. Who is known as the 'Father of Indian Renaissance'? Examine his role.
5. Explain the role of various leaders in changing social scenario of India.
6. Describe the causes of Indian renaissance.
7. Write short notes on the following:
    (a) Brahm Samaj
    (b) Prarthana Samaj
    (c) Arya Samaj
    (d) Theosophical Society
8. Bring out the features of Indian renaissance.

SUGGESTED READINGS

Andrews, C.F.: *The Renaissance in India,* London, 1912.
Bose, Nemai Sadhan: *The Indian National Movement,* Calcutta, 1965.
Bose, N.S.: *The Indian Awakening and Bengal,* Calcutta, 1960.
Buch, M.A.: *Rise and Growth of Indian Nationalism,* Baroda, 1939.
Chatterjee, Nand Lal: *India's Freedom Struggle,* Allahabad, 1958.
Datta, B.N.: *Vivekananda, Patriot, Prophet,* Calcutta, 1954.
Datta, K.K.: *Dawn of Renascent India,* Nagpur, 1950.
Desai, A.R.: *Social Background of Indian Nationalism,* Bombay, 1948.
Gambhirananda, Swami: *History of the Ramakrishna Math and Mission,* Calcutta, 1957.
Ghose, Aurobindo: *The Renaissance in India,* Calcutta, 1946.
Ghose, N.N.: *England's Work in India,* Calcutta, 1909.
Griffiths, Sir Percival: *The British Impact on India,* London, 1952.
Heimsath, Charles H.: *Indian Nationalism and Hindu Social Reforms,* Bombay, 1964.
Iqbal Singh: *Life of Raja Rammohan Roy,* Bombay, 1958.
Karvc, D.G.: *Ranade, the Prophet of Liberated India,* Poona, 1942.
MacDonald, J.R.: *The Awakening of India,* London, 1911.
Majumdar, R.C.: *On Rammohan Roy,* Calcutta, 1972.
Mehrotra, S.R.: *Towards India's Freedom and Partition,* New Delhi, 1979.
Nag, Jamuna: *Raja Rammohan Roy,* 1972.
Nevinson, H.W.: *The New Spirit in India,* London, 1908.
O' Malley, L.S.S.: *Modern India and the West,* London, 1941.
Pal, B.C.: *Brahmo Samaj and the Battle of Swaraj in India,* Calcutta, 1926.
Pal, B.C.: *The New Spirit,* Calcutta, 1907.
Romain Rolland: *Life of Ramakrishna,* Calcutta, 1931.
Romain Rolland: *The Life of Vivekananda and the Universal Gospel,* Almora, 1947.
Sharma, S.R.: *Renaissance of Hinduism.*
Zacharias, H.C.E.: *Renascent India,* London, 1933.

40 Political, Cultural and Social Impact of British Rule

 LEARNING OBJECTIVES

- Know the true nature of the British rule in India
- Assess the impact of the British rule on Indian polity, society and culture

The nature of British rule in India and its impact did not remain the same throughout but continued to change with the social, economic and political developments in England. The rise of a powerful class of manufacturers as a result of the Industrial Revolution in England had an important impact on Indian administration and politics. Another result of the Industrial Revolution was that large amounts of capital were accumulated in England which came to be invested in India, in railways, tea plantations, coal mining, jute mills, shipping, trade and banking.

POLITICAL EFFECTS

The expansion of British dominions in India left behind a blazing trail of discontent and disaffection throughout India. This was not confined to the ruling chiefs and royal families of the states conquered by the British or annexed by them on various grounds and not even to the immediate entourage and dependants of those royal courts. British rule was not favourably looked upon even by the people at large in any region where it was newly introduced. The question of welcoming it did not arise. Discontent and disaffection were particularly strong in Burma, Assam, Coorg, Sindh, the Punjab and Avadh. The deposition of the ruler of Satara, the despotic coercion of Sindhia and other such acts created a feeling of hatred and hostility against the British. The Doctrine of Lapse, particularly applied by Lord Dalhousie, produced great discontentment in the states directly affected and created a sense of alarm among the other Indian states.

The policy of wholesale annexation did not unnerve the native rulers alone but affected the people as well. The fall of the royal houses of Peshwa, Bhonsle, Avadh, Jhansi, Punjab and Satara and the precarious existence of the rest on the mere sufferance of the British, not only gave a rude shock to the sentiments of the people, but cast adrift in the world a huge body of people, both high and low, who had hitherto earned their livelihood by service, both civil and military, in those defunct states Proud aristocracies were reduced to beggary and servitude. Artisans and crafts men who flourished upon the luxury of the court and the wealthy people were faced with utter ruin. Old ideas, traditions and pageants of pomp and glory which were dear to the common people, rapidly passed away. There was fear and bewilderment on all sides. There was a state of uneasy suspense about the future which was aggravated by the new system of administration introduced by the British in India.

There was an inherent dislike of the people of a foreign rule. The people found it difficult to adjust themselves to the new system of administration which was radically different from the system to which they were accustomed for centuries. It affected the vested interests of the classes and individuals who had profited under the old system. A large number of pious and learned men and religious and educational institutions flourished under the patronage of the Indian States mainly by the grant of rent-free lands. The new Government established by the British in India resumed the rent-free lands on a massive scale through the Inam Commission. That ruined a large number of individuals and institutions.

The changes and experiments in the land revenue system brought misery and ruin both upon the landlords and tenants. The cultivators suffered on account of excessive land rent. The landlords were dissatisfied as they were deprived of the authority which they were accustomed to exercise for the maintenance of law and order. They were reduced in practice to the position of mere farmers of revenue who would be ejected if they failed to pay the land revenue.

Even the introduction of the rule of law in place of personal rule dictated by whims and caprices of individuals, gave rise to discontent. It involved the principle of equality in the eye of law. It was resented by persons who claimed a privileged position or a preferential treatment which they had enjoyed for ages. The poor and the weaker sections of society did not derive much material benefit from them because they were not familiar with the complicated procedure laid down for the rule of law. As a matter of fact, it was not intelligible to the masses and involved long delay and heavy expenses which the poor could not afford. The people did not find much difference in practice between the rough and ready method of justice of the old days and the new judicial machinery.

The new system of police was highly inefficient and there was a general sense of insecurity of life and property. A Committee of Parliament reported in 1813 that the police committed "degradations on the peaceable inhabitants of the same nature as those practiced by the dacoits whom they were employed-to suppress." Lord William Bentinck wrote in 1832, "As for the police, so far from being a protection to the people, I cannot better illustrate the public feeling regarding it, than by the following fact, that nothing can exceed the popularity of a recent regulation by which, if a robbery has been committed, the police are prevented from making any inquiry into it except upon the requisition of the persons robbed, that is to say, the shepherd is a more ravenous beast of prey than the wolf."

The inefficiency and corruption of the police were vividly described in the following passage quoted in the Calcutta Gazette of 30 April 1827: "It is common in the country when any case of burglary-occurs in the house of any person, to prevent, if possible, its coming to the knowledge of the Magistrate, and the person robbed generally contrives to fill up the hole privately, in the course of the night and gives some bribe to the Chowkidars who may discover it: the reason of this is, that were he to give publicity to his loss, and make complaint before any public authority, he would seldom recover his property, but only have to pay the Amla something from the remainder. When a case of theft occurs, the Amla consider it an occasion of profit, and give full vent to their disposition for pillage and plunder."

The following is an extract from a letter published in the Calcutta Gazette of 10 June 1830, "To detect theft, and to prevent the violence of rogues and robbers, the Magistrates have appointed in the various zillas, Police Darogas, Buksees, Muhuris and Peons; but these men inflicted far greater distress on the poor inhabitants than either thieves or robbers can do, for when they come with great power and pomp, they seldom refrain from theft. Thieves use some caution in their villainy, but the Darogas and more particularly those belonging to the Police, plunder with violence."

There were certain aspects of British administration, which made it highly unpopular. The English officials were not accessible to the people who could not lay their grievances personally before them, as they were accustomed to under the native rule. The English system of administration operated like a machine. There was a lack of personal element in it which was disliked by the people.

The English laws introduced in India by British officials were strange and not intelligible to the people. The British substituted English in place of Persian as the court language. This was highly disliked by the Muslims. The exclusion of Indians from all high offices, both in civil administration and the army, was resented as it left no avenues of growth and even maintenance. The exclusion of Indians from high offices was resented particularly by the Muslims who had held those offices very recently. The view of Sir Syed Ahmed Khan was that the permanence and prosperity of the Government depended on an accurate knowledge of the manners, customs, usages, habits, hopes and aspirations and temper and ability of the people and a foreign Government could not possess such knowledge as long as the people were not allowed to participate in the administration of the country.

One illustration will suffice to show that Englishmen were not willing to allow any Indian to occupy any important position in the administration. Raja Ram Roy was the adopted son of Raja Rammohan Roy. After the death of his father in 1833, he was appointed an extra clerk in the offices of the Board of Control by Hobhouse, President of Board of Control, in the hope that his action would have "a beneficial effect on the natives of India generally" by showing them that there was "every disposition on the part of the supreme authority to furnish them with the means and motives of rendering themselves capable of assisting to a much greater extent than at present, in the administration of India." Hobhouse also proposed to nominate Raja Ram as a writer in the service of the English East India Company. It was merely a practical application of the principle laid down in Section 87 of the Charter Act of 1833 that no Indian "shall, by reason only of religion, place of birth, descent, colour, or any of them, be disabled from holding any place, office or employment under the East India Company." In spite of that, there was a lot of opposition from British bureaucracy and ultimately the proposal had to be dropped.

As a general rule, the British officials treated the Indians with undisguised contempt. Sir Syed Ahmed Khan who himself was an official of the East India Company, tells us about the British officials that "their pride and arrogance led them to consider the natives of India as undeserving the name of human beings." Such treatment was "more offensive to Muslims who for centuries past have received special honour and enjoyed special immunities in Hindustan."

Another cause of discontent was the denial of any political right to the Indians. The Indians who received English education were enthusiastic about British rule in the hope that with the progress of education, the political status of the Indians would be raised and they would get their rightful position in the administration of their country. When their hopes were not fulfilled, they felt disappointed and frustrated. They failed to get even a single seat in the Legislative Council or a single appointment in the Covenanted Service of the East India Company. They resented the rejection of all their demands for reform in the administration. When individuals failed to get redress of their grievances, political organisations were set up for that purpose. Even then, the British Government held out no hopes of conceding any political reform in a liberal spirit.

The administration of the East India Company was corrupt. It has been pointed out that "no civilised Government ever existed on the face of the earth which was more corrupt, more perfidious and more rapacious than the Government of East India Company from the year 1765 to 1784." Richard Becher, a servant of the East India Company, wrote in May 1769, "It must give pain to every Englishman to have reason to think that since the accession of the Company to the Dewani, the condition of the people of the country has been worse than it was before and yet I am afraid the fact is undoubted. This fine country which flourished under the most despotic and arbitrary Government is verging towards ruin."

The legal system established by the British in India was extremely expensive. The parties had to engage lawyers who demanded high fees. They had also to pay a high stamp fee in advance for filing a case. The procedure of the courts established by the East India Company was highly complicated. There was a lot of delay in the decision of cases. Many people were ruined by litigation. The English language in which the proceedings of the courts were conducted was not intelligible to the people.

About the administrative system of the East India Company, Dr. R. C. Majumdar writes that there was security against foreign aggression but not against theft, robbery and crimes and oppressions of other kinds. The law courts had not yet become efficient instruments of impartial justice. The police served as agencies of oppression rather than protection. The prison house was as wretched as it could be. The District Magistrate was determined that the prison should be a distinctly uncomfortable place. The medical officers made a determined effort to keep down the terrible death rate in jail. About the amenities of life in Bengal in 1854, Sir John Stretchy wrote, "There were almost no roads, no bridges or schools, and there was no protection to life or property. The police was worthless and robberies and violent crimes by gangs of armed men which were unheard of in other provinces, were common not far from Calcutta". (*British Paramountcy and Indian Renaissance*, p. 401.)

Dr. R. C. Majumdar sums up the position in these words, "All the while the Indians were mere passive onlookers — they had no place or power in the administration of their own country. The curse of slavery with all the attendant evils, so pithily described by Munro, was exercising a ruinous and degenerating influence upon the character of the people at large. The early dreams and enthusiastic hopes of the small band of English-educated Indians were giving place to disillusion and despair, while the common people, full of discontent and disaffection, bided their time in sullen resentment, marked by occasional outburst of violence. By the time the British completed the first hundred years of their rule, they gained the whole of India, but lost their hold upon the hearts of the Indians. The Government were fully aware of this and made full allowance for this important factor in devising plans for the safety of their Indian Empire". (*Ibid.*)

IMPACT IN CULTURAL AND SOCIAL FIELDS

British rule in India brought this country into contact with the West and thus Western ideas spread in this country. The intellectual life of the people of India began to undergo revolutionary changes through the ideas of democracy, sovereignty of the people, rationalism and humanism. These new ideas helped the people of India to examine critically their own society, economy and the true nature of British imperialism in India. Modern ideas were spread by the press, pamphlets, lectures and political parties. Modern education was introduced in India after 1813 and it continued to spread through the efforts of the Government, missionaries and private individuals. However, the spread of education was very limited. Primary education was practically neglected. Higher education was left to private institutions and the Government merely gave grants-in-aid which were insufficient. The main object of the education was to help the Government to recruit enough of Indians to fill in the lower branches of the administration. The Government was able to pay low salaries to Indians. However, modern technical education was completely neglected. Emphasis was put on English as the medium of instruction. The result was that education could not spread to the masses. That also created a linguistic and cultural gulf between the educated and the masses. The standard of education in the country was not high as adequate funds were not available for that purpose. Education was a monopoly of the middle and upper classes and those living in cities and towns.

The orthodox and socially reactionary sections of Indian society opposed the introduction of modern education and culture in the country. The middle- and upper-class Indians blindly imitated Western life and culture. They copied European manners and customs and became Europeans in every way except in blood. The British also made every effort to impose their culture on India in order to make Indians better customers for their goods. That enabled the economic penetration of the country and consolidation of British rule.

Indian society was very much influenced by British impact. This was particularly so in the cities. Modern industries, new means of transport, growing urbanisation and increasing employment of women in factories, offices, hospitals and schools promoted social change. The penetration of capitalism made social status dependent mainly on money and profit-making became the most desirable social activity.

The humanitarian instincts if some of the British officials were aroused by the glaring defects in Indian society. The Christian missionaries also played their part. The result was that in 1829, Lord William Bentinck. abolished the practice of burning widows along with their husbands known as Sati. The two laws of 1832 and 1850 removed disabilities due to a change of religion, particularly conferring the right of inheritance on Christian converts. The Act of 1850 was offensive both to Hindus and Muslims who regarded it as an incentive to conversion to Christianity. The Widow Remarriage Act, 1856 allowed the remarriage of widows. It was not likely to affect more than a few Hindu widows but a cry was raised that Hinduism was in danger. Sir Syed Ahmed Khan refers to the genuine apprehension of the Indians regarding mass conversion to Christianity. To quote him, "All persons, whether intelligent or ignorant, respectable or otherwise, believe that the Government was really and sincerely desirous of interfering with the religion and customs of the people, converting them all, whether Hindus or Mahommedans to Christianity and forcing there to adopt European manners and habits.

Up to 1813, missionaries were not allowed to come to India. However, the Charter Act of 1813 compelled the East India Company to permit the Christian missionaries to come to India under licence. The result was that a large number of missionaries came to India. They set up schools, colleges and hospitals which were used as nurseries of conversion to Christianity. The teaching of Christian doctrines was made compulsory in the girls' schools started by Christian missionaries. The main object was to use those institutions for preaching Christianity. The Bible was introduced not only in missionary institutions but also in Government schools and colleges. Some schools, mainly supported by the Government, were actually run by clergymen for the spread of Christianity. All the evils and abuses of Hinduism were painted in the blackest colours and the blessings of Christianity were described in glowing phrases and salvation was offered to those who became the followers of Jesus Christ. Public prison houses were used as instruments for conversions to Christianity. Filthy abuses were showered on Hindu gods and goddesses. Sir Syed Ahmed Khan tells us that civil and military officers helped the missionaries in their activities. The latter openly preached in mosques and temples and abused other religions because a Chaprasi or a policeman accompanied them. A series of letters were written and widely distributed by Mr. Edmond. Those letters were addressed generally to the public and particularly to those Indians who held respectable appointments in the service of the state. It was stated in those letters that as the railway system united the different extremes of India, it was necessary that there should be only one religion in India and that was possible if everyone embraced Christianity. Sir Syed Ahmed Khan writes, "These letters so terrified the natives that they were as people struck blind, or from under whose feet the ground had suddenly slipped away. All felt convinced that the hour so long anticipated had at last arrived, and that the servants of the Government first and then the whole population would have to embrace Christianity."

When railways and telegraphs were first introduced in India, the people considered them as ingenious devices for breaking the social order and caste-rules, and thus prepare the way for mass conversion to Christianity. In the case of railway where people of all classes and castes had to sit together and it was not possible to observe proper rules about bath and food, the intention of the Christian Government to convert the Hindus to Christianity was clear.

Sir Syed Ahmed Khan tells us that during the general famine of 1837, orphans were converted to Christianity and that confirmed the fears of the Indians.

Industrial development in India resulted in the growth of two new social classes viz., the industrial capitalist class and modern working class. These two classes were entirely new because modern mines, industries and means of transport were new. These classes represented a new system of economic organisation, new social relations, new ideas and a new outlook. They possessed an all-India outlook.

To begin with, the British encouraged the social and religious reformers but later on withdrew their support from them and gradually sided with the socially orthodox and conservative element of society. To meet the growing challenge of nationalism in the country, Englishmen followed the policy of divide and rule and actively encouraged communalism and casteism which strengthened the reactionary forces in society.

There were powerful forces for social change among the lower castes and women. Led by men such as Jotiba Phule, the lower castes built up powerful movements from the end of the 19th century. The lower castes in Kerala and other parts of South India organised themselves during the 1920's and 1930's to fight against the socio-economic oppression by the upper castes. Women and tribal people rose in defence of their rights. Common participation in demonstrations, public meetings, popular movements, trade unions and Kisan Sabhas weakened the notions of caste and male superiority.

It was a result of British impact on India that a large number of social and religious movements such as the Brahmo Samaj, the Prarthana Samaj, the Arya Samaj, the Theosophical Society and the Rama Krishna Mission were started. They did a lot of work to change Indian society and its outlook.

The basic colonial character of British rule and its harmful impact on the lives of the Indian people led to the rise and development of a powerful nationalist movement in the country. It embraced within its fold all the different classes and groups of Indian society. They sank their mutual differences and worked for the freedom of the country.

REVIEW QUESTIONS

1. Write an essay on the nature of the British rule in India.
2. Analyse the impact of the British rule on the political, cultural and social conditions of India.
3. Assess the impact of Industrial revolution on Indian administration and politics.
4. The expansion of the British dominions in India left behind a blazing trail of discontent and disaffection throughout India. Comment.
5. Assess the impact of the British rule on the polity and society of India.

SUGGESTED READINGS

Bearce, S.D.: *British Attitude Towards India (1748-1848)*, Oxford, 1961.
Bose, N.S.: *The Indian Awakening and Bengal*, 1960.
Chatterjee, Nandlal: *India's Freedom Struggle*, Allahabad, 1958.
Desai, A.R.: *Social Background of Indian Nationalism*, Bombay, 1948.
Ghose, Sankar: *The Renaissance to Militant Nationalism in India*, Allied Publishers, Calcutta, 1969.
Griffiths, Sir Percival: *The British Impact on India*, London, 1952.
Hutchins, Francis G.: *The Illusion of Permanence: British Imperialism in India*, Princeton, 1967.
Majumdar, R.C.: *History of Freedom Movement in India*.
Majumdar, R.C.: *British Paramountcy and Indian Renaissance*, Bombay, 1970.
Srinivasachari, C.S.: *Social and Religious Movements in the Nineteenth Century*, 1947.
Vyas, K.C.: *The Social Renaissance in India*, Bombay, 1957.

41 Changes in Land Revenue Settlement

LEARNING OBJECTIVES

- Discuss the land revenue systems of British India
- Highlight the salient features of the Permanent Settlement of Bengal

PERMANENT SETTLEMENT OF BENGAL

The period between 1765 and 1793 was characterised by many experiments in land revenue administration. The English East India Company adopted the method of trial and error and in this process attempted many experiments. In 1772, Warren Hastings instituted a Five-Year settlement of land revenue by farming out estates to the highest bidders. He acted on the presumption that the Zamindars were merely tax gatherers and had no proprietary right in the settlement and no preference was given to them. In some cases, they were actually discouraged. In 1773, changes were made in the machinery of revenue collection. The Collectors, who had found to be corrupt or indulging in private trade, were replaced by Indian Diwans. The trend of Warren Hastings' thinking was towards centralisation. The Five-year settlement was a miserable failure and hence in 1777, Warren Hastings reverted to the system of annual settlement, though the basis of open auction to the highest bidder was retained. Preference was given to Zamindars if their bids were high enough. On the whole, Warren Hastings failed to devise a satisfactory system of revenue settlement. He is said to have left behind "a dark trail of misery, insurrection and famine". Lord Cornwallis observed in 1789 that "one-third of the Company's territory in Hindustan is now jungle, inhabited only by wild beasts".

When Lord Cornwallis came to India, he was directed to cleanse the Augean stables and to make a settlement which combined the consideration of the Company's interest with the happiness of the natives and the security of the landholders. He ordered an inquiry into the question of usages, tenures and rents. The inquiry was headed by John Shore who submitted his report in June 1789. The view of John Shore was that the Zamindars were the proprietors of the soil and they succeeded to it by right of inheritance. The sovereign authority could not justly exercise the power of depriving them of the succession, nor of altering it, when there were any legal heirs. The privilege of deposing of the land, by sale or mortgage, was derived from their fundamental right and was exercised by the Zamindars before the English East India Company got the Diwani. Lord Cornwallis stamped it with the seal of his approval.

Originally, the revenue settlement was made for ten years in 1789 but the same was made permanent by the following Proclamation of Lord Cornwallis on 22 March 1793: "The Governor-

General-in-Council accordingly declares to the Zamindars, independent Talookdars and other actual proprietors of land, with or in behalf of whom a settlement has been concluded under the Regulations above-mentioned, that at the expiration of the terms of the settlement, no alteration will be made in the assessment which they have engaged to pay, but that they and their heirs and lawful successors will be allowed to **hold their estates forever**".

There were four classes of Zamindars in Bengal with whom the revenue was settled permanently in 1793. (1) There were the original independent chiefs such as the Rajas of Cooch-Bihar, Assam and Tripura who retained possession of their territories on payment of revenue as tribute to the Mughal rulers, (2) There were the old established land-holding families such as the Rajas of Rajshahi, Burdwan and Dinajpur who paid a fixed land tax to the ruling powers. (3) There were the Collectors of revenue who had been inducted by the Mughal Government and whose office had tended, after several generations, to become hereditary. (4) There were the farmers who had been incharge of the collection of revenue after the grant of Diwani to the English East India Company who had come to be known by the general term Zamindar.

There were three parties concerned in sharing the produce of land and those where the Government, the Zamindars and the Cultivators or Ryots. The Permanent Settlement defined the position of the first two and fixed permanently the share of the Government in the produce of the land. It conferred the greatest benefit on the Government as the land revenue demand was fixed at the highest pitch and the share of the Government was fixed at 89% of the estimated rent of the land which left only 11% to the landlord for his duties connected with the collection of revenue. The Government was assured a certain and steady revenue. While the revenue demand on lands already under cultivation was fixed, the Government could still look forward to an increase in its income with the extension of cultivation. There was an additional financial advantage for the Government from the abolition of the entire revenue-collecting machinery consisting of Tehsildars, Qanungos, Patwaris and other revenue officers. There was also a political advantage for the Government. Under the Mughal rule, the Zamindars exercised magisterial and executive authority and for all practical purposes and to all outward appearance, they enjoyed the appurtenances of sovereignty in their respective areas. Cornwallis took political powers from them and gave them unlimited powers of ownership of land which did not belong to them in the past. While the political authority and power of creating trouble by the Zamindars disappeared, their economic powers over the peasantry were enormously increased. However, the interests of the Ryots were neglected by the Settlement. The Court of Directors admitted that "the right of the Bengal Ryots had passed sub-silentio and they had become to all purposes tenants-at-will". There was no definition of the claims to be made by the Zamindars on their tenants. Except in a few special cases, the Zamindars exacted from the Ryots as much as they could be made to pay. There is no doubt that what was left to the actual cultivator, after all exactions, was little more than sufficient to keep the souls and bodies of the peasants together. It is rightly said that the Ryot had no rights and the was left to fight it out himself with the Zamindars.

The high rate of land revenue pressed so hard upon the Zamindars that about half of the landed property in Bengal was reported to have been put on sale and changed hands in a period of 22 years from 1793 to 1815. Prior to 1793, more than 50% of the land revenue of the Company was paid by twelve great Zamindars, the largest held by the Burdwan Raj that accounted for 17%. Those Zamindars were not men of entrepreneurial inclination eager to manage their massive estates optimally for increasing agricultural productivity. They were leaders whose social and ceremonial obligation as required by the customs and traditions of their community, precluded the development of those calculating and maximising propensities essential for economic development. The Zamindars delegated economic functions to his officers, managers and under-tenants. He was dependent on his Amla who took advantage of his ignorance and tried to enrich themselves at the expense of their master. The proprietary rights acquired by the Zamindars carried with them the duty to pay the agreed taxes of the Company and if that was not done in time the Company had the power of summary seizure and sale of assets for the payment of arrears. The Amla with their eye on the main chance, contrived to entangle the financial affairs of the Zamindar and hoped that if the property was sold on account of failure to pay the tax in time, they might add to their holdings and enhance their status. Historians have noted the intriguing fact that the purchasers of the properties of the old Zamindars very largely resided in the districts where the large estates were located. That was due to the fact that the Amlas took advantage of the distress of their masters. Land was also purchased by loyal retainers, under-tenants, families of the old Zamindars and outsiders with liquid interests.

In 1796, lands carrying a rental of ₹28,70,061 on the roll and representing one-tenth of the three provinces were sold in one year. According to Baden-Powell, in the two years between 1796-97 and 1797-98, the sale of estates yielding 14 lakhs and 22.7 lakhs respectively were affected and "by the end of the century the greater portion of the estates of the Nadiya, Rajshahi, Bishnpur and Dinajpur Rajas had been alienated. The Burdwan estate was seriously crippled and Birbhum Zamindars completely ruined. A host of smaller Zamindars shared the same fate. In fact, it is scarcely too much to say that, within ten years that immediately followed the Permanent Settlement, a complete revolution took place in the constitution and ownership of the estates which formed the subject of that settlement".

However, the distress of the Zamindar was removed by the Regulations of 1799 which invested the Zamindar with arbitrary powers to eject the cultivator, attach his agricultural stock and implements for non-payment of arrears and start other proceedings against him with a view to pressing him to his utmost capacity. The law of 1799 opened the floodgates of exploitation of the helpless peasants who were absolutely at the mercy of the Zamindar.

The Permanent Settlement led to the sub-infeudation of Zamindari rights. In the 39 Districts of Bengal and Bihar, the number of estates multiplied in twenty years to the high figure of 1,10,456. In twenty years, the number of estates had doubled in the Patna Division and trebled in the Tirhut Division.

Not only the units of cultivation, even the rent-collecting rights were sub-divided. The new Zamindari rights proved valuable property and within twenty years of the Permanent Settlement, the Zamindar's interests which amounted to 11% in 1793, were being sold for nearly 28 years' purchase. The rent-receiving rights came to have a value which they did not possess before and became a commodity to be freely bought and sold in the market. The Zamindar farmed out his revenue to a middleman (Patnidar) who, in turn, contracted with a sub-farmer (Dar Patnidar) and the latter also entered into dealings with a number of under-links (Seh Patnidars) and so on. A chain of rent-receiving interests was created and the evil became so great that when the Zamindari was abolished in India, after her Independence in 1947, there were in one case as many as 150 intermediary interests 'between the original landlord and the actual cultivator'. Each sub-agent tried to squeeze the next man in the chain to the utmost and the burden of all exactions ultimately fell on the cultivator. The intermediaries were not all rich. The interest of each was small and their economic position was only slightly better than that of the cultivator. The result was that sub-infeudation levelled the Zamindar, the intermediary and the cultivator.

There was a clash of interests between the rich landlords who looked upon the land as their private property to be used for maximum monetary return and the dispossessed cultivators who were left with, nothing but their labour to sell to earn their livelihood. In most cases, the new landlords were businessmen who purchased land in search for profitable investment of surplus funds. They were not familiar with the affairs of cultivation and were not interested in the work of agricultural improvement which was left to the cultivator, who had neither the means, nor the knowledge, nor the will to carry it out. The landlords were merely rent-receiving absentee businessmen who cared more for their rents than for the improvement of agriculture. Instead of being natural leaders of rural population, the landlords of that period played the role of agents to the foreign political power. Against a guarantee of regular payment of a fixed amount of land revenue to the Government, they purchased the right of exacting whatever they could from the politically defenceless and economically weak peasantry.

One of the consequences of the Regulations of 1799 was that the condition of the cultivator became miserable. The new landlords were different from the old Zamindars. They had no roots in the village. They were a class of rentiers who were only interested in the realisation of the profits on their investments. They were unjust to their Ryots. At one stroke, they wiped out the traditional rights of occupancy of the cultivators, reduced them to the position of tenants-at-will and subjected them to rack-renting and ejectment. They appropriated the whole surplus of land leaving just enough for the subsistence of the tenant.

As Zamindaris were sold to those who possessed ready cash, new families of moneylenders, merchants and others appeared on the rural scene. Unlike the families of Laws and Tagores, new Zamindars had no roots in the soil and behaved in an irresponsible manner. They were not interested in agriculture as such. Their primary interest was to get the maximum from their tenants. Unmitigated hardships were inflicted on the tenants who had cultivated land for generations and were now left at the mercy of their new Zamindars. The cultivators were the greatest sufferers. They were constantly exposed to the ever-increasing demands of rent, etc. There was much wealth in the country but the same was not equitably distributed. The result was that the new Zamindars became richer and the cultivators became poorer. That accounts for the glaring disparity in the economic condition of the people in whose areas the Permanent Settlement was introduced. As the future interests of the state were unwittingly sacrificed, the Government had no share in the increased agricultural prosperity of the country. That also explains why the Government of Bengal was perennially afflicted with recurring deficits although Bengal itself was the richest province of India. The development of that province with regard to public works was severely handicapped.

Certain laws were passed to remedy the defects in the Permanent Settlement of Bengal. The Bengal Tenancy Act was passed in 1822 whereby tenants were given protection against ejectment or enhancement of their rent. The Bengal Rent Act, 1859 ensured for the farmers a fixity of rent and security of tenure. Under that Act, a Ryot who had held land for twenty years at the same rent was treated as if he had held it since 1793 and was given rights and privileges accordingly. Occupancy rights were given to the tenants who held land for twelve years and their rent could be raised after an inquiry by a court of law.

RYOTWARI SYSTEM

When the wars in South India brought new territories under British control where Zamindari tenure was not in general use, the advisability of settling lands on the model of Bengal was seriously questioned. Moreover, the expectations from the Zamindari system had not been justified. It had been argued at the time of the Permanent Settlement of Bengal that the landlords with whom the settlement was made permanently, would prove a bulwark of order and stability and would entertain a warm and zealous attachment to the Government founded on the solid basis of their own interest. However, what actually happened was different. Immediately after the Permanent Settlements in Bengal and Northern Sarkars, a struggle started between the local Governments and the Zamindars which was not always confined to chicanery and falsehood on one side, nor to the utmost exercise of civil rigours on the other. The bailiffs of the Collectors supported by their armed force and sometimes the regular troops and the Zamindars with their own courts, police and means of private defence, faced each other. Instead of cooperating with the Government in the task of administration, the Zamindars embarrassed the Government. They resented enquiry into their relations with the cultivators. They foiled attempts to determine their rights. They prevented the Ryot from seeking justice outside their courts. They promoted bribery and corruption and connived at crime. There were robbers and dacoits in the Zamindari areas. There were frequent rebellions of Zamindars in the Northern Sarkars. So long as the Zamindars paid the fixed rents, the Government did not interfere. The Government machinery did not come into direct touch with the people and that weakened the position of the Government to control the country. It was also felt that the Permanent Settlement deprived the state of a share in the increase of rent which resulted from the general improvement of the economic condition and the Zamindar got the entire unearned increment. It was also realised that the Permanent Settlement favoured a handful of Zamindars and completely ignored the interests of the peasants who were really in a very bad shape.

Captain Read and Sir Thomas Munro led the attack on the Permanent Settlement and gradually convinced the Home authorities of the unwisdom of extending it to other parts of India. The result was that the Select Committee of the House of Commons which reviewed the affairs of the English East India Company before the renewal of the Charter of the Company in 1813, decided in favour of the Ryotwari system.

The argument of Munro was that when the settlement of a great province was in view, the prosperity of the body of the people should be the grand object to which everything else should be made to yield. That could be best achieved under a Ryotwari settlement. The Ryotwari settlement was supposed to perpetuate the agrarian relations which had existed for centuries in the past. It proposed to confirm the proprietary rights of the cultivator in the land cultivated by him, subject to the payment of the government demand and thus to combine in him the characters of the labourer, the farmer and the landlord. The system was advantageous both to the Government and the cultivator. To the Government it ensured the benefit of all future increases of revenue resulting from the extension of cultivation and the rise of prices of agricultural produce. It helped to win over the mass of the cultivating population to the support of British rule and free it from dependence upon the support of a few big Zamindars. The strength of British rule would lie more in the contentment of the masses than in the loyalty of a few big Zamindars who exploited the cultivators. The Ryotwari system was better than the Zamindari system even for the future progress of cultivation. Once the peasant was confirmed in his hereditary rights in land, he would apply his energy and resources to the improvement and extension of cultivation. The magic of property would help to raise the standard of farming. Ryotwari system was the only land system that was possible under the circumstances outside Bengal. It was the system which had always prevailed in India.

The Ryotwari system would establish the closest relations between the people and the Government as the rent was to be realised by the Government officials directly from each holding. It was necessary that each field should be measured and surveyed and its boundaries determined and boundary-marks set up. It involved the preparation of field maps, village maps and Taluq maps and a whole Department of the Surveyor-General to carry out those duties.

The two broad features of the Ryotwari system were the direct settlement between the Government and the Ryot (cultivator) and assessment for a temporary period. No intermediary, whether a Zamindar or Taluqdar, was recognised. The Ryot had no right of ownership. He was given the right of occupancy which was both hereditary and transferable.

What distinguished the Ryotwari from the Zamindari system was that it substituted for the multiplicity of landholders one Zamindar which was the Government. It brought the cultivators into direct relations with the Government which was the sole landlord. There was no intermediary agency between the workers on the soil and the rulers of the country.

The land settlements of Munro operated for nearly thirty years and caused widespread oppression and agricultural distress. The cultivator became poorer. He fell in the clutches of the Chetty or the moneylender for the payment of land revenue. The machinery of collection was very oppressive and torture was normally resorted for the collection of state dues. The result was that in 1855 an extensive survey and settlement plan was decided upon the basis of 30% of the gross produce. The actual work began in 1861. The Rule of 1864 limited the state demand to 50% of the rental. However, those instructions remained more on paper and not in practice.

After the incorporation of the Peshwa's territory in the Bombay Presidency in 1818, Mountstuart Elphinstone, its Governor, introduced a revenue system which had a general resemblance to the Ryotwari system of the Madras Presidency. Elphinstone emphasized two important features of Maratha Government viz., the existence of village communities as units of local administration and existence of Mirasi tenure. Mirasdars were hereditary peasant proprietors who cultivated their own fields and paid land revenue to the state at fixed rates. Chaplain, Commissioner of the Deccan, submitted two reports in 1821 and 1822 in which he made valuable suggestions. A regular survey of the land was conducted by Pringle during 1824-8. The state demand was fixed at 55% of the net produce. Unfortunately, most of the surveys were faulty. In 1835, Wingate was appointed the Superintendent of Survey. He submitted his report in 1847. Broadly speaking, the state demand for a district was first determined on the basis of the past history of the district and past condition of the people which means their paying capacity. Then the total district demand was distributed among the fields. The earlier system of equitable basis of field produce was substituted by a geological basis of assessment. The assessment was placed upon each field instead of the holdings of a cultivator so that a cultivator could give up any field he liked or take up other fields which may have remained unoccupied. The settlement was made for 30 years. Resettlement work began after 30 years in 1866.

The introduction of the Ryotwari system in Madras and Bombay Presidencies made the peasant, instead of the Zamindar, the proprietor of the land. The recognition of private property in land gave him the rights of lease, mortgage and sale. Unfortunately, these rights failed to improve the condition of the peasant. The reason was that the Government loaded him with heavy demands. The Government realised the folly of exorbitant assessments and undertook a process of downward revision so that eventually the peasant came to enjoy a surplus of rent over the revenue paid to the Government. The result was an increase in the value of land. Property began to yield profit and attract investors. The moneyed class in Madras and Bombay bought the lands and crops under control by loan. The reason was that the cultivator had to pay the Government demand even when his crop failed. His ignorance and improvidence were also exploited by the moneylender who kept him in perpetual debt by offering him facilities of credit. Interest rates were very high and the cultivator was able to pay only the interest on loan and not the principal. Accounts were manipulated by moneylender and documents were forged so that interest continued to mount in spite of payments by the debtor. The courts of the country accepted the documents and account books of the moneylender as valid proof of the debt and awarded decrees in favour of the moneylender. The rent laws introduced by the British were responsible for the disruption of the old agrarian structure and the creation of a new social order. The new rent-receiving landlords, moneylenders and businessmen came to form the nucleus of the new middle class that emerged in the country in the 19th century. The dispossessed cultivators, the village artisans and menials came to constitute the landless wage-earning class, the proletariat.

MAHALWARI SYSTEM

In 1801, seven districts were acquired by the British from the Nawab of Oudh which came to be known as Ceded Districts. Five more districts which were surrendered by the Marathas after their defeat in 1805 were also added. The administration of all those districts was separated from Bengal and the new province was later on called the North-Western Province. The system adopted in the beginning was to make the District Officer the Collector of Revenues, civil judge and magistrate. Later on, the office of the judge was separated. Gradually, the Regulations of Bengal were introduced. In the matter of revenues, the Governor-General-in-Council desired to adopt the permanent settlement on the Bengal model and the Commissioners were required to make a settlement with the Zamindars for three years which was to be repeated for another three years and then four years. After ten years, the settlement was to be declared permanent.

The declaration of policy to introduce permanent settlement in 1802 was made without adequate knowledge of the conditions regarding land tenure and the capacity of land. The Regulations of 1793 which were applied to the new territories were divorced from reality. The big Zamindars and the headman of the village were brought to the same level in the matter of acknowledging proprietary rights in land. There was a tendency to treat harshly the bigger landholders and leniently the smaller ones. The Bengal Government was keen to hasten the permanent settlement which in normal course would be due in 1812-13 for the Ceded and 1815-16 for the conquered provinces. The Bengal Government asked for the confirmation of the Court of Directors. A Commission was appointed for the full control of the revenue administration in the province. On the basis of the reports of the Collectors, the Commissioners recommended the postponement of Permanent Settlement. There was fresh thinking among the Court of Directors and ultimately the idea of Permanent Settlement was given up in 1817. It appears that the Directors had become conscious of the possible loss of revenue and were not prepared to forego all future increase in it. They decided on the compromise of periodical settlements. The experiments made in Madras in respect of settling directly with the actual cultivators also influenced the thinking of the authorities who were impressed by the advantages of the system. Therefore, there was need for reorientation of the revenue policy. Discussions, finally leading to the Memorandum of Holt Mackenzie, culminated in the adoption of a type of settlement in 1822 which combined the features of Zamindari and Ryotwari systems.

The essence of the Mackenzie's proposals was the gradual elimination of the "intermediate proprietors" created by the British laws and the protection of the rights of the actual cultivators, namely village Zamindars and resident Ryots. These inclined to the establishment of direct relations between the state and the cultivator, with the limitation that it should not undermine the structure of the village community which he desired to sustain. Mackenzie would not recognise the rights of proprietors in land of the Taluqdars, but held that they possessed only the right to collect revenues which the Government may continue or withdraw. He suggested a thorough inquiry before undertaking the settlement. His suggestions were incorporated into the Regulation of 1822 which formed the basis of the new settlement and had the effect of introducing a major revolution in the socio-economic relationships of the community.

The new Rules invested the Government with the right to absorb the "entire rent of the land, viz., the surplus of agricultural produce left after payment of the wages of labour and the profits of stock". However, the Government decided to take only 80% of the rental, leaving 20% as remuneration to the agency appointed for the collection of revenue. The rental value was to be assessed Mahal wise which was to be the revenue unit and comprised the whole village or part of it. For such an assessment, it was necessary to determine the total extent of land in the Mahal, the proportion of cultivated, cultivable and waste land, quality of soil, its productive power, nature of crops grown, cost of cultivation and the average prices. The Government was inclined "to supersede the rights of all Taluqdars, Rajas, Pergunna Zamindars". Wherever they were allowed to continue, a detailed settlement was to be made "with each of the proprietors or occupants possessing a heritable and transferable property in the soil or a hereditary right of occupancy subject to the payment of a fixed rent. The rights of the parties were to be carefully ascertained and recorded", and Pattas granted to prevent extortion by Taluqdars. At the same time, the rights of the resident Ryots were also to be protected, as they were entitled to "perpetual occupancy, subject to the payment of the fixed rent". In their care, the Regulation provided for specifying the amount or rate of rent which they were liable to pay during the tendency of a settlement and limiting the right of the Zamindar to enhance it by means of the requirement of the grant of Patta. These rights of the Ryots were justifiable by the Collector who could restore or confirm the rights when interfered with by the Zamindar.

The detailed enquiries involved in the process of settlement were both Pine-consuming and expensive. The Collectors were not able to bestow their whole attention to it. The result was that there was very little progress in the next ten years. That prompted Lord William Bentinck to suggest radical changes in the procedure to save time, energy and money. Bentinck called a conference at Allahabad in January 1833 and on the basis of its deliberations passed Regulation IX of 1833 which removed some defects of the existing system and facilitated early settlement of the province under the guidance of Robert Mertins Bird.

Bird's method was not very much different from that of Mackenzie. Bird determined the fiscal unit known as Mahal and fixed the land tax on it. The gross amount was to be distributed among the individual holders who were made responsible for its payment, through the Headman or Lambardar in the Pattidari village or the Zamindar where he held the land individually. Revenue was fixed not as a share of the produce of land but as a proportion of rent. Initially the state share had been fixed at 80% of the gross rental which was considered to be extortionate by Bird. Bentinck reduced it to 66%, leaving the balance as the profit of the Zamindar. However, even that did not bring belief to the landholder and the cultivator. Bird could not complete the settlement of the whole province before he left in 1842 and it was left to Robertson and Thomason to bring the whole province under it. Thomason introduced a further change in the rate of revenue collection, which was fixed at 50% of the rental by the Saharanpur Rules in 1855. Many alterations were made in the procedure which was simplified. The cultivator was protected from being ejected from his holdings if he had been cultivating the same for a period of 12 years and agreed to pay a fixed rent. During the pendency of the settlement, rent could not be enhanced. While assessing the increase at the time of the next settlement, amounts paid by the tenant were taken into account. The duration of the settlement was fixed at 20 years and subsequently 30 years. The above Rules formed the basis of revenue policy during the 19th century and the system adopted in the North-Western Province was applied to the territories acquired in Northern India and in the Central Provinces.

It is worthy of notice that under the Mahalwari system, the state did not fix land revenue for ever but for a limited period of 20 or 30 years. The settlement was not made with individual landlords but with the village as a whole which was held responsible for its payment. An agreement on behalf of the entire village to pay the stipulated amount of revenue was signed by the village Headman known as Lambardar. Whatever amount of revenue the whole village was required to pay was paid by the villagers according to their respective holdings. The Government Settlement Officers were made responsible for the assessment of land revenue which they did in consultation with the Lambardar and the village bodies. The tenants had with them their records of right and the village was in possession of land charts, maps and settlement of individual holdings. While fixing the land revenue, the yielding capacity of the soil, the nature of the crop it produced and the price of that crop were taken into account. The assessment once made was continued for the full term of the settlement.

There were certain shortcomings in the Mahalwari system. The Lambardar and the village Headman enjoyed privileges which they misused for their self-interest. The Lambardar and Headman acted as intermediaries between the Government and the villagers. The result was that small tenants were reduced to an inferior position and very often opposed by powerful Headman. They were uses at cultivators for their lands. The sub-ordinate cultivators "actually got just a subsistence remuneration and the rest of the produce went into the hands of the big owners.

TALUQDARI SYSTEM

The Mahalwari system did not cover the whole of Uttar Pradesh. In the district of Avadh, there existed another system known as the Taluqdari system. A number of villages were put under the Taluqdari system. The Government entered into an agreement with the Taluqdari for a period of 30 years and he collected the stipulated revenue from different villages under his charge and deposited them with the Government after deducting the cost of collection of revenue, and his own remuneration for the work. The Taluqdars of Avadh had no real rights over the lands under their charge. They worked as revenue collectors for the fixed period of the settlement and not in perpetuity.

In the Punjab, the assessments made by the British Government were lower than the demands made during the rule of the Sikhs in the Punjab. However, the payment of land revenue was to be made in cash and not in the form of a share of the crops as before. The collection of revenue was also strict.

It is worthy of notice that the changes in the land revenue system brought many changes in village life. The old rural society was broken up. As population increased, the lands of a family were divided among a large number of persons. The small plots did not produce enough to maintain their owners. Cottage industries disappeared on account of the import of British goods and the peasants had nothing to supplement their income. The landless labourers found no employment for a large part of the year. Poverty compelled the villagers to take loans from moneylenders at high rates of interest and that resulted in the exploitation of the villagers. The Zamindars, moneylenders and lawyers exploited the poor peasants.

REVIEW QUESTIONS

1. Discuss the salient features of the permanent settlement of Bengal.
2. What were the problems created by the permanent settlement? Elaborate.
3. Describe the merits and demerits of the permanent settlement.
4. Bring out the features of the Ryotwari system.
5. Write short notes on the following:
    (a) Mahalwari system
    (b) Taluqdari system
6. Describe the merits and demerits of the Mahalwari system.
7. How did the land revenue policies of the British affected the life of the peasants? Explain.

SUGGESTED READINGS

Aspinall, A.: *Cornwallis in Bengal,* 1931.
Baden-Powell, B.H.: *The Land Systems of British India,* 2 Vols.
Banerji, D.N.: *Early Administrative System of the East India Company.*
Boulger, D.C.: *Lord William Bentinck,* 1897.
Brown, D.D.: *Agricultural Development in India's Districts,* Cambridge, 1971.
Dutt, R.C.: *Economic History of India,* Vols. I and II.
Frykenberg, Robert E. (Ed.): *Land Tenure and Peasant in South Asia,* New Delhi, 1977.
Gupta, Sulekh Chandra: *Agrarian Relations and Early British Rule in India.*
Impious Hussain: *Land Revenue Policy in Northern India.*
Kay, J.W.: *The Administration of the East India Company.*
Marshall, P.J.: *Problems of Empire, Britain and India, 1712-1813,* London, 1968.
Philips. C.H.: *The East India Company, 1784-1834,* Manchester, 1940.
Ranajit Guha: *A Rule of Property for Bengal, an Essay on the Idea of Permanent Settlement.*
Report from the Select Committee on the Affairs of East India Company, 1833, General Appendix.
Report of the Bengal Land Revenue Commission, 1943.
Ruthnaswamy, M.: *Some Influences that made the British Administrative System in India,* 1939.
Schweinitz, Karl de: *The Rise and Fall of British India,* London, 1985.
Seton-Karr, W.S.: *The Marquis Cornwallis,* 1898.
Sinha, N.K.: *Economic History of Bengal,* 3 Vols.
Siraj-ul-Islam: *The Permanent Settlement in Bengal: A Study of its Operation,* Oxford, 1976.
Tara Chand: *History of the Freedom Movement in India,* Vol. I.

Chronological Table

1498	Vasco da Gama reached Calicut.
1505-9	De Almedia as first Viceroy of the Portuguese possessions in India.
1509-15	Albuquerque as second Viceroy of the Portuguese possessions in India.
1510	Conquest of Goa by Albuquerque.
1600	Queen Elizabeth granted a charter to the English East India Company on 31 December.
1602	Dutch East India Company started.
1664	The French East India Company started.
1714-20	Peshwa Balaji Vishwanath.
1720-40	Peshwa Baji Rao.
1727-94	Mahadji Scindhia.
1740-61	Peshwa Balaji Baji Rao.
1742-1800	Nana Phadnavis.
1746-8	First Carnatic War.
1746	Madras surrendered to the French in September.
1748	Treaty of Aix-La-Chapelle.
1748-54	Second Carnatic War.
1748	Death of Asaf Jah Nizam-ul-Mulk in May.
1751	Capture of Arcot by Clive.
1756-63	Third Carnatic War.
1757	Battle of Plassey.
1757-60	Mir Jafar as Nawab of Bengal.
1760	Battle of Wandiwash in January in which Sir Eyre Coote defeated Count Lally.
1760-63	Mir Kasim as Nawab of Bengal.
1761	Fall of Pondicherry in January. Third Battle of Panipat between the Marathas and Ahmed Shah Abdali.
1761-72	Peshwa Madhavrao I.
1763	Peace of Paris.
1764	Battle of Buxer in October. Munro defeated Mir Kasim and Nawab of Oudh.
1765	Shuja-ud-Daula finally defeated in May.
1765	Second Governorship of Bengal by Clive.
1765-72	Dual Government of Bengal.
1767-9	Verelst as Governor of Bengal.
1767-9	First Mysore War.
1770	Famine in Bengal.
1770-2	Cartier as Governor of Bengal.
1772-3	Warren Hastings as Governor of Bengal.
1772	Abolition of Dual Government of Bengal by Warren Hastings.
1772	Peshwa Narayanrao.
1773-85	Warren Hasting as Governor-General.
1773	The Regulating Act passed.
1774-95	Peshwa Madhavrao Narayan.
1775	Treaty of Surat entered into by Raghoba with the Government of Bombay.
1776	Death of Monson. Treaty of Purandar entered into by Warren Hastings.
1777	Death of Clavering.
1778-82	First Maratha War.
1780	Francis left India for England
1780-4	Second Mysore War.
1781	The Judicature Act.
1782	Treaty of Salbai between the Peshwa and Warren Hastings.
1783	Fox India Bill.
1784	Pitt's India Act. Treaty of Mangalore between Sultan Tipu of Mysore and English East India Company.
1788	Declaratory Act.
1786-93	Cornwallis as Governor-General.
1790-02	Third Mysore War.
1792	Treaty of Seringapatam between Sultan Tipu and Cornwallis
1793	Permanent Settlement of Bengal.
1793-8	Sir John Shore as Governor-General.
1793	The Charter of the English East India Company renewed for 20 years.
1796-1818	Peshwa Baji Rao II.
1796-1805	Lord Wellesley as Governor-General.
1799	Fourth Mysore War and death of Sultan Tipu.
1800	Death of Nana Phadnavis in March.
1801	Wellesley took over the civil and military administration of Carnatic.

1802	Treaty of Bassein entered into between the Peshwa and the English East India Company.
1802	Second Maratha War.
1804	Treaty of Deogaon between Raja of Berar and English East India Company.
	Treaty of Surji Arjangaon between English East India Company and Maharaja Scindhia.
1805	Lord Cornwallis as Governor-General.
1805-7	Sir George Barlow as Governor-General.
1817-13	Lord Minto as Governor-General.
1809	Treaty of Amritsar between Maharaja Ranjit Singh and English East India Company.
1813	The Charter of English East India Company renewed for 20 years.
1813-23	Lord Hastings as Governor-General.
1814-6	War between English East India Company and Nepal.
1816	Treaty of Sagauli signed between Gorkhas of Nepal and English East India Company.
1817-8	Pindari War.
	Third Maratha War.
1823-28	Lord Amherst as Governor-General.
1824-06	First Burmese War.
1826	Treaty of Yandaboo between Government of India and Burma.
1828-35	Lord William Bantinck as Governor-General.
1828	Brahmo Samaj founded by Raja Ram Mohan Roy.
1829	Abolition of Sati in December.
1833	Charter of the English East India Company renewed for 20 years.
1835-6	Sir Charles Metcalfe as Governor-General.
1836-42	Lord Auckland as Governor-General.
1838	Tripartite Treaty between Maharaja Ranjit Singh, Shah Shuja and Government of India.
1838-42	First Afghan War.
1839	Death of Maharaja Ranjit Singh.
1840	Death of Kharak Singh in November.
1841-43	Sher Singh as ruler of the Punjab.
1842-4	Lord Ellenborough as Governor-General.
1843	Annexation of Sind.
1845-6	First Sikh War.
1845	Battle of Ferozshah fought on 21 December between the Sikhs and Government of India.
1846	Battle of Aliwal in which the Sikhs were defeated. Battle of Subraon.
	Treaty of Lahore signed in March between the Sikhs and Government of India.
	Treaty of Bhairowal signed in December between Government of India and Lahore Durbar.
1848-9	Second Sikh War.
1848-56	Lord Dalhousie as Governor-General.
1848	Annexation of the State of Satara.
1849	Battle of Chillianwala on 13 January.
	Battle of Gujarat in February.
	The Punjab annexed on 29 March.
	Parmahans Sabha started in Maharashtra.
1852	Second Burmese War and annexation of Pegu.
1853	Annexation of Jhansi.
1853	Annexation of Berar.
	The Charter of the Company renewed.
1854	Annexation of Nagpur.
	Wood's Despatch on education.
1856	Annexation of Oudh.
1856-8	Lord Canning as Governor-General.
1857-8	The Revolt.
1858-62	Lord Canning as Governor-General and Viceroy of India.
1858	Government of India Act.
	The Queen's Proclamation.
1861	Indian Councils' Act.
	Indian Civil Service Act.
1862-3	Lord Elgin.
1864-9	Lord Lawrence as Governor-General and Viceroy.
1869-72	Lord Mayo as Governor-General and Viceroy.
1872-6	Lord Northbrook as Governor-General and Viceroy.
1875	The Theosophical Society started by Blavatsky and Olcott.
	Arya Samaj founded by Swami Dayanand.
1876-80	Lord Lytton as Governor-General and Viceroy.
1877	Lord Lytton held Durbar at Delhi where Queen Victoria was proclaimed Empress of India.
1878	Vernacular Press Act passed.
1879-81	Second Afghan War.
1880-4	Lord Ripon as Governor-General and Viceroy.
1882	Lord Ripon issued his famous Resolution on Local Self-Government.
	Hunter Commission on education appointed.
	Decentralisation of Finance under Lord Ripon.

1883	Ilbert Bill Controversy. Circular issued by Hume to graduates of Calcutta University on 1 March.
1884-6	Lord Dufferin as Governor-General and Viceroy.
1884	Punjdeh Affair.
1885-6	Third Burmese War and annexation of Upper Burma in 1886. First Session of Indian National Congress held on 28 December at Bombay.
1886	Aitchison Commission appointed.
1887	Dev Samaj founded.
1888-93	Lord Lansdowne as Governor-General and Viceroy.
1892	Indian Councils' Act passed.
1894-9	Lord Elgin II as Governor-General and Viceroy.
1896	Ramakrishna Mission started.
1897	Tilak arrested and sentenced. Famine in the Deccan. Outbreak of Plague.
1899-1905	Lord Curzon as Governor-General and Viceroy.
1899	Official Secrets Act passed.
1900	The Calcutta Corporation Act.
1902	Lord Curzon appointed a Commission on Education in January.
1904	Treaty of Lhasa imposed on Dalai Lama by the Government of India. Decentralisation of Finance under Lord Curzon Indian Universities Act.
1905	Partition of Bengal.
1905-10	Lord Minto II Governor-General and Viceroy.
1907	Seditious Meetings Act passed. Lajpat Rai and Ajit Singh deported from the Punjab. Surat Split.
1908	The Newspaper (Incitement to Offences) Act passed. Explosive Substances Act passed. Tilak sentenced to six years imprisonment.
1909	Minto-Morely Reforms.
1910	Death of King Edward VII and accession of George V.
1910-06	Lord Hardinge an Governor-General and Viceroy.
1910	The Indian Press Act passed.
1911	The Delhi Durbar in which Partition of Bengal was cancelled.
1912	A bomb thrown on Lord Hardinge on 23 December when he was entering Delhi.
1914	Komagata Maru ship reached on 22 May the port of Vancouver but not allowed to enter the harbour by the Government.
1915	Gokhale's Political Testament. 21 February fixed by Ghadar Party for an All-India revolt.
1916-21	Lord Chelmsford as Governor-General and Viceroy.
1916	Congress-League Scheme. Indian Home Rule League started by Tilak with its headquarters at Poona on 28 April. Home Rule League started on 15 September by Annie Besant.
1917	Declaration made on 20 August by Montagu, Secretary of State for India, regarding the goal of the British Government in India.
1918	Montagu-Chelmsford Report published on 8 July.
1919	Government of India Act passed. Calcutta University Commission submitted its Report. Jallianwala Bagh tragedy on 13 April.
1920	Non Co-operation Resolution passed at Calcutta Congress Session in September.
1921-06	Lord Hardinge as Governor-General and Viceroy.
1921	Chamber of princes set up on 8 February by a royal proclamation. Visit to India by Prince of Wales in November.
1922	Arrest of Mahatma Gandhi on 13 March in Non-Cooperation Movement.
1923	Appointment of the Lee commission on superior civil services in India. Swarajist Party formed on 1 January.
1925	Looting of train on 9 August near Kakori railway station.
1926-31	Lord Irwin as Governor-General and Viceroy.
1927	Appointment of the Simon Commission in November. Butler Committee appointed by Government of India
1928	The Nehru Report. All-Parties Conference held at Delhi in February-March Simon Commission visited Lahore on 20 October and Lajpat Rai assaulted by police. Death of Lala Lajpat Rai on 17 November
1929	Fourteen points of Mr. Jinnah. Statement issued by Lord Irwin on 31 October regarding the goal of British Government. Resolution passed by the Indian National Congress in 31 December declaring,

	complete independence for India. Tricolour flag of Independence hoisted on banks of the river Ravi near Lahore on 31 December. Bomb thrown in Central Assembly by Sardar Bhagat Singh on 8 April. Bomb attempt on train of Lord Irwin near New Delhi oh 23 December.	1940	Congress session held at Ramgarh in March. Pakistan Resolution passed by Muslim League at Lahore 23 March. August Offer by the Viceroy.
1930	First Independence Day observed on 26 January Mahatma Gandhi started Dandi march on 12 March. Simon commission Report published in May.	1941	Subhash Chandra Bose escaped on 26 January from India. Cripps came to India with his proposals in March. Congress rejected Cripps Proposals on 11 April. "Quit India" resolution passed on 8 August by the Congress and arrest of Congress leaders.
1930-01	First Round Table Conference.		
1931	Gandhi-Irwin Pact signed on 5 March. Bhagat Singh, Sukh Dev and Raj Guru hanged on 28 March.	1944-07	Lord Wavell as Governor-General and Viceroy.
1931-06	Lord Willingdon as Governor-General and Viceroy	1945	Desai-Liaquat Formula released in January. Surrender of Germany on 5 May. All members of the Congress Working Committee released on 15 June. The Simla Conference opened by Lord Wavell on 25 June. Labour Party came to power in Britain on 10 July. Simla Conference declared a failure on 14 July. Japan surrendered on 14 August. Elections to Central Assembly held in November-December.
1931	Second Round Table Conference attended by Mahatma Gandhi in London. The Indian Press (Emergency Powers) Act passed.		
1932	Government of India issued four ordinances on 4 January. Communal Award announced on 16 August by British Prime Minister. Poona Pact signed in September. Third Round Table Conference held in London from 17 November to 24 December. Foreign Relations Act passed.		
		1946	Parliamentary Delegation came to India from London in January. Prime Minister Attlee declared on 19 February that Government had decided to send a Cabinet Mission of India. Cabinet Mission reached Delhi on 24 March. Cabinet Mission Scheme announced on 16 May. Direct Action Day celebrated on 16 August by the Muslim Langue. Interim Government formed on 2 September by the Congress Mr. Jinnah agreed on 13 October to the Muslim League joining the Interim Government. First session of the Constituent Assembly of India started on 9 December but boycotted by the Muslim League.
1933	The White Paper issued in March. Joint Select Committee appointed in April.		
1934	Indian States (Protection) Act passed. Joint Select Committee submitted its report on 22 November.		
1935	Government of India Bill published on 22nd January. Government of India Act received royal assent on 2 August.		
1936-44	Lord Linlithgow as Governor-General and Viceroy.		
1937	Elections held in India in February.		
1938	Haripura session of the Congress on 19-20 February. Press Laws Inquiry Committee appointed.		
1939	Tripuri session of the Congress. World War II started on 1 September. Viceroy of India declared war against Germany on 3 September. All Congress ministries in the Provinces resigned by the end of October.	1947	Prime Minister Attlee declared on 20 February that British Government would leave India not later than June 1948.
		1947-08	Lord Mountbatten as Governor-General. Lord Mountbatten reached India on 22 March.

	3 June Plan for Partition of India.		Shah Commission appointed on 28 May 1977.
	Indian Independence Act passed by British Parliament on 18 July.	1978	President Carter of America visited India in January.
	India became independent on 15 August.		Forty-third Amendment of the Constitution on 13 April.
1947-64	Jawaharlal Nehru as Prime Minister of India.	1979	Forty-fourth Amendment of the Constitution on 30 April.
1948	Appointment of the University Commission under Chairmanship of Sir S. Radhakrishnan.		Fall of Janata Government on 15 July.
1950	The Constitution of India came into force on 26 January.		Charan Singh became Prime Minister on 28 July.
1951	The Press (Objectionable Matters) Act passed.	1980	Lok Sabha elections in January.
1952	The Press Commission appointed by Government of India on 23 September.		Mrs. Indira Gandhi became Prime Minister on 14 January.
1952-62	Dr. Rajendra Prasad as President of India.	1981	Meeting of Non-Aligned Conference in New Delhi in February.
1956	University Grants Commission Act passed.		Anandpur Sahib Resolution adopted on 13 April.
1962-07	Dr. S. Radhakrishnan as President of India.	1982	Mrs. Indira Gandhi on official visit to the United States in July.
1964-06	Lal Bahadur Shastri as Prime Minister of India.	1983	Non-Aligned Summit held in New Delhi in March.
1965	War-between India and Pakistan.	1984	Army entered the Golden Temple at Amritsar on 5 June.
1966	Mrs. Indira Gandhi as Prime Minister of India.		Mrs. Indira Gandhi assassinated on 31 October and Rajiv Gandhi became Prime Minister.
1967-09	Dr. Zakir Husain as President of India.		
1969-74	V. V. Giri as President of India.		
	Indo-Soviet Treaty signed in August.		Elections to Lok Sabha held. Congress won overwhelming majority.
	War between India and Pakistan in December.	1985	Elections held in the States.
1972	The Simla Agreement signed between India and Pakistan.		Fifty-first and Fifty-second Amendments of the Constitution.
1974	Fakhruddin Ali Ahmed as President of India.		Rajiv-Longowal Accord on 24 July.
1975	Emergency declared in India in June.		Assam Accord on 15 August.
1976	India and Pakistan agreed in May to re-establish old diplomatic relations at ambassadorial level and restoration of other severed links such as air links including over flights, road and air links and that was done in July.		Assassination of Longowal on 20 August.
			Akali Dal formed the Ministry in Punjab.
			Elections in Assam in December and formation of the Ministry by Asom Gana Parishad.
	Prime Minister Indira Gandhi visited the Soviet Union in June 1976.		
1977	Elections to Lok Sabha held in March and Janta Party formed the Ministry.		

Index

Afghan War I, 558
Afghanistan and Curzon, 289
Ahmed Shah (1748-1754), 16
Ahmad Shah Abdali, invasions of, 23
Aitchison Commission, 502
Akbar II, 28
Alamgir II (1754-59), 27
Albuquerque, 83
Ali Gohour, 111
The Aligarh Scheme of Pakistan 476
Amherst, Lord, 179
Amherst and First Burmese War, 179
Anand Math, 428
Anglo-Afghan Relations, 556
Anglo-French Struggle for Supremacy in the Deccan, 94
Anglo-Oudh Relations, 242
Anglo-Russian Convention, 300
Anglo-Sikh Relations (1809-39), 223
Annexation of the Punjab, 237
Arya Samaj, 548
Auckland, Lord, 214
August, Declaration of 1917, 385
Avadh, 43

Badan Singh, 51
Bahadur Shah I(1707-12), 4
Bahadur Shah II(1837-57), 28
Baji Rao (1720-40), 185
Bajirao II (1796-1818), 691
Balaji Baji Rao, 61, 189
Balaji Vishwanath, 60,182
Bankim Chandra Chatterjee, 667
Barlow, Sir George, 170
Battle of Panipat, third, 188
Battle of Plassey (1757), 191
Beck, Work of, 466
Begums of Oudh, 134
Bengal from 1767 to 1772, 127
Bharatpur, Capture of, 179
Bentinck, Lord William, 206
Bentinck, Estimate of, 213

Bhandarkar, Sir R.G., 667
Black-hole , 109
Brahmo Samaj, 546
British Impact in India, 664
Burmese War I, 179
Burmese War II, 241
Burmese War III, 284
Butler Committee, 584

Cabinet Mission Scheme, 402
Calcutta University Commission, 540
Canning, Lord, 268
Carnatic, 64
Carnatic War I, 95
Carnatic War II, 98
Carnatic War III, 99
Causes of Nationalist Movement in India, 426
Causes of Pakistan Demand, 474
Chamber of Princes, 583
Charter Act of 1793, 322
Charter Act of 1813, 323
Charter Act of 1833, 212, 324, 418
Charter Act of 1853, 327, 418, 423
Chelmsford, Lord, 303
Chet Singh, 133
Chiplunkar, Vishnu Krishna, 668
Clive's Second Governorship of Bengal, 118
Communal Award, 379
Congress-League Scheme, 347
Cornwallis completed the work of Hastings, 154
Cornwallis, Lord, 146
Cornwallis, Reforms of, 148, 500
Cripps Proposals, 398
Curzon's Foreign Policy, 288
Curzon, Internal Administration of, 292
Curzon, Famine Policy of, 292
Curzon, Agriculture, 293
Curzon, Railways, 293
Curzon, Lord, 288
Curzon, Police Reforms of, 293
Curzon, Military Reforms of, 294
Curzon and Decentralisation of Finance, 295

Curzon and Indian Universities Act, 295
Curzon and Reform of the Bureaucratic Machinery, 295
Curzon and the Calcutta Corporation, 296
Curzon and Partition of Bengal, 297
Curzon, Estimate of, 298

Dadabhai Naoroji, 480
Dalhousie, Lord, 240
Dalhousie and Conquest of Punjab 240
Dalhousie and Second Burmese War, 241
Dalhousie and Doctrine of Lapse, 241
Dalhousie and Annexation of Berar, 242
Dalhousie, Administrative Reforms of, 247
Dalhousie and Abolition of Titles and Pensions, 247
Dalhousie's Responsibility for the Mutiny, 248
Dalhousie, Estimate of, 249
Dayanand and Arya Samaj 548, 670
De Almeida, 83
Debendranath Tagore, 669
Decentralisation Commission Report, 518
Decentralisation of Finance in India, 492
Decentralisation of Finance and Ripon, 280
Declaratory Act of 1788, 322
Delhi Durbar, 301
Dev Samaj, 548
Disintegration of the Mughal Empire, 2
Downfall of 'the Mughals, Causes of the, 28
Dufferin and Panjdeh Affair, 284
Dufferin and Third Burmese War, 284
Dundas's Bill, 319
Durga Das, 28
Dutch in India, 88
Dyarchy, Working of, 363

Education, History of, 535
Elgin, Lord, 270
Ellenborough, Lord, 216
Ellenborough and Sindh, 216
Ellenborough and War with Gwalior, 220

Farrukhabad, 48
Farrukh-siyar, 19
Fine Arts, 673
Fox India Bill, 319
French East India Company, 92

Gandhi-Irwin Pact (1931), 300
Gokhale, Gopal Krishan, 481
Gokhale's Political Testament, 350

Government of India Act, (1858), 328
Government of India Act, 1919, 359
Government of India Act, 1935, 505, 587

Hardinge, Lord, 220, 301
Home Rule Movement, 443
Hunter Commission,1882, 538
Hyderabad, State of, 597
Hyder Ali, Rise of, 139

Ilbert Bill, 281
India and World War I, 449
Indian Civil Service Act, 501
Indian Councils Act, 1861, 332
Indian Councils Act, 1892, 335
Indian Independence Act, 405
Indian National Army, 460
Indian Press Act, 1910, 526
Indian Press (Emergency Powers) Act, 1931, 528
Indian States(Protection) Act,1934, 530
Indian Universities Act, 1904, 295
Indologists and Renaissance in India, 666
Infanticide, Abolition of, 553
Integration and Democratisation of States, 605
Irwin, Lord, 304
Ishwar Chandra Vidyasagar and Widow Remarriage, 554
Islington Commission, 503

Jahandar Shah (1712-13), 7
Jallianwala Bagh Tragedy, 450
Jammu and Kashmir, State of, 601
Jats, the, 49
Javid Khan, 27
Judicature Act of 1781, 318
Junagadh, State of, 594

Keshab Chandra Sen, 427, 669
Kunwar Singh, 262

Lansdowne, Lord, 285
Latif's Scheme-on Pakistan, 476
Lawrence, Lord, 271, 562
Lee Commission (1923), 504
Legacy of British Rule in India, 614
Licensing Act of 1857, 524
Linlithgow, Lord, 305
London Company, 90
Lucknow Pact, 1916, 469
Lytton, Lord, 274, 566
Lytton, Estimate of, 275

Macpherson, Sir John, 145
Madhavrao I, 192
Madhavrao Narayan, 194
Mahadji Scindhia, 194
Mahatma Gandhi, 486
Marathas, The, 60
Maratha War I, 136
Maratha War II, 166
Maratha War III, 174
Maratha Administration under Peshwas, 197
Marathas, Causes of Downfall, 201
Mayo, Lord, 272
Mayo's Resolution of 1870, 493, 514
Memorandum of the Nineteen (1916), 346
Metcalfe, Sir Charles, 214
Meston Settlement, 496
Minto II, Lord, 300
Minto-Morley Reforms, 301, 338
Mir Jafar, 43, 110
Mir Kasim, 112
Mountbatten, Lord, 306
Muddiman Committee Report, 370
Mughul Empire, Disintegration of, 2
Muhammad Shah, 12
Munro's Recommendations regarding the Press, 523
Mysore, 63
Mysore War I, 140
Mysore War II, 141
Mysore War III, 146
Mysore War IV, 163

Nadir Shah's Invasion of India, 18
Nana Phadnavis, 197
Nand Kumar, Trial of, 133
Narayanrao, 194
Nehru Report, 372
The Newspapers (Incitement to Offences) Act, 1908, 525
Nizam-ul-Mulk, Asaf Jah, 104
Non-Cooperation Movement, 451
North-Western Frontier Policy, 570

Pakistan, Establishment of, 464
Pakistan Resolution, 473
Paramountcy in India, 579
Partition of Bengal and its effects, 297, 440, 466
Partition of India, 406
Permanent Settlement of Bengal, 151, 682
Persian Gulf arid Curzon, 290
Peshwas, Rise and fall of 182

Pindari War, 173
Pitt's India Act, 145, 320
Policy of Masterly Inactivity, 562
Policy of Subordinate Isolation, 577
Policy of Subordinate Union, 578
Poona Pact, 380
Portuguese Empire in India, causes of failure of, 86
Portuguese in India, 82
Prarthana Samaj, 547, 669
Press in India, History of the, 522
Press Commission, 532
Press (Objectionable Matter) Act, 1951, 531
Press Laws Inquiry Committee, 1948, 530
Punjab Frontier, 572
Punjab Politics from 1839 to 1845, 233
Punjab Reorganisation Act, 1966, 611
Panjdeh Affair, 284
Public Service Commissions, 507
Public Services in India, 500

Queen's Proclamation of 1858, 331

Rabindranath Tagore, 667
Radhakrishnan, Dr., 307
Radhakrishnan Commission, 541
Rajagopalachariar, C., 307
Raja Ram Mohan Roy, 544
Rajendra Prasad, 307
Rajput States, 52
Rammohan Roy, 668
Ramakrishna Mission, 547
Ramakrishna Paramhans, 671
Ranjit Singh, Maharaja, 222
Ranjit Singh, Civil Administration of, 225
Ranjit Singh, Army of, 228
Ranjit Singh, Personality of, 231
Ranjit Singh, Estimate of, 232
Ranjit Singh's responsibility for ultimate decline of sikh power, 232
Reading, Lord, 304
Regulating Act, 1773, 312
Renaissance, meaning of, 662
Renaissance in India, 662
Renaissance in India, nature of, 662
Renaissance in India, condition before, 663
Renaissance in India, British impact on, 664
Renaissance in India and Indologists, 666
Renaissance in India and Indian Writers, 667
Renaissance in India and Rammohan Roy and Brahmo Samaj, 668

Renaissance in India and Prarthana Samaj, 669
Renaissance in India and Arya Samaj, 670
Renaissance in India and Theosophical Society, 670
Renaissance in India and Ramakrishna Paramhans, 671
Renaissance in India and Vivekananda, 671
Renaissance in India and Vernacular Literature, 672
Renaissance in India and Spirit of Research and Discovery, 673
Renaissance in India and Fine Arts, 673
Ring Fence Policy, 576
Ripon, Lord, 278
Ripon's Resolution on Local Self-Government, 279
Rohilkhand, 47
Round Table Group, 351

Sayyid Brothers, 14
Sergeant Scheme for Education, 541
Shah Alam II (1759-1806), 27
Shore, Sir John, 157
Sikhs, The, 54, 222, 550
Sikh War I, 234
Sikh War II, 236
Simon Commission, 370
Sindh, Annexation of, 216
Sri Aurobindo, 549, 663
States Reorganisation Commission, 607
Suraj Mal, 51
Sir Syed Ahmed Khan, Work of, 465
Swarajist Party, 453

Terrorist Movement in India, 444
Theosophical Society, 547, 670

Tibet and Curzon, 290
Tilak, Lokmanya Bal Gangadhar, 483
Tipu, Sultan, 164
Treaty of Lahore, 236

Universities Act of 1904, 295, 539
University Grants Commission, 542

Vernacular Press Act, 1878, 524
Vivekananda, Swami 671

Wajid Ali Shah, 245
War with Nepal, 172
Warren Hastings, 130
Warren Hastings' reforms, 130
Warren Hastings and Rohilla war, 132
Warren Hastings and Trial of Nand Kumar, 133
Warren Hastings and Chet Singh, 133
Warren Hastings and Begums of Oudh, 134
Warren Hastings and Supreme Court, 135
Warren Hastings and First Maratha War, 136
Warren Hastings and First Mysore War, 140
Warren Hastings and Second Mysore War, 141
Warren Hastings, Estimate of 142
Wavell, Lord, 306
Wellesley, Lord, 160, 501, 522
Wellesley and Subsidiary System, 161
Wellesley and Fourth Mysore War, 163
Wellesley and Tipu, 164
Wellesley and Oudh, 165
Wellesley, Estimate of, 167
Why England gave India Independence, 460
Willingdon, Lord, 305
Wood's Despatch of 1854, 248, 537